W9-DFL-357

The Facts On File
DICTIONARY OF
PUBLIC
ADMINISTRATION

The Facts On File
DICTIONARY OF
PUBLIC
ADMINISTRATION

JAY M. SHAFRITZ

Graduate School of Public Affairs
University of Colorado at Denver

Facts On File Publications
New York, New York ● Oxford, England

The Facts On File Dictionary of Public Administration

Library of Congress Cataloging-in-Publication Data

Shafritz, Jay M.
    The Facts on File dictionary of public administration.

    1. Public administration—Dictionaries. I. Facts on
File, Inc. II. Title. III. Title: Dictionary of public
administration.
JA61.S54   1986   350′.0003′21   85-27542
ISBN 0-8160-1266-0

Printed in U.S.A.
10 9 8 7 6 5 4 3 2 1

CONTRIBUTORS

M. A. Aleem
Osmania University
Hyderabad, India

Joseph D. Atkinson, Jr.
Johnson Space Center
National Aeronautics and Space Administration

Harry A. Bailey, Jr.
Department of Political Science
Temple University

James S. Bowman
Department of Public Administration
Florida State University

Sarah Y. Bowman
Graduate School of Business Administration
University of Colorado at Denver

Ronald S. Calinger
School of Arts and Sciences
The Catholic University of America

Fred D. Coe
Gates Rubber Company
Denver, Colorado

Kay Smith Cormier
Auraria Library
University of Colorado at Denver

Robert W. Gage
Graduate School of Public Affairs
University of Colorado at Denver

Richard P. Hiskes
Department of Political Science
University of Connecticut

Albert C. Hyde
Public Administration Department
San Francisco State University

Bernard A. Karshmer
Health Science Center
University of Colorado

Lawrence F. Keller
College of Urban Affairs
Cleveland State University

Betty L. McCummings
Graduate School of Public Affairs
University of Colorado at Denver

Howard E. McCurdy
School of Government and Public Administration
The American University

Dail A. Neugarten
Graduate School of Public Affairs
University of Colorado at Denver

Daniel Oran
Falls Church, Virginia

J. Steven Ott
Applied Management Corporation
Denver, Colorado

E. Samuel Overman
Graduate School of Public Affairs
University of Colorado at Denver

Robert E. Quinn
Institute for Government and Policy Studies
Rockefeller College
State University of New York at Albany

David H. Rosenbloom
The Maxwell School
Syracuse University

Frank J. Thompson
Department of Political Science
University of Georgia

E. C. Wakham
Western Executive Seminar Center
U.S. Office of Personnel Management

Jonathan P. West
Department of Politics and Public Affairs
University of Miami

FOREWORD

The publication of this *Dictionary of Public Administration* is a professional and intellectual event of great magnitude. It is a work that truly fulfills the concept of an encyclopedia as a compendium of all that is known about a particular subject. Within its pages, one can find information about virtually every aspect of contemporary public administration—concepts, terms, organizations, statutes and judicial decisions, processes and practices, slang, journals, and the people who have been the leading contributors to the development of the field. The names and addresses of organizations are included, as are legal citations and sources for further reading. Importantly, its contents are not confined to the formal aspects of public administration; rather, descriptions of standard, but unofficial, practices are also included.

Yet there is much more. Professor Shafritz has not only compiled and organized the subject matter of public administration into a readily usable format, he has done so accurately, succinctly, and with the subtlety gained from a deep understanding of the field. The amount of work that went into this volume is daunting, but it is likely to be more than matched by the utility of the book. In my mind, there is no doubt that the *Dictionary* will rapidly become the most used book in public administration. Practitioners, professors, students, public officials, journalists, and others will soon wonder how anyone ever got along without it. Indeed, I hope that copies of this volume soon find their way into government offices throughout the nation. The amount of time saved in searching for information on items and the degree of understanding the book will impart would certainly contribute to the operating efficiency of public agencies. Similarly, the *Dictionary* will be of immense value to students seeking professional degrees in public administration.

The intellectual importance of this volume goes well beyond its immediate utility. Professor Shafritz has done nothing less than codify and provide standard definitions and descriptions of the items and elements that comprise the field of public administration. He has clarified the language of public administration and identified its central ideas. He has explained the contributions of numerous individuals and organizations to thinking about public administration. Consequently, the *Dictionary* will serve as a central force in the further development of knowledge of public administration. It will also be a benchmark for measuring our progress at some future time.

In sum, I believe the *Dictionary* to be an extremely important book—one that marks a turning point in the development of the field of public administration as a practice, profession, and academic discipline. It is also one that no practitioner, teacher, or student of the field should be without.

July 1985

David H. Rosenbloom
The Maxwell School
Syracuse University

PREFACE

This dictionary is a tool for all those who must be knowledgeable about the theory, concepts, practices, laws, institutions, literature, and people of the academic discipline and professional practice of public administration. Any such compendium is inherently a "work in progress." Unless a subject is a dead language or an outdated technology, its terminology is constantly changing. Nevertheless, the author has sought to capture and codify the language of public administration fully aware that, even when finished, it will remain incomplete. A living language does not wait on publisher's deadlines.

The goal was to present herein all words, terms, names, phrases, and processes with which a student or practitioner of public administration should be familiar, and then some: some because they are historically important; some just because! The criteria for including entries had to be rather loosely defined because the subject, public administration, is so loosely defined.

The boundaries of the field are so wide and overlap so many other fields that judgment calls constantly had to be made about just how far to go into related fields, such as law, economics, psychology, statistics, management, history, and medicine. As a rule of thumb, if a term was found in any of several score standard texts, it is included here. Generally excluded were those terms whose meaning in the context of public administration did not differ from definitions to be found in any standard English dictionary.

In general, those items which are more central to the concerns of public administration tend to be given more detailed coverage than those that are more on the periphery of the subject. There are basically two types of definitions: (1) those that are given brief glossary descriptions, and (2) those that are given more comprehensive coverage. The length of each entry reflects a judgment of how important each topic was considered.

The references at the end of entries serve as an example of the usage of the term as well as to provide sources for further information. The citations, for the most part, can be found in any university library; fugative materials, those sources that exist only in the most specialized collections, were generally avoided. Because such references have been given as often as is possible or practical, they are in their totality a comprehensive bibliography. Perhaps the greatest single source of information was the U.S. government. Extensive use was made of materials printed by a variety of federal agencies, and the legions of anonymous public servants who over the years have produced the various manuals, glossaries, directories, and guidelines that were so useful are hereby acknowledged.

In order to find all of the entries in any given subset of public administration, one need only find a logical large entry—bureaucracy, civil service reform, management, pay, etc.—and follow the cross-references. In addition to the entries that the reader might expect to find in a dictionary of public administration, there are some categories of entries that warrant a word of explanation:

Biographical entries. There are a great many identifications of individuals, both living and dead, who have been significant in the history, writing, and practice of public administration. Such entries are designed merely to identify an individual. The author readily concedes that some notable individuals may have been excluded or that other individuals may have been described in words too brief to do them justice, but the principal object was identification. Of course, other things might have been said if the object was to do them justice.

Court cases. There are several hundred legal decisions, mostly those of the U. S. Supreme Court, that are especially significant to public administrators. As a whole the cases focus on public management and labor relations issues. (This limitation was imposed because summaries of all major public policy cases would have required many volumes this size.) Such judicial decisions are usually many pages long for good reason. So be cautious! A brief summary of a case, no matter how succinct, may not be sufficient information upon which to base formal action. These summaries were written to identify the case and its significance, not necessarily to make less work for lawyers. The full legal citation is given with each entry of this type so that the reader may readily locate the full text of any of these court cases.

Journals. A list of *all* of the journals and magazines that bear upon public administration would be almost as large as this entire work. Only those periodicals that most consistently address the concerns of public administration specialists are included. Each periodical entry contains a statement of purpose as well as an appropriate address. A master list of all journal entries can be found under "public administration journals."

Laws. Many laws that directly impact public administrative practices are summarized. The reader must keep in mind that these entries are necessarily brief summaries of complicated laws that are constantly subject to amendment.

Organizations. All of the major federal government agencies have been included. Many private organizations and professional societies that bear upon public administration also have individual entries. All of these organizational entries contain a statement of the purpose of the organization as well as its address and phone number.

No one writes a large reference book without help from others. The list of contributors which follows the title page names those who came to my assistance. I asked this helpful bunch for draft material which I could freely edit, revise, or ignore without consulting them further. They were all gracious enough to provide me with such "raw data" and trusting enough to believe that I would not abuse it. While they all helped in various ways, a few of the contributors must be thanked for a specific series of entries:

Harry A. Bailey, Jr. of Temple University drafted many of the entries related to the American Presidency;

James S. Bowman of The Florida State University drafted many of the entries concerned with environmental and energy issues;

Robert W. Gage of the University of Colorado drafted many of the entries concerned with federalism and intergovernmental relations;

Richard P. Hiskes of the University of Connecticut drafted many of the entries concerned with science and technology policy;

Albert C. Hyde of San Francisco State University drafted many of the entries concerned with public budgeting and finance;

Lawrence F. Keller of Cleveland State University drafted many of the entries concerned with city management;

Robert F. Quinn of the State University of New York at Albany drafted many of the methodological entries; and

David H. Rosenbloom of Syracuse University drafted many of the entries concerned with constitutional law.

There is one debt that is so large that a mere acknowledgement seems hardly enough. Had it not been for the generous help and encouragement of my friend and sometime writing companion, Albert C. Hyde, this book not only would not be finished, it would not even have been begun. I also gratefully acknowledge the assistance of Elizabeth Boris, Patricia Breivik, Betty Calinger, Mary Lou Goodyear, Stanley Goldstein, F. William Heiss, Franklin James, Cora Hurwitz, Marshall Kaplan, Robert Leduc, John W. Moore, Mark Pogrebin, Cheryl Walker Ryan, John Sweeney, Eileen Tynan and Beth Forrest Warner.

Finally, I must acknowledge the very real assistance and forbearance provided by my family. My wife, Luise, at great cost to her personal growth, typed much of the manuscript. My sons Todd and Noah turned out to be able research assistants. In a sense, this was a family project.

While I had considerable assistance in producing this book, all mistakes, omissions, or other flaws to be found herein are solely my responsibility. Yet I remain hopeful that as the years go by, this work will warrant a subsequent edition. I would therefore encourage those of you who might care enough to help me do it "right" the next time around to let me hear from you.

Jay M. Shafritz
Graduate School of Public Affairs
University of Colorado at Denver
Denver, CO 80202

A

AA, see AFFIRMATIVE ACTION.

AACSB, see AMERICAN ASSEMBLY OF COLLEGIATE SCHOOLS OF BUSINESS.

AAG, see AFFIRMATIVE ACTION GROUPS.

AAO, see AFFIRMATIVE ACTION OFFICER.

AAP, see AFFIRMATIVE ACTION PLAN or AFFIRMATIVE ACTION PROGRAM.

abandonment of position, quitting a job without formally resigning.

abdication, giving up a public office by ceasing to perform its function rather than by formally resigning.

Abbott Laboratories v. Gardner, 387 U.S. 136 (1967), U.S. Supreme Court case which allowed drug companies to contest the legality of a regulation issued by the commissioner of the Food and Drug Administration prior to the date of the regulation's effectiveness. By holding that the Declaratory Judgment Act was intended for such a purpose, the court created a greater measure of judicial review of the rules issued by administrative agencies.

Abilene Paradox, a phenomenon of organizational behavior in which members assume that others favor an action or strategy, and no one questions or challenges it. Therefore, dysfunctional decisions are made and implemented. The Abilene Paradox is a form of "pluralistic ignorance." See Jerry B. Harvey, "The Abilene Paradox: The Management of Agreement," *Organizational Dynamics* (Summer 1974).

ability, the present power to perform a physical or mental function. *See* Stephen Dakin and A. John Arrowood, "The Social Comparison of Ability," *Human Relations* (February 1981).

ability test, performance test designed to reveal a measure of present ability (*e.g.,* a typing test).

ability to pay (labor relations), concept from collective bargaining referring to an employer's ability to tolerate the costs of requested wage and benefit increases. Factfinders and arbitrators frequently use the "ability to pay" concept for justifying their decisions.
See also NATIONAL LABOR RELATIONS BOARD V. TRUITT MANUFACTURING.

ability to pay (taxation), the principle that the tax burden should be distributed according to a person's wealth. It is based on the assumption that as a person's income increases, the person can and should contribute a larger percentage of his/her income to support government activities. The progressive income tax is based on this principle.
See also DIMINISHING MARGINAL UTILITY OF INCOME.

Abood v. Detroit Board of Education, 431 U.S. 209 (1977), U.S. Supreme Court case which held that public sector agency shops requiring nonunion employees to pay a service fee equivalent to union dues were constitutional. The court declared unconstitutional a union's use of such service fees for political and ideological purposes unrelated to collective bargaining. See Charles M. Rehmus and Benjamin A. Kerner, "The Agency Shop After *Abood:* No Free Ride, But What's the Fare?" *Industrial and Labor Relations Review* (October 1980).

abrogation of agreement, formal cancellation of a collective bargaining agreement or portion thereof.

absence, short-term unavailability for work, lasting at least one day or normal tour of duty. If an employee is absent from the job for a lesser period, it is usually considered a lateness. For an analysis of the relationship between absence and job satisfaction, see Nigel Nicholson, Colin A. Brow, and J. K. Chadwick-Jones, "Absence From Work and Job Satisfaction," *Journal of Applied Psychology* (December 1976). *See also* Donald L. Hawk, "Absenteeism and Turnover," *Personnel Journal* (June 1976). For some comparative statistics, see Janice Neipert Hedges, "Absence from Work—A Look at Some National Data," *Monthly Labor Review* (July 1973); Carol Boyd Leon, "Employed But Not At Work: A Review of Unpaid Absences," *Monthly Labor Review* (November 1981).

absence rate, amount of absence, calculated by the U.S. Bureau of Labor Statistics using the following formula:

Absence rate =
$$\frac{\text{work days lost (per month)}}{\text{days worked plus days lost}} \times 100$$

absence without leave, absence without prior approval.

absentee, any worker not present for one or more scheduled days of work. See John Scherba and Lyle Smith, "Computerization of Absentee Control Programs," *Personnel Journal* (May 1973).

absenteeism, as defined by the U.S. Bureau of Labor Statistics:

the failure of workers to appear on the job when they are scheduled to work. It is a broad term which is applied to time lost because sickness or accident prevents a worker from being on the job, as well as unauthorized time away from the job for other reasons. Workers who quit without notice are also counted as absentees until they are officially removed from the payroll.

Generally, "absenteeism" is associated with unnecessary, unexcused, or habitual absences from work. For academic analyses of the problem, see R. Oliver Gibson, "Toward a Conceptualization of Absence Behavior of Personnel in Organizations," *Administrative Science Quarterly* (June 1966); J. K. Chadwick-Jones, Nigel Nicholson and Colin Brown, *Social Psychology of Absenteeism* (New York: Praeger Publishers, 1982); Jacob Wolpin and Ronald J. Burke, "Relationships Between Absenteeism and Turnover: A Function of the Measures?" *Personnel Psychology* (Spring 1985); John M. Ivancevich, "Predicting Absenteeism From Prior Absence and Work Attitudes," *Academy of Management Journal* (March 1985). For "nuts-and-bolts" presentations of the problem, see Frederick J. Gaudet, *Solving the Problem of Employee Absence* (New York: American Management Associations, 1963); Dan R. Dalton and James L. Perry, "Absenteeism and the Collective Bargaining Agreement: An Empirical Test," *Academy of Management Journal* (June 1981); Ronald J. Bula, "Absenteeism Control," *Personnel Journal* (June 1984); Steve Markham and Dow Scott, "Controlling Absenteeism: Union and Nonunion Differences," *Personnel Administrator* (February 1985). For a bibliography, see Paul M. Muchinsky, "Employee Absenteeism: A Review of the Literature," *Journal of Vocational Behavior* (June 1977). For the "no-fault" perspective, see Darrell Olson and Ruth Bangs, "No-Fault Attendance Control: A Real World Application," *Personnel Administrator* (June 1984); Frank E. Kuzmits, "Is Your Organization Ready for No-Fault Absenteeism?" *Personnel Administrator* (December 1984).

See also REINFORCEMENT.

absolute advantage, an international trade concept formulated by Adam Smith which holds that one nation has an *absolute advantage* over another when it can produce more of a product using the same amount of resources than the other can. *See also* ADAM SMITH, COMPARATIVE ADVANTAGE.

abstract objective, *see* OBJECTIVE.

abuse, also FRAUD, furnishing excessive services to beneficiaries, violating program regulations or performing improper practices, none of which involves prosecutable fraud. *Fraud* is the obtaining of something of value by unlawful means through willful misrepresentation. *See* John D. Young, "Reflections on the Root Causes of Fraud, Abuse, and Waste in Federal Social Programs," *Public Administration Review* ((July/August 1983); James S. Larson, "Fraud in Government Programs: A Secondary Analysis," *Public Administration Quarterly* (Fall 1983).

Academy of Management, nonprofit organization founded in 1941 with primary objectives of advancing research, learning, teaching, and practice in the field of management and encouraging the extension and unification of knowledge pertaining to management. The Academy, most of whose members are college teachers, views itself as America's academic "voice" in U.S. management.

Academy of Management Journal, quarterly that publishes articles in the fields of business policy and planning, international management, management consulting, management education and development, management history, manpower management, organizational behavior, organization and management theory, organization development, production-operations management, social issues in management, organizational communication, and health care administration.

The *Journal* publishes original research of an empirical nature either in the form of articles or as research notes. Although studies which serve to test either theoretical propositions or hypotheses derived from practice are of particular interest, exploratory work and survey research findings are also included. The *Journal* does not publish purely conceptual papers which do not contain any original data. Conceptual articles of this kind are published in the *Academy of Management Review*.

Academy of Management Journal
P.O. Box KZ

Mississippi State University
Mississippi State, MS 39762

Academy of Management Review, quarterly which seeks distinguished original manuscripts that (a) move theoretical conceptualization forward in the field of management and/or (b) indicate new theoretical linkages that have rich potential for theory and research in management and (c) provide clear implications of theory for problem-solving in administrative and organizational situations.

Academy of Management Review
P.O. Box KZ
Mississippi State University
Mississippi State, MS 39762

Academy of Political Science, nonprofit organization founded in 1880 to promote the understanding of political science and its application to government, political, social, economic, and related problems. Publishes the *Political Science Quarterly*.

Academy of Political Science
2852 Broadway
New York, NY 10025
(212) 866-6752

accelerating premium pay, bonus incentive system in which pay rates rise as production standards are exceeded. For example, an employee who exceeds standard production by two percent may get just a two percent bonus, while an employee who exceeds by five percent may get a ten percent bonus.

acceptable level of unemployment, the individual to whom it is acceptable still has a job.

acceptance theory of authority, *see* ZONE OF ACCEPTANCE.

accession, any addition to the workforce of an organization.

accession rate, also called HIRING RATE, number of employees added to a payroll during a given time period, usually expressed as a percentage of total employment. The accession rate is a significant indicator of economic growth—an increase (decrease) tends to indicate economic recovery (recession). Statistics on the accession rates of major industries are gathered monthly by the Bureau of Labor Statistics of the U.S. Department of Labor. Accession rates can be computed using the following formula:

$$\text{accession rate} = \frac{\text{total accessions} \times 100}{\text{total number of workers}}$$

accidental death benefit, feature found in some life insurance policies that provides for payment of additional amounts to the beneficiary if the insured party dies as a result of an accident. When such provisions allow for an accidental death benefit that is twice the normal value of the policy, they are known as "double-indemnity" provisions.

accident and sickness benefits, variety of regular payments made to employees who lose time from work due to off-the-job disabilities occasioned by accidents or sickness.

accident frequency rate, as computed by the Bureau of Labor Statistics, the accident frequency rate is the total number of disabling injuries per million hours worked. See Paul C. Rohan and Bernard Brody, "Frequency and Costs of Work Accidents in North America, 1971-80," *Labour and Society* (April-June 1984).

accident prevention, total planned effort on the part of labor, management, and government regulators to eliminate the causes and severity of workplace injuries and accidents. For a text, see Willie Hammer, *Occupational Safety Management and Engineering* (Englewood Cliffs, N.J.: Prentice-Hall, 1976). See also Robert A. Reber, Jerry A. Wallin and Jagdeep S. Chhokar, "Reducing Industrial Accidents: A Behavioral Experiment," *Industrial Relations* (Winter 1984).

accident-proneness, concept that implies that certain kinds of personalities are more likely to have accidents than others. However, psychological research supports the assertion that accident-proneness is more related to situational factors than personality factors. For the classic analysis on the subject, see A. G. Arbous and J. E. Kerrich, "The Phenomenon of Accident-Proneness," *Industrial Medicine and Surgery* (April 1953). Nevertheless, Joseph T. Kunce established a relationship between "Vocational Interest and Accident Proneness," in the *Journal of Applied Psychology* (June 1967).

accident severity rate, generally computed as the number of work days lost because of accidents per thousand hours worked.

acculturation, the process by which individuals or groups acquire the cultural characteristics of an organizational or social unit through extensive contact and interaction. See ORGANIZATIONAL CULTURE.

accountability, extent to which one is responsible to higher authority—legal or organizational—for one's actions in society at large or within one's particular organizational position. For discussion in a public administration context, see Bruce L. R. Smith and D. C. Hague, eds., *The Dilemma of Accountability in Modern Government: Independence Versus Control* (New York: St. Martin's Press, 1971); Jerome B. McKinney and Lawrence C. Howard, *Public Administration: Balancing Power and Accountability* (Oak Park, Ill.: Moore Publishing Co., 1979); Bernard Rosen, *Holding Government Bureaucracies Accountable* (New York: Praeger Publishers, 1982); Bruce L. R. Smith and James D. Carroll, eds., *Improving the Accountability and Performance of Government* (Washington, D.C.: The Brookings Institution, 1982); Frank J. Sorauf, "Who's In Charge? Accountability in Political Action Committees," *Political Science Quarterly* (Winter 1984-85).
See also the following entries:
ADMINISTRATIVE ACCOUNTABILITY
BUTZ V. ECONOMOU
CONTROL FEEDBACK

accounting, also CASH ACCOUNTING and ACCRUAL ACCOUNTING, process of classifying, measuring, and interpreting financial transactions. *Cash accounting* is the recording of transactions at the time the payment is actually made. *Accrual accounting* means that revenues are recorded when they are earned and expenses are recorded as they are incurred. For texts, *see* Edward B. Deakin and Michael W. Maher, *Cost Accounting:* (Homewood, Ill.: Richard D. Irwin, Inc., 1984) and Leon E. Hay, *Accounting for Governmental and Nonprofit Entities*, 6th ed. (Homewood, Ill.: Richard D. Irwin, Inc., 1980).

accounting systems, the total structure of records and procedures that record, classify, and report information on the financial position and operations of a governmental unit or any of its funds, balanced accounts groups, and organizational components.

accounts payable, amounts owed to others for goods and services received and assets acquired.

accounts receivable, amounts due from others for goods furnished and services rendered.

accreditation, the process by which an agency or organization evaluates and recognizes a program of study or an institution as meeting certain predetermined standards. The recognition is called accreditation. Similar assessment of individuals is called *certification*.

accrual accounting, *see* ACCOUNTING.

accrued expenditures, charges during a given period that reflect liabilities incurred and the need to pay for: (a) services performed by employees, contractors, other government accounts, vendors, carriers, grantees, lessors, and other payees; (b) goods and other tangible property received; and (c) amounts becoming owed under programs for which no current service or performance is required (such as

annuities, insurance claims, other benefit payments, and some cash grants, but excluding the repayment of debt, which is considered neither an obligation nor an expenditure). Expenditures accrue regardless of when cash payments are made, whether invoices have been rendered, or, in some cases, whether goods or other tangible property have been physically delivered.

See also ACCOUNTING and LIABILITIES.

achievement battery, *see* ACHIEVEMENT TEST.

achievement drive, also called ACHIEVEMENT NEED, motivation to strive for high standards of performance in a given area of endeavor. For the classic work on achievement motivation, *see* David C. McClelland, *The Achieving Society* (Princeton, N.J.: Van Nostrand Reinhold Co., 1961). *Also see* David C. McClelland, "Achievement Motivation Can be Developed," *Harvard Business Review* (November-December 1965); Perry Pascarella, *The New Achievers* (New York: The Free Press, 1984).

achievement need, *see* ACHIEVEMENT DRIVE.

achievement test, test designed to measure an individual's level of proficiency in a specific subject or task. A collection of achievement tests designed to measure levels of skill or knowledge in a variety of areas is called an achievement battery. *See* Norman E. Gronlund, *Constructing Achievement Tests*, 2nd ed. (Englewood Cliffs, N.J.: Prentice-Hall, 1977).

ACIPP, *see* ADVISORY COUNCIL ON INTERGOVERNMENTAL PERSONNEL POLICY.

ACIR, *see* ADVISORY COMMISSION ON INTERGOVERNMENTAL RELATIONS.

across-the-board increase, increase in wages, whether expressed in dollars or percentage of salary, given to an entire workforce.

5

act, written bill formally passed by a legislature, such as the U.S. Congress. An act is a "bill" from its introduction until its passage by a legislature. An act becomes a law when it is signed by a chief executive, such as the U.S. President.

The Stages of a Bill in the U.S. Congress

Following in brief are the usual steps by which a bill becomes a law.

1. Introduction by a member, who places it in the "hopper", a box in the House chamber; the bill is given a number and printed by the Government Printing Office so that copies are available the next morning.

2. Referral to one or more standing committees of the House by the speaker, at the advice of the parliamentarian.

3. Report from the committee or committees, after public hearings and "markup" meetings by subcommittee, committee, or both.

4. House approval of a special rule, reported by the House Rules Committee, making it in order for the House to consider the bill.

5. Consideration of the bill in Committee of the Whole, in two stages: first, a time for general debate on the bill; and second, a time for amending the bill, one part at a time, under a rule that limits speeches on amendments to five minutes each.

6. Passage by the House after votes on amendments adopted in Committee of the Whole.

7. Transmittal to the Senate, by message.

8. Consideration by the Senate—usually after referral to, and report from a Senate committee, and after debate and amendment on the Senate floor.

9. Transmission from the Senate back to the House, with or without Senate amendments to the bill.

10. Resolution of differences between the House and the Senate, either through additional amendments or the report of a conference committee.

11. Enrollment on parchment paper and then signing by the speaker and by the president of the Senate.

12. Transmittal to the president of the United States.

13. Approval or disapproval by the president; if the president disapproves, he usually returns the bill with a veto message that explains his reasons.

14. House and Senate action to override the veto by two-thirds votes; both chambers must vote to override the veto if the bill is to become law.

15. Filing with the administrator of the General Services Administration after approval by the President or passage by Congress over his veto.

Action, federal agency that provides centralized coordination and administration of domestic volunteer activities sponsored by the federal government. Action is the administrative home of Volunteers in Service to America (VISTA), the Foster Grandparent Program, the Retired Senior Volunteer Program (RSVP), and related programs.

Action
806 Connecticut Avenue, N.W.
Washington, D.C. 20525
(202) 254-3958

actionable, refers to an act or occurrence that provides adequate reason for a grievance or lawsuit.

action plan, a description of the specific steps involved in achieving a goal. See Waldron Berry, "An Action Planning Process for All," *Supervisory Management* (April 1984).

action research, in its broadest context, the application of the scientific method to practical problems. As the basic model underlying organization development, action research, according to Wendell L. French and Cecil H. Bell, Jr., in *Organization Development: Behavioral Science Interventions for Organization Improvement* (Englewood Cliffs, N.J.: Prentice-Hall, 1973), is:

the process of systematically collecting research data about an ongoing system relative to some objective, goal, or need of that system; feeding these data back into the system; taking actions by altering selected variables within the system based both on the data and on hypotheses; and evaluating the results of actions by collecting more data. This definition characterizes action research in terms of the activities comprising the

process: first a static picture is taken of an organization; on the basis of "what exists" hunches and hypotheses suggest actions; these actions typically entail manipulating some variable in the system that is under the control of the action researcher (this often means doing something differently from the way it has always been done); later, a second picture is taken of the system to examine the effects of the actions taken.
For a book-length study of action research in action, see William F. Whyte and Edith L. Hamilton, *Action Research for Management* (Homewood, Ill.: Irwin-Dorsey Press, 1964). See also Mark A. Frohman, Marshall Sashkin, and Michael J. Kavanagh, "Action Research As Applied to Organization Development," *Organization and Administrative Sciences* (Spring/ Summer 1976); Melvin Blumberg and Charles D. Pringle, "How Control Groups Can Cause Loss of Control in Action Research: The Case of Rushton Coal Mine," *The Journal of Applied Behavioral Science*, Vol. 19, No. 4 (1983); Michael Peters and Viviane Robinson, "The Origins and Status of Action Research," *The Journal of Applied Behavioral Science*, Vol. 20, No. 2 (1984).

action theory, a mode of analysis which seeks to unite theory and practice by taking the face-to-face encounter as the primary analytical unit. See Bayard L. Catron and Michael M. Harmon, "Action Theory in Practice: Toward Theory Without Conspiracy," *Public Administration Review* (September/October 1981); Michael M. Harmon, *Action Theory for Public Administration* (New York: Longman, 1981).

active listening, counseling technique in which the counselor listens to both the facts and the feelings of the speaker. Such listening is called "active" because the counselor has the specific responsibilities of showing interest, of not passing judgment, and of helping the speaker to work out his problems. For a discussion, see Carl R. Rogers and Richard E. Farson, "Active Listening," *Readings in Management: An Organizational Perspective,* edited by C. R.

Anderson and M. J. Gannon (Boston: Little, Brown and Co., 1977).

activity, a specific and distinguishable line of work performed by one or more organizational components of a governmental unit for the purpose of discharging a function or subfunction for which the governmental unit is responsible. For example, food inspection is an activity performed in the discharge of the health function.
See also BUDGET ACTIVITY and FUNCTIONAL CLASSIFICATION.

actuarial projections, mathematical calculations involving the rate of mortality for a given group of people. See Robert W. Batten, *Mortality Table Construction* (Englewood Cliffs, N.J.: Prentice-Hall, 1978) and Howard E. Winklevoss, *Pension Mathematics with Numerical Illustrations* (Homewood, Ill.: Richard D. Irwin, 1977).

actuary, specialist in the mathematics of insurance. See John H. Flittie and Andrea Feshbach, "Ten Questions to Ask Your Actuary," *Governmental Finance* (June 1981).

Adamson Act of 1916, federal law that provided the eight-hour day for interstate railroad employees. Its constitutionality was upheld by the U.S. Supreme Court in *Wilson* v. *New,* 243 U.S. 332 (1917).

addiction, see DRUG ADDICTION.

ad hoc, Latin phrase meaning "for this special purpose," "for this one time."

ad hoc arbitrator, arbitrator selected by the parties involved to serve on one case. Nothing prevents the arbitrator from being used again if both parties agree. *Ad hoc* or temporary, single-case arbitration is distinguished from "permanent" arbitration where arbitrators are named in an agreement to help resolve disputes about the agreement that may arise during the life of the agreement.
See also ARBITRATION.

ad hoc committee, committee created for a specific task or purpose, whose existence ceases with the attainment of its goal.

ad-hocracy, Alvin Toffler's term, in *Future Shock* (New York: Random House, 1970), for "the fast-moving, information-rich, kinetic organization of the future, filled with transient cells and extremely mobile individuals." Ad-hocracy is obviously a contraction of *ad hoc* (Latin for "to this" or temporary) and *bureaucracy.*
See also FUTURE SHOCK.

adjournment, the putting off of business to another time or place; the decision of a court, legislature, or other group to stop meeting either temporarily or permanently.

adjudication, resolution of a dispute by means of judicial or quasi-judicial proceedings.

adjusted case, according to the National Labor Relations Board, a case that is closed when an informal settlement agreement is executed and compliance with its terms is secured. A central element in an "adjusted" case is the agreement of the parties to settle differences without recourse to litigation.

adjusted gross income, federal income tax term referring, in general, to the money a person earns minus allowable deductions for certain expenses for travel, work, business, moving, etc.

adjustment assistance, financial and technical assistance to firms, workers, and communities to help them adjust to rising import competition. While the benefits of increased trade to the importing country generally exceed the costs of adjustments, the benefits are widely shared while the adjustment costs are sometimes narrowly concentrated on a few domestic producers and communities. Both import restraints and adjustment assistance are designed to reduce these hardships. But adjustment assistance, unlike import restraints, allows the economy to enjoy the full benefits of trade expansion. Adjustment assistance is designed to facilitate structural shifts of resources from less productive to more productive industries, contributing further to improved standards of living. Under U.S. law, qualified workers adversely affected by increased import competition can receive special unemployment compensation, retraining to develop new skills, and job search and relocation assistance; affected firms can receive technical assistance and loan guarantees to finance their modernization or shift to other product lines, and communities threatened by expanding imports can receive loans and other assistance to attract new industry or to enable existing plants to move into more competitive fields. *See* Steve Charnovitz, "Trade Adjustment Assistance: What Went Wrong?" *The Journal of the Institute for Socioeconomic Studies* (Spring 1984).

Adkins* v. *Children's Hospital, *see* WEST COAST HOTEL V. PARRISH.

administered prices, prices determined by other than market forces such as those set by monopolies, cartels, or governments.

administration, management and direction of the affairs of governments and institutions. Administration can also refer to administrators collectively or to the execution of public policy. For analyses of fifteen different meanings of the word, *see* A. Dunsire, *Administration: The Word and the Science* (New Yorkj: Halsted Press, John Wiley, 1973).

Administration, Irish journal of public administration.
Administration
Institute of Public Administration
57-61 Lansdowne Road
Dublin 4, Ireland

Administration & Society, quarterly that seeks to further the understanding of public and human service organizations, their administrative processes, and their impacts upon the larger society. Most articles are written by academics and government employees.

Administration & Society
Sage Publications, Inc.
275 South Beverly Drive
Beverly Hills, CA 90212

administrative accountability, that aspect of administrative responsibility by which officials are held answerable for general notions of democracy and morality as well as for specific legal mandates. *See* Herbert Finer, "Administrative Responsibility in Democratic Government," *Public Administration Review* (Summer 1941); Arch Dotson, "Fundamental Approaches to Administrative Responsibility," *Western Political Quarterly* (September 1957); Herbert J. Storing, *Responsibility in Government* (New York: Van Nostrand Reinhold, 1969); Charles J. Fox, "Civil Service Reform and Ethical Accountability," *Public Personnel Management* (1981).

See also the following entries:
ACCOUNTABILITY
ADMINISTRATIVE MORALITY
CODE OF ETHICS
ETHICS

administrative advocacy, the recognition that public administration is a highly political process involving severe differences of judgment in which the most feasible course of action is likely to emerge from the competition produced when each group pleads for the cause which it represents, whether that cause be more funds to carry out agency policies, the survival of a program, a particular piece of advice, or the desire for a more efficient system of administrative decision making. *See* Paul Davidoff, "Advocacy and Pluralism in Planning," *Journal of the American Institute of Planners* (December 1965) and Nancy A. Moore, "The Public Administrator as Policy Advocate," *Public Administration Review* (September/October 1978).

administrative agency, a sub-branch of the government set up to carry out the laws. In the context of labor relations, any impartial private or governmental organization that oversees or facilitates the labor relations process.

The contemporary pattern of labor relations in both the public and private sectors relies on administrative agencies to provide ongoing supervision of the collective bargaining process. While generally headed by a board of three to five members, these agencies make rulings on unfair labor practices, on the appropriateness of bargaining units, and sometimes on the proper interpretation of a contract or the legitimacy of a scope of bargaining. They also oversee representation elections and certify the winners as the exclusive bargaining agents for all of the employees in a bargaining unit. The National Labor Relations Board is the prototype of administrative agencies dealing with labor relations. The NLRB model has been adapted to the public sector by the federal government and several states. The equivalent agency for federal employees is the Federal Labor Relations Authority. In the states such agencies are generally called Public Employment Relations Boards (or PERBs). Typically, their functions parallel those of the NLRB, as do the methods by which they are appointed, their terms of office, and their administrative procedures. One important difference in the public sector is that binding arbitration over interests may be used instead of strikes as the final means of resolving disputes. When this is the case, the PERB may have a role in overseeing the use of arbitration and even the substance of the arbitrators' rulings when they raise serious issues about the scope of bargaining or public policy.

administrative analysis, totality of the approaches and techniques that allow an organization to assess its present condition in order to make adjustments that enhance the organization's ability to achieve its goals.

See also SYSTEMS ANALYSIS and STRATEGIC MANAGEMENT.

administrative behavior, human behavior in an organizational context. While *administrative behavior* tends to be used interchangeably with *organizational behavior,* the latter by implication restricts itself to work organizations while the

9

former is rightly concerned with all of the organizations of society. The classic work on this subject is Herbert A. Simon, *Administrative Behavior: A Study of Decision-Making Processes in Administrative Organizations*, 3rd ed. (New York: Macmillan, 1976). *See also* Herbert Kaufman, *The Forest Ranger: A Study in Administrative Behavior* (Baltimore: Johns Hopkins Press, 1960) and Sidney Malick and Edward H. Van Ness, eds., *Concepts and Issues in Administrative Behavior* (Englewood Cliffs, N.J.: Prentice-Hall, 1962).

See also BUREAUCRACY and ORGANIZATIONAL BEHAVIOR.

Administrative Conference of the United States, a permanent independent agency established by the Administrative Conference Act of 1964. The purpose of the Administrative Conference is to develop improvements in the legal procedures by which federal agencies administer regulatory, benefit, and other government programs. As members of the Conference, agency heads, other federal officials, private lawyers, university professors, and other experts in administrative law and government are provided with a forum in which they can conduct continuing studies of selected problems involving administrative procedures and combine their experience and judgment in cooperative efforts toward improving the fairness and effectiveness of such procedures.

Administrative Conference of the
United States
2120 L Street, N.W.
Washington, D.C. 20037
(202) 254-7020

administrative discretion, general principle of administration encompassing a number of points in administrative law; the requirement that the actions of any public official be based upon a specific, legal grant of authority which establishes strict limits on official action. *See* Clark C. Havighurst, ed., *Administrative Discretion: Problems of Decision-Making by Governmental Agencies* (Dobbs Ferry, N.Y.: Oceana Publications, 1974).

administrative due process, term encompassing a number of points in administrative law which require that the administrative procedures of government agencies and regulatory commissions, as they affect private parties, be based upon written guidelines that safeguard individual rights and protect against the arbitrary or inequitable exercise of bureaucratic power. *See* J. S. Fuerst And Roy Petty, "Due Process—How Much is Enough?" *The Public Interest* (Spring 1985).

See also DUE PROCESS.

administrative law, as defined by the man who has written the standard texts on the subject, Kenneth Culp Davis:

Administrative law is the law concerning the powers and procedures of administrative agencies, including especially the law governing judicial review of administrative action. An administrative agency is a governmental authority, other than a court and other than a legislative body, which affects the rights of private parties through either adjudication, rulemaking, investigating, prosecuting, negotiating, settling, or informally acting. An administrative agency may be called a commission, board, authority, bureau, office, officer, administrator, department, corporation, administration, division, or agency. Nothing of substance hinges on the choice of name, and usually the choices have been entirely haphazard. When the President, or a governor, or a municipal governing body exercises powers of adjudication or rulemaking, he or it is to that extent an administrative agency.

See Kenneth Culp Davis, *Administrative Law Text,* 3rd ed. (St. Paul, Minn.: West Publishing Co., 1972). *Also see* Bernard Schwartz and H. W. R. Wade, *Legal Control of Government: Administrative Law in Britain and the United States* (New York: Oxford-Clarendon Press, 1972); Donald P. Rothschild and Charles H. Koch, Jr., *Fundamentals of Administrative Practice and Procedure: Cases and Procedure* (Charlottesville, Va.: Michie Bobbs-Merrill Law Publishing, 1981); Kenneth F.

Warren, *Administrative Law in the American Political System* (St. Paul, Minn.: West Publishing, 1982); Richard C. Cortner, *The Bureaucracy in Court: Commentaries and Case Studies in Administrative Law* (Port Washington, N.Y.: Kennikat Press, 1982); Lief H. Carter, *Administrative Law and Politics: Cases and Comments* (Boston: Little, Brown, 1983); Michael W. Dolan, "Administrative Law and Public Administration," *Public Administration Review* (January/February 1984).

administrative law judge, also called HEARING EXAMINER and HEARING OFFICER, governmental official who conducts hearings in the place of and in behalf of a more formal body, such as the National Labor Relations Board or the Merit Systems Protection Board. *See* Paul N. Pfeiffer, "Hearing Cases Before Several Agencies—Odyssey of an Administrative Law Judge," *Administrative Law Review* (Summer 1975).

administrative morality, use of religious, political, or social precepts to create standards by which the quality of public administration may be judged; in the main, the standards of honesty, responsiveness, efficiency, effectiveness, competence, effect on individual rights, adherence to democratic procedures, and social equity. *See* Paul H. Appleby, *Morality and Administration in American Government* (Louisiana State University Press, 1952); Robert T. Golembiewski, *Men, Management, and Morality: Toward A New Organizational Ethic* (New York: McGraw-Hill, 1965); Dwight Waldo, "Reflections on Public Morality," *Administration and Society* (November 1974); Joel L. Fleishman, Lance Liebman and Mark H. Moore, eds., *Public Duties: The Moral Obligations of Government Officials* (Cambridge, Mass.: Harvard University Press, 1981); Gregory D. Foster, "Legalism, Moralism and the Bureaucratic Mentality," *Public Personnel Management* (1981).

administrative order, a directive carrying the force of law issued by an administrative agency.

administrative planning, totality of deciding what an organization will do, who will do it, and how it will be done.

administrative presidency, Richard Nathan's descriptive term for how Richard M. Nixon sought to use administrative tactics—reorganization, decentralization and impoundment—to assert presidential authority over the federal bureaucracy. *See* Nathan's *The Plot That Failed: Nixon and the Administrative Presidency* (New York: Wiley, 1975) and Nathan's "The Administrative Presidency," *The Public Interest* (Summer 1976).

Administrative Procedure Act of 1946, basic law of how U.S. Government agencies must operate in order to provide adequate safeguards for agency clients and the general public.

administrative process, according to Stephen P. Robbins, *The Administrative Process: Integrating Theory and Practice* (Englewood Cliffs, N.J.: Prentice-Hall, 1976), the "planning, organizing, leading, and evaluating of others so as to achieve a specific end." However, in the context of public administration, the administrative process also involves exercising the formal authority of the state. *See* Louis C. Gawthrop, ed., *The Administrative Process and Democratic Theory* (Boston: Houghton Mifflin Co., 1970).

administrative reform, according to Gerald Caiden, *Administration Reform* (Chicago: Aldine, 1969):

Administrative reform—the artificial inducement of administrative transformation against resistance—has existed ever since men conceived better ways of organizing their social activities. . . . Administrative reform is power politics in action; it contains ideological rationalizations, fights for control of areas, services, and people, political participants and institutions, power drives, campaign strategies and obstructive tactics, compromises and concessions.

See also I. M. Destler, *Presidents, Bureaucrats, and Foreign Policy: The*

Politics of Organizational Reform (Princeton, N.J.: Princeton University Press, 1972); Robert Packoff, "Operationalizing Administrative Reform for Improved Governmental Performance," *Administration and Society* (May 1974); William G. Scott, "Administrative Reform: The Revolutionary Renewal of America," *Public Administration Review* (March/April 1983); Robert Miewald and Michael Steinman, eds., *Problems in Administrative Reform* (Chicago: Nelson-Hall Publishers, 1985).

administrative remedy, a means of enforcing a right by going to an administrative agency either for help or for a decision. People are often required to "exhaust all administrative remedies" by submitting their problems to the proper agency before taking their case to court.

Administrative Science Quarterly, the premier scholarly journal of its kind, dedicated to advancing the understanding of administration through empirical investigation and theoretical analysis. Articles cover all phases of management, human relations, organizational behavior, and organizational communications.
   Administrative Science Quarterly
   Graduate School of Management
   Cornell University
   Malott Hall
   Ithaca, NY 14853

administrative workweek, period of seven consecutive calendar days designated in advance by the head of the agency. Usually an administrative workweek coincides with a calendar week.

administrator, any manager; the head of a government agency; or someone appointed by a court to handle a deceased person's estate.
   See also MANAGEMENT.

admonition, simple reproval of an employee by a supervisor.
   See also REPRIMAND.

ADO, *see* ALLEGED DISCRIMINATORY OFFICIAL.

ad valorem tax, *see* TAX BASE.

advance appropriation, appropriation provided by the Congress for use in a fiscal year or more beyond the fiscal year for which the appropriation act is passed (*e.g.,* the 1976 appropriation for use in fiscal year 1976 for the Washington Metropolitan Area Transit Authority contained in the Department of Transportation and Related Agencies Appropriation Act, 1975, which was passed on August 28, 1974). Advance appropriations allow state and local governments and others sufficient time to develop plans with assurance of future federal funding. An advance appropriation is sometimes mistakenly referred to as "forward funding," which permits an agency to obligate funds in the current year for programs that are to operate in subsequent fiscal years.
   See also ADVANCE FUNDING.

advance funding, budget authority provided in an appropriation act to obligate and disburse funds during a fiscal year from a succeeding year's appropriation. The funds so obligated increase the budget authority for the fiscal year in which obligated, and reduce the budget authority of the succeeding fiscal year. Advance funding is a device for avoiding supplemental requests late in the fiscal year for certain entitlement programs should the appropriations for the current year prove to be too low.
   See also ADVANCE APPROPRIATION.

advance on wages, wages/salaries drawn in advance of work performance or earned commissions. Also applies to payments in advance of the regular pay day for sums already earned.

advances, amounts of money prepaid pursuant to budget authority in contemplation of the later receipt of goods, services, or other assets. Advances are ordinarily made only to payees to whom an agency has an obligation, and not in excess of the amount of the obligation. A common example is travel advances, which are amounts made available to employees prior to the beginning of a trip for costs incurred.

adversary proceeding, a formal hearing with both sides appropriately represented.

adversary system, the American system of law where a judge (or jury) acts as a decision maker between opposite sides. This is in contrast to inquisitorial systems where the prosecutor and the judge are the same person and individuals must exonerate themselves or be condemned.

adverse action, personnel action considered unfavorable to an employee, such as discharge, suspension, demotion, etc.
    See also DISCIPLINARY ACTION.

adverse effect, differential rate of selection (for hire, promotion, etc.) that works to the disadvantage of an applicant subgroup, particularly subgroups classified by race, sex, and other characteristics on the basis of which discrimination is prohibited by law.
    See also WASHINGTON V. DAVIS.

adverse impact, term applied when a selection process for a particular job or group of jobs results in the selection of members of any racial, ethnic, or sex group at a lower rate than for members of other groups; that process is said to have adverse impact. Federal EEO enforcement agencies generally regard a selection rate for any group that is less than four fifths (4/5) or eighty percent of the rate for other groups as constituting evidence of adverse impact. *See* John Klinefelter and James Thompkins, "Adverse Impact in Employment Selection," *Public Personnel Management* (May-June 1976); Irwin Greenberg, "An Analysis of the EEOC 'Four-Fifths' Rule," *Management Science* (August 1979); Gail F. Jones, "Usefulness of Different Statistical Techniques for Determining Adverse Impact in Small Jurisdictions," *Review of Public Personnel Administration* (Fall 1981); Robert J. Haertel, "The Statistical Procedures for Calculating Adverse Impact," *Personnel Administrator* (February 1984).

See also SYSTEMIC DISCRIMINATION and WASHINGTON V. DAVIS.

adverse-inference rule, an analytical tool used by the Equal Employment Opportunity Commission (EEOC) in its investigations. The EEOC holds that when relevant evidence is withheld by an organization and the EEOC feels that there is no valid reason for such a withholding, the EEOC may presume that the evidence in question is adverse to the organization being investigated. The EEOC Compliance Manual permits use of the adverse-inference rule only if "the requested evidence is relevant," the evidence was requested "with ample time to produce it and with notice that failure to produce it would result in an adverse inference," and the "respondent produced neither the evidence nor an acceptable explanation."

advisory arbitration, arbitration that recommends a solution of a dispute but is not binding upon either party.

Advisory Commission on Intergovernmental Relations (ACIR), federal commission created by the Congress in 1959 to monitor the operation of the U.S. federal system and to recommend improvements. The ACIR is a permanent national bipartisan body representing the executive and legislative branches of federal, state, and local government and the public.

The commission is composed of 26 members—nine representing the federal government, fourteen representing state and local government, and three representing the public. The President appoints twenty—three private citizens and three federal executive officials directly and four governors, three state legislators, four mayors, and three elected county officials from slates nominated by the National Governors' Conference, the Council of State Governments, the National League of Cities/U.S. Conference of Mayors, and the National Association of Counties. The three Senators are chosen by the President of the Senate and the three Congressmen by the Speaker of the House. Each Commission member serves a two-year term and may be reappointed.

As a continuing body, the commission approaches its work by addressing itself to specific issues and problems, the resolution of which would produce improved cooperation among the levels of government and more effective functioning of the federal system. In addition to dealing with the all-important functional and structural relationships among the various governments, the ACIR has also extensively studied critical stresses currently being placed on traditional governmental taxing practices. One of the long-range efforts of the commission has been to seek ways to improve federal, state, and local governmental taxing practices and policies to achieve equitable allocation of resources, increased efficiency in collection and administration, and reduced compliance burdens upon the taxpayers. *See* Samuel K. Grove, J. Fred Giertz and James W. Fossett, "ACIR: A Mixed Review," *Publius* (Summer 1984).

ACIR
1111 Twentieth Street, N.W.
Washington, D.C. 20575
(202) 653-5536

Advisory Council on Intergovernmental Personnel Policy (ACIPP), organization created to advise the President on intergovernmental personnel matters. It was established on January 5, 1971 by President Nixon's Executive Order 11607, in accordance with the requirements of the Intergovernmental Personnel Act of 1970 Public Law 91-648. The Council was abolished June 25, 1974 by Executive Order 11792.

advisory opinion, statement by a judge or regulatory agency about a question that has been informally submitted. The U.S. Supreme Court never issues advisory opinions.

advocacy, administrative, *See* AD-MINISTRATIVE ADVOCACY.

AEI, *see* AMERICAN ENTERPRISE INSTITUTE FOR PUBLIC POLICY RESEARCH.

affected class, according to the U.S. Department of Labor's Office of Federal Contract Compliance:

persons who continue to suffer the present effects of past discrimination. An employee or group of employees may be members of an affected class when, because of discrimination based on race, religion, sex, or national origin, such employees, for example, were assigned initially to less desirable or lower paying jobs, were denied equal oportunity to advance to better paying or more desirable jobs, or were subject to layoff or displacement from their jobs.

Employees may continue to be members of an "affected class" even though they may have been transferred or advanced into more desirable positions if the effects of past discrimination have not been remedied. For example, if an employee who was hired into a lower paying job because of past discriminatory practices has been subsequently promoted, further relief may be required if the employee has not found his or her "rightful place" in the employment structure of a federal government contractor.

affidavit, written statement made under oath before a person permitted by law to administer such an oath (*e.g.*, a notary public). Such statements are frequently used in labor arbitration and other formal hearings.

affirmative action, term that first gained currency in the 1960s, when it meant the removal of "artificial barriers" to the employment of women and minority group members. Toward the end of that decade, however, the term got lost in a fog of semantics and came out meaning the provision of compensatory opportunities for hitherto disadvantaged groups. In a formal, legal sense, affirmative action now refers to specific efforts to recruit, hire, and promote disadvantaged groups for the purpose of eliminating the present effects of past discrimination. For an official treatment, *see* U.S. Equal Employment Opportunity Commission, *Affirmative Action and Equal Employment: A Guide-*

book for Employers (Washington, D.C.: U.S. Government Printing Office, 1974). For a hostile critique, see Nathan Glazer, *Affirmative Discrimination: Ethnic Inequality and Public Policy* (New York: Basic Books, 1975). *Also see* Margery M. Milnick, "Equal Employment Opportunity and Affirmative Action: A Managerial Training Guide," *Personnel Journal* (October 1977); Diane P. Jackson, "Affirmative Action for the Handicapped and Veterans: Interpretative and Operational Guidelines," *Labor Law Journal* (February 1978); Carl J. Bellone and Douglas H. Darling, "Implementing Affirmative Action Programs: Problems and Strategies," *Public Personnel Management* (1980); Michael A. Hitt and Barbara W. Keats, "Empirical Identification on the Criteria for Effective Affirmative Action Programs," *The Journal of Applied Behavioral Science*, Vol. 20, No. 3 (1984); Nelson C. Dometrius and Lee Sigelman, "Assessing Progress Toward Affirmative Action Goals in State and Local Government: A New Benchmark," *Public Administration Review* (May-June 1984); David H. Rosenbloom, "The Declining Salience of Affirmative Action in Federal Personnel Management," *Review of Public Personnel Administration* (Summer 1984).

See also the following entries:
DEFUNUS V. ODEGAARD
EQUAL EMPLOYMENT OPPORTUNITY
PHILADELPHIA PLAN
REGENTS OF THE UNIVERSITY OF
   CALIFORNIA V. ALLAN BAKKE
REVERSE DISCRIMINATION
RIGHTFUL PLACE
TITLE VII
TOKENISM
UNITED STEELWORKERS OF AMERICA
   V. WEBER ET AL.
UPWARD-MOBILITY PROGRAM
VOCATIONAL REHABILITATION ACT OF
   1973

Affirmative Action Compliance Manual for Federal Contractors, publication of the Bureau of National Affairs, Inc., which includes a "News and Developments" report, plus the manual used by the Office of Federal Contract Compliance Programs (OFCCP), the OFCCP Construction Compliance Program Operations Manual, and material taken from the official compliance manuals used by the Department of Defense, the Department of the Treasury, the Department of Housing and Urban Development, and the Department of Health and Human Services—with appropriate excerpts from other official compliance manuals.

affirmative action groups, also called PROTECTED GROUPS, segments of the population that have been identified by federal, state, or local laws to be specifically protected from employment discrimination. Such groups include women, identified minorities, the elderly, and the handicapped.

affirmative action officer, individual in an organization who has the primary responsibility for the development, installation, and maintenance of the organization's affirmative action program.

affirmative action plan, an organization's written plan to remedy past discrimination against, or underutilization of, women and minorities. The plan itself usually consists of a statement of goals, timetables for achieving milestones, and specific program efforts.

affirmative action program, formal course of action undertaken by employers to hire and promote women and minorities in order to remedy past abuses or maintain present equity. The most basic tool of an affirmative action program is the affirmative action plan.

affirmative discrimination, see AFFIRMATIVE ACTION.

affirmative order, order issued by the National Labor Relations Board (NLRB) or similar state agency demanding that an employer or union take specific action to cease performing and/or undo the effects of an unfair labor practice. For example, the NLRB might issue an affirmative order to a company to "make whole" a wrongfully discharged employee by reinstating the employee with full back pay and re-establishing the employee's seniority and other rights.

affirmative recruitment, recruiting efforts undertaken to assure that adequate numbers of women and minorities are represented in applicant pools for positions in which they have been historically under-utilized.

affirmative zoning, land use regulations which seek to require the construction of low income housing or other construction of use to the disadvantaged.

AFGE, *see* AMERICAN FEDERATION OF GOVERNMENT EMPLOYEES.

AFL-CIO, *see* AMERICAN FEDERATION OF LABOR-CONGRESS OF INDUSTRIAL ORGANI-ZATIONS.

AFSCME, *see* AMERICAN FEDERATION OF STATE, COUNTY AND MUNICIPAL EMPLOYEES.

age discrimination, disparate or un-favorable treatment of an individual in an employment situation because of age. The Age Discrimination in Employment Act of 1967 makes most age discrimination il-legal, except where a bona fide occupa-tional qualification (BFOQ) is involved. Executive Order 11141 prohibits age dis-crimination in the federal government. *See* W. L. Kendig, *Age Discrimination in Employment* (New York: American Man-agement Associations, 1978); Frank P. Doyle, "Age Discrimination and Organi-zational Life," *Industrial Gerontology* (Summer 1973); Donald P. Schwab and Herbert G. Heneman III, "Age Stereotyp-ing in Performance Appraisal," *Journal of Applied Psychology* (October 1978); James W. Walker and Daniel E. Lupton, "Performance Appraisal Programs and Age Discrimination Law," *Aging and Work* (1978); Paul S. Greenlaw and John P. Kohl, "Age Discrimination in Employment Guidelines," *Personnel Journal* (March 1982); Robert H. Faley, Lawrence S. Kleiman and Mark L. Lengnick-Hall, "Age

Discrimination and Personnel Psychology: A Review and Synthesis of the Legal Literature with Implications for Future Re-search," *Personnel Psychology* (Summer 1984).

Age Discrimination in Employment Act of 1967 (ADEA), as amended, prohibits discrimination on the basis of age against any person between the ages of forty and seventy. There is no upper age limit with respect to employment in the federal gov-ernment. The law applies to all public employers, private employers of twenty or more employees, employment agencies serving covered employers, and labor unions of more than twenty-five members. Employers may not fail or refuse to hire, discharge, or otherwise discriminate against any individual with respect to com-pensation or terms or conditions of em-ployment because of age. Employment agencies may not fail or refuse to refer an individual because of age, and labor unions may not exclude or expel a person because of age, or otherwise discriminate regarding terms or conditions of employ-ment. The ADEA prohibits help wanted advertisements which indicate preference, limitation, specification or discrimination based on age. For example, terms such as "girl" and "35-55" may not be used be-cause they indicate the exclusion of quali-fied applicants based on age. The law does not prohibit discharge or discipline of an employee for good cause.

The ADEA does not cover situations in which age is a bona fide occupational qualification, such as modeling "junior miss" fashions; differences which are based on reasonable factors other than age, such as the use of physical examinations where heavy physical demands are made upon the worker; registered apprenticeship pro-grams; and differences based on bona fide seniority systems or employee benefit plans such as retirement, pension, or in-surance plans. However, the act prohibits using employee benefit plans as a basis for refusing to hire older applicants or retiring older employees. The law does not per-mit the involuntary retirement of workers under age seventy, except for certain senior executive and high-level policy-making employees.

In addition to the federal law, many states have age discrimination laws or provisions in their fair employment practices law that prohibit discrimination based on age. Some of these laws have no upper limit in protections against age discrimination in employment, others protect workers until they reach sixty, sixty-five, or seventy years of age. *See* Cynthia E. Gitt, "The 1978 Amendments to the Age Discrimination in Employment Act—A Legal Overview," *Marquette Law Review* (Summer 1981); Michael H. Schuster and Christopher S. Miller, "Performance Appraisal and the Age Discrimination in Employment Act," *Personnel Administrator* (March 1984); Michael Schuster and Christopher S. Miller, "An Empirical Assessment of the Age Discrimination in Employment Act," *Industrial and Labor Relations Review* (October 1984).

See also the following entries:
EQUAL EMPLOYMENT OPPORTUNITY COMMISSION V. WYOMING
OSCAR MAYER & CO. V. EVANS
RETIREMENT AGE
UNITED AIRLINES V. MCMANN

ageism, in the tradition of racism and sexism, ageism is discrimination against those who are considered old.

agency, any department, office, commission, authority, administration, board, government-owned corporation, or other independent establishment of any branch of government in the United States.

agency, employment, *see* EMPLOYMENT AGENCY.

agency and private trust transactions, receipt, holding, and disbursement of moneys by a government as agent or trustee for other governments or private persons, such as collection of local government taxes, collection of federal income taxes and social security "taxes," receipt and return of guarantee deposits, and the like.

Agency for International Development (AID), unit of the U.S. International Development Cooperation Agency that carries out assistance programs designed to help the people of certain less developed countries develop their human and economic resources, increase productive capacities, and improve the quality of life. AID was a part of the U.S. Department of State until 1979.

AID
320 21st Street, N.W.
Washington, D.C. 20523
(202) 655-4000

agency missions, responsibilities assigned to a specific agency. Agency missions are expressed in terms of the purpose to be served by the programs authorized to carry out functions or subfunctions which, by law, are the responsibility of that agency and its component organizations.

agency shop, union security provision, found in some collective bargaining agreements, which requires that non-union employees of the bargaining unit must pay the union a sum equal to union dues as a condition of continuing employment. The agency shop was designed as a compromise between the union's desire to eliminate "free riders" by means of compulsory membership and management's wish that union membership be voluntary. Its constitutionality was upheld by the U.S. Supreme Court in *Abood* v. *Detroit Board of Education*. For legal analyses, *see* Norman E. Jones, "Agency Shop," *Labor Law Journal* (November 1959); Raymond N. Palombo, "The Agency Shop in a Public Service Merit System," *Labor Law Journal* (July 1975).

See also ABOOD V. DETROIT BOARD OF EDUCATION, ELLIS V. BROTHERHOOD OF RAILWAY CLERKS, and NATIONAL LABOR RELATIONS BOARD V. GENERAL MOTORS.

agent, person who is formally designated to act on behalf of either an employer or a union.
See also BARGAINING AGENT and BUSINESS AGENT.

Age of Scarcity, period in U.S. history that began in the mid-1970s and was characterized by very slow economic growth, small increases in national productivity, and marginal gains in per capita income. Prior to this time, tensions between political equality and economic inequality had been dealt with by rapid growth where nearly everyone's share of the nation's resources increased. Societal tensions increased since political disputes had to be resolved by redistributing income from one group to another. One form of reaction to the Age of Scarcity was the passage of referendum Proposition 13 (also known as the Jarvis-Gann Amendment) in California during 1978. Proposition 13 became a symbol of the nation's tax revolt against big government, inflation, and erosion of personal income in the late 1970s. *See* William Ophus, *Ecology and the Politics of Scarcity* (San Francisco: Freeman, 1977) and Richard J. Barnet, *The Lean Years: Politics in the Age of Security* (New York: Simon and Schuster, 1980).

aggregate cost method, also called AGGREGATE METHOD, projected funding technique that computes pension benefits and costs for an entire plan rather than for its individual participants.

AGPA, *see* AMERICAN GROUP PSYCHOTHERAPY ASSOCIATION.

agreement, *see* the following entries:
  BLANKET AGREEMENT
  FAIR-SHARE AGREEMENT
  GENTLEMEN'S AGREEMENT
  INDEX OF AGREEMENT
  INDIVIDUAL AGREEMENT
  INTERIM AGREEMENT
  LABOR AGREEMENT
  MASTER AGREEMENT
  MODEL AGREEMENT
  OPEN-END AGREEMENT
  SWEETHEART AGREEMENT

Agriculture, Department of (USDA), department of U.S. government that works to improve and maintain farm income, to develop and expand markets abroad for agricultural products, to en-

hance the environment, and to maintain our production capacity by helping landowners protect the soil, water, forests, and other natural resources. The department, through inspection and grading services, safeguards and assures standards of quality in the daily food supply.
  U.S. Department of Agriculture
  14th St. & Independence Avenue, S.W.
  Washington, D.C. 20250
  (202) 447-2791

AID, *see* AGENCY FOR INTERNATIONAL DEVELOPMENT.

AIM, *see* AMERICAN INSTITUTE OF MANAGEMENT.

air pollution, presence of contaminant substances or particulates in the atmosphere that do not disperse properly and that interfere with human, animal or plant life.

air quality control region, geographic area designated by a common air pollution situation.

air quality standards, levels measured by the amount of pollutants in the air prescribed by law or regulation that can not be exceeded in a defined area over a specific period of time. *Primary standards* are numerical levels of air pollution required to protect the public health. *Secondary standards* are numerical levels that would protect the public welfare and include effects on all geographic, social, and economic aspects.

Air Traffic Controllers Strike, strike of the Professional Air Traffic Controllers Organization (PATCO) in 1981 that resulted in the complete destruction of the union and the dismissal of eleven thousand air traffic controllers. On July 29, 1981, 95 percent of PATCO's thirteen thousand members voted to reject the government's final offer. As one striking controller put it: "Where are they going to get thirteen thousand controllers and train them before the economy sinks? The reality is, we are it.

They have to deal with us." The government was equally determined in its resolve to keep the planes flying. First it cut back scheduled flights and reduced staff at smaller airports. Then it brought supervisors and retired controllers back to service and ordered military controllers to civilian stations. Finally, President Reagan addressed the nation on television. After reminding viewers that it is illegal for federal government employees to strike and that each controller signed an oath asserting that he or she would never strike, he proclaimed: "They are in violation of the law, and if they do not report for work within forty-eight hours, they have forfeited their jobs and will be terminated." Just over one thousand controllers reported back. Most thought that the president was bluffing, but he wasn't. Over eleven thousand former controllers received formal letters of dismissal. The union's assets were frozen by the courts, some PATCO leaders were literally hauled away to jail in chains, and the Department of Transportation started formal proceedings to decertify the union. In late October the Federal Labor Relations Authority formally decertified PATCO—the first time that it had ever done so to any union of government workers. In December PATCO filed for bankruptcy. In the end over eleven thousand controllers who stayed on strike lost their jobs permanently. See David B. Bowers, "What Would Make 11,500 People Quit Their Jobs?" *Organizational Dynamics* (Winter 1983); Herbert R. Northrup, "The Rise and Demise of PATCO," *Industrial and Labor Relations Review* (January 1984).

AJPA, see AUSTRALIAN JOURNAL OF PUBLIC ADMINISTRATION.

Alabama Power Company v. Davis, 431 U.S. 581 (1977), U.S. Supreme Court case which held that employers who rehire a returning veteran are required to credit the employee's military service toward the calculation of pension benefits. A unanimous court concluded that "pension payments are predominantly rewards for continuous employment with the same employer," rather than deferred compensation for services rendered. Thus, the purpose of Section 9 of the Selective Service Act, as explained by Justice Thurgood Marshall for the Court, is to protect veterans "from the loss of such rewards when the break in their employment resulted from their response to the country's military needs."

Albemarle Paper Co. v. *Moody,* 422 U.S. 405 (1975), U.S. Supreme Court case that established the principle that once discrimination has been proven in a Title VII (of the Civil Rights Act of 1964) case, the trial judge ordinarily does not have discretion to deny back pay. For analyses, see William H. Warren, "*Albemarle* v. *Moody:* Where It All Began," *Labor Law Journal* (October 1976); Thaddeus Holt, "A View from Albemarle," *Personnel Psychology* (Spring 1977); James Ledvinka and Lyle F. Schoenfeldt, "Legal Developments in Employment Testing: Albemarle and Beyond," *Personnel Psychology* (Spring 1978).

alcoholism, detrimental dependency on alcoholic beverages. It was only in 1956 that the American Medical Association first recognized alcoholism as a disease. However, it is still not universally recognized as such. Almost all large organizations have some program to deal with alcoholic employees. For a comprehensive reference on employee alcoholism, see Joseph F. Follman, Jr., *Alcoholics and Business: Problems, Costs, Solutions* (New York: Amacom, 1976). Also see Marilyn C. Regier, *Social Policy in Action: Perspectives on the Implementation of Alcoholism Reforms* (Lexington, Mass.: Lexington Books, 1979); Tia Schneider Denenberg and R. V. Denenberg. *Alcohol and Drugs: Issues in the Workplace* (Washington: The Bureau of National Affairs, Inc., 1983); Robert O'Brien and Dr. Morris Chafetz, eds., *The Encyclopedia of Alcoholism* (New York: Facts on File, 1983); Joseph Madonia, "Managerial Responses to Alcohol and Drug Abuse Among Employees," *Personnel Administrator* (June 1984); Tim Bornstein,

"Drug and Alcohol Issues in the Workplace: An Arbitrator's Perspective," *Arbitration Journal* (September 1984).

alderman, title for some members of local legislatures.

Alexander v. *Gardner-Denver Company,* 415 U.S. 36 (1974), U.S. Supreme Court case that held the prior submission of a claim to arbitration under the nondiscrimination clause of a collective bargaining agreement does not foreclose an employee from subsequently exercising his right to a trial *de novo* under Title VII of the Civil Rights Act of 1964. For analyses, *see* Gary R. Siniscalco, "Effect of the Gardner-Denver Case on Title VII Disputes," *Monthly Labor Review* (March 1975); Sanford Cohen and Christian Eaby, "The Gardner-Denver Decision and Labor Arbitration," *Labor Law Journal* (January 1976); M. M. Hoyman and L. E. Stallworth, "Arbitrating Discrimination Cases After *Gardner-Denver,*" *Monthly Labor Review* (October 1983); Karen Elwell and Peter Feuille, "Arbitration Awards and *Gardner-Denver* Lawsuits: One Bite or Two?" *Industrial Relations* (Spring 1984); Michele Hoyman and Lamont E. Stallworth, "The Arbitration of Discrimination Grievances in the Aftermath of *Gardner-Denver,*" *Arbitration Journal* (September 1984); Aubrey R. Fowler, Jr., "Arbitration, the Trilogy, and Individual Rights: Developments Since *Alexander* v. *Gardner-Denver,*" *Labor Law Journal* (March 1985).

alienation, a concept originally from Marxism which held that industrial workers would experience feelings of disassociation because they lacked control of their work (and would thus be ripe for revolution). The word has lost its Marxist taint and now refers to any feelings of estrangement from one's work, family, society, etc. *See* Michael P. Smith, "Alienation and Bureaucracy: The Role of Participatory Administration," *Public Administration Review* (November/December 1971); Robert P. Vecchio, "Worker Alienation as a Moderator of the Job Quality-Job

Satisfaction Relationship: The Case of Racial Differences," *Academy of Management Journal* (September 1980); John F. Witte, *Democracy, Authority, and Alienation in Work* (University of Chicago Press, 1980); Abraham K. Korman, Ursula Wittig-Berman and Dorothy Lang, "Career Success and Personal Failure: Alienation in Professionals and Managers," *Academy of Management Journal* (June 1981); Beverly H. Burris, *No Room at the Top: Underemployment and Alienation in the Corporation* (New York: Praeger Publishers, 1983).

aliens, *see* the following entries:
AMBACH V. NORWICK
CITIZENSHIP, U.S.
ESPINOZA V. FARAH MANUFACTUR-
ING COMPANY
EXAMINING BOARD V. FLORES DeOTERO
FOLEY V. CONNELIE
HAMPTON V. MOW SUN WONG
SUGARMAN V. DOUGALL

Alien Registration Act of 1940, also called the SMITH ACT, U.S. law that requires the annual registration of aliens. It also prohibits advocating the violent overthrow of the U.S. government.

alleged discriminatory official (ADO), individual charged in a formal equal employment opportunity complaint with having caused or tolerated discriminatory actions. For an analysis of the due process procedures to which ADOs are entitled, *see* Glenn E. Schweitzer, "The Rights of Federal Employees Named as Alleged Discriminatory Officials," *Public Administration Review* (January-February 1977).
See also Bush v. *Lucas.*

Allied Chemical Workers v. *Pittsburgh Plate Glass Co.,* 404 U.S. 157 (1971), case in which the U.S. Supreme Court held that unions have no right to bargain over retirees' benefits because retired persons are neither employees nor members of a bargaining unit.

allied health personnel, specially trained

and licensed (when necessary) health workers other than physicians, dentists, podiatrists and nurses. The term has no constant or agreed-upon detailed meaning, sometimes being used synonymously with paramedical personnel; sometimes meaning all health workers who perform tasks which must otherwise be performed by a physician; and sometimes referring to health workers who do not usually engage in independent practice.

Allis-Chalmers decision, see NATIONAL LABOR RELATIONS BOARD V. ALLIS-CHALMERS.

Allison, Graham T., Jr. (1940-   ), author of a classic study of government policymaking, *Essence of Decision: Explaining the Cuban Missile Crisis* (Boston: Little, Brown, 1971), which demonstrated the inadequacies of the view that the decisions of a government are made by a "single calculating decisionmaker" who has control over the organizations and officials within his government. Allison's book is an expansion of his "Conceptual Models and the Cuban Missile Crisis," *American Political Science Review* (September 1969). *See also Remaking Foreign Policy: The Organizational Connection*, with Peter Szanton (New York: Basic Books, 1976).

allocate, also REALLOCATE, to assign a position or class to a particular salary grade in the salary schedule, based on an evaluation of its relative worth. To reallocate is to change the existing allocation of a position or class to a different salary grade in the schedule.

allocation, for purposes of government accounting, the amount of obligational authority transferred from one agency, bureau, or account that is set aside in a transfer appropriation account to carry out the purposes of the parent appropriation or fund. (The account to which the appropriation is made is called the parent account.) For example, allocations are made when one or more agencies share the administration of a program for which ap-

propriations are made to only one of the agencies or to the president.

allocation formula, quantitative formula by which grant funds are distributed to eligible recipients. Usually it is specified in legislation, but sometimes is provided by regulations.

allotment, system by which departments control spending by lower units; a legal authorization to incur expenditures for a given amount of money for a specific purpose made on a monthly or quarterly basis.

allowable charge, generic term referring to the maximum fee that a third party will use in reimbursing a provider for a given service. An allowable charge may not be the same as either a reasonable, customary, or prevailing charge as the terms are used under the Medicare program.

allowance, financial payment to compensate an employee for the extra expense of living at a hardship post, for special clothing such as uniforms, or for some other benefit that personnel policy allows. *See also* the following entries:

CLOTHING ALLOWANCE
COST-OF-LIVING ALLOWANCE
FAMILY ALLOWANCE
FATIGUE ALLOWANCE
HARDSHIP ALLOWANCE
HOUSING ALLOWANCE
MILEAGE ALLOWANCE
RELOCATION ALLOWANCE
SUBSISTENCE ALLOWANCE

allowances, amounts included in a budget request or projection to cover possible additional proposals, such as statutory pay increases and contingencies for relatively uncontrollable programs and other requirements. As used by Congress in the concurrent resolutions on the budget, allowances represent a special functional classification designed to include amounts to cover possible requirements, such as civilian pay raises and contingencies. Allowances remain undistributed until they occur or become firm, then they are distributed to the appropriate functional classification(s).

See also CONTROLLABILITY.

allowed time, also called NORMAL TIME, time given an employee to perform a task. Normally includes an allowance for fatigue and personal and/or unavoidable delays.

alphabetism, discrimination against those whose names begin with letters at the end of the alphabet.

alternate form, also called EQUIVALENT FORM or COMPARABLE FORM, any of two or more versions of a test that are the same with respect to the nature, number, and difficulty of the test items and that are designed to yield essentially the same scores and measures of variability for a given group.

alternate-form reliability, measure of the extent to which two parallel or equivalent forms of a test are consistent in measuring what they purport to measure.

alternation ranking, technique used in job evaluation and performance appraisal that ranks the highest and the lowest, then the next highest and the next lowest, etc., until all jobs have been ranked.

alternative costs, *see* OPPORTUNITY COST.

alternative technology, *see* APPROPRIATE TECHNOLOGY.

AMACOM, *see* AMERICAN MANAGEMENT ASSOCIATIONS.

Amalgamated Association of Street, Electric Railway, and Motor Coach Employees of America **v.** *Lockridge,* 403 U.S. 274 (1971), case in which the U.S. Supreme Court held that a complaint from a union member that his union had wrongfully interfered with his employment (he was suspended from his union because of dues arrearage) was a matter within the exclusive jurisdiction of the National Labor Relations Board.

Ambach **v.** *Norwick,* 441 U.S. 68 (1979), U.S. Supreme Court decision which held that barring aliens from permanent certification as public school teachers did not violate the 14th Amendment's equal protection clause. The ruling upheld the New York Education Law's citizenship requirement for public (but not private) school teachers.

See also the following entries:
    CITIZENSHIP, U.S.
    FOLEY V. CONNELIE
    HAMPTON V. MOW SUN WONG
    SUGARMAN V. DOUGALL

American Academy of Political and Social Science, nonprofit organization formed in 1889 to promote the progress of political and social science, especially through publications and meetings.
    American Academy of Political and
      Social Science
    3937 Chestnut Street
    Philadelphia, PA 19104
    (215) 386-4594

American Arbitration Association, (AAA), formed in 1926, a public service, nonprofit organization dedicated to the resolution of disputes of all kinds through the use of arbitration, mediation, democratic election and other voluntary methods. The AAA does not act as arbitrator. Its function is to submit to parties selected lists from which disputants may make their own choices and to provide impartial administration of arbitration. The association's National Panel of Arbitrators consists of some forty thousand men and women, each an expert in some field or profession, who have been nominated for their knowledge and reputation for impartiality. In nonlabor cases, these arbitrators serve without compensation except under unusual circumstances. They offer their time and skill as a public service. AAA's panels also include impartial experts in labor-management relations for arbitrating disputes arising out of the application and interpretation of collective bargaining agreements.

The AAA's access to impartial experts, its reputation for impartiality, and its experience in dispute-settling techniques of all kinds are put at the disposal of the public in ways other than the administration of arbitrations. Its Community Dispute Services division applies the techniques of arbitration, mediation, and factfinding to the solution of conflicts of all kinds in urban areas. AAA's Election Department conducts impartial polls to choose union officers, to determine the appropriate representatives for school teachers, to select committee members in local anti-poverty programs, and for many other purposes.

The AAA is the most important single center of information, education and research on arbitration. Among the association's periodicals are three monthly publications summarizing labor arbitration awards in private industry, in schools, and in other agencies of government; a monthly news bulletin for members and arbitrators; a quarterly journal, *The Arbitration Journal*, containing reports of arbitration court cases and authoritative articles on arbitration; a bimonthly report of no fault automobile arbitration awards; a quarterly law letter on arbitration; various specialized pamphlets on arbitration practice and procedure; and outlines for teaching labor-management arbitration and arbitration law courses. The AAA's library serves other educational institutions as a clearinghouse of information and answers the research inquiries of AAA members and of students.

Although headquartered in New York, the AAA has regional offices throughout the United States. For further information, *see* Robert Coulson, *Labor Arbitration — What You Need To Know*, 2nd ed. (New York: American Arbitration Association, 1978).

American Arbitration Association
140 West 51st Street
New York, NY 10020
(212) 484-4000
See also NATIONAL ACADEMY OF ARBITRATORS.

American Assembly of Collegiate Schools of Business (AACSB), an organization of institutions devoted to higher education for business and administration, formally established in 1916. Its membership has grown to encompass not only educational institutions but business, government, and professional organizations as well, all seeking to improve and promote higher education for business and working to solve problems of mutual concern. Through its accrediting function, the AACSB provides guidelines to educational institutions in program, resource, and faculty planning. The Accreditation Council of AACSB is recognized by the Council on Postsecondary Accreditation and by the U.S. Department of Education, as the sole accrediting agency for bachelors and masters programs in business administration.

AACSB
605 Old Ballas Road
Suite 220
St. Louis, MS 63141
(314) 872-8481

1755 Massachusetts Avenue, N.W.
Suite 320
Washington, D.C. 20036
(202) 483-0400

American Association for Counseling and Development, a professional association of forty thousand members concerned with personnel and guidance work at all educational levels from kindergarten through higher education, in community agencies, correction agencies, rehabilitation programs, government, business/industry, and research facilities. Formerly (until 1983) the American Personnel and Guidance Association.

American Association for Counseling
    and Development
5999 Stevenson Ave.
Alexandria, VA 22304
(703) 823-9800

American Center for Quality of Work Life, organization that promotes greater work force involvement in quality of work and safety issues through training and research.

American Center for Quality of Work
Life
1411 K Street, N.W., Suite 930
Washington, D.C. 20005
(202) 338-2933

American City and County, trade
magazine (formerly *American City*) for
municipal managers.
American City and County
Morgan-Grampian, Inc.
Berkshire Common
Pittsfield, MA 01201

**American Enterprise Institute for Public
Policy Research (AEI),** independent,
nonprofit, nonpartisan research and
educational organization whose basic purpose is to promote the competition of
ideas. AEI, which tends to favor deregulation, decentralization, and a market
economy, provided the Reagan administration with a fair share of both ideas and
advisors.
AEI
1150 17th Street, N.E.
Washington, D.C. 20036
(202) 862-5800

**American Federation of Government
Employees (AFGE),** the largest union of
federal government employees. Founded
in 1932 it has grown to 700,000 members
in 1,380 locals around the world.
AFGE
1325 Massachusetts Ave., N.W.
Washington, D.C. 20005
(202) 737-8700

*American Federation of Government
Employees* v. *Phillips,* 358 F. Supp. 60
(1973), U.S. district court case that reaffirmed the constitutional principle that the
president does not have discretionary
power to execute the laws, with special
reference to the impoundment of congressionally appropriated funds.

American Federation of Labor (AFL),
organized in 1881 as a federation of craft
unions, the Federation of Organized Trade
and Labor Unions, it changed its name to
the American Federation of Labor in 1886

after merging with those craft unions that
had become disenchanted with the Knights
of Labor. In 1955, the AFL merged with
the Congress of Industrial Organizations to
become the AFL-CIO (*see* AMERICAN
FEDERATION OF LABOR-CONGRESS OF IN-
DUSTRIAL ORGANIZATIONS).

**American Federation of Labor-
Congress of Industrial Organizations**
(AFL-CIO), a voluntary federation of over
100 national and international unions
operating in the United States. The AFL-
CIO is not itself a union; it does no bargaining. It is perhaps best thought of as a
union of unions. The affiliated unions
created the AFL-CIO to represent them
in the creation and execution of broad national and international policies and in
coordinating a wide range of joint activities.
Each member union of the AFL-CIO
remains autonomous, conducting its own
affairs in the manner determined by its own
members. Each has its own headquarters,
officers, and staff. Each decides its own
economic policies, carries on its own contract negotiations, sets its own dues and
provides its own membership services.
Each of the affiliated unions is free to withdraw at any time. But through its voluntary participation, it plays a role in
establishing overall policies for the U.S.
labor movement, which in turn advance
the interests of *every* union.
The AFL-CIO serves its constituent
unions by:
1. Speaking for the whole labor move-
    ment before Congress and other
    branches of government.
2. Representing U.S. labor in world af-
    fairs, through its participation in
    international labor bodies and
    through direct contact with the cen-
    tral labor organizations of free coun-
    tries throughout the world.
3. Helping to organize the unorganized
    workers of the United States.
4. Coordinating such activities as com-
    munity services, political education
    and voter registration for greater
    effectiveness.
While retaining control over their own
affairs, member unions have ceded a

degree of authority to the AFL-CIO in certain matters. These include:

1. *Ethical practices.* Every affiliated union must comply with the AFL-CIO Ethical Practices Codes, which establish basic standards of union democracy and financial integrity.
2. *Totalitarian domination.* No union controlled by Communists, fascists or other totalitarians can remain in the AFL-CIO.
3. *Internal disputes.* Each union has agreed to submit certain types of disputes with other affiliated unions to the mediating and judicial processes of the AFL-CIO.

AFL-CIO
815 16th Street, N.W.
Washington, D.C. 20006
(202) 637-5000

American Federation of Labor v. National Labor Relations Board, 308 U S 401 (1940), U.S. Supreme Court case which held that the National Labor Relations Board under Section 9 (d) of the National Labor Relations (Wagner) Act of 1935 had the discretion to determine appropriate bargaining units and that such a certification is not subject to review by federal appellate courts.

American Federation of Labor v. Swing, 312 U.S. 321 (1941), U.S. Supreme Court case which held that stranger picketing is lawful. Justice Felix Frankfurter wrote that "a State cannot exclude working men from peacefully exercising the right of free communication by drawing the circle of economic competition between employers and workers so small as to contain only an employer and those directly employed by him."

American Federation of Musicians v. Wittstein, 379 U.S. 171 (1964), U.S. Supreme Court case, which held that Section 101 (a) (3) (B) of the Labor-Management Reporting and Disclosure (Landrum-Griffin) Act of 1959 permits a weighted-voting system under which delegates cast a number of votes equal to the membership of their local union.

American Federation of State, County and Municipal Employees (AFSCME), the largest union of state and local government employees. Founded in 1936 it has grown to 1,200,000 members in 3,000 locals.
AFSCME
1625 L Street, N.W.
Washington, D.C. 20036
(202) 452-4800

American Group Psychotherapy Association (AGPA), professional association organized in 1942 to provide a forum for the exchange of ideas among qualified professional persons interested in group psychotherapy; to publish and to make publication available on all subjects relating to group psychotherapy; to encourage the development of sound training programs in group psychotherapy for qualified mental health professionals; to establish and maintain high standards of ethical, professional group psychotherapy practice; and to encourage and promote research in group psychotherapy.
American Group Psychotherapy Association
1995 Broadway
New York, NY 10023
(212) 787-2618

American Institute of Management (AIM), founded in 1948 to conduct studies in management research and to enhance the development of the managerial sciences as an educational discipline, AIM serves as a professional association for managers. Its purpose is to improve management thinking, practices, performance, and results through pertinent comments, studies, meetings, and publications that contribute to managerial knowledge, skill, and theory.
American Institute of Management
45 Willard Street
Quincy, MA 02169
(617) 472-0277

American Journal of Public Health, official monthly journal of the American Public Health Association that is concerned with both health policy and administration. *American Journal of Public Health*

1015 Eighteenth Street, N.W.
Washington, D.C. 20036

American Management Associations (AMA), with over eighty-five thousand members, the largest organization for professional managers. AMA programs operate principally through its divisions: Finance, General Management, Information Systems and Technology, Insurance and Employee Benefits, Manufacturing, Marketing, Management Systems, Research and Development, Human Resources, Packaging, International Management, Purchasing, Transportation and Physical Distribution, and General Administrative Services. AMACOM is its in-house publishing division.

American Management Associations
135 West 50th Street
New York, NY 10020
(212) 586-8100

American Municipal Association, *see* NATIONAL LEAGUE OF CITIES.

American Newspaper Publishers Association v. National Labor Relations Board, 345 U.S. 100 (1953), U.S. Supreme Court case in which it was held that requiring employers to pay printers for setting "bogus" type was not an unfair labor practice on the part of the union under Section 8(b) (6) of the National Labor Relations Act. The court said that Section 8(b) (6) "condemned only the exactment by a union of pay from an employer in return for services not performed and not to be performed, but not the exactment of pay for work done by an employee with the employer's consent."
See also FEATHERBEDDING.

American Personnel and Guidance Association, *see* AMERICAN ASSOCIATION FOR COUNSELING AND DEVELOPMENT.

American Planning Association (APA), professional association of planning agency officials, professional planners, and planning educators formed in 1978 through a merger of the American Institute of Planners and the American Society of Planning Officials.

APA
1313 East 60th Street
Chicago, IL 60637
(312) 955-9100

American Political Science Association (APSA), leading academic organization for American political scientists.

APSA
1527 New Hampshire Avenue, N.W.
Washington, D.C. 20036
(202) 483-2512

American Political Science Review (APSR), quarterly published by the American Political Science Association. The *Review* is the most prestigious of the academic political science journals.

APSR
1527 New Hampshire Avenue, N.W.
Washington, D.C. 20036

American Productivity Center, Inc., created in 1977, a privately funded, nonprofit organization dedicated to strengthening the free enterprise system by developing practical programs to improve productivity and the quality of working life in the United States.

American Productivity Center, Inc.
123 North Post Oak Lane
Houston, TX 77024
(713) 681-4020

American Psychological Association (APA), founded in 1892 and incorporated in 1925, the major psychological organization in the United States. With more than fifty-eight thousand members, it includes most of the qualified psychologists in the country.

The purpose of the APA is to advance psychology as a science and a profession and as a means of promoting human welfare by the encouragement of psychology in all its branches in the broadest and most liberal manner. It does so by the promotion of research in psychology and the improvement of research methods and conditions; by the continual improvement of the qualifications and competence of psychologists through high standards of ethical conduct, education, and achievement; and by the dissemination of psychological knowledge through meetings, psychological journals, and special reports.

American Psychological Association
1200 Seventeenth Street, N.W.
Washington, D.C. 20036
(202) 955-7600

American Public Welfare Association (APWA), professional association of welfare agencies and administrators.

APWA
1125 15th Street, N.W.
Washington, D.C. 20036
(202) 293-7550

American Public Works Association (APWA), professional association for city engineers and others involved in the construction, management or maintenance of public works.

APWA
1313 E. 60th Street
Chicago, IL 60637
(312) 667-2200

American Review of Public Administration (ARPA), quarterly, formerly (until 1981) *Midwest Review of Public Administration,* which is "devoted to fostering a dialogue between the theoretician and the practitioner of public administration."

ARPA
Park College
Parkville, MO 64152

American Shipbuilding Co. v. National Labor Relations Board, 380 U.S. 300 (1965), U.S. Supreme Court case which held that an employer, in the face of a bargaining impasse, could temporarily shut down his plant and lay off his employees for the sole purpose of bringing pressure to bear in support of his bargaining position.

See also LOCKOUT.

American Society for Personnel Administration (ASPA), a nonprofit professional association of personnel and industrial relations managers. Founded in 1948, ASPA today serves over thirty-three thousand members with 380 chapters in the United States and thirty-seven other countries. It is the largest professional association devoted exclusively to human resource management.

ASPA's purpose is (1) to provide assistance for the professional development of members, (2) to provide international leadership in establishing and supporting standards of excellence in human resource management, (3) to provide the impetus for research to improve management techniques, (4) to serve as a focal point for the exchange of authoritative information, and (5) to publicize the human resource management field to create a better understanding of its functions and importance.

American Society for Personnel
    Administration
606 N. Washington Street
Alexandria, VA 22314
(703) 548-3440

American Society for Public Administration (ASPA), a nationwide, nonprofit educational and professional organization dedicated to improved management in the public service through exchange, development, and dissemination of information about public administration. ASPA has over seventeen thousand members and subscribers representative of all governmental levels, program responsibilities, and administrative interests. Its membership includes government administrators, teachers, researchers, consultants, students and civic leaders. Since its inception in 1939, ASPA has provided national leadership in advancing the "science, processes, and art" of public administration. It is the only organization of its kind in the U.S. aiming broadly to improve administration of the public service at all levels of government and in all functional and program fields. Society members are located in every state as well as overseas. Many activities are carried out through more than 117 chapters in major governmental and educational centers. The ASPA program includes publications, meetings, education, research, and various special services, all aimed at improved understanding and strengthened administration of the public service.

ASPA has the following membership sections:

Conference on Minority Public Administrators Section

National Young Professionals Forum

Section on Budgeting and Financial Management

Section on Criminal Justice Administration

Section on Government and Business

Section on Human Resources Administration

Section on Intergovernmental Administration and Management

Section on International and Comparative Administration

Section on Management Science and Policy Analysis

Section on National Security and Defense Administration

Section on Natural Resources and Environmental Administration

Section on Personnel Administration and Labor Relations

Section for Professional Development

Section on Public Administration Education

Section on Science and Technology in Government

Section for Women in Public Administration

For a history, see Donald C. Stone, "Birth of ASPA—A Collective Effort in Institution Building," *Public Administration Review* (January/February 1975).

American Society for Public Administration
1120 G Street, N.W.
Washington, D.C. 20005
(202) 393-7878

American Society for Training and Development (ASTD), national professional society of twenty-two thousand persons with training and development responsibilities in business, industry, government, public service organizations, and educational institutions. Founded in 1944, ASTD is the only organization devoted exclusively to the comprehensive education, development, and expansion of the skills and standards of professionals in training and human resource development. Formerly (until 1964) the American Society of Training Directors.

American Society for Training and Development
P.O. Box 5307
Madison, WI 53705
(608) 274-3440

American Steel Foundries* v. *Tri-City Central Trades Council, 257 U.S. 184 (1921), U.S. Supreme Court case which held that the rights of pickets are restricted to "observation, communication and persuasion"; and required that strikebreakers be given "clear passage."

amicus curiae, literally, "friend of the court"; any person or organization allowed to participate in a lawsuit who would not otherwise have a right to do so. Participation is usually limited to filing a brief on behalf of one side or the other. *See* Samuel Krislov, "The *Amicus Curiae* Brief: From Friendship to Advocacy," *Yale Law Journal* (March 1963).

amortization, gradual reduction of the principal of a loan, together with payment of interest, according to a known schedule of payments at regular intervals. By the end of the life of a loan, its principal balance will be fully paid off, in contrast to a loan involving a balloon payment.

Amtrak, *see* NATIONAL RAILROAD PASSENGER CORPORATION.

analogies test, test that asks a whole series of questions such as: a foot is to a man as a paw is to what? The examinee is usually given four or five answers to choose from.

analogue, individual's counterpart or opposite number in another organization.

analysis of variance, statistical procedure

for determining whether the change noted in a variable that has been exposed to other variables exceeds what may be expected by chance.

analytical estimating, work measurement technique whereby the time required to perform a job is estimated on the basis of prior experience.

anarchism, the belief that government and its administrative institutions are intrinsically evil; therefore, they should be abolished (typically by violence) so that they can be replaced by more benign and natural arrangements that have not been "corrupted" by exploitative and oppressive governments.

anarcho-syndicalism, late nineteenth century movement which advocated that trade unions oppose, destroy and replace government.

andragogy, an orientation to teaching adults which uses student-centered rather than instructor-centered learning experiences, problem solving-based rather than content-oriented curriculum, and an active rather than a passive learning environment. Andragogy is the opposite of pedagogy, and is becoming accepted as a more effective orientation for causing adults to learn. *See* M. S. Knowles & Associates, *Andragogy in Action: Applying Modern Principles of Adult Learning* (San Francisco: Jossey-Bass Publishers, 1984).

Annals, The, bimonthly journal of the American Academy of Political and Social Science. Each issue focuses on a prominent social or political problem.

    The Annals
    Editorial Office:
    3937 Chestnut Street
    Philadelphia, PA 19104

    Subscriptions:
    Sage Publications, Inc.
    275 South Beverly Drive
    Beverly Hills, CA 90212

annexation, acquisition of adjacent settlements by a city. After annexation the area is part of the city. Though most cities grew by annexation, it is difficult for most to annex now, as the suburbs are typically composed of already incorporated entities not usually subject to involuntary annexation. *See* Leo F. Schnore, "Municipal Annexations and the Growth of Metropolitan Suburbs," *American Journal of Sociology* (January 1962).

annual arrangements, tool to facilitate coordination among grant programs and to increase a city's capacity to set priorities. Involves negotiations between HUD field offices and cities aimed at packaging categorical programs into community development activities.

annual earnings, employee's total compensation during a calendar year— includes basic salary or wages, all overtime and premium pay, vacation pay, bonuses, etc.

annualized cost, cost of something for a twelve-month period. Annualized costs may be figured on the calendar year, the fiscal year, the date a contract becomes effective, etc.

annuitant, one who is the recipient of annuity benefit payments.
    See also REEMPLOYED ANNUITANT.

annuity, annual sum payable to a former employee who has retired; an agreement or contract by which a person purchases a claim to a future series of payments made at fixed intervals over a specified time period, often in the form of payments made by an insurance company during the remainder of a lifetime.
    See also the following entries:
        DEFERRED ANNUITY
        DEFERRED LIFE ANNUITY
        FIXED ANNUITY
        GROUP ANNUITY
        TAX-DEFERRED ANNUITY

antideficiency acts, laws enacted by Congress to prevent the incurring of obligations or the making of expenditures (outlays) in excess of amounts available in appropriations or funds.

Anti-Kickback Act of 1934, *see* KICKBACK.

anti-labor legislation, any law at any level of government that organized labor perceives to be to its disadvantage and to the disadvantage of prime union interests— better hours, wages, and working conditions. Leading examples would be "right-to-work" laws and "anti-strike" laws.

Anti-Racketeering Act of 1934, also called the HOBBS ACT, a federal law that, as amended, prohibits the use of extortion or violence that in any way obstructs, delays, or affects interstate commerce. Thus, it is a federal crime for union leaders to either blackmail employers or accept bribes for not calling strikes.
See also LABOR RACKETEER.

Anti-Strikebreaker Act of 1936, also called the BYRNES ACT, federal statute that prohibits employers from transporting strikebreakers across state lines. As amended in 1938, it also forbids the interstate transportation of persons for the purpose of interfering with peaceful picketing (common carriers excluded).

Anti-Trust Act of 1914, *see* CLAYTON ACT.

antitrust laws, those federal and state statutes which limit the ability of businesses and unions to exercise monopoly control and cause the restraint of trade. The Sherman Anti-Trust Act of 1890 was the first significant American break with the economic philosophy of laissez-faire. It asserted that law could create and control conditions in the marketplace and that it was sometimes in the public interest for government to exercise substantial indirect control over economic conditions. *See* William J. Bigoness, Richard A. Mann, and Barry S. Roberts, "Does Your Collective Bargaining Agreement Violate Antitrust Law?" *Personnel Administrator* (Oc-

tober 1981); James P. Watson, "Antitrust Claims in Labor Disputes After Associated General Contractors: A Prognosis," *Labor Law Journal* (June 1983); Edward B. Miller, *Antitrust Laws and Employee Relations: An Analysis of Their Impact on Management and Union Policies* (Philadelphia, PA: The Wharton School's Industrial Research Unit, University of Pennsylvania, 1984); Garry D. Fisher, "Salary Surveys— An Antitrust Perspective," *Personnel Administrator* (April 1985).

APA, *see* (1) AMERICAN PLANNING ASSOCIATION and (2) AMERICAN PSYCHOLOGICAL ASSOCIATON.

APGA, *see* AMERICAN PERSONNEL AND GUIDANCE ASSOCIATION.

Appalachian Regional Commission (ARC), federal-state compact concerned with the economic, physical, and social development of the thirteen-state Appalachian region.
ARC
1666 Connecticut Avenue, N.W.
Washington, D.C. 20235
(202) 673-7835

apparatchik, Russian word for a bureaucrat, now used colloquially to refer to any administrative functionary. The word as used in English seems to have no political connotations; it merely implies that the individual referred to mindlessly follows orders.

appeal, any proceeding or request to a higher authority that a lower authority's decision be reviewed.

appellant, one who appeals a case to a higher authority.

appellate jurisdiction, power of a tribunal to review cases that have previously been decided by a lower authority.

Appleby, Paul H. (1891-1963), most influential advocate of the notion that politics and administration are intertwined. Appleby worked to destroy the myth that politics was separate or could somehow be taken out of public administration. Public administrators, Appleby said, made policy; they were involved in the political process; and this political involvement acted as a check on the arbitrary exercise of bureaucratic power in a democratic state. Major works include: *Big Democracy* (New York: Alfred Knopf, 1945), *Policy and Administration* (University of Alabama Press, 1949), *Morality and Administration in Democratic Government* (Baton Rouge: Louisiana State University Press, 1952), *Public Administration for a Welfare State* (New Delhi: Asia Publishing House, 1961), and *Citizens as Sovereigns* (Syracuse: Syracuse University Press, 1962). For a complete review of Appleby's work and influence, *see* Roscoe C. Martin, ed., *Public Administration and Democracy: Essays in Honor of Paul H. Appleby* (Syracuse University Press, 1965).

apple polishers, as defined in Edward M. Cook, "The High Cost of Promoting Apple Polishers," *Personnel Administration* (May-June 1966):

There are two major categories of apple polishers: (a) *Hard-Core Apple Polisher*—The compulsive yes man; never known to disagree with a superior; seldom supports his subordinates if conflict develops; pleasant personality; has many good qualities but close study of performance reveals the apple polishing syndrome. He seldom seeks real responsibility, contributes little that is creative, has seldom actually fought for his ideas or grasped a nettlesome problem with his bare hands; he may be valuable on the lower rungs of the corporate ladder, dangerous as he ascends, murder if allowed to select, cultivate, and proliferate subordinates in his own image. (2) *Skin-Deep Apple Polisher*—This category includes many younger people who are ambitious and have been led to believe that polishing is somehow almost as important as performance; many of these individuals are salvageable if the right kind of supervisor influences them in time. Unfortunately, some may become hard-core eventual-

ly, depending on organization climate; included in this group are many good, creative men of integrity who don't enjoy polishing and eventually move on to organizations which don't require it.

applicant, an individual seeking initial employment or an in-house promotional opportunity.

applicant pool, all those individuals who have applied for a particular job over a given period.

applicant population, the set of individuals within a geographical area, with identifiable characteristics or a mix of such characteristics, from which applicants for employment are obtained. Changes in recruiting practices may change certain characteristics of those who apply for work and therefore may change the nature of the applicant population.

applicant tally, tally system by which the EEO status of applicants is recorded at the time of application or interview. By periodically comparing applicant tally rates with rates of appointment and/or rejection, the progress of affirmative action recruitment efforts can be measured.

application blank, frequently the first phase of the selection process. Properly completed it can serve three purposes: (1) it is a formal request for employment; (2) it provides information that indicates the applicant's fitness for the position; and (3) it can become the basic personnel record for those applicants who are hired. Application blanks must conform to all EEOC guidelines; requested information must be a valid predictor of performance. For additional information, *see* C. C. Kessler and G. J. Gibbs, "Getting the Most from Application Blanks and References," *Personnel* (January-February 1975); Ernest C. Miller, "An EEO Examination of Employment Applications," *The Personnel Administrator* (March 1980); Debra D. Purrington, "A Review of State Government Employment Application Forms for Suspect Inquiries," *Public Personnel*

Management (Spring 1982).
See also WEIGHTED APPLICATION BLANK.

applied costs, the financial measure of resources consumed or applied within a given period of time to accomplish a specific purpose, such as performing a service, carrying out an activity, or completing a unit of work or a specific project, regardless of when ordered, received, or paid for.

applied psychology, generally, the practical use of the discoveries and principles of psychology. *See* Harry W. Hepner, *Psychology Applied to Life and Work,* 6th ed. (Englewood Cliffs, N.J.: Prentice-Hall, 1979); Wayne F. Casio, *Applied Psychology in Personnel Management,* 2nd ed. (Reston, VA: Reston/Prentice-Hall, 1982).

appointing authority, *see* APPOINTING OFFICER.

appointing officer, also APPOINTING AUTHORITY, person having power by law, or by lawfully delegated authority, to make appointments to positions in an organization.

appointment, non-elective government job. Most jurisdictions offer several different kinds of appointments. For example, the federal government offers the following four varieties in its merit system:
1. *Temporary appointment*—does not ordinarily last more than one year. A temporary worker can't be promoted and can't transfer to another job. Temporary employees are not under the retirement system. Persons over seventy can be given only temporary appointments, but the appointments can be renewed.
2. *Term appointment*—made for work on a specific project that will last more than one year but less than four years. A term employee can be promoted or reassigned to other positions within the project for which that employee was hired. He is not under the retirement system. If you accept a temporary or term appoint-

ment, your name will stay on the list of eligibles from which you were appointed. This means that you will remain eligible for permanent jobs that are normally filled by career-conditional or career appointments.
3. *Career-conditional appointment*—leads after three years' continuous service to a career appointment. For the first year, the employee serves a probationary period. During this time, it must be demonstrated that the employee can do a satisfactory job and he or she may be dismissed for failure to do so. Career-conditional employees have promotion and transfer privileges. After career-conditional employees complete their probation, they cannot be removed except for cause. However, in reduction-in-force (layoff) actions, career-conditional employees are dismissed ahead of career employees.
4. *Career appointment*—employee serves a probationary period, as described above, and has promotion, reinstatement and transfer privileges. After completion of the probation, this type of employee is in the last group to be affected in layoffs.

See also NONCOMPETITIVE APPOINTMENT and PROVISIONAL APPOINTMENT.

appointment clause, portion of Article II, Section 2, of the U.S. constitution that reads in part that the president,
by and with the Advice and Consent of the Senate, shall appoint Ambassadors, other public Ministers and Consuls, Judges of the Supreme Court, and all other officers of the United States, whose Appointments are not herein otherwise provided for, and which shall be established by Law: but the Congress may by Law vest the Appointment of such inferior Officers, as they think proper, in the President alone, in the Courts of Law, or in the Heads of Departments.

Thus offices and, by implication, departments and agencies must be provided for by law. This means that the creation of the structures of the executive branch rests largely with Congress.

The appointment clause was placed in the Constitution very late during the debates in Philadelphia and was intended as a check on the president. Without it he could have created office after office, department after department without congressional authorization. While the president still would have been dependent upon Congress for the funding of such an endeavor, constitutionally his authority could have been shared with such officers and departments without any effective congressional oversight or check. As it stands in the Constitution, however, Congress creates the structure of the executive branch and obviously has the power to check up on its handiwork. Since all units of the executive branch other than the president rest upon statutory foundations, Congress can, if it so desires, abolish any federal agency. Congress can also assign independent functions to executive branch officials and can create administrative agencies outside the presidential domain. Today's federal bureaucracy is dependent upon the legislative will.

The appointment clause is also significant because it allows the Congress to vest the authority to make "inferior" appointments with the president, the courts, or department heads. The number of such presidential appointments has varied throughout U.S. political history. Today, with over 90 percent of all federal servants having a merit appointment of one type or another, presidential appointments, while not inconsequential, are decidedly limited in scope. The most important group of these appointments are those in the Executive Office of the President. The fact that the Constitution allows appointments to be made by department heads, when deemed appropriate by Congress, has had important consequences for federal personnel administration. The fact that the Congress can condition such appointments has given it considerable authority and control over the federal personnel system. Indeed, the federal merit

system as well as the other fundamental features of federal personnel administration are based on statute. In addition, the "rule of three"—the practice of allowing appointing officials to choose from among the top three eligibles for any given position—is a direct outgrowth of the constitutional presumption that department heads must be given some choice in making appointments and cannot be compelled to choose any given individual, no matter how well qualified.

All of this adds up to what might at first seem like a startling conclusion: the Congress clearly has a great deal of authority over federal administrative processes. Not only must appropriations be granted by law, but the size, structure, mission, and authority of executive branch agencies are all solidly within the domain of congressional power. So is federal personnel administration and the oversight, or evaluation, of the bureaucracy. Having had a bad experience with a king, the founders feared executive power. This is nowhere more evident than in the constitutional clauses that bear upon public administration. While charged with the faithful execution of the laws, the president's constitutional authority over the administrative structures necessary to implement statutes is severely limited. How, then, has the president become the nation's "administrative chief"? In part through the power of dismissal and in part through congressional delegation of administrative power to him.

See also the following entries:
HUMPHREY'S EXECUTOR V. UNITED
  STATES
MYERS V. UNITED STATES
PATRIONAGE
PRESIDENTIAL POWER

apportionment (budgeting), executive budget function that takes place after passage of an appropriations bill when a jurisdiction's budget office creates a plan for expenditures to reconcile agency or department programs with available resources.

apportionment (personnel), a requirement, written into the Pendleton Act of 1883, that all federal government merit system jobs in headquarters offices of agencies in the metropolitan Washington, D.C., area are to be distributed among the residents of the states, territories and the District of Columbia. Each state or territory is allocated a certain number of these competitive positions on the basis of population. Residents of the states which have not filled their allocations are considered for appointment to these apportioned positions ahead of residents of states which have exceeded their allocations.

apprentice, according to the U.S. Department of Labor's *Dictionary of Occupational Titles* (Fourth Edition, 1977):

a worker who learns, according to written or oral contractual agreement, a recognized skilled craft or trade requiring one or more years of on-the-job training through job experience supplemented by related instruction, prior to being considered a qualified skilled worker. High school or vocational school education is often a prerequisite for entry into an apprenticeship program. Provisions of apprenticeship agreement regularly include length of apprenticeship; a progressive scale of wages; work processes to be taught; and amount of instruction in subjects related to the craft or trade, such as characteristics of materials used, physics, mathematics, estimating, and blueprint reading. Apprenticeability of a particular craft or trade is best evidenced by its acceptability for registration as a trade by a State apprenticeship agency or the Federal Bureau of Apprenticeship and Training. Generally, where employees are represented by a union, apprenticeship programs come under the guidance of joint apprenticeship committees composed of representatives of the employers or the employer association and representatives of the employees. These committees may determine need for apprentices in a locality and establish minimum apprenticeship standards of education, experience, and training. In

instances where committees do not exist, apprenticeship agreement is made between apprentice and employer, or an employer group.

While the title "apprentice" is often loosely used as a synonym for any beginner, helper, or trainee, this is technically incorrect. For an evaluation of current practices, *see* Norman Parkin, "Apprenticeships: Outmoded or Undervalued?" *Personnel Management* (May 1978).

apprentice rate, also APPRENTICE SCALE, usually a schedule of rates for workers in formal apprenticeship programs that gradually permits the attainment of the minimum journeyman rate.

apprentice scale, *see* APPRENTICE RATE.

Apprenticeship Act of 1937, also called the FITZGERALD ACT, Public Law 77-308, law that authorized the Secretary of Labor to formulate and promote the furtherance of labor standards necessary to safeguard the welfare of apprentices and to cooperate with the states in the promotion of such standards.

appropriate bargaining unit, *see* APPROPRIATE UNIT.

appropriate technology, also ALTERNATIVE TECHNOLOGY, concepts that involve the rejection of centralized control or direction for the use of technology, and the replacement of it with local determination of which technologies best fit the local environment. Proponents stress the democratizing, populist thrust of appropriate/alternative technology, as opposed to the current centralized decision-making process for science and technology through federal agencies. *See* David Dickson, *Alternative Technology and the Politics of Technical Change* (New York: Universe, 1975); Richard C. Dorf and Yvonne L. Hunter, eds., *Appropriate Visions: Technology, the Environment, and the Individual* (San Francisco: Boyd & Fraser, 1978); John Hagel, *Alternative Energy Strategies: Constraints and Oppor-*

tunities (New York: Praeger, 1976); Karl Hess, *Community Technology* (New York: Harper & Row, 1978).

appropriate unit, also known as BARGAINING UNIT and APPROPRIATE BARGAINING UNIT, group of employees that a labor organization seeks to represent for the purpose of negotiating agreements; an aggregation of employees that has a clear and identifiable community of interest and that promotes effective dealings and efficiency of operations. It may be established on a plant or installation, craft, functional or other basis.

appropriation, act of Congress that permits federal agencies to incur obligations and to make payments out of the Treasury for specified purposes. An appropriation usually follows enactment of authorizing legislation. An appropriation act is the most common form of budget authority, but in some cases the authorizing legislation provides the budget authority. There are several types of appropriations that are not counted as budget authority, for example:
1. Appropriation to liquidate contract authority—congressional action to provide moneys to pay obligations incurred against contract authority.
2. Appropriation to reduce outstanding debt—congressional action to provide moneys for debt retirement.
3. Appropriation for refund of receipts.

Appropriations are categorized in a variety of ways, such as by their period of availability (one-year, multiple-year, no-year), the timing of congressional action (current, permanent), and the manner of determining the amount of the appropriation (definite, indefinite). *See* Richard F. Fenno, Jr., "The House Appropriations Committee as a Political System: The Problem of Integration," *American Political Science Review* (June 1962); Richard F. Fenno, Jr., *The Power of the Purse: Appropriations Politics in Congress* (Boston: Little, Brown, 1966); David Lowery, Samual Bookheimer and James Malachowski, "Partisanship in the Appropriations Process: Fenno Revisited," *American Politics Quarterly* (April 1985).

See also the following entries:
ADVANCE APPROPRIATION
ADVANCE FUNDING
BUDGETING
SUPPLEMENTAL APPROPRIATION

appropriation account, also called FUND ACCOUNT, a summary account for each appropriation and/or fund showing transactions to such accounts. Each such account provides the framework for establishing a set of balanced accounts on the books of the agency concerned.

appropriation limitations, a statutory restriction in appropriation acts that establishes the maximum or minimum amount that may be obligated or expended for specified purposes.

approximation of laws, the process whereby governments align their laws concerning commercial transactions in order to facilitate international trade.

APSA, *see* AMERICAN POLITICAL SCIENCE ASSOCIATION.

APSR, *see* AMERICAN POLITICAL SCIENCE REVIEW.

aptitude, capacity to acquire knowledge, skill, or ability with experience and/or a given amount of formal or informal education or training.

aptitude test, usually a battery of separate tests designed to measure an individual's overall ability to learn. A large variety of specialized aptitude tests has been developed to predict an applicant's performance on a particular job or in a particular course of study. *See* Edwin E. Ghiselli, *The Validity of Occupational Aptitude Tests* (New York: John Wiley & Sons, 1966).

APWA, *see* (1) AMERICAN PUBLIC WELFARE ASSOCIATION and (2) AMERICAN PUBLIC WORKS ASSOCIATION.

arbiter, also ARBITRATOR, one chosen to decide a disagreement. In a formal sense an *arbiter* is one who has the power to decide while an *arbitrator* is one who is chosen to decide by the parties to the dispute; but the words tend to be used interchangeably. *See* Murray Greenberg and Philip Harris, "The Arbitrator's Employment Status as a Factor in the Decision Making Process," *Human Resource Management* (Winter 1981); John Smith Herrick, "Labor Arbitration as Viewed by Labor Arbitrators," *The Arbitration Journal* (March 1983); Orley Ashenfelter and David E. Bloom, "Models of Arbitrator Behavior: Theory and Evidence," *The American Economic Review* (March 1984).

arbitrability, whether or not an issue is covered by a collective bargaining agreement and can be heard and resolved in arbitration. The U.S. Supreme Court held, in *United Steelworkers* v. *Warrior & Gulf Navigation Co.,* 363 U.S. 574 (1960), that any grievance is arbitrable unless there is an express contract provision excluding the issue from arbitration; doubts "should be resolved in favor of coverage." *See* Mark M. Grossman, *The Question of Arbitrability: Challenges to the Arbitrator's Jurisdiction and Authority* (Ithaca, NY: Cornell University, New York State School of Industrial and Labor Relations, 1984).

See also UNITED STEELWORKERS OF AMERICA V. WARRIOR AND GULF NAVIGATION CO.

arbitrary, an action decided by personal whim that was not guided by general principles or rules.

arbitration, means of settling a labor dispute by having an impartial third party (the arbitrator) hold a formal hearing and render a decision that may or may not be binding on both sides. The arbitrator may be a single individual or a board of three, five, or more. When boards are used, they may include, in addition to impartial members, representatives from both of the disputants. Arbitrators may be selected jointly by labor and management or recommended by the Federal Mediation and Conciliation Service, by a state or local agency offering similar referrals, or by the private American Arbitration Association. *See* Henry S. Farber, "Role of Arbitration in Dispute Settlement," *Monthly Labor Review* (May 1981); Harry Graham, "Arbitration Results in the Public Sector," *Public Personnel Management* (Summer 1982); Owen Fairweather, *Practice and Procedure in Labor Arbitration,* 2nd ed. (Washington, D.C.: BNA Books, 1983); Aubrey R. Fowler, Jr., "Responsibilities in Arbitration: A Tripartite View," *Personnel Administrator* (November 1984); Richard L. Kanner, "The Dynamics of the Arbitration Process," *Arbitration Journal* (June 1984); Frank Elkouri and Edna Asper Elkouri, *How Arbitration Works,* 4th ed. (Washington, D.C.: Bureau of National Affairs, Inc., 1985).

See also the following entries:
AD HOC ARBITRATOR
BINDING ARBITRATION
COMPULSORY ARBITRATION
DICTA
EXPEDITED ARBITRATION
FINAL OFFER ARBITRATION
FUNCTUS OFFICIO
GRIEVANCE ARBITRATION
INTEREST ARBITRATION
OBLIGATORY ARBITRATION
TERMINAL ARBITRATION
TEXTILE WORKERS V. LINCOLN MILLS
UNITED STEELWORKERS OF AMERICA
    V. AMERICAN MANUFACTURING CO.
UNITED STEELWORKERS OF AMERICA
    V. ENTERPRISE WHEEL AND CAR
    CORP.
VOLUNTARY ARBITRATION
WAGE ARBITRATION
ZIPPER CLAUSE

arbitration acts, laws that help (and sometimes require) the submission of certain types of problems (often labor disputes) to an arbitrator.

arbitration clause, provision of a collective bargaining agreement stipulating that disputes arising during the life of the contract over its interpretation are subject to arbitration. The clause may be broad enough to include "any dispute" or restricted to specific concerns.

Arbitration Journal, quarterly journal of

the American Arbitration Association, Inc.; includes articles written by practitioners and academics on all phases of arbitration and labor relations as well as reviews of related legal decisions.

Arbitration Journal
American Arbitration Association, Inc.
140 West 51st Street
New York, NY 10020

arbitration standards, the four fundamental criteria that arbitrators must be concerned with in making their judgments: acceptability, equity, the public interest, and ability to pay. The mix of these factors that will be applied in any particular case of arbitration will depend upon the arbitrator's proclivities, the nature of the dispute, and, if it is in the public sector, the standards, if any, set forth in the pertinent legislation.

arbitration tribunal, panel created to decide a dispute that has been submitted to arbitration.

arbitrator, one who conducts an arbitration.
See also NATIONAL ACADEMY OF ARBITRATORS and PERMANENT ARBITRATOR.

architectural barriers, physical aspects of a building that might hinder or prevent the employment of a physically handicapped person. The lack of a ramp, for example, may prevent a person in a wheelchair from entering a building having only stairways for access. The Architectural Barriers Act of 1968 (Public Law 90-480), as amended, requires that buildings constructed with federal funds be accessible to and usable by the physically handicapped.

Architectural Barriers Act of 1968, see ARCHITECTURAL BARRIERS.

archives, permanently available records created or received by an organization for its formal/official purposes.

area agreement, collective bargaining agreement that covers a variety of employers and their workers in a large geographic area.

area labor-management committees, groups of local labor and business leaders who seek to solve problems affecting the economic well-being of an entire community, rather than just a particular worksite or industry. See Richard D. Leone and Michael F. Eleey, "The Origins and Operations of Area Labor-Management Committees," *Monthly Labor Review* (May 1983).

area of consideration, geographic or organizational area within which all candidates who meet the basic requirements for promotion to a position are given the opportunity to be considered.

area standards picketing, picketing to demand that the primary employer pay "area standards" wages; that is, wages that are paid to union labor by other employers in the same geographic area.

area wage differences, differing pay rates for various occupations in differing geographic areas.

area wage survey, *see* WAGE SURVEY.

Argyris, Chris (1923-   ), one of the most influential advocates of the use of organization development (OD) techniques. His writings have provided the theoretical foundations for innumerable empirical research efforts dealing with the inherent conflict between the personality of a mature adult and the needs of modern organizations. Major works include: *Personality And Organization* (New York: Harper & Row, 1957); *Understanding Organizational Behavior* (Homewood, Ill.: Dorsey, 1960); *Interpersonal Competence And Organization Effectiveness* (Homewood, Ill.: Dorsey, 1962); *Integrating the Individual and the Organization* (New York: Wiley, 1964); *Intervention Theory and Method* (Reading, Mass.: Addison-Wesley, 1970); *Management and Organizational Development* (New York: McGraw-Hill, 1971); *Organizational Learning: A Theory of Action Perspective,* with Donald A. Schon (Reading, Mass.: Addison-Wesley, 1978).
See also PSEUDO-EFFECTIVENESS.

arithmetic mean, *see* MEAN.

Arizona v. Norris, U.S. Supreme Court case, 77 L. Ed. 2d 1236 (1983), which held that employers may not require female employees to make the same contributions to a pension plan as men while giving the males a larger benefit. The Court limited its ruling to plan contributions made after July 31, 1983, and did not specify how equalization of benefits must be achieved, which meant that it could be attained by raising women's benefits, lowering men's benefits, or a combination of the two approaches.

Army Alpha and Beta Tests, developed in 1917 by a special committee of the American Psychological Association to help the U.S. Army classify the abilities of its recruits. The committee developed the Army Alpha Intelligence Test (a verbal test for literate recruits) and the Army Beta Intelligence Test (a nonverbal test suited for illiterate and foreign-born recruits). After World War I, the tests were released for civilian use and became the progenitors of modern industrial and educational group intelligence/aptitude testing.

Arnett v. Kennedy, 416 U.S. 134 (1974), U.S. Supreme Court case which held that the administrative procedures afforded federal employees discharged "for such cause as will promote the efficiency of the service" neither violated the due process rights of such employees nor were unconstitutionally vague.

Arnold Co. v. Carpenters District Council of Jacksonville, *see* WILLIAM E. ARNOLD CO. V. CARPENTERS DISTRICT COUNCIL OF JACKSONVILLE.

artificial barriers to employment, limitations (such as age, sex, race, national origin, parental status, credential requirements, criminal record, lack of child care, and absence of part-time or alternative working patterns/schedules) in hiring, firing, promotion, licensing, and conditions of employment which are not directly related to an individual's fitness or ability to perform the tasks required by the job.

Ash Council, President Nixon's Advisory Council on Executive Organization, chaired by Roy Ash of Litton Industries, whose efforts led to the transformation of the Bureau of the Budget into the Office of Management and Budget. *See* Roger G. Noll, *Reforming Regulation: An Evaluation of the Ash Council Proposals* (Washington, D.C.: The Brookings Institution, 1971).

Ashurst-Sumners Act of 1935, federal law that forbids the interstate shipping of goods produced by convict labor into states that prohibit convict labor.

ASPA, *see* AMERICAN SOCIETY FOR PERSONNEL ADMINISTRATION or AMERICAN SOCIETY FOR PUBLIC ADMINISTRATION.

ASQ, *see* ADMINISTRATIVE SCIENCE QUARTERLY.

assembly line, production method requiring workers to perform a repetitive task on a product as it moves along on a conveyor belt or tract. Although much has been written about the "inhuman" demands of machine-paced work, the classic study remains Charles R. Walker and Robert H. Guest's *The Man on the Assembly Line* (Cambridge, Mass.: Harvard University Press, 1952).

Assembly of Governmental Employees, an umbrella organization for state and local public employee groups dedicated to the maintenance of merit principles and the extension of collective bargaining.
Assembly of Governmental Employees
1730 Rhode Island Ave., N.W.
Washington, D.C. 20036
(202) 347-5628

assertiveness training, training program designed to help less assertive people communicate and express their ideas and feelings more effectively. The ideal level of assertiveness lies midway between passivity and aggressiveness. The concept was pioneered by J. Wolpe in his *Psychotherapy by Reciprocal Inhibition* (Stanford, Calif.: Stanford University Press, 1958).

For a general discussion, *see* Harold H. Dawley, Jr., and W. W. Wenrich, *Achieving Assertive Behavior: A Guide to Assertive Training* (Belmont, Calif.: Wadsworth Publishing Co., 1976). For the obverse, *see* Michael D. Ames, "Non-Assertion Training Has Value Too," *Personnel Journal* (July 1977). Also *see* Madelyn Burley-Allen, *Managing Assertively: How to Improve Your People Skills* (New York: John Wiley, 1983).

assessed valuation, tax value assigned to property.

assessment center, a process consisting of the intense observation of a subject undergoing a variety of simulations and stress situations over a period of several days. The term "assessment center" does not refer to a particular place. Assessment centers have proven to be an increasingly popular way of identifying individuals with future executive potential so that they may be given the appropriate training and development assignments.

As the assessment center concept is more widely adopted, one question will become more and more commonplace: If the door to management development and advancement goes through the assessment center, who will be the gatekeeper? Unless the organization can afford to process its entire management cadre through assessment centers, those individuals not selected for attendance might justifiably conclude they have been negatively evaluated. The decision, or nondecision, not to send an individual to an assessment center while peers are being sent could even have considerable legal ramifications. Because management development funds will continue to be a scarce resource, any organization implementing an assessment center program must also be concerned with designing an equitable nomination process.

For accounts of assessment center methodologies, *see* Douglas W. Bray, "The Assessment Center Method," *Training and Development Handbook,* 2nd ed., Robert L. Craig, ed. (New York: McGraw-Hill, 1976); William C. Byham and Carl Wettengel, "Assessment Centers for Supervisors and Managers: An Introduction and Overview," *Public Personnel Management* (September-October 1974); Wayne F. Cascio and Val Silbey, "Utility of the Assessment Center as a Selection Device," *Journal of Applied Psychology* (April 1979); William C. Byham, "Starting an Assessment Center the Correct Way," *Personnel Administrator* (February 1980); Task Force on Assessment Center Standards, "Standards and Ethical Considerations for Assessment Center Operations," *Personnel Administrator* (February 1980); Paul R. Sackett, "A Critical Look at Some Common Beliefs About Assessment Centers," *Public Personnel Management* (Summer 1982); Linda L. Kolb, "Use of Assessment Center Methodology for Appraising Performance," *Personnel Administrator* (October 1984).

See also IN-BASKET EXERCISE.

assessments, amounts paid by union members in addition to their regular dues when a union needs funds urgently in order to support a strike or some other union-endorsed cause. The amount of these assessments are usually limited by a union's constitution and/or bylaws.

assessor, official of a jurisdiction who determines the value of property for the purpose of taxation.

asset-linked annuity, *see* VARIABLE ANNUITY.

assets, also CURRENT ASSETS and FIXED ASSETS, book value of items owned by an enterprise or jurisdiction as reflected on a balance sheet. *Current assets* are cash or those highly liquid items which are convertible to a known amount of cash, usually within a year (*i.e.,* accounts receivable, securities, inventory, and amounts due from other funds). *Fixed assets* are those items which normally are not convertible into cash within a year (*i.e.,* buildings, equipment and machinery).

assignment of wages, also called AT-TACHMENT OF WAGES, procedure that has an employer, upon the authorization of the employee, automatically deduct a portion of the employee's wages and pay it to a third party, usually a creditor. When this is ordered by a court, the process is known as garnishment.

See also GARNISHMENT.

assumption-of-risk doctrine, common-law concept that an employer should not be held responsible for an accident to an employee if the employer can show that the injured employee had voluntarily accepted the hazards associated with a given job.

ASTD, see AMERICAN SOCIETY FOR TRAINING AND DEVELOPMENT.

Atomic Energy Commission, see NUCLEAR REGULATORY COMMISSION.

at-risk populations, those identifiable groups that have been systematically denied on an economic, social, and political basis the opportunity for and access to public and private goods and resources.

attachment of wages, see ASSIGNMENT OF WAGES.

attendance bonus, also called ATTENDANCE MONEY, payment to an employee that serves as an inducement to regular attendance.

attitude, learned predisposition to act in a consistent way toward particular persons, objects, or conditions.

attitude scale, any series of attitude indices that have given quantitative values relative to each other.

attitude survey, questionnaire, usually anonymous, that elicits the opinion of employees or clients. Once completed they are summarized and analyzed to determine compliance with and attitudes towards current personnel management or other policies. See Martin Fishbein, ed., *Readings in Attitude Theory and Measure-*

ment (New York: John Wiley, 1967); Price Pritchett, "Employee Attitude Surveys: A Natural Starting Point for Organization Development," *Personnel Journal* (April 1975); Stuart M. Klein, Allen I. Kraut, and Alan Wolfson, "Employee Reactions to Attitude Survey Feedback: A Study of the Impact of Structure and Process," *Administrative Science Quarterly* (December 1971); Randall B. Dunham and Frank J. Smith, *Organizational Surveys* (Glenview, Ill.: Scott, Foresman and Co., 1979); Wallace Martin, "What Management Can Expect From an Employee Attitude Survey," *Personnel Administrator* (July 1981); Mitchell Lee Marks, "Conducting an Employment Attitude Survey," *Personnel Journal* (September 1982).

attrition, reduction in the size of a workforce through normal processes, such as voluntary resignations, retirements, discharges for cause, transfers, and deaths. See Jack Frye, "Attrition in Job Elimination," *Labor Law Journal* (September 1963); James A. Feldt and David F. Andersen, "Attrition Versus Layoffs: How to Estimate the Costs of Holding Employees on Payroll When Savings are Needed," *Public Administration Review* (May/June 1982).

audio-visual media, those things that communicate information through human sight or sound sensors—films, slides, recordings, maps, etc. See James E. Holbrook, "Here's How to Sell Your Ideas for Audio-Visual Training Programs to Top Management." *Personnel Administrator* (July 1981).

audit, final phase of the budgetary process. An audit is a review of the operations of the agency, especially its financial transactions, to determine whether the agency has spent the money in accordance with the law, in the most efficient manner, and with desired results. See Elmer B. Staats, "GAO Audit Standards: Development and Implementation," *Public Management* (February 1974); Richard E. Brown and Ralph Craft, "Auditing and

Public Administration: The Unrealized Partnership," *Public Administration Review* (May/June 1980); and Roger H. Hermanson, Stephen E. Loeb, John M. Saada, and Robert H. Strawser, *Auditing Theory and Practice* (Homewood, Ill.: Richard D. Irwin, Inc., third edition, 1983).

See also the following entries:
COMPLIANCE
CONTRACT AUDIT
DESK AUDIT
ECONOMY AND EFFICIENCY AUDITS
FINANCIAL AUDIT
GENERALLY ACCEPTED ACCOUNTING
  PRINCIPLES
PROGRAM EVALUATION
PROGRAM RESULTS AUDIT
REPORT (AUDIT)
SOCIAL AUDIT

auditing, expanded scope of, according to the Comptroller General of the United States, *Standards For Audit of Governmental Organizations, Programs, Activities, And Functions* (Washington, D.C.: U.S. General Accounting Office, 1981), the expanded scope of auditing a government organization, a program, an activity, or a function should include:

1. *Financial and compliance*—determines (a) whether the financial statements of an audited entity present fairly the financial position and the results of financial operations in accordance with generally accepted accounting principles and (b) whether the entity has complied with laws and regulations that may have a material effect upon the financial statements.
2. *Economy and efficiency*—determines (a) whether the entity is managing and utilizing its resources (such as personnel, property, space) economically and efficiently, (b) the causes of inefficiencies or uneconomical practices, and (c) whether the entity has complied with laws and regulations concerning matters of economy and efficiency.
3. *Program results*—determines (a) whether the desired results or bene-

fits established by the legislature or other authorizing body are being achieved and (b) whether the agency has considered alternatives that might yield desired results at a lower cost.

auditor, person or organization conducting an audit.

auditor's opinion, an expression in an auditor's report as to whether the information in the financial statement of a jurisdiction is presented fairly in accordance with generally accepted accounting principles (or with other specified accounting principles applicable to the auditee) applied on a basis consistent with that of the preceding reporting period.

audit program, detailed steps and procedures to be followed in conducting the audit and preparing the report. A written audit program should be prepared for each audit and it should include such information as the purpose and scope, background information needed to understand the audit objectives and the entity's mission, definition of unique terms, objectives, and reporting procedures.

audit standards, general measures of the quality and adequacy of the work performed. They also relate to the auditor's professional qualities.

Australian Journal of Public Administration, formerly *Public Administration,* quarterly publication of the Royal Institute of Public Administration's Australia Regional Groups.
AJPA
G.P.O. Box 904
Sydney 2001
Australia

authoritarian theory, see THEORY X.

authority, power inherent in a specific position or function that allows an incumbent to perform assigned duties and assume assigned responsibilities. *See* Richard Bendix, *Work and Authority in Indus-*

try: Ideologies of Management in the Course of Industrialization (New York: Wiley, 1956); Robert L. Peabody, Organizational Authority: Superior-Subordinate Relationships in Three Public Service Organizations (New York: Atherton, 1964); Richard Sennett, Authority (New York: Knopf, 1980); and Richard E. Flathman, The Practice of Political Authority (University of Chicago Press, 1980).

See also the following entries:
BUDGET AUTHORITY
FUNCTIONAL AUTHORITY
POWER

authorization, also called AUTHORIZING LEGISLATION, basic substantive legislation enacted by Congress which sets up or continues the legal operation of a federal program or agency, either indefinitely or for a specific period of time, or sanctions a particular type of obligation or expenditure within a program. Such legislation is normally a prerequisite for subsequent appropriations or other kinds of budget authority to be contained in appropriation acts. It may limit the amount of budget authority to be provided subsequently or may authorize the appropriation of "such sums as may be necessary"; in a few instances, budget authority may be provided in the authorization.

See also BACKDOOR AUTHORITY.

authorization card, form signed by a worker to authorize a union to represent the worker for purposes of collective bargaining. The U.S. Supreme Court held, in National Labor Relations Board v. Gissel Packing Co., 395 U.S. 575 (1969), that the National Labor Relations Board had the power to require an employer to bargain with a union which had obtained signed authorization cards from a majority of the employees. In such circumstances a secret ballot election is considered unnecessary. See Daniel F. Gruender and Philip M. Prince, "Union Authorization Cards: Why Not Laboratory Conditions?" Labor Law Journal (January 1981).

See also SHOWING OF INTEREST.

authorization election, or REPRESENTA-

TION ELECTION, polls conducted by the National Labor Relations Board (or other administrative agency) to determine if a particular group of employees will be represented by a particular union or not. See Dean S. Ellis, Laurence Jacobs, and Cary Mills, "A Union Authorization Election: The Key to Winning," Personnel Journal (April 1972); Julius G. Getman, Stephen B. Goldberg, and Jeanne B. Herman, Union Representation Elections: Law and Reality (New York: Russell Sage Foundation, 1976); Ronald L. Seeber and William N. Cooke, "The Decline in Union Success in NLRB Representation Elections," Industrial Relations (Winter 1982); Gary L. Tidwell, "The Supervisor's Role in a Union Election," Personnel Journal (August 1983); John J. Lawler, "The Influence of Management Consultants on the Outcome of Union Certification Elections," Industrial and Labor Relations Review (October 1984).

See also the following entries:
JOY SILK MILLS V. NATIONAL LABOR
RELATIONS BOARD
NATIONAL LABOR RELATIONS BOARD
V. EXCHANGE PARTS
RUN-OFF ELECTION
SHOWING OF INTEREST

authorizing committee, a standing committee of the House or Senate with legislative jurisdiction over the subject matter of those laws, or parts of laws, that set up or continue the legal operations of federal programs or agencies. An authorizing committee also has jurisdiction in those instances where backdoor authority is provided in the substantive legislation.

See also SELECT COMMITTEE and STANDING COMMITTEE.

authorizing legislation, see AUTHORIZATION.

automatic checkoff, also called COMPULSORY CHECKOFF, illegal procedure whereby the employer deducts union dues and assessments from the pay of all employees in the bargaining unit without the prior consent of each individual employee. Section 302 of the Labor-Management Relations (Taft-Hartley) Act of 1947 provides that checkoffs must be voluntary and initiated only upon the the written authorization of each employee on whose account such deductions would be made.

automatic stabilizer, also called BUILT-IN STABILIZER, a mechanism having a countercyclical effect that automatically moderates changes in incomes and outputs in the economy without specific decisions to change government policy. Unemployment insurance and the income tax are among the most important of the automatic stabilizers in the United States.
    See also COUNTERCYCLICAL.

automatic wage adjustment, raising or lowering of wage rates in direct response to previously determined factors such as an increase/decrease in the Consumer Price Index.

automatic wage progression, the increasing of wages premised on length of service.

automation, sometimes called MECHANIZATION, use of machines to do work that would otherwise have to be done by humans. While examples of automation go back to ancient times, the term itself was only coined in the mid-1930s by D. S. Harder, then of General Motors. As a word, automation has a considerable emotional charge since its manifestations have tended to create technological unemployment.
    Automation tends to be popularly used interchangeably with mechanization—the use of machines. However, a production system is not truly automated unless the machinery is to some degree self-regulated—that is, capable of adjusting itself in response to feedback from its earlier outputs. This attribute lessens the need for human attendants. According to Herbert A. Simon, in *The Shape of Automation for Men and Management* (New York: Harper & Row, 1965),
    the term "mechanization" has nearly been replaced by its newer synonym, "automation." Automation is nothing new; it is simply the continuation of that trend toward the use of capital in production that has been a central characteristic of the whole Industrial Revolution. What is possibly new, if anything, is the extension of mechanization to wider and wider ranges of productive processes, and the growing prospect of complete mechanization—that is, the technical feasibility of productive processes that do not require human participation.
    See George E. Biles and Richard A. Bassler, "Low-Priced Automation for Personnel Management Functions," *Personnel Administrator* (August 1984); Zane Quible and Jane N. Hammer, "Office Automation's Impact on Personnel," *Personnel Administrator* (September 1984); David F. Noble, *Forces of Production: A Social History of Industrial Automation* (New York: Knopf, 1984).

automaton, person acting mechanically in a monotonous routine without the need to use any intellectual capacities. The thrust of the scientific management movement was to make workers the most efficient possible automatons. A significant portion of modern industrial unrest is directly related to the work force's resentment at being treated in such a manner.

autonomous work group, collection of individuals who have all the resources and abilities necessary to produce a particular product or service.

auxiliary agency, also called HOUSEKEEPING AGENCY or OVERHEAD AGENCY, administrative unit whose prime responsibility is to serve other agencies of the greater organization. Personnel agencies are usually auxiliary, housekeeping, or overhead agencies.

average deviation, also called MEAN DEVIATION, measure of dispersion that provides information on the extent of scatter, or the degree of clustering, in a set of data.

average earned rate, total earnings for a given time period divided by the number of hours worked during the period.

average hourly earnings, wages earned by an employee per hour of work during a specific time period. The average hourly earnings are computed by dividing total pay received by the total hours worked.

average incumbents, average workforce strength figure found by adding the workforce strengths at the beginning and end of a specified report period and dividing this sum by two. This type of computation is widely used in turnover analysis.

average straight-time hourly earnings, average wages earned per hour exclusive of premium payments and shift differentials.

award, at the end of the arbitration process, the final decision of the arbitrator(s) when such arbitration is binding on both parties.

award, incentive, *see* INCENTIVE AWARD.

AWOL, absent without official leave. This term is usually restricted to the military.

B

Babbage, Charles (1792-1871), English mathematician and inventor. Best known as the "father" of the modern computer, he is also acclaimed for building upon the assembly line concepts of Adam Smith and anticipating the scientific management techniques of Frederick W. Taylor. Major works include: *On the Economy of Machinery and Manufactures* (London: Charles Knight, 1832); *Passages from the Life of a Philosopher* (London: Longman & Green, 1864). For modern biographies, *see* Maboth Moseley, *Irascible Genius: A Life of Charles Babbage, Inventor* (London: Hutchinson & Co., 1964); Philip and Emily Morrison, eds., *Charles Babbage and His Calculating Engines* (New York:

Dover Publications, 1961); Anthony Hyman, *Charles Babbage, Pioneer of the Computer* (Princeton: Princeton University Press, 1982).

QUANTIFYING THE UNQUANTIFIABLE?

Letter From Charles Babbage to Alfred, Lord Tennyson

(c. 1850)

Although Babbage never strayed very long from his calculating Engines, his tremendous scientific curiosity led him into many byways—some stemming directly from the main line of his machines, and some that were far afield . . .

He even extended his demand for statistical accuracy to poetry; it is said that he sent the following letter to Alfred, Lord Tennyson about a couplet in "The Vision of Sin":

"Every minute dies a man, / Every minute one is born": I need hardly point out to you that this calculation would tend to keep the sum total of the world's population in a state of perpetual equipoise, whereas it is a well-known fact that the said sum total is constantly on the increase. I would therefore take the liberty of suggesting that in the next edition of your excellent poem the erroneous calculation to which I refer should be corrected as follows: "Every moment dies a man / And one and a sixteenth is born." I may add that the exact figures are 1.167, but something must, of course, be conceded to the laws of metre.

From Introduction to *Charles Babbage and his Calculating Engines*, Dover Publications, New York, 1961.

Babbitt v. United Farm Workers, 60 L. Ed. 2d 895 (1979), U.S. Supreme Court case which held that a state's regulation of union election procedures did not violate First Amendment rights.

Babcock and Wilcox decision, *see* NATIONAL LABOR RELATIONS BOARD V. BABCOCK AND WILCOX.

backdoor authority, term generally used

to denote legislation enacted outside the normal appropriation process that permits the obligation of funds. The most common forms of backdoor authority are *borrowing authority* (authority to spend debt receipts) and *contract authority*. In other cases (*e.g.,* interest on the public debt) a permanent appropriation is provided that becomes available without any current action by the Congress. *Entitlement authority* may sometimes take the form of backdoor authority, since the enactment of the basic benefit legislation may, in effect, mandate the subsequent enactment of the appropriations to pay the statutory benefits. Section 401 of the Congressional Budget and Impoundment Control Act of 1974 specifies certain limits on the use of backdoor authority. Examples of accounts that have backdoor authority are the federal-aid highways trust fund, the Environmental Protection Agency's construction grants, and the Social Security trust funds.

See also AUTHORIZATION.

back loaded, a labor agreement providing for a greater wage increase in its later years; for example, a three year contract that provides for a two percent increase in the first year and six percent in each of the remaining two years.

See also FRONT LOADED.

back pay, delayed payment of wages for a particular time period.

See also ALBEMARLE PAPER CO. V. MOODY.

back-to-work movement, striking employees returning to their jobs before their union has formally ended the strike.

backward bending supply curve, the graphic depiction of the assumption that as wages increase, workers will continue to offer to work only to a point; thereafter the amount of offered labor will decline as the demand for more leisure increases relative to the demand for more income.

bafflegab, *see* GOBBLEDYGOOK.

Baggett v. *Bullitt,* 377 U.S. 360 (1960), U.S. Supreme Court case that held two sections of a State of Washington loyalty oath unconstitutional on the grounds that the oath was too broad and too vague.

See also LOYALTY.

Bailey v. *Richardson,* 182 F. 2d 46 (1950), affirmed by an equally divided Supreme Court, 341 U.S. 918 (1951), U.S. Court of Appeals (District of Columbia Circuit) case that upheld the constitutionality of the loyalty program in the federal government. The majority decision held that there is no prohibition against dismissal of government employees because of their political beliefs, activities, or affiliation and that "the First Amendment guarantees free speech and assembly, but it does not guarantee governmental employ."

The case became a *cause célèbre* when it became known that during a hearing on Ms. Bailey's loyalty she was asked "did you ever write a letter to the Red Cross about the segregation of blood?" Traditional notions of due process were also violated in hearings not providing for confrontation and cross-examination. Eventually, the "doctrine of privilege" upon which the court's reasoning was based was abandoned by the judiciary. *See* David H. Rosenbloom, *Federal Service and the Constitution* (Ithaca: Cornell University Press, 1971) and William Van Alstyne, "The Demise of the Right-Privilege Distinction in Constitutional Law," *Harvard Law Review,* Vol. 81 (1968).

Bakke, E. Wight (1903–1971), social scientist most noted for his pioneering empirical research on the problem-solving behavior of groups in organizations. Major works include: *Bonds of Organization* (New York: Harper & Row, 1950); *The Fusion Process* (New Haven, Conn.: Labor and Management Center, Yale University, 1953).

Bakke decision, *see* REGENTS OF THE UNIVERSITY OF CALIFORNIA V. ALLAN BAKKE.

balanced budget, a budget in which receipts are equal to or greater than outlays. *See* L. Douglas Lee, "Balancing the Budget: Does It Matter?" *Journal of the Institute of Socioeconomic Studies* (Winter 1980).

balance of payments, tabulation of a nation's debt and credit transactions with foreign countries and international institutions.

balance of trade, the amount by which the value of merchandise exports exceeds (trade surplus) or falls short of (trade deficit) the value of merchandise imports.

balance sheet, itemized accounting statement that reflects total assets, total liabilities, and fund balances as of a given date. *See* Charles W. Bastable, "On a Federal Balance Sheet," *Government Accountants Journal* (Winter 1977-1978).

balances of budget authority, balances that result from the fact that not all budget authority enacted in a fiscal year is obligated and paid out in that same year. Balances are classified as follows:
  obligated balance, the amount of obligations already incurred for which payment has not yet been made. This balance can be carried forward indefinitely until the obligations are paid.
  unobligated balance, the portion of budget authority that has not yet been obligated. In one-year accounts the unobligated balance expires (ceases to be available for obligation) at the end of the fiscal year. In multiple-year accounts the unobligated balance may be carried forward and remain available for obligation for the period specified. In no-year accounts the unobligated balance is carried forward indefinitely until (1) specifically rescinded by law, or (2) the purposes for which it was provided have been accomplished, or (3) such time as disbursements have not been made against the appropriation for two full consecutive years.
  unexpended balance, the sum of the obligated and unobligated balances.

band curve chart, or, CUMULATIVE BAND CHART, chart on which the bands of a graph are plotted one above the other.

bank holiday, any of the traditional legal holidays or other special occasions when banks and some other businesses remain closed. The six essentially "standard" paid holidays are: Christmas Day, Thanksgiving Day, New Year's Day, Independence Day, Labor Day, and Memorial Day. Many business and government jurisdictions offer as many as twice this number of paid holidays for their employees, but the specific days vary with local customs. In addition to the six listed above, all federal employees have paid holidays for Washington's Birthday, Columbus Day, and Veteran's Day.

Bankruptcy Act, *see* WAGE EARNER PLAN.

BANs, *see* BOND ANTICIPATION NOTES.

bar examination, written test that new lawyers must pass in order to practice law.

bargaining, *see* the following entries:
  BLUE SKY BARGAINING
  COALITION BARGAINING
  COLLECTIVE BARGAINING
  CRISIS BARGAINING
  GOOD-FAITH BARGAINING
  JOINT BARGAINING
  MULTIEMPLOYER BARGAINING
  PATTERN BARGAINING
  PRODUCTIVITY BARGAINING
  REGIONAL BARGAINING
  SUNSHINE BARGAINING

bargaining agent, the union organization (not an individual) that is the exclusive representative of all the workers, union as well as non-union, in a bargaining unit. Employers may voluntarily agree that a particular union will serve as the bargaining agent for their employees, or the decision on representation can be settled by secret ballot election conducted by the Federal Labor Relations Authority, the National Labor Relations Board or a counterpart state agency.

bargaining agreement, *see* LABOR AGREEMENT.

bargaining chip, a phrase that came out of the Strategic Arms Limitations Talks of the 1970s meaning a military resource that one nation might discard or downgrade in return for a concession from a rival nation. But the term was so widely bandied about by the news media that it now refers to anything one might be willing to trade in a negotiation.

bargaining item, illegal, *see* ILLEGAL BARGAINING ITEM.

bargaining rights, legal rights that most workers have to bargain collectively with their employers.
See also EXCLUSIVE BARGAINING RIGHTS.

bargaining strength, relative power that each of the parties holds during the negotiating process. The final settlement often reflects the bargaining power of each side. *See* Samuel B. Bacharach and Edward J. Lawler, "Power and Tactics in Bargaining," *Industrial and Labor Relations Review* (January 1981).

bargaining theory, the sum of several approaches to the study of how people negotiate and how to negotiate successfully. These approaches include mathematical modeling, game theory, various schools of psychology, and the study of bargaining in many different settings.

bargaining theory of wages, theory that wages are based on the supply and demand for labor, that wages can never be higher than a company's break-even point or lower than bare subsistence for the workers, and that the actual "price" of labor is determined by the relative strengths—the bargaining power—of employers and workers. While the bargaining theory does not explain wage determination over the long run, it is generally accepted as the most pragmatic explanation of short-run wage determination. The beginnings of the bargaining theory are found in Adam Smith's *The*

Wealth of Nations (1776), but its modern formulation dates from John Davidson's *The Bargaining Theory of Wages* (New York: G.P. Putnam's Sons, 1898). *Also see* John T. Dunlop, ed., *Theory of Wage Determination* (New York: St. Martin's Press, 1957).

bargaining unit, or simply UNIT, group of employees, both union members and others, that an employer has recognized and/or an administrative agency has certified as appropriate for representation by a union for purposes of collective bargaining. All of the employees in a bargaining unit are subsequently covered in the labor contract that the union negotiates on their behalf. Bargaining units may be as small as the handful of workers in a local shop or as large as the workforce of an entire industry. The size of a bargaining unit is important in that it significantly affects the relative bargaining strength of both labor and management. *See* James L. Perry and Harold L. Angle, "Bargaining Unit Structure and Organizational Outcomes," *Industrial Relations* (Winter 1981).
See also the following entries:
   AMERICAN FEDERATION OF LABOR V.
      NATIONAL LABOR RELATIONS BOARD
   APPROPRIATE UNIT
   NATIONAL LABOR RELATIONS BOARD
      V. MAGNAVOX
   UNION SECURITY

Barnard, Chester I. (1886–1961), a Bell System executive closely associated with the Harvard Business School, best known for his sociological analyses of organizations that encouraged and foreshadowed the post-World War II behavioral revolution. Barnard viewed organizations as cooperative systems where "the function of the executive" was to maintain the dynamic equilibrium between the needs of the organization and the needs of its employees. In order to do this, management had to be aware of the interdependent nature of the formal and informal organization. Barnard's analysis of the significance and role of informal organizations provided the theoretical foundations for a whole generation of empirical research. Major works include: *The Functions of the Executive* (Cambridge, Mass.: Harvard University Press, 1938); *Organization and Management: Selected Papers* (Cambridge, Mass.: Harvard University Press, 1948). For biography, *see* William B. Wolf, *How to Understand Management: An Introduction to Chester I. Barnard* (Los Angeles: Lucus Brothers Publishers, 1968); William B. Wolf, *The Basic Barnard: An Introduction to Chester I. Barnard and His Theories of Organization and Management* (Ithaca, N.Y.: New York State School of Industrial and Labor Relations, Cornell University, 1974).

Barr v. Matteo, 360 U.S. 564 (1959), U.S. Supreme Court case concerning the immunity of federal administrators from civil suits for damages in connection with their official duties. The court, without majority opinion, held that the acting director of the Office of Rent Stabilization had such an immunity. By implication, other federal employees would be immune from civil suits depending upon the nature of their responsibilities and duties.

See also the following entries:
BUTZ V. ECONOMOU
SPALDING V. VILAS
WOOD V. STRICKLAND

BARS, *see* BEHAVIORALLY ANCHORED RATING SCALES.

base, point from which budgetary calculations usually begin, generally the appropriation the agency received in the preceding fiscal year.
See also ZERO-BASE BUDGETING.

base period, time that an employee must work before becoming eligible for state unemployment insurance benefits.

base points, minimum point values given to the factors in a job evaluation system.

base rate, *see* BASE SALARY.

base salary, or BASE RATE, standard earnings before the addition of overtime or premium pay.

base time, time required for an employee to perform an operation while working normally with no allowance for personal/unavoidable delays or fatigue.

basic rate of pay, employee's hourly wage. The regular rate of pay upon which overtime and other wage supplements would be computed.

basic workday, number of hours in a normal workday, as established by collective bargaining agreements or statutory law. Premium payments must usually be paid for time worked in excess of the basic workday. The eight-hour day is widely accepted as the standard basic workday.

basic workweek, number of hours in a normal workweek, as established by collective bargaining agreements or statutory law. Premium payments must usually be paid for time worked in excess of the basic workweek. The forty-hour week is widely accepted as the standard basic workweek.
See also FAIR LABOR STANDARDS ACT.

Batterton v. Francis, 432 U.S. 416 (1977), U.S. Supreme Court case which held that a state could deny welfare benefits for families of unemployed fathers if the father is unemployed as a result of a strike.

battery, or TEST BATTERY, two or more tests administered together and standardized on the same population so that the results on the various tests are comparable. The term battery is also used to refer to any tests administered as a group. *See* W. Considine, *et al.,* "Developing a Physical Performance Test Battery for Screening Chicago Fire Fighter Applicants," *Public Personnel Management* (January-February 1976).

Bauer, Raymond A. (1916-1977), social psychologist best known to public administration for co-authoring (with Ithiel de Sola Pool and Lewis A. Dexter) a classic study in policy analyses, *American Business and Public Policy: The Politics of Foreign Trade* (New York: Atherton, 1963; 2nd ed., 1972). Other policy-related works include: *Social Indicators*, ed. (Cambridge, Mass.: MIT Press, 1966); *The Study of Policy Formation*, ed. with Kenneth Gergen (New York: The Free Press, 1968); *Second Order Consequences: Methodological Essays on the Impact of Technology*, ed. with others (Cambridge, Mass.: MIT Press, 1969).

Bay Ridge Company* v. *Aaron, 334 U.S. 446 (1948), U.S. Supreme Court case which held that premium payments provided for in collective bargaining agreements had to be considered in computing the "regular rate" of pay for overtime computations.

Bedford Cut Stone Company* v. *Journeyman Stone Cutters' Association, 174 U.S. 37 (1927), U.S. Supreme Court case which held that union members cannot, without being in violation of the Sherman Anti-Trust Act of 1890, refuse to work on work that had previously been worked on by non-union labor.

beggar-thy-neighbor policy, a course of action through which a country tries to reduce unemployment and increase domestic output by raising tariffs and instituting non-tariff measures that impede imports. Countries that pursued such policies in the early 1930s found that other countries retaliated by raising barriers against the first country's exports, which tended to worsen the economic difficulties that precipitated the initial protectionist action.

beginner's rate, or TRAINEE RATE, wage rate for an inexperienced employee. Once a previously established training period is completed, an employee is entitled to the regular rate of pay for the job.

behaviorally anchored rating scales (BARS), performance evaluation technique that is premised upon the scaling of critical incidents of work performance. For the methodology, *see* Donald Schwab, Herbert Heneman III, and Thomas DeCotiis, "Behaviorally Anchored Scales: A Review of the Literature," *Personnel*

Psychology, Vol. 28 (1975); Frank J. Landy, *et al.*, "Behaviorally Anchored Scales for Rating the Performance of Police Officers," *Journal of Applied Psychology* (December 1976); Michael Loar, Susan Mohrman and John R. Stock, "Development of a Behaviorally Based Performance Appraisal System," *Personnel Psychology* (Spring 1982).

behavioral sciences, general term for all of the academic disciplines that study human and animal behavior by means of experimental research.

See also NATIONAL TRAINING LABORA TORIES INSTITUTE FOR APPLIED BEHAVIORAL SCIENCE.

behavioral technology, emerging discipline that seeks to meld together both the technical and human aspects of the workplace. It places equal emphasis on the social as well as the technological sciences in order to foster the individual's fullest use as both a human and technical resource. *See* James G. Brianas, "Behavioral Technology: A Challenge to Modern Management," *Public Personnel Management* (July-August 1973).

behaviorism, school of psychology which holds that only overt behavior is the proper subject matter for the entire discipline. According to the foremost exponent of behaviorism, B. F. Skinner, "behaviorism is not the science of human behavior; it is the philosophy of that science." *About Behaviorism* (New York: Alfred A. Knopf, 1974).

behavior modeling, training, usually for first or second line supervisors, that uses videotapes and/or roleplaying sessions to give supervisors an opportunity to improve their supervisory abilities by imitating "models" who have already mastered such skills. For summaries of the technique, *see* Bernard L. Rosenbaum, "New Uses for Behavior Modeling," *The Personnel Administrator* (July 1978); Scott B. Parry and Leah R. Reich, "An Uneasy Look at Behavior Modeling," *Training and Development Journal* (March 1984); John T.

Clifford, Frank Petrock and James Davisson, "Behavior Modeling for Quality Assurance," *SAM Advanced Management Journal* (Summer 1984).

behavior models, diagrams used by social scientists to better explain their theories of human behavior. For examples, *see* JOHARI WINDOW and MANAGERIAL GRID.

behavior modification (BMod), use of positive or negative reinforcements to change the behavior of individuals or groups. *See* C. E. Schneider, "Behavior Modification: Training the Hard Core Unemployed," *Personnel* (May–June 1973); C. Ray Gullett and Robert Reisen, "Behavior Modification: A Contingency Approach to Employee Performance," *Personnel Journal* (April 1975); W. Clay Hamner and Ellen P. Hamner, "Behavior Modification on the Bottom Line," *Organizational Dynamics* (Spring 1976); Jerry L. Gray, "The Myths of the Myths About Behavior Mod in Organizations," *Academy of Management Review* (January 1979); James C. Robinson, "Will Behavior Modeling Survive the '80s?" *Training and Development Journal* (January 1980); Donald T. Tosti, "Behavior Modeling: A Process," *Training and Development Journal* (August 1980).

Bell, Daniel (1919-   ), sociologist whose critiques of modern industrial societies have touched upon their politics and their management. Bell is considered to be both a major critic of the "machine civilization" of the scientific management era and a pioneer in social forecasting. Major works include: *Work and Its Discontents: The Cult of Efficiency in America* (Boston: Beacon Press, 1956); *The End of Ideology* (Glencoe, Ill.: The Free Press, 1960); *The Coming of Post-Industrial Society* (New York: Basic Books, 1973). *See also* POST-INDUSTRIAL SOCIETY.

beltway bandits, term applied to consulting firms in the Washington, D.C., area because so many of them are located on the interstate beltway, Route 495, which surrounds the metro area.

benchmark, any standard that is identified with sufficient detail so that other similar classifications can be compared as being above, below, or comparable to the "benchmark" standard.

benchmark position, position used as a frame of reference in the evaluation of other positions.

beneficiary, person, group, or organization to whom an insurance policy is payable.

benefit, a sum of money provided in an insurance policy payable for certain types of loss, or for covered services, under the terms of the policy. The benefits may be paid to the insured or on his or her behalf to others.

benefit, death, *see* DEATH BENEFIT.

benefit-cost analysis, *see* COST-BENEFIT ANALYSIS.

benefit district, method for financing construction of public works in which those who directly benefit are charged for the construction costs. For example, sidewalks are often financed through increases in property taxes of residents through whose property the sidewalk passes; that is, those owners are members of a sidewalk or benefit district that levies a tax and is dissolved when the construction costs have been recovered.

benefit period, the period of time for which payments for benefits covered by an insurance policy are available. The availability of certain benefits may be limited over a specified time period; for example, two well-baby visits during a one-year period. While the benefit period is usually defined by a set unit of time, such as a year, benefits may also be tied to a spell of illness.

benefit plans, welfare programs administered by a union for its members and paid for out of dues, voluntary contributions, or special assessments.

See also the following entries:
CAFETERIA BENEFITS PLAN
FLAT-BENEFIT PLAN
FRINGE BENEFITS
HEALTH BENEFITS

benefit seniority, use of seniority in computing an employee's economic fringe benefits such as pensions, vacations, bonuses, etc.

Benge, Eugene J. (1896-   ), generally credited with having "invented" the factor-comparison method of job evaluation in the 1920s. Major works include: *Manual of Job Evaluation* with S. Burk and E. N. Hay (New York: Harper Bros., 1941); *How To Manage for Tomorrow* (Homewood, Ill.: Dow Jones-Irwin, 1975); *Elements of Modern Management* (New York: AMACOM, 1976).

benign neglect, *see* MOYNIHAN, DANIEL PATRICK.

Bennis, Warren G. (1925-   ), a leading proponent of organization development, is perhaps best known for his continuous sounding of the death knell of bureaucratic institutions. Bennis has indicted most present organizational formats as inadequate for a future that will demand rapid organizational and technological changes, participatory management, and the growth of a more professionalized workforce. Organizations of the future, Bennis maintains, will be more responsive to these needs and, in consequence, decidedly less bureaucratic, less structured, and less rigid. Major works include: *Changing Organizations* (New York: McGraw-Hill, 1966); *The Temporary Society*, with Philip E. Slater (New York: Harper & Row, 1968); *Organization Development: Its Nature, Origins, and Prospects* (Reading, Mass.: Addison-Wesley, 1969); *The Leaning Ivory Tower*, with P. W. Biederman (New York: Jossey-Bass, 1973).
    See also POSTBUREAUCRATIC ORGANIZATIONS.

Bentham, Jeremy (1748-1832), Utili-tarian philosopher who held that self-interest was the prime motivator and that a government should strive to do the greatest good for the greatest numbers. *See* J. A. W. Gunn, "Jeremy Bentham and the Public Interest," *Canadian Journal of Political Science* (December 1968).

bereavement leave, *see* FUNERAL LEAVE.

Berne, Eric (1910-1970), the psychoanalyst who founded the field of transactional analysis. Major works include: *Games People Play: The Psychology of Human Relationship* (New York: Grove Press, 1964); *Principles of Group Treatment* (New York: Oxford University Press, 1966); *What Do You Say After You Say Hello?* (New York: Grove Press, 1972); *Intuition & Ego States: The Origins of Transactional Analysis* (New York: Harper & Row, 1977). For biography, *see* Warren D. Cheney, "Eric Berne: Biographical Sketch," in *Eric Berne: Beyond Games and Scripts* (New York: Grove Press, 1976).

Bertalanffy, Ludwig von (1901-1972), Austrian-Canadian biologist considered to be the "father of general systems theory." His basic statement on the subject is *General System Theory: Foundations, Development, Applications,* rev. ed. (New York: George Braziller, 1968). For a biography, *see* Mark Davidson, *Uncommon Sense: The Life and Thought of Ludwig von Bertalanffy (1901-1972), Father of General Systems Theory* (Boston: Houghton Mifflin, 1983).

Beth Israel Hospital* v. *National Labor Relations Board, 437 U.S. 483 (1978), U.S. Supreme Court case which upheld a National Labor Relations Board determination that employees seeking to organize a bargaining unit of hospital employees could not be prohibited from distributing leaflets in a hospital cafeteria patronized predominantly by hospital employees. To a limited extent, the court gave its approval to the NLRB's attempt to permit a substantial range for union communication to actual and potential

51

members, provided such communication does not disrupt employer's business activities.

BFOQ, *see* BONA FIDE OCCUPATIONAL QUALIFICATION.

bias, tendency of a selection device to err in a particular direction.
See also CULTURAL BIAS.

biased sample, sample that does not truly represent the total population from which it was selected.

bicameral, *also* UNICAMERAL, a legislature that consists of two separate chambers or houses. A unicameral legislature has only one. Nebraska is the only unicameral state.

bidding, means by which an employee of an organization makes known his or her interest in a vacant position in that same organization. *See* Elaine Gale Wrong, "Arbitrators, the Law, and Women's Job Bids," *Labor Law Journal* (December 1982).

Big Blue, the International Business Machines Corporation (IBM).

Big Eight, slang term for the eight largest public accounting firms: Arthur Anderson and Co.; Coopers and Lybrand; Ernst and Ernst; Haskins and Sells; Peat, Marwick, Mitchell and Company; Price Waterhouse and Company; Touche Ross and Company; and Arthur Young and Company. *See* Mark Stevens, *The Big Eight: An Inside View of America's Eight Most Powerful and Influential Accounting Firms* (New York: Macmillan, 1981).

bigotry, *see* DISCRIMINATION.

Big Seven, *see* PUBLIC INTEREST GROUPS.

bilateralism, joint policies between states; specifically, the agreement to extend to each other privileges (usually relating to trade) that are not available to others.

bill, *see* ACT.

Bill of Rights, first ten amendments to the U.S. Constitution.

Only a few individual rights were specified in the Constitution when it was ratified in 1788. Shortly after its adoption, however, ten amendments—called the Bill of Rights—were added to the Constitution to guarantee basic individual liberties. These liberties include freedom of speech, freedom of press, freedom of religion, and freedom to assemble and petition the government.

The guarantees of the Bill of Rights originally applied only to actions of the federal government and did not prevent state and local governments from taking action which might threaten an individual's civil liberty. States had their own constitutions, some of which contained their own bills of rights guaranteeing the same or similar rights. These rights, however, were not guaranteed by all the states; and where they did exist, they were subject to varying interpretations. In short, citizens were protected only to the extent that the states themselves recognized their rights.

In 1868, the Fourteenth Amendment was added to the Constitution. In part, it provides that no state shall "deprive any person of life, liberty, or property without due process of law." It was not until 1925 in the case of *Gitlow* v. *New York*, 268 U.S. 652, that the Supreme Court interpreted the phrase "due process of law" to mean in effect "without abridgement of certain of the rights guaranteed by the Bill of Rights." Since that decision, the Supreme Court has ruled that a denial by a state of certain of the rights contained in the Bill of Rights actually represents a denial of due process of law. While the court has not ruled that all rights in the Bill of Rights are contained in the notion of "due process," neither has it limited that notion to the rights enumerated in the Bill of Rights. It simply has found that there are concepts in the Bill of Rights so basic to a democratic society that they must be recognized as part of "due process of law" and made applicable to the states as well as the federal government.

At present, the following guarantees of the Bill of Rights have been applied to the states under the terms of the Fourteenth Amendment: Amendments I, IV, and VI; the self-incrimination, double jeopardy, and just compensation clauses of Amendment V; and the guarantee against cruel and unusual punishment of Amendment VIII. Only Amendments II and III, the right to indictment by grand jury in Amendment V, the right to jury trial in a civil suit in Amendment VII, and the prohibition against excessive bail or fines in Amendment VIII have not yet been applied to the states.

To place these rights in a broader perspective, one should realize that they make up only the core of what are considered to be our civil rights—those privileges and freedoms that are accorded all Americans by virtue of their citizenship. There are many other "civil" rights which are not specifically mentioned in the Constitution but which nonetheless have been recognized by the courts, guaranteed by statute and now are embedded in our democratic traditions. The right to buy, sell, own, and bequeath property; the right to enter into contracts; the right to marry and have children; the right to live and work where one desires; and the right to participate in the political, social and cultural processes of the society in which one lives are a few of those rights that are considered as fundamental to a democratic society as those specified by the Constitution. *See* Irving Brant, *The Bill of Rights: Its Origin and Meaning* (Indianapolis: Bobbs Merrill, 1965); Robert A. Rutland, *The Birth of the Bill of Rights: 1776-1791*, revised ed. (Middletown, CT: Wesleyan University Press, 1983).

See also the following entries:

bimodal distribution, frequency distribution in which there are two modes—two most frequently occurring scores. A graphic presentation would show two peaks.

binding arbitration, actually a redundancy! Arbitration, unless it is advisory, is by its nature binding upon the parties. *See* Susan A. MacManus, "State Mandated Collective Bargaining and Compulsory Binding Arbitration: The Fiscal Effect on Municipal Governments," *Public Administration Quarterly* (Winter 1984).

Binet, Alfred (1857-1911), French psychologist who originated the first modern intelligence test. For a biography, *see* Theta Holmes Wolf, *Alfred Binet* (Chicago: University of Chicago Press, 1973).

bi-partite board, labor-management committee established as part of a grievance process in order to resolve a dispute short of arbitration.

birth leave, paid time off upon the birth of a child. This is generally available only to men. Women, should the occasion warrant, would necessarily take maternity leave. *See* Nancy Norman and James T. Tedeschi, "Paternity Leave: The Unpopular Benefit Option," *Personnel Administrator* (February 1984).
See also MATERNITY LEAVE.

biserial correlation, correlation between the score on a particular item and the total test score.

Bishop v. Wood, 426 U.S. 341 (1976), U.S. Supreme Court case, which held that an employee's discharge did not deprive him of a property interest protected by the Due Process Clause of the U.S. Constitution's 14th Amendment. The court further asserted that even assuming a false explanation for the employee's discharge, he was still not deprived of an interest in liberty protected by the clause if the reasons for his discharge were not made public.

Bivens v. Six Unknown Named Federal Narcotics Agents, 403 U.S. 388 (1971), U.S. Supreme Court case establishing the principle that individuals could sue public officials for damages in connection with the violation of their constitutional rights under the Fourth Amendment. By implication, the same principle would apply to violations of other constitutional rights.

See also CARLSON V. GREEN.

black-lung disease, scientific name PNEUMOCONIOSIS, chronic and disabling occupational disease (mostly of miners) resulting from the inhalation of dusts over a long period of time. Its popular name results from the tendency of the inhaled dusts to blacken lung tissue. See Carvin Cook, "The 1977 Amendments to the Black Lung Benefits Law," *Monthly Labor Review* (May 1978).

See also USERY V. TURNER ELKHORN MINING CO.

Blake, Robert R. (1918-   ) **and Jane S. Mouton,** (1930-   ), industrial psychologists best known for their conceptualization of the "managerial grid"— a graphic description of the various managerial approaches. The grid itself represents leadership styles that reflect two prime dimensions, "concern for people" on the vertical axis, and "concern for production" on the horizontal axis. For a complete presentation of the grid concept, see any of their books: *The Managerial Grid* (Houston: Gulf Publishing, 1964); *Corporate Excellence Through Grid Organization Development* (Houston: Gulf Publishing, 1968); *Building a Dynamic Organization Through Grid Organization Development* (Reading, Mass.: Addison-Wesley, 1969).

blanketing-in, term for large-scale importation of previously noncareer jobs into the regular civil service. In the short run, "blanketing-in" can be (and has been) used to protect political favorites from the next administration. In the long run, blanketing-in is one of the major means through which the career civil service has been enlarged. For a comprehensive discussion of the process, see Hugh Heclo, *A Government of Strangers: Executive Politics in Washington,* (Washington, D.C.: The Brookings Institution, 1977), pp. 41-46.

Blau, Peter M. (1918-   ), sociolgist who has specialized in the study of formal organizations and bureaucracies and produced pioneering empirical as well as theoretical analyses of organizational behavior. Major works include: *The Dynamics of Bureaucracy* (Chicago: University of Chicago Press, 1955, revised 1963); *Bureaucracy in Modern Society* (New York: Random House, 1956); *Formal Organizations,* with W. Richard Scott (San Francisco: Chandler Publishing, 1962); *Exchange and Power in Social Life* (New York: Wiley, 1964); *The American Occupational Structure* (New York: Wiley, 1967); *The Structure of Organizations* (New York: Basic Books, 1971); *The Organization of Academic Work* (New York: Wiley, 1973).

bleeding shark, an employee in trouble at work who is attacked by others instead of helped.

block grant, see GRANT.

BLS, see BUREAU OF LABOR STATISTICS.

blue-circle rate, see GREEN-CIRCLE RATE.

blue-collar workers, those workers, both skilled and unskilled, engaged primarily in physical labor. For example, the U.S. Bureau of the Census considers all craftsmen, construction workers, machine operators, farm workers, transportation equipment operators, factory production and maintenance workers to fit into the blue-collar category. For an analysis of blue-collar angst, see Irving Howe, ed., *The World of the Blue-Collar Worker* (New York: Quadrangle Books, 1972). *Also see* Nancy R. Brunner, "Blue-Collar

Women," *Personnel Journal* (April 1981); Robert Schrank, "Horse-Collar Blue-Collar Blues," *Harvard Business Review* (May-June 1981); Mary Russell, "Career Planning in a Blue Collar Company," *Training and Development Journal* (January 1984); Loren M. Solnick, "The Effect of Blue-Collar Unions on White Collar Wages and Fringe Benefits," *Industrial & Labor Relations Review* (January 1985).

Blue Cross and Blue Shield, non-profit group health insurance plans for, respectively, hospital and physician's fees.

Blue Eagle, *see* NATIONAL INDUSTRIAL RECOVERY ACT OF 1933.

blue flu, when police officers informally strike by calling in sick, they are said to be suffering from a disease so unique that it affects only police—the blue flu. *See* Casey Ichniowski, "Arbitration and Police Bargaining: Prescriptions for the Blue Flu," *Industrial Relations* (Spring 1982).

blue laws, state and local legislation banning commercial and related activities on particular days, usually Sunday.

Blue Shield, *see* BLUE CROSS AND BLUE SHIELD.

blue sky bargaining, unreasonable and unrealistic negotiating demands by either side, usually made at the beginning of the negotiating process. The only "useful" purposes of such bargaining are to (1) satisfy an outside audience that their concerns are being attended to, (2) delay the "real" negotiations because such a delay is thought to hold a tactical advantage, and (3) provide a basis for compromise as the negotiations progress.

BMod, *see* BEHAVIOR MODIFICATION.

BNA, *see* BUREAU OF NATIONAL AFFAIRS, INC.

BNA Pension Reporter, Bureau of National Affairs, Inc., information service that provides weekly notification of develop-

ments under the Employee Retirement Income Security Act of 1974, including enforcement actions, court decisions, labor and industry activities, and employee benefit trust fund regulation; activities of the Department of Labor, the Internal Revenue Service, the Pension Benefit Guaranty Corporation, and Congress; and state and local government actions.

BNA Policy and Practice Series, "common sense" guide on the handling of employer-employee relations published by the Bureau of National Affairs, Inc. Covers personnel management, labor relations, fair employment practices, wages and hours, and compensation.

board, also COMMISSION, a group charged with directing a governmental function. Boards or commissions are used when it is desirable to have bipartisan leadership or when their functions are of a quasi-judicial nature.

Board of Regents* v. *Roth, 408 U.S. 564 (1972), U.S. Supreme Court case which established the principle that a dismissed or nonrenewed public employee had no general constitutional right to either a statement of reasons or a hearing. However, both of these might be constitutionally required, the court ruled, in individual instances where any of the following four conditions existed:

1. Where the removal or non-renewal was in retaliation for the exercise of constitutional rights such as freedom of speech or association.
2. Where the adverse action impaired the individual's reputation.
3. Perhaps not fully distinguishable from the above, where a dismissal or nonrenewal placed a stigma or other disability upon the employee which foreclosed his or her freedom to take advantage of other employment opportunities.
4. Where one had a property right or interest in the position, as in the case of tenured or contracted public employees.

bod biz, slang term for sensitivity training programs.

body chemistry, nebulous concept that refers to the fact that strangers, upon meeting, react to a variety of irrational and subliminal signals, which, in turn, determine whether they like each other or not.

***Boeing* decision,** *see* NATIONAL LABOR RELATIONS BOARD V. BOEING.

bogey, easily exceeded informal standard that employees may establish in order to restrict production.

bona fide occupational qualification (BFOQ or BOQ), *bona fide* is a Latin term meaning "in good faith," honest, or genuine. A BFOQ, therefore, is a *necessary* occupational qualification. Title VII of the Civil Rights Act of 1964 allows employers to discriminate against applicants on the basis of religion, sex, or national origin when being considered for certain jobs if they lack a BFOQ. However, what constitutes a BFOQ has been interpreted very narrowly by the EEOC and the federal courts. Legitimate BFOQ's include female sex for a position as an actress or male sex for a sperm donor. There are no generally recognized BFOQ's with respect to race or color. Overall, a BFOQ is a job requirement that would be discriminatory and illegal were it not for its necessity for the performance of a particular job. For analyses, *see* Jeffery M. Shaman, "Toward Defining and Abolishing the Bona Fide Occupational Qualification Based on Class Status," *Labor Law Journal* (June 1971); Thomas Stephen Neuberger, "Sex as a Bona Fide Occupational Qualification Under Title VII," *Labor Law Journal* (July 1978).
See also DOTHARD V. RAWLINSON.

bona fide union, union that was freely chosen by employees and that is not unreasonably or illegally influenced by their employer.

bond, certificate of indebtedness issued by a borrower to a lender that constitutes a legal obligation to repay the principal of the loan plus accrued interest.
See also the following entries:
CALLABLE BONDS
MUNICIPAL BONDS
REVENUE BONDS
SERIAL BONDS

bond anticipation notes (BANs), form of short-term borrowing used to accelerate progress on approved capital projects. Once the revenues for a project have been realized from the sale of long-term bonds the BANs are repaid. BANs may also be used to allow a jurisdiction to wait until the bond market becomes more favorable for the sale of long-term securities.

bond bank, an arrangement whereby small units of government within a state are able to pool their long-term debt in order to create a larger bond issue at more advantageous rates. *See* David S. Kidwell and Robert J. Rogowski, "Bond Banks: A State Assistance Program that Helps Reduce New Issue Borrowing Costs," *Public Administration Review* (March/April 1983).

bond funds, funds established to account for the proceeds of bond issues pending their disbursement.

bonus, also called SUPPLEMENTAL COMPENSATION, any compensation that is in addition to regular wages and salary. Because "bonus" has a mildly paternalistic connotation, it has been replaced in some organizations by "supplemental compensation."
See also the following entries:
DANGER-ZONE BONUS
NONPRODUCTION BONUS
PRODUCTION BONUS
STEP BONUS

boondoggle, slang term for any wasteful and/or unproductive program.

Booster Lodge No. 405, Machinists v. National Labor Relations Board, 412 U.S. 84 (1973), U.S. Supreme Court case which held that a union's attempt to collect fines from strikers who had resigned from the union before crossing picket lines was an unfair labor practice.

bootleg wages, wages above union scale that an employer might pay in a tight labor market in order to retain and attract employees, as well as wages below union scale that an employee might accept in lieu of unemployment.

BOQ, see BONA FIDE OCCUPATIONAL QUALIFICATION.

border tax adjustments, the remission of taxes on exported goods, including sales taxes and value added taxes, designed to ensure that national tax systems do not impede exports. The GATT permits such frontier adjustments on exports for indirect taxes on the grounds that these are passed on to consumers, but not for direct taxes (*e.g.*, income taxes assessed on producing firms). The United States makes little use of border tax adjustments, since it relies more heavily on income (or direct) taxes than most other governments.

Boren, James H., see INTERNATIONAL ASSOCIATION OF PROFESSIONAL BUREAUCRATS.

Borg-Warner case, see NATIONAL LABOR RELATIONS BOARD V. WOOSTER DIVISION OF BORG-WARNER CORP.

borough, local government unit generally smaller than a city. New York City, for example, is divided into five boroughs: Manhattan, Brooklyn, Bronx, Queens, and Richmond.
See also TOWN.

borrowing authority, statutory authority (substantive or appropriation) that permits a federal agency to incur obligations and to make payments for specified purposes out of borrowed moneys. Section 401 of the Congressional Budget and Impoundment Control Act of 1974 limits new borrowing authority (except for certain instances) to the extent or amount provided in appropriation acts. Borrowing

authority, also called "Authority to Spend Debt Receipts," may be either of two types:
1. *Public debt authority.* The authority to obligate and spend amounts borrowed from the Treasury that in turn are derived from the sale of public debt securities.
2. *Agency debt authority.* The authority to obligate and spend amounts derived from the sale of agency debt securities, assumption of mortgages, loans, etc.
See also BACKDOOR AUTHORITY.

boss, slang term used by subordinates to refer to anyone from whom they are willing to take orders. *See* John J. Gabarro and John P. Kotter, "Managing Your Boss," *Harvard Business Review* (January-February 1980); William P. Anthony, *Managing Your Boss* (New York: AMACOM, 1983).

bossism, also POLITICAL MACHINE, informal system of local government in which political power is concentrated in the hands of a central figure, called a political boss, who may not have a formal government position. The power is concentrated through the use of a political machine whereby a hierarchy is created and maintained through the use of patronage and government largesse to assure compliance with the wishes of the boss. It was a dominant system in American city government after the Civil War and was the main target of the American urban reform effort. *See* Harold Zink, *City Bosses in the United States* (Durham, N.C.: Duke University Press, 1930); Lyle W. Dorsett, "The City Boss and the Reformer: A Reappraisal," *Pacific Northwest Quarterly* (October 1962); Lee S. Greene, ed., "City Bosses and Political Machines," *The Annals of the American Academy of Political and Social Science* (May 1964); Seymour J. Mandlebaum, *Boss Tweed's (New York* (New York: John Wiley and Sons, 1965); Alexander Callow, Jr., *The Tweed Ring* (New York: Oxford University Press, 1966); Harold F. Gosnell, *Machine Politics: Chicago Model,* 2nd ed.,

(Chicago: University of Chicago Press, 1968); Alfred Steinberg, *The Bosses* (New York: Macmillan, 1972); Alexander B. Callow, Jr., ed., *The City Boss in America* (New York: Oxford University Press, 1976); Thomas M. Guterbock, *Machine Politics in Transition: Party and Community in Chicago* (Chicago: University of Chicago Press, 1980).

Boston Police Strike of 1919, the nation's first taste of large-scale municipal labor problems. While the patrolmen struck for a variety of reasons, including the right to form a union and affiliate with the AFL, the strike brought chaos to the city. Samuel Gompers protested the police commissioner's refusal to allow the union to affiliate with the AFL. Calvin Coolidge, then Governor of Massachusetts, responded with his famous assertion that "there is no right to strike against the public safety by anybody, anywhere, anytime." These words so captured the public's imagination that a tidal wave of support gained him the Republican vice-presidential nomination in 1920 (and when Harding died in 1923, Coolidge became president). The failure of the Boston Police Strike of 1919 was a lesson that would inhibit municipal unionization for many decades.

For a history, see Francis Russell, *A City in Terror—1919—The Boston Police Strike* (New York: The Viking Press, 1975).

bottom line, the profit or loss for an activity; the final result of an activity; a final conclusion or responsibility. *See* Michael O'Keefe, "The Link to Bottom-Line Results," *Training and Development Journal* (January 1981).

bottom-line concept, in the context of equal employment opportunity, a concept that suggests that an employer whose total selection process has no adverse impact can be assured that EEO enforcement agencies will not examine the individual components of that process for evidence of adverse impact. However, not all EEO enforcement agencies subscribe to the concept.

bottom-up management, catch-phrase describing a philosophy of participative management designed "to release the thinking and encourage the initiative of all those down from the bottom up." For the original presentation, *see* W. B. Given, Jr., *Bottom Up Management* (New York: Harper & Row, 1949).

Boulding, Kenneth E. (1910-   ), economist, social scientist, and prolific author best known to organizational analysts for his classic article, "General Systems Theory—The Skeleton of Science," *Management Science* (April 1956), and his book *The Organizational Revolution* (New York: Harper & Row, 1953), which deal with the relationships between organizations and ethical systems.

Boulwareism, approach to collective bargaining in which management makes a final "take it or leave it" offer that it believes is both fair and the best it can do. The concept is named for Lemuel R. Boulware, a vice president of the General Electric Company, who pioneered the tactic in the 1950s. If the final offer is rejected by the union, management grants the benefits of the offer to all non-union workers and assures the union that there will be no retroactive benefits when the union finally accepts the "final" offer. Because this tactic called for management to communicate directly to the workers, circumventing the union, it was challenged as an unfair practice. Boulwareism, as used by General Electric, was found in violation of the National Labor Relations Act in a 1969 ruling of the U.S. Circuit Court of Appeals in New York. The company's appeal to the U.S. Supreme Court was denied. The major defense of Boulwareism is: Lemuel R. Boulware, *The Truth About Boulwareism: Trying To Do Right Voluntarily* (Washington, D.C.: Bureau of National Affairs, 1969).

bounded rationality, *see* SATISFICING.

bourgeois, in the context of Marxism, a member of the ruling class in capitalistic societies; one of the owners of the means of production. The plural is *bourgeoisie*. Marx distinguished between the *haute bourgeoisie*, the real leaders of industry, and the *petit bourgeoisie*, the small businessmen, whom he felt really belonged with the proletariat.

boycott, during the mid-19th century, Charles C. Boycott, a retired English army captain, was in Ireland managing the estate of an absentee owner. His methods were so severe and oppressive that the local citizens as a group refused to deal with him in any manner. When Captain Boycott was forced to flee home to England, the first boycott or nonviolent intimidation through ostracism was a success.

In the context of labor relations, a boycott is any refusal to deal with or buy the products of a business as a means of exerting pressure in a labor dispute. The U.S. Supreme Court has consistently held that boycotts are an illegal "restraint of trade" under the Sherman Antitrust Act of 1890. *Also see* Robert S. Jordan, "Boycott Diplomacy: The U.S., the U.N. and UNESCO," *Public Administration Review* (July/August 1984).

See also the following entries:
LAWLOR V. LOEWE
NATIONAL WOODWORK MANUFACTURES
ASSOCIATION V. NATIONAL LABOR
RELATIONS BOARD
PRIMARY BOYCOTT
SECONDARY BOYCOTT
UNITED STATES V. HUTCHESON

Boys Market* v. *Retail Clerks' Local 770, 398 U.S. 235 (1970), U.S. Supreme Court case which held that when a labor contract has a no-strike provision and provides an arbitration procedure, a federal court may, upon the request of an employer, issue an injunction to terminate a strike by employees covered by such a contract. This reversed an earlier decision, *Sinclair Refining* v. *Atkinson,* 370 U.S. 195 (1962), that forbade federal courts from issuing injunctions to stop a strike in violation of a no-strike clause. For an analysis, *see* John A. Relias, "The Developing Law Under Boys Markets," *Labor Law Journal* (December 1972).

See also ARBITRATION, INJUNCTION and STRIKE.

bracero program, or BRACERO SYSTEM, practice arising during World War II. The farm manpower shortage was so great that Mexican field hands or *braceros* were imported as seasonal farm workers. The practice, sanctioned by law in 1951, was long opposed by organized labor and was terminated by Congress in 1964. Since that time, however, an informal and unofficial bracero program has evolved from the large numbers of illegal aliens coming into the United States from Mexico.
See also UNDOCUMENTED WORKERS.

Bradford, Leland P. (1905-   ), director of the National Training Laboratories from 1947 to 1967, who pioneered the development of "sensitivity" training. Major works include: *T-Group Theory and Laboratory Method: Innovation in Re-Education*, co-editor (New York: John Wiley, 1964); *Making Meetings Work: A Guide for Leaders & Group Members* (San Diego, Calif.: University Associates, 1976).

Bradley* v. *Fisher, *see* STUMP V. SPARKMAN.

brain drain, pejorative term referring to the unfortunate flow of human capital—talent—from a country or an organization. While historically used to describe the exodus of doctors, scientists, and other professionals from a particular country, it is colloquially used to refer to the departure of any valued employee or group of employees. *See* Walter Adams, ed., *The Brain Drain* (New York: Macmillan, 1968).

brainstorming, frequently used to describe any group effort to generate ideas. It has a more formal definition—a creative conference for the sole purpose of producing suggestions or ideas that can serve as leads to problem solving. The concept has been most developed by Alex Osborn. See his *Applied Imagination* (New York: Charles Scribner's Sons, 1963). For a how-to account, *see* Ronald H. Gorman and H. Kent Baker, "Brainstorming Your Way to Problem-Solving Ideas," *Personnel Journal* (August 1978). *Also see* Toby Katz, "Brainstorming Updated," *Training and Development Journal* (February 1984).

Branti v. Finkel, 445 U.S. 507 (1980), Supreme Court case expanding on the Court's earlier ruling in *Elrod* v. *Burns* (1976) that the dismissal of nonpolicymaking, nonconfidential public employees for their partisan affiliation violates the First and/or Fourteenth Amendments. The burden is on the hiring authority to demonstrate that partisan affiliation is an appropriate requirement for effective performance in office, which could not be done in this instance involving the position of assistant public defender.

brass, slang term of military origin which now refers to the key executives in an organization.

breach of contract, violation of a collective bargaining agreement by either party. If established grievance machinery is not adequate to deal with the dispute, traditional lawsuits remain as a remedy.

bread-and-butter unions, *see* BUSINESS UNIONS.

breakdown, *see* NERVOUS BREAKDOWN.

break in service, the time between separation and reemployment that may cause a loss of rights or privileges.

Bretton Woods System, international monetary system devised by a conference of leading world economists in 1944 at Bretton Woods, New Hampshire. In order to abolish the economic ills believed to be responsible for the 1929 depression and World War II, a new international monetary system was created that established rules for an exchange rate system, balance-of-payments adjustments, and supplies of reserve assets; the conference also founded the International Monetary Fund and the International Bank for Reconstruction and Development. The Bretton Woods system is generally perceived to have collapsed in August 1971 when the United States suspended the convertibility of dollars into gold. *See* Lawrence B. Krause, *Sequel to Bretton Woods: A Proposal to Reform the World Monetary System* (Washington, D.C.: The Brookings Institution, 1971).

bridge job, position specifically designed to facilitate the movement of individuals from one classification and/or job category to another classification and/or category. Such bridge jobs are an integral part of many career ladders and upward mobility programs.

brief, a written statement prepared by each side in a formal lawsuit or hearing which summarizes the facts of the situation and makes arguments about how the law should be applied.

broken time, or SPLIT SHIFT, daily work schedule that is divided by a length of time considerably in excess of the time required for a normal meal break. For example, a school bus driver may work from 6 to 10 A.M. and then from 2 to 6 P.M.

Brookings Institution, nonprofit organization devoted to research, education, and publication in economics, government, foreign policy, and the social sciences generally. In its research, it functions as an independent analyst and critic, committed to publishing its findings for the information of the public. In its conferences and other activities, it serves as a bridge between scholarship and public policy, bringing new knowledge to the attention of decision makers and affording scholars a better insight into policy issues. The Institution's Advanced Study Program is devoted to public policy education of leaders in both government and business.

Brookings Institution
1775 Massachusetts Avenue, N.W.
Washington, D.C. 20036
(202) 797-6000

brotherhood, term used by some of the older unions as an indication of solidarity and common interests. For example, the Brotherhood of Railroad Signalmen.

Brownlow, Louis (1879-1963), major figure in the development of city management as a profession, best remembered as chairman of the President's Committee on Administration Management (1936-37). Major works include: *The President and the Presidency* (Chicago: Public Administration Service, 1949); *A Passion for Politics: The Autobiography of Louis Brownlow, First Half* (Chicago: University of Chicago Press, 1955), *A Passion For Anonymity: The Autobiography of Louis Brownlow, Second Half* (Chicago: University of Chicago Press, 1958). For an appreciation, *see* Barry D. Karl, "Louis Brownlow," *Public Administration Review* (November/December 1979).

Brownlow Committee, also called PRESIDENT'S COMMITTEE ON ADMINISTRATIVE MANAGEMENT, appointed by President Franklin Roosevelt in 1936 for the purpose of diagnosing the manpower support needs of the president and making appropriate recommendations for the reorganization of the executive branch. The committee of three, chaired by Louis Brownlow, included Charles Merriam and Luther Gulick. The committee reported to the president in January 1937. It found that the president needed help in carrying out his work and proposed enhanced presidential instruments for management and rationalized organization in the executive branch. Heavily influenced by the committee's report, Congress in 1939 passed a reorganization act authorizing the president, subject to congressional veto, to redistribute and restructure executive branch agencies. President Roosevelt subsequently created the Executive Office of the President. The EOP began with six top-level assistants in 1939, but has expanded to several offices and over 100 top-level assistants. *See* Richard Polenberg, *Reorganizing Roosevelt's Government: The Controversy over Executive Reorganization, 1936-1939*

(Cambridge, Mass.: Harvard University Press, 1966) and Barry Karl, *Executive Reorganization and Reform in the New Deal* (Cambridge, Mass.: Harvard University Press, 1963).

See also EXECUTIVE OFFICE OF THE PRESIDENT.

The Brownlow Committee Reports

The president needs help. His immediate staff assistance is entirely inadequate. He should be given a small number of executive assistants who would be his direct aides in dealing with the managerial agencies and administrative departments of the government. These assistants, probably not exceeding six in number, would be in addition to his present secretaries, who deal with the public, with the Congress, and with the press and the radio. These aides would have no power to make decisions or issue instructions in their own right. They would not be interposed between the president and the heads of his departments. They would not be assistant presidents in any sense. Their function would be, when any matter was presented to the president for action affecting any part of the administrative work of the government, to assist him in obtaining quickly and without delay all pertinent information possessed by any of the executive departments so as to guide him in making his responsible decisions; and then when decisions have been made, to assist him in seeing to it that every administrative department and agency affected is promptly informed. Their effectiveness in assisting the president will, we think, be directly proportional to their ability to discharge their functions with restraint. They would remain in the background, issue no orders, making no decisions, emit no public statements. Men for these positions should be carefully chosen by the president from within and without the government. They should be men in whom the president has personal confidence and whose character and attitude is such that they would not attempt to exercise power on their own account. They should be possessed of high competence, great physical vigor, and a passion for anonymity.

Source: President's Committee on Administrative Management, *Administrative Management in the Government of the United States, January 8, 1937* (Washington, D.C.: United States Government Printing Office, 1937).

Brown v. Board of Education of Topeka, Kansas, 347 U.S. 483 (1954), landmark Supreme Court decision holding that the separation of children by race and according to law in public schools "generates a feeling of inferiority as to their [the minority group's] status in the community that may affect their hearts and minds in a way unlikely ever to be undone." Consequently, it held that "separate educational facilities are inherently unequal" and therefore violate the equal protection clause of the Fourteenth Amendment. *See* Richard Kluger, *Simple Justice: The History of Brown v. Board of Education and Black America's Struggle for Equality* (New York: Knopf, 1976); Raymond Wolters, *The Burden of Brown: Thirty Years of School Desegregation* (Knoxville, Tenn.: University of Tennessee Press, 1984).

Brown v. General Services Administration, 425 U.S. 820 (1976), U.S. Supreme Court case which held that Congress intended Title VII of the Civil Rights Act of 1964 to provide the sole statutory protection against employment discrimination for federal employees—even though it is not the sole protection for workers in the private sector.

buckology, basis technique for evading responsibility. *See* R. C. Burkholder, "Buckology: The Art and Science of Passing the Buck," *Supervision* (March 1978).

buddy system, on-the-job training technique that has a trainee assigned to work closely with an experienced worker until the trainee has gained enough experience to work alone.

budget, financial plan serving as a pattern for and control over future operations—hence, any estimate of future costs or any systematic plan for the utilization of the workforce, material, or other resources.

Budget, Bureau of the, central budget agency of the United States from 1921 to 1970. For histories, *see* Fritz Marx Morstein, "The Bureau of the Budget: Its Evolution and Present Role," *The*

American Political Science Review (October 1945) and Allen Schick, "The Budget Bureau That Was: Thoughts on the Rise, Decline and Future of a Presidential Agency," *Law and Contemporary Problems,* Vol. 25 (1970).

See also CONGRESSIONAL BUDGET AND IMPOUNDMENT CONTROL ACT OF 1974.

budget, current services, budget that projects estimated budget authority and outlays for the upcoming fiscal year at the same program level (and without policy changes) as the fiscal year in progress. To the extent mandated by existing law, estimates take into account the budget impact of anticipated changes in economic conditions (such as unemployment or inflation), beneficiary levels, pay increases, and benefit changes. The Congressional Budget and Impoundment Control Act of 1974 requires that the President submit a current services budget to the Congress by November 10 of each year.

budget, envelope, a budgeting practice used in Canada whereby programs are divided into "envelopes" to be managed by appropriate cabinet committees. *See* Jerry McCaffery, "Canada's Envelope Budget: A Strategic Management System," *Public Administration Review* (July/August 1984).

budget, executive, process by which agency requests for appropriations are prepared and submitted to a budget bureau under the chief executive for review, alteration, and consolidation into a single budget document that can be compared to expected revenues and executive priorities before submission to the legislature; also refers to the methods for controlling departmental spending after the legal appropriations have been made.

budget, full-employment, estimated receipts, outlays, and surplus or deficit that would occur if the economy were continually operating at a rate defined as being at full capacity (traditionally defined as a certain percentage unemployment rate for the civilian labor force).

budget, line-item, classification of budgetary accounts according to narrow, detailed objects of expenditure (such as motor vehicles, clerical workers, or reams of paper) used within each particular agency of government, generally without reference to the ultimate purpose or objective served by the expenditure.

budget, operating, short-term plan for managing the resources necessary to carry out a program. "Short-term" can mean anything from a few weeks to a few years. Usually an operating budget is developed for each fiscal year with changes made as necessary.

budget, president's, budget for a particular fiscal year transmitted to the Congress by the president in accordance with the Budget and Accounting Act of 1921, as amended. Some elements of the budget, such as the estimates for the legislative branch and the judiciary, are required to be included without review by the Office of Management and Budget or approval by the president.

budget, tax-expenditures, enumeration of revenue losses resulting from "tax expenditures" under existing law for each fiscal year. Section 601 of the Congressional Budget and Impoundment Control Act of 1974 requires that estimated levels of tax expenditures be presented in the president's budget.

budget, unified, present form of the budget of the federal government in which receipts and outlays from federal funds and trust funds are consolidated. When these fund groups are consolidated to display budget totals, transactions which are outlays of one fund group to the other fund group (interfund transactions) are deducted to avoid double counting. The fiscal activities of off-budget federal agencies are not included in the unified budget.

budget activities, categories within most accounts that identify the purposes, projects, or types of activities financed.

budget amendment, proposal, submitted to the Congress by the president after his formal budget transmittal but prior to completion of appropriation action by the Congress, that revises previous requests, such as the amount of budget authority.

Budget and Accounting Act of 1921, act that created the Bureau of the Budget (later OMB) and the General Accounting Office.

budgetary reserves, portions of budget authority set aside under authority of the Antideficiency Act (31 U.S.C. 665), as amended by the Congressional Budget and Impoundment Control Act of 1974, for contingencies or to effect savings whenever savings are made possible by or through changes in requirements or greater efficiency of operations. Section 1002 of the Congressional Budget and Impoundment Control Act of 1974 restricts the establishment of budgetary reserves and requires that all reserves be reported to the Congress.

budget authority, authority provided by law to enter into obligations which generally result in immediate or future outlays of government funds. The authority to insure or guarantee the repayment of indebtedness incurred by another person or government is usually not considered to be budget authority. The basic forms of budget authority are: appropriations, contract authority, and borrowing authority. Budget authority may be classified by the period of availability (one-year, mulitple-year, no-year), by the timing of legislative action (current or permanent), or by the manner of determining the amount available (definite or indefinite).

1. Period of Availability. *One-year (annual) authority* — budget authority that is available for obligation only during a specified fiscal year and expires at the end of that time. *Multiple-year authority* — budget authority that is available for a specified period of time in excess of one fiscal year. *No-year authority* — budget authority that remains avail-

able for obligation for an indefinite period of time, usually until the objectives have been obtained.

2. Timing of Congressional Action. *Current authority*—budget authority enacted by a legislature in or immediately preceding the fiscal year in which it becomes available. *Permanent authority*—budget authority that becomes available as the result of previously enacted legislation (substantive legislation or prior appropriations act), and does not require current action by the legislature. Authority created by such legislation is considered to be "current" in the first year in which it is provided and "permanent" in succeeding years. It is possible to distinguish between "fully permanent" (such as interest on the public debt) and "conditionally permanent" where authority expires after a set period of time (such as general revenue sharing).

3. Determination of Amount. *Definite authority*—authority which is stated as a specific sum at the time the authority is granted. This includes authority stated as "not to exceed" a specified amount. *Indefinite authority*—authority for which the amount is not stated, but is to be determined by subsequent circumstances such as an appropriation of all or part of the receipts from a certain source.

budget call, *see* BUDGET GUIDANCE.

budget cycle, timed steps of the budget process including preparation, approval, execution, and audit.

budget deficit, amount by which a government's budget outlays exceed its budget receipts for any given period. Deficits are financed primarily by borrowing from the public.

budget estimates, estimates of budget authority, outlays, receipts, or other budget measures that cover the current and budget years, as reflected in the executive's budget and budget updates.

budget guidance, also BUDGET CALL, direction given by a jurisdiction's budget bureau or equivalent unit at the time of the call for budget estimates for the forthcoming budget period. Guidance frequently includes specific instructions regarding the format and timing of the budget submissions as well as statements of executive policy concerning scope of requests and program emphasis for the coming year.

budgeting, no less than the single most important decision-making process in U.S. public institutions today. The budget itself is also a jurisdiction's most important reference document. In their increasingly voluminous formats budgets simultaneously record policy decision outcomes, cite policy priorities as well as program objectives, and delineate government's total service effort.

A public budget has four basic dimensions. *First,* it is a political instrument that allocates scarce public resources among the social and economic needs of the jurisdiction. *Second,* a budget is a managerial and/or administrative instrument. It specifies the ways and means of providing public programs and services; it establishes the costs and/or criteria by which activities are evaluated for their efficiency and effectiveness. It is the budgeting process that ensures all of the programs and activities of a jurisdiction will be reviewed or evaluated at least once during each year (or cycle). *Third,* a budget is an economic instrument that can direct a nation's or a state's economic growth and development. Certainly at the national level—and to a lesser extent at the state and regional levels—government budgets are primary instruments for redistributing income, stimulating economic growth, promoting full employment, combating inflation, and maintaining economic stability. *Fourth,* a budget is an accounting instrument that holds government officials responsible for the expenditure of the funds with which they have been entrusted. Budgets also hold governments accountable in the aggregate. The very concept of a budget implies that there is a ceiling or a spending limitation, which literally (but theoretically) requires governments to live within their means.

Budgets as we know them today are relatively new phenomena. Prior to this century they were little more than compilations of piecemeal appropriations reports passed by a legislature. The Budget and Accounting Act that began the establishment of today's federal budgeting mechanisms was not passed until 1921. Earlier budgeting efforts at the state and local levels go back to experiments and developments in New York City and other localities in the early 1900s. Prior to this time there was little perceived need for sophisticated budgeting mechanisms because government expenditures were relatively insignificant. Federal "budgeting"—if it can even be called that—was primarily an exercise in getting rid of "surplus funds" accumulated by tariff revenues or finding ways to fund major land purchases. In retrospect, the nation's first great public administrator, Alexander Hamilton, may perhaps have succeeded too well in putting the new republic on a solid financial footing. However, there were instances throughout the 19th century, such as the financial panic of 1837 and Abraham Lincoln's efforts to finance the Civil War, that generated some concern that there might be a need for a budgeting system. Later social forces, such as the progressive reform movement, the scientific management movement, and the emergence of more diverse and specialized government programs, provided the impetus for more effective advocation of a budgeting system. The pioneering work done in some states and municipalities provided the federal government with further examples of the direction to go in budgeting. Indeed, the federal nature of the U.S. system of government has proven to be an essential factor in budgetary reform. Such reforms often emerge from "experiments" in state and local "laboratories," whether they be in New York City in the 1900s or Georgia in the 1970s.

The thrust for reform came to a head in the report of the Taft Commission of 1912, which argued strenuously for a national budgeting system to serve the executive branch. Even in its infancy, a recurring theme of governmental budgeting was already apparent—the conflict between the legislative and executive branch as to who would control the budgeting process—and Congress quickly rejected the Taft Commission recommendations. After World War I, President Wilson rekindled the idea of an executive budget mechanism, but Congress proposed its own legislation, which Wilson promptly vetoed because of lack of control by the executive. Finally, in 1921, the Budget and Accounting Act was signed into law. It established a Bureau of the Budget (to be lodged in the Treasury Department), a formal budgeting mechanism to be controlled by the executive branch, and a General Accounting Office accountable to Congress.

It would be another eighteen years, however, before the Bureau of the Budget would become a direct staff branch of the chief executive. During this period, budgeting processes focused primarily on accountability and control, and the initial technology of budgeting was the line-item budget—a systematic, accounting-oriented method of recording public expenditures against various classification categories, such as salaries, travel, supplies, equipment, etc.

Above all, budgeting is a legislative process. Whatever the executive branch does in the budgeting process, it is in the end subjected to legislative review. The extent to which this process represents a rubber-stamp ratification or a zealous, totally independent and often contradictory restructuring of a entire budget submission depends on two considerations: (1) the strength of the legislature, and (2) the nature of the legislature's budgeting powers. Over the years, much research has focused on the politics of the legislative process. That is, the strengths of the legislature vis-à-vis the executive, the bureaucracy, the public, the interest groups, the media, or any other conceivable group that seeks to influence or exert pressure on legislatures. Extensive consideration of the legislative budgetary process has only just begun, in large measure a result of the recent Congressional Budget and Impoundment Control Act of 1974. But the research focus is still national. Little systematic attention is being given to legislatures at the state, county, municipal, and town levels, or even to parliaments and assemblies in developing countries or international organizations. Yet all of these legislatures approve budgets and they add to or subtract from executive recommendations to suit their own wills.

It doesn't seem realistic to expect legislatures to be able to confront and totally oversee budget submissions, nor, it is argued, would we want them to do so, since that role is being performed by the central budget office or budget officer. What we do expect is a selective, sharply focused review with corresponding modifications of the most controversial or most expendable aspects of the budget. This the legislatures do, but the degree of effectiveness among different legislatures may vary greatly.

Legislative budgeting as a process is generally concerned with authorizations and appropriations. The U.S. Congress, for example, has numerous committees with responsibility for designing and recommending bills that would establish various public policies and programs. However, the lifeblood of any policy or program is public funding. With the exception of treaties and testimonials, legislation without the approval or appropriation of funds is of dubious value. When an authorization committee recommends a bill for a program, they will include a price tag—what they authorize for supporting and establishing that program. Authorizations generally carry over certain periods of time from one to several years. Another committee must decide exactly how much funding will be provided in any given fiscal year. This, the appropriation, is determined by an appropriations committee that has the primary responsibility for budgetary oversight. Generally, appropriations committees split up the executive budget submission into the respective areas

of their subcommittees. They conduct hearings with the responsible program officials or budget officials as part of their review of the budget recommendations of the executive.

However, the power of the appropriations process, or legislative budgeting, is strongly affected by the legal rules and procedures that have been established. Two generally accepted models represent the two extremes in legislative-executive budgeting relationships. In the strong executive model, the chief executive is allowed to have the more formidable budgeting powers, foremost among them being the line-item veto, which sets executive budget recommendations as a ceiling. The legislature can reduce a program's budget, and this must be accepted by the executive. If the legislature attempts to increase the spending recommendations for a program, however, the executive may veto anything over the initial recommendation. This veto power can extend to each individual budget line item.

At the other end of the scale is the strong legislature-weak executive model. Here the line-item veto is forbidden. Legislatures can virtually rewrite the entire budget to their own liking, submit it as one package incorporating all of a government's expenses, and present it to the chief executive on a take-it-or-leave-it basis. Weak executive models have one other major characteristic—the extensive use of earmarking, whereby tax revenues from specific sources must be used solely for certain programs, such as gas tax revenues for road repairs or alcoholic beverage taxes for mental health institutions, etc. States with half of their budgetary revenues tied up in uncontrollable earmarked funds have general funds (for all other uses) and general budgets that are characteristically short of both funds and flexibility. Still, a chief executive's control of information and available specialized expertise can frequently offset the inherent executive handicap in the strong legislative model. The best example of the strong legislative model is the U.S. Congress. With its new budgetary process established by the Congressional Budget and Impoundment Control Act of 1974, it may provide the first successful example of a fully systematized legislative budgeting process.

For texts, see Jesse Burkhead, *Government Budgeting* (New York: Wiley Press, 1956); John P. Crecine, *Government Problem-Solving; A Computer Simulation of Municipal Budgeting* (Chicago: Rand McNally, 1969); Kenneth S. Howard, *Changing State Budgeting* (Lexington, Ky.: Council of State Governments, 1973); Albert C. Hyde and Jay M. Shafritz, eds., *Government Budgeting: Theory, Process, Politics* (Oak Park, Ill.: Moore Publishing Co., 1978); Dennis S. Ippolito, *The Budget and National Politics* (San Francisco: W. H. Freeman, 1978); Fred A. Kramer, ed., *Contemporary Approaches to Public Budgeting* (Cambridge, Mass.: Winthrop Publishers, 1979); Robert D. Lee and Ronald W. Johnson, *Public Budgeting Systems*, 2nd ed. (Baltimore: University Park Press, 1977); Lance T. LeLoup, *Budgetary Politics* (Brunswich, Ohio: King's Court, 1977); Thomas D. Lynch, *Public Budgeting in America* (Englewood Cliffs, N.J.: Prentice-Hall, 1979); John Wanat, *Introduction to Budgeting* (North Scituate, Mass.: Duxbury, 1978); Aaron Wildavsky, *The Politics of the Budgetary Process*, 4th ed. (Boston: Little, Brown and Co., 1984); Thomas Lynch, ed., *Contemporary Public Budgeting* (New Brunswick, N.J.: Transaction Books, 1981); Jack Rabin and Thomas D. Lynch, eds., *Handbook on Public Budgeting and Financial Management* (New York: Marcell Dekker, 1983).

See also the following entries:

APPROPRIATION
AUDIT
BACKDOOR AUTHORITY
BALANCED BUDGET
CROSSWALK
CURRENT SERVICES ESTIMATES
DISBURSEMENTS
DEBT FINANCING
FEDERALISM, FISCAL
FISCAL POLICY
FISCAL INTEGRITY
MISSION BUDGETING
OFF-BUDGET FEDERAL AGENCIES
OFFSETTING RECEIPTS
PLANNING, PROGRAMMING, BUDGETING SYSTEMS
PUBLIC FINANCE
RECONCILIATION
RESCISSION
RIVLIN, ALICE, M.
SHICK, ALLEN
SPENDING AUTHORITY
TOTAL OBLIGATIONAL AUTHORITY
TRANSFER AUTHORITY
UNCONTROLLABLE EXPENSES
ZERO-BASE BUDGETING

budgeting, capital, a budget process that deals with planning for large expenditures for capital items. Capital expenditures should be for long-term investments (such as bridges and buildings) which yield returns for years after they are completed. Capital budgets typically cover five- to ten-year periods and are updated yearly. Items included in capital budgets may be financed through borrowing (including tax-exempt municipal bonds), savings, grants, revenue sharing, special assessments, etc.

A capital budget provides for separating financing of capital or investment expenditures from current or operating expenditures. The federal government has never had a capital budget in the sense of financing capital or investment-type programs separately from current expenditures. See Richard Musgrave, "The Nature of Budgetary Balance and the Case for the Capital Budget," *American Economic Review* (June 1939); Alan Walter Steiss, *Local Government Finance: Capital Facilities Planning and Debt Administration* (Lexington, Mass.: Lexington Books, 1975); John J. Clark, Thomas J. Hindeland and Robert E. Pritchard, *Capital Budgeting: Planning and Control of Capital Expenditures* (Englewood Cliffs, N.J.: Prentice-Hall, 1979); C. Don Wiggins, "A Case in Governmental Capital Budgeting," *Governmental Finance* (June 1980); John Matzer, Jr., ed., *Capital Financing Strategies for Local Governments* (Washington, D.C.: International City Management Association, 1983); Ronald W. Chapman, "Capital Financing: An Old Approach Reapplied," *Public Productivity Review* (December 1983); J. Lisle Bozeman, "The Capital Budget: History and Future Directions," *Public Budgeting & Finance* (Autumn 1984).

budgeting, comparative. Budgeting necessarily deals with political, economic, administrative-managerial, evaluative and accountabilitative factors all in one process. Only with a comparative approach to the study of budgeting can the details and features of various budgeting processes and systems be understood in the context of the organizational and societal environments in which they function. Aaron Wildavsky maintains that budgeting is explicitly comparative and that the students of budgeting ought to have available various comparisons of budgeting processes among different jurisdictions. *See* Wildavsky's *Budgeting: A Comparative Theory of Budgetary Processes* (Boston: Little, Brown & Co., 1975). *Also see* Naomi Caiden, "Budgeting in Poor Counties: Ten Assumptions Re-examined," *Public Administration Review* (January-February 1980).

budgeting, continuous, an approach to financial management advocated for poor, unstable countries in which budgetary and financial decisions are made on an ad hoc rather than a long-range basis according to the current level of revenues and expenditures.

budgeting, cost-based, also OBLIGATION-BASED BUDGETING, budgeting in terms of costs to be incurred; that is, the resources to be consumed in carrying out a program, regardless of when the funds to acquire the resources were obligated or paid, and without regard to the source of funds (*i.e.*, appropriation). For example, inventory items become costs when they are withdrawn from inventory and the cost of buildings is distributed over time, through periodic depreciation charges, rather than in a lump sum when the buildings are acquired.

budgeting, incremental, method of budget review focusing on the increments of increase or decrease in the budget of existing programs. *See* Aaron Wildavsky and Arthur Hammon, "Comprehensive vs. Incremental Budgeting in the Department of Agriculture," *Administrative Science Quarterly* (December 1965); John Wanat, "Bases of Budgetary Incrementalism," *American Political Science Review* (September 1974); Lance T. LeLoup, "The Myth of Incrementalism: Analytical Choices in Budgetary Theory," *Polity* (Summer 1978); Bernard T. Pitsvada and Frank D. Draper, "Making Sense of the Federal Budget the Old Fashioned Way—Incrementally," *Public Administration Review* (September/October 1984).

budgeting, obligation-based, *see* BUDGETING, COST-BASED.

budgeting, performance, also PROGRAM BUDGETING. Budgeting systems concerned with performance work data and efficiency concepts were first developed just before World War I in the New York City Bureau of Municipal Research. The first federal efforts at performance budgeting were in the Department of Agriculture and the Tennessee Valley Authority during the 1930s, and then, under the auspices of the Hoover Commission of 1949, the designation "performance budgeting" was officially sanctioned as the preferred budgeting method. The Hoover Commission stated its recommendation bluntly: "A program or performance budget should be substituted for the present budget, thus presenting in a document of much briefer compass the Government's expenditure requirements in terms of services, activities, and work projects rather than in terms of the things bought."

A specific definition of performance budgeting has long been elusive. Jesse Burkhead, in his text, *Government Budgeting* (New York: John Wiley, 1956), maintains there can be no precise definition of performance budgeting because performance budgeting systems tend to be so varied in their operations. Nevertheless, a general definition of performance budgeting is both possible and useful: performance budgeting presents purposes and objectives for which funds are being allocated, examines costs of programs and activities established to meet these objectives, and identifies and analyzes quantitative data measuring work performed and accomplishments.

One problem of no small significance must be clarified. The terms performance budgeting and program budgeting tend to be used interchangeably, but they are not synonymous. In performance budgeting, programs are generally linked to the various higher levels of an organization and serve as labels that encompass and structure the subordinate performance units. These units—the central element of performance budgeting—are geared to an organization's operational levels, and information about them is concrete and meaningful to managers at all levels. Program budgeting, on the other hand, might or might not incorporate performance measurement, yet might still be useful for delineating broad functional categories of expenditure for review at higher levels. Overall, performance budgeting tends to be retrospective—focusing on previous performance and work accomplishments—while program budgeting tends to be forward-looking—involving policy planning and forecasts.

While the predominant orientation of performance budgeting was for the purpose of better management and enhanced efficiency, most of its early advocates expressed hope that its associated processes would further executive-legislative budgeting relationships. Indeed, the generally recognized success of performance budgeting was instrumental in obtaining Congressional approval of the Budgeting and Accounting Procedures Act of 1950, which gave the president greater discretion over the format and content of executive budget submissions. See Catherine Seckler-Hudson, "Performance Budgeting in Government," *Advanced Management* (March 1953); Ali Eghtedari and Frank Sherwood, "Performance Budgeting in Los Angeles," *Public Administration Review* (Spring 1960); Marion L. Henry and Willis Proctor, "New York State's Performance Budget Experiment," *Public Administration Review* (Spring 1960); Harley H.

Hinrichs and Graeme M. Taylor, eds., *Program Budgeting and Benefit-Cost Analysis* (Pacific Palisades, Calif.: Goodyear, 1969); Charles W. Binford, "Reflections on the Performance Budget: Past, Present and Future," *Governmental Finance* (November 1972).

budgeting, planning programming, *see* PLANNING PROGRAMMING BUDGETING SYSTEMS.

budgeting, program, *see* BUDGETING, PERFORMANCE.

Budgeting and Accounting Procedures Act of 1950, passed in response to the report of the first Hoover Commission, this act called for the use of performance budgeting throughout the federal government and gave the president broader authority to specify budget content, arrangements, etc.

budget receipts, moneys received by a government from its public. The federal government's budget receipts arise from:

1. The exercise of governmental or sovereign power (consisting primarily of tax revenues, but also including receipts from premiums on compulsory social insurance programs, court fines, certain license fees, and the like).

2. Premiums from voluntary participants in federal social insurance programs (such as deposits by states for unemployment insurance and for social security for their employees) that are closely related to compulsory social insurance programs.

3. Gifts and contributions.

budget surplus, amount by which a government's budget receipts exceed its budget outlays for any given period.

budget update, statement summarizing amendments to or revisions in budget authority requested, estimated outlays, and estimated receipts for a fiscal year that has not been completed. The president may submit updates at any time but is required by the Congressional Budget and Impoundment Control Act of 1974 to transmit such statements to the Congress by April 10 and July 15 of each year.

budget year, fiscal year for which the budget is being considered; the fiscal year following the current year.

Buffalo Forge Co. v. *United Steelworkers,* 423 U.S. 911 (1976), U.S. Supreme Court case which held that federal courts were permitted to enjoin a strike over a nonarbitrable issue pending an arbitrator's decision on whether the strike violates a no-strike pledge in a collective bargaining contract.

buffer, organizational procedures or structures that absorb disruptive inputs and thus protect the continuity or equilibrium of some core group. For example, people in positions near the boundaries of organizations often absorb a wide variety of messages and demands. These inputs are filtered, processed, and passed to the "technical core" of the organization in a sequential and routine form. Because the inputs have been buffered the central work processes are not disrupted.

built-in stabilizers, features of the economy (such as unemployment benefits, welfare payments, etc.) that automatically act to modify the severity of economic downturns.
See also AUTOMATIC STABILIZER.

bump, or BUMPING, layoff procedure that gives an employee with greater seniority the right to displace or "bump" another employee. Sometimes bumping rights are restricted to one plant, office, or department. Because of legally guaranteed bumping rights, the laying off of a single worker can lead to the sequential transfers of a dozen others. *See* Wilbur C. Rich, "Bumping, Blocking and Bargaining: The Effect of Layoffs on Employees and

Unions," *Review of Public Personnel Administration* (Fall 1983).

burden of proof, requirement that a party to an issue show that the weight of evidence is on his or her side in order to have the issue decided in his or her favor.

Burdine Case; Texas Department of Community Affairs v. *Burdine,* U.S. Supreme Court case, 450 U.S. 248 (1980), which held that employers charged with discrimination do not have to prove that a person hired or promoted was better qualified than the person passed over. Instead, the employer need only provide adequate evidence that race or sex was not a factor in the decision.

The unanimous opinion of the Supreme Court, written by Justice Lewis F. Powell, Jr., said that although Federal law prohibits discrimination, it does not demand that an employer give preferential treatment to minorities or women; that an employer does not have to prove that its action is lawful; rather, the employer need only produce evidence which would allow a judge to conclude that the decision had not been motivated by discriminatory animus.

bureau, government department, agency, or subdivision of same.

bureaucracy, used as a general invective to refer to any inefficient organization, its more formal usage refers to a specific set of structural arrangements. The dominant structural definition of bureaucracy, indeed the point of departure for all further analyses on the subject, is that of the German sociologist Max Weber. Drawing upon studies of ancient bureaucracies in Egypt, Rome, China, and the Byzantine Empire, as well as on the more modern ones emerging in Europe during the 19th and early part of the 20th centuries, Weber used an "ideal type" approach to extrapolate from the real world the central core of features that would characterize the most fully developed bureaucratic form of organization. This "ideal type" is neither a description of reality nor a statement of normative preference. It is merely an identification of the major variables or features that characterize bureaucracy. The fact that such features might not be fully present in a given organization does not necessarily imply that the organization is "non-bureaucratic." It may be an immature rather than a fully developed bureaucracy. At some point, however, it may be necessary to conclude that the characteristics of bureaucracy are so lacking in an organization that it could neither reasonably be termed bureaucratic nor be expected to produce patterns of bureaucratic behavior.

Weber's "ideal type" bureaucracy possesses the following characteristics:

1. The bureaucrats must be personally free and subject to authority only with respect to the impersonal duties of their offices.
2. They are arranged in a clearly defined hierarchy of offices.
3. The functions of each office are clearly specified.
4. Officials accept and maintain their appointments freely—without duress.
5. Appointments are made on the basis of technical qualifications which ideally are substantiated by examinations—administered by the appointing authority, a university, or both.
6. Officials should have a money salary as well as pension rights. Such salaries must reflect the varying levels of positions in the hierarchy. While officials are always free to leave the organization, they can be removed from their offices only under previously stated specific circumstances.
7. An incumbent's post must be his sole or at least his major occupation.
8. A career system is essential. While promotion may be the result of either seniority or merit, it must be premised on the judgment of hierarchical superiors.
9. The official may not have a property right to his position nor any personal claim to the resources which go with it.

10. An official's conduct must be subject to systematic control and strict discipline.

While Weber's structural identification of bureaucratic organization (first published in 1922) is perhaps the most comprehensive statement on the subject in the literature of the social sciences, it is not always considered satisfactory as an intellectual construct. For example, Anthony Downs, in *Inside Bureaucracy* (Boston: Little, Brown, 1967), argues that at least two elements should be added to Weber's definition. First, the organization must be large. According to Downs, "any organization in which the highest ranking members know less than half of the other members can be considered large." Second, most of the organization's output cannot be "directly or indirectly evaluated in any markets external to the organization by means of voluntary *quid pro quo* transactions."

Definitions of bureaucracy apply equally to organizations in the public and the private sector. However, public sector bureaucracies tend to operate in a somewhat different climate from those in the private sector. What has come to be known as the "third sector"—not-for-profit organizations such as hospitals, universities, and foundations—would analytically be classed with public organizations because of the lack of free-market forces upon them. In short, bureaucracy is best conceptualized as a specific form of organization, and public bureaucracy should be considered a special variant of bureaucratic organization.

The literature on bureaucracy is immense. The following is a representative sample: Alan A. Altshuler and Norman C. Thomas, *The Politics of the Federal Bureaucracy*, 2nd ed. (New York: Harper & Row, 1977); Martin Albrow, *Bureaucracy* (New York: Praeger, 1970); Warren G. Bennis, ed., *American Bureaucracy* (New Brunswick, N.J.: Transaction Books, E. P. Dutton, 1970); Peter Blau and Marshall Meyer, *Bureaucracy in Modern Society* (New York: Random House, 1971); William W. Boyer, *Bureaucracy on Trial: Policy Making by*

Government Agencies (Indianapolis: Bobbs-Merrill Co., 1964); Michel Crozier, *The Bureaucratic Phenomenon* (Chicago: University of Chicago Press, 1964); Michael T. Dalby and Michael S. Werthman, *Bureaucracy in Historical Perspective* (Glenview, Ill.: Scott, Foresman, & Co., 1971); Eugene P. Dvorin and R. H. Simmons, *From Amoral to Humane Bureaucracy* (San Francisco: Canfield Press, 1972); Virginia B. Ermer and John H. Strange, eds., *Blacks and Bureaucracy* (New York: Crowell, 1972); Douglas M. Fox, *The Politics of City and State Bureaucracy* (Pacific Palisades, Calif.: Goodyear Publishing Co., 1974); Louis C. Gawthrop, *Bureaucratic Behavior in the Executive Branch: An Analysis of Organizational Change* (New York: Free Press, 1969); Wolf V. Heydebrand, *Hospital Bureaucracy: A Comparative Study of Organizations* (New York: Dunellen, 1973); Mathew Holden, Jr., "Imperialism in Bureaucracy," *American Political Science Review* (December 1966); Ralph P. Hummel, *The Bureaucratic Experience*, 2nd ed. (New York: St. Martin's, 1982); Henry Jacoby, *The Bureaucratization of the World* (Berkeley: University of California Press, 1973); Herbert Kaufman, "Fear of Bureaucracy: A Raging Pandemic," *Public Administration Review* (January–February 1981); Daniel Katz, *et al.*, *Bureaucratic Encounters* (Ann Arbor, Mich.: Institute for Social Research, 1975); Fred A. Kramer, *Perspectives on Public Bureaucracy: A Reader on Organization*, 2nd ed. (Cambridge, Mass.: Winthrop Publishers, 1977); Joseph LaPalombara, *Bureaucracy and Political Development* (Princeton, N.J.: Princeton University Press, 1963); Eugene Lewis, *American Politics in a Bureaucratic Age: Citizens, Clients, Constituents and Victims* (Englewood Cliffs, N.J.: Prentice-Hall, 1977); Lewis C. Mainzer, *Political Bureaucracy* (Glenview, Ill.: Scott, Foresman, 1973); Arnold J. Meltsner, *Policy Analysis in the Bureaucracy* (Berkeley: University of California Press, 1976); James A. Medeiros and David E. Schmitt, *Public Bureaucracy: Values and Perspectives* (North Scituate, Mass.: Duxbury Press, 1977); Kenneth J. Meier, *Politics and Bureaucracy: Policymaking in the Fourth Branch of Government* (North Scituate, Mass.: Duxbury Press, 1979); Robert K. Merton, *et al.*, *Reader in Bureaucracy* (New York: Free Press, 1952); Marshall W. Meyer, *Change in Public Bureaucracies* (New York: Cambridge University Press, 1979); Nicos P. Mouzelis, *Organization and Bureaucracy* (Chicago: Aldine, 1973); B. Guy Peters, *The Politics of Bureaucracy: A Comparative Approach* (New York: Longman, 1978); Charles Peters and Michael Nelson, eds., *The Culture of Bureaucracy* (New York: Holt, Rinehart & Winston, 1979); Norman J. Powell, *Responsible Public Bureaucracy in the United States* (Boston: Allyn & Bacon, 1967); Randall B. Ripley and Grace A. Franklin, *Congress, the Bureaucracy, and Public Policy* (Homewood, Ill.: Dorsey Press, 1976); Francis E. Rourke, *Bureaucracy, Politics and Public Policy* (Boston: Little, Brown, 1969); Francis E. Rourke, ed., *Bureaucracy, Politics, and the Public Interest* (Boston: Little, Brown and Co., 1972); Francis E. Rourke, ed., *Bureaucratic Power in National Politics* (Boston: Little, Brown and Co., 1972); Clarence N. Stone, Robert K. Whelan, and William J. Murin, *Urban Policy and Politics in a Bureaucratic Age* (Englewood Cliffs, N.J.: Prentice-Hall, 1979); J. A. Stockfish, *The Political Economy of Bureaucracy* (New York: General Learning Press, 1972); Victor A. Thompson, *Bureaucracy and Innovation* (University: University of Alabama Press, 1969); Victor A. Thompson, *Bureaucracy and the Modern World* (Morristown, N.J.: General Learning Press, 1976); Gordon Tullock, *The Politics of Bureaucracy* (Washington, D.C.: The Public Affairs Press, 1965); Ludwig Von Mises, *Bureaucracy* (New Haven, Conn.: Yale University Press, 1944); Carol H. Weiss and Allen H. Barton, eds., *Making Bureaucracies Work* (Beverly Hills, Calif.: Sage Publications, 1980); James Q. Wilson, "The Bureaucracy Problem," *Public Interest* (Winter 1967); and Peter Woll, *American Bureaucracy* (New York: W.W. Norton & Co., Inc., 1963).

See also the following entries:

bureaucrat, denizen of a bureaucracy. *See also* APPARATCHIK.

Bureaucrat, The, quarterly journal of the National Area Chapter of the American Society for Public Administration and the Federal Executive Alumni Association.
The Bureaucrat
P.O. Box 347
Arlington, VA 22210

How the Bureaucracy Won the War!

The sense of bungling and futility cast a shadow over Washington and over political life generally. In the country at large, said one observer, a profound cynicism had developed toward "the system." Roosevelt was still popular, but not the major political and economic institutions which affected people's lives. In the late months of 1942 a joke was being told of a Japanese spy sent to discover which agencies of American government could be sabotaged and thereby cripple the American war effort. He reported back: "Suggested plan hopeless. Americans brilliantly prepared. For each agency we destroy two more are already fully staffed and doing exactly the same work."

Source: Geoffrey Perrett, Days of Sadness, Years of Triumph: The American People 1939–1945 (Penguin Books, 1973), p. 247.

---

bureaucratic impersonality, as Max Weber held, bureaucracy's "special virtue" was "dehumanization." Hardly anyone would argue that bureaucracy does not have dehumanizing consequences for its employees and, to a lesser extent, for its clients as well. By dehumanization, Weber meant the elimination "from official business [of] love, hatred, and all purely per-

sonal, irrational, and emotional elements." In Weber's view, formalization, hierarchy, and the other central features of bureaucracy render the individual bureaucrat "only a single cog in an ever-moving mechanism which prescribes to him an essentially fixed route of march." Consequently, "the individual bureaucrat is forged to the community of all functionaries who are integrated into the mechanism." He cannot "squirm out of the apparatus in which he is harnessed." Today the term "impersonality" is generally used in referring to this aspect of bureaucratic behavior. Viewed against an historical background of administrative organizations characterized by such "irrational" elements as nepotism, personal subjugation, and capricious and uninformed judgment, impersonality can be seen as a step in the direction of greater rationality; a step further in the direction of Aristotle's ideal of "a government of laws; not of men." *See* David Nachmias and David H. Rosenbloom, *Bureaucratic Governnment USA* (New York: St Martin's Press, 1980); Norma M. Williams, Gideon Sjoberg and Andree F. Sjoberg, "The Bureaucratic Personality: An Alternative View," *Journal of Applied Behavioral Science* (July–August–September 1980).

bureaucratic policymaking. What sets bureaucratic policymaking apart from other sources of policymaking has been its possession of certain attributes, or what Francis E. Rourke calls "the skills of bureaucracy." Principal among such skills is expertise, or what Max Weber noted as "its purely technical superiority." Technical expertise is not automatic, nor is it the sole province of the bureaucracy. But according to Peter Woll in *Public Policy* (Cambridge, Mass.: Winthrop, 1974), it has become well developed because of the existence of three characteristics: specialization, fragmentation, and access and group action.

Specialization stems from the increasing frequency of complexity and technicality of policy issues and problems. The fact is that more and more modern public problems can not be solved by the lay person. Executive branch departments, and specifically the administrative agencies, have taken the lead in policy formulation in many areas because their staffs have the specific expertise, the most extensive preparatory backgrounds, and the cumulative experience and information bases in dealing with similarly specific and complex policy problems to react best and direct effective responses. So many problems are related to previous problems or result directly from previous policy solutions that policy continuity has become one of the most compelling arguments for specialization. For this reason and because the legislative branch would be hard pressed to develop such expertise, our political system has been modified by Congressional delegation of legal responsibilities (that is, policymaking power) to administrative agencies.

A second characteristic is fragmentation, which in part greatly encouraged functional specialization. Fragmentation originates with the emphasis on checks and balances and separation of powers among the branches of government. This fragmentation characteristic manifests itself inside the bureaucracy where public policy issues require the inputs of various agencies and departments, each possessing potentially conflicting views on issues and acting as checks on one another's policy recommendations and final actions. The result of this fragmentation is a process in which agencies, indeed all parts of government, act as interest groups in pursuit of their own objectives. David B. Truman describes this in *The Governmental Process* (New York: Knopf, 1951), as a "web of relationships" in which administrative agencies will attempt to exert influence on other agencies just as other groups and agencies will attempt to pressure them.

A third characteristic of administrative agencies—"access and group action"—refers to the roles that administrative agencies play in providing channels of contact and inquiry through which groups or organized segments of the public can pursue and influence policy formulation by making their views known. Agencies will react to groups that attempt to play roles in pursuit of an interest or any particular issue. Such reaction is the essence of the concept of "bureaucratic responsiveness." While there are a number of factors that will shape how responsive an agency will be, agencies will tend to be cognizant of these interests. But any assumption that the access and group action characteristic of the bureaucratic policy formulation process will lead to representation of all interests should be questioned. The scope and bias of the pressure system are as limited as the small number of real pressure groups that exist. The result is that only a few participate and have significant influence.

bureaucratic risk taking, extraordinary action, generally resisted by the persons in charge, taken by a public servant who commits the government to a profitable course of action, blocks the execution of an illegal or immoral order, or exposes corruption, deceit, or an unlawful act taking place within the bureaucracy. .

Bureau of Labor Statistics (BLS), agency responsible for the economic and statistical research activities of the Department of Labor. The BLS is the government's principal fact-finding agency in the field of labor economics, particularly with respect to the collection and analysis of data on manpower and labor requirements, living conditions, labor-management relations, productivity and technological developments, occupational safety and health, structure and growth of the economy, urban conditions and related socioeconomic issues, and international aspects of certain of these subjects.

It has no enforcement or administrative functions. Practically all of the basic data it collects from workers, businesses, and governmental agencies are supplied through voluntary cooperation based on interest in and need for the analyses and summaries that result. The research and statistical projects planned grow out of the needs of these groups, as well as the needs of Congress and the federal and state governments. The information collected is issued in monthly press releases, in special publications, and in its official publication, the *Monthly Labor Review*. Other major BLS periodicals include: *The Consumer Price Index, Wholesale Prices and Price Indexes, Employment and Earnings, Current Wage Developments, Occupational Outlook Handbook,* and *Occupational Outlook Quarterly.* For histories, *see* Jonathan Grossman and Judson MacLaury, "The Creation of the Bureau of Labor Statistics," *Monthly Labor Review* (February 1975); J.P. Goldberg and W. T. Moye, "The AFL and a National BLS: Labor's Role is Crystallized" *Monthly Labor Review* (March 1982); Edgar Weinberg, "BLS and the Economy: A Centennial Timetable," *Monthly Labor Review* (November 1984).

Bureau of Labor Statistics
200 Constitution Avenue, NW
Washington, D.C. 20210
(202) 523-1327

Bureau of Municipal Research, *see* IN-STITUTE OF PUBLIC ADMINISTRATION.

Bureau of National Affairs, Inc. (BNA), the largest private employer of information specialists in the nation's capital. Its function is to report, analyze, and explain the activities of the federal government and the courts to those persons who are directly affected—educators, attorneys, labor relations practitioners, business executives, accountants, union officials, personnel administrators, and scores of others. The BNA organization is universally recognized as a leading source of authoritative information services.

BNA Communications, Inc., produces employee communication, motivational, and supervisory and sales training films, case studies for management development, and related instructional materials.

Bureau of National Affairs, Inc.
1231 25th Street, N.W.
Washington, D.C. 20037
(202) 452-4500

bureaupathology, term used by Victor A. Thompson in *Modern Organization* (New York: Knopf, 1960) to describe the pathological or dysfunctional aspects of bureaucracy. According to Thompson, the bureaupathic official usually exaggerates the official, non-technical aspects of relationships and suppresses the technical and the informal. He stresses rights, not abilities. Since his behavior stems from insecurity, he may be expected to insist on petty rights and prerogatives, on protocol, on procedure—in short, on those things least likely to affect directly the goal accomplishment of the organization. For example, a rather functionless reviewing officer will often insist most violently on his right to review and scream like an injured animal if he is bypassed. He will often insist on petty changes, such as minor changes in the wording of a document. If he has a counterpart at a higher organizational level, he will probably insist on exclusive contact with that higher clearance point. By controlling this particular communication channel he protects his authority and influence.

Also see George West, "Bureau-pathology and the Failure of MBO," *Human Resource Management* (Summer, 1977).

burnout, worker's feeling of mental and physical fatigue that causes indifference and emotional disengagement from his or her job. *See* Harry Levinson, "When Executives Burn Out," *Harvard Business Review* (May-June 1981); Oliver L. Niehouse, "Burnout: A Real Threat to Human Resources Managers," *Personnel* (September-October 1981); Whiton Stewart Paine, ed., *Job Stress and Burnout: Research, Theory, and Intervention Perspectives* (Beverly Hills, Calif.: Sage Publications, Inc., 1982); Morley D. Glicken and Katherine Janka, "Executives Under Fire: The Burnout Syndrome," *California Management Review* (Spring 1982).

Bush v. Lucas, 462 U.S. 367 (1983), U.S. Supreme Court case which held that federal employees cannot sue their supervisors for violations of their First Amendment rights because Congress has provided an alternative remedy, namely appeals through the civil service system to the Merit Systems Protection Board.

business agent, full-time officer of a local union, elected or appointed, who handles grievances, helps enforce agreements, and otherwise deals with the union's financial, administrative, or labor-management problems.

business cycles, the recurrent phases of expansion and contraction in overall business activity. Although no two business cycles are alike, they are all thought to follow a pattern of prosperity, recession (or depression), and recovery. See Donald A. Larson, "Labor Supply Adjustment Over the Business Cycle," *Industrial and Labor Relations Review* (July 1981); George Sayers Bain and Farouk Elsheikh, "Union Growth and the Business Cycle: A Disaggregated Study," *British Journal of Industrial Relations* (March 1982).

business games, see MANAGEMENT GAMES.

business necessity, the major legal defense for using an employment practice that effectively excludes women and/or minorities. The leading court case, *Robinson* v. *Lorrilard Corp.*, 444 F.2d 791 (4th Cir. 1971); *cert. denied,* 404 U.S. 1006 (1971), holds that the test of the business necessity defense

> is whether there exists an overriding legitimate business purpose such that the practice is necessary to the safe and efficient operation of the business. Thus, the business purpose must be sufficiently compelling to override any racial impact; the challenged practice must effectively carry out the business purpose it is alleged to serve; and there must be available no acceptable alternative policies or practices which would better accomplish the business purpose advanced, or accomplish it equally well with a lesser differential racial impact.

business unions, also called BREAD-AND-BUTTER UNIONS, the comparatively con-servative U.S. trade unions, so-called because they have tended to concentrate on gaining better wages and working conditions for their members rather than devote significant efforts on political action as many European unions have done. The classic description of business unionism was given by Adolph Strasser (1871-1910), president of the Cigar Makers Union and one of the founders of the AFL, when he told a congressional committee: "We have no ultimate ends. We are going from day to day. We fight only for immediate objectives—objectives that will be realized in a few years. We are all practical men." For a historical analysis, see Philip Taft, "On the Origins of Business Unionism," *Industrial and Labor Relations Review* (October 1963).

busing, see MILLIKEN V. BRADLEY.

Butz* v. *Economou, 438 U.S. 478 (1978), Supreme Court case that provided an immunity from suit for civil damages to federal administrative officials exercising adjudicatory functions. See Gerald J. Miller, "Administrative Malpractice before and after *Butz* v. *Economou,*" *Bureaucrat* (Winter 1980-81); Michael W. Dolan, "Government Employee Accountability and the Federal Tort Claims Act," *Bureaucrat* (Fall 1980); Robert G. Vaughn, "The Personal Accountability of Civil Servants," *Bureaucrat* (Fall 1980).

buy American acts, various state and national laws that require government agencies to give a preference to American-made goods when making purchases. Similar "buy national" practices are also being used by all the major trading partners of the United States. They are counted among the nontariff barriers to trade.

buzz group, device that seeks to give all the individuals at a large meeting an equal opportunity to participate by breaking the larger meeting into small groups of six to eight persons. These "buzz groups" each designate one person to report on their consensus (and dissents, if any) when the total group reconvenes.

buzzwords, according to Robert Kirk Mueller, in *Buzzwords: A Guide to the Language of Leaderships* (New York: Van Nostrand Reinhold Co., 1974), "those phrases that have a pleasant buzzing sound in your ears while you roll them on your tongue and that may overwhelm you into believing you know what you're talking about when you don't." Mueller credits the late Professor Ralph Hower of Harvard for first using the term in this context. In spite of this "formal" definition, the technical vocabularies of any occupational specialty are often referred to as buzzwords.

Byrnes Act: *see* ANTI-STRIKE-BREAKER ACT OF 1936.

C

CAB, *see* CIVIL AERONAUTICS BOARD.

Cabell* v. *Shavez-Salido, 70 L.Ed. 2d 677 (1982), U.S. Supreme Court case which held that a state statute requiring peace officers, including deputy probation officers, to be U.S. citizens did not violate the equal protection clause of the 14th Amendment.

cabinet, heads of the executive departments of a jurisdiction who report to and advise its chief executive. For example, the president's cabinet, the mayor's cabinet, etc.

The "President's Cabinet" is an institution whose existence rests upon custom rather than law. The cabinet came into being because President Washington found it useful to meet with the chiefs of the several executive departments. While all subsequent presidents have considered it necessary to meet with the cabinet, their attitudes toward the institution and its members have varied greatly. Some presidents have convened their cabinet only for the most formal and routine matters while others have relied upon it for advice and support.

The President's Cabinet differs from the cabinet in the British parliamentary system in that, in the United States, the executive power is constitutionally vested in the president, so that the cabinet members are responsible to him; whereas in the British system, the cabinet as a whole, rather than only the prime minister who heads it, is considered the executive, and the cabinet is collectively responsible to the parliament for its performance. In addition, whereas in the United States the cabinet secretaries are parts only of the executive branch, in Britain the cabinet ministers are typically drawn from among the majority party's members in parliament.

Traditionally, membership of the cabinet has consisted of the secretaries of the several executive departments. At the present time cabinet membership consists of the secretaries of thirteen executive departments, the two newest members being the Secretary of Energy and the Secretary of Education. It should be remembered that a substantial part of the executive branch is not represented in the cabinet.

From the earliest days, presidents have accorded to others the privilege of attending and participating in cabinet meetings. In recent years, the ambassador of the United States to the United Nations and the director of the Office of Management and Budget, among others, have been accorded cabinet rank.

See Richard F. Fenno, Jr., *The President's Cabinet* (Cambridge, Mass.: Harvard University Press, 1959); Nelson W. Polsby, "Presidential Cabinet Making: Lessons for the Political System," *Political Science Quarterly* (Spring 1978); James J. Best, "Presidential Cabinet Appointments: 1953-1976," *Presidential Studies Quarterly* (Winter 1981); R. Gorden Hoxie, "The Cabinet in the American Presidency, 1789-1984," *Presidential Studies Quarterly* (Spring 1984).

cafeteria benefits plan, also called SMORGASBORD BENEFITS PLAN, any program that allows employees to choose their fringe benefits within the limits of the total benefit dollars for which they are eligible. This allows each employee to have, in effect, his own individualized benefit program. Because such programs cost more to administer, they tend to exist mainly as part of high-level managerial compensation packages. However, increasing computer capabilities will make it increasingly likely that such plans will be more widely offered. *See* George W. Hettenhouse, "Conpensation Cafeteria for Top Executives," *Harvard Business Review* (September-October 1971); Robert V. Goode, "Complications at the Cafeteria Checkout Line," *Personnel* (November-December 1974); Berwyn N. Fragner, "Employees' 'Cafeteria' Offfers Insurance Options," *Harvard Business Review* (November-December 1975); David J. Thomsen, "Introducing Cafeteria Compensation in Your Company," *Compensation Review* (First Quarter 1978); Peter W. Stonebraker, "A Three-Tier Plan for Cafeteria Benefits," *Personnel Journal* (December 1984).

CAG, *see* COMPARATIVE ADMINISTRATION GROUP

California Management Review **(CMR),** quarterly that seeks to serve as a bridge between creative thought about management and executive action. An authoritative source of information and ideas contributing to the advancement of management science, it is directed to active managers, scholars, teachers, and others concerned with management.

California Management Review
Graduate School of Business
  Administration
350 Barrows Hall
University of California
Berkeley, CA 94720

callable bonds, also NONCALLABLE BONDS, so designated because the issuing jurisdiction may repay part or all of the obligation prior to the maturity date. For this reason "callable" bonds ordinarily carry higher interest rates. *Noncallable bonds*, on the other hand, may not be repurchased until the date of maturation.

call-back pay, compensation, often at premium rates, paid to workers called back on the job after completing their normal shift. Contract provisions often provide for a minimum number of hours of call-back pay regardless of the number of hours actually worked.

call-in pay, wages or hours of pay guaranteed to workers (usually by contract provision) who, upon reporting to work, find no work to do.

call memorandum, a memorandum requesting the submission of a document such as the program plan by a specified date.

camel's nose, one of the principal strategies bureaucrats use to obtain funding for a new program. They begin with an appropriation request that appears insignificant until it becomes part of the agency's base and must be funded at a much higher level in order to complete the program.

Campbell, Alan K. (1923-   ), nickname SCOTTY, the last chairman of the U.S. Civil Service Commission, who became the first director of the Office of Personnel Management during 1979-80.

Canadian Public Administration **(CPA),** journal that focuses primarily on Canadian and comparative aspects of public administration.

CPA
Institute of Public Administration of
  Canada
1205 Fewster Drive, Unit 14
Mississauga, Ontario L4W 1A2
CANADA

candidate, applicant for a position.

candidate population, all of the individuals who apply for a particular position.

Cannon v. Guste, 423 U.S. 918 (1975), U.S. Supreme Court case which held that a Louisiana statute requiring state civil service employees to retire at age sixty-five violated neither the due process nor the equal protection clause of the 14th Amendment.

CAO, see GENERAL MANNAGER.

CAP, see COMMUNITY ACTION PROGRAMS.

capacity building, term used to refer to any system, effort, or process—including a federal grant or contract—which includes among its major objectives strengthening the capability of elected chief executive officers, chief administrative officers, department and agency heads, and program managers in general purpose government to plan, implement, manage or evaluate policies, strategies, or programs designed to impact on social conditions in the community. See William A. Jones, Jr., and C. Bradley Doss, Jr., "Local Officials' Reaction to Federal 'Capacity Building'," *Public Administration Review* (January–February 1978); Charles R. Warren and Leanne R. Aronson, "Sharing Management Capacity: Is There a Federal Responsibility," *Public Administration Review* (May–June 1981); Beth Walter Honadle, "A Capacity-Building Framework: A Search for Concept and Purpose," *Public Administration Review* (September–October 1981); John W. Ostrowski, Louise G. White and John D.R. Cole, "Local Government Capacity Building: A Structured Group Process Approach," *Administration & Society* (May 1984).

CAPE, see COALITION OF AMERICAN PUBLIC EMPLOYEES.

capital, the designation applied in economic theory to one of the three major factors of production, the others being land and labor. Capital can refer either to physical capital, such as plant and equip-

ment, or to the financial resources required to purchase physical capital.

capital assets, almost all property owned by an individual or organization other than things held for sale.

capital budgeting, see BUDGETING, CAPITAL.

capital depreciation, the decline in value of *capital* assets (assets of a permanent or fixed nature, goods and plant) over time with use. The rate and amount of depreciation is calculated by a variety of different methods (e.g., straight line, sum of the digits, declining balance) which often give quite different results.

capital gains tax, tax on the income derived from the sale of a capital asset (i.e., real estate, stocks, etc.).

capital intensive, any production process requiring a large proportion of capital relative to labor.

capitalism, private ownership of most means of production and trade combined with a generally unrestricted marketplace of goods and services.

capital outlay, directed expenditure for construction of buildings, roads, and other improvements, and for purchase of equipment, land, and existing structures. Includes amounts for additions, replacements, and major alterations to fixed works and structures.

capitation, a method of payment for health services in which an individual or institutional provider is paid a fixed per capita amount for each person served without regard to the actual number or nature of services provided to each person.

career, total work history of an individual. Harold L. Wilensky has defined career in structural terms as "a succession of related jobs, arranged in a hierarchy of prestige, through which persons move in an ordered (more or less predictable) sequence," in his article, "Orderly Careers and Social Participation: The Impact of Work History on Social Integration in the Middle Mass," from the *American Sociological Review* (August 1961). For an analysis of the career interactions between individuals and their organizations, *see* Edgar H. Schein, "The Individual, the Organization, and the Career: A Conceptual Scheme," *Journal of Applied Behavioral Science* (July-August 1971).

career appointment, *see* APPOINTMENT.

career change, occurs when individuals break with their present careers in order to enter other fields. For analyses, *see* Marie R. Haug and Marvin B. Sussman, "The Second Career—Variant of a Sociological Concept," *Journal of Gerontology,* Vol. 23 (1967); Dale L. Hiestand, *Changing Careers after Thirty-five* (New York: Columbia University Press, 1971); Rimantas Vaitenas and Yoash Weiner, "Developmental, Emotional, and Interest Factors in Voluntary Mid-Career Change," *Journal of Vocational Behavior,* Vol. 11 (1977); Harry Levinson, "A Second Career: The Possible Dream," *Harvard Business Review* (May-June 1983).

career-conditional appointment, *see* APPOINTMENT.

career counseling, guidance provided to employees in order to assist them in achieving occupational training, education, and career goals. Career counseling services available to federal employees may include: (1) assessing their skills, abilities, interests, and aptitudes; (2) determining qualifications required for occupations within the career system and how the requirements relate to their individual capabilities; (3) defining their career goals and developing plans for reaching the goals; (4) identifying and assessing education and training opportunities and enrollment procedures; (5) identifying factors which may impair career development; and (6) learning about resources, inside or outside the agency, where additional help is available. *See* Ted R. Gambill, "Career Counseling: Too Little, Too Late?" *Training and Development Journal* (February 1979); Andre G. Beaumont, Alva C. Cooper and Raymond H. Stockard, *A Model Career Counseling and Placement Program,* 3rd ed. (Bethlehem, Pa.: College Placement Services, Inc., 1980); Russell B. Flanders and Neale Baxter, "The Sweat of Their Brows: A Look Back Over Occupational Information and Career Counseling," *Occupational Outlook Quarterly* (Fall 1981); Karen Raskin-Young, "Career Counseling in a Large Organization," *Training and Development Journal* (August 1984).

career curve, *see* MATURITY CURVE.

career decisionmaking, or OCCUPATIONAL DECISIONMAKING, evaluation process that leads to a choice of an occupation for an individual to pursue. *See* Martin Katz, "A Model of Guidance for Career Decision-Making," *Vocational Guidance Quarterly* (September 1966); Donald R. Kaldor and Donald G. Zytowski, "A Maximizing Model of Occupational Decision-Making," *Personnel and Guidance Journal* (April 1969).

career development, systematic development designed to increase an employee's potential for advancement and career change. It may include classroom training, reading, work experience, etc. *See* Meryl R. Louis, "Managing Career Transition: A Missing Link in Career Development," *Organizational Dynamics* (Spring 1982); I. Marlene Thorn, Francis X. Fee and Jane O'Hara Carter, "Career Development: A Collaborative Approach," *Management Review* (September 1982); Beverly L. Kaye, "Performance Appraisal and Career Development: A Shotgun Marriage," *Personnel* (March-April 1984); Caela Farren and Beverly Kaye, "The Principles of Program Design: A Successful Career Development Model," *Personnel Administrator* (June 1984).

career earnings formula, a formula which bases pension benefits on average earnings in all years of credited service.

career ladder, series of classifications in which an employee may advance through training and/or on-the-job experience into successively higher levels of responsibility and salary. *See* Russ Smith and Margret Waldie, "Multi-Track Career Ladders: Maximizing Opportunities," *Review of Public Personnel Administration* (Spring 1984).

career lattice, a term that identifies horizontal and/or diagonal paths of occupational mobility leading from the entry level. Most often these paths link parallel paths of vertical or upward occupational mobility. A horizontal path of occupational mobility is often called a job transfer while a diagonal path is often referred to as a transfer-promotional path. This "lateral" mobility usually occurs within an occupational field (*e.g.*, engineering, accounting) but usually not in the same specific occupational classification.

career management, aspect of personnel management that is concerned with the occupational growth of individuals within an organization. *See* Marion S. Kellogg, *Career Management* (New York: American Management Association, Inc., 1972); Douglas T. Hall and Francine S. Hall, "What's New in Career Management," *Organizational Dynamics* (Summer 1976); Edward O. Joslin, "Career Management: How to Make it Work," *Personnel* (July–August 1977).

career mobility, also called JOB MOBILITY, degree to which an individual is able to move or advance from one position to another. *See* Yoav Vardi, "Organizational Career Mobility: An Integrative Model," *Academy of Management Review* (July 1980); Terry A. Beehr, Thomas D. Taber, and Jeffrey T. Walsh, "Perceived Mobility Channels: Criteria for Intraorganizational Job Mobility," *Organizational Behavior and Human Performance* (October 1980); George J. Borjas, "Job Mobility and Earnings Over the Life Cycle," *Industrial and Labor Relations Review* (April 1981); Sheldon E. Haber, "The Mobility of Professional Workers and Fair Hiring," *Industrial and Labor Relations Review* (January 1981); Sue Estler, "Evolving Jobs as a Form of Career Mobility: Some Policy Implications," *Public Personnel Management* (Winter 1981).

career negotiation, that aspect of career planning that has both the individual employee and the organization, in the light of their respective interests and needs, develop (negotiate) a career plan that serves both parties. *See* James F. Wolf and Robert N. Bacher, "Career Negotiation: Trading Off Employee and Organizational Needs," *Personnel* (March–April 1981).

career path, direction of an individual's career as indicated by career milestones. An employee following a career path may proceed up a single career ladder and then beyond it into a supervisory or executive position, or an employee may move from one career ladder to another. *See* Joseph J. Wnuk, Jr., "Career Paths," *Training and Development Journal* (May 1970); James W. Walker, "Let's Get Realistic About Career Paths," *Human Resource Management* (Fall 1976); Donald Grass, "A Guide to R & D Career Pathing," *Personnel Journal* (April 1979).

career pattern, sequence of occupations of an individual or group of individuals. The study of career patterns has spawned the theory that an individual's work history is a good predictor of future vocational behavior. For the pioneering research, *see* William H. Form and Delbert C. Miller, "Occupational Career Pattern as a Sociological Instrument," *American Journal of Sociology* (January 1949); Donald E. Super, "Career Patterns as a Basis for Vocational Counseling," *Journal of Counseling Psychology*, Vol. 1, No. 1 (1954).

career planning, according to James W. Walker, "Does Career Planning Rock the Boat," *Human Resources Management* (Spring 1978),

is the personal process of planning one's life work. It entails evaluating abilities and interests, considering alternative

career opportunities, establishing career goals and planning practical development activities. The process results in decisions to enter a certain occupation, join a particular company, accept or decline job opportunities (relocations, promotions, or transfers, etc.) and ultimately leave a company for another job or for retirement.
Also see Charles E. Okosky, "Career Planning," *Personnel Journal* (November 1973); Sam Gould, "Career Planning in the Organization," *Human Resource Management* (Spring 1978); John J. Leach, "The Career Planning Process," *Personnel Journal* (April 1981); Jonathan P. West, *Career Planning, Development, and Management: An Annotated Bibliography* (New York: Garland Publishing Co., 1983).

career promotion, promotion made on the basis of merit, but without competition with other employees. An example is the promotion of an employee who, as he or she learns more about the job, can do more difficult kinds of work and assume greater responsibility, so that he or she is performing duties classified at a higher grade level.

career reserved position, position within the U.S. federal Senior Executive Service that has a specific requirement for political impartiality; may be filled only by career appointment.

career system, sequence of progressively more responsible positions in the same general occupation that an organization makes available to qualified individuals.

Carlson v. Green, 446 U.S. 14 (1980), Supreme Court case which held that the Eighth Amendment's prohibition against cruel and unusual punishment gives federal prisoners or their survivors a direct right to bring suits for damages against prison officials on charges of mistreatment. The decision is an expansion of the court's ruling in *Bivens v. Six Unknown Named Federal Narcotics Agents.*

See also BIVENS V. SIX UNKNOWN NAMED FEDERAL NARCOTICS AGENTS.

Carter v. United States, 407 F. 2d 1238 (1968), U.S. Court of Appeals, District of Columbia Circuit case which held that a Federal Bureau of Investigation employee whose job tenure was within the ambit of the Universal Military Training and Service Act (1964) could not be dismissed for allegedly "sleeping with young girls and carrying on" without a trial to determine whether such activities, to the extent that they occurred, presented sufficient "cause" within the meaning of that statute.

Cary v. Westinghouse Electric Corp., 375 U.S. 261 (1964), U.S. Supreme Court case which held that disputes involving work assignments were arbitrable.

casebook, collection of case studies on a given topic. The following are casebooks in public administration: Joseph L. Bower and Charles J. Christenson, *Public Management: Text and Cases* (Homewood, Ill.: Richard D. Irwin, 1978); Robert T. Golembiewski and Michael White, eds., *Cases in Public Management,* 2nd ed. (Chicago: Rand McNally, 1976); Carl E. Lutrin and Allen K. Settle, *American Public Administration: Concepts & Cases,* 2nd ed. (Palo Alto, Calif.: Mayfield Publishing, 1980); R. Joseph Novogrod, Marshall Edward Dimock and Gladys Ogden Dimock, *Casebook in Public Administration* (New York: Holt, Rinehart and Winston, 1969); Harold Stein, *Public Administration and Policy Development: A Casebook* (New York: Harcourt, Brace, 1952); Joseph A. Uveges, Jr., *Cases in Public Administration: Narratives in Administrative Problems* (Boston: Holbrook Press, 1978); Marc Holzer and Ellen Doree Rosen, *Current Cases in Public Administration* (New York: Harper & Row, 1981); Paul Dryfoos, editor, *Cases in Public Policy and Management,* 4th edition (Boston: Public Policy and Management Program for Case and Course Development, Boston University School of Management, June 1984).

Case Co. v. National Labor Relations

Board, see J. I. CASE CO. V. NATIONAL LABOR RELATIONS BOARD.

case law, all recorded judicial and administrative agency decisions.

case study, research design that focuses upon the in-depth analysis of a single subject. It is particularly useful when the researcher seeks an understanding of dynamic processes over time. A case study is usually more qualitative than quantitative in methodological approach and is more appropriate for generating hypotheses than for testing hypotheses. In a case study the researcher usually collects data through the review of records, interviews, questionnaires, and observations. It is particularly appropriate for generating insights in new areas of research. See Chris Argyris, "Some Limitations of the Case Method: Experiences in a Management Development Program," *Academy of Management Review* (April 1980).

cash accounting, see ACCOUNTING.

cash assistance, direct cash payments to beneficiaries of public welfare programs.

casual labor, employees that are (1) essentially unskilled, (2) used only a few days at a time, or (3) needed seasonally.

catalyst, see CHANGE AGENT.

catastrophic health insurance, health insurance which provides protection against the high cost of treating severe or lengthy illnesses or disabilities. Generally such policies cover all or a specified percentage of medical expenses above an amount that is the responsibility of the insured himself (or the responsibility of another insurance policy up to a maximum limit of liability).

catchmenting, designation of a geographic area whose residents will be provided specific government services. See Gary L. Tischler *et al.*, "The Impact of Catchmenting," *Administration in Mental Health* (Winter 1972).

categorical grant, see GRANT.

Cato Institute, a conservative-oriented public policy research organization.
Cato Institute
224 Second Street, S.E.
Washington, D.C. 20003
(202) 546-0200

caucus, a private meeting of political party members in order to seek agreement on a common course of action.

cause, short form of "just cause," reason given for removing someone from an office or job. The cause cited may or may not be the real reason for the removal.
See also CARTER V. UNITED STATES.

CBO, see CONGRESSIONAL BUDGET OFFICE.

CCH, see COMMERCE CLEARING HOUSE, INC.

CEA, see COUNCIL OF ECONOMIC ADVISERS.

cease-and-desist order, ruling, frequently issued in unfair labor practice cases, which requires the charged party to stop conduct held to be illegal and take specific action to remedy the unfair labor practice.

CED, see COMMITTEE FOR ECONOMIC DEVELOPMENT.

ceiling, upper limit of ability measured by a test. A test has a low ceiling for a given population if many examinees obtained perfect scores; it has a high ceiling if there are few or no perfect scores.

ceiling, job or **position,** see JOB CEILING.

census, in ancient Rome this was the registration of citizens and their property so that it could be determined who owed what taxes and who was entitled to vote. The modern census seeks a vast array of statistical information and is not directly concerned with taxation or suffrage. Article 1, Section 2, of the U.S. Constitution requires that a census be conducted every ten years so that members of the House of Representatives shall be appropriately apportioned among the states.

Census, Bureau of the, general purpose statistical agency of the U.S. federal government that collects, tabulates, and publishes a wide variety of statistical data about the people and the economy of the nation. These data are utilized by the Congress, by the executive branch, and by the public generally in the development and evaluation of economic and social programs.

Bureau of the Census
Department of Commerce
Washington, D.C. 20233
(301) 763-4051

Center for Political Studies, see IN-STITUTE FOR SOCIAL RESEARCH.

Center for Research on Utilization of Scientific Knowledge, see INSTITUTE FOR SOCIAL RESEARCH.

central bank, in most countries, the central monetary authority. Functions may include issuing a country's currency, carrying out a nation's monetary policy, and managing the level of the country's foreign exchange reserves and the external value of its currency. In the United States, the Federal Reserve System functions as the nation's central bank.

central city, see CITY.

central clearance, the Office of Management and Budget's (OMB) coordination and assessment of recommendations and positions taken by the various federal departments and agencies on legislative matters as they relate to a president's program.

The first form of central clearance is *substantive bill clearance.* Departmental and agency drafts of bills en route to Congress must clear OMB for approval. Congressional committees also solicit views from interested agencies on substantive legislative bills emanating from sources other than the executive branch. However,

executive agency responses are expected to be cleared by OMB.

The second form of central clearance is *financial bill clearance.* Since the Budget and Accounting Act of 1921, federal agencies have not had the authority to decide for themselves what appropriations to ask of Congress. A department or agency's proposed spending measure must clear OMB.

The third form of central clearance is *enrolled bill clearance.* When enrolled bill enactments come from Congress to the president for signature or veto, OMB solicits agency opinion on the merits of the congressionally approved legislation. OMB evaluates agency opinion and prepares its own report to the president recommending either approval or veto and the reasons why. For the classic account of the development of central clearance, see Richard E. Neustadt, "Presidency and Legislation: The Growth of Central Clearance," *American Political Science Review* (September 1954). For an update, see Robert S. Gilmour, "Central Legislative Clearance: A Revised Perspective," *Public Administration Review* (March–April 1971).

central hiring hall, see HIRING HALL.

Central Intelligence Agency (CIA), federal agency responsible for coordinating the various intelligence activities of the United States. The CIA has no police, subpoena, or law enforcement powers, and has no internal security functions.

CIA
Washington, D.C. 20505
(703) 351-1100

centralization, also DECENTRALIZATION, any process by which the power and authority in an organization or polity is concentrated. *Decentralization* is the reverse—power and authority are distributed more widely in an organization or polity. *See* James Fesler, "Approaches to Understanding Decentralization," *The Journal of Politics* (August 1965); Irving Kristol, "Decentralization for What?" *The Public Interest* (Spring 1968); Herbert Kaufman,

"Administrative Decentralization and Political Power," *Public Administration Review* (January-February 1969); Dwight Ink and Alan L. Dean, "A Concept of Decentralization," *Public Administration Review* (January-February 1970); Adam W. Herbert, "Management Under Conditions of Decentralization and Citizen Participation," *Public Administration Review* (October 1972); Henry J. Schmandt, "Municipal Decentralization: An Overview," *Public Administration Review* (October 1972); Mario Fantini and Marilyn Gittel, *Decentralization: Achieving Reform* (New York: Praeger Publishers, 1973); Norman Furniss, "The Practical Significance of Decentralization," *The Journal of Politics* (November 1974); David O. Porter and Eugene A. Olsen, "Some Critical Issues in Government Centralization and Decentralization," *Public Administration Review* (January-February 1976); Allen Barton *et al.*, *Decentralizing City Government: An Evaluation of the New York City Manager Experiment* (Lexington, Mass.: Lexington Books, 1977); G. Guibert and B. Lanvin, "Decentralization in Government: The United States and France Compared," *Journal of Policy Analysis and Management* (Winter 1984); D. Conyers, "Decentralization and Development: A Review of the Literature," *Public Administration and Development* (April-June 1984).

central labor union, association of local labor unions in a specific geographic region.

central tendency, series of statistical measures that provide a representative value for a distribution, or, more simply, that refer to how scores tend to cluster in a distribution. The most common measures of central tendency are the mean, median, and mode.

CEO, *see* CHIEF EXECUTIVE OFFICER.

certificate, list of eligibles ranked according to regulations for appointment or promotion consideration. A more useful term is "candidate list."

certification, formal determination by the National Labor Relations Board or other administrative agency that a particular union is the majority choice of, and thus the exclusive bargaining agent for, a group of employees in a given bargaining unit. *Decertification* is the opposite process, where an administrative agency withdraws a union's official designation as the exclusive bargaining agent. In both cases, these actions are usually preceded by a formal polling of the union membership. *See* Arthur P. Brief and Dale E. Rude, "Voting in Union Certification Elections: A Conceptual Analysis," *Academy of Management Review* (April 1981); William E. Fulmer and Tamara A. Gilman, "Why Do Workers Vote for Union Decertification?" *Personnel* (March-April 1981); William E. Fulmer, "Decertification: Is the Current Trend a Threat to Collective Bargaining?" *California Management Review* (Fall 1981); John C. Anderson, Gloria Busman, Charles A. O'Reilly, III, "The Decertification Process: Evidence from California," *Industrial Relations* (Spring 1982); Richard Block and Myron Roomkin, "Determinants of Voter Participation in Union Certification Elections," *Monthly Labor Review* (April 1982); William N. Cooke, "Determinants of the Outcomes of Union Certification Elections," *Industrial and Labor Relations Review* (April 1983); James P. Swann, Jr., "The Decertification of a Union," *Personnel Administrator* (January 1983).

See also ACCREDITATION and OCCUPATIONAL CERTIFICATION.

certification, selective, certifying only the names of eligibles who have special qualifications required to fill particular vacant positions.

certification of eligibles, procedure whereby those who have passed competitive civil service examinations have their names ranked in order of score and placed on a list of those eligible for appointment. When a government agency has a vacancy, it requests its personnel arm to provide a list of eligibles for the class to which the vacant position has been allocated. The personnel agency then "certifies" the names of the highest ranking eligibles to the appointing authority for possible selection. Usually, only a limited number of the qualified eligibles are certified. When a jurisdiction requires that three eligibles be certified to the appointing authority, this is referred to as the "rule of three." For an overview, *see* Carmen D. Saso and Earl P. Tanis, *Selection and Certification of Eligibles: A Survey of Policies and Practices* (Chicago: International Personnel Management Association, 1974).

certification proceeding, process by which the National Labor Relations Board or other administrative agency discovers whether or not the employees of an organization want a particular union to represent them.

certified employee organization, union that an administrative agency has certified as the official representative of the employees in a bargaining unit for the purpose of collective negotiations. Such certification is usually the direct result of a representation election.

Certified Public Accountant (CPA), accountant certified by a state government as having met specific educational and experience requirements. *See* Phillip E. Rogers, "Individual State Experience Requirements for Obtaining the CPA Certificate," *Government Accountants Journal* (Spring 1982).

certiorari, order or writ from a higher court demanding that a lower court send up the record of a case for review. Except for a few instances of original jurisdiction, most cases that reach the U.S. Supreme Court do so because the Supreme Court itself has issued such a writ or "granted certiorari." If certiorari is denied by the Supreme Court, it means that the justices are content to let the lower-court decision stand. *See* S. Sidney Ulmer, "The Supreme Court's Certiorari Decisions: Conflict as a Predictive Variable," *American Political Science Review* (December 1984).

CETA, *see* COMPREHENSIVE EMPLOYMENT AND TRAINING ACT OF 1973.

CFR, *see* CODE OF FEDERAL REGULATIONS.

chain picketing, continuous, moving human chain sometimes formed by striking workers to prevent anyone from crossing their picket line.

chance score, score that has a significant probability of occurring on the basis of random selection of answers.

Chandler v. Roudebush, 425 U.S. 840 (1976), U.S. Supreme Court case which held federal employees, after exhausting all administrative remedies concerning a claim of sexual and/or racial discrimination, have the same right to a trial *de novo* in the federal courts as is enjoyed by other employees under the Civil Rights Act of 1964 as amended.

change agent, or CATALYST, descriptive ways of referring to organization development consultants or facilitators. *See* Lee Grossman, *The Change Agent* (New York: AMACOM, 1974). *See also* Stephen R. Michael, *et al.,* *Techniques of Organizational Change* (New York: McGraw-Hill Book Co., 1981); Stephen R. Michael, "Organizational Change Techniques: Their Present, Their Future," *Organizational Dynamics* (Summer 1982).

change in duty station, personnel action that changes an employee from one geographical location to another in the same agency.

charging party, any individual who formally asserts that he or she is aggrieved because of an unlawful employment practice.

charismatic leadership, leadership that is based on the compelling personality of the leader rather than upon formal position. *See* Robert J. House, "A 1976 Theory of Charismatic Leadership," in James G. Hunt and Lars L. Larson, eds., *Leadership: The Cutting Edge* (Carbondale, Ill.: Southern Illinois University Press, 1977); Ann Ruth Willner, *The Spellbinders: Charismatic Political Leadership* (New Haven, Conn.: Yale University Press, 1984); Arthur Schweitzer, *The Age of Charisma* (Chicago, IL: Nelson-Hall Publishers, 1985).

charter, also CITY CHARTER and MODEL CHARTER, document that spells out the purposes and powers of the municipal corporation. In order to operate, a municipal corporation must have a charter like any other corporation. The municipality can perform only those functions and exercise only those powers that are in the charter. If the particular state permits home rule, a city can develop and implement its own charter. Otherwise it is limited to statutory charters spelled out by the state legislature. The National Municipal League has developed a *model charter* which it advocates for all cities.

checkoff, union security provision, commonly provided for in the collective bargaining agreement, that allows the employer to deduct union dues, assessments, and initiation fees from the pay of all union members. The deducted amounts are delivered to the union on a prearranged schedule. The Labor-Management Relations (Taft-Hartley) Act of 1947 requires that union members must give written permission for these fees to be deducted.

checkoff, compulsory, *see* AUTOMATIC CHECKOFF.

checks and balances, the notion that constitutional devices can prevent any power within a state from becoming absolute by being balanced against, or checked by, another source of power within that same state. First put forth by the French philosopher Charles de Montesquieu (1689-1755) in his *The Spirit of the Laws* (1734), this notion was further developed by Thomas Jefferson (1743-1826) in his *Notes on the State of Virginia* (1784) where he asserted that "the powers of government should be so divided and balanced among several bodies of magistracy, as that none could transcend their legal limits, without being effectively checked and restrained by the others." The U.S. Constitution is often described as a system of "checks and balances."

Chicago School, a loose term for those economists associated with the University of Chicago who advocate laissez-faire capitalism. Milton Friedman and George Stigler are the best known members of this "school."

chief executive officer (CEO), individual who is personally accountable to the board of directors or the electorate for the activities of the organization or the jurisdiction. *See* Chris Argyris, "The CEO's Behavior: Key to Organizational Development," *Harvard Business Review* (March–April 1973): Robert H. Rock, *The Chief Executive Officer* (New York: D.C. Heath-Lexington Books, 1977); Harry Levinson, "Criteria for Choosing Chief Executives," *Harvard Business Review* (July–August 1980); John F. Rockart and Michael E. Treacy, "The CEO Goes On-Line," *Harvard Business Review* (January–February 1982).
See also GENERAL MANAGER.

chief steward, union representative who supervises the activities of a group of shop stewards.

childbirth, *see* PREGNANCY.

child care, *see* DAY CARE.

child labor, originally meant employing children in a manner that was detrimental to their health and social development; but now that the law contains strong child labor prohibitions, the term refers to the employment of children below the legal age limit.

Efforts by the labor movement and social reformers to prevent the exploitation of children in the workplace date back well into the nineteenth century. As early as 1842, some states (Connecticut and Massachusetts) legislated a maximum ten-hour work day for children. In 1848,

Pennsylvania established a minimum working age of twelve for factory jobs. But it wold be twenty years more before any state had inspectors to enforce child labor laws. And it would not be until the late 1930s that federal laws would outlaw child labor (mainly through the Fair Labor Standards Act). The practice was so entrenched that earlier federal attempts to outlaw child labor were construed by the Supreme Court as being unconstitutional infringements on the power of the states to regulate conditions in the workplace.

For histories of the horrendous conditions that led to the passage of federal and state child labor prohibitions, see Jeremy P. Felt, *Hostages of Fortune: Child Labor Reform in New York State* (Syracuse, N.Y.: Syracuse University Press, 1965); Walter I. Trattner, *Crusade for the Children: A History of the National Child Labor Committee and Child Labor Reform in America* (Chicago: Quadrangle Books, 1970); Ronald B. Taylor, *Sweatshops in the Sun: Child Labor on the Farm* (Boston: Beacon Press, 1973). For present-day impact, see Daniel J. B. Mitchell and John Clapp, "The Impact of Child-Labor Laws on the Kinds of Jobs Held by Young School-Leavers," *The Journal of Human Resources* (Summer 1980); Lee Swepston, "Child Labour: Its Regulation by ILO Standards and National Legislation," *International Labour Review* (September–October 1982); Thomas A. Coens, "Child Labor Laws: A Viable Legacy for the 1980s," *Labor Law Journal* (October 1982).

See also FAIR LABOR STANDARDS ACT and WORKING PAPERS.

chilling effect, result of employment practices, government regulations, court decisions, or legislation (or the threat of these) that may create an inhibiting atmosphere that prevents the free exercise of individual employment rights. A chilling effect tends to keep minorities and women from seeking employment and advancement in an organization even in the absence of formal bars. Other chilling effects may be positive or negative, depending upon the "chillee's" perspective. For example, even discussion of proposed regulations can "chill" employers or unions into compliance.

chi-square, statistical procedure that estimates whether the observed values in a distribution differ from the expected distribution and thus may be attributable to the operation of factors other than chance. Particular values of chi-square are usually identified by the symbol χ^2.

Christmas bonus, *see* NONPRODUCTION BONUS.

chronic unemployment, unemployment lasting longer than six months.

CIA, *see* CENTRAL INTELLIGENCE AGENCY.

CIO, *see* (1) CONGRESS OF INDUSTRIAL ORGANIZATIONS and (2) AMERICAN FEDERATION OF LABOR-CONGRESS OF INDUSTRIAL ORGANIZATIONS.

circuit court of appeals, *see* COURT OF APPEALS.

circuit rider, government official who travels from jurisdiction to jurisdiction providing any of a variety of technical services.

citizen, an individual who owes allegiance to and, in turn, receives protection from a state; a person born or naturalized in the United States. All U.S. citizens are also citizens of the state in which he or she has a permanent residence; corporations are citizens of the state in which they were legally created.

citizen participation, means of empowering individuals/groups with bargaining power to represent their own interests and to plan and implement their own programs with a view towards social, economic, and political power and control. *See* Sherry R. Arnstein, "A Ladder of Citizen Participation," *Journal of the American Institute of Planners* (July 1969); Edgar S. Cahn and Barry A. Passett, eds., *Citizen Participation: Effecting Community Change* (New York: Praeger, 1971); Richard Cole,

Citizen Participation and the Urban Policy Process (Lexington, Mass.: Lexington Books, 1974); Lloyd C. Irland, "Citizen Participation—A Tool for Conflict Management on the Public Lands," *Public Administration Review* (May–June 1975); David M. Lenny, "The Case for Funding Citizen Participation in the Administrative Process," *Administrative Law Review* (Summer 1976); D. Stephen Cupps, "Emerging Problems of Citizen Participation," *Public Administration Review* (September–October 1977); Judy B. Rosener, "Citizen Participation: Can We Measure Its Effectiveness?" *Public Administration Review* (September–October 1978); Joan B. Aron, "Citizen Participation at Government Expense," *Public Administration Review* (September–October 1979); Mary Grisez Kweit and Robert W. Kweit, *Implementing Citizen Participation in a Bureaucratic Society: A Contingency Approach* (New York: Praeger Publishers, 1982); Curtis Ventriss, "Emerging Perspectives on Citizen Participation," *Public Administration Review* (May–June 1985).

See also INTEREST GROUP and LOBBYING.

citizenship, U.S., a requirement for public employment in some jurisdictions. For a discussions of recent court rulings, *see* Arnold L. Steigman, "Public Administration by Litigation: The Impact of Court Decisions Concerning Citizenship on Public Personnel Management," *Public Personnel Management* (March–April 1979); Charles O. Agege, "Employment Discrimination Against Aliens: the Constitutional Implications," *Labor Law Journal* (February 1985).

See also the following entries:
AMBACH V. NORWICK
CABELL V. SHAVEZ-SALIDO
FOLEY V. CONNELIE
HAMPTON V. MOW SUN WONG
SUGARMAN V. DOUGALL

city, also CENTRAL CITY and INDEPENDENT CITY, municipal corporation chartered by its state. A *central city* is the core of a metropolitan area, while an *independent city* is outside of or separate from a met-

ropolitan area. The standard history is Lewis Mumford, *The City in History* (New York: Harcourt, Brace and World, 1961).

For histories of city government, *see* Lawrence J. R. Herson, "The Lost World of Municipal Government," *American Political Science Review* (June 1957); Ernest S. Griffith, *A History of American City Government: The Conspicuous Failure, 1870–1900* (New York: Praeger, 1974); Ernest S. Griffith, *A History of American City Government: The Progressive Years and Their Aftermath, 1900–1920* (New York: Praeger, 1974); Jon Teaford, *The Municipal Revolution in America: Origins of Modern Urban Government, 1630–1825* (Chicago: University of Chicago Press, 1975); Edward C. Banfield, *The Unheavenly City Revisited: A Revision of the Unheavenly City* (Boston: Little, Brown & Co., 1974); Gunther Barth, *City People: The Rise of Modern City Culture in Nineteenth-Century America* (New York: Oxford University Press, 1980).

city charter, *see* CHARTER.

city-county consolidation, merger of all governments within a county to form one government unit. *See* Brett W. Hawkins, *Nashville Metro: The Politics of City-County Consolidation* (Nashville, Tenn.: Vanderbilt University Press, 1966); Vincent L. Marando, "The Politics of City-County Consolidation," *National Civic Review* (February 1975); Thomas W. Fletcher, "Is Consolidation the Answer?" *Public Management* (May 1980).

city engineer, professional position in local government dealing with local public works. Most of the early city managers were engineers.

city management, *see* the following entries:
AMERICAN CITY AND COUNTY
BOROUGH
BOSSISM
CHARTER
CITIZEN PARTICIPATION
CITY

CITY-COUNTY CONSOLIDATION
CITY MANAGER
CITY PLANNER
COMMISSION FORM OF GOVERNMENT
COMMUNITY CONTROL
CORPORATION COUNSEL
COUNCIL-MANAGER PLAN
COUNCIL OF GOVERNMENT
COUNTY
DILLON'S RULE
ENABLING ACT
FEDERAL ASSISTANCE PROGRAMS
GARDEN CITY
GRANT
GREEN RIVER ORDINANCE
HOME RULE
ICMA RETIREMENT CORPORATION
INTERNATIONAL CITY MANAGEMENT
   ASSOCIATION
LAKEWOOD PLAN
LITTLE CITY HALL
MAYOR-COUNCIL SYSTEM
METROPOLITAN GOVERNMENT
MODEL CITIES PROGRAM
MUNICIPAL BONDS
MUNICPAL COMMERCIAL PAPER
MUNICIPAL CORPORATION
MUNICIPAL FINANCE OFFICERS
   ASSOCIATION
NATIONAL LEAGUE OF CITIES
NATIONAL MUNICIPAL LEAGUE
NATIONAL URBAN LEAGUE
NATION'S CITIES
NEIGHBORHOOD ASSOCIATION
PROGRESSIVE MOVEMENT
PROPOSITION 2½
PROPOSITION 13
REVENUE SHARING
RING THEORY OF URBAN DEVELOPMENT
SERVICE CONTRACT
706 AGENCY
STANDARD METROPOLITAN STATISTICAL
   AREA
TOWN
TOWN MEETING
UNINCORPORATED AREA
UNITED STATES CONFERENCE OF MAYORS
URBAN AFFAIRS QUARTERLY
URBAN ENTERPRISE ZONE
URBAN HOMESTEADING
URBAN INSTITUTE
URBAN PARK MOVEMENT
URBAN PLANNING

URBAN RENEWAL
ZONING

city manager, chief executive of the council/manager (originally commission/manager) system of local government. In contrast to other types of government, the city manager is an appointed chief executive serving at the pleasure of the council. The concept was created by Richard Childs, an urban reformer, who wanted to replace political bosses with municipal experts. To do this effectively, he created the concept of an administrative chief executive armed with the critical administrative powers such as appointment and removal of administrative officials but denied any political powers such as the veto. The dichotomy between administration and politics upon which the system was premised was implemented by putting all of the policymaking and political functions into the city council. This essentially abolished any separation of powers in the traditional sense at the local level. The decision-making ability of the council was assured by: (1) creating a small council, typically from five to nine elected through at-large, non-partisan elections; and (2) permitting the council to hire and fire the city manager, their expert in the implementation of community policies.

Present council/manager systems, found in about one half of all U.S. cities, often deviate from this traditional model. Many have large councils, partisan elections, and separately elected mayors, and some if not all of the council people are elected from wards. In fact, some recent national court decisions have required ward elections in some cities. The system has been criticized by some political scientists as being unresponsive to some elements of the community and supported by public administrationists for its effective management in the public interest. In some larger cities a variant of the system has evolved, utilizing a chief administrative officer often appointed by the mayor. The best history of the city manager profession is Richard J. Stillman II, *The Rise of the City Manager, A Public Professional in Local Government* (Albuquerque: Univer-

sity of New Mexico Press, 1974). *Also see* Harold A. Stone, Don K. Price and Katherine H. Stone, *City Manager Government in the United States* (Chicago: Public Administration Service, 1940); John C. Bollens and John C. Ries, *The City Manager Profession, Myths and Realities* (Chicago: Public Administration Service, 1969); Keith F. Mulrooney, Symposium Editor, "The American City Manager: An Urban Administrator in a Complex and Evolving Situation," *Public Administration Review* (January-February 1971); Ronald O. Loveridge, *City Managers in Legislative Politics* (Indianapolis: The Bobbs-Merrill Co., 1971); Fremont J. Lyden and Ernest G. Miller, "Why City Managers Leave the Profession: A Longitudinal Study in the Pacific Northwest," *Public Administration Review* (March-April 1976); Frank Aleshire and Fran Aleshire, "The American City Manager: New Style, New Game," *National Civic Review* (May 1977); LeRoy R. Harlow, *Without Fear or Favor: Odyssey of a City Manager* (Provo, Utah: Brigham Young University Press, 1977); Alan L. Saltzstein, "City Managers and City Councils: Perceptions of the Division of Authority," *Western Political Quarterly* (June 1974); Harmon Zeigler, Ellen Kehoe and Jane Reisman, *City Managers and School Superintendents: Response to Community Conflict* (New York: Praeger Publishers, 1984); William R. Fannin and Don Hellriegel, "Policy Roles of City Managers," *American Politics Quarterly* (April 1985).
See also GENERAL MANAGER.

City of Los Angeles, Department of Water & Power v. Manhart, 435 U.S. 703 (1978), U.S. Supreme court case, which held that a pension plan requiring female employees to contribute more from their wages to gain the same pension benefits as male employees was in violation of Title VII of the Civil Rights Act of 1964. While the actual statistics were undisputed (women live longer than men), the court reasoned that Title VII prohibits treating individuals "as simply components of a racial, religious, sexual or national class." See Linda H. Kistler and Richard C. Healy, "Sex Discrimination in Pension Plans Since *Manhart,*" *Labor Law Journal* (April 1981).

City of Newport v. Fact Concerts, Inc., 69 L.Ed. 2d 616 (1981), U.S. Supreme Court case which held that municipalities are not subject to punitive damages in civil suits.

city planner, also CITY PLANNING, administrative official charged with the development of blueprints for the planned growth of a political unit, such as a city. The office and the concept of city planning arose during the reform movement, reflecting the belief that science should rule political life and that trained planners could create the best plans for the future development of a city. See John W. Reps, *The Making of Urban America: A History of City Planning in the United States* (Princeton, N.J.: Princeton University Press, 1964); Alan A. Altshuler, *The City Planning Process: A Political Analysis* (Ithaca, N.Y.: Cornell University Press, 1965); David C. Ranney, *Planning and Politics in the Metropolis* (Columbus, Ohio: Merrill, 1969); Francine Rabinovitz, *City Politics and Planning* (Chicago: Aldine, 1969); Ralph E. Thayer, "The Local Government Annual Report as a Policy Planning Opportunity," *Public Administration Review* (July-August 1978).

Civil Aeronautics Board (CAB), federal agency that promoted and regulated the civil air transport industry within the U.S. and between the U.S. and foreign countries. Created in 1938, it was abolished on January 1, 1985.

civil disobedience, Henry David Thoreau's (1817-1962) notion from his essay *On the Duty of Civil Disobedience* (1849) that one should not support a government (by paying taxes) if it sanctions policies (slavery) with which one disagrees. Now the phrase is used to refer to acts of lawbreaking designed to bring public attention to laws of questionable morality and legitimacy. The most famous practioners of civil disobedience in this century were Mohandas K. Gandhi (1869-1948) in India and Martin Luther King, Jr. (1929-1968) in the United States.

civilian labor force, *see* LABOR FORCE.

civil rights, generally, the protections and privileges given to all citizens by the U.S. Constitution. However, "civil rights" frequently is used to refer to those positive acts of government that seek to make constitutional guarantees a reality for all citizens. *See* Richard E. Morgan, *Disabling America: The "Rights Industry" in Our Time* (New York: Basic Books, 1985).

Civil Rights Act of 1964, the most far-reaching regulation of labor relations since the National Labor Relations Act of 1935. Designed to eliminate racial and sexual discrimination in most areas of U.S. life, it affected employers of fifteen or more employees engaged in interstate commerce by providing for the withholding of federal funds from programs administered in a discriminatory manner and establishing a right to equal employment opportunity without regard to race, color, religion, sex, or national origin. It also created the Equal Employment Opportunity Commission (EEOC) to assist in implementing this right. Its provisions were extended to public sector employers in 1972 (*see* EQUAL EMPLOYMENT OPPORTUNITY ACT OF 1972).

See also EQUAL EMPLOYMENT OPPORTUNITY COMMISSION and TITLE VII.

Civil Rights Acts of 1866, 1870, and 1971, laws that insure equality before the law in a variety of functional areas (ability to enter into contracts, sue, give evidence, and secure equal protection of persons and property) and establish that individuals or governments denying any rights or privileges shall be liable for legal action. These acts are often used in conjunction with, but are not replaced by, the Civil Rights Act of 1964 as the basis for suits.

Civil Rights Acts of 1957 and 1960, the Civil Rights Act of 1957 (Public Law 85-135) is generally considered to be the beginning of contemporary civil rights legislation. It established the U.S. Commission on Civil Rights and strengthened the judiciary's ability to protect civil rights. The Civil Rights Act of 1960 (Public Law 86-449) served mainly to plug legal loopholes in the 1957 law. For a broad history of the civil rights movement, *see* Richard Bardolph, ed., *The Civil Rights Record: Black Americans and the Law, 1849-1970* (New York: Thomas Y. Crowell Co., 1970).

Civil Rights Commission, *see* COMMISSION ON CIVIL RIGHTS.

civil service, collective term for all of those employees of a government who are not members of the military services. For histories of the U.S. civil service, *see* Paul P. Van Riper, *History of the United States Civil Service* (Evanston, Ill.: Row, Peterson, 1958); Jay M. Shafritz, *Public Personnel Management: The Heritage of Civil Service Reform* (New York: Praeger, 1975). *Also see* W. D. Heisel, "Alternatives to Traditional Civil Service," *Public Personnel Management Journal* (Fall 1983); Bruce L. R. Smith, ed., *The Higher Civil Service in Europe and Canada: Lessons for the United States* (Washington, D.C.: The Brookings Institution, 1984); Ellen M. Bussey, ed., *Federal Civil Service Law and Procedures: A Basic Guide* (Washington, D.C.: Bureau of National Affairs, Inc., 1985); David H. Rosenbloom, editor, *Public Personnel Policy: The Politics of Civil Service* (Port Washington, N.Y.: Associated Faculty Press, 1985).

See also INTERNATIONAL CIVIL SERVICE.

Civil Service Assembly of the United States and Canada, *see* INTERNATIONAL PERSONNEL MANAGEMENT ASSOCIATION.

civil service commission, government agency charged with the responsibility of promulgating the rules and regulations of the civilian personnel management system. Depending upon its legal mandate, a civil service commission may hear employee appeals and take a more active (or passive) role in the personnel management process. Influenced by the example of the 1883 Pendleton Act, state and local jurisdictions began to institute civil service commissions. But this was a very slow process. While New York State adopted a merit system that same year and Massachusetts did so during the following year, it would be more than twenty years before another state did so (in 1905). By 1935 only twelve states had formally instituted merit systems. These early efforts weren't all successes. Connecticut had its first civil service law repealed while Kansas kept its statute as law but refused to vote appropriations for it. Nor were these laws necessarily effective even when kept on the books. For example, New York State, which had the most stringent prohibitions against political assessments on the salaries of public employees since 1883, had widespread "voluntary" contributions to the party at least through the 1930s.

Perhaps the most striking difference in public personnel management found among different jurisdictional levels in the United States is that the merit system and the commission form of administering it have been far less successful in state and local governments than at the federal level. The reasons for this have been largely political. Although national politicians once relied dearly upon patronage for securing and maintaining their positions, the federal government never fell under the control of a unified political machine. At most it was dominated by a coalition of state and local political "bosses." At the state and local levels, however, another picture was once common. While less important in recent decades, political machines once ruled supreme at these levels, and especially in local politics. Even where this was not the case, the "spoils" tradition was often strong. Consequently, with some exceptions, until the post-World War II period, the politics of patronage was largely able to forestall the adoption of effective merit-oriented reforms.

While some cities, including New York, Albany, Buffalo, Syracuse, Chicago, Evanston, and Seattle, introduced merit systems during the 1880s and 1890s, the vast number of local jurisdictions were left untouched by the first wave of civil service reform. During the Progressive Era of the early 1900s, when corruption and "bossism" were among the prime targets of muckrakers and reform politicians, progress was also made in many cities, including Los Angeles, San Francisco, Pittsburgh, Cincinnati, Cleveland, St. Louis, and Baltimore. Overall, only sixty-five cities had created civil service commissions by 1900. By 1930 that number had risen to 250. Today less than 12 percent of cities with populations exceeding fifty-thousand still lack merit systems.

The reader should be aware that all statistics concerning merit system coverage are inherently deceptive. While such figures may be numerically accurate, they merely indicate that merit systems are "on the books," not that they exist in practice. The surveys of merit system coverage that are annually undertaken by a variety of good-government groups are typically administered by mailed questionnaire. These statistics are by no means ascertained by empirical investigation. Consequently, while the arithmetic of these surveys may be impeccable, the resulting summaries frequently belie the true extent of merit system coverage. Remember, the city of Chicago has an excellent merit system on the books, yet it has managed to retain its well-earned reputation as the most famous large American city with patronage abuses.

Subnational jurisdictions followed the federal merit system example in many respects: bipartisan civil service commissions became common, examining methods and related administrative detail were frequently similar, and prohibitions concerning political assessments and other varieties of inference were legally binding many years before a general pattern of compliance appeared. In some areas such as position classifications programs and retirement provisions, a variety of local jurisdictions were many years ahead of the federal service. However, at the local level the pattern of reform that evolved contained a crucial difference—the civil service commission was made administratively and presumably politically independent of the jurisdiction's chief executive officer. The commission format was mandated by political, not administrative, considerations. Then, as now, the illogic of divorcing the control of personnel from programmatic authority was recognized. Nevertheless, the more immediate goal of defeating the influences of spoils was paramount, and thus the rationale for the commission device was quite reasonable. Not only would it be independent from the party-controlled government, but its three- or five-part membership would be in a better position to resist political pressures than could any single administrator. Appellate functions, especially, are better undertaken by a tribunal than by a solitary judge. Not insignificantly, a commission provides a political safety valve by making room for special-interest representation, such as racial, religious, or employee groups.

It wasn't very long before the rationale for the independent commission was seriously challenged. As the city manager movement developed early in this century, managers—nonpartisan reform-type managers at that—found themselves burdened with the same kinds of restrictions upon their authority over personnel that had been designed to thwart the spoilsmen. These managers thus asserted that the original reason for establishing an independent personnel agency—namely, lack of confidence in the appointing authority—did not exist with regard to them. They felt, quite reasonably, that the personnel function should be integrated with the other administrative functions under the executive. While this line of reasoning made considerable headway where the city manager concept was firmly entrenched, it had little applicability for most of the larger cities where merit system provisions implemented only a few years earlier had degenerated into a sham. This was achieved by the dual process of appointing persons unsympathetic to merit system ideals as civil service commissioners and by restricting the work of the commission by denying adequate appropriations. In response to such "starve 'em out" tactics, many jurisdictions later enacted ordinances providing that a fixed percentage of each year's budget would be for the administration of the merit system.

Despite these rather inauspicious beginnings, the merit system has now taken a firm hold on most sizable public jurisdictions. Two basic factors have accounted for the continued growth of merit systems at the state and local level. First, as the scope and nature of state and local employment changed it was almost inevitable that patronage appointees would have to give way to those with greater technical training and an interest in public service careers. It should be remembered in this context that even in the federal government at its worst, the spoils system never substantially abused positions requiring technical skills. For the most part, then, the complex functions of government, rather than the ideas of civil service reformers, have led to the relative demise of spoils practices.

Second, the federal government threw its weight in favor of the development of forceful merit systems at the state and local levels. Beginning in the 1930s, it has adopted a variety of measures to coerce or induce states to use merit procedures where federal funding is involved. Federal standards for this purpose were issued in 1939 and revised in 1948 and 1971.

Ironically, at the same time that the federal government has been pressuring state and local governments to adopt and strengthen merit systems, the commission form of administering them has been on the wane for reasons similar to the abolition of the commission format at the federal level. Put simply, independent, structurally and politically isolated personnel agencies of a regulatory nature have great difficulty in serving the needs of elected executives and public managers. *See* Donald R. Harvey, *The Civil Service Commission* (New York: Praeger, 1970); Winston W. Crouch, *A Guide for Modern Personnel Commissions* (Chicago: International Personnel Management Association, 1973).

See also GRANT'S CIVIL SERVICE COMMISSION.

Civil Service Commission, U.S., see the following entries:

GRANT'S CIVIL SERVICE COMMISSION
MERIT SYSTEMS PROTECTION BOARD
OFFICE OF PERSONNEL MANAGEMENT
UNITED STATES CIVIL SERVICE COMMISSION

Civil Service Commission v. National Association of Letter Carriers, see UNITED STATES CIVIL SERVICE COMMISSION V. NATIONAL ASSOCIATION OF LETTER CARRIERS.

Civil Service Journal, official quarterly of the U.S. Civil Service Commission. It ceased publication in 1979.

civil service reform, generally dated from the post-Civil War period, but the political roots of the reform effort go back much earlier—to the beginning of the republic. As John Adams tended to maintain the appointments of George Washington, Thomas Jefferson was the first president who had to face the problem of a philosophically hostile bureaucracy. While sorely pressed by his supporters to remove Federalist officeholders and replace them with Republican partisans, Jefferson was determined not to remove officials for political reasons alone. Jefferson rather courageously maintained that only "malconduct is a just ground of removal: mere difference of political opinion is not." With occasional defections from this principle, even by Jefferson himself, this policy was the norm rather than the exception down through the administration of Andrew Jackson.

President Jackson's rhetoric on the nature of public service was far more influential than his administrative example. In claiming that all men, especially the newly enfranchised who did so much to elect him, should have an equal opportunity for public office, Jackson played to his plebeian constituency and put the patrician civil service on notice that they had no natural monopoly on public office. Jackson's concept of rotation in office was basically conceived as a sincere measure of reform. As such it was enthusiastically supported by contemporary reformers. While Jackson's personal indulgence in spoils were more limited than commonly thought, he nevertheless established the intellectual and political rationale for the unmitigated spoils system that was to follow. Of course, Jackson's spoils doctrine would hardly have taken as it did were it not for the fact that the country was well prepared to accept it. Indeed, much of the venality of the spoils process was in full flower in state and local governments a full generation before it crept into federal office.

The spoils system flourished under Jackson's successors. The doctrine of rotation of office progressively prevailed over the earlier notion of stability in office. Presidents even began turning out of office appointees of previous presidents of the same party. President Millard Fillmore had dissident Whigs turned out in favor of "real" Whigs. When James Buchanan, a Democrat, succeeded Franklin Pierce, also a Democrat, it was announced that no incumbents appointed by Pierce would be retained. This development led William Marcy to remark, "they have it that I am the author of the office seeker's doctrine, that 'to the victors belong the spoils,' but I certainly should never recommend the policy of pillaging my own camp."

Abraham Lincoln as president followed the example of his predecessors and was an unabashed supporter and skillful user of the spoils system; his highly partisan exploitation of federal patronage was a great aid to the war effort. Paradoxically, while the spoils system reached its zenith under Lincoln, its decline may also be dated from his administration; for Lincoln refused to accede to the hitherto observed principle of quadrennial rotation after his reelection in 1864. This was the first significant setback that the principle of rotation had received since Jackson laid out its theoretical justifications. Yet through the height of the spoils period, there existed what some historians have called a "career service." Many clerks had continuous tenure all through this period, retaining their positions through competence, custom, and neutrality.

The chronology of civil service reform is easily delineated. A variety of specific events and documents have provided a convenient framework for analysis. However, the motivations of those who led the reform movement have remained a clouded issue, lending themselves to considerable speculations. Historians tend to agree that the leaders of the reform movement represented a socioeconomic class that was both out of power and decidedly antagonistic to those elements of society who were in power. In simplistic terms, it was the WASP (white Anglo-Saxon Protestant) patricians versus the ethnic plebians. The social upheavals that accompanied the Civil War left in its wake what Richard Hofstadter has described as a displaced class of old gentry, professional men, and the civic leaders of an earlier time. This displacement, this alienation, did much to establish the "ins" versus the "outs" pattern of the politics of reform. Because the reformers blamed the professional politician for their own political impotence, they struck at the source of his strength—the spoils system. President Grant inadvertently accelerated the demand for reform when, upon obtaining office, he not only excluded from patronage appointments the old gentry, but denied office to the editors of influential newspapers and journals. This was in contrast to Lincoln's policy of courting the press by bestowing lavish patronage upon them. As a result, the press of both parties started speaking out more strongly than ever before in favor of reform.

As the American economy expanded during the last half of the nineteenth century, the orientation of the business community became less and less focused on parochial interests bounded by the neighborhood and more and more oriented toward urban, regional, and international markets. Economic determinists could well argue that the death knell of the spoils system was sounded when the ineptness of government began to hamper the expansion of business. It is noteworthy in this respect that the federal government made some efforts to institute merit system concepts in both the New York Post Office and the New York Customhouse several years before the passage of the Pendleton Act. Such reform measures, limited as they were, were a direct result of pressure from a business community that had grown increasingly intolerant of ineptness in the postal service and extortion by the customs service.

Depending upon your point of view, the advent of modern merit systems is either an economic, political, or moral development. Economic historians would maintain that the demands of industrial expansion—a dependable postal service, a viable transportation network, and so on—necessitated a government service based upon merit. Political analysts could argue rather persuasively that it was the demands of an expanded suffrage and democratic rhetoric that sought to replace favoritism with merit. Economic and political considerations are so intertwined that it is impossible to say which factor is the true midwife of the merit system. The moral impetus behind reform is even more difficult to define. As moral impulses tend to hide economic and political motives, the weight of moral concern which is undiluted by other considerations is impossible to measure. Nevertheless, the cosmetic effect of moral overtones was of significant aid to the civil service reform movement in the United States because it accentuated the social legitimacy of the reform proposals.

With the ever-present impetus of achieving maximum public services for minimum tax dollars, the businessman was quite comfortable in supporting civil service reform. Support for reform was just one of a variety of strategies employed by the business interests to have power pass from the politicos to themselves. The political parties of the time were almost totally dependent for a financial base upon assessments made on the wages of their members in public office. The party faithful had long been expected to kick back a percentage of their salary in order to retain their positions. A good portion of the Pendleton Act is devoted to forbidding this and other related methods of extortion. With the decline of patronage the parties had to seek out new funding sources. The business interests were more than willing to assume this new financial burden and its concomitant influence.

There is no doubt that civil service reform would have come about without the 1881 assassination of President James A. Garfield. There is also no doubt that the assassination helped. While Garfield's assassination was certainly instrumental in creating the appropriate climate for the passage of "An Act to regulate and improve the Civil Service of the United States," popularly known as the Pendleton Act after George H. Pendleton, the otherwise obscure senator from Ohio who sponsored it, historians maintain that the Republican reversals during the mid-term elections of 1882 had the more immediate effect on enactment. Civil service reform had been the deciding issue in a number of congressional contests. The state that harbored the greatest excesses of the spoils system, New York, even elected as governor the reform-minded mayor of Buffalo, Grover Cleveland. Thus when President Arthur signed the Pendleton Act into law on January 16, 1883 and created the United States Civil Service Commission it was essentially a gesture by reluctant politicians to assuage public opinion and the reform elements.

One of the lasting legacies of the reform movement, with its emphasis upon the creation of independent civil service commissions, was the divorcing of personnel administration from general management. How did this unfortunate situation develop? It was certainly not the intent of the reformers that the public service should become dominated by those seeking small jobs and great security. The impetus of the reform movement was of necessity essentially negative—destroy the spoils system—rather than positive. In the last century the scope of governmental operations was of such a dimension that the managerial implications of reform were hardly relevant. Besides, for the time, the abolition of spoils alone was a major managerial improvement in itself as it frequently implied that the incumbent would actually perform the duties of his position. By and large, the extent of concern for

positive personnel management was evidenced by the impetus for position classification programs which offered the radical idea of equal pay for equal work. But classification programs did not come into fashion until the 1920s and 1930s. Personnel management during the early reform period was limited to the essentials: discovering who was on the payroll, providing equitable salaries, and recording attendance. The reform task was so immense that the emphasis had to be on the negative or policing aspects of personnel management—and that in itself was positive.

See William Seal Carpenter, *The Unfinished Business of Civil Service Reform* (Princeton, N.J.: Princeton University Press, 1952); Charles Cook, *Biography of an Ideal: The Diamond Anniversary History of the Federal Civil Service* (Washington, D.C.: U.S. Government Printing Office, 1959); Carl Russell Fish, *The Civil Service and the Patronage* (New York: Russell & Russell, 1904, 1963); Ari Hoogenboom, *Outlawing the Spoils: A History of the Civil Service Reform Movement, 1865-1883* (Urbana, Ill.: University of Illinois Press, 1961); Matthew Josephson, *The Politicos, 1865-1896* (New York: Harcourt, Brace, 1938); Frederick C. Mosher, *Democracy and the Public Service* (New York: Oxford University Press, 1968); Paul P. Van Riper, *History of the United States Civil Service* (Evanston, Ill.: Row, Peterson, 1958); Leonard D. White, *The Federalists* (New York: Macmillan, 1948), *The Jeffersonians* (New York: Macmillan, 1951), *The Jacksonians* (New York: Macmillan, 1954), and *The Republican Era* (New York: Macmillan, 1958).

See also the following entries:
BLANKETING-IN
GARFIELD, JAMES
LLOYD-LAFOLLETTE ACT OF 1912
NATIONAL CIVIL SERVICE LEAGUE
PENDLETON ACT OF 1883
SENIOR CIVIL SERVICE

Civil Service Reform Act of 1978, act that mandated that (in January of 1979) the U.S. Civil Service Commission would

97

be divided into two agencies—an Office of Personnel Management (OPM) to serve as the personnel arm of the chief executive and an independent Merit Systems Protection Board (MSPB) to provide recourse for aggrieved employees. In addition, the act created a Federal Labor Relations Authority (FLRA) to oversee federal labor-management policies.

On March 2, 1978, President Carter, with the enthusiastic support of his Civil Service Commission leadership, submitted his civil service reform proposals to Congress. On that same day, before the National Press Club, he further called his proposals to Congress' attention by charging that the present federal personnel system had become a "bureaucratic maze which neglects merit, tolerates poor performance, and permits abuse of legitimate employee rights, and mires every personnel action in red tape, delay, and confusion."

The reform bill faced considerable opposition from federal employee unions (who thought the bill was too management oriented) and from veterans' groups (who were aghast at the bill's curtailment of veterans' preferences). The unions lost. The veterans won. The bill passed almost totally intact. The major exception was the deletion of strong veterans' preference curtailments. The Senate passed the bill by voice vote and the House endorsed it with the wide margin of 365 to 8. On October 13, 1978—only six months after he had submitted it to the Congress—President Carter signed the Civil Service Reform Act of 1978 into law.

While the act includes provisions for new performance appraisal systems, mandates new adverse action and appeals procedures, and requires a trial period for new managers and supervisors, probably its greatest management innovation is the creation of the Senior Executive Service (SES). The SES will pool the most senior-level managers (GS 16 and up) into an elite eleven-thousand-member executive corps that the Office of Personnel Management will have wide latitude in rewarding and punishing. See Kenneth W. Kramer. "Seeds of Success and Failure: Policy

Development and Implementation of the 1978 Civil Service Reform Act," *Review of Public Personnel Administration* (Spring 1982); Carl J. Bellone, "Structural vs. Behavioral Change: The Civil Service Reform Act of 1978," *Review of Public Personnel Administration* (Spring 1982); Patricia W. Ingraham and Carolyn Ban, editors, *Legislating Bureaucratic Change: The Civil Service Reform Act of 1978* (Albany, N.Y.: State University of New York Press, 1984).

See also the following entries:
FEDERAL LABOR RELATIONS AUTHORITY
MERIT SYSTEMS PROTECTION BOARD
OFFICE OF PERSONNEL MANAGEMENT
SENIOR EXECUTIVE SERVICE

Civil Service Retirement and Disability Fund, the accumulation of money held in trust by the U.S. Treasury for the purpose of paying annuity, refund, and death benefits to persons entitled to them. The Fund's moneys come from five main sources: (1) deductions from the pay of employees who are members of the Civil Service Retirement System; (2) contributions by the employing agencies in amounts which match the deductions from their employees; (3) payments from the U.S. Treasury for interest on the existing unfunded liability of the system and for the cost of allowing credit for military service; (4) appropriations to meet liabilities that result from changes in the system; and (5) interest earned through investment of money received from the first four sources. The money is invested by the U.S. Treasury in government securities.

Clark, John Bates (1847-1938), The first major American economist and a leading exponent of marginal analysis. His *Distribution of Wealth* (1899) presents the *marginal productivity theory of distribution* "to show that the distribution of the income of society is controlled by a natural law, and that this law, if it worked without friction, would give to every agent of production the amount of wealth which that agent creates."

class, unique position or a group of positions sufficiently similar in respect to duties and responsibilities that the same title may be used to designate each position in the group, the same salary may be equitably applied, the same qualifications required, and the same examination used to select qualified employees.

See also the following entries:
GROUP OF CLASSES
SERIES OF CLASSES
SPECIFICATION
TITLE

class action, search for judicial remedy that one or more individuals may undertake on behalf of themselves and all others in similar situations. Rule 23(b) of the Federal Rules of Civil Procedure establishes the technical legal requirements for the definition of a class in federal court proceedings:

One or more members of a class may sue or be sued as representative parties on behalf of all only if (1) the class is so numerous that joinder of all members is impractical, (2) there are questions of laws or facts common to the class, (3) the claims or defenses of the representative parties are typical of the claims or defenses of the class, and (4) the representative parties will fairly and adequately protect the interests of the class.

See James W. Loewen, *Social Science in the Courtroom: Statistical Techniques and Research Methods for Winning Class-Action Suits* (Lexington, Mass.: Lexington Books, 1982).

classical economics, the economic theories of the 19th century that are usually associated with the works of Adam Smith, Thomas Malthus, David Ricardo, and John Stuart Mill.

classical organization theory, *see* OR-GANIZATION THEORY.

classification, *see* POSITION CLASSIFICATION.

Classification Acts, *see* POSITION CLASSIFICATION.

Classification and Compensation Society, founded in 1969 to promote and improve classification and compensation as a professional field. The Society's goals are to provide for the exchange of ideas, information, and experiences for the benefit of members and employing organizations; provide perspective on events and problems; and stimulate creative efforts to improve or develop concepts, techniques, programs, and systems. Advancement of these objectives is accomplished through work study groups; open forums such as seminars and conferences; and publication of articles, studies, reports, and technical papers.

Classification and Compensation
  Society
810 18th Street, N.W.
Suite 601
Washington, D.C. 20006
(202) 783-4847

classification standards, descriptions of classes of positions that distinguish one class from another in a series. They are, in effect, the yardstick or benchmark against which positions are measured to determine the proper level within a series of titles to which a position should be assigned.

classified service, all those positions in a governmental jurisdiction that are included in a formal merit system. Excluded from the classified service are all exempt appointments. Classified service is a term that predates the concept of position classification and has no immediate bearing on position classification concepts or practices.

classify, group positions according to their duties and responsibilities and assign a class title. To reclassify is to reassign a position to a different class, based on a reexamination of the duties and responsibilities of the position.

See also the following entries:
DESK AUDIT
JOB ANALYSIS
POSITION CLASSIFICATION

Clayton Act of 1914, the federal law that extended the Sherman Act's prohibition against monopolies and price discrimination. It also sought to exempt labor unions from antitrust laws and to limit the jurisdiction of courts in issuing injunctions against labor organizations. Subsequent judicial construction limited its effectiveness in this area and new laws were necessary to achieve the original intent.

Clean Air Act, federal statute (passed in 1963 and amended in 1965, 1967, 1970, and 1977) intended to protect public health and welfare from the effects of air pollution. The act established national air quality standards and specific automobile emission standards to achieve these goals. *See* Peter Navarro, "The 1977 Clean Air Act Amendments: Energy, Environmental, Economic, and Distributional Impacts," *Public Policy* (Spring 1981); R. Shep Melnick, *Regulation and the Courts: The Case of the Clean Air Act* (Washington, D.C.: The Brookings Institution, 1983).

clean-up time, time during the normal work day when employees are allowed to cease production in order to clean themselves, their clothing, or their workplace. Clean-up time allowances are frequently written into union contracts.

Cleveland Board of Education v. Lafleur, 414 U.S. 632 (1974), U.S. Supreme Court case, which held that arbitrary mandatory maternity leaves were unconstitutional. The court held that requiring pregnant teachers to take unpaid maternity leave five months before expected childbirth was in violation of the due process clause of the 14th Amendment.

clientele, individuals or groups who benefit from the services provided by an agency.

clientele agency, loose term for government organizations whose prime mission is to promote, serve or represent the interest of a particular group.

clique, informal organizational subgroup whose members prefer to associate with each other on the basis of common interests. Melville Dalton, in *Men Who Manage* (New York: Wiley, 1959), offers an extensive analysis of organizational cliques and concludes that they

are both an outgrowth and instrument of planning and change. They fall into recognizable types shaped by, and related to, the official pattern of executive positions. Cliques are the indispensable promoters and stabilizers—as well as resisters—of change; they are essential both to cement the organization and to accelerate action. They preserve the formalities vital for moving to the goal, and they provoke but control the turmoil and adjustment that play about the emerging organization.

clock card, form designed to be used with a time clock.

closed-end program, also OPEN-END PROGRAM, program which has a limited legislative appropriation. A program for which Congress has established no limit on the amount of federal funds available for matching recipient expenditures is considered an *open-end* program. Examples are the AFDC and Medicaid programs.

closed shop, union security provision that would require an employer to hire and retain only union members in good standing. The Labor-Management Relations (Taft-Hartley) Act of 1947 made closed shops illegal. *See* Charles G. Goring and others, *The Closed Shop: A Comparative Study of Public Policy and Trade Union Security in Britain, the USA, and West Germany* (New York: St. Martin's Press, 1981).

closed union, union that formally bars new members or makes becoming a member practically impossible in order to protect the job opportunities of its present members.

closing date, the deadline for submitting applications for a civil service exam. When a civil service examination is announced, applications are accepted as long as the announcement is "open." The closing date is usually stated on the exam announcement.

clothing allowance, funds provided by employers to employees so that they can buy special clothing, such as uniforms or safety garments.

clout, slang term for political influence and/or power. *See* Susan and Martin Tolchin, *Clout — Womanpower and Politics* (New York: G. P. Putnam's Sons, 1973); Len O'Connor, *Clout: Mayor Daley and His City* (Chicago: Regnery, 1975).

cluster laboratory, laboratory training experience for a group of people from the same organization. The group consists of several subgroups of individuals whose work in the larger organization is related.

CMR, *see* CALIFORNIA MANAGEMENT REVIEW.

coaching, also COACHING ANALYSIS, face-to-face discussions with a subordinate in order to effect a change in his or her behavior. *Coaching analysis* consists of analyzing the reasons why unsatisfactory performance is occurring. According to Ferdinand F. Fournies, in *Coaching for Improved Work Performance* (New York: Van Nostrand Reinhold, 1978), there are five steps in the coaching technique:
1. Getting the employee's agreement that a problem exists.
2. A mutual discussion of alternative solutions.
3. Mutual agreement on the action to be taken to solve the problem.
4. Measuring the results of subsequent performance.
5. Recognize achievement and improved performance when it occurs.

Also see Neil Rackham, "The Coaching Controversy," *Training and Development Journal* (November 1979); Jack Kon-drasuk, "The Coaching Controversy Revisited," *Training and Development Journal* (February 1980); James F. Wolf and Frank P. Sherwood, "Coaching: Supporting Public Executives on the Job," *Public Administration Review* (January-February 1980).

coalition bargaining, also COORDINATED BARGAINING, negotiation between an employer and a group of unions whose goal is to gain one agreement covering all, or identical agreements for each. *Coordinated bargaining* differs only in that bargaining sessions take place simultaneously at different locations. *See* George H. Hildebrand, "Cloudy Future for Coalition Bargaining," *Harvard Business Review* (November-December 1968); Stephen B. Goldberg, "Coordinated Bargaining: Some Unresolved Questions," *Monthly Labor Review* (April 1969); David Lewin and Mary McCormick, "Coalition Bargaining in Municipal Government: The New York City Experience," *Industrial and Labor Relations Review* (January 1981).

Coalition of American Public Employees (CAPE), formed in 1972 by leaders of public employee organizations in an effort to coordinate programs of political, legal, and legislative action and public education at the national and state level. Members included the American Federation of State, County and Municipal Employees (AFSCME); the National Education Association (NEA); the American Nurses Association (ANA); the Physicians National Housestaff Association (PNHA); and the National Association of Social Workers (NASW). Representing nearly four million workers, CAPE was the largest organization of public employees in the nation. It ceased to exist on August 31, 1982.

Coal Mine Health and Safety Act of 1969, *see* USERY V. TURNER ELKHORN MINING CO.

Codd v. Velger, 429 U.S. 624 (1977), Supreme Court case which held that public employees are not constitutionally entitled to a hearing in dismissals where no issue of fact is at stake.

code of ethics, statement of professional standards of conduct to which the practitioners of many professions say they subscribe. In the wake of the Watergate scandals, the National Academy of Public Administration prepared guidelines that sought "to summarize the rules of the game by which men and women, who regard themselves as professional administrators in the public service, try to conduct themselves." The chart below, reprinted from Jerome B. McKinney and Lawrence C. Howard, *Public Administration: Balancing Power and Accountability* (Oak Park, Ill.: Moore Publishing, 1979), summarizes these guidelines. *Also see*

James S. Bowman, "The Management of Ethics: Codes of Conduct in Organizations," *Public Personnel Management* (1981); Gerald E. Caiden, "Ethics in the Public Service: Codification Misses the Real Target," *Public Personnel Management* (1981); Steven W. Hays and Richard R. Gleissner, "Codes of Ethics in State Government: A Nationwide Survey," *Public Personnel Management* (1981); Ralph Clark Chandler, "The Problem of Moral Reasoning in American Public Administration: The Case for a Code of Ethics," *Public Administration Review* (January–February 1983); Guy Benveniste, "Ethics and Policy Experts: On a Code of Ethics for Policy Experts," *Journal of Policy Analysis and Management* (Summer 1984).

NAPA CODE OF ETHICS

Inputs to Decisions	Limits of Compromise	Implementing Decisions
1. Inform others participating in the decision of significant information.	1. Resist decisions before they are final even by going to the legislature if the pending mistake warrants this action and the risk of losing future usefulness in the agency is a price worth paying.	1. Ask no subordinate to take any illegal action.
2. Interpret data not only unbiased by conflict of interest but also with one's value base revealed.	2. While one may be required to prepare a disputed document on an objectionable subject, he is not required to sign it.	2. Do not suppress significant public information.
3. Be guided in advocacy by the importance of the issue, one's competence, and by one's place in the hierarchy.	3. Uphold the law in your sphere of responsibility and discretion.	3. Carry out legal decisions in good faith despite your disagreement with their merit.
4. Accept decisions made within the rules even though one regards them as unwise.	4. Resign if interpretations of the law by superiors are unacceptable.	4. Underlying all guidelines is that all administrators are bound by the law of the land and are obligated to use their power in the public interest.
5. Defend decisions which have been properly made even though personally objectionable.		

SOURCE: *Adapted from George A. Graham, "Ethical Guidelines for Public Administrators: Observations on Rules of the Game,"* Public Administration Review *(January–February 1974), pp. 90-92.*

See also ETHICS and STANDARDS OF CONDUCT.

Code of Federal Regulations (CFR), annual cumulation of executive agency regulations published in the daily *Federal Register,* combined with regulations issued previously that are still in effect. Divided into fifty titles, each representing a broad subject area, individual volumes of the CFR are revised at least once each calendar year and issued on a staggered quarterly basis. An alphabetical listing by agency of subtitle and chapter assignments in the CFR is provided in the back of each volume under the heading "Finding Aids" and is accurate for the revision date of that volume.

codetermination, in German *MITBESTIMMUNGSRECHT,* union participation in all aspects of management even to the extent of having union representatives share equal membership on an organization's board of directors. In Germany, where codetermination is often legally required, the process is called *Mitbestimmungsrecht,* literally meaning "the right of codetermination." See Svetozar Pejovich, ed., *The Codetermination Movement in the West: Labor Participation in the Management of Business Firms* (Lexington, Mass.: Lexington Books, 1978); Robert J. Kuhne, *Co-Determination in Business: Workers' Representatives in the Boardroom* (New York: Praeger, 1980); Alfred L. Thimm, *The False Promise of Codetermination: The Changing Nature of European Workers' Participation* (Lexington, Mass.: Lexington Books, 1980).

coefficient of correlation, see CORRELATION COEFFICIENT.

coffee break, also called TEA BREAK, popular term for any brief rest period for workers. While work breaks for refreshments and socializing go back to ancient times, it wasn't until after World War II that coffee breaks became a national institution: first, because millions of workers brought the custom with them from World War II military service, and second, because by this time considerable research on worker fatigue had consistently shown that beverage breaks reduce fatigue while improving alertness and productivity. The British, of course, have tea breaks. For a brief history of the coffee break, see William J. Tandy, "Tempest in a Coffee Pot," *Public Personnel Review* (October 1953). See also Steven Habbe, "Coffee, Anyone?" *The Conference Board Record* (July 1965).

COG, see COUNCIL OF GOVERNMENT.

cognitive dissonance, theory first postulated by Leon Festinger in A *Theory of Cognitive Dissonance* (Evanston, Ill.: Row, Peterson Co., 1957) which holds that when an individual finds himself in a situation where he is expected to believe two mutually exclusive things, the subsequent tension and discomfort generates activity designed to reduce the dissonance or disharmony. For example, an employee who sees himself in an inequitable wage situation could experience cognitive dissonance. The theory of cognitive dissonance assumes that a worker performing the same work as another but being paid significantly less will do something to relieve his dissonance. Among his options are asking for a raise, restricting output, or seeking another job. For studies on wage inequity, see J. Stacy Adams, "Wage Inequities, Productivity and Work Quality," *Industrial Relations* (October 1963); William M. Evan and Roberta G. Simmons, "Organizational Effects of Inequitable Rewards in Two Experiments in Status Inconsistency," *Administrative Science Quarterly* (June 1969). For further studies in cognitive dissonance, see J. W. Brehm and A. R. Cohn, *Explorations in Cognitive Dissonance* (New York: John Wiley, 1962).
See also INEQUITY THEORY.

cohesiveness, commitment on the part of group members to group membership—a sense of belonging, of unity and collectivity.

COLA, see COST-OF-LIVING ADJUSTMENT.

cold-storage training, the preparation of employees for jobs in advance of the need for them in those particular jobs.

Cole v. *Richardson,* 405 U.S. 676 (1971), U.S. Supreme Court case which upheld the right of Massachusetts to exact from its employees a promise to "oppose the overthrow of the government of the United States of America or of this Commonwealth by force, violence or by any illegal or unconstitutional method." A public employer may legitimately require employees to swear or affirm their allegiance to the Constitution of the United States and of a particular state. Beyond that, the limits of constitutional loyalty oaths are unclear.

See also LOYALTY.

collections, amounts received by a government during the fiscal year. Collections are classified into two major categories: (1) budget receipts, collections from the public and from payments by participants in voluntary social insurance programs, and (2) offsetting collections, collections from government accounts or from transactions with the public that are of a business type or market-oriented nature.

collective bargaining, a comprehensive term that encompasses the negotiating process that leads to a contract between labor and management on wages, hours, and other conditions of employment as well as the subsequent administration and interpretation of the signed contract. Collective bargaining is, in effect, the continuous relationship that exists between union representatives and employers. The four basic stages of collective bargaining are: (1) the establishment of organizations for bargaining, (2) the formulation of demands, (3) the negotiation of demands, and (4) the administration of the labor agreement.

Collective bargaining is one of the keystones of the National Labor Relations Act, which declares that the policy of the United States is to be carried out

by encouraging the practice and pro-

cedure of collective bargaining and by protecting the exercise by workers of full freedom of association, self-organization, and designation of representatives of their own choosing, for the purpose of negotiating the terms and conditions of their employment or other mutual aid or protection.

The predominant public sector labor relations model comes from the private sector. But this fit has been long recognized as far from perfect. This is one reason why public sector labor relations were at first opposed and then organized as a meet-and-confer rather than a collective bargaining process. The term "collective negotiations" was often used to further avoid the suggestion of actual bargaining. But today, those jurisdictions with well developed labor relations programs rely upon the private sector model. The ramifications are considerable.

Instead of accepting the "public interest" or some equally saccharine goal as the watchword of the negotiating process, the public sector unions readily accepted the adversary model of negotiations so common in the private sector. This model assumes that for one side to win the other must lose. Essentially, each side is haggling over its share of the organization's profits. There being no legal profits as such in government, the question must be asked: Has the private sector model, based on conflict and individual acquisitiveness, been appropriately applied to the public sector?

This private sector model of labor relations was consolidated by the National Labor Relations Act, as amended. It provides for bargaining between workers and management on the assumption that the outcome will reflect the inherent strength of each. Rules for fair labor relations practices were established and the National Labor Relations Board was created to adjudicate disputes over their application. Workers retain the right to strike and to bargain as equals with management over virtually all employment-related issues not constrained by law. Although relations are assumed to be adversarial, the model is based on the belief that the free market imposes an ultimate harmony of interest between employer and employee: neither party favors the economic demise of the employer.

Employing this basic model in the public sector is problematic because some of its crucial assumptions do not fit. It is difficult to assume coequality between the parties in public sector collective bargaining. What does it mean to say that a union is equal to the government, or to the people as a whole? Elected legislative bodies and elected executives are generally considered the appropriate policymaking bodies in American government. Public managers bargaining with organized employees are not. The basic adjustment to the inequality of the parties to labor disputes has been to recognize the government's greater authority by restricting the scope of bargaining.

Since it is not assumed that the parties in public sector collective bargaining are equal in principle, it follows that the outcome of disputes should not depend upon their relative strengths. Consequently, there should be no need to strike. But public sector strikes are not necessarily intended to harm the employer economically. They tend to do more political than economic damage, at least in the short run. This is because the governmental employer is likely to derive its revenues from taxation, rather than exclusively from user fees. Yet, when a strike interrupts a government service, tax dollars are not refunded; nor are they paid out in compensation to striking employees. So a strike may temporarily enhance a government's economic position. In short, the function of a strike in the public sector is substantially different from that in the private sector.

The most common effort to adjust public sector collective bargaining to the absence of the legalized strike has been to introduce some form of binding arbitration. But this raises a host of different problems. Arbitration inherently undercuts the bargaining process itself. Where both sides are convinced a dispute will go to arbitration, they will tend to spend most of their time posturing rather than negotiating or compromising. Moreover, arbitration cannot resolve the concern that the sovereign make public policy. And arbitrators' decisions are not automatically sensible or in the public interest. Sometimes, they may even disregard a jurisdiction's ability to pay for the awards they authorize.

The nature of arbitration of public sector labor disputes is also related to the remoteness of the "market" as a constraint on the total compensation of employees. In fact, the economic aspects of public sector labor relations tend to work best when cities are on the threshold of bankruptcy and therefore the "market" is not so remote. Since the market does not serve as a constraint as directly in the public sector as in the private sector, some substitute for it must be devised to resolve labor disputes. Unfortunately, arbitration has not always fared well in this context. Often, arbitrators will look to comparable jurisdictions to determine what is equitable. But there is a built-in redundance in this approach and the selection of "comparable" jurisdictions is always somewhat arbitrary. In the private sector, an arbitration award is sometimes based on the relative strength of the parties, but this approach is not very meaningful in the public sector since the parties are fundamentally so unequal. In other words, the remoteness of the market has required arbitrators to develop other standards for reaching their awards— standards that are fraught with difficulty.

Overall, the public sector is incredibly fragmented in terms of collective bargaining. There is no national law on the subject. States and cities vary widely in their practices. The law differs from one to another, placing substantial burdens on national labor unions and dispute resolution personnel who work in different jurisdictions. While the opportunity to experiment and to adapt to local conditions is valuable, such fragmentation makes it hard to speak of "public sector collective bargaining" without engaging in overgeneralization.

See Benjamin Aaron, Joseph R. Grodin, and James L. Stern, *Public Sector Bargaining* (Washington, D.C.: Bureau of National Affairs, 1979); Alan Edward

Bent and T. Zane Reeves, *Collective Bargaining in the Public Sector* (Menlo Park, CA: Benjamin/Cummings, 1978); Charles Feigenbaum, "Civil Service and Collective Bargaining: Conflict or Compatibility?" *Public Personnel Management* (May–June 1974); Randell W. Eberts and Joe A. Stone, *Unions and Public Schools: The Effects of Collective Bargaining on American Education* (Lexington, Mass.: Lexington Books, 1984); Marvin J. Levine and Eugene C. Hagburg, *Public Sector Labor Relations* (St. Paul, Minn.: West Publishing, 1979); Marvin J. Levine and Eugene C. Hagburg, eds., *Labor Relations in the Public Sector* (Salt Lake City: Brighton, 1979); David Lewin, Raymond D. Horton and James W. Kuhn, *Collective Bargaining and Manpower Utilization in Big City Governments* (Montclair, N.J.: Allanheld, Osmun and Co., 1979); J. Joseph Loewenberg and Michael H. Moskow, *Collective Bargaining in Government* (Englewood Cliffs, N.J.: Prentice-Hall, 1972); Lanning S. Mosher, "Facing the Realities of Public Employee Bargaining," *Public Personnel Management,* (July–August 1978); Michael Moskow, Jr., Joseph Lowerberg, and Edward C. Koziara, *Collective Bargaining in Public Employment* (New York: Random House, 1970); Joyce M. Najita and Helene S. Tanimoto, *Guide to Statutory Provisions in Public Sector Collective Bargaining: Characteristics, Functions, and Powers of Administrative Agencies* (Honolulu: Industrial Relations Center, University of Hawaii, 1981); Charles A. Salerno, *Police at the Bargaining Table* (Springfield, Ill.: Charles C. Thomas, 1981); Richard P. Schick and Jean J. Couturier, *The Public Interest in Government Labor Relations* (Cambridge, MA: Ballinger, 1977); Russel A. Smith, Harry T. Edwards, and R. Theodore Clark, Jr., *Labor Relations Law in the Public Sector* (Indianapolis: Bobbs-Merrill, 1974); Clyde W. Summers, "Public Employee Bargaining: A Political Perspective," *Yale Law Journal* (May 1974).

See also the following entries:

ABILITY TO PAY

H. J. HEINZ CO. V. NATIONAL LABOR RELATIONS BOARD

INLAND STEEL CO. V. NATIONAL LABOR RELATIONS BOARD

NATIONAL LABOR RELATIONS ACT

PORTER CO. V. NATIONAL LABOR RELATIONS BOARD

POSTAL REORGANIZATION ACT OF 1970

PRODUCTIVITY BARGAINING

REGIONAL BARGAINING

REOPENER CLAUSE

RETIREMENT AGE

REVERSE COLLECTIVE BARGAINING

SPLIT-THE-DIFFERENCE

SUNSHINE BARGAINING

TEXTILE WORKERS V. LINCOLN MILLS

UNFAIR LABOR PRACTICES (EMPLOYERS)

UNFAIR LABOR PRACTICES (UNIONS)

UNION SECURITY CLAUSE

WELFARE FUNDS

ZIPPER CLAUSE

Collective Bargaining Negotiations & Contracts, biweekly reference service published by the Bureau of National Affairs, Inc., which presents comprehensive coverage of wage rates and data and cost-of-living figures; bargaining issues, demands, counterproposals, and significant settlements; strategy, techniques, industry facts and figures; and equal employment opportunity activities as they affect collective bargaining.

collective negotiations, an alternate term for "collective bargaining," which, in the public sector, may sometimes be legally and/or semantically unacceptable; *see* Robert T. Woodworth and Richard B. Peterson, *Collective Negotiation for Public and Professional Employees* (Glenview, Ill.: Scott, Foresman, 1969).

College Placement Annual, *see* COLLEGE PLACEMENT COUNCIL, INC.

College Placement Council, Inc., nonprofit corporation that provides professional services to career planning and placement directors at four-year and two-year colleges and universities in the United States, as well as to employers who hire graduates of these institutions. Each year the Council publishes the *College Place-*

ment Annual, which includes the occupational needs anticipated by approximately 1,300 corporate and government employers who normally recruit college graduates.

College Placement Council, Inc.
P.O. Box 2236
Bethlehem, PA 18001

Collyer **doctrine,** the predisposition of the National Labor Relations Board to defer to arbitral awards in disputes involving unfair labor practices if certain conditions are met—one of them being that the arbitrator must have considered and resolved the statutory issues, if any, present in the case. This was first enunciated in the case of *Collyer Insulated Wire,* 192 NLRB 837 (1971). *See* Dennis K. Reischl, "Applying *Collyer* in the Federal Sector: Past Due Remedy," *Labor Law Journal* (June 1982).

comer, slang term for younger managers who seem to have the potential of assuming top management responsibilities. For how to find and best use your organization's "comers," *see* Robert A. Pitts, "Unshackle Your 'Comers,' " *Harvard Business Review* (May–June 1977).

comity, the constitutional provision that "the citizens of each state shall be entitled to all privileges and immunities of citizens in the several states."

Commerce Business Daily, a daily publication of the U.S. Department of Commerce that identifies upcoming federal government contracts (requests for proposals) in excess of $25,000.

Commerce, Department of, created in 1913 when the Congress split the Department of Commerce and Labor (founded in 1903) into two cabinet level departments. The Department of Commerce encourages, serves, and promotes the nation's economic development and technological advancement. It offers assistance and information to domestic and international business; provides social and economic statistics and analyses for busi-

ness and government planners; assists in the development and maintenance of the U.S. merchant marine; provides research for and promotes the increased use of science and technology in the development of the economy; provides assistance to speed the development of the economically underdeveloped areas of the nation; seeks to improve understanding of the earth's physical environment and oceanic life; promotes travel to the United States by residents of foreign countries; assists in the growth of minority businesses; and seeks to prevent the loss of life and property from fire.

Department of Commerce
14th St. Between Constitution Ave.
and E Street, N.W.
Washington, D.C. 20230
(202) 377-2000

commerce clause, the part of the U.S. Constitution that allows Congress to control trade with foreign countries and from state to state. This is called the *commerce power* (Article One, Section Eight of the Constitution). If anything "affects interstate commerce" (such as labor unions, product safety, etc.), it is fair game for the federal government to regulate what goes on or even to take over all regulation.

Commerce Clearing House, Inc. (CCH), publishers of a variety of loose-leaf information services concerned with law, taxes, business, urban affairs, etc.

Commerce Clearing House, Inc.
4025 W. Peterson Ave.
Chicago, IL 60646
(312) 583-8500

commercial market strategy, approach whereby government subsidizes the delivery of goods or services to a target group by serving as bill payer as clients seek designated benefits from existing market outlets. For example, in the case of Medicare, beneficiaries seek medical care from a broad range of physicians and hospitals and government pays a portion of their bills.

commission, *see* BOARD.

Commissioners of Conciliation, *see* MEDIATION.

commission form of government, the original reform structure of urban governance which put all the executive, legislative and administrative powers into a commission, which replaced the council. As a collective group, the commission is the local legislature, while each member individually is an administrator of a department or a set of departments. The obvious problem of coordinating administration in such a system led to its decline. It was first used in 1900 in Galveston, Texas, following a devastating hurricane. In this instance, many of the original commissioners were appointed by the governor. *See* Bradley R. Rice, *Progressive Cities: The Commission Government Movement in America, 1901-1920* (Austin, Texas: University of Texas Press, 1977); and Bradley R. Rice, "The Galveston Plan of City Government by Commission: The Birth of a Progressive Idea," *Southwestern Historical Quarterly* (April 1975).

Commission on Civil Rights, also called CIVIL RIGHTS COMMISSION, body whose role is to encourage constructive steps toward equal opportunity for all. The Commission investigates complaints, holds public hearings, and collects and studies information on denials of equal protection of the laws because of race, color, religion, sex, or national origin. Voting rights, administration of justice, and equality of opportunity in education, employment, and housing are among the many topics of specific Commission interest.

The Commission on Civil Rights, created by the Civil Rights Act of 1957, makes findings of fact but has no enforcement authority. Findings and recommendations are submitted to both the president and the Congress. Many of the Commission's recommendations have been enacted by statute, executive order, or regulation. The Commission evaluates federal laws and the effectiveness of government equal opportunity programs. It also serves as a national clearinghouse for civil rights information.

Commission on Civil Rights
1121 Vermont Avenue, N.W.
Washington, D.C. 20425
(202) 376-8177

Commission on Intergovernmental Relations, *see* KESTNBAUM COMMISSION.

Commission on the Organization of the Executive Branch, *see* (1) HOOVER COMMISSION OF 1947-1949 and (2) HOOVER COMMISSION OF 1953-1955.

Committee for Economic Development (CED), nonpartisan organization of business leaders and scholars who conduct research and formulate policy recommendations on economic and public policy issues.
CED
477 Madison Avenue
New York, NY 10022
(212) 688-2063

Committee for Industrial Organization, committee established within the American Federation of Labor in 1935 that grew to be the Congress of Industrial Organizations in 1938. *See* (1) CONGRESS OF INDUSTRIAL ORGANIZATIONS and (2) AMERICAN FEDERATION OF LABOR-CONGRESS OF INDUSTRIAL ORGANIZATIONS.

committeeman, or COMMITTEEWOMAN, worker (usually) elected by co-workers to represent the union membership in the handling of grievances and the recruitment of new union members, among other duties.

Committee on Political Education (COPE), nonpartisan organization of the AFL-CIO, made up of members of the AFL-CIO's Executive Council. COPE has the responsibility spelled out in the AFL-CIO Constitution of "encouraging workers to register and vote, to exercise their full rights and responsibilities of citizenship, and to perform their rightful part in the political life of the city, state and national communities."

COPE is not a political party, nor is it committed to the support of any particular party. From the first convention of the

AFL-CIO (in 1955) to the most recent, COPE has been instructed to work in support of candidates who support issues of concern to the AFL-CIO regardless of the party affiliation of the candidate. The policies of COPE are determined by its national committee in line with the policies and programs adopted by the AFL-CIO conventions.

COPE reports facts about issues and candidates. It publishes voting records of elected officials to help AFL-CIO members inform themselves in order to vote intelligently. Candidates for political offices are recommended to the membership in the appropriate area by state and local COPE bodies, representing affiliated unions at the local and state level. The basis for the endorsement is the record and the program of the candidates compared to the policies of the AFL-CIO.

For a critical review of COPE's activities, see Terry Catchpole, *How to Cope with COPE: The Political Operations of Organized Labor* (New Rochelle, N.Y.: Arlington House, 1968).

> Committee on Political Education
> 815 16th Street, N.W.
> Washington, D.C. 20006
> (202) 637-5101

Committee on the Civil Service, *see* FULTON COMMITTEE.

Common Cause, leading public interest lobby. *See* Andrew S. McFarland, *Common Cause: Lobbying in the Public Interest* (Chatham, N.J.: Chatham House, 1984).

> Common Cause
> 2030 M Street, N.W.
> Washington, D.C. 20036
> (202) 833-1200

common labor rate, wage rate for the least skilled physical or manual labor in an organization. This is usually an organization's lowest rate of pay.

common law of the shop, or INDUSTRIAL RELATIONS COMMON LAW, that portion of the common law that applies to the work-

place. Common law is the total body of law established by judicial precedent.

common situs picketing, picketing of an entire construction site by members of a single union to increase their strike's impact and to publicize a dispute with one or more contractors or subcontractors. In 1976, President Ford vetoed a bill that would have made common situs picketing legal.

commonwealth, the notion from Thomas Hobbes (1588-1679) and other philosophers of his era that the members of a social order have a "common weal" which is in their collective interest to preserve and protect. "Common weal" evolved into commonwealth which came to mean "the state." Thus the republic established in Britain under Oliver Cromwell from 1649 to 1660 was called the Commonwealth. Several American states, such as Pennsylvania, are also formally "commonwealths" rather than states.

Commonwealth v. Hunt, *see* SHAW, LEMUEL.

communication, process of exchanging information, ideas, and feelings between two or more individuals or groups. *Horizontal communication* refers to such an exchange among peers or people at the same organizational level. *Vertical communication* refers to such an exchange between individuals at differing levels of the organization. For a text, *see* William V. Haney, *Communications and Interpersonal Relations,* 4th ed. (Homewood, Ill.: Richard D. Irwin, 1979). *Also see* Robert B. Highsaw and Don L. Bowen, eds., *Communication in Public Administration* (Montgomery, Ala.: University of Alabama Press, 1965).

See also GRAPEVINE and NONVERBAL COMMUNICATION.

Community Action Programs (CAP). The Economic Opportunity Act of 1964 provided for Community Action Programs which would be funded by the federal government but operated by community agencies exempt from political review or control at the state or local level. These programs were effectively abandoned by the Nixon administration. See Daniel P. Moynihan, *Maximum Feasible Misunderstanding: Community Action in the War on Poverty* (New York: Free Press, 1969); Harold Wolman, "Organization Theory and Community Action Agencies," *Public Administration Review* (January–February 1972); John H. Strange, "Citizen Participation in Community Action and Model Cities Programs," *Public Administration Review* (October 1972); and Gary English, "The Trouble with Community Action," *Public Administration Review* (May–June 1972).

community control, extreme form of citizen participation in which democratically selected representatives of a neighborhood-sized governmental jurisdiction are given administrative and financial control over such local programs as education, land use, and police protection. See Alan Altshuler, *Community Control: The Black Demand for Participation in Large American Cities* (New York: Pegasus Books, 1970); Joseph F. Zimmerman, *The Federated City: Community Control in Large Cities* (New York: St. Martin's, 1972); Norman I. Fainstein and Susan S. Fainstein, "The Future of Community Control," *American Political Science Review* (September 1976).

community development, approach to the administration of social and economic development programs in which government officials are dispatched to the field to act as catalysts at the local level, encouraging local residents to form groups, define their own needs, and develop self-help projects. The government provides technical and material assistance and helps the community establish institutions (such as farm cooperatives) to carry on the development programs after the officials have left. See Leanne M. Lachman, "Planning for Community Development: A Proposed Approach," *Journal of Housing* (February 1975); Hayden Roberts, *Community Development: Learning and Action* (Toronto: University of Toronto Press, 1979).

Community Dispute Services, *see* AMERICAN ARBITRATION ASSOCIATION.

community health care, activities and programs intended to improve the healthfulness of, and general health status in, a specified community. The term is widely used with many different definitions, and thus must be used with caution. It is variously defined, as above, in a manner similar to public health; synonymously with environmental health; as all health services of any kind available to a given community; or even synonymously with a community's ambulatory care.

community health center, an ambulatory health care program usually serving a catchment area with scarce or nonexistent health services or a population with special health needs. Often known as neighborhood health centers.

community of interest, criterion used to determine if a group of employees make up an appropriate bargaining unit.

community power, usually the study or description of the political order, both formal and informal, of a segment of U.S. local governance. See Floyd Hunter, *Community Power Structure* (Chapel Hill: University of North Carolina Press, 1953); Robert A. Dahl, *Who Governs? Democracy and Power in an American City* (New Haven, Conn.: Yale University Press, 1961); Nelson W. Polsby, *Community Power and Political Theory* (New Haven, Conn.: Yale University Press, 1963); Robert E. Agger, Daniel Goldrich and Bert Swanson, *The Rulers and the Rules: Political Power and Impotence in American Communities* (New York: Wiley, 1964); Robert V. Presthus, *Men at the Top: A Study in Community Power* (New York: Oxford University Press, 1964); C. W. Gilbert, *Community Power Structure: Propositional Inventory, Tests, and Theory* (Gainesville, Fla.: University of Florida Press, 1972); Will D. Hawley and Frederick Wirt, *The Search for Community Power,* 2nd ed. (Englewood Cliffs, N.J.: Prentice-Hall, 1974). For an update of a classic study, *see* Floyd Hunter, *Community Power Succession: Atlanta's Policy-Makers Revisited* (Chapel Hill: University of North Carolina Press, 1980).

Community Services Administration (CSA), federal agency whose overall purpose was to reduce poverty in the U.S. Agency guidelines fixed the incomes which qualified a family or person for participation in anti-poverty programs. The Community Services Administration was created in 1974 as the successor to the Office of Economic Opportunity, the prime mover in the Johnson administration's "war on poverty." Abolished in 1981, its close-out functions were assigned to the Office of Community Services of the Department of Health and Human Services.

community wage survey, any survey whose purpose is to ascertain the structure and level of wages among employees in a local area.

company store, store operated by an organization for the exclusive use of employees and their families. The largest company store in the world is the U.S. military's PX (Post Exchange) system.

company town, slang term for any community whose economy is dominated by one employer. True company towns, where the company literally owned all of the land, buildings, and stores are practically nonexistent in the modern U.S.— with the possible exception of remote areas of Alaska. For history, *see* James B. Allen, *The Company Town in the American West* (Norman, Okla.: University of Oklahoma Press, 1966); Christopher Norwood, "The Bittersweet Story of the First Company Town," *Business and Society Review* (Summer 1976).

company union, an historical term that described unions organized, financed, or otherwise dominated by an employer. The National Labor Relations (Wagner) Act of 1935 outlawed employer interference with unions, thus relegating company unions to history.

See also TEXAS AND NEW ORLEANS RAILWAY V. BROTHERHOOD OF RAILWAY AND STEAMSHIP CLERKS and UNFAIR LABOR PRACTICES (EMPLOYERS).

comparable form test, *see* ALTERNATE FORM.

comparable worth, providing equitable compensation for performing work of a comparable value as determined by the relative worth of a given job to an organization. The basic issue of comparable worth is whether Title VII of the Civil Rights Act of 1964 makes it unlawful for an employer to pay one sex at a lesser rate than the other when job performance is of comparable worth or value. For example, should graduate nurses be paid less than gardeners? Or should beginning librarians with a master's degree be paid less than beginning managers with a master's degree? Historically, nurses and librarians have been paid less than occupations of "comparable worth" because they were considered "female" jobs. Comparable worth as a legal concept and as a social issue directly challenges traditional and market assumptions about the worth of a job. *See* Bruce A. Nelson, *et al.*, "Wage Discrimination and the 'Comparable Worth' in Perspective," *University of Michigan Journal of Law Reform* (Winter 1980); Donald J. Treiman and Heidi I. Hartmann, eds., *Women, Work and Wages: Equal Pay for Jobs of Equal Value* (Washington, D.C.: National Academy Press, 1981); Helen Remick, "The Comparable Worth Controversy," *Public Personnel Management* (Winter 1981); Mary Helen Doherty and Ann Harriman, "Comparable Worth: The Equal Employment Issue of the 1980s," *Review of Public Personnel Administration* (Summer 1981); John R. Schnebly, "Comparable Worth: A Legal Overview," *Personnel Administrator* (April 1982); Stanley C. Wisniewski, "Achieving Equal Pay for Comparable Worth Through Arbitration," *Employee Relations Law Journal* (Autumn 1982); Clarence Thomas, "Pay Equity and Comparable Worth," *Labor Law Journal* (January 1983); Elaine Johansen,

"Managing the Revolution: The Case for Comparable Worth," *Review of Public Personnel Administration* (Spring 1984); Sean DeForrest, "How Can Comparable Worth Be Achieved?" *Personnel* (September-October 1984); Helen Remick, ed., *Comparable Worth and Wage Discrimination: Technical Possibilities and Political Realities* (Philadelphia, Pa.: Temple University Press, 1984).

See also EQUAL PAY FOR EQUAL WORK and COUNTY OF WASHINGTON V. GUNTHER.

compa-ratio, a person's current salary as a percentage of the midpoint of his or her salary range.

Comparative Administration Group (CAG), organization of scholars who served on technical assistance missions to Third World countries during the 1960s. For a history, *see* Brian Loveman, "The Comparative Administration Group, Development Administration and Antidevelopment," *Public Administration Review* (November-December 1976).

comparative advantage, the position a country or a region has in the production of those goods it can produce relatively more efficiently than other goods. Modern trade theory says that regardless of the general level of the country's productivity or labor costs relative to those of other countries, it should produce for export those goods in which it has the greatest *comparative advantage* and import those goods in which it has the greatest *comparative disadvantage.* The country that has few economic strengths will find it advantageous to devote its productive energies to those lines in which its disadvantage is least marked, provided the opportunity to trade with other areas is open to it. *The comparative advantage theory* was first proposed by David Ricardo in 1817.

comparative budgeting, *see* BUDGETING, COMPARATIVE.

comparative-norm principle, as defined in Arthur A. Sloane and Fred Witney, *Labor Relations,* 3rd ed. (Englewood Cliffs, N.J.: Prentice-Hall, 1977):

To a great extent, company and union negotiators make use of the "comparative-norm principle" in wage negotiations. The basic idea behind this concept is the presumption that the economics of a particular collective bargaining relationship should neither fall substantially behind nor be greatly superior to that of other employer-union relationships; that, in short, it is generally a good practice to keep up with the crowd, but not necessarily to lead it.

compassionate leave, any leave granted for urgent family reasons. This term, which is mainly used by the military, is sometimes informally abbreviated to "passionate leave."

compensable factors, various elements of a job that, when put together, both define the job and determine its value to the organization.

compensable injury, work injury that qualifies an injured worker for workers' compensation benefits.

compensation, *also* PAY or REMUNERATION, generic terms that encompass all forms of organizational payments and rewards. For general discussions, *see* Patrick R. Pinto and Benjamin H. Lowenberg, "Pay: A Unitary View," *Personnel Journal* (June 1973); Edward E. Lawler III, "New Approaches To Pay: Innovations That Work," *Personnel* (September-October 1973); Thomas A. Mahoney, ed., *Compensation and Reward Perspectives* (Homewood, Ill.: Richard D. Irwin, Inc., 1979); Robert W. Hartman and Arnold R. Weber, eds., *The Rewards of Public Service: Compensating Top Federal Officials* (Washington, D.C.: The Brookings Institution, 1980); Sara M. Freedman, Robert T. Keller and John R. Montanari, "The Compensation Program: Balancing Organizational and Employee Needs," *Compensation Review,* Vol. 14, No. 4 (1982); Benson Rosen and Sara

Rynes, "Compensation, Jobs and Gender," *Harvard Business Review* (July–August 1983).
See also the following entries:
BONUS
DEFERRED COMPENSATION
DUAL COMPENSATION ACT OF 1964
EXECUTIVE COMPENSATION
INDIRECT WAGES
PAY
TOTAL COMPENSATION COMPARABILITY
UNEMPLOYMENT BENEFITS

compensation management, the facet of management concerned with the selection, development, and direction of the programs that implement an organization's financial reward system. For surveys of the subject, *see* Richard I. Henderson, *Compensation Management: Rewarding Performance in the Modern Organization* (Reston, Va.: Reston Publishing Co., 1976); Thomas H. Patten, Jr., *Pay: Employee Compensation and Incentive Plans* (New York: The Free Press, 1977); George T. Milkovich and Jerry M. Newman, *Compensation* (Plano, Tex.: Business Publications, Inc., 1984).

Compensation Review, quarterly journal covering all aspects of employee compensation. Also contains "condensations of noteworthy articles" from other business and professional publications that relate to compensation.
Compensation Review
Editorial Adress:
AMACOM
Division of American Management
Associations
135 West 50th Street
New York, NY 10020
Subscriptions:
Compensation Review
Trudeau Road
Saranac Lake, NY 12983

compensatory time, time off in lieu of overtime pay.

competence, ability to consistently perform a task or job to an acceptable standard.
See also INTERPERSONAL COMPETENCE.

competitive area, term used to describe the commuting area to which employees are restricted to competing for retention during layoffs or reductions-in-force.

competitive level, all positions of the same grade within a competitive area which are sufficiently alike in duties, responsibilities, pay systems, terms of appointment, requirements for experience, training, skills, and aptitudes that the incumbent of any of them could readily be shifted to any of the other positions without significant training or undue interruption to the work program. In the federal government, the job to which an employee is officially assigned determines his competitive level.

competitive promotion, selection for promotion made from the employees rated *best* qualified in competition with others, all of whom have the *minimum* qualifications required by the position.

competitive seniority, use of seniority in determining an employee's right, relative to other employees, to job related "rights" that cannot be supplied equally to any two employees.

competitive service, a general term for those civilian positions in a governmental jurisdiction that are not specifically excepted from merit system regulations.

competitive wages, rates of pay that an employer, in competition with other employers, must offer if he or she is to recruit and retain employees.

complaint examiner, official designated to conduct discrimination complaint hearings.

completion item, test question that calls for the examinee to complete or fill in the missing parts of a phrase, sentence, etc.

compliance, inducing individuals and/or organizations to act in accordance with governmentally prescribed rules or goals; a determination of whether (1) there is compliance with laws and regulations that could materially affect a jurisdiction's financial position and statements, (2) there is compliance with laws and regulations that could significantly affect the acquisition, management, and utilization of resources, and (3) programs are being carried out in conformity with laws and regulations.

compliance agency, generally, any government agency that administers laws and/or regulations relating to equal employment opportunity. Specifically, a federal agency delegated enforcement responsibilities by the U.S. Department of Labor's Office of Federal Contract Compliance Programs (OFCCP) to ensure that federal contractors adhere to EEO regulations and policies. *See* Kenneth C. Marino, "Conducting an Internal Compliance Review of Affirmative Action," *Personnel* (March–April 1980).

complimentary interview, according to Joseph P. Cangemi and Jeffrey C. Claypool, "Complimentary Interviews: A System for Rewarding Outstanding Employees," *Personnel Journal* (February 1978),

the general purpose of a complimentary interview is to positively evaluate personnel and to give them performance feedback, recognition and praise, to highlight potential, and to enhance organizational planning.

composite score, score derived by combining scores obtained by an applicant on two or more tests or other measures.

Comprehensive Employment and Training Act of 1973 (CETA), law that, as amended, established a program of financial assistance to state and local governments to provide job training and employment opportunities for economically disadvantaged, unemployed, and underemployed persons. CETA provided funds for state and local jurisdictions to hire unemployed and underemployed persons in public service jobs. The CETA reauthorization legislation expired in September 1982. It was replaced by the Job Training Partnership Act of 1982, which

was signed into law in October 1982. The legislation provides for job training programs which are planned and implemented under the joint control of local elected government officials and private industry councils in service delivery areas designated by the governor of each state. The new law took effect October 1, 1983, providing for a one-year transition period under the CETA system. *See* William Mirengoff and Lester Rindler, *The Comprehensive Employment and Training Act: Impact on People, Places, Programs – An Interim Report* (Washington, D.C.: National Academy of Sciences, 1976): William Mirengoff et al., *CETA: Accomplishments, Problems, Solutions* (Kalamazoo, Mich.: The W.E. Upjohn Institute for Employment Research, 1982); Pawan K. Sawhney, Robert H. Jantzen and Irwin L. Herrnstadt, "The Differential Impact of CETA Training," *Industrial and Labor Relations Review* (January 1982); Laurie J. Bassi, "The Effect of CETA on the Postprogram Earnings of Participants," *The Journal of Human Resources* (Fall 1983); Grace A. Franklin and Randall B. Ripley, *CETA: Politics and Policy, 1973-1982* (Knoxville, TN: University of Tennessee Press, 1984); Royal S. Dellinger, "Implementing the Job Training Partnership Act," *Labor Law Journal* (April 1984); Camille Robinson and Relmond Van Daniker, "Financial Management Issues in the Job Training Partnership Act," *State Government* (Spring 1985).

compressed time, the same number of hours worked in a week spread over fewer days than normal.

comp time, *see* COMPENSATORY TIME.

comptroller, *see* CONTROLLER.

compulsory arbitration, negotiating process whereby the parties are required by law to arbitrate their dispute. Some state statutes concerning collective bargaining impasses in the public sector mandate that parties who have exhausted all other means of achieving a settlement must submit their dispute to an arbitrator. The intent of such requirements for compulsory arbitration is to induce the parties to reach agreement by presenting them with an alternative that is both certain and unpleasant. *See* Carl M. Stevens, "Is Compulsory Arbitration Compatible with Bargaining," *Industrial Relations* (February 1966); Mollie H. Bowers, "Legislated Arbitration: Legality, Enforceability, and Face-Saving," *Public Personnel Management* (July-August 1974).

See *also* LOCAL 174, TEAMSTERS V. LUCAS FLOUR CO.

compulsory check-off, *see* AUTOMATIC CHECK OFF.

compulsory retirement, cessation of employment at an age specified by a union contract or company policy.

computer data bases, *see* DATA BASES.

conciliation, *see* MEDIATION.

Conciliation, Commissioners of. *see* MEDIATION.

conciliator, individual who is assigned or who assumes the responsibility for maintaining disputing parties in negotiations until they reach a voluntary settlement. The Federal Mediation and Conciliation Service (FMCS) has Commissioners of Conciliation located in its various regional offices available to assist parties in the settlement of labor-management disputes.

concrete objective, *see* OBJECTIVE.

concurrent power, a power held jointly by both federal and state governments. Taxation is a major example.

concurrent resolution on the budget, resolution passed by both Houses of Congress, but not requiring the signature of the president, setting forth, reaffirming, or revising the Congressional Budget for the United States Government for a fiscal year. There are two such resolutions required preceding each fiscal year. The first required concurrent resolution, due by May

15, establishes the Congressional Budget. The second required concurrent resolution, due by September 15, reaffirms or revises it. Other concurrent resolutions may be adopted at any time following the first required concurrent resolution.

concurrent validity, measure of the usefulness of a prospective employment examination. First the exam must be given to individuals already performing successfully on the job. Each incumbent must then be independently rated by supervisors on actual job performance. The test scores and the ratings are correlated; if the better workers also obtain the better test scores, then the examination can be said to have concurrent validity. *See* Bruce A. Fournier and Paul Stager, "Concurrent Validation of a Dual-Task Selection Test," *Journal of Applied Psychology* (October 1976); Marvin H. Trattner, "Task Analysis in the Design of Three Concurrent Validity Studies of the Professional and Administrative Career Examination," *Personnel Psychology* (Spring 1979).

Conference Board, Inc., The, independent, nonprofit business research organization. Since 1916 it has continuously served as an institution for scientific research in the fields of business economics and business management. Its sole purpose is to promote prosperity and security by assisting in the effective operation and sound development of voluntary productive enterprise. The Board has more than four thousand associates and serves forty thousand individuals throughout the world. It does continuing research in the fields of economic conditions, marketing, finance, personnel administration, international activities, public affairs, antitrust, and various other related areas.

The Conference Board, Inc.
845 Third Ave.
New York, NY 10022
(212) 759-0900

conference committee, *see* SELECT COMMITTEE.

confidence testing, testing approach that

allows the subject to express his or her attraction to or confidence in possible answers in percentage terms. *See* Ernest S. Selig, "Confidence Testing Comes of Age," *Training and Development Journal* (July 1972).

conflict, situation in which individuals or collectivities adhere to and act upon incompatible values, perceptions, or feelings.

conflict of interest, any situation where a decision that may be made (or influenced) by an office holder may (or may appear to) be to that office holder's personal benefit. *See* Common Cause, *Serving Two Masters: A Common Cause Study of Conflicts of Interest in the Executive Branch* (Washington, D.C.: Common Cause, 1976) and Robert G. Vaughn, *Conflict-of-Interest Regulation in the Federal Executive Branch* (Lexington, Mass.: Lexington Books, 1979).

conflict resolution, according to Kenneth E. Boulding, in *Conflict and Defense: A General Theory* (New York: Harper & Bros., 1962), the attempt to see that conflicts, which are inevitable, remain constructive rather than destructive. Traditional administrative theory, having been based on the models provided by the military and the Catholic Church, viewed organizational conflict as deviancy. But the growing recognition that reasonable conflict can produce organizational benefits is leading to changes in administrative structure that will permit and control conflict. Since it has been the hierarchical structure of organizations that has commonly suppressed the potential value of confict, that hierarchical structure must be altered before conflict can come into its full beneficent flower. The implications of this for the future of personnel management are awesome. *See* A. C. Filley, "Some Normative Issues in Conflict Management," *California Management Review* (Winter 1978); Eleanor Phillips and Ric Cheston, "Conflict Resolution: What Works?" *California Management Review* (Summer 1979); Michele Stimac, "Strategies for

Resolving Conflict: Their Functional and Dysfunctional Sides," *Personnel* (November–December 1982); Paul Joyce and Adrian Woods, "The Management of Conflict: A Quantitative Analysis," *British Journal of Industrial Relations* (March 1984); Dean Tjosvold, "Making Conflict Productive," *Personnel Administrator* (June 1984); Vincent L. Ferraro and Sheila A. Adams, "Interdepartmental Conflict: Practical Ways to Prevent and Reduce It," *Personnel* (July–August 1984); M. Afzalur Rahim, "A Strategy for Managing Conflict in Complex Organizations," *Human Relations* (January 1985).

conformity, expression or enactment of similar feelings or behaviors by the members of a collectivity.

confrontation, process in which opposing parties exchange information on points of difference in order to move towards compromise or resolution.

confrontation meeting, organization development technique that has an organizational group (usually the management corps) meet for a one-day effort to assay their organizational health. *See* Richard Beckhard, "The Confrontation Meeting," *Harvard Business Review* (March–April 1967).

Congress, that legislative institution of the U.S. government created and defined by Article 1 of the Constitution.

congressional budget, budget as set forth by Congress in a concurrent resolution on the budget. These resolutions include: (1) the appropriate level of total budget outlays and of total new budget authority; (2) an estimate of budget outlays and new budget authority for each major functional category; (3) the amount, if any, of the surplus or deficit in the budget; (4) the recommended level of federal revenues; and (5) the appropriate level of the public debt.

Congressional Budget and Impoundment Control Act of 1974, law regarding congressional budgeting responsibilities. The act's "Declaration of Purposes" states the reasons for its passage:

The Congress declares that it is essential—

1. to assure effective congressional control over the budgetary process;
2. to provide for the congressional determination each year of the appropriate level of federal revenues and expenditures;
3. to provide a system of impoundment control;
4. to establish national budget priorities; and
5. to provide for the furnishing of information by the executive branch in a manner that will assist the Congress in discharging its duties.

The significant features of the act include:

1. creation of two new budget committees: the House and Senate Budget Committees;
2. creation of a Congressional Budget Office to support Congress just as

the OMB serves the President.

3. adoption of a new appropriations process for Congress;
4. adoption of a new budget calendar for Congress;
5. establishment of a new fiscal year (October 1 through September 30) to more rationally deal with the timing of budget cycles;
6. creation of a Current Services Budget; and
7. creation of two new forms of impoundments: recissions and deferrals, both of which must be submitted to the Congess.

See James J. Finley, "The 1974 Congressional Initiative in Budget Making," *Public Administration Review* (May-June 1975); Jerome A. Miles, "The Congressional Budget and Impoundment Control Act—A Departmental Budget Officer's View," *The Bureaucrat* (January 1977); John Dumbrell, "Strengthening the Legislative Power of the Purse: The Origins of the 1974 Budgetary Reforms in the U.S. Congress," *Public Administration* (Winter

CONGRESSIONAL BUDGET TIMETABLE

On or before:	Action to be completed:
November 10	President transmits current services budget.
15th day after Congress convenes	President transmits his budget.
March 15	Committees submit reports to budget committees.
April 1	Congressional Budget Office submits report to budget committees.
April 15	Budget committees report first concurrent resolution on the budget to their Houses.
May 15	Committees report bills authorizing new budget authority.
May 15	Congress adopts first concurrent resolution on the budget.
7th day after Labor Day	Congress completes action on bills providing budget authority.
September 15	Congress completes actions on second required concurrent resolution on the budget.
September 25	Congress completes action on reconciliation bill or resolution, or both, implementing second concurrent resolution.
October 1	Fiscal year begins.

1980); Douglas H. Shumavon, "Policy Impact of the 1974 Congressional Budget Act," *Public Administration Review* (May-June 1981); Bernard T. Pitsvada and Frank D. Draper, "The Budget and Impoundment Act and the Budget Process," *Government Accountants Journal* (Summer 1984).

Congressional Budget Office (CBO), support agency of the U.S. Congress created in 1974 by the Congressional Budget and Impoundment Act. It provides Congress with basic budget data and with analyses of alternative fiscal, budgetary, and programmatic policy issues. The CBO has specific responsibility for the following:

1. *Economic Forecasting and Fiscal Policy Analysis.* The federal budget both affects and is affected by the national economy. The Congress considers the federal budget in the context of the current and projected state of the national economy. The CBO therefore provides periodic forecasts and analyses of economic trends and alternative fiscal policies.
2. *Scorekeeping.* Under the new budget process the Congress establishes, by concurrent resolution, targets (or ceilings) for overall expenditures, budget authority, and budget outlays, and for broad functional categories. The Congress also establishes targets (or ceilings) for the levels of revenues, the deficit, and the public debt. The CBO "keeps score" for the Congress by monitoring the results of congressional action on individual authorization, appropriation, and revenue bills against the targets or ceilings specified in the concurrent resolutions.
3. *Cost Projections.* The CBO is required to develop five-year cost estimates for carrying out any public bill or resolution reported by congressional committees. At the start of each fiscal year, the CBO also provides five-year projections on the costs of continuing current federal spending and taxation policies.
4. *An Annual Report on the Budget.*

The CBO is responsible for furnishing the House and Senate Budget Committees by April 1 of each year with a report that includes a discussion of alternative spending and revenue levels and alternative allocations among major programs and functional categories, all in the light of major national needs and the effect on the balanced growth and development of the United States.

5. *Special Studies.* The CBO undertakes studies requested by the Congress on budget-related areas.

CBO
Second and D Streets, S.W.
Washington, D.C. 20515
(202) 226-2621

congressional committees, *see* STANDING COMMITTEES.

congressional exemption, exclusion of the approximately eighteen thousand congressional staff employees from coverage of the large variety of laws regulating working conditions that the U.S. Congress has passed throughout the years. Each member of Congress has complete autonomy over the pay and working conditions of his or her staff and need not comply with laws on labor relations, equal pay, civil rights, occupational safety, etc.
See also DAVIS V. PASSMAN.

congressional government, that type of government in which the legislature is separate from the executive and each is independent of the other. This is in contrast to a cabinet form of government in which an executive is chosen by, and responsible to, a legislature.

congressional power, *see* APPOINTMENT CLAUSE.

Congressional Record, publication containing the proceedings of Congress. Issued daily when Congress is in session, publication of the *Record* began March 4, 1873. It was the first series officially reported, printed, and published directly by the federal government.

congressional veto, also known as the LEGISLATIVE VETO, is a statutory measure that allows the president to put forth a proposal subject to the approval or disapproval of Congress. Either action must usually be taken within either sixty or ninety days. The congressional veto may take the form of a committee-veto, a simple resolution passed by either house or a concurrent resolution.

The congressional veto was first provided for in the Economy Act of June 30, 1932, when Congress authorized President Herbert Hoover to reorganize executive departments and agencies subject to disapproval by a simple majority of either house within sixty days.

Since 1932, but especially since 1972, several hundred pieces of legislation have included some version of the congressional veto. But in 1983 the Supreme Court ruled in *Immigration and Naturalization Service* v. *Chadha,* 454 U.S. 812 (1983), that the congressional veto violated the separation of powers and was therefore unconstitutional.

See also VETO.

Congress of Industrial Organizations (CIO), labor organization that originated in 1935, when the Committee for Industrial Organization was formed within the American Federation of Labor (AFL) to foster the organization of workers in mass production industries. The activities of the Committee precipitated a split in the AFL because many of the older union leaders refused to depart from the craft union concept. In 1937, those unions associated with the committee were formally expelled from the AFL. One year later, those unions formed their own federation—the Congress of Industrial Organizations—with John L. Lewis as its first president. In 1955, the CIO formally merged with the AFL to form the present AFL-CIO. For a history of the split, *see* Walter Galenson, *The CIO Challenge to the AFL: A History of the American Labor Movement, 1935-1941* (Cambridge, Mass.: Harvard University Press, 1960); Nelson Lichtenstein, *Labor's War at Home: The CIO in*

World War II (New York: Cambridge University Press, 1982).

See also AMERICAN FEDERATION OF LABOR and AMERICAN FEDERATION OF LABOR-CONGRESS OF INDUSTRIAL ORGANIZATIONS.

Connell v. **Higginbotham,** 403 U.S. 207 (1971), U.S. Supreme Court case which held that it was unconstitutional to require public employees to swear that they "do not believe in the overthrow of the Government of the United States or of the State of Florida by force or violence." The court reasoned that at the very least, the Constitution required that a hearing or inquiry be held to determine the reasons for refusal.

See also LOYALTY OATH.

consensual validation, procedure of using mutual agreement as the criterion for validity.

consent decree, approach to enforcing equal employment opportunity involving a negotiated settlement that allows an employer to not admit to any acts of discrimination yet agree to greater EEO efforts in the future. Consent decrees are usually negotiated with the Equal Employment Opportunity Commission or a federal court. See Lewis J. Ringler, "EEO Agreements and Consent Decrees May be Booby-Traps," *The Personnel Administrator* (February 1977); Ichniowski Casey, "Have Angels Done More? The Steel Industry Consent Decree," *Industrial and Labor Relations Review* (January 1983).

consent order, regulatory agency procedure to induce voluntary compliance with its policies. A consent order usually takes the form of a formal agreement whereby an industry agrees to stop a practice in exchange for the agency's cessation of legal action against the industry.

consolidated decision packages, packages prepared at higher organizational and program levels that summarize and supplement information contained in decision packages received from subordinate units in an agency. Consolidated packages may reflect different priorities, including the addition of new programs or the abolition of existing ones.

See also DECISION PACKAGES and ZERO-BASE BUDGETING.

consolidated government, see METROPOLITAN GOVERNMENT.

conspiracy doctrine, see SHAW, LEMUEL.

constant dollar, a dollar value adjusted for changes in prices. Constant dollars are derived by dividing current dollar amounts by an appropriate price index, a process generally known as deflating. The result is a constant dollar series as it would presumably exist if prices and transactions were the same in all subsequent years as in the base year. Any changes in such a series would reflect only changes in the real volume of goods and services. Constant dollar figures are commonly used for computing the gross national product and its components and for estimating total budget outlays.

See also CURRENT DOLLAR.

constituency, individuals or groups having an interest in the activities of a public official or agency.

constitution, document that prescribes the rules by which a government operates. The Constitution of the United States is reprinted in **Appendix A.**

constitutional, consistent with and reflective of the Constitution.

The U.S. Constitution lies at the very heart of our political system and establishes the framework and rules of the game within which that system operates. It defines the roles and powers of the legislative, judicial and executive branches, delineates the extent of federal political power, and places limitations on the authority of the states. Moreover, our politics have grown up around the Constitution and have become "constitutionalized." Many, if not virtually all, domestic political issues are eventually treated in consti-

tutional terms. In recent years we have witnessed this phenomenon with reference to civil rights, crime, pornography, abortion, women's rights, and impeachment, to name but some of the more obvious cases. Only the realm of foreign affairs has substantially escaped this tendency. Consequently, in addressing matters of government and politics, Americans are likely to pose as the first question, "Is it constitutional?" Only subsequently do we consider the desirability of policies and governmental arrangements on their own merits. The importance of the Constitution in U.S. politics poses a serious problem for the student and practitioner of public administration because it offers precious little guidance on administrative arrangements and practices. To put it bluntly, the founding fathers simply failed to anticipate the rise of the administrative state; and big, burgeoning government bureaucracies raise perplexing constitutional problems.

As every school child knows, the Constitution provides for three branches of government. This division of political labor and separation of powers subsumes administrative power and responsibility under the powers of the executive. Little heed is given to the notion that independent administrative authority might arise. Thus, when we look to the founding fathers for guidance on public administration we find that while they anticipated some amount of administration, they failed to provide directly for it. They did not consider how administrative power could be effectively integrated into the political system they were designing.

See Norton E. Long, "Bureaucracy and Constitutionalism," *American Political Science Review* (September 1952); Frank M. Coleman, *Politics, Policy and the Constitution* (New York: St. Martin's Press, 1982).

See also BILL OF RIGHTS.

constitutional government, a form of limited government in which a constitution delineates the exercise of power and in which any officer who violates constitutional provisions ceases to hold power legitimately and thus is removable from office.

constitutional law, that area of the law concerned with the interpretation and application of the nation's highest law— the Constitution. *See* David H. Rosenbloom, "The Sources of Continuing Conflict Between the Constitution and Public Personnel Management," *Review of Public Personnel Administration* (Fall 1981); Donald D. Barry, *The Legal Foundations of Public Administration* (St. Paul, Minn.: West Publishing, 1981).

constitutional right, prerogative guaranteed to the people by the Constitution.

construct, an idea or concept created or synthesized ("constructed") from available information and refined through scientific investigation. In psychological testing, a construct is usually dimensional, an attribute of people that varies in degree from one person to another. Tests are usually intended to be measures of intellectual, perceptual, psychomotor, and personality constructs (*e.g.,* a clerical test may measure the construct known as "perceptual speed and accuracy" or the performance of invoice clerks may be measured in terms of "ability to recognize errors").

constructive discharge theory, a basis for civil rights suits. If an employer makes conditions of continued employment so intolerable that it results in a "constructive discharge" whereby the employee "voluntarily" leaves, the employer may still be subject to charges that he violated Title VII of the Civil Rights Act of 1964, which generally prohibits employers from discharging employees because of their race, color, sex, or national origin.

construct validity, measure of how adequate a test is for assessing the possession of particular psychological traits or qualities.

consultant, individual or organization temporarily employed by other individuals or organizations because of some presumed

expertise. *See* Garry D. Brewer, *Politicians, Bureaucrats, and the Consultant: A Critique of Urban Problem Solving* (New York: Basic Books, 1973); Don L. Bowen and Merril J. Collett, "When and How to Use a Consultant: Guidelines for Public Managers," *Public Administration Review* (September–October 1978); Richard L. Pattenaude, Symposium Editor, "Consultants in the Public Sector," *Public Administration Review* (May–June 1979); Robert E. Kelley, "Should You Have an Internal Consultant?" *Harvard Business Review* (November–December 1979); Anthony J. Tasca, "Developing Internal Consultants," *Training and Development Journal* (December 1979); George Barbour, Jr., "How To Get the Most Out of Your Consultant," *Public Management* (April 1981); Michael A. Tita, "Internal Consultants: Captive Problem Solvers," *Management Review* (June 1981); Peter Szanton, *Not Well Advised* (New York: Basic Books, 1981); Arthur N. Turner, "Consulting is More Than Giving Advice," *Harvard Business Review* (September–October 1982); Gerald L. Moore, *The Politics of Management Consulting* (New York: Praeger Publishers, 1984); Danielle B. Nees and Larry E. Greiner, "Seeing Behind the Look-Alike Management Consultants," *Organizational Dynamics* (Winter 1985).

Consumer Credit Protection Act of 1970, act that limits the amount of an employee's disposable income which may be garnished and protects employees from discharge because of one garnishment.

Consumer Price Index (CPI), also called COST-OF-LIVING INDEX, monthly statistical measure of the average change in prices over time in a fixed market basket of goods and services. Effective with the January 1978 index, the Bureau of Labor Statistics began publishing CPI's for two population groups: (1) a new CPI for all Urban Consumers (CPI-U) which covers approximately 80 percent of the total noninstitutional civilian population; and (2) a revised CPI for Urban Wage Earners and Clerical Workers (CPI-W) which represents about half the population covered by the CPI-U. The CPI-U includes, in addition to wage earners and clerical workers, groups which historically have been excluded from CPI coverage, such as professional, managerial, and technical workers, the self-employed, short-term workers, the unemployed, and retirees and others not in the labor force.

BLS introduced an important improvement in the CPI-U with release of the January 1983 data. The Bureau changed the homeownership component from an "asset" approach to a "flow of services" approach. The change was implemented by a rental equivalence technique. The CPI-W will continue to use the old homeownership method until January 1985, when it also will be changed to incorporate a rental equivalence measure of homeownership costs.

The CPI is based on prices of food, clothing, shelter, fuels, transportation fares, charges for doctors' and dentists' services, drugs, and other goods and services that people buy for day-to-day living. Prices are collected in eighty-five urban areas across the country from over eighteen thousand tenants, eighteen thousand housing units for property taxes, and about twenty-four thousand establishments—grocery and department stores, hospitals, filling stations, and other types of stores and service establishments. All taxes directly associated with the purchase and use of items are included in the index. Prices of food, fuels, and a few other items are obtained every month in all eighty-five locations. Prices of most other commodities and services are collected every month in the five largest geographic areas and every other month in other areas. Prices of most goods and services are obtained by personal visits of the Bureau's trained representatives. Mail questionnaires are used to obtain public utility rates, some fuel prices, and certain other items.

In calculating the index, price changes for the various items in each location are averaged together with weights which represent their importance in the spending of the appropriate population group. Local data are then combined to obtain a U.S. city average. Separate indexes are also published for twenty-eight local areas. Area indexes do not measure differences in the level of prices among cities; they only measure the average change in prices for each area since the base period.

The index measures price changes from a designated reference date—1967—which equals 100.0. An increase of 22 percent, for example, is shown as 122.0. This change can also be expressed in dollars as follows: The prices of a base period "market basket" of goods and services in the CPI has risen from $10 in 1967 to $12.20.

For a brief history, see Julius Shiskin, "Updating the Consumer Price Index—An Overview," *Monthly Labor Review* (July 1974). *Also see* Robert J. Gordon, "The Consumer Price Index: Measuring Inflation and Causing It," *The Public Interest* (Spring 1981); P. Cagan and G. H. Moore, "Some Proposals to Improve the Consumer Price Index," *Monthly Labor Review* (September 1981); Daniel J. B. Mitchell, "Should The Consumer Price Index Determine Wages?" *California Management Review* (Fall 1982); John L. Marcout, "Revisions of the Consumer Price Index Now Under Way," *Monthly Labor Review* (April 1985).

Consumer Product Safety Commission (CPSC), federal commission created to protect the public against unreasonable risks of injury from consumer products; to assist consumers to evaluate the comparative safety of consumer products; to develop uniform safety standards for consumer products and minimize conflicting state and local regulations; and to promote research and investigation into the causes and prevention of product-related deaths, illnesses, and injuries.

CPSC
1111 Eighteenth St., N.W.
Washington, D.C. 20207
(202) 634-7740

consumer taxes, taxes levied by all levels of government against the tax base of consumer spending. The two most prevalent types of consumer taxes are taxes on retail sales and taxes on selected commodities. Consumer taxes are the largest revenue source for state governments and the second most productive source for the federal government and local jurisdictions. These taxes have been found objectionable to many as they are regressive in nature, only moderately elastic and have a more negative impact on the poor because they spend a larger portion of their income on taxed commodities. Consumer taxes tend to be popular because (1) they produce high levels of revenue at low apparent rates of taxation, (2) small increases have generally been politically acceptable and (3) such increases produce significant revenue returns. Additionally, consumer taxes offer the advantage of being collectible at the point of sale by the seller rather than by the jurisdiction. Examples of state and local consumer taxes include retail sales taxes, liquor and tobacco taxes, utilities taxes, lodging taxes, entertainment and admissions taxes, automotive taxes including license and registration fees, etc. Federal consumer taxes include firearms taxes, transportation taxes, gambling taxes, narcotics taxes, and taxes on manufactured goods and imports.

See also TAXATION.

contact counseling, according to Len Sperry and Lee R. Hess, *Contact Counseling: Communication Skills for People in Organizations* (Reading, Mass.: Addison-Wesley, 1974), "the process by which the manager aids the employee to effectively problem-solve and develop."

contempt, a willful disobeying of a judge's command or an official court order.

content validity, refers to a selection device that measures the specific abilities needed to perform the job. Examinations that require applicants to perform an actual, representative sample of the work done on the job would obviously have content validity. *See* Stephen Wollack, "Content Validity: Its Legal and Psychometric Basis," *Public Personnel Management* (November–December 1976); Lyle F. Schoenfeldt *et al.,* "Content Validity

Revisited," *Journal of Applied Psychology* (October 1976); Erich P. Prien, "The Function of Job Analysis in Content Validation," *Personnel Psychology* (Summer 1977); Stephen J. Mussio and Mary K. Smith, *Content Validity: A Procedural Manual* (Chicago: International Personnel Management Association, 1973); Robert M. Guion, " 'Content Validity' in Moderation," *Personnel Psychology* (Summer 1978); Lawrence S. Kleinman and Robert H. Faley, "Assessing Content Validity: Standards Set by the Court," *Personnel Psychology* (Winter 1978); Dwight R. Norris and James A. Buford, Jr., "A Content Valid Writing Test: A Case Study," *The Personnel Administrator* (January 1980).

contextual variable, a condition that may affect the validity of a test.

contingency management, also called SITUATIONAL MANAGEMENT, any management style that recognizes that the application of theory to practice must necessarily take into consideration, and be contingent upon, the given situation. *See* Henry L. Tosi and W. Clay Hamner, *Organizational Behavior and Management: A Contingency Approach* (Chicago, Ill.: St. Clair Press, 1974); Robert P. Vecchio, "A Dyadic Interpretation of the Contingency Model of Leadership Effectiveness," *Academy of Management Journal* (September 1979); Donald D. White and Bill Davis, "Behavioral Contingency Management: A Bottom-Line Alternative for Management Development," *The Personnel Administrator* (April 1980); John Prooslin Goodman and William R. Sandberg, "A Contingency Approach to Labor Relations Strategies," *Academy of Management Review* (January 1981).

contingency model of leadership effectiveness, Fred E. Fiedler's theory of leadership effectiveness. According to Fiedler, the appropriate leadership style is determined by three critical elements in the leader's situation: (1) the power position of the leader; (2) the task structure; (3) the leader-member personal relationships. The nature of these three factors determines the "favorableness" of the situation for the leader, which in turn requires a particular leadership style. Fiedler views leader behavior as a single dimension ranging from "task-oriented" to "relationship-oriented." He contends that task-oriented leaders perform best in very favorable or very unfavorable situations, whereas relationship-oriented leaders are best in mixed situations. Fiedler suggests that it may be to an organization's advantage to try to design jobs to fit leaders' styles rather than attempting to change leaders' behavior to fit the situation. For the original presentation, see Fred E. Fiedler, *A Theory of Leadership Effectiveness* (New York: McGraw-Hill, 1967). For a critique of Fiedler's concepts, see George Green, James Orris, and Kenneth M. Alvares, "Contingency Model of Leadership Effectiveness: Some Methodological Issues," *Journal of Applied Psychology* (June 1971).

contingent liability, existing condition, situation, or set of circumstances involving uncertainty as to a possible loss to an agency that will ultimately be resolved when one or more future events occur or fail to occur. For the purpose of federal credit programs, a contingent liability is a conditional commitment that may become an actual liability because of a future event beyond the control of the government. Contingent liabilities include such items as loan guarantees and bank deposit insurance.

See also LIABILITIES.

continuing education, general term that usually refers to graduate or undergraduate course work undertaken on a part-time basis in order to keep up to date on new developments in one's occupational field, learn a new field, or contribute to one's general education. See Irwin M. Rubin and Homer G. Morgan, "A Projective Study of Attitudes Toward Continuing Education," *Journal of Applied Psychology* Vol. 51, No. 6 (1967); Philip T. Crotty, "Continuing Education and the Experienced Manager," *California Management Review* (Fall 1974); Richard

Morano, "Continuing Education in Industry," *Personnel Journal* (February 1973).

continuing plans, *see* STANDING PLANS.

continuing resolution, legislation that provides budget authority for specific ongoing activities in cases where the regular fiscal year appropriation for such activities has not been enacted by the beginning of the fiscal year. The continuing resolution usually specifies a maximum rate at which the agency may incur obligations based on the rate of the prior year, the president's budget request, or an appropriation bill passed by either or both houses of the Congress.

continuous budgeting, *see* BUDGETING CONTINUOUS.

continuous negotiating committee, laobr-management committee established to review a collective bargaining agreement on a continuous basis.

contraband, things that are illegal to import or export or that are illegal to possess.

contract, *see* the following entries:
  BREACH OF CONTRACT
  EMPLOYMENT CONTRACT
  INCENTIVE CONTRACT
  INDIVIDUAL CONTRACT
  IRON-CLAD OATH
  LABOR AGREEMENT
  MASTER AGREEMENT
  SWEETHEART CONTRACT
  TERMINATION CONTRACT
  YELLOW-DOG CONTRACT

contract audit, an examination and evaluation of government contracts for goods and services with private as well as nonprofit organizations.

contract authority, form of budget authority under which contracts or other obligations may be entered into prior to an appropriation. Contract authority does not provide funds to pay the obligations and thus requires a subsequent appropriation or the realization of revenues to liquidate the obligations. To avoid double counting, appropriations to liquidate contract authority are not considered as budget authority. The Congressional Budget and Impoundment Control Act of 1974 limits new contract authority (except in certain instances) to the extent or amount provided by appropriation acts.

See also BACKDOOR AUTHORITY.

contract bar, an existing collective bargaining agreement that bars a representation election sought by a competing union.

contract employees, private sector employees who work indirectly for government because of their employer's government contract.

contracting, legal process by which the government enters into relationships with firms in the private sector that administer public programs or provide the government with goods or services. The contract may provide that the government reimburse the firm for the costs it incurs or that the government pay a fixed price for the product; both types of contracts may contain incentive provisions that reward the contractor for meeting deadlines and staying within cost estimates.

See Clarence H. Danhof, *Government Contracting and Technological Change* (Washington, D.C.: The Brookings Institution, 1968); Roger S. Ahlbrandt, Jr., "Implications of Contracting for a Public Service," *Urban Affairs Quarterly* (March 1974); Patricia S. Florestano and Stephen B. Gordon, "Public vs. Private: Small Government Contracting with the Private Sector," *Public Administration Review* (January–February 1980); Ira Sharkansky, "Policy Making and Service Delivery on the Margins of Government: The Case of Contractors," *Public Administration Review* (March–April 1980); Phillip J. Cooper, "Government Contracts in Public Administration: The Role and Environment of the Contracting Officer," *Public Administration Review* (September–October 1980).

contracting-out, having work performed outside an organization's own work force. Contracting-out has often been an area of union-management disagreement. While many unions recognize management's right to occasionally subcontract a job requiring specialized skills and equipment not possessed by the company or its employees, they oppose the letting of work that could be done by the organization's own work force. In particular, unions are concerned if work normally performed by its members is contracted to firms having inferior wages or working conditions or if such action may result in reduced earnings or layoffs of regular employees. See Daniel D. Brener and Danial W. Fitzpatrick, "An Experience in Contracting Out for Services," *Governmental Finance* (March 1980); Ronald Donovan and Marsha J. Orr, *Subcontracting in the Public Sector: The New York State Experience* (Ithaca, N.Y.: Cornell University, New York State School of Industrial and Labor Relations, 1982).

See also FIBREBOARD PAPER PRODUCTS CORPORATION V. NATIONAL LABOR RELATIONS BOARD.

contributory pension plan, any pension program that has employees contributing a portion of the cost.

control, that aspect of management concerned with the comparison of actual versus planned performance as well as the development and implementation of procedures to correct substandard performance. Control, which is inherent in all levels of management, is a feedback process which should ideally report only unexpected situations. This is the essence of management by exception. Some management control systems regularly report critical indicators of performance so that management will have advance notice of potential problems.

As the term is used in organization theory and behavior, control is an aspect of management in which it is assumed that cause-effect relationships are known and there is a high level of certainty. In *Management or Control? The Organizational Challenge* (Bloomington, Ind.: Indiana

University Press, 1980) Russell Stout, Jr. asserts that there is a managerial tendency toward inappropriate use of control, particularly in public organizations. Preoccupation with accountability and avoidance of errors leads to increased controls and often "overcontrol," when a more experimental management orientation is needed.

control group, in a research design, a group with characteristics similar to the experimental or subject group, which is not exposed to the experimental treatment and which is used for comparative purposes.

controllability, ability of the Congress or the president under existing law to control outlays during a given fiscal year. "Relatively uncontrollable" usually refers to spending that cannot be increased or decreased without changes in existing substantive law. Such spending is usually the result of open-ended programs and fixed costs, such as social security and veterans' benefits, but also includes payments due under obligations incurred during prior years.

controller or comptroller, the financial officer of a company or a government agency. For example, the *Comptroller General* of the U.S. heads the Government Accounting Office, which audits government agencies. *See* Jacques C. Leger, "The Departmental Comptroller," *Government Accountants Journal* (Winter 1983–1984).

convalescent leave, leave for civilian employees on duty abroad who are injured as a result of "war, insurgency, mob violence, or other similar hostile action." Such leave with pay is completely separate from an employee's sick-leave benefits and can be granted by federal government agencies.

convergent validity, in testing, evidence that different measures of a construct will produce similar results.

converted score, general term referring to any of a variety of "transformed" scores, in terms of which raw scores on a test may be expressed for such reasons as facilitating interpretation and permitting comparison with scores on other test forms. For example, the raw scores obtained by candidates on the various College Board tests are converted to scores on a common scale that ranges from two-hundred to eight-hundred.

convict labor, *see* ASHURST-SUMNERS ACT OF 1935.

coolie labor, originally a term for unskilled Asian labor in the 19th-century U.S., the phrase is now applied—typically in a jocular or derisive manner—to any cheap labor.

cooling-off period, any legal provision that postpones a strike or lockout for a specific period of time in order to give the parties an additional opportunity to mediate their differences. While the device has great popular appeal, it has proven to be of doubtful value because "more time" will not necessarily resolve a labor dispute. The first federal requirements for a cooling-off period were set forth in the War Labor Disputes (Smith-Connally) Act of 1943. This was superseded by the national emergency provisions of the National Labor-Management Relations (Taft-Hartley) Act of 1947, which called for an eighty-day cooling-off period in the event of a "national emergency."

cooperative agreement, a form of assistance award from the federal government to a state or local government or other recipient to support and stimulate an activity or venture to accomplish a public purpose, and in which the federal government will be substantially involved during the performance of the contemplated activity.

cooperative education, an educational process wherein students alternate formal studies with actual work experiences. It is distinguished from other part time employment in that successful completion of the off-campus experiences becomes a prerequisite for graduation. For an account of one company's experiences over twenty years, see Jack J. Phillips, "Is Cooperative Education Worth It? One Company's Answer," *Personnel Journal* (October 1977). For a text, see Ronald W. Stadt and Bill G. Gooch, *Cooperative Education* (Indianapolis: Bobbs-Merrill Co., Inc., 1977).

cooperative federalism, see FEDERALISM, COOPERATIVE.

cooptation, efforts of an organization to bring and subsume new elements into its policymaking process in order to prevent such elements from being a threat to the organization or its mission. The classic analysis of cooptation is found in Philip Selznick's *TVA and the Grass Roots* (Berkeley, Calif.: University of California Press, 1949). Also see Ronald S. Burt, *Corporate Profits and Cooptation: Networks of Market Constraints and Directorate Ties in the American Economy* (New York: Academic Press, 1983).

coordinated bargaining, see COALITION BARGAINING.

coordination of benefits (COB), provisions and procedures used by insurers to avoid duplicate payment for losses insured under more than one insurance policy. For example, some people have a duplication of benefits for their medical costs arising from an automobile accident in their automobile and health insurance policies. A coordination of benefits or antiduplication clause in one or the other policy will prevent double payment for the expenses by making one of the insurers the primary payer and assuring that no more than 100 percent of the costs are covered. There are standard rules for determining which of two or more plans, each having COB provisions, pays its benefits in full and which pays a sufficiently reduced benefit to prevent the claimant from making a profit.

copayment, a type of cost sharing whereby insured or covered persons pay a specified flat amount per unit of service or unit of time (*e.g.,* $2 per visit, $10 per inpatient hospital day), their insurer paying the rest of the cost. The copayment is incurred at the time the service is used. The amount paid does not vary with the cost of the service (unlike coinsurance, which is payment of some percentage of the cost).

COPE, see COMMITTEE ON POLITICAL EDUCATION.

Copeland Act, see KICKBACK.

coproduction, according to Jeffrey L. Brudney and Robert E. England, "Toward a Definition of the Coproduction Concept," *Public Administration Review* (January–February 1983), "an emerging conception of the service delivery process which envisions direct citizen involvement in the design and delivery of city services with professional service agents." Also see Charles Levine, "Citizenship and Service Delivery: The Promise of Coproduction," *Public Administration Review* (March 1984); Stephen L. Percy, ed., "Symposium: Coproduction," *Urban Affairs Quarterly* (June 1984).

Corning Glass Works* v. *Brennan, 417 U.S. 188 (1974), U.S. Supreme Court case which held that it was a violation of the Equal Pay Act of 1963 to continue to pay some men at a higher rate ("red circle") than women for the same work even though all new hires for these same positions would receive the same salary regardless of sex.

Coronado Coal* v. *United Mine Workers, 268 U.S. 295 (1925), U.S. Supreme Court case which held that unincorporated organizations such as labor unions could be sued and held liable for damages.

corporation counsel, attorney for a municipal corporation.

correctional institution, prison, reformatory, house of correction, or other institution for the confinement and correction of convicted persons and juveniles.

correction for guessing, reduction in a test score for wrong answers—sometimes applied in scoring multiple-choice questions—that is intended to discourage guessing and to yield more accurate ranking of examinees in terms of their true knowledge.

corrections, generic term that includes all government agencies, facilities, programs, procedures, personnel, and techniques concerned with the investigation, intake, custody, confinement, supervision, or treatment of alleged or adjudicated adult offenders, delinquents, or status offenders.

correlation, relationship or "going-to-getherness" between two sets of scores or measures; the tendency of one score to vary concomitantly with the other.

correlation, biserial, see BISERIAL CORRELATION.

correlation coefficient, number expressing the degree to which two measures tend to vary together. A correlation coefficient can range from -1.00 (a perfect negative relationship) to $+1.00$ (a perfect positive relationship). When there is no correlation between two measures, the coefficient is 0. A correlation coefficient only indicates concomitance; it does not indicate causation.

The values of the correlation coefficient are easily misinterpreted since they do not fall along an ordinary, absolute scale. For example, a correlation coefficient of .20 does not signify twice as much relationship as does one of .10, nor can a correlation coefficient be interpreted as a percentage statement. A correlation coefficient is a mathematical index number which requires for its interpretation some knowledge of that branch of mathematical statistics known as correlation theory. As a very rough guide to interpretation, however, a correlation between a single employment test and a measure of job performance of approximately .20 often is high enough to be useful (such correlations rarely exceed .50), a correlation of .40 is ordinarily considered very good, and most personnel research workers are usually pleased with a correlation of .30.

The mathematical symbol for the correlation coefficient is r.

cosmic search, in the context of equal employment opportunity, an endless search by an employer for an alternative selection procedure with less adverse impact.

cosmopolitanism, the belief in the ancient ideal of a world-state to which all human beings would belong. This later became a term of abuse in the Soviet Union for internal expressions of admiration for any aspect of external bourgeois capitalistic culture.

cosmopolitan-local construct, two latent social roles that manifest themselves in organizational settings, according to Alvin W. Gouldner. The first role, *cosmopolitan,* tends to be adopted by true professionals. It assumes a small degree of loyalty to the employing organization, a high commitment to specialized skills, and an outer-reference group orientation. The second role, *local,* tends to be adopted by non-professionals. It assumes a high degree of loyalty to the employing organization, a low commitment to specialized skills, and an inner-reference group orientation. These role models are extremes and represent the two ends of a continuum. *See* Alvin W. Gouldner, "Cosmopolitans and Locals: Toward an Analysis of Latent Social Roles—I," *Administrative Science Quarterly* (December 1957). While Gouldner's construct has received substantial empirical testing and criticism, its value as a general model remains evident. For a critical examination of the construct, *see* Andrew J. Grimes and Philip K. Berger, "Cosmopolitan-Local: Evaluation of a Construct," *Administrative Science Quarterly* (December 1970). *See also* Timothy A. Almy, "Local-Cosmopolitanism and

U.S. City Managers," *Urban Affairs Quarterly* (March 1975).

cost-based budgeting, *see* BUDGETING, COST-BASED.

cost-benefit analysis, also BENEFIT-COST ANALYSIS, any process by which organizations seek to determine the effectiveness of their spending, in relation to costs, in meeting policy objectives. *See* E. J. Mishan, *Cost-Benefit Analysis*, new and expanded edition (New York: Praeger Publishers, 1976); Logan Cheek, "Cost Effectiveness Comes to the Personnel Function," *Harvard Business Review* (May–June 1973); Harold S. Luft, "Benefit-Cost Analysis and Public Policy Implementation," *Public Policy* (Fall 1976); P. G. Sassone and William Schaffer, *Cost-Benefit Analysis: A Handbook* (New York: Academic Press, 1978); Elizabeth David, "Benefit-Cost Analysis in State and Local Investment Decisions," *Public Administration Review* (January–February 1979); Edward M. Gramlich, *Benefit-Cost Analysis of Government Programs* (Englewood Cliffs, N.J.: Prentice-Hall, 1981).

cost center, accounting device whereby all related costs attributable to some "center" within an institution, such as an activity, department, or program (*e.g.,* a hospital burn center), are segregated for accounting or reimbursement purposes. Contrasts with segregating costs of different types, such as nursing, drugs or laundry, regardless of which "center" incurred them.

cost-effectiveness analysis, an analytical technique used to choose the most efficient method for achieving a program or policy goal. The costs of alternatives are measured by their requisite estimated dollar expenditures. Effectiveness is defined by the degree of goal attainment, and may also (but not necessarily) be measured in dollars. Either the net effectiveness (effectiveness minus costs) or the cost-effectiveness ratios of alternatives are compared. The most cost-effective method

chosen may involve one or more alternatives. The limited view of costs and effectiveness distinguishes this technique from cost-benefit analysis, which encompasses society-wide impacts of alternatives. *See* Henry M. Levin, *Cost-Effectiveness: A Primer* (Beverly Hills, CA: Sage, 1983).
See also COST-BENEFIT ANALYSIS.

costing-out, determining the actual cost of a contract proposal (wages and fringe benefits). *See* W. D. Heisel and Gordon S. Skinner, *Costing Union Demands* (Chicago: International Personnel Management Association, 1976); Robert E. Allen and Timothy J. Keaveny, "Costing Out a Wage and Benefit Package," *Compensation Review* (Second Quarter 1983).

cost of insurance, the amount which a policyholder pays to the insurer minus what he gets back from it. This should be distinguished from the rate for a given unit of insurance (*e.g.,* $10 for a $1000 life insurance policy).

cost of living adjustment (COLA), also COST-OF-LIVING ALLOWANCE, an increase in compensation in response to increasing inflation. A *cost-of-living allowance* is additional compensation for accepting employment in high costs-of-living areas. *See* Robert J. Thorton, "A Problem with the 'COLA' Craze," *Compensation Review* (Second Quarter 1977); Clarence R. Deitsch and David A. Dilts, "The COLA Clause: An Employer Bargaining Weapon?" *Personnel Journal* (March 1982); Wallace E. Hendricks and Lawrence M. Kahn, "Cost-of-Living Clauses in Union Contracts: Determinants and Effects," *Industrial and Labor Relations Review* (April 1983).

Cost of Living Council, federal agency authorized by the Economic Stabilization Act of 1970 which monitored inflation. Created by Executive Order 11615 in 1971, it was abolished by Executive Order 11788 in 1974.

cost-of-living escalator, *see* ESCALATOR CLAUSE.

Cost-of-Living Index, see CONSUMER PRICE INDEX.

cost-push inflation, see INFLATION, COST-PUSH.

cost-revenue analysis, systematic comparison of a local community's costs of providing services to each type of land use (e.g., single-family residential) with the amount of revenue received from that source.

cost-sharing, provisions by which the costs of assisted programs are shared between the grantor and the recipient (and sometimes by third parties).

council-manager plan, also COUNTY-MANAGER SYSTEM, form of municipal government in which an elected city council appoints a professional city manager to administer the city government. A county-manager system offers the same essential structure at the county level. See Richard S. Childs, *The First Fifty Years of the Council-Manager Plan of Municipal Government* (New York: National Municipal League, 1965); John Porter East, *Council-Manager Government: The Political Thought of its Founder, Richard S. Childs* (Chapel Hill: University of North Carolina Press, 1965); Orin F. Nolting, *Progress and Impact of the Council-Manager Plan* (Chicago: Public Administration Service, 1969); David A. Booth, comp., *Council-Manager Government 1940-1964: An Annotated Bibliography* (Chicago: International City Management Association, 1965); Robert Boynton and Deil Wright, "Mayor-Manager Relationships in Large Council-Manager Cities: A Reinterpretation," *Public Administration Review* (January-February 1971).

Council of Economic Advisers (CEA), established in the Executive Office of the President by the Employment Act of 1946, the CEA consists of three economists (one designated chairman) appointed by the president with the advice and consent of the Senate who formulate proposals to "maintain employment, production and purchasing power." The CEA, as the president's primary source of economic advice, assists the president in preparing various economic reports. For a history, see Edward S. Flash, *Economic Advice and Presidential Leadership: The Council of Economic Advisors* (New York: Columbia University Press, 1965).

Council of Economic Advisers
Executive Office Building
Washington, D.C. 20500
(202) 395-5084

council of government (COG), multijurisdictional cooperative arrangements to permit a comprehensive approach to planning, development, transportation, environment and similar problems that affect a region as a whole. They are comprised of designated policymaking representatives from each participating government within the region. COGs are substate regional planning agencies established by states and are responsible for areawide review of projects applying for federal funds and for development of regional plans and other areawide special purpose arrangements. See "COGs—Governing for the 21st Century," *Public Management* (January 1969); Nelson Wikstrom, *Councils of Governments: A Study of Political Incrementalism* (Chicago: Nelson-Hall Publishers, 1985).

Council of State Governments (CSG), joint agency of all state governments—created, supported, and directed by them. Its purpose is to strengthen all branches of state government and preserve the state governmental role in the federal system through catalyzing the expression of states' views on major issues, conducting research on state programs and problems, assisting in federal-state liaison and state-regional-local cooperation, offering training, reference and consultation services to state agencies, officials and legislators, and serving as a broad instrument for bringing together all elements of state government.

CSG
Ironworks Pike
P.O. Box 11910

Lexington, KY 40511
(606) 252-2291

Council on Environmental Quality, federal agency that develops and recommends to the president national policies which further environmental quality, performs a continuing analysis of changes or trends in the national environment, administers the environmental impact statement process, provides an ongoing assessment of the nation's energy research and development from an environmental and conservation standpoint, and assists the president in the preparation of the annual environmental quality report to the Congress.
Council on Environmental Quality
722 Jackson Place, N.W.
Washington, D.C. 20006
(202) 395-5700

Council on Wage and Price Stability, body established in 1974 within the Executive Office of the President. The Council monitored the economy as a whole with respect to key indicators such as wages, costs, productivity, profits, and prices. The council became inactive in 1981.

council ward, legislative district from which a person is elected to a city council.

counseling, crisis, see CRISIS INTERVENTION.

counseling, employee, see EMPLOYEE COUNSELING.

countercyclical, actions aimed at smoothing out swings in economic activity. Countercyclical actions may take the form of monetary and fiscal policy (such as countercyclical revenue sharing or jobs programs). Automatic (built-in) stabilizers have a countercyclical effect without necessitating changes in governmental policy.
See also AUTOMATIC STABILIZER.

counterproposal, offer made by a party in response to an earlier offer made by another party.

countervailing duty, a retaliatory extra charge that a country places on imported goods to counter the subsidies or bounties granted to the exporters of the goods by their home governments.

countervailing power, concept developed by John Kenneth Galbraith which holds that large industries have an inherent tendency to generate the development of large buyers and unions which seek to *countervail* their power; in effect both buyers and sellers are prevented from abusing power by the development of countervailing powers in the economy.
See his *American Capitalism: The Concept of Countervailing Power* (Boston: Houghton Mifflin, 1956).

county, also PARISH, unit for administrative decentralization of state government. With the exception of a few sparsely settled areas in the western states, the county was geographically created to enable anyone to get to the county seat in one day. It is typically governed by an elected board or commission. There is a present movement toward a county administrator or executive (sometimes elected). In Louisiana, the comparable unit is called a *parish. See* Herbert Sydney Duncombe, *Modern County Government* (Washington, D.C.: National Association of Counties, 1977); John C. Bollens, *American County Government, with an Annotated Bibliography* (Beverly Hills, Calif.: Sage Publications, 1969); and Susan Walker Torrence, *Grass Roots Government: The County in American Politics* (Washington, D.C.: Robert B. Luce, 1974).

county-manager system, see COUNCIL-MANAGER PLAN.

County of Washington v. Gunther, 68 L. Ed. 2d 751 (1981), U.S. Supreme Court case which held that a claim of sex-based wage discrimination was not precluded by a failure to allege performance of work equal to that performed by male counterparts. This case involved female matrons of a county jail who performed substantially equal work to that performed by male guards, but were compensated less. Although they alleged in their complaint a violation of the equal pay standard of the Equal Pay Act as between themselves and the male guards, they did not allege that job performance was "substantially equal" as required under the Act. Suing under Title VII, the matrons' argument was that even if their job content was not substantially equal to that of the male guards, some of the difference in compensation paid to them was because of sex discrimination. While the Court agreed with the matrons, it dodged the issue of comparable worth. Justice Brennan in his majority opinion wrote that "respondent's claim is not based on the controversial concept of 'comparable worth'." *See* Laura N. Gasaway, "Comparable Worth: A Post *Gunther* Overview," *The Georgetown Law Journal* (June 1981); Barbara N. McLennan, "Sex Discrimination in Employment and Possible Liabilities of Labor Unions: Implications of *County of Washington* v. *Gunther*," *Labor Law Journal* (January 1982).

See also COMPARABLE WORTH.

coup d'etat, a change in the leadership of a government by force brought about by those who already held some form of power (either military or political). This technically differs from a revolution in that revolutions are usually brought about by those who are not presently in power.

court, agency of the judicial branch of government authorized or established by statute or constitution and consisting of one or more judicial officers, which has the authority to decide upon controversies in law and disputed matters of fact brought before it.

court of appeals, also called FEDERAL COURT OF APPEALS and U.S. COURT OF APPEALS, appellate court below the U.S. Supreme Court which hears appeals from cases tried in federal district courts. In most cases, a decision by a court of appeals is final since only a small fraction of their decisions are ever reviewed by the U.S. Supreme Court. Before 1948 the court of appeals was called the circuit court of appeals.

The courts of appeals are intermediate appellate courts created in 1891 to relieve the Supreme Court of considering all appeals in cases originally decided by the federal trial courts.

The decisions of the courts of appeals are final except as they are subject to discretionary review or appeal in the Supreme Court.

The United States is divided into twelve judicial circuits, including the District of Columbia as a circuit, in each of which there is a United States court of appeals. At present each United States court of appeals has from four to twenty-three permanent circuit judgeships (132 in all), depending upon the amount of judicial work in the circuit. The judge senior in commission who has not reached his seventieth birthday is the chief judge. One of the justices of the Supreme Court is assigned as circuit justice for each circuit. Each court of appeals usually hears cases in divisions consisting of three judges, but they may sit *en banc* with all judges present.

cousin laboratory, a laboratory training experience for people who have no direct working relationship with each other but come from the same organization.

Couturier, Jean J. (1927-   ), professional reformer. As the executive director of the National Civil Service League, he was the single individual most responsible for the League's promulgation of its 1970 "Model Public Personnel Administration Law," which called for the abolition of traditional civil service commissions. For an account of this abolition movement, *see* Jean J. Couturier, "The Quiet Revolution in Public Personnel Laws," *Public Personnel Management* (May-June 1976).

coverage, the guarantee against specific losses provided under the terms of an insurance policy. Frequently used interchangeably with *benefits* or *protection*. Refers to the extent of the insurance afforded by a policy. Often used to mean insurance or an insurance contract.

covered jobs, all those positions that are affected and protected by specific labor legislation.

cover your ass (CYA), any bureaucratic technique that serves to hold the individual bureaucrat blameless for policies or actions with which he or she was once associated.

CPA, see CERTIFIED PUBLIC ACCOUNTANT.

CPI, see CONSUMER PRICE INDEX.

CPI Detailed Report, U.S. Bureau of Labor Statistics' monthly publication featuring detailed data and charts on the Consumer Price Index.

CPI Detailed Report
Superintendent of Documents
Government Printing Office
Washington, D.C. 20402

CPM, see CRITICAL PATH METHOD.

CPSC, see CONSUMER PRODUCT SAFETY COMMISSION.

cradle-to-the-grave, also WOMB-TO-TOMB, slang phrases that refer to the total security offered citizens in the fully realized welfare state.

craft, any occupation requiring specific skills that must be acquired by training.

craft guild, see GUILD.

craft union, also called HORIZONTAL UNION and TRADE UNION, labor organization that restricts its membership to skilled craft workers (such as plumbers, carpenters, etc.), in contrast to an industrial union that seeks to recruit all workers in a particular industry. The U.S. labor movement has its origins in small craft unions. For a history, see Lloyd Ulman, The Rise of the National Trade Union (Cambridge, Mass.: Harvard University Press, 1966). For an international perspective, see E. Owen Smith, ed., Trade Unions in the Developed Economies (New York: St. Martin's Press, 1981).

craft unit, bargaining unit that consists only of workers with the same specific skill (such as electricians, plumbers, or carpenters).

creative federalism, see FEDERALISM, CREATIVE.

creativity test, test that stresses divergent thinking or the ability to create new or original answers; considered useful for examining the culturally disadvantaged and certain ethnic groups whose command of English is not highly developed. Such tests utilize common and familiar objects in order to sample the testee's originality, flexibility, and fluency of thinking. Tasks include suggesting improvements in familiar devices such as telephones or listing many possible uses for a broom handle. The tests are scored simply on the number of acceptable answers given by the subject. See John A. Hattie, "Conditions for Administering Creativity Tests," Psychological Bulletin (November 1977).

credentialism, an emphasis on paper manifestations, such as college degrees, instead of on actual ability to accomplish the tasks of a job. For two attacks on the value of the credentials offered by higher education, see John Keats, The Sheepskin Psychosis (Philadelphia: J. B. Lippincott, 1965); Caroline Bird, The Case Against College (New York: David McKay Co., 1975). For how to avoid the problem, see H. Dudley Dewhirst, "It's Time to Put the Brakes on Credentialism," Personnel Journal (October 1973). For a history, see Randall Collins, The Credential Society: An Historical Sociology of Education and Stratification (New York: Academic Press, 1979).
See also RESTRICTIVE CREDENTIALISM.

credit budget, a proposed federal budget process which would place ceilings on the total volume of direct loan obligations and loan guarantee commitments which could be extended by the federal government for the fiscal year. According to this proposal, Congress would include in its concurrent budget resolutions target ceilings for federal credit activities. Furthermore, the authority to guarantee or insure loans would be limited for each program annually in appropriations actions. The president's budgets include a recommended credit budget.

credit check, reference check on a prospective employee's financial standing. Such checks are usually conducted only when financial status may bear upon the job, as with bank tellers, for example.

credited service, employment time that an employee has for benefit purposes.

credit rating, assessment of the credit of a bond issuer. The ability of a jurisdiction to sell its bonds is often a function of the credit rating it enjoys. This credit rating translates into a rating for each issue which in turn determines the level of interest the jurisdiction must pay to entice buyers. The two major municipal bond rating services are Standard and Poors Corporation and Moody's Investors Service.

credit union, not a labor union, but a cooperative savings and loan association.

crisis bargaining, collective bargaining negotiations conducted under the pressure of a strike deadline.

crisis intervention, a formal effort to help an individual experiencing a crisis to reestablish equilibrium. A crisis is a turning point in a person's life. It can be the death of a child, spouse, or parent. It can be a heart attack. It can be anything that tests the limits of an individual's ability to cope. *See* Mike Berger, "Crisis Intervention in Personnel Administration," *Personnel Journal* (November 1969); William Getz *et al., Fundamentals of Crisis Counseling: A Handbook* (Lexington, Mass.: Lexington Books, 1974); Romaine V. Edwards, *Crisis Intervention and How it Works* (Springfield, Ill.: Charles C. Thomas, 1977); Morley D. Glicken,

"Managing a Crisis Intervention Program," *Personnel Journal* (April 1982).

criterion, plural CRITERIA, measure of job performance or other work-related behavior against which performance on a test or other predictive measure is compared.

criterion contamination, influence on criterion measures of variables or factors not relevant to the work behavior being measured. If the criterion is, for example, a set of supervisory ratings of competence in job performance and if the ratings are correlated with the length of time the supervisor has known the individual people he/she rates, then the length of acquaintance is a contaminant of the criterion measure. Similarly, if the amount of production on a machine is counted as the criterion measure and if the amount of production depends in part on the age of the machine being used, then age of machinery is a contaminant of production counts.

criterion objective, *see* PERFORMANCE OBJECTIVE.

criterion-referenced test, test by which a candidate's performance is measured according to the degree a specified criterion has been met. *See* W. James Popham, *Criterion-Referenced Measurement* (Englewood Cliffs, N.J.: Prentice-Hall, 1978); Frank L. Schmidt and John E. Hunter, "The Future of Criterion-Related Validity," *Personnel Psychology* (Spring 1980); Leonard Berger, "The Promise of Criterion-Referenced Performance Appraisal (CRPA)," *Review of Public Personnel Administration* (Summer 1983).

criterion related validation, *see* STATISTICAL VALIDATION.

criterion relevance, judgment of the degree to which a criterion measure reflects the important aspects of job performance. Such a judgment is based on an understanding of the measurement process itself, of the job and worker requirements as revealed through careful job analysis, and of the needs of the organization.

critical-incident method, also called CRITICAL-INCIDENT TECHNIQUE, identifying, classifying and recording significant examples—critical incidents—of an employee's behavior for purposes of performance evaluation. The theory behind the critical-incidents approach holds that there are certain key acts of behavior that make the difference between success and failure. After the incidents are collected they can be ranked in order of frequency and importance and assigned numerical weights. Once scored, they can be equally as useful for employee development and counseling as for formal appraisals. For the pioneering work on the concept, *see* John C. Flanagan, "The Critical Incident Technique," *Psychological Bulletin* (July 1954); John C. Flanagan and Robert K. Burns, "The Employee Performance Record: A New Approach and Development Tool," *Harvard Business Review* (September–October 1957). *Also see* John M. Champion and John H. James, *Critical Incidents in Management,* 4th ed. (Homewood, Ill.: Richard D. Irwin, Inc., 1980).

critical path method (CPM), network-analysis technique for planning and scheduling. The "critical path" is a sequence of activities that connect the beginning and end of events or program accomplishments. *See* J. D. Wiest and F. K. Levy, *A Management Guide to PERT/CPM,* 2nd ed. (Englewood Cliffs, N.J.: Prentice-Hall, 1977).

critical score, *see* CUTTING SCORE.

cross agency ranking, a process of ranking, on a government-wide basis, the decision packages that fall within a specified margin of a budget total. The purpose of cross agency ranking is to help assure that diverse programs of the same priority are considered for inclusion within the budget total.
    See also DECISION PACKAGE and ZERO-BASE BUDGETING.

cross-check, procedure by which the National Labor Relations Board or some other appropriate agency compares union authorization cards to an employer's payroll to determine whether a majority of the employees wish union representation. With the employer's consent, such a cross-check can bring union recognition and certification without a formal hearing and election.

cross picketing, picketing by more than one union when each claims to represent the work force.

cross validation, process which seeks to apply the results of one validation study to another. As such, it is a check on the accuracy of the original validation study.

crosswalk, any procedure for expressing the relationship between budgetary data from one set of classifications to another, such as between appropriation accounts and authorizing legislation.

crowding out, commonly refers to the displacement of private investment expenditures by increases in public expenditures financed by sales of government securities. The extent of the displacement depends on such factors as the responsiveness of private savings and investment to changes in interest rates and the degree to which the Federal Reserve monetizes the increase in public debt.

Crozier, Michel J., (1922-   ), French sociologist whose book, *The Bureaucratic Phenomenon* (Chicago: University of Chicago Press, 1964), is considered by Howard E. McCurdy to be "the best empirical study of bureaucratic behavior since the Hawthorne studies." *Also see The Stalled Society* (New York: Viking Press, 1973).

crude score, *see* RAW SCORE.

CSA, *see* COMMUNITY SERVICES ADMINISTRATION.

CSG, *see* COUNCIL OF STATE GOVERNMENTS.

cult of personality, a concertration of political power and authority in one individual rather than in the office that is occupied. The phrase came from the 1956 meeting of the Russian Communist Party where Stalin was denounced for his excesses in office.

cultural bias, in the context of employee selection, the indirect and incidental (as opposed to direct and deliberate) bias of individuals and instruments making selection decisions. Also, the propensity of a test to reflect favorable or unfavorable effects of certain types of cultural backgrounds. *See* Ollie A. Jensen, "Cultural Bias in Selection," *Public Personnel Review* (April 1966).

culturally disadvantaged, groups that do not have full participation in U.S. society because of low incomes, substandard housing, poor education, and other "atypical" environmental experiences.

culture-fair test, also called CULTURE-FREE TEST, a test yielding results that are not culturally biased. For an analysis, *see* R. L. Thorndike, "Concepts of Culture-Fairness," *Journal of Educational Measurement* (Summer 1971).

cumulative band chart, *see* BAND CURVE CHART.

cumulative frequency, sum of successively added frequencies (usually) of test scores.

cumulative frequency chart, graphic presentation of a cumulative frequency distribution which has the frequencies expressed in terms of the number of cases or as a percentage of all cases.

cumulative percentage, cumulative frequency expressed as a percentage.

current assets, *see* ASSETS.

current dollar, the dollar value of a good or service in terms of prices current at the time the good or service was sold. This is in contrast to the value of the good or service in constant dollars.
See also CONSTANT DOLLAR.

current liabilities, *see* LIABILITIES.

current services budget, *see* BUDGET, CURRENT SERVICES.

current services estimates, estimates of budget authority and outlays for the ensuing fiscal year based on continuation of existing levels of service. These estimates reflect the anticipated costs of continuing programs and activities at present spending levels without policy changes; that is, ignoring all new initiatives that are not yet law. Such estimates of budget authority and outlays, accompanied by the underlying economic and programmatic assumptions upon which they are based (such as the rate of inflation, the rate of real economic growth, the unemployment rate, program caseloads, and pay increases) are required to be transmitted by the president to the Congress with the president's budget.

Current Wage Developments, U.S. Bureau of Labor Statistics' monthly report about collective bargaining settlements and unilateral management decisions about wages and benefits.
Current Wage Developments
Superintendent of Documents
Government Printing Office
Washington, D.C. 20402

current year, the fiscal year in progress.

curricular validity, degree to which an examination is representative of the body of knowledge for which it is testing.

curriculum vita, *see* RESUMÉ.

custom duties, taxes on imports or exports. *See also* DUTY.

Customs Service, United States, agency of the Department of the Treasury which collects revenue from imports and enforces customs and related laws.

U.S. Customs Service
1301 Constitution Avenue, N.W.
Washington, D.C. 20229
(202) 566-8195

customs union, a group of nations that has eliminated trade barriers among themselves and imposed a common tariff on all goods imported from all other countries. The European Common Market is a customs union.

cutback, work force reduction that results in layoffs.

cutback management, *see* MANAGEMENT, CUTBACK.

cutting score, also called CRITICAL SCORE, PASSING SCORE, or PASSING POINT, test score used as an employment requirement. Those at or above such a score are eligible for selection or promotion, whereas those below the score are not.

There are many approaches to establishing the cutting score. Perhaps the most defensible is one of the job-related approaches (*e.g.,* using data from a criterion-related validity study). A common and practical approach is the *flexible passing score,* which is established for each test on the basis of a number of factors (some of which, such as the number of positions to be filled, may not be job-related). Arbitrarily establishing a cutting score of seventy percent in an attempt to be certain all eligibles possess the traits desired for a job (the *70-percent syndrome*) is not defensible from a psychometric point of view and has resulted in the costly situation where no applicants are eligible after taking a difficult test. *See* Glenn G. McClung, *Considerations in Developing Test Passing Points* (Chicago: International Personnel Management Association, 1974).

See also MULTIPLE CUTTING SCORE.

CYA, *see* COVER YOUR ASS.

cycle time, *see* JOB SCOPE.

cyclical unemployment, unemployment caused by a downward trend in the business cycle.

D

DAF, *see* DECISION-ANALYSIS FORECASTING.

Dahl, Robert A. (1915-   ), one of the most influential U.S. political scientists who was (1) an early proponent of pluralism and interest group participation in the political process and (2) an early advocate of a science of public administration. Major works include: "The Science of Public Administration: Three Problems," *Public Administration Review* (Winter 1947); *Politics, Economics, and Welfare,* with Charles E. Lindblom (New York: Harper & Bros., 1953); *A Preface to Democratic Theory* (Chicago: University of Chicago Press, 1956); *Who Governs? Democracy and Power in an American City* (New Haven, Conn.: Yale University Press, 1961); *Modern Political Analysis* (Englewood Cliffs, N.J.: Prentice-Hall, 1963; 3rd edition, 1976); *Pluralist Democracy in the United States* (Chicago: Rand McNally, 1967); *After the Revolution?: Authority in a Good Society* (New Haven, Conn.: Yale University Press, 1970); and *Polyarchy: Participation and Opposition* (New Haven, Conn.: Yale University Press, 1971).

Daily Labor Report, Bureau of National Affairs, Inc., report that gives Monday through Friday notification of all significant developments in the labor field. Covers congressional activities, court and NLRB decisions, arbitration, union developments, key contract negotiations, and settlements.

daily rate, basic pay earned by an employee for a standard work day.

137

Dale, Ernest (1917-   ), a leading authority on management and leadership who asserted that executive ability is not necessarily transferable among organizations and cultures. Major works include: *The Great Organizers* (New York: McGraw-Hill, 1960); *Staff in Organization,* with L. F. Urwick (New York: McGraw-Hill, 1960); *Management: Theory and Practice* (New York: McGraw-Hill, 1965); *Modern Management Methods,* with C. C. Michelon (Cleveland: World Publishing, 1965).

Danbury Hatters' **case,** *see* LAWLOR V. LOEWE.

danger-zone bonus, bonus paid to employees as an inducement to get them to work in an area that is especially hazardous.

Darby Lumber **case,** *see* UNITED STATES V. DARBY LUMBER.

Darlington **case,** *see* TEXTILE WORKERS V. DARLINGTON MANUFACTURING COMPANY.

data, plural of *datum; datum* is a single bit of information. Some economists derisively define a political scientist as someone who thinks that the plural of anecdote is data.

data bank, also called DATA BASE, information stored in a computer system so that any particular item or set of items could be extracted or organized as needed. Data bank (or data base) is also used to refer to any data-storage system.

data bases (library), computer accessible information files which usually contain bibliographic citations and abstracts that provide quick subject access to journal articles, conference papers, and other original sources. Most academic and some large public libraries provide access to data bases. Below is a representative list of data bases in many areas of public administration:

- *ABI/Inform* (August 1971-present), designed to meet the information needs of executives by covering all phases of business management and administration. Articles from approximately 200 U.S. and foreign journals, proceedings, and transactions are indexed and abstracted to provide information in the areas of accounting, decision sciences, finance, industrial relations, managerial economics, marketing, operations research, organization behavior, and public administration.
- *American Statics Index* (1973-present), a comprehensive index of the statistical publications from more than four-hundred central or regional issuing agencies of the U.S. Government; provides abstracts and indexing of all federal statistical publications, including non-GPO publications, which contain social, economic, demographic, or natural resources data.
- *BLS Consumer Price Index* (dates of coverage vary from record to record), contains time series of consumer price indexes calculated by the U.S. Bureau of Labor Statistics (BLS).
- *BLS Employment, Hours and Earnings* (dates of coverage vary from record to record), contains time series on employment, hours of work, and earnings information for the United States organized by industry. National, state, and local data are provided.
- *BLS Labor Force* (dates of coverage vary from record to record), contains time series on U.S. employment, unemployment, and non-participation in the labor force. The data are classified by a variety of demographic, social and economic characteristics.
- *CIS* (1970-present), the machine-readable form of the Congressional Information Service's *Index to Publications of the United States Congress. CIS* provides current, comprehensive access to the contents of the entire spectrum of Congressional working papers published by the nearly three-hundred House, Senate and Joint committees and subcommittees each year.
- *Comprehensive Dissertation Index*

(1861-present), a definitive subject, title, and author guide to virtually every American dissertation accepted at an accredited institution since 1861, when academic doctoral degrees were first granted in the United States.

- *Criminal Justice Periodicals Index* (1975-present), provides comprehensive cover-to-cover indexing of 120 administration of justice and law enforcement periodicals and journals.
- *Federal Index* (October 1976-present), provides coverage of such federal actions as proposed rules, regulations, bill introductions, speeches, hearings, roll calls, reports, vetoes, court decisions, executive orders, and contract awards. *The Washington Post* and federal documents such as the *Congressional Record, Federal Register,* and Presidential documents are indexed as well as other publications covering government activities.
- *Federal Register Abstracts* (March 1977-present), comprehensive coverage of federal regulatory agency actions as published in the *Federal Register,* the official U.S. Government publication of regulations, proposed rules, and legal notices.
- *Government Printing Office Monthly Catalog* (July 1976-present), contains records of reports, studies, fact sheets, maps, handbooks, conference proceedings, etc., issued by all U.S. federal government agencies, including the U.S. Congress. Included are records of all of the Senate and House hearings on private and public bills and laws.
- *Legal Resource Index* (1980-present), provides cover-to-cover indexing of over 660 law journals and five law newspapers plus legal monographs.
- *Magazine Index* (1976-present), covers over 370 popular magazines.
- *Management Contents* (September 1974-present), covers contents of two hundred business- and management-related journals.
- *National Newspaper Index* (1979-present), provides front page to back page indexing of *The Christian*

Science Monitor, The New York Times, and *The Wall Street Journal.*

- *National Criminal Justice Reference Service* (1972-present), covers all aspects of law enforcement and criminal justice.
- *National Technical Information Service* (1964-present), consists of government-sponsored research, development, and engineering plus analyses prepared by federal agencies, their contractors or grantees.
- *Newsearch* (current month only, daily updates), a daily index of more than two thousand news stories, information articles and book reviews from over fourteen hundred newspapers, magazines and periodicals. At the end of each month the magazine article data is transferred to the *Magazine Index* data base; the newspaper indexing data is transferred to the *National Newspaper Index* data base.
- *PAIS International* (1976-present), contains references to information in all fields of social science including political science, banking, public administration, international relations, economics, law, public policy, social welfare, sociology, education and social anthropology.
- *Social Scisearch* (1972-present), a multidisciplinary data base indexing every significant item from the one thousand most important social sciences journals throughout the world and social sciences articles selected from twenty-two hundred additional journals in the natural, physical, and biomedical sciences.
- *Sociological Abstracts* (1963-present), covers the world's literature in sociology and related disciplines in the social and behavioral sciences.
- *United States Political Science Documents* (1975-present), coverage includes such specific areas as foreign policy, international relations, behavioral sciences, public administration, economics, law and contemporary problems, world politics, and all areas of political science including theory and methodology.

datum, see DATA.

Davis, Keith (1918-), sometimes called "Mr. Human Relations" because his work marks the beginning of the modern view of human relations with its empirical approach to understanding organizational behavior. Major works include: *Human Relations in Business* (New York: McGraw-Hill, 1957); *Human Relations at Work* (New York: McGraw-Hill, 1962); *Business and Its Environment,* with R. L. Blomstron (New York: McGraw-Hill, 1966); *Human Behavior at Work* (New York: McGraw-Hill, 1977).

Davis-Bacon Act of 1931, also called PREVAILING WAGE LAW, federal law passed in 1931 which requires contractors on federal construction projects to pay the rates of pay and fringe benefits that prevail in their geographic areas. Prevailing rates are determined by the Secretary of Labor and must be paid on all federal contracts and subcontracts of $2,000.00 or more. For an economic analysis of the impact of the act, see Armand J. Thieblot, Jr. *et al., The Davis-Bacon Act* (Philadelphia: The Wharton School of the University of Pennsylvania, 1975). *Also see* Robert S. Goldfarb and John F. Morrall III, "The Davis-Bacon Act: An Appraisal of Recent Studies," *Industrial and Labor Relations Review* (January 1981).

Davis v. *Passman,* 442 U.S. 229 (1979), U.S. Supreme Court case which held that a woman discharged from employment by a U.S. congressman had the Fifth Amendment right to seek to recover damages from the congressman for alleged sex discrimination.
See also CONGRESSIONAL EXEMPTION.

day care, a newly emerging employee fringe benefit increasingly coming about because more than half of all mothers with children under six are now in the labor force. *See* Oscar Ornato and Carol Buckham, "Day Care: Still Waiting its Turn as a Standard Benefit," *Management Review* (May 1983); Sheila B. Kamerman, "Child-Care Services: A National Picture,"

Monthly Labor Review (December 1983); Sandra L. Burud, Pamela R. Aschbacher and Jacquelyn McCroskey, *Employer-Supported Child-Care: Investing in Human Resources* (Dover, Mass.: Auburn House Publishing Co., 1984); Thomas I. Miller, "The Effects of Employer-Sponsored Child Care on Employee Absenteeism, Turnover, Productivity, Recruitment or Job Satisfaction: What is Claimed and What is Known," *Personnel Psychology* (Summer 1984).

day wage, earnings for a set number of hours per day.

daywork, regular day shift that is paid on the basis of time rather than output.

day worker, casual, usually unskilled, worker hired by the day.

dead time, time on the job lost by a worker through no fault of his own.

dead work, mining term that refers to required work (removing debris, rocks, etc.) that does not directly produce the material being mined.

Dean v. *Gadsden Times Publishing Corp.,* 412 U.S. 543 (1973), Supreme Court case which upheld an Alabama law providing that an employee called to serve on a jury "shall be entitled to his usual compensation received from such employment less the fee or compensation he received for serving" as a juror.

death and gift taxes, taxes imposed on transfer of property at death, in contemplation of death, or as a gift.

death benefit, benefit provided under a pension plan that is paid to an employee's survivors or estate. Payments may be made in monthly installments or in a lump sum.

debt, general obligation, long-term full-faith-and-credit obligations other than those payable initially from nontax revenue. Includes debt payable in the first instance from particular earmarked taxes, such as motor fuel sales taxes or property taxes.

debt, nonguaranteed, long-term debt payable solely from pledged specific sources—e.g., from earnings of revenue-producing activities (university and college dormitories, toll highways and bridges, electric power projects, public building and school building authorities, etc.) or from specific nonproperty taxes. Includes only debt that does not constitute an obligation against any other resources if the pledged sources are insufficient.

debt financing, paying for government programs or capital improvements by borrowing.

Fiscal organizations have revenue options other than taxation. They can charge fees for service, run lotteries, or lease or sell public lands. While these and other tax alternatives can sweeten the revenue picture considerably, the major tax alternative is to borrow—to sell public bonds. Of course, there are constraints to borrowing. Many jurisdictions have fixed ceilings on the amount of debt they can incur. Various legal limitations exist regarding issuance and whether or not voter approval is necessary. Market limitations also exist in terms of how much money a jurisdiction can borrow; or conversely, how much of a bond issuance the public will buy. Certainly New York City will testify that distinct market limitations exist, regardless of how much interest you are willing to pay. Finally, there used to be, and supposedly still is, a political aversion to borrowing—a feeling that it is somehow a poor financial management practice.

While the federal debt presents one set of economic considerations, the mechanics of state and local government borrowing is of more administrative interest. For the most part, debt finance is tied to various forms of capital construction, such as buildings, highways, bridges, dams, and so on. The theoretical justification for such borrowing is that as future generations will benefit from such capital improvements, they should also have the privilege of sharing the financial burden.

State and local governments begin with a major advantage on the borrowing market. The interest paid on their bonds is tax exempt—a powerful incentive for purchase. Still, all state and local governments acquire a separate credit rating which determines in part the interest rate that must be paid. When a state, for example, wants to sell bonds, it will put out a request for bids from bond brokers who, once their bid is accepted, will sell the bond issue on the open market. Various types of bonds may be issued. Full-faith-and-credit bonds are the most secure in that the government entity guarantees the bond. Other types of bonds cascade down from this pinnacle. General-obligation bonds carry a pledge of repayment from the general revenues of the government. Special-tax or revenue bonds have repayment premised upon an earmarked special tax or a special revenue source.

Given the public's ever-present aversion to debt financing, many fiscal organizations have resorted to some imaginative new concepts for debt financing. Whether or not some of the practices constitute outright deceit or are in fact constructive responses to a very demanding political environment is debatable. To illustrate, it it useful to recount the tale of the uncrowned champion of debt financing—former New York governor Nelson A. Rockefeller.

In the Rockefeller gubernatorial period, the State of New York embarked on some unprecedented capital construction projects. It built scores of new college dormitories, office buildings, highways, bridges, hospitals, and the like. It did this without a voter referendum on bond issues because it never used the state's full-faith-and-credit bonding authority. Instead, it created special agencies or authorities such as one for state university building construction or the Mental Health Facility Construction Fund that took responsibility for capital construction projects. Special bonding agencies such as the Housing Finance Agency were set up that issued the bonds and borrowed the money to finance the project. The construction funds then turned over tuition payments or patient fees to repay the financing agency. The new buildings, in the meantime, were turned over to the appropriate agencies for operation.

Rockefeller's most ambitious single project was Empire State Plaza government center in Albany, the state capital. The project was financed by the County of Albany, which authorized thirty-year bonds for the construction. The state simply pays a yearly rent to the county for the use of the buildings. This rent equals the annual bond payment plus a 1 percent "fee." At the end of thirty years the county will turn the buildings over to the state permanently. The state got their government center, no voter approval was required, and the only extra costs to the public were the higher interest rates that must still be paid because the bonds could not offer the full faith and credit of the state. As much as 40 percent of all state and local bonds are not guaranteed and consequently have higher interest rates than would full-faith-and-credit bonds. *See* Lennox L. Moak, *Administration of Local Government Debt* (Chicago: Municipal Finance Officers' Association, 1970).

See also FEDERALISM, FISCAL, and PUBLIC FINANCE.

debt outstanding, all debt obligations remaining unpaid on the date specified.

debt service, regular payments of principal, interest, and other costs (such as insurance) made to pay off a financial obligation.

debugging, process of detecting, locating, and removing mistakes or imperfections from a computer program or any new system.

De Canas v. *Bica,* 424 U.S. 351 (1976), U.S. Supreme Court case which upheld a California statute penalizing those who employed illegal aliens when such employment decreased the employment of citizens and other aliens.

decentralization, *see* CENTRALIZATION.

decertification, *see* CERTIFICATION.

decile, division that contains one tenth of whatever is being divided.

decision analysis, a discipline for "systematic evaluation of alternative actions as a basis for choice among them," according to Rex V. Brown, Andrew S. Kahr and Cameron Peterson, *Decision Analysis: An Overview* (New York: Holt, Rinehart & Winston, 1974). *Also see* Howard Raiffa, *Decision Analysis* (Reading, Mass.: Addison-Wesley, 1968); E. S. Quade, *Analysis for Public Decisions* (New York: Elsevier, 1975); Jacob W. Ulvila and Rex V. Brown, "Decision Analysis Comes of Age," *Harvard Business Review* (September–October 1982).

decision-analysis forecasting (DAF), variant of the Delphi Technique developed by the U.S. Civil Service Commission to assist senior management in forecasting manpower and organizational needs. It is specifically designed for use on problems where the experience and judgments of top-level policymakers comprise the basic and often the only information.

DAF develops its forecasts by (1) "decomposing" each manpower planning problem into its relevant factors, (2) quantifying subjective preferences and probability judgments for each problem factor, and (3) combining the available data plus these quantified judgments into a table of predictions. The methodology draws largely on decision analysis theory, using "decision trees" and some simple mathematics from probability theory.

For the complete methodology, *see* Bureau of Executive Manpower, U.S. Civil Service Commission, *Decision Analysis Forecasting for Executive Manpower Planning* (Washington, D.C.: U.S. Government Printing Office, June 1974).

See also DELPHI TECHNIQUE.

decision-making, process of selecting the most desirable course of action from among alternatives. In a larger sense decision-making is the total process by which managers act to achieve organizational goals. *See* Herbert A. Simon, "Theories of Decision-Making in Economics and Behavioral Science," *American Economic Review* (June 1959); Martin Landau, "The Concept of Decision-Making in the Field of Public Administration" in S. Mailick and E. H. Van Ness, eds., *Concepts and Issues in Administrative Behavior* (Englewood Cliffs, N.J.: Prentice-Hall, 1962); David Braybrooke and Charles E. Lindblom, *A Strategy of Decision* (New York: Free Press, 1963); Theodore C. Sorensen, *Decision-Making in the White House* (New York: Columbia University Press, 1963); William J. Gore, *Administrative Decision-Making: A Heuristic Model* (New York: Wiley, 1964); William J. Gore and James W. Dyson, eds., *The Making of Decisions: A Reader in Administrative Behavior* (New York: The Free Press, 1964); Charles E. Lindblom, *The Intelligence of Democracy: Decision Making Through Mutual Adjustment* (New York: The Free Press, 1965); Herbert A. Simon, "Administrative Decision-Making," *Public Administration Review* (March 1965); Amitai Etzioni, "Mixed Scanning: A 'Third' Approach to Decision-Making," *Public Administration Review* (December 1967); Graham T. Allison, *Essence of Decision: Explaining the Cuban Missile Crisis* (Boston: Little, Brown & Co., 1971); Henry Mintzberg *et al.*, "The Structure of 'Unstructured' Decision Processes," *Administrative Science Quarterly* (June 1976); Charles A. Holloway, *Decision Making Under Uncertainty: Models and*

Henry Kissinger on Decision-making

I have seen it happen more often than not that when one asks for choices one is always given three: two absurd ones and the preferred one. And the experienced bureaucrat, which I am slowly becoming, can usually tell the preferred one because it is almost always the one that is typed in the middle.

Source: The New York Times Magazine (October 28, 1973), p. 93.

Choices (Englewood Cliffs, N.J.: Prentice-Hall, 1979); Robert A. Dunn and Kenneth D. Ramsing, *Management Science: A Practical Approach to Decision Making* (New York: Macmillan, 1981); Mark Funkhouser, "Current Issues in Legislative Decision Making," *Public Administration Review* (May–June 1984).

See also BUREAUCRATIC POLICYMAKING and POLICYMAKING.

decision-making, career or occupational, *see* CAREER DECISIONMAKING.

decision packages, mechanisms used in zero-base budgeting to look at the effects on programmatic resource requirements, products, and levels of performance of alternative levels of funding.

decision rule, any directive established to make decisions in the face of uncertainty. For example, a payroll office might be given a decision rule to deduct one hour's pay from an employee's wages for each lateness that exceeds ten minutes but is less than one hour.

decision table, a tabular presentation of the various factors associated with, as well as the decision options for, a given problem.

decision theory, a body of knowledge concerned with the nature and processes of decisionmaking. Decision theory abstracts given situations into a more structured problem which calls for the decision maker to deal with the situation by an objective judgment. Frequently dependent upon quantitative analysis, decision theory is also called *statistical decision theory* and *Bayesian decision theory.* Bayesian refers to Thomas Bayes (1702-1761), who provided a mathematical basis for probability inference. *See* John W. Boudreau, "Decision Theory Contributions to HRM Research and Practice," *Industrial Relations* (Spring 1984).

decision tree, graphic method of presenting various decisional alternatives so that the various risks, information needs, and courses of action are visually available to the decision maker. The various decisional alternatives are displayed in the form of a tree with nodes and branches. Each branch represents an alternative course of action or decision, which leads to a node which represents an event. Thus, a decision tree shows both the different courses of action available and their possible outcomes. According to John F. Magee, in "Decision Trees for Decision Making," *Harvard Business Review* (July–August 1964), making a decision tree requires management to:

1. identify the points of decision and alternatives available at each point;
2. identify the points of uncertainty and the type or range of alternative outcomes at each point;
3. estimate the values needed to make the analysis, especially the probabilities of different events or results of action and the costs and gains of various events and actions; and
4. analyze the alternative values to choose a course.

declining-block pricing, the pricing of a service (*e.g.*, electricity) so that its unit price decreases as the consumption level increases.

deconstitutionalization, tendency of the U.S. Supreme Court to refuse to hear cases even though they may involve constitutional questions.

decruitment, slang term for the process of recycling older middle- and top-level managers into lower-level, lower-paying positions. The concept was pioneered in Denmark, where some employers freeze promotions for managers at age fifty and start recruiting them at age sixty. *See* Yitzchak M. Shkop and Esther M. Shkop, "Job Modification as An Alternative to Retirement," *Personnel Journal* (July 1982).

deductible, the amount of loss or expense that must be incurred by an insured or otherwise covered individual before an insurer will assume any liability for all or part of the remaining cost of covered services.

Deductibles may be either fixed dollar amounts or the value of specified services (such as two days of hospital care or one physician visit).

deduction, any amount for any reason that is withheld from an employee's pay and credited toward a legitimate purpose, such as taxes, insurance, United Fund, etc.

default, failure to pay legal debts. *See* Richard Rose and B. Guy Peters, *Can Government Go Bankrupt?* (New York: Basic Books, 1978).

See also PUBLIC FINANCE.

**A 20th Century Fable
Is There Life After Default?**

Revenues plummeted and interest requirements mounted. It seemed only a matter of time. The precarious situation existed for nearly two years. Attempts were made to refinance the governmental bonds in an effort to relieve the financial strain. But it became increasingly difficult to convince new creditors to buy the bond issues. Although the refunding efforts were premised upon sufficient taxes to service the bonds at all times, the bonds themselves could not pledge the full faith and credit of the government. Many claimed default was inevitable. No assistance was forthcoming from the federal government. Finally, on March 1, the first of the major defaults on bond obligations occurred when the government could not make its regular interest payment.

How it came to this was less certain. Many claimed that the situation had been untenable from the start given the demographics of the area. Others assessed it as a miscalculation of revenue capacities balanced against an impulsive borrowing spree. One analysis noted that the jurisdiction's financial policy seemed designed to get along without paying enough taxes to cover its expenses. Every possible financial expedient was used in order to "get by." While the citizens had an apparent horror of paying interest they were neither willing to pay taxes sufficient to furnish the services that they demanded. In effect, they were "trying to follow a pay-as-you-go policy without paying." Other analysts were quick to note the impact of graft and corruption on the fiscal problem. It was easy to cite numerous examples of inefficiency, fraud, and outright thievery.

The legislative body was called into session and a Refunding Act was passed which reduced the bond interest rates by nearly 35% and extended their maturation dates.

These revised bonds were made full faith and credit obligations of the government. At the same time new constitutional amendments were passed that prohibited any increase in tax rates or future bond issues except by voter approval. Irate bondholders lost little time in filing a host of suits against the government. Several asked for receiverships of toll bridges so that their revenues could be exclusively used to pay off their bonds. The State Supreme Court rejected such requests. Undaunted, the bondholders appealed to the federal courts and began winning appeals. A receiver was actually appointed for one toll bridge.

The issue became even more acute when several state governments who held the jurisdiction's bonds for trust funds filed suit in federal court to compel the government to raise its taxes in order to pay off its obligations. When confronted with this pressure, a special session of the legislature agreed to pay off, in full, all interest on bonds held by state governments only. In the meantime the private bondholders continued their suits and by November 1 had obtained a federal injunction against disbursement of government funds for certain purposes. Finally, a federal court produced a landmark ruling which set a major precedent for future cases. The court found the refunding law unconstitutional and forbade the jurisdiction's treasurer from paying out funds to service the new bonds. The court held that if officials invade contractual rights guaranteed by the federal Constitution, they are bound by federal court remedies available to the injured parties.

Now the government was in total chaos. Its funds were tied up; the refunding law was void; and, it could not even service bonds at the new 35% less interest rate. Another legislative session was called. A second refunding law was passed. This time the bonds were given their old higher interest rates and a 10 year extension of their maturation dates. Certain revenue sources were legislatively earmarked to pay off interest obligations and a variety of tax increases were passed. While the government was operating, it was at a considerably reduced level. Taxpayer unhappiness was evident and new proposals for refunding and reducing taxes were being circulated. Almost needless to say—the government's credit rating was a shambles.

As our modern day fable comes to an end, the reader is asked to guess the identity of the jurisdiction that suffered this terrible fate. No, it is not New York City or Cleveland. But our fable is a true story. The events recounted above actually happened to the State of Arkansas in 1933, when it went "bankrupt" by excessive borrowing used to finance highways and the pensions of confederate civil war veterans and their de-

pendents. Caught up in the depths of the Depression, its falling revenues resulted in default of its debt. For further gory details, see B. U. Ratchford's *American State Debts* (Durham, N.C.: Duke University Press, 1941). Unlike the private sector, where a corporate default results in the end of the corporation and division of all remaining assets, fiscal organizations inevitably live on. There is life after default; but it is a hell of litigation.

Defense, Department of (DOD), federal agency responsible for providing the military forces needed to deter war and protect U.S. security. The major elements of these forces are the Army, Navy, Marine Corps, and Air Force, consisting of about two million men and women on active duty. Of these, some 475,000—including about 50,000 on ships at sea—are serving outside the United States. They are backed, in case of emergency, by the 2.5 million members of the reserve components. In addition, there are about one million civilian employees in the Defense Department.

Department of Defense
The Pentagon
Washington, D.C. 20301
(202) 545-6700

defensive program evaluation, see PROGRAM EVALUATION.

deferred annuity, annuity that does not start until after a specified period or until the annuitant reaches a specified age.

deferred compensation, withholding of a portion of current earnings until a later time, usually retirement, when the receiver would likely be in a lower income tax bracket. *See* George H. Cauble, "Deferred Compensation: An Employee Income and Tax Deferral Plan That is as Good as it Sounds," *Public Personnel Management* (Summer 1983).

deferred full vesting, pension plan that provides that an employee retains rights to accrued benefits if he or she is terminated after a specified age and/or after he or she completes a specified period of service in the organization.

deferred graded vesting, pension plan that provides that an employee acquires a right to a specified percentage of accrued benefits if and when he or she meets the participation requirements stipulated by the plan.

deferred life annuity, annuity that becomes effective at a specified future date. If death occurs before the specified date, no benefits are paid. Once the annuity has started, it continues only for the life of the insured.

deferred rating system, system used to fill most federal government positions at GS-9 and above and most scientific positions. There are no "standings" on one of these registers and no numerical score is assigned at time of application, since applications are not rated until specific vacancies become available. Candidates are rated and referred for appointment consideration on the basis of their relative qualifications for a particular position. The best qualified applicants will be placed at the top of the list of eligibles and will be referred to the agency for employment consideration on the basis of their qualifications and according to the laws regarding veterans' preference and appointment. The names of all other applicants will be returned to the register for possible consideration at a later time.

deferred wage increase, negotiated pay increase that does not become effective until a specified future date.

deficiency bill, also SUPPLEMENTAL BILL, bill carrying appropriations to supplement appropriations that have proved insufficient. Appropriations are normally made on the basis of estimates for a year, but conditions may arise that exhaust the appropriations before the end of the fiscal year.

deficit, amount by which a government's expenditures are exceeded by its revenues.

deficit financing, a situation in which a government's excess of outlays over receipts for a given period is financed primarily by borrowing from the public. *See* Robert Eisner and Paul J. Pieper, "How To Make Sense of the Deficit," *The Public Interest* (Winter 1985); Ali F. Darrat, "Inflation and the Federal Budget Deficits: Some Empirical Results," *Public Finance Quarterly* (April 1985).

defined benefit plan, a pension plan which includes a formula for calculating retirement benefits (such as a specified percent of earnings or flat dollar amount per year of service) and obligates the employer to provide the benefits so determined. Therefore, employer contributions are not fixed, but are whatever is needed, together with earnings of pension fund investments, to finance the required benefits.

defined contribution plan, a pension plan that obligates the employer to contribute money to a pension fund according to a formula (such as a specified percent of earnings). Benefits are not fixed, but depend on the amount of employer contributions and the earnings of pension fund investments.

deflation, *see* INFLATION.

DeFunis* v. *Odegaard, 416 U.S. 312 (1974), U.S. Supreme Court case concerning a white male who was denied admission to law school at the same time minority applicants with lesser academic credentials were accepted. DeFunis challenged the school's action on the grounds that it denied him equal protection of the laws in violation of the fourteenth amendment. He was successful in local court and was admitted. On appeal, the school won a reversal in the state supreme court. Nevertheless, DeFunis remained in law school pending further action by the U.S. Supreme Court. As the nation awaited a definitive resolution of the issue of reverse discrimination, the Supreme Court sought to avoid the problem. Since DeFunis had completed all but his last quarter of law school and was not in danger of being denied his diploma no matter what was decided, a majority of the justices seized upon this fact and declared that the case was consequently "moot"—that it was beyond the court's power to render decisions on hypothetical matters of only potential constitutional substance. *See* Allan P. Sindler, *Bakke, DeFunis, and Minority Admissions: The Quest for Equal Opportunity* (New York: Longman, 1978). *See also* the following entries:

REGENTS OF THE UNIVERSITY OF CALIFORNIA V. ALLEN BAKKE
REVERSE DISCRIMINATION
UNITED STEELWORKERS OF AMERICA V. WEBER, ET AL.

degrees, gradations used in the point-rating method of job evaluation to differentiate among job factors

dehiring, generally, any means of encouraging a marginal or unsatisfactory employee to quit as an alternative to being fired. This face-saving technique allows an organization to (1) avoid the distasteful aftermath of firing an employee, (2) avoid the implication that someone made a mistake in hiring the employee, (3) avoid the adverse effect of the public thinking that the organization is not a secure place in which to be employed, and (4) protect the feelings of the employee involved. *See* Lawrence L. Steinmetz, *Managing the Marginal and Unsatisfactory Performer* (Reading, Mass.: Addison-Wesley Publishing Company, 1969).

See also QUIT.

deinstitutionalization, removal of individuals from institutional settings and returning them to community life. *See* Steven P. Segal, "Community Care and Deinstitutionalization: A Review," *Social Work* (November 1979).

delegation, designating or appointing of a person with the power to act as one's representative or agent in specified matters. A delegation of authority in an organizational sense may be implied in statements of responsibility for functional entities or group endeavors but can also be documented by other methods. Certain delegations that are granted to a single individual may be restricted as to any further redelegations (*e.g.*, it could restrict a senior clerk from delegating some disagreeable task that clerk was responsible for to a junior clerk). Delegation of authority begins at the executive level and filters down through an organization to workers themselves who must have enough authority to make decisions called for in their daily tasks.

delegation of power, empowering one to act for another. The delegation of power from one branch of government to another and from one official to another is fundamental to our form of government. Article I, Section 8 of the Constitution enumerates the powers of Congress and then grants to Congress the power "To make all laws which shall be necessary and proper for carrying into Execution the foregoing Powers, and all other Powers vested by this Constitution in the Government of the United States, or in any Department or Officer thereof." But how explicit must such laws be? If Congress were to attempt to legislate in such a fashion so as to give complete direction to administrative officials, it would result in unworkable government. Every contingency would have to be anticipated in advance; the legislature would have to be expert in all phases of all policy areas. Moreover, changes in the nature of implementing statutes would have to be accomplished by new laws. The congressional workload would be crushing. Consequently, Congress typically avoids writing highly detailed legislation, preferring to state broad policy objectives and allowing administrators to choose the means of attaining them. While administrative discretion is clearly necessary, it can raise important constitutional questions. If the delegation is so broad as to allow administrators to exercise legislative power without congressional guidance or standards, then the requirements of the separation of powers may be breached. This issue is of great importance because Congress does tend to delegate important questions of public policy to administrative officials rather than come to grips with the questions itself. Excellent examples of this can be found in the areas of equal opportunity for minorities, women, and the handicapped. Certainly, the administratively chosen "means" of affirmative action have been more controversial and politicized than the legislatively enacted "end" of equal opportunity. *See* Sotirios A. Barber, *The Constitution and the Delegation of Congressional Power* (Chicago: University of Chicago Press, 1975); Benjamin Jones, "Public Employee Labor Arbitration and the Delegation of Governmental Powers," *State Government* (Spring 1978).

See also REGULATION.

Wholesale Delegations Become the Rule

In the next decade and a half, the Supreme Court all but abandoned the view exemplified in the 1935 decisions—that the courts must invalidate laws delegating power unless they contain limiting standards. The change in the judicial attitude was but a reflection in the field of administrative law of the deference toward the legislator in economic affairs which marked American public law at mid-century. Judges who upheld legislative interventions in the economic area, even in fields previously ruled beyond the scope of governmental authority, were bound to take a more lenient attitude toward delegations of power in the same area.

At the same time, the changed judicial attitude encouraged Congress and the state legislatures to make broader delegations to administrative agencies than had formerly been their wont. Wholesale delegations became the rule rather than the exception; the broad grants made during the later New Deal, World War II, and the Cold War period were all sustained by the courts. Even a statute such as the Communications Act of 1934, which limits the authority conferred on the Federal Communications Commission only by the requirement that the Commission act in the "public interest"—plainly no limitation at all—was sustained.

Bernard Schwartz, *The Law in America: A History* (New York: McGraw-Hill Book Co., 1974), p. 178.

---

delphi method, a procedure for forecasting specific technological and social events. Experts are asked to give their best judgment as to the probability of a specific event occurring. The results are collated and then returned to the original experts for their perusal along with an opportunity to revise their own predictions. Revised estimates with supporting arguments are then recorded and recirculated again and again; in theory, the feedback always narrows the range of answers. In the end, a group prophecy will have been arrived at without the possibility of distortion from face-to-face contact, leadership influences, or the pressures of group dynamics.

See Harold A. Linstone and Murray Turoff, eds., *The Delphi Method: Techniques and Applications* (Reading, Mass.: Addison-Wesley Publishing Co., 1975); John Rohrbaugh, "Improving the Quality of Group Judgment: Social Judgment

---

THE DELPHI TECHNIQUE:
A HYPOTHETICAL EXAMPLE

The figure below presents a hypothetical decision tree designed to predict the probability of an increase in staffing for an agency that is considering a new training office. The question of the new staff seems to hinge on whether or not the organization's budget is to be cut. In the example, the group of organizational influentials consists of twenty individuals who "vote" on one of four outcomes. But the final outcome shows that sixteen of twenty voters believe the training office will be established anyway. This Delphi exercise concludes that the probability of new training being established is .8—and the organization would do well to begin plans for staffing this new office.

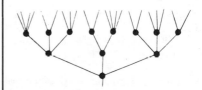

SOURCE: Adapted from John W. Vincent, *Decision Analysis Forecasting For Executive Manpower Planning* (Washington, D.C.: Bureau of Executive Manpower, U.S. Civil Service Commission, June 1974).

Analysis and the Delphi Technique," *Organizational Behavior and Human Performance* (August 1979); Gregory W. Fischer, "When Oracles Fail—A Comparison of Four Procedures for Aggregating Subjective Probability Forecasts," *Organizational Behavior and Human Performance* (August 1981).

de minimus, short form of *de minimus non curat lex*; Latin for "the law does not bother with trifles."

Demonstration Cities and Metropolitan Development Act of 1966, *see* MODEL CITIES PROGRAM.

demotion, reassignment of an employee to a job of lower status, responsibility, and pay. There are three basic kinds of demotions: (1) *voluntary demotion*, usually the result of a reduction in force; the employee takes a job of lower status and pay rather than being laid off; (2) *involuntary demotion*, resulting from a worker's inability to perform adequately on the job; (3) *disciplinary demotion*, which usually takes place after an employee has been repeatedly warned to stop some kind of misconduct or disruptive behavior. For the classic analysis of the problem, *see* F. H. Goldner, "Demotion in Industrial Management," *American Sociological Review* (October 1965). *Also see* Lynn Isabella and Douglas T. Hall, "Demotions and Career Growth," *Training and Development Journal* (April 1984).

dental plan, also called DENTAL INSURANCE, group insurance program, either contributory or noncontributory, that typically pays for some portion of the following dental services for an employee and his/her family:
1. diagnostic and preventive services (oral examinations and prophylaxis)
2. oral surgery
3. restorative services (fillings and inlays)
4. endodontic treatment (root canal therapy)
5. periodontic treatment (treatment of gums)
6. prosthodontic services (dentures and bridgework)
7. orthodontic services (straightening of teeth)

See Richard A. Harvey, "Designing a Corporate Dental Plan," *Compensation Review* (Third Quarter 1975).

See also SUPPLEMENTAL MEDICAL INSURANCE.

departmental seniority, also called UNIT SENIORITY, seniority based on years of service in a particular subsection of a larger organization as opposed to seniority based simply on total years of service to the larger organization, company, or governmental jurisdiction.

dependent variable, factor in an experimental relationship which has or shows variation that is hypothesized to be caused by another independent factor or variable.

depletion allowance, tax credit sometimes granted to owners of exhaustible natural resources.

depreciation, the systematic and rational allocation of the costs of equipment and buildings (having a life of more than one year) over their useful lives. To match costs with related revenues in measuring income or determining the costs of carrying out program activities, depreciation reflects the use of the asset(s) during specific operating periods.

deregulation, efforts to lift restrictions on business that have been imposed over the years by various government regulatory agencies. *See* Susan J. Tolchin and Martin Tolchin, *Dismantling America: The Rush to Deregulate* (Boston: Houghton Mifflin, 1983). *See also* REGULATION.

derivative violation, *see* UNFAIR LABOR PRACTICES (EMPLOYERS).

derived score, any test score that is obtained after some statistical treatment or manipulation of the raw score.

descriptive average, estimate of a mean based upon incomplete data.

desk audit, also called JOB AUDIT, review of the duties and responsibilities of a position through an interview with the incumbent and/or the incumbent's supervisor made at the employee's desk or regular place of work.

See also POSITION CLASSIFICATION.

detail, temporary assignment of a employee to a different position for a specified period with the assumption that the employee will return to "normal" duties at the end of the detail. Technically, a position cannot be "filled" by a detail, as the employee continues to be the incumbent of the position from which he was detailed.

Detroit Edison Company v. National Labor Relations Board, 440 U.S. 301 (1979), U.S. Supreme Court case which held that the NLRB could not order an employer to provide testing information to a union without the examinee's consent.

devaluation, the lowering of the value of a nation's currency in relation to gold, or to the currency of other countries, when this value is set by government intervention in the exchange market. Devaluation normally refers to fixed exchange rates. In a system of flexible rates, if the value of the currency falls, it is referred to as depreciation; if the value of the currency rises, it is referred to as appreciation.

development administration, see PUBLIC ADMINISTRATION, COMPARATIVE.

deviation, amount by which a score differs from a reference value such as the mean or the norm.

dexterity test, also called PSYCHOMOTOR TEST, any testing device that seeks to determine the motor/mechanical skills of an individual.

DHHS, see HEALTH and HUMAN SERVICES, DEPARTMENT OF.

diagnostic test, any testing device that is primarily designed to identify the nature and/or source of an individual's disabilities.

dialectical organization, postbureaucratic form of organization designed to be responsive to clientele needs; *dialectical* refers to the permanent state of tension between the tendency toward bureaucratization and the tendency toward responsiveness to clients, a tension the organization uses to continually renew itself. *See* Orin F. White, Jr., "The Dialectical Organization: An Alternative to Bureaucracy," *Public Administration Review* (January–February 1969).

Dickson, William J. (1904–), chief of the Employee Relations Research Department at the Hawthorne Works of the Western Electric Company during the famous Hawthorne experiments. As such, he collaborated with the Harvard research group led by Elton Mayo. He was co-author, with F. J. Roethlisberger, of the definitive account of the experiments, *Management and the Worker* (Cambridge, Mass.: Harvard University Press, 1939). He also wrote, again with Roethlisberger, *Counseling in An Organization* (Cambridge, Mass.: Harvard University Press, 1966).

dicta, in its most common usage, that portion of the opinion of a judge that is not the essence of the judge's decision. In the context of arbitration, dicta becomes any opinion or recommendation an arbitrator expresses in making an award that is not necessarily essential to the resolution of the dispute. According to Anthony V. Sinicropi and Peter A. Veglahn, in "Dicta in Arbitration Awards: An Aid or Hindrance?" *Labor Law Journal* (September 1972),

> by using dicta, the arbitrator can clarify obligations of the parties in their collective bargaining relationship. Conversely, the arbitrator may upset a mutually acceptable understanding by the parties with his gratuitous advice on an issue. Dicta can either strengthen and stabilize a collective bargaining relationship or emasculate that relationship. Obviously, the parties are free to disregard the arbitrator's views as expressed in dicta.

Dictionary of Occupational Titles (DOT), an outgrowth of the needs of the public employment service system for a comprehensive body of standardized occupational information for purposes of job placement, employment counseling, and occupational career guidance. Now in its fourth edition, the DOT includes standardized and comprehensive descriptions of job duties and related information for twenty thousand occupations, covers nearly all jobs in the U.S. economy, groups occupations into a systematic occupational classification structure based on interrelationships of job tasks and requirements, and is designed as a job placement tool to facilitate matching job requirements and worker skills. *See* Employment and Training Administration, U.S. Department of Labor, *Dictionary of Occupational Titles,* 4th ed. (Washington, D.C.: Government Printing Office, 1977). *Also see* Ann R. Miller et al., *Work, Jobs, and Occupations: A Critical Review of the Dictionary of Occupational Titles* (Washington, D.C.: National Academy Press, 1980); Pamela S. Cain and Donald J. Treiman, "The Dictionary of Occupational Titles as a Source of Occupational Data," *American Sociological Review* (June 1981).

See also UNITED STATES EMPLOYMENT SERVICES.

differential, displacement, see DISPLACEMENT DIFFERENTIAL.

differential piece work, also DIFFERENTIAL PIECE RATE, wage program in which the money rate per piece is determined by the total number of pieces produced over a time period—usually a day.

See also TAYLOR DIFFERENTIAL PIECE-RATE PLAN.

differentials, increases in wage rates because of shift work or other conditions generally considered to be undesirable. *See* Graef S. Crystal, "The Re-emergence of Industry Pay Differentials," *Compensation Review* (Third Quarter 1983).

See also the following entries:
    NIGHT DIFFERENTIAL
    SKILL DIFFERENTIAL
    WAGE DIFFERENTIAL

differential user charge, any user charge scaled to meet the requirements of different kinds of customers, levels of usage, time or season of use, etc.

differential validation, also called DIFFERENTIAL PREDICTION, assumption which holds that different tests or test scores might predict differently for different groups. Some social groups, because of a variety of sociological factors, tend to score lower (higher) than other groups on the same test.

difficulty index, any of a variety of indexes used to indicate the difficulty of a test question. The percent of some specified group, such as students of a given age or grade, who answer an item correctly is an example of such an index.

diffusion index, a statistical measure of the overall behavior of a group of economic time series. It indicates the percentage of series expanding in the selected group. If one half of the series in the group are rising over a given time span, the diffusion index value equals 50. The limits of a diffusion index are 0 and 100. As an analytical measure, the diffusion index is helpful in indicating the spread of economic movements from one industry to another and from one economic process to another.

diffusion theory of taxation, assertion that the real burden of an increase in taxes of any kind is eventually distributed throughout the population because of price changes.

Dillon's Rule, criteria developed by state courts to determine the nature and extent of powers granted to municipal corporations. It is a very strict and limiting rule, stating that municipal corporations have only those powers (1) expressly granted in the charter, (2) necessarily or fairly implied by or incidental to the express powers, and (3) essential to the declared purposes of the corporation. "Any fair, reasonable, substantial doubt" about a power is to result in denying that power to the corporation. The rule was formulated by John F. Dillon in his *Commentaries on the Law of Municipal Corporations,* 5th ed. (Boston: Little, Brown, 1911). In some states the rule has been relaxed, especially in dealing with home rule cities.

See also HOME RULE and MUNICIPAL CORPORATION.

diminishing marginal utility of income, also ABILITY TO PAY PRINCIPLE OF TAXATION, the principle that suggests that the marginal value of an additional dollar of income to a rich person is less than to a poor person. This concept is a mainstay of progressive taxation because it suggests that graduated income taxes will have less of a negative effect on wealthier members of the community than on those with less wealth. Proportionally larger tax payments by those with higher incomes recognizes the diminishing marginal utility of income. *See* Walter J. Blum and Harry Kalven, Jr., *The Uneasy Case for Progressive Income Taxation* (Chicago: University of Chicago Press, 1953), and Joseph Pechman, *Federal Tax Policy* (Washington, D.C.: The Brookings Institution, 1971).

directed interview, also NONDIRECTIVE INTERVIEW, *interview* where the interviewer has full control of the interview content, typically soliciting answers to a variety of specific questions. In the *nondirective interview,* in contrast, it is more the responsibility of the interviewee to determine the subjects to be discussed.

direct labor, also INDIRECT LABOR, work performed on a product that is a specific contribution to its completion. *Indirect labor* consists of all overhead and support activities that do not contribute directly to the completion of a product. *See* Robert V. Penfield, "A Guide to the Computation and Evaluation of Direct Labor Costs," *Personnel Journal* (June 1976).

director of personnel, *see* PERSONNEL DIRECTOR.

direct relief, *see* RELIEF.

direct tax, also INDIRECT TAX. A direct tax (e.g., an income tax) is paid to a government directly by a taxpayer. An indirect tax (e.g., a sales tax) is paid to a third party who in turn pays it to a government.

disability, also called WORK DISABILITY, according to Sar A. Levitan and Robert Taggart, *Jobs for the Disabled* (Baltimore: Johns Hopkins University Press, 1977), "There are essentially two interrelated dimensions of work disability: the presence or perception of physical or mental handicaps and a reduced work capacity." *See* Robert B. Nathanson, "The Disabled Employee: Separating Myth from Fact," *Harvard Business Review* (May–June 1977); Robert B. Nathanson and Jeffrey Lambert, "Integrating Disabled Employees into the Workplace," *Personnel Journal* (February 1981); Nancy J. Schweitzer and John Deely, "Interviewing the Disabled Job Applicant," *Personnel Journal* (March 1982).

Also see HANDICAPPED.

disability insurance, insurance designed to compensate individuals who lose wages because of illness or injuries.

disability retirement, retirement caused by a physical inability to perform on the job.

disabled veteran, veteran of the armed services who has a service-connected disability and is rated 10 percent or more disabled by the Veterans Administration. Disabled veterans generally have the right to a 10-point bonus on federal government entrance examinations. Many state and local governments offer similar advantages.

See also VETERANS PREFERENCE.

disadvantaged, culturally, *see* CULTURALLY DISADVANTAGED.

disadvantaged workers, usually denotes unemployed or underemployed workers who are either members of a minority group, handicapped, or over forty-five years of age. They tend to have lower education rates and higher criminal-arrest rates than the rest of the population. *See* Lloyd Zimpel, ed., *The Disadvantaged Worker: Readings in Developing Minority Manpower* (Reading, Mass.: Addison-Wesley, 1971); James L. Koch, "Employing the Disadvantaged: Lessons from the Past Decade," *California Management Review* (Fall 1974); Daphne Williams Nitri, "Training the Economically Disadvantaged," *Training and Development Journal* (September 1980); Robert H. Haveman & John L. Palmer, eds., *Jobs for Disadvantaged Workers: The Economics of Employment Subsidies* (Washington, D.C.: The Brookings Institution, 1982).

disaffiliation, withdrawal of a local union from its national or international union membership or the withdrawal of a national or international union from its federation membership. When a federation or national union initiates disaffiliation, the process is more properly called suspension or expulsion.

disbursements, payments. In budgetary usage, gross disbursements represent the amount of checks issued, cash, or other payments made less refunds received. Net disbursements represent gross disbursements less income collected and credited to the appropriation or fund account, such as amounts received for goods and services provided.

discharge, *see* DISMISSAL.

discharge, discriminatory, *see* DISCRIMINATORY DISCHARGE.

discharge warning, formal notice to an employee that he or she will be discharged if unsatisfactory work behavior continues.

disciplinary action, any action short of dismissal taken by an employer against an employee for a violation of organizational policy. *See* Walter E. Baer, *Discipline and Discharge Under the Labor Agreement* (New York: American Management Associations, 1972); Edward L. Harrison, "Legal Restrictions on the Employer's Author-

ity to Discipline," *Personnel Journal* (February 1982); Ira G. Asherman, "The Corrective Discipline Process," *Personnel Journal* (July 1982); Dan Cameron, "The When, Why and How of Discipline," *Personnel Journal* (July 1984).

See also ADVERSE ACTION and NATIONAL LABOR RELATIONS BOARD V. J. WEINGARTEN, INC.

disciplinary demotion, *see* DEMOTION.

disciplinary fine, fine that a union may levy against a member for violating a provision of the union's bylaws. *See* Dell Bush Johannesen, "Disciplinary Fines as Interference with Protected Rights: Section 8(6)(1) (A)," *Labor Law Journal* (May 1973).

disciplinary layoff, suspension of an employee as punishment for violating some rule or policy.

discipline, *see* the following entries:
ADMONITION
ADVERSE ACTION
DISCIPLINARY ACTION
PREVENTIVE DISCIPLINE
PROGRESSIVE DISCIPLINE
REPRIMAND
SLIDE-RULE DISCIPLINE

discipline clause, provision of a collective bargaining agreement that stipulates the means for disciplining workers who violate management or union rules.

discount rate, the interest rate that a commercial bank pays when it borrows from a Federal Reserve Bank. The discount rate is one of the tools of monetary policy used by the Federal Reserve System. The Federal Reserve customarily raises or lowers the discount rate to signal a shift toward restraining or easing its money and credit policy.

discouraged workers, also called HIDDEN UNEMPLOYED, persons who want to work but are not seeking employment because of a belief that such an effort would be fruitless. For analyses, *see* Paul O. Flaim, "Dis-

Discrimination

When last worked and reason for leaving last job	1979	1980	1981	1982	1983
Discouraged workers by when last worked and, for those who worked the previous year, reasons for leaving last job, 1979–83 (Numbers in thousands)					
Total	766	993	1,103	1,567	1,641
Never worked	101	155	141	223	229
Last worked more than 5 years ago	158	217	221	339	332
Last worked 1 to 5 years ago	251	288	366	536	625
Worked last year	255	334	375	469	454
Left job because of					
School family	40	54	63	62	57
Health	16	10	15	12	10
Retirement	8	8	11	17	16
Economic problems	125	180	202	268	280
Other reasons	67	82	83	109	92

Source: Paul O. Flaim, "Discouraged Workers: How Strong Are Their Links to the Job Market?" Monthly Labor Review *(August 1983).*

couraged Workers and Changes in Unemployment," *Monthly Labor Review* (March 1973); Joseph L. Gastwirth, "Estimating the Number of 'Hidden Unemployed'," *Monthly Labor Review* (March 1973); T. Aldrich Finegan, "Discourged Workers and Economic Fluctuations," *Industrial and Labor Relations Review* (October 1981); Donald R. Williams, "Young Discouraged Workers: Racial Differences Explored," *Monthly Labor Review* (June 1984).

discretionary function, *see* MINISTERIAL FUNCTION.

discretionary grant, *see* GRANT.

discriminant validity, evidence that a measure of a construct is indeed measuring that construct.

discrimination, in the context of employment, the failure to treat equals equally. Whether deliberate or unintentional, any action that has the effect of limiting employment and advancement opportunities because of an individual's sex, race, color, age, national origin, religion, physical handicap, or other irrelevant criterion is discrimination. Because of the EEO and civil rights legislation of recent years, individuals aggrieved by unlawful discrimination now have a variety of administrative and judicial remedies open to them. Employment discrimination has its origins in the less genteel concept of bigotry. For the standard history, *see* Gustavus Myers, *History of Bigotry in the United States,* edited and revised by Henry M. Christman (New York: Capricorn Books, 1943, 1960). *Also see* William P. Murphy, Julius G. Getman and James E. Jones, Jr., *Discrimination in Employment,* 4th ed. (Washington, D.C.: Bureau of National Affairs, Inc., 1979).

See also the following entries:
AGE DISCRIMINATION
CIVIL RIGHTS ACT OF 1964
EQUAL EMPLOYMENT OPPORTUNITY
EQUAL EMPLOYMENT OPPORTUNITY ACT OF 1972
IMPACT THEORY OF DISCRIMINATION
INTERNATIONAL BROTHERHOOD OF TEAMSTERS V. UNITED STATES
MCDONNELL DOUGLAS CORP. V. GREEN
NATIONAL ORIGIN DISCRIMINATION
RELIGIOUS DISCRIMINATION
REVERSE DISCRIMINATION
RIGHTFUL PLACE
SEX DISCRIMINATION
SYSTEMIC DISCRIMINATION
THIRD-PARTY ALLEGATIONS OF DISCRIMINATION
UNFAIR LABOR PRACTICES (EMPLOYERS)

UNFAIR LABOR PRACTICES (UNIONS)
WASHINGTON V. DAVIS

discrimination index, any of a variety of indexes used to indicate the extent to which a test item differentiates among examinees with respect to some criterion (such as the test as a whole).

discriminatory discharge, dismissal of an employee for union activity. This is an unfair labor practice.

dishonest graft, see HONEST GRAFT.

dismissal, also called DISCHARGE, management's removal of an employee from employment. *See* Robert W. Fisher, "When Workers Are Discharged—An Overview: A Special Report on the Handling of Dismissal Cases in U.S. Law, Contract and Custom," *Monthly Labor Review* (June 1973); Erwin S. Stanton, "The Discharged Employee and the EEO Laws," *Personnel Journal* (March 1976); Clyde W. Summers, "Protecting *All* Employees Against Unjust Dismissal," *Harvard Business Review* (January–February 1980); Frederick Brown, "Limiting Your Risks in the New Russian Roulette—Discharging Employees," *Employee Relations Law Journal* (Winter 1982-83); Gail Frommer Brod, "The NLRB Changes Its Policy on the Legality of an Employer's Discharge of a Disloyal Supervisor," *Labor Law Journal* (January 1983); Larry D. Farley and Joseph J. Allotta, "Standards of Proof in Discharge Arbitration: A Practitioner's View," *Labor Law Journal* (July 1984).
See also the following entries:
BISHOP V. WOOD
CODD V. VELGER
BOARD OF REGENTS V. ROTH
GARRITY V. NEW JERSEY
HINES V. ANCHOR MOTOR FREIGHT
MYERS V. UNITED STATES
NORTON V. MACY
MCDONALD V. CITY OF WEST
  BRANCH, MICHIGAN
SAMPSON V. MURRAY
UNFAIR LABOR PRACTICES
  (EMPLOYERS)

dismissal pay, see SEVERANCE PAY.

disparate effect, tendency of an employment screening device or criteria to limit the appointment opportunities of women and minorities at a greater rate than for non-minority males.

displaced employee, employee of the federal government who is serving or who last served under career or career-conditional appointment or an employee with competitive status who is serving or who last served with Group I or Group II tenure in an excepted position, when (1) the employee has received a reduction-in-force notice and the employing agency determines that he or she cannot be placed on another position in his or her competitive area; (2) the employee declines to transfer within his or her function, or to accept a new assignment to another commuting area, and the employing agency determines that he or she will not be placed in another position in his or her own commuting area; (3) the employee is receiving compensation for injuries (under subchapter 1, chapter 81, of title 5, U.S. Code); or (4) the employee is under age sixty and is a recovered disability annuitant or a disability annuitant restored to earning capacity. Federal civil service regulations require agencies to have in operation a positive program of placement assistance for their displaced employees.
See also GROUP I TENURE/GROUP II TENURE/GROUP III TENURE.

displaced homemaker, usually a woman who has been caring for a family and has lost her means of support through divorce, separation, death, or the disabling of a spouse and has only the briefest work experience outside the home. *See* Tish Sommers and Laurie Shields, "Displaced Homemakers: 'Forced Retirement' Leaves Many Penniless," *Civil Rights Digest* (Winter 1978); Nancy C. Baker, *New Lives for Former Wives: Displaced Homemakers* (Garden City, N.Y.: Doubleday, 1980); Laurie Shields, *Displaced Homemakers: Organizing for a New Life* (New York: McGraw-Hill, 1980); Eileen Applebaum, *Back to Work: Determinants of Women's Successful Re-entry* (Boston,

Mass.: Auburn House Publishing Co., 1981).

displacement differential, compensation equal to the difference between an employee's regular pay and the rate of a temporary assignment caused by layoff or technological displacement. Such differentials are usually available only for a limited time.

disposable personal income, personal income less personal taxes and nontax payments to governments. It is the income available to persons for consumption or saving.

distractors, also called FOILS, in multiple-choice examinations, the incorrect alternatives which serve the function of being distractors.

distribution, bimodal, see BIMODAL DISTRIBUTION

district, subdivision of many different types of areas (such as countries, states, or counties) for judicial, political or administrative purposes. *Districting* is the process of drawing a district's boundary lines for purposes of apportionment.

district council, a level of labor organization below the national union but above the locals. The district council is composed of local unions in a particular industry within a limited geographic area.

district court, also called FEDERAL DISTRICT COURT and U.S. DISTRICT COURT, court of original jurisdiction for most federal cases. This is the only federal court that holds trials where juries and witnesses are used. Each state has at least one district court. When equal employment opportunity problems cannot be resolved within an organization, they frequently spill over into the local federal district court.

Altogether there are eighty-nine district courts in the fifty states, plus the one in the District of Columbia. In addition, the Commonwealth of Puerto Rico has a United States district court with jurisdiction corresponding to that of district courts in the various states.

At present, each district court has from one to twenty-seven federal district judgeships, depending upon the amount of judicial work within its territory. In districts with more than one judge, the judge senior in commission who has not reached his seventieth birthday acts as the chief judge. There are altogether 485 permanent district judgeships in the fifty states and fifteen in the District of Columbia. There are seven district judgeships in Puerto Rico.

districting, see DISTRICT.

division of labor, also called FACTORY SYSTEM, production process that has individual workers specializing in the varying aspects of a larger task. The most famous and influential statement on the economic rationale of the factory system is found in Adam Smith's *The Wealth of Nations* (1776). Smith discusses the optimum organization of a pin factory and finds that while traditional pin makers could produce a few dozen pins a day, pin workers organized in a factory with each performing a limited operation could produce tens of thousands a day. *See* Charles F. Sabel, *Work and Politics: The Division of Labor in Industry* (New York: Cambridge University Press, 1982).

dock, deduct a part of an employee's wages as a penalty for tardiness, absenteeism, breakage, etc.

doctrine, legal principle or rule.

doctrine of mutuality, according to Julius Rezler and S. John Insalata, "Doctrine of Mutuality: A Driving Force in American Labor Legislation," *Labor Law Journal* (May 1967),

doctrine that basically contends that whenever a legal burden or restriction is imposed by a legislative act on a party to industrial relations, either the same burden or restriction should be imposed upon the other party or the restriction should be removed from the first party, too. The doctrine also implies that whenever a right or privilege is conferred by a legislative act on one of the parties, the same right or privilege should be conferred on the other party or be withdrawn from the first party, too.

document and stock transfer taxes, taxes on the recording, registering, and transfer of documents such as mortgages, deeds, and securities.
See also TAXATION.

DOD, *see* DEFENSE, DEPARTMENT OF.

DOE, *see* (1) EDUCATION, DEPARTMENT OF and (2) ENERGY, DEPARTMENT OF.

do gooders, also GOO-GOOs, derisive terms for social and political reformers. "Goo-Goos" stood for "good government."

DOI, *see* INTERIOR, DEPARTMENT OF THE.

DOL, *see* LABOR, DEPARTMENT OF.

Domestic Council, also DOMESTIC POLICY STAFF, president's primary advisors on domestic issues. In 1970 President Nixon established the Domestic Council, a nineteen-member body, "as a domestic counterpart to the National Security Council." In 1977 President Carter supplanted it with the Domestic Policy Staff. The primary change has been in title. *See* Raymond J. Waldman, "The Domestic Council: Innovation in Presidential Government," *Public Administration Review* (May–June 1976); Ronald C. Moe, "The Domestic Council in Perspective," *The Bureaucrat* (October 1976); and John Helmer and Louis Maisel, "Analytical Problems in the Study of Presidential Advice: The Domestic Council Staff in Flux," *Presidential Studies Quarterly* (Winter 1978).

domicile, an individual's permanent legal residence. While an individual can legally have many residences, he or she can have only one domicile. Some government jurisdictions have residency requirements that require employees to be domiciled within the bounds of the jurisdiction. *See*

Stephen L. Hayford, "Local Government Residency Requirements and Labor Relations: Implications and Choices for Public Administrators," *Public Administration Review* (September–October, 1978).
See also MCCARTHY V. PHILADELPHIA CIVIL SERVICE COMMISSION.

Dorchy v. Kansas, 272 U.S. 306 (1926), U.S. Supreme Court case which held that there is no constitutional right to strike.

DOT, *see* (1) DICTIONARY OF OCCUPATIONAL TITLES and (2) TRANSPORTATION, DEPARTMENT OF.

Dothard v. Rawlinson, 433 U.S. 321 (1977), U.S. Supreme Court case which upheld an Alabama regulation that prohibits the employment of women as prison guards in "contact positions" (requiring continual close physical proximity to inmates) within the state's correctional facilities.
See also BONA FIDE OCCUPATIONAL QUALIFICATION.

dotted-line responsibility, a customer's obligations after signing. Where? On the "dotted line." Or an obligation that organizational members have to consult with, but not report to, each other. This is reflective of the "dotted line" connections that exist on organization charts.

double-dipper, one of the hundred thousand retired military personnel who are employed by the federal government as civilian workers. Because they draw two government incomes, they are colloquially called double-dippers. The term is sometimes applied, with an intentional or unintentional lack of precision, to state and local government employees—even to elected officials—who also hold private sector jobs while occupying what are or are held to be full time positions. More recently the term has been applied to civil service pensioners who also become eligible for social security retirement benefits. *See* Robert Dalrymple, Susan Grad and Duke Wilson, "Civil Service Retirement System Annuitants and Social Security," *Social*

Security Bulletin (February 1983).
See also DUAL COMPENSATION ACT OF 1964.

double entry, method of bookkeeping that shows each transaction as both a debit and a credit by using both horizontal rows and vertical columns of numbers. The totals of the rows and columns should always be the same. This makes it easier to find out where mistakes are than if the records were kept with only one "entry" for each item.

double indemnity, *see* ACCIDENTAL DEATH BENEFIT.

double taxation, either the illegal imposition of two taxes on the same property by the same government during the same time period for the same purpose, or any time the same money is taxed twice. A *legal* form of *double taxation* is taxing a corporation on its profits, then taxing its stockholders on their dividends from the corporation. *See* Charles K. Coe, "Double Taxation: Identifying the Hidden Tax Burden in America's Cities," *Urban Affairs Quarterly* (December 1983).

double time, penalty or premium rate of pay for overtime work, for holiday or Sunday work, etc., amounting to twice the employee's regular hourly wage.

downgrading, reassignment of an employee to a position having a lower rate of pay and/or lesser responsibilities.

Downs, Anthony (1930-), economist and policy analyst whose classic book on bureaucracy, *Inside Bureaucracy* (Boston: Little, Brown, 1967), sought to justify bureaucratic government on economic grounds and develop laws and propositions that would aid in predicting the behavior of bureaus and bureaucrats. Other major works include: *An Economic Theory of Democracy* (New York: Harper & Bros., 1957); *Urban Problems and Prospects* (Chicago: Markham, 1970); *Federal Housing Subsidies: How Are They Working* (Lexington, Mass.: Lexington Books, 1973); and *Opening Up The*

Suburbs (New Haven, Conn.: Yale University Press, 1973).
See also BUREAUCRACY and ISSUE ATTENTION CYCLE.

down time, periods of inactivity while waiting for the repair, setup or adjustment of equipment.

down-time pay, payments for time spent idle because of equipment failures (or routine maintenance) that are clearly beyond the responsibility of the employee.

draft registration, *see* ROSTKER V. GOLDBERG.

dramaturgy, manner in which an individual acts out or theatrically stages his or her organizational role. All organization members are involved in such impression management, as Victor A. Thompson, in *Modern Organization* (New York: Alfred A. Knopf, 1961), indicates:

> We must try to control the information or cues imparted to others in order to protect our representations of self and to control the impressions others form about us. We are all involved, therefore, in dramaturgy.

Dror, Yehezkel (1928-), a leading proponent of a more rational approach to policy formulation and evaluation. Dror advocates an optimal approach to policy making that seeks out the best possible policy, regardless of the past. Dror is a major critic of incremental approaches to policymaking. Major works include: "Policy Analysts: A New Professional Role in Government Service," *Public Administration Review* (September 1967); *Public Policymaking Reexamined* (Scranton, Pa.: Chandler Co., 1968); "Prolegomena to the Policy Sciences," *Policy Sciences* (September 1970); *Design for Policy Sciences* (New York: American Elsevier, 1971); and *Ventures in Policy Sciences* (New York: American Elsevier, 1971).

Drucker, Peter F. (1909-), the preeminent philosopher of management, the world's best-selling management author, and the man usually credited with having invented "management by objectives." Major works include: *The Concept of the Corporation* (New York: John Day Co., 1946); *The New Society* (New York: Harper & Row, 1950); *The Practice of Management* (New York: Harper & Row, 1954); *Managing for Results* (New York: Harper & Row, 1964); *The Effective Executive* (New York: Harper & Row, 1967); *The Age of Discontinuity* (New York: Harper & Row, 1969); *Management: Tasks, Responsibilities, Practices* (New York: Harper & Row, 1974). For a biography, *see* John J. Tarrant, *Drucker: The Man Who Invented Corporate Society* (New York: Warner Books, 1976). *Also see* Alan M. Kantrow, "Why Read Peter Drucker?" *Harvard Business Review* (January–February 1980).

See also the following entries:
KNOWLEDGE WORKER
MANAGEMENT BY OBJECTIVES
PENSION FUND SOCIALISM

drug addiction, also DRUG ABUSE, any habitual use of a substance which leads to psychological and/or physiological dependence. *Drug abuse* consists of using drugs to one's physical, emotional and/or social detriment without being "formally" addicted. For the dimensions of the problem, *see* Pasquale A. Carone and Leonard W. Krinsky, eds., *Drug Abuse in Industry* (Springfield, Ill.: Charles C. Thomas Publishers, 1973); Rolf E. Rogers and John T. C. Colbert, "Drug Abuse and Organizational Response: A Review and Evaluation," *Personnel Journal* (May 1975); Ken Jennings, "The Problem of Employee Drug Use and Remedial Alternatives," *Personnel Journal* (November 1977); Peter A Susser, "Legal Issues Raised by Drugs in the Workplace," *Labor Law Journal* (January 1985). For how drug abuse cases have been handled in arbitration, *see* Kenneth Jennings, "Arbitrators and Drugs," *Personnel Journal* (October 1976). For the public employer's perspective, *see* George W. Noblit, Paul H. Radtke, and James G. Ross, *Drug Use and Public Employment: A Personnel Manual* (Chicago: International Personnel Management Association, 1975).

dry promotion, slang term for a promotion that offers an increase in status but no monetary increase.

dual-career couple, a husband and wife pursuing professional careers that both feel are equally important. This has important implications for recruitment and transfer policies: for example, one spouse may be unwilling to accept a move unless an appropriate job is also found for the other. *See* Francine S. Hall and Douglas T. Hall, *The Two-Career Couple* (Reading, Mass.: Addison-Wesley, 1979); Carole K. Holahan and Lucia A. Gilbert, "Conflict Between Major Life Roles: Women and Men in Dual-Career Couples," *Human Relations* (June 1979); Richard E. Kopelman, Lyn Rosenweig and Laura H. Lally, "Dual-Career Couples: The Organizational Response," *Personnel Administrator* (September 1982); Howard Hayghe, "Married Couples: Work and Income Patterns," *Monthly Labor Review* (December 1983); Maria Helene Sekas, "Dual-Career Couples—A Corporate Challenge," *Personnel Administrator* (April 1984); Patricia A. Mathews, "The Changing Work Force: Dual-Career Couples and Relocation," *Personnel Administrator* (April 1984).

Dual Compensation Act of 1964, (Public Law 88–448), law that provides that civilian employees of the federal government shall not be entitled to receive basic compensation from more than one civilian office for more than an aggregate of forty hours of work in any one calendar week (Sunday through Saturday). The act also contains a variety of exemptions.
See also DOUBLE-DIPPER.

dual federalism, *see* FEDERALISM, DUAL.

dual ladder, also called PARALLEL LADDER, a variant of a career ladder, provides dual or parallel career hierarchies so that both professional and managerial employees will be afforded appropriate career advancement. *See* Bertram Schoner and Thomas Harrell, "The Questionable Dual Ladder," *Personnel* (January-February 1965); Fred Goldner and R. R. Ritti, "Professionalism as Career Immobility," *American Journal of Sociology* (March 1967); Carl L. Bellas, "The Dual Track Career System within the Internal Revenue Service," *Public Personnel Management* (September-October 1972).

dual unionism, situation where two rival unions claim the right to organize workers in a particular industry or locality.

due process, U.S. Constitution requirement that "no person shall be deprived of life, liberty, or property without due process of law." While the specific requirements of due process vary with new Supreme Court decisions, the essence of the idea is that individuals must be given adequate notice and a fair opportunity to present their side in a legal dispute and that no law or government procedure should be arbitrary or unfair. *See* Joseph Shane, "Due Process and Probationary Employees," *Public Personnel Management* (September-October 1974); Lewis R. Amis, "Due Process in Disciplinary Procedures," *Labor Law Journal* (February 1976); Deborah D. Goldman, "Due Process and Public Personnel Management," *Review of Public Personnel Administration* (Fall 1981).

See also the following entries:
ARNETT V. KENNEDY
GOSS V. LOPEZ
MATHEWS V. ELDRIDGE

due process of law, a guarantee of fundamental fairness. While administrative officials are afforded substantial protections under the concept of immunity, their action vis-a-vis the citizen or corporation is generally limited by the requirements of due process. The provision that no person "shall be deprived of life, liberty, or property, without due process of law" is considered to be a powerful restraint on the procedures by which governments in the U.S. limit the rights or property interests of their citizens. However, the con-

cept raises considerable questions regarding both the procedures deemed "fair" and the kinds of rights and interests protected by it. For the most part, these two elements are related in that the more fundamental the right or interest, the greater the procedural protections afforded the citizen when the state seeks to abridge it. The degree of protection ranges from a jury trial and appellate processes to a hearing of some sort, perhaps including a right to counsel, confrontation, and cross-examination of adverse witnesses before an impartial examiner. Of course, there are instances in which citizens are adversely affected by administrative decisions but nevertheless have no right or opportunity to be heard.

In recent years the most interesting developments in this area of constitutional law have been (1) the extension of the procedural safeguards afforded citizens at the hearing stage and (2) the extension of the right to have a hearing to situations previously not deemed sufficiently important to warrant such protections. Consider the procedural protections afforded public employees in dismissals. It has now been found that where constitutionally protected rights and interests are at stake, there may be a right to an open hearing including counsel, confrontation, and cross-examination. *See* John D. Aram and Paul F. Salipante, Jr., "An Evaluation of Organizational Due Process in the Resolution of Employee/Employer Conflict," *Academy of Management Review* (April 1981).

dues, fees that must be periodically paid by union members in order for them to remain in good standing with their union. The dues are used to finance all of the activities of the union and its affiliates. For a survey of who pays what, *see* Charles W. Hickman, "Labor Organizations' Fees and Dues," *Monthly Labor Review* (May 1977).

See also UNFAIR LABOR PRACTICES (UNIONS).

dues checkoff, *see* CHECKOFF.

dues picket line, a common union practice before the checkoff was in widespread use. The union officers and their close supporters formed a *dues picket line* at the factory gate on paydays in order to encourage union members to pay their dues. Any union member seeking to cross the line without paying might find himself in a situation with violent overtones.

dumping, term used in international trade meaning to sell a product in export markets below the selling price for the same product in domestic markets. Rules created by countries to protect themselves from this practice are called *anti-dumping laws.* Additional tariffs that may be imposed on imports that have been dumped are called *dumping duties.*

dumping ground of management, *see* TRASHCAN HYPOTHESIS.

Dunlop v. Bachowski, 421 U.S. 560 (1975), U.S. Supreme Court case which held that while a decision of the Secretary of Labor to initiate or not initiate civil action to set aside a union's election of officers is not excepted from judicial review, the reviewing court's review must be limited to determining whether the "Secretary's decision is so irrational as to be arbitrary and capricious, and the court's review may not extend to an adversary trial of a complaining union member's challenges to the factual basis for the Secretary's decision."

Dunnette, Marvin D. (1926-), industrial psychologist, one of the most prolific researchers and writers in the areas of personnel selection and organizational effectiveness. Major works include: *Psychology Applied to Business and Industry,* with W. K. Kirchner (New York: Appleton-Century-Crofts, 1965); *Personnel Selection and Placement* (Belmont, Calif.: Wadsworth Publishing Company, 1966); *Managerial Behavior, Performance, and Effectiveness,* with J. P. Campbell, E. E. Lawler III, and K. E. Weick, Jr. (New York: McGraw-Hill, 1970); *Handbook of Industrial and Organizational Psychology* (Chicago, Ill.: Rand McNally, 1976).

duty, large segment of the work done by one individual. A job is made up of one or more duties.

duty, also TARIFF, a tax imposed on imported products. A duty is distinguished from a tariff solely by the fact that the duty is the actual tax imposed or collected, while the tariff, technically speaking, is the schedule of duties. However, in practice the words are often used interchangeably. Various types of duties include: 1. *Import duties,* imposed on goods entering a nation or political unit. 2. *Export duties,* imposed on goods leaving a nation or political unit. Export duties are expressly forbidden in the United States by our Constitution which provides that "no tax or duty shall be laid on articles exported from any state." Other countries, however, lay export duties even on their chief exports for revenue purposes, to bolster domestic manufacture of some article, or to encourage the keeping of scarce raw materials within the country for home use. 3. *Transit duties,* imposed by a country simply for allowing goods to pass through its territory en route from one country to another. The United States does not levy transit duties. 4. *Ad valorem duties,* imposed on goods on the basis of value. The advantage of ad valorem duties is that they fluctuate with economic conditions—that is, the duty rises and falls in relationship to prices. The disadvantage of the ad valorem system is that it presents a valuation problem, is an expensive system to maintain, and opens the doors to corruption. 5. *Specific duties,* imposed on the basis of some unit of measurement—so much per pound, per bushel, per dozen, etc. Specific duties avoid the problems of appraisement involved in the collection of ad valorem taxes. The disadvantages of specific duties are that they require a minute detailing of rates for the many products imported and that they do not reflect changes in economic conditions. 6. *Compound duties,* which have the combined attributes of ad valorem and specific duties. Fifty cents per pound plus 10 per cent ad valorem is the way that a combined duty would be imposed. 7. *Subsidies* *and bounties,* amounts paid by governments on the export of certain goods from their countries for the purpose of stimulating the export of those goods. A *bounty* is given gratuitously. A *subsidy* is given in exchange for the meeting of some condition or other. Subsidies and bounties may be given either in the form of direct cash payments based on the number of units of the product exported, or they may take the form of especially low freight rates on the particular article, or of special tax exemption or low-interest government loans, etc. 8. *Countervailing duties,* imposed in addition to the regular duty for the purpose of counteracting the effect of a bounty or subsidy in another country. 9. *Anti-dumping duties,* calculated to offset the advantage gained by exporters when they sell their products in a foreign country at a price lower than that at which the same article sells at home, or at a price even lower than the cost of production.

duty of fair representation, obligation of a labor union to represent all of the members in a bargaining unit fairly and without discrimination. *See* Jean T. McKelvey, ed., *The Duty of Fair Representation* (Ithaca, N.Y.: New York State School of Industrial and Labor Relations, Cornell University, 1977); George W. Bohlander, "Fair Representation: Not Just a Union Problem," *The Personnel Administrator* (March 1980); Stanley J. Schwartz, "Different Views of the Duty of Fair Representation," *Labor Law Journal* (July 1983); Stephen Allred, "The *Bowen* Decision: Mandate for Reexamination of Apportionment of Damages in Fair Representation Cases," *Labor Law Journal* (July 1983).

See also ELECTRICAL WORKERS V. FOUST and UNFAIR LABOR PRACTICES (UNIONS).

duty station, the specific geographical area to which an employee is permanently assigned.

duty to bargain, positive obligation under various state and federal laws that employers and employees bargain with each other in good faith. Section 8 (d) of the Labor-Management Relations (Taft-Hartley) Act of 1947 holds that the duty to bargain collectively

is the performance of the mutual obligation of the employer and the representative of the employees to meet at reasonable times and confer in good faith with respect to wages, hours, and other terms and conditions of any employment, or the negotiation of an agreement, or any question arising thereunder, and the execution of a written contract incorporating any agreement reached if requested by either party, but such obligation does not compel either party to agree to a proposal or require the making of a concession.

For legal analyses, *see* Archibald Cox, "The Duty to Bargain in Good Faith," *Harvard Law Review* (June 1958); Stanley A. Gacek, "The Employer's Duty to Bargain on Termination of Unit Work," *Labor Law Journal* (October 1981).

dyad, interpersonal encounter or relationship between two people or two groups. Dyads are frequently artificially (as opposed to spontaneously) created for sensitivity training purposes. *See* David M. Herold, "Two Way Influence Processes in Leader-Follower Dyads," *Academy of Management Journal* (June 1977).

Dye, Thomas R. (1935–), political scientist specializing in American government, public policy, and political elites. Major works include: *Politics, Economics and the Public: Policy Outcomes in the American States* (Chicago: Rand McNally, 1966); *Politics in the Metropolis,* with Brett W. Hawkins (Columbus, Ohio: Charles E. Merrill, 1967); *Politics in States and Communities* (Englewood Cliffs, N.J.: Prentice-Hall, 1969; 3rd ed., 1977); *American Government: Theory, Structure, and Process,* with others (Belmont, Calif.: Wadsworth, 1969); *The Irony of Democracy,* with L. Harmon Zeigler (North Scituate, Mass.: Duxbury Press, 1970; 3rd ed., 1975); *The Politics of Equality* (Indianapolis: Bobbs-Merrill, 1971); *Understanding Public Policy* (Englewood Cliffs, N.J.: Prentice-Hall,

1972; 3rd ed., 1978); *Who's Running America: Institutional Leadership in America* (Englewood Cliffs, N.J.: Prentice-Hall, 1976); and *Policy Analysis* (University, Alabama: University of Alabama Press, 1976).

dynamic psychology, school of psychology that is primarily concerned with motivation.

dynamic system, any system that has its parts interrelated in such a way that a change in one part necessarily affects other parts of the system. This is in contrast to a *static system,* whose parts can be affected independently of the rest of its system.

E

EAP, see EMPLOYEE ASSISTANCE PROGRAM.

earmark, also RED CIRCLE, terms used to designate a position for restudy when vacant to determine its proper classification before being refilled.

earmarked tax, see TAX, EARMARKED.

earnings, total remuneration of an employee or group of employees for work performed, including wages, bonuses, commissions, etc.
    See also GUARANTEED EARNINGS.

earthquake manager, one who shakes everything up.

easement, see RIGHT-OF-WAY.

Eastex, Inc.* v. *National Labor Relations Board, 437 U.S. 556 (1978), U.S. Supreme Court case which affirmed a National Labor Relations Board ruling that union members have the right to distribute,

on their employers' property, leaflets containing articles pertaining to political issues (such as right-to-work laws and minimum wages) as well as those directly connected to the union-employer relationship.

econometric model, a set of related equations used to analyze economic data through mathematical and statistical techniques. Such models are devised in order to depict the essential quantitative relationships that determine the behavior of output, income, employment, and prices. Econometric models are used for forecasting, estimating the likely quantitative impact of alternative assumptions, including those pertaining to government policies, and for testing various propositions about the way the economy works. *See* W. Patrick Beaton, ed., *Municipal Expenditures, Revenues, and Services: Economic Models and Their Use by Planners* (New Brunswick, N.J.: Center for Urban Policy Research/Rutgers University, 1983).

econometrics, a subdiscipline of economics which is known by its use of mathematical techniques such as regression analysis and modeling to test economic theories and forecast economic activity. *See* Brigitte H. Sellekaerts and Stephen W. Welch, "An Econometric Analysis of Minimum Wage Noncompliance," *Industrial Relations* (Spring 1984).

Economic Advisers, Council of, *see* COUNCIL OF ECONOMIC ADVISERS.

economic analysis, a systematic approach to the problem of choosing how to employ scarce resources and an investigation of the full implications of achieving a given objective in the most efficient and effective manner. The determination of efficiency and effectiveness is implicit in the assessment of the cost effectiveness of alternative approaches.

economic determinism, doctrine holding that economic concerns are the primary motivating factors of human behavior.

economic efficiency, the mix of alternative factors of production which results in maximum outputs, benefits, or utility for a given cost. Also, that mix of productive factors which represents the minimum cost at which a specified level of output can be obtained.

economic growth, increase in a nation's productive capacity leading to an increase in the production of goods and services. Economic growth usually is measured by the annual rate of increase in real (constant dollars) gross national product.

economic man, concept that finds humans motivated *solely* by economic factors—always seeking the greatest reward at the least possible cost. Any management philosophy assuming that workers are motivated by money and can be further motivated only by more money is premised on the "economic man" concept. *See* Harvey Leibenstein, *Beyond Economic Man: A New Foundation for Microeconomics* (Cambridge, Mass.: Harvard University Press, 1976).

economic indicators, measurements of various economic and business movements and activities in a community, such as employment, unemployment, hours worked, income, savings, volume of building permits, volume of sales, etc., whose fluctuations affect and may be used to determine overall economic trends. The economic time series can be segregated into leaders, laggers, and coinciders in relation to movements in aggregate economic activity.

Economic Opportunity Act of 1964, the keystone of the Johnson Administration's "war on poverty." The act created the Job Corps and other work incentive programs. For histories, *see* Sar A. Levitan, *The Great Society's Poor Law* (Baltimore: The Johns Hopkins Press, 1969); Robert H. Haveman, ed., *A Decade of Federal Anti-Poverty Programs: Achievements, Failures, and Lessons* (New York: Academic Press, 1977); James T. Patterson, *America's Struggle Against Poverty, 1900-1980*

(Cambridge, Mass.: Harvard University Press, 1981).
See also GREAT SOCIETY.

economic policy, process by which a government manages its economy. Economic policy generally consists of three dimensions—fiscal policy, monetary policy, and any other facet of public policy that has economic implications (e.g., energy policy, farm policy, labor union policy, etc.). The interaction of these dimensions of economic policy becomes crucial since none can operate in a vacuum. While monetary policy basically exercises control over the quantity and cost (interest rates) of money and credit in the economy, fiscal policy deals with the size of budgets, deficits, and taxes. Other policy areas, such as housing policy (also dependent upon interest rates) and programs dependent upon deficit spending involve aspects of both monetary and fiscal policy and vice versa. However, their interrelationship does not exist with regard to implementation. Monetary policy, while receiving major inputs from the President and other executive agencies, is the responsibility of the Federal Reserve Board, an independent agency. Fiscal policy, while receiving similar inputs from the Federal Reserve Board, is primarily the responsibility of the president and Congress. The degree of equality and subsequent share of responsibility here varies within a stable range. While a president may wish to spend this or that amount, only Congress has the constitutional ability to levy taxes. *See* Charles Schultze, *The Politics and Economics of Public Spending* (Washington, D.C.: The Brookings Institution, 1968); Edward R. Tufte, *Political Control of the Economy* (Princeton, N.J.: Princeton University Press, 1979); and Robin W. Broadway, *Public Sector Economics* (Englewood Cliffs, N.J.: Prentice-Hall, 1979).
    See also the following entries:
    FISCAL POLICY
    MONETARY POLICY
    POLITICAL ECONOMY

Economic Policy Board, President Ford's

cabinet-level committee on foreign and domestic economic policy. *See* Roger Porter, *Presidential Decision Making: The Economic Policy Board* (New York: Cambridge University Press, 1980).

Economic Report of the President, economic assessment and forecast which is prepared by the Council of Economic Advisors for presentation to the Congress each January.

Economic Stabilization Program, federal program established to control wages and prices. On August 15, 1971, all wages and prices were frozen for a period of ninety days. During that period a system of wage and price controls administered through a Cost of Living Council was implemented. Controls continued, with periodic changes in the flexibility and the intensity with which they were enforced, until their legislative authority ultimately expired in April 1974.

economic strike, strike that is undertaken for economic gain; that is, for better wages, hours, and working conditions.
See also NATIONAL LABOR RELATIONS BOARD V. MACKAY RADIO & TELEGRAPH COMPANY.

economic time series, a set of quantitative data collected over regular time intervals (*e.g.,* weekly, monthly, quarterly, annually) which measures some aspect of economic activity. The data may measure a broad aggregate such as the gross national product or a narrow segment such as the sale of trucks or the price of labor.

economies of scale, cost savings resulting from aggregation of resources and/or mass production. In particular, the term refers to decreases in average cost when all factors of production are expanded proportionately. For example, hospital costs for a unit of service are generally less in three hundred- than in thirty-bed hospitals.

economy and efficiency audits, audits that seek to determine (a) whether an organizational entity is managing and utilizing its resources (such as personnel, proper-

ty, space) economically and efficiently, (b) the causes of inefficiencies or uneconomical practices, and (c) whether the entity has complied with laws and regulations concerning matters of economy and efficiency.

EDP, *see* ELECTRONIC DATA PROCESSING.

educable retarded person, individual who is only mildly retarded and thus employable in many simple jobs, usually requiring repetitive tasks.

education, cooperative, *see* COOPERATIVE EDUCATION.

Education, Department of (DOE), cabinet-level department that establishes policy for, administers, and coordinates most federal assistance to education. Created on October 17, 1979, when the Department of Health, Education and Welfare was divided in two.
> DOE
> 400 Maryland Ave., S.W.
> Washington, D.C. 20202
> (202) 245-3192

EEO, *see* EQUAL EMPLOYMENT OPPORTUNITY.

EEO Act of 1972, *see* EQUAL EMPLOYMENT OPPORTUNITY ACT OF 1972.

EEOC, *see* EQUAL EMPLOYMENT OPPORTUNITY COMMISSION.

EEOC Compliance Manual, publication of the Bureau of National Affairs, Inc., which provides a summary of the latest Equal Employment Opportunity Commission (EEOC) developments and the photographic text of the official operations manual that is followed by the staff of the EEOC.

EEO Counselor, *see* EQUAL EMPLOYMENT OPPORTUNITY COUNSELOR.

EEO Officer, *see* EQUAL EMPLOYMENT OPPORTUNITY OFFICER.

EEO-1, the annual report on the sex and minority status of various work force categories that is required of all employers with one hundred or more employees. The report must be filed with the Joint Reporting Committee of the Equal Employment Opportunity Commission and the Office of Federal Contract Compliance.

effective labor market, labor market from which an employer actually draws applicants, as distinct from the labor market from which an employer attempts to draw applicants.

effectiveness, traditionally, the extent to which an organization accomplishes some predetermined goal or objective; more recently, the overall performance of an organization from the viewpoint of some strategic constituency. Effectiveness is not entirely dependent upon the efficiency of a program because program outputs may increase without necessarily increasing effectiveness. Effectiveness is increased by strategies which employ resources to take advantage of changes in unmanageable factors in such a way that the greatest possible advancement of whatever one is seeking is achieved. See P. S. Goodman and J. M. Pennings, *New Perspectives on Organizational Effectiveness* (San Francisco: Jossey-Bass, 1977); Philip B. Coulter, "Organizational Effectiveness in the Public Sector: The Example of Municipal Fire Protection," *Administrative Science Quarterly* (March 1979); Kim Cameron, "Critical Questions in Assessing Organizational Effectiveness," *Organizational Dynamics* (Autumn 1980); Leonard Greenhalgh, "Maintaining Organizational Effectiveness During Organizational Retrenchment," *The Journal of Applied Behavioral Science,* Vol. 18, No. 2 (1982); Raymond F. Zammuto, *Assessing Organizational Effectiveness* (Albany: State University of New York Press, 1982); Edward E. Lawler III, "Education, Management Style, and Organizational Effectiveness," *Personnel Psychology* (Spring 1985).

Also see PERSONNEL EFFECTIVENESS GRID.

efficacy, commonly used synonym for effectiveness, but may usefully be distinguished from it by using efficacy for the results of actions undertaken under ideal circumstances and effectiveness for their results under usual or normal circumstances. Actions can thus be efficacious and effective, or efficacious and ineffective, but not the reverse.

efficiency, also EFFICIENCY RATIO, measure determined by seeking the ratio of output to input, which is called the *efficiency ratio.*

$$\text{efficiency} = \frac{\text{output}}{\text{input}}$$

Generally speaking, efficiency refers to the promotion of administrative methods that will produce the largest store of results for a given objective at the least cost; the reduction of material and personnel costs while maximizing precision, speed, and simplicity in administration. According to the traditional view, efficiency is the primary aim of the administrative sciences. See Aaron Wildavsky, "The Political Economy of Efficiency: Cost-Benefit Analysis, Systems Analysis and Program Budgeting," *Public Administration Review* (December 1966); Selwyn W. Becker and Duncan Neuhauser, *The Efficient Organization* (New York: Elsevier, 1975); Joseph L. Bower, "Managing for Efficiency, Managing for Equity," *Harvard Business Review* (July-August 1983); Robert P. McGowan, "Improving Efficiency in Public Management: The Torment of Sisyphus," *Public Productivity Review* (Summer 1984); Robert E. Goodin and Peter Wilenski, "Beyond Efficiency: The Logical Underpinnings of Administrative Principles," *Public Administration Review* (November-December 1984).

See also PRODUCTIVITY.

efficiency expert, mildly pejorative and decidedly dated term for a management or systems analyst.

efficiency rating, now dated term for performance appraisal. The Civil Service Reform Act of 1978 mandates that each federal agency will install employee "performance appraisal" systems. For an account of the old ways, *see* Mary S. Schinagl, *History of Efficiency Ratings in the Federal Government* (New York: Bookman Associates, 1966).

See also PERFORMANCE APPRAISAL.

efficiency ratio, *see* EFFICIENCY.

egalitarianism, *see* EQUALITY.

80-percent rule, *see* ADVERSE IMPACT.

elasticity, a numerical measure of the responsiveness of one variable to changes in another. If greater than one, it indicates that the first variable is relatively elastic to changes in the second (*i.e.*, when the second changes by one percent, the first changes by more than one percent). If the numerical value of elasticity is equal to or less than one (*i.e.*, unitary elasticity or less) the first variable is said to be *inelastic* to changes in the second (a one percent change in the second variable will cause a one percent or less change in the first).

Efficiency in the Foreign Service

There seemed to be little reason to maintain a large staff in our embassy in Prague. I recommended to Washington that my inherited complement of eighty Americans (almost microscopic by today's embassy standards) be reduced, as a start, by one half. That is to say, that the roster be cut from eighty to forty, with the major part of the reduction to be from agencies other than the State Department, since those agencies were the ones supplying the soap-bubble blowers.

Pentagon personnel, for instance, accounted for thirty-three of my eighty colleagues. I suggested to Washington that ten soldiers ought henceforth to be sufficient to advise one Ambassador about military developments in Czechoslovakia. I also suggested that since Czechoslovakia was a landlocked country, lacking seacoast or navy, my naval attaché might just as well be assigned to Switzerland or Bolivia.

The State Department, after meditation, informed me that my recommendations were "interesting" and there was "agreement in principle" that they ought to be implemented.

I was thus encouraged to embark on a campaign of the utmost frustration. The outraged squawks of my American colleagues in Prague quickly reverberated beside the Potomac, where every agency represented in my embassy demanded of the State Department that the proposed reductions be borne by every other agency.

The State Department, which had instigated my investigation, and encouraged my recommendations, promptly went into a tailspin. After six months, and an expenditure of effort on my part sufficient to have built, singlehanded, a bridge across the Vitava River, I had managed to reduce my overblown staff by two persons—from eighty to seventy-eight.

At which point, the Communists, ignorant of my hassle with Washington over personnel, and believing that they were doing the American government in general and the American ambassador in particular the greatest possible disservice, suddenly declared five sixths of the embassy personnel *persona non grata*. That is to say, unwelcome people. Czechoslolvakia gave the embassy two weeks in which to evacuate sixty-six of my seventy-eight colleagues, together with all their families, pets, and belongings.

A *persona non grata* declaration is not debatable, and the State Department had no choice but to comply. We got the sixty-sixth member of the staff across the border at Rosvadov within the prescribed time limit, and I sat back to enjoy the first unobstructed view from my chancery since reaching Czechoslovakia the previous autumn.

The American embassy in Prague then consisted of thirteen people, including the ambassador. . . .

The Pentagon had three persons on my reduced staff, instead of ten they had earlier insisted upon. Two colonels, one from the army and one from the Air Force, competed unhappily for the services of one sergeant.

It was an efficient embassy. It was probably the most efficient embassy I ever headed.

Source: Ellis Briggs, *Farewell to Foggy Bottom: The Recollections of a Career Diplomat* (New York: David McKay, 1964), pp. 169–171.

---

elasticity of demand, measure of the sensitivity of demand for a product or service to changes in its price (price elasticity) or the income of the people demanding the product or service (income elasticity). Price elasticity is the ratio of the resulting percentage change in demand to a given percentage change in price. *See* Kim B. Clark and Richard B. Freeman, "How Elastic Is The Demand for Labor?" *The Review of*

Economics and Statistics (November 1980).

Electrical Workers v. Foust, 442 U.S. 42 (1979), U.S. Supreme Court case which held that an award of punitive damages for a union's breach of its duty of fair representation in processing an employee's grievance was prohibited by the Railway Labor Act.

See also DUTY OF FAIR REPRESENTATION.

electronic data processing (EDP), computer manipulation of data. The term is gradually being supplanted by "management information systems."

See also MANAGEMENT INFORMATION SYSTEM.

element, also called JOB ELEMENT, smallest unit into which a job can be divided without analyzing the physical and mental processes necessarily involved. See Ronald A. Ash, "Job Elements for Task Clusters," *Public Personnel Management* (Spring 1982).

Elfbrandt v. Russell, 384 U.S. 11 (1966), Supreme Court case holding an Arizona loyalty oath unconstitutional in violation of freedom of association since, coupled with a perjury statute, it proscribed membership in any organization having for one of its purposes the overthrow of the government of the State of Arizona. The Court reasoned that one might join such an organization without supporting its illegal purposes.

See also LOYALTY.

Elgin, Joliet & Eastern Railway v. Burley, 325 U.S. 711 (1945), U.S. Supreme Court case which upheld the right of employees to object to a compromise settlement of a grievance committee when they had not formally authorized the committee to act for them.

eligibility, legislative and administrative criteria for determining which units of government (or other potential beneficiaries—*e.g.,* Indian tribes, non-profits, universities, individuals, etc.) are entitled

to be recipients of Federal Assistance Programs.

eligible, any applicant for appointment or promotion who meets the minimum qualification requirements.

eligible list, also called ELIGIBLE ROSTER and ELIGIBLE REGISTER, list of qualified applicants in rank order established from the test score results of competitive examinations.

See also REEMPLOYMENT LIST.

Ellis v. Brotherhood of Railway Clerks, 80 L Ed 2d 428 (1984), U.S. Supreme Court case in which the Court restricted activities that unions in the railroad and airline transportation industries may finance using fees obtained from workers who object to the expenditures. The Court's interpretation of the Railway Labor Act applies only to workers who are represented by a union in collective bargaining but are not members of the union. The money at question is the so-called "agency shop fee" paid by "non-members" in lieu of the dues paid by fellow employees who are members of the union.

In the ruling, written by Justice Byron White, the Court said that if an employee objects, the employee's agency shop payments cannot be used for organizing other workers or for paying union legal expenses for lawsuits over issues not specifically related to the bargaining agreement covering the workers. See Jan W. Henkel and Normal J. Wood, "Limitations on the Use of Union Shop Funds After *Ellis*: What Activities are 'Germane' to Collective Bargaining?" *Labor Law Journal* (December 1984).

Elrod v. Burns, 427 U.S. 347 (1976), U.S. Supreme Court case which held that the First Amendment, which safeguards the rights of political beliefs and association, prevents political firings of state, county, and local workers below the policymaking level.

Emergency Employment Act of 1971, federal statute that authorized federal funds for state and local government public service jobs during times of high unemployment. It was superseded by the Comprehensive Employment and Training Act of 1973. For a history, see Howard W. Hallman, *Emergency Employment: A Study in Federalism* (University, Ala.: University of Alabama Press, 1977).

emergency management, that aspect of public administration concerned with reducing the risk to life and property "posed by intermittently occurring natural and man-made hazardous events." See William J. Petak, "Emergency Management: A Challenge for Public Administration," *Public Administration Review* (January 1985).

Also see FEDERAL EMERGENCY MANAGEMENT AGENCY.

eminence grise, "gray eminence," the power behind the throne. Staff officers are sometimes accused of exercising such power.

eminent domain, a government's right to take private property for the public's use.

emolument, any monetary gain or other advantage achieved from employment; a more comprehensive term than wages and/or salaries.

emotionally handicapped employees, also EMOTIONAL REHABILITANTS, a polite way of referring to employees who have had or are having a problem with mental illness. *Emotional rehabilitant,* a more formal label, has been defined in Charles A. Burden and Russell Faulk, "The Employment Process for Rehabilitants: Two Studies of the Hiring of Emotional Rehabilitants," *Personnel Journal* (October 1975), as "a person who has suffered an emotional illness serious enough to require hospitalization, but has since recovered and has been judged by medical and social authorities to be ready to reenter the customary, competitive work situation."

empirical, findings or conclusions derived from direct and repeated observations of a phenomenon under study.

empirical validity, validity of a test according to how well the test actually measures what it was designed to measure. Most other kinds of validity are efforts to achieve empirical validity.

employ, hire the services of an individual and/or his or her equipment.

employee, general term for all those who let themselves for hire.

See also DISPLACED EMPLOYEE and PROBATIONARY EMPLOYEE.

employee assistance program (EAP), formal program designed to assist employees with personal problems through both (1) internal counseling and aid and (2) a referral service to outside counseling resources. The thrust of such programs is to increase productivity by correcting distracting outside personal problems. See Richard T. Hellan and Carl R. Tisone, "Employee Assistance Programming: Personnel's Sobering Influence on the Bottom Line," *The Personnel Administrator* (May 1976); Paul M. Roman, "Employee Assistance Programs in Australia and the United States: Comparisons of Origin, Structure, and the Role of Behavioral Science Research," *The Journal of Applied Behavioral Science*, Vol. 19, No. 3 (1983); Harvey Shore, "Employee Assistance Programs—Reaping the Benefits," *Sloan Management Review* (Spring 1984); Dale A. Masi, *Designing Employee Assistance Programs* (New York: AMACOM, 1984); Donna R. Kemp, "State Employee Assistance Programs: Organization and Services," *Public Administration Review* (May–June 1985); Assistance Programs: Managing Troubled Employees," *Public Administration Review* (May–June 1985).

Employee Assistance Quarterly, a journal of research on work-based alcoholism, drug and mental health programs.

Employee Assistance Quarterly
The Haworth Press
28 East 22nd Street
New York, NY 10010

employee benefits, *see* FRINGE BENEFITS.

employee counseling, formal efforts on the part of an organization to help its members deal with their personal and professional problems and concerns so that they will be more effective in both their personal and organizational lives. For the classic work on employee counseling, *see* William J. Dickson and F. J. Roethlisberger, *Counseling In An Organization: A Sequel to the Hawthorne Researches* (Boston: Graduate School of Business Administration, Harvard University, 1966). *Also see* John H. Meyer and Teresa C. Meyer, "The Supervisor as Counselor—How to Help the Distressed Employee," *Management Review* (April 1982); Stephen J. Holoviak and Sharon Brookens Holoviak, "The Benefits of In-House Counseling," *Personnel* (July-August 1984).

See also PRE-RETIREMENT COUNSELING.

employee development, term that may include career development and upward mobility. It may be oriented toward development for better performance on an employee's current job, for learning a new policy or procedure, or for enhancing an employee's potential for advancement. *See* Donald B. Miller, "Training Managers to Stimulate Employee Development," *Training and Development Journal* (February 1981).

employee relations, personnel function that centers upon the relationship between the supervisor and individual employees.

Employee Retirement Income Security Act of 1974 (ERISA), popularly known as PENSION REFORM ACT OF 1974, federal statute enacted to protect "the interest of participants in employee benefit plans and their beneficiaries . . . by establishing standards of conduct, responsibility and obligations for fiduciaries of employee benefit plans, and by providing for appropriate remedies, sanctions, and ready access to the Federal courts." The basic intent of ERISA is to insure that employees will eventually gain appropriate benefits from the pension plans in which they participate. *See* Peter Henle and Raymond Schmitt, "Pension Reform: The Long Hard Road to Enactment," *Monthly Labor Review* (November 1974); Donald G. Carlson, "Responding to the Pension Reform Law," *Harvard Business Review* (November-December 1974); Bruce M. Stott, "How Will ERISA Affect Your Pension Plan?" *Personnel Journal* (June 1977); Raymond J. Donovan, "Effective Administration of ERISA," *Labor Law Journal* (March 1982); Kathleen D. Gill, ed., *ERISA: The Law and the Code* (Washington, D.C.: Bureau of National Affairs, Inc., 1985).

See also LABOR-MANAGEMENT SERVICES ADMINISTRATION.

employee selection, *see* PERSONNEL SELECTION.

employees, exempt, *see* EXEMPT EMPLOYEES.

employer paternalism, *see* PATERNALISM.

employer unit, any bargaining unit that holds all of the eligible employees of a single employer.

employment, occupational activity usually, but not necessarily, for pay. In economic statistics, employment refers to all persons who, during the week when the employment survey was taken, did any work for pay or profit, or who worked for fifteen hours or more without pay on a farm or in a business operated by a member of the person's family. Also included as employed are those who did not work or look for work, but had a job or business from which they were temporarily absent during the week.

See also FULL EMPLOYMENT and SEASONAL EMPLOYMENT.

Employment Act of 1946, federal statute that created the Council of Economic Advisors in the Executive Office of the President and asserted that it was the federal government's responsibility to maintain economic stability and promote full employment. For a legislative history of the act, *see* Stephen K. Bailey, *Congress Makes a Law* (New York: Columbia University Press, 1950). *Also see* Hugh S. Norton, *The Employment Act and the Council of Economic Advisors, 1946-1976* (Columbia, S.C.: University of South Carolina Press, 1977).

employment agency, private agency that provides brokerage services between employers and individuals seeking work. Fees or commissions are charged the employer, the worker, or both. *See* Terry L. Dennis and David P. Gustafson, "College Campuses vs. Employment Agencies as Sources of Manpower," *Personnel Journal* (August 1973); John M. Malloy, "Employment Agency Fees: An Area of Continued Litigation?" *Taxes* (February 1974); Tomas Martinez, *The Human Marketplace: An Examination of Private Employment Agencies* (New Brunswick, N.J.: Transaction Books, 1976).

Employment and Earnings, U.S. Bureau of Labor Statistics' comprehensive monthly report on employment, hours, earnings, and labor turnover by industry, area, occupation, etc.

> *Employment and Earnings*
> Superintendent of Documents
> Government Printing Office
> Washington, D.C. 20402

Employment and Training Administration (ETA), agency of the Department of Labor that encompasses a group of offices and services. Major units include: the U.S. Employment Service; the Office of Employment and Training; and the Bureau of Apprenticeship and Training.

> Employment and Training Administration
> Department of Labor
> 200 Constitution Ave., N.W.
> Washington, D.C. 20210
> (202) 376-7032

employment-at-will, the common law concept that an employment having no specific term may be terminated by either party with or without notice or cause. In recent years discharged employees have increasingly challenged what they consider to be wrongful discharges. They have based their court suits on claims of violation of public policy, the existence of an implied contract, and the covenant of good faith and fair dealing. Generally speaking, only those employees protected by collective bargaining, antidiscrimination laws, civil service, and teacher tenure laws are not subject to "at-will" discharges. *See* Anthony T. Oliver Jr., "The Disappearing Right to Terminate Employees at Will," *Personnel Journal* (December 1982); Marco L. Colosi, "Who's Pulling the Strings on Employment at Will?" *Personnel Journal* (May 1984); Lawrence Z. Lorber, "Basic Advice on Avoiding Employment-At-Will Troubles," *Personnel Administrator* (February 1984); Emily A. Joiner, "Erosion of the Employment-at-Will Doctrine," *Personnel* (September-October 1984); Brian Heshizer, "The New Common Law of Employment: Changes in the Concept of Employment at Will," *Labor Law Journal* (February 1985).

employment contract, generally a promise or set of promises for which the law offers a remedy if the promise(s) is breached. According to John J. Villarreal, "Employment Contracts for Managers and Professionals," *Personnel Journal* (October 1974), an employment contract specifically refers to

> the agreed-upon contributions/inducements between employer and employee for the services of each. These promises must be legally enforceable and they must be made by mature, knowledgeable and consenting individuals. . . . For each employment contract there must be agreements between the organization and the individual on goals to be accomplished, units of measurement, performance targets and organizational rewards.

Employment Cost Index (ECI), measures the rate of change in employee compensation, which includes wages, salaries, and employers' cost for employee benefits.

171

Several elements distinguish the ECI from other surveys of employee compensation. It is comprehensive in that it (1) includes costs incurred by employers for employee benefits in addition to wages and salaries; and (2) covers all establishments and occupations in both the private nonfarm and public sectors. It measures the change in a fixed set of labor costs so that it is not affected over time by changes in the composition of the labor force. See Beth Levin, "The Employment Cost Index: Recent Trends and Expansion," *Monthly Labor Review* (May 1982).

employment interview, *see* INTERVIEW.

employment manager, job title sometimes given to managers who function as personnel directors.

employment parity, *see* PARITY.

employment-population ratio (E-P ratio), also called EMPLOYMENT RATIO, ratio of employment to working-age population. Some economists think that the E-P ratio is more useful for diagnosing the severity of an economic slowdown than is the unemployment rate. See Christopher Green, "The Employment Ratio as an Indicator of Aggregate Demand Pressure," *Monthly Labor Review* (April 1977); Carol Boyd Leon, "The Employment-Population Ratio: Its Value in Labor Force Analysis," *Monthly Labor Review* (February 1981).

employment practice, in the context of equal employment opportunity, any screening device operating at any point in the employment cycle. If an employment practice is not related to job performance, it will not be able to withstand a court challenge.

employment ratio, *see* EMPLOYMENT-POPULATION RATIO.

employment relations, general term for all relationships that occur in a worker-manager context. While used synonymously with labor relations and industrial relations, it is often applied in non-union

situations in order to emphasize "non-union."

employment standard, a specific requirement for employment. An employment standard can be based on a wide variety of things. For example, if assessment is based on tests, the standard might be a specific cutting score. If education is assessed, the standard might be a specific class standing, or grades of B or better in certain courses of study.

Employment Standards Administration (ESA), agency of the Department of Labor that administers laws and regulations setting employment standards, providing workers' compensation to those injured on their jobs and requiring federal contractors to provide equal employment opportunity. Its major divisions include the Wage and Hour Division, the Office of Federal Contract Compliance, and the Office of Workers' Compensation.

Employment Standards Administration
Department of Labor
200 Constitution Ave., N.W.
Washington, D.C. 20210
(202) 523-8165

employment taxes, also called PAYROLL TAXES, any of a variety of taxes levied by governments on an employer's payroll. The most common employment tax is the employer's contribution to social security known as FICA taxes (after the Federal Insurance Contribution Act). There are also FUTA taxes (after the Federal Unemployment Tax Act) and sometimes other unemployment insurance contributions required by state law. See Samuel S. Ress, "Payroll Taxes and Controls," *CPA Journal* (April 1977); Julian Block, "How to Save on Employment Taxes," *Administrative Management* (February 1976).

employment testing, any means of measuring the qualifications of applicants for employment in specific positions. See Robert M. Guion, *Personnel Testing* (New York: McGraw-Hill, 1965); J. M. Thyne, *Principles of Examining* (New York: John Wiley, 1974); M. T. Matteson, "Employment Testing: Where Do We Stand?" *The Personnel Administrator* (January 1975).

Emporium Capwell Co. v. *Western Addition Community Organization,* 420 U.S. 50 (1975), U.S. Supreme Court case which held that employees have no right to bypass union-management grievance procedures in order to protest alleged racial discrimination.

enabling act, legislation permitting cities and/or districts to engage in particular programs. Such enabling acts prescribe some of the administrative details of implementation. As cities are the creatures of the state, their ability to participate in particular types of programs, especially those of the national government, depends upon state law.

encounter group, form of group psychotherapy in which body contact and/or emotional expression are the primary forms of interaction as opposed to traditional verbal interaction. Encounter groups seek to produce experiences which force individuals to examine themselves in new and different ways, aided by others. Part of the emphasis on body movement includes attention to nonverbal communications. An individual should learn to be more conscious of his/her own nonverbal communications, to read others' signs more adequately and to practice being more adept in his/her body language. *See* A. Burton, ed., *Encounter* (San Francisco: Jossey-Bass, 1969); Dianna Hartley, Howard B. Roback, and Stephen I. Abramowitz, "Deterioration Effects on Encounter Groups," *American Psychologist* (March 1976); Kurt W. Back, *Beyond Words: The Story of Sensitivity Training and the Encounter Movement* (New York: Russell Sage Foundation, 1972); Carl A. Bramlette and Jeffrey H. Tucker, "Encounter Groups: Positive Change or Deterioration?" *Human Relations* (April 1981).

end-testing, examining individuals who have just completed a course of training on the subject in which they were trained in order to measure the individual's attain-

ments and/or the effectiveness of the training.

Energy, Department of (DOE), cabinet-level department that provides the framework for a national energy plan through the coordination and administration of the energy functions of the federal government. DOE is responsible for the research, development, and demonstration of energy technology; the marketing of federal power; energy conservation; regulation of energy production and use; pricing and allocation; and a central energy data collection and analysis program.

DOE
1000 Independence Ave., S.W.
Washington, D.C. 20585
(202) 252-5000

Energy Act of 1976, an omnibus federal law containing provisions for conservation, production, and allocation of energy supplies. Its parts include (1) executive branch authority to order major fuel-burning plants to switch from oil to coal, (2) fuel economy standards for automobiles and efficiency measures for major appliances, (3) standby presidential power to allocate supplies in a crisis and creation of an oil reserve, (4) presidential authority to adjust oil prices, and (5) Congressional review of presidential actions and General Accounting Office audits of energy producers and consumers.

See also NATIONAL ENERGY ACT OF 1978.

energy lobby, businesses, trade associations, and some unions that engage in information dissemination, lobbying, and litigation in order to develop energy supplies, relax environmental restrictions, and obtain governmental assistance. Generally consists of industries involved in resource extraction and power production such as oil and gas, coal, and electric utilities. Members of the lobby are principally industry public relations specialists.

energy policy, efforts that encourage energy development, protect against energy shortages, conserve energy resources, and safeguard the environment from damage caused by expansion of energy supplies. Although most observers predict that by the year 2000 Americans will use twice as much energy as they do now, the U.S. does not have a comprehensive energy policy.

Until the 1973–74 Arab oil embargo, U.S. energy policy was dominated by a doctrine of unlimited growth and use of oil. Indeed, extremely cheap petroleum products displaced other energy sources. With the quadrupling of the price of oil since 1969 and the eventual depletion of reserves, a transition from dependence on oil and gas to other fossil fuels and renewable energy sources will have to occur. These sources include coal, nuclear energy, and various forms of renewable energy such as solar power. However, because of problems associated with each of these alternatives, oil will remain the mainstay of U.S. energy for the near future. In the long run, all energy sources will be more expensive than the cheap oil and gas of the past.

Proposals to manage the energy crisis can be divided into hard and soft energy paths. The hard strategy emphasizes large investments in nuclear fission, electrical power, coal extraction, and other capital intensive, high technology, centralized systems. Advocates maintain that given sufficient economic incentives, energy supplies will be increased. Through conservation measures and production relevant to end use needs, the soft path emphasizes labor intensive, appropriate technology, and decentralized systems.

For a thorough overview of energy legislation, see Energy Policy (Washington, D.C.: Congressional Quarterly, Inc., 1979). The landmark book on hard and soft energy strategies is Amory Lovins, Soft Energy Paths (San Francisco, Calif.: Friends of the Earth International, 1977). A definitive work on future energy policy is Robert Stobaugh and Daniel Yergin, eds., Energy Future (New York: Random House, 1979). Also see Gregory A. Daneke and George K. Lagassa, Energy Policy and Public Administration (Lexington, Mass.: Lexington Books, 1980); Jack N. Barkenbus, "Federal Energy Policy Paradigms and State Energy Roles," Public Administration Review (September–October 1982); Max Neiman and Barbara J. Burt, eds., The Social Constraints on Energy-Policy Implementation (Lexington, MA: Lexington Books, 1983); Richard H. K. Vietor, Energy Policy in America Since 1945: A Study of Business-Government Relations (New York: Cambridge University Press, 1984); Douglas R. Bohi and William B. Quandt, Energy Security in the 1980s: Economic and Political Perspectives (Washington, D.C.: The Brookings Institution, 1984).

Engraving and Printing, Bureau of, federal bureau that designs, engraves, and prints all major items of financial character issued by the U.S. government. It produces paper currency; Treasury bonds, bills, notes, and certificates; postage, revenue, and certain customs stamps.

Bureau of Engraving and Printing
Fourteenth and C Streets, S.W.
Washington, D.C. 20228
(202) 447-1380

enjoin, require or command. A court's injunction directs (enjoins) a person or persons to do or not do certain acts.

enrolled bill, one that has been passed by Congress and is awaiting action by the president.

Prior to arrival of the formal parchment version of a bill at the White House for the president's approval or disapproval, the Government Printing Office sends a number of facsimiles of the legislation to the Office of Management and Budget (OMB). The Legislative Reference Division of the OMB in turn sends facsimiles of the bill to all executive departments and agencies that have a legitimate interest in its subject matter. The recommendations of appropriate departments and agencies with proposed approval or veto statements are delivered to the OMB within two days after receipt of the bill. These views along with those of the OMB are sent to the White House within five of the constitutional days that a president has to sign a bill. The president may accept or reject the recommendations of the agency or department or the OMB as he deems appropriate.

The requirements and procedures for department and agency compliance with the enrolled bill process are detailed in OMB Circular No. A-19 Revised, Transmittal Memorandum No. 1, dated September 20, 1979.

enrolled bill clearance, see CENTRAL CLEARANCE.

enterprise zone, also called URBAN ENTERPRISE ZONE, area of high unemployment and poverty which is granted business tax reductions by a state in order to lure industry and concomitant prosperity. See Neal R. Pierce, "Enterprise Zones Open Urban Opportunities," Public Administration Times (February 1, 1981); Lawrence Revzan, "Enterprise Zones: Present Status and Potential Impact," Governmental Finance (December 1983); David Boeck, "The Enterprise Zone Debate," The Urban Lawyer (Winter 1984).

entitlement authority, legislation that requires the payment of benefits to any person or government meeting the requirements established by such law (e.g., social security benefits and veterans' pensions). Section 401 of the Congressional Budget and Impoundment Control Act of 1974 places certain restrictions on the enactment of new entitlement authority.

See also BACKDOOR AUTHORITY.

entitlement program, any government program which pays benefits to individuals, organizations or other governments who meet eligibility requirements set by law. See Eleanor Chelimsky, "Reducing Fraud and Abuse in Entitlement Programs: An Evaluative Perspective," The GAO Review (Summer 1981).

entrance level position, position in an occupation at the beginning level grade.

entrance rate, also called PROBATIONARY RATE and HIRING RATE, hourly rate of pay at which new employees are hired.

entrapment, inducing a person to commit a crime that the person would not have committed without such inducement. When done by government agents, usually police, for the purposes of prosecuting an individual, it is generally unlawful. In most cases a criminal charge based on entrapment will fail.

entropy, term from thermodynamics that is applicable to all physical systems and sometimes applied to social systems. It refers to the inherent tendency of all closed systems, which do not interact with their environments, to move toward a chaotic state in which there is no further potential for work. According to James G. Miller, in "Living Systems: Basic Concepts," Behavioral Science (July 1965), "the disorder, disorganization, lack of patterning, or randomness of organization of a system is known as its entropy."

Negative entropy, an arresting of the entropy process, can be acquired by an open system, according to Daniel Katz and Robert L. Kahn, in The Social Psychology of Organizations (New York: John Wiley & Sons, 1966):

The open system, however, by importing more energy from its environment than it expends, can store energy and can acquire negative entropy.

For an expansive view of the concept, see Jeremy Rifkin, Entropy: A New World View (New York: Bantam, 1980).

environmental differential, additional pay authorized for a duty involving unusually severe hazards or working conditions.

environmental impact statement, see ENVIRONMENTAL POLICY.

environmental lobby, citizen groups that engage in information dissemination, public discussion, lobbying, litigation, and demonstrations on behalf of environmental protection. Generally consists of preservationists (who want to save the natural environment from man's use except for aesthetic and controlled recreational enjoyment) and utilitarians (who advocate the prudent use and renewal of environmental resources). In 1979, the combined membership of all environmental groups was estimated at eight million. The single largest group is the National Wildlife Federation; perhaps the best known is the Sierra Club. *See* Odom Fanning, *Man and His Environment: Citizen Action* (New York: Harper & Row, 1975.

environmental movement, a spontaneous grassroots mobilization of citizens that grew out of the earlier conservation movement, which is concerned with the quality of natural and human environment. The movement receives its organizational expression through the formation of interest groups that engage in lobbying, court litigation, and public information activities.

According to sociologist Allan Schnarberg, *The Environment: From Surplus to Scarcity* (New York: Oxford University Press, 1979), individuals interested in environmental problems may be classified into four categories based on their definition of the causes and extent of environment problems:

1. Cosmetologists define the crisis in terms of the most conspicuous consequences of consumption; groups such as garden clubs, the Boy Scouts, or industry representatives are frequently concerned with litter disposal, but ignore the fundamental causes of litter.

2. Meliorists are similar to cosmetologists in their perception of the social and economic origins of pollution in society—*i.e.*, they focus primarily on consumption-related activities; however, such people may have a greater knowledge of environmental problems and may be, for example, less interested in anti-litter campaigns and more concerned with recycling of wastes.

3. Reformists consider the consumption and production aspects of environmental degradation; these individuals are likely to be members of environmental groups that lobby for change within the system (*e.g.*, regulation and controls on municipal and corporate polluters).

4. Radicals see the present political system as fundamentally inimical to environmental quality and concentrate on identifying new goals for society and the changes required to move in a different direction; radicals may be members of some of the more extremist environmental groups or activists in more general groups on the far right or left of the political spectrum.

A significant event in the history of the movement was Earth Day, celebrated on April 22, 1970, with parades, teach-ins, clean-up projects, and demonstrations across the nation.

environmental policy, also NATIONAL ENVIRONMENTAL POLICY ACT OF 1969 and ENVIRONMENTAL IMPACT STATEMENT. The National Environmental Policy Act of 1969 declared a federal responsibility for the protection of the environment. The act, which created the President's Council on Environmental Quality, provides for the preparation of an *environmental impact statement* (a document which assesses the impact of a new program upon the environment) on all major federal actions significantly affecting the quality of the human environment. During the 1970s, in what was known as the Environmental Decade, it became evident that if the nation was going to improve the quality of the environment a new legal framework would be necessary. Thus, landmark legislation was passed dealing with most forms of pollution, endangered species, wilderness, and strip mining. Comparable activities occurred at the state and local level.

For year-end summaries of the state of the environment, *see* Council on Environmental Quality, *Annual Report* (Washington, D.C.: Government Printing Office, annual, beginning 1970). *Also see* Neil Orloff, *The Environmental Impact Statement Process: A Guide to Citizen Action* (Washington, D.C.: Information Resources Press, 1978); Joseph Lee Rodgers, Jr., *Environmental Impact, Assessment, Growth Management, and the Comprehensive Plan* (Cambridge, Mass.: Ballinger Publishing Co., 1977);

Robert Dorfman, "Incidence of the Benefits and Costs of Environmental Programs," *American Economic Review* (February 1977); Bernard J. Frieden, *The Environmental Protection Hustle* (Cambridge, Mass.: MIT Press, 1979); Laura M. Lake, *Environmental Regulation: The Political Effects of Implementation* (New York: Praeger Publishers, 1982); Lynton K. Caldwell, *Science and the National Environmental Policy Act* (University, Ala.: University of Alabama Press, 1982); Norman J. Vig and Michael E. Kraft, editors, *Environmental Policy in the 1980s: Reagan's New Agenda* (Washington, D.C.: Congressional Quarterly Press, 1984).

Environmental Impact Statement

As the story is told, Moses led the tribes of Israel from bondage in Egypt to the shores of the Red Sea. Looking behind him, he saw the rapidly approaching armies and chariots of the pharaoh and became alarmed. Looking then to the heavens, he called out for assistance. A voice from the heavens promptly answered: "Moses, be calm, for I have good news and bad news."

Moses replied, "Tell me quickly, for the armies grow nearer."

The voice answered: "The good news is that when you raise your staff to the sky, the Red Sea will open, creating a path for your people to cross over in safety. Then the walls of the sea shall come crashing down and destroy the armies."

Moses then queried, "That is marvelous, and the bad news?"

The voice replied, "The bad news is that you will first have to prepare an environmental impact statement."

Environmental Protection Agency (EPA), federal agency created to permit coordinated and effective governmental action on behalf of the environment. EPA endeavors to abate and control pollution systematically, by proper integration of a variety of research, monitoring, standard setting, and enforcement activities. As a complement to its other activities, EPA coordinates and supports research and antipollution activities by state and local

governments, private and public groups, individuals, and educational institutions.
EPA
401 M Street, S.W.
Washington, D.C. 20460
(202) 382-2090

EOP, see EXECUTIVE OFFICE OF THE PRESIDENT.

EPA, see ENVIRONMENTAL PROTECTION AGENCY.

E-P ratio, see EMPLOYMENT-POPULATION RATIO.

equal employment opportunity (EEO), concept fraught with political, cultural, and emotional overtones. Generally, it applies to a set of employment procedures and practices that effectively prevent any individual from being adversely excluded from employment opportunities on the basis of race, color, sex, religion, age, national origin, or other factors that cannot lawfully be used in employment efforts. While the ideal of EEO is an employment system that is devoid of both intentional and unintentional discrimination, achieving this ideal may be a political impossibility because of the problem of definition. One man's equal opportunity may be seen by another as tainted with institutional racism or by a woman as institutional sexism. Because of this problem of definition, only the courts have been able to say if, when, and where EEO exists.

It was not until the Kennedy administration that EEO became a central and major aspect of federal personnel administration. Between 1961 and 1965, the civil rights movement reached the pinnacle of its political importance and became a dominant national issue. Indeed, it was a sign of the times when Kennedy declared, "I have dedicated my administration to the cause of equal opportunity in employment by the Government." Accordingly he issued yet another executive order, this time creating the President's Committee on Equal Employment Opportunity. The new committee gained prestige and some measure of political clout by including the vice president as its chairman. It stressed "affirmative action" in the sense of making special efforts to bring more members of minority groups into the federal service. These included recruitment drives at high schools and colleges heavily attended by minorities. Agencies were encouraged to provide better training opportunities for minority group members. The committee also began the practice of taking an annual census of minority employment in the government. Although it deemphasized the importance of complaints, believing that they were of only remedial importance, it nevertheless took steps to strengthen the complaint system. Finally, and most importantly, the committee developed a new sense of realism in recognizing that "full equality of employment opportunity requires that we face up to the whole problem of equality itself." Accordingly, it began thinking along compensatory lines.

The Kennedy program was carried forward by President Johnson until 1965, when another reorganization occurred and a longer-lived program was initiated. The change was a result of many factors. The Civil Rights Act of 1964 declared that "it shall be the policy of the United States to ensure equal employment opportunities for Federal employees." It also created the Equal Employment Opportunity Commission to combat discrimination in the private sphere and, consequently, the coordination of all federal civil rights activities became increasingly complex and difficult. Funding for the President's Committee on EEO ran into difficulty in Congress, and it was decided to shift its responsibilities to the Civil Service Commission, where the program remained until 1979.

The Civil Rights Act also required EEO for women by prohibiting discrimination on the basis of sex. Prior to its enactment, Kennedy had created a Commission on the Status of Women and subsequently issued a memorandum requiring that appointments and promotions be made without regard to sex except under circumstances where the Civil Service Commission found differentiated treatment justifiable. In 1967, the Women's Program was incorporated into the overall EEO program for the first time.

The next major development in the evolution of the EEO program came in 1969, when President Nixon issued an executive order requiring agency heads to "establish and maintain an affirmative program of equal employment opportunity." The following year, Nixon changed the nature of EEO activities still further by creating a Spanish-Speaking Program within the overall EEO program. Designed to bring more members of the Spanish-speaking population into the federal service, it is now called the Hispanic Employment Program and constitutes an integral part of the government's EEO efforts. It has been effective in turning attention to the special circumstances of the Hispanic segment of the population.

The Equal Employment Opportunity Act of 1972 solidified the Civil Service Commission's authority in this area and placed the program on a solid statutory basis for the first time. It reaffirmed the traditional policy of nondiscrimination and empowered the Commission to enforce its provisions "through appropriate remedies, including reinstatement or hiring of employees with or without back pay . . . and issuing such rules, regulations, orders and instructions as it deems necessary and appropriate." It also made the Commission responsible for the annual review and approval of agency EEO plans and for evaluating agency EEO activities. The act also brought state and local governments under the federal EEO umbrella for the first time. The Equal Employment Opportunity Commission, hithertofore primarily concerned with the private sector, was given equal authority over the nonfederal public sector.

In 1979, as a part of the overall federal civil service reforms then taking place, the enforcement aspects of the federal EEO program were transferred to the Equal Employment Opportunity Commission. But while the EEOC gained responsibility for reviewing affirmative action plans and processing complaints of discrimination, the newly created Office of Personnel Management contained an Office of Affirmative Employment Programs which had responsibility for the Federal Women's Program, the Hispanic Employment Program, and programs for veterans, the handicapped, and the "upward mobility" of members of these groups and minorities generally.

There are several lessons of contemporary relevance to be learned from the past. Foremost among these is the simple fact that the government had engaged in widespread discriminatory practices. Blacks, members of other minority groups, and women were not excluded on the basis of their qualifications, but rather on the basis of their social characteristics. The merit system, once created, did not fully apply to them. In addition, the development of the federal EEO program indicated that while organizational change came frequently, substantive change has been evasive. Although the first-stage problem of equalizing the opportunity of members of minority groups and women to gain entrance to the federal service has been more or less resolved, these government employees remain overwhelmingly and disproportionately concentrated in the lower grades of the bureaucracy. Whether equal opportunity has been created remains debatable.

For the law of EEO, see Charles A. Sullivan, Michael J. Zimmer and Richard F. Richards, *Federal Statutory Law of Employment Discrimination* (Indianapolis, Ind.: Michie Bobbs-Merrill, 1980); Daniel B. Edelman, *EEO in the Judicial Branch: An Outline of Policy and Law* (Williamsburg, Va.: National Center for State Courts, 1981); Barbara Lindemann Schlei and Paul Frossman, *Employment Discrimination Law*, 2nd ed. (Washington, D.C.: Bureau of National Affairs, Inc., 1983). For the history of EEO in the federal government, see David H. Rosenbloom, *Federal Equal Employment Opportunity: Politics and Public Personnel Administration*(New York: Praeger, 1977).

See also the following entries:
ADVERSE EFFECT
ADVERSE IMPACT
ADVERSE-INFERENCE RULE
AFFECTED CLASS

AFFIRMATIVE ACTION
BONA FIDE OCCUPATIONAL QUALIFICATION
BOTTOM-LINE CONCEPT
BUSINESS NECESSITY
CHILLING EFFECT
CONSENT DECREE
DISCRIMINATION
DISPARATE EFFECT
EMPLOYMENT PRACTICE
FAIR EMPLOYMENT PRACTICE COMMISSION
FAIR EMPLOYMENT PRACTICE COMMITTEE
GOALS
HISHON V. KING AND SPALDING
MAKE WHOLE
NATIONAL ASSOCIATION FOR THE ADVANCEMENT OF COLORED PEOPLE V. FEDERAL POWER COMMISSION
READING ASSISTANT
REASONABLE ACCOMMODATION
REHABILITATED OFFENDER PROGRAM
RELIGIOUS DISCRIMINATION
REPRESENTATIVE BUREAUCRACY
REVERSE DISCRIMINATION
RIGHTFUL PLACE
SCHLESINGER V. BALLARD
SEX PLUS
TEXAS DEPARTMENT OF COMMUNITY AFFAIRS V. JOYCE ANN BURDINE
THIRD PARTY
TITLE VII
TOKENISM
UNDERUTILIZATION
UNFAIR LABOR PRACTICES (EMPLOYERS)
UNFAIR LABOR PRACTICES (UNIONS)
UPWARD MOBILITY PROGRAM

Equal Employment Opportunity Act of 1972, also called EEO ACT OF 1972, amends Title VII of the 1964 Civil Rights Act by strengthening the authority of the Equal Employment Opportunity Commission and extending anti-discrimination provisions to state and local governments and labor organizations with fifteen or more employees and public and private employment agencies. See William Brown III, "The Equal Employment Opportunity Act of 1972—The Light at the Top of the Stairs," *Personnel Administration* (June 1972); Harry Grossman, "The Equal Employment Opportunity Act of 1972, Its Implications for the State and Local Government Manager," *Public Personnel Management* (September–October 1973).

See also HAZELWOOD SCHOOL DISTRICT V. UNITED STATES.

Equal Employment Opportunity Commission (EEOC), created by Title VII of the Civil Rights Act of 1964. The EEOC is composed of five members (one designated chair) appointed for five-year terms by the president, subject to the advice and consent of the Senate. The EEOC's mission is to end discrimination based on race, color, religion, sex, or national origin in hiring, promotion, firing, wages, testing, training, apprenticeship, and all other conditions of employment and to promote voluntary action programs by employers, unions, and community organizations to make equal employment opportunity an actuality.

The EEOC's operations are decentralized in forty-eight field offices which receive written charges of discrimination against public and private employers, labor organizations, joint labor-management apprenticeship programs, and public and private employment agencies. EEOC members may also initiate charges alleging that a violation of Title VII has occurred. Charges of Title VII violation must be filed with the EEOC within 180 days of the alleged violation. The EEOC is responsible for notifying persons so charged within ten days of the receipt of a new charge. Before investigation, a charge must be deferred for sixty days to a local fair employment practices agency in states and municipalities where an enforceable fair employment practices law is in effect. (The deferral period is 120 days for an agency which has been operating less than one year.) After an investigation, if there is reasonable cause to believe the charge is true, the district office attempts to remedy the alleged unlawful practices through the informal methods of conciliation, conference, and persuasion.

Unless an acceptable conciliation agreement has been secured, the EEOC may, after thirty days from the date the charge was filed, bring suit in an appropriate federal district court. (The U.S. Attorney General brings suit when a state government, governmental agency, or political subdivision is involved.) If the EEOC or the Attorney General does not proceed in this manner, at the conclusion of the administrative procedures, or earlier at the request of the charging party, a "Notice of Right to Sue" is issued, which allows the charging party to proceed within ninety days in a federal district court. In appropriate cases, the EEOC may intervene in such civil action if the case is of general public interest. The investigation and conciliation of charges having an industrywide or national impact are coordinated or conducted by the EEOC's Office of Systemic Programs.

If it is concluded after a preliminary investigation that prompt judicial action is necessary to carry out the purposes of the act, the EEOC or the Attorney General, in a case involving a state government, governmental agency, or political subdivision, may bring an action for appropriate temporary or preliminary relief pending final disposition of a charge.

The EEOC encourages and assists in voluntary action by employers, unions, and employment agencies through affirmative action programs, providing the EEOC's services in developing multiplant and industrywide programs and in identifying discriminatory systems and devising ways to change them. Such programs are designed to help those organizations achieve EEO goals through nondiscriminatory recruiting, fair employee selection procedures, expanded training programs, and job upgrading.

Federal employees or applicants who want to file complaints of job discrimination based on race, color, national origin, sex, religion, age, or physical or mental handicap must first consult an equal employment opportunity counselor within their agency within thirty calendar days of the alleged act. If the complaint cannot be resolved informally, the person may file a formal complaint within fifteen calendar days following the final interview with the counselor.

The EEOC has direct liaison with state and local governments, employer and union organizations, trade associations, civil rights organizations, and other agencies and organizations concerned with employment of minority-group members and women. The EEOC engages in and contributes to the cost of research and other mutual interest projects with state and local agencies charged with the administration of fair employment practices laws. Furthermore, the Commission enters into work-sharing agreements with the state and local agencies in order to avoid duplication of effort by identifying specific charges to be investigated by the respective agencies. *See* William A. Webb, "The Mission of the Equal Employment Opportunity Commission," *Labor Law Journal* (July 1983); Frank J. Thompson, "Deregulation at the EEOC: Prospects and Implications," *Review of Public Personnel Administration* (Summer 1984).

    Equal Employment Opportunity Commission
    2401 E St., N.W.
    Washington, D.C. 20507
    (202) 634-6922
    See also 706 AGENCY.

Equal Employment Opportunity Commission v. Wyoming, 75 L Ed 2d 18 (1983), U.S. Supreme Court case which upheld the federal government's 1974 extension of the Age Discrimination in Employment Act to cover state and local government workers.

equal employment opportunity counselor, specifically designated individual within an organization who provides an open and systematic channel through which employees may raise questions, discuss real and imagined grievances, and obtain information on their procedural rights. Counseling is the first stage in the discrimination complaint process. The counselor attempts through interviews and inquiries to resolve informally problems related to equal employment opportunity. *See* U.S. Civil Service Commission, *Equal Employment Opportunity Counseling: A* *Guidebook* (Washington, D.C.: Government Printing Office, October 1975).

equal employment opportunity officer, official within an organization who is designated responsible for monitoring EEO programs and assuring that both organizational and national EEO policies are being implemented.

equality, also EGALITARIANISM, philosophic disposition toward the greater political and social equality of the citizens within a state; this is, all citizens would have an equal claim on the political and economic rewards of the society. However, economists warn that "any insistence on carving the pie into equal slices would shrink the size of the pie." Arthur M. Okun, *Equality and Efficiency: The Big Tradeoff* (Washington, D.C.: The Brookings Institution, 1975). *See also* Terry Eastland and William J. Bennett, *Counting by Race: Equality from the Founding Fathers to Bakke and Weber* (New York: Basic Books, 1979).

equalization, adjustment of assessments and taxes on real estate to make sure that properties are properly valued and are taxed fairly according to value.

Equal Pay Act of 1963, basically an amendment to the Fair Labor Standards Act of 1938. The Equal Pay Act of 1963 (Public Law 88-38) prohibits pay discrimination because of sex and provides that men and women working in the same establishment under similar conditions must receive the same pay if jobs require equal (similar) skill, effort, and responsibility. *See* John E. Burns and Catherine G. Burns, "An Analysis of the Equal Pay Act," *Labor Law Journal* (February 1973).
    See also the following entries:
    COMPARABLE WORTH
    CORNING GLASS WORKS V. BRENNAN
    COUNTY OF WASHINGTON V. GUNTHER

equal pay for equal work, principle that salary rates should not be dependent upon factors unrelated to the quantity or quality of work. *See* Francine D. Blau, *Equal*

Pay in the Office (Lexington, Mass.: Lexington Books, 1977); Barrie O. Pettman, ed., *Equal Pay For Women: Progress and Problems in Seven Countries* (New York: McGraw-Hill, 1977); Raymond L. Hogler, "Equal Pay, Equal Work, and the United States Supreme Court," *Labor Law Journal* (November 1981); Winn Newman, "Pay Equity Emerges as a Top Labor Issue in the 1980's," *Monthly Labor Review* (April 1982); Paul S. Greenlaw and John P. Kohl, "The EEOC's New Equal Pay Guidelines," *Personnel Journal* (July 1982); Judith A. Alexander, *Equal-Pay-for-Equal-Work Legislation in Canada* (Ottawa, Ontario: Economic Council of Canada, 1984).

equal protection clause, *see* BROWN V. BOARD OF EDUCATION OF TOPEKA, KANSAS.

equal protection of laws, constitutional requirement that the government will in no way fail to treat equals equally, set up illegal categories to justify treating persons unfairly, or give unfair or unequal treatment to a person based on that person's race, religion, etc.

Equal Rights Amendment (ERA), amendment passed by Congress in 1972 that never became law because too few states ratified it. The proposed Twenty-seventh Amendment read: "Equality of rights under the law shall not be denied or abridged by the United States or any state on account of sex." *See* Bruce E. Altschuler, "State ERAs: What Have They Done," *State Government* Vol. 56, No. 4 (1983); Gilbert Y. Steiner, *Constitutional Inequality: The Political Fortunes of the Equal Rights Amendment* (Washington, D.C.: The Brookings Institution, 1985).

equated scores, scores from different tests of the same variable which are reduced by weighting in order to have a common basis for comparison.

equating, process of adjusting the raw statistics obtained from a particular sample to corresponding statistics obtained for a base group or reference population.

equipercentile equating, process that treats as equivalent those raw scores that fall at the same percentile in different samples although the raw scores themselves may be different.

equity, external/internal, *see* EXTERNAL EQUITY.

equity theory, *see* INEQUITY THEORY.

equivalent form, *see* ALTERNATE FORM.

ergonomics, *see* HUMAN-FACTORS ENGINEERING.

ERISA, *see* EMPLOYEE RETIREMENT INCOME SECURITY ACT OF 1974.

ESA, *see* EMPLOYMENT STANDARDS ADMINISTRATION.

escalator clause, also called COST-OF-LIVING ESCALATOR, provision of a collective bargaining agreement which allows for periodic wage adjustments in response to changes in the cost of living, usually as determined by the Consumer Price Index of the Bureau of Labor Statistics. *See* Francis S. Cunningham, "The Use of Price Indexes in Escalator Contracts," *Monthly Labor Review* (August 1963); Robert H. Ferguson, *Cost-of-Living Adjustments in Union-Management Agreements* (Ithaca, N.Y.: New York State School of Industrial and Labor Relations, Cornell University, 1976); Wayne Vroman, "Cost-of-Living Escalators and Price-Wage Linkages in the U.S. Economy, 1968-1980," *Industrial & Labor Relations Review* (January 1985).

escape clause, in a maintenance-of-membership shop, part of a union contract that provides for a period of time during which union members may withdraw (escape) from the union without affecting their employment.

Espinoza v. Farah Manufacturing Company, 414 U.S. 86 (1973), U.S. Supreme Court case which held that an employer who refused to hire a lawfully admitted resident alien because of a long-standing policy against the employment of aliens could not be held liable under Title VII of the Civil Rights Act of 1964 if the company already employed a significant percentage of other employees who were of the same national origin but were also U.S. citizens.

esprit de corps, strong feelings of unity and common purpose on the part of a group.

estates analysis, paradigm for describing the federal government's science/technology policymaking process. Developed by Don K. Price, estates analysis posits four estates or groups involved in science/technology policymaking: (1) the "political estate" of elected public officials; (2) the "administrative estate" comprised of private and public sector managers; (3) the "professional estate" made up of the organized professions such as medicine or engineering; and (4) the "scientific estate" of scientists in government, universities, or corporations involved with basic research. The interactions between these groups or estates is the process from which policy emerges. See Don K. Price, *The Scientific Estate* (Cambridge, Mass.: Belknap Press of Harvard University Press, 1965).

estate tax, see TAX, ESTATE.

estimated tax, portion of income tax which individuals with income other than salaries must "declare" and pay every three months.
   See also TAXATION.

ETA, see EMPLOYMENT AND TRAINING ADMINISTRATION.

ethics, a set of moral principles or values.
   There are many ethical individuals involved in public administration. However, their ethical standards tend to reflect their personal background rather than some abstract standards of professional conduct. Analyses of the ethical issues in public administration range from the "always-plead-innocent" school of venality to the philosophic concerns of providing equitable public services to each member of the community. *See* Wayne A. R. Leys, "Ethics and Administrative Discretion," *Public Administration Review* (Winter 1943); Robert C. Wood, "Ethics in Government as a Problem in Executive Management," *Public Administration Review* (Winter 1955); Paul H. Douglas, *Ethics in Government* (Cambridge, Mass.: Harvard University Press, 1957); Abraham Kaplan, *American Ethics and Public Policy* (New York: Oxford University Press, 1963); Stephen K. Bailey, "Ethics and the Public Service," *Public Administration Review* (December 1964); James P. Clarre, "Code of Ethics: Waste of Time or Important Control?" *Public Management* (August 1967); George A. Graham, "Ethical Guidelines for Public Administrators: Observations on Rules of the Games," *Public Administration Review* (January–February 1974); F. J. Tickner, "Ethical Guidelines for Administrators: Comparison with Whitehall," *Public Administration Review* (November–December 1974); John A. Rohr, "The Study of Ethics in the P. A. Curriculum," *Public Administration Review* (July–August 1976); Susan Wakefield, "Ethics and the Public Service: A Case for Responsibility," *Public Administration Review* (November–December 1976); John Rohr, *Ethics for Bureaucrats* (New York: Dekker, 1978); Jeremy F. Plant and Harold F. Gortner, "Ethics, Personnel Management, and Civil Service Reform," *Public Personnel Management,* Vol. 10, No. 1 (1981); Terry L. Cooper, *The Responsible Administrator: An Approach to Ethics for the Administrative Role* (Port Washington, N.Y.: Kennikat Press, 1982); Debra W. Stewart, "Managing Competing Claims: An Ethical Framework for Human Resources Decision Making," *Public Administration Review* (January–February 1984); York Willbern, "Types and Levels of Public Morality," *Public Administration Review* (March–April 1984); Theodore R. Vallance, editor, *Values and Ethics in Human Development Professions* (Dubuque, Iowa: Kendall-Hunt, 1984).
   See also CODE OF ETHICS and WHISTLEBLOWING.

Code Of Ethics
of the
American Society for Public Administration

ASPA members share with their neighbors all of the responsibilities and rights of citizenship in a democratic society. However, the mission and goals of ASPA call every member to additional dedication and commitment. Certain principles and moral standards must guide the conduct of ASPA members not merely in preventing wrong, in pursuing right through timely and energetic execution of responsibilities.

To this end, we, the members of the Society, recognizing the critical role of conscience in choosing among courses of action and taking into account the moral ambiguities of life, commit ourselves to:

1. demonstrate the highest standards of personal integrity, truthfulness, honesty and fortitude in all our public activities in order to inspire public confidence and trust in public institutions;

2. serve the public with respect, concern, courtesy, and responsiveness, recognizing that service to the public is beyond service to oneself;

3. strive for personal professional excellence and encourage the professional development of our associates and those seeking to enter the field of public administration;

4. approach our organization and operational duties with a positive attitude and constructively support open communication, creativity, dedication and compassion;

5. serve in such a way that we do not realize undue personal gain from the performance of our official duties;

6. avoid any interest or activity which is in conflict with the conduct of our official duties;

7. respect and protect the privileged information to which we have access in the course of official duties;

8. exercise whatever discretionary authority we have under law to promote the public interest;

9. accept as a personal duty the responsibility to keep up to date on emerging issues and to administer the public's business with professional competence, fairness, impartiality, efficiency and effectiveness;

10. support, implement, and promote merit employment and programs of affirmative action to assure equal opportunity by our recruitment, selection, and advancement of qualified persons from all elements of society;

11. eliminate all forms of illegal discrimination, fraud, and mismanagement of public funds, and support colleagues if they are in difficulty because of responsible efforts to correct such discrimination, fraud, mismanagement or abuse;

12. respect, support, study, and when necessary, work to improve federal and state constitutions, and other laws which define the relationships among public agencies, employees, clients and all citizens.
Approved by National Council April, 8, 1984

Ethics in Government Act of 1978, federal statue that seeks to deal with possible conflicts of interest by former federal executive branch employees by imposing post-employment prohibitions on their activities. The restrictions in the law are concerned with former government employees' representation or attempts to influence federal agencies, not with their employment by others. What is prohibited depends on how involved a former employee was with a matter while with the government and whether he or she was one of a specified group of senior employees. *See* J. Jackson Walter, "The Ethics in Government Act, Conflict of Interest Laws and Presidential Recruiting," *Public Administration Review* (November-December 1981).

ethnic categories, *see* RACE CATEGORIES

ethnic group, social, biological, or (sometimes) political division of humankind. *See* David Nachmias and David Rosenbloom, "Bureaucracy and Ethnicity," *American Journal of Sociology* (January 1978); Joseph Rothschild, *Ethnopolitics: A Conceptual Framework* (New York: Columbia University Press, 1981); Thomas Sowell, *Ethnic America: A History* (New York: Basic Books, 1981); Stephen Steinberg, *The Ethnic Myth: Race, Ethnicity, and Class in America* (New York: Atheneum, 1981).

Etzioni, Amitai W. (1929-), sociologist and author of a variety of books on international relations, best known to organizational analysts for his studies of how organizations interact with the larger society and how the various parts of organizations interact, change, and survive. Major works include: *A Comparative Analysis of Complex Organizations* (Glencoe, Ill.: The Free Press, 1961); *Modern Organizations* (Englewood Cliffs, N.J.: Prentice-Hall, 1964).

See also MIXED-SCANNING

Euclidian zoning, zoning laws that keep all apartment houses, shops, businesses, etc., out of single-home residential areas.

eupsychian management, term originated by Abraham H. Maslow, in *Eupsychian Management: A Journal* (Homewood, Ill.: Richard D. Irwin, Inc., 1965), to describe an ideal situation with respect to workers motivation, productivity, and mental health. Relating eupsychian management to his more famous "hierarchy of needs," Maslow defines it as "the culture that would be generated by one thousand self-actualizing people on some sheltered island."

See also NEEDS HIERARCHY and SELF-ACTUALIZATION.

Eurodollars, refers to a deposit denominated in U.S. dollars held in commercial banks outside the United States. The international trade in Eurodollars functions as a source of international short-term capital which tends to flow to countries offering the highest interest rates. Other currencies have also filled this role and are called Eurocurrencies. *See* W. P. Hogan and Ivor F. Pearce, *The Incredible Eurodollar, Or Why the World's Money System is Collapsing,* 3rd ed. (Winchester, MA: Allen & Unwin, 1984).

evaluation. *Evaluation research* is an attempt to assess specific policy options by conducting experiments, assessing their outcomes, and recommending whether the new concept should be broadly applied. *Policy evaluation* analyzes policy alternatives in advance of a decision. *Program evaluation* is the use of research techniques to measure the past performance of a specific program—in particular, the program's impact on the conditions it seeks

to modify—for the purpose of changing the operation of the program so as to improve its effectiveness at achieving its objectives. *See* Fred D. Baldwin, "Evaluating Evaluators," *Public Administration Review* (January–February 1972); Joseph S. Wholey, "The Role of Evaluation in Improving Public Programs," *Public Administration Review* (November–December 1976); Albert C. Hyde and Jay M. Shafritz, eds., *Program Evaluation in the Public Sector* (New York: Praeger, 1979); Theodore H. Poister *et al., Applied Program Evaluation in Local Government* (Lexington, Mass.: Lexington Books, 1979); David Nachmias, *Public Policy Evaluation* (New York: St. Martin's, 1979); Erwin C. Hargrove, "The Bureaucratic Politics of Evaluation: A Case Study of the Department of Labor," *Public Administration Review* (March–April 1980); Mark R. Daniels and Clifford J. Wirth, "Paradigms of Evaluation Research," *American Review of Public Administration* (Spring 1983).

See also PROGRAM EVALUATION.

examination, *see* EMPLOYMENT TESTING.

examination, assembled, examination that includes as one of its parts a written or performance test for which applicants are required to take at appointed times and places.

examination, group oral, *see* GROUP ORAL INTERVIEW.

examination, unassembled, examination in which applicants are rated on their education, experience, and other qualifications as shown in the formal application and any supportive evidence that may be required, without assembling for a written or performance test.

Examining Board v. Flores de Otero, 426 U.S. 572 (1976), U.S. Supreme Court case which held that a Puerto Rican statute permitting only U.S. citizens to practice privately as civil engineers was unconstitutional and that resident aliens could not be denied the same opportunity.

Excelsior rule, ruling by the National Labor Relations Board that an employer must provide a list of the names and addresses of all employees eligible to vote in a forthcoming representation election. While the list is given to the NLRB, it is made available to employee organizations. The U.S. Supreme Court, in *NLRB* v. *Wyman-Gordon Co.,* 394 U.S. 759 (1969), upheld the NLRB's right to demand such a list.

excepted positions, also called EXEMPTED POSITIONS, U.S. civil service positions that have been excepted or exempted from merit system requirements. Most of the excepted positions in the U.S. Civil Service are excluded by statute and are under merit systems administered by agencies such as the Tennessee Valley Authority, the Federal Bureau of Investigation, the U.S. Foreign Service, and the U.S. Postal Service. Excepted position has the same meaning as *unclassified position,* or *position excepted by law,* or *position excepted by executive order,* or *position excepted by civil service rule,* or *position outside the competitive service* as used in existing statutes and executive orders.

excepting language, language relied on to establish an exception from the competitive service. The Attorney General of the United States has held that such language must be so plain and unequivocal as to admit of no doubts. When acts are silent on how appointments shall be made, the civil service laws, rules, and regulations apply.

excess profits tax, *see* TAX, EXCESS PROFITS.

Exchange Parts decision, *see* NATIONAL LABOR RELATIONS BOARD V. EXCHANGE PARTS.

exchange rate, the price of one currency in terms of another currency. For example, if $1 = 2 Deutsche Marks, the DM exchange rate for the dollar is DM 2, while the dollar exchange rate for the DM is $.50. *See* Ralph C. Bryant, *Financial Interdependence and Variability in Exchange Rates* (Washington, D.C.: The Brookings Institution, 1980).

excise tax, *see* TAX, EXCISE.

exclusionary clause, that part of a contract that tries to restrict the legal remedies available to one side if the contract is broken.

exclusive recognition, also called EXCLUSIVE BARGAINING RIGHTS, in the private sector, the only form of recognition available to a union representing a specific bargaining unit. An employer is required to negotiate in good faith and to give exclusive bargaining rights to a union holding such recognition. In fact, a private employer may not bargain or consult with a union that does not hold exclusive recognition without committing an unfair labor practice.

As a term, exclusive recognition has had its greatest usage in the federal service. The Civil Service Reform Act of 1978 provides that in order to obtain exclusive recognition, a union must (1) qualify as a bona fide union, (2) submit to the agency a roster of its officers and representatives, a copy of its constitution and bylaws, and a statement of its objectives, and (3) show that it has majority support solely by means of a secret ballot election in which it receives a majority of the votes cast. Exclusive recognition entitles the union to act for, and to negotiate agreements covering, all the employees in the unit. It guarantees the union the opportunity to be represented at discussions between management and employees concerning grievances and personnel policies.

ex-con, *see* EX-OFFENDER.

executive, any of the highest managers in an organization; that branch of government concerned with the implementation of the policies and laws created by a legislature.

See also GROUP EXECUTIVE and PLURAL EXECUTIVE.

executive agreement, term that covers a wide variety of international agreements and understandings that are reached by the governments concerned in the course of administering their relationships.

The executive agreement device permits a president to enter into open and/or secret arrangements with a foreign government without the advice and consent of the Senate.

There are two broad categories of executive agreements: presidential agreements and congressional-executive agreements. Presidential agreements are those made solely on the basis of the constitutional authority of the president; congressional-executive agreements cover all international agreements entered into under the combined authority of the president and the Congress.

The executive agreement is used for significant political agreements, such as an aid-for-naval-bases agreement with Spain, as well as routine, non-political agreements such as reciprocal postal arrangements with England. The former are usually made under the president's sole power to faithfully execute the laws, or his diplomatic or commander-in-chief powers. The latter agreements are usually made under authority of Congress and the president. The vast majority of executive agreements are entered into in pursuit of specific congressional authority.

The Supreme Court, in *U.S.* v. *Belmont,* 301 U.S. 324 (1937), unanimously held an executive agreement to be a valid international compact, state policy not withstanding. The court said in part:

In respect of all international negotiations and compacts, and in respect of our foreign relations generally, state lines disappear.

The court has ruled, however, that the president is not free to enter into executive agreements that violate constitutional provisions. *See U.S.* v. *Guy W. Capps, Inc.,* 204 F. 2d 655 (4th Cir. 1953), aff'd on other grounds, 348 U.S. 296 (1955), and *Reid* v. *Covert,* 354 U.S. 1 (1957).

By the Case Act of 1972, PL 92-403, Congress required that the Secretary of State transmit to Congress all executive agreements to which the United States is a party no later than sixty days after such agreement has entered into force. The president need report secret agreements only to the foreign relations committees of the two Houses. The law did not give Congress authority to disapprove an executive agreement.

Executive agreements have been published since 1950 in a series entitled *United States Treaties and Other International Agreements.*

executive budget, *see* BUDGET, EXECUTIVE.

executive compensation, totality of the benefits paid to the members of the upper levels of the organizational hierarchy. According to William H. Cash, "Executive Compensation," *The Personnel Administrator* (September 1977),

executive compensation programs are generally viewed as being made up of five basic elements—base salary, short-term (annual) incentives or bonuses, long-term incentives and capital appreciation plans, fringe benefits, and prerequisites.

For a bibliography, *see* Karen B. Tracy, "On Executive Compensation," *Harvard Business Review* (January–February 1977).

executive development, *see* MANAGEMENT DEVELOPMENT.

Executive Interchange Program, *see* PRESIDENT'S EXECUTIVE INTERCHANGE PROGRAM.

Executive Office of the President (EOP), umbrella office consisting of the top presidential staff agencies that provide the president help and advice in carrying out his major responsibilities. The EOP was created by President Franklin Roosevelt under authority of the Reorganization Act of 1939. Since then, presidents have used executive orders, reorganization plans and legislative initiatives to reorganize, expand, or contract the EOP. For an excellent study of the growth of the EOP, *see* Thomas E.

187

Cronin, "The Swelling of the Presidency," *Saturday Review* (February 1973). *Also see* Emmette S. Redford and Marlan Blisset, *Organizing the Executive Branch: The Johnson Presidency* (Chicago: University of Chicago Press, 1981).

> The White House Office
> 1600 Pennsylvania Ave., N.W.
> Washington, D.C. 20500
> (202) 456-1414
> *See also* the following entries:
> BROWNLOW COMMITTEE
> PRESIDENCY, AMERICAN
> PRESIDENTIAL POWER

executive order, any rule or regulation issued by a chief administrative authority that, because of precedent and existing legislative authorization, has the effect of law. Executive orders are the principal mode of administrative action on the part of the president of the United States.

The power of a president to issue executive orders emanates from the constitutional provision requiring him to "take care that the laws be faithfully executed," the Commander-in-Chief clause, and express powers vested in him by congressional statutes. *See* William D. Neighbors, "Presidential Legislation By Executive Order," *University of Colorado Law Review* (Fall 1964); William Hebe, "Executive Orders and the Development of Presidential Power," *Villanova Law Review* (March 1972); E. Lee Bernick, "Discovering a Governor's Powers: The Executive Order," *State Government,* Vol. 57, No. 3 (1984).

Executive Order 8802, presidential executive order of June 25, 1941 which (1) required that defense contractors not discriminate against any worker because of race, creed, or national origin and (2) established a Committee on Fair Employment Practice to investigate and remedy violations.

Executive Order 10925, presidential executive order of March 6, 1961 which for the first time required that "affirmative action" be used to implement the policy of nondiscrimination in employment by the federal government and its contractors.

Executive Order 10988, presidential executive order of January 17, 1962 which first established the right of federal employees to bargain with management over certain limited issues. Considered the "Magna Carta" of labor relations in the federal government, it was superseded by Executive Order 11491.

Executive Order 11141, presidential executive order of February 12, 1964 which prohibits employment discrimination because of age by federal government contractors.

Executive Order 11246, presidential executive order of September 24, 1965 which requires federal government contracts to contain provisions against employment discrimination because of race, color, religion, or national origin.

See also PHILADELPHIA PLAN.

Executive Order 11375, presidential executive order of October 17, 1967 which requires federal government contracts to contain provisions against employment discrimination because of sex.

Executive Order 11451, *see* PRESIDENT'S EXECUTIVE INTERCHANGE PROGRAM.

Executive Order 11478, presidential executive order of August 8, 1969 which prohibits discrimination in federal government employment because of race, color, religion, sex, or national origin.

Executive Order 11491, presidential executive order of October 29, 1969 which granted each federal employee the right to join or not join a labor organization, created the Federal Labor Relations Council (which was superseded by the Federal Labor Relations Authority), and generally expanded the scope of bargaining for federal employees. *See* Ed D. Roach and Frank W. McClain, "Executive Order 11491: Prospects and Problems," *Public Personnel Review* (July 1970).

Executive Order 11914, presidential executive order of April 28, 1976 which extends nondiscrimination with respect to the handicapped provisions of the Vocational Rehabilitation Act of 1973 to all federal departments and agencies.

Executive Order 11935, see HAMPTON V. MOW SUN WONG.

Executive Order 12008, see PRESIDENTIAL MANAGEMENT INTERN PROGRAM.

executive oversight, total process by which an executive attempts to exercise control over his organization and hold individual managers responsible for the implementation of their programs. See Lance T. LeLoup and William B. Moreland, "Agency Strategies and Executive Review: The Hidden Politics of Budgeting," *Public Administration Review* (May–June 1978).

executive privilege, presidential claim that the executive branch may withhold information from the Congress or its committees and the courts to preserve confidential communications within the executive branch or to secure the national interest.

Although the Constitution does not explicitly grant the executive a privilege to withhold information from Congress, presidents have from the beginning of the Republic claimed it. President George Washington withheld from the House of Representatives papers and documents connected with the Jay Treaty because, he argued, the House had no constitutional role in the treaty making process.

The presidential claim of executive privilege was not seriously challenged until President Richard Nixon sought to use executive privilege to sustain immunity from the judicial process. In 1974 the U.S. Supreme Court restricted the privilege when it held that in a criminal case before a court a concrete need for evidence takes precedence over a generalized assertion of executive privilege unrelated to defense or diplomacy.

The Supreme Court did acknowledge a constitutional protection for the "presi-

dent's need for complete candor and objectivity from [his] advisors" and for "military, diplomatic, or sensitive national security secrets." See U.S. v. Nixon, 418 U.S. 683 (1974). For a listing of previous presidential uses of the executive privilege, see *The Power of the President to Withhold Information from the Congress*, compiled by the Subcommittee on Constitutional Rights of the Senate Committee on the Judiciary, 85th Congress, 2nd Session (1958). For the view that the presidential claim of executive privilege is without historical foundation see Raoul Berger, *Executive Privilege: A Constitutional Myth* (Cambridge, Massachusetts: Harvard University Press, 1974). Also see Adam C. Breckenridge, *The Executive Privilege: Presidential Control Over Information* (University of Nebraska Press, 1974).

The Supreme Court Limits Executive Privilege

In support of his claim of absolute privilege, the President's counsel urges two grounds, one of which is common to all governments and one of which is peculiar to our system of separation of powers. The first ground is the valid need for protection of communications between high Government officials and those who advise and assist them in the performance of their manifold duties; the importance of this confidentiality is too plain to require further discussion. Human experience teaches that those who expect public dissemination of their remarks may well temper candor with a concern for appearances and for their own interests to the detriment of the decisionmaking process. Whatever the nature of the privilege of confidentiality of Presidential communications in the exercise of Art II powers, the privilege can be said to derive from the supremacy of each branch within its own assigned area of constitutional duties. Certain powers and privileges flow from the nature of enumerated powers; the protection of the confidentiality of Presidential communications has similar constitutional underpinnings.

The second ground asserted by the President's counsel in support of the claim of absolute privilege rests on the doctrine of separation of powers. Here it is argued that the independence of the Executive Branch within its own sphere, *Humphrey's Executor v. United States*, 295 U.S. 602, 629-630, 79 L Ed 1611, 55 S. Ct. 869 (1935); *Kilbourn v Thompson*, 103 U.S. 168, 190-191, 26 L Ed 377 (1881), insulates a President from a judicial subpoena in an ongoing criminal prosecution, and thereby protects confidential Presidential communications.

However, neither the doctrine of separation of powers, nor the need for confidentiality of high-level communications, without more, can sustain an absolute, unqualified Presidential privilege of immunity from judicial process under all circumstances. The President's need for complete candor and objectivity from advisers calls for great deference from the courts. However, when the privilege depends solely on the broad, undifferentiated claim of public interest in the confidentiality of such conversations, a confrontation with other values arises. Absent a claim of need to protect military, diplomatic, or sensitive national security secrets, we find it difficult to accept the argument that even the very important interest in confidentiality of Presidential communications is significantly diminished by production of such material for in camera inspection with all the protection that a district court will be obliged to provide.

The impediment that an absolute, unqualified privilege would place in the way of the primary constitutional duty of the Judicial Branch to do justice in criminal prosecutions would plainly conflict with the function of the courts under Art III. In designing the structure of our Government and dividing and allocating the sovereign power among three co-equal branches, the Framers of the Constitution sought to provide a comprehensive system, but the separate powers were not intended to operate with absolute independence.

Source: United States v. *Richard M. Nixon,* 418 U.S. 683 (1974).

executive recruiter, *see* HEAD-HUNTER.

Executive Schedule, scale under which key management and policymaking positions in the federal service are compensated. Secretaries of cabinet departments, heads of agencies and their principal deputies, assistant secretaries, members of boards and commissions—a total of nearly 700 positions—are assigned to one of the five levels of the Executive Schedule, largely on the basis of protocol and interorganizational alignment. Virtually all the positions covered by the Executive Schedule are created by statute and carry specific statutory responsibilities and authorities.

executive session, any meeting of a legislative group or subgroup that is not open to the public.

exempted positions, *see* EXCEPTED POSITIONS,

exempt employees, employees who, because of their administrative, professional or executive status, are not covered by the overtime provisions of the Fair Labor Standards Act. In consequence, their employing organizations are not legally required to pay them for overtime work. For an analysis of the problem, *see* Robert A. Sbarra, "Exempt Employee Overtime," *Compensation Review* (First Quarter 1976).

exemption, deduction from gross income for income tax purposes allowed for the support of one's self and dependents.

exit interview, also called SEPARATION INTERVIEW, tool to monitor employee terminations that seeks information on why the employee is leaving and what he or she liked or disliked about his or her job, working conditions, company policy, etc. Exit interviews are usually, and most desirably, conducted by the personnel department and not by the supervisor of the exiting employee. When interviews are not possible, *exit questionnaires* seek to gather the same information. *See* Charles Bahn, "Expanded Use of the Exit Interview," *Personnel Journal* (December 1965); Martin Hilb, "The Standardized Exit Interview," *Personnel Journal* (June 1978); Laura Garrison and Jacqueline Ferguson, "Separation Interviews," *Personnel Journal* (September 1977); Wanda R. Embrey, R. Wayne Mondy, and Robert M. Noc, "Exit Interview: A Tool for Personnel Development," *Personnel Administrator* (May 1979); Pamela Garretson and Kenneth S. Teel, "The Exit Interview: Effective Tool or Meaningless Gesture?" *Personnel* (July–August 1982).

ex-offender, anyone who has been convicted of a crime or served time in prison. For an analysis of the problem of employing ex-offenders, *see* Marvin A. Jolson, "Are Ex-Offenders Successful Employees?" *California Management Review* (Spring 1975); Frederick Englander, "Helping Ex-Offenders Enter the Labor Market," *Monthly Labor Review* (July 1963); P. K. Lattimore and A. D. Witte, "Programs to Aid Ex-offenders: We Don't Know 'Nothing Works'," *Monthly Labor Review* (April 1985).

ex officio, Latin phrase ("by virtue of his office"). Many individuals hold positions on boards, commissions, councils, etc., because of an office that they temporarily occupy. For example, the mayor of a city may be an *ex officio* member of the board of trustees of a university in his or her city.

expectancy, probability of success on the job in terms of a specific criterion and associated with a known fact about an individual such as a test score, level of education, etc.

expectancy theory, also VALENCE, holds that individuals have cognitive "expectancies" regarding outcomes that are likely to occur as a result of what they do, and that individuals have preferences among these various outcomes. Consequently, motivation occurs on the basis of what the individual expects to occur as a result of what he chooses to do. An "expectancy" in this context refers to an employee's perceived probability that a given level of effort will result in a given outcome, such as a promotion or raise in salary. The value that an employee places on this outcome, the strength of the employee's preference for it, has been termed *valence* by Victor H. Vroom, *Work and Motivation* (New York: John Wiley, 1964). Valence can be positive or negative, depending on whether an individual is attracted to or repelled by a possible outcome. *See* Robert J. House, H. Jack Shapiro, and Mahmoud A. Wahba, "Expectancy Theory as a Predictor of Work Behavior and Attitude: A Reevaluation of Empirical Evidence," *Decision Sciences* (July 1974); Daniel R. Ilgen, Delbert N. Nebeker and Robert D. Pritchard, "Expectancy

Theory Measures: An Empirical Comparison in an Experimental Simulation," *Organizational Behavior and Human Performance* (October 1981); Gedaliahu H. Harel and Loretta K. Conen, "Expectancy Theory Applied to the Process of Professional Obsolescence," *Public Personnel Management* (Spring 1982); Samuel B. Pond, III, Achilles A. Armenakis and Samuel B. Green, "The Importance of Employee Expectations in Organizational Diagnosis," *The Journal of Applied Behavioral Science*, Vol. 20, No. 2 (1984). *See also* PSYCHOLOGICAL CONTRACT.

expedited arbitration, new streamlined process that is being increasingly incorporated into union contracts in an effort to cut down the backlog of grievance cases, because conventional arbitration is frequently so time consuming and expensive. In 1971, in response to the concern of parties over rising costs and delays in grievance arbitration, the Labor-Management Committee of the American Arbitration Association recommended the establishment of expedited procedures under which cases could be scheduled promptly and awards rendered no later than five days after the hearings. In return for giving up certain features of traditional labor arbitration (such as transcripts, briefs, and extensive opinions) the parties utilizing simplified procedures can get quick decisions and realize certain cost savings. While the term expedited arbitration can be applied to any "fast" method of resolving disputes through the use of an arbitrator, it is usually characterized by on-site hearings and the minimal involvement of the hierarchies of both union and management. For details of the technique, *see* Lawrence Stessin, "Expedited Arbitration: Less Grief Over Grievances," *Harvard Business Review* (January-February 1977).

expenditures, term generally used interchangeably with *outlays.*

experience-based learning, *see* LABORATORY TRAINING.

experienced unemployed, term from the U.S. Bureau of the Census that refers to "unemployed persons who have worked at any time in the past."

experience rating, insurance term which refers to a review of a previous year's group claims experience in order to establish premium rates for the following year. *See* Joseph M. Becker, *Experience Rating in Unemployment Insurance: An Experiment in Competitive Socialism* (Baltimore: The Johns Hopkins University Press, 1972).

experimental group, a group in a research design that is exposed to the treatment or manipulation called for in that design.

experimenter effect, any distortion in an experiment's findings because of the behavior or attitudes of the experimenters.
    See also HAWTHORNE EFFECT.

expert, efficiency, *see* EFFICIENCY EXPERT.

expiration date, time established by a collective bargaining agreement for the agreement to terminate.

expired account, an account in which authority to incur obligations has lapsed but from which outlays may be made to pay existing obligations and liabilities previously incurred, as well as valid adjustments thereto.

exported tax, *see* TAX EXPORTED.

Export-Import Bank (Eximbank), an autonomous agency of the U.S. government created to facilitate export-import trade. Under various programs, the *Eximbank* provides export credits and direct loans to foreign buyers and sells insurance and export guarantees to U.S. manufacturers.
    Eximbank
    811 Vermont Avenue, N.W.
    Washington, D.C. 20571
    (202) 566-8990

external alignment, relationship of positions within an organization to similar positions in the near environment. In theory, the most desirable external alignment calls for compensation programs similar to those provided by other employers in the local labor market.

external equity, also INTERNAL EQUITY, a measure of the justice of an employee's wages when the compensation for his/her position is compared to the labor market as a whole within a region, profession, or industry. *Internal equity* is a measure of the justice of an employee's wages when the compensation for his/her position is compared to similar positions within the same organization. *See* Thomas A. Mahoney, "Justice and Equity: A Recurring Theme in Compensation," *Personnel* (September–October 1975).

external house organ, *see* HOUSE ORGAN.

externalities, *see* SPILLOVER EFFECT.

external labor market, geographic region from which employers reasonably expect to recruit new workers.

extrinsic motivation, motivation not an inherent part of the work itself. When one works solely for the monetary rewards, one is extrinsically motivated.

F

face amount, in life insurance, the amount, stated on the front of the policy, that is payable upon the death of the insured. The actual amount payable to the beneficiary may differ according to the policy's specific provisions, such as double indemnity or subsequent riders.

face validity, also called FAITH VALIDITY, measure of the degree to which a test *ap-*

pears to be valid. While this is the most superficial kind of validity, it may contribute significantly to the legitimacy of the test in the eyes of the candidates (an important consideration in avoiding legal challenges). However, it can also deceive employers who may be tempted to save the time and money required for genuine validation. According to Raymond B. Cattell, "Validity and Reliability: A Proposed More Basic Set Of Concepts," *Journal of Educational Psychology* (February 1964),

in some trivial sense face or faith validity perhaps still has a role, but in diplomacy rather than psychology, as when an industrial psychologist is pressured to make tests which a chief executive will, from the depths of his ignorance commend or sanction as measuring what he conceives to be this or that trait.

facilitator, individual who serves as a catalyst, usually in a formal organization development effort, in order to improve the interactions and interpersonal relationships of a group.

factfinding, an impartial review of the issues in a labor dispute by a specially appointed third party, whether it be a single individual, panel, or board. The factfinder holds formal or informal hearings and submits a report to the administrative agency and/or the parties involved. The factfinder's report, usually considered advisory, may contain specific recommendations. According to Robert E. Doherty, "On Factfinding: A One-Eyed Man Lost Among the Eagles," *Public Personnel Management* (September-October 1976),

factfinding nowadays seems to be regarded as a way station in the onward march toward the strike, unilateral management determination, or (in most instances) further haggling which eventually ends up in a settlement—a settlement which may or may not bear a relationship to the factfinder's report. The factfinder is only rarely treated with deference—and rightfully so. It takes considerable audacity to believe that after a few hours of testimony any in-

dividual whose talents are somewhat less than those of a Solomon can come to understand the issues well enough to render a report that is sufficiently clear and logical to impress both parties.

factor analysis, any of several methods of analyzing the intercorrelations among test scores or other sets of variables. *See* Wayne K. Kirchner and June A. Lucas, "Using Factor Analysis to Explore Employee Attitudes," *Personnel Journal* (June 1970); Richard L. Gorsuch, *Factor Analysis* (Philadelphia: W. B. Saunders, 1974); T. Gregory Morton, "Factor Analysis, Multicollinearity, and Regression Appraisal Models," *The Appraisal Journal* (October 1977).

factor evaluation system, also called FACTOR COMPARISON SYSTEM, a hybrid of traditional duties or position classification systems. With traditional duties classification, different combinations of factors are used for different positions; the factor evaluation system uses the same factors for all positions. With traditional duties classification, grade levels are ascertained by the weight and eloquence of narrative descriptions; the factor evaluation system determines grade levels by comparing positions directly to one another. The main ingredient of a factor evaluation system is, obviously, the factor—any of the various key elements individually examined in the evaluation process. Once the factors of a position have been identified, they can be ranked—the factors of one position are compared to another. Such a factor comparison can have only three outcomes. Any given factor must be higher, lower, or equal to the factor of another position. When positions are ranked by factors, all of the factors of each position are compared and an overall ranking is achieved. *See* Lawrence L. Epperson, "The Dynamics of Factor Comparison/Point Evaluation," *Public Personnel Management* (January-February 1975).

See also POSITION CLASSIFICATION.

factors, *see* JOB FACTORS.

factory system, see DIVISION OF LABOR.

fair day's work, generally, the amount of work produced in a work day by a qualified employee of average skill exerting average effort.

Fair Employment Practice Commission (FEPC), generic term for any state or local government agency responsible for administering/enforcing laws prohibiting employment discrimination because of race, color, sex, religion, national origin, or other factors.

Fair Employment Practice Committee (FEPC), former federal committee. In 1941, President Franklin D. Roosevelt issued Executive Order 8802, which called for the elimination of discrimination based upon race, color, religion, or national origin within the defense production industries and the federal service. A newly created Fair Employment Practice Committee was charged with implementing the order. By almost all accounts, however, the committee was weak and even somewhat disinterested in combating discrimination in the federal service. In 1946, it met its demise through an amendment to an appropriations bill. For its history, see Louis C. Kesselman, *The Social Politics of FEPC* (Chapel Hill, N.C.: University of North Carolina Press, 1948); Will Maslow, "FEPC—A Case History in Parliamentary Maneuver," *University of Chicago Law Review* (June 1946).

fair employment practice laws, all government requirements designed to prohibit discrimination in the various aspects of employment. See James S. Russell, "A Review of Fair Employment Cases in the Field of Training," *Personnel Psychology* (Summer 1984).

Fair Employment Practice Service, reference service published by the Bureau of National Affairs, Inc., which covers federal and state laws dealing with equal opportunity in employment, full texts of federal and state FEP laws, orders, and regulations, as well as federal, state, and local court opinions and decisions of the Equal Employment Opportunity Commission.

Fair Labor Standards Act (FLSA), also called WAGES AND HOURS ACT, federal statute of 1938 which, as amended, establishes minimum-wage, overtime-pay, equal-pay, recordkeeping, and child-labor standards affecting more than fifty million full-time and part-time workers.

For histories of FLSA, see Jonathan Grossman, "Fair Labor Standards Act of 1938: Maximum Struggle for a Minimum Wage," *Monthly Labor Review* (June 1978); P. K. Elder and H. D. Miller, "The Fair Labor Standards Act: Changes of Four Decades," *Monthly Labor Review* (July 1979); Horst Brand, "The Evolution of Fair Labor Standards: A Study in Class Conflict," *Monthly Labor Review* (August 1983).

See also the following entries:
CHILD LABOR
GARCIA V. SAN ANTONIO METROPOLITAN TRANSIT AUTHORITY
NATIONAL LEAGUE OF CITIES V. USERY
OVERTIME
UNITED STATES V. DARBY LUMBER

fair representation, see DUTY OF FAIR REPRESENTATION.

fair-share agreement, arrangement whereby both the employer and the union agree that employees are not obligated to join the union, but that all employees must pay the union a prorated share of bargaining costs as a condition of employment.

faith validity, see FACE VALIDITY.

false negative, any incidence whereby an individual, who is in fact qualified, is excluded by a test or some other screening criteria.

false positive, any incidence whereby an individual, who is in fact unqualified, is selected because of a test or some other screening criteria.

family allowances, payments to workers,

in addition to regular wages, based on the number of dependent children that a worker may have. Almost all of the major industrial countries except the United States have family-allowance programs financed by their governments. For an analysis, *see* George E. Rejda, "Family Allowances as a Program for Reducing Poverty," *The Journal of Risk and Insurance* (December 1970).

family-expense policy, health insurance policy that insures both the individual policyholder and his or her immediate dependents (usually spouse and children).

family T-group, work team that undertakes a T-group effort as a unit.
See also T-GROUP.

fatigue, weariness caused by physical or mental exertion that lessens the capacity to, and the will for, work. For an analysis, *see* R. A. McFarland, "Fatigue In Industry: Understanding Fatigue in Modern Life," *Ergonomics*, Vol. 14, No. 1 (1971).

fatigue allowance, in production planning, that additional time added to "normal" work time to compensate for the factor of fatigue.

fatigue curve, also MONOTONY CURVE, graphic representation of productivity increases and decreases influenced by fatigue. As workers "warm up" or practice their tasks, productivity increases; thereafter fatigue sets in and productivity decreases. After lunch or coffee breaks, productivity should rise again slightly, but thereafter continuously decline until the end of the day. This pattern varies with differing kinds of work. Fatigue curve measurements are essential in establishing realistic work standards.

A *monotony curve* is characterized by a drop in productivity in the middle of the work period, great variability in the rate of productivity, and a tendency to "end spurt"—show an increase in productivity at the end of the work period due to a feeling of relief that the work period is almost over.

The classic work on fatigue and monotony curves was done as part of the Hawthorne experiments. *See* F. J. Roethlisberger and William J. Dickson, *Management and the Worker* (Cambridge, Mass.: Harvard University Press, 1939). *See also* HAWTHORNE STUDIES.

fat work, slang term for work that offers more money for no more than normal effort; also work that offers regular wages but requires a less than normal effort.

favoritism, according to John E. Fisher in "Playing Favorites in Large Organizations," *Business Horizons* (June 1977),

one way authoritarian executives control subordinates is by permitting favorites to enjoy opportunities for highly visible accomplishments while making it difficult, if not impossible, for those who are in disfavor to do so. Then when the favorite is promoted or meritoriously cited, his sponsor can point with pride to how impressive his achievements look on paper. If a nonfavorite has the temerity to complain about the choice, he is confronted with his own predictable paucity of accomplishments. Often the latter is puzzled by his lack of accomplishments despite his application of hard work, initiative and resourcefulness. If he reflects, however, he may recall that his soundest recommendations have been turned down and his initiative curbed at every turn.

Fayol, Henri (1841-1925), French executive engineer who developed the first comprehensive theory of management. His *Administration Industrielle et Générale* (published in France in 1916) was almost ignored in the U.S. until Constance Storrs' English translation, *General and Industrial Management* (London: Pitman, 1949), appeared. Today his theoretical contributions are generally considered as significant as those of Frederick W. Taylor.

FBI, *see* FEDERAL BUREAU OF INVESTIGATION.

FCC, see FEDERAL COMMUNICATIONS COMMISSION.

FDIC, see FEDERAL DEPOSIT INSURANCE CORPORATION.

featherbedding, term meaning an easy or superfluous job; originated in the U.S. Army in the 1850s. Those frontier soldiers who had easy jobs at headquarters and could sleep in comfortable featherbeds were called "featherbed soldiers." So featherbedding grew to mean any job that required little or no work.

Today featherbedding connotes any labor practice that requires an employer to pay for more workers than are truly needed for a job, or to pay for work that is not performed. Featherbedding provisions in labor contracts usually have their origin in work rules that were once efficient but have become obsolete due to newer technology. Union leaders often insist on maintaining the older practices in order to protect the jobs of those whose livelihoods are threatened by the new technology.

The Labor-Management Relations (Taft-Hartley) Act of 1947 makes it an unfair labor practice "to cause or attempt to cause an employer to pay or deliver or agree to pay or deliver any money or other thing of value in the nature of an exaction, for services which are not performed." This provision has not had much effect, however, because of the legal subtleties of defining featherbedding practices. See Robert D. Leiter, *Featherbedding and Job Security* (New York: Twayne Publishers, 1964); Paul A. Weinstein, ed., *Featherbedding and Technological Change* (Boston: D.C. Heath, 1965).

See also AMERICAN NEWSPAPER PUBLISHERS ASSOCIATION V. NATIONAL LABOR RELATIONS BOARD and UNFAIR LABOR PRACTICES (UNIONS).

Fed, see FEDERAL RESERVE SYSTEM.

federal assistance programs, term used to refer to the variety of federal programs available to state and local governments including counties, cities, metropolitan and regional governments; schools, colleges, and universities; health institutions; nonprofit and for profit organizations; and individuals and families. Current federal assistance programs are listed in the annual *Catalogue of Federal Domestic Assistance.*

Federal Bureau of Apprenticeship and Training, see APPRENTICE.

Federal Bureau of Investigation (FBI), principal investigative arm of the U.S. Department of Justice. It is charged with gathering and reporting facts, locating witnesses, and compiling evidence in matters in which the federal government is, or may be, a party in interest. Cooperative services of the FBI for other duly authorized law enforcement agencies include fingerprint identification, laboratory services, police training, and the National Crime Information Center.
> FBI
> Ninth Street & Pennsylvania Avenue, N.W.
> Washington, D.C. 20535
> (202) 324-3000

Federal Communications Commission (FCC), body that regulates interstate and foreign communications by radio, television, wire, and cable. It is responsible for the orderly development and operation of broadcast services and the provision of nationwide and worldwide telephone and telegraph service at reasonable rates.
> FCC
> 1919 M Street, N.W.
> Washington, D.C. 20554
> (202) 655-4000

Federal Council on the Arts and Humanities, see NATIONAL FOUNDATION ON THE ARTS AND THE HUMANITIES.

federal court of appeals, see COURT OF APPEALS.

federal debt, consists of public debt and agency debt.
> *Public Debt.* That portion of the federal debt representing borrowing by the Treasury Department and the Fed-

eral Financing Bank (except its borrowings from the Treasury).

Agency Debt. That portion of the federal debt arising when a federal agency authorized by law, other than Treasury or the Federal Financing Bank (FFB), borrows funds directly from the public. To avoid double-counting, when a federal agency borrows funds from Treasury or the FFB, the transaction is not included in federal debt; the Treasury or FFB borrowing required to obtain the money to lend to the agency is already part of the public debt. Agency debt may be incurred by agencies within the federal budget (such as the Tennessee Valley Authority) or by off-budget federal agencies (such as the Postal Service). Debt of government-sponsored, privately owned enterprises (such as the Federal National Mortgage Association) is not included in the federal debt.

There are three basic concepts or tabulations of federal debt: gross federal debt, debt held by the public, and debt subject to statutory limit.

Gross Federal Debt. The sum of all public and agency debt issues outstanding.

Debt Held by the Public. That part of the gross federal debt held by the public. (The Federal Reserve System is included in "the public" for this purpose.) Debt held by government trust funds (*e.g.*, Social Security Trust Fund), revolving funds, and off-budget federal agencies is excluded from debt held by the public.

Debt Subject to Statutory Limit. Defined by the Second Liberty Bond Act of 1917, as amended. At present virtually all public debt but only a small portion of agency debt is included in debt subject to statutory limit.

See also PUBLIC FINANCE and DEBT FINANCING.

Federal Deposit Insurance Corporation (FDIC), body established to promote and preserve public confidence in banks and to protect the money supply through provision of insurance coverage for bank deposits.

FDIC
550 Seventeenth Street, N.W.
Washington, D.C. 20429
(202) 389-4221

federal district court, *see* DISTRICT COURT.

Federal Emergency Management Agency (FEMA), the single point of accountability for emergency preparedness and response for all levels of government and for all kinds of emergencies—natural, man-made, and nuclear. *See* Peter J. May, "FEMA's Role in Emergency Management: Examining Recent Experience," *Public Administration Review* (January 1985).

FEMA
500 C Street, S.W.
Washington, D.C. 20472
(202) 287-0300

Federal Employee's Compensation Act of 1916, federal statute administered by the U.S. Department of Labor that provides compensation for disability and death, medical care, and rehabilitation services for all civilian employees and officers of the United States who suffer injuries while in the performance of their duties.

Federal Employees Part-Time Career Employment Act of 1978, federal statute that requires federal agencies to implement employment programs for part-timers (persons working between sixteen and thirty-two hours per week).

federalese, *see* GOBBLEDYGOOK.

Federal Executive Institute, The (FEI), established by Executive Order in 1968, the federal government's primary in-residence training facility for executive development. *See* Paul Lorentzen, "Role of the Federal Executive Institute," *The Bureaucrat* (Summer 1981).

FEI
Route 29 North

Federal Financing Bank

Charlottesville, VA 22903
(804) 296-0181

Federal Financing Bank, (FFB), unit located within the U.S. Department of the Treasury. The FFB was created to centralize federal agency borrowing. Instead of selling debt directly in the financial markets, agencies would sell their obligations to the FFB at lower cost. Originally, the FFB was to sell its own obligations to the public to raise funds for its operations, but the FFB currently obtains all of its capital by borrowing directly from the Treasury.

federal funds, funds collected, owned, and used by the federal government for the general purposes of the government. There are four types of federal fund accounts: general funds, special funds, public enterprise (revolving) funds, and intragovernmental funds. Each is discussed in a separate entry.

federal funds rate, the interest rate at which depository institutions such as banks lend each other reserve funds on an overnight or temporary basis.

Federal Home Loan Bank Board, also FEDERAL SAVINGS AND LOAN INSURANCE CORPORATION, body that supervises and regulates savings and loan associations, which specialize in lending out money on homes and are the country's major private source of funds to pay for building and buying homes. The Board operates the *Federal Savings and Loan Insurance Corporation*, which protects savings of the more than seventy-five million Americans with savings accounts in FSLIC-insured savings and loan associations. The Board also directs the *Federal Home Loan Bank System* which, like the Federal Reserve System for banks, provides reserve credit and the assurance that member savings and loan associations will continue to be a source of financing for homes.

Federal Home Loan Bank Board
1700 G Street, N.W.
Washington, D.C. 20552
(202) 377-6000

federal intrafund transactions, *see* OFFSETTING RECEIPTS

federalism, according to Daniel J. Elazar, *American Federalism: A View From the States* (New York: Thomas Y. Crowell, 1966),

federalism can be defined as the mode of political organization that unites smaller polities within an overarching political system by distributing power among general and constituent governments in a manner designed to protect the existence and authority of both national and subnational political systems, enabling all to share in the overall system's decision-making and executing processes. In its simplest form, federalism means national unification through the maintenance of subnational systems.

A federal government is a device by which the federal qualities of a society are articulated and protected. The essential nature of federalism is to be sought in the many forces—economic, social, political, cultural—that have made the outward forms of federalism necessary. Federalism, like most institutional forms is a solution of, or an attempt to solve, a certain kind of problem of political organization. Viable federal systems accommodate regional or subsystem diversity, thereby enhancing the strength of the greater federation.

History indicates clearly that the principal factor in the formation of federal systems of government has been a common external threat. Tribes, cities, colonies, or states have joined together in voluntary unions to defend themselves. However, not all systems so formed have been federal; a federal system has the following features: (1) a constitution which divides governmental powers between the central government and the constituent governments, giving substantial powers and sovereignty to each; (2) levels of government that act through their own instrumentalities to exercise power *directly* over citizens (unlike a confederation, in which only regional units act directly on citizens while the central government acts only on regional governments); and (3) a constitutional distribution of powers that *cannot* be changed *unilaterally* by either level of government, or by the ordinary process of legislation.

The classic commentary on U.S. federalism, *The Federalist Papers* (1787–88), is considered by many political scientists to be the most important work of political science written in the United States, the one product of the American mind that is rightly counted among the classics of political theory. Authored by Alexander Hamilton, James Madison, and John Jay, they reflect the genius of the balance achieved in the American system between the views of Madison, an exponent of limited government, and Hamilton, an admirer of an energetic national government.

See Walter H. Bennett, *American Theories of Federalism* (University, Ala.: University of Alabama Press, 1964); William H. Riker, *Federalism: Origin, Operation, Significance* (Boston: Little, Brown & Co., 1964); Morton Grodzins, *The American System: A New View of Government in the United States* (Chicago: Rand McNally, 1966); Aaron Wildavsky, *American Federalism in Perspective* (Boston: Little, Brown, 1967); James T. Patterson, *The New Deal and the States: Federalism in Transition* (Princeton, N.J.: Princeton University Press, 1969); James L. Sundquist, *Making Federalism Work* (Washington, D.C.: Brookings Institution, 1969); Richard H. Leach, *American Federalism* (New York: W. W. Norton, 1970); Daniel J. Elazar, *American Federalism: A View from the States*, 2nd ed. (New York: Crowell, 1972); Arthur W. MacMahon, *Administering Federalism in a Democracy* (New York: Oxford University Press, 1972); Parris N. Glendening and Marvis M. Reeves, *Pragmatic Federalism: An Intergovernmental View of the American Government* (Pacific Palisades, Calif.: Palisades Publishing, 1977); Robert D. Newton, "Administrative Federalism," *Public Administration Review* (May–June 1978); David B. Walker, *Toward a Functioning Federalism* (Cambridge, Mass.: Winthrop Publishers, 1981); Stephen David and Paul Kantor, "Urban Policy in the Federal System: A Reconceptualization of Federalism," *Polity* (Winter 1983); Deil S. Wright and Harvey L. White, eds., *Federalism and Intergovernmental Relations* (Washington, D.C.: American Society for Public Administration, 1984).

federalism, cooperative, the notion that the national, state, and local governments are cooperating, interacting agents jointly working to solve common problems, rather than acting as conflicting and sometimes hostile competitors pursuing the same or similar ends.

While some cooperation has always been evident in the mix of conflict, competition, and complexity of intergovernmental relationships, cooperation has been most prominent between the 1930s and the 1950s. The emergency funding arrangements of the post-depression years known collectively as the "New Deal," and the cooperative government of federal-state-local authorities during World War II to administer civilian defense, rationing, and other wartime programs are noteworthy examples of cooperative federalism in the United States. *See* Daniel J. Elazar, *The American Partnership: Intergovernmental Cooperation in the 19th Century United States* (Chicago: University of Chicago Press, 1962).

federalism, creative, the Johnson administration's term for its approach to intergovernmental relations, which was characterized by joint planning and decisionmaking among all levels of government (as well as the private sector) in the management of intergovernmental programs.

Many new programs of this period had an urban-metropolitan focus and much attention was given to antipoverty issues. Creative federalism sought to foster the development of a singular "Great Society" by reintegrating the poor into "mainstream" America. Its efforts were marked by the rapid development of categorical grant programs to state and local governments and direct federal grants to cities, frequently bypassing state governments entirely. *See* James L. Sundquist, *Mak-*

ing Federalism Work (Washington, D.C.: Brookings Institution, 1969).

federalism, dual, 19th century concept, now discredited, that the functions and responsibilities of the federal and state governments were theoretically distinguished and functionally separate from each other.

The basic idea of dual federalism was expressed succinctly by James Bryce, a British scholar who visited the United States in the 1880s to observe its political system. He described relations between the national and state and local governments as follows:

The characteristic feature and special interest of the American Union is that it shows us two governments covering the same ground yet distinct and separate in their action. It is like a great factory wherein two sets of machinery are at work, their revolving wheels apparently intermixed, their bands crossing one another, yet each doing its own work without touching or hampering the other.

See James Bryce, *The American Commonwealth, Vol. 1,* 2nd ed. (London: Macmillan, 1891), p. 318.

federalism, fiscal, refers to fiscal relationships that exist between and among units of government in a federal system. The theory of fiscal federalism, or multi-unit governmental finance, is one part of the branch of applied economics known as public finance.

The theory of fiscal federalism addresses the question of the optimal design of governments in a multi-level (or federal) governmental system. The public sector, according to the theory of fiscal federalism, has three principal economic problems to solve: the attainment of the most equitable distribution of income; the maintenance of high employment with stable prices; and the establishment of an efficient pattern of resource allocation.

The theory of fiscal federalism postulates that a federal form of government can be especially effective in solving these problems because of the flexibility it has in dealing with some problems at the national or central level and some at the local or regional levels. It argues that, for a variety of reasons, the first two problems, equitable distribution of income and maintenance of high employment with stable prices, are problems that the national level of government is best equipped to handle. However, according to the theory, the decentralized regional or local units of government can more efficiently deal with the third problem, allocation of resources, because such units of government are more familiar than the central or national government with local needs and the desires of citizens for public services. Even so, grants-in-aid from the national level of government to local levels may be needed to stimulate local government spending for national purposes, to provide for uniform or minimum service levels (as in education), or to compensate citizens of one area for benefits from services they finance that spill over to residents of another area. Spillover benefits are especially frequent in such programs as clean water and air pollution control, health, and education.

For the public administrator, fiscal federalism refers, first and foremost, to the politics and administration of complex intergovernmental grant-in-aid systems; these systems include federal grants to state and local governments and to other organizations and state grants to their local governments.

Modern grant systems contain complex and often perplexing laws and regulations that apply to eligibility, receipt, and administration of funds granted by one level of government to another. Total federal aid as a percentage of state and local revenues has increased dramatically since the middle of the 20th century, from 11 percent in 1955 to more than 32 percent in 1980. The major portion of federal aid has been distributed through narrowly defined or specific grants-in-aid called categorical grants, and is concentrated in such areas as education, highways, public welfare, and housing programs. Federal funds have also been distributed through less restrictive block grants and through general revenue sharing.

Fiscal federalism also includes the complex matter of taxation. Governments in the U.S. federal system have specialized with respect to types of taxes they utilize for obtaining their major revenues. The federal government obtains most of its revenue from income taxation. State governments have relied more heavily on consumption taxes (primarily sales taxes), while local governments have depended principally on the property tax. An important area of fiscal federalism involves tax policy: which governments should specialize in what types of taxation and why? Another area involves tax overlap and coordination: vertical coordination as between federal and state income taxes, and horizontal coordination as necessary with state taxation on the income of multi-state corporations. Other matters of fiscal federalism apply to limitations in taxing and expenditure authority that may be imposed by one level of government upon another.

See Richard Musgrave, *Essays on Fiscal Federalism* (Washington, D.C.: Brookings Institution, 1965); George F. Break, *Intergovernmental Fiscal Relations in the United States* (Washington, D.C.: Brookings Institution, 1967); Richard E. Wagner, *The Fiscal Organization of American Federalism* (Chicago: Markham Publishing Company, 1971); Daniel J. Elazar, "Fiscal Questions and Political Answers in Intergovernmental Finance," *Public Administration Review* (September-October 1972); Wallace E. Oates, *Fiscal Federalism* (New York: Harcourt Brace Jovanovich, 1972); Advisory Commission on Intergovernmental Relations, *Trends in Fiscal Federalism 1954-1974* (Washington, D.C.: Government Printing Office, 1975); Advisory Commission on Intergovernmental Relations, *Significant Features of Fiscal Federalism: 1976 Edition* (Washington, D.C.: Government Printing Office, June 1976); Wallace E. Oates, ed., *The Political Economy of Fiscal Federalism* (Lexington, Mass.: Lexington Books, 1977); George F. Break, *Financing Government in a Federal System* (Washington, D.C.: Brookings Institution, 1980); David H. McKay, "Fiscal Federalism, Professionalism and the Transformation of American State Government," *Public Ad-*

ministration (Spring 1982); Charles E. McLure, Jr., and Peter Mieszkowski, eds., *Fiscal Federalism and the Taxation of Natural Resources* (Lexington, MA: Lexington Books, 1983).

See also the following entries:
INTERGOVERNMENTAL EXPENDITURE
INTERGOVERNMENTAL REVENUE
INTERGOVERNMENTAL FUNDS

federalism, horizontal, also VERTICAL FEDERALISM, state-to-state interactions and relationships. Interstate relationships take many forms, including compacts and commissions which have been established for specific purposes: river basin management, transportation, extradition of criminals, conservation of forests and wildlife, and administration of parks and recreation.

Horizontal relationships between and among state and local governments also are numerous. Cities frequently contract for services from neighboring state and local governments. The Lakewood Plan, established in southern California in 1954, has been the most comprehensive example of interlocal contracting for services to date. Under this plan, the City of Lakewood contracted for a rather comprehensive package of services from Los Angeles County, where Lakewood is located.

State-national government interactions are examples of vertical federalism. These interactions are not limited to the executive branches of our national and state governments. Close coordination exists between the federal and state court systems. Criss-crossing vertical relationships also have become more common. For example, the executive branch of the national government embarked upon several programs for assistance to state courts and state legislatures in the 1970s.

federalism, marble-cake, concept that the cooperative relationships among the varying levels of government result in an intermingling of activities. This was in contrast to the more traditional view of layer cake federalism, which held that the three levels of government were totally separate.

Marble-cake federalism is usually associated with Morton Grodzins. His marble-cake metaphor is used to refer to the fact that there are numerous functions which are shared by the different levels of government in the U.S. system. Grodzins pointed out, with the case of a rural county health official called a sanitarian, that the sanitarian is appointed by the state government under merit standards established by the federal government, and while his base salary comes from state and federal funds, the county provides him with an office and office amenities and pays a portion of his expenses. *See* his *The American System,* edited by Daniel J. Elazar (Chicago: Rand McNally, 1966).

federalism, new, a reconceptualization of federalism as intergovernmental relations; also refers to the actual relationships between the levels of government as they shared in the performance of expanding governmental functions in the early 1970s. As it was applied during the Nixon years, new federalism referred to the style of decentralized management at the federal level symbolized by such programs as Federal Assistance Review, General Revenue Sharing, and decentralization of federal regional management to ten coterminous regions, each with a common regional center. New federalism as developed by the Reagan administration disregarded the Nixon approach of decentralized federal regional management entirely, and turned to development of direct relationships of the federal government to state governments. The intent of new federalism under the Reagan administration has been to return power and responsibility to the state and to dramatically reduce the role of the federal government in domestic programs. As articulated by the Reagan White House, new federalism has two phases. Phase one consists of the President's Economic Recovery Program, which includes reductions in the federal budget, the use of new block grant programs to give states greater flexibility in using federal monies, and the reduction of the volume of new federal regulations and tax reductions to stimulate the economy. Phase two of new federalism is the return from the federal to state governments of

some authority to tax, thereby increasing the revenue capacity of state governments. *See* Michael D. Reagan, *The New Federalism* (New York: Oxford University Press, 1972); Leigh E. Grosenick, ed., *The Administration of the New Federalism: Objectives and Issues* (Washington, D.C.: American Society for Public Administration, 1973); Carl E. Van Horn, "Evaluating the New Federalism: National Goals and Local Implementors," *Public Administration Review* (January-February 1979); Neil R. Peirce, "New Panels to Move Quickly to Help Reagan 'Unbend' The Federal System," *National Journal* (May 2, 1981); Rochelle L. Stanfield, "Ready for 'New Federalism,' Phase II? Turning Tax Sources Back to the States," *National Journal* (August 22, 1982); Terry Nichols Clark, "Local Fiscal Dynamics Under Old and New Federalism," *Urban Affairs Quarterly* (September 1983); Thomas Luce and Janet Rothenberg Pack, "State Support Under the New Federalism," *Journal of Policy Analysis and Management* (Spring 1984); Sarah F. Liebschutz, "New Federalism Modified: Jobs and Highways in New York," *Publius* (Summer 1984); Richard P. Nathan and Fred C. Doolittle, "The Untold Story of Reagan's 'New Federalism'," *The Public Interest* (Fall 1984).

See also FEDERAL REGIONAL COUNCILS.

federalism, picket-fence, concept that implies that bureaucratic specialists at the various levels of government exercise (along with clientele groups) considerable power over the nature of intergovernmental programs. Bureaucratic or program specialists at national, state, and local government levels for such fields as public housing, vocational education, health and hospitals, and higher education, among others, represent the pickets in the picket fence. They communicate with each other in daily work, belong to the same professional organizations, and have similar professional training. They are likely to be in conflict with general purpose government officials (mayors, governors, the president) who attempt to coordinate the various vertical power structures or pickets. The general purpose officials are the "cross pieces" of the fence. The metaphor is credited to Terry Sanford, then governor of the state of North Carolina. *See* Terry Sanford, *Storm Over the States* (New York: McGraw-Hill, 1967).

Federal Judicial Center, the judicial branch's agency for policy research, systems development, and continuing education.

Federal Judicial Center
Dolley Madison House,
1520 H Street, N.W.
Washington, D.C. 20005
(202) 633-6011

Federal Labor Relations Authority (FLRA), created by the Civil Service Reform Act of 1978 to oversee the creation of bargaining units, supervise elections, and otherwise deal with labor-management issues in federal agencies. The FLRA is headed by a chairman and two members who are appointed on a bipartisan basis to staggered five-year terms. The FLRA replaces the Federal Labor Relations Council (FLRC).

Within the FLRA, a general counsel, appointed to a five-year term, will investigate alleged unfair labor practices and prosecute them before the FLRA. Also within the FLRA and acting as a separate body, the Federal Service Impasses Panel (FSIP) acts to resolve negotiation impasses.

See Kenneth A. Kovach, "The F.L.R.A. and Federal Employee Unionism," *Public Personnel Management* (January–February 1980).

Federal Labor Relations Authority
500 C Street, S.W.
Washington, D.C. 20424
(202) 382-0711

Federal Labor Relations Council (FLRC), unit established in 1969 by Executive Order 11491 and supplanted by the Federal Labor Relations Authority pursuant to provisions of the Civil Service Reform Act of 1978.

federal labor union, a local union affiliated directly with the AFL-CIO rather than with a national or international union.

Federal Law Enforcement Training Center, interagency training center serving over thirty federal law enforcement agencies representing ten executive departments. The center conducts common recruit, advanced, specialized, and refresher law enforcement training for the special agents and police officers from the participating agencies, and provides the necessary facilities, equipment, and support for the accomplishment of that training.

Federal Law Enforcement Training
Center
Department of the Treasury
Glynco, GA 31520
(912) 267-2100

Federal Maritime Commission (FMC), body that regulates the waterborne foreign and domestic offshore commerce of the United States, assures that U.S. international trade is open to all nations on fair and equitable terms, and guards against unauthorized monopoly in the waterborne commerce of the United States.

FMC
1100 L Street, N.W.
Washington, D.C. 20573
(202) 523-5773

Federal Mediation and Conciliation Service (FMCS), unit created by the Labor-Management Relations (Taft-Hartley) Act of 1947 as an independent agency of the federal government. FMCS helps prevent disruptions in the flow of interstate commerce caused by labor-management disputes by providing mediators to assist disputing parties in the resolution of their differences. FMCS can intervene on its own motion or by invitation of either side in a dispute. Mediators have no law enforcement authority and rely wholly on persuasive techniques. FMCS also helps provide qualified third-party neutrals as factfinders or arbitrators.

The mediator's efforts are directed toward the establishment of sound and stable labor-management relations on a continuing basis. FMCS mediators assist representatives of labor and management in settling disputes about wages, hours, and other aspects of the employment relationship that arise in the course of negotiations. In this work, the mediator has a more basic function—encouraging and promoting better day-to-day relations between labor and management. He/she thereby helps to reduce the incidence of work stoppages. Issues arising in negotiations may then be faced as problems to be settled through mutual effort rather than issues in dispute.

FMCS offers its facilities in labor-management disputes in any industry affecting interstate commerce, either upon its own motion or at the request of one or more of the parties to the dispute, whenever in its judgment such dispute threatens to cause a substantial interruption of commerce. Employers and unions are required to file with FMCS a notice of every dispute affecting commerce not settled within thirty days after prior service of a notice to terminate or modify an existing contract. FMCS is required to avoid the mediation of disputes that would have only a minor effect on interstate commerce if state or other conciliation services are available to the parties. FMCS is directed to make its mediation and conciliation facilities available only as a last resort and in exceptional cases in the settlement of grievance disputes arising over the application or interpretation of existing collective bargaining agreements.

On the joint request of employers and unions, FMCS will also assist in the selection of arbitrators from a roster of private citizens who are qualified as neutrals to adjudicate matters in dispute.

FMCS has offices in seventy-nine principal cities, with meeting facilities available for labor-management negotiations. See Jerome T. Barrett and Lucretia Dewey Tanner, "The FMCS Role in Age Discrimination Complaints: New Uses of Mediation," Labor Law Journal (November 1981); Kay McMurray, "The Federal Mediation and Conciliation Service: Serving Labor-Management Relations in the Eighties," Labor Law Journal (February 1983).

> Federal Mediation and Conciliation Service
> 2100 K Street, N.W.
> Washington, D.C. 20427
> (202) 653-5290

Federal Open Market Committee, the seven members of the Federal Reserve Board and five of the twelve Federal Reserve Bank Presidents. They meet every four to six weeks to set Federal Reserve guidelines regarding purchases and sales of Government securities in the open market as a means of influencing the volume of credit and money. The FOMC also sets Federal Reserve policy relating to foreign exchange markets.

Federal Pay Comparability Act of 1970, federal statute that placed the initiative for maintaining pay comparability for federal employees with the president rather than with the Congress. See Raymond Jacobson, "Pay Comparability," Civil Service Journal (April–June 1974); George L. Stelluto, "Federal Pay Comparability: Facts to Temper the Debate," Monthly Labor Review (June 1979).

Federal Personnel Manual **(FPM),** publication of the Office of Personnel Management (OPM) that contains all OPM personnel regulations and instructions to federal agencies.

Federal Regional Councils (FRCs), bodies established by Executive Order 11647 of February 10, 1972. A Council was created for each of the ten standard federal regions and an Under Secretaries Group for Regional Operations was established to provide policy guidance to Federal Regional Councils. The Councils were mandated to improve coordination of the categorical grant system and to develop closer working relationships among themselves and with state and local governments. Executive Order 11731 of July 23, 1973 broadened the Federal Regional Council mandate, including coordination of direct federal program assistance to state and local governments.

Federal Regional Councils were composed of the principal regional officials of the Departments of Agriculture, Commerce, Energy, Health and Human Services, Housing and Urban Development, Interior, Labor, and Transportation, and the Environmental Protection Agency. They were abolished by Executive Order 12407 of February 22, 1983. *See* Melvin B. Mogulof, "Federal Interagency Action and Inaction: The Federal Regional Council Experience," *Public Administration Review* (May–June 1972); U.S. General Accounting Office, *Assessment of Federal Regional Councils* (Washington, D.C.: Government Printing Office, January 1974); Robert W. Gage, "Federal Regional Councils: Network Organizations for Policy Management in the Intergovernmental System," *Public Administration Review* (March–April 1984).

See also FEDERALISM, NEW.

Federal Register, daily publication that is the medium for making available to the public federal agency regulations and other legal documents of the executive branch. These documents cover a wide range of government activities—environmental protection, consumer product safety, food and drug standards, occupational health and safety, and many more areas of concern to the public. Perhaps more importantly, the *Federal Register* includes *proposed* changes in regulated areas. Each proposed change published carries an invitation for any citizen or group to participate in the consideration of the proposed regulation through the submission of written data, views, or arguments, and sometimes by oral presentations. For further information on the *Federal Register,* write to the Office of the Federal Register, National Archives and Records Service, Washington, D.C. 20408.

Federal Register System, system established in 1935 by the Federal Register Act. Administrative rules and regulations issued by executive departments and agencies under authority of law are codified and made known to the public through the system. It consists of the *Federal Register,* published daily Tuesday through Saturday except for the day following a legal holiday; the *Code of Federal Regulations,* an annually issued multi-volume cumulation of administrative regulations in force; and the annually published *United States Government Manual.* The system is administered by the National Archives and Records Service of the General Services Administration.

There are four basic kinds of documents which must be published in the *Federal Register* before they are considered legally binding: (1) presidential proclamations and executive orders of general interest, and any other document the president submits or orders to be published; (2) every document issued under proper authority which prescribes a penalty or course of conduct; confers a right, privilege, authority, or immunity; or imposes an obligation, and which is relevant or applicable to the general public, members of a class of people, or persons of a locality; (3) documents or classes of documents required by act of Congress to be filed and published; and (4) other documents deemed by the Director of the Federal Register to be of sufficient interest. Although the *Federal Register* is unknown to many citizens, it constitutes a major means of regulating and governing in the U.S.

Federal Regulation of Lobbying Act of 1946, see LOBBY.

Federal Reserve Notes, obligations of the Federal Reserve backed by the full faith and credit of the U.S. Government. Nearly all of the nation's circulating paper currency consists of Federal Reserve notes printed by the Treasury Department and issued to the Federal Reserve Banks, which put them into circulation through depository institutions.

Federal Reserve System, colloquially known as the FED, central bank of the U.S., charged with administering and making policy for the nation's credit and monetary affairs. Run by a seven-member

Board of Governors appointed by the president (who also appoints their chairman), the system includes twelve Federal Reserve Banks, twenty-four branches, all national banks, and many state banking institutions. Three major monetary tools are available to the Federal Reserve System to control the economy's supply of money and credit:

1. *Open market operations* which, through the purchase or sale of government bonds, increase or decrease the availability of dollars to member banks.
2. *Discount rate adjustments* which increase or decrease the interest rate charged to member banks for the money they borrow.
3. *Reserve requirements* which, through changes in levels of reserve, increase or decrease the number of dollars a bank may make available for loan.

Two less significant tools, moral suasion and selective controls over stock purchase margin requirements, are also used to help manage the economy. *See* Ralph C. Bryant, *Controlling Money: The Federal Reserve and Its Critics* (Washington, D.C.: The Brookings Institution, 1983).

Federal Reserve System
20th Street and Constitution Avenue, N.W.
Washington, D.C. 20551
(202) 452-3000

Federal Salary Reform Act of 1962, *see* SALARY REFORM ACT OF 1962.

Federal Savings and Loan Insurance Corporation, *see* FEDERAL HOME LOAN BANK BOARDS.

Federal Service Entrance Examination (FSEE), from 1955 through 1974, the U.S. Civil Service Commission's most basic means of selecting new college graduates for over two hundred different occupational specialties. In the early 1970s, the FSEE came under increasing attack because of its adverse impact on equal employment opportunity. In 1975, it was replaced by the Professional and Ad-

ministrative Careers Examination (PACE). *See* Robert Sadacca, *The Validity and Discriminatory Impact of the Federal Service Entrance Examination* (Washington, D.C.: The Urban Institute, 1971).

See also PROFESSIONAL AND ADMINISTRATIVE CAREERS EXAMINATION.

Federal Service Impasses Panel (FSIP), body located within the Federal Labor Relations Authority. The Federal Service Impasses Panel has the responsibility of aiding federal agencies and their labor organizations in settling their negotiation impasses when voluntary efforts have failed. The FSIP may authorize binding arbitration, third-party factfinding, or other appropriate measures.

Federal Service Impasses Panel
500 C Street, S.W.
Washington, D.C. 20424
(202) 382-0711

Federal Supplemental Compensation, a program enacted in 1982 to provide benefits to individuals who exhaust all of their rights to benefits under the regular and extended Unemployment Insurance programs. In states where extended benefits are not in effect, exhaustees of regular unemployment insurance immediately become eligible for Federal Supplemental Compensation. In states on extended benefits, an individual must exhaust those benefits before collecting Federal Supplemental Compensation. *See* Arlene Holen, "Federal Supplemental Compensation and Unemployment Insurance Recipients," *Monthly Labor Review* (April 1984).

Federal Times, weekly newspaper that covers pending civil service legislation, compensation problems, corruption, labor/management concerns, and other issues of interest to federal government employees.

Federal Times
Springfield, VA 22159

Federal Trade Commission (FTC), body whose objective is to prevent the free enterprise system from being stifled, substantially lessened, or fettered by monopoly or restraints on trade, or corrupted by unfair or deceptive trade practices. As an administrative agency, acting quasi-judicially and quasi-legislatively, the commission was established to deal with trade practices on a continuing and corrective basis. It has no authority to punish; its function is to "prevent," through cease-and-desist orders and other means, those practices condemned by the law of federal trade regulation; however, court ordered civil penalties up to $10,000 may be obtained for each violation of a commission order. For a critical history, see Edward F. Cox, Robert C. Fellmuth, and John E. Schulz, *The Nader Report on the Federal Trade Commission* (New York: Grove Press, 1969). *Also see* Kenneth W. Clarkson and Timothy J. Muris, *The Federal Trade Commission Since 1970: Economic Regulation and Consumer Welfare* (New York: Cambridge University Press, 1981).

FTC
Pennsylvania Avenue at Sixth
  Street, N.W.
Washington, D.C. 20580
(202) 523-3598

Federal Trade Commission v. Sperry Hutchinson Co., 405 U.S. 233 (1972), Supreme Court case stating the principle that the adjudicatory decisions of administrative agencies show a "rational connection between the facts found and the choice made." The case signaled a wider scope of judicial review of the substance of such adjudicatory decisions.

Federal Wage System, the basic pay system for the almost half a million trade, craft, and labor (blue-collar) employees of the federal government, established by Public Law 92-392.

Rates of pay for Federal Wage System employees are maintained in line with prevailing levels of pay for comparable work within each local wage area. Within each local wage area there is a single set of wage schedules applicable to the blue-collar employees of all agencies in the area. Each nonsupervisory schedule consists of fifteen grades. A single grade structure applies na-

tionwide. Individual positions are graded on the basis of job evaluation in accordance with a uniform set of job-grading standards. There are separate leader and supervisory schedules for each area.

Uniform policies and procedures for the Federal Wage System are established by the Office of Personnel Management, but significant roles in policymaking and operation of the system are played by both agencies and employee unions.

The prevailing rate principle on which federal blue-collar pay rates are based dates from the 1860's. While there have been many changes in the determination of blue-collar pay since then, with respect to occupational and agency coverage, agency authorities, and administrative procedures, the basic principle is over one hundred years old. *See* M. Frank Barton, Jr., and Thomas S. O'Connor, "Are Federal Wage-Board Employees Overpaid?" *Government Accountants Journal* (Fall 1978).

Federal Women's Program, program established in 1967 by the U.S. Civil Service Commission to enhance the employment and the advancement of women. Executive Order 11478, signed by president Nixon on August 8, 1969, integrated the Federal Women's Program with other equal employment opportunity programs. Federal agencies must designate a Federal Women's Program coordinator to provide advice on special concerns of women and to insure that agency affirmative action plans are designed to eliminate barriers to the full employment of women at all levels and in all occupations For a histories, see Helene S. Markoff, "The Federal Women's Program," *Public Administration Review* (March-April 1972); Janice Mendenhall, "Roots of the Federal Women's Program," *Civil Service Journal* (July-September 1977).

federated governments, *see* METROPOLITAN GOVERNMENT.

federation, national and/or international unions joined together for common purposes. The AFL-CIO is the major U.S. union federation.

feedback, information about the effect and/or results of the behavior of a person or system that is communicated back to that person or system so that human behavior or organization (mechanical) performance might be modified. For accounts of how to use organization feedback, *see* David A Nadler, *Feedback and Organization Development: Using Data-Based Methods* (Reading, Mass.: Addison-Wesley Publishing Co., 1977); Robert T. Golembiewski and Richard J. Hilles, *Toward the Responsive Organization: The Theory and Practice of Survey/Feedback* (Salt Lake City: Brighton Publishing, 1979); David A. Nadler, Cortlandt Cammann, and Philip H. Mirvis, "Developing a Feedback System for Work Units: A Field Experiment in Structural Change," *Journal of Applied Behavioral Science* (January-February-March 1980); Daniel R. Ilgen and William A. Knowlton, Jr., "Performance Attributional Effects on Feedback from Superiors," *Organizational Behavior and Human Performance* (June 1980); Alan Brown and Frank Heller, "Usefulness of Group Feedback Analysis as a Research Method: Its Application to a Questionnaire Study," *Human Relations* (February 1981). For how it relates to productivity, *see* Peter G. Kirby, "Productivity Increases Through Feedback Systems," *Personnel Journal* (October 1977). For information on handling negative feedback, *see* Thomas B. Wilson, "Making Negative Feedback Work," *Personnel Journal* (December 1978). *See also* Herbert Kaufman, *Administrative Feedback: Monitoring Subordinates' Behavior* (Washington, D.C.: Brookings Institution, 1973).

feeder account, those appropriation and revolving fund accounts whose resources are available only for transfer to other specified appropriation or revolving fund accounts.

FEI, *see* FEDERAL EXECUTIVE INSTITUTE.

fellow servant doctrine, common-law concept that an employer should not be held responsible for an accident to an employee if the accident resulted from the negligence of another employee.

FEMA, *see* FEDERAL EMERGENCY MANAGEMENT AGENCY.

FEPC, *see* (1) FAIR EMPLOYMENT PRACTICE COMMITTEE and (2) FAIR EMPLOYMENT PRACTICE COMMISSION.

Fibreboard Paper Products Corporation v. National Labor Relations Board, 379 U.S. 203 (1965), U.S. Supreme Court case which held that a company was obligated to bargain over an economically motivated decision to subcontract work previously performed by union members.

fiduciary, a person who manages money or property for others. Anyone who has discretionary authority or responsibility for the administration of a pension plan is a fiduciary.

Fiedler, Fred E. (1922-), psychologist most noted for his contingency theory of leadership effectiveness, which holds that leadership is a function of both the leader and the leadership situation. Major works include: *A Theory of Leadership Effectiveness* (New York: McGraw-Hill, 1967); *Leadership and Effective Management,* with Martin Chemers (Glenview, Ill.: Scott, Foresman & Co., 1974).

field examiner, administrative agency employee who conducts certification elections and investigates charges of unfair labor practices.

field review, method of employee appraisal whereby a representative of the personnel department visits an employee's work site in order to gather the information necessary for a written evaluation.

field survey, research method in which data are collected through interviews or questionnaires from a sample of people selected to represent some larger population. The selection process saves time and energy because it is not necessary to contact every member of the population. The method is most appropriate for gathering information about topics of which the respondents are consciously aware.

field theory, theory developed by Kurt Lewin which holds that an individual's behavior at any given time is the result of his/her basic personality interacting with the psychological forces of the environment. *See* Kurt Lewin, "Behavior and Development as a Function of the Total Situation," in Dorwin Cartwright, ed., *Field Theory in Social Science* (New York: Harper & Bros., 1951).

See also GROUP DYNAMICS and LEWIN, KURT.

final offer arbitration, also called LAST OFFER ARBITRATION, negotiating stratagem that has an arbitrator choose from among the disputing parties' final or last offers. Peter Feuille, in *Final Offer Arbitration: Concepts, Development, Techniques* (Chicago: International Personnel Management Association, 1975), describes its intended role in the collective bargaining process:

Since the arbitrator will not be free to compromise between the parties' positions, the parties will be induced to develop ever more reasonable positions prior to the arbitrator's decision in the hope of winning the award. And, the theory goes, these mutual attempts to win neutral approval should result in the parties being so close together that they will create their own settlement. In other words, the final offer procedure was purposefully designed to contain the seeds of its own destruction.

For a case study, *see* Gary Long and Peter Feuille, "Final Offer Arbitration: 'Sudden Death' in Eugene," *Industrial and Labor Relations Review* (January 1974). *Also see* Angelo S. DeNisi and James B. Dworkin, "Final-Offer Arbitration and the Naive Negotiator," *Industrial and Labor Relations Review* (October 1981).

financial administration, activities in-

volving finance and taxation. Includes managing central agencies for accounting, auditing, and budgeting; the supervision of government finance; tax administration; collection, custody, and disbursement of funds; administration of employee-retirement systems; debt and investment administration; and the like. *See* J. Richard Aronson and Eli Schwartz, eds., *Management Policies in Local Government Finance* (Washington, D.C.: International City Management Association, 1981); John Mikesell, *Fiscal Administration: Analysis and Applications for the Public Sector* (Homewood, Ill.: Dorsey Press, 1982).

financial audit, determination of (1) whether financial operations are properly conducted, (2) whether the financial reports of an audited entity are presented fairly, and (3) whether the entity has complied with applicable laws and regulations. *See* Comptroller General of the United States, *Standards for Audit of Governmental Organizations, Programs, Activities and Functions, rev ed.* (Washington, D.C.: General Accounting Office, 1981).

financial bill clearance, see CENTRAL CLEARANCE.

financial core member, someone who pays a union's initiation fees and monthly dues, but does not actually join. Such employees are entitled to fair representation in collective bargaining and grievances by the union, but they have no right to political participation in its affairs. By the same token, however, the union has no disciplinary authority over them.

fink, slang term for a strikebreaker—any individual who hires out to help an employer break a strike. According to H. L. Mencken, "fink" is a perversion of "pink" for "Pinkerton." The Pinkertons were employees of the Pinkerton Detective Agency who were frequently hired to harass and otherwise oppose strikes in the latter part of the 19th century. As Pinkerton's, Inc., the agency is still in business selling guard and security services.

See also SCAB.

Finnegan v. Leu, 456 U.S. 431 (1982), U.S. Supreme Court case which upheld the right of a successful challenger for the leadership of a union to dismiss all the business agents who had supported the incumbent in the election. The Court reasoned that democracy itself would be served by enabling elected union leaders to carry out their programs and policies without resistance from business agents who were in opposition to them. The Court also maintained that the removal of a business agent on these grounds, which was allowed under the union's constitution, was not an act of discipline that interfered with the agent's rights of freedom of speech.

fire, discharge from employment. The word has such a rude connotation that it is hardly ever used for formal purposes. It seems so much more genteel and antiseptic to terminate, discharge, dismiss, sever, or lay off an employee. For two "self-help" books on firing, see John J. Tarrant, *Getting Fired: An American Ordeal* (New York: Van Nostrand Reinhold Co., 1974); Auren Uris and Jack Tarrant, *How to Keep from Getting Fired* (Chicago: Henry Regnery Co., 1975). *See also* Stephen S. Kaagen, "Terminating People from Key Positions," *Personnel Journal* (February 1978); Frederic D. Homer and Garth Massey, "On Being Canned: Personnel Decisions in Democratic Bureaucracies," *Bureaucrat* (Spring 1979); Edward J. Mandt, "Employee Termination: Proceed with Care," *Management Review* (December 1980); Laurence J. Stybel, Robin Cooper, and Maryanne Peabody, "Planning Executive Dismissals: How to Fire a Friend," *California Management Review* (Spring 1982); David W. Ewing, "Your Right to Fire," *Harvard Business Review* (March–April 1983); Daniel T. Kingsley, *How to Fire an Employee* (New York: Facts on File, 1984).

Fire Fighters Local Union No. 1784 v. Stotts, U.S. Supreme Court case, 81 L. Ed. 483 (1984), which held that courts may not interfere with seniority systems to protect newly hired black employees from layoff. The case began in 1977 when black firefighters charged that the Memphis, Tenn., fire department had violated Title VII of the Civil Rights Act of 1964 by engaging in racial discrimination in hiring and promotion of employees. In 1980 the city and the black employees agreed on an affirmative action plan that was approved by a Federal district judge. In 1981, when the city was suffering from budget problems, some of the newly hired black firefighters were among those scheduled for layoff because the city's contract with the union contains a "last hired, first fired" provision. In response to a request from the threatened black workers, the district court ordered the city not to follow seniority in determining who was to be laid off "insofar as it will decrease the percentage" of black firefighters. The result was that seventy-two whites were laid off or demoted along with only eight blacks. They were all rehired or promoted six months later.

The union and the city appealed the seniority ruling to the U.S. Court of Appeals but lost, leading to their appeal to the Supreme Court.

Writing for the majority, Justice Byron R. White said that the law permits remedies only for individuals who can prove they are "actual victims" of job discrimination, rather than groups of disadvantaged minorities who may not have suffered specific wrongs in a specific job situation. To back this holding, he cited a 1964 memorandum issued by sponsors of Title VII which said "Title VII does not permit the ordering of racial quotas in business or unions." Justice White also said that it is "inappropriate to deny an innocent employee the benefit of seniority." *See* Louis P. Britt III, "Affirmative Action: Is There Life After Stotts?" *Personnel Administrator* (September 1984).

First Concurrent Resolution on the Budget, the resolution containing government-wide budget targets of receipts, budget authority, and outlays that guides Congress in its subsequent consideration of appropriations and revenue measures. It is required to be adopted by both houses of Congress no later than May 15, pursuant to the Congressional Budget and Impoundment Control Act of 1974. *See also* CONCURRENT RESOLUTION ON THE BUDGET.

first-dollar coverage, coverage under an insurance policy which begins with the first dollar of expense incurred by the insured for the covered benefits.

First Hoover Commission, *see* HOOVER COMMISSION OF 1947-1949.

first-line management, level of management that is just above the workers (for example, a foreman). *See* W. Earl Sasser, Jr., and Frank S. Leonard, "Let First-Level Supervisors Do Their Job," *Harvard Business Review* (March-April 1980); Ernest A. Doud, Jr., and Edward J. Miller, "First-Line Supervisors: The Key to Improved Performance," *Management Review* (December 1980), Lawrence L. Steinmetz and H. Ralph Todd, Jr., *First-Line Management: Approaching Supervision Effectively,* 3rd ed. (Plano, Texas: Business Publications, 1983).

fiscal, having to do with taxation, public revenues, or public debt.

fiscal federalism, see FEDERALISM, FISCAL.

fiscal impact analysis, a projection of the public cost and revenues associated with residential or nonresidential growth in a given jurisdiction.

fiscal integrity, also FISCAL RESPONSIBILITY, reliability in fiscal matters. You will be deemed to have fiscal integrity when the person so deeming agrees with your fiscal policies. If that same person disagrees with your policies you may be deemed so lacking in fiscal responsibility as to be considered fiscally irresponsible.

fiscal policy, the manipulation of government finances by raising or lowering taxes or levels of spending to promote economic stability and growth. Stability and growth must be combined since stability without growth is stagnation. The use of fiscal policy for economic objectives is a decidedly recent phenomenon. For the greater part of our two-hundred-year history as a nation, fiscal policy was not a factor. The national budgetary policy was premised upon having expenditures equal revenues (a balanced budget). In fact, with the exception of war years, budgeting prior to the 1900s was primarily an exercise in deciding how to get rid of excess revenues, generated primarily by tariffs. This is not to say that modern fiscal policies would not have saved the nation considerable distress from assorted recessions and depressions, but the 19th century held that the economy followed a "natural" order. The first major tampering with the "natural" order of things came in 1913 with the advent of the federal income tax and the establishment of the Federal Reserve System. In 1921, the Budget and Accounting Act provided for a unified federal executive budget. The Great Depression of the 1930s, along with the initiation of social security and unemployment compensation programs, provided the first recognitions of the need for a national economic policy. However, legitimization of the goal of a national economic policy came with the passage of the Full Employment Act of 1946. The act not only created a council of economic advisors for the president, but it prescribed objectives for economic prosperity and charged the president with insuring their achievement.

Basically, fiscal policy offers two courses of action: discretionary and built-in. The first involves changing policy decisions. Discretionary fiscal policy has two major facets—the level of receipts and the level of expenditures. The major fiscal policy actions of recent years are replete with various tax cuts and temporary reductions. Given the time lags involved in legislating tax changes, it is easy to see why presidents have preferred to wage fiscal policy battles in terms of government spending.

The second dimension of fiscal policy involves built-in fiscal stabilizers—that is, preset or automatic policy. These are the transfer payments, the progressive tax rates, and the changing federal budget

deficits and surpluses that move automatically to counter economic downturns or control excessive periods of demand and business activity. For example, if more people are laid off from work in a recessionary period, payments for unemployment compensation will mount automatically. This increases the federal budget deficit, which in turn stimulates the economy and moves to offset the economic downswing. If the economy heats up, wages and overtime increase and personal income increases. This fuels demands for goods and services and creates inflation. As personal income increases, however, more and more people will find themselves in higher tax brackets. The tax structure thus functions as an automatic stabilizer by taxing people more heavily and creating a budget surplus. This acts as a restraint on the economy because it absorbs more personal income and in consequence restrains demand for goods and services. *See* Lawrence C. Pierce, *The Politics of Fiscal Policy Formation* (Pacific Palisades, Calif.: Goodyear Publishing Co., 1971); James C. Snyder, *Fiscal Management and Planning in Local Government* (Lexington, Mass.: Lexington Books, 1977); David C. Mowery, Mark S. Kamlet, and John P. Crecine, "Presidential Management of Budgetary and Fiscal Policymaking," *Political Science Quarterly* (Fall 1980); James N. Danziger and Peter Smith Ring, "Fiscal Limitations: A Selective Review of Recent Research," *Public Administration Review* (January–February 1982); John J. Kirlin, *The Political Economy of Fiscal Limits* (Lexington, Mass.: Lexington Books, 1982).
    See also the following entries:

    BUDGETING
    DEBT FINANCING
    FEDERALISM, FISCAL
    INTERGOVERNMENTAL REVENUE
    MONETARY POLICY
    PUBLIC FINANCE
    POLITICAL ECONOMY

fiscal responsibility, *see* FISCAL INTEGRITY.

fiscal stress, see MANAGEMENT, CUT-BACK.

fiscal year, any yearly accounting period without regard to a calendar year. The fiscal year for the federal government through fiscal year 1976 began on July 1 and ended on June 30. Since fiscal year 1977, fiscal years for the federal government begin on October 1 and end on September 30. The fiscal year is designated by the calendar year in which it ends (*e.g.*, fiscal year 1982 is the fiscal year ending September 30, 1982.)

Fitzgerald, A. Ernest (1926–), famous "whistle blower."
    Fitzgerald was the GS-17 Deputy for Management Systems in the Office of the Assistant Secretary of the Air Force who in 1968 first testified to cost overruns on the Air Force's giant C-5A military cargo plane. The Air Force, which had not acknowledged the cost overruns, stripped him of his primary duties of overseeing cost reports on the major weapons systems and assigned him to essentially clerical tasks. A year later the Air Force reorganized Fitzgerald's office and abolished his job. Fitzgerald appealed the Air Force action. After almost four years of litigation, Fitzgerald was reinstated to his original civil service position and given back pay.
    The Fitzgerald affair triggered a great deal of discussion in the media and the government about the need to protect "whistle-blowers." For Fitzgerald's own account, *see* A. Ernest Fitzgerald, *The High Priests of Waste* (New York: W. W. Norton, 1972).
    See also WHISTLE BLOWER.

Fitzgerald Act, *see* APPRENTICESHIP ACT OF 1937.

Fitzpatrick* v. *Bitzer, 424 U.S. 953 (1976), U.S. Supreme Court case which ruled that the Equal Employment Opportunity Act of 1972 amendments to Title VII of the Civil Rights Act of 1964 created an exception to the immunity of states to back pay suits. The court held that this exception was authorized by the 14th Amendment's grant of power to Congress to enforce that amendment's ban on state denials of equal protection.

fixed annuity, annuity that provides constant, periodic dollar payments for its entire duration.

fixed assets, see ASSETS.

fixed-benefit retirement plan, retirement plan whose benefits consist of a fixed amount or fixed percentage.

fixed shift, work shift to which an employee is assigned indefinitely.

flagged rate, also called OVERRATE, compensation rates paid to employees whose positions warrant lower rates.

Flast v. Cohen, 392 U.S. 83 (1968), Supreme Court case concerning the expenditure of federal funds for instructional purposes in religious schools under the Elementary and Secondary Education Act of 1965. The court found that parties had standing to challenge these expenditures if they could show that (1) they were taxpayers, and (2) the challenged enactment exceeded specific constitutional limitations imposed on the exercise of the congressional power to tax and spend.

flat-benefit plan, pension plan whose benefits are unrelated to earnings. Such a plan might provide a stipulated amount per month per year of service.

flat organization, also TALL ORGANIZATION, one whose structure has comparatively few levels. In contrast, a *tall organization* is one whose structure has many levels. See Rocco Carzo, Jr., and John N. Yanovzas, "Effects of Flat and Tall Organization Structure," *Administrative Science Quarterly* (June 1969); Edwin E. Ghiselli and Jacob P. Siegel, "Leadership and Managerial Success in Tall and Flat Organization Structures," *Personnel Psychology* (Winter 1972).
See also PYRAMID.

flat rate, also called STANDARD RATE and SINGLE RATE, pay structure offering only one rate of pay for each pay level.

Fleetwood Trailer Co. decision, *see* NATIONAL LABOR RELATIONS BOARD V. MACKAY RADIO & TELEGRAPH COMPANY.

flexible passing score, *see* CUTTING SCORE.

flexible working hours, *see* FLEXI-TIME.

flexi-time, flexible work schedule in which workers can, within a prescribed band of time in the morning and again in the afternoon, start and finish work at their discretion as long as they complete the total number of hours required for a given period, usually a month. That is, the workday can vary from day to day in its length as well as in the time that it begins and ends. The morning and evening bands of time often are designated as "quiet time." Telephone calls and staff meetings are confined to "core time," which generally runs from midmorning to midafternoon. Time clocks or other mechanical controls for keeping track of the hours worked usually are a part of flexi-time systems.
For discussions of the concept, *see* Janice Neipert Hedges, "New Patterns for Working Time," *Monthly Labor Review* (February 1973); Alvar O. Elbing, Herman Gadon, and John R. M. Gordon, "Flexible Working Hours: It's About Time," *Harvard Business Review* (January–February 1974); Richard S. Rubin, "Flexitime: Its Implementation in the Public Sector," *Public Administration Review* (May–June 1979); Robert T. Golembiewski and Carl W. Proehl, Jr., "Public Sector Applications of Flexible Workhours: A Review of Available Experience," *Public Administration Review* (January–February 1980); Simcha Ronen and Sophia B. Primps, "The Impact of Flexitime on Performance and Attitudes in Twenty-five Public Agencies," *Public Personnel Management* (Vol. 9, No. 3, 1980); Cary B. Barad, "Flexitime Under Scrutiny: Research on Work Adjustment and Organizational Performance," *The Personnel Administrator* (May 1980); Halcyone H. Bohen and Anamaria Viveros-Long, *Balancing Jobs and Family Life: Do Flexible Work Schedules Help?* (Philadelphia, Pa.: Tem-

ple University Press, 1981); William D. Hicks and Richard J. Klimoski, "The Impact of Flexitime on Employee Attitudes," *Academy of Management Journal* (June 1981); Richard A. Wheat, "The Federal Flexitime System: Comparison and Implementation," *Public Personnel Management* (Spring 1982); Glenn W. Rainey, Jr., and Lawrence Wolf, "The Organizationally Dysfunctional Consequences of Flexible Work Hours: A General Overview," *Public Personnel Management* (Summer 1982); Robert C. Wender and Ronald L. Sladky, "Flexible Plans Are Not Just For Large Firms," *Personnel Administrator* (December 1984).

See also FOUR-DAY WORKWEEK.

Florida Power & Light Co. v. Brotherhood of Electrical Workers, 417 U.S. 790 (1974), U.S. Supreme Court case which held that supervisors who are union members may be disciplined by their unions for performing nonsupervisory tasks so long as the supervisors do not act as management bargainers or grievance adjusters.

flowchart, graphic representation of an analysis of, or solution to, a problem that uses symbols to indicate various operations, equipment, and data flow.

FLRA, see FEDERAL LABOR RELATIONS AUTHORITY.

FLRC, see FEDERAL LABOR RELATIONS COUNCIL.

FLSA, see FAIR LABOR STANDARDS ACT.

FLSA Decision see NATIONAL LEAGUE OF CITIES V. USERY.

FMC, see FEDERAL MARITIME COMMISSION.

FMCS, see FEDERAL MEDIATION AND CONCILIATION SERVICE.

focus job area, a unit of an establishment's work force (such as a seniority unit, job title, etc.) in which minorities or women are concentrated or underrepresented relative to their overall representation in the relevant work force sector or to their availability for the jobs in question. This concept is more related to determining the existence of discrimination rather than to finding underutilization for the purpose of setting goals as part of an affirmative action program.

Foggy Bottom, slang term for the U.S. State Department because its present building is located on a site that was once considered close to a swamp (now drained). The term continues in use because "foggy" aptly describes the kinds of pronouncements so often necessitated by diplomacy. See Charles Frankel, *High on Foggy Bottom* (New York: Harper & Row, 1968).

See also STATE, DEPARTMENT OF.

foils, see DISTRACTORS.

Foley v. Connelie, 435 U.S. 291 (1978), U.S. Supreme Court case which upheld a New York law requiring state police to be U.S. citizens. The court reasoned that because state police exercise considerable discretion in executing the laws, a state may exclude aliens from such positions without unconstitutionally denying them equal protection of the laws.

See also the following entries:
AMBACH V. NORWICK
CITIZENSHIP, U.S.
HAMPTON V. MOW SUN WONG
SUGARMAN V. DOUGALL

Follett, Mary Parker (1868-1933), early social psychologist who anticipated, in the 1920s, many of the conclusions of the Hawthorne experiments of the 1930s and the post-World War II behavioral movement. In calling for "power with," as opposed to "power over," she anticipated the movement toward more participatory management. Her "law of the situation" is contingency management in its humble origins. Major works include: *The New State* (New York: Longmans, Green, 1918); *Creative Experience* (New York: Longmans, Green, 1924). For her collected papers, see Henry C. Metcalf and

Lyndall Urwick, eds., *Dynamic Administration: The Collected Papers of Mary Parker Follett* (New York: Harper and Bros., 1940). For an appreciation of her contributions, *see* Elliot M. Fox, "Mary Parker Follett: The Enduring Contribution," *Public Administration Review* (November–December 1968).

See also LAW OF THE SITUATION and POWER.

forced choice, testing technique that requires the subject to choose from among a given set of alternatives.

forced-distribution method, performance appraisal technique that predetermines the percentage of ratees to be placed in the various performance categories.

force-field analysis, procedure for determining what factors, or forces, seem to be contributing to a problem.

forecasting, attempt to evaluate observable or known facts and from them predict a future environment or project a range of future possibilities or happenings.

foreign aid, refers to all official grants and concessional loans (*i.e.,* loans made on "softer" than commercial terms), in currency or in kind, which are broadly aimed at transferring resources from developed to less developed countries for the purposes of economic development and/or income distribution.

Foreign aid may be bilateral (from one country to another) or multilateral (distributed through international financial institutions such as the World Bank or the IMF). Foreign aid, which is also referred to as economic assistance, may be given as project aid (where the donor provides money for a specific project such as a dam or a school) or as program aid (where the donor does not know on which projects the money will be spent). Economic assistance consists of both "hard" loans (*i.e.,* at commercial bank interest rates) and "soft" loans (concessional or low-interest loans). Aid may be "tied" by multilateral aid agencies (*e.g.,* the loans must

be partially financed by the recipient country) or aid may be "tied" in bilateral arrangements (*e.g.,* the money must be spent on procurement in the donor country or must be used on shipping by the donor country). Countries give foreign aid for various reasons: for humanitarian purposes after wars or natural disasters; to strengthen allies militarily against external and/or internal threats; to promote the economic development of the recipient country; or to meet the basic human needs of the poor citizens of the recipient country.

foreign currency account, account established in the U.S. Treasury for foreign currency that is acquired without payment of United States dollars primarily in payment for commodities (such as through the Agricultural Trade Development Assistance Act, P.L. 480). These currencies may be expended without charge to dollar appropriations. They may be available for obligation without further congressional action or Congress may appropriate these foreign currencies.

foreign service, a corps of professional diplomats. The U.S. Foreign Service is the diplomatic corps responsible for administering U.S. foreign policies.

See also STATE, DEPARTMENT OF.

Foreign Service pay system, system that actually consists of four different pay schedules that apply to the Department of State:

1. *Foreign Service Officer schedule* consists of eight levels. Individual Foreign Service Officers are assigned to levels on a rank-in-person basis similar to that of the military personnel system.
2. *Foreign Service Information Officer schedule* of the U.S. Information Agency is identical in structure and operation to the Foreign Service Officer schedule.
3. *Foreign Service Reserve schedule* also consists of eight levels, and is used for temporary appointments of people who are not part of the regular Foreign Service career system.

4. *Foreign Service Staff Officer schedule* covers the administrative and support employees of the Foreign Service. It consists of ten grades.

See also EXECUTIVE SCHEDULE and GENERAL SCHEDULE.

foreign trade zones (FTZs), designated areas in the United States, usually near ports of entry, considered to be outside the Customs territory of the United States. Foreign and domestic merchandise may be moved into these areas for storage, exhibition, assembly, manufacturing, or processing without incurring any state or federal duties and without involving any quota restrictions. If the finished product is exported, no U.S. duty is paid; if the product is to be sold in the United States, no duty is paid until the product is ready to leave the zone. Typically, FTZs are fenced-in areas with warehouse facilities and easy access to all forms of transportation. Outside the United States, such areas are called free trade zones.

foreman, first-line supervisor—the first level of management responsible for securing adequate production and the managerial employee who supervises the work of nonmanagerial employees. The extent to which the foreman is responsible for the traditional functions of management varies considerably from one organization to another. For a complete analysis, *see* Thomas H. Patten, Jr., *The Foreman: Forgotten Man of Management* (New York: American Management Association, 1968). For a classic account of the role of the foreman, *see* F. J. Roethlisberger, "The Foreman: Master and Victim of Double Talk," *Harvard Business Review* (Spring 1945; reprinted September–October 1965).

Present-day foremen work under a fading occupational title. It has fallen victim to the U.S. Department of Labor's effort to "de-sex" the nature of work and has been retired as an officially acceptable job title by the fourth edition of the *Dictionary of Occupational Titles* (1977).

Forest Service, agency with the Department of Agriculture that has the federal responsibility for national leadership in forestry. The Forest Service manages 154 national forests and 19 national grasslands comprising 187 million acres in 41 states and Puerto Rico, under the principles of multiple use and sustained yield.

Forest Service
P.O. Box 2417
Washington, D.C. 20013
(202) 447-3760

formal organization, *see* INFORMAL ORGANIZATION.

Form 171, *see* STANDARD FORM 171.

formula-based categorical grant, *see* GRANT.

formula-project categorical grant, *see* GRANT.

formula score, raw score on a multiple-choice test after a correction for guessing has been applied. With five-choice items, for example, the formula score is the number of correct answers minus one-fourth the number of wrong answers. This makes zero the score that would most likely be obtained by random guessing.

Form W-2, also called W-2 FORM and WAGE AND TAX STATEMENT, form showing earnings for the preceding year and various deductions. By the end of January of each year, employers must provide each employee with at least two copies of his or her withholding statement, officially a Wage and Tax Statement or Internal Revenue Service Form W-2. Employees must file one copy of their Form W-2 with their federal income tax return.

forward funding, practice of obligating funds in one fiscal year for programs that are to operate in a subsequent year.

Foster v. Dravo Corp., 420 U.S. 92 (1975), U.S. Supreme Court case which held that a veteran, upon being restored to his former civilian position under the Military Selective Service Act, is not entitled to full vacation benefits for the years he was in military service if the vacation scheme was intended as a form of short-term deferred compensation for work performed and not as accruing automatically as a function of continued association with the company.

See also VETERANS REEMPLOYMENT RIGHTS.

four-day workweek, reallocation of the standard forty-hour workweek over four days instead of five. By lengthening the workday, employees get a three-day weekend every week with no loss of pay. This concept differs from the four-day/thirty two-hour workweek that some union leaders advocate. For the basic work on this subject, *see* Riva Roor, ed., *Four Days, Forty Hours and Other Forms of the Rearranged Workweek* (New York: Mentor Books, 1973).

See also FLEXI-TIME.

four-fifths rule, *see* ADVERSE IMPACT.

FPM, *see* FEDERAL PERSONNEL MANUAL.

Franks v. Bowman Transportation Co., *see* RETROACTIVE SENIORITY.

fraud, *see* ABUSE.

FRCs, *see* FEDERAL REGIONAL COUNCILS.

Frederickson, H(orace) George (1934-), scholar most associated with the call for a "new public administration." Major works include: "Toward A New Public Administration," in *Toward A New Public Administration: The Minnowbrook Perspective,* ed. by Frank Marini (Scranton, Pa.: Chandler, 1971); *Power, Public Opinion and Policy in a Metropolitan Community: A Case Study of Syracuse* (New York: Praeger, 1973); "Social Equity and Public Administration," symposium editor, *Public Administration Review* (January–February 1974); "The Lineage of the New PA," *Administration and Society* (August 1977); and *New Public Administration* (University, Ala.: University of Alabama Press, 1980).

Freedom of Information Act of 1966, (Public Law 89-487, as amended by Public Law 93-502), law that provides for making information held by federal agencies available to the public unless it comes within one of the specific categories of matters exempt from public disclosure. The legislative history of the act (particularly the recent amendments) makes it clear that the primary purpose was to make information maintained by the executive branch of the federal government more available to the public. At the same time, the act recognized that records that cannot be disclosed without impairing rights of privacy or important government operations must be protected from disclosure.

Virtually all agencies of the executive branch of the federal government have issued regulations to implement the Freedom of Information Act. These regulations inform the public where certain types of information may be readily obtained, how other information may be obtained on request, and what internal agency appeals are available if a member of the public is refused requested information. To locate specific agency regulations pertaining to freedom of information, consult the *Code of Federal Regulations* index under "Information Availability." For an analysis of possible conflicts between the Freedom of Information Act and the National Labor Relations Act, *see* Stephen J. Cabot, "'Freedom of Information' vs. the NLRB: Conflicts and Decisions," *Personnel Journal* (June 1977). *Also see* Robert L. Saloschin, "The Freedom of Information Act: A Governmental Perspective," *Public Administration Review* (January–February 1975); Harold C. Relyea, Symposium Editor, "The Freedom of Information Act a Decade Later," *Public Administration Review* (July–August 1979).

For a comparative perspective, *see* Donald C. Rowat, ed., *Administrative Secrecy in Developed Countries* (New York: Columbia University Press, 1979).

See also NATIONAL LABOR RELATIONS BOARD V. ROBBINS TIRE AND RUBBER CO. and NATIONAL TECHNICAL INFORMATION SERVICE.

free-response test, technique used in psychological testing that places no restriction on the kind of response an individual is to make (so long as it relates to the situation presented).

free rider, derogatory term for a person working in a bargaining unit and receiving substantially all of the benefits of union representation without belonging to the union.

free trade zones, see FOREIGN TRADE ZONES.

frequency distribution, tabulation of scores (or other data) from high to low, or low to high, showing the number of individuals who obtain each score or fall in each score interval.

frictional unemployment, unemployment that is due to the inherent time lag involved with the reemployment of labor.

Friedman, Milton (1912-), Nobel Prize-winning conservative economist generally considered the leading proponent of a return to laissez-faire economics. As a leading advocate of positive economics, he has been a major influence on thinking about monetary policy, consumption, and government regulation. Major works include: *A Theory of the Consumption Function* (Princeton, NJ: Princeton University Press, 1957); *Capitalism and Freedom* (Chicago: University of Chicago Press, 1962); *Essays in Positive Economics* (Chicago: University of Chicago Press, 1966); *Free to Choose: A Personal Statement,* with Rose Friedman (New York: Harcourt, Brace, Jovanovich, 1980).

friend of the court, see AMICUS CURIAE.

fringe benefits, also called EMPLOYEE BENEFITS, general term used to describe any of a variety of nonwage or supplemental benefits (such as pensions, insurance, vacations, paid holidays, etc.) that employees receive in addition to their regular wages. For an economic analysis, *see*

Bevars Mabry, "The Economics of Fringe Benefits," *Industrial Relations* (February 1973). For discussions, *see* Ralph L. Harris, "Let's Take the 'Fringe' out of Fringe Benefits," *Personnel Journal* (February 1975); Richard C. Huseman, John D. Hatfield, and Richard B. Robinson, "The MBA and Fringe Benefits," *The Personnel Administrator* (July 1978); Richard B. Freeman, "The Effects of Unionism on Fringe Benefits," *Industrial and Labor Relations Review* (July 1981); R. Frumkin and W. Wistrowski, "BLS Takes a New Look at Employee Benefits," *Monthly Labor Review* (August 1982); Donald C. Platten, "The Employee Benefits—Does the Company Also?" *Harvard Business Review* (September-October 1983); Henry Saveth, "Benefit Programs After Tax Reform," *Personnel Journal* (October 1984); Kenneth Gagala and Gene Daniels, *Labor Guide to Negotiating Wages and Benefits* (Reston, Va.: Reston/Prentice-Hall, 1985).
See also PERQUISITES.

frontage assessment, a tax to pay for improvements (such as sidewalks or sewer lines) that is charged in proportion to the frontage (number of feet bordering the road) of each property.

front loaded, a labor agreement providing for a greater wage increase in its early period; for example, a three-year contract that provides for a ten percent increase in the first year and four percent in each of the remaining two years. *See* John B. Beare, "Uncertainty and Front-End Loading of Labor Agreements," *Journal of Labor Research,* Vol. VI (1985).

front pay, compensation provided to an individual or group which begins when a remedy for alleged discrimination is agreed to and ends when the individual or group attains its "rightful place."

Fry v. United States, 421 U.S. 542 (1975), U.S. Supreme Court case which held that state governments had to abide by federal wage and salary controls even though the enabling legislation did not expressly refer to the states. Such legislation was ruled constitutional because general raises to state employees, even though purely intrastate in character, could significantly affect interstate commerce, and thus could be validly regulated by Congress under the Constitution's Commerce Clause.

FSEE, see FEDERAL SERVICE ENTRANCE EXAMINATION.

FSIP, see FEDERAL SERVICE IMPASSES PANEL.

FTC, see FEDERAL TRADE COMMISSION.

FTZs, see FOREIGN TRADE ZONES.

full-crew rule, safety regulation requiring a minimum number of workers for a given operation.

full employment, economic situation where all those who want to work are able to. In recent years, economists have been telling the public that "full" employment really means from 3 to 6 percent unemployment. See Marilyn Wilson, "What Is 'Full Employment'?" *Dun's Business Month* (February 1983).

Full Employment and Balanced Growth Act of 1977, see HUMPHREY-HAWKINS ACT OF 1977.

full-employment budget, see BUDGET, FULL-EMPLOYMENT.

full faith and credit, the descriptive term for those obligations that have first claim upon the resources of the state.

full field investigation, personal investigation of an applicant's background to determine whether he/she meets fitness standards for a critical-sensitive federal position.

full funding, providing budgetary resources to cover the total cost of a program or project at the time it is undertaken. Full funding differs from incremental funding, where budget authority is provided or recorded for only a portion of total estimated obligations expected to be incurred during a single fiscal year. Full funding is generally discussed in terms of multi-year programs, whether or not obligations for the entire program are made in the first year.

Fullilove v. Klutznick, U.S. Supreme Court case, 448 U.S. 448 (1980), which held that Congress has the authority to use quotas to remedy past discrimination, reasoning that the 14th Amendment's requirement of equal protection means that groups historically denied this right may be given special treatment. See Peter G. Kilgore, "Racial Preferences in the Federal Grant Programs: Is There a Basis for Challenge After *Fullilove v. Klutznick?*" *Labor Law Journal* (May 1981).

full responsibility, total responsibility for an action. Nowhere is primitive ritual or Machiavellian feigning more apparent than in the periodic assumption of full responsibility by an organization's chief executive. Although one of the advantages of delegating a problem is the ease with which the cunning manager can shift the blame for the situation if it sours, modern executives are seldom so crude as to lay blame. The appropriate tactic would be to assume "full" responsibility for the situation. Paradoxically, in "assuming" full responsibility, the manager is seemingly relieved of it. It is expected that the top management of any organizational unit will occasionally declare its willingness, indeed eagerness, to take personal responsibility for the actions and especially the mistakes of subordinates. Murray Edelman observes in his *The Symbolic Uses of Politics* (Urbana, Ill.: University of Illinois Press, 1967) that whenever this ritual is enacted, all of the participants tend to experience "a warm glow of satisfaction and relief that responsibility has been assumed and can be pinpointed. It once again conveys the message that the incumbent is the leader, that he knows he is able to cope, and that he should be followed." In reality, however, this ritual proves to have no substance. It "emphatically does not mean that the chief executive will be penalized for the mistakes of subordinates or that the latter will not be penalized." This is the tactic that President Nixon employed when he first addressed the nation concerning the Watergate scandals in the spring of 1973. He boldly proclaimed that all of the possibly illegal actions of White House officials were his responsibility and that he fully accepted that responsibility. Certainly Nixon did not mean to imply—at that point in time—that he should be punished for the transgressions of his underlings. Government officials of lesser rank are no less sophisticated with their manipulations of rituals and symbols.

See also SYMBOLS.

full-time-worker rate, wage rate of regular full-time employees, as distinguished from the wage rate of temporary or part-time employees performing the same job.

full-time workers, also PART-TIME WORKERS, according to the Bureau of Labor Statistics, those employed at least thirty-five hours a week. *Part-time workers* are those who work fewer hours. Workers on part-time schedules for economic reasons (such as slack work, terminating or starting a job during the week, material shortages, or inability to find full-time work) are among those counted as being on full-time status, under the assumption that they would be working full time if conditions permitted. The BLS classifies unemployed persons in full-time or part-time status by their reported preferences for full-time or part-time work. For a discussion of what the terms mean, *see* Janice Neipert Hedges and Stephen J. Gallogly, "Full and Part Time: A Review of Definitions," *Monthly Labor Review* (March 1977).

fully funded pension plan, pension plan whose assents are adequate to meet its obligations into the foreseeable future.

Fulton Committee, formally COMMITTEE ON THE CIVIL SERVICE, 1966-1968, British committee whose charge was to "examine the structure, recruitment and management, including training, of the Home Civil Service and to make recommendations." The committee, whose 1968 report recommended major reforms, was popularly known after its chairman, Lord Fulton. The Spring 1969 issue of *Public Administration* is devoted to summaries of the report's many volumes.

function, all, or a clearly identifiable segment, of an agency's mission, including all the parts of that mission (*e.g.*, procurement), regardless of how performed.

functional analysis, a research perspective in which the analyst attempts to discover those antecedent structures and processes that tend to cause, bring about, or reinforce a given pattern of behavior.

functional authority, authority inherent to a job or work assignment.

functional classification, a means of presenting budget authority, outlay, and tax expenditure data in terms of the principal purposes which federal programs are intended to serve. The Congressional Budget and Impoundment Control Act of 1974 requires the Congress to estimate outlays, budget authority, and tax expenditures for each function. Each account is generally placed in the single function (*e.g.*, national defense, health) that best represents its major purpose, regardless of the agency administering the program. Functions are generally subdivided into narrower categories called *subfunctions*.

functional illiterate, individual whose reading and writing skills are so poor that he/she is incapable of functioning effectively in the most basic business, office, or factory situations. Because many functional illiterates are high school graduates, the value of such diplomas is being increasingly discounted by personnel offices.

functional job analysis, technology of work analysis that measures and describes a position's specific requirements. Functional job analysis can discard traditionally restrictive labels for positions. In their place, a variety of component descriptions are used to more accurately illustrate the specific and varied duties actually performed by an incumbent. Functional job analysis data readily lend themselves to computerized personnel management information systems. *See* Sidney A. Fine, "Functional Job Analysis: An Approach to a Technology for Manpower Planning," *Personnel Journal* (November 1974); Steven Spirn and Lanny Solomon, "A Key Element in EDP Personnel Management: Functional Job Analysis," *Personnel Journal* (November 1976).

functional leadership, concept holding that leadership emerges from the dynamics associated with the particular circumstances under which groups integrate and organize their activities, rather than from the personal characteristics or behavior of an individual. *See* Robert G. Lord, "Functional Leadership Behavior: Measurement and Relation to Social Power and Leadership Perceptions," *Administrative Science Quarterly* (March 1977).

functus officio, Latin term that can be applied to an officer who has fulfilled the duties of an office that has expired and who, in consequence, has no further formal authority. Arbitrators are said to be *functus officio* concerning a particular case after they have declared their awards on it. According to Israel Ben Scheiber, in "The Doctrine of Functus Officio with Particular Relation to Labor Arbitration," *Labor Law Journal* (October 1972),

the need to plead the doctrine of "functus officio" cannot be regarded as a major problem or one that occurs with any significant degree of regularity. However, to an arbitrator who is asked to interpret, modify or clarify the language of his award (usually by the losing party) because of a claim that he has overlooked some fact or, in any event, not worded his opinion and/or award with sufficient clarity, a request to reopen the case and to issue a supplemental award can be a source of considerable embarrassment. This is so, in part, be-

cause to the aggrieved party, being told that an arbitrator is "functus officio" often appears as a senseless refuge and a convenient and unsatisfactory excuse given by the arbitrator for refusing to correct or make clear something which he has written and therefore should be able to clarify to the satisfaction of the applicant.

fund, accounting device established to control receipt and disbursement of income from sources set aside to support specific activities or attain certain objectives. *See* Regina E. Herzlinger and H. David Sherman, "Advantages of Fund Accounting in 'Nonprofits'," *Harvard Business Review* (May-June 1980).

fund account, *see* APPROPRIATION ACCOUNT.

funded pension plan, pension plan that provides for the periodic accumulation of money to meet the pension plan's obligations in future years.

funding method, any of the procedures by which money is accumulated to pay for pensions under a pension plan.

funeral leave, also called BEREAVEMENT LEAVE, paid time off for an employee at the time of a death in his/her immediate family. The majority of all employers offer such time off, usually three or four days. The biggest problem with administering such a benefit is defining just what constitutes a member of the "immediate" family.

fungible, a description for things that are easily substituted for one another. For example, bushels of wheat are fungible because one may easily be substituted for another. A grant is "fungible" when the recipient is able to use the grant funds for purposes other than those specified in the grant authorization.

furlough, period of absence from work, initiated either by the employer as a layoff or the employee as a leave of absence.

Furnco Construction Corp. v. Waters, 438 U.S. 567 (1978), U.S. Supreme Court case which held that the initial burden of proving a case of employment discrimination rests upon the complainant.

future shock, as defined in the leading work on the subject, Alvin Toffler's *Future Shock* (New York: Random House, 1970), "the distress, both physical and psychological, that arises from an overload of the human organism's physical adaptive systems and its decision making processes. Put more simply, future shock is the human response to over-stimulation." Also *see* James M. Mitchell and Rolfe E. Schroeder, "Future Shock for Personnel Administration," *Public Personnel Management* (July-August 1974). For one man's antidote to the problem, *see* George S. Odiorne, "Management by Objectives: Antidote to Future Shock," *Personnel Journal* (April 1974).

futuristics, fledgling discipline that seeks to anticipate future societal developments and present alternative courses of action for the polity's consideration. Within this discipline, there is a growing literature on the future of work. For two examples, *see* Paul Dickson, *The Future of the Workplace: The Coming Revolution in Jobs* (New York: Weybright and Talley, 1975); William T. Morris, *Work and Your Future: Living Poorer, Working Harder* (Reston, Va.: Reston Publishing Co., 1975); Barry O. Jones, *Sleepers, Wake! Technology and the Future of Work* (New York: Oxford University Press, 1982); Delores Hayden, *Redesigning the American Dream: The Future of Housing, Work, and Family Life* (New York: W.W. Norton, 1984).

G

gag rules, or GAG ORDERS, colloquial term for any formal instructions from a compe-tent authority, usually a judge, to refrain from discussing and/or advocating something. One of the most famous gag rules/orders is President Theodore Roosevelt's executive orders in 1902 and 1904 which forbade federal employees, on pain of dismissal, either as individuals or as members of organizations, to seek any pay increases or to attempt to influence legislation before Congress, except through the heads of their departments. Roosevelt's gag orders were repealed by the Lloyd-LaFollette Act of 1912, which granted public employees the right to organize unions.

gain sharing, any of a variety of wage payment methods in which the worker receives additional earnings due to increases in productivity. *See also:*
INDUSTRIAL DEMOCRACY
SCANLON PLAN
WORKERS' COUNCILS

Galbraith, John Kenneth (1908-), 20th century's most readable economist who has long called for the public ownership of those private corporations doing most of their business with the government. Galbraith finds public administration to be a major impediment to his socialist vision: "No argument against public ownership is so much used or so effective as the allegation that it is incompetent" ("Tasks for the Democratic Left," *The New Republic*, August 16, 1975). Galbraith concludes that the "extension of the area of public ownership is only possible politically or economically as the reputation for efficient public management is affirmed." During the long wait for this to happen, the reader will surely have time to read all of Galbraith's major works: *American Capitalism: The Concept of Countervailing Power* (Boston: Houghton Mifflin, 1952; revised 1956); *A Theory of Price Control* (Cambridge, Mass.: Harvard University Press, 1952); *The Great Crash* (Boston: Houghton Mifflin, 1954; 3rd ed., 1972); *Economics and the Art of Controversy* (New Brunswick, N.J.: Rutgers University Press, 1955); *The Affluent Society* (Boston: Houghton Mifflin, 1958;

3rd ed., 1976); *Journey to Poland and Yugoslavia* (Cambridge, Mass.: Harvard University Press, 1958); *The Liberal Hour* (Boston: Houghton Mifflin, 1960); *Economic Development in Perspective* (Cambridge, Mass.: Harvard University Press, 1962); *The Scotch* (Boston: Houghton Mifflin, 1964); *The New Industrial State* (Boston: Houghton Mifflin, 1967; 3rd ed., 1978); *The Triumph: A Novel of Modern Diplomacy* (Boston: Houghton Mifflin, 1968); *Ambassador's Journal* (Boston: Houghton Mifflin, 1969); *How to Control the Military* (Garden City, N.Y.: Doubleday, 1969); *A China Passage* (Boston: Houghton Mifflin, 1973); *Economics and the Public Purpose* (Boston: Houghton Mifflin, 1973); *Money: Whence it Came, Where it Went* (Boston: Houghton Mifflin, 1975); *The Age of Uncertainty* (Boston: Houghton Mifflin, 1977); *Almost Everyone's Guide to Economics*, with Nicole Salinger (Boston: Houghton Mifflin, 1978). For biographies, see John S. Gambs, *John Kenneth Galbraith* (Boston: Twayne, 1975); Charles H. Hession, *John Kenneth Galbraith and I Its Critics* (New York: New American Library, 1972); C. Lynn Monro, *The Galbrathian Vision* (Washington, D.C.: University Press of America, 1977).

games, *see* MANAGEMENT GAMES.

game theory, a mathematical approach to decision-making in situations involving two or more players with presumably conflicting interests. Because the theory of games assumes rationality on the part of the players, the strategies and decisions of one player are heavily dependent upon the anticipated behavior of the opposition. The possible outcomes of a two-person game are frequently presented in a *payoff matrix* consisting of numbers arranged in rows and columns with the degrees of preference that each player assigns to each outcome. Of course, a player's overall strategy is a *game plan*.

gaming simulation, a model of reality with dynamic parts that can be manipulated to teach the manipulator(s) how to better cope with the represented processes in real life. *See* John G. H. Carlson and Michael J. Misshauk, *Introduction to Gaming: Management Decision Simulations* (New York: John Wiley, 1972); Gilbert B. Siegel, "Gaming Simulation in the Teaching of Public Personnel Administration," *Public Personnel Management* (July–August 1977).

Gantt, Henry L(awrence) (1861-1919), contemporary and protege of Frederick W. Taylor; a pioneer in the scientific management movement and inventor of the "Gantt Chart." For a collection of his major works, *see* Alex W. Rathe, ed., *Gantt on Management* (New York: American Management Association, 1961). For a biography, *see* Leon R. Alford, *Henry Lawrence Gantt: Leader in Industry* (New York: Harper & Bros., 1934).

Gantt Chart, chart developed during World War I by Henry L. Gantt. The Gantt Chart's distinguishing feature is that work planned and work done are shown in the same space in their relation to each other and in their relation to time. Today any chart which uses straight lines to compare planned and actual progress over time could be called a Gantt Chart.

GAO, *see* GENERAL ACCOUNTING OFFICE.

GAO Review, quarterly publication of the U.S. General Accounting Office.
GAO Review
Superintendent of Documents
Washington, D.C. 20402

Garcia v. San Antonio Metropolitan Transit Authority, 83 L. Ed. 2d 1016 (1985), U. S. Supreme Court case that held that the application of the minimum wage and overtime requirements of the Fair Labor Standards Act to public agency employment does not violate any constitution provision. This reversed *National League of Cities v. Usery* (1976), which held that the Tenth Amendment prohibited the federal government from establishing wages and hours for state employees.

garden city, an urban setting, including gardens for inhabitants, surrounded by green belts. Around the turn of the century, the general belief in the efficacy of science led to a series of movements based on ideal cities which could be and should be created. One of the earliest such models was Ebenezer Howard's concept of a garden city. *See* Ebenezer Howard, *Garden Cities of Tomorrow* (Cambridge, Mass.: M.I.T. Press, 1965).

Gardner, John W. (1912-), former president of the Carnegie Corporation (1955-65), former Secretary of Health, Education and Welfare (1965-68), and former chairman of the National Urban Coalition (1968-70), who founded Common Cause—the public interest lobby— in 1970. Gardner is the author of a variety of books criticized for their "sermonizing" qualities by some but praised for their sincere moral tone by others. Major works include: *Excellence: Can We Be Equal and Excellent Too?* (New York: Harper & Row, 1961); *Self-Renewal: The Individual and the Innovative Society* (New York: Harper & Row, 1964); *No Easy Victories* (New York: Harper & Row, 1968); *The Recovery of Confidence* (New York: W. W. Norton, 1970); *In Common Cause* (New York: W. W. Norton, 1972).

Gardner-Denver case, *see* ALEXANDER V. GARDNER-DENVER COMPANY.

Gardner v. Broderick, 392 U.S. 273 (1968), and companion case *Uniformed Sanitation Men's Ass'n. v. Commissioner of Sanitation of the City of New York,* 392 U.S. 280 (1968), Supreme Court decisions holding the dismissals of public employees for refusing to waive immunity from prosecution or testify at grand jury hearings to be unconstitutional.

Garfield, James A(bram) (1831-1881), twentieth president of the United States, assassinated on July 2, 1881, by Charles Guiteau, an insane attorney who had worked for Garfield's election and was angry about not receiving a patronage appointment. Garfield's death gave new life to the reform movement, culminating in the passage of the Pendelton or Civil Service Act of 1883.

Garfield's Martyrdom

Every President who dies in office, whether from bacteria or bullets, is regarded as a martyr to the public weal, at least in some degree. James A. Garfield, whose troubled six months were marred by officemongering, was probably helped, as far as reputation was concerned, by his assassination. One recalls George Bernard Shaw's cutting remark, "Martyrdom is the only way in which a man can become famous without ability."

Source: Thomas A. Bailey, *Presidential Greatness* (New York: Appleton-Century-Crofts, 1966), p. 116.

Garner v. Board of Public Works of Los Angeles, 341 U.S. 716 (1951), Supreme Court case upholding the constitutionality of a municipal loyalty oath requiring employees to disclose whether they were or ever had been a member of the Communist Party and to take an oath to the effect that for five years prior to the effective date of the ordinance they had not advocated the overthrow of the government by force or belonged to any organization so advocating.

See also LOYALTY.

garnishment, any legal or equitable procedure through which earnings of any individual are required to be withheld for the payment of any debt. Most garnishments are made by court order.

The Federal Wage Garnishment Act limits the amount of an employee's disposable earnings subject to garnishment in any one week and protects the employee from discharge because of garnishment for any one indebtedness. It does not change other matters related to garnishment, such as the right of a creditor to collect the full amount owed and most garnishment procedures established by state laws or rules. The largest amount of total disposable earnings subject to garnishment in any workweek may not exceed the lesser of: (1) 25 percent of the disposable earnings for that week or (2) the amount by which disposable earnings for that week exceeds thirty times the federal minimum hourly wage.

No court of the United States, or any state, may make, execute, or enforce any order or process in violation of these restrictions.

The restrictions on the amount that may be garnisheed in a week do not apply to: (1) court orders for the support of any person, such as child support and alimony; (2) bankruptcy court orders under Chapter XIII of the Bankruptcy Act: and (3) debts due for state or federal taxes. A levy against wages for a federal tax debt by the Internal Revenue Service is not restricted by this law.

The Federal Wage Garnishment Act is enforced by the Secretary of Labor, acting through the Wage and Hour Division, U.S. Department of Labor.

Garrity v. New Jersey, 385 U.S. 493 (1967), Supreme Court case holding that a New Jersey practice of dismissing public employees who relied upon the Fifth Amendment privilege against self-incrimination was unconstitutional.

GATB, see GENERAL APTITUDE TEST BATTERY.

Gateway Coal Company v. United Mine Workers, 414 U.S. 368 (1974), U.S. Supreme Court case which held that disputes over safety issues can be submitted to arbitration and that courts can issue injunctions against work stoppages provoked by such disputes.

GAW, see GUARANTEED ANNUAL WAGE.

Geduldig v. Aiello, 417 U.S. 484 (1974), U.S. Supreme Court case which held that the State of California's temporary disability insurance program, which denied benefits for pregnancy-related disabilities, was not in violation of the equal protection clause of the 14th Amendment.

General Accounting Office (GAO), independent agency created by the Budget and Accounting Act of 1921 to audit federal government expenditures and assist Congress with its legislative oversight responsibilities. The GAO is directed by the Comptroller General of the United States, who is appointed by the president with the advice and consent of the Senate for a term of fifteen years. *See* Keith E. Marvin and James L. Hedrick, "GAO Helps Congress Evaluate Programs," *Public Administration Review* (July-August 1974); Martin J. Fitzgerald, "The Expanded Role of the General Accounting Office in Support of a Strengthened Congress," *Bureaucrat* (January 1975); John T. Rourke, "The GAO: An Evolving Role," *Public Administration Review* (September-October 1978); Erasmus H. Kloman, ed., *Cases in Accountability: The Work of the GAO* (Boulder, Colo.: Westview Press, 1979); and Frederick C. Mosher, *The GAO: The Quest for Accountability* (Boulder, Colo.: Westview Press, 1979).

General Accounting Office
441 G Street, N.W.
Washington, D.C. 20548
(202) 275-2812

General Agreement on Tariffs and Trade (GATT), a multilateral trade agreement containing guidelines for conduct of international trade based on three basic principles: nondiscriminatory treatment of all signatories in trade matters; eventual elimination of tariff and non-tariff barriers to trade, mostly through negotiations; and resolution of conflicts or damages arising from trade actions of another signatory through consultation. The agreement, however, contains many practical exceptions to these principles and no sanctions for their violation. GATT has sponsored multilateral trade negotiations at various times.

General Aptitude Test Battery (GATB), group of tests designed by the United States Employment Service and used extensively in state employment offices. The series of twelve tests measure nine aptitude areas: intelligence, verbal aptitude, numerical aptitude, spatial aptitude, form perception, clerical perception, motor coordination, finger dexterity, and manual dexterity. Scores from the tests are combined to create measures of individual aptitudes and general intelligence. The GATB has demonstrated impressive validity. *See* Stephen E. Bennis, "Occupational Validity of the General Aptitude Test Battery," *Journal of Applied Psychology* (June 1968).

See also NONREADING APTITUDE TEST BATTERY.

General Electric Co. v. Gilbert, 429 U.S. 125 (1976), U.S. Supreme Court case which held that excluding pregnancies from sick leave and disability benefit programs is not "discrimination based on sex" and so is not a violation of Title VII of the Civil Rights Act of 1964. This decision led to a Title VII amendment (the Pregnancy Discrimination Act of 1978) that reversed the court's decision. *See* Steven C. Kahn, "*General Electric Co.* v. *Gilbert:* Retreat from Rationality?" *Employee Relations Law Journal* (Summer 1977).

See also PREGNANCY and PREGNANCY DISCRIMINATION ACT OF 1978.

general fund, fund credited with all receipts not earmarked by law for a specific purpose and from general borrowing. It is used for the general purposes of a government through various general fund accounts.

general increase, any upward salary adjustment governing the pay of most employees.

general labor union, any labor organization that accepts as members workers in every category of skill.

generally accepted accounting principles, rules and procedures established by authoritative bodies or conventions that have evolved through custom and common usage. The National Council on Governmental Accounting's Statement 1, "Governmental Accounting and Financial Reporting Principles," is generally acknowledged as the authoritative publication in the area of accounting for state and

local government units. GAO's publication, "Accounting Principles and Standards for Federal Agencies," contains generally accepted accounting principles for the federal agencies.

general manager, also CITY ADMINISTRATOR and CHIEF ADMINISTRATIVE OFFICER (CAO), administrative official appointed in council/mayor system of government. They are typically appointed by the mayor and share powers with that office.

General Motors decision, see NATIONAL LABOR RELATIONS BOARD V. GENERAL MOTORS.

general obligation debt, *see* DEBT, GENERAL OBLIGATION.

general revenue sharing, *see* (1) GRANT and (2) REVENUE SHARING.

General Schedule (GS), basic pay system for federal white-collar employees. It is the largest of the civilian pay systems, covering approximately 1.4 million of the total of 2.8 million civilian employees.

The General Schedule, established by the Classification Act of 1949, consists of eighteen grades or "levels of work" which are described broadly. Virtually any job can be accommodated within the schedule by evaluation of its level of duties, responsibilities, and qualification requirements. As befits its title, the General Schedule exhibits great occupational diversity: messengers, typists, secretaries, engineers, administrative personnel, research scientists, as well as occupations which are neither white-collar nor blue-collar in the traditional sense (police and fire fighters, for example).

A single pay table, nationwide in its applicability, sets forth the pay rates for the General Schedule. From 1949, when the General Schedule was enacted, until 1962, pay rates were adjusted by Congress on an irregular basis, largely in response to the pressures of inflation on employees' salaries. In 1962, Congress established the principle that pay rates would be maintained on the basis of com-

GS Pay Schedule for Federal White-Collar Workers, 1985

GS	1	2	3	4	5	6	7	8	9	10
1	$9,339	$9,650	$9,961	$10,271	$10,582	$10,764	$11,071	$11,380	$11,393	$11,686
2	10,501	10,750	11,097	11,393	11,521	11,860	12,199	12,538	12,877	13,216
3	11,458	11,840	12,222	12,604	12,986	13,368	13,750	14,132	14,514	14,896
4	12,862	13,291	13,720	14,149	14,578	15,007	15,436	15,865	16,294	16,723
5	14,390	14,870	15,350	15,830	16,310	16,790	17,270	17,750	18,230	18,710
6	16,040	16,575	17,110	17,645	18,180	18,715	19,250	19,785	20,320	20,855
7	17,824	18,418	19,012	19,606	20,200	20,794	21,388	21,982	22,576	23,170
8	19,740	20,398	21,056	21,714	22,372	23,030	23,688	24,346	25,004	25,662
9	21,804	22,531	23,258	23,985	24,712	25,439	26,166	26,893	27,620	28,347
10	24,011	24,811	25,611	26,411	27,211	28,011	28,811	29,611	30,411	31,211
11	26,381	27,260	28,139	29,018	29,897	30,776	31,655	32,534	33,413	34,292
12	31,619	32,673	33,727	34,781	35,835	36,889	37,943	38,997	40,051	41,105
13	37,599	38,852	40,105	41,358	42,611	43,864	45,117	46,370	47,623	48,876
14	44,430	45,911	47,392	48,873	50,354	51,835	53,316	54,797	56,278	57,759
15	52,262	54,004	55,746	57,488	59,230	60,972	62,714	64,456	66,198	67,940
16	61,296	63,339	65,382	67,425	69,468*	71,511*	73,554*	75,597*	77,640*	
17	71,804*	74,197*	76,590*	78,983*	81,376*					
18	84,157*									

*In most cases, the maximum salary payable is $68,700.

227

parability with rates paid in the private sector, as these rates were arrived at through the interplay of market forces. Authority to adjust the pay rates remained with the Congress, however, and full comparability was not achieved in theory until the passage of the Federal Pay Comparability Act of 1970, which delegated to the President authority for making annual adjustments of General Schedule pay rates under the principle of comparability.

General Services Administration (GSA), federal agency that establishes policy and provides for the management of the federal government's property and records, including construction and operation of buildings, procurement and distribution of supplies, utilization and disposal of property, transportation, traffic, and communications management, stockpiling of strategic materials, and the management of a government-wide automatic data processing resources program.

GSA
General Services Building
18th and F Streets, N.W.
Washington, D.C. 20405
(202) 655-4000

general strike, work stoppage by a substantial portion of the total work force of a locality or country. Because general strikes have tended to be more political than pragmatic in their goals, they have historically been more popular in Europe than in the United States. General strikes have been decidedly infrequent since World War II. *See* Christopher Farman, *The General Strike, May, 1926* (London: Hart-Davis, 1972); David Jay Bercuson, *Confrontation at Winnipeg: Labour, Industrial Relations, and the General Strike* (Montreal: McGill-Queen's University Press, 1974); Gordon Ashton Phillips, *The General Strike: The Politics of Industrial Conflict* (London: Weidenfeld and Nicolson, 1976); Mick Jenkins, *The General Strike of 1842* (London: Lawrence and Wishart, 1980).

general systems theory, term that describes efforts to build theoretical models

that are conceptually, as Kenneth E. Boulding, "General Systems Theory—The Skeleton of Science," *Management Science* (April 1956), puts it, "somewhere between the highly generalized constructions of pure mathematics and the specific theories of the specialized disciplines." For the work of the man who sought a unity of science by introducing this notion, *see* Ludwig von Bertalanffy, *General Systems Theory: Foundations, Development, Applications* (New York: George Braziller, 1968).

See also SYSTEMS ANALYSIS and SYSTEMS APPROACH.

generic management, those areas and concerns of management that are of common concern to both the public, nonprofit and private sectors. *See* Myron D. Fottler, "Is Management Really Generic?" *Academy of Management Review* (January 1981).

gentlemen's agreement, any agreement or understanding based solely on oral communications. It is usually unenforceable if one party reneges.

gentrification, the gradual replacement of the poor by people with middle and upper class incomes in a given neighborhood. *See* J. John Palen and Bruce London, eds., *Gentrification, Displacement, and Neighborhood Revitalization* (Albany, N.Y.: State University of New York Press, 1983).

geographical differential, also called INTER-CITY DIFFERENTIAL, differences in wage rates for the same work in various regions or cities. *See* Richard J. Cebula, *Geographic Living-Cost Differentials* (Lexington, Mass: Lexington Books, 1983).

George, Henry (1839-1897), an economist whose *Progress and Poverty (1879)* advocated a single tax on land which would replace all other taxes.

geriatrics, also GERONTOLOGY and INDUSTRIAL GERONTOLOGY, that branch of medicine concerned with the special medical problems of older people. *Gerontology* is that branch of biology which is concerned with the nature of the aging process. *Industrial gerontology* is a far more comprehensive term that summarizes all of those areas of study concerned with the employment and retirement problems of workers who are middle-aged and beyond. *See* Harold L. Sheppard, ed., *Towards an Industrial Gerontology: An Introduction to a New Field of Applied Research and Service* (Cambridge, Mass.: Schenkman Publishing Company, 1970); Arthur N. Schwartz and James A. Peterson, *Introduction to Gerontology* (New York: Holt, Rinehart and Winston, 1979); Robert L. Kane *et al., Geriatrics in the United States: Manpower Projections and Training Considerations* (Lexington, Mass.: Lexington Books, 1981); Louis Lowy, *Social Policies and Programs on Aging* (Lexington, Mass.: Lexington Books, 1980); Mildred Doering, Susan R. Rhodes and Michael Schuster, *The Aging Worker: Research and Recommendations* (Beverly Hills, CA: Sage, 1983); Bennett M. Rich and Martha Baum, *The Aging: A Guide to Public Policy* (Pittsburgh, Pa.: University of Pittsburgh Press, 1985).

gerontology, *see* GERIATRICS.

GERR, *see* GOVERNMENT EMPLOYEE RELATIONS REPORT.

GERT, acronym for GRAPHICAL EVALUATION AND REVIEW TECHNIQUE, process that provides a framework for modeling real-world research and development projects requiring many false starts, redoings, and multiple outcomes. For a text, *see* Lawrence J. Moore and Edward R. Clayton, *GERT Modeling and Simulation: Fundamentals and Applications* (New York: Petrocelli-Charter, 1976). For a specific application to personnel, *see* T. W. Bonham, Edward R. Clayton, and Lawrence J. Moore, "A GERT Model to Meet Future Organizational Manpower Needs," *Personnel Journal* (July 1975).

Gestalt therapy, psychotherapy technique pioneered by Frederic S. Perls which emphasizes the treatment of a person as a biological and perceptual whole. "Gestalt" is a German word for a configuration, pattern, or otherwise organized whole whose parts have different qualities than the whole. According to William R. Passons, "Gestalt Therapy Interventions for Group Counseling," *Personnel and Guidance Journal* (November 1972):

> in Gestalt therapy the principal means for facilitating responsibility and integration is the enhancement of self-awareness. These changes, however, are not forced or programmed. Rather they are allowed. As Perls stated it: 'This is the great thing to understand: that awareness per se—by and of itself—can be curative.'
>
> Necessarily, then, Gestalt interventions are designed to enhance awareness of the person's 'now' experience—emotionally, cognitively, and bodily. As such, many of the interventions lend themselves to group counseling.

The classic work on this subject is F. S. Perls, R. F. Hefferling and P. Goodman, *Gestalt Therapy* (New York: Julian Press, 1951).

GETA, *see* GOVERNMENT EMPLOYEES TRAINING ACT OF 1958.

get the sack, be fired. At the dawn of the industrial revolution, factory workers had to use their own tools. When a worker was fired, he was given a sack in which to gather up his tools.

ghetto, area of a city inhabited exclusively by members of an ethnic, racial, religious or social group. It often carries connotations of low income. *See* William K. Tabb, *The Political Economy of the Ghetto* (New York: Norton, 1970); Garth L. Mangum and Stephen F. Seninger, *Coming of Age in the Ghetto: A Dilemma of Youth Unemployment* (Baltimore: Johns Hopkins University Press, 1978); David A. Snow and Peter J. Leahy, "The Making of a Black Slum-Ghetto: A Case Study of Neighborhood Transition," *Journal of Applied Behavioral Science* (October-

November–December 1980); Daniel R. Fusfeld and Timothy Bates, *The Economics of the Urban Ghetto* (Middletown, Conn.: Wesleyan University Press, 1984).

Gilbert **case,** *see* GENERAL ELECTRIC CO. V. GILBERT.

Gilbreth, Frank Bunker (1868–1924) **and Lillian Moller** (1878–1972), husband and wife team who were the pioneers of time-and-motion study.

Frank and Lillian Gilbreth's influence on the scientific management movement was rivaled only by that of Frederick W. Taylor. Frank Gilbreth became the archtypical "efficiency expert." Two of their twelve children illustrated his mania for efficiency in their memoir, *Cheaper By the Dozen*, Frank B. Gilbreth, Jr., and Ernestine Gilbreth Carey (New York: Grosset & Dunlap, 1948):

> Yes, at home or on the job, Dad was always the efficiency expert. He buttoned his vest from the bottom up, instead of from the top down, because the bottom-to-top process took him only three seconds, while the top-to-bottom took seven. He even used two shaving brushes to lather his face, because he found that by doing so he could cut seventeen seconds off his shaving time. For a while he tried shaving with two razors, but he finally gave that up.
>
> "I can save forty-four seconds," he grumbled, "but I wasted two minutes this morning putting this bandage on my throat."
>
> It wasn't the slashed throat that really bothered him. It was the two minutes.

For more serious biographies, *see* Edna Yost, *Frank and Lillian Gilbreth: Partners for Life* (New Brunswick, N.J.: Rutgers University Press, 1949); Lillian Moller Gilbreth, *The Quest for the One Best Way: A Sketch of the Life of Frank Bunker Gilbreth* (Easton, Pa.: Hive Publishing, 1973). For their collected works, *see* William R. Spriegel and Clark E. Meyers, eds., *The Writings of the Gilbreths* (Homewood, Ill.: Richard D. Irwin, 1953).

See also SCIENTIFIC MANAGEMENT and THERBLIG.

Ginzberg, Eli (1911–), political economist and leading authority on manpower research and employment and training policy. Major works include: *Human Resources: The Wealth of a Nation* (New York: Simon and Schuster, 1958); *The American Worker in the Twentieth Century,* with Hyman Berman (Glencoe, Ill.: The Free Press of Glencoe, 1963); *The Development of Human Resources* (New York: McGraw-Hill, 1966); *Manpower Agenda for America* (New York: McGraw-Hill, 1968); *Manpower Strategy for the Metropolis* (New York: Columbia University Press 1968); *The Human Economy* (New York: McGraw-Hill, 1976). For biographical sketch, *see* Gloria Stevenson, "Eli Ginzberg: Pioneer in Work Force Research," *Worklife* (May 1976).

girl Firday, *see* MAN FRIDAY.

giveback, any demand by management that a union accept a reduction in the present terms of employment. *See* The Bureau of National Affairs Editorial Staff, "Give-Backs Highlight Three Major Bargaining Agreements," *Personnel Administrator* (January 1983); Scott A. Kruse, "Giveback Bargaining: One Answer to Current Labor Problems" *Personnel Journal* (April 1983).

Givhan* v. *Western Line Consolidated School District, 435 U.S. 950 (1979), Supreme Court decision upholding the constitutional right of an employee (here a teacher) to privately express his or her views to a supervisor (here a school principal).

GNP, *see* GROSS NATIONAL PRODUCT.

goals, also QUOTAS and TIMETABLE, within the context of equal employment opportunity, realistic objectives which an organization endeavors to achieve through affirmative action. A *quota*, in contrast, restricts employment or development opportunities to members of particular groups by establishing a required number or proportionate representation which managers are obligated to attain without regard to "equal" employment opportunity. To be meaningful, any program of goals or quotas must be associated with a specific *timetable*—a schedule of when the goals or quotas are to be achieved. *See* Daniel Seligman, "How 'Equal Opportunity' turned into Employment Quotas," *Fortune* (March 1973); Neil C. Churchill and John K. Shank, "Affirmative Action and Guilt-Edged Goals," *Harvard Business Review* (March-April 1976). For a case study of how the nation's largest private employer met its government mandated goals and timetables, *see* Carol J. Loomis, "A.T.& T. in the Throes of 'Equal Employment,' " *Fortune* (January 15, 1979). *Also see* David H. Rosenbloom, "The Civil Service Commission's Decision to Authorize the Use of Goals and Timetables in the Federal Equal Employment Opportunity Program," *Western Political Quarterly* (June 1973).

See also FULLILOVE V. KLUTZNICK and KIRKLAND V. NEW YORK STATE DEPARTMENT OF CORRECTIONAL SERVICES.

gobbledygook, also OFFICIALESE, FEDERALESE, and BAFFLEGAB. slang terms for the obtuse language so frequently used by bureaucrats. *See* John O'Hayre, *Gobbledygook Has Gotta Go* (Washington, D.C.: Government Printing Office, 1966); Alan Siegel, "Fighting Business Gobbledygook: How to Say It in Plain English," *Management Review* (November 1979).

Example of Gobbledygook

We respectfully petition, request, and entreat that due and adequate provision be made, this day and the date hereinafter subscribed, for the satisfying of these petitioners' nutritional requirements and for the organizing of such methods of allocation and distribution as may be deemed necessary and proper to assure the reception by and for said petitioners of such quantities of baked cereal products as shall, in the judgment of the aforesaid petitioners, constitute a sufficient supply thereof.

Translation: "Give us this day our daily bread."

Goesaert v. *Cleary,* 335 U.S. 464

(1948), U.S. Supreme Court case which found state laws denying women the right to practice certain occupations to be unconstitutional under the 14th Amendment's equal protection clause.

going rate, wage rate most commonly paid to workers in a given occupation.

Goldberg v. *Kelly,* 397 U.S. 254 (1970), U.S. Supreme Court case which held that the due process clause of the Constitution requires government agencies to provide welfare recipients with an opportunity for an evidentiary hearing before terminating their benefits.

goldbricking, shirking or giving the appearance of working. A "goldbrick" was a slang term for something that had only a surface appearance of value. The word has now come to imply industrial work slowdowns whether they be individual initiatives (or the lack of individual initiative) or group efforts (organized or otherwise).

gold-circle rate, pay rate that exceeds the maximum rate of an employee's evaluated pay level.

golden handcuffs, the feeling of being bound to remain in a job because financial benefits would be forfeited upon resignation.

golden handshake, the dismissal of an employee with provision of a large cash bonus.

golden parachute, being able to leave a company with a substantial financial benefit; or a no-cut contract given to executives of a company facing a takeover bid. *See* Philip L. Cochran and Steven L. Wartick, "Golden Parachutes: A Closer Look," *California Management Review* (Summer 1984).

goldfish-bowl bargaining, *see* SUNSHINE BARGAINING.

gold standard, system in which all forms of money, paper and otherwise, are held at a parity with a coined monetary unit defined by its gold content and are convertible into this gold coin on demand. This monetary unit is coined freely, without an appreciable charge for the process; gold coins circulate freely and may be freely exported, imported, or melted down; gold is unlimited legal tender; and gold constitutes a large part of the nation's reserve. Because of the first two conditions this is referred to as the *gold coin standard*. A close cousin is the *gold bullion standard*. This differs only in that a special condition of convertibility is imposed: a stipulated minimum of bullion must be purchased with paper money for the act of redemption to take place. On March 10, 1933, President Franklin D. Roosevelt, relying on the Emergency Banking Act, prohibited by executive order the export of gold and gold certificates as well as payments in gold by banks. The United States was then off the gold standard.

Gompers, Samuel (1850-1924), one of the founders of the American Federation of Labor in 1886. He was the first president of the AFL and held that post, except for one year, until his death. For his autobiography, *see Seventy Years of Life and Labor: An Autobiography* (New York: E. P. Dutton, 1925). Other biographies include: Bernard Mandel, *Samuel Gompers: A Biography* (Yellow Springs, Ohio: The Antioch Press, 1963); Stuart Bruce Kaufman, *Samuel Gompers and the Origins of the American Federation of Labor: 1848-1896* (Westport, Conn.: Greenwood Press, 1973); Harold C. Livesay, *Samuel Gompers and Organized Labor in America* (Boston: Little, Brown, 1978).

good faith, in the context of equal employment opportunity, the absence of discriminating intent. The "good faith" of an employer is usually considered by the courts in fashioning an appropriate remedy to correct the wrongs of "unintentional" discrimination.

good-faith bargaining, sincere negotiation. Section 8(a) (5) of the National Labor Relations Act makes it illegal for an employer to refuse to bargain in good faith about wages, hours, and other conditions of employment with the representative selected by a majority of the employees in a unit appropriate for collective bargaining. A bargaining representative seeking to enforce its right concerning an employer under this section must show that it has been designated by a majority of the employees, that the unit is appropriate, and that there has been both a demand that the employer bargain and a refusal by the employer to do so.

The duty to bargain covers all matters concerning rates of pay, wages, hours of employment, or other conditions of employment. These are called "mandatory" subjects of bargaining about which the employer, as well as the employees' representative, must bargain in good faith, although the law does not require "either party to agree to a proposal or require the making of a concession." These mandatory subjects of bargaining include, but are not limited to, such matters as pensions for present and retired employees, bonuses, group insurance, grievance procedure, safety practices, seniority, procedures for discharge, layoff, recall, or discipline, and the union shop. On "nonmandatory" subjects—that is, matters that are lawful but not related to "wages, hours, and other conditions of employment"—the parties are free to bargain and to agree, but neither party may insist on bargaining on such subjects over the objection of the other party.

An employer who is required to bargain under this section must, as stated in Section 8(d), "meet at reasonable times and confer in good faith with respect to wages, hours, and other terms and conditions of employment, or the negotiation of an agreement, or any question arising thereunder, and the execution of a written contract incorporating any agreement reached if requested by either party."

An employer, therefore, will be found to have violated Section 8 (a) (5) if its conduct in bargaining, viewed in its entirety, indicates that the employer did not negotiate with a good-faith intention to reach agreement. However, the employer's good faith is not at issue where its conduct constitutes an out-and-out refusal to bargain on a mandatory subject. For example, it is a violation for an employer, regardless of good faith, to refuse to bargain about a subject it believes is not a mandatory subject of bargaining, when in fact it is.

See also the following entries:

NATIONAL LABOR RELATIONS BOARD V. INSURANCE AGENTS' INTERNATIONAL UNION
NATIONAL LABOR RELATIONS BOARD V. TRUITT MANUFACTURING
UNFAIR LABOR PRACTICES (EMPLOYERS)
UNFAIR LABOR PRACTICES (UNIONS)

Goodnow, Frank J. (1859–1939), one of the founders and first president (in 1903) of the American Political Science Association. Goodnow is now best known as one of the principal exponents, along with Woodrow Wilson, of public administration's politics/administration dichotomy. His most enduring work is *Politics and Administration: A Study in Government* (New York: Macmillan, 1900). For an appreciation, see Charles G. Haines and Marshall E. Dimock, eds., *Essays on the Law and Practice of Governmental Administration: A Volume in Honor of Frank J. Goodnow* (Baltimore: Johns Hopkins Press, 1935). *Also see* Lurton W. Blassingame, "Frank J. Goodnow: Progressive Urban Reformer," *North Dakota Quarterly* (Summer 1972).

good standing, state of compliance. For example, a union member is in "good standing" with his union if he or she meets all of the requirements for membership and his or her dues and other fees are current.

goo-goos, see DO-GOODERS.

gopher, lackey. While this is not formally listed as a job title on anybody's resume, many a successful manager will admit to having worked his way up from gopher— go for coffee, go for this, go for that, etc.

Gouldner, Alvin W. (1920–1981), a leading sociologist who has made some of the most significant contributions to the field of industrial sociology. Major works include: *Patterns of Industrial Bureaucracy* (Glencoe, Ill.: The Free Press, 1954); *Wildcat Strikes*, with R. A. Peterson (Yellow Springs, Ohio: Antioch Press, 1954); *Notes on Technology and the Moral Order,* with Richard A. Peterson (Indianapolis: Bobbs-Merrill, 1962); *Enter Plato* (New York: Basic Books, 1965); *The Coming Crisis of Western Sociology* (New York: Basic Books, 1970).

governmental accountability, the duty of those governments and agencies that are entrusted with public resources and the authority for applying them to render a full accounting of their activities to the public.

Governmental Finance, quarterly journal of the Municipal Finance Officers Association devoted to budgetary and financial management policies and procedures.
Governmental Finance
180 North Michigan Avenue
Chicago, IL 60601

government corporation, government-owned corporation or an agency of government that administers a self-supporting enterprise. Such a structure is used (1) when an agency's business is essentially commercial, (2) when an agency can generate its own revenue, and (3) when the agency's mission requires greater flexibility than government agencies normally have. Examples of federal government corporations include the Saint Lawrence Seaway Development Corporation, the Federal Deposit Insurance Corporation, the National Railroad Passenger Corporation (AMTRAK), and the Tennessee Valley Authority. At the state and municipal levels, corporations, often bearing different names, such as "authorities," operate enterprises such as turnpikes, airports, and harbors (such as the Port of New York Authority). See Harold Seidman, "The Government Corporation in the United States," *Public Administration* (Summer 1959); Annmarie Hauck Walsh, *The Public's Business: The Politics and Practices of Government Corporations*

(Cambridge, Mass.: M.I.T. Press 1980); Ronald C. Moe, "Government Corporations and the Erosion of Accountability: The Case of the Proposed Energy Security Corporation," *Public Administration Review* (November–December 1979); Lloyd Musolf, *Uncle Sam's Private, Profit-seeking Corporations: Comsat, Fannie Mae, Amtrak and Conrail* (Lexington, Mass.: Lexington Books, 1983).

Government Employee Relations Report (GERR), report published by the Bureau of National Affairs, Inc. This is a weekly notification and reference service designed solely for the public sector. Provides comprehensive coverage of all significant developments affecting public employee relations on the federal, state and local levels.

Government Employees Training Act of 1958, federal statute (Public Law 85–507) which held that

in order to promote efficiency and economy in the operation of the Government and provide means for the development of maximum proficiency in the performance of official duties by employees thereof, to establish and maintain the highest standards of performance in the transaction of the public business, and to install and utilize effectively the best modern practices and techniques which have been developed, tested, and proved within or outside of the Government, it is necessary and desirable in the public interest that self-education, self-improvement, and self-training by such employees be supplemented and extended by Government-sponsored programs, provided for by this Act, for the training of such employees in the performance of official duties and for the development of skills, knowledge, and abilities which will best qualify them for performance of official duties.

GETA (1) was a clear-cut mandate that the federal workforce should be trained to its most effective level, (2) authorized expenditures for training, (3) provided for both centralized training by the U.S. Civil

Service Commission and departmental training programs, and (4) authorized agencies to buy training from existing educational and professional institutions.

Government Executive, trade magazine for public managers.
  Government Executive
  Executive Publications, Inc.
  1725 K Street, N.W.
  Washington, D.C. 20006

Government Printing Office (GPO), federal agency that executes orders for printing and binding placed by Congress and the departments and establishments of the federal government. It sells through mail orders and government bookstores over twenty-five thousand different publications that originated in various government agencies. It also administers the depository library program through which selected government publications are made available in libraries throughout the country.
  GPO
  North Capitol and H Streets, N.W.
  Washington, D.C. 20401
  (202) 275-2051

government-sponsored enterprises, federal budget term which refers to enterprises with completely private ownership established and chartered by the federal government to perform specialized credit functions. Examples include the Federal National Mortgage Association, institutions in the Farm Credit System, Federal Home Loan Banks, and the Federal Home Loan Mortgage Corporation. These enterprises are not included in the budget totals, but financial information on their operation is published in a separate part of the appendix to the president's budget.

GPO, *see* GOVERNMENT PRINTING OFFICE.

Grace Commission, formally the President's Private Sector Survey on Cost Control. Chaired by J. Peter Grace, it was created in 1982 to examine the federal government's operations and policies from a business perspective. Its final report, prepared by over 1,500 volunteer private-

234

sector executives, contained over two thousand recommendations for improving the efficiency of the federal government. See Charles T. Goodsell, "The Grace Commission: Seeking Efficiency for the Whole People?" *Public Administration Review* (May-June 1984); J. Peter Grace, *Burning Money: The Waste of Your Tax Dollars* (New York: Macmillan, 1984); Steven Kelman, "The Grace Commission: How Much Waste in Government?" *The Public Interest* (Winter 1985).

grade, established level or zone of difficulty. Positions of the same difficulty and responsibility tend to be placed in the same grade even though the content of the work differs greatly.

grade creep, also called GRADE ESCALATION, long-term tendency for positions to be reallocated upward. For an analysis of the problem, see Seymour S. Berlin, "The Manager, the Classifier, and Unwarranted Grade Escalation," *Civil Service Journal* (July-September 1964).

gradual pressure strike, concerted effort by employees to influence management by gradually reducing production until their objectives are met. See Michael L. Broorshire and J. Fred Holly, "Resolving Bargaining Impasses Through Gradual Pressure Strikes," *Labor Law Journal* (October 1973).

graduated wages, wages adjusted on the basis of length of service and performance.

Graduate School, U.S. Department of Agriculture, nonprofit school for adults. It is self-supporting and does not receive direct appropriated funds from Congress or the Department of Agriculture. The faculty is mostly part time and is drawn from throughout government and the community at large. Faculty members are paid an honorarium and take annual leave or leave without pay when they teach during normal working hours. The school does not grant degrees but does provide planned sequences of courses leading to certificates of accomplishment in a number of occupational fields important to government.

The Graduate School's objective is to help improve government services by providing needed continuing education and training opportunities for government employees and agencies. The Graduate School, administered by a director and governed by a General Administration Board appointed by the Secretary of Agriculture, was established by the Secretary of Agriculture in 1921.

USDA Graduate School
600 Maryland Ave., S.W.
Washington, D.C. 20250
(202) 447-4419

graft, honest/dishonest, see HONEST GRAFT.

Grand Canyon management, described by William Thomas in "Humor for Hurdling the Mystique in Management," *Management of Personnel Quarterly* (Winter 1970):

Few sights in the world are like the Grand Canyon. It is one of nature's most splendid scenarios. To see it from close up one can take advantage of a certain kind of tour—renting a mule and riding through the canyon itself. Mules are used on these tours instead of horses because they are surefooted and the tourist can sit relaxed, concentrating on the surroundings, secure in the knowledge that his mount will miss nary a step. That accurately describes the Grand Canyon Manager. He sits on his (mule) and watches everything going on around him. Staff people, particularly those in areas like Personnel, are frequent practitioners of Grand Canyon Management.

grandfather clause, originally a device used by some states of the Old South to disenfranchise black voters. Grandfather clauses, written into seven state constitutions during the Reconstruction era, granted the right to vote only to persons whose ancestors—"grandfathers"—had voted prior to 1867. The U.S. Supreme Court ruled, in *Guinn* v. *United States,*

238 U.S. 347 (1915), that all grandfather clauses were unconstitutional because of the 15th Amendment. Today, a grandfather clause is a colloquial expression for any provision or policy that exempts a category of individuals from meeting new standards. For example, if a company were to establish a policy that all managers had to have a master's degree as of a certain date, it would probably exempt managers without such degrees who were hired prior to that date. This statement of exemption would be a grandfather clause. *See* Christopher Leman, "How to Get There from Here: The Grandfather Effect and Public Policy," *Policy Analysis* (Winter 1980).

grant, an intergovernmental transfer of funds. The Advisory Commission on Intergovernmental Relations has identified the following types of grants:

1. *Block Grant.* A grant that is distributed in accordance with a statutory formula for use in a variety of activities within a broad functional area largely at the recipient's discretion.

2. *Categorical Grant.* A grant that can be used only for specific, narrowly defined activities. Usually legislation details the parameters of the program and specifies the types of eligible activities, but sometimes these may be determined by administrators.

3. *Conditional Grant.* A grant that is awarded with limitations (conditions) attached to use of the funds. Both categorical and block grants are conditional, although the categorical grant generally has a greater number and severity of conditions.

4. *Formula-Based Categorical Grant.* A categorical grant under which funds are allocated among recipients according to factors specified in legislation or in administrative regulations.

5. *Project Categorical Grant.* Nonformula categorical grants awarded on a competitive basis to recipients who submit specific, individual applications in the form and at the times indicated by the grantor agency.

6. *Formula-Project Categorical Grant.*

A project grant for which a formula specified in statutes or regulations is used to determine the amount available for a state area, and then funds are distributed at the discretion of the administrator in response to project applications submitted by substate entities.

7. *Open-end Reimbursement Grant.* Often regarded as a formula grant, but characterized by an arrangement wherein the federal government commits itself to reimbursing a specified portion of state-local program expenditures with no limit on the amount of such expenditures.

8. *Discretionary Grant.* A grant awarded at the discretion of a federal administrator, subject to conditions specified by legislation. Generally used interchangeably with project grant.

9. *General Revenue Sharing.* A financial assistance program for states and their general purpose political subdivisions under which funds are distributed by formula with few or no limits on the purposes for which they may be spent and few restrictions on the procedures by which they are spent.

10. *Special Revenue Sharing.* Usually used interchangeably with the term block grant. The term was employed by the Nixon administration in connection with its grant consolidation proposals. Those who consider special revenue sharing a separate form usually differentiate it from the block grant by its lack of a matching requirement and imposition of fewer conditions on recipient performance.

11. *Target Grant.* A grant which "packages" and coordinates funds for wide-ranging public services directed at a specific clientele group or geographic area. Major examples include the Appalachian Regional Development Program, the Community Action Program, and the Model Cities Program.

See V. O. Key, Jr., *The Administration of Federal Grants to the States* (Chicago: Public Administration Clearing House, 1937); B. Douglas Harman, "The Bloc Grant: Readings from a First Experiment," *Public Administration Review* (March–April 1970); Martha Derthick, *The Influence of Federal Grants: Public Assist-*

ance in Massachusetts (Cambridge, Mass.: Harvard University Press, 1970); Thomas H. Kiefer, *The Political Impact of Federal Aid to State and Local Governments* (Morristown, Pa.: General Learning Press, 1974); Sar A. Levitan and Joyce K. Zickler, "Block Grants for Manpower Programs," *Public Administration Review* (March-April 1975); Robert D. Newton, "Towards an Understanding of Federal Assistance," *Public Administration Review* (July-August 1975); Advisory Commission on Intergovernmental Relations, *The Intergovernmental Grant System As Seen by Local, State and Federal Officials* (Washington, D.C.: Government Printing Office, 1977); Carl W. Stenberg and David B. Walker, "The Block Grant: Lessons from Two Early Experiments," *Publius* (Spring 1977); Catherine H. Lovell, "Coordinating Federal Grants from Below," *Public Administration Review* (September-October 1979); Raymond A. Rosenfeld, "Local Implementation Decisions for Community Development Block Grants," *Public Administration Review* (September-October 1979); George E. Hale and Marian Lief Palley, *The Politics of Federal Grants* (Washington, D.C.: Congressional Quarterly Press, 1981); Robert M. Stein, "The Allocation of Federal Aid Monies: The Synthesis of Demand-Side and Supply-Side Explanations," *American Political Science Review* (June 1981); James W. Fossett, *Federal Aid to Big Cities: The Politics of Dependence* (Washington, D.C.: The Brookings Institution, 1983); David Swain, "Block Grants Make Little or No Difference: A Local Perspective," *Public Administration Quarterly* (Spring 1983); Catherine Lovell, "Community Development Block Grants: The Role of Federal Requirements," *Publius* (Summer 1983); Fred C. Doolittle, "State Legislatures and Federal Grants: An Overview," *Public Budgeting & Finance* (Summer 1984); Lawrence D. Brown, James W. Fossett, and Kenneth T. Palmer, *The Changing Politics of Federal Grants* (Washington, D.C.: The Brookings Institution, 1984); David R. Morgan and Robert E. England, "The Small Cities Block Grant Program:

An Assessment of Programmatic Change Under State Control," *Public Administration Review* (November-December 1984); Richard P. Nathan and Fred C. Doolittle, "Federal Grants: Giving and Taking Away," *Political Science Quarterly* (Spring 1985).

See also the following entries:
ANNUAL ARRANGEMENTS
FEDERALISM, FISCAL
FUNGIBLE
STIMULATIVE
TARGETED

grantee, a recipient of grant funds.

grant-in-aid, federal transfers of payments to states or federal or state transfers to local governments for specified purposes usually subject to a measure of supervision and review by the granting government or agency in accordance with prescribed standards and requirements. *See* Deil S. Wright, *Federal Grants-in-Aid: Perspectives and Alternatives* (Washington, D.C.: American Enterprise Institute, 1968); Helen Ingram, "Policy Implementation Through Bargaining: The Case of Federal Grants-in-Aid," *Public Policy* (Fall 1977); and Charles L. Vehorn, *The Regional Distribution of Federal Grants-in-Aid* (Washington, D.C.: Academy for Contemporary Problems, 1978).

Grant's Civil Service Commission, the reform-minded commission appointed by Ulysses S. Grant. On the last day of the legislative session of the 41st Congress in 1871, a rider was attached to an otherwise unrelated appropriations bill authorizing President Grant to make rules and regulations for the civil service. The rider itself was only one sentence long and did not formally require the president to do anything. It certainly would not have passed had it been thought to be anything more than a symbolic sop to the reformers. The rider authorized the president "to prescribe such rules and regulations for the admission of persons into the civil service of the United States as will best promote the efficiency thereof, and ascertain the fitness of each candidate." To the surprise of almost everyone, Grant proceeded to appoint a civil service commission. He authorized them to establish and implement appropriate rules and regulations. The commission required boards of examiners in each department who worked under the commission's general supervision. All things considered, a viable program existed during 1872 and 1873. Several thousand persons were examined and several hundred were actually appointed. But once the Congress realized that Grant was serious about reform and intent upon cutting into their patronage powers, the program was terminated. Congress simply refused to appropriate funds for the work of the commission and the president formally abolished it in 1875.

For an exhaustive history, *see* Lionel V. Murphy, "The First Federal Civil Service Commission: 1872-1875," *Public Personnel Review* (October 1942).

See also CIVIL SERVICE REFORM.

grants-in-kind, donations of surplus property or commodities.

grapevine, informal means by which organizational members give or receive information. According to Keith Davis, in "The Care and Cultivation of the Corporate Grapevine," *Dun's* (July 1973),

Wherever people congregate in groups, the grapevine is sure to grow. It may manifest itself in smoke rings, jungle tom-toms, taps on prison walls or just idle chitchat, but it will always be there. Indeed, the word grapevine has been part of our jargon ever since the Civil War, when telegraph lines were strung loosely from tree to tree in vine-like fashion and resulted in messages that were frequently garbled.

For a more scholarly analysis by Keith Davis, see "Management Communication and the Grapevine," *Harvard Business Review* (September-October 1953). *Also see* Roy Rowan, "Where Did *That* Rumor Come From?" *Fortune* (August 13, 1979).

graphical evaluation and review technique, *see* GERT.

graphic rating scale, performance appraisal chart that lists traits (such as promptness, knowledge, helpfulness, etc.) with a range of performance to be indicated with each (unsatisfactory, satisfactory, etc.).

graveyard shift, also called LOBSTER SHIFT, slang term for the tour of duty of employees who work from 11 P.M. or midnight until dawn.

Great Society, label for the 1960s domestic policies of the Johnson administration that were premised on the belief that social and/or economic problems could be solved by new federal programs. *See* Sar Levitan, *The Great Society's Poor Law* (Baltimore: The Johns Hopkins Press, 1969); Henry J. Aaron, *Politics and the Professors: The Great Society in Perspective* (Washington, D.C.: The Brookings Institution, 1978); Sar A. Levitan and Robert Taggart, "The Great Society Did Succeed," *Political Science Quarterly* (Winter 1977); Michael K. Brown and Stephen P. Erie, "Blacks and the Legacy of the Great Society: The Economic and Political Impact of Federal Social Policy," *Public Policy* (Summer 1981); John E. Schwartz, *America's Hidden Success: A Reassessment of Twenty Years of Public Policy* (New York: W. W. Norton, 1983); Charles Murray, *Losing Ground: American Social Policy 1950-1980* (New York: Basic Books, 1984).

green card, a small document which identifies an alien as a permanent resident of the U.S. The "green card" was originally green but is now white and salmon.

green-circle rate, also called BLUE-CIRCLE RATE, pay rate that is below the minimum rate of an employee's evaluated pay level.

green hands, slang term for inexperienced workers.

green revolution, term that refers to the development of new hybrid grain seeds and the application of scientific methods to agriculture in developing countries in order to achieve higher food production. After the new seed varieties (which produced grain that was highly responsive to fertilizer, was less sensitive to growing conditions, and matured early) were introduced in the mid-1960s, grain production in many developing countries approached self-sufficiency for the first time.

Green River Ordinance, legal provision allowing local government to control soliciting. Named for the Wyoming city in which it was initiated.

Gresham's Law, Thomas Gresham's (1519-1579) advice to Queen Elizabeth that bad (or cheap) money will drive good (or dear) money out of circulation. This is a major argument against bimetallic money standards.

grievance, any dissatisfaction felt by an employee in connection with his/her employment. The word generally refers to a formal complaint initiated by an employee, by a union, or by management concerning the interpretation or application of a collective bargaining agreement or established employment practices. For a discussion of how to avoid grievances, see W. B. Werther, Jr., "Reducing Grievances Through Effective Contract Administration," *Labor Law Journal* (April 1974). *Also see* Stephen B. Goldberg and Jeanne M. Brett, "An Experiment in the Mediation of Grievances," *Monthly Labor Review* (March 1983); Donald S. McPherson, Conrad J. Gates, and Kevin N. Rogers, *Resolving Grievances: A Practical Approach* (Reston, Va.: Reston/Prentice-Hall, 1983); Michael E. Gordon and Sandra J. Miller, "Grievances: A Review of Research and Practice," *Personnel Psychology* (Spring 1984).

grievance arbitration, also called RIGHTS ARBITRATION, arbitration concerned with disputes that arise over the interpretation/appplication of an existing collective bargaining agreement. The grievance arbitrator interprets the contract for the parties. *See* Richard Mittenthal, "Making Arbitration Work: Alternatives in Designing the Machinery," *The Arbitration Journal* (September 1981).

grievance committee, those union and/or management representatives who are formally designated to review grievances left unresolved by lower elements of the grievance machinery.

See also ELGIN, JOLIET & EASTERN RAILWAY V. BURLEY.

grievance machinery, totality of the methods, usually enumerated in a collective bargaining agreement, used to resolve the problems of interpretation arising during the life of an agreement. Grievance machinery is usually designed so that those closest to the dispute have the first opportunity to reach a settlement. According to Walter E. Baer, *Grievance Handling* (New York: American Management Associations, 1970),

the grievance machinery is the formal process, preliminary to any arbitration, that enables the parties to attempt to resolve their differences in a peaceful, orderly, and expeditious manner. It permits the company and the union to investigate and discuss their problems without interrupting the continued, orderly operation of the business. And, when the machinery works effectively, it can satisfactorily resolve the overwhelming majority of disputes between the parties.

grievance procedure, specific means by which grievances are channeled for their adjustment through progressively higher levels of authority in both an organization and its union. Grievance procedures, while long considered the "heart" of a labor contract, are increasingly found in nonunionized organizations as managers realize the need for a process to appeal the decisions of supervisors that employees consider unjust. For a how-to, see Maurice S. Trotta, *Handling Grievances: A Guide for Management and Labor* (Washington, D.C.: Bureau of National Affairs, 1976). *Also see* Steven Briggs, "The Grievance Procedure and Organizational Health,"

Personnel Journal (June 1981); David Lewin and Richard Peterson, "A Model for Measuring Effectiveness of the Grievance Process," *Monthly Labor Review* (April 1982).

For non-union grievance procedures, *see* Donald A. Drost and Fabius P. O'Brien, "Are There Grievances Against Your Non-Union Grievance Procedure?" *Personnel Administrator* (January 1983); Alan Balfour, "Five Types of Non-Union Grievance Systems," *Personnel* (March–April 1984); Fabius P. O'Brien and Donald A. Drost, "Non-Union Grievance Procedures: Not Just an Anti-Union Strategy," *Personnel* (September–October 1984); James K. McCollum and Dwight R. Norris, "Nonunion Grievance Machinery in Southern Industry," *Personnel Administrator* (November 1984).

See also EMPORIUM CAPWELL CO. V. WESTERN ADDITION COMMUNITY ORGANIZATION, MCDONALD V. CITY OF WEST BRANCH, MICHIGAN, and SMITH V. ARKANSAS STATE HIGHWAY EMPLOYEES, LOCAL 1315.

grievant, one who files a formal grievance; the one who does so *grieves*. This person is not in a state of mourning, but one of complaining. A study of grievants and non-grievants in one company found that the grievants were more likely to be (1) better educated, (2) younger in terms of seniority, (3) more active in union matters, (4) lower paid, and (5) more likely to be absent or tardy. *See* Howard A. Sulkin and Robert W. Pranis, "Comparison of Grievants with Non-grievants in a Heavy Machinery Company," *Personnel Psychology* (Summer 1967).

Griffenhagen, Edwin O. (1886–), management engineer who became one of the pioneers in the development of position classification and job analysis. For his history of the origin of modern duties-classification systems, *see* "The Origin of Modern Occupation Classification in Personnel Administration," *Public Personnel Studies* (September 1924).

Griggs et al. v. *Duke Power Company,* 401 U.S. 424 (1971), the most significant single Supreme Court decision concerning the validity of employment examinations. The court unanimously ruled that Title VII of the Civil Rights Act of 1964 "proscribes not only overt discrimination but also practices that are discriminatory in operation." Thus, if employment practices operating to exclude minorities "cannot be shown to be related to job performance, the practice is prohibited." The ruling dealt a blow to restrictive credentialism, stating that, while diplomas and tests are useful, the "Congress has mandated the commonsense proposition that they are not to become masters of reality." In essence, the court held that the law requires that tests used for employment purposes "must measure the person for the job and not the person in the abstract."

The *Griggs* decision applied only to the private sector until the Equal Employment Opportunity Act of 1972 extended the provisions of Title VII of the Civil Rights Act of 1964 to cover public as well as private employees. *See* Hugh Steven Wilson, "A Second Look at *Griggs* v. *Duke Power Company:* Ruminations on Job Testing, Discrimination and the Role of the Federal Courts," *Virginia Law Review* (May 1972); Alfred W. Blumrosen, "Strangers in Paradise: *Griggs* v. *Duke Power Co.* and the Concept of Employment Discrimination," *Michigan Law Review* (November 1972).

Griner, John F. (1907–), president of the American Federation of Government Employees (AFGE) from 1962 to 1973).

gross domestic product (GDP), the value of the total output of final goods and services produced in a country in a specific period, usually a year. It differs from gross national product in that GDP excludes (and GNP includes) the value of net income accruing to factors of production from abroad.

gross national product (GNP), monetary value of all of the goods and services produced in a nation in a given year.

gross national product gap, the difference between the economy's output of goods and services and its potential output at full employment—that is, the difference between actual GNP (gross national product) and potential GNP.

group, *see* SMALL-GROUP RESEARCH.

group annuity, any of a variety of pension plans designed by insurance companies for a group of persons to cover all of those qualified under one contract.

group cohesiveness, measure of the degree of unity and solidarity that a group possesses.

group development, loose term concerned with the various processes and circumstances that occur when individuals organize themselves into goal oriented groups. For a survey of the theory and research, *see* John M. Ivancevich and J. Timothy McMahon, "Group Development, Trainer Style and Carry-over Job Satisfaction and Performance," *Academy of Management Journal* (September 1976).

group dynamics, field "invented" by Kurt Lewin (that is, he was responsible, either directly or indirectly, for most of the pioneering research on group dynamics). Two of Lewin's close associates, Dorwin Cartwright and Alvin Zander, went on to produce what was for many years the standard text on the subject—*Group Dynamics: Research and Theory,* 3rd ed. (New York: Harper & Row, 1968). They defined "group dynamics" as the field of inquiry dedicated to advancing knowledge about the nature of groups, how they develop, and their relationships to individuals, other groups, and larger institutions. *See* Kurt Lewin, "Frontiers in Group Dynamics: Concept, Method and Reality in Social Science," *Human Relations* (June 1947).
    See also the following entries:
      FIELD THEORY
      GROUPTHINK
      ORGANIZATION DEVELOPMENT

group executive, manager responsible for the work of two or more organizational divisions.

group incentive plan, *see* INCENTIVE-WAGE PLAN.

group insurance, also GROUP HEALTH INSURANCE and GROUP LIFE INSURANCE, term that refers to any insurance plan that covers individuals (and usually their dependents) by means of a single policy issued to the employer or association with which the insured individuals are affiliated. The cost of group insurance is usually significantly lower than the costs for equivalent individual policies. Group insurance policies are written in the name of the employer so that individual employees are covered only as long as they remain with the insuring employer. Sometimes group insurance policies provide that an employee can continue his/her coverage upon resignation by buying an individual policy. The most common kinds of group insurance are *group health insurance* and *group life insurance.* Many employers pay a substantial portion or all of the cost of group insurance.

group of classes, two or more closely related job classes having a common basis of duties, responsibilities, and qualification requirements but differing in some particular (such as the nature of specialization) that is essential from the standpoint of recruitment and selection and requires that each class in the group be treated individually. Such classes have the same basic title but may be distinguished by a parenthetic. For example: Engineer (Chemical), Engineer (Electrical), etc.

Group I Tenure/Group II Tenure/Group III Tenure, federal government terms for the tenure groupings of its employees. Employees who are serving in competitive positions are grouped as follows:
    Group I. Career employees who have completed their probationary period and who are not serving in obligated positions. (An obligated position is a position to which a former

employee has mandatory reemployment or restoration rights.)

Group II. Career-conditional employees and career employees who have not completed probationary periods or who occupy obligated positions.

Group III. Employees serving under temporary appointments pending establishment of a register, employees serving under indefinite appointments, etc.

Employees serving under appointments to excepted positions, aliens, and attorneys are grouped according to their tenure of employment as follows:

Group I. Permanent employees whose appointments carry no restrictions or conditions.

Group II. Employees serving trial periods, those whose tenure is indefinite solely because they are occupying obligated positions, and those serving under conditional appointments who have not completed the three-year service requirement for appointment without condition or limitation.

Group III. This group includes all employees serving under appointments specifically identified as indefinite. It also includes employees serving under temporary excepted appointments limited to one year or less who have completed one year or more of current continuous employment in the excepted service.

group oral interview, also called GROUP ORAL EXAMINATION, measurement tool that involves a group of candidates (ideally five to seven) discussing a job-related problem. The evaluators do not actively participate in the group discussion; their role is to observe and evaluate the behavior of the participants. The value of this technique is heavily dependent on the ability of the evaluators.

group psychotherapy, any form of psychological treatment involving more than one subject. Organization development efforts can be considered a form of group psychotherapy. *See* Robert R. Dies, "Group Psychotherapy: Reflections on Three Decades of Research," *Journal of Applied Behavioral Science* (July-Au-

gust-September 1979); George M. Gazda, *Basic Approaches to Group Psychotherapy and Group Counseling,* 3rd ed. (Springfield, Ill.: Charles C. Thomas, 1982).

See also ENCOUNTER GROUP and INTERNATIONAL JOURNAL OF GROUP PSYCHOTHERAPY.

group theory, *see* INTEREST GROUP THEORY.

groupthink, psychological drive for consensus at any cost which tends to suppress both dissent and the appraisal of alternatives in small decision-making groups. Groupthink, because it refers to a deterioration of mental efficiency and moral judgment due to in-group pressures, has an invidious connotation. For the basic work on the subject, *see* Irving L. Janis, *Victims of Groupthink: A Psychological Study of Foreign-Policy Decisions and Fiascoes* (Boston: Houghton Mifflin Co., 1972).

GS, *see* GENERAL SCHEDULE.

GSA, *see* GENERAL SERVICES ADMINISTRATION.

guaranteed annual wage (GAW), any of a variety of plans whereby an employer agrees to provide employees with a predetermined minimum (1) number of hours of work or (2) salary each year.

guaranteed base rate, *see* GUARANTEED RATE.

guaranteed earnings, provision in some union contracts that employees will be paid (guaranteed) a specified minimum wage, even when production must cease because of a machinery breakdown or some other cause beyond the control of the employee.

guaranteed rate, also called GUARANTEED BASE RATE, minimum wage guaranteed to an employee working under an incentive pay program.

guaranteed workweek, provision in some

union contracts that an employee will be paid a full week's wages even when there is not enough actual work available to otherwise warrant a full week's pay.

Guest, Robert H. (1916-   ), known for his pioneering studies of life on the assembly line and of job design. Major works include: *The Man on the Assembly Line,* with Charles R. Walker (Cambridge, Mass.: Harvard University Press, 1952); *Organizational Change: The Effect of Successful Leadership* (Homewood, Ill.: Dorsey Press, 1962).

guide chart, tool used by a factor-ranking system of job evaluation which contains a narrative description and point value for each degree of each factor.

guideline method, job evaluation technique that determines the value of a position in an organization not by an analysis of the position's content but by what the labor market says it is worth.

guidelines, also called GUIDEPOSTS, (1) general standards, usually expressed as a percentage, by which the federal government measures wage and price increases to determine if they are consistent with the national economic interest, or (2) published outlines for action or suggested courses of conduct that many federal agencies issue for the guidance of their clients.

guideposts, see GUIDELINES.

guild, also called CRAFT GUILD, in medieval Western Europe, an association for mutual aid and/or for the furtherance of religious and business interests. Merchant guilds date from the 11th century. Although there was a craft guild movement in ancient Rome, the modern union movement usually traces its lineage to the craft guilds of the Middle Ages, which paralleled the merchant guilds of the time. Craft guilds were associations of individual workers who sought to regulate production, establish standards, and fix prices. These craft guilds gave us the now familiar

rankings for their classes of membership— apprentice, journeyman, and master.

Gulick, Luther (1892-   ), highly honored reformer, researcher, and practitioner of public administration, best known to management generalists for having invented POSDCORB *(see entry).* Major works include: *Papers on the Science of Administration,* edited with Lyndall Urwick (New York: Institute of Public Administration, 1937); *Administrative Reflections from World War II* (University of Alabama Press, 1948); *The Metropolitan Problem and American Ideas* (New York: Knopf, 1962). *See* Stephen K. Blumberg, "Seven Decades of Public Administration: A Tribute to Luther Gulick," *Public Administration Review* (March-April 1981).

H

Hall v. *Cole,* 412 U.S. 1 (1973), U.S. Supreme Court case which held that union members who successfully challenge a union action in court can be awarded attorneys' fees if it could be shown that litigant's victory benefited the entire union.

halo effect, bias in ratings arising from the tendency of a rater to be influenced in his/her rating of specific traits by his general impression of the person being rated. The concept was "discovered" by Edward L. Thorndike in "A Constant Error in Psychological Ratings," *Journal of Applied Psychology* (March 1920). *Also see* Larry M. King, John E. Hunter, and Frank L. Schmidt, "Halo in a Multi-dimensional Forced-Choice Performance Evaluation Scale," *Journal of Applied Psychology* (October 1980); Rich Jacobs and Steven W. J. Kozlowski, "A Closer Look at Halo Error in Performance Ratings," *Academy of Management Journal* (March 1985).

Hammer v. **Dagenhart,** 247 U.S. 251 (1918), U.S. Supreme Court case which held unconstitutional a federal statute barring goods made by child labor from interstate commerce. The court would not concede that the federal government could regulate child labor in interstate commerce until 1941, when it upheld the Fair Labor Standards Act of 1938 that put restrictions on the use of child labor. The landmark case was *United States* v. *Darby Lumber Company,* 312 U.S. 100 (1941).

Hampton v. **Mow Sun Wong,** 426 U.S. 88 (1976), U.S. Supreme Court case which held that a U.S. Civil Service Commission regulation excluding resident aliens from the federal competitive service had been adopted in violation of the due process clause of the Fifth Amendment. Because the court expressly decided only the validity of the regulations promulgated by the Civil Service Commission and reserved comment on the appropriateness of a citizenship requirement instituted by the president, on September 2, 1976 President Ford issued Executive Order 11935, which provides that only U.S. citizens and nationals may hold permanent positions in the federal competitive service except when necessary to promote the efficiency of the service. For a legal analysis, *see* Eric C. Scoones, "Procedural Due Process and the Exercise of Delegated Power: The Federal Civil Service Employment Restriction on Aliens," *The Georgetown Law Journal* (October 1977).
    See also SUGARMAN V. DOUGALL.

handicapped employees, emotionally, *see* EMOTIONALLY HANDICAPPED EMPLOYEES.

handicapped individual, also QUALIFIED HANDICAPPED INDIVIDUAL, any person who (1) has a physical or mental impairment which substantially limits one or more of such person's major life activities, (2) has a record of such an impairment, or (3) is regarded as having such an impairment. A *qualified handicapped individual*, with respect to employment, is one who with reasonable accommodation can perform the essential functions of a job in question. According to the Vocational Rehabilitation Act of 1973 (as amended), federal contractors and subcontractors are required to take affirmative action to seek out qualified handicapped individuals for employment.
    See Robert B. Nathanson, "The Disabled Employee: Separating Myth from Fact," *Harvard Business Review* (May-June 1977); Sar A. Levitan and Robert Taggart, "Employment Problems of Disabled Persons," *Monthly Labor Review* (March 1977); Gopal C. Pati, "Countdown on Hiring the Handicapped," *Personnel Journal* (March 1978); Vigdor Grossman, *Employing Handicapped Persons: Meeting EEO Obligations* (Washington, D.C.: Bureau of National Affairs, Inc., 1980); Gopal C. Pati and John J. Adkins, "Hire the Handicapped—Compliance is Good Business," *Harvard Business Review* (January-February 1980); Ray B. Bressler and A. Wayne Lacy, "An Analysis of the Relative Job Progression of the Perceptibly Physically Handicapped," *Academy of Management Journal* (March 1980); Donald J. Peterson, "Paving the Way for Hiring the Handicapped," *Personnel* (March-April 1981); Sara M. Freedman and Robert T. Keller, "The Handicapped in the Workforce," *Academy of Management Review* (July 1981); Harriet McBryde Johnson, "Who is Handicapped? Defining the Protected Class Under the Employment Provisions of Title V of the Rehabilitation Act of 1973," *Review of Public Personnel Administration* (Fall 1981); Anne Waltz, "Integrating Disabled Workers into Your Workforce," *Public Personnel Management* (Winter 1981); Sara M. Freedman and Robert T. Keller, "The Handicapped in the Workforce," *The Academy of Management Review* (July 1981).
    See also the following entries:
    ARCHITECTURAL BARRIERS
    NATIONAL REHABILITATION ASSOCIATION
    READING ASSISTANT
    REASONABLE ACCOMMODATION
    REHABILITATED OFFENDER PROGRAM
    SHELTERED WORKSHOP

VOCATIONAL REHABILITATION ACT OF 1973
WAGNER-O'DAY ACT
WORK-ACTIVITIES CENTERS
WORK-READY

hands-on test, performance test that uses the actual tools of the job.

Hanna Mining Co. v. District 2, Marine Engineers, 382 U.S. 181 (1965), U.S. Supreme Court case which held that while supervisory personnel are not employees for purposes of the National Labor Relations Act, the act does not preempt state labor laws affecting supervisors.

hard cases, cases where fairness may require judges to be loose with legal principles; that's why "hard cases make bad law."

hard-core unemployed, those individuals who, because of racial discrimination, an impoverished background, or the lack of appropriate education, have never been able to hold a job for a substantial length of time. *See* Leonard Nadler, "Helping the Hard-Core Adjust to the World of Work," *Harvard Business Review* (March-April 1970); Keith C. Weir, "Hard Core Training and Employment," *Personnel Journal* (May 1971); Daniel M. Seifer, "Continuing Hard Problems: The 'Hard-Core' and Racial Discrimination," *Public Personnel Management* (May-June 1974); Albert A. Blum, "Hard-Core Unemployment: A Long-Term Problem," *Business and Society* (Spring 1983).

hardship allowance, additional money paid to an employee who accepts an assignment that offers difficult living conditions, physical hardships, unattractive climate, and/or a lack of the usual amenities found in the United States.

hardware, formally, the mechanical, magnetic, electrical, and electronic devices or components of a computer. Informally, any piece of computer or automatic data processing equipment.
See also SOFTWARE.

Harvard Business Review **(HBR),** journal for professional managers, published bimonthly by the faculty of the Harvard University Graduate School of Business Administration. The editors modestly state that, in selecting articles for publication, they "try to pick those that are timeless rather than just timely." The *Harvard Business Review* is almost universally considered the foremost business journal in the United States.
   Editorial Address:
   Harvard Business Review
   Boston, MA 02163
   Subscriptions:
   Harvard Business Review
   Subscription Service Department
   P.O. Box 3000
   Woburn, MA 01888

Harvard Business School (HBS), the most prestigious of the prestigious "B" schools. Robert Townsend, in *Up the Organization* (New York: Knopf, 1970), suggests that you "don't hire Harvard Business School graduates. This worthy enterprise confesses that it trains its students for only three posts—executive vice-president, president, and board chairman. The faculty does not blush when HBS is called the West Point of capitalism." For the "inside" story about the education of the managerial elite in the U.S., *see* Peter Cohn, *The Gospel According to the Harvard Business School* (Garden City, N.Y.: Doubleday & Co., 1973).

Harvard Fatigue Laboratory (HFL), research organization that existed within the Harvard Business School from 1927 to 1947. According to Steven M. Horvath and Elizabeth C. Horvath, in *The Harvard Fatigue Laboratory: Its History and Contributions* (Englewood Cliffs, New Jersey: Prentice-Hall, 1973), its highly influential research efforts tended to focus on the notion that "group psychology, social problems and the physiology of fatigue of normal man must be studied, not only as individual factors in determining physical and mental health, but more especially to determine their interrelatedness and the effect upon work."

Hatch Act, collective popular name for two federal statutes. The Hatch Act of 1939, 53 Stat. 410 (1939), restricted the political activities of almost all federal employees, whether in the competitive service or not. The impetus for this legislation came primarily from a decrease in the proportion of federal employees who were in the competitive service. This was a direct result of the creation of several New Deal agencies that were placed outside the merit system. Senator Carl Hatch, a Democrat from New Mexico, had worked for several years to have legislation enacted that would prevent federal employees from being active in political conventions. He feared that their involvement and direction by politicians could lead to the development of a giant national political machine.

A second Hatch Act in 1940, 54 Stat. 640 (1940), extended these restrictions to positions in state employment having federal financing. Penalties for violation of the Hatch Act by federal employees have been softened considerably over time. Originally, removal was mandatory, but, by 1962, the minimum punishment was suspension for thirty days.

It has never been possible to define completely the political activities prohibited by the Hatch Act. However, the following are among the major limitations:

1. serving as a delegate or alternate to a political party convention;
2. soliciting or handling political contributions;
3. being an officer or organizer of a political club;
4. engaging in electioneering;
5. with some exceptions, being a candidate for elective political office; and
6. leading or speaking to partisan political meetings or rallies.

The constitutionality of these regulations was first upheld by the Supreme Court in *United Public Workers* v. *Mitchell*, 330 U.S. 75 (1947), and reaffirmed in *Civil Service Commission* v. *National Association of Letter Carriers*, 413 U.S. 548 (1973). Repeal of the Hatch Act (or relax- ation of some of its provisions) has been high on the legislative agenda of unions, especially since union legal challenges to the act have been unsuccessful. *See* Philip L. Martin, "The Hach Act: The Current Movement for Reform," *Public Personnel Management* (May-June 1974); Henry Rose, "A Critical Look at the Hatch Act," *Harvard Law Review* (January 1962); Steven W. Hayes and Luther F. Carter, "The Myth of Hatch Act Reform," *Southern Review of Public Administration* (December 1980).

See also UNITED STATES CIVIL SERVICE COMMISSION V. NATIONAL ASSOCIATION OF LETTER CARRIERS.

hatchet man, according to Qass Aquarius, *The Corporate Prince: A Handbook of Administrative Tactics* (New York: Van Nostrand Reinhold Co., 1971),

> when dirty work must be done, the wise administrator tries to keep his hands clean. Perhaps he may have a subordinate, a hatchet man, to do his dirty work for him, thereby avoiding the displeasure of those who do not approve of the actions. For this reason many administrators prefer to have their subordinates do their firing for them. Sometimes a board of directors deliberately brings in a president as a hatchet man to clean house, prune the corporate tree of its deadwood, thereby incurring great displeasure among people within the organization. After all the bloodletting has taken place, the board can find other work for the hatchet man and a new man can be brought in who immediately bestows benefits upon a grateful, relieved organization.

Hawkins* v. *Bleakly, 243 U.S. 210 (1917), U.S. Supreme Court case which upheld the constitutionality of state workmen's compensation laws.

Hawthorne Effect, any production increase due to known presence of benign observers. Elton Mayo and his associates, while conducting their now famous Hawthorne Studies, discovered that the researchers' concern for and attention to the workers led to increases in production. For Mayo's account, *see* Elton Mayo, *The Human Problems of an Industrial Civilization* (New York: Viking Press, 1933, 1960).

Hawthorne Studies, also called HAW-THORNE EXPERIMENTS, studies conducted at the Hawthorne Works of the Western Electric Company near Chicago; probably the most important single management study yet reported. Beginning in the late 1920s, a research team led by Elton Mayo of the Harvard Business School started a decade-long series of experiments aimed at determining the relationship between work environment and productivity. The experimenters, because they were initially unable to explain the results of their findings, literally stumbled upon what today seems so obvious—that factories and other work situations are first of all social situations. The Hawthorne Studies are generally considered to be the genesis of the human relations school of management thought. The definitive account of the experiments is given in F. J. Roethlisberger and William J. Dickson's *Management and the Worker* (Cambridge, Mass.: Harvard University Press, 1939).

Work group behavior, output restriction, supervisory training, personnel research, interviewing methodology, employee counseling, socio-technical systems theory, small group incentive plans, and organizational theory became prime concerns of management because, in one way or another, they were brought to the fore or elucidated by the Hawthorne Studies. For a reexamination of the studies a generation later, *see* Henry A. Landsberger, *Hawthorne Revisited* (Ithaca, N.Y.: Cornell University Press, 1958).

See also MAYO, ELTON.

Hay, Edward N. (1891-1958), editor and publisher of the *Personnel Journal* from 1947 to 1958 who pioneered the development of modern testing and job evaluation techniques. Major works include: *Manual of Job Evaluation: Procedures of Job Analysis And Appraisal*, with Eugene J.

Benge and Samuel L. H. Burk (New York: Harper & Bros., 1941); *Psychological Aids in the Selection of Workers,* with G. W. Wadsworth, Jr., D. W. Cook, and C. L. Shartle (New York: American Management Association, 1941).

See also HAY SYSTEM.

Hayek, Friedrick A. von (1899-), Nobel Prize-winning economist who advocated laissez-faire capitalism and advanced the theory of business cycles.

Hay Guide Chart-Profile Method, *see* HAY SYSTEM.

Hay System, one of the best known job evaluation methods, developed by Edward N. Hay. Essentially a modification of the factor-comparison technique, Hay's Guide Chart-Profile Method is based on three factors: knowhow, problem-solving and accountability. Many organizations have adopted variations of the Hay System for job evaluation. For an analysis, *see* Charles W. G. Van Horn, "The Hay Guide Chart-Profile Method," *Handbook of Wage and Salary Administration,* Milton L. Rock, ed. (New York: McGraw-Hill, 1972).

See also POINT SYSTEM.

hazard pay, compensation paid to an employee above regular wages for work that is potentially dangerous to his/her health. *See* Craig A. Olson, "An Analysis of Wage Differentials Received by Workers on Dangerous Jobs," *The Journal of Human Resources* (Spring 1981).

Hazelwood School District* v. *United States, 433 U.S. 299 (1977), U.S. Supreme Court case which held that a public employer did not violate Title VII of the Civil Rights Act of 1964 if, from March 24, 1972 (when Title VII became effective for public employers), all of its employment decisions were made in a "non-discriminatory way," even if it had "formerly maintained an all-white workforce by purposefully excluding Negroes."

HBR, *see* HARVARD BUSINESS REVIEW.

HBS, see HARVARD BUSINESS SCHOOL.

health, defined by the World Health Organization as "a state of complete physical, mental, and social wellbeing and not merely the absence of disease or infirmity." Experts recognize, however, that health has many dimensions (anatomical, physiological, and mental) and is largely culturally defined. The relative importance of various disabilities will differ depending upon the cultural milieu and the role of the affected individual in that culture. Most attempts at measurement have taken a negative approach in that the degree of ill health has been assessed in terms of morbidity and mortality. In general, the detection of changes in health status is easier than the definition and measurement of the absolute level of health.

Health and Human Services, Department of (DHHS), cabinet-level department of the federal government most concerned with health, welfare, and income security plans, policies, and programs. It was created on October 17, 1979, when the Department of Health, Education and Welfare was divided in two.
> DHHS
> 200 Independence Avenue, S.W.
> Washington, D.C. 20201
> (202) 245-6296

health benefits, total health service and health insurance programs that an organization provides for its employees.

Health, Education and Welfare, Department of (HEW), former cabinet-level department of the federal government. Created in 1953, HEW was reorganized into the Department of Education and the Department of Health and Human Services in 1979.
See also (1) EDUCATION, DEPARTMENT OF and (2) HEALTH AND HUMAN SERVICES, DEPARTMENT OF.

health facilities, collectively, all buildings and facilities used in the provision of health services. Usually limited to facilities which were built for the purpose of providing health care, such as hospitals and nursing homes, and thus does not include an office building which includes a physician's office.

health insurance, group, see GROUP INSURANCE.

health maintenance organization (HMO), according to Robert Gumbiner, "Selection of a Health Maintenance Organization," *Personnel Journal* (August 1978),

> a nonprofit organization which maintains clinics and hospitals and supplies physicians, health care specialists and medication at little or no additional cost. It differs from indemnity insurance in that for a monthly fee, total health and medical care are provided. That is, indemnity insurance pays only in case of illness or accident, but an HMO allows a person to see a doctor for preventive care, and without extra charges. (Since an HMO commits itself to paying all medical expenses, it is in its own interest to keep people healthy.) Thus its subscribers are sometimes able to avoid serious illness.

Also see Jeffery Cohelan, "HMO's—How They Can Keep the Lid on Escalating Health Care Costs," *Pension World* (March 1978); Deborah H. Harrison and John R. Kimberly, "HMOs Don't Have to Fail," *Harvard Business Review* (July-August 1982); Allan Blostin and William Marclay, "HMOs and Other Health Plans: Coverage and Employee Premiums," *Monthly Labor Review* (June 1983).

Health Maintenance Organization Act of 1973, federal statute that sets standards of qualifications for an HMO and mandates that employers of twenty-five or more who currently offer a medical benefit plan offer the additional option of joining a qualified HMO, if one exists in the area. *See* Lawrence D. Brown, *Politics and Health Care Organization: HMOs as Federal Policy* (Washington, D.C.: The Brookings Institution, 1983).

hearing, legal or quasi-legal proceedings

in which arguments, witnesses, or evidence are heard by a judicial officer, administrative body, or legislative committee.

hearing examiner/officer, see ADMINISTRATIVE LAW JUDGE.

HEARS, see HIGHER EDUCATION ADMINISTRATION REFERRAL SERVICE.

Heinz case, see H.J. HEINZ CO. V. NATIONAL LABOR RELATIONS BOARD.

helping interview, interview that consists of a genuine dialogue between the interviewer and the interviewee; the interviewer is an empathic listener rather than a mere technician recording information. See Alfred Benjamin, The Helping Interview, 2nd ed. (Boston: Houghton Mifflin, 1974).

Helvering v. Davis, 301 U.S. 619 (1937), U.S. Supreme Court case which held constitutional the Social Security Act of 1935.

Herring, E. Pendleton (1903-), one of the most influential of the pre-World War II scholars of public administration who later served as president (from 1948 to 1968) of the Social Science Research Council. Herring's Group Representation Before Congress (New York: Russell, 1929, 1967) was one of the pioneering works in the study of pressure groups. Federal Comissioners: A Study of Their Careers and Qualifications (Cambridge, Mass.: Harvard University Press, 1936) was one of the first studies of the relationship between a manager's background and behavior in office. Public Administration and the Public Interest (New York: Russell & Russell, 1936) remains a major analysis of the relationships between government agencies and their formal and informal constituencies.

Herzberg, Frederick (1923-), a major influence on the conceptualization of job design, especially job enrichment. His motivation-hygiene or two-factor theory of motivation is the point of departure and a common reference point for analyses of the subject. Major works include: The

Motivation To Work, with Bernard Mausner and Barbara Snyderman (New York: John Wiley & Sons, 1959); Work And The Nature of Man (Cleveland: World Publishers, 1966); and The Managerial Choice (Homewood, Ill.: Dow Jones-Irwin, 1976).
See also JOB ENRICHMENT and MOTIVATION-HYGIENE THEORY.

heuristic, short-cut process of reasoning that searches for a satisfactory, rather than an optimal, solution to a very large, complex, and/or poorly defined problem. See Charles L. Hinkle and Alfred A. Kuehn, "Heuristic Models: Mapping the Maze for Management," California Management Review (Fall 1967) and William J. Gore, Administrative Decisionmaking: A Heuristic Model (New York: John Wiley & Sons, Inc., 1964).

Hicklin v. Orbeck, 434 U.S. 919 (1978), U.S. Supreme Court case which held unconstitutional an Alaska law granting employment preferences to Alaskan residents. The law violated the constitutional requirement that states grant all U.S. citizens the same "privileges and immunities" granted to their own citizens.

hidden agenda, unannounced or unconscious goals, personal needs, expectations, and strategies that each individual brings with his/her participation in a group. Parallel to the group's open agenda are the private or hidden agendas of each of its members. See Michael B. McCaskey, "The Hidden Messages Managers Send," Harvard Business Review (November-December 1979); Priscilla Elfrey, The Hidden Agenda: Recognizing What Really Matters at Work (New York: Wiley, 1982).

hidden unemployed, see DISCOURAGED WORKERS.

hierarchy, any ordering of persons, things, or ideas by rank or level. See Arnold S. Tannenbaum, Hierarchy in Organizations (San Francisco: Jossey-Bass, 1974); Neely Gardner, "The Non-Hierarchical Organization of the

Future: Theory vs. Reality," *Public Administration Review* (September–October 1976); Thomas A. Mahoney, "Organizational Hierarchy and Position Worth," *Academy of Management Journal* (December 1979); John F. Padgett, "Managing Garbage Can Hierarchies," *Administrative Science Quarterly* (December 1980); Jon S. Ebeling and Michael King, "Hierarchical Position in the Work Organization and Job Satisfaction," *Human Relations* (July 1981); Patricia Yancey Martin, Dianne Harrison, and Diana DiNitto, "Advancement for Women in Hierarchical Organizations: A Multilevel Analysis of Problems and Prospects," *The Journal of Applied Behavioral Science,* Vol. 19, No. 1 (1983).

Higher Education Administration Referral Service (HEARS), nonprofit organization that helps institutions locate qualified individuals for nonacademic administrative vacancies. HEARS is cosponsored by nineteen major higher education associations.

    HEARS
    Suite 510
    One Dupont Circle
    Washington, D.C. 20036
    (202) 293-6440

high match, *see* MATCHING SHARE.

Hines v. Anchor Motor Freight, 424 U.S. 554 (1976), U.S. Supreme Court case which held that, if a union member can prove that he was erroneously discharged and that his union's representation tainted the decision of the arbitration committee which upheld the discharge, then he is entitled to take legal action against both the employer and the union.

hire, *see* EMPLOY.

hiring, preferential, *see* PREFERENTIAL HIRING.

hiring hall, also called UNION HIRING HALL and CENTRAL HIRING HALL, employment office usually run by the union to coordinate the referral of its members to jobs.

Sometimes hiring halls are operated jointly with management and/or state government assistance. Hiring halls are especially important for casual or seasonal trades (such as construction and maritime work). For an analysis of the hiring-hall process, *see* Stuart B. Philpott, "The Union Hiring Hall as a Labor Market: A Sociological Analysis," *British Journal of Industrial Relations* (March 1965). For a history, *see* Philip Ross, "Origin of the Hiring Hall in Construction," *Industrial Relations* (October 1972).

hiring rate, *see* ACCESSION RATE and ENTRANCE RATE.

Hishon v. King and Spalding, 81 L. Ed. 2d 59 (1984), U.S. Supreme Court case which held that a law firm must comply with federal anti-discrimination laws when deciding which members of the firm should be elevated to partners.

Hispanic Employment Program, *see* SPANISH SPEAKING PROGRAM.

histogram, bar graph of a frequency distribution.

hit the bricks, slang phrase for going out on strike.

H. J. Heinz Co. v. National Labor Relations Board, 311 U.S. 514 (1941), U.S. Supreme Court case which held that a company had to sign a collective bargaining agreement, even when wages, hours, and other terms and conditions of employment were not in dispute.

HMO, *see* HEALTH MAINTENANCE ORGANIZATION.

Hobbs Act, *see* ANTI-RACKETEERING ACT OF 1934.

holdback, the amount of money withheld from periodic payments to contractors to assure compliance with contract terms. Usually the amount to be withheld is expressed as a percentage in the contract provisions. The amounts withheld are paid to the contractor after a designated official certifies that the contractor has completed work pursuant to the contract terms.

Holden v. Hardy, 169 U.S. 336 (1898), U.S. Supreme Court case which held that a state, in exercising its police power to protect the public health, had the right to legislate hours of work.

holiday pay, premium rate, usually provided for in union contracts, paid for work performed on holidays.

Hollerith cards, punched cards used by computers, first developed by Herman Hollerith of the U.S. Bureau of the Census in 1889.

Homans, George C. (1910-   ), industrial sociologist best known for his early application of "systems" to organizational analysis. Major works include: *An Introduction to Pareto: His Sociology,* with C. P. Curtis, Jr. (New York: Knopf, 1934); *The Fatigue of Workers: Its Relation to Industrial Production* (New York: Reinhold Publishing Company, 1941); *The Human Group* (New York: Harcourt Brace Jovanovich, 1950); *Sentiments and Activities* (New York: The Free Press, 1962); *Nature of Social Science* (New York: Harcourt Brace Jovanovich, 1967); *Social Behavior: Its Elementary Forms,* rev. ed. (New York: Harcourt Brace Jovanovich, 1974).

home health agency, an agency which provides home health care. To be certified under Medicare an agency must provide skilled nursing services and at least one additional therapeutic service (physical, speech, or occupational therapy, medical social services, or home health aide services) in the home.

home health care, health services rendered to an individual as needed in the home. Such services are provided to aged, disabled, sick, or convalescent individuals who do not need institutional care. The services may be provided by a visiting nurse association, home health agency, hospital, or other organized community group. They may be quite specialized or comprehensive (nursing services; speech, physical, occupational, and rehabilitation therapy; homemaker services; and social services). Under Medicare, such services must be provided by a home health agency. Under Medicaid, states may, but do not have to, restrict coverage of home health care to services provided by home health agencies.

homemaker services, non-medical support services (*e.g.*, food preparation, bathing) given a homebound individual who is unable to perform these tasks himself. Such services are not covered under the Medicare and Medicaid programs, or most other health insurance programs, but may be included in the social service programs developed by the states under title XX of the Social Security Act. Homemaker services are intended to preserve independent living and normal family life for the aged, disabled, sick, or convalescent.

homeostasis, maintenance of equilibrium among bodily and systemic processes. The normal functioning of the body or system is dependent upon maintaining such internal stability. For an introduction to the concept, *see* L. L. Langley, *Homeostasis* (New York: Reinhold Publishing, 1965).

home rule, ability of a municipal corporation to develop and implement its own charter. It resulted from the urban reform movement of the turn of the century, which hoped to remove urban politics from the harmful influence of state politics. Home rule can be either a statutory or a constitutional system and varies in its details from state to state. *See* Frank J. Goodnow, *Municipal Home Rule* (New York: Macmillan, 1895); Howard L. McBain, *The Law and Practice of Municipal Home Rule* (New York: Columbia University Press, 1916); J. D. McGoldrick, *Law and Practice of Municipal Home Rule, 1916-1930* (New York: Columbia University Press, 1933); Lyle E. Schaller, "Home Rule—A Critical Appraisal," *Political Science Quarterly* (September 1961);

Eugene C. Lee, "Home Rule Appraised," *National Civil Review* (October 1962); and Charles Hoffman, "Pennsylvania Legislation Implements Home Rule," *National Civic Review* (September 1972).

homogeneity principle, principle of administration that advises the executive to group the major functions of an organization together according to their purpose, the process used, the persons served, or the places where it takes place, with each constituted as a single unit under the direction of a single administrator guided by a single plan of action.

honcho, slang word for a boss or any person in charge of a work detail. U.S. soldiers first adopted the term from the Japanese word *hancho* ("group leader").

honest graft, also DISHONEST GRAFT, the classic distinction between the two genres of graft was made by George Washington Plunkitt, a politico associated with New York's Tammany Hall early in this century. *Dishonest graft*, as the name implies, involves bribery, blackmailing, extortion, and other obviously illegal activities. As for *honest graft*, let Plunkitt speak:

> Just let me explain by examples. My party's in power in the city, and it's goin' to undertake a lot of public improvements. Well, I'm tipped off, say, that they're going to lay out a new park at a certain place.
>
> I see my opportunity and I take it, I go to that place and I buy up all the land I can in the neighborhood. Then the board of this or that makes its plan public, and there is a rush to get my land, which nobody cared particular for before.
>
> Ain't it perfectly honest to charge a good price and make a profit on my investment and foresight? Of course, it is. Well, that's honest graft.

For more of Plunkitt's wisdom, *see* William Riordon, *Plunkitt of Tammany Hall* (New York: E. P. Dutton & Co., 1963).

honeymoon period, that period of time immediately following a major agreement between management and labor when both sides may seek to de-emphasize the normal difficulties inherent in their relationships.

Hoover Commission of 1947-1949, also known as the COMMISSION ON THE ORGANIZATION OF THE EXECUTIVE BRANCH and the FIRST HOOVER COMMISSION, twelve-member commission created by Congress via the Lodge-Brown Act of 1947 for the ostensible purpose of integrating and reducing the number of governmental agencies generated by World War II. The act creating the commission required the president, the Senate majority leader and the speaker of the House each to appoint four members of the commission. Two of each of these four were to be public representatives; two were to be public officials. By the same token, two of each of these four would be Democrats and two would be Republicans. Finally, the Commission would select a chairman from among its own members. Former President Herbert Hoover was appointed to the Commission by Republican speaker of the House Joseph Martin. Subsequently, Hoover was unanimously chosen by the commission to be its chairman.

The Commission made its report in 1949. Instead of calling for a reduction of governmental agencies, the commission made a vigorous call for increased managerial capacity in the Executive Office of the President (EOP) through (1) unlimited discretion over presidential organization and staff, (2) a strengthened Bureau of the Budget, (3) an office of personnel located in the EOP, and (4) the creation of a staff secretary to provide liaison between the president and his subordinates. In addition, the commission recommended that executive branch agencies be reorganized to permit a coherent purpose for each department and better control by the president. Many of its recommendations were adopted, including the passage of the Reorganization Act of 1949 and the establishment of the Department of Health, Education and Welfare in 1953. For a comprehensive review of the accomplishments of the Commission, *see* Peri E. Arnold, "The First Hoover Commission and the Managerial Presidency," *Journal of Politics* (February 1976).

Hoover Commission of 1953-1955, also known as the COMMISSION ON THE ORGANIZATION OF THE EXECUTIVE BRANCH OF THE GOVERNMENT and the SECOND HOOVER COMMISSION, like the First Hoover Commission, a twelve-member commission created by Congress. The Ferguson-Brown Act of July 10, 1953 created the Second Hoover Commission for three ostensible purposes: (1) the promoting of economy, efficiency and improved service in the transaction of the public business; (2) the defining and limiting of executive functions; and (3) the curtailment and abolition of governmental functions and activities which are competitive with private enterprise. The latter purpose constituted the major difference between the enabling authority of the first and second Hoover commissions.

The act creating the commission required that its twelve members be composed as follows:
1. four appointed by the president of the United States, two from the executive branch and two from private life;
2. four appointed by the president of the Senate, two from the Senate and two from private life;
3. four appointed by the speaker of the House of Representatives, two from the House of Representatives and two from private life.

In contrast to the First Hoover Commission, the enabling legislation of the Second Hoover Commission did not require bipartisanship in the selection of commission members. Finally, the commission would select a chairman from among its own members.

Former President Herbert Hoover was appointed to the commission by President Dwight D. Eisenhower. Subsequently, Hoover was unanimously chosen by the commission to be its chairman.

The commission made a progress report to Congress on December 31, 1954. The commission made its regular substantive report to Congress in the form of eighteen volumes which were submitted between February and June 1955. A final report to Congress was made in the form of a volume entitled *Final Report to the Congress*. Instead of emphasizing improving the management of the executive branch, the commission dealt more extensively with questions of policy. Among its major recommendations was a call for eliminating nonessential government services and activities competitive with private enterprise. The commission's recommendations were based on the assumption that the federal government had grown beyond appropriate limits and that this growth should be reversed. Harvey C. Mansfield reports that "this Commission's recommendations got nowhere." *See* his "Federal Executive Reorganization: Thirty Years of Experience," *Public Administration Review* (July-August 1969). For comprehensive analyses of Hoover II, *see* William R. Devine, "The Second Hoover Commission Reports: An Analysis," *Public Administration Review* (Autumn 1955); James W. Fesler "Administrative Literature and the Second Hoover Commission Reports," *American Political Science Review* (March 1967); Ronald C. Moe, "A New Hoover Commission: A Timely Idea or Misdirected Nostalgia?" *Public Administration Review* (May-June 1982)

Hopf, Harry Arthur (1882-1949), management theorist who did pioneering work on executive compensation systems and the measurement of managerial performance. For the case that he originated many of the concepts of "management by objectives," *see* Edmund R. Gray and Richard J. Vahl, "Harry Hopf: Management's Unheralded Giant," *Southern Journal of Business* (April 1971).

horizontal communication, *see* COMMUNICATION.

horizontal conflict, bureaucratic conflict

between units of an agency that are located at similar hierarchical levels.

horizontal equity, *see* TAX EQUITY.

horizontal federalism, *see* FEDERALISM, HORIZONTAL.

horizontal loading, *see* JOB LOADING.

horizontal occupational mobility, *see* OCCUPATIONAL MOBILITY.

horizontal promotion, advancement for an employee within his/her basic job category. For example, a promotion from Window Washer I to Window Washer II or from Junior Accountant to Intermediate Accountant.

horizontal union, *see* CRAFT UNION.

horizontal work group, work group that contains individuals whose positions are essentially the same in terms of rank, prestige, and level of skill.

hospitalization, group insurance program that pays employees for all or part of their hospital, nursing, surgical, and other related medical expenses due to injury or illness to them or their dependents.

hot-cargo provisons, contract clauses that allow workers to refuse to work on or handle "unfair goods" or "hot cargo" — products coming from a factory where there is a labor dispute. The Labor-Management Reporting and Disclosure (Landrum-Griffin) Act of 1959 outlawed such provisons (except for those affecting suppliers or subcontractors in construction work and jobbers in the garment industry). For a legal analysis, *see* Paul A. Brinker, "Hot Cargo Cases Since 1958," *Labor Law Journal* (September 1971).

See also UNFAIR LABOR PRACTICES (UNIONS).

hot stove discipline, disciplinary practices that are immediate, painful, and impersonal.

hourly-rate workers, employees whose weekly pay is determined solely by the actual number of hours worked during a week.

housekeeping agency, *see* AUXILIARY AGENCY.

House of Labor, informal term for the AFL-CIO. *See* AMERICAN FEDERATION OF LABOR-CONGRESS OF INDUSTRIAL ORGANIZATIONS.

house organ, also INTERNAL HOUSE ORGAN and EXTERNAL HOUSE ORGAN, any publication — magazine, newspaper, newsletter, etc. — produced by an organization to keep its employees informed about the activities of the organization and its employees. *Internal house organs* are directed primarily to an organization's employees; *external house organs* find a wider distribution as part of the organization's public relations program. *See* Jim Mann, "Is Your House Organ A Vital Organ?" *Personnel Journal* (September 1977).

housing allowance, either (1) special compensation, consisting of a flat rate or a salary percentage, for the purpose of subsidizing the living expenses of an employee, usually paid only to employees sent overseas, or (2) subsidy paid directly or indirectly to citizens whose incomes are below a certain standard in order to enable them to live in conventional, non-public housing. *See* Katharine L. Bradbury and Anthony Downs, eds., *Do Housing Allowances Work?* (Washington, D.C.: Brookings Institution, 1981).

Housing and Urban Development, Department of (HUD), principal federal agency responsible for programs concerned with housing needs and improving and developing the nation's communities.

For a history, *see* Dwight A. Ink, "Establishing the New Department of Housing and Urban Development," *Public Administration Review* (September 1967).
HUD
451 Seventh Street, S.W.

Washington, D.C. 20410
(202) 655-4000

HRM, see HUMAN RESOURCES MANAGE-MENT.

H.R. 10 Plan, see KEOGH PLAN.

HUD, see HOUSING AND URBAN DEVELOP-MENT, DEPARTMENT OF.

HUD "701", refers to Section 701 of the Housing Act of 1954 (and subsequent amendments), which provides for grants to strengthen the "planning and decision-making capabilities of the chief executives of State, area-wide, and local agencies to promote more effective use of the Nation's physical, economic, and human resources."

human capital, a concept that views employees as assets in the same sense as financial capital. It presupposes that an investment in human potential will yield significant returns for the organization. See Theodore W. Schultz, *Investment in Human Capital* (New York: The Free Press, 1971); Thomas K. Connellan, "Management as a Capital Investment," *Human Resource Management* (Summer 1972); Stanley A. Horowitz and Allan Sherman, "A Direct Measure of the Relationship Between Human Capital and Productivity," *Journal of Human Resources* (Winter 1980); William A. Darity, Jr., "The Human Capital Approach to Black-White Earnings Inequality: Some Unsettled Questions," *The Journal of Human Resources* (Winter 1982); R.U. Miller and M.A. Zaidi, "Human Capital and Multinationals: Evidence From Brazil and Mexico," *Monthly Labor Review* (June 1982).

human-factors engineering, also called ERGONOMICS, design for human use. The objective of human factors engineering, usually called ergonomics in Europe, is to increase the effective use of physical objects and facilities by people at work, while at the same time attending to concerns such as health, safety, job satisfaction, etc.

These objectives are sought by the systematic application of relevant information about human behavior to the design of the things (usually machines) that people use and to the environments in which they work. The leading text is Ernest J. McCormick, *Human Factors Engineering,* 3rd ed. (New York: McGraw-Hill, 1970). *Also see* Roy J. Shepard, *Men at Work: Applications of Ergonomics to Performance and Design* (Springfield, Ill.: Charles C. Thomas, 1974); Vico Henriques and Charlotte LeGates, "Special Report: A Look at VDT's and Their Impact on the Workplace and an Overview of a New Science Called Ergonomics," *Personnel Administrator* (September 1984).

human relations, discipline concerned with the application of the behavioral sciences to the analysis and understanding of human behavior in organizations.

Personnel operations still tend to live in the shadow of the old-style human-relations approach to management that emphasized sympathetic attitudes on the part of managers. Its critics contended that the human-relations approach (most popular during the late 1940s and 1950s) was little more than a gimmick—that there was sincere interest in the workers only to the extent that they could be manipulated for management's ends. The goal was to adjust the worker—the same old interchangeable part of the scientific management movement—so that he or she would be content in the industrial situation, not to change the situation so that the workers would find more contentment in their work.

Today, human relations is in a more mature period. Like the caterpillar that turned into the butterfly, it simply evolved into something much more desirable. By expropriating advances in the behavioral sciences as its own, it grew into its current definition. For texts, *see* Keith Davis, *Human Behavior at Work: Human Relations and Organizational Behavior* (New York: McGraw-Hill, 1972); Aubrey C. Sanford, *Human Relations: Theory and Practice* (Columbus, Ohio: Charles E.

Merrill, 1973); Robert M. Fulmer, *Practical Human Relations* (Homewood, Ill.: Richard D. Irwin, 1983).

Human Relations, monthly journal founded on the belief that social scientists in all fields should work toward integration in their attempts to understand the complexities of human problems. Articles tend to be theoretical analyses of human interactions in the workplace as well as society in general.
  Editorial Address:
  Editor
  Human Relations
  Tavistock Centre
  120 Belsize Lane
  London NW3 5BA
  Subscriptions:
  Plenum Publishing Corp.
  233 Spring Street
  New York, NY 10013

human resource accounting, concept that views the employees of an organization as capital assets similar to plant and equipment. While the concept is intuitively attractive, calculating the value, replacement cost, and depreciation of human assets poses significant problems. Consequently, it is viewed with considerable skepticism by managers and accountants. For the methodology, *see* Eric G. Flamholtz, "Human Resources Accounting: Measuring Positional Replacement Costs," *Human Resource Management* (Spring 1973); Robert Wright, "Managing Man as a Capital Asset," *Personnel Journal* (April 1970). For a text, *see* Edwin H. Caplan and Stephen Landekich, *Human Resource Accounting: Past, Present and Future* (New York: National Association of Accountants, 1974). *Also see* Sue A. Ebersberger, "Human Resource Accounting: Can We Afford It?" *Training and Development Journal* (August 1981); Blair Y. Stephenson and Stephen G. Franklin, "Human Resource Accounting: Dollars and Sense for Management," *Business and Society* (Winter–Spring 1981–82); Bruce G. Meyers and Hugh M. Shane, "Human Resource Accounting for Managerial Decisions: A Capital Budgeting Ap-

proach," *Personnel Administrator* (February 1984).

Human Resource Management, previously titled MANAGEMENT OF PERSONNEL QUARTERLY, quarterly whose articles deal with a variety of topics related to personnel practices and human resource management. Most articles are written by academics and tend to be either theoretical analyses and/or reports of research.
  Editorial Address:
  Human Resource Management
  Graduate School of Business
    Administration
  University of Michigan
  Ann Arbor, MI 48109
  Subscriptions:
  Subscription Department
  John Wiley & Sons
  605 Third Avenue
  New York, NY 10157

Human Resource Planning, quarterly journal of the Human Resource Planning Society, which is devoted to the advancement of the practice, technology, and theory of planning for human resources.
  Human Resource Planning
  P.O. Box 2553
  Grand Central Station
  New York, NY 10163

Human Resource Planning Society, nonprofit organization devoted to the advancement of the practice, technology, and theory of planning for human resources. Its quarterly journal is *Human Resource Planning*.
  Human Resource Planning Society
  P.O. Box 2553
  Grand Central Station
  New York, NY 10163
  (617) 837-0630

human resources, also called MANPOWER, general term for all of the employees in an organization or the workers in a society. It is gradually replacing the more sexist "manpower."

Human Resources Abstracts, formerly POVERTY AND HUMAN RESOURCES AB-

STRACTS, quarterly publication that contains abstracts of current literature on human, social, and manpower problems and solutions ranging from slum rehabilitation and job development training to compensatory education, minority group problems, and rural poverty.

Human Resources Abstracts
Sage Publications, Inc.
275 South Beverly Drive
Beverly Hills, CA 90212

human resources administration, increasingly popular euphemism for the management of social welfare programs. Many jurisdictions that had Departments of Welfare have replaced them with Departments of Human Resources.

human resources development, a more impressive-sounding phrase for the training and development function of personnel management. *See* Lue Rachelle Brim-Donohoe, "A Case for Human Resources Development," *Public Personnel Management* (Winter 1981); Leonard Nadler, ed., *The Handbook of Human Resource Development* (New York: John Wiley & Sons, 1984).

human resources management (HRM), term often used synonymously with personnel management. HRM transcends traditional personnel concerns, taking the most expansive view of the personnel department's mandate. Instead of viewing the personnel function as simply that collection of disparate duties necessary to recruit, pay, and discharge employees, the HRM approach assumes that personnel's appropriate mission is the maximum utilization of its organization's human resources. Recent textbooks are beginning to reflect this larger vision of the personnel function. *See* Andrew F. Sikula, *Personnel Administration and Human Resources Management* (New York: John Wiley, 1976); William P. Anthony and Edward A. Nicholson, *Management of Human Resources: A Systems Approach to Personnel Management* (Columbus, Ohio: Grid, Inc., 1977); Lawrence A. Klatt, Robert G. Murdick, and Fred E.

Schuster, *Human Resources Management: A Behavioral Systems Approach* (Homewood, Ill.: Richard D. Irwin, 1978); Richard B. Peterson and Lane Tracy, *Systematic Management of Human Resources* (Reading, Mass.: Addison-Wesley, 1979); Andrew J. DuBrin, *Personnel and Human Resources Management* (New York: D. Van Nostrand, 1981). *Also see* Joyce D. Ross, "A Definition of Human Resources Management," *Personnel Journal* (October 1981); Raymond E. Miles and Howard R. Rosenberg, "The Human Resources Approach to Management: Second-Generation Issues," *Organizational Dynamics* (Winter 1982); Donald Summers, "Human Resources Specialists: Working with Managers to Improve Productivity," *Personnel* (September–October 1984); John A. Hooper, "A Strategy for Increasing the Human Resource Department's Effectiveness," *Personnel Administrator* (June 1984).

human resources planning, also called MANPOWER PLANNING, projecting and managing the supply and demand of human resources. There is no universally accepted definition of what human resources planning (or its more sexist equivalent, "manpower planning") is or consensus on what activities should be associated with it. Organizations claiming that they do such planning appear to use a wide variety of methods to approach their own unique problems.

Historically, manpower planning was most associated with the Johnson Administration's Great Society Programs of the 1960s. It was and remains an integral part of numerous government programs whose objective was to affect the labor market in order to improve the employment status and welfare of individuals. All such programs have a macro focus—they deal with the aggregate labor force of the country (all employed and unemployed individuals). At roughly the same time of the new manpower initiatives of the Johnson Administration, parallel thinking on human resources planning began to emerge at the firm and organizational level. Both situations are concerned with future demand aspects; that is, what will be the requirements for the future work force. At the macro level, this means projecting what skills will be in demand to service the economy. At the micro level, this entails projecting specific requirements for the work force of the organization, or what quantities and qualities of personnel will be needed to carry out organizational objectives. Both levels are concerned with future supply aspects. At the macro level this means that projections must be made on what the national work force will consist of in terms of future skills, both surpluses and deficits. For the micro level, the organization must forecast what its future force work will consist of as well as evaluate its competitive position in order to decide what quantities and qualities of personnel it can encourage to enter the organization as replacements.

Some of the better works on human resources planning include D.J. Bell, *Planning Corporate Manpower* (London: Longman Group, 1974); Elmer H. Burack and James H. Walker, *Manpower Planning and Programming* (Boston: Allyn and Bacon, 1972); Edward B. Jakubauskas and Neil A. Palomba, *Manpower Economics* (Reading, Mass.: Addison-Wesley, 1973); Ray A. Killian, *Human Resource Management* (New York: American Management Association, 1976); James W. Walker, *Human Resources Planning* (New York: McGraw-Hill, 1980).

human resources planning models, also called MANPOWER PLANNING MODELS, according to Richard G. Grinold and Kneale T. Marshall, *Manpower Planning Models* (New York: Elsevier North-Holland, 1977), models that use systems analysis to (a) *Forecast* the future manpower requirements that will be satisfied by the current inventory of personnel; forecast the future manpower budget commitments represented by the current stock of personnel. (b) *Analyze* the impact of proposed changes in policy, such as changes in promotion or retirement rules, changes in salary and benefits, changes in transfers into and out of the organization, and changes in the organ-

ization's rate of growth. (c) *Test* the rationale of historical policy for consistency, and establish the relations among operating rules of thumb. (d) *Explore* regions of possible policy changes and allow a planner to experiment with and perhaps discover new policies. (e) *Understand* the basic flow process, and thus aid in assessing the relative operational problems. (f) *Design* systems that balance the flows of manpower, requirements, and costs. (g) *Structure* the manpower information system in a manner suitable for policy analysis and planning.

human resources requirements analysis, also called MANPOWER REQUIREMENTS ANALYSIS, analysis and projection of (a) the personnel movements and (b) the numbers and kinds of vacancies to be expected during each stage of management's work force plan. According to the Office of Personnel Management, the essential steps in manpower requirements analysis are:

- *First,* to estimate what portion of the work force present at the start of the planning period, or hired during the period, will leave their positions during the period.
- *Second,* to estimate how many of these position leavers will move to other positions in the work force during the period and how many will leave the service entirely.
- *Third,* to estimate the positions to be occupied by in-service movers at the end of the planning period.
- *Fourth,* by comparison of this retained work force with the work force specified in management's work force plan, to identify the numbers and kinds of positions to be filled during the planning period.

See Richard B. Frantzreb, "Human Resource Planning: Forecasting Manpower Needs," *Personnel Journal* (November 1981); Norman Scarborough and Thomas W. Zimmerer, "Human Resources Forecasting: Why and Where to Begin," *Personnel Administrator* (May 1982).

human resources utilization, also called MANPOWER UTILIZATION, general terms for the selection, development, and placement of human resources within an economic or organizational system in order to use these resources in the most efficient manner. *See* Edward B. Jakubauskas and Neil A. Palomba, *Manpwer Economics* (Reading, Mass.: Addison-Wesley, 1973); Edward J.Giblin and Oscar A. Ornati, "Optimizing the Utilization of Human Resources," *Organizational Dynamics* (Autumn 1976).

human services, general term for organizations that seek to improve the quality of their client's lives by providing counseling, rehabilitative, nutritional, informational, and related services. *See* Wayne F. Anderson, Bernard J. Frieden, and Michael J. Murphy, eds., *Managing Human Services* (Washington, D.C.: International City Management Association, 1977); S. B. Sarason *et al., Human Services and Resource Networks: Rationale Possibilities and Public Policy* (San Francisco: Jossey-Bass, 1977); Frank Benest, "One City's Commitment to a Comprehensive Human Services Delivery System: A Case History of Gardena, California," *Public Administration Review* (March-April 1977); Laurence E. Lynn, Jr., *The State and Human Services: Organizational Change in a Political Context* (Cambridge, Mass.: The M.I.T. Press, 1980); Roger A. Lohmann, *Breaking Even: Financial Management in Human Service Organizations* (Philadelphia, Pa.: Temple University Press, 1980); Murray L. Gruber, ed., *Management Systems in the Human Services* (Philadelphia, Pa.: Temple University Press, 1981); Eli Glogow, "Reforming Human Services: Change Through Participation," *Public Administration Review* (September-October 1984).

See also PENNHURST STATE SCHOOL V. HALDERMAN.

Humphrey-Hawkins Act of 1977, formally the FULL EMPLOYMENT AND BALANCED GROWTH ACT OF 1977, federal statute that asserts it is the policy of the federal government to reduce overall unemployment to a rate of 4 percent by 1983, while reducing inflation to a rate of 3 percent. The act explicitly states that it is the "right of all Americans able, willing and seeking to work" to have "full opportunities for useful paid employment." However, the discussion of the act in the *Congressional Record* of December 6, 1977 states that "there is clearly no right to sue for legal protection of the right to a job." The popular name of the act comes from its co-sponsors, former Senator Hubert H. Humphrey (D-Minn.) and Representative Augustus F. Hawkins (D-Calif.).

Humphrey's Executor* v. *United States, 295 U.S. 602 (1935), Supreme Court case prohibiting the dismissal of commissioners of the Federal Trade Commission by the president for reasons of disagreement over policy. The court reasoned that an FTC commissioner "occupies no place in the executive department and . . . exercises no part of the executive power," thereby distinguishing the case from *Myers* v. *United States*. By implication, the decision would apply to positions in any federal agency exercising predominantly quasi-judicial and/or quasi-legislative functions.

See also (1) MYERS V. UNITED STATES and (2) WIENER V. UNITED STATES.

hypothesis, testable assertion, statement, or proposition about the relationship between two variables that are in some way related to each other. For example, a personnel manager might hypothesize that a specific kind of job performance can be predicted from a particular kind of knowledge about an applicant (such as scores on tests or grades in school). Hypotheses of this kind are proven—one way or another—by validation studies.

I

IAG, *see* INTERAGENCY ADVISORY GROUP.

IAPB, *see* INTERNATIONAL ASSOCIATION OF PROFESSIONAL BUREAUCRATS.

IAPES, *see* INTERNATIONAL ASSOCIATION OF PERSONNEL IN EMPLOYMENT SECURITY.

IAPW, *see* INTERNATIONAL ASSOCIATION OF PERSONNEL WOMEN.

ICC, *see* INTERSTATE COMMERCE COMMISSION.

ICMA, *see* INTERNATIONAL CITY MANAGEMENT ASSOCIATION.

ICMA Retirement Corporation, nonprofit, tax-exempt organization providing a deferred compensation retirement plan for the mobile employees of state and local government. The Retirement Corporation was organized because of the inability of state and local governments to provide retirement security for those types of public servants whose careers require a periodic change in employment from one government or agency to another. State and local governments and agencies may also use the plan as a supplement to existing employee benefit programs.

The plan was developed by the International City Management Association, which underwrote the Retirement Corporation. In recognition of the plan's importance, most of the major public interest and professional associations related to state and local government have become sponsors of the plan.

ICSC, *see* INTERNATIONAL CIVIL SERVICE COMMISSION.

idle time, time for which employees are paid but not able to work because of mechanical malfunctions or other factors not within their control.

IDP, *see* INDIVIDUAL DEVELOPMENT PLAN.

IIAS, *see* INTERNATIONAL INSTITUTE OF ADMINISTRATIVE SCIENCES.

IJPA, *see* (1) INDIAN JOURNAL OF PUBLIC ADMINISTRATION and (2) INTERNATIONAL JOURNAL OF PUBLIC ADMINISTRATION.

illegal aliens, also called UNDOCUMENTED WORKERS, individuals from other countries who are living/working in the United States unlawfully. The U.S. Department of Labor prefers to refer to these individuals as "undocumented workers." *See* Jose A. Rivera, "Aliens Under the Law: A Legal Perspective," *Employee Relations Law Journal* (Summer 1977); Joanne G. Minarcini, "Illegal Aliens: Employment Restrictions and Responses," *The Personnel Administrator* (March 1980); G. G. Gutierrez, "The Undocumented Immigrant: The Limits of Cost-Benefit Analysis," *Public Management* (October 1980); Ellen Sehgal and Joyce Violet, "Documenting the Undocumented," *Monthly Labor Review* (October 1980); Joan M. McCrea, "Illegal Labor Migration from Mexico to the United States," *Labour and Society* (October–December 1981); Jean Baldwin Grossman, "Illegal Immigrants and Domestic Employment," *Industrial and Labor Relations Review* (January 1984).

See also ALIENS, DE CANAS V. BICA, and IMMIGRATION AND NATURALIZATION SERVICE V. HERMAN DELGATO.

illegal bargaining items, any proposal made during the collective bargaining process that is expressly forbidden by law. For example, a union shop in a "right-to-work" state.

illegal strike, strike that violates existing law. While most public sector strikes are illegal, so are strikes that violate a contract, that are not properly authorized by the union membership, and that violate a court injunction.

ILO, see INTERNATIONAL LABOR ORGANIZATION.

immediate full vesting, pension plan that entitles an employee to all of the retirement income—both his/her contributions as well as those of his/her organization—accrued during his/her time of participation in the plan.

Immigration and Naturalization Service (INS), federal agency responsible for administering the immigration and naturalization laws relating to the admission, exclusion, deportation, and naturalization of aliens. Specifically, the INS inspects aliens to determine their admissibility into the U.S.; adjudicates requests of aliens for benefits under the law; guards against illegal entry into the United States; investigates, apprehends, removes aliens in this country in violation of the law; and examines alien applicants wishing to become citizens. See Milton D. Morris, *Immigration The Beleaguered Bureaucracy* (Washington, D.C.: The Brookings Institution, 1985).

INS
425 I Street, N.W.
Washington, D.C. 20536
(202) 633-4316

Immigration and Naturalization Service v. Herman Delgato, 80 L. Ed. 247 (1984), U.S. Supreme Court case which held that it is constitutional for federal agents to conduct "factory surveys" to enforce immigration laws.

During each survey, which lasted from one to two hours, some agents were stationed near the exits, while other agents moved systematically through the factory approaching employees and, after identifying themselves, asking from one to three questions relating to their citizenship. If an employee gave a credible reply that he or she was a U.S. citizen or produced immigration papers, the agent moved to another employee. During the survey, employees continued with their work and were free to walk around within the factory. The surveys resulted in the arrests of 164 of the 590 workers.

In the majority opinion, written by Justice Rehnquist, the Supreme Court held that the factory surveys did not result in the seizure of the entire work force and the individual questioning of the employees who initiated the case did not amount to a detention or seizure under the Fourth Amendment. Justice Rehnquist said that a "consensual encounter" between a police officer and a citizen could be transformed into a violation of the Fourth Amendment if, in view of all the circumstances surrounding the incident, a reasonable person would have believed that he was not free to leave. According to the Court, this did not occur during the surveys because employees were free to move about in the normal course of their duties, and the INS agents were stationed at the exits to insure that all employees were questioned, not to prevent them from leaving.

Finally, the Court said that because there was no seizure of the entire work force, the respondents could litigate only what happened to them, which, based on their own description of their encounters with the agents, were "classic consensual encounters," rather than violations of the Fourth Amendment.

immunity, an exemption from ordinary legal culpability while holding public office. Governmental officials generally need some protections against law suits, whether frivolous or not, which might be brought against them by individuals who are dissatisfied with their actions or adversely affected by them. Otherwise government could be brought to a standstill by such suits or crippled by the threat of them. In general, judges, executives, and legislators are well protected by judicial doctrines concerning immunities, whereas police officers, sheriffs, and similar officials are not. See David H. Rosenbloom, "Public Administrators' Official Immunity and the Supreme Court: Developments During the 1970's," *Public Administration Review* (March-April 1980); Walter S. Groszyk, Jr., and Thomas J. Madden,

"Managing Without Immunity: The Challenge for State and Local Government Officials in the 1980s," *Public Administration Review* (March–April 1981).
See also the following entries:

impact evaluation, *see* PROCESS EVALUATION.

impact ratio, in employment decisions that offer people employment opportunities (such as hiring, training, promotion, etc.), the selection rate for that group divided by the selection rate for the group with the highest selection rate. For any adverse employment decision (such as disciplinary action, layoff, termination, etc.), the impact ratio is the rate for the group in question. Impact ratios are compared to the 80 percent rule of thumb to determine adverse impact.

impact theory of discrimination, concept that asserts it is the consequences of employment practices that are relevant, not their intent. Even though an intent is benign, its consequences could foster systemic discrimination.

impasse, a condition that exists during labor-management negotiations when either party feels that no further progress can be made toward reaching a settlement.

TYPES OF IMPASSE RESOLUTION

	Mediation	Fact-Finding	Arbitration
Process	Intervention by Federal Mediation and Conciliation Service or other appropriate third party at request of negotiating parties or on own proffering of services	A procedure for compelling settlement, frequently a final alternative to arbitration	A terminal procedure alternative to or following fact-finding
Subject Matter	Terms of new agreement being negotiated	Terms of agreement being negotiated	Terms of agreement being negotiated (also final step in grievance procedure)
Setting	*Mediator* tries to determine basis for agreement and persuade parties to reach agreement	*Parties* try to persuade fact-finder by arguments	*Parties* try to persuade arbitrator by arguments (same as fact-finding)
Third Party	*Mediator*—a Federal Commissioner of Mediation and Conciliation or other third party	*Fact-finder*—a public employee or a private citizen selected by parties or by an administrative agency	*Arbitrator*—a public employee or a private citizen selected by parties or by an administrative agency
Power Factor	*Mediator* limited to persuasion and ability to find compromise	*Fact-finder* may make recommendations for impasse resolution	*Arbitrator* makes binding decision
Publicity	Confidential process—no public record kept	Quasi-public process with recommendations recorded and reported	Quasi-public process with decisions recorded and reported

Impasses are resolved either by strikes or by the helpful intervention of neutral third parties. *See* Karl A. Van Asselt, "Impasse Resolution," *Public Administration Review* (March-April 1972); Jonathan Brock, *Bargaining Beyond Impasse: Joint Resolution of Public Sector Labor Disputes* (Boston, Mass.: Auburn House Publishing Co., 1982).

impeachment, a quasi-judicial process for removing public officials from office. *See* Raoul Berger, *Impeachment: The Constitutional Problems* (Cambridge, Mass.: Harvard University Press, 1973).

implementation, also POLICY IMPLEMENTATION, from the perspective of Pressman and Wildavsky, "a process of interaction between the setting of goals and actions geared to achieving them" as well as "an ability to forge subsequent links in the causal chain so as to obtain the desired results." Yet Eugene Bardach holds that implementation is "a process of assembling the elements required to produce a particular programmatic outcome" as well as "the playing out of a number of loosely interrelated games whereby these elements are withheld from or delivered to the program assembly process on particular terms." Meanwhile, Charles O. Jones maintains that implementation consists of "those activities directed toward putting a program into effect." This involves interpretation or the "translation of program language into acceptable and feasible directives," organization or "the establishment of units and methods for putting a program into effect," and application or "the routine provision of services, payments or other agreed-upon program objectives or instruments."

Each of these definitions tends to highlight a somewhat different and important aspect of the process. The first definition usefully calls attention to the interaction between setting goals and carrying them out. This helps clarify that implementation is political in a very fundamental sense in that the activities that go on under its banner shape who gets what, when, and where from government. Like lawmakers, administrators and those with whom they interact during the implementation process exert power over program objectives and influence program outputs and outcomes.

The second definition's portrayal of implementation as the playing out of interrelated games appropriately directs attention to the strategic aspect of the process. Implementation involves administrators, interest groups, and other actors with diverse values, mobilizing power resources, forming coalitions, consciously plotting strategies, and generally engaging in strategic behavior designed to assure that their point of view prevails. The terrain may be different from that found in Congress or elsewhere but the basic staples of the political process are very much present.

A major virtue of the final definition is that it explicitly points to the role of routine and other aspects of organizational structure in implementation. In order to conserve time and energy, reduce the burdens of calculation, promote equal treatment of clients, and accomplish related functions, organizations develop standard operating procedures. These procedures plus other informal decision rules greatly simplify choices for administrators. Decisions can be made almost unthinkingly. Certainly, they are often made without the strategic consciousness suggested by the game metaphor. Moreover, these procedures serve to structure attention. Administrators with an intense interest in an implementation issue and with ample resources to influence its resolution often remain inert because standard operating procedures load up their agendas with so many other (often trivial) issues that they lack the time to get involved. An official with strong convictions about some issue need not, therefore, become an active player in the implementation game. Any effort to comprehend how implementation processes affect program outputs and outcomes cannot, then, ignore the collective impact of countless procedures and simple decision rules. Implementation mixes the consciously strategic with the routine.

The literature on implementation is relatively new but rapidly growing. A sample follows: Douglas R. Bunker, "Policy Sciences Perspectives on Implementation Processes," *Policy Sciences* (March 1972); Jeffrey L. Pressman and Aaron B. Wildavsky, *Implementation* (Berkeley, Calif.: University of California Press, 1973); Donald S. Van Meter and Carl E. Van Horn, "The Policy Implementation Process: A Conceptual Framework," *Administration and Society* (February 1975); Walter Williams, "Implementation Analysis and Assessment," *Policy Analysis* (Summer 1975); Erwin C. Hargrove, *The Missing Link: The Study of the Implementation of Social Policy* (Washington, D.C.: Urban Institute, 1975); Walter Williams and Richard Elmore, eds., *Social Program Implementation* (New York: Academic Press, 1976); Harold S. Luft, "Benefit-Cost Analysis and Public Policy Implementation," *Public Policy* (Fall 1976); Richard R. Nelson and Douglas Yates, eds., *Innovation and Implementation in Public Organizations* (Lexington, Mass.: Lexington Books, 1977); Charles O. Jones, *An Introduction to the Study of Public Policy*, 2nd ed. (North Scituate, Mass.: Duxbury Press, 1977); Eugene Bardach, *The Implementation Game* (Cambridge, Mass.: M.I.T. Press, 1977); Paul Berman, "The Study of Macro- and Micro-Implementation," *Public Policy* (Spring 1978); Richard Elmore, "Organizational Implementation," *Public Policy* (Spring 1978); Janice M. Beyer and Harrison M. Trice, *Implementing Change: Alcoholism Policies in Work Organizations* (New York: Free Press, 1978); Carol E. Van Horn, *Policy Implementation in the Federal System: National Goals and Local Implementors* (Lexington, Mass.: Lexington Books, 1979); Robert S. Montjoy and Laurence J. O'Toole, Jr., "Toward a Theory of Policy Implementation: An Organizational Perspective," *Public Administration Review* (September-October 1979); Daniel Mazmanian and Paul A. Sabatier, eds., *Effective Policy Implementation* (Lexington, Mass.: Lexington Books, 1980); Robert T. Nakamura and Frank Smallwood, *The Politics of Policy Implementation* (New York: St. Martin's Press, 1980); George C. Edwards III, *Implement-

ing Public Policy* (Washington, D.C.: Congressional Quarterly Press, 1980); Walter Williams *et al.*, *Studying Implementation: Methodological and Administrative Issues* (Chatham, N.J.: Chatham House Publishers, 1982); Daniel A. Mazmanian and Paul A. Sabatier, *Implementation and Public Policy* (Glenview, IL: Scott, Foresman, 1983).

implicit price deflator, a price index for the gross national product (GNP); the ratio of GNP in current prices to GNP in constant prices.

impoundment, tactic available to fiscal strategists—the withholding by the executive branch of funds authorized and appropriated by law. There are several types of impoundment decisions. The earliest example traces back to Thomas Jefferson, who impounded funds designed to finance gunboats for the Mississippi River. A primary and accepted mode of impoundment is for emergencies, as in the case of war. President Franklin Roosevelt impounded funds slated for numerous programs that were "superseded" by the events of late 1941. Another mode of impoundment is to confiscate funds when the program objective has been accomplished. Presidents Eisenhower and Truman both made use of impoundment to take back "extra" funds from programs whose objectives had been met or were clearly not in need of funds. Another mode of impoundment is for legal compliance. President Lyndon Johnson impounded and threatened to impound funds for local governments and school districts who were in violation of the Civil Rights Act or federal court orders.

The case for fiscal impoundment was made by the Nixon administration as being necessary for economic stabilization and to enable the president to accomplish his legal responsibilities under the Full-Employment Act of 1946. However, fiscal impoundment really amounts to a form of line-item veto. Several state governments empower their governors with the *right* to specify a budgetary figure for each program in the budget. If the legislature exceeds the recommended sum, the governor may veto any legislatively added sum above the original recommendation. Of course, any cuts made by the legislature are binding. However, the line-item veto is not an executive power granted by either the U.S. Constitution or subsequent legislation.

The arguments in favor of impoundment made by the Nixon administration focused on the difficulties that the executive had in planning a budget (based on their revenue estimates) and then having Congress essentially tack on $20-30 billion more for "favorite programs" which were not planned for. As a direct result of the impoundment controversy, the Congress set up its own parallel budget machinery in 1974 under the new Congressional Budget and Impoundment Control Act. Significant for fiscal policy is the fact that the act incorporated a congressional ceiling on expenditures. In essence, the new congressional budget process requires the Congress to set a maximum limit (recognizing the fiscal implications) and to make the various subcommittees keep the total final budget under that ceiling. Of course, this doesn't prevent Congress from establishing a very high ceiling, but it does force Congress to face the total fiscal issue directly. See Louis Fisher, "Funds Impounded by the President: The Constitutional Issue," *George Washington Law Review* (July 1970); Louis Fisher, "The Politics of Impounded Funds," *Administrative Science Quarterly* (September 1970); Vivian Vale, "The Obligation to Spend: Presidential Impoundment of Congressional Appropriations," *Political Studies* (December 1977).

See also AMERICAN FEDERATION OF GOVERNMENT EMPLOYEES V. PHILLIPS.

impoundment resolution, a resolution by either the House of Representatives or the Senate that expresses disapproval of a proposed deferral of budget authority. Whenever all or part of any budget authority provided by Congress is deferred, the president is required to transmit a special message to Congress describing the deferrals. Either house may, at any time, pass a resolution disapproving this deferral of budget authority, thus requiring that the funds be made available for obligation. When no congressional action is taken, deferrals may remain in effect until, but not beyond, the end of the fiscal year.

in-basket exercise, training technique and type of test frequently used in management assessment centers to simulate managerial problems by presenting the subject with an array of written materials (the kinds of items that might accumulate in an "in-basket") so that responses to the various items and problems can be evaluated. See F. M. Lopez, Jr., *Evaluating Executive Decision Making— The In-Basket Technique* (New York: American Management Association, 1966); Cabot L. Jaffee, *Problems in Supervision: An In-Basket Training Exercise* (Reading, Mass.: Addison-Wesley Publishing Co., 1968); Betty Salem, Don Ellis, and Douglas Johnson, "Development and Use of an In-Basket Promotional Exam for Police Sergeant," *Review of Public Personnel Administration* (Spring 1981).

See also ASSESSMENT CENTER.

incentive, reward, whether monetary or psychic, that motivates and/or compensates an employee for performance above standard.

incentive awards, also called INCENTIVE SCHEME, formal plan or program designed to motivate individual or group efforts to improve the economy and efficiency of organizational operations. There are essentially two kinds of awards—monetary and honorary.

incentive contract, that portion or clause of a collective bargaining agreement that establishes the terms and conditions of an incentive-wage system.

incentive pay, wage-system that rewards a worker for productivity above an established standard.

incentive plan, individual/group, *see* INCENTIVE-WAGE PLAN.

incentive rate, special wage rate for production above a previously fixed standard of performance.

incentive scheme, *see* INCENTIVE AWARD.

incentive-wage plan, also GROUP INCENTIVE PLAN, wage program that has wages rise with increases in productivity. Individual incentive plans are based on the performance of the individual employee while *group incentive plans* are based on the performance of the total work group. For a survey of the relevant research in both the U.S. and the U.K., *see* R. Marriott, *Incentive Payment Systems: A Review of Research and Opinion,* 4th ed. (London: Staples, 1971). For a how-to approach, *see* H. K. Von Kaas, *Making Incentives Work* (New York: American Management Association, 1971). For a critique of their faults, *see* Arch Patton, "Why Incentive Plans Fail," *Harvard Business Review* (May-June 1972). *See also* Michael Schuster and Gary Florkowski, "Wage Incentive Plans and the Fair Labor Standards Act," *Compensation Review,* Vol. 14, No. 2 (1982); G. David Garson and D. S. Brenneman, "Incentive Systems and Goal Displacement in Personnel Resource Management," *Review of Public Personnel Administration* (Spring 1981); Bernard Dwortzan, "The ABCs of Incentive Programs," *Personnel Journal* (June 1982).

incidental learning, also called LATENT LEARNING, learning that takes place without formal instruction, intent to learn, or ascertainable motive. The information obtained tends to lie dormant until an occasion for its use arises.

income, indirect, *see* INDIRECT WAGES.

incomes policy, general term for the totality of the federal government's influence upon wages, prices and profits. *See* Orley Ashenfelter and Richard Layard, "Incomes Policy and Wage Differentials," *Economica* (May 1983).

incompetence, demonstrated failure of an employee to meet minimum standards of job performance. For the classic analysis of why such people manage to hang in there despite their poor performance, *see* William J. Goode, "The Protection of the Inept," *American Sociological Review* (February 1967). For how to remove incompetents in the federal service, *see The Other Side of the Merit Coin: Removals for Incompetence in the Federal Service* (Washington, D.C.: U.S. Merit Systems Protection Board, 1982). *See also* D. Keith Denton, "Survival Tactics: Coping with Incompetent Bosses," *Personnel Journal* (April 1985).

increment, also called STEP INCREASE, established salary increase between steps of a given salary grade, marking a steady progression from the minimum of the grade to the maximum.

incremental budgeting, *see* BUDGETING, INCREMENTAL.

incremental funding, the provision (or recording) of budgetary resources for a program or project based on obligations estimated to be incurred within a fiscal year when such budgetary resources will cover only a portion of the obligations to be incurred in completing the program or project as programmed. This differs from full funding, where budgetary resources are provided or recorded for the total estimated obligations for a program or project in the initial year of funding. For distinction, *see* FULL FUNDING.

incrementalism, an approach to decision making in government in which executives begin with the current situation, consider a limited number of changes in that situation based upon a restricted range of alternatives, and test those changes by instituting them one at a time; a normative theory of government that views policymaking as a process of bargaining and competition involving the participation of different persons with conflicting points of view. *See* Yehezkel Dror, "Muddling Through—Science or Inertia," *Public Administration Review* (September 1964);

John J. Bailey and Robert J. O'Connor, "Operationalizing Incrementalism: Measuring the Muddles," *Public Administration Review* (January-February 1975); Anthony J. Balzer, "Reflections on Muddling Through," *Public Administration Review* (November-December 1979); Bruce Adams, "The Limitations of Muddling Through: Does Anyone in Washington Really Think Anymore?" *Public Administration Review* (November-December 1979).

See also LINDBLOM, CHARLES E.

incumbent, person presently serving in a position.

indemnify, compensate insured individuals for their losses.

indemnity, insurance contract to reimburse an individual or organization for possible losses of a particular type.

independent agency, also REGULATORY COMMISSION, federal executive agency not included under the executive departments or within the Executive Office of the President. Some, such as the Smithsonian Institution, are of long standing. Many others have been created in recent years, as the responsibilities of the government have increased. A *regulatory commission* is an independent agency established by Congress to regulate some aspect of U.S. economic life. Among these are the Securities and Exchange Commission, the Interstate Commerce Commission, and others. Such agencies are, of course, not independent of the U.S. government. They are subject to the laws under which they operate as these laws are enacted by Congress and executed by the president.

Independent agencies and commissions within the executive branch of the government can be divided into those units that are under the direct supervision and guidance of the president, and are therefore responsible to him; and those that are not under such supervision and guidance, and therefore are not responsible to him. The units in the first group can be categorized as independent executive agencies, while those in the second group can be subdivided into independent regulatory commissions and government-sponsored enterprises.

Independent executive agencies, with rare exceptions, are headed by single administrators appointed by the president and confirmed by the senate. These administrators serve at the pleasure of the president and can be removed by him whenever he wishes. In addition, they must submit their budget requests to the Office of Management and Budget (OMB), which is located within the Executive Office of the President, for review and clearance. Examples of independent executive agencies are the Commission on Civil Rights, the Environmental Protection Agency, the General Services Administration, the Small Business Administration, and the Veterans Administration.

Independent regulatory commissions and government-sponsored enterprises are bodies headed by several commissioners, directors, or governors who also are appointed by the president and confirmed by the senate. Unlike administrators of independent executive agencies, they serve for fixed terms and cannot be removed at the pleasure of the president. In some cases government-sponsored enterprises may also have directors who are private citizens. While all of the independent regulatory commissions and most of the government-sponsored enterprises submit their budget requests to OMB for review and clearance, the degree of dependence on these budgets varies considerably. Nearly all of the government-sponsored enterprises generate a considerable part of their financial resources from outside sources, while the independent regulatory commissions (except for the Federal Reserve Board and the Federal Home Loan Bank Board) rely on the government for their funding.

Activities of all of the above units are presented in public reports which are prepared annually. In addition, those units that are subject to periodic authorization and appropriations hearings (all of the independent executive agencies, independent regulatory commissions, and most of the Government-sponsored enterprises) must undergo a review of their activities at those hearings.

See Robert E. Cushman, *The Independent Regulatory Commissions* (New York: Oxford University Press, 1941); Marver Bernstein, *Regulating Business by Independent Commissions* (Princeton, N.J.: Princeton University Press, 1955); Louis M. Kohlmeier, Jr., *The Regulators, Watchdog Agencies and the Public Interest* (New York: Harper & Row, 1969); William L. Cary, *Politics and the Regulatory Agencies* (New York: McGraw-Hill, 1967); Elmer Smead, *Governmental Promotion and Regulation of Business* (New York: Appleton-Century-Crofts, 1969); Nicholas Johnson, "A New Fidelity to the Regulatory Ideal," *Georgetown Law Journal* (March 1971); Roger G. Noll, *Reforming Regulation* (Washington, D.C.: Brookings, 1971); James Q. Wilson, ed., *The Politics of Regulation* (New York: Basic Books, 1970); Jeffrey E. Cohen, "Presidential Control of Independent Regulatory Commissions Through Appointment: The Case of the ICC," *Administration and Society* (May 1985).

See also REGULATION and RULEMAKING.

independent city, *see* CITY.

independent union, union that is not affiliated with the AFL-CIO.

independent variable, a factor in a hypothesized relationship that is thought to cause or bring about variation in the performance of the dependent factor.

indexing, system by which salaries, pensions, welfare payments, and other kinds of income are automatically adjusted to account for inflation. *See* Geoffrey Brennan, "Inflation, Taxation, and Indexation," *Policy Studies Journal* (Spring 1977); Robert S. Kaplan, *Indexing Social Security: An Analysis of the Issues* (Washington, D.C.: American Enterprise Institute, 1977); Theodore Turnasella, "Market Indexed Compensation," *Personnel Administrator* (May 1984).

index number, measure of relative value compared with a base figure for the same series. In a time series in index form, the base period usually is set equal to 100, and data for other periods are expressed as percentages of the value in the base period. Many indexes published by government agencies are presently expressed in terms of a 1967 = 100 base.

Index numbers possess a number of advantages over the raw data from which they are derived. First, they facilitate analysis by their simplicity. Second, they are a more useful basis for comparison of changes in data originally expressed in dissimilar units. Third, they permit comparisons over time with some common starting point—the index base period.

index of agreement, index, usually expressed as a percentage, showing the extent to which examiners agree on a candidate's scores.

Indian Journal of Public Administration **(IJPA),** quarterly of comparative and development administration focusing on south Asia.

IJPA
Indian Institute of Public Administration
Indraprastha Estate
Ring Road
New Delhi, 11002
INDIA

indirect compensation/income, *see* INDIRECT WAGES.

indirect cost, any cost incurred for common objectives that therefore cannot be directly charged to any single cost objective. These costs are allocated to the various classes of work in proportion to the benefit to each class. Indirect cost is also referred to as overhead or burden cost.

indirect labor, *see* DIRECT LABOR.

indirect labor costs, loose term for the wages of nonproduction employees.

indirect tax, *see* DIRECT TAX.

indirect validity, see SYNTHETIC VALIDITY.

indirect wages, also called INDIRECT IN-
COME and INDIRECT COMPENSATION, non-
financial benefits employees receive from
their work situations—favorable organizational environment, nontaxable benefits,
perquisites, and the authority, power,
and/or status that may come with their
jobs.

individual agreement, also called INDI-
VIDUAL CONTRACT, formal agreement between a single employee and his/her
employer that determines the employee's
conditions and terms of employment.

individual-contract pension trust, pension plan that creates a trust to buy and
hold title to employees' individual insurance and/or annuity contracts. The
employer makes payments to the trust,
which then pays the insurance premiums
on its various contracts.

individual development plan (IDP),
periodically prepared schedule of developmental experiences, including both work
assignments and formal training, designed
to meet particular developmental objectives needed to improve current performance and/or to prepare the individual for
positions of greater responsibility.

Individual Retirement Account (IRA), individual pension that the Pension Reform
Act of 1974, as amended, allows each person to create in order to put aside money
that builds up tax-free until retirement.
Funds can be invested in savings accounts,
mutual funds, annuities, government
bonds, etc. Individuals *may* start withdraw-
ing funds at age 59½ and *must* begin with-
drawals by age 70½. Funds are taxed in
the year they are withdrawn.

individual test, testing device designed to
be administered (usually by a specially
trained person) to only one subject at a
time.

industrial accident insurance, see WORK-
ERS' COMPENSATION.

Industrial and Labor Relations Review,
scholarly quarterly containing theoretical
articles and research reports in the areas
of labor-management relations; labor
organizations; labor law; politics, government, and industrial relations; international and comparative industrial relations;
labor market; income security, insurance,
and benefits; labor conditions; manpower;
personnel; management; organization;
and work performance and satisfaction.
Industrial and Labor Relations Review
The New York State School of
Industrial and Labor Relations
Cornell University
Ithaca, NY 14853

**industrial and organizational psycholo-
gy,** see INDUSTRIAL PSYCHOLOGY.

industrial democracy, also PARTICIPATIVE
MANAGEMENT, any of a variety of efforts
designed to encourage employees to participate in an organization's decision-
making processes by identifying problems
and suggesting solutions to them in a formal manner. While the terms "industrial
democracy" and "participative management" tend to be used almost interchangeably, there is a distinction. Industrial
democracy was used as far back as 1897
by Beatrice and Sidney Webb to describe
democratic practices within the trade union
movement. The term's modern usage to
cover innumerable types of joint or cooperative management programs dates from
World War I. Then it connoted a scheme
to avoid labor-management disputes which
might adversely affect war production. Today industrial democracy connotes joint
action by management and workers'
representatives. *Participative management*, in contrast, connotes cooperative
programs that are unilaterally implemented
from on high. Nevertheless, both terms
seem to be rapidly losing their distinctive
connotations. The most comprehensive
survey of the state of industrial democracy
throughout the world is David Jenkins, *Job
Power: Blue and White Collar Democracy*
(Garden City, N.Y.: Doubleday, 1973).
For a bibliography, see Ronald L. Weiher,
"Sources on Industrial Democracy," *Har-*

vard Business Review (September-October 1975). For a review of practices in Sweden, Great Britain, and the United States, see Nancy Foy and Herman Gadon, "Worker Participation: Contrasts in Three Countries," Harvard Business Review (May-June 1976). For more on participative management, see William P. Anthony, Participative Management (Reading, Mass.: Addison-Wesley, 1978); Rosabeth Moss Kanter, "Dilemmas of Managing Participation," Organizational Dynamics (Summer 1982); Henry Mintzberg, "Why America Needs, But Cannot Have, Corporate Democracy," Organizational Dynamics (Spring 1983); William Foote Whyte, "Worker Participation: International and Historical Perspectives," The Journal of Applied Behavioral Science, Vol. 19, No. 3 (1983); Henry P. Guzda, "Industrial Democracy: Made in the U.S.A.," Monthly Labor Review (May 1984); Janice A. Klein, "Why Supervisors Resist Employee Involvement," Harvard Business Review (September-October 1984); S.A. Levitan and D. Werneke, "Work Participation and Productivity Change," Monthly Labor Review (September 1984).

See also SCANLON PLAN and WORKERS' COUNCILS.

industrial gerontology, see GERIATRICS.

industrial health services, health services provided by physicians, dentists, nurses, or other health personnel in an industrial setting for the appraisal, protection, and promotion of the health of employees while on the job. Occupational health services is now the preferred term.

industrial medicine, that branch of medicine that is concerned with protecting workers from hazards in the workplace and with dealing with health problems/emergencies that may occur during working hours. See Diana Chapman Walsh, "Is There a Doctor In-House?" Harvard Business Review (July-August 1984).

industrial paternalism, see PATERNALISM.

industrial policy, government regulation of industrial planning and production through law, tax incentives, and subsidies. See Richard P. Nielsen, "Industrial Policy: Review and Historical Perspective," Public Administration Review (September-October 1983); Alan M. Kantrow, ed., "The Political Realities of Industrial Policy," Harvard Business Review (September-October 1983); J. L. Badaracco, Jr., and D. B. Yoffie, "'Industrial Policy:' It Can't Happen Here," Harvard Business Review (November-December 1983); Arthur Levitt, Jr., "Industrial Policy: Slogan or Solution," Harvard Business Review (March-April 1984).

industrial psychiatry, see OCCUPATIONAL PSYCHIATRY.

industrial psychology, also called OCCUPATIONAL PSYCHOLOGY, INDUSTRIAL AND ORGANIZATIONAL PSYCHOLOGY, and I/O PSYCHOLOGY, concerned with those aspects of human behavior related to work organizations; its focus has been on the basic relations in organizations between (1) employees and their co-workers, (2) employees and machines, and (3) employees and the organization. Because the term industrial psychology holds a restrictive connotation, the field is increasingly referred to as industrial and organizational psychology or I/O Psychology. For the most comprehensive summary of the state of the art, see Marvin D. Dunnette, ed., Handbook of Industrial and Organizational Psychology (Chicago: Rand McNally, 1976). Also see Earl C. Pence, Douglas Cederblom and Daniel L. Johnson, "The Image of Industrial/Organizational Psychologists," Personnel Administrator (April 1984).

industrial relations, generally used to refer to all matters of mutual concern to employers and employees and their representatives. In a more technical sense, its use should be limited to labor-management relationships in private sector manufacturing organizations. See Keith Bradley and Alan Gleb, Worker Capitalism: The New Industrial Relations (Cambridge,

Mass.: The MIT Press, 1983); Joseph W. Garbarino, "Unionism Without Unions: The New Industrial Relations?" *Industrial Relations* (Winter 1984); Thomas A. Kochan, Robert B. Mckersie, and Peter Cappelli, "Strategic Choice and Industrial Relations Theory," *Industrial Relations* (Winter 1984); Sanford M. Jacoby, "The Future of Industrial Relations," *California Management Review* (Summer 1984); Jack Barbash, *The Elements of Industrial Relations* (Madison: University of Wisconsin Press, 1984).

Industrial Relations, thrice-yearly journal of scholarly articles and symposia on all aspects of the employment relationship, with special attention given to pertinent developments in the fields of labor economics, sociology, psychology, political science, and law.

Industrial Relations
Institute of Industrial Relations
University of California
Berkeley, CA 94720

industrial relations common law, *see* COMMON LAW OF THE SHOP.

industrial relations research, *see* PERSONNEL RESEARCH.

industrial revolution, a very general term that refers to a society's change from an agrarian to an industrial economy. The Industrial Revolution of the western world is considered to have begun in England in the 18th century. For the case that it actually began much earlier, *see* Jean Gimpel, *The Industrial Revolution of the Middle Ages* (New York: Holt, Rinehart and Winston, 1976). *Also see* Gene Bylinsky, "A New Industrial Revolution Is on the Way," *Fortune,* (Oct. 5, 1981); Joseph Finkelstein and David A. H. Newman, "The Third Industrial Revolution: A Special Challenge to Managers," *Organizational Dynamics* (Summer 1984).

industrial sociology, *see* OCCUPATIONAL SOCIOLOGY.

industrial union, also called VERTICAL UNION, union whose members work in the same industry and encompass a whole range of skilled and unskilled occupations. *See* Harold W. Aurand, *From the Molly Maguires to the United Mine Workers: The Social Ecology of an Industrial Union, 1869-1897* (Philadelphia, Pa.: Temple University Press, 1971).

inequity theory, also EQUITY THEORY, theory most fully developed by J. Stacy Adams (he premised his work upon Leon Festinger's theory of cognitive dissonance), who holds that inequity exists for Worker A whenever his/her perceived job inputs and outcomes are inconsistent with Worker B's job inputs and outcomes. Inequity would exist if a person perceived that he/she was working much harder than another person who received the same pay. Adams suggests that the presence of inequity creates tension within Person A to reduce the inequity by, for example, increasing (or decreasing) one's effort if it is perceived to be low (or high) relative to others' work effort. *See* J. Stacy Adams, "Toward an Understanding of Inequity," *Journal of Abnormal and Social Psychology* (November 1963); Paul S. Goodman and Abraham Friedman, "An Examination of Adams' Theory of Inequity," *Administrative Science Quarterly* (December 1971); Michael R. Carrell and John Dittrich, "Equity Theory: The Recent Literature, Methodological Considerations, and New Directions," *Academy of Management Review* (April 1978); John E. Dittrich and Michael R. Carrell, "Organizational Equity Perceptions, Employee Job Satisfaction, and Departmental Absence and Turnover Rates," *Organizational Behavior and Human Performance* (August 1979).

See also COGNITIVE DISSONANCE.

inflation, also DEFLATION, a rise in the costs of goods and services which is equated to a fall in the value of a nation's currency. *Deflation* is the reverse, a fall in costs and a rise in the value of money. Cost-push inflation is inflation caused by increases in the costs of production which are independent of the state of demand.

Demand-pull inflation is inflation caused by increased demand rather than by increases in the cost of production. Hidden inflation is a price increase achieved by selling smaller quantities (or a poorer quality) of a product for the same price as before. Hyperinflation is inflation so extreme that it practically destroys the value of paper money. *See* Henry J. Aaron, ed., *Inflation and the Income Tax* (Washington, D.C.: Brookings Institution, 1976); Arthur M. Okun, *Curing Chronic Inflation* (Washington, D.C.: Brookings Institution, 1978); John Case, *Understanding Inflation* (New York: William Morrow, 1981); T. Kristensen, *Inflation and Unemployment in Modern Society* (New York: Praeger, 1981); David P. Calleo, "Inflation and American Power," *Foreign Affairs* (Spring 1981); Thomas J. Dougherty, *Controlling the New Inflation* (Lexington, Mass.: Lexington Books, 1981); William E. Klay, "Combating Inflation Through Wage Negotiations: A Strategy for Public Administration," *Public Administration Review* (September–October 1981); Wayne Vroman, *Wage Inflation: Prospects for Deceleration* (Washington, D.C.: The Urban Institute Press, 1983).

informal organization, also FORMAL ORGANIZATION, spontaneously developed relationships and patterns of interaction between employees. According to Chester I. Barnard's classic statement on the subject, "Informal Organizatons and Their Relation to Formal Organizations," Chapter IX from his *The Functions of the Executive* (Cambridge, Mass.: Harvard University Press, 1938),

> informal organization, although comprising the processes of society which are unconscious as contrasted with those of formal organization which are conscious, has two important classes of effects: (a) it establishes certain attitudes, understandings, customs, habits, institutions; and (b) it creates the condition under which formal organization may arise.

initiation fees, payments required by unions of all new members and/or of employees who having once left the union wish to return. Initiation fees serve several purposes: (1) they are a source of revenue, (2) they force the new member to pay for the advantages secured by those who built the union, and (3) when the fees are high enough they can be used as a device to restrict membership.

initiative, procedure that allows citizens, as opposed to legislators, to propose the enactment of laws.

injunction, also called LABOR INJUNCTION, court order forbidding specific individuals or groups from performing acts the court considers injurious to property or other rights of an employer or community. There are two basic types of injunctions: (1) *temporary restraining order,* which is issued for a limited time prior to a formal hearing, and (2) *permanent injunction,* which is issued after a full formal hearing. Once an injunction is in effect, the court has contempt power to enforce its rulings through fines and/or imprisonment. For an analysis, *see* Richard D. Sibbernsen, "New Developments in the Labor Injunction," *Labor Law Journal* (October 1977).

See also BOYS MARKET V. RETAIL CLERKS LOCAL 770 and MUNIZ V. HOFFMAN.

injury, traumatic, under the Federal Employee's Compensation Act, for continuation of pay purposes, a wound or other condition of the body caused by external force, including stress or strain. The injury must be identifiable by time and place of occurrence and member or function of the body affected, and be caused by a specific event or incident or series of events or incidents within a single day or work shift.

injury, work related, for compensation under the Federal Employees' Compensation Act, a personal injury sustained while in the performance of duty. The term "injury" includes diseases proximately caused by the employment.

ink-blot test, see RORSCHACH TEST.

in-kind match, also called SOFT MATCH, grant recipient's fulfilling of its cost-sharing obligation by a contribution other than cash, such as the rental of space or equipment or staff services.

Inland Steel Co. v. National Labor Relations Board, decision by the U.S. Court of Appeals, 7th Circuit (1948) which held that a company was required to bargain with its union over retirement and pension matters. The decision was indirectly upheld by the U.S. Supreme Court when it denied certiorari in the case, 336 U.S. 960 (1949).

input, raw material of any process.

input-output table, a matrix table in which each of the producing (output) sectors of an economy is shown to be a consumer (input) of the output of one of the other producing sectors of the economy. The table consists of a vertical array (output sectors) mapped against a horizontal array (input sectors). Each one of the producers is also listed as a consumer. The table shows the high degree of interrelatedness and interdependence between the various sectors of an economy: a change in the figure in any one "box" of the table will precipitate an almost endless series of adjustments and readjustments in the other figures (boxes). The analysis of an input-output table reveals for each sector or industry what inputs it buys from every other industry in the table and how much of its output it sells to every other industry. *See also* LEONTIEF, WASSILY.

INS, *see* IMMIGRATION AND NATURALIZATION SERVICE.

in-service training, term used mainly in the public sector to refer to job-related instruction and educational experiences made available to employees. In-service training programs are usually offered during normal working hours. However, some programs, especially those offering college credit, are available to the employee only on his/her own time.

inspector general, job title (of military origin) for the administrative head of an inspection/investigative unit of a larger agency. *See* Jarold A. Kieffer, "The Case for an Inspector General of the United States," *Bureaucrat* (Summer 1980).

Institute for Social Research (ISR), established at the University of Michigan in 1946. The ISR conducts research on a broad range of subjects within its four constituent research centers: (1) *Survey Research Center*—concerned primarily with the study of large populations, organizations, and special segments of society, and generally utilizes interview surveys; (2) *Research Center for Group Dynamics*—concerned with the development of the basic science of behavior in groups, seeking to explain the nature of the social forces which affect group behavior, the relations among members, and the activities of the group as a whole; (3) *Center for Research on Utilization of Scientific Knowledge*—studies the processes required for the full use of research findings and new knowledge; and (4) *Center for Political Studies*—investigates political behavior, focusing on national politics in many countries, and maintains a rich collection of election data.

Institute for Social Research
The University of Michigan
426 Thompson Street
Ann Arbor, MI 48104
(313) 764-8363

Institute of Public Administration, formerly the BUREAU OF MUNICIPAL RESEARCH, founded in 1906 as the New York *Bureau of Municipal Research*. One of the most influential forces for urban reform and technical innovation in public administration. Today, the Institute of Public Administration remains a private research organization providing consultation, technical services, and training in many areas of public administration. For a history, *see* Jane S. Dahlberg, *The New York Bureau of Municipal Research* (New York: New

York University Press, 1966).
Institute of Public Administration
55 West 44th Street
New York, NY 10036
(212) 730-5480

institutional discrimination, practices contrary to EEO policies that occur even though there was no intent to discriminate. Institutional discrimination exists whenever a practice or procedure has the effect of treating one group of employees differently from another.

institution building, approach to technical assistance in developing countries that promotes developmental changes by identifying a particular organization possessing technical capability, managerial skill, and an internal commitment to change and then forging linkages between this organization and the groups in its environment that provide the organization with resources, support, and outlets for its products or services. See Melvin G. Blase, *Institution Building: A Source Book* (Beverly Hills, Calif.: Sage Publications, 1973) and D. Woods Thomas *et al., Institution Building* (Cambridge, Mass.: Schenkman Publishing Co., 1973).

instrumented laboratory, laboratory training experience that uses feedback from measurements taken during laboratory sessions of the behavior and feelings of the group and/or its component individuals. See Jay Hall, "The Use of Instruments in Laboratory Training," *Training and Development Journal* (May 1970).

insubordination, disobedience of higher authorities in an organization; refusal to take orders from those who are properly designated to give them.

insurable risk, a risk which has the following attributes: it is one of a large homogeneous group of similar risks; the loss produced by the risk is definable and quantifiable; the occurrence of loss in individual cases is accidental or fortuitous; the potential loss is large enough to cause

hardship; the cost of insuring is economically feasible; the chance of loss is calculable; and it is sufficiently unlikely that loss will occur in many individual cases at the same time.

insurance, also INSURANCE PREMIUM, contractual arrangement that has a customer pay a specified sum, the insurance premium, in return for which the insurer will pay compensation if specific events occur (*e.g.,* death for life insurance, fire for fire insurance, hospitalization for health insurance, etc.). The insurance premiums are calculated so that their total return to the insurance company is sufficient to cover all policyholder claims plus administrative costs and profit. For texts, see Mark S. Dorfman, *Introduction to Insurance* (Englewood Cliffs, N.J.: Prentice-Hall, 1978) and Robert I. Mehr and Emerson Cammack, *Principles of Insurance*, 7th ed. (Homewood, Ill.: Richard D. Irwin, Inc., 1980).
See also the following entries:
DENTAL INSURANCE
DISABILITY INSURANCE
GROUP INSURANCE
LIFE INSURANCE
PLAN TERMINATION INSURANCE

insurance commissioner, the state official charged with the enforcement of laws pertaining to insurance in the respective states. The commissioner's title, status in government, and responsibilities differ somewhat from state to state but all states have an official having such reponsibilities regardless of the title. Sometimes called superintendent or director.

insurance pool, an organization of insurers or reinsurers through which particular types of risks are shared or pooled. The risk of high loss by any particular insurance company is transferred to the group as a whole (the insurance pool) with premiums, losses, and expenses shared in agreed amounts. The advantage of a pool is that the size of expected losses can be predicted for the pool with much more certainty than for any individual party to it. Pooling arrangements are often used for catastrophic coverage or for certain high risk populations like the disabled. Pooling may also be done within a single company by pooling the risks insured under various different policies so that high losses incurred by one policy are shared with others.

insurance premium, *see* INSURANCE.

insurance trust contributions, amounts derived from contributions, assessments, premiums, "taxes," etc., required of employers and employees for financing of compulsory or voluntary social insurance programs operated by a government.

insured, person who buys insurance on property or the person whose life is insured.

insurer, person, company, or governmental agency that provides insurance.

intangible objective, *see* OBJECTIVE.

intangible rewards, satisfactions of no monetary value that an individual gains from a job.

intangibles, those benefits and costs which cannot be converted into dollar values.

integrative bargaining, *see* PRODUCTIVITY BARGAINING.

intelligence, an individual's ability to cope with his/her environment and deal with mental abstractions. The military, as well as some other organizations, use the word "intelligence" in its original Latin sense— as information.

intelligence function, use of techniques that encourage organizational advocacy and competitiveness in the gathering, interpreting, and communicating of information in order to give executives accurate and up-to-date information for use in decision making and administration.

intelligence quotient (IQ), measure of an individual's general intellectual capability.

IQ tests have come under severe criticism because of their declining relevancy as a measurement tool for individuals past the age of adolescence and because of their inherent cultural bias, which has tended to discriminate against minorities. *See* Ashley Montagu, ed., *Race and IQ* (New York: Oxford University Press, 1975); Brigitte Berger, "A New Interpretation of the I.Q. Controversy," *The Public Interest* (Winter 1978).

IQ Classifications		
The following table illustrates a traditional classification of IQ's and indicates the percentage of persons in a normal population who would fall into each classification.		
Classification	**IQ**	**Percentage of Population**
Gifted	140 and above	1
Very Superior	130–139	2.5
Superior	120–129	8
Above Average	110–119	16
Average	90–109	45
Below Average	80–89	16
Dull or Borderline	70–79	8
Moron	60–69	2.5
Imbecile, idiot	59 and under	1

intelligence test, any of a variety of standardized tests that seek to measure a range of mental abilities and social skills. *See* Charles Bahn, "Can Intelligence Tests Predict Executive Competence?" *Personnel* (July–August 1979).

Interagency Advisory Group (IAG), the Office of Personnel Management's key link for the purposes of communication, consultation, and coordination with the rest of the federal personnel community. Its members are the top personnel officials from the departments and agencies of the federal government.

Interagency Committee on Handicapped Employees, *see* VOCATIONAL REHABILITATION ACT OF 1973.

intercity differential, *see* GEOGRAPHICAL DIFFERENTIAL.

interdisciplinary team, *see* TASK GROUP.

interest, community of, *see* COMMUNITY OF INTEREST.

interest arbitration, arbitration of a dispute arising during the course of contract negotiations where the arbitrator must decide what will or will not be contained in the agreement. *See* Ronald W. Haughton, "Some Successful Uses of 'Interest' Arbitration," *Monthly Labor Review* (September 1973); Betty Southard Murphy, "Interest Arbitration," *Public Personnel Management* (September-October 1977); Henry S. Farber, "Splitting-the-Difference in Interest Arbitration," *Industrial and Labor Relations Review* (October 1981); Richard Johnson, "Interest Arbitration Examined," *Personnel Administrator* (January 1983); Patricia Compton-Forbes, "Interest Arbitration Hasn't Worked Well in the Public Sector," *Personnel Administrator* (February 1984); John Delaney and Peter Feuille, "Police Interest Arbitration: Awards and Issues," *Arbitration Journal* (June 1984); I. B. Helburn and Robert C. Rodgers, "Hesitancy of Arbitrators to Accept Interest Arbitration Cases: A Test of the Conventional Wisdom," *Public Administration Review* (May-June 1985).

interest group, *see* PUBLIC INTEREST GROUP.

interest group liberalism, a theory of policymaking maintaining that public authority is parceled out to private interest groups resulting in weak, decentralized government incapable of long-range planning. Powerful interest groups operate to promote private goals, but do not compete to promote the public interest. Government becomes not an institution that makes hard choices among conflicting values, but a holding company for interests. These interests are promoted by alliances of interest groups, relevant government agencies, and the appropriate congressional committees in each issue area. The major book expounding this view is Theodore Lowi, *The End of Liberalism,* 2nd ed. (New York: Norton, 1979).

See also (1) AGE OF SCARCITY and (2) PLURALISM.

interest group theory, also GROUP THEORY, theory essentially based on the premise that individuals function primarily through groups and that these groups will act as appropriate and necessary to further group goals (based on common interest). The group process, including formulation of group objectives and development of specific group actions and response, is seen as a fundamental characteristic of the political process.

The significance of groups in the political process has been recognized for over two thousand years. Aristotle was one of the first to note that political associations were both significant and commonplace because of the "general advantages" members obtained.

One of the first specific references to groups in the American political process was Madison's famous discussion of factions in the *Federalist Papers* No. 10. Madison defined the group or faction as "a number of citizens whether amounting to a majority or minority of the whole, who are united and activated by some common impulse of passion, or of interest, adverse to the rights of other citizens, or to the permanent and aggregate interests of the community." In Madison's view, the group was inherent in the nature of people and its causes were unremovable. The only choice then was to control the effects of group pressure and power. A more elaborate discussion of group theory can be traced to John C. Calhoun's treatise on governance, *A Disquisition on Government* (New York: Peter Smith, 1853). While essentially an argument for the protection of minority interests, the treatise suggests that ideal governance must deal with all interest groups since they represent the legitimate interests of the citizens. If all the groups participated on some level of parity within the policymaking process, then all individual interests would be recognized by the policymakers.

While the work of Calhoun represents

the development of early group theory, modern political science group theory has taken greater impetus from the work of Arthur F. Bentley. In *The Process of Government* (Cambridge, Mass.: Harvard University Press, 1908, 1967), Bentley explained that political analysis has had to shift its focus from forms of government to the actions of individuals in the context of groups. Groups are action mechanisms that enable numbers of individuals to achieve political, economic, and social purposes and desires.

It remained for David Truman and Earl Latham to conceptualize the theoretical implications of group action and to begin assembling a theory of the group process. Truman's principal work—*The Governmental Process* (New York: Knopf, 1951)—views group interaction as the real determinant of public policy which should constitute the primary focal point of study. Truman defines the interest group as "a shared attitude group that makes certain claims upon other groups in the society. If and when it makes its claims through or upon any of the institutions of government, it becomes a political interest group." Group pressure is assured through the establishment of lines of access and influence. Truman notes that the administrative process provides a multitude of points of access comparable to the legislature. What Truman provides for group theory is a complete description and analysis of how groups interact, function, and influence in the overall political system.

There are two types of group concept identified by Truman: existing groups and potential groups. The potential group is constituted by people who have common values and attitudes, but do not yet see their interests being threatened. Should such a possibility occur, Truman argues that potential groups will form and attempt to protect their interests. Truman's social-pluralism concept envisions in group competition a high degree of social equilibrium and resultant stability, which is ensured by the "multiplicity of coordinate or nearly coordinate points of access to government decisions." Open access is coterminous with open participation in policy formulation.

Earl Latham's *The Group Basis of Politics* (Ithaca, N.Y.: Cornell University Press, 1952) provides another basis for examining the theory of the group process. What is particularly significant about Latham's work is his conceptualization that government itself was a group just like the various private groups attempting to access the policy process. Latham ascribes to government the same characteristics and concern for power that is associated with all organized private groups. Since this study is concerned foremost with government's role in the policy process, Latham's work is a more appropriate basis for elaboration of the group theory model.

Latham contends that the basic structure of the political community is associational. The state or political community will establish "norms of permissible behavior in group relations and enforce these norms." In essence, the state becomes more than a referee between groups in conflict because it is also developing goals as well as overseeing activity. As for the dynamics of group interaction which formulate public policy, Latham sees three primary modes of action which represent a group's mastery of its environment: placing restraints on the environment such as establishing jurisdictions; neutralizing the environment by using counterclaims or "propaganda"; or by conciliating the environment by constantly amassing points and credits for future actions. Latham visualizes these modes as the primary ways by which organized groups attempt to survive and effect their objectives.

Latham views the legislature as the referee of the group struggle, responsible for "ratifying the victories of the successful coalitions, and recording the terms of the surrenders, compromises, and conquests in the form of statutes." The function of the bureaucrat is quite different, however. The bureaucrats, according to Latham, are like "armies of occupation left in the field to police the rule won by the victorious coalition." Although Latham's description is aimed primarily at regulatory agencies, he sees the bureaucrat being deluged by the losing coalitions of groups for more favorable actions despite the general rules established. The result is that "regulatory agencies are constantly besought and importuned to interpret their authorities in favor of the very groups for the regulation of which they were originally granted." Obviously, this brief quotation does not explicitly recognize the crucial significance of the initiating role played by administrative agencies in public policymaking. Still, the description of the resulting process is remarkably apt.

Latham completes his overview of government as official groups by examining the judiciary. The judge will function much like the bureaucrat since judges are a critical part of the administrative process. The role of judges will be "to develop a more or less homogenous and objective system out of statutes, administrative decrees, and the causes of private clients." This task makes the judiciary superior and different from bureaucratic agencies. However, Latham notes the transferal of quasi-judicial power to regulatory agencies which has left executive agencies with a wide range of discretion and power.

Latham distinguishes among three types of groups based on phases of development: incipient, conscious, and organized. An incipient group is one "where the interest exists but is not recognized by the members of the putative association"; a conscious group is one "in which the community sense exists but which has not become organized"; and finally, an organized group is "a conscious group which has established an objective and formal apparatus to promote the common interest." Latham's "incipient" and "conscious" groups are essentially the same as Peter Woll's concept of "potential groups," based on his definition that "there always exist within society potential political interests below the surface which can be activated when people sharing those interests are brought to a condition of awareness about the need to take action," in *Public Policy* (Cambridge, Mass.: Winthrop, 1974).

The concept of "potential groups" keeps the bureaucratic policymaking process honest (or perhaps more balanced) given the possibility that new groups might surface or some issues may influence decision-making. The "potential groups" concept also serves as a counter-argument to the claim that group theory is undemocratic. Once the concept of potential group is married to the active role of organized groups, the claim can be made, in David Truman's words, that "all interests of society by definition are taken into account in one form or another by the institutions of government." *See* Jeffrey M. Berry, *The Interest Group Society* (Boston, Mass.: Little, Brown, 1984).

See also PRESSURE GROUP and LOBBY.

interest inventory, questionnaire designed to measure the intensity of interest that an individual has in various objects and activities. Interest inventories are widely used in vocational guidance. *See* Donald G. Zytowski, *Contemporary Approaches to Interest Measurement* (Minneapolis: University of Minnesota Press, 1973).

interest test, battery of questions designed to determine the interest patterns of an individual, particularly with regard to vocational choice.

interexaminer reliability, *see* INTERRATER RELIABILITY.

interface, point of contact, or the boundary between organizations, people, jobs, and/or systems. For analyses, *see* Frank T. Paine, "The Interface Problem," *The Personnel Administrator* (January–February 1965); Daniel A. Wren, "Interface and Interorganizational Coordination," *Academy of Management Journal* (March 1967); L. David Brown, *Managing Conflict at Organizational Interfaces.* (Reading, Mass.: Addison-Wesley, 1983).

interfund transactions, *see* OFFSETTING RECEIPTS.

intergovernmental expenditure, amount paid to other governments as fiscal aid in the form of shared revenues and grants-in-aid, as reimbursements for performance of general government activities, and for specific services for the paying government (*e.g.*, care of prisoners and contractual research), or in lieu of taxes. Excludes amounts paid to other governments for purchase of commodities, property, or utility services, any tax imposed and paid as such, and employer contributions for social insurance (*e.g.*, contributions to the federal government for old age, survivors, disability, and health insurance for state employees).

See also FEDERALISM and FISCAL POLICY.

Intergovernmental Personnel Act of 1970 (IPA) (Public Law 91-648), federal statute designed to strengthen the personnel resources of state and local governments by making available to them a wide range of assistance. The act contains a declaration of policy that (1) the quality of public service at all levels can be improved through personnel systems that are consistent with merit principles, and (2) it is in the national interest for federal assistance to be directed toward strengthening state and local personnel systems in line with merit principles.

Specifically, IPA:

1. authorizes the U.S. Civil Service Commission (now the Office of Personnel Management) to make grants to help meet the costs of strengthening personnel management capabilities of state and local governments in such areas as recruitment, selection, and pay administration, and for research and demonstration projects;
2. authorizes grants to help states and localities develop and carry out training programs for employees, particularly in such core management areas as financial management, automatic data processing, and personnnel management (the grant programs of the IPA Act were eliminated in 1981);
3. authorizes awards for Government Service Fellowship grants to support graduate-level study by employees selected by state and local governments;
4. authorizes a wide range of technical

assistance in personnel management to be made available to state and local governments on a reimbursable, nonreimbursable, or partly reimbursable basis;
5. provides for the temporary assignment of personnel between federal agencies and state and local governments or institutions of higher education;
6. allows employees of state and local governments to benefit from training courses conducted for federal employees, by federal agencies;
7. fosters cooperative recruitment and examining efforts; and
8. makes the Office of Personnel Management the sole federal agency responsible for prescribing and maintaining merit system standards required under federal grant programs.

intergovernmental relations (IGR), fiscal and administrative processes by which higher units of government share revenues and other resources with lower units of government, generally accompanied by special conditions that the lower units must satisfy as prerequisites to receiving the assistance.

IGR has been described by former Senator Edmund Muskie, while chairman of the Senate Subcommittee on Intergovernmental Relations, as the "hidden dimension of government," "performing as almost a fourth branch of government," but having "no direct electorate, . . . no set perspective, . . . no special control," and moving "in no particular direction."

IGR is held by scholars to have certain distinctive features or characteristics. Among these has been the central role of public officials, elected officials, and senior civil servants. A second feature of IGR is its focus on the informal, practical, goal-oriented arrangements that can be realized within the public institutional environment to "get things done." Another feature of IGR is its policy component, consisting of the official intentions and actions (or inactions) of public officials, the consequences of these actions in the intergovernmental context, and the systematic analysis of these actions.

See W. Brook Graves, *American Intergovernmental Relations: Their Origins, Historical Development and Current Status* (New York: Charles Scribner's Sons, 1964); H. Clyde Reeves, "Role of State Governments in our Intergovernmental System," *Public Adminstration Review* (May-June 1968); David J. Kennedy, "The Law of Appropriateness: An Approach to a General Theory of Intergovernmental Relations," *Public Administration Review* (March-April 1972); Donald H. Haider, *When Governments Come to Washington: Governors, Mayors, and Intergovernmental Lobbying* (New York: Free Press, 1974); Allen Schick, "The Intergovernmental Thicket: The Questions are Still Better than the Answers," *Public Administration Review* (December 1975); Deil S. Wright, *Understanding Intergovernmental Relations,* 2nd ed. (Monterey, California: Brooks/Cole Publishing Co., 1982); Richard H. Leach, *Intergovernmental Relations in the 1980s* (New York: Marcel Dekker, 1983); Arnold M. Howitt, *Managing Federalism: Studies in Intergovernmental Relations* (Washington, D.C.: Congressional Quarterly Press, 1984); Thomas J. Kane, Jr., "City Managers View Intergovernmental Relations," *Publius* (Summer 1984).

See also ADVISORY COMMISSION ON INTERGOVERNMENTAL RELATIONS and FEDERALISM.

intergovernmental revenue, amounts received from other governments as fiscal aid in the form of shared revenues and grants-in-aid, as reimbursements for performance of general government functions and specific services for the paying government (*e.g.,* care of prisoners and contractual research), or in lieu of taxes.

Revenue has also been supplied by the federal government to offset the import of large federal programs upon state and local governments. Impact funds have been provided, for example, for elementary and secondary education in the vicinity of large military institutions where enrollment of children from military families in local schools has been significant.

The flow of intergovernmental revenues, particularly that due to grants-in-aid from the federal government to other governments, has increased dramatically since 1949. The flow of federal aid (in 1967 dollars) increased from $21 per capita in 1949 to $181 per capita in 1978, and has fallen somewhat since that time, decreasing to $158 per capita in 1980.

See Deil S. Wright, *Federal Grants-in-aid: Perspectives and Alternatives* (Washington, D.C.: American Enterprise Institute, 1968); Thomas H. Kiefer, *The Political Impact of Federal Aid to State and Local Governments* (Morristown, N.J.: General Learning Press, 1974); Advisory Commission on Intergovernmental Relations, *Significant Features of Fiscal Federalism, 1979-80* (Washington, D.C.: U.S. Government Printing Office, October, 1980).

See also FEDERALISM, FISCAL and PUBLIC FINANCE.

interim agreement, collective bargaining agreement designed to avoid a strike and/or to maintain the current conditions of employment while the settlement of a dispute or the signing of a final comprehensive contract is pending.

Interior, Department of the (DOI), cabinet-level federal department. As the nation's principal conservation agency, the DOI has responsibility for most of our nationally-owned public lands and natural resources; also has a major responsibility for American Indian reservation communities and for people who live in island territories under U.S. administration.

DOI
C Street between 18th & 19th
  Streets, N.W.
Washington, D.C. 20240
(202) 343-3171

intermittent, less than full-time employment requiring irregular work hours that cannot be prescheduled.

intern, *see* INTERNSHIP.

internal alignment, relationship among positions in an organization in terms of rank and pay. In theory, the most desirable internal alignment calls for similar treatment of like positions, with the differences in treatment in direct proportion to differences in the difficulty, responsibilities, and qualifications for a position.

internal consistency reliability, measure of the reliability of a test based on the extent to which items in the test measure the same traits.

internal control, the plan of organization and all of the coordinate methods and measures adopted within an agency to safeguard the agency's assets, check the accuracy and reliability of its accounting data, promote operational efficiency, and encourage adherence to prescribed managerial policies. *See* Frederic A. Heim, Jr., and Harold Steinberg, "Implementing the Internal Control Process in the Federal Government," *Government Accountants Journal* (Winter 1983-1984).

internal equity, *see* EXTERNAL EQUITY.

internal house organ, *see* HOUSE ORGAN.

Internal Revenue Service (IRS), federal agency within the Treasury Department. The IRS is responsible for administering and enforcing the internal revenue laws, except those relating to alcohol, tobacco, firearms, and explosives (which is the responsibility of the Bureau of Alcohol, Tobacco and Firearms). The IRS mission is to encourage and achieve the highest possible degree of voluntary compliance with the tax laws and regulations. Basic IRS activities include providing taxpayer service and education; determination, assessment, and collection of internal revenue taxes; determination of pension plan qualifications and exempt organization status; and preparation and issuance of rulings and regulations to supplement the provisions of the Internal Revenue Code.

IRS
1111 Constitution Avenue, N.W.

Washington, D.C. 20224
(202) 566-5000

International Association of Personnel in Employment Security (IAPES), organization founded in 1913 for individuals working in job placement and unemployment compensation in the public sector. It now claims over 26,000 members.

IAPES
1101 Louisville Road
Frankfort, KY 40601
(502) 223-4459

International Association of Personnel Women (IAPW), a professional association of women personnel workers in business, government, and education established to expand and improve the professionalism of women working in personnel management.

IAPW
5820 Wilshire Blvd.
Suite 500
Los Angeles, CA 90036
(213) 937-9000

International Association of Professional Bureaucrats (IAPB), group founded in 1968 and headed by James H. Boren (a former college professor, congressional staffer, and State Department official). IAPB is an organization dedicated to bureaucratic reform and maintaining the status quo. Its motto is: "When in charge, ponder. When in trouble, delegate. When in doubt, mumble." In addition to conducting seminars on fingertapping and eloquent mumbling, IAPB sponsors a number of annual awards banquets at which the organization's highest award, "The Order of the Bird," has been presented to leading bureaucrats in the governmental, corporate, and academic fields. The U.S. Postal Service was presented The Order of the Bird in recognition of its orderly postponement patterns in delivering special delivery mail. *See* James H. Boren, *When In Doubt, Mumble: A Bureaucrat's Handbook* (New York: Van Nostrand Reinhold, 1972); James H. Boren, *Have*

Your Way With Bureaucrats (Radnor, Pa.: Chilton Books Co., 1975).
IAPB
National Press Building
Washington, D.C. 20045
(202) 347-2490

International Brotherhood of Teamsters v. United States, 431 U.S. 324 (1977), U.S. Supreme Court case which held that a seniority system is not unlawful merely because it perpetuates an employer's previous discriminatory policies. The majority found that Title VII protects "bona fide" seniority systems—those designed without discriminatory intent—even though they lock in the effects of illegal employment discrimination. The congressional judgment, the court said, was that Title VII should not "destroy or water down the vested seniority rights of employees simply because their employer had engaged in discrimination prior to the passage of the Act." For an analysis, *see* Stephen L. Swanson, "The Effect of the Supreme Court's Seniority Decisions," *Personnel Journal* (December 1977).
See also RETROACTIVE SENIORITY.

International City Management Association (ICMA), professional organization for appointed chief executives in cities, counties, towns, and other local governments. Its primary goals include strengthening the quality of urban government through professional management and developing and disseminating new concepts and approaches to management through a wide range of information services, training programs, and publications.

As an educational and professional association, ICMA is interested in the dissemination and application of knowledge for better urban management. To further these ends, ICMA utilizes a comprehensive research, data collection, and information dissemination program to facilitate reference and research by local government officials, university professors and students, researchers, and others concerned with urban affairs. Among ICMA publications are: *The Municipal Year Book, The County*

Year Book, and its monthly magazine, *Public Management.*
ICMA
1120 G St., N.W.
Washington, D.C. 20005
(202) 626-4600
See also ICMA RETIREMENT CORPORATION.

international civil service, term that does not refer to any particular government entity, but to any bureaucratic organization that is by legal mandate composed of differing citizenships and nationalities. Examples include the United Nations Secretariat, the International Labour Organization, and the Commission of the European Communities. Sometimes the term is used to collectively refer to the employees of all international bureaucracies. For a symposium, *see* Sidney Mailick, ed., "Toward an International Civil Service," *Public Administration Review* (May–June 1970). For the standard work on the legal aspects of the subject, *see* M. B. Akehurst, *The Law Governing Employment in International Organizations* (Cambridge, England: Cambridge University Press, 1967). *See also* Robert S. Jordan, "What Has Happened to Our International Civil Service: The Case of the United Nations," *Public Administration Review* (March–April 1981).

International Civil Service Commission (ICSC), fifteen-member commission created by the United Nations in 1974 to make recommendations concerning the personnel policies of the various United Nations secretariats. For a history and analysis, *see* John P. Renninger, "Staffing International Organizations: The Role of the International Civil Service Commission," *Public Administration Review* (July–August 1977).

International Institute of Administrative Sciences (IIAS), the only international non-governmental organization that aims at formulating and disseminating the general principles of public administration as a comparative science and practice. Its journal is the *International Review of Administrative Sciences.*

IIAS
25 Rue de la Charite
1040 Brussels, Belgium

International Journal of Government Auditing, quarterly of the International Organization of Supreme Audit Institutions. Text in English, French, and Spanish.

International Journal of Government
  Auditing
Box 1138, Postal Station Q
Toronto, Ontario M4T 2P4
CANADA

International Journal of Group Psychotherapy, official quarterly of the American Group Psychotherapy Association. Devoted to reporting and interpreting research and practice in group psychotherapy in various settings in the United States and in other countries, it reflects the types of group psychotherapy now employed, and helps stimulate the study of validation of practice and results. It also serves as a forum of ideas and experiences, with a view toward clarifying and enlarging the scope of group psychotherapy techniques.

International Journal of Group Psychotherapy
American Group Psychotherapy Association, Inc.
1995 Broadway—14th Floor
New York, NY 10023

International Journal of Public Administration (IJPA), quarterly journal serving "all areas" of public administration.

IJPA
Marcel Dekker Journals
P.O. Box 11305
Church Street Station
New York, NY 10249

International Labor Organization (ILO), specialized agency associated with the United Nations, created by the Treaty of Versailles in 1919 as a part of the League of Nations. The United States joined this autonomous intergovernmental agency in 1934 and is currently one of 132 member countries that finance ILO operations. Governments, workers, and employers share in making the decisions and shaping its policies. This tripartite representation gives the ILO its balance and much of its strength and makes it distinct from all other international agencies.

The purpose of the ILO is to improve labor conditions, raise living standards, and promote economic and social stability as the foundation for lasting peace throughout the world. The standards developed by the annual ILO Conference are guides for countries to follow and form an international labor code that covers such questions as employment, freedom of association, hours of work, migration for employment, protection of women and young workers, prevention of industrial accidents, workmen's compensation, conditions of seamen, and social security. The only obligation on any country is to consider these standards; no country is obligated to adopt, accept, or ratify them. For a history, *see* Antony Alcock, *History of the International Labor Organization* (New York: Octagon Books, 1972). *See also* Walter Galenson, *The International Labor Organization: An American View* (Madison: University of Wisconsin Press, 1981).

International Labor Organization
International Labor Office:
Geneva, Switzerland
Washington Branch:
1750 New York Ave., N.W.
Washington, D.C. 20006
(202) 376-2315

International Labour Review, monthly journal that has published original research, comparative studies, and articles of interest to the international labor community since 1897.

International Labour Review
International Labour Office
CH—1211 Geneva 22
SWITZERLAND

International Personnel Management Association (IPMA), organization established in January 1973 through the consolidation of the Public Personnel Association (successor to the Civil Service Assembly of the United States and Canada) and the Society for Personnel Administration. IPMA is a nonprofit membership organization for agencies and persons in the public personnel field. Its members are located in federal, state, provincial, and local governments throughout the United States, Canada, and elsewhere around the world. Among IPMA's continuing purposes are the improvement of personnel administration, promotion of merit principles of employment, and assistance for persons and agencies engaged in personnel work.

IPMA is divided into national sections (for example, the U.S. section is "International Personnel Management Association-United States"), geographic regions, and local chapters.

IPMA
1850 K Street, N.W.
Washington, D.C. 20006
(202) 833-5860

international representative, title sometimes used by agents of international unions.

International Trade Commission, United States, formerly the UNITED STATES TARIFF COMMISSION, commission that furnishes studies, reports, and recommendations involving international trade and tariffs to the president, the Congress, and other government agencies. It was created in 1916 as the *United States Tariff Commission* and changed to its present name in 1974.

U.S. I.T.C.
701 E Street, N.W.
Washington, D.C. 20436
(202) 523-0161

internship, any of a variety of formal training programs for new employees or students that allows them to learn by working closely with professionals in their field. Almost all professional educational programs at universities require or allow their students to undertake internships of one kind or another. *See* Daniel S. Golmmen and Francis B. Atkinson, "The Business Intern—New Source of Employees," *Management World* (January 1978); Thomas P. Murphy, *Government Management Internships and Executive Development* (Lexington, Mass.: Lexington Books, 1973); Nicholas Henry, Symposium Editor, "Internships in Public Administration," *Public Administration Review* (May-June 1979); "NASPAA Guidelines for Public Service Internships," *Southern Review of Public Administration* (September 1979); Sigmund G. Ginsburg, "Try Before You Hire: Business Internship Programs," *Management Review* (January 1981); Edgar Mills, Richard J. Harris, and Robert Brischetto, "Internships in an Instant Bureaucracy: Some Organizational Lessons," *The Journal of Applied Behavioral Science,* Vol. 19, No. 4 (1983); Daniel F. Griswold, "Student Internships," *Personnel Administrator* (July 1984).

See also PRESIDENTIAL MANAGEMENT INTERN PROGRAM.

interpersonal competence, measure of an individual's ability to work with other people in a variety of situations. To have interpersonal competence while occupying any given position, one would have to be proficient in meeting all of a position's role demands. *See* David Moment and Abraham Zaleznik, *Role Development and Interpersonal Competence* (Boston: Harvard University Graduate School of Business Administration, 1963); Chris Argyris and Roger Harrison, *Interpersonnal Competence and Organizational Effectiveness* (Homewood, Ill.: Richard D. Irwin, 1962).

interpolation, process of estimating intermediate values between two known values.

interrater reliability, also called INTEREXAMINER RELIABILITY, extent to which examiners give the same score to like performing candidates. *See* J. M. Greenwood and W. J. McNamara, "Interrater Reliability in Situational Tests," *Journal of Applied Psychology* (April 1967).

Interstate Commerce Commission

(ICC), federal commission that regulates interstate surface transportation, including trains, trucks, buses, inland waterway and coastal shipping, freight forwarders, and express companies. The regulatory laws vary with the type of transportation; however, they generally involve certification of carriers seeking to provide transportation for the public, rates, adequacy of service, purchases, and mergers. For a critical history, see Robert Fellmeth, *The Interstate Commerce Omission* (New York: Grossman, 1970).

ICC
Twelfth Street & Constitution Avenue, N.W.
Washington, D.C. 20423
(202) 275-7252

interstate compacts, formal arrangements entered into by two or more states, with the approval of Congress, to operate joint programs. See M. Wendell, *The Interstate Compact Since 1925* (Chicago: Council of State Governments, 1951); V. V. Thursby, *Interstate Cooperation: A Study of the Interstate Compact* (Washington, D.C.: Public Affairs Press, 1953); Richard H. Leach and Redding S. Sugg, Jr., *The Administration of Interstate Compacts* (Baton Rouge, La.: Louisiana State University Press, 1959); Weldon V. Barton, *Interstate Compacts in the Political Process* (Chapel Hill, N.C.: University of North Carolina Press, 1967); Martha Derthick and Gary Bombardier, *Between State and Nation: Regional Organizations of the United States* (Washington, D.C.: Brookings Institution, 1974); Paul Hardy, *Interstate Compacts: The Ties That Bind* (Athens, Ga.: Institute of Government, University of Georgia, 1982); Richard C. Kearney and John J. Stucker, "Interstate Compacts and the Management of Low Level Radioactive Wastes," *Public Administration Review* (January–February 1985).

intervention, one of the most basic techniques of organization development. According to Chris Argyris, *Intervention Theory and Method: A Behavioral Science*

View (Reading, Mass.: Addison-Wesley, 1970),

to intervene is to enter into an ongoing system of relationships, to come between or among persons, groups, or objects for the purpose of helping them. There is an important implicit assumption in the definition that should be made explicit: the system exisits independently of the intervenor. There are many reasons one might wish to intervene. These reasons may range from helping the clients make their own decisions about the kind of help they need to coercing the clients to do what the intervenor wishes them to do. Examples of the latter are . . . executives who invite interventionists into their system to manipulate subordinates for them; trade union leaders who for years have resisted systematic research in their own bureaucratic functioning at the highest levels because they fear that valid information might lead to entrenched interests—especially at the top—being unfrozen.

Also see Iain Mangham, *Interactions and Interventions in Organizations* (New York: John Wiley, 1979); William G. Dyer, "Selecting an Intervention for Organizational Change," *Training and Development Journal* (April 1981); James Ledvinka and W. Bartley Hildreth, "Integrating Planned-Change Intervention and Computer Simulation Technology: The Case of Affirmative Action," *The Journal of Applied Behavioral Science*, Vol. 20, No. 2 (1984).

interview, also called EMPLOYMENT INTERVIEW and SELECTION INTERVIEW, conversation between two or more persons for a particular purpose. The purpose of an employment or selection interview is evaluation. According to Richard A. Fear, *The Evaluation Interview,* 2nd ed. (New York.: McGraw-Hill, 1978), "the interview is designed to perform three basic functions; (1) to determine the relevance of the applicant's experience and training to the demands of a specific job, (2) to appraise his personality, motivation, and character, and (3) to evaluate his intellectual functioning." For texts, *see* J. D. Drake, *Interviewing for Managers* (New York: AMACOM, 1972); R. L. Gordon, *Interviewing*, rev. ed. (Homewood, Ill.: Richard D. Irwin, 1975); Felix M. Lopez, *Personnel Interviewing*, 2nd ed. (New York: McGraw-Hill, 1975); Richard F. Olsen, *Managing the Interview* (New York: Wiley 1980).

Interviewers who ask questions that are not job related could inadvertently violate EEO provisions. *See* Robert D. Gatewood and James Ledvinka, "Selection Interviewing and EEO: Mandate for Objectivity," *The Personnel Administrator* (May 1976); James G. Goodale, "Tailoring the Selection Interview to the Job," *Personnel Journal* (February 1976).

See also the following entries:

  COMPLIMENTARY INTERVIEW
  DIRECTED INTERVIEW
  EXIT INTERVIEW
  GROUP ORAL INTERVIEW
  HELPING INTERVIEW
  PATTERNED INTERVIEW
  SCREENING INTERVIEW
  STRESS INTERVIEW

interview schedule, formal list of questions that an interviewer puts to an interviewee.

interbudgetary transactions, *see* OFFSETTING RECEIPTS.

intragovernmental funds, federal funds that facilitate financing of transactions within and between federal agencies. These are two types of intragovernmental funds:

1. *Intragovernmental Revolving Funds* are funds credited with collections from other agencies and accounts that are authorized by law to carry out a cycle of intragovernmental business-type operations.
2. *Management Funds* (including working funds) are funds authorized by law in which money from two or more appropriations are merged in order to carry out a common purpose or project not involving a cycle of operations.

intragovernmental transactions, *see* OFFSETTING RECEIPTS.

intrinsic reward, also called PSYCHIC INCOME, reward contained in the job itself, such as personal satisfaction, a sense of achievement, and the prestige of office. *See* William E. Reif, "Intrinsic Versus Extrinsic Rewards: Resolving The Controversy," *Human Resource Management* (Summer 1975); Lee Dyer and Donald F. Parker, "Classifying Outcomes in Work Motivation Research: An Examination of the Intrinsic-Extrinsic Dichotomy," *Journal of Applied Psychology* (August 1975).

See also TITLES.

inventory, questionnaire designed to obtain non-intellectual information about a subject. Inventories are often used to gain information on an individual's personality traits, interests, attitude, etc. *See* Robert C. Droege and John Hawk, "Development of a U.S. Employment Service Interest Inventory," *Journal of Employment Counseling* (June 1977).

inventory, interest, *see* INTEREST INVENTORY.

inverse seniority, concept that allows workers with the greatest seniority to elect temporary layoff so the most recently hired (who would normally be subject to layoff) can continue working. The key to making the concept practical is the provision that senior workers who are laid off receive supplementary compensation in excess of state unemployment compensation and have the right to return to their previous jobs. *See* R. T. Lund, D. C. Bumstead, and S. Friedman, "Inverse Seniority: Timely Answer to the Layoff Dilemma?" *Harvard Business Review* (September–October 1975); S. Friedman, D. C. Bumstead, and R. T. Lund, "Inverse Seniority as an Aid to Disadvantaged Groups," *Monthly Labor Review* (May 1976).

involuntary demotion, *see* DEMOTION.

I/O psychology, *see* INDUSTRIAL PSY-CHOLOGY.

IPA, *see* INTERGOVERNMENTAL PERSONNEL ACT OF 1970.

IPMA, *see* INTERNATIONAL PERSONNEL MANAGEMENT ASSOCIATION.

IQ, *see* INTELLIGENCE QUOTIENT.

iron law of oligarchy, Robert Michels' theory, stated in *Political Parties* (Glencoe, Ill.: The Free Press, 1915, 1949), that organizations are by their nature oligarchic because majorities within an organization are not capable of ruling themselves:

Organization implies the tendency to oligarchy. In every organization, whether it be a political party, a professional union, or any other association of the kind, the aristocratic tendency manifests itself very clearly. The mechanism of the organization, while conferring a solidity of structure, induces serious changes in the organized mass, completely inverting the respective position of the leaders and the led. As a result of organization, every party or professional union becomes divided into a minority of directors and a majority of directed.

iron law of wages, also called SUB-SISTENCE THEORY OF WAGES, concept, variously stated as a law or theory, which holds that in the long run workers will be paid merely the wages that they require for bare survival. It is premised upon the notion that as wages rise, workers have larger families. This increases the labor force and, in turn, drives down wages. The ensuing poverty causes family sizes to decline and, in turn, drives wages higher. Then the cycle begins again. While various writers popularized these notions in the last century, they are most fully stated in David Ricardo's *Principles of Political Economy and Taxation* (New York: E. P. Dutton & Co., 1817, 1962).

IRS, *see* INTERNAL REVENUE SERVICE.

ISR, *see* INSTITUTE FOR SOCIAL RESEARCH.

issue attention cycle, a model developed by Anthony Downs that attempts to explain how many policy problems evolve on the political agenda. The cycle is premised on the proposition that the public's attention rarely remains focused on any one issue for a very long period of time—regardless of the objective nature of the problem.

The cycle consists of five steps: the pre-problem stage (an undesirable social condition exists, but has not captured public attention); alarmed discovery and euphoric enthusiasm (a dramatic event catalyzes the public attention accompanied by an enthusiasm to solve the problem); recognition of the cost of change (gradual realization of the difficulty of implementing meaningful change); decline of public interest (people become discouraged or bored and/or new issue claims attention); and the post-problem stage (although the issue has a higher level of attention than in stage one, it has been displaced, but not solved, on the nation's agenda). *See* Anthony Downs, "Ups and Downs with Ecology—the Issue Attention Cycle," *Public Interest* (Summer 1972).

See also DOWNS, ANTHONY.

item, smallest unit of an employment test; a test question.

See also RECALL ITEM and RECOGNITION ITEM.

item analysis, statistical description of how a particular question functioned when used in a particular test. An item analysis provides information about the difficulty of the question for the sample on which it is based, the relative attractiveness of the options, and how well the question discriminated among the examinees with respect to a chosen criterion. The criterion most frequently used is the total score on the test of which the item is a part. However, the criterion may be the score on a subtest, on some other test, or, in general, on any appropriate measure that ranks the examinees from high to low.

item validity, extent to which a test item measures what it is supposed to measure.

item veto, *see* VETO.

J

Jackson, Andrew (1767-1845), president of the United States from 1829-1837 who has been blamed for inventing the spoils system. Prior to Jackson, the federal service was a stable, long-tenured corps of officials decidedly elitist in character and remarkably barren of corruption. Jackson, for the most part, continued with this tradition in practice, turning out of office about as many appointees as had Jefferson. In his most famous statement on the character of public office, Jackson asserted that the duties of public office are "so plain and simple that men of intelligence may readily qualify themselves for their performance; and I cannot but believe that more is lost by the long continuance of men in office than is generally to be gained by their experience." Jackson was claiming that all men, especially the newly enfranchised who did so much to elect him, should have an equal opportunity for public office. In playing to his plebeian constituency, Jackson put the patrician civil service on notice that they had no natural monopoly on public office. His rhetoric on the nature of the public service was to be far more influential than his administrative example. While Jackson's personal indulgence in spoils was more limited than popularly thought, he did establish the intellectual and political rationale for the unmitigated spoils system that was to follow.

The classic work on Jackson's patronage policies is Erik M. Eriksson, "The Federal Civil Service Under President Jackson," *Mississippi Valley Historical Review* (March 1927). For later studies, *see* Sidney H. Aronson, *Status and Kinship in the Higher Civil Service* (Cambridge, Mass.: Harvard University Press, 1964); Leonard D. White, *The Jacksonians* (New York: Macmillan, 1954); Matthew A. Crenson, *The Federal Machine: Beginnings of Bureaucracy in Jacksonian America* (Baltimore: Johns Hopkins University Press, 1975).

jargon, *see* BUZZWORDS.

jargonaphasia, physiological disorder manifested by the intermingling of correct words with unintelligible speech. Many writers of organization memoranda and government regulations seem to suffer from this ailment.

Jarvis-Gann Amendments, *see* (1) AGE OF SCARCITY and (2) PROPOSITION 13.

jawboning, any presidential pressure on labor, management, or both to make their behavior more compatible with the national interest. The jawbone in jawboning refers to the biblical "jawbone of an ass" with which Samson "slew a thousand men." According to Theodore C. Sorenson, in *Kennedy* (New York: Harper & Row, 1965), the term was first used by Walter Heller (then Chairman of the Council of Economic Advisors) in reference to President Kennedy's efforts to impose his economic guidelines on price-setting and collective bargaining. While President Kennedy never used the term itself, his successor, President Johnson, admittedly used jawboning extensively because it neatly complemented both his policies and personality. Subsequent presidents have tried to avoid the term but have stuck with the practice.

J. I. Case Co. v. ***National Labor Relations Board,*** 321 U.S. 332 (1944), U.S. Supreme Court case which held that individual contracts—no matter what the circumstances that justify their execution or what their terms—cannot be used to defeat or delay any procedures or rights under the National Labor Relations Act.

Jim Crow, a name given to any law requiring the segregation of the races. All such statutes are now unconstitutional.

See Comer Vann Woodward, *The Strange Career of Jim Crow*, 3rd ed. (New York: Oxford University Press, 1974).

job, word with three common usages: (1) colloquial term for one's position or occupation, (2) group of positions that are identical with respect to their major duties and responsibilities, (3) discrete unit of work within an occupational specialty. Historically, jobs were restricted to manual labor. Samuel Johnson's *English Dictionary* (1755) defines a job as "petty, piddling work; a piece of chance work." Anyone not dwelling in the lowest strata of employment had a position, a profession, a calling, or (at the very least) an occupation. However, our language strives ever toward egalitarianism and now even an executive at the highest level would quite properly refer to his position as a job.

job, bridge, see BRIDGE JOB.

job, covered, see COVERED JOB.

job action, a strike or work slowdown, usually by public employees. Russell K. Schutt, "Models of Militancy: Support for Strikes and Work Actions Among Public Employees," *Industrial and Labor Relations Review* (April 1982).

job analysis, determination of a position's specific tasks and of the knowledges, skills, and abilities that an incumbent should possess. This information can then be used in making recruitment and selection decisions, creating selection devices, developing compensation systems, approving training needs, etc. See Clement J. Berwitz, *The Job Analysis Approach to Affirmative Action* (New York: John Wiley, 1975); Eugene Rouleau and Burton F. Krain, "Using Job Analysis to Design Selection Procedures," *Public Personnel Management* (September–October 1975); Edwin T. Cornelius III, Theodore J. Carron, and Marianne N. Collins, "Job Analysis Models and Job Classification," *Personnel Psychology* (Winter 1979); Jai Ghropade and Thomas J. Atchison, "The Concept of Job Analysis: A Review and

Some Suggestions," *Public Personnel Management* (Vol. 9, No. 3, 1980), Richard D. Arvey, *et al.*, "Potential Sources of Bias in Job Analytic Processes," *Academy of Management Journal* (September 1982); Stephen E. Bennis, Ann Holt Belenky, and Dee Ann Soder, *Job Analysis: An Effective Management Tool* (Washington, D. C.: BNA Books, 1983); Sidney Gael, *Job Analysis* (San Francisco: Jossey-Bass, 1983).

job analysis, functional, see FUNCTIONAL JOB ANALYSIS.

job audit, see DESK AUDIT.

job bank, tool first developed in the late 1960s by the U.S. Employment Service so that its local offices could provide applicants with greater access to job openings and employers with a greater choice of workers from which to choose. The job bank itself is a computer. Each day the computer is fed information on new job openings and on jobs just filled. Its daily printout provides up-to-the-minute information for all job seekers, greater exposure of employers' needs, and a faster referral of job applicants.

job categories, the nine designated categories of the EEO-1 report: officials and managers, professionals, technicians, sales workers, office and clerical, craft workers (skilled), operatives (semiskilled), laborers (unskilled), and service workers.

job ceiling, maximum number of employees authorized at a given time.

job classification evaluation method, method by which jobs are grouped into classes based on the job's level of difficulty. See also POSITION CLASSIFICATION.

job coding, numbering system used to categorize jobs according to their job families or other areas of similarity. For example, all positions in a clerical series might be given numbers from 200 to 299 or all management positions might be numbered from 500 to 599. Higher numbers usually indicate higher skill levels within a series.

job content, duties and responsibilities of a specific position.

Job Corps, federal training program offering comprehensive development for disadvantaged youth through centers with the unique feature of residential facilities for all or most enrollees. Its purpose is to prepare these youth for the responsibilities of citizenship and to increase their employability by providing them with education, vocational training, and useful work experience in rural, urban, or inner-city centers. Enrollees may spend a maximum of two years in the Job Corps. However, a period of enrollment from six months to a year is usually sufficient to provide adequate training and education to improve employability to a substantial degree.

Job Corps recruiting is accomplished primarily through state employment services.

For the early history, see Christopher Weeks, *Job Corps: Dollars and Dropouts* (Boston: Little, Brown & Co., 1967); Sar A. Levitan, "Job Corps Experience with Manpower Training," *Monthly Labor Review* (October 1975); David A. Long, Charles D. Mallar, and Craig V. D. Thornton, "Evaluating the Benefits and Costs of the Job Corps," *Journal of Policy Analysis and Management* (Fall 1981).

job cycle, amount of time required for an employee to perform a discrete unit of work.

job definition, formal statement of the task requirements of a job. The term is frequently used interchangeably with job description.

job depth, measure of the relative freedom that the incumbent of a position has in the performance of assigned duties.

job description, also called POSITION GUIDE, summary of the duties and responsibilities of a job. According to Robert Townsend, in *Up the Organization* (New York: Knopf, 1970),

at best, a job description freezes the job as the writer understood it at a particular instant in the past. At worst, they're prepared by personnel people who can't write and don't understand the jobs.

For how-to treatments, see W. J. Walsch, "Writing Job Descriptions: How and Why," *Supervisory Management* (February 1972); R. I. Henderson, "Job Descriptions—Critical Documents, Versatile Tools," *Supervisory Management* (December 1975); Mark A. Jones, "Job Descriptions Made Easy," *Personnel Journal* (May 1984).

See also SPECIFICATION.

job design, also called JOB REDESIGN, a general term for increasing job satisfaction or productivity by making jobs more interesting and efficient. It is one of the central concerns of industrial society. In addition to providing all of our goods and services, work provides our social identities and is the single most significant determinant of our physical and emotional health. Organizing work in a manner consistent with societal goals has been the basic task of management since prehistory. This task is made more difficult today by the ever-increasing educational levels and expectations of employees. During the first phase of industrialization, workers were content to be interchangeable human parts of machines (it was more desirable than the alternative of subsistence agriculture). But the modern-day archetypical industrial citizens are highly educated individuals who exhibit little resemblance to their illiterate forebears. The scientific management movement, which grew up as an adjunct of industrial engineering, concerned itself solely with the physical considerations of work; it was human engineering. The research findings of medicine and the behavioral sciences in the last half-century have thoroughly demonstrated that the social and psychological basis of work is as significant to long-term productivity and efficiency as are the traditional physiological factors. A modern job design purview seeks to address the totality of these concerns. *See* Harold M. F. Rush, *Job Design for Motivation* (New York: The Conference Board, 1971); Louis E. Davis and James C. Taylor, eds., *The Design of Jobs*, 2nd ed. (Santa Monica, Calif.: Goodyear Publishing Co., 1979); Sar A. Levitan and William B. Johnston, "Job Redesign, Reform, Enrichment—Exploring the Limitations," *Monthly Labor Review* (July 1973); Richard W. Woodman and John J. Sherwood, "A Comprehensive Look at Job Design," *Personnel Journal* (August 1977); Robert A. Karasek, Jr., "Job Demands, Job Decision Latitude, and Mental Strain: Implications for Job Redesign," *Administrative Science Quarterly* (June 1979); Russ Smith, "Job Redesign in the Public Sector: The Track Record," *Review of Public Personnel Administration* (Fall 1981); Allan R. Cohen, "Lucid Design for Work Redesign," *The Journal of Applied Behavioral Science*, Vol. 18, No. 1 (1982).

job diagnostic survey, research instrument developed by Hackman and Oldham to measure job characteristics and outcomes that might result from job redesign. The Hackman and Oldham approach is particularly concerned with the level of skill variety, task identity, task significance, autonomy, and feedback that characterize a job. *See* J. R. Hackman and G. R. Oldham, "Development of the Job Diagnostic Survey," *Journal of Applied Psychology* (April 1975).

job dilution, dividing a relatively sophisticated job into parts that can be performed by less skilled labor.

job element, *see* ELEMENT.

job enrichment, also JOB ENLARGEMENT, term often confused or used interchangeably with *job enlargement*. However, enlarging a job—adding more but similar duties—does not substantively change and by no means enriches it. For example, an assembly-line worker performing two menial tasks is not going to have his/her attitudes affected in any significant way if he/she is allowed to perform additional menial tasks. Job enrichment can only occur when motivational factors are designed into the work. Job enlargement is nothing more than horizontal loading—similar tasks laid alongside one another. But job enrichment comes only with vertical loading—building into lower level jobs the very factors that make work at the higher levels of the organization more satisfying, more responsible, even more fun. Two such factors would be personal responsibility for discrete units of work and the ability to set one's own pace within an overall schedule.

The most influential individual in the movement towards more enriched jobs has been Frederick Herzberg. For summaries of his work, *see* "One More Time: How Do You Motivate Employees?" *Harvard Business Review* (January-February 1968); "The Wise Old Turk," *Harvard Business Review* (September-October 1974). *Also see* Robert N. Ford, "Job Enrichment Lessons from AT&T," *Harvard Business Review* (January-February 1973); J. Richard Hackman *et al.*, "A New Strategy for Job Enrichment," *California Management Review* (Summer 1975); Roy W. Walters and Associates, *Job Enrichment for Results* (Reading, Mass.: Addison-Wesley, 1975); Antone Alber and Melvin Blumberg, "Team vs. Individual Approaches to Job Enrichment Programs," *Personnel* (January-February 1981).

job evaluation, process that seeks to determine the relative worth of a position. It implies a formal comparison of the duties and responsibilities of various positions in order to ascertain the worth, rank, or classification of one position relative to all others in an organization. While job content is obviously the primary factor in evaluation, market conditions must also be considered. *See* Bryan Livy, *Job Evaluation: A Critical Review* (New York: John Wiley, 1975); Philip M. Oliver, "Modernizing A State Job Evaluation and Pay Plan," *Public Personnel Management* (May-June 1976); Thomas H. Patten, Jr., "Job Evaluation and Job Enlargement: A Collision Course?" *Human Resource Manage-*

ment (Winter 1977); Committee on Occupational Classification and Analysis, National Research Council, *Job Evaluation: An Analytic Review* (Washington, D.C.: National Academy Press, 1979); Howard Risher, "Job Evaluation: Problems and Prospects," *Personnel* (January–February 1984); Edward C. Brett and Charles M. Cumming, "Job Evaluation and Your Organization: An Ideal Relationship?" *Personnel Administrator* (April 1984); Kenneth E. Foster and Sheryll Gimplin-Poris, "Job Evaluation: It's Time to Face the Facts," *Personnel Administrator* (October 1984).

See also WHOLE-JOB RANKING.

Job Evaluation and Pay Review Task Force, group created by the Job Evaluation Policy Act of 1970 (Public Law 91-216), which asserted that it was the sense of the Congress that there be a coordinated position classification system for all civilian positions and which authorized the Civil Service Commission to establish a temporary planning unit that would submit a report within two years. The unit became known as the Job Evaluation and Pay Review Task Force. Its final report, released in January, 1972, is popularly known as the *Oliver Report* after the task force director, Philip M. Oliver. The report found the federal government's classification and ranking systems to be obsolete and recommended a new job evaluation system. The new system was field-tested and revised and became the Civil Service Commission's factor evaluation system. For the report, *see Report of the Job Evaluation and Pay Review Task Force to the United States Civil Service Commission* (Committee on Post Office and Civil Service, Subcommittee on Employee Benefits, 92d Cong., 2d Sess., House Committee Print No. 16., January 12, 1972).

job factors, also called FACTORS, an infinite number of specific factors that pertain to differing jobs. The factors themselves can usually be categorized within the following groupings:

1. *Job Requirements*—the knowledge, skills, and abilities needed to perform the duties of a specific job.
2. *Difficulty of Work*—the complexity or intricacy of the work and the associated mental demands of the job.
3. *Responsibility*—the freedom of action required by a job and the impact of the work performed upon the organizational mission.
4. *Personal Relationships*—the importance of interpersonal relationships to the success of mission accomplishment.
5. *Other Factors*—Specific job-oriented elements which should be considered in the evaluation process. For example, physical demands, working conditions, accountability, number of workers directed.

job family, group or series of jobs in the same general occupational area, such as accounting or engineering. *See* L. R. Taylor, "The Construction of Job Families Based on the Component and Overall Dimensions of the PAQ," *Personnel Psychology* (Summer 1978).

job freeze, formal halt to an organization's discretionary hiring and promoting. Such an action is inherently temporary.

job grading, *see* POSITION RANKING.

job hopper, person who frequently changes jobs. *See* Larry Lang, "The Impact of Job-Hopping on Retirement Benefits," *Personnel Administrator* (May 1984).

job loading, also HORIZONTAL LOADING and VERTICAL LOADING, assigning a greater variety of duties and responsibilities to a job. It is *horizontal loading* when the newly assigned tasks are at the same level of interest and responsibility as the job's original tasks. It is *vertical loading* when the newly assigned tasks allow for increased responsibility, recognition, and personal achievement. The horizontal/vertical terminology comes from Frederick Herzberg, "One More Time: How Do You Motivate Employees?"

Harvard Business Review (January–February 1968).

See also JOB ENRICHMENT.

job mobility, a measure of the degree to which an individual can move from job to job within one organization; or the degree to which an individual can market his or her skills to another organization. *See* John C. Anderson, George T. Milkovich and Anne Tsui, "A Model of Intra-Organizational Mobility," *Academy of Management Review* (October 1981); William M. Pearson, "Organizational Mobility Among State Executives," *Review of Public Personnel Administration* (Fall 1984).

job posting, system that allows and encourages employees to apply for other jobs in their organization. According to Dave R. Dahl and Patrick R. Pinto, in "Job Posting: An Industry Survey," *Personnel Journal* (January 1977),

it is also a complicated system for employee self-development, which embraces internal recruitment, counseling regarding realistic job expectations, encouragement of training and development experiences, and support for the personal risk that any change incurs.

Also see Lawrence S. Kleiman and Kimberly J. Clark, "User's Satisfaction With Job Posting," *Personnel Administrator* (September 1984).

job preview, *see* WORK PREVIEW.

job pricing, determining the dollar value of a particular job.

job range, a measure of the number of different tasks that a job has.

job ranking, also called RANKING, most rudimentary method of job evaluation, which simply ranks jobs in order of their importance to an organization.

job redesign, *see* JOB DESIGN.

job-relatedness, degree to which an applicant appraisal procedure's knowledges,

skills, abilities, and other qualification requirements have been determined to be necessary for successful job performance through a careful job analysis.

job restructuring, also called WORK RESTRUCTURING, element of job analysis that involves the identification of jobs within the context of the system of which they are a part and the analysis and rearrangement of their tasks to achieve a desired purpose. Although the term is relatively new, the concept is familiar. Employers frequently find it necessary to rearrange or adjust the contents (tasks performed) of jobs within a system because of economic conditions, technological changes, and the inability to fill vacant positions, among other reasons. Because the interdependencies and relationships among jobs in a system cannot be ignored, job restructuring should be thought of not as changing one job but rather as rearranging the contents of jobs within a system. *See* Manpower Administration, U.S. Department of Labor, *A Handbook for Job Restructuring* (Washington, D.C.: U.S. Government Printing Office, 1970); Leonard A. Schlesinger and Richard E. Walton, "The Process of Work Restructuring, and Its Impact on Collective Bargaining," *Monthly Labor Review* (April 1977); Ernesto J. Poza and M. Lynn Markus, "Success Story: The Team Approach to Work Restructuring," *Organizational Dynamics* (Winter 1980); William A. Pasmore, "Overcoming the Roadblocks in Work-Restructuring Efforts," *Organizational Dynamics* (Spring 1982).

job rotation, transfer of a worker from one assignment to another in order to minimize boredom and/or enhance skills. *See* Martin J. Gannon, Brian A. Poole, and Robert E. Prangley, "Involuntary Job Rotation and Worker Behavior," *Personnel Journal* (June 1972).

job sample, *see* WORK SAMPLE.

job sampling, *see* WORK SAMPLING.

job satisfaction, the totality of an employee's feelings about the various aspects of his or her work; an emotional appraisal of whether one's job lives up to one's values. *See* Edwin A. Locke, "The Nature and Causes of Job Satisfaction," in Marvin D. Dunnette, ed., *Handbook of Industrial and Organizational Psychology* (Chicago: Rand McNally, 1976); Philip Janson and Jack K. Martin, "Job Satisfaction and Age: A Test of Two Views," *Social Forces* (June 1982); Jack F. McKenna and Paul L. Oritt, "Job Dissatisfaction: A Social Disease," *Business and Society* (Winter-Spring 1981-82); A. Chelte, J. Wright, and C. Tausky, "Did Job Satisfaction Really Drop During the 1970's?" *Monthly Labor Review* (November 1982).

job scope, also CYCLE TIME, relative complexity of a particular task. This is usually reflected by the *cycle time*—the time it takes to complete the task.

job security, presence of safeguards that protect an employee from capricious assignments, demotion, or discharge. *See* Edward Yemin, "Job Security: Influence of ILO Standards and Recent Trends," *International Labour Review* (January-February 1976); Frederick V. Fox and Barry M. Staw, "The Trapped Administrator: Effects of Job Insecurity and Policy Resistance on Commitment to a Course of Action," *Administrative Science Quarterly* (September 1979); Kevin Williams and David Lewis, "Legislating for Job Security: The British Experience of Reinstatement and Reengagement," *Employee Relations Law Journal* (Winter 1982-83); James F. Bolt, "Job Security: Its Time Has Come," *Harvard Business Review* (November-December 1983); Marta Mooney, "Let's Use Job Security as a Productivity Builder," *Personnel Administrator* (February 1984).

job-sharing, concept that has two persons—each working part-time—sharing the same job. *See* Barney Olmsted, "Job-Sharing—A New Way to Work," *Personnel Journal* (February 1977); Gretl S. Meier, *Job Sharing: A New Pattern for Quality of Work and Life* (Kalamazoo,

Mich.: W. E. Upjohn Institute for Employment Research, 1979); Michael Frease and Robert A. Zawacki, "Job-Sharing: An Answer to Productivity Problems," *The Personnel Administrator* (October 1979); Patricia Lee, *The Complete Guide to Job Sharing* (New York: Walker and Co., 1983).

See also WORKSHARING.

job specifications, *see* SPECIFICATION.

job spoiler, *see* RATEBUSTER.

Job Training Partnership Act of 1983, *see* COMPREHENSIVE EMPLOYMENT AND TRAINING ACT OF 1973.

job upgrading, reclassifying a position from a lower to a higher classification.

job vacancy, also JOB-VACANCY RATE, an available job for which an organization is actively seeking to recruit a worker. The *job-vacancy rate* is the ratio of the number of job vacancies to the sum of actual employment plus job vacancies. *See* Daniel Creamer, *Measuring Job Vacancies* (New York: National Industrial Conference Board, 1967).

Johari Window, model, frequently used in laboratory training, for examining the mirror image of one's self. The window, developed by Joseph Luft and Harry Ingham (Joe + Harry = Johari), consists of the following four quadrants:
1. The first quadrant, the *public self*, contains knowledge that is known to both the subject and others.
2. The second quadrant, the *blind self*, contains knowledge that is known to others and unknown to the subject.
3. The third quadrant, the *private self*, contains all of those things that a subject keeps secret.
4. The fourth quadrant, the *unknown area*, contains information that neither the subject nor others know.

The Johari Window model is usually used as a visual aid for explaining the concepts of interpersonal feedback and disclosure. *See* Joseph Luft, *Group Processes: An Introduction to Group Dynamics* (Palo Alto, Calif.: National Press Books, 1963).

joint bargaining, two or more unions united to negotiate with a single employer.

joint committee, *see* SELECT COMMITTEE.

joint council, labor-management committee established to resolve disputes arising during the life of a contract.

Joint Funding Simplification Act of 1974, federal legislation that seeks to enable states, local governments, and other public or private organizations and agencies to use federal assistance more effectively by drawing upon resources from more than one federal agency, program, or appropriation. The act encourages federal-state arrangements to combine state and federal resources in support of projects of common interest.

joint resolution, a resolution that requires the approval of both houses of Congress and the signature of the president, just as a bill does, and that has the force of law if approved. There is no real difference between a bill and a joint resolution. The latter is generally used in dealing with limited matters, such as a single appropriation for a specific purpose.

joint training, training program that brings management and union officials together in a learning situation focusing on some aspect of labor relations.

***Jones and Laughlin* decision,** *see* NATIONAL LABOR RELATIONS BOARD V. JONES AND LAUGHLIN STEEL CORP.

Journal of Applied Behavioral Science, quarterly directed at those interested in inducing social/organizational changes by means of the behavioral sciences.
Journal of Applied Behavioral Science
Editorial Address:
NTL Institute for Applied Behavioral Science

P.O. Box 9155
Rosslyn Station
Arlington, VA 22209
Subscriptions:
36 Sherwood Place
P.O. Box 1678
Greenwich, CT 06836

Journal of Collective Negotiations in the Public Sector, quarterly that emphasizes practical strategies for resolving impasses and preventing strikes in the public sector.
Journal of Collective Negotiations in the Public Sector
Baywood Publishing Company
120-17 Marine Street
P. O. Box D
Farmingdale, NY 11735

Journal of Counseling and Development, monthly journal of the American Association for Counseling and Development which publishes articles of common interest to counselors and personnel workers in schools, colleges, community agencies, and government.
Journal of Counseling and Development
5999 Stevenson Avenue
Alexandria, VA 22304

Journal of Human Resources, quarterly that provides a forum for analysis of the role of education and training in enhancing production skills, employment opportunities, and income, as well as of manpower, health, and welfare policies as they relate to the labor market and to economic and social development. It gives priority to studies having empirical content.
Journal of Human Resources
Editorial Office:
Social Science Building
1180 Observatory Drive
Madison, WI 53706
Subscriptions and Advertising Office:
Journals Department
The University of Wisconsin Press
114 North Murray Street
Madison, WI 53701

Journal of Policy Analysis and Management, scholarly quarterly, the official publication of the Association for Public Policy and Management and the successor journal to both *Public Policy* and *Policy Analysis*.

Editorial address
Professor Raymond Vernon
Journal of Policy Analysis and Management
John F. Kennedy School of Government
Harvard University
Cambridge, MA 02138
Subscriptions
John Wiley & Sons
605 Third Avenue
New York, NY 10158

Journal of Political Economy, the bimonthly journal of the Department of Economics and the Graduate School of Business of the University of Chicago.
Editorial Address:
Editor of the *Journal of Political Economy*
1126 East 59th Street
Chicago, IL 60637
Subscriptions:
University of Chicago Press
Journals Division
P.O. Box 37005
Chicago, IL 60637

Journal of Public Policy, quarterly of public policy analysis that offers an international, interdisciplinary perspective.
Cambridge University Press
32 East 47th Street
New York, NY 10022

journeyman, also called JOURNEY WORKER, originally one of the three grades of workers recognized by the medieval guilds—masters, journeymen, and apprentices. The journeyman had completed apprenticeship training and was considered a fully skilled worker who was eligible to be hired by a master and receive specified wages. A master was a journeyman who was enterprising enough to "open his own store" and hire others as journeymen and apprentices.

Today, a *journey worker* (the desexed designation) is any worker who has completed a specified training program as an apprentice in learning a trade or craft or who can provide evidence of having spent a number of years qualifying for his/her trade or craft.

journeyman pay, also called JOURNEYMAN RATE and UNION SCALE, minimum wages paid to all journeymen/journey workers in a given community. Craft unions tend to refer to this minimum rate of pay as union scale.

Joy Silk Mills **v.** *National Labor Relations Board,* 185 F. 2d 732, decision of the U.S. Court of Appeals which held that a company would have to bargain with a union that lost a representation election if it could be shown that the union's loss of strength was due to the employer's coercive activities. The decision was indirectly upheld by the U.S. Supreme Court when it denied certiorari in the case, 341 U.S. 914 (1951). For an analysis, *see* William A. Krupman, "The Joy Silk Rule—The Courts Weave A New Fabric," *Labor Law Journal* (October 1968).

judge, judicial officer who has been elected or appointed to preside over a court of law, whose position has been created by statute or by constitution, and whose decisions in criminal and juvenile cases may only be reviewed by a judge of a higher court and may not be reviewed de novo.

judicial officer, any person exercising judicial powers in a court of law.

judicial review, power of the U.S. Supreme Court to declare actions by the president or the Congress to be invalid or unconstitutional; any court's power to review legislative acts or decisions of lower courts (or quasi-judicial entities such as arbitration panels) in order to either confirm or overturn them. It was first asserted by the Supreme Court in *Marbury* v. *Madison,* 1 Cranch 137 (1803). *See* Jesse H. Chopper, *Judicial Review and the National Political Process* (University of Chicago Press, 1980).

See also the following entries:

ABBOTT LABORATORIES V. GARDNER
DUNLOP V. BACHOWSKI
FEDERAL TRADE COMMISSION V. SPERRY
HUTCHINSON COMPANY
MARBURY V. MADISON

judiciary, the courts in general.

jurisdiction, either (1) a union's exclusive right to represent particular workers within specified industrial, occupational, or geographical boundaries, or (2) a territory, subject matter, or person over which lawful authority may be exercised.

jurisdictional dispute, disagreement between two unions over which should control a particular job or activity. *See* F. Bruce Simmons III, "Jurisdictional Disputes: Does the Board Really Snub the Supreme Court?" *Labor Law Journal* (March 1985).
See also UNITED STATES V. HUTCHESON.

jurisdictional strike, strike that results when two unions have a dispute over whose members should perform a particular task and one or the other strikes in order to gain its way. For example, both electricians and carpenters may claim the right to do the same task at a construction site. Because the employer is caught in the middle, the Labor-Management Relations (Taft-Hartley) Act of 1947 makes jurisdictional strikes illegal.
See also STRIKE and UNFAIR LABOR PRACTICES (UNIONS).

jury-duty pay, the practice of giving employees leave with pay if they are called to jury duty. Many organizations reduce such pay by the amount the employee is paid by the court for jury service. *See* T. J. Halatin and Jack D. Eure, Jr., "What to Do About Employee Absences for Jury Duty," *Supervisory Management* (May 1981).
See also DEAN V. GADSDEN TIMES PUBLISHING CORP.

Justice, Department of, cabinet-level department of the U.S. federal government. As the largest law firm in the nation, the Department of Justice is supposed to represent the citizens of the United States in enforcing the law in the public interest. The department conducts all suits in the Supreme Court in which the U.S. is concerned. It represents the government in legal matters generally, rendering legal advice and opinions, upon request, to the president and to the heads of the executive departments. The attorney general supervises and directs these activities, as well as those of the U.S. attorneys and U.S. marshals in the various judicial districts around the country.

Department of Justice
Constitution Avenue and Tenth Street, N.W.
Washington, D.C. 20530
(202) 633-2000

K

Kafkaesque, bureaucratic to a ridiculous extreme. Franz Kafka's (1883-1924) novels and short stories often dealt with the theme of bureaucratic frustration.

Kahn, Robert L. (1918-   ), psychologist and a leading authority on organizational behavior. Major works include: *The Dynamics of Interviewing,* with Charles F. Cannell (New York: John Wiley, 1957); *Organizational Stress: Studies in Role Conflict and Ambiguity,* with others (New York: Wiley, 1964); *The Social Psychology of Organizations,* 2nd ed., with Daniel Katz (New York: John Wiley, 1978).

Kaiser Aluminum & Chemical Corp. v. Weber, et al., *see* UNITED STEELWORKERS OF AMERICA V. WEBER, ET AL.

Katz, Daniel (1903-   ), psychologist and a leading authority on organizational behavior. Major works include: *Bureaucratic Encounters : A Pilot Study in the Evaluation of Government Services* (Ann Arbor, Mich.: Institute for Social Research,

University of Michigan, 1975); *The Social Psychology of Organizations*, 2nd ed., with Robert L. Kahn (New York: John Wiley, 1978).

Kaufman, Herbert (1922-   ), a major voice in public administration who wrote the classic study of administrative behavior in the U.S. Forest Service, *The Forest Ranger: A Study in Administrative Behavior* (Baltimore: Johns Hopkins Press, 1960). Other major works include: "Emerging Conflicts in the Doctrines of Public Administration," *American Political Science Review* (December 1956); *Governing New York City*, with Wallace S. Sayre (New York: W. W. Norton, 1960); *Politics and Policies in State and Local Government* (Englewood Cliffs, N.J.: Prentice-Hall, 1963); "Organization Theory and Political Theory," *American Political Science Review* (March 1964); "Administrative Decentralization and Political Power," *Public Administration Review* (January-February 1969); *The Limits of Organizational Change* (University, Ala.: University of Alabama Press, 1971); *Administrative Feedback: Monitoring Subordinates' Behavior* (Washington, D.C.: The Brookings Institution, 1973); *Are Government Organizations Immortal?* (Washington, D.C.: The Brookings Institution, 1976); *Red Tape: Its Origins, Uses, and Abuses* (Washington, D.C.: The Brookings Institution, 1977); *The Administrative Behavior of Federal Bureau Chiefs* (Washington, D.C.: Brookings Institution, 1981).

Kelley v. *Johnson,* 425 U.S. 238 (1976), U.S. Supreme Court case which upheld a municipal regulation limiting the hair length of police.

Keogh Plan, also called H.R. 10 PLAN, the Self-Employed Individuals Tax Retirement Act of 1962 which encourages the establishment of voluntary pension plans by self-employed individuals. Congressman Eugene J. Keogh was the prime sponsor of the Act. H.R. 10 was the number assigned to the bill prior to its passage.

Kepner-Tregoe model, a model for organizational decision making that includes four major components: (1) situational appraisal, (2) problem analysis, (3) decision analysis, and (4) potential problem analysis. See C. H. Kepner and B. B. Tregoe, *The New Rational Manager* (Princeton, N.J.: Kepner-Tregoe, Inc., 1981).

Kerr-Mills, popular name for the Social Security Amendments of 1960 which expanded and modified the federal government's existing responsibility for assisting the states in paying for medical care for the aged poor.

Kestnbaum Commission, the Commission on Intergovernmental Relations created (in 1953) by President Eisenhower and chaired by Meyer Kestnbaum whose report (submitted in 1955) led to the creation of the permanent Advisory Commission on Intergovernmental Relations in 1959.

Key, V. O. Jr. (1908-1963), political scientist who did pioneering work in developing more empirical methods to explore political and administrative behavior. Major works include: "Police Graft," *American Journal of Sociology* (March 1935); "The Lack of a Budgetary Theory," *American Political Science Review* (December 1940); *Politics, Parties and Pressure Groups* (New York: Crowell, 1942; 5th ed., 1964); *Southern Politics in State and Nation* (New York: Knopf, 1949); *A Primer of Statistics for Political Scientists* (New York: Crowell, 1954); *American State Politics: An Introduction* (New York: Knopf, 1956); *Public Opinion and American Democracy* (New York: Knopf, 1961); *The Responsible Electorate*, edited by Milton C. Cummings, Jr. (Cambridge, Mass.: Harvard University Press, 1966). This last work was published posthumously.

key classes, occupations or positions for which data are gathered from other employers (via a salary survey) in order to serve as a basis for establishing wage rates.

Keyishian v. *Board of Regents,* 385 U.S. 589 (1967), U.S. Supreme Court case which held that laws "which make Communist Party membership, as such, prima facie evidence of disqualification for employment in the public school system are overbroad and therefore unconstitutional."

Keynes, John Maynard (1883-1946), English economist who wrote the most influential book on economics of this century, *The General Theory of Employment, Interest and Money* (London: Macmillan, 1936). Keynes founded a school of thought known as *Keynesian economics,* which called for using a government's fiscal and monetary policies to positively influence a capitalistic economy, and developed the framework of modern macroeconomic theory. Keynes observed that "practical men, who believe themselves to be quite exempt from any intellectual influences, are usually the slaves of some defunct economist" and provided the definitive economic forecast when he asserted that "in the long run we are all dead." For biography, see Robert Lekachman, *The Age of Keynes* (New York: Random House, 1975); John Fender, *Understanding Keynes: An Analysis of "The General Theory"* (New York: Wiley, 1981); Charles H. Hession, *John Maynard Keynes: A Personal Biography of the Man Who Revolutionized Capitalism and the Way We Lived* (New York: Macmillan, 1984). *Also see* Amar Bhide, "Beyond Keynes: Demand-Side Economics," *Harvard Business Review* (July-August 1983); James Tobin, "A Keynesian View of the Budget Deficit," *California Management Review* (Winter 1984).

kickback, money extorted from employees or contractors by employers or third parties who threaten to sever the employment relationship. Most kickbacks are obviously unethical if not illegal. The Anti-Kickback Act of 1934 (or the Copeland Act, as amended) prohibits kickbacks by federal contractors and subcontractors.

kicked upstairs, slang term for the removal of an individual from a position where his or her performance is not thought satisfactory by promoting him or her to a higher position in the organization.

kick-in-the-ass motivation, *see* KITA.

Kingsley, J. Donald (1908-), formerly Director-General of the United Nations' International Refugee Organization, co-author of the first full-scale text on public personnel administration, and creator of the concept "representative bureaucracy." Major works include: *Public Personnel Administration,* with William E. Mosher (New York: Harper & Bros., 1936); *Representative Bureaucracy: An Interpretation of the British Civil Service* (Yellow Springs, Ohio: Antioch Press, 1944).

Kirkland, Lane (1922-), president of the AFL-CIO beginning in 1979.

Kirkland v. *New York State Department of Correctional Services,* federal court of appeals case, 520 F. 2d 420 (2d Cir. 1975), cert. denied, 429 U.S. 974 (1976), which dealt with the permissible range of remedies for illegal employment discrimination. While approving portions of a lower court ruling ordering New York State to develop an unbiased, job-related test for hiring correctional officials and instituting temporary hiring and promotion quotas until such a test could be developed, the appeals court overturned the portion of the order requiring a "permanent" quota to be followed until members of minority groups reached a specified proportion of correctional sergeants. *See* Roscoe W. Wisner, "The Kirkland Case—Its Implications for Personnel Selection," *Public Personnel Management* (July-August 1975).

KITA, acronym used by Frederick Herzberg to refer to "kick-in-the-ass" attempts at worker motivation. Variants of KITA include "negative physical KITA" (literally using physical force); "negative psychological KITA" (hurting someone with a psychic blow); and "positive KITA" (offering rewards for performance). Herzberg states that KITA cannot create motivation; its only ability is to create movement. *See* Frederick Herzberg, "One More Time: How Do You Motivate Employees?" *Harvard Business Review* (January-February 1968).

kitchen cabinet, informal advisors of a chief executive. First used as a derisive term for some of President Andrew Jackson's advisors. The word "kitchen" originally implied that such advisors were not respectable enough to visit in the more formal rooms of the White House. Over the years the term has lost its derisive quality.

knowledge, understanding of facts or principles relating to a particular subject or subject area.

knowledge worker, Peter F. Drucker's term, in *The New Society: The Anatomy of Industrial Order* (New York: Harper Torchbooks, 1949, 1962), for the largest and most rapidly growing group in the working population of the developed countries, especially the United States.

It is a group of "workers" though it will never identify itself with the "proletariat," and will always consider itself "middle-class" if not "part of management." And it is an independent group because it owns the one essential resource of production: knowledge. . . . It is this group whose emergence makes ours a "new" society. Never before has any society had the means to educate large numbers of its citizens, nor the opportunities for them to make their education productive. Our society however, cannot get enough educated people, nor can it really effectively utilize any other resource but the educated man who works with his knowledge rather than with his animal strength or his manual skill.

Also see Donald B. Miller, "How to Improve the Performance and Productivity of the Knowledge Worker," *Organizational Dynamics* (Winter 1977); Edward Mandt, "Managing the Knowledge Worker of the Future," *Personnel Journal* (March 1978).

See also DRUCKER, PETER.

Krislov, Samuel (1929-), constitutional law scholar who is best known outside of that field for his analyses of the link between broader political questions of representative bureaucracy and those emanating from equal employment opportunity concerns. Major works include: *The Negro in Federal Employment: The Quest for Equal Opportunity* (University of Minnesota Press, 1967); *The Supreme Court and Political Freedom* (New York: The Free Press, 1968); *The Judicial Process and Constitutional Law* (Boston: Little, Brown, 1972); *Representative Bureaucracy* (Englewood Cliffs, N.J.: Prentice-Hall, 1974); *Representative Bureaucracy and the American Political System*, with David H. Rosenbloom (New York: Praeger, 1981).

L

labor, collective term for an organization's work force exclusive of management.

See also the following entries:
    CASUAL LABOR
    CHILD LABOR
    CONTRACT LABOR
    DIRECT LABOR
    DIVISION OF LABOR
    SKILLED LABOR

Labor, Department of (DOL), U.S. federal agency whose purpose is to foster, promote, and develop the welfare of the wage earners of the United States, to improve their working conditions, and to advance their opportunities for profitable employment. In carrying out this mission, DOL administers more than 130 federal labor laws guaranteeing workers' rights to safe and healthful working conditions, a minimum hourly wage and overtime pay, unemployment insurance, workers' compensation, and freedom from employment discrimination. DOL also protects workers' pension rights, sponsors job training programs, helps workers find jobs, works to strengthen free collective bargaining, and keeps track of changes in employment, prices, and other national economic measurements.

Department of Labor
200 Constitution Ave., N.W.
Washington, D.C. 20210
(202) 523-8165

labor agreement, formal results achieved by collective bargaining. *See* Arnold M. Zack and Richard I. Block, *Labor Agreement in Negotiation and Arbitration* (Washington, D.C.: BNA Books, 1983); James Suchan and Clyde Scott, "Readability Levels of Collective Bargaining Agreements," *Personnel Administrator* (November 1984).

laboratory education, also called LABO-RATORY METHOD, method of learning about human behavior through experiencing group activities. According to Clayton P. Alderfer, in "Understanding Laboratory Education: An Overview," *Monthly Labor Review* (December 1970):

the various forms of laboratory education include a number of common elements such as acceptance of experience-based learning technology, recognition of the role of emotions in human relationships, and utilization of the small group (10 to 12 persons) as a central component in training designs.

The learning laboratory usually takes place on a "cultural island." Participants are taken away from their normal day-to-day activities to a setting where the learning experiences occur. Frequently this new setting is naturally beautiful, but at the very least it is different and thereby provides the participant with both safety from former distractions and a setting that does not necessarily reinforce his usual ways of behaving. A second component of the laboratory involves the use of unstructured or semistructured learning tools. The staff usually attempts to design a set of experiences that serve to heighten certain aspects of human behavior and emotions. Participants learn by becoming actively in-

volved in these activities and by developing skills which allow them to observe both themselves and others during these experiences. A person is asked to engage himself in the unfolding events and later to step back and try to see the patterns in his own and others' behavior. Much of the sense of excitement and high level of emotionality comes from the participant's becoming involved. Experiential learning is based on the assumption that experience precedes intellectual understanding.

laboratory experiment, research method in which a researcher consciously manipulates an independent variable in order to observe the effects of the manipulation on a dependent variable. While a laboratory experiment maximizes control over the research process, it is often questioned in terms of generalizability to normal conditions in the real world.

laboratory training, also SENSITIVITY TRAINING and T-GROUP, generic term for those educational/training experiences that are designed (1) to increase an individual's sensitivity to his/her own motives and behavior, (2) to increase sensitivity to the behavior of others, and (3) to ascertain those elements of interpersonal interactions that either facilitate or impede a group's effectiveness. While laboratory training and *sensitivity training* tend to be used interchangeably, sensitivity training is the subordinate term (being the most common method of laboratory training) and the popular name given to almost all experience-based learning exercises. The basic vehicle for the sensitivity training experience is the *T-Group* (T for Training). According to Chris Argyris, in "T-Groups for Organizational Effectiveness," *Harvard Business Review* (March–April 1964), the T-Group experience is

designed to provide maximum possible opportunity for the individuals to expose their behavior, give and receive feedbacks, experiment with new behavior, and develop everlasting awareness and acceptance of self and others. The T-group, when effective, also provides individuals with the opportunity to learn the nature of effective group functioning. They are able to learn how to develop a group that achieves specific goals with minimum possible human cost.

See Robert T. Golembiewski and Arthur Blumberg, eds., *Sensitivity Training and the Laboratory Approach,* 3rd ed. (Itasca, Ill.: Peacock, 1977); Henry Clay Smith, *Sensitivity Training: The Scientific Understanding of Individuals* (New York: McGraw-Hill, 1973); C. L. Cooper and I. L. Mangham, *T-Groups: A Survey of Research* (New York: Wiley, 1971); Dee G. Appley and Alvin E. Winder, *T-Groups and Therapy Groups in A Changing Society* (San Francisco: Jossey-Bass, 1973); Peter B. Smith, "The T-Group Trainer—Group Facilitator or Prisoner of Circumstance?" *Journal of Applied Behavioral Science* (January-February-March 1980).

See also the following entries:
INSTITUTE FOR APPLIED BEHAVIORAL SCIENCE
INSTRUMENTED LABORATORY
NATIONAL TRAINING LABORATORIES
ROLE
TRAINERLESS LABORATORY

labor certification, certification by the U.S. Department of Labor which certain aliens (such as foreign medical graduates) seeking to immigrate to the United States in order to work must obtain before they may obtain a visa.

labor cost, that part of the cost of a product or service that is attributable to wages.

labor costs, also UNIT LABOR COST, total expenses an employer must meet in order to retain the services of employees. The *unit labor cost* is the expense for labor divided by the number of units of output produced.

labor costs, indirect, see INDIRECT LABOR COSTS.

labor court, permanent court of industrial arbitration available in some European countries to settle labor disputes. See

Joseph J. Shutkin, "One Nation Indivisible—A Plea for a U.S. Court of Labor Relations," *Labor Law Journal* (February 1969).

Labor Day, U.S. holiday. In 1894, the U.S. Congress mandated that the first Monday after the first Tuesday in September would be a federal holiday honoring the nation's workers.

labor dispute, according to Section 2(9) of the National Labor Relations Act, as amended, term that covers
any controversy concerning terms, tenure or conditions of employment, or concerning the association or representation of persons in negotiating, fixing, maintaining, changing, or seeking to arrange terms or conditions of employment.

See also LAUF V. E. G. SHINNER AND COMPANY and LINN V. UNITED PLANT GUARD WORKERS.

labor economics, the subfield of economics concerned with wages and the supply/allocation of manpower. See F. Ray Marshall, Vernon M. Briggs, Jr., and Allan G. King, *Labor Economics: Wages, Employment, Trade Unionism and Public Policy,* 5th ed. (Homewood, Ill.: Richard D. Irwin, 1984); Gordon F. Bloom and Herbert R. Northrup, *Economics of Labor Relations* 9th ed. (Homewood, Ill.: Richard D. Irwin, 1981); Paul J. McNulty, *The Origins and Development of Labor Economics* (Cambridge, MA: MIT Press, 1980). Robert M. Fearn, *Labor Economics: The Emerging Synthesis* (Cambridge, Mass.: Winthrop Publishers, 1981). For a how-to approach, see George S. Odiorne, "How to Become Your Company's Labor Economist," *Management of Personnel Quarterly* (Spring 1968).

labor force, also CIVILIAN LABOR FORCE and TOTAL LABOR FORCE, according to the Bureau of Labor Statistics, all employed or unemployed persons in the civilian non-institutional population. The *total labor force* includes military personnel.

Persons not in the labor force are those not classified as employed or unemployed; this group includes persons retired, those engaged in their own housework, those not working while attending school, those unable to work because of long-term illness, those discouraged from seeking work because of personal or job market factors, and those who are voluntarily idle. The noninstitutional population comprises all persons sixteen years and older who are not inmates of penal or mental institutions, sanitariums, or homes for the aged, infirm, or needy. See Howard N. Fullerton, Jr. and Paul O. Flaim, "New Labor Force Projections to 1990," *Monthly Labor Review* (December 1976); H. N. Fullerton, Jr. and J. Tschetter, "The 1995 Labor Force: A Second Look," *Monthly Labor Review* (November 1983).

labor-force participation, rate at which a given group (women, blacks, handicapped, etc.) is represented (either nationally, regionally, or locally) in the labor force.

labor grade, one of a series of steps in a wage rate structure established by a process of job evaluation or collective bargaining.

labor injunction, see INJUNCTION and BOYS MARKET V. RETAIL CLERKS' LOCAL 770.

labor intensive, any production process requiring a large proportion of human effort relative to capital investment.

labor law, body of law applied to concerns of employment, wages, conditions of work, unions, labor-management relations, etc. See Ronald A. Wykstra and Eleanour V. Stevens, *Labor Law and Public Policy* (New York: Odyssey Press, 1970); Benjamin J. Taylor and Fred Witney, *Labor Relations Law,* 4th ed. (Englewood Cliffs, N.J.: Prentice-Hall, 1983); Bruce Feldacker, *Labor Guide to Labor Law,* 2nd ed. (Reston, Va.: Reston/Prentice-Hall, 1983); James B. Atleson, *Values and Assumptions in American Labor Law* (Amherst: The

University of Massachusetts Press, 1983); Benjamin Aaron, "Future Trends in Industrial Relations Law," *Industrial Relations* (Winter 1984).

Labor Law Journal, monthly devoted to legislative, administrative, and judicial developments pertaining to legal problems in the labor field.
   Editorial Address:
   Editor, *Labor Law Journal*
   Suite 1100
   1301 Pennsylvania Ave., N.W.
   Washington, D.C. 20004
   Subscriptions:
   Commerce Clearing House, Inc.
   4025 W. Peterson Ave.
   Chicago, IL 60646

labor-management relations, general term referring to the formal and informal dealings and agreements between employees or employee organizations and managers.

Labor-Management Relations Act of 1947 (LMRA), also called TAFT-HARTLEY ACT, federal statute that modified what the Congress thought was a pro-union bias in the National Labor Relations (Wagner) Act of 1935. Essentially a series of amendments to the National Labor Relations Act, Taft-Hartley provided:
   1. that "National Emergency Strikes" could be put off for an eighty-day cooling-off period during which the president might make recommendations to Congress for legislation that might cope with the dispute;
   2. a list of unfair labor practices by unions, which balanced the list of unfair labor practices by employers delineated in the Wagner Act;
   3. that the "closed shop" was illegal (this provision allowed states to pass "right-to-work" laws);
   4. that supervisory employees be excluded from coverage under the act;
   5. that suits against unions for contract violations were allowable (judgments enforceable only against union assets);
   6. that a party seeking to cancel an

existing collective bargaining agreement is required to give sixty days' notice;

7. that employers have the right to seek a representation election if a union claimed recognition as a bargaining agent;

8. that the National Labor Relations Board be reorganized and enlarged from three to five members; and

9. that the Federal Mediation and Conciliation Service be created to mediate labor disputes.

The Taft-Hartley Act was passed over the veto of President Truman.

See also NATIONAL LABOR RELATIONS BOARD V. WOOSTER DIVISION OF BORG-WARNER CORP. and UNFAIR LABOR PRACTICES (UNIONS).

Labor-Management Reporting and Disclosure Act of 1959, also called LANDRUM-GRIFFIN ACT, federal statute enacted in response to findings of corruption in the management of some unions. The purpose of the act is to provide for

the reporting and disclosure of certain financial transactions and administrative practices of labor organizations and employers, to prevent abuses in the administration of trusteeships by labor organizations, to provide standards with respect to the election of officers of labor organizations and for other purposes.

Congress determined that certain basic rights should be assured to members of labor unions, and these are listed in Title I of the act as a Bill of Rights. Existing rights and remedies of union members under other federal or state laws, before any court or tribunal, or under the constitution and bylaws of their unions are not limited by the provisions of Title I. Executive Order 11491 made these rights applicable to members of unions representing employees of the executive branch of the federal government.

Titles II through VI of the act deal primarily with the following: reporting by unions, by union officers and employees, by employers, by labor relations consultants, and by surety companies; union trusteeships; union safeguards. The Secre-

tary of Labor has varying administrative and enforcement responsibilities under these titles. In addition, Titles II through VI contain a number of criminal provisions which involve enforcement responsibilities of the U.S. Department of Justice. Title VII contains amendments to the Labor-Management Relations Act of 1947.

See Doris B. McLaughin and Anita L. W. Schoomaker, *The Landrum-Griffin Act and Union Democracy* (Ann Arbor: University of Michigan Press, 1978); Janice R. Bellace and Alan D. Berkowitz, *The Landrum-Griffin Act: Twenty Years of Federal Protection of Union Members' Rights* (Philadelphia: Wharton School, University of Pennsylvania, 1979); John Lawler, "Wage Spillover: The Impact of Landrum-Griffin," *Industrial Relations* (Winter 1981).

See also the following entries:
AMERICAN FEDERATION OF MUSICIANS V. WITTSTEIN
TRUSTEESHIP

Labor-Management Services Administration (LMSA), agency of the U.S. Department of Labor that provides a framework within which workers and employees can resolve their differences together. It helps both labor and management through special studies of collective bargaining problems and research on labor-management policy development. Unions are required to make annual reports to it and to comply with standards for union elections under the Labor-Management Reporting and Disclosure Act of 1959. Under the Employee Retirement Income Security Act of 1974, the agency administers reporting and disclosure, fiduciary, and minimum standards that protect the benefits and rights of pension and welfare plan participants and beneficiaries. LMSA also administers the veterans' reemployment rights provisions of the Veterans' Readjustment Assistance Act of 1974 and similar earlier laws.

LMSA
Department of Labor
200 Constitution Ave., N.W.
Washington, D.C. 20210
(202) 523-6231

labor market, according to Everett Johnson Burtt, Jr., in *Labor Markets, Unions, and Government Policies* (New York: St. Martin's Press, 1963),

consists of those forces of demand and supply that establish a single price and the quantity sold of a particular labor service. Most labor markets can be defined spatially as local in character: the supply of machinists in Springfield, Vermont, for example, does not influence the price of machinists in Cleveland, Ohio. National markets can, however, be said to exist for some occupations, such as transistor engineers, airplane pilots, or certain types of government administrators. The factors determining the geographical size of a labor market depend upon the concentration demand in certain centers and upon the degree of mobility of labor supplies.

See Paul D. Montagna, *Occupations and Society: Toward A Sociology of the Labor Market* (New York: John Wiley & Sons, 1977); Ivar Berg, ed., *Sociological Perspectives on Labor Markets* (New York: Academic Press, 1981); R. Bednarzik and R. Tiler, "Area Labor Market Response to National Unemployment Patterns," *Monthly Labor Review* (January 1982); Denis Maillat, "Mobility Channels: An Instrument for Analyzing and Regulating the Local Labour Market," *International Labour Review* (May–June 1984).

See also the following entries:
EFFECTIVE LABOR MARKET
EXTERNAL LABOR MARKET
SPLIT LABOR MARKET

labor mobility, degree of ease with which workers can change jobs and occupations.

labor monopoly, dominance over the supply of labor by a union or group of unions.

labor movement, inclusive term for the progressive history of U.S. unionism. Sometimes it is used in a broader sense to encompass the fate of the "workers." For histories, *see* Leon Litwack, *The American Labor Movement* (Englewood Cliffs, N.J.:

Prentice-Hall, 1962); Joel Seidman, "The Labor Movement Today: A Diagnosis," *Monthly Labor Review* (February 1965); Jack Barbash, "Labor Movement Theory and the Institutional Setting," *Monthly Labor Review* (September 1981); Maurice F. Neufeld, "The Persistence of Ideas in the American Labor Movement: The Heritage of the 1830s," *Industrial and Labor Relations Review* (January 1982).

labor organization, as defined by Section 2(5) of the National Labor Relations act (as amended), a labor organization

means any organization of any kind, or any agency or employee representation committee or plan, in which employees participate and which exists for the purpose, in whole or part, of dealing with employers concerning grievances, labor disputes, wages, rates of pay, hours of employment, or conditions of work.

For the names, sizes, addresses, phone numbers, etc., of all U.S. labor organizations, *see* Courtney D. Gifford, *Directory of U.S. Labor Organizations: 1984–85 Edition* (Washington, D.C.: Bureau of National Affairs, Inc., 1984).

labor organizer, *see* ORGANIZER.

labor piracy, attracting employees away from one organization and into another by offering better wages and other benefits.

labor pool, set of trained workers from which prospective employees are recruited.

labor racketeer, broad term that applies to a union leader who uses his/her office as a base for unethical and illegal activities. For a history, *see* John Hutchinson, *The Imperfect Union: A History of Corruption in American Trade Unions* (New York: E. P. Dutton & Co., 1972).

See also ANTI-RACKETEERING ACT OF 1934 and UNFAIR LABOR PRACTICES (UNIONS).

labor relations, totality of the interactions between an organization's management and organized labor. For texts, *see* Gordon F. Bloom and Herbert R. Northrup,

THE LABOR RELATIONS LEGAL SYSTEM

Sector	Legal Base	Administrative Agency
Private industry	National Labor Relations Act, as amended	National Labor Relations Board
Railroads and airlines	Railway Labor Act, as amended	National Mediation Board
Postal Service	Postal Reorganization Act of 1970	National Labor Relations Board
Federal government	Civil Service Reform Act of 1978	Federal Labor Relations Authority
State and local government	Public employee relations acts	Public employment relations boards

Economics of Labor Relations, 9th ed. (Homewood, Ill.: Richard D. Irwin, 1981); John A. Fossum, *Labor Relations: Development, Structure, Process* (Dallas: Business Publications, 1982); Edward E. Herman and Alfred Kuhn, *Collective Bargaining and Labor Relations* (Englewood Cliffs, N.J.: Prentice-Hall, 1981); Raymond D. Horton, *Municipal Labor Relations in New York City: Lessons of the Lindsay-Wagner Years* (New York: Praeger, 1973); Hugh D. Jascourt, ed., *Government Labor Relations* (Oak Park, Ill.: Moore Publishing, 1979); David Lewin, Peter Feuille, and Thomas A. Kochan, eds., *Public Sector Labor Relations: Analysis and Readings* (Sun Lakes, Ariz.: Thomas Horton & Daughters, 1982); Murray B. Nesbitt, *Labor Relations in the Federal Government Service* (Washington, D.C.: Bureau of National Affairs, 1976); David H. Rosenbloom and Jay M. Shafritz, *Essentials of Labor Relations* (Reston, Va.: Reston/Prentice-Hall, 1985); Arthur A. Sloane and Fred Witney, *Labor Relations,* 4th ed. (Englewood Cliffs, N.J.: Prentice-Hall, 1981); Russel A. Smith, Harry T. Edwards, and R. Theodore Clark, Jr., *Labor Relations Law in the Public Sector* (Indianapolis: Bobbs-Merrill, 1974).

See also COLLECTIVE BARGAINING.

labor reserve, general term that refers to potential members of the work force. Historically the concept has been applied to the least skilled and the least able. For a modern definition, see Christopher G.

Gellner, "Enlarging the Concept of a Labor Reserve," *Monthly Labor Review* (April 1975).

labor slowdown, see SLOWDOWN.

Labor Statistics, Bureau of, see BUREAU OF LABOR STATISTICS.

labor studies, formal academic degree concentrations or certificate programs concerned with the various aspects of labor relations. See Lois S. Gray, "Academic Degrees for Labor Studies—A New Goal for Unions," *Monthly Labor Review* (1977).

Labor Studies Journal, journal published three times a year by the University and College Labor Education Association which offers articles and reviews on all aspects of labor studies.

Labor Studies Journal
Subscription Address:
Transaction Periodicals Consortium
Rutgers University
Box L
New Brunswick, NJ 08903
Editorial Address:
George Meany Center for Labor Studies
10,000 New Hampshire Ave.
Silver Springs, MD 20903

labor surplus area, an area of high unemployment for which the federal government sets aside procurement contracts for competition among firms that agree to perform a substantial portion of the production of the contract in the labor surplus area.

labor theory of value, notion that the value of a product is dependent or determined by the amount (or value) of the labor needed to produce it. Karl Marx used this concept (developed earlier by Adam Smith and David Ricardo) to denounce capitalists who exploited the working class by selling products at higher prices than the cost of the labor that went into them.

Laffer curve, purported relationship between tax rates and government revenues "discovered" by economist Arthur B. Laffer. According to Laffer, higher taxes reduce government revenues because high tax rates discourage taxable activity. Following this logic, a government can raise its total revenues by cutting taxes. This should stimulate new taxable activity, and the revenue from this should more than offset the loss from lower tax rates. *See* Michael Kinsley, "Alms for the Rich," *The New Republic* (August 19, 1978); Jude Wanniski, *The Way the World Works* (New York: Simon and Schuster, 1978); Arthur B. Laffer and Jan P. Seymour, *The Economics of the Tax Revolt* (New York: Harcourt Brace Jovanovich, 1979).

laissez-faire, "hands off" style of leadership that emphasizes loose supervision.

Lakewood Plan, *see* SERVICE CONTRACT.

lame duck, in U.S. politics, any office-holder who is serving out the remainder of a fixed term after declining to run, or being defeated, for reelection. Since he/she will soon be leaving, his/her authority is considered impaired or "lame." The term is used in an organizational sense to refer to anyone whose leaving has been announced, whether for retirement, promotion, transfer, etc.

Lame Duck Amendment, the Twentieth Amendment to the Constitution, proclaimed by the Secretary of State on February 6, 1933 to have been ratified by sufficient states to make it a part of the Constitution. This amendment provides, among other things, that the terms of the president and vice president shall end at noon on January 20, the terms of senators and representatives shall end at noon on January 3 instead of March 4, and the terms of their successors shall then begin. Prior to this amendment, the annual session of Congress began on the first Monday in December (Constitution, Art. I, Sec. 4). Since the terms of new members formerly began on March 4, this meant that members who had been defeated or did not stand for reelection in November continued to serve during the "lame duck" session from December through March 4.

Landrum-Griffin Act, *see* LABOR-MANAGEMENT REPORTING AND DISCLOSURE ACT OF 1959.

lapsed funds, unobligated budget authority that by law has ceased to be available for obligation because of the expiration of the period for which it was available.

Lasswell, Harold D. (1902–1978), one of the most influential and prolific of social scientists. While he made major contributions to the fields of communications, psychology, political science, sociology, and law, he may be best known to public administration for having pioneered the concept and methodology of "the policy sciences." Major works include: *Propaganda Technique in World War I* (Cambridege, Mass.: M.I.T. Press, 1927, 1971); *Psychopathology and Politics* (New York: Viking, 1930, 1960); *Politics: Who Gets What, When, How* (New York: Peter Smith, 1936, 1950); *Power and Society,* with Abraham Kaplan (New Haven, Conn.: Yale University Press, 1950, 1963); *The Policy Sciences,* edited with David Lerner (Stanford University Press, 1951, 1968); *Power, Corruption, and Rectitude,* with Arnold A. Rogow (Englewood Cliffs, N.J.: Prentice-Hall, 1963); *Pre-view of Policy Sciences* (New York: American Elsevier, 1971). For an appreciation, *see* Arnold A. Rogow, *Politics, Personality, and Social Science in the Twentieth Century: Essays in Honor of*

Harold D. Lasswell (Chicago: University of Chicago Press, 1969).

last dollar coverage, insurance coverage without upper limits or maximums no matter how great the benefits payable.

last offer arbitration, *see* FINAL OFFER ARBITRATION.

latent learning, *see* INCIDENTAL LEARNING.

lateral entry, appointment of an individual from outside the organization to a position above the bottom level of a generally recognized career ladder.

lateral transfer, *see* TRANSFER.

Lauf* v. *E. G. Shinner and Company, 303 U.S. 323 (1938), U.S. Supreme Court case which held that organizational picketing was a "labor dispute" within the meaning of the Norris-LaGuardia Act of 1932. This meant the employer could not seek an injunction in a federal court to stop the picketing.

law, *see* ACT.

law enforcement agency, federal, state, or local criminal justice agency of which the principal functions are the prevention, detection, and investigation of crime and the apprehension of alleged offenders.

Law Enforcement Assistance Administration (LEAA), federal agency within the Department of Justice that assisted state and local governments in strengthening and improving law enforcement and criminal justice. Projects funded by LEAA touched virtually every aspect of criminal justice and included court administration, organized crime, white collar crime, public corruption, disorders and terrorism, the rehabilitation of offenders, victim assistance, and the implementation of criminal justice standards and goals.

LEAA operations have been closed out and remaining functions transferred to the Office of Justice Assistance.

Lawler, Edward E., III (1938-), psychologist who has written widely in the area of organizational behavior; a leading authority on the relationship between pay and organizational effectiveness. Major works include: *Managerial Attitudes and Performance,* with L. W. Porter (Homewood, Illinois: Richard D. Irwin, 1968); *Managerial Behavior, Performance and Effectiveness,* with J. P. Campbell, M. D. Dunnette, and K. E. Weick, Jr. (New York: McGraw-Hill, 1970); *Pay and Organizational Effectiveness: A Psychological View* (New York: McGraw-Hill, 1971); *Motivation in Work Organizations* (Monterey, California: Brooks/Cole Publishing Company, 1973); *Behavior in Organizations,* with L. W. Porter and J. R. Hackman (New York: McGraw-Hill, 1975).

Lawlor* v. *Loewe, also called DANBURY HATTERS' CASE, 235 U.S. 522 (1908), U.S. Supreme Court case which held that the hatter's union which was seeking to organize a factory in Danbury, Connecticut was in violation of the Sherman Anti-Trust Act of 1890 when it successfully organized a boycott against the company. The court ruled against the union because its boycott had the assistance of other affiliates of the American Federation of Labor and the Sherman Act prohibited "any combination whatever to secure action which essentially obstructs the free flow of commerce between the states, or restricts in that regard, the liberty of a trader to engage in business." The uproar over this decision led to the passage of the Clayton Act of 1914, which disallowed the application of the Sherman Act to combinations of labor.

Law of Bureaucratic Assimilation, law defined as "the length of time in weeks required for the acceptance and internalization of a new idea in a government bureaucracy varies as $T = 2 + 2(n-3)^2$ in which n is the number of individuals or discrete organizational elements involved in agreeing upon the fact and form of the idea and required for its adoption." *See* Robert B. Lee, "The Law of Bureaucratic Assimilation," *Public Administration Review* (March–April 1969).

Law of Effect, fundamental concept in learning theory that holds that, other things being equal, an animal will learn those habits leading to satisfaction and will not learn (or learn only slowly) those habits causing annoyance. It was first formulated by Edward L. Thorndike in *Education: A First Book* (New York: Macmillan, 1920) as follows:

The greater the satisfyingness of the state of affairs which accompanies or follows a given response to a certain situation, the more likely that response is to be made to that situation in the future. Conversely, the greater the discomfort or annoyingness of the state of affairs which comes with or after a response to a situation, the more likely that response is not to be made to that situation in the future.

Law of the Situation, Mary Parker Follett's notion, in Henry C. Metcalf and Lyndall Urwick, eds., *Dynamic Administration The Collected Papers of Mary Parker Follett* (New York: Harper & Bros., 1940), that

one person should not give orders to another person, but both should agree to take their orders from the situation. If orders are simply part of the situation, the question of someone giving and someone receiving does not come up.
See also FOLLETT, MARY PARKER.

Law of Triviality, C. Northcote Parkinson's discovery that "the time spent on any item of the agenda will be in inverse proportion to the sum involved." Parkinson attempted to head off his critics by asserting the statement that this law has never been investigated is not entirely accurate. Some work has actually been done in this field, but the investigators pursued a line of inquiry that led them nowhere. They assumed that the greatest significance should attach to the order in which items of the agenda are taken. They assumed, further, that most of the available time will be spent on

items one to seven and that the latter items will be allowed automatically to pass. The result is well known. . . . We realize now that position on the agenda is a minor consideration.

For more, *see* C. Northcote Parkinson, *Parkinson's Law and other Studies in Administration* (Boston: Houghton Mifflin Co., 1957). For a methodological analysis, *see* Ross Curnow, "An Empirical Examination of the Parkinsonian Law of Triviality," *Public Personnel Review* (January 1971).
See also PARKINSON'S LAW.

layoff, temporary or indefinite separation from employment, without prejudice or loss of seniority, resulting from slack work, a shortage of materials, decline in product demand, or other factors over which the worker has no control. The Bureau of Labor Statistics compiles monthly layoff rates by industry. For an account of how a General Electric division sought to do it "nicely," *see* Ken Leinweber, "Showing Them the Door," *Personnel* (July–August 1976). *Also see* Robert W. Bednarzik, "Layoffs and Permanent Job Losses: Workers' Traits, Patterns," *Monthly Labor Review* (September 1983); R. Wayne Mondy and Shane R. Preameaux, "Management/Union Perceptions of Recent Layoffs," *Personnel Administrator* (November 1984).

The "last hired-first fired" policy of layoffs has come under increasing criticism because of the unequal impact that it has had upon minorities. For analyses of layoffs dealing with this problem, *see* William R. Walter and Anthony J. Obadal, "Layoffs: The Judicial View," *Personnel Administrator* (May 1975); James Ledvinka, "EEO, Seniority, and Layoffs," *Personnel* (January–February 1976); Robert N. Roberts, " 'Last-Hired, First-Fired' and Public Employee Layoffs: The Equal Employment Opportunity Dilemma," *Review of Public Personnel Administration* (Fall 1981).

See also the following entries:
DISCIPLINARY LAYOFF
RECALL
RE-EMPLOYMENT LIST

RETENTION STANDING
RIF

LEAA, *see* LAW ENFORCEMENT ASSISTANCE ADMINISTRATION.

lead agency, under the Federal Wage System, the federal agency with the largest number of federal wage workers in a geographical area. The lead agency has the primary role for determining wage rates for all federal employees who work in that area and are covered by the system.

leadership, exercise of authority, whether formal or informal, in directing and coordinating the work of others. The literature on the concept of leadership is immense. The best one-volume summary is Ralph M. Stogdill, *Handbook of Leadership: A Survey of Theory and Research,* rev. ed. (New York: The Free Press, 1981). The best quote on the problems of leadership comes from Harry S. Truman, who said while discoursing on his job as president of the United States: "I sit here all day trying to persuade people to do the things they ought to have sense enough to do without my persuading them." *Also see* James M. Burns, *Leadership* (New York: Harper & Row, 1978); John B. Miner, "The Uncertain Future of the Leadership Concept: Revisions and Clarifications," *The Journal of Applied Behavioral Science,* Vol. 18, No. 3 (1982); Bert A. Rockman, *The Myth of Leadership: The Presidency in the American System* (New York: Praeger Publishers, 1983).

See *also* the following entries:
CHARISMATIC LEADERSHIP
CONTINGENCY MODEL OF LEADERSHIP
EFFECTIVENESS
FULL RESPONSIBILITY
FUNCTIONAL LEADERSHIP
LIFE CYCLE THEORY OF LEADERSHIP
PATH-GOAL THEORY OF LEADERSHIP

leadership, transformational, leadership that strives to change organizational culture and directions, rather than continuing to move along historical paths. It reflects the ability of a leader to develop a values-based vision for the organization, convert the vision into reality, and maintain it over time. Transformational leadership is a 1980's concept, closely identified with the concepts of symbolic management and organizational culture. *See* W. G. Bennis, "Transformative Power and Leadership," in T. J. Sergiovanni and J. E. Corbally, eds., *Leadership and Organizational Culture* (Urbana, Ill.: University of Illinois Press, 1984); and N. M. Tichy and D. O. Ulrich, "The Leadership Challenge—A Call for the Transformational Leader," *Sloan Management Review* (Fall 1984).

leadership style, patterns of a leader's interactions with his/her subordinates.

leading indicators, statistics that generally precede a change in a situation. For example, an increase in economic activity is typically preceded by a rise in the prices of stocks. Each month the Bureau of Economic Analysis of the Department of Commerce publishes data on hundreds of economic indicators in its *Business Conditions Digest.* Several dozen of these are classified as "leading." The Bureau's composite index of twelve leading indicators is a popular means of assessing the general state of the economy.

learning, generally, any behavior change occurring because of interaction with the environment. *See* Lee Hess and Len Sperry, "The Psychology of the Trainee as Learner," *Personnel Journal* (September 1973).

See *also* INCIDENTAL LEARNING and PROGRAMMED LEARNING.

learning curve, the concept that when workers repeatedly perform a task, the amount of labor required per unit of output decreases according to a constant pattern. Of course, as production processes become more dependent upon machines, the learning curve becomes less and less significant. *See* Raymond B. Jordan, *How To Use The Learning Curve* (Boston: Materials Management Institute, 1965). For a critique of its limitations, *see* William J. Abernathy and Kenneth Wayne, "Limits of the Learning Curve," *Harvard Business*

Review (September-October 1974).

The learning curve as a concept in training describes a learning process in which increases of performance are large at the beginning but become smaller with continued practice. Learning of any new thing eventually levels off as mastery is attained, at which point the curve becomes horizontal. For further details, *see* Bernard M. Bass and James A. Vaughn, *Training in Industry: The Management of Learning* (Belmont, Calif.: Wadsworth Publishing Co., 1966). *Also see* Winfred B. Hirschmann, "Profit from the Learning Curve," *Harvard Business Review* (January-February 1964).

learning plateau, that flat part of a learning curve that indicates there has been little or no additional learning.

leave, birth, *see* BIRTH LEAVE.

leave of absence, *see* FURLOUGH and LEAVE WITHOUT PAY.

leave without pay, a temporary non-pay status and short-term absence from duty, granted upon the employee's request. The permissive nature of leave without pay distinguishes it from absence without leave. A *leave of absence* is the same as leave without pay except for duration. A leave of absence implies a more substantial amount of time away from one's position.

L. Ed., abbreviation for *Lawyer's Edition* of the *U.S. Supreme Court Reports.*

Leffingwell, William Henry (1876-1934), the first person to apply the principles of scientific management to office management. His pioneering book, *Scientific Office Management* (Chicago: A. W. Shaw Co., 1917), is the forerunner of all subsequent studies of office work.

legislative history, the written record of the writing of an act of Congress. It may be used in writing rules or by courts in interpreting the law, to ascertain or detail the intent of the Congress if the act is ambiguous or lacking in detail. The legislative history is listed in the slip law and consists of the House, Senate, and conference committee reports (if any), and the House and Senate floor debates on the law. The history, particularly the committee reports, often contains the only available complete explanation of the meaning and intent of the law.

legislative intent, supposed real meaning of a statute as it can be interpreted from the legislative history.

legislative oversight, total means by which a legislature monitors the activities of agencies in order to see that laws are faithfully executed. *See* Cortus T. Koehler, "Policy Development and Legislative Oversight in Council-Manager Cities: An Information and Communications Analysis," *Public Administration Review* (September-October 1973); Alan Rosenthal, "Legislative Oversight and the Balance of Power in State Government," *State Government,* Vol. 56, No. 3 (1983); Morris S. Ogul, *Congress Oversees the Bureaucracy: Studies in Legislative Supervision* (Pittsburgh, Pa.: University of Pittsburgh Press, 1985).

legislative veto, *see* CONGRESSIONAL VETO.

legitimacy, characteristic of a social institution such as a government or a family whereby it has both a legal and a perceived right to make binding decisions for its members. Legitimacy is granted to an institution by its public. *See* Seymour Martin Lipset, "Some Social Requisites of Democracy: Economic Development and Political Legitimacy," *American Political Science Review* (March 1959); Edgar H. Schein and J. Steven Ott, "The Legitimacy of Organizational Influence," *American Journal of Sociology* (May 1962); John Dowling and Jeffrey Pfeffer, "Organizational Legitimacy: Social Values and Organizational Behavior," *Pacific Sociological Review* (January 1975); Peter L. Berger, "New Attack on the Legitimacy of Business," *Harvard Business Review* (September-October 1981).

Leontief, Wassily (1906–), Nobel Prize-winning developer of input-output analysis, which has played an increasingly important role in econometric forecasting. *See* Wassily Leontief, *Input-Output Economics* (New York: Oxford University Press, 1966).

leptokurtic, frequency distribution or curve that is more peaked, as opposed to flat-topped, than a normal curve.

lese majesty, in French LÈSE-MAJESTÉ, literally injured majesty, originally an offense against one's sovereign or ruler. Now it quite properly refers to an insolent or slighting behavior towards one's bureaucratic superiors.

Letter Carriers **decision,** *see* UNITED STATES CIVIL SERVICE COMMISSION V. NATIONAL ASSOCIATION OF LETTER CARRIERS.

Letter Carriers **v.** *Austin, see* OLD DOMINION BRANCH NO. 496, NATIONAL ASSOCIATION OF LETTER CARRIERS V. AUSTIN.

level annual premium funding method, method in which, after the pension costs for a new employee are actuarially determined, pension contributions or premiums are paid into a fund (or to an insurance company) in equal installments during the employee's remaining working life so that upon retirement the pension benefit is fully funded.

level of difficulty, classification term used to indicate the relative ranking of duties and responsibilities.

Levinson, Harry (1922–), psychologist and leading authority on organizational mental health and work motivation. Major works include: *Men, Management and Mental Health,* with C. R. Price, H. J. Munden & C. M. Solley (Cambridge, Mass.: Harvard University Press, 1962); *Emotional Health in the World of Work* (New York: Harper & Row, 1964); *Organizational Diagnosis* (Cambridge, Mass.: Harvard University Press, 1972); *The Exceptional Executive: A Psychological Conception* (Cambridge, Mass.: Harvard University Press, 1968); *Executive Stress* (New York: Harper & Row, 1970); *The Great Jackass Fallacy* (Boston: Harvard Graduate School of Business Administration, 1973).

Lewin, Kurt (1890–1947), psychologist popularly noted for his assertion that "there is nothing so practical as a good theory." He was the most influential experimental psychologist of the twentieth century. His research originated the modern concepts of group dynamics, action research, field theory, and sensitivity training. Major works include: *Principles of Topological Psychology* (New York: McGraw-Hill, 1936); *Resolving Social Conflicts: Selected Papers on Group Dynamics* (New York: Harper & Row, 1948); *Field Theory In Social Science: Selected Theoretical Papers,* edited by Dorwin Cartwright (London: Tavistock, 1963). For a biography, *see* Alfred J. Marrow, *The Practical Theorist: The Life and Work of Kurt Lewin* (New York: Basic Books, 1969).

liabilities, also CURRENT LIABILITIES and LONG-TERM LIABILITIES, the current and long-term debts owed by a jurisdiction or enterprise. *Current liabilities* are due and payable within a year and include such items as accounts payable, wages, and short-term debt. *Long-term liabilities* are payable more than a year hence and include items such as bonds.
See also CONTINGENT LIABILITY.

Library of Congress, library established under the law approved April 24, 1800, appropriating $5,000 "for the purchase of such books as may be necessary for the use of Congress." The library's scope of responsibility has been widened by subsequent legislation. One department, the Congressional Research Service, functions exclusively for the legislative branch of the government. As the library has developed, its range of service has come to include the entire governmental establishment in all its branches and the public at large, so that it has become a national library for the United States.

Library of Congress
10 First Street, S.E.
Washington, D.C. 20540
(202) 287-5000

license, a permission granted to an individual organization by competent authority, usually public, to engage in a practice, occupation, or activity otherwise unlawful. Licensure is the process by which the license is granted. Since a license is needed to begin lawful practice, it is usually granted on the basis of examination and/or proof of education rather than measures of performance. License when given is usually permanent but may be conditioned on annual payment of a fee, proof of continuing education, or proof of competence. Common grounds for revocation of a license include incompetence, commission of a crime (whether or not related to the licensed practice), or moral turpitude.

See also OCCUPATIONAL LICENSING.

lie detector, also called POLYGRAPH, also VOICE STRESS ANALYZER and PSYCHOLOGICAL STRESS ANALYZER, an instrument for recording physiological phenomena such as blood pressure, pulse rate, and the respiration rate of individuals as they answer questions put to them by an operator. The technique is based on the assumption that when an individual experiences apprehension, fear, or emotional excitement, his/her respiration rate, blood pressure, etc., will sharply increase. These physiological data are then interpreted by an operator who makes judgments on whether or not a subject is lying. Only one thing is certain about polygraph tests: they are not 100 percent accurate. Lie detectors have been used in police investigations since the 1920s, and have been increasingly used for employee screening since World War II. However, the authority of employers to use polygraph tests in personnel investigations has been challenged. Many state and local legislative actions have placed legal limitations on the public and private employers' use of lie detectors. Thirteen states prohibit the use of polygraphs as a condition of employment or continued employ-

ment. In addition, labor arbitrators often refuse to admit test results as evidence of "just cause" for discharge and have upheld a worker's right to refuse to take such a test. According to David T. Lykken, in "Psychology and The Lie Detector Industry," *American Psychologist* (October 1974), "the general use of lie detectors in employee screening cannot be justified . . . and psychologists have a professional responsibility to oppose this growing practice." For other analyses, *see* Burke M. Smith, "The Polygraph," *Scientific American* (January 1967); Mary Ann Coghill, *The Lie Detector In Employment,* rev. ed. (Ithaca, N.Y.: New York State School of Industrial and Labor Relations, Cornell University, 1973); John A. Beit and Peter B. Holden, "Polygraph Usage Among Major U.S. Corporations," *Personnel Journal* (February 1978); Phillip W. Davis and Pamela McKenzie-Rundle, "The Social Organization of Lie Detector Tests," *Urban Life* (July–October 1984); David J. Carr, "Employer Use of the 'Lie Detector': The Arbitration Experience," *Labor Law Journal* (November 1984).

The voice stress analyzer or psychological stress analyzer is a lie detector that can be used without the subject knowing that he/she is being tested. By simply analyzing the stress in the subject's voice it purports to tell whether or not the truth is being told. As such devices have only been available since the mid-1970s, their use should still be considered experimental.

life cycle theory of leadership, theory put forth by Paul Hersey and Kenneth R. Blanchard which suggests that the appropriate leadership style for a particular situation should be primarily dependent upon the task maturity level of the follower(s). Maturity is defined as a function of task-relevant education and experience, achievement motivation, and willingness and ability to accept responsibility. Leadership is seen as a combination of two types of behavior: "Task Behavior" (Directive), ranging from low to high, and "Relationships Behavior" (Supportive), ranging from low to high. If a follower is assessed to be extremely "immature," the theory suggests that high task-low relationships is the appropriate leadership style. As the follower matures, the theory suggests that the leader's behavior should move from high task-low relationships (Quadrant I), to high task-high relationships (Quadrant II), to high relationship-low task (Quadrant III), to low task-low relationships (Quadrant IV).

Life Cycle Theory of Leadership

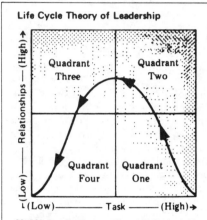

SOURCE: From Paul Hersey and Kenneth H. Blanchard, "Life Cycle Theory of Leadership." Reproduced by special permission from the May 1969 TRAINING AND DEVELOPMENT JOURNAL. Copyright 1969 by the American Society for Training and Development, Inc.

life insurance, insurance that provides for the payment of a specific amount to a designated beneficiary in the event of the death of the insured. See Viviana A. Rotman Zelizer, *Morals and Markets: The Development of Life Insurance in the United States* (New York: Columbia University Press, 1979); Allan P. Blostin, "Is Employer-Paid Life Insurance Declining Relative to Other Benefits?" *Monthly Labor Review* (September 1981).

See also the following entries:
ACCIDENTAL DEATH BENEFIT
GROUP LIFE INSURANCE
INSURANCE
SPLIT-DOLLAR LIFE INSURANCE
TERM LIFE INSURANCE
VARIABLE LIFE INSURANCE

Likert, Rensis (1903-1981), one of the pioneers of organizational survey research and director of the Institute of Social Research at the University of Michigan from 1948 to 1970. He is perhaps best known for his linking-pin theory and his concepts of Systems 1, 2, 3, and 4. Major works include: *New Patterns of Management* (New York: McGraw-Hill, 1961); *The Human Organization: Its Management and Value* (New York: McGraw-Hill, 1967); *New Ways of Managing Conflict,* with Jane Gibson Likert (New York: McGraw-Hill, 1976).

Likert Scale, also called LIKERT-TYPE SCALE, one of the most widely used scales in social research. Named after Rensis Likert, who first presented it in "A Technique for the Measurement of Attitudes," *Archives of Psychology* (No. 140, 1932), the scale presents a subject with a statement to which the subject expresses his/her reaction or opinion by selecting one of five (or more) possible responses arranged at equidistant intervals.

Questions Using a Likert Scale

1. The sick-leave policies of this company are not liberal enough.
   (a) strongly agree
   (b) agree
   (c) no opinion
   (d) disagree
   (e) strongly disagree
2. My supervisor is a good leader.
   (a) strongly agree
   (b) agree
   (c) uncertain
   (d) disagree
   (e) strongly disagree

Lilienthal, David E. (1899-   ), former chairman of the Tennessee Valley Authority (1941-46) and the Atomic Energy Commission (1946-50) who wrote widely of the advantages offered a democratic society by the intermingling of politics and administration. Major works include: *TVA: Democracy on the March* (New York: Harper & Bros., 1944); *This I Do Believe* (New York: Harper & Bros., 1949); *Big Business: A New Era* (New York: Harper & Bros., 1953); *Change, Hope and the Bomb* (Princeton, N.J.: Princeton University Press, 1963); *The Journals of David*

E. *Lilienthal* (New York: Harper & Row, vols. I & II, 1964; vol. III, 1966; vol. IV, 1969; vol. V, 1971; vol. VI, 1976).

Lindblom, Charles E. (1917-), the leading proponent of the incremental approach to policy/decision-making. In his most famous work, "The Science of Muddling Through," *Public Administration Review* (Spring 1959), Lindblom took a hard look at the rational models of the decisional processes of government. He rejected the notion that most decisions are made by rational—total information—processes. Instead he saw such decisions—indeed, the whole policymaking process—as dependent upon small incremental decisions that tend to be made in response to short-term political conditions. Lindblom's thesis, essentially, held that decisionmaking was controlled infinitely more by events and circumstances than by the will of those in policymaking positions. His thesis encouraged considerable work in that area of the discipline that sits most on the boundary between political science and public administration—public policy. Lindblom restated his "muddling" thesis in "Still Muddling, Not Yet Through," *Public Administration Review* (January-February 1980). Other major works include: *Unions and Capitalism* (New Haven, Conn.: Yale University Press, 1949); *Politics, Economics, and Welfare,* with Robert A. Dahl (New York: Harper & Row, 1953); *A Strategy of Decision,* with D. Braybrooke (New York: The Free Press, 1963); *The Intelligence of Democracy: Decision Making Through Mutual Adjustment* (New York: The Free Press, 1965); *The Policy-Making Process,* 2nd ed. (Englewood Cliffs, N.J.: Prentice-Hall, 1980); *Politics and Markets* (New York: Basic Books, 1978).

line-item budget, *see* BUDGET, LINE-ITEM.

line-item veto, *see* VETO.

line of authority, *see* SCALAR CHAIN.

line organization, those segments of a larger organization that perform the ma-jor functions of the organization and have the most direct responsibilities for achieving organizational goals.

line-staff conflict, organizational conflict described by Charles Coleman and Joseph Rich in "Line, Staff and the Systems Perspective," *Human Resources Management* (Fall 1973):

> One of the pillars of traditional organization theory is the concept that line officers possess command authority in core areas of the organization and that staff officers provide them with specialized assistance. However, empirical studies have shown time and again that the traditional line-staff idea leads to large amounts of conflict.

See Melville Dalton, "Conflict Between Staff and Line Management Officers," *American Sociological Review* (June 1950); Robert T. Golembiewski, *Organizing Men and Power: Patterns of Behavior and Line-Staff Models* (Chicago: Rand McNally, 1967); Philip J. Browne and Robert T. Golembiewski, "The Line-Staff Concept Revisited: An Empirical Study of Organizational Images," *Academy of Management Journal* (September 1974); Vivian Nossiter, "A New Approach Toward Resolving the Line and Staff Dilemma," *Academy of Management Review* (January 1979).

linkage, an international political strategy relating two or more issues in negotiations, and then using them as tradeoffs or pressure points, much as in a "carrot and stick" technique.

linking pin, concept developed by Rensis Likert in his *New Patterns of Management* (New York: McGraw-Hill, 1961). A "linking pin" is anyone who belongs to two groups within the same organization, usually as a superior in one and as a subordinate in the other. *See* George Graen *et al.,* "Effects of Linking-Pin Quality on the Quality of Working Life of Lower Participants," *Administrative Science Quarterly* (September 1977).

See also LIKERT, RENSIS.

Linn v. *United Plant Guard Workers,*
383 U.S. 53 (1966), U.S. Supreme Court
case which held that the National Labor
Relations Act does not bar libel actions
brought by either party to a labor dispute
who alleges the circulation of false and defamatory statements during a union organizing campaign as long as the
complainant pleads and proves that the
statements were made with malice and injured him/her.

listening, one of the oldest and most useful of personnel management techniques.
According to John A. Wilson, *The Culture
of Ancient Egypt* (Chicago: University of
Chicago Press, 1951), the ancient Egyptians advised their leaders to

> be calm as thou listenest to what the
> petitioner has to say. Do not rebuff him
> before he has swept out his body or be-
> fore he has said that for which he
> came. . . .It is not [necessary] that
> everything about which he has peti-
> tioned should come to pass, [for] a good
> hearing is soothing to the heart.

Some things haven't changed much in
4000 years! For modern pep talks on how
to be a good listener, *see* Thomas G. Ban-
ville, *How to Listen—How to be Heard*
(Chicago: Nelson-Hall, 1978); A.W.
Clausen, "Listening and Responding to
Employees' Concerns," *Harvard Business
Review* (January-February 1980); Robert
L. Montgomery, *Listening Made Easy:
How to Improve Listening on the Job, at
Home and in the Community* (New York:
AMACOM, 1981).

list of eligibles, *see* ELIGIBLE LIST.

little city hall, a branch office of municipal
government. *See* Eric A. Nordlinger, *Decentralizing the City: A Study of Boston's
Little City Halls* (Cambridge, Mass.: The
M.I.T. Press, 1972).

living wage, also STARVATION WAGES,
subsistence wage. Although one might
suspect that *starvation wages* would be
necessarily of limited duration, many a
union leader will assert that the workers
have been putting up with them far too

long. A *living wage,* in contrast, wards off
starvation and even provides for some of
the comforts of life. However, the ultimate
goal of the union must be a "decent living
wage," which affords a standard of luxury
that can hardly be imagined by those on
starvation wages.

Lloyd-LaFollette Act of 1912, federal
statute that guarantees civilian employees
of the federal government the right to petition Congress, either individually or
through their organizations. The act was
the only statutory basis for the organization of federal employees until the Civil
Service Reform Act of 1978. In addition,
it provided the first statutory procedural
safeguards for federal employees facing
removal. It states that "no person in the
classified civil service of the United States
shall be removed or suspended without
pay therefrom except for such cause as will
promote the efficiency of such service and
for reasons given in writing."

LMRA, *see* LABOR-MANAGEMENT RELA-
TIONS ACT OF 1947.

loading, in insurance, the amount added
to the actuarial value of the coverage (expected or average amounts payable to the
insured) to cover the expense to the insurer of securing and maintaining the business: *i.e.,* the amount added to the pure
premium needed to meet anticipated liabilities for expenses, contingencies, profits,
or special situations.

loading, job/horizontal/vertical, *see*
JOB LOADING.

loan guarantee, an agreement by which
the government pledges to pay part or all
of the loan principal and interest to a
lender or holder of a security in the event
of default by a third party borrower. The
purpose of a guaranteed loan is to reduce
the risk borne by a private lender by shifting all or part of the risk to the federal government. If it becomes necessary for the
government to pay part or all of the loan
principal or interest, the payment is a direct
outlay. Otherwise, the guarantee does not
directly affect federal budget outlays.

loan insurance, a type of loan guarantee whereby a government agency operates a program of pooled risks, pledging the use of accumulated insurance premiums to secure a lender against default on the part of the borrower.

lobby, also FEDERAL REGULATION OF LOBBYING ACT OF 1946, any individual, group, or organization that seeks to influence legislation or administrative action. The term arose from the use of lobbies, or corridors, in legislative halls as places to meet with and persuade legislators to vote a certain way. Lobbying in general is not an evil; many lobbies provide legislatures with reliable firsthand information of considerable value. However, some lobbies have given the practice an undesirable connotation.

The Federal Regulation of Lobbying Act of 1946 requires that persons who solicit or accept contributions for lobbying purposes keep accounts, present receipts and statements to the clerk of the House, and register with the clerk of the House and the secretary of the Senate. The information received is published quarterly in the *Congressional Record*. The purpose of this registration is to disclose the sponsorship and source of funds of lobbyists, but not to curtail the right of persons to act as lobbyists. *See* Donald R. Hall, *Cooperative Lobbying—The Power of Pressure* (Tucson: University of Arizona Press, 1969); Harmon Zeigler and Michael Baer, *Lobbying: Interaction and Influence in American State Legislatures* (Belmont, Calif.: Wadsworth, 1969); Suzanne Farkas, *Urban Lobbying: Mayors in the Federal Arena* (New York: New York University Press, 1971); Donald H. Haider, *When Governments Come to Washington: Governors, Mayors, and Intergovernmental Lobbying* (New York: The Free Press, 1974); Jeffrey M. Berry, *Lobbying for the People* (Princeton, N.J.: Princeton University Press, 1977); and Carol S. Greenwald, *Group Power: Lobbying and Public Policy* (New York: Praeger, 1977).

local, *see* COSMOPOLITAN-LOCAL CONSTRUCT.

Local Affairs, Department of, generic name of a state agency with oversight responsibilities for local government. Sometimes local governments are required to submit audit and budget reports to such an agency, with the exact requirements varying from state to state.

local independent union, local union not affiliated with a national or international union.

local industrial union, local union consisting of workers in a variety of occupations in an industry.

Local 174, Teamsters v. *Lucas Flour Co.,* 369 U.S. 95 (1962), U.S. Supreme Court case which held that a strike to settle a dispute which a collective bargaining agreement provides shall be settled by compulsory arbitration is a violation of the agreement.

local union, regional organization of union members who are part of a national or international union. A local union is chartered by the national or international union with which it is affiliated.

Lochner v. *New York,* 198 U.S. 45 (1905), U.S. Supreme Court case which declared unconstitutional a New York law which sought to regulate the hours of employment.

lockout, employer's version of a strike—the closing of a business in order to pressure the employees and/or the union to accept the employer's offered terms of employment. This early weapon against the union movement lost much of its effect when locked-out employees became eligible for unemployment compensation. Almost all union contracts with a no-strike clause contain a similar ban against lockouts. For an analysis, *see* Willard A. Lewis, "The 'Lockout as Corollary of Strike' Controversy Reexamined," *Labor Law Journal* (November 1972).

See also AMERICAN SHIPBUILDING CO. V. NATIONAL LABOR RELATIONS BOARD and TEXTILE WORKERS V. DARLINGTON MANUFACTURING COMPANY.

lodge, organizational unit of some labor unions, equivalent to a local union.

Lodge 76, International Association of Machinists* v. *Wisconsin Employment Relations Commission, 427 U.S. 132 (1976), U.S. Supreme Court case which held that a state cannot interfere with a union's power to collectively refuse overtime during contract negotiations or to engage in other partial strike activities unregulated by federal labor laws.

logistics, those inventory, production and traffic management activities which seek the timely placement of goods (and associated services) at the proper place and in the appropriate quantities. *See* Joseph E. Boyett, Jr., "Logistics: DOD's Achilles Heel? *The Bureaucrat* (Spring 1982).

Long, Norton E. (1910-), political scientist who wrote classic accounts of the political dimensions of public administration. The beginning of his article, "Power and Administration," *Public Administration Review* (Autumn 1949), is perhaps the most poetic paragraph in the literature of public administration:

> There is no more forlorn spectacle in the administrative world than an agency and a program possessed of statutory life, armed with executive orders, sustained in the courts, yet stricken with paralysis and deprived of power. An object of contempt to its enemies and of despair to its friends.

Long's major essays have been collected in *The Polity* (Chicago: Rand McNally, 1962). *Also see The Unwalled City: Rebuilding the Urban Community* (New York: Basic Books, 1972).

longevity pay, also called LONGEVITY RATE, salary additions based on length of service. Contracts or pay plans frequently state specific time periods to qualify for such upward wage adjustments.

longitudinal survey, study of a group of subjects that follows them through time. *See* Herbert S. Parnes, "Longitudinal Surveys: Prospects and Problems," *Monthly Labor Review* (February 1972); Mary Corcoran, Greg J. Duncan, and Michael Ponza, "A Longitudinal Analysis of White Women's Wages," *The Journal of Human Resources* (Fall 1983).

long-range planning, consideration in the present time period (today) of what capability must be provided in the future to meet the anticipated objectives that are inherent in a predicted situation, condition, or event and the courses of action that might be involved.

long-term debt, debt payable more than one year after date of issue.

long-term debt offsets, cash and investment assets of sinking funds and other reserve funds, however designated, which are specifically held for redemption of long-term debt.

long-term debt retired, par value of long-term debt obligations liquidated by repayment or exchange, including debt retired by refunding operations.

long-term liabilities, *see* LIABILITIES.

long-term original issues, all long-term debt issued other than that issued to refund existing long-term debt. Includes long-term debt issued for funding of existing short-term obligations.

Lordstown strike, three-week wildcat strike at the General Motors automobile assembly plant at Lordstown, Ohio in April, 1972. One of the most technically sophisticated plants of its kind in the world, the plant could produce about one hundred Chevrolet Vega cars per hour. In 1971, assembly-line workers began to purposely disrupt production, while claiming that management was seeking to "speed up" the assembly line. This problem festered and led to the strike. While the strike gained no economic benefits for the workers, it did focus national attention on the problems of job monotony and worker alienation. For accounts, *see* Barbara Garson, "Luddites in Lordstown," *Harpers*

(June 1972); Stanley Aronwitz, *False Promise: The Shaping of American Working Class Consciousness* (New York: McGraw-Hill, 1973); James O'Toole, "Lordstown: Three Years Later," *Business and Society Review* (Spring 1975).

Lordstown syndrome, workers' perception that they are required to perform dehumanized and monotonous work. Among the dysfunctional aspects of this syndrome are high absenteeism, low productivity, sabotage, and wildcat strikes. While the term has its origins in the 1972 strike at the General Motors plant in Lordstown, Ohio, the phenomenon itself is more widespread. For a discussion, *see* "The Spreading Lordstown Syndrome," *Business Week* (March 4, 1972).

Lorenz curve, graphic device most commonly used in macroeconomics to show the unequal distribution of national income. The Lorenz curve can be applied to wage and salary structures to demonstrate the spread of wages from the lowest paid employee to the highest paid. A curve is constructed by plotting the cumulative percentage of employees against the cumulative percentage of wages and salaries. This curve is compared to a 45° line and the area between the two computed as a value L. The greater the L value, the greater the inequality of wages. *See* T. M. Husband and A. P. Schofield, "The Use of the Lorenz Curve and the Pareto Distribution in Internal Pay Structuring: A Research Note," *The Journal of Management Studies* (October 1976).

Los Angeles Department of Water and Power v. Manhart, *see* CITY OF LOS ANGELES, DEPARTMENT OF WATER & POWER V. MANHART.

love, also called OFFICE ROMANCE, strong affection. When individuals working in the same organization discover that they have an emotional and/or physical attraction for each other, that may be very nice for them but it is a potential problem for their organization's management. For general advice on handling this kind of situation, *see* Auren Uris, *The Blue Book of Broadminded Business Behavior* (New York: Thomas Y. Crowell Co., 1977). For scholarly analyses, *see* Robert E. Quinn, "Coping with Cupid: The Formation, Impact, and Management of Romantic Relationships in Organizations," *Administrative Science Quarterly* (March 1977); Eliza G. C. Collins, "Managers and Lovers," *Harvard Business Review* (September-October 1983).
See also SEXUAL HARASSMENT.

Lowi, Theodore J. (1931-), a leading critic of interest group pluralism often noted for his classifying of all public policies as either distributive, regulatory, or redistributive. Major works include: *At the Pleasure of the Mayor: Patronage and Power in New York City, 1898-1958* (New York: The Free Press, 1964); "American Business, Public Policy, Case-Studies, and Political Theory," *World Politics* (July 1964); *Private Life and Public Order*, ed. (New York: W. W. Norton, 1968); *The End of Liberalism: The Second Republic of the United States* (New York: W. W. Norton, 1969; 2nd ed., 1979); "Decision-Making versus Policy-Making," *Public Administration Review* (May-June 1970); *The Politics of Disorder* (New York: Basic Books, 1971); "Four Systems of Policy, Politics, and Choice," *Public Administration Review* (July-August 1972); *Poliscide*, with others (New York: Macmillan, 1976); *American Government: Incomplete Conquest* (Hinsdale, Ill.: The Dryden Press, 1976).
See also PUBLIC POLICYMAKING.

low man on the totem pole, refers to the lowest person in any organizational hierarchy. The phrase is credited to Fred Allen who, while writing an introduction to a book by H. Allen Smith, said, "If Smith were an Indian, he would be low man on any totem pole." Smith then used the phrase as the title of his next book, *Low Man on A Totem Pole* (Garden City, N.Y.: Doubleday Doran and Co., 1941).

low match, *see* MATCHING SHARE.

319

loyalty, also LOYALTY OATH, allegiance. A *loyalty oath* is an affirmation of allegiance. Many public employers may legitimately require their employees to swear or affirm their allegiance to the Constitution of the United States and to that of a particular state. *See* Paul E. Donnelly, "The Pervasive Effect of McCarthyism on Recent Loyalty Oath Cases," *St. Louis University Law Journal* (Spring 1972); T. W. Fletcher, "The Nature of Administrative Loyalty," *Public Administration Review* (Winter 1958); O. Glenn Stahl, "Loyalty, Dissent, and Organizational Health," *Bureaucrat* (July 1974); Paul M. Sniderman, *A Question of Loyalty* (Berkeley, Calif.: University of California Press, 1981).

See also the following entries:
> BAGGETT V. BULLITT
> BAILEY V. RICHARDSON
> COLE V. RICHARDSON
> CONNELL V. HIGGINBOTHAM
> ELFBRANDT V. RUSSELL
> GARNER V. BOARD OF PUBLIC
>   WORKS OF LOS ANGELES
> KEYISHIAN V. BOARD OF REGENTS
> SHELTON V. TUCKER

loyalty program, *see* BAILEY V. RICHARDSON.

Luddite, originally, member of a group that appeared in Nottingham, England, in 1811. Luddites were organized bands of handicraftsmen who, masked and operating at night, sought to destroy the new textile machinery that was displacing them. Their name is thought to have come from Ned Ludd, a village idiot who gained local notoriety in 1779 by destroying some stocking frames belonging to his employer. While Ned Ludd has the same historical stature as Robin Hood (that is, more likely to be mythical than real), his namesakes today would include anyone who seeks to destroy machinery in order to protect a job. For a history, *see* Malcolm I. Thomis, *The Luddites: Machine-Breaking in Regency England* (New York: Schocken Books, 1972).

M

Machiavelli, Niccolo (1469–1527), most famous management analyst of the Italian Renaissance, often credited with having established the moral foundations of modern personnel management. In *Discorsi sopra la prima deca di Tito Livio* ("Discourses on the First Decade of Tito Livy") he offers his advice to all staff specialists:

> If you tender your advice with modesty, and the opposition prevents its adoption, and, owing to someone else's advice being adopted, disaster follows, you will acquire very great glory. And, though you cannot rejoice in the glory that comes from disasters which befall your country or your prince, it at any rate counts for something.

For a modern appreciation, *see* Anthony Jay, *Management and Machiavelli: An Inquiry into the Politics of Corporate Life* (New York: Holt, Rinehart, and Winston, 1967). *Also see* Mark Hulliung, *Citizen Machiavelli* (Princeton, N.J.: Princeton University Press, 1983).

MacKay Rule, *see* NATIONAL LABOR RELATIONS BOARD V. MACKAY RADIO & TELEGRAPH COMPANY.

macroeconomics, study of the relationships between broad economic aggregates such as national income, consumer savings and expenditures, capital investment, employment, money supply, prices, and balance of payments. Macroeconomics is especially concerned with government's role in affecting these aggregates. For texts, *see* Robert L. Heilbroner and Lester C. Thurow, *Understanding Macroeconomics*, 6th ed. (Englewood Cliffs, N.J.: Prentice-Hall, 1978); Paul Wonnacott, *Macro-*

economics, 3rd ed. (Homewood, Ill.: Richard D. Irwin, Inc., 1984); Michael R. Edgmand, *Macroeconomics: Theory and Policy* (Englewood Cliffs, N.J.: Prentice-Hall, 1979); Jan Walter Elliott, *Macroeconomic Analysis,* 2nd ed. (Englewood Cliffs, N.J.: Prentice-Hall, 1979).

Magna Charta, the charter of liberties that English nobles forced from King John in 1215. Now the term is also used to refer to any document offering fundamental guarantees of rights.

Magnavox decision, *see* NATIONAL LABOR RELATIONS BOARD V. MAGNAVOX.

Maier, Norman R. F. (1900–1977), psychologist best known for his research in industrial psychology, human relations, and executive development. Major works include: *Principles of Human Relations* (New York: John Wiley, 1952); *The Appraisal Interview* (New York: John Wiley, 1958); *Psychology in Industrial Organizations,* 4th ed. (Boston: Houghton Mifflin, 1973).

maintenance of effort, a federal requirement that grant recipients maintain the level of program expenditures financed from their own resources prior to receipt of a grant and use the grant funds to supplement state-local expenditures for the aided activities.

maintenance-of-membership shop, union security provision found in some collective bargaining agreements which holds that employees who are members of the union at the time the agreement is negotiated, or who voluntarily join the union subsequently, must maintain their membership for the duration of the agreement as a condition of employment.

maintenance-of-standards clause, a contract provision that prevents an employer from changing the conditions of employment unless such changes are negotiated with the union.

maintenance review, formal, periodic review (usually annual) of all positions in an organization, or portion of an organization, to insure that classifications are correct and position descriptions are current.

major duty, any duty or responsibility of a position that (1) determines qualification requirements for the position, (2) occupies a significant amount of the employee's time, and (3) is a regular or recurring duty.

major-medical insurance, insurance designed to offset the heavy medical expenses resulting from catastrophic or prolonged illness or injury. Generally, such policies do not provide first dollar coverage, but do provide benefit payments of 75 to 80 percent of all types of medical expenses above a certain base amount paid by the insured. Most major medical policies sold as private insurance contain maximums on the total amount that will be paid (such as $50,000); thus, they do not provide last dollar coverage or complete protection against catastrophic costs. However, there is a trend toward $250,000 limits or even unlimited plans. In addition, benefit payments are often 100 percent of expenses after the individual has incurred some large amounts ($500 to $2,000) of out-of-pocket expenses.

make-up pay, allowances paid to piece workers to make up the difference between actual piece work earnings and guaranteed rates (or statutory minimum wages).

make whole, legal remedy that provides for an injured party to be placed, as near as may be possible, in the situation he or she would have occupied if the wrong had not been committed. The concept was first put forth by the U.S. Supreme Court in the 1867 case of *Wicker* v. *Hoppock.* In 1975, the Court held, in the case of *Albermarle Paper Company* v. *Moody* (422 U.S. 405), that Title VII of the Civil Rights Act of 1964 (as amended) intended a "make whole" remedy for unlawful discrimination.

See also RETROACTIVE SENIORITY and RIGHTFUL PLACE.

make-work, any effort to reduce or limit labor output so that more labor must be employed.

Malek Manual, guidebook concerning the operations of the federal personnel system that was prepared for Fred Malek, the manager of the White House Personnel Office during the early part of the Nixon Administration. Its Machiavellian character (it asserted that "There is no merit in the merit system") gave it tremendous notoriety. For a dispassionate analysis, *see* Frank J. Thompson and Raymond G. Davis, "The Malek Manual Revisited," *The Bureaucrat* (Summer 1977). For Malek Manual excerpts, *see* Frank J. Thompson, ed., *Classics of Public Personnel Policy* (Oak Park, Ill.: Moore Publishing Company, 1979).

MALEK MANUAL EXCERPT

The best way to appreciate the usefulness of the Malek Manual is to read its own "example of the rape of the merit system."

Let us assume that you have a career opening in your Department's personnel office for a Staff Recruitment Officer. Sitting in front of you is your college roommate from Stanford University in California who was born and raised in San Francisco. He received his law degree from Boalt Hall at the University of California. While studying for the bar he worked at an advertising agency handling newspaper accounts. He also worked as a reporter on the college newspaper. Your personnel experts judge that he could receive an eligibility rating for a GS-11.

The first thing you do is tear up the old job description that goes with that job. You then have a new one written, to be classified at GS-11, describing the duties of that specific Staff Recruitment Officer as directed toward the recruitment of recent law graduates for entry level attorney positions, entry level public information officers for the creative arts and college news liaison sections of your public information shop, and to be responsible for general recruiting for entry level candidates on the West Coast. You follow that by listing your selective criteria as follows: Education: BA and LLB, stating that the candidate should have extensive experience and knowledge by reason of employment or residence on the West Coast. Candidate should have at-

tended or be familiar with law schools, and institutions of higher education, preferably on the West Coast. The candidate should also possess some knowledge by reasons of education or experience of the fields of college journalism, advertising, and law.

You then trot this candidate's Application for Federal Employment over to the Civil Service Commission, and shortly thereafter he receives an eligibility rating for a GS-11. Your personnel office then sends over the job descriptions (GS-11) along with the selective criteria which was based on the duties of the job description. When the moment arrives for the panel to "spin the register" you insure that your personnel office sends over two "friendly" bureaucrats. The register is then spun and your candidate will certainly be among the only three who even meet the selective criteria, much less be rated by your two "friendly" panel members as among the "highest qualified" that meet the selection criteria. In short, you write the job description and selective criteria around your candidate's Form 171.

There is no merit in the merit system!

SOURCE: *Executive Session Hearings Before the Select Committee on Presidential Campaign Activities of the United States Senate, Watergate and Related Activities,* BOOK 19 (Washington, D.C.: U.S. Government Printing Office, 1974).

---

malpractice, professional misconduct or lack of ordinary skill in the performance of a professional act. A practitioner is liable for damages or injuries caused by malpractice. Such liability for some professions (like medicine) can be covered by malpractice insurance against the costs of defending suits instituted against the professional and/or any damages assessed by the court, usually up to a maximum limit.

malpractice insurance, insurance against the risk of suffering financial damage because of malpractice.

Malthus, Thomas Robert (1766–1834), English economist whose *Essay on Population* held that the world's population must ultimately outstrip food supply because, left unchecked, population increases geometrically while food production increases arithmetically.

management, term that can refer to both (1) the people responsible for running an organization and (2) the running process itself—the utilizing of numerous resources to accomplish an organizational goal. For general histories, *see* Claude S. George, Jr., *The History of Management Thought* (Englewood Cliffs, N.J.: Prentice-Hall, 1972); Daniel A. Wren, *The Evolution of Management Thought*, 2nd ed. (New York: John Wiley & Sons, 1979).

See also the following entries:

CAREER MANAGEMENT
CONTINGENCY MANAGEMENT
EUPSYCHIAN MANAGEMENT
FIRST-LINE MANAGEMENT
GRAND CANYON MANAGEMENT
INDUSTRIAL DEMOCRACY
MUSHROOM MANAGEMENT
PRINCIPLES OF MANAGEMENT
PROJECT MANAGEMENT
REACTION MANAGEMENT
SANDWICH MANAGEMENT
SCIENTIFIC MANAGEMENT
STRATEGIC MANAGEMENT
SYSTEMS MANAGEMENT

Management, quarterly magazine for government managers published by the U.S. Office of Personnel Management.

Management
Government Printing Office
Washington, D.C. 20402

management, cutback, phrase that describes the decline of public organizations in times of fiscal stress. *See* Charles H. Levine, ed., *Managing Fiscal Stress: The Crisis in the Public Sector* (Chatham, N.J.: Chatham House, 1980); Charles H. Levine, ed., "Symposium on Organizational Decline and Cutback Management," *Public Administration Review* (July–August 1978); James M. Howell and Charles F. Stamm, *Urban Fiscal Stress: A Comparative Analysis of 66 U.S. Cities* (Lexington, Mass.: Lexington Books, 1979); Charles H. Levine and Irene Rubin, eds., *Fiscal Stress and Public Policy* (Beverly Hills, Calif.: Sage Publications, 1980); Leonard Greenhalgh and Robert B. McKersie, "Cost-Effectiveness of Alternative Strategies for Cut-back Management," *Public Administration Review* (November–December 1980); Carol W.

Lewis and Anthony T. Logalbo, "Cutback Principles and Practices: A Checklist for Managers," *Public Administration Review* (March–April 1980); Charles H. Levine, Irene S. Rubin and George G. Wolohojian, "Resource Scarcity and the Reform Model: The Management of Retrenchment in Cincinnati and Oakland," *Public Administration Review* (November–December 1981); Carol W. Lewis, W. Wayne Shannon, and G. Donald Ferree, Jr., "The Cutback Issue: Administrators' Perceptions, Citizen Attitudes, and Administrative Behavior," *Review of Public Personnel Administration* (Fall 1983); Irene S. Rubin, *Shrinking the Federal Government: The Effect of Cutbacks on Five Federal Agencies* (New York: Longman, 1985); Perry Moore, "The Problems and Prospects of Cutback Management," *Personnel Administrator* (January 1985).

management, risk, *see* RISK MANAGEMENT.

management audit, any comprehensive examination of the administrative operations and organizational arrangements of a company or government agency which uses generally accepted standards of practice for the purposes of evaluation. The pioneering work on this is Jackson Martindell, *The Scientific Appraisal of Management* (New York: Harper and Row, 1950). *Also see* William P. Leonard, *The Management Audit* (Englewood Cliffs, N.J.: Prentice-Hall, 1962); M. J. V. Bell, "Management Audit in the Ministry of Defence," *Public Administration* (Autumn 1984).

management by exception, management control process that has a subordinate report to an organizational superior only exceptional or unusual events that might call for decision-making on the part of the superior. In this way, a manager may avoid unnecessary detail that only confirms that all is going according to plan. This concept originated with Frederick Taylor. For an update, *see* Lester R. Bittel, *Man-*

agement by Exception (New York: McGraw-Hill, 1964).

management by objectives (MBO), approach to managing whose hallmark is a mutual—by both organizational subordinate and superior—setting of measurable goals to be accomplished by an individual or team over a set period of time. According to George S. Odiorne, in *Management by Objectives* (New York: Pitman Publishing Company, 1965),

> The superior and subordinate managers of an organization jointly define its common goals, define each individual's major areas of responsibility in terms of the results expected of him and use these measures as guides for operating the unit and assessing the contribution of each of the members.

The phrase and concept of MBO was first popularized by Peter F. Drucker, in his *The Practice of Management* (New York: Harper & Row, 1954).

One of the major uses of MBO is for formal performance appraisals. For an assertion that this use is dysfunctional, *see* Harry Levinson, "Management by Whose Objectives?" *Harvard Business Review* (July–August 1970).

For analysis of MBO in the public sector, *see* Dale D. McConkey, *MBO for Nonprofit Organizations* (New York: AMACOM, 1975); George L. Morrisey, *Management by Objectives and Results in the Public Sector* (Reading, Mass.: Addison-Wesley Publishing Co., 1976). In addition, there is a symposium on MBO in *Public Administration Review* (January–February 1976); *also see* Jack N. Kondrasuk, "Studies in MBO Effectiveness," *Academy of Management Review* (July 1981); Perry D. Moore and Ted Staton, "Management by Objectives in American Cities," *Public Personnel Management* (Summer 1981); Richard Gruner, "Employment Discrimination in Management by Objectives Systems," *Labor Law Journal* (June 1983).

management clause, *see* MANAGEMENT RIGHTS CLAUSE.

management development, also called EXECUTIVE DEVELOPMENT, any conscious effort on the part of an organization to provide a manager with skills that might be needed for future duties, such as rotational assignments or formal educational experiences. The semantic difference between training workers and developing managers is significant. A manager is trained so that he can be of greater organizational value not only in his present but in his future assignments as well. In such a context the development investment made by the organization in a junior manager may only pay off when and if that individual grows into a bureau or division chief. For an analysis, *see* Edgar H. Schein, "Management Development: Full Spectrum Training," *Training and Development Journal* (March 1975); Raymond Pomerleau, "The State of Management Development in the Federal Service," *Public Personnel Management* (January–February 1974); John Sauter, "Purchasing Public Sector Executive Development," *Training and Development Journal* (April 1980); Robert E. Boynton, "Executive Development Programs: What Should They Teach?" *Personnel* (March–April 1981); David Bresnick, "University/Agency Collaboration in Management Development Efforts," *Public Administration Review* (November–December 1981); Stanley D. Truskie, "Guidelines for Conducting in-House Management Development," *Personnel Administrator* (July 1981); Stanley D. Truskie, "Getting the Most From Management Development Programs," *Personnel Journal* (January 1982); H. Wayne Smith and Clay E. George, "Evaluating Internal Advanced Management Programs," *Personnel Administrator* (August 1984); Fred E. Fiedler and Joseph E. Garcia, "Comparing Organization Development and Management Training," *Personnel Administrator* (March 1985).

management games, also called BUSINESS GAMES, any of a variety of simulation exercises used in management development and education. *See* Joel M. Kibbee, Clifford J. Craft, and Burt Nanus,

Management Games: A New Technique for Executive Development (New York: Van Nostrand Reinhold, 1961); Robert G. Graham and Clifford F. Gray, *Business Games Handbook* (New York: American Management Association, 1969); David W. Zukerman and Robert E. Horn, *The Guide to Simulations/Games for Education and Training* (Lexington, Mass.: Information Resources, 1973). For a view of all of modern business as a game, *see* John McDonald, *The Games of Business* (Garden City, N.Y.: Doubleday, 1975). For an analysis of the players, *see* Michael Maccoby, *The Gamesman: The New Corporate Leaders* (New York: Simon & Schuster, 1976).

management information system (MIS), any formal process in an organization that provides managers with facts that they need for decision-making. Modern management information systems are almost invariably dependent upon computers. For the theory behind a modern MIS, *see* Jaglit Singh, *Great Ideas in Information Theory, Language and Cybernetics* (New York: Dover Publications, 1966). For what can go wrong, *see* Russell L. Ackoff, "Management Misinformation Systems," *Management Science* (December 1967); *also see* Eric J. Eno, "The Administrative Generalist and MIS," *Public Administration Review* (September–October 1979); Gilbert W. Fairholm, "A Reality Basis for Management Information System Decisions," *Public Administration Review* (March–April 1979); Forest W. Horton, Jr., and Donald A. Marchand, *Information Management in Public Administration* (Arlington, Va.: Information Resources Press, 1982); Robert V. Head, *Federal Information Systems Management: Issues and New Directions* (Washington, D.C.: The Brookings Institution, 1982).

management movement, the totality of events, starting in the last century, that led to the recognition of *management* as a professional discipline. The movement is usually dated from 1886 when Henry R. Towne told the American Society of Mechanical Engineers that "the matter of shop management is of equal importance with that of engineering."

management official, individual employed by an agency in a position whose duties and responsibilities require or authorize the individual to formulate, determine, or influence the policies of the agency.

Management of Personnel Quarterly, *see* HUMAN RESOURCE MANAGEMENT.

management prerogatives, *see* MANAGEMENT RIGHTS.

management rights, also called MANAGEMENT PREROGATIVES and RESERVED RIGHTS, those rights reserved to management that management feels are intrinsic to its ability to manage and, consequently, not subject to collective bargaining. According to Paul Prasow and Edward Peters, "New Perspectives on Management's Reserved Rights," *Labor Law Journal* (January 1967),

management's authority is supreme in all matters except those it has expressly conceded in the collective agreement, or in those areas where its authority is restricted by law. Put another way, management does not look to the collective agreement to ascertain its rights; it looks to the agreement to find out which and how much of its rights and powers it has conceded outright or agreed to share with the union.

For further analyses of management rights, *see* George Bennett, "Management Rights in the Public Sector," *Labor Law Journal* (September 1977); Bruno Stein, "Management Rights and Productivity," *The Arbitration Journal* (December 1977).

management rights clause, also called MANAGEMENT CLAUSE, that portion of a collective bargaining agreement that defines the scope of management rights, functions, and responsibilities—essentially all those activities which management can undertake without the consent of the union. A typical management rights clause might read: "It is the intention hereof that all of the rights, powers, prerogatives, authorities that the company had prior to the signing of this agreement are retained by the company except those that are specifically abridged, delegated, granted, or modified by the agreement." See Richard F. Groner and Leon E. Lunden, "Management Rights Provisions in Major Agreements," *Monthly Labor Review* (February 1966); Frank P. Zeidler, *Management's Rights Under Public Sector Collective Bargaining Agreements* (Washington, D.C.: International Personnel Management Association, 1980).

mangement science, also called OP-ERATIONS RESEARCH, approach to management dating from World War II that seeks to apply the scientific method to managerial problems. Because of its emphasis on mathematical techniques, management science as a term is frequently used interchangeably with operations research. Management science should not be confused with Frederick W. Taylor's Scientific Management Movement. For an elementary introduction, *see* Stafford Beer, *Management Science: The Business Use of Operations Research* (New York: Doubleday and Co., 1968). For a governmental perspective, *see* Michael J. White, *Management Science in Federal Agencies: The Adoption and Diffusion of a Socio-Technical Innovation* (Lexington, Mass.: Lexington Books, 1975). *Also see* Jack Byrd, *Operations Research Models for Public Administration* (Lexington, Mass.: Lexington Books, 1975); Charles E. Pinkus and Anne Dixson, *Solving Local Government Problems: Practical Applications of Operations Research in Cities and Regions* (London: Allen & Unwin, 1981).

Management Science, leading monthly management journal for those who are mathematically oriented.
Management Science
Graduate School of Business
Columbia University
401 Uris Hall
New York, NY 10027

"Management Theory Jungle," title of an article by Harold Koontz that appeared in the *Journal of the Academy of Management* (December 1961), wherein Koontz sought to classify the major schools of management theory into six groupings: (1) the management process school, (2) the empirical school, (3) the human behavior school, (4) the social system school, (5) the decision theory school, and (6) the mathematical school. Koontz noted that the terminology and principles of the various schools of management thought have resulted in a "semantics jungle." For an update, *see* Harold Koontz, "The Management Theory Jungle Revisited," *Academy of Management Review* (April 1980).

management trainee, administrative job title loosely assigned to a wide variety of entry-level positions that are usually reserved for new college graduates. *See* Hal Anderson, "Selecting Management Trainees," *Personnel Journal* (November 1976).

manager, generally speaking, any organization member whose job includes supervising others. A *top manager* is one of those who makes policy for, and is responsible for, the overall success of the organization. A *middle manager* is responsible for the execution and interpretation of top management policies and for the operation of the various departments. A *supervisory manager* is responsible for the final implementation of policies by rank and file employees.

manager, project, *see* PROJECT MANAGER.

managerial grid, the basis of Robert R. Blake and Jane S. Mouton's widely implemented organization development program. By using a graphic gridiron format, which has an X axis locating various degrees of orientation toward production and a Y axis locating various degrees of orientation toward people, individuals scoring this "managerial grid" can place themselves at one of eighty-one available positions that register their relative orientations toward people or production. Grid scores can then be used as the point of departure for a discussion of individual and organizational growth needs. *See* Robert R. Blake and Jane S. Mouton, *The Managerial Grid* (Houston: Gulf Publishing, 1964).

managerial obsolescence, *see* OCCUPATIONAL OBSOLESCENCE.

managerial philosophy, the guiding philosophy of an organization. It need not be formally expressed. Indeed, many managers would deny that they have one. But it's always there, somewhere—whether stated or unstated, conscious or unconscious, intentional or unintentional. It is this philosophy that facilitates management's decision-making process. Of course, different managerial philosophies have evolved in reflection of differing organizational environments and work situations. For example, a managerial philosophy appropriate for a military combat unit would hardly be suitable for a medical research team seeking to find a cure for cancer. The sincerity and rigor of an employee's motivation toward his or her duties is a direct reflection of the host organization's managerial philosophy. *See* Michael Albert and Murray Silverman, "Making Management Philosophy A Cultural Reality, Part I: Get Started," *Personnel* (January–February 1984); Michael Albert and Murray Silverman, "Making Management Philosophy A Cultural Reality, Part 2: Design Human Resources Programs Accordingly," *Personnel* (March–April 1984).

managerial psychology, generally, all those concepts of human behavior in organizations that are relevant to managerial problems. A standard text is Harold J. Leavitt, *Managerial Psychology: An Introduction to Individuals, Pairs, and Groups in Organizations*, 3rd ed. (Chicago: University of Chicago Press, 1972).

managerial revolution, term that refers to James Burnham's concept that as the con-

trol of the large corporations passes from the hands of the owners into the hands of professional administrators, the society's new governing class will be the possessors not of wealth but of technical administrative expertise. *See* James Burnham, *The Managerial Revolution* (New York: The John Day Co., 1941). For a history of this new managerial class, *see* Alfred D. Chandler, Jr., *The Visible Hand: The Managerial Revolution in American Business* (Cambridge, Mass.: Harvard University Press, 1977).

mandamus, also called WRIT OF MANDAMUS, court order that compels the performance of an act.

mandatory bargaining items, those collective bargaining items that each party must bargain over if introduced by the other party.

man-day, amount of work that can be accomplished in a single normal day of work.

man Friday or GIRL FRIDAY, helper. In Daniel Defoe's 1719 novel, *Robinson Crusoe*, the hero, a castaway on a desolate island, was fortunate to find a black man who developed into a hardworking helper. He was named Friday because that was the day of the week when Crusoe rescued him from acquaintances who thought he was good enough to eat. Over time, a man Friday or girl Friday became synonymous with a general and cheerful helper.

***Manhart* decision,** *see* CITY OF LOS ANGELES, DEPARTMENT OF WATER & POWER V. MANHART.

Manhattan Project, federally financed research project during World War II which resulted in the development of the atomic bomb. This project is generally referred to as the first major involvement with science by the federal government in a policymaking role.

manit, contraction for man-minute.

man-machine systems, according to W. T. Singleton, in his *Man-Machine Systems* (Baltimore: Penguin Books, 1974), systems that have

to do with the design of work, on the assumption that work nowadays is never done by men, nor is it done by machine, it is always done by man-machine systems. The man-machine system has proved enormously successful because men and machines are so different, each compensates for the weaknesses of the other. There are therefore, problems of deciding what men should do and what machines should do in the pursuit of any objective. That is what the man-machine allocation function is about.

Also see Henry M. Parsons, *Man-Machine System Experiments* (Baltimore: Johns Hopkins Press, 1972).

manning table, also called PERSONNEL INVENTORY, listing of all of the employees in an organization by job and personal characteristics which serves as a basic reference for planning and other purposes.

manpower, *see* HUMAN RESOURCES.

Manpower Development and Training Act of 1962 (MDTA), federal statute that authorized the U.S. Department of Labor to identify the skills and capability needs of the economy and to initiate and find appropriate training programs. It was superseded by the Comprehensive Employment and Training Act of 1973. *See* Garth L. Mangum, *MDTA: Foundation of Federal Manpower Policy* (Baltimore: Johns Hopkins Press, 1968).

manpower planning, *see* HUMAN RESOURCES PLANNING.

manpower planning models, *see* HUMAN RESOURCES PLANNING MODELS.

manpower requirements analysis, *see* HUMAN RESOURCES REQUIREMENTS ANALYSIS.

manpower utilization, *see* HUMAN RESOURCES UTILIZATION.

marble-cake federalism, *see* FEDERALISM, MARBLE-CAKE.

Marbury v. *Madison,* 1 Cranch 137 (1803), a preeminent Supreme Court case that established the court's power of judicial review—the power to declare federal legislation unconstitutional and consequently unenforceable through the courts. Judicial review extends to activities of state and local governments as well as to those of executive and administrative officials of the federal government.

March, James G. (1928-   ), social psychologist best known for his application of behavioral science concepts to organizational concerns. He wrote (with Herbert A. Simon) a landmark book in organizational behavior, *Organizations* (New York: John Wiley & Sons, 1958). Other major works include: *A Behavioral Theory of the Firm*, with R. M. Cyert (Englewood Cliffs, N.J.: Prentice-Hall, 1963); *Handbook of Organizations,* ed. (Chicago: Rand McNally, 1965).

marginal analysis, any technique that seeks to determine the point at which the cost of something (for example, an additional employee or machine) will be worthwhile or pay for itself.

marginal cost pricing, pricing equal to the marginal (additional) costs to a government of the last unit of a good or service produced.

marginal employees, those members of an organization who contribute least to the organization's mission because of their personal sloth or the inherent nature of their duties. *See* Charles A. O'Reilly III and Barton A. Weitz, "Managing Marginal Employees: The Use of Warnings and Dismissals," *Administrative Science Quarterly* (September 1980).

marginal productivity theory of wages, theory holding that the wages of workers will be determined by the value of the productivity of the marginal worker; additional workers will not be hired if the value of the added production is less than the wages that must be paid them. Consequently, wages will tend to equal the value of the product contributed by the last (the marginal) worker hired. The theory, first formulated by John Bates Clark in 1899, has been severely criticized for being premised upon business circumstances that tend to be uncommon in real life. For the original source, see John Bates Clark, *The Distribution of Wealth* (New York: Macmillan, 1899). For analysis, see J. R. Hicks, *The Theory of Wages*, 2nd ed. (London: Macmillan, 1963).

marginal tax rate, the tax rate or percentage which is applied on the last increment of income for purposes of computing federal or other income taxes.

Marshall, Alfred (1842-1924), English economist who provided many of the foundations of modern microeconomic theory.

Marshall Plan, aid program proposed by George Catlett Marshall (1880-1959) U.S. Army Chief of Staff during World War II. In 1947 President Harry S. Truman made him Secretary of State. In June of that year he proposed the European Recovery Program, a massive aid program that became known as the Marshall Plan. The plan worked so well and became so well known that the phrase entered the language, meaning any massive use of federal funds to solve a major social problem. See Norton E. Long, "A Marshall Plan for Cities?" *Public Interest* (Winter 1977); Charles L. Mee, Jr., *The Marshall Plan: The Launching of Pax Americana* (New York: Simon & Schuster, 1984).

Marshall v. Barlow's, Inc., 436 U.S. 307 (1978), U.S. Supreme Court case which interpreted the Fourth Amendment's prohibition on unreasonable searches to impose a warrant requirement on Occupational Safety and Health Administration inspections. The court ruled that such warrants do not require evidence establishing probable cause that a violation has occurred on the premises. Rather, a judge can issue an OSHA warrant upon a showing that the inspection follows a reasonable administrative or legislative plan for enforcing the Occupational Safety and Health Act.

martinet, strict disciplinarian. The word comes from an inspector general in the army of France's Louis XIV, Jean Martinet, who was so despised for his spit-and-polish discipline that he was "accidentally" killed by his own soldiers while leading an assault in 1672.

Maryland v. Wirtz, see NATIONAL LEAGUE OF CITIES V. USERY.

Marxism, the doctrine of revolution based on the writings of Karl Marx (1818-1883) and Friedrich Engels (1820-1895) which maintains that human history is a history of struggle between the exploiting and exploited classes. They wrote the *Communist Manifesto* (1848) "to do for history what Darwin's theory has done for biology." The basic theme of Marxism holds that the proletariat will suffer so from alienation that they will rise up against the bourgeoisie who own the means of production and overthrow the system of capitalism which has so neglected the labor theory of value. After a brief period of rule by "the dictatorship of the proletariat," the classless society of communism would be forthcoming. While Marxism currently has a strong influence on the economies of the second, third, and fourth worlds, its intent has never been fully achieved. Indeed, because Marx's writings are so vast and often contradictory, serious Marxists spend considerable time arguing about just what Marx "really" meant. Marx's magnum opus, *Das Kapital* (1867), is frequently referred to as the "bible of socialism."

Maslow, Abraham H. (1908-1970), psychologist best known for his theory of human motivation, which was premised upon a "needs hierarchy" within which an individual moved up or down as the needs of each level were satisfied or threatened. Major works include: *Motivation and Personality* (New York: Harper & Row, 1954;

2nd ed., 1970); *Eupsychian Management* (Homewood, Ill.: Richard D. Irwin, 1965). For a biography, *see* Frank G. Goble, *The Third Force: The Psychology of Abraham Maslow* (New York: Grossman Publishers, 1970).

See also SELF-ACTUALIZATION.

Massachusetts Board of Retirement v. Murgia, 427 U.S. 307 (1976), U.S. Supreme Court case which held that a state statute requiring uniformed state police to retire at age fifty was not a violation of equal protection. The court ruled that the state had met its burden of showing some rational relationship between the statute and the purpose of maintaining the physical condition of its police.

Massachusetts v. Mellon, Frothingham v. Mellon, 262 U.S. 447 (1923), Supreme Court decision holding that federal taxpayers do not have standing to sue the government in federal court by virtue of the "injury" they bear due to taxation.

mass picketing, tactic used when a union wants to indicate broad support for a strike. A "mass" of strikers picket a place of business in order to discourage nonstrikers from entering the premises.

mass transit, the public provision of transportation in an urban area, typically governed by a special district.

master, skilled worker in a trade who is qualified to train apprentices.

See also JOURNEYMAN.

master agreement, also called MASTER CONTRACT, collective bargaining contract that serves as a model for an entire industry or segment of that industry. While the master agreement serves to standardize the economic benefits of all of the employees covered by it, it is often supplemented by a local contract which deals with the varying circumstances of the various local unions.

mastery, perfect performance on a test.

Mastro Plastics Corp. v. National Labor Relations Board, 350 U.S. 270 (1956), U.S. Supreme Court case which held that in the absence of contractual or statutory provision to the contrary, an employer's unfair labor practices provide adequate grounds for an orderly strike. In such circumstances, the striking employees "do not lose their status and are entitled to reinstatement with back pay, even if replacements for them have been made."

matching funds, those funds provided for a specific purpose by one level of government as a condition for receiving funds for this same purpose from another level of government.

matching item, test item that asks which one of a group of words, pictures, etc., matches up with those of another group.

matching share, also HIGH MATCH and LOW MATCH, the contribution that grant recipients are required to make to supplement the grantor's grant moneys. A *high match* is a recipient's contribution that is 50 percent or greater. A *low match* is a recipient's contribution that is less than 50 percent of the total cost.

maternity leave, formally approved temporary absence from work for childbirth and its aftermath.

See also the following entries:
BIRTH LEAVE
CLEVELAND BOARD OF EDUCATION V. LAFLEUR
MONELL V. DEPT. OF SOCIAL SERVICES, NEW YORK CITY
NASHVILLE GAS CO. V. SATTY
PREGNANCY DISCRIMINATION ACT OF 1978

Mathews v. Eldridge, 424 U.S. 319 (1976), U.S. Supreme Court case which held that while due process requires pretermination hearings for recipients of welfare benefits, it does not require such hearings for those who receive disability benefits.

matrix diamond, basic structural form of

matrix organizations; this is in contrast to the pyramid—the basic structural form of traditional organizations.

matrix manager, any manager who shares formal authority over a subordinate with another manager.

matrix organization, any organization using a multiple command system whereby an employee might be accountable to one superior for overall performance as well as to one or more leaders of particular projects. "Matrix" is a generic term that is used to refer to various organizational structures. For an exhaustive analysis, see Stanley M. Davis and Paul R. Lawrence, *Matrix* (Reading, Mass.: Addison-Wesley Publishing Co., 1977). For critiques, see Kenneth Knight, "Matrix Organization: A Review," *Journal of Management Studies* (May 1976); Harvey F. Kolodny, "Evolution to a Matrix Organization," *Academy of Management Review* (October 1979); Mary Ellen Simon, "Matrix Management at the U.S. Consumer Product Safety Commission," *Public Administration Review* (July-August 1983).

See also PROJECT MANAGEMENT and TASK FORCE.

Matthew Effect, Robert Merton's concept that refers to communications and reward systems in the scientific community and how they affect priorities in government sponsorship of scientific research. Drawing from the biblical book of Matthew a verse which states, "for every one that hath shall be given," Merton describes the "Matthew Effect" as an influence in the reward system of science which provides honor, recognition, and financial support for established scientists to the exclusion of new or young scientists and scientific ideas. The policy effect is inertial in that the same scientists, research, and ideas are given federal money in the form of grants, fellowships, etc., to the exclusion of others. See Robert K. Merton, "The Matthew Effect in Science," *Science* (January 5, 1968).

maturity curve, also called CAREER CURVE and SALARY CURVE, technique for determining the salaries of professional and technical employees that relates the employee's education and experience to on-the-job performance. For example, after it is determined what the average compensation for a professional employee is for each of various categories of experience, the individual employee is assigned a salary based upon whether he or she is considered average, below average, or above average in performance. See H. C. Rickard, "Maturity Curve Surveys," *Handbook of Wage and Salary Administration*, M. L. Rock, ed. (New York: McGraw-Hill, 1972); Robert L. McCormack, "A New Method for Fitting Salary Curves," *Personnel Journal* (October 1967).

May Day, day selected in 1889 by the International Socialist Congress as the day to publicize the eight-hour day. The American Federation of Labor planned a major demonstration on May 1, 1890. Since then May Day has become a major holiday in socialist countries. In 1955, President Eisenhower proclaimed May 1 as "Loyalty Day."

Mayo, Elton (1880-1949), principal organizer and researcher of the famous Hawthorne experiments, considered the founder of the human relations approach in industry. Major works include: *The Human Problems of An Industrial Civilization* (New York: The Viking Press, 1933); *The Social Problems of An Industrial Civilization* (New York: The Viking Press, 1945). For a biography, see Lyndall F. Urwick, *The Life and Work of Elton Mayo* (London: Urwick, Orr & Partners, Ltd., 1960).

mayor-council system, also STRONG MAYOR and WEAK MAYOR, system of urban government with a separately elected executive, the mayor, and an urban legislature, council, usually elected in partisan ward elections. It is called a *strong mayor* system if the office of mayor is filled by separate city-wide elections and has powers, such as veto, appointment and removal, etc. In contrast, where the office of mayor lacks such powers it is called a *weak mayor* system. This designation does not take into account any informal powers possessed by the incumbent mayor, only the formal powers of the office. Hence, Richard Daley of Chicago was a strong mayor in a weak mayor system. *See* Jeffrey L. Pressman, "Preconditions of Mayoral Leadership," *American Political Science Review* (June 1972); Paul Hain, Chris Garcia, and Judd Conway, "From Council-Manager to Mayor-Council: The Case of Albuquerque," *Nation's Cities* (October 1975).

MBA, *see* MPA.

MBO, *see* MANAGEMENT BY OBJECTIVES.

McAuliffe v. Mayor of New Bedford, 155 Mass. 216 (1892), Massachusetts Supreme Court case concerning the constitutionality of a city rule prohibiting policemen from joining labor unions. Justice Oliver Wendell Holmes' immortal words were:

> The petitioner may have a constitutional right to talk politics, but he has no constitutional right to be a policeman. There are few employments for hire in which the servant does not agree to suspend his constitutional right of free speech, as well as of idleness, by the implied terms of his contract. The servant cannot complain, as he takes the employment on the terms which are offered him.

The logic of this decision has been rejected by the Supreme Court in more recent years. *See* David H. Rosenbloom, *Federal Service and the Constitution* (Ithaca: Cornell University Press, 1971).

McCarthyism, extreme anti-communism. Senator Joseph R. McCarthy of Wisconsin rose to fame and influence during the 1950s by recklessly charging that individuals or organizations were communist or communist influenced. Today any actions by public officials which flout individual rights would be considered examples of McCarthyism except by those totally insensitive to the concept of due process of law.

McCarthy v. Philadelphia Civil Service Commission, 424 U.S. 645 (1976), U.S. Supreme Court case which upheld an ordinance requiring that city employees live within city limits.

McClellan Committee, Senate Committee on Improper Activities in Labor-Management Relations, chaired by Senator John L. McClellan (1896–1977) of Arkansas. The committee's findings of violence and corruption spurred the passage of the Labor-Management Reporting and Disclosure (Landrum-Griffin) Act of 1959. For accounts of the committee's work by its chairman and legal counsel, *see* John L. McClellan, *Crime Without Punishment* (New York: Duell, Sloan and Pearce, 1962); Robert F. Kennedy, *The Enemy Within* (New York: Harper & Row, 1960).

McClelland, David C. (1917–), psychologist widely considered the foremost authority on achievement motivation. The body of McClelland's work asserts that achievement motivation can be developed within individuals, provided that the environment in which they live and work is supportive. Major works include: *The Achievement Motive,* with J. W. Atkinson, R. A. Clark, and E. A. Lowell (New York: Appleton-Century-Crofts, 1953); *The Achieving Society* (Princeton, N.J.: Van Nostrand, 1961); *Motivating Economic Achievement,* with D. G. Winter (New York: The Free Press, 1969).

McConnell v. Anderson, 451 F.2d 193 (1971), certiorari denied 405 U.S. 1046 (1972), U.S. Court of Appeals for the Eighth Circuit case holding the dismissal of a state university employee for personal conduct involving the public application for a marriage license with another male to be constitutional.

McDonald v. City of West Branch, Michigan, 80 L. Ed. 2d 302 (1984), U.S. Supreme Court case which held that a discharged police officer could seek redress in court even though he had fully utilized the grievance procedure in his union's contract, culminating in an arbitrator's ruling that the discharge was warranted.

McDonald v. Santa Fe Trail Transportation Co., 424 U.S. 952 (1976), U.S. Supreme Court case which held an employer could not impose racially discriminatory discipline on employees guilty of the same offense.

McDonnell Douglas Corporation v. Green, 411 U.S. 792 (1973), U.S. Supreme Court case which held that an employee could establish a prima facie case of discrimination by initially showing (1) that he or she was a member of a racial minority; (2) that he or she applied and was qualified for an opening for which the employer sought applicants; (3) that despite qualifications he or she was rejected; (4) that after rejection the position remained open and the employer continued to seek applicants.

McGregor, Douglas M. (1906-1964), organizational humanist and managerial philosopher who is best known for his conceptualization of Theory X and Theory Y. Major works include: *The Human Side of Enterprise* (New York: McGraw-Hill, 1960); *The Professional Manager* (New York: McGraw-Hill, 1967). For an evaluation of McGregor's impact and contribution, *see* Warren G. Bennis, "Chairman Mac in Perspective," *Harvard Business Review* (September-October 1972).

MDTA, *see* MANPOWER DEVELOPMENT AND TRAINING ACT OF 1962.

mean, simple average of a set of measurements, obtained by summing the measurements and dividing by the number of them.

mean deviation, *see* AVERAGE DEVIATION.

means test, criterion used to determine if someone is eligible for government welfare or other benefits. For example, a family might only be allowed certain welfare benefits if their annual cash income is less than $10,609 a year (the federal government's definition of poverty for a family of four). The means test would then be income below that level.

Meany, George (1894-1979), labor leader who started out as a plumber in a Bronx local and was president of the AFL-CIO from its creation in 1955 to 1979. For a biography, *see* Joseph C. Goulden, *Meany* (New York: Atheneum, 1972); Archie Robinson, *George Meany and His Times: A Biography* (New York: Simon and Schuster, 1981).

measured day work, also called MEASURED DAY RATE, an incentive wage plan that is premised upon a guaranteed base wage rate that is based upon previous job performance. *See* Andrew J. Waring, "The Case for the Measured Day Rate Plan," *Personnel Journal* (October 1961).

measure of dispersion, also called MEASURE OF VARIABILITY, any statistical measure showing the extent to which individual test scores are concentrated about or spread out from a measure of central tendency.

mechanical aptitude tests, tests designed to measure how well an individual can learn to perform tasks that involve the understanding and manipulation of mechanical devices. Classified into two subgroups—mechanical reasoning and spatial relations.

mechanistic system, organization form, proven to be most appropriate under stable conditions, which is characterized by: (1) a high degree of task differentiation and specialization with a precise delineation of rights and responsibilities; (2) a high degree of reliance on the traditional hierarchical structure; (3) a tendency for the top of the hierarchy to control all incoming and outgoing communications; (4) an emphasis on vertical interactions between superiors and subordinates; (5) a demand for loyalty to the organization and to superiors; and

(6) a greater importance placed on internal (local) knowledge, skill, and experience, in contrast to more general (cosmopolitan) knowledge, experience, and skill. The classic analysis of mechanistic systems is to be found in Tom Burns and G. M. Stalker, *The Management of Innovation* (Chicago: Quadrangle Books, 1961).

See also ORGANIC SYSTEM.

mechanization, *see* AUTOMATION.

med-arb, a combination of mediation and arbitration which engages a third party neutral in both mediation and arbitration. The main idea is to mediate in an effort to resolve the impasse or at least reduce the number of issues going to arbitration. Then, where mediation is unsuccessful, some form of binding arbitration is used. *See* James L. Stern, "The Mediation of Interest Disputes by Arbitrators Under the Wisconsin Med-Arb Law for Local Government Employees," *Arbitration Journal* (June 1984).

median, middle score in a distribution, the 50th percentile, the point that divides the group into two equal parts. Half of a group of scores fall below the median and half above it.

mediation, also CONCILIATION, any attempt by an impartial third party to help settle disputes between labor and management. A mediator has no power but that of persuasion. The mediator's suggestions are advisory in nature and may be rejected by both parties. Mediation and conciliation tend to be used interchangeably to denote the entrance of an impartial third party into a labor dispute. However, there is a distinction. *Conciliation* is the less active term. It technically refers simply to efforts to bring the parties together so that they may resolve their problems themselves. *Mediation,* in contrast, is a more active term. It implies that an active effort will be made to help the parties reach agreement by clarifying issues, asking questions, and making specific proposals. However, the usage of the two terms has been so blurred that the only place where it is absolutely necessary to distinguish between them is in a dictionary. For a text, *see* William E. Simkin, *Mediation and the Dynamics of Collective Bargaining* (Washington, D.C.: Bureau of National Affairs, 1971). For a legal analysis, *see* Lon L. Fuller, "Mediation—Its Forms and Functions," *Southern California Law Review* (Winter 1971). For a public sector perspective, *see* Paul D. Staudohar, "Some Implications of Mediation for Resolution of Bargaining Impasses in Public Employment," *Public Personnel Management* (July-August 1973); Ronald Hoh, "The Effectiveness of Mediation in Public Sector Arbitration Systems: The Iowa Experience," *Arbitration Journal* (June 1984). For a bibliography, *see* Edward Levin and Daniel V. DeSantis, *Mediation: An Annotated Bibliography* (Ithaca, N.Y.: New York State School of Industrial and Labor Relations, Cornell University, 1978). *Also see* Ahmad Karim and Richard Pegnetter, "Mediator Strategies and Qualities and Mediation Effectiveness," *Industrial Relations* (Winter 1982); John R. Stepp *et al.,* "Helping Labor and Management See and Solve Problems," *Monthly Labor Review* (September 1982); Deborah M. Kolb, "Roles Mediators Play: State and Federal Practice," *Industrial Relations* (Winter 1981); Perry A. Zirkel and J. Gary Lutz, "Characteristics and Functions of Mediators: A Pilot Study," *The Arbitration Journal* (June 1981); Deborah M. Kolb, *The Mediators* (Cambridge, Mass.: M.I.T. Press, 1983); Arnold M. Zak, *Public Sector Mediation* (Washington, D.C.: Bureau of National Affairs, Inc., 1985).

See also PREVENTIVE MEDIATION.

Mediation Service, abbreviated way of referring to the Federal Mediation and Conciliation Service or state agencies performing a similar function.

mediator, individual who acts as an impartial third party in order to help resolve labor-management disputes. Appointed by an administrative agency or by the parties involved, the mediator's role is to help the parties reach an agreement short of a strike. *See* Arthur S. Meyer, "Function of the Mediator in Collective Bargaining," *Industrial and Labor Relations Review* (January 1960).

Medicaid, federal-state program to pay for medical care for the poor.

medical insurance, supplemental, *see* SUPPLEMENTAL MEDICAL INSURANCE.

Medicare, the national health insurance program for the elderly and the disabled. The two parts of Medicare—hospital insurance and medical insurance—help protect people sixty-five and over from the high costs of health care. Also eligible for Medicare are disabled people under sixty-five who have been entitled to social security disability benefits for twenty-four or more consecutive months (including adults who are receiving benefits because they have been disabled since childhood). Insured workers and their dependents who need dialysis treatment or a kidney transplant because of permanent kidney failure also have Medicare protection. For a history of how the Medicare bill passed, *see* Max J. Skidmore, *Medicare and the American Rhetoric of Reconciliation* (University, Ala.: University of Alabama Press, 1970). *Also see* Theodore Marmor, *The Politics of Medicare* (Chicago: Aldine, 1973).

meet-and-confer discussions, technique used mostly in the public sector for determining conditions of employment whereby the representatives of the employer and the employee organization hold periodic discussions to seek agreement on matters within the scope of representation. Any written agreement is in the form of a nonbinding memorandum of understanding. This technique is often used where formal collective bargaining is not authorized.

megatrends, term popularized by John Naisbitt in his 1982 book bearing the same title. Megatrends are basic socio/economic/technological trends that are—and will continue—influencing basic public, non-profit and for-profit organization strategies at least through the 1980's.

Member of Congress, person elected to either the Senate or the House of Representatives. A member of the Senate is usually referred to as Senator and a member of the House of Representatives as Representative or Congressman or Congresswoman.

A member of the House of Representatives must be at least twenty-five years of age, must have been a United States citizen for at least seven years, and must reside in the state from which he or she is sent to Congress.

A member of the United States Senate must be at least thirty years of age, must have been a citizen of the United States for nine years, and must be a resident of the state he or she will represent in Congress.

In the Senate, when a vacancy occurs for any reason, the 17th Amendment directs the governor of the state to call an election to fill such vacancy, and authorizes the legislature to make provision for an immediate appointment pending such election. In the event that state law does allow for such an appointment made by the governor, the person so appointed serves only until the next general election, or the special election called for the purpose of filling the vacancy. In such an election, the person chosen serves only the remainder of the original term.

In the House of Representatives vacancies may be filled only by election.

menial, originally a household servant. For centuries, it has been used as a term of disparagement and contempt used to describe work of degrading drudgery. According to Albert L. Porter, "Repugnance for 'Menial Jobs'," *Management of Personnel Quarterly* (Winter 1971),

a man's sense of well-being and meaningfulness in work is not so much a matter of external circumstances—the kind of job he has—as it is of his deepdown belief that he is a worthy human being. If he lacks that, any job can seem dissatisfying and "menial." Executives may suffer from this (or related behaviors) as much as assembly-line workers.

mentally handicapped employees, also called MENTALLY RETARDED EMPLOYEES, individuals with less than normal intellectual ability. On standard tests, an intelligence quotient of 70 is usually thought to be the upper borderline for those who are classified as retarded. Until comparatively recently, the retarded had only the most limited opportunities in the open job market. But more enlightened attitudes towards dealing with retarded individuals and an employment climate influenced by the concept of equal employment opportunity for all are rapidly improving the employment prospects for the mentally handicapped/retarded. Mental deficiency and vocational deficiency are not synonymous. According to Donn E. Prolin, in *Vocational Preparation of Retarded Citizens* (Columbus, Ohio: Charles E. Merrill, 1976), "one of the greatest problems that persons with mental retardation encounter is the continual underestimation of their potentials by the general public and professional workers." *Also see* Howard F. Rudd, "Supervising the Mentally Handicapped: The Procedures, the Rewards," *Supervisory Management* (December 1976); The National Association for Retarded Citizens, "Mentally Retarded Persons in the Open Job Market," *Personnel Journal* (May 1977).

See also PENNHURST STATE SCHOOL V. HALDERMAN.

mentally ill employees, *see* EMOTIONALLY HANDICAPPED EMPLOYEES.

mentally retarded employees, *see* MENTALLY HANDICAPPED EMPLOYEES.

mentor, wise counselor. The word comes from Homer's *The Odyssey.* When Odysseus set off for the war at Troy, he left his house and wife in the care of a friend named Mentor. When things got rough at home for Odysseus' family, Athena, the goddess of wisdom, assumed the shape of Mentor and provided Telemachus, the son of Odysseus, with some

very helpful advice about how to deal with the problems of his most unusual adolescence. For an analysis of the importance of mentoring in organizational careers, *see* Eileen C. Shapiro, Florence P. Haseltine, and Mary P. Rowe, "Moving Up: Role Models, Mentors and the 'Patron System'," *Sloan Management Review* (Spring 1978). For a case study, *see* Barbara Kellerman, "Mentoring in Political Life: The Case of Willy Brandt," *American Political Science Review* (June 1978). *Also see* Mary C. Johnson, "Speaking From Experience: 'Mentors—The Key to Development and Growth,'" *Training and Development Journal* (July 1980); Gerald R. Roche, "Much Ado About Mentors," *Harvard Business Review* (January-February 1979); T. J. Halatin, "Why Be a Mentor," *Supervisory Management* (February 1981); Kathy E. Kram, *Mentoring at Work: Developmental Relationships in Organizational Life* (Glenview, Ill.: Scott, Foresman, 1985); Laura L. Vertz, "Women, Occupational Advancement, and Mentoring: An Analysis of One Public Organization," *Public Administration Review* (May-June 1985).

merchant guild, *see* GUILD.

merit increase, raise in pay based upon a favorable review of an employee's performance. This is the way most organizations seek to relate quality of performance to financial rewards. *See* A. Mikalachki, "There Is No Merit in Merit Pay!" *The Business Quarterly* (Spring 1976); Ernest C. Miller, "Top- and Middle-Management Compensation—Part 2: Incentive Bonus and Merit Increase Plans," *Compensation Review* (Fourth Quarter 1976); Douglas L. Fleuter, "A Different Approach to Merit Increases," *Personnel Journal* (April 1979); James T. Brinks, "Is There Merit in Merit Increases?" *The Personnel Administrator* (May 1980); Jeffrey D. Schwartz, "Maintaining Merit Compensation in a High Inflation Economy," *Personnel Journal* (February 1982); Robert A. Printz and David A. Waldman, "The Merit of Merit Pay," *Personnel Administrator* (January 1985).

meritocracy, word coined by Michael Young, in his *The Rise of the Meritocracy, 1870-2033* (London: Thames & Hudson, 1958; Penguin Books, 1961). Referred to a governing class that was both intelligent and energetic, yet sowed the seeds of its own destruction because of its obsession with test scores and paper qualifications that eventuallly forced those deemed to have lesser IQs to revolt. A favorite slogan of the revolutionaries was, "Beauty is achievable by all." Today meritocracy is often used to refer to any elitist system of government or education. The grisly connotation of the word's original use has been effectively forgotten.

merit pay system, also called MERIT PAY PROGRAM, set of procedures designed to reward employees with salary increases reflective of their on-the-job performance. According to Myles H. Goldberg, "Another Look at Merit Pay Programs," *Compensation Review* (Third Quarter 1977),

many merit pay programs are built around the concept of a fixed pool of merit increase dollars. This pool is derived usually by applying a percentage merit increase factor to the salaries of currently employed staff. Administrative guidelines define the average merit increase (usually as a percentage of salary) and restrict the increase to an amount within a set range. Typically, satisfactory or acceptable performance merits an average pay increase, better-than-acceptable performance merits a larger increase, and less-than-acceptable performance merits a lower increase.

Also see Edward E. Lawler, "Merit Pay: Fact or Fiction?" *Management Review* (April 1981); Richard E. Kopelman and Leon Reinharth, "Research Results: The Effect of Merit Pay Practices on White Collar Performance," *Compensation Review* (Fourth Quarter 1982); Jone L. Pearce and James L. Perry, "Federal Merit Pay: A Longitudinal Analysis," *Public Administration Review* (July-August 1983).

merit principle, the concept that members of an organization are selected and promoted based on achievements measured in a standard way through open competition.

merit promotion, selection to a higher grade made solely on the basis of job-related qualifications without regard to factors such as race, color, religion, national origin, sex, age, political belief, marital status, or physical handicap.

merit raise, *see* MERIT INCREASE.

merit system, a public sector concept of staffing which implies that no test of party membership is involved in the selection, promotion, or retention of government employees and that a constant effort is made to select the best qualified individuals available for appointment and advancement. For a classic analysis of why it ain't necessarily so, *see* E. S. Savas and Sigmund G. Ginsburg, "The Civil Service: A Meritless System?" *The Public Interest* (Summer 1973). *Also see* Nicholas P. Lovrich, Jr., *et al.,* "Do Public Servants Welcome or Fear Merit Evaluation of Their Performance?" *Public Administration Review* (May-June 1980); Lawrence D. Greene, "Federal Merit Requirements: A Retrospective Look," *Public Personnel Management* (Spring 1982).

merit system principles, nine basic merit principles that the Civil Service Reform Act of 1978 put into law. They should govern all personnel practices in the federal government and define prohibited practices.

Personnel Practices and Actions in the Federal Government Require:
- Recruitment from all segments of society, and selection and advancement on the basis of ability, knowledge, and skills, under fair and open competition.
- Fair and equitable treatment in all personnel management matters, without regard to politics, race, color, religion, national origin, sex, marital status, age, or handicapping condition, and with proper regard for individual privacy and constitutional rights.

- Equal pay for work of equal value, considering both national and local rates paid by private employers, with incentives and recognition for excellent performance.
- High standards of integrity, conduct, and concern for the public interest.
- Efficient and effective use of the federal work force.
- Retention of employees who perform well, correcting the performance of those whose work is inadequate, and separation of those who cannot or will not meet required standards.
- Improved performance through effective education and training.
- Protection of employees from arbitrary action, personal favoritism, or political coercion.
- Protection of employees against reprisal for lawful disclosures of information.

Officials and Employees Who Are Authorized to Take Personnel Actions Are Prohibited From:
- Discriminating against any employee or applicant.
- Soliciting or considering any recommendation on a person who requests or is being considered for a personnel action unless the material is an evaluation of the person's work performance, ability, aptitude, or general qualifications, or character, loyalty, and suitability.
- Using official authority to coerce political actions, to require political contributions, or to retaliate for refusal to do these things.
- Willfully deceiving or obstructing an individual as to his or her right to compete for federal employment.
- Influencing anyone to withdraw from competition, whether to improve or worsen the prospects of any applicant.
- Granting any special preferential treatment or advantage not authorized by law to a job applicant or employee.
- Appointing, employing, promoting, or advancing relatives in their agencies.
- Taking or failing to take a personnel action as a reprisal against employees who exercise their appeal rights; refuse to engage in political activity; or lawfully disclose violations of law, rule, or regulation, or mismanagement, gross waste of funds, abuse of authority, or a substantial and specific danger to public health or safety.
- Taking or failing to take any other personnel action violating a law, rule, or regulation directly related to merit system principles.

Merit Systems Protection Board (MSPB), independent federal government agency created by the Civil Service Reform Act of 1978 and designed to safeguard both the merit system and individual employees against abuses and unfair personnel actions. The MSPB is headed by three board members, appointed on a bipartisan basis to seven-year nonrenewable terms. The MSPB hears and decides employee appeals and orders corrective and disciplinary actions against an employee or agency when appropriate. It also oversees the merit system and reports annually to Congress on how the system is functioning.

Within the MSPB is an independent special counsel, appointed by the president for a five-year term. The special counsel has the power to investigate charges of prohibited personnel practices (including reprisals against whistleblowers), to ask MSPB to stop personnel actions in cases involving prohibited personnel practices, and to bring disciplinary charges before the MSPB against those who violate merit system law.

Merit Systems Protection Board
1120 Vermont Ave., N.W.
Washington, D.C. 20419
(202) 653-7124

Merrick differential piece rate, also called MERRICK MULTIPLE PIECE RATE, incentive wage plan that establishes three different piece rates on the basis of performance— one for beginners, one for average workers, and one for superior workers.

Merton, Robert K. (1910-   ), sociologist who did pioneering work on the concepts of bureaucratic goal displacement and bureaucratic dysfunctions. Major works include: "Bureaucratic Structure and Personality," *Social Forces* 18 (1940); *Social Theory and Social Structure* (New York: The Free Press, 1949; rev. ed., 1957); *Reader in Bureaucracy*, edited with others (New York: The Free Press, 1952); *The Focused Interview*, with others (New York: The Free Press, 1956); *The Sociology of Science: Theoretical and Empirical Investigations* (Chicago: University of Chicago Press, 1973); *Sociological Ambivalence and Other Essays* (New York: The Free Press, 1976).

Metcalf, Henry C. (1867-1942), a leading advocate of a "humanized industrialism" and co-author of one of the earliest and most influential texts on personnel administration. Major works include: *Personnel Administration: Its Principles and Practices*, with Ordway Tead (New York: McGraw-Hill, 1920); *Scientific Foundations of Business Administration* (Baltimore: The Williams & Wilkins Co., 1926); *Dynamic Administration: The Collected Papers of Mary Parker Follett*, edited with Lyndall Urwick (New York: Harper & Bros., 1942).

Metcalfe, Henry (1847-1917), a Captain in the U.S. Army who developed pioneering concepts of shop management at the Frankford Arsenal. *See* his *The Cost of Manufactures and the Administration of Workshops, Public and Private* (New York: Wiley & Sons, 1885).

metropolitan government, also CONSOLIDATED GOVERNMENT and FEDERATED GOVERNMENT, a central government for a metropolitan area. It is a *consolidated government* if all the existing local governments at the time of its formation were abolished. In contrast, under a *federated*

government each local unit retains its identity and some of its functions while other functions are transferred to the metropolitan government. *See* Joseph F. Zimmerman, *The Federated City: Community Control in Large Cities* (New York: St. Martins Press, 1972); John C. Bollens and Henry J. Schmandt, *The Metropolis: Its People, Politics, and Economic Life,* 3rd ed. (New York: Harper & Row, 1975); Charles Adrian and Charles Press, *Governing Urban America,* 5th ed. (New York: McGraw-Hill, 1977).

MFOA, *see* MUNICIPAL FINANCE OFFICERS ASSOCIATION.

M-Form Society, normative concept of U.S. society popularized by William Ouchi in 1984. The M-Form Society conceptually parallels a multi-divisional corporation in structure and method of functioning. See W. Ouchi, *The M-Form Society: How American Teamwork Can Recapture the Competitive Edge* (Reading, Mass.: Addison-Wesley Publishing Company, 1984).

MGD data, *see* MINORITY GROUPS DESIGNATOR DATA.

Mickey Mouse, pejorative term for many aspects of governmental administration. When Walt Disney's famous mouse made it "big" in the 1930s, he appeared in a variety of cartoon shorts that had him building something that would later fall apart (such as a house or boat), or generally going to a great deal of trouble for little result. So Mickey Mouse gradually gave his name to anything requiring considerable effort for slight result, including many of the Mickey Mouse requirements of personnel. The term is also applied to policies or regulations felt to be needless, silly, or mildly offensive.

microeconomics, the study of how small economic units (*i.e.,* the consumer, the household, etc.) interrelate with the market in determining the relative price of goods and the factors of production. For texts, see Robert L. Heilbroner and Lester C. Thurow, *Understanding Microeconomics*, 4th ed. (Englewood Cliffs, N.J.: Prentice-Hall, 1978); R. Stephen Polkinghorn, *Micro-Theory and Economic Choices* (Homewood, Ill.: Richard D. Irwin, Inc., 1979); William P. Albrecht, Jr., *Microeconomic Principles* (Englewood Cliffs, N.J.: Prentice-Hall, 1979); J. P. Gould, *Microeconomic Theory*, 5th ed. (Homewood, Ill.: Richard D. Irwin, Inc., 1980).

mid-career change, see CAREER CHANGE.

mid-career crisis, also MID-LIFE CRISIS, terms used to refer to a period in a person's life, usually during his/her 30s, which is marked by feelings of personal frustration and professional failure. Such feelings may or may not have a basis in fact. For general accounts of mid-life crises, see Gail Sheehy, *Passages: Predictable Crises of Adult Life* (New York: E. P. Dutton, 1976); Roger Gould, *Transformations* (New York: Simon and Schuster, 1978). For analyses of the problem of mid-career crises, see Harry Levinson, "On Being a Middle-Aged Manager," *Harvard Business Review* (July-August 1969); Robert T. Golembiewski, "Mid-Life Transition and Mid-Career Crisis: A Special Case For Individual Development," *Public Administration Review* (May-June 1978); Daniel J. Levinson et al., *The Seasons of a Man's Life* (New York: Knopf, 1978); Barbara S. Lawrence, "The Myth of the Midlife Crisis," *Sloan Management Review* (Summer 1980); Raymond E. Hill and Edwin L. Miller, "Job Change and the Middle Seasons of a Man's Life," *Academy of Management Journal* (March 1981); Richard A. Payne, "Mid-Career Block," *Personnel Journal* (April 1984).

See also STRESS.

middle management, vague delineation of organizational authority and leadership that lies below top management and above first-level supervisors. *See* Emmanuel Kay, *The Crises in Middle-Management* (New York: American Management Association, 1974); Steven H. Appelbaum, "The Mid-

dle Manager: An Examination of Aspirations and Pessimism," *The Personnel Administrator* (January 1977); Rosabeth Moss Kanter, "The Middle Manager as Innovator," *Harvard Business Review* (July-August 1982); Bernard Keys and Robert Bell, "Four Faces of the Fully Functioning Middle Manager," *California Management Review* (Summer 1982).

mid-level managers, see MIDDLE MANAGEMENT.

mid-life crisis, see MID-CAREER CRISIS.

midnight shift, tour of duty that usually runs from midnight to 8 A.M.

Midwest Review of Public Administration, see AMERICAN REVIEW OF PUBLIC ADMINISTRATION.

migratory worker, individual whose principal income is earned from temporary employment (typically in agriculture) and who, in order to find work, moves several times a year through many states. For accounts of the life of migrant workers, see Robert Coles, *Uprooted Children: The Early Life of Migrant Farm Workers* (New York: Harper & Row, 1971); Carey McWilliams, *Ill Fares the Land: Migrants and Migratory Labor in the United States* (New York: Barnes & Noble, 1967); Ronald L. Goldfarb, *Migrant Farm Workers: A Caste of Despair* (Ames, Ia.: Iowa State University Press, 1981).

mileage allowance, specific amount an employee is reimbursed for each mile for which his personal automobile is used on company business. For how to determine a mileage allowance rate, see Joseph A. Capolarello, "Employee Mileage Allowances: Too High or Too Low?" *Personnel Journal* (February 1975).

Miles' Law, "Where you stand depends on where you sit," Rufus E. Miles, Jr., "The Origin and Meaning of Miles' Law," *Public Administration Review* (September-October 1978). *Also see* Rufus E. Miles, Jr., "Miles's Six Other Maxims of

Management," *Organizational Dynamics* Summer 1979).

NEW YORK MAYOR DISCOVERS MILES' LAW

"There is no question that there is a decided difference in what I did as a congressman and what I am doing as mayor when it comes to spending money. It isn't a difference in philosophy. It is that I didn't understand what I was doing when I was in Congress because you spend other people's money. In Congress you are not aware of the costs of the programs because either the federal government is spending it and they print the dollars or, worse, you impose the cost on the cities. You just tell them what to do but don't give them the money to do it.

"So now I'm an executive. I look at what has to be done and I say to myself, how could I have voted for those dumb programs?"

SOURCE: *Wall Street Journal* (March 10, 1981)

---

military-industrial complex, a nation's armed forces and their industrial suppliers. President Dwight D. Eisenhower warned during his farewell address in 1961 that "in the councils of government we must guard against the acquisition of unwarranted influence, whether sought or unsought, by the military-industrial complex. The potential for the disastrous rise of misplaced power exists and will persist."

military leave, lengthy leave of absence for service in the armed forces of the United States or a short-term leave of absence for service in the military reserves.

military service, service in the armed forces. Military service for civil service retirement purposes is creditable provided it was active service, was terminated under honorable conditions, and was performed before separation from a civilian position under the retirement system. The federal government defines military service for retirement purposes as "service in the Army, Navy, Air Force, Marine Corps, and Coast Guard, including the service academies, and, after June 30, 1960, in the Regular Corps or Reserve Corps of the Public Health Service and, after June 30, 1961,

as a commissioned officer of the Coast and Geodetic Survey."

See also ALABAMA POWER CO. V. DAVIS and ROSTKER V. GOLDBERG.

Mill, John Stuart (1806–1873), English philosopher of utilitarianism and economist whose *Principles of Political Economy* (1848) advanced the theory of international trade.

Miller v. Wilson, 236 U.S. 373 (1915), U.S. Supreme Court case which held that a state law limiting the employment of women to eight hours a day was constitutional.

Milliken v. Bradley, 418 U.S. 717 (1974), Supreme Court case holding that de facto racial segregation in the Detroit metropolitan area public schools, in which minorities were heavily concentrated in the city as opposed to the suburbs, was not unconstitutional since it did not develop from the specific activities of the suburban school districts or any other public authority. The decision largely foreclosed court ordered busing between cities and their suburbs.

minimum wage, smallest hourly rate that may be paid to a worker. While many "minimum wages" are established by union contracts and organizational pay policies, "the" minimum wage usually refers to the federal minimum wage law — the Fair Labor Standards Act (FLSA). The minimum wage at any given time is established by Congress via FLSA amendments. The Secretary of Labor regulates some exceptions to the minimum wage. Persons with impaired earning or production capacity because of age, physical or mental deficiencies, or injury may be paid as low as 50 percent of the wage paid to a nonhandicapped worker for the same type, quality, and quantity of work.

Forty-one states, the District of Columbia, and Puerto Rico have minimum wage laws for adults with minimun rates currently in effect. State minimum wage laws are of two basic types: those that contain a minimum in the law itself (a statutory rate) and those that authorize an administrator or wage board to set minimum rates by occupation or industry. Several states combine the two types and have both a statutory minimum for most employment and provisions for wage orders to establish rates and/or working conditions for certain occupations or industries. Only the legislature can change statutory rates, but wage orders can be modified by the administrator or wage board. Under both types of minimum wage law, lower rates are generally payable to learners and apprentices, handicapped persons, and minors.

Statutory state minimum wage rates for experienced adults varied widely in mid-1982—from a low of $1.25 an hour in Georgia to a high of $3.85 in Alaska. Some states provide for automatic upward adjustment if the federal minimum wage rate is increased. When workers are covered by both the federal minimum wage law (the Fair Labor Standards Act, or FLSA) and a state law, they are entitled to the higher rate.

Full-time students may be employed at 85 percent of the minimum wage under certain conditions. For an analysis of how youth unemployment, particularly black youth, would be reduced if a lower minimum wage was available for teenagers, see "Would the 'Teenwage' Cut Unemployment?" Business Week (September 19, 1977). Also see Peyton Elder, "The 1977 Amendments to the Federal Minimum Wage Law," Monthly Labor Review (January 1978); Sar A. Levitan and R. S. Belous, "The Minimum Wage Today: How Well Does It Work?" Monthly Labor Review (July 1979); D. Quinn Mills and Shirley Frobes, "Impact of Increases in the Federal Minimum Wage on Target Groups in Urban Areas," Public Policy (Summer 1981); Robert Swidinsky and David A. Wilton, "Minimum Wages, Wage Inflation, and the Relative Wage Structure," The Journal of Human Resources (Spring 1982); John Z. Drabicki and Akira Takayama, "Minimum Wage Regulation and Economic Growth," Journal of Economics and Business, Vol. 34, No. 3 (1982); Curtis L. Gilroy, "The Effects of the Minimum Wage on Farm Employment: A New Model," Monthly Labor Review (June 1982); Brigitte H. Sellekaerts and Stephen W. Welch, "An Econometric Analysis of Minimum Wage Noncompliance," Industrial Relations (Spring 1984).

See also NATIONAL LEAGUE OF CITIES V. USERY and WEST COAST HOTEL V. PARRISH.

mini-shift, tour of duty for a permanent part-time employee. For an analysis of its utility, see William B. Werther, Jr., "Mini-Shifts: An Alternative to Overtime," Personnel Journal (March 1976).

FLSA Minimum Wage Standards

Legislation	Hourly Rate	Effective Date
Act of 1938	$ .25	Oct. 24, 1938
	.30	Oct. 24, 1939
	.40	Oct. 24, 1945
Amendments of:		
1949	.75	Jan. 25, 1950
1955	1.00	Mar. 1, 1956
1961	1.15	Sept. 3, 1961
	1.25	Sept. 3, 1963
1966	1.40	Feb. 1, 1967
	1.60	Feb. 1, 1968
1974	2.00	May 1, 1974
	2.10	Jan. 1, 1975
	2.30	Jan. 1, 1976
1977	2.65	Jan. 1, 1978
	2.90	Jan. 1, 1979
	3.10	Jan. 1, 1980
	3.35	Jan. 1, 1981

ministerial function, also DISCRETIONARY FUNCTION, required action. In determining liability of government agents for the consequences of their actions, courts have created a distinction between ministerial and discretionary functions. Though often blurred in specific cases, the distinction attempted to limit liability to acts done by the agents' volition, hence called discretionary, in comparison to those actions called ministerial which were viewed as compelled by the constitution, a statute, charter or other law.

minority groups designator data, also called MGD DATA, data base or system which provides statistical employment information by race or national origin. In theory, such data should only be used in studies and analyses that evaluate an organization's equal employment opportunity programs.

MIS, *see* MANAGEMENT INFORMATION SYSTEM.

misery index, the total of the rates of inflation and unemployment.

mission agency, any government department or agency whose legislation gives it responsibility for promotion of some cause or operation of some system as its primary reason for existence (mission) and which is appropriated funds for the conduct of this mission.

mission budgeting, an end-purpose approach to budgeting. Mission budgeting was prompted by congressional dissatisfaction with budgetary submissions containing voluminous detail on what expenditures were to be made as opposed to explaining who would be spending what, and why. Consequently, the Congressional Budget and Impoundment Act of 1974 (Section 601) requires that agency budgets will be presented in terms of agency missions in addition to more traditional budget presentations. The basic idea is that a mission budget would categorize programs and activities by end-purposes so that the Congress would be better able to examine all similar programs and activities. *See* U.S. General Accounting Office, *Mission Budgeting: Discussion and Illustration of the Concept in Research and Development Programs* (Washington, D.C.: Government Printing Office, July 27, 1977).

Mitbestimmungsrecht, *see* CODETERMINATION.

mixed economy an economic system that lies somewhere in the middle of laissez-faire capitalism and socialism. All of the industrialized countries of the free world have mixed economies; some are just more mixed up than others.

mixed-scanning, decision-making model that uses both incrementalism and the rational-comprehensive approach to seek best short-term solutions. *See* Amitai Etzioni, "Mixed Scanning: 'Third' Approach to Decision Making," *Public Administration Review* (December 1967).

mobility, *see* OCCUPATIONAL MOBILITY.

mobility assignment, term generally used for the sharing of talent between the federal government and states, local governments, and institutions of higher education, as authorized by Title IV of the Intergovernmental Personnel Act of 1970, Public Law 91-648. Title IV is designed to: (1) improve the delivery of government services at all levels of government by bringing the specialized knowledge and experience of skilled people to bear on problems that are of mutual concern to state or local jurisdictions and the federal government; (2) strengthen intergovernmental understanding, broaden perspective, and increase capacity of personnel resources; and (3) help preserve the rights and benefits of employees so they will be better able to accept temporary assignments.

The ground rules for IPA Mobility Assignments are as follows:

1. Assignments can be made to or from federal agencies and states, local governments, and private and public colleges and universities for any period up to two years. They must be with the consent of the employee and for work of mutual benefit to the jurisdictions involved.
2. Employees can be assigned on a "detail" or leave without pay basis. If on detail, the employee is considered to continue on active duty with the organization from which detailed. If on leave, the employee goes on the rolls of the receiving organization.
3. No person-for-person exchange is required, although this can and does happen.
4. Federal employee salary, job rights, and benefits are protected, and travel and moving expenses are authorized.

5. For state, local, and university employees, Title IV permits federal agencies to pay the employee's share of certain fringe benefits where this is appropriate, but job rights and continuation of benefit coverage remain the responsibility of the state or local employer.
6. Program officials of participating governments arrange assignments. Costs of the assignment, including salary, may be shared or borne entirely by either jurisdiction. This is subject to negotiation.

For further information contact the Office of Personnel Management.

mode, score or value that occurs most frequently in a distribution.

model, a simplification of reality, a reduction in time and space that allows for a better understanding of reality. The representation may be expressed in words, numbers, or diagrams. For example, a textbook may have several paragraphs describing a model of leadership. In the next chapter it may have several diagrams representing a model of motivation. These are both simplified representations of more complex phenomena and are intended to facilitate understanding.

model agreement, collective bargaining agreement developed by a national or international union to serve as a standard for its locals.

model charter, see CHARTER.

Model Cities Program, also DEMONSTRATION CITIES AND METROPOLITAN DEVELOPMENT ACT OF 1966, national government program creating demonstration cities which would designate particular areas for intensive use of coordinated federal programs. Though originally programmed for only a dozen or so cities as part of Lyndon Johnson's Great Society, it quickly grew to include more than 150 cities. It was dismantled under Richard Nixon and replaced by revenue sharing. See Marshall

Kaplan, *The Model Cities Program* (New York: Praeger, 1970); Robert A. Aleshire, "Power to the People: An Assessment of the Community Action and Model Cities Experience," *Public Administration Review* (September 1972).

modeling, identification of the fixed and variable components in a system, assigning them numerical or economic values and relating them to each other in a logical fashion so that one can derive optimal solutions to operational problems by manipulating the components of the model.

modified union shop, variation of the union shop that exempts certain classes of employees from joining the union. Such exemptions might include employees who were employed before a certain date, seasonal workers, work study students, etc.

Monell v. *Dept. of Social Services, New York City,* 436 U.S. 658 (1978), U.S. Supreme Court case which held that cities and municipalities may be held liable when their official policies (in this case a mandatory maternity leave policy) or customs violate a person's constitutional rights.

See also OWEN V. CITY OF INDEPENDENCE.

monetary policy, a government's formal efforts to manage the money in its economy in order to realize specific economic goals. Three basic kinds of monetary policy decisions can be made: (1) decisons about the amount of money in circulation; (2) decisions about the level of interest rates; and (3) decisions about the functioning of credit markets and the banking system.

Controlling money is, of course, the key variable. In 1913 the United States passed into law the Federal Reserve Act which created a strong central bank for the country, similarly titled—the Federal Reserve. Like most central banks, the Federal Reserve is empowered to control the amount of money in circulation by either creating or canceling dollars. Implementation of money control is achieved through the process of putting up for sale or buying government securities. This is usually termed Open Market Operations—which means that the Federal Reserve competes with other bidders in the purchasing or selling of securities. The difference is that when the Federal Reserve buys securities, it pays in the form of new currency in circulation. If it sells some of its securities, it decreases money available, since in effect it absorbs currency held by others. This does not mean, however, that the money stock fluctuates greatly. It steadily increases. It is in the margin of the increase that money supply has its impact.

The other major tools involve interest rates and the amount of credit made available by banks. By varying interest rates and controlling bank reserve requirements, the Federal Reserve can attempt to affect investments and loans. It does this in two ways: first, by changing its discount rate—the interest rate it charges other banks for loans of money which these banks can use to make loans; and second, by changing the reserve requirement—the amount of money a bank must have on hand in comparison to the amount of money they have out on loan. See Milton Friedman, "The Role of Monetary Policy," American Economic Review (March 1968); Thomas F. Cargill, Money, The Financial System, and Monetary Policy (Englewood Cliffs, N.J.: Prentice-Hall, 1979); Paul M. Horvitz, Monetary Policy and the Financial System, 4th ed. (Englewood Cliffs, N.J.: Prentice-Hall, 1979); Douglas Fisher, Money, Banking, and Monetary Policy (Homewood, Ill.: Richard D. Irwin, Inc., 1980); Martin Feldstein, Inflation, Capital Taxation and Monetary Policy (Cambridge, Mass.: National Bureau of Economic Research, 1981); George Macesich, The Politics of Monetarism: Its Historical and Institutional Development (Totowa, N.J.: Rowman & Allanheld, 1984).

See also FISCAL POLICY and RESERVE REQUIREMENTS.

monetary targets, monetary policy intentions stated in terms of projections of monetary aggregate and credit growth which the Federal Reserve announces in semi-annual reports submitted to the Congress pursuant to the Full Employment and Balanced Growth Act of 1978. The growth rate projections are stated as ranges with upper and lower bounds, covering the annual periods from the fourth quarter of one year to the fourth quarter of the following year.

money purchase benefit, pension that is entirely dependent on contributions made to an individual's account.

money supply, the amount of money in the economy. There are several definitions of money. M1-A consists of currency (coin and paper notes) plus demand deposits at commercial banks, exclusive of demand deposits held by other domestic banks, foreign banks, and official institutions and the U.S. government. M1-B is M1-A plus other checkable accounts, including negotiable orders of withdrawal and automatic transfers from savings accounts at commercial banks and thrift institutions, credit union share draft accounts, and demand deposits at mutual savings banks. M-2 consists of M1-B plus savings and small denomination time deposits at all depository institutions, overnight repurchase agreements at commercial banks, overnight Eurodollars held by U.S. residents other than Caribbean branches of member banks, and money market mutual fund shares. M-3 is M-2 plus large denomination time deposits at all depository institutions and term repurchase agreements at commercial banks and savings and loan associations.

monopoly, situation in which there is only a single producer/seller of a product. See E. S. Savas, "Municipal Monopoly," Harper's (December 1971); Robert L. Bish and Robert Warren, "Scale and Monopoly Problems in Urban Government Services," Urban Affairs Quarterly (September 1972).

monotony curve, see FATIGUE CURVE.

Monte Carlo techniques, operations research processes premised upon the laws of probability.

Monthly Labor Review (MLR)

Monthly Labor Review (MLR), major publication of the U.S. Bureau of Labor Statistics. Articles deal with labor relations, trends in the labor force, new laws and court decisions affecting workers, etc. Lists the major labor agreements expiring each month and gives monthly current labor statistics on employment, unemployment, wages and prices, and productivity.

Monthly Labor Review
Editorial Address:
Bureau of Labor Statistics
U.S. Department of Labor
Washington, D.C. 20210
Subscriptions:
Superintendent of Documents
Government Printing Office
Washington, D.C. 20402

moonlighting, in the 19th century, any illicit nighttime activity. In the mid-1950s, it gained currency as a slang term for a second job. Employee moonlighting may impede primary job productivity and otherwise cause problems when there are questions about sick leave claims, absenteeism, tardiness, overtime scheduling, and potential conflicts of interest. Many employers—because of union contracts, civil service regulations, or company policy—formally restrict moonlighting by their employees. Typically, such restrictions require advance approval and stipulate that moonlighting be done outside of regularly scheduled work periods. According to the Bureau of Labor Statistics of the U.S. Department of Labor, 4.7 percent of all employed persons hold two or more jobs. Men employed in the protective services (primarily police and fire) and as teachers (except college) had the highest rates of moonlighting—10.4 percent and 16.3 percent respectively. For a complete analysis, *see* Kopp Michelotti, "Multiple Jobholding in May 1975," *Monthly Labor Review* (November 1975). *Also see* Lawrence Stessin, "Moonlighting: The Employer's Dilemma," *Personnel* (January–February 1981).

morale, collective attitude of the work force toward their work environment and a crude measure of the organizational climate. Peter F. Drucker insists that the only true test of morale is performance. As such, morale is one of the most significant indicators of organizational health. "What physical health is to a physical organization, morale is to a cooperative system," said Fritz J. Roethlisberger in *Management and Morale* (Cambridge, Mass.: Harvard University Press, 1941). *Also see* Louis C. Schroeter, *Organizational Elan* (New York: American Management Association, 1970); Robert G. Pajer, "The Relationship of Morale to Productivity," *Public Personnel Review* (October 1970); Christian F. Paul and Albert C. Gross, "Increasing Productivity and Morale in a Municipality: Effects of Organization Development," *Journal of Applied Behavioral Science* (January–February–March 1981); Robert H. Garin and John F. Cooper, "The Morale-productivity Relationship: How Close?" *Personnel* (January–February 1981).

morality, administrative, *see* ADMINISTRATIVE MORALITY.

more-favorable-terms clause, *see* MOST-FAVORED-NATION CLAUSE.

morphological analysis, any technique which seeks to systematically find all of the possible means for achieving a goal. *See* Lucien Geradin, "Morphological Analysis: Method for Creativity," in James S. Bright and Milton E. F. Schoeman, *A Guide to Practical Technological Forecasting* (Englewood Cliffs, N.J.: Prentice-Hall, 1973).

Moses, Robert (1881–1981), New York State and New York City official who had the greatest influence on the physical development of modern New York City and its environs. For a biography, *see* Robert A. Caro, *The Power Broker: Robert Moses and the Fall of New York* (New York: Random House, 1974). For a more affectionate portrait, *see* Herbert Kaufman, "Robert Moses: Charismatic Bureaucrat," *Political Science Quarterly* (Fall 1975).

Mosher, Frederick C. (1913–   ), a major voice in public administration who wrote the standard historical analysis of the civil service in the United States, *Democracy and the Public Service* (New York: Oxford University Press, 1968). Other works include: *Governmental Reorganizations: Cases and Commentary* (Indianapolis, Indiana: Bobbs-Merrill, 1967); *Programming Systems and Foreign Affairs Leadership* (New York: Oxford University Press, 1970); *American Public Administration: Past, Present, and Future* (University, Alabama: University of Alabama Press, 1975).

Mosher, William E. (1877-1945), founder and first president (1940-1941) of the American Society for Public Administration. Co-author, with J. Donald Kingsley, of the first public personnel text, *Public Personnel Administration* (New York: Harper Bros., 1936).

most-favored nation, trade policy whereby countries agree to give each other the most favorable trade concessions that they might separately give to any other country.

most-favored-nation clause, also called MORE-FAVORABLE-TERMS CLAUSE, that portion of a collective bargaining agreement where a union agrees not to sign contracts with any other employers under more favorable terms.

motion study, according to Benjamin W. Niebel, *Motion and Time Study*, 6th ed. (Homewood, Ill.: Richard D. Irwin, 1976), the study of the body motions used in performing an operation, with the thought of improving the operation by eliminating unnecessary motions and simplifying necessary motions, and then establishing the most favorable motion sequence for maximum efficiency. *See also* TIME STUDY.

motivation, also WORK MOTIVATION, an emotional stimulus that causes a person to act. *Work motivation* is an amalgam of all of the factors in one's working environment that foster (positively or negatively) productive efforts. Classic analyses of worker motivation include: A. H. Maslow, *Motivation and Personality* (New York: Harper & Row, 1954); F. Herzberg, B. Mausner, and B. Snyderman, *The Motivation to Work* (New York: John Wiley, 1959); V. H. Vroom, *Work and Motivation* (New York: John Wiley, 1964). *See also* Kae H. Chung, *Motivational Theories and Practices* (Columbus, Ohio: Grid, Inc., 1977); Gene Milbourn, Jr., "The Relationship of Money and Motivation," *Compensation Review* (Second Quarter 1980); Philip C. Grant, "Why Employee Motivation Has Declined in America," *Personnel Journal* (December 1982); William Rabinowitz, Kenneth Falkenbach, Jeffrey R. Travers, C. Glenn Valentine and Paul Weener, "Worker Motivation: Unsolved Problem or Untapped Resource?" *California Management Review* (January 1983); Larry L. Cummings, "Compensation, Culture and Motivation: A Systems Perspective," *Organizational Dynamics* (Winter 1984); Michael E. Cavanagh, "In Search of Motivation," *Personnel Journal* (March 1984); Leonard Ackerman and Joseph P.

Theorist	Assumptions of man	Contribution
Scientific management (Taylor)	Economic man	Man primarily motivated by financial reward
Human Relations School (Mayo)	Social man	Importance of informal organizations on human behavior
Maslow	Self-actualizing man	Hierarchy of needs
Herzberg	Self-actualizing man	Motivation-hygiene theory
McGregor	Self-actualizing man	Theory X, Theory Y views of man
Vroom	Complex man (Contingency view)	Expectancy theory

Major contributors to theories of motivation.

Source: P. Bryans and T. P. Cronin, Organization Theory *(London: Mitchell Beazley, 1983), p. 54.*

Grunenwald, "Help Employees Motivate Themselves," *Personnel Journal* (July 1984).
> See also the following entries:
> EXTRINSIC MOTIVATION
> REINFORCEMENT
> SELF-ACTUALIZATION
> STROKING

Motivation-Hygiene Theory, also called TWO-FACTOR THEORY, theory put forth in a landmark study by Frederick Herzberg, Bernard Mausner, and Barbara Snyderman in *The Motivation to Work* (New York: John Wiley & Sons, 1959). It was one of the first extensive empirical demonstrations of the primacy of internal worker motivation. Five factors were isolated as determiners of job satisfaction: achievement, recognition, work itself, responsibility, and advancement. Similarly, the factors associated with job dissatisfaction were realized: company policy and administration, supervision, salary, interpersonal relations, and working conditions. The satisfying factors were all related to job content, the dissatisfying factors to the environmental context of the job. The factors that were associated with job satisfaction were quite separate from those factors associated with job dissatisfaction. According to Herzberg, in "The Motivation-Hygiene Concept and the Problems of Manpower," *Personnel Administration* (January-February 1964),

> since separate factors needed to be considered depending on whether job satisfaction or job dissatisfaction was involved, it followed that these two feelings were not the obverse of each other. The opposite of job satisfaction would not be job dissatisfaction, but rather NO job satisfaction; and similarly the opposite of job dissatisfaction is NO job dissatisfaction—not job satisfaction.

Because the environmental context of jobs, such as working conditions, interpersonal relations, and salary, served primarily as preventatives, they were termed hygiene factors, as an analogy to the medical use of hygiene meaning preventive and environmental. The job-content factors such as achievement, advance-ment, and responsibility were termed motivators because these are the things that motivate people to superior performance. Again according to Herzberg, in *Work and the Nature of Man* (Cleveland: World Publishers, 1966),

> the principal result of the analysis of this data was to suggest that the hygiene or maintenance events led to job dissatisfaction because of a need to avoid unpleasantness; the motivator events led to job satisfaction because of a need for growth or self-actualization. At the psychological level, the two dimensions of job attitudes reflected a two-dimensional need structure: one need system for the avoidance of unpleasantness and a parallel need system for personal growth.

Since its original presentation, a considerable number of empirical investigations by a wide variety of researchers has tended to confirm the Motivation-Hygiene Theory. Its chief fault seems to be its rejection of the view that pay is a unique incentive capable, in differing circumstances, of being a hygiene as well as a motivator factor. But the theory's main holding—that worker motivation is essentially internal—remains largely unchallenged.
See also HERZBERG, FREDERICK.

Motor Coach Employees v. Lockridge, *see* AMALGAMATED ASSOCIATION OF STREET, ELECTRIC RAILWAY, AND MOTOR COACH EMPLOYEES OF AMERICA V. LOCKRIDGE.

Mountain Timber Company v. Washington, 343 U.S. 238 (1917), U.S. Supreme Court case which held constitutional state workmen's compensation laws.

Mouton, Jane S., *see* BLAKE, ROBERT R. AND JANE S. MOUTON.

Moynihan, Daniel Patrick (1927-), U.S. Senator from New York elected in 1976, former Ambassador to the United Nations (1975-76), former Ambassador to India (1973-75), former urban affairs advisor to President Nixon (1969-73). Moynihan first came to national attention in 1965 when as an Assistant Secretary of Labor he wrote a report suggesting instability in black families—"The Negro Family: The Case for National Action." For a full account of the ensuing controversy, see Lee Rainwater and William Yancey, *The Moynihan Report and the Politics of Controversy* (Cambridge, Mass.: M.I.T. Press, 1967). Moynihan once again ran afoul of black leaders when in 1970 he wrote in a memorandum to President Nixon that "the time may have come when the issue of race could benefit from a period of 'benign neglect'." When the memorandum was leaked to the press, its misinterpretation once again made Moynihan a *persona non grata* with the black community. Despite his active public life, Moynihan has earned a substantial scholarly reputation. Major works include: *Beyond the Melting Pot,* with Nathan Glazer (Cambridge, Mass.: M.I.T. Press, 1964); *On Understanding Poverty,* ed. (New York: Basic Books, 1969); *Maximum Feasible Misunderstanding: Community Action in the War on Poverty Toward a National Urban Policy,* ed. (New York: Basic Books, 1970); *The Politics of a Guaranteed Income* (New York: Random House, 1973); *Coping: Essays on the Practice of Government* (New York: Random House, 1973). *Also see* Douglas Schoen, *Pat: A Biography of Daniel Patrick Moynihan* (New York: Harper & Row, 1979).

MPA or MBA, Master of Public Administration and Master of Business Administration, respectively. These are the leading managerial degrees for practitioners in the private and public sectors. While such degrees are obviously helpful, it has long been established that there is no direct relationship between scholastic performance and success in management. For an analysis of this seeming contradiction, see J. Sterling Livingston, "Myth of the Well-Educated Manager," *Harvard Business Review* (January-February 1971). *Also see* Philip T. Crotty, "The Value of MBA and Executive Development Programs," *Training and Development Journal* (May 1972); George Grode and Marc Holzer,

"The Perceived Utility of MPA Degrees," *Public Administration Review* (July-August 1975); J. N. Behrman and R. I. Levin, "Are Business Schools Doing Their Job?" *Harvard Business Review* (January-February 1984); R. L. Jenkins, R. C. Reizenstein, and F. G. Rodgers, "Reports Cards on the MBA," *Harvard Business Review* (September-October 1984); Robert F. Durant and William A. Taggart, "Mid-Career Students in MPA Programs: Implications for Pre-Service Student Education," *Public Administration Review* (March-April 1985).

Ms., title of courtesy for a woman which is used without regard to her marital status. On January 26, 1977, the U.S. Civil Service Commission announced that it would revise all of its personnel forms—including job application forms—to make "Ms." available for those who prefer it. As present stocks are depleted and the forms are reprinted, the change will be incorporated in all forms that require a title. The commission also instructed all federal agencies under its jurisdiction to incorporate "Ms." in addition to "Miss," "Mrs.," and "Mr." on their internal personnel forms.

MSPB, *see* MERIT SYSTEMS PROTECTION BOARD.

Mt. Healthy Board of Education v. Doyle, 429 U.S. 274 (1977), U.S. Supreme Court case which held that the first amendment does not demand that a discharged employee be placed "in a better position as a result of the exercise of constitutionally protected activity than he would have occupied had he done nothing." An employer should not be inhibited from evaluating an employee's performance and "reaching a decision not to rehire on the basis of that record, simply because the protected conduct makes the employer more certain of the correctness of its decison." *See* William H. DuRoss III, "Toward Rationality in Discriminatory Cases: The Impact of *Mt. Healthy Board of Education* v. *Doyle* Upon the NLRA," *The Georgetown Law Journal* (April 1978).

muckrakers, journalists who, in the early part of this century, wrote exposés of business and governmental corruption. Some of the most famous muckrakers were Lincoln Steffens, Ida M. Tarbell, and Upton Sinclair. Today, anyone who writes an exposé of governmental corruption or incompetence might be called a muckraker. For anthologies of representative muckraking, see Harvey Swados, ed., *Years of Conscience: The Muckrakers* (New York: World Publishing, 1962); Arthur & Lila Weinberg, eds., *The Muckrakers* (New York: Capricorn Books, 1964).

muddling through, see (1) INCREMENTALISM and (2) LINDBLOM, CHARLES E.

multicraft union, craft union that encompasses several different skilled occupations.

multiemployer bargaining, collective bargaining involving more than one company, usually in the same industry. *See* Richard Pegnetter, *Multiemployer Bargaining in the Public Sector: Purposes and Experiences* (Chicago: International Personnel Management Association, 1975); Robert B. Hoffman, "The Trend Away from Multiemployer Bargaining," *Labor Law Journal* (February 1983).

multiple-choice test, test consisting entirely of multiple-choice items, which require the examinee to choose the best or correct answer from several that are given as options. *See* J. Marshall Trieber, "The Use of Multiple-Choice for Testing," *Training and Development Journal* (October 1980).

multiple cutting score, assignment of a cutting score to each of several tests (or other standards) and the requirement that an applicant achieve a passing score on each of them to be hired or eligible for hire.

multiple regression analysis, see REGRESSION ANALYSIS.

multiple time plan, wage incentive plan that provides for higher base rates as progressively higher levels of production are reached.

municipal bonds, also TAX-EXEMPT MUNICIPAL BONDS, the debt instruments of subnational governments; terms used interchangeably with public borrowing and debt financing. This causes some confusion because they appear to refer only to bonds issued by local government. Yet bonds issued by states, territories, or possessions of the United States, or by any municipality, political subdivison (including cities, counties, school districts, and special districts for fire prevention, water, sewer, irrigation, and other purposes), or public agency or instrumentality (such as an authority or commission) are subsumed under the rubric "municipal bonds." While the interest on municipal bonds is exempt from federal taxes, state and local exemptions may vary. *See* Gordon L. Calvert, *Fundamentals of Municipal Bonds* (Washington, D.C.: Securities Industry Association, 1972); Michael D. Joehnk and David S. Kidwell, "A Look at Competitive and Negotiated Underwriting Costs in the Municipal Bond Market," *Public Administrative Review* (May-June 1980); Earl D. Benson, "Municipal Bond Interest Cost, Issue Purpose and Proposition 13," *Governmental Finance* (September 1980); Robert M. Nauss and B. R. Keeler, "Minimizing Net Interest Cost in Municipal Bond Bidding," *Management Science* (April 1981); Jay H. Abrams, "Financial Capital Expenditures: A Look at the Municipal Bond Market," *Public Administration Review* (July-August 1983); L. R. Jones, "The WPPSS Default: Trouble in the Municipal Bond Market," *Public Budgeting & Finance* (Winter 1984); Robert B. Inzer and Walter J. Reinhart, "Rethinking Traditional Municipal Bond Sales," *Governmental Finance* (June 1984); Robert L. Bland, "The Interest Cost Savings from Experience in the Municipal Bond Market," *Public Administration Review* (January-February 1985). *See also* REVENUE BONDS.

municipal commercial paper, short-term promissory notes issued by local jurisdictions. *See* Byron Klapper, "Municipal Commercial Paper," *Governmental Finance* (September 1980).

municipal corporation, city. Cities are legally corporations, bound by their charters and any relevant state and federal legislation. As a charter, even if developed and implemented through a home rule process, is a document bestowed by the state, cities are not legally comparable to state governments, which have the ability to obtain powers from the people.
See also DILLON'S RULE.

Municipal Finance Officers Association (MFOA), professional association of governmental fiscal agencies and officers.
MFOA
180 North Michigan Avenue
Chicago, IL 60601
(312) 977-9700

municipal revenue bonds, state and local government debt securities whose interest and principal are paid from the revenues of rents, tolls, or other user charges flowing from specific projects financed by the bonds.

Muniz v. *Hoffman,* 422 U.S. 454 (1975), U.S. Supreme Court case which held that a union did not have a statutory or constitutional right to a jury trial on charges of criminal contempt stemming from its violation of an injunction issued under the authority of the National Labor Relations Act.

Munsterberg, Hugo (1863-1916), German psychologist who spent his later years at Harvard and earned the title of "father" of industrial or applied psychology by proposing the use of psychology for practical purposes. His major book is *Psychology and Industrial Efficiency* (Boston: Houghton Mifflin, 1913). For a sympathetic biography, *see* Margaret Munsterberg, *Hugo Munsterberg: His Life and Work* (New York: Appleton-Century-Crofts, 1922). *Also see* Merle J. Moskowitz, "Hugo Munsterberg: A Study in the History of Applied Psychology,"

American Psychologist (October 1977); Matthew Hale, Jr., *Human Science and Social Order: Hugo Munsterberg and the Origins of Applied Psychology* (Philadelphia, Pa.: Temple University Press, 1980).

Murgia **decision,** *see* MASSACHUSETTS BOARD OF RETIREMENT V. MURGIA.

Murphy's Law, cosmic law. *Public Administration Review* (July 1976) published the following Murphy's Laws:
1. Anything that can go wrong will go wrong.
2. Anything that can go wrong will—at the worst possible time.
3. Nothing is as easy as it seems.
4. If there is a possibility of several things going wrong, the one that will go wrong is the one that will do the most damage.
5. Everything takes longer than it should.
6. Left to themselves, things will go from bad to worse.
7. Nature always sides with the hidden flaw.
8. If everything seems to be going well, you have obviously overlooked something.

Murphy seems related to that famous literary wit, Anonymous. Only one thing seems certain—Murphy's laws were not written by Murphy, but by another person with the same name. *Also see* Robert D. Behn, "Why Murphy Was Right," *Policy Analysis* (Summer 1980); William C. Waddell, *Overcoming Murphy's Law* (New York: AMACOM, 1981).

mushroom management, poor management technique. All that mushrooms need in order to grow is to be left undisturbed in the dark and fed fertilizer frequently. Mushroom managers keep subordinates in the dark and feed them lots of manure. Unfortunately, this technique works better on real mushrooms than it does on subordinates—they cease to grow at all. *Source:* William Thomas, "Humor for Hurdling the Mystique in Management,"

Management of Personnel Quarterly (Winter 1970).

mutuality, *see* DOCTRINE OF MUTUALITY.

mutual rating, *see* PEER RATING.

Myers, M. Scott (1922-), industrial psychologist and leading authority on job design and motivation. Major works include: *Every Employee a Manager: More Meaningful Work Through Job Enrichment,* 2nd ed. (New York: McGraw-Hill, 1981); "Overcoming Union Opposition to Job Enrichment," *Harvard Business Review* (May-June 1971); *Managing with Unions* (Reading, Mass.: Addison-Wesley, 1978).

Myers v. United States, 272 U.S. 52 (1926), U.S. Supreme Court case that presented the question of "whether under the Constitution the President has the exclusive power of removing executive officers of the United States whom he has appointed by and with the advice and consent of the Senate." The opinion of the Court was delivered by Chief Justice Taft, who had previously been president. Not surprisingly, he argued that the removal power is an executive power, vested by the Constitution in the president alone. In Taft's view, the power to dismiss the officials in the executive branch was necessary for presidential control of administration and the ability to make sure that the laws are faithfully executed.

See also (1) HUMPHREY'S EXECUTOR V. UNITED STATES and (2) WIENER V. UNITED STATES.

N

N, mathematical symbol commonly used to represent the number of cases in a distribution, study, etc. The symbol of the number of cases in a subgroup of N is n.

NAACP, *see* NATIONAL ASSOCIATION FOR THE ADVANCEMENT OF COLORED PEOPLE.

NAACP v. Federal Power Commission, *see* NATIONAL ASSOCIATION FOR THE ADVANCEMENT OF COLORED PEOPLE V. FEDERAL POWER COMMISSION.

NAB, *see* NATIONAL ALLIANCE OF BUSINESS.

NACI, *see* NATIONAL AGENCY CHECK AND INQUIRY.

NACo, *see* NATIONAL ASSOCIATION OF COUNTIES.

NALC decision, *see* UNITED STATES CIVIL SERVICE COMMISSION V. NATIONAL ASSOCIATION OF LETTER CARRIERS.

NAPA, *see* NATIONAL ACADEMY OF PUBLIC ADMINISTRATION.

NAS, *see* NATIONAL ACADEMY OF SCIENCES.

NASA, *see* NATIONAL AERONAUTICS AND SPACE ADMINISTRATION.

NASDA, *see* NATIONAL ASSOCIATION OF STATE DEVELOPMENT AGENCIES.

Nashville Gas Co. v. Satty, 434 U.S. 136 (1977), U.S. Supreme Court case which held that pregnant women forced to take maternity leave cannot be denied their previously accumulated seniority rights when they return to work.

NASPAA, *see* NATIONAL ASSOCIATION OF SCHOOLS OF PUBLIC AFFAIRS AND ADMINISTRATION.

NASS, *see* NATIONAL ASSOCIATION OF SUGGESTION SYSTEMS.

NATB, *see* NONREADING APTITUDE TEST BATTERY.

national, a union composed of a variety of widely dispersed affiliated local unions. The Bureau of Labor Statistics defines a national union as one with agreements with different employers in more than one state.

National Academy of Arbitrators, organization founded in 1947 "to establish and foster high standards and competence among those engaged in the arbitration of labor-management disputes on a professional basis; to adopt canons of ethics to govern the conduct of arbitrators; to promote the study and understanding of the arbitration of labor-management disputes." The Academy is not an agency for the selection or appointment of arbitrators. It does invite and sponsor activities designed to improve general understanding of the nature of arbitration and its use as a means of settling labor disputes.

In considering applications for membership, the Academy applies the following standards: (1) the applicant should be of good moral character, as demonstrated by adherence to sound ethical standards in professional activities; (2) the applicant should have substantial and current experience as an impartial arbitrator of labor-management disputes, so as to reflect general acceptability by the parties; and (3), as an alternative to (2), the applicant with limited but current experience in arbitration should have attained general recognition through scholarly publication or other activities as an impartial authority on labor-management relations. Membership will not be conferred upon applicants who serve partisan interests as advocates or consultants for labor or management in labor-management relations or who are associated with or are members of a firm which performs such advocate or consultant work. The Academy had about six hundred members in 1984. See J. Timothy Sprehe and Jeffrey Small, "Members and Nonmembers of the National Academy of Arbitrators: Do They Differ?" *Arbitration Journal* (September 1984).

National Academy of Arbitrators
Office of the Secretary
Graduate School of Business
  Administration
University of Michigan
Ann Arbor, MI 48109
(313) 763-9714

National Academy of Conciliators, an organization of about one thousand members founded in 1979 to foster alternatives to litigation through dispute settlement consultation and training.

National Academy of Conciliators
5530 Wisconsin Ave.
Suite 1130
Chevy Chase, MD 20815
(301) 654-6515

National Academy of Public Administration (NAPA), organization of more than three hundred distinguished practitioners and scholars in public administration, supported by a small staff and dedicated to improving the role of public management in a democratic society. The Academy was founded in 1967 to serve as a source of advice and counsel to government and public officials on problems of public administration; to help improve the policies, processes, and institutions of public administration through early identification of important problems and significant trends; to evaluate program performance and assess administrative progress; and to increase public understanding of public administration and its critical role in a democratic society.

National Academy of Public
  Administration
1120 G Street, N.W.
Washington, D.C. 20004
(202) 347-3190
See also AMERICAN SOCIETY FOR PUBLIC ADMINISTRATION.

National Academy of Sciences (NAS), organization of distinguished scientists and engineers dedicated to the furtherance of science and its use for the general welfare. Although not a governmental agency, the academy has long enjoyed close relations with the federal government. Its congressional charter of 1863 specifies that the Academy shall, whenever called upon by any department of the Government, investigate, examine, experiment, and report upon any subject of science or art, the actual expense of such investigations, examinations, experiments, and reports to be paid from appropriations which may be made for the purpose, but the Academy shall receive no compensation whatever for any service to the Government of the United States. Thus, no federal funds are appropriated directly to the academy, the principal funding mechanism typically being the negotiation of contracts with government agencies.

NAS
2101 Constitution Avenue, N.W.
Washington, D.C. 20418
(202) 334-2000

National Aeronautics and Space Administration (NASA), federal agency whose principal statutory functions are to conduct research for the solution of problems of flight within and outside the earth's atmosphere and to develop, construct, test, and operate aeronautical and space vehicles; to conduct activities required for the exploration of space with manned and unmanned vehicles; to arrange for the most effective utilization of the scientific and engineering resources of the United States with other nations engaged in aeronatical and space activities for peaceful purposes; and to provide for the widest practicable and appropriate dissemination of information concerning NASA's activities and their results.

NASA
400 Maryland Avenue, S.W.
Washington, D.C. 20546
(202) 453-1000

national agency check and inquiry (NACI), investigation of applicants for nonsensitive federal positions by means of a name check through national investigative files and voucher inquiries.

National Alliance of Business (NAB), business group formed in 1968 to work in partnership with the federal government in order to find permanent jobs for the hard core unemployed.

National Alliance of Business
1015 15th Street, N.W.

Washington, D.C. 20005
(202) 457-0040

National Association for the Advancement of Colored People (NAACP), the largest and historically most influential of the black interest groups, founded in 1909.

NAACP
270 W. 96th Street
New York, NY 10014
(212) 749-2323

National Association for the Advancement of Colored People v. Federal Power Commission, 425 U.S. 663 (1976), U.S. Supreme Court case which held that the Federal Power Commission is authorized to consider the consequences of discriminatory employment practices on the part of its regulatees only insofar as such consequences are directly related to its establishment of just and reasonable rates in the public interest. To the extent that illegal, duplicative, or unnecessary labor costs are demonstrably the product of a regulatee's discriminatory employment practices and can be or have been demonstrably quantified by judicial decree or the final action of an administrative agency the Federal Power Commission should disallow them.

National Association of Counties (NACo), major organization of county government and management officials. NACo provides research, reference, and lobbying services for its members.

NACo
440 1st. Street, N.W.
Washington, D.C. 20001
(202) 393-6226

National Association of Regional Councils (NARC), national organization of councils of governments and similar agencies.

NARC
1700 K Street, N.W.
Washington, D.C. 20036
(202) 457-0710

National Association of Schools of Public Affairs and Administration

(NASPAA), organization of academic programs in public administration and public affairs with a stated objective of advancing education and training in public affairs and public administration. NASPAA serves as a national center for information on programs and developments in this field, and represents the concerns and interests of member institutions in the formulation and support of national policies for education in public affairs and public administration.

NASPAA member schools collectively represent public administration education and scholarship in the United States. **Appendix B** contains a complete list of NASPAA member names and addresses.
NASPAA
1120 G Street, N.W.
Washington, D.C. 20005
(202) 628-8965

National Association of State Development Agencies (NASDA), clearinghouse organization of state economic development agencies.
NASDA
One Skyline Place
5205 Leesburg Pike
Falls Church, VA 22041

National Association of Suggestion Systems (NASS), non-profit organization founded in 1942 to promote and develop suggestion systems in industry and government. NASS seeks to develop new technology and disseminate information about suggestion systems to its more than eight hundred members and to all others interested in suggestion systems.
National Association of Suggestion
Systems
230 North Michigan Ave.
Chicago, IL 60601
(312) 372-1770

National Center for Productivity and Quality of Working Life, federal agency that existed from 1975 to 1978. In 1970, the National Commission on Productivity was formed to focus public attention on the importance of productivity and to enlist the cooperation of labor, management, government, and the public in a sustained effort to improve the economy's performance. In 1975, Public Law 94-136 created the National Center for Productivity and Quality of Working Life as an independent agency with no regulatory authority to work with Congress and federal agencies to develop a national policy for greater productivity, improved worker morale, and work quality. The new National Center thereupon assumed much of the work and the staff of the expired National Commission. After publishing a variety of reports, the National Center expired on September 30, 1978.

National Civic Review, monthly journal of the National Municipal League.
National Civic Review
55 W. 44th Street
New York, NY 10036

National Civil Service League (NCSL), a good-government lobby formed in 1881 by patrician reformers concerned with the debilitating and corrupting effects of patronage and the "spoils system" on the efficiency and moral stature of government. The Pendleton Act, drawn up by the League and sponsored by a League member, Senator George Pendleton of Ohio, introduced merit principles into federal employment.

The League has continued its reform efforts. Its Model Public Personnel Administration Law of 1970, which advocates replacing civil service commissions with personnel directors appointed by the chief executive, has been adopted in whole or in part by hundreds of governmental jurisdictions. The Civil Service Reform Act of 1978 was heavily influenced by the League's model law.
National Civil Service League
3600 Gunston Road
Alexandria, VA 22302
See also CIVIL SERVICE REFORM, COUTURIER, JEAN J., and PENDLETON ACT OF 1883.

National Commission on Productivity, *see* NATIONAL CENTER FOR PRODUCTIVITY AND QUALITY OF WORKING LIFE.

National Commission on State Workmen's Compensation Laws, *see* WORKMEN'S COMPENSATION.

National Conference of State Legislatures (NCSL), body that came into existence in January, 1975, replacing three previously-existing organizations (National Legislative Conference, National Conference of State Legislative Leaders, National Society of State Legislators). The NCSL is the only nationwide organization representing all state legislators (7,600) and their staffs (approximately 10,000), and it seeks to advance the effectiveness, independence, and integrity of the state legislature as an equal coordinate branch of government. It also fosters interstate cooperation and represents states and their legislatures with Congress and federal agencies.
NCSL
1125 17th St.
Denver, CO 80202
(303) 292-6600

national consultation rights, rights accorded a union of federal government employees if it holds exclusive recognition for either 10 percent or more, or five thousand or more, of the employees of an agency. According to Section 7113 of the Civil Service Reform Act of 1978:

> When a labor organization holds national consultation rights, the agency must give the labor organization notice of proposed new substantive personnel policies and proposed changes in established personnel policies and an opportunity to comment on such proposals. The labor organization has a right to suggest changes in personnel policies and to have those suggestions carefully considered. The labor organization also has a right to consult, in person at reasonable times, upon request, with appropriate officials on personnel policy matters and a right to submit its views in writing on personnel policy matters at any time. National consultation rights do not include the right to negotiate. Further, the agency is not required to consult with a labor organization on any matter which would be outside the

scope of negotiations if the labor organization held national exclusive recognition in that agency.

National consultation rights were first granted to federal employees under Executive Order 11491 of October 29, 1969.

National Credit Union Administration (NCUA), body responsible for chartering, insuring, supervising, and examining federal credit unions and for administering the National Credit Union Share Insurance Fund.
NCUA
1776 G Street, N.W.
Washington, D.C. 20456
(202) 357-1000

national debt, the total outstanding debt of a central government.

National Employ the Handicapped Week, also called NETH WEEK, the first full week in October, which has been set aside by the U.S. Congress to emphasize the employment of the handicapped.

National Endowment for the Arts/Humanities, *see* NATIONAL FOUNDATION ON THE ARTS AND THE HUMANITIES.

National Energy Act of 1978, federal statute composed of five separate pieces of legislation including (1) the National Energy Conservation Policy Act (establishes regulatory, grant, and loan programs to encourage conservation), (2) the Energy Tax Act (includes provisions to reduce dependence on imported oil, increase conservation, and encourage development of solar energy), (3) the Natural Gas Policy Act (decontrols price of new natural gas), (4) the Public Utility Regulatory Policies Act (encourages pricing of energy to reflect replacement costs), and (5) the Power Plant and Industrial Use Act (provides incentives for the increased use of coal).
See also ENERGY ACT OF 1976 and ENERGY LOBBY.

National Environmental Policy Act of 1969, *see* ENVIRONMENTAL POLICY.

National Foundation on the Arts and the Humanities, an independent federal agency created in 1965. The foundation consists of national endowments for the arts and humanities as well as a *Federal Council on the Arts and Humanities.*

The activities of the *National Endowment for the Arts* are designed to foster the growth and development of the arts in the U.S. The endowment awards grants to individuals, state and regional arts agencies, and nonprofit organizations representing the highest quality in the fields of architecture and environmental arts, crafts, dance, education, expansion arts, folk arts, literature, museums, music, media arts (film, radio, and television), theatre, and the visual arts.

National Endowment for the Arts
1100 Pennsylvania Ave., N.W.
Washington, D.C. 20506
(202) 682-5400

The activities of the *National Endowment for the Humanities* are designed to promote and support the production and dissemination of knowledge in the humanities, especially as it relates to the serious study and discussion of contemporary values and public issues. The endowment makes grants to individuals, groups or institutions—schools, colleges, universities, museums, public television stations, libraries, public agencies, and private nonprofit groups—to increase understanding and appreciation of the humanities. It makes grants in support of research productive of humanistic knowledge of value to the scholarly and general public.

National Endowment for the Humanities
1100 Pennsylvania Ave., N.W.
Washington, D.C. 20506
(202) 786-0438

National Governors Association (NGA), formerly the NATIONAL GOVERNORS CONFERENCE, membership organization that includes governors of the states, territories, and Puerto Rico. The NGA seeks to improve state government, addresses problems requiring interstate cooperation, and endeavors to facilitate intergovernmental relations at the federal/state and state/local levels. *See* Carol S. Weissert, "The

National Governors' Association: 1908-1983." *State Government,* Vol. 56, No. 2 (1983).

NGA
444 North Capitol Street
Washington, D.C. 20001
(202) 624-5300

National Governors Conference, *see* NATIONAL GOVERNORS ASSOCIATION.

National Industrial Recovery Act of 1933 (NIRA), federal statute that guaranteed employees "the right to organize and bargain collectively through representatives of their own choosing . . . free from the interference, restraint or coercion of employers." The act, which created the National Recovery Administration (NRA) to administer its provisions, was designed to establish self-government of industry through codes of fair competition which tended to eliminate competitive practices. Companies adopting their industries' codes of fair practice were entitled to display the "Blue Eagle," a flag or poster indicating compliance. The Supreme Court declared the act to be unconstitutional in 1935, but the Wagner Act of that year provided employees with even stronger collective bargaining guarantees.

National Institute for Occupational Safety and Health (NIOSH), body established under the provisions of the Occupational Safety and Health Act of 1970. NIOSH is the federal agency responsible for formulating new or improved occupational safety and health standards.

Under the Occupational Safety and Health Act, NIOSH has the responsibility for conducting research designed to produce recommendations for new occupational safety and health standards. These recommendations are transmitted to the Department of Labor, which has the responsibility for the final setting, promulgation, and enforcement of the standards.

National Institute for Occupational Safety and Health
1600 Clifton Road, N.E.

Atlanta, GA 30333
(404) 329-3644

National Labor Relations Act of 1935 (NLRA), also called WAGNER-CONNERY ACT and WAGNER ACT, the nation's principal labor relations law applying to all interstate commerce except railroad and airline operations (which are governed by the Railway Labor Act). The NLRA seeks to protect the rights of employees and employers, to encourage collective bargaining, and to eliminate certain practices on the part of labor and management that are harmful to the general welfare. It states and defines the rights of employees to organize and to bargain collectively with their employers through representatives of their own choosing. To ensure that employees can freely choose their own representatives for the purpose of collective bargaining, the act establishes a procedure by which they can exercise their choice at a secret ballot election conducted by the National Labor Relations Board. Further, to protect the rights of employees and employers, and to prevent labor disputes that would adversely affect the rights of the public, Congress has defined certain practices of employers and unions as unfair labor practices. The NLRA is administered and enforced principally by the National Labor Relations Board, which was created by the act.

In common usage, the National Labor Relations Act refers not to the act of 1935, but to the act as amended by the Labor-Management Relations (Taft-Hartley) Act of 1947 and the Labor-Management Reporting and Disclosure (Landrum-Griffin) Act of 1959.

See also the following entries:

National Labor Relations Board (NLRB), federal agency that administers the nation's laws relating to labor relations in the private and nonprofit sectors. (There are some public sector organizations also under its jurisdiction, most notably the U.S. Postal Service.) The NLRB is vested with the power to safeguard employees' rights to organize, to determine through elections whether workers want unions as their bargaining representatives, and to prevent and remedy unfair labor practices (*see also* AMERICAN FEDERATION OF LABOR V. NATIONAL LABOR RELATIONS BOARD).

The NLRB is an independent agency created by the National Labor Relations Act of 1935 (Wagner Act), as amended in 1947 (Taft-Hartley Act) and 1959 (Landrum-Griffin Act). The Postal Reorganization Act of 1971 conferred jurisdiction upon the NLRB over unfair labor practice charges and representation elections affecting U.S. Postal Service employees. Jurisdiction over all privately operated health care institutions was conferred on the NLRB by an amendment to the act in 1974.

The NLRB has two principal functions—preventing and remedying unfair labor practices by employers and labor organizations or their agents, and conducting secret ballot elections among employees in appropriate collective bargaining units to determine whether or not they desire to be represented by a labor organization. The NLRB also conducts secret ballot elections among employees who have been covered by a union-shop agreement to determine whether or not they wish to revoke their union's authority to make such agreements; in jurisdictional disputes, decides and determines which competing group of workers is entitled to perform the work involved; and conducts secret ballot elections among employees concerning employers' final settlement offers in national emergency labor disputes.

Under general supervision of the general counsel, thirty-three regional directors and their staffs process representation, unfair labor practice, and jurisdictional dispute cases. (Some regions have subregional or resident offices.) They issue complaints in unfair labor practice cases; seek settlement of unfair labor practice charges; obtain compliance with Board orders and court judgments; and petition district courts for injunctions to prevent or remedy unfair labor practices. The regional directors also direct hearings in representation cases; conduct elections pursuant to agreement or the decision-making authority delegated to them by the NLRB, or pursuant to NLRB directions; and issue certifications of representatives when unions win or certify the results when unions lose employee elections. They process petitions for bargaining unit clarification, for amendment of certification, and for rescission of a labor organization's authority to make a union-shop agreement. They also conduct national emergency employee referendums.

The NLRB can act only when it is formally requested to do so. Individuals, employers, or unions may initiate cases by filing charges of unfair labor practices or petitions for employee representation elections with the NLRB field offices serving the area where the case arises.

In the event a regional director declines to proceed on a representation petition, the party filing the petition may appeal to the NLRB. Where a regional director declines to proceed on an unfair labor practice charge, the filing party may appeal to the general counsel. Administrative law judges conduct hearings in unfair labor practice cases, make findings, and recommend remedies for violations found. Their decisions are reviewable by the NLRB if exceptions to the decision are filed. *See* James A. Gross, *The Making of the National Labor Relations Board: A Study in Economics, Politics, and the Law* (Albany, N.Y.: State University of New York Press, 1974); James A. Gross, *The Reshaping of the National Labor Relations Board: National Labor Policy in Transition, 1937-1947* (Albany, N.Y.: State University of New York Press, 1981); John R. Van de Water, "New Trends in NLRB Law," *Labor Law Journal* (October 1982).

National Labor Relations Board
1717 Pennsylvania Ave., N.W.
Washington, D.C. 20570
(202) 655-4000
See also the following entries:
MASTRO PLASTICS CORP. V. NATIONAL

LABOR RELATIONS BOARD
NEWPORT NEWS SHIPBUILDING AND DRY DOCK CO. V. SCHAUFFLER
PORTER CO. V. NATIONAL LABOR RELATIONS BOARD
SEARS, ROEBUCK, & CO. V. SAN DIEGO COUNTY DISTRICT COUNCIL OF CARPENTERS

National Labor Relation Board v. *Allis-Chalmers,* 388 U.S. 175 (1967), U.S. Supreme Court case which held that a union could fine its members for breaking a lawful strike and could obtain a judgment in court in order to enforce payment of the fine.

National Labor Relations Board v. *Babcock and Wilcox,* 351 U.S. 105 (1956), U.S. Supreme Court case which held that non-employee union organizers may have access to an employer's grounds for organizational purposes only if there is no other practical means of access to the employees.

National Labor Relations Board v. *Boeing,* 412 U.S. 67 (1973), U.S. Supreme Court case which held that the validity of a fine imposed by a union upon a member does not depend upon the fine being reasonable in amount.

National Labor Relations Board v. *Exchange Parts,* 375 U.S. 405 (1964), U.S. Supreme Court case which held that the conferral of employee benefits while a representation election is pending, for the purpose of inducing employees to vote against the union, interferes with the right to organize guaranteed by the National Labor Relations Act.

National Labor Relations Board v. *Fansteel Metallurgical Corp., see* SIT-DOWN STRIKE.

National Labor Relations Board v. *General Motors,* 373 U.S. 734 (1963), U.S. Supreme Court case which held that the agency shop is not an unfair labor practice.

National Labor Relations Board v. Gissel Packing Co., see AUTHORIZATION CARD.

National Labor Relations Board v. Granite State Joint Board, Textile Workers, 409 U.S. 213 (1972), U.S. Supreme Court case which held that a union could not collect fines imposed upon employees who had returned to work after resigning their membership during a strike. Since at the time there were no valid restraints on their freedom of resignation, the employees' action was an exercise of their statutory rights. "When a member lawfully resigns from the union, its power over him ends," said Justice Douglas in delivering the court's opinion.

National Labor Relations Board v. Jones and Laughlin Steel Corp., 301 U.S. 1 (1937), U.S. Supreme Court case that upheld the National Labor Relations (Wagner) Act of 1935, which gave labor the right to organize and bargain collectively. The NLRB, created by the act to enforce its provisions, ordered the Jones and Laughlin Steel Corporation to reinstate some employees it had discharged because of their union activities. The corporation responded by challenging both the authority of the NLRB to issue such an order and the legality of the act itself. The court ruled that

> employees have as clear a right to organize and select their representatives for lawful purposes as the respondent to organize its business and select its own officers and agents. Discrimination and coercion to prevent the free exercise of the right of employees to self-organization and representation is a proper subject for condemnation by competent legislative authority.

National Labor Relations Board v. J. Weingarten, Inc., 420 U.S. 251 (1975), U.S. Supreme Court case which held that an employee under company investigation for misconduct has a right to the presence of a union representative while being interrogated by a company investigator. *See* Lewis H. Silverman and Michael J. Soltis,

"Weingarten: An Old Trumpet Plays the Labor Circuit," *Labor Law Journal* (November 1981).

National Labor Relations Board v. MacKay Radio & Telegraph Company, 304 U.S. 33 (1938), U.S. Supreme Court case which held that an employer could hire permanent replacements for workers on strike for economic reasons. The court expanded the *Mackay* rule in the *Fleetwood Trailer Co.* decision, 389 U.S. 375 (1967), when it held that if a striker has been replaced and no suitable employment is available, the status of a striker as an employee continues until he has obtained "other regular and substantially equivalent employment. Until then, the striker remains on a preferred hiring list, unless there is a 'legitimate and substantial business justification' for not hiring him at all."

National Labor Relations Board v. Magnavox, 415 U.S. 322 (1974), U.S. Supreme Court case which held that a union cannot waive the distribution rights of employees who seek to distribute literature in support of the bargaining unit.

National Labor Relations Board v. Robbins Tire and Rubber Co., 57 L. Ed. 2d 159 (1978), U.S. Supreme Court case which held that witness' statements in pending unfair labor practice cases are exempt from disclosure under the Freedom of Information Act.

National Labor Relations Board v. Truitt Manufacturing, 351 U.S. 149 (1956), U.S. Supreme Court case which held that a refusal by an employer to attempt to substantiate a claim of inability to pay increased wages may support a finding of a failure to bargain in good faith.

National Labor Relations Board v. Wooster Division of Borg-Warner Corp., 356 U.S. 342 (1958), U.S. Supreme Court case which held there were three categories of bargaining proposals under the Labor-Management Relations (Taft-Hartley) Act of 1947—illegal subjects, mandatory subjects, and voluntary subjects.

National Labor Relations Board v. Wyman-Gordon Co., see EXCELSIOR RULE.

National Labor Relations Board v. Yeshiva University, 444 U.S. 672 (1980), U.S. Supreme Court case which held that university faculty members who were involved in the governance (management) of their institutions were excluded from the protections and rights offered nonmanagerial employees by the National Labor Relations Act. See Joel M. Douglas, "Distinguishing *Yeshiva*: A Troubling Task for the NLRB," *Labor Law Journal* (February 1983); Clarence R. Deitsch and David A. Dilts, "*NLRB v. Yeshiva University*: A Positive Perspective," *Monthly Labor Review* (July 1983).

National League of Cities (NLC), formerly AMERICAN MUNICIPAL ASSOCIATION, organization founded in 1924 by and for reform-minded state municipal leagues. Membership in NLC was opened to individual cities in 1947, and NLC now has more than 1100 direct member cities. The twenty-seven U.S. cities with populations greater than 500,000 are all NLC direct members, as are 87 percent of all cities with more than 100,000 residents. NLC is an advocate for municipal interests before Congress, the executive branch, and the federal agencies and in state capitals across the nation where other matters of importance to cities are decided.

National League of Cities
1301 Pennsylvania Ave., N.W.
Washington, D.C. 20004
(202) 626-3000

National League of Cities v. Usery, 426 U.S. 833 (1976), U.S. Supreme Court case which held that the doctrine of federalism as expressed in the Tenth Amendment invalidates the 1974 amendments to the Fair Labor Standards Act (FLSA) extending minimum-wage and overtime provisions to state and local employees performing traditional governmental functions. This decision reversed the Court's decision in *Maryland* v. *Wirtz*, 392 U.S. 183 (1968), which approved the extension of the FLSA to certain state-operated hospitals, institutions, and schools. *NLC* v. *Usery* was, in turn, reversed in 1985 by *Garcia* v. *San Antonio Metropolitan Transit Authority*.

National Mediation Board, federal agency that provides the railroad and airline industries with specific mechanisms for the adjustment of labor-management disputes; that is, the facilitation of agreements through collective bargaining, investigation of questions of representation, and the arbitration and establishment of procedures for emergency disputes. First created by the Railway Labor Act of 1934, today the board's major responsibilities are: (1) the mediation of disputes over wages, hours, and working conditions which arise between rail and air carriers and organizations representing their employees, and (2) the investigation of representation disputes and certification of employee organizations as representatives of crafts or classes of carrier employees.

National Mediation Board
1425 K Street, N.W.
Washington, D.C. 20572
(202) 523-5920

National Municipal League, membership organization that serves as a clearinghouse and lobby for urban concerns. For a history, see Frank Mann Stewart, *A Half Century of Municipal Reform: The History of the National Municipal League* (Berkeley and Los Angeles: University of California Press, 1950).

National Municipal League
55 W. 44th St.
New York, NY 10036
(212) 730-7930

national origin discrimination, type of discrimination prohibited by Title VII of the Civil Rights Act of 1964. Title VII prohibits disparate treatment, whether overt or covert, of any individual or group of individuals because of their national origin except when such treatment is necessary because of a bona fide occupational qualification; for example, it might be lawful to require native fluency in Spanish for a position as a translator. The Equal Employment Opportunity Commission (EEOC) gives as examples of national origin discrimination

the use of tests in the English language where the individual tested came from circumstances where English was not that person's first language or mother tongue, and where English language skill is not a requirement of the work to be performed; denial of equal opportunity to persons married to or associated with persons of a specific national origin; denial of equal opportunity because of membership in lawful organizations identified with or seeking to promote the interests of national groups; denial of equal opportunity because of attendance at schools or churches commonly utilized by persons of a given national origin; denial of equal opportunity because their name or that of their spouse reflects a certain national origin, and denial of equal opportunity to persons who as a class of persons tend to fall outside national norms for height and weight where such height and weight specifications are not necessary for the performance of the work involved.

Some states have laws prohibiting the employment of noncitizens in varying circumstances. According to the EEOC, "where such laws have the purpose or effect of discriminating on the basis of national origin, they are in direct conflict with and are, therefore, superseded by Title VII of the Civil Rights Act of 1964, as amended." *See* Charles J. Hollon and Thomas L. Bright, "National Origin Harassment in the Work Place: Recent Guideline Development from the EEOC," *Employee Relations Law Journal* (Autumn 1982).

National Panel of Arbitrators, *see* AMERICAN ARBITRATION ASSOCIATION.

national planning, the concept of centralized, government conducted or coor-

dinated, economic planning and development. The concept has been highly controversial because of its identification with socialistic and communistic approaches to government management of national economies. National planning was advocated by Frederick Winslow Taylor in the 1920's, but he was unsuccessful in gaining acceptance for it in the United States. In the 1980's, various forms, approaches, and government and industry roles in national planning have been suggested for revitalizing the U.S. industrial economy. *Also see* INDUSTRIAL POLICY and PLANNING.

National Planning Association (NPA), nonpartisan, nonprofit organization whose goal is to encourage joint economic planning and cooperation by leaders from business, labor, agriculture, and the professions.

NPA
1606 New Hampshire Avenue,
N.W.
Washington, D.C. 20009
(202) 265-7685

National Public Employer Labor Relations Association (NPELRA), professional association of state and local government labor relations specialists who solely represent management.

NPELRA
55 E. Monroe Street
Chicago, IL 60603
(312) 782-1752

National Railroad Adjustment Board, federal agency created by the Railway Labor Act of 1934. The National Railroad Adjustment Board has the responsibility of deciding disputes growing out of grievances or out of interpretation or application of agreements concerning rates of pay, rules, or working conditions in the railroad industry.

National Railroad Adjustment
Board
10 West Jackson Blvd.
Chicago, IL 60604
(312) 886-7300

National Railroad Passenger Corpora-

tion, also called AMTRAK, a for-profit corporation created by the Rail Passenger Service Act of 1970 to provide a balanced transportation system by improving and developing intercity rail passenger service.

Amtrak
400 North Capitol Street, N.W.
Washington, D.C. 20001
(202) 383-3000

National Recovery Administration, *see* NATIONAL INDUSTRIAL RECOVERY ACT OF 1933.

National Rehabilitation Association (NRA), founded in 1925, a private, nonprofit organization of 18,000 people whose purpose is to advance the rehabilitation of all handicapped persons.

National Rehabilitation
   Association
633 S. Washington Street
Alexandria, VA 22314
(703) 836-0850

National Right to Work Committee, also NATIONAL RIGHT TO WORK LEGAL DEFENSE FOUNDATION, INC., advocate of legislation to prohibit all forms of forced union membership. The *National Right to Work Legal Defense Foundation, Inc.,* seeks to establish legal precedents protecting workers against compulsory unionism.

National Right to Work Committee
8001 Braddock Road
Springfield, VA 22160
(703) 321-9820

National Safety Council, non-governmental, nonprofit public service organization dedicated to reducing the number and severity of all kinds of accidents by gathering and distributing information about the causes of accidents and ways to prevent them.

National Safety Council
444 North Michigan Avenue
Chicago, IL 60611
(312) 527-4800

National Science Foundation (NSF), organization whose purposes are to: increase the nation's base of scientific knowl-

edge and strengthen its ability to conduct scientific research; encourage research in areas that can lead to improvements in economic growth, energy supply and use, productivity, and environmental quality; promote international cooperation through science; and develop and help implement science education programs. In its role as a leading federal supporter of science, NSF also has an important role in national science policy planning.

NSF
1800 G Street, N.W.
Washington, D.C. 20550
(202) 655-4000
See also RANN.

National Science Foundation Act of 1950, act that established the National Science Foundation and granted it a threefold mandate: (1) to financially support important scientific research, both basic and applied; (2) to promote better education in scientific fields; and (3) to function as an oversight agency coordinating and directing all research projects being carried out under the direction of other federal agencies. The NSF never attempted to carry out the third aspect of its original mandate. *See* Luther J. Carter, "A New and Searching Look at NSF," *Science* (June 8, 1979).

National Security Council (NSC), body whose statutory function is to advise the president with respect to the integration of domestic, foreign, and military policies relating to national security.

NSC
Old Executive Office Building
Washington, D.C. 20506
(202) 395-4974

National Technical Information Service (NTIS), body established in 1970 to simplify and improve public access to Department of Commerce publications and to data files and scientific and technical reports sponsored by federal agencies. It is the central point in the United States for the public sale of government-funded research and development reports and other analyses prepared by federal agencies, their contractors, or grantees.

National Technical Information
Service
5285 Port Royal Road
Springfield, VA 22161
(703) 487-4600

National Training Laboratories Institute for Applied Behavioral Science (NTL), also called NTL INSTITUTE, organization founded as the National Training Laboratories in 1947 in Bethel, Maine. The early years at Bethel were devoted to the development of human relations laboratories. It was during this period that NTL proved the effectiveness of the new concept of the T-Group ("T" for training). NTL's concept of the T-Group—in which individuals, working in small groups, develop new insights into self and others— is still an important element in NTL programs and has been widely imitated. During the 1950s and 1960s, major areas for experimentation and development were expanded to include group dynamics, organization development, and community development. During the 1960s and early 1970s, the development of individual potential in personal growth programs became an added thrust, as did innovation in working with large systems. In the late 1970s, NTL helped men and women recognize and develop their potential in response to the array of alternatives in lifestyles, careers, and patterns of interaction available to them. It works toward keeping change from becoming chaos by promoting flexibility and innovation and by providing help in planning for individuals, organizations, and large systems.

Today, NTL Institute is internationally recognized as a focal agency for experience-based learning programs. It is also known as the institution which has had most to do with developing the new profession of laboratory education, with exploring new means of relating, with new approaches to social change, and with new methods of managing organizations. Interest in laboratory education has grown rapidly, and NTL defines as one of its roles helping to maintain professional standards in a field now popularized and often misunderstood.

National Training Laboratories
Institute
Mailing Address:
P.O. Box 9155
Rosslyn Station
Arlington, VA 22209
Address:
1501 Wilson Blvd.
Arlington, VA 22209
(703) 527-1500

National Transportation Safety Board (NTSB). The NTSB seeks to assure that all types of transportation in the United States are conducted safely. The board investigates accidents and makes recommendations to government agencies, the transportation industry, and others on safety measures and practices. The board also regulates the procedures for reporting accidents and promotes the safe transport of hazardous materials by government and private industry.

NTSB
800 Independence Avenue, S.W.
Washington, D.C. 20594
(202) 382-6600

National Urban League, also called the URBAN LEAGUE, nonpartisan community service agency (115 local units) devoted to the economic and social concerns of blacks.

National Urban League
500 East 62nd Street
New York, NY 10021
(212) 310-9000

National Woodwork Manufactures Association v. National Labor Relations Board, 386 U.S. 612 (1967), U.S. Supreme Court case which held that when a boycott is used as a shield to preserve customary jobs, rather than as a sword to gather new ones, it does not violate the National Labor Relations Act's proscription against secondary boycotts, Section 8(6)(4)(B).

Nation's Cities, monthly magazine of the National League of Cities.

Nation's Cities
1301 Pennsylvania Ave., N.W.
Washington, D.C. 20004

native ability, actual ability. A test score is usually interpreted to mean that an individual's native ability lies somewhere in a range (plus or minus fifty points, for example) surrounding the score.

Natural Gas Policy Act, *see* NATIONAL ENERGY ACT OF 1978.

NCSL, *see* NATIONAL CIVIL SERVICE LEAGUE.

needs analysis, any of a variety of approaches that seek to establish the requirements of a particular situation in order to determine what, if any, program activity should be initiated. *See* Ralph R. Drtina and R. Allen Morgan, "The Use of Needs Assessment Data by Managers of Human Service Delivery Organizations: Some Empirical Findings," *Public Productivity Review* (December 1983).

needs hierarchy, a psychological concept. In the July 1943 issue of *Psychological Review*, Abraham H. Maslow published his now classic "A Theory of Human Motivation," in which he put forth his hierarchical conception of human needs. Maslow asserted that humans had five sets of goals or basic needs arranged in a hierarchy of prepotency: physiological needs, safety needs, love or affiliation needs, esteem needs and the need for self-actualization—the desire "to become everything that one is capable of becoming." Once lower needs are satisfied, they cease to be motivators of behavior. Conversely, higher needs cannot motivate until lower needs are satisfied. It is commonly recognized that there are some inescapable incongruities in Maslow's needs hierarchy. Some lower needs in some people, such as security, love, and status, never seem to be satiated. However, this does not take away from the importance of the desire for higher level needs as a motivational force in others. *See* Abraham Maslow, *Motivation and Personality*, 2nd ed. (New York:

Harper & Row, 1970); Edwin C. Nevis, "Using An American Perspective in Understanding Another Culture: Toward a Hierarchy of Needs for the People's Republic of China," *The Journal of Applied Behavioral Science*, Vol. 19, No. 3 (1983).
See also SELF-ACTUALIZATION.

MASLOW'S HIERARCHY OF NEEDS

SELF-ACTUALIZATION

EGO NEEDS

AFFILIATION NEEDS

SAFETY NEEDS

PHYSIOLOGICAL NEEDS

negative entropy, *see* ENTROPY.

negatively skewed, *see* SKEWNESS

negative reinforcement, *see* REINFORCEMENT.

negative strike, *see* POSITIVE STRIKE.

negative stroking, *see* STROKING.

negative transfer, *see* TRANSFER OF LEARNING.

negotiating committee, continuous, *see* CONTINUOUS NEGOTIATING COMMITTEE.

negotiation, process by which representatives of labor and management bargain—directly discuss proposals and counterproposals—in order to establish the conditions of work (wages, hours, benefits, the machinery for handling grievances, etc.). For general theories on the negotiating process, *see* Gerald I. Nierenberg, *The Art of Negotiating: Psychological Strategies for Gaining Advantageous Bargains* (New York: Hawthorn Books, 1968); Otomar J. Bartos, *Process and Outcome of Negotiations* (New York:

Columbia University Press, 1974); Jeffrey Z. Rubin and Bert R. Brown, *The Social Psychology of Bargaining and Negotiation* (New York: Academic Press, 1975). For a specific application to labor relations, *see* Richard E. Walton and Robert B. McKersie, *A Behavioral Theory of Labor Negotiations* (New York: McGraw-Hill, 1965). *Also see* William E. Klay, "Combating Inflation Through Wage Negotiations: A Strategy for Public Administration," *Public Administration Review* (September–October 1981); John J. Hoover, "Negotiating the Initial Union Contract," *Personnel Journal* (September 1982); David W. Ewing, "How To Negotiate With Employee Objectors," *Harvard Business Review* (January–February 1983); Michael E. Gordon, Neal Schmitt, and Walter G. Schneider, "Laboratory Research on Bargaining and Negotiations: An Evaluation," *Industrial Relations* (Spring 1984); Colette A. Frayne and Phillip L. Hunsaker, "Strategies for Successful Interpersonal Negotiating," *Personnel* (May–June 1984).

negotiation, career, *see* CAREER NEGOTIATION.

negotiations, collective, *see* COLLECTIVE NEGOTIATIONS.

neighborhood association, also NEIGHBORHOOD MOVEMENT, organization of residents of a neighborhood. In many American cities, neighbors in a particular area have formally organized into associations. These associations often play important political roles, lobbying local government and protecting neighborhood interests at all levels of government. They often reflect a movement calling for a decentralization of local government. At the extreme are advocates for neighborhood self-sufficiency, seeing both economic and political power possible for poorer neighborhoods only to the extent they can become independent of the dominant urban government. *See* Milton Kolter, *Neighborhood Government: The Local Foundation of Political Life* (Indianapolis: Bobbs-Merrill, 1969); Howard W. Hallman, *The Organi-*

zation and Operation of Neighborhood Councils: A Practical Guide (New York: Praeger, 1977); Sandra Perlman Schoenberg and Patricia L. Rosenbaum, *Neighborhoods that Work: Sources for Viability in the Inner City* (New Brunswick, N.J.: Rutgers University Press, 1980); Anthony Downs, *Neighborhoods and Urban Development* (Washington, D.C.: Brookings Institution, 1981).

neoclassical organization theory, *see* ORGANIZATION THEORY.

nepotism, any practice by which officeholders award positions to members of their immediate family. It is derived from the Latin *nepos,* meaning nephew or grandson. The rulers of the medieval church were often thought to give special preference to their nephews in distributing churchly offices. At that time, "nephew" became a euphemism for an illegitimate son. *See* Leonard Bierman and Cynthia D. Fisher, "Antinepotism Rules Applied to Spouses: Business and Legal Viewpoints," *Labor Law Journal* (October 1984).

nervous breakdown, catch-all expression for mental illness that does not refer to any particular disorder. Individuals in high pressure jobs who can no longer cope with the associated mental strains are frequently said to have had nervous breakdowns, but the actual clinical reason for their incapacity could be any of a large variety of mental and/or physical maladies.
   See also OCCUPATIONAL NEUROSIS and STRESS.

NETH Week, *see* NATIONAL EMPLOY THE HANDICAPPED WEEK.

net pay, *see* TAKE-HOME PAY.

net social benefit, the social benefits minus the social costs of a proposed program or project.

network, pattern of "interrelated and interconnected individuals, groups and/or organizations that form a system of communication." At present more is

known about the structure of networks than is known about the dynamics of network interaction. Large networks are known to show great complexity and structural variation with actors performing specialized functions as gatekeepers or linking pins. *See* Jeffalyn Johnson, "Networking: A Management Tool," *The Bureaucrat* (Winter 1977); James R. Lincoln and Jon Miller, "Work and Friendship Ties in Organizations: A Comparative Analysis of Relational Networks," *Administrative Science Quarterly* (June 1979); Noel M. Tichy, Michael L. Tushman, and Charles Fombrun, "Social Network Analysis for Organizations," *Academy of Management Review* (October 1979); Michael K. Moch, "Job Involvement, Internal Motivation, and Employees' Integration into Networks of Work Relationships," *Organizational Behavior and Human Performance* (February 1980); Joseph Galaskiewicz and Deborah Shatin, "Leadership and Networking Among Neighborhood Human Service Organizations," *Administrative Science Quarterly* (September 1981); Margaret Nemec, " 'Networking': Here's How at Equitable," *The Personnel Administrator* (April 1980); Philomena D. Warihay, "The Climb to the Top: Is the Network the Route for Women?" *The Personnel Administrator* (April 1980); Jessica Lipnack and Jeffrey Stamps, *Networking: The First Report and Directory* (Garden City, N.Y.: Doubleday, 1982).
See also OLD BOYS' NETWORK.

neutral, any third party who is actively engaged in labor-management negotiations in order to facilitate a settlement.

neutral competence, concept that envisions a continuous, politically uncommitted cadre of bureaucrats at the disposal of elected or appointed political executives. *See* Herbert Kaufman, "Emerging Conflicts in the Doctrines of Public Administration," *American Political Science Review* (December 1956); Hugh Heclo, "OMB and the Presidency—the Problem of 'Neutral Competence,' " *Public Interest* (Winter 1975).

New Deal, the domestic programs and policies of the administration of President Franklin D. Roosevelt (1933-1945).

new federalism, *see* FEDERALISM, NEW.

new girls' network, *see* OLD BOYS' NETWORK.

new hire, individual who has just joined an organization as an employee.
See also PROBATIONARY EMPLOYEE.

new industrial state, John Kenneth Galbraith's concept (from his 1967 book of the same name) which holds that modern organizations have become so complex that traditional leaders are no longer able to "make" major decisions; they can only ratify the decisions made for them by a technostructure of specialists who may be more interested in maintaining themselves than in generating profits.

Newport News Shipbuilding and Dry Dock Co. **v.** *EEOC,* 77 L. Ed. 2d 18 (1983), U.S. Supreme Court case which ruled that the company had discriminated against a male employee by providing limited health insurance coverage of his wife's pregnancy costs, while providing full coverage of health costs for the spouses of female employees. Writing for the majority, Justice John Stevens said that the Newport News plan violated the Pregnancy Discrimination Act of 1978. Continuing, Justice Stevens said that in enacting the law, the Congress had "unambiguously expressed its disapproval" of the Court's 1976 ruling in *General Electric Co.* v. *Gilbert* that the exclusion of disabilities caused by pregnancy from an employer's disability plan did not constitute discrimination based on sex.

Newport News Shipbuilding and Dry Dock Co. **v.** *Schauffler,* 303 U.S. 54 (1938), U.S. Supreme Court case which held that a company was subject to the authority of the National Labor Relations Board even if its participation in interstate commerce was limited to receiving goods from other states.

new public administration, *see* PUBLIC ADMINISTRATION, NEW.

New York Telephone Co. v. *New York State Department of Labor,* 440 U.S. 519 (1979), U.S. Supreme Court case which held that the payment of unemployment compensation to strikers was not in conflict with the policy of free collective bargaining established by the National Labor Relations Act.

New York Times v. *Sullivan,* 376 U.S. 254 (1964), U.S. Supreme Court case which held that a state cannot, under the 1st and 14th Amendments, award damages to a public official for defamatory falsehood relating to his official conduct unless he proves "actual malice"—that the statement was made with the knowledge of its falsity or with reckless disregard of whether it was true or false.

NCSL, *see* NATIONAL CONFERENCE OF STATE LEGISLATURES.

NCUA, *see* NATIONAL CREDIT UNION ADMINISTRATION.

NGA, *see* NATIONAL GOVERNORS ASSOCIATION.

nibbling, also called PIECE RATE NIBBLING, practice of cutting the piece rates paid to employees upon an increase in their output.

night premium, also called NIGHT DIFFERENTIAL, additions to regular wage rates that are paid to employees who work on shifts other than the regular day shift.

NIOSH, *see* NATIONAL INSTITUTE FOR OCCUPATIONAL SAFETY AND HEALTH.

NIRA, *see* NATIONAL INDUSTRIAL RECOVERY ACT OF 1933.

NLC, *see* NATIONAL LEAGUE OF CITIES.

NLC v. *Usery,* *see* NATIONAL LEAGUE OF CITIES V. USERY.

NLRA, *see* NATIONAL LABOR RELATIONS ACT OF 1935.

NLRB, *see* NATIONAL LABOR RELATIONS BOARD.

Nolde Brothers, Inc. v. *Local No. 358, Bakery Workers,* 430 U.S. 243 (1977), U.S. Supreme Court case which held that a "party to a collective-bargaining contract may be required to arbitrate a contractual dispute over severance pay pursuant to the arbitration clause of that agreement even though the dispute, although governed by the contract, arises after its termination." *See* Irving M. Geslewitz, "Case Law Development Since *Nolde Brothers:* When Must Post-Contract Disputes Be Arbitrated?" *Labor Law Journal* (April 1984).

nominating officer, subordinate officer of an agency to whom authority has been delegated by the head of the agency to nominate for appointment but not actually appoint employees.

noncallable bonds, *see* CALLABLE BONDS.

noncompetitive appointment, government employment obtained without competing with others, in the sense that it is done without regard to civil service registers. Includes reinstatements, transfers, reassignments, demotions, and some promotions.

noncontributory pension plan, pension program that has the employer paying the entire cost.

nondirective interview, *see* DIRECTED INTERVIEW.

nonguaranteed debt, *see* DEBT, NONGUARANTEED.

nonproduction bonus, also called CHRISTMAS BONUS and YEAR-END BONUS, payments to workers that are, in effect, gratuities upon which employees cannot regularly depend. Richard P. Helwig, "The Christmas Bonus: A Gift or a Give-Away?"

Personnel Journal (November 1973), warns that

> it is an unfair labor practice if an employer refuses to bargain as to wages, hours of employment, or other conditions of employment. The factual question to be determined is whether a Christmas gift constitutes a condition of employment such as compensation for service, as distinguished from a mere discretionary gift? If so, the discontinuance of such a program is a bargainable matter and must be discussed with the union prior to taking such action.

nonprofit sector, all those businesses and organizations set up for religious, charitable, educational, or other purposes that would entitle them to a special tax exempt status. *See* P. H. Mirvis and E. J. Hackett, "Work and the Work Force in the Nonprofit Sector," *Monthly Labor Review* (April 1983).

Nonreading Aptitude Test Battery (NATB), form of the General Aptitude Test Battery designed by the United States Employment Service for individuals so disadvantaged that testing premised upon literacy would be inappropriate. *See* Patricia Marshall, "Tests Without Reading," *Manpower* (May 1971).

nonsuability clause, that portion of a labor contract where a company agrees that it will not sue a labor union because of a wildcat strike, provided that the union lives up to its obligation to stop the strike.

nonsupplant provision, provision in grant agreements that does not clearly specify an actual level of spending to be maintained (as in a maintenance of effort provision) but merely stipulates that recipients shall maintain spending from their own resources at the level that would have existed in the absence of aid.

nonverbal communication, any means of projecting opinion, attitudes, and desires through the use of body postures, movements, expressions, gestures, eye contact, use of space and time, or other means of expressing such ideas short of written and/or verbal communications. For the classic work, *see* Edward T. Hall, *The Silent Language* (Garden City, N.Y.: Doubleday, 1959). For a text, *see* Mark L. Knapp, *Nonverbal Communication In Human Interaction* (New York: Holt, Rinehart and Winston, Inc., 1972). For more, *see* Constance E. Obudho, *Human Nonverbal Behavior — An Annotated Bibliography* (Westport, Conn.: Greenwood Press, 1979). *Also see* Fernando Poyatos, *New Perspectives in Nonverbal Communication* (New York: Pergamon Press, 1983); Peter Bull, *Body Movement and Interpersonal Communication* (New York: Wiley, 1983); Walburga Von Raffler-Engel, *The Perception of Nonverbal Behavior in the Career Interview* (Amsterdam: John Benjamins Publishing, 1983).

norm, standard or criteria against which an individual's test score or production rate can be compared and evaluated.

normal distribution, frequency distribution that follows the pattern of the normal "bell shaped" curve, characterized by symmetry about the mean and a standard relationship between width and height of the curve.

normal time, *see* ALLOWED TIME.

normative, those findings or conclusions that are premised upon morally established norms of right or wrong. *See* Michael Harmon, "Normative Theory and Public Administration," in *Toward A New Public Administration,* edited by Frank Marini (Scranton, Pa.: Chandler Publishing Co., 1971).

normative standard, standard of performance obtained by examining the relative performance of a group or sample of candidates.

norm-referenced test, any test that describes a candidate's performance in terms of its relation to the performance of other candidates.

norms, in psychological testing, tables of scores from a large number of people who have taken a particular test. For an analysis of norm referenced test scores, see H. B. Lyman, *Test Scores and What They Mean,* 2nd ed. (Englewood Cliffs, N.J.: Prentice-Hall, 1971).

In a more general sense, norms are socially enforced requirements and expectations about basic responsibilities, behavior and thought patterns of members in their organizational roles. Edgar H. Schein distinguishes between two types of organizational norms based on their centrality to the organization's values: pivotal and relevant. *See* E. H. Schein, "Organizational Socialization and the Profession of Management," *Sloan Management Review* (Winter 1968).

Norris-LaGuardia Act of 1932, federal statute that generally removed the power of the federal courts to prevent coercive activities by unions if such actions did not involve fraud or violence. The act was significant because it finally allowed unions to exert effective economic pressures against employers. It also declared yellow-dog contracts to be unenforceable. Many states have "Little Norris-LaGuardia" acts that cover industries not engaged in interstate commerce.

See also YELLOW-DOG CONTRACT.

Northwest Airlines v. Air Line Pilots & Transport Workers, 447 U.S. 920 (1981), U.S. Supreme Court case which held that an employer found guilty of job bias does not have the right to force a union to pay part of the damages, even though the discrimination results from provisions of a collective bargaining agreement.

Norton v. Macy, 417 F. 2d 1161 (1969), U.S. Court of Appeals, District of Columbia Circuit, case holding that a federal employee could not legally be dismissed for allegedly immoral conduct unless it could be shown that such conduct had an adverse effect on the efficiency of the federal service.

no-show jobs, government positions for which the incumbent collects a salary but is not required to report to work. While no-show jobs are by their nature illegal, they are not uncommon. In 1975, when a New York State assemblyman was tried in Albany County Court for authorizing no-show jobs on his legislative payroll, he claimed discriminatory prosecution and asked that his case be dismissed because the practice was so commonplace. The judge concurred and the case was dismissed. *See* Albany, N.Y., *Times-Union,* September 23-28, 1975.

no-solicitation rule, employer's rule that prohibits solicitation of employees for any purpose during working hours.

notary public, semi-public official who can administer oaths, certify the validity of documents, and perform a variety of formal witnessing duties.

nothing job, a job that offers nothing (no satisfaction, prestige, etc.) to a worker except wages; or an easy task that can be quickly done.

NPA, *see* NATIONAL PLANNING ASSOCIATION.

NRA, *see* (1) NATIONAL INDUSTRIAL RECOVERY ACT OF 1933 or (2) NATIONAL REHABILITATION ASSOCIATION.

NRC, *see* NUCLEAR REGULATORY COMMISSION.

NSC, *see* NATIONAL SECURITY COUNCIL.

NSF, *see* NATIONAL SCIENCE FOUNDATION.

NTIS, *see* NATIONAL TECHNICAL INFORMATION SERVICE.

NTL, *see* NATIONAL TRAINING LABORATORIES FOR APPLIED BEHAVIORAL SCIENCE.

NTSB, *see* NATIONAL TRANSPORTATION SAFETY BOARD.

Nuclear Regulatory Commission

(NRC), formerly the ATOMIC ENERGY COMMISSION, body that licenses and regulates the uses of nuclear energy to protect the public health and safety and the environment. It does that by licensing persons and companies to build and operate nuclear reactors and to own and use nuclear materials. The NRC makes rules and sets standards for these types of licenses. The NRC also inspects the activities of the persons and companies licensed to ensure that they do not violate the safety rules of the commission. The NRC was created in 1975 and supplanted the Atomic Energy Commission.

NRC
1717 H Street, N.W.
Washington, D.C. 20555
(301) 492-7000

null hypothesis, hypothesis used in statistics that asserts there is no difference between two populations that cannot be explained by chance.

O

OASDI, see OLD AGE, SURVIVORS, AND DISABILITY INSURANCE.

object classification, uniform classification identifying the transactions of the federal government by the nature of the goods or services purchased (such as personnel compensation, supplies and materials, equipment) without regard to the agency involved or the purpose of the programs for which they are used.

objective, also ABSTRACT OBJECTIVE, INTANGIBLE OBJECTIVE, CONCRETE OBJECTIVE, and TANGIBLE OBJECTIVE, a point to be reached, the end result of an action or the broad overall purposes of an agency.

Abstract or *intangible objectives* are the qualities one seeks to attain in people and the environment that exemplify the appli-

cation of the highest management principles. They are the broad, general goals cited by management as theoretical considerations, ideals, or qualities to be attained. These abstractions or ideals are found in such objectives as: improve employee morale, increase individual employee productivity, be cost conscious, provide better on-the-job training, etc.

Concrete or *tangible objectives* are the translation of broad, strategic goals into specific, realistic goals containing identifiable and/or measurable performance from the application of resources.

objective test, any examining device whose scoring is not dependent upon the discretion of the examiners.

objectivity, fairness. An applicant appraisal procedure is objective if it elicits observable responses that can be recorded and reported in a precise, specified way. Objectivity seeks to remove personal opinion by reducing the impact of individual judgment.

obligational authority, the sum of (a) budget authority provided for a given fiscal year, (b) balances of amounts brought forward from prior years that remain available for obligation, and (c) amounts authorized to be credited to a specific fund or account during that year, including transfers between funds or accounts.

obligation budgeting, see BUDGETING, COST-BASED.

obligations, amounts of orders placed, contracts awarded, services rendered, or other commitments made by government agencies during a given period which will require outlay during the same or some future period. (General instructions to federal agencies are contained in OMB Circular A-34.)

obligatory arbitration, arbitration requested by one party in a situation where the other party is obligated (for example, by a contract provision) to accept it.

obsolescence, see OCCUPATIONAL OBSOLESCENCE.

occupation, relatively continuous pattern of activity that (1) provides a livelihood for an individual and (2) serves to define an individual's general social status.

occupational career, career that, according to Walter L. Slocum, in "Occupational Careers in Organizations: A Sociological Perspective," *Personnel and Guidance Journal* (May 1965), "consists of entry into a position at the lowest rung of a career ladder, followed by an orderly sequence of promotions to positions at successively higher status levels and finally to retirement."

occupational certification, also called CERTIFICATION, practice that permits practitioners in a particular occupation to claim minimum levels of competence. While certification enables some practitioners to claim a competency which others cannot, this type of regulation does not prevent uncertified people from supplying the same services as certified people. *See* Kenneth K. Henning, "Certification as a Recognition of Professional Development," *State and Local Government Review* (May 1981).
See also OCCUPATIONAL LICENSING.

occupational decision-making, see CAREER DECISION-MAKING.

occupational disease, see OCCUPATIONAL ILLNESS.

occupational grouping, grouping of classes within the same broad occupational category, such as engineering, nursing, accounting, etc.

occupational hazard, any danger directly associated with one's work. *See* Nicholas A. Ashford, *Crisis in the Workplace: Occupational Disease and Injury—A Report to the Ford Foundation* (Cambridge, Mass.: The MIT Press, 1976); N. Root and D. Sebastian, "BLS Develops Measure of Job Risk by Occupation," *Monthly Labor Review* (October 1981).

occupational health, all the activities related to protecting and maintaining the health and safety of employees. *See* Joseph A. Page and Mary-Win O'Brien, *Bitter Wages: Ralph Nader's Study Group Report on Disease and Injury on the Job* (New York: Grossman, 1973); John Mendeloff, *Regulating Safety: An Economic and Political Analysis of Occupational Safety and Health Policy* (Cambridge, Mass.: The M.I.T. Press, 1979); Steven Deutsch, ed., "Theme Issue: Occupational Safety and Health," *Labor Studies Journal* (Spring 1981); W. B. Creighton and E. J. Micallef, "Occupational Health and Safety as an Industrial Relations Issue: The Rank-General Electric Dispute, 1981," *The Journal of Industrial Relations* (September 1983).

occupational illness, also called OCCUPATIONAL DISEASE, any abnormal condition or disorder, other than one resulting from an occupational injury, caused by exposure to environmental factors associated with employment. It includes acute and chronic illnesses or diseases which may be caused by inhalation, absorption, ingestion, or direct contact. *See* H. J. Hilaski and C. L. Wang, "How Valid are Estimates of Occupational Illness?" *Monthly Labor Review* (August 1982).

occupational injury, any injury (such as a cut, fracture, sprain, amputation, etc.), that results from a work accident or from exposure involving a single incident in the work environment. *See* Fred Siskind, "Another Look at the Link Between Work Injuries and Job Experience," *Monthly Labor Review* (February 1982).

occupational licensing, also called LICENSING, according to Clifford Elliott and Vincent H. Smith, "Occupational Licensing: An Empirical Approach," *University of Michigan Business Review* (July 1978), act that

requires that all non-licensed persons cease to practice and be excluded from future participation in the licensed occupation. The additional benefit provided to the community from licensing occupations is to protect the community from the spillover costs that might result if individual consumers choose low quality services. A classic example of this possibility is to be found in medicine. A man with a contagious disease who hires the services of a low-cost quack and consequently fails to be cured, may impose the disease on people who might not have caught it if he had been forced to utilize the services of a more competent person.

Also see Alex Maurizi, "Occupational Licensing and the Public Interest," *Journal of Political Economy* (March-April 1974); Barbara F. Esser, Daniel H. Kruger, and Benjamin Shimberg, *Occupational Licensing: Practices and Politics* (Washington, D.C.: Public Affairs Press, 1973); Stuart Dorsey, "The Occupational Licensing Queue," *Journal of Human Resources* (Summer 1980).

See also OCCUPATIONAL CERTIFICATION.

occupational mobility, also HORIZONTAL and VERTICAL OCCUPATIONAL MOBILITY, the movement of individuals from one occupation to another. A change from one occupation to another of similar occupational status is an example of *horizontal occupational mobility.* A change of occupational status levels within the same occupation is an example of *vertical occupational mobility. See* Dixie Sommers and Alan Eck, "Occupational Mobility in the American Labor Force," *Monthly Labor Review* (January 1977); Harrison C. White, *Chains of Opportunity: System Models of Mobility in Organizations* (Cambridge, Mass.: Harvard University Press, 1970); Marshall I. Pomer, *Intergenerational Occupational Mobility in the United States: A Segmentation Perspective* (Gainesville, Fla.: University Presses of Florida, 1981); Ellen Sehgal, "Occupational Mobility and Job Tenure in 1983," *Monthly Labor Review* (October 1984).

occupational neurosis, development of incapacitating physical symptoms that make it impossible to continue one's work.

occupational obsolescence, concept usually associated with professional employees who lack currency with their discipline. For example, an engineer who has served as an administrator for a significant number of years may, in consequence, be unable to function in his/her engineering speciality because the "state of the art" has moved too far. For thorough analyses of the concept and the problem, *see* H. G. Kaufman, *Obsolescence and Professional Career Development* (New York: AMACOM, 1974); Samuel S. Dubin, "Obsolescence or Lifelong Education: A Choice for the Professional," *American Psychologist* (May 1972); Clayton Reeser, "Managerial Obsolescence—An Organization Dilemma," *Personnel Journal* (January 1977); Benson Rosen and Thomas H. Jerdee, "A Model Program for Combatting Employee Obsolescence," *Personnel Administrator* (March 1985).

Occupational Outlook Handbook, the Bureau of Labor Statistics' biennial survey of employment trends that contains descriptive information and employment prospects for hundreds of occupational categories.

Occupational Outlook Quarterly, the U.S. Bureau of Labor Statistics' magazine designed to help high school students and guidance counselors assess career opportunities.

> Occupational Outlook Quarterly
> Superintendent of Documents
> Government Printing Office
> Washington, D.C. 20402

occupational parity, *see* PARITY.

occupational prestige, also called OCCUPATIONAL STATUS, ascribed status associated with an individual's employment. Opinion surveys typically find physicians, college professors, psychologists, bankers, and architects at the top of a hierarchy of occupational prestige, while unskilled farm workers and garbage collectors compete for the lowest rankings. According to Donald J. Treiman, in *Occupational Prestige in Comparative Perspective* (New York: Academic Press, 1977),

people in all walks of life share understandings about occupations—how much skill they require, how physically demanding they are, whether they are considered men's work or women's work, and so on—but particularly about their prestige. Every adult member of society ordinarily is able to locate occupations on a hierarchy of prestige. These perceptions form part of the *conscience collective*. This permits one to rank oneself and others with respect to the social honor derived from occupational status.

Also see Andre L. Delebec and James Vigen, "Prestige Ratings of Business and Other Occupations," *Personnel Journal* (February 1970); Anthony P. M. Coxon and Charles L. Jones, *Class and Hierarchy: The Social Meaning of Occupations* (New York: St. Martin's Press, 1979).

occupational psychiatry, also called IN-DUSTRIAL PSYCHIATRY, any of the professional activities of psychiatry conducted at the workplace of the clients. *See* W. E. Powles and W. D. Ross, "Industrial and Occupational Psychiatry," in S. Arieti, ed., *American Handbook of Psychiatry*, 2nd ed. (New York: Basic Books, 1975).

occupational psychology, *see* IN-DUSTRIAL PSYCHOLOGY.

occupational registration, simple requirement that persons active in a particular occupation file their names with an appropriate authority. As such regulations place no restrictions upon the persons engaged in the particular occupation, registration is no indication of competence.

Occupational Safety and Health Act of 1970, also called WILLIAMS-STEIGER ACT, federal government's basic legislation for providing for the health and safety of employees on the job. The act created the Occupational Safety and Health Review Commission, the Occupational and Health Administration, and the National Institute for Occupational Safety and Health. *See* George C. Guenther, "The Significance of the Occupational Safety and Health Act to the Worker in the United States," *International Labor Review* (January 1972); Judson MacLaury, "The Job Safety Law of 1970: Its Passage was Perilous," *Monthly Labor Review* (March 1981).

See also WORKERS' COMPENSATION.

Occupational Safety and Health Administration (OSHA), body established by the Occupational Safety and Health Act of 1970. OSHA develops and promulgates occupational safety and health standards, develops and issues regulations, conducts investigations and inspections to determine the status of compliance with safety and health standards and regulations, and issues citations and proposes penalties for noncompliance with safety and health standards and regulations. The Assistant Secretary for Occupational Safety and Health has responsibility for occupational safety and health activities. OSHA has ten regional offices. *See* Albert L. Nichols and Richard Zeckhauser, "Government Comes to the Workplace: An Assessment of OSHA," *The Public Interest* (Fall 1977); Frank J. Thompson, "The Substitution Approach to Intergovernmental Relations: The Case of OSHA," *Publius* (Fall 1983); Benjamin W. Mintz, *OSHA: History, Law, and Policy* (Washington, D.C.: Bureau of National Affairs, Inc., 1985).

OSHA
U.S. Department of Labor
Washington, D.C. 20210
(202) 523-8017
See also MARSHALL V. BARLOW'S, INC.

Occupational Safety & Health Reporter, weekly notification and reference service published by the Bureau of National Affairs, Inc. Covers significant legislative, administrative, judicial, and industrial developments under the Occupational Safety and Health Act. Includes information on standards, legislation, regulations, enforcement, research, advisory committee recommendations, union activities, and state programs.

See also BUREAU OF NATIONAL AFFAIRS, INC.

Occupational Safety and Health Review Commission (OSHRC), independent adjudicatory agency established by the Occupational Safety and Health Act of 1970 to adjudicate enforcement actions initiated under the act when they are contested by employers, employees, or representatives of employees.

Within OSHRC there are two levels of adjudication. All cases which require a hearing are assigned to an OSHRC judge who will decide the case. Each such decision is subject to discretionary review by the three OSHRC members upon the motion of any one of the three. However, approximately 90 percent of the decisions of the judges become final orders without any change whatsoever.

The Occupational Safety and Health Act covers virtually every employer in the country. It requires employers to furnish their employees with employment and a place of employment free from recognized hazards that are causing or are likely to cause death or serious physical harm to employees and to comply with occupational safety and health standards promulgated under the act.

The Secretary of Labor has promulgated a substantial number of occupational safety and health standards which, pursuant to the act, have the force and effect of law. He has also initiated a regular program of inspections in order to check upon compliance. A case for adjudication by OSHRC arises when a citation is issued against an employer as the result of such an inspection and it is contested within fifteen working days thereafter.

When a case is docketed, it is assigned for hearing to an OSHRC judge. The hearing will ordinarily be held in or near the community where the alleged violation occurred. At the hearing, the Secretary of Labor will have the burden of proving his case.

After the hearing, the judge must issue a report, based on findings of fact, affirming, modifying, or vacating the secretary's citation or proposed penalty, or directing other appropriate relief. His report will become a final order of OSHRC thirty days thereafter unless, within such period, any OSHRC member directs that such report shall be reviewed by OSHRC itself. When that occurs, the OSHRC members will thereafter issue their own decision on the case.

Once a case is decided, any person adversely affected or aggrieved thereby may obtain a review of such a decision in a United States court of appeals.

OSHRC
1825 K Street, N.W.
Washington, D.C. 20006
(202) 634-7943

occupational socialization, process by which an individual absorbs and adopts the values, norms, and behavior of the occupational role models with whom he/she interacts. Occupational socialization is complete when an individual internalizes the values and norms of the occupational group. *See* Wilbert E. Moore, "Occupational Socialization," in David A. Goslin, ed., *Handbook of Socialization Theory and Research* (Chicago: Rand McNally & Co., 1969).

occupational sociology, also called INDUSTRIAL SOCIOLOGY and SOCIOLOGY OF WORK, subspecialty of sociology concerned with examining the social structures and institutions which a society develops to facilitate its work. For texts, *see* Walter S. Neff, *Work and Human Behavior* (Chicago: Aldine Publishing Company, 1968); Lee Taylor, *Occupational Sociology* (New York: Oxford University Press, 1968); Elliott A. Krause, *The Sociology of Occupations* (Boston: Little, Brown, 1971).

occupational status, *see* OCCUPATIONAL PRESTIGE.

occupational survey, an organization's study of all positions in a given class, series of classes, or occupational group in whatever departments or divisions they may be located.

OD, *see* ORGANIZATION DEVELOPMENT.

Odiorne, George S. (1920-   ), one of the foremost authorities on MBO. Major works include: *Management by Objectives — A System of Management Leadership* (New York: Pitman, 1965); *Management Decisions by Objectives* (Englewood Cliffs, N.J.: Prentice-Hall 1969); *Personnel Policy: Issues and Practices* (Columbus, Ohio: Charles E. Merrill, 1963); *Training by Objectives* (New York: Macmillan, 1970); *Personnel Administration by Objectives* (Homewood, Ill.: Richard D. Irwin, 1971).

OFCCP, *see* OFFICE OF FEDERAL CONTRACT COMPLIANCE PROGRAMS.

off-budget federal agencies, agencies, federally owned in whole or in part whose transactions have been excluded from the budget totals under provisions of law (*e.g.*, the Federal Financing Bank). The fiscal activities of these agencies are not included in either budget authority or outlay totals, but are presented in the Budget Appendix as "Annexed Budgets." *See* James T. Bennett and Thomas J. DiLorenzo, *Underground Government: The Off-Budget Public Sector* (Washington, D.C.: The Cato Institute, 1983).

office, *see* OPEN OFFICE and TURKEY FARM.

office automation, a loose term for any significant use of machines in offices. In the 1960s, it referred to any use of computers to process paperwork. Today it refers to word processing and other information retrieval equipment, but it has also taken on a larger connotation—the "office of the future"—in which electronic office devices are linked by telecommunications to other offices throughout a company, a region, or the world.

Office of Federal Contract Compliance Programs (OFCCP), agency within the Department of Labor delegated the responsibility for ensuring that there is no employment discrimination by government contractors because of race, religion, color, sex, or national origin, and to ensure affirmative action efforts in employing Vietnam Era veterans and handicapped workers. *See* Frank Erwin, "The New OFCCP Guidelines: What Happened?" *The Personnel Administrator* (February 1977).

OFCCP
200 Constitution Ave., N.W.
Washington, D.C. 20210
(202) 523-9475

Office of Management and Budget (OMB), office that supplanted the Bureau of the Budget in the Executive Office of the President on July 1, 1970. According to the *United States Government Manual*, the functions of OMB include:

To assist the President in his program to develop and maintain effective government by reviewing the organizational structure and management procedures of the executive branch to ensure that they are capable of producing the intended results;

To assist in developing efficient coordinating mechanisms to implement Government activities and to expand interagency cooperation;

To assist the President in the preparation of the budget and the formulation of the fiscal program of the Government;

To supervise and control the administration of the budget;

To assist the President by clearing and coordinating departmental advice on proposed legislation and by making recommendations as to Presidential action on legislative enactments, in accordance with past practice;

To assist in the development of regulatory reform proposals and in programs for paperwork reduction, especially reporting burdens of the public;

To assist in the consideration and clearance and, where necessary, in the preparation of proposed Executive orders and proclamations;

To plan and develop information

systems to provide the President with program performance data;

To plan, conduct, and promote evaluation efforts to assist the President in the assessment of program objectives, performance, and efficiency;

To keep the President informed of the progress of activities by agencies of the Government with respect to work proposed, work actually initiated, and work completed, together with the relative timing of work between the several agencies of the Government all to the end that the work programs of the several agencies of the executive branch of the Government may be coordinated and that the moneys appropriated by the Congress may be expended in the most economical manner with the least possible overlapping and duplication of effort.

For a history, see Larry Berman, *The Office of Management and Budget and the Presidency, 1921-1979* (Princeton University Press, 1979). *Also see* Shelley Lynne Tomkin, "Playing Politics in OMB: Civil Servants Join the Game," *Presidential Studies Quarterly* (Winter 1985).

OMB
Executive Office Buildling
Washington, D.C. 20503
(202) 395-3080

Office of Management and Budget (OMB) Circular A-95, a regulation first issued by the OMB, July 24, 1969, in partial implementation of Title IV of the Intergovernmental Cooperation Act of 1968. Major revisions of the circular were promulgated on February 9, 1971, November 13, 1973, and January 2, 1976.

Circular A-95 is designed to promote maximum coordination of federal programs and projects with state, areawide, and local plans and programs by providing an opportunity to governors, mayors, county elected officials, and other state and local officials, through clearinghouses, to influence federal decisions on proposed projects that may affect their own plans and programs.

The circular sets forth procedures under which federal agencies and applicants for federal assistance give state and local governments, through state and areawide clearinghouses, an opportunity to assess the relationship of their proposals to state, areawide, and local plans and programs for the development of their area. Federal agencies are required to consider these assessments in deciding whether or not to proceed with a proposed project. However, clearinghouse recommendations on federal or federally assisted development proposals are advisory only.

OMB Circular A-95 was published in the *Federal Register* of January 13, 1976. For the significance of Circular A-95 in intergovernmental relations, *see* George Gordon, "OMB Circular A-95: Perspectives and Implications," *Publius* (Winter 1974).

Office of Personnel Management (OPM), the central personnel agency of the federal government, created by the Civil Service Reform Act of 1978. OPM took over many of the responsibilities of the U.S. Civil Service Commission, including central examining and employment operations, personnel investigations, personnel program evaluation, executive development, and training. OPM administers the retirement and insurance programs for federal employees and exercises management leadership in labor relations and affirmative action. As the central personnel agency, OPM develops policies governing civilian employment in executive branch agencies and in certain agencies of the legislative and judicial branches. Subject to its standards and review, OPM delegates certain personnel powers to agency heads.

Office of Personnel Management
1900 E Street, N.W.
Washington, D.C. 20415
(202) 632-5491

Office of Science and Technology Policy, body that serves as a source of scientific, engineering, and technological analysis and judgment for the president with respect to major policies, plans and programs of the federal government.

Office of Science and Technology Policy
Old Executive Office Building

Office of Technology Assessment (OTA)

Washington, D.C. 20506
(202) 395-4692

Office of Technology Assessment (OTA), also TECHNOLOGY ASSESSMENT ACT OF 1972, office created by the Technology Assessment Act of 1972 to help the Congress anticipate and plan for the consequences of uses of technology. The OTA provides an independent and objective source of information about the impacts, both beneficial and adverse, of technological applications, and identifies policy alternatives for technology-related issues.

OTA
600 Pennsylvania Avenue, S.E.
Washington, D.C. 20510
(202) 224-8713

office romance, *see* LOVE.

office title, job title that differs from the classified title assigned to a job and is used to describe a particular position for other than payroll, budget, or official purposes. For example, a head clerk position might have an "office" title of office supervisor.

officialese, *see* GOBBLEDYGOOK.

official personnel folder (OPF), official repository of employment records and documents affecting personnel actions during an employee's federal civilian service.

off-line, computer system whose operations are not under the control of a central processing unit, or a computer system that does not process information as it is received, but stores and processes it at a later time.

offsetting receipts, all federal government collections and deposits into receipt accounts which are offset against budget authority and outlays rather than reflected as budget receipts in computing budget totals. Under current budgetary usage, cash collections not deposited into receipt accounts (such as revolving fund receipts, refunds, and reimbursements) are deducted from outlays at the account level.

These items are not considered "offsetting receipts" and are not included in compilations of offsetting receipts.

Offsetting receipts are generally deducted at the budget function or subfunction level; any offsetting receipts deducted at the function or subfunction level are also deducted from agency budget authority and outlays. In three cases—(1) employer share, employee retirement; (2) intragovernmental interest received by trust funds; and (3) rents and royalties from the Outer Continental Shelf lands—the deductions, referred to as undistributed offsetting receipts, are made from budget totals rather than being offset by function and subfunction and by agency.

Offsetting receipts are subdivided into two major categories—proprietary receipts from the public and intragovernmental transactions.

1. *Proprietary Receipts from the Public.* Those collections from the public deposited in receipt accounts which arise from the conduct of business-type activities.
2. *Intragovernmental Transactions.* All collections or deposits into receipt accounts in which the payment is made by a federal agency.

Intragovernmental transactions may represent either receipts from off-budget federal agencies where a payment comes from a federal agency whose funds are excluded from the budget totals, or *intrabudgetary transactions* where both the paying and the receiving accounts are within the budget. Intrabudgetary transactions in turn are further subdivided into three groups:

1. *Interfund Transactions*, where the payment is from a federal to a trust fund or vice versa.
2. *Federal Intrafund Transactions,* where both the paying and receiving accounts are federal funds.
3. *Trust Intrafund Transactions,* where both the paying and receiving accounts are trust funds.

ogive, a cumulative frequency graph.

Ohio Bureau of Employment Services

v. *Hodory,* 431 U.S. 471 (1977), U.S. Supreme Court case which ruled that a "State can withhold jobless benefits from workers laid off as a result of a strike against their employer even when they are not involved in the strike because it occurs at another location."

Oil Workers v. *Mobil Oil Co.,* 426 U.S. 407 (1976), U.S. Supreme Court case which considered the express authorization in the National Labor Relations Act for states to enact "right-to-work" laws forbidding union shops. Texas, a right-to-work state, tried to apply its statute to oil-tanker workers who were hired and often based in Texas. Because the workers spent the bulk of their working time on the high seas, however, the court decided that Texas law should not govern these workers and upheld a union-shop clause in their contract.

Old Age, Survivors, and Disability Insurance (OASDI), federal program created by the Social Security Act which taxes both workers and employers to pay benefits to retired and disabled people, their dependents, widows, widowers, and children of deceased workers.
See also SOCIAL SECURITY.

old boys' network, also NEW GIRLS' NETWORK, colloquial way of referring to the fact that men who went to school together or belong to the same clubs tend to help each other in the business world as the occasion arises. Many a career was advanced because a college roommate was in a critical position twenty years later. In an effort to develop similar ties for similar advantages, some women have been purposely trying to create a "new girls' network" by sponsoring appropriate social events. As Sarah Weddington, President Carter's "women's advisor," told one such group, "where you are tomorrow may well depend upon whom you meet tonight." *See* Stephen L. Slavin, "The Old Boy Network at Six Big Banks," *Business and Society Review* (Fall 1977).
See also NETWORK.

Old Dominion Branch No. 496, National Association of Letter Carriers v. *Austin,* 418 U.S. 264 (1974), U.S. Supreme Court case which held use of the epithet "scab," which was literally and factually true and in common parlance in labor disputes, was protected under federal law.

Older Americans Act of 1965, federal statute that as amended attempts to provide a national policy for assisting older Americans in securing equal opportunity and an enhanced quality of life. The act provides assistance to states for new and improved programs, planning, training, and research.

oligarchy, *see* IRON LAW OF OLIGARCHY.

Oliver Report, see JOB EVALUATION AND PAY REVIEW TASK FORCE.

OMB, *see* OFFICE OF MANAGEMENT AND BUDGET.

OMB Circular A-95, see OFFICE OF MANAGEMENT AND BUDGET.

ombudsman, also ORGANIZATION OMBUDSMAN, official whose job is to investigate the complaints of the citizenry concerning public services. Originally a Swedish word meaning "representative of the King," ombudsmen are now found in many countries at a variety of jurisdictional levels. For a comprehensive discussion, *see* Stanely V. Anderson, ed., *Ombudsmen for American Government?* (Englewood Cliffs, N.J.: Prentice-Hall, 1968). *Also see* William B. Gwyn, "The Ombudsman in Britain: A Qualified Success in Government Reform," *Public Administration* (Summer 1982).

An *organization ombudsman* is a high-level staff officer who receives complaints and grievances about his organization directly from the employees. Such an officer mainly serves as an open channel of communication between employees and top management. *See* Isidore Silver, "The Corporate Ombudsman," *Harvard Business Review* (May-June 1967); Marshall

Dimock, "The Ombudsman and Public Administration," *Public Administration Review* (September–October 1983).

on-line, computer system whose operations are under the control of a central processing unit or a computer system in which information is processed as received.

on-the-job training, any training that takes place during regular working hours and for which normal wages are paid. *See* Earl R. Gomersall and M. Scott Myers, "Breakthrough in On-the-Job Training," *Harvard Business Review* (July–August 1966); Martin M. Broadwell, "It Pays to Increase Your Support of On-the-Job Training," *Training* (October 1977); Delbert W. Fisher, "Educational Psychology Involved in On-the-Job Training," *Personnel Journal* (October 1977).
See also UNDERSTUDY.

open-book test, test that allows candidates to consult textbooks or other relevant material while the examination is in progress.

open-end agreement, collective bargaining agreement providing for a contract that will remain in effect until one of the parties wants to reopen negotiations.

open-end program, entitlement program for which eligibility requirements are determined by law (*e.g.*, Medicaid). Actual obligations and resultant outlays are limited only by the number of eligible persons who apply for benefits and the actual benefits received.
See also CLOSED-END PROGRAM.

open-end reimbursement grant, *see* GRANT.

open enrollment, a period when new subscribers may elect to enroll in a health insurance plan or prepaid group practice. Open enrollment periods may be used in the sale of either group or individual insurance and may be the only period of a year when insurance is available.

open-market operations, the purchase and sale of various securities, chiefly marketable federal government securities, by the Federal Reserve System in the open market for the purpose of implementing Federal Reserve monetary policy. Open-market operations, one of the most flexible instruments of monetary policy, affect the reserves of member banks, and thus the supply of money and the availability and cost of credit.

open office, completely open room without walls, doors, or dividers; room with partitions and potted plants where walls once were; room with partitioned cubicles that curve and connect; and/or an office laid out according to how information flows from one person to the next.

open shop, any work organization that is not unionized. The term also applies to organizations that have unions but do not have union membership as a condition of employment. Historically, an "open shop" was one that tended to discriminate against unions.

open system, any organism or organization that interacts with its environment.

open union, union willing to admit any qualified person to its membership upon payment of initiation fees.

operating budget, *see* BUDGET, OPERATING.

operational planning, decision-making that implements the larger goals and strategies of an organization.
See also PLANNING and STRATEGIC PLANNING.

operational validity, quality of test administration, interpretation, and application. According to William C. Byham and Stephen Temlock, in "Operational Validity—A New Concept in Personnel Testing," *Personnel Journal* (September 1972), "operational validity includes everything that happens with and to a test after test research has been completed.

Operational validity can never make invalid tests predictive; it can only assure maximum prediction within the limits of the tests used." According to Dennis M. Groner, in "A Note on 'Operational' Validity," *Personnel Journal* (March 1977), "in the strictest sense of the word, operational validity is not validity at all, but a source of error which reduces the correlation between a predictor and a criterion."

operations research, a group of mathematical methods for the efficient allocation of scarce resources such as capital, labor, and materials. *See also* MANAGEMENT SCIENCE for partially overlapping definitions. For history, *see* Russell L. Ackoff, "The Development of Operations Research as a Science," *Operations Research* (June 1956).

OPF, *see* OFFICIAL PERSONNEL FOLDER.

OPM, *see* OFFICE OF PERSONNEL MANAGEMENT.

opportunity cost, also called ALTERNATIVE COST, true cost of choosing one alternative rather than another; represents the implicit cost of the highest foregone alternative.

oral board, committee formed for the purpose of interviewing candidates for employment, promotion, or evaluation.

oral examination, group, *see* GROUP ORAL INTERVIEW.

oral interview, group, *see* GROUP ORAL INTERVIEW.

oral test, any test that has an examiner ask a candidate a set of questions, as opposed to a paper-and-pencil test.

organic system, the organization form that has proved to be most appropriate under changing conditions. It is characterized by: (1) constant reassessment of tasks, assignments, and the use of organizational expertise; (2) authority,

control, and communication that are frequently *ad hoc*, depending upon specific commitments and tasks; (3) communications and interactions between members that are both very open and extensive; (4) leadership stressing consultation and group decisional processes; and (5) greater commitment to the organization's tasks and goals than to traditional hierarchical loyalty. The classic analysis of organic systems is to be found in Tom Burns and G. M. Stalker, *The Management of Innovation* (Chicago: Quadrangle Books, 1961).
See also MECHANISTIC SYSTEM.

organization, any structure and process of allocating jobs so that common objectives may be achieved. *See* James G. March and Herbert A. Simon, *Organizations* (New York: John Wiley, 1958); James G. March, ed., *Handbook of Organizations* (Chicago: Rand McNally, 1965); Harold J. Leavitt, William R. Dill, and Henry B. Eyring, *The Organizational World* (New York: Harcourt Brace Jovanovich, 1973).

organization, flat/tall, *see* FLAT ORGANIZATION.

organization, formal/informal, *see* INFORMAL ORGANIZATION.

organizational behavior, academic discipline consisting of those aspects of the behavioral sciences that focus on the understanding of human behavior in organizations. *See* Walter E. Natemeyer, ed., *Classics of Organizational Behavior* (Oak Park, Ill.: Moore Publishing Co., 1979); William B. Eddy, *Public Organization Behavior and Development* (Cambridge, Mass.: Winthrop Publishers, 1981); Debra W. Stewart and G. David Garson, *Organizational Behavior and Public Management* (New York: Marcel Dekker, 1983).

organizational conflict, *see* CONFLICT RESOLUTION.

organizational culture, the pattern of fundamental beliefs and attitudes which powerfully affects members' behaviors in and around the organization, persists over extended periods of time, and pervades the organization (to different extents and with varying intensity). The organizational culture is transmitted to new members through socialization (or enculturation) processes; is maintained and transmitted through a network of rituals, rites, myths, communication, and interaction patterns; is enforced and reinforced by group norms and the organization's system of rewards and controls. Organizational cultures vary in intensity, content, and compatibility with the primary pattern of attitudes.

Sources of organizational culture include the attitudes and behaviors of dominant, early organization "shapers" and "heroes"; the organization's nature of work (or business), including its functions and interactions with the external environment; attitudes, values and "willingness to act" of new members. The organizational culture serves useful purposes including, for example, (1) providing a framework for shared understanding of events, (2) defining behavioral expectations, (3) providing a source of and focus for members' commitment, and (4) functioning as an organizational "control system" (i.e., through group norms). According to Stanley M. Davis in *Managing Corporate Culture* (Cambridge, Mass.: Ballinger, 1984), "The culture of an organization is the point of contact at which philosophy comes to bear on the problems of organizations . . . the culture is the meeting place of ethics with organization."

Although organizational culture has similarities to the concept of organizational climate, the latter typically is limited in use to the "feeling tone" or the "psychological climate." In contrast, organizational culture typically is used more as it is in the traditional anthropological sense. *See*, for example, E.H. Schein, "Coming to a New Awareness of Organizational Culture," *Sloan Management Review* (Winter 1984). For comprehensive introductions to the concepts, *see* Fritz Steele and Stephen Jenks, *The Feel of the Work Place: Understanding and Improving Organization Climate* (Reading,

Mass.: Addison-Wesley Publishing Co., 1977); Terrence E. Deal and Allan A. Kennedy, *Corporate Cultures: The Rituals of Corporate Life* (Reading, Mass.: Addison-Wesley, 1982).

For how to evaluate the climate in your organization, *see* William R. LaFollette, "How Is the Climate in Your Organization," *Personnel Journal* (July 1975); Alan L. Wilkins, "The Culture Audit: A Tool for Understanding Organizations," *Organizational Dynamics* (Autumn 1983); Daniel R. Denison, "Bringing Corporate Culture to the Bottom Line," *Organizational Dynamics* (Autumn 1984). *Also see* Allan P. Jones and Lawrence R. James, "Psychological Climate: Dimensions and Relationships of Individual and Aggregated Work Environment Perceptions," *Organizational Behavior and Human Performance* (April 1979); Andrew M. Pettigrew, "On Studying Organizational Cultures," *Administrative Science Quarterly* (December 1979); Benjamin Schneider, "The Service Organization: Climate Is Crucial," *Organizational Dynamics* (Autumn 1980); Edgar H. Schein, "The Role of the Founder in Creating Organizational Culture," *Organizational Dynamics* (Summer 1983); Vijay Sathe, "Some Action Implications of Corporate Culture: A Manager's Guide to Action," *Organizational Dynamics* (Autumn 1983).

See also POLITICAL CULTURE.

Organizational Dynamics, quarterly publication of the American Management Associations that is a review of organizational behavior for professional managers.

Organizational Dynamics
Editorial Address:
American Management Associations
135 West 50th Street
New York, NY 10020
Subscriptions:
Box 319
Saranac Lake, NY 12983

organizational humanism, movement to create more humane work environments.

organizational iceberg, concept that the

formal or overt aspects of an organization are just the proverbial tip of the iceberg. The greater part of the organization—the feelings, attitudes, and values of its members, for example—remain covert or hidden from obvious view. In short, the formal organization is visible, while the informal is hidden and waiting to sink any ship that ignores it.

organizational identification, according to Douglas T. Hall, Benjamin Schneider, and Harold T. Nygren, in "Personal Factors in Organizational Identification," *Administrative Science Quarterly* (July 1970), "the process by which the goals of the organization and those of the individual become increasingly integrated or congruent."

organizational mirror, according to Jack K. Fordyce and Raymond Weil, in *Managing with People* (Reading, Mass.: Addison-Wesley, 1971),
a particular kind of meeting that allows an organizational unit to collect feedback from a number of key organizations to which it relates (e.g., customers, suppliers, users of services within the larger organization). The meeting closes with a list of specific tasks for improvement of operations, products, or services.

organizational picketing, picketing an employer in order to encourage union membership. The Landrum-Griffin Act severely limited such picketing.

organizational politics, the use of influence and power to influence the allocation of organization resources, typically through the informal organization. B.T. Mayes and R. W. Allen limit the definition to those actions in which the desired ends may not be sanctioned by the organization or, if the ends are sanctioned, the influence means may not be sanctioned. *See* their "Toward a Definition of Organizational Politics," *The Academy of Management Review* (October 1977).
Also see REALPOLITIK.

organizational pyramids, *see* PYRAMIDS.

organizational socialization, the implicit and/or explicit processes used by formal and informal organizations to prepare (or shape) members to conform (preferably voluntarily) to the organization or sub-organization's values and desired patterns of behavior. Organizational socialization processes are activated whenever a member crosses organizational boundaries, vertically or horizontally. *See* E. H. Schein, "Organizational Socialization and the Profession of Management," *Sloan Management Review* (Winter 1968); J. Van Mannen, "People Processing: Strategies of Organizational Socialization," *Organizational Dynamics* (Summer 1978).

Organizational Behavior & Human Performance, journal published bimonthly (beginning each year in February). This journal of fundamental research and theory in applied psychology seeks papers describing original empirical research and theoretical developments in all areas of human performance theory and organizational psychology. Preference is given to those articles contributing to the development of theories relevant to human performance or organizational behavior.
Organizational Behavior &
Human Performance
Academic Press, Inc.
111 Fifth Avenue
New York, NY 10003

organization chart, graphic description of the structure of an organization, usually in the form of a diagram.

organization design, formal structure of the organization. Organization design is a relatively new term that implies that the structure is a consciously manipulatable variable. The term emerges from a resurgence of concern about the question, "What is the most appropriate structure in a given situation?" *See* J. Galbraith, *Organization Design* (Reading, Mass.: Addison-Wesley, 1977); Henry Mintzberg, "Organization Design: Fashion or Fit?" *Harvard Business Review* (January-February 1981).

organization development (OD), activity premised upon the notion that any organization wishing to survive must periodically divest itself of those parts or characteristics that contribute to its malaise. OD is a process for increasing an organization's effectiveness; as a process it has no value bias, yet it is usually associated with the idea that maximum effectiveness is to be found by integrating an individual's desire for personal growth with organizational goals. Wendell L. French and Cecil H. Bell, Jr., in *Organization Development: Behavioral Science Interventions for Organization Improvement* (Englewood Cliffs, N.J.: Prentice-Hall, 1973), provide a formal definition:

> organization development is a long-range effort to improve an organization's problem-solving and renewal processes, particularly through a more effective and collaborative management of organization culture—with special emphasis on the culture of formal work teams—with the assistance of a change agent, or catalyst, and the use of the theory and technology of applied behavioral science, including action research.

Other major texts include: Warren Bennis, *Organization Development: Its Nature, Origin, and Prospects* (Reading, Mass.: Addison-Wesley, 1969); Chris Argyris, *Management and Organizational Development: The Path From XA to YB* (New York: McGraw-Hill, 1971); Edgar F. Huse, *Organization Development and Change* (St. Paul, Minn.: West Publishing, 1975); Stanley P. Powers, F. Gerald Brown, and David S. Arnold, *Developing the Municipal Organization* (Washington, D.C.: International City Management Association, 1974). *Also see* Robert T. Golembiewski and William B. Eddy, eds., *Organization Development in Public Administration* (New York: Marcel Dekker, 1978); Wendell L. French, Cecil H. Bell, Jr., and Robert A. Zawacki, eds., *Organization Development: Theory, Practice, and Research* (Dallas, Texas: Business Publications, Inc., 1978); Glen H. Varney, *Organization Development for Managers* (Reading, Mass.: Addison-Wesley, 1977); Warner Woodworth and Reed Nelson, "Witch Doctors, Messianics, Sorcerers, and OD Consultants: Parallels and Paradigms," *Organizational Dynamics* (Autumn 1979); Dennis D. Umstot, "Organization Development Technology and the Military: A Surprising Merger?" *Academy of Management Review* (April 1980); W. Warner Burke, "Organization Development and Bureaucracies in the 1980s," *Journal of Applied Behavioral Science* (July–August–September 1980); Anthony T. Cobb and Newton Margulies, "Organization Development: A Political Perspective," *Academy of Management Review* (January 1981); David A. Nadler, "Managing Organization Change: An Integrative Perspective," *Journal of Applied Behavioral Science* (April–May–June 1981); Robert T. Golembiewski, Carl W. Proehl, Jr., and David Sink, "Success of OD Applications in the Public Sector: Toting Up the Score for a Decade, More or Less," *Public Administration Review* (November–December 1981); W. Warner Burke, *Organization Development: Principles and Practices* (Boston: Little, Brown and Co., 1982).

See also the following entries:
ACTION RESEARCH
ARGYRIS, CHRIS
BENNIS, WARREN
BLAKE, ROBERT R. AND JANE S. MOUTON
CONFRONTATION MEETING
NATIONAL TRAINING LABORATORIES INSTITUTE FOR APPLIED BEHAVIORAL SCIENCE
PROCESS CONSULTATION
SMALL-GROUP RESEARCH
TEAM BUILDING

organization man, generic term to describe any individual within an organization who accepts the values of the organization and finds harmony in conforming to its policies. The term was popularized by William H. Whyte, Jr., in his best selling book, *The Organization Man* (New York: Simon & Schuster, 1956). Whyte wrote that these individuals were "the ones of our middle class who have left home, spiritually as well as physically, to take the vows of organization life, and it is they who are the mind and soul of our great self-perpetuating institutions." For the organization man's replacement, see Robert Stephen Silverman and D. A. Heming, "Exit The Organization Man: Enter the Professional Person," *Personnel Journal* (March 1975); Edith L. Highman, *The Organization Woman: Building a Career—An Inside Report* (New York: Human Sciences Press, 1985).

organization ombudsman, see OMBUDSMAN.

organization theory, also CLASSICAL ORGANIZATION THEORY and NEOCLASSICAL ORGANIZATION THEORY, theory that seeks to explain how groups and individuals behave in varying organizational structures and circumstances.

Classical organization theory, as its name implies, was the first theory of its kind, is considered traditional, and will continue to be the base upon which subsequent theories are built. The development of any theory must be viewed in the context of its time. The beliefs of early management theorists about how organizations worked or should work was a direct reflection of the social values of their times. And the times were harsh. Individual workers were not viewed as individuals, but as the interchangeable machine parts made of flesh when it was impractical to make them of steel. Consequently, the first theories of organizations were concerned with the anatomy—the structure—of formal organizations. This is the hallmark of classical organization theory—a concern for organizational structure that is premised upon the assumed rational behavior of its human parts.

There is no firm definition as to just what "neoclassical" means in *neoclassical organization theory,* but the general connotation is that of a theoretical perspective that revises and/or is critical of traditional (classical) organization theory because it does not pay enough attention to the needs and interactions of organizational members. The watershed between classical and neoclassical organization theory is

World War II. The major writers of the classical school (Taylor, Fayol, Weber, Gulick, etc.) did their most significant work before World War II. The major neoclassical writers (Simon, March, Selznick, Parsons, etc.) gained their reputations as organization theorists by attacking the classical writers after the war.

For the historical evolution of organization theory, see William G. Scott, "Organization Theory: An Overview and an Appraisal," *Academy of Management Journal* (April 1961); Charles Perrow, "The Short and Glorious History of Organizational Theory," *Organizational Dynamics* (Summer 1973); Jay M. Shafritz and Philip H. Whitbeck, *Classics of Organization Theory* (Oak Park, Illinois: Moore Publishing Company, 1978); Hal G. Rainey, "Public Organization Theory: The Rising Challenge," *Public Administration Review* (March–April 1983); Jeffrey Pfeffer, *Organizations and Organization Theory* (Marshfield, Mass.: Pittman Publishing, 1984).

See also REALPOLITIK.

organized labor, collective term for members of labor unions. See Sanford Cohen, *Labor in the United States,* 5th ed. (Columbus, Ohio: Charles E. Merrill, 1979).

organizer, also called LABOR ORGANIZER and UNION ORGANIZER, individual employed by a union who acts to encourage employees of a particular plant or organization to join the union that the organizer represents. See Stephen I. Scholossberg and Judith A. Scott, *Organizing and the Law: A Handbook for Union Organizers,* 3rd ed. (Washington, D.C.: Bureau of National Affairs, Inc., 1983); James H. Hopkins and Robert D. Binderup, "Employee Relations and Union Organizing Campaigns," *The Personnel Administrator* (March 1980); William E. Fulmer, *Union Organizing: Management and Labor Conflict* (New York: Praeger Publishers, 1982); John J. Hoover, "Union Organization Attempts: Management's Response," *Personnel Journal* (March 1982); Kenneth Gagala, *Union*

Organizing and Staying Organized (Reston, Va.: Reston/Prentice-Hall, 1983); Paula B. Voos, "Does It Pay to Organize? Estimating the Cost to Unions," *Monthly Labor Review* (June 1984).

See also the following entries:
BETH ISRAEL HOSPITAL V. NATIONAL LABOR RELATIONS BOARD
NATIONAL LABOR RELATIONS BOARD V. BABCOCK AND WILCOX
PANDOL & SONS V. AGRICULTURAL LABOR RELATIONS BOARD

orientation, formal introduction and guided adjustment of new employees to their new job, new co-workers, and new working environment. See Murray Lubliner, "Employee Orientation," *Personnel Journal* (April 1978); Daniel N. Kanouse and Philomena Warihay, "A New Look at Employee Orientation," *Training and Development Journal* (July 1980); Mark S. Tauber, "New Employee Orientation: A Comprehensive Systems Approach," *Personnel Administrator* (January 1981); Edmund J. McGarrell, Jr., "An Orientation System that Builds Productivity," *Personnel Administrator* (October 1984); Ronald E. Smith, "Employee Orientation: 10 Steps to Success," *Personnel Journal* (December 1984).

orientation checklist, a listing in an orderly and logical sequence of all of the items about which a new employee should be informed or which he must do as part of the orientation process.

Oscar Mayer & Co.* v. *Evans, 441 U.S. 750 (1979), U.S. Supreme Court case which held an employee must exhaust state remedies for age discrimination before bringing federal action under the Age Discrimination in Employment Act.

OSHA, see OCCUPATIONAL SAFETY AND HEALTH ADMINISTRATION.

OSHRC, see OCCUPATIONAL SAFETY AND HEALTH REVIEW COMMISSION.

outlaw strike, see WILDCAT STRIKE.

outlays, checks issued, interest accrued on the public debt, or other payments, net of refunds and reimbursements. Total budget outlays consist of the sum of the outlays from appropriations and funds included in the unified budget, less offsetting receipts. Off-budget federal agencies are not included in the unified budget and, for purposes of the budget, they are treated as private entities. See U.S. General Accounting Office, *Federal Budget Outlay Estimates: A Growing Problem* (Washington, D.C.: Government Printing Office, February 1979); Rodney L. Clouser and David L. Debertin, "Regional Distributors of Federal Outlays in the U.S.," *State Government,* Vol. 56, No. 1 (1983).

out-of-title work, also called OUT-OF-CLASS EXPERIENCE, duties performed by an incumbent of a position that are not appropriate to the class to which the position has been assigned.

outplacement, according to John Scherba, in "Outplacement: An Established Personnel Function," *The Personnel Administrator* (July 1978),

the extension of services to a terminated employee to: 1) minimize the impact of termination, 2) reduce the time necessary to secure a new position, 3) improve the person's job search skills and 4) ultimately bring about the best possible match between the person and available jobs.

Also useful is J. D. Erdlen, "Guidelines for Retaining an Outplacement Consultant," *The Personnel Administrator* (January 1978); Dick Schaaf, "Training for Outplacement and Retirement," *Training* (May 1981); Dane Henriksen, "Outplacement: Guidelines That Ensure Success," *Personnel Journal* (August 1982); Lawrence M. Brammer and Frank E. Humberger, *Outplacement and Inplacement Counseling* (Englewood Cliffs, N.J.: Prentice-Hall, 1984).

See also DEHIRING.

output, end result of any process.

output curve, see WORK CURVE.

outreach, process of systematically extending resources and activities to identified populations at risk for the purpose of enhancing their level and quality of participation and their utilization of specified services.

outstationing, placement of direct service personnel of one organization into another organization's physical facility. However, the service personnel remain accountable to and are paid by their own organization.

overachievement, also UNDERACHIEVEMENT, psychological concepts that describe a discrepancy between predicted and actual achievement/performance. Individuals whose performance exceeds or goes below expectations are described as overachievers or underachievers. *See* Robert L. Thorndike, *The Concepts of Over and Underachievements* (New York: Columbia University Press, 1963).

overhead agency, *see* AUXILIARY AGENCY.

overrate, *see* FLAGGED RATE.

oversight, *see* LEGISLATIVE OVERSIGHT.

overtime, work performed in excess of the basic workday/workweek as defined by law, collective bargaining, or company policy. For an economic analysis, *see* Ronald G. Ehrenberg, *Fringe Benefits and Overtime Behavior: Theoretical and Econometric Analysis* (Lexington, Mass.: D.C. Heath, 1971); Ronald G. Ehrenberg and Paul L. Schumann, "Compliance With the Overtime Provisions of the Fair Labor Standards Act," *Journal of Law and Economics* (April 1982).

See also BAY RIDGE COMPANY V. AARON and LODGE 76, INTERNATIONAL ASSOCIATION OF MACHINISTS V. WISCONSIN EMPLOYMENT RELATIONS COMMISSION.

overtime computations, calculations of overtime pay. For employees covered by the Fair Labor Standards Act, overtime must be paid at a rate of at least 1½ times the employee's regular pay rate for each hour worked in a workweek in excess of the maximum allowable in a given type of employment. Generally, the regular rate includes all payments made by the employer to or on behalf of the employee (excluding certain statutory exceptions). The following examples are based on a maximum forty-hour workweek:

1. **Hourly rate** (regular pay rate for an employee paid by the hour). If more than forty hours are worked, at least 1½ times the regular rate for each hour over forty is due. *Example:* An employee paid $3.80 an hour works forty-four hours in a workweek. The employee is entitled to at least 1½ times $3.80, or $5.70, for each hour over forty. Pay for the week would be $152 for the first forty hours, plus $22.80 for the four hours of overtime—a total of $174.80.

2. **Piece rate.** The regular rate of pay for an employee paid on a piecework basis is obtained by dividing the total weekly earnings by the total number of hours worked in the same week. The employee is entitled to an additional ½ of this regular rate for each hour over forty, besides the full piecework earnings. *Example:* An employee paid on a piecework basis works forty-five hours in a week and earns $162. The regular pay rate for that week is $162 divided by 45, or $3.60 an hour. In addition to the straight time pay, the employee is entitled to $1.80 (half the regular rate) for each hour over forty. Another way to compensate pieceworkers for overtime, if agreed to before the work is performed, is to pay 1½ times the piece rate for each piece produced during overtime hours. The piece rate must be the one actually paid during non-overtime hours and must be enough to yield at least the minimum wage per hour.

3. **Salaries.** The regular rate for an employee paid a salary for a regular or specified number of hours a week

is obtained by dividing the salary by the number of hours. If, under the employment agreement, a salary sufficient to meet the minimum wage requirement in every work-week is paid as straight time for whatever number of hours are worked in a workweek, the regular rate is obtained by dividing the salary by the number of hours worked each week. To illustrate, suppose an employee's hours of work vary each week and the agreement with the employer is that the employee will be paid $200 a week for whatever number of hours of work are required. Under this pay agreement, the regular rate will vary in overtime weeks. If the employee works fifty hours, the regular rate is $4 ($200 divided by fifty hours). In addition to the salary, 1/2 the regular rate, or $2, is due for each of the ten overtime hours, for a total of $220 for the week. If the employee works fifty-four hours, the regular rate will be $3.70 ($200 divided by 54). In that case, an additional $1.85 is due for each of the fourteen overtime hours, for a total of $225.90 for the week.

In no case may the regular rate be less than the minimum wage required by the Act. If a salary is paid on other than a weekly basis, the weekly pay must be determined in order to compute the regular rate and overtime. If the salary is for a half month, it must be multiplied by twenty-four and the product divided by fifty-two weeks to get the weekly equivalent. A monthly salary should be multiplied by twelve and the product divided by fifty-two.

Owen, Robert (1771–1858), Welsh industrialist, social reformer and utopian socialist who was one of the first writers to consider the importance of the human factor in industry. His model factory communities, New Lanark in Scotland and New Harmony in Indiana, were among the first to take a modern approach to personnel management. For biographies, *see*

J. F. C. Harrison, *Quest for the New Moral World: Robert Owen and the Owenites in Britain and America* (New York: Scribner, 1969); Arthur L. Morton, *The Life and Ideas of Robert Owen* (New York: International Publishers, 1969); and Sidney Pollard, ed., *Robert Owen, Prophet of the Poor* (Lewisburg, Pa.: Bucknell University Press, 1971).

Owen v. City of Independence, 445 U.S. 622 (1980), Supreme Court case expanding an earlier ruling in *Monell* v. *New York City Department of Social Services* (1978) concerning individuals' suits against cities under 42 U.S. Code section 1983 for damages in connection with the violation of constitutional rights. The court held that a municipality cannot rely upon a "good faith" defense in such cases since "the knowledge that a municipality will be liable for all of its injurious conduct, whether committed in good faith or not, should create an incentive for officials who may harbor doubts about the lawfulness of their intended actions to err on the side of protecting citizen's constitutional rights."

See also MONELL V. NEW YORK CITY DEPARTMENT OF SOCIAL SERVICES.

P

PACE, *see* PROFESSIONAL AND ADMINISTRATIVE CAREERS EXAMINATION.

package settlement, term that describes the total money value (usually quoted as cents per hour) of an increase in wages and benefits achieved through collective bargaining. For example, a new contract might give employees an increase of 50¢ an hour. However, when the value of increased medical and pension benefits are included, the "package settlement" might come to 74¢ an hour. See John G. Kilgour, " 'Wrapping the Package' of Labor Agreement Costs," *Personnel Journal* (June 1977).

PAIR, acronym for "personnel and industrial relations"; or for "personnel administration/industrial relations."

Panama Refining Co.* v. *Ryan, 293 U.S. 388 (1935), U.S. Supreme Court case invalidating a statute allowing the president to exclude from interstate commerce oil produced in excess of state regulations. The court held that the statute was an unconstitutional breach of the separation of powers.

Pandol & Sons* v. *Agricultural Labor Relations Board, 429 U.S. 802 (1976), U.S. Supreme Court case which upheld state regulations permitting union organizers access to private property for the purpose of organizing California's farm workers.

PAQ, see POSITION ANALYSIS QUESTIONNAIRE.

PAR, see PUBLIC ADMINISTRATION REVIEW.

paradigm, model that refers to a conception of a situation or condition. *See* Emanuel Wald, "Toward a Paradigm of Future Public Administration," *Public Administration Review* (July-August 1973); Nicholas Henry, "Paradigms of Public Administration," *Public Administration Review* (July-August 1975); Richard J. Stillman II, "Professor Ostrom's New Paradigm for American Public Administration: Adequate or Antique?" *Midwest Review of Public Administration* (December 1976); Alan Sheldon, "Organization Paradigms: A Theory of Organizational Change," *Organizational Dynamics* (Winter 1980); Phillip Ein-Dor and Eli Seger, *A Paradigm for Management Information Systems* (New York: Praeger, 1981).

paradox of thrift, paradox that holds that while individual increases in savings may be good for the individual, the totality of such increases can lead to an overall reduction in income and employment if not offset by an increase in investment.

paradox of value, the fact that so many of the absolute necessities of life (such as water) are cheap or relatively inexpensive compared to the price of luxury items (such as diamonds); in effect, great utility does not necessarily yield economic value and economic value does not mean that an item is useful.

paralegal, see PARAPROFESSIONAL.

parallel forms, two or more forms of a test that are assembled as closely as possible to the same statistical and content specifications so that they will provide the same kind of measurement at different administrations.

parallel ladder, see DUAL LADDER.

paramedic, see PARAPROFESSIONAL.

paraprofessional, any individual with less than standard professional credentials who assists a fully credentialed professional with the more routine aspects of his/her professional work. For example, paralegals assist lawyers and paramedics assist medical doctors. *See* Robert Cohen, *"New Careers" Grows Older: A Perspective on the Paraprofessional Experience, 1965-1975* (Baltimore: Johns Hopkins Press, 1976); Charlotte Mugnier, *The Paraprofessional and the Professional Job Structure* (Chicago: American Library Association, 1980); Greg H. Firth, *The Role of the Special Education Paraprofessional* (Springfield, Ill.: Charles C. Thomas, 1982).

Pareto, Vilfredo (1848-1923), Italian sociologist and economist who is considered the "father" of the idea of social systems. The *Pareto optimality* is an equilibrium point reached in a society when resource allocation is most efficient; that is, no further changes in resource allocation can be made that will increase the welfare of one person without decreasing the welfare of other persons. *Pareto's law* holds that the pattern of income tends to become distributed in the same proportion in every country no matter what political or taxation conditions exist. Thus, the only way to increase the income of the poor is to increase overall production. Another of Pareto's laws is the *law of the trivial many and the critical few* (also called the *80-20 rule*), which holds that 80 percent of the traffic in a group of items is accounted for by only 20 percent of the items themselves. *See* Warren J. Samuels, *Pareto on Policy* (New York: Elsevier Scientific, 1974); Renato Cirillo, *The Economics of Vilfredo Pareto* (Totowa, N.J.: Cass, 1979).

parish, *see* COUNTY.

parity, also EMPLOYMENT PARITY, OCCUPATIONAL PARITY, and WAGE PARITY, long term goal of all affirmative action efforts, which will be achieved after all categories of an organization's employees are proportionately representative of the population in the organization's geographic region. *Employment parity* exists when the proportion of protected groups in the external labor market is equivalent to their proportion in an organization's total work force without regard to job classifications. *Occupational parity* exists when the proportion of an organization's protected group employees in all job classifications is equivalent to their respective availability in the external labor market.

Wage parity requires that the salary level of one occupational classification be the same as for another. The most common example of wage parity is the linkage between the salaries of police and firefighters. Over two-thirds of all cities in the United States have parity policies for their police and firefighters. But according to David Lewin, in "Wage Parity and the Supply of Police and Firemen," *Industrial Relations* (February 1973),

> parity contributes to the problem of attracting and retaining qualified personnel in police ranks; it also inflates wages in the fire services beyond the level necessary to secure adequate staffing, thus imposing a heavy burden on local taxpayers. Furthermore, parity implies that police and fire occupations are similar in nonpay characteristics when,

in fact, policemen and firemen not only perform substantially different functions, but also have different promotional opportunities. Thus, from the perspective of the external labor market and from considerations of internal equity, wage parity is a deficient policy and should no longer guide the wage setting process for the protective services.

For legal analyses of the police/fire parity issue, *see* Hoyt N. Wheeler, Richard Berger, and Stephen McGarry, "Parity: An Evaluation of Recent Court and Board Decisions," *Labor Law Journal* (March 1978); Paul A. Lafranchise, Sr., and Michael T. Leibig, "Collective Bargaining for Parity in the Public Sector," *Labor Law Journal* (September 1981).

parity, farm, also PRICE SUPPORTS, the price designed to allow a farmer to maintain a purchasing power equal to a previous base period. In theory the parity price that the government is willing to pay gives a farmer a fair return on his investment when contrasted with his costs. Since the 1930s the federal government has been using price supports (accompanied with production controls) to stabilize the prices of agricultural commodities. In this context a price support is a guarantee to buy farm products at set prices. The Congress determines what parity support prices will be in general while parity prices for specific commodities are the responsibility of the U.S. Department of Agriculture.

Parkinson's Law, C. Northcote Parkinson's famous law that "work expands so as to fill the time available for its completion." It first appeared in his *Parkinson's Law and Other Studies in Administration* (Boston: Houghton Mifflin Co., 1957). With mathematical precision, he "discovered" that any public administrative department will invariably increase its staff an average of 5.75 percent per year. In anticipation of suggestions that he advise what might be done about this problem, he asserted that "it is not the business of the botanist to eradicate the weeds.

Enough for him if he can tell us just how fast they grow."

See also LAW OF TRIVIALITY.

Parsons, Talcott (1902-1979), preeminent sociologist whose theories of social action and structural-functionalism furthered the .development of organization theory. Major works include: *The Structure of Social Action* (New York: McGraw-Hill, 1937); *The Social System* (New York: The Free Press, 1951); *Structure and Process in Modern Societies* (New York: The Free Press, 1960); *Social Structure and Personality* (New York: The Free Press, 1964); *Politics and Social Structure* (New York: The Free Press, 1969); *Social Systems and the Evolution of Action Theory* (New York: The Free Press, 1977).

participative management, *see* INDUSTRIAL DEMOCRACY.

part-time workers, *see* FULL-TIME WORKERS.

passing point, *see* CUTTING SCORE.

passing score, *see* CUTTING SCORE.

passing the buck, *see* BUCKOLOGY.

passionate leave, *see* COMPASSIONATE LEAVE.

pass rate, proportion of candidates who pass an examination.

pass-through, process by which a state government receives federal grants and passes the money through to substate jurisdictions. Such action may be mandated by the grant statute or result from a state decision.

past practice, manner in which a similar issue was resolved before the occasion of a present grievance.

past year, fiscal year immediately preceding the current year; the last completed fiscal year.

PATCO, *See* AIR TRAFFIC CONTROLLERS' STRIKE.

paternalism, also called INDUSTRIAL PATERNALISM and EMPLOYER PATERNALISM, in the United States, a derogatory reference to an organization's "fatherly" efforts to better the lot of its employees. Historically, the U.S. labor movement has considered paternalistic efforts to be a false and demeaning charity which inhibited the growth of union membership. In other societies where there are well established paternalistic traditions, the derogatory connotations of the word may be absent. Japan is undoubtedly the most paternalistic of all the major industrial societies. For a history and analysis of the concept, *see* John W. Bennett, "Paternalism," David L. Sills, ed., *International Encyclopedia of the Social Sciences* (New York: Macmillan Co. & The Free Press, 1968). *Also see* John Kleinig, *Paternalism* (Totowa, N.J.: Rowman & Allanheld, 1983).

paternity leave, *see* BIRTH LEAVE.

path-goal theory of leadership, a leadership style that has the leader indicate to his or her followers the "path" by which to accomplish their individual and organizational goals, then help to make that "path" as easy to follow as possible. According to Robert J. House, in "A Path-Goal Theory of Leader Effectiveness," *Administrative Science Quarterly* (September 1971),

The motivational function of the leader consists of increasing personal pay-offs to subordinates for work-goal attainment, and making the path to these pay-offs easier to travel by clarifying it, reducing roadblocks and pitfalls, and increasing the opportunities for personal satisfaction in route.

Also see Robert J. House and T. R. Mitchell, "Path-Goal Theory of Leadership," *Journal of Contemporary Business* (Autumn 1974); Charles N. Greene, "Questions of Causation in the Path-Goal Theory of Leadership," *Academy of Management Journal* (March 1979).

patronage, the power of elected officials

to make partisan appointments to office or to confer contracts, honors, or other benefits on their political supporters. For the most comprehensive survey of U.S. patronage practices, *see* Martin and Susan Tolchin, *To the Victor: Political Patronage from the Clubhouse to the White House* (New York: Random House, 1971). *Also see* Frank Sorauf, "The Silent Revolution in Patronage," *Public Administration Review* (Winter 1960); James Q. Wilson, "The Economy of Patronage," *Journal of Political Economy* (August 1961); Kenneth J. Meier, "Ode to Patronage: A Critical Analysis of Two Recent Supreme Court Decisions," *Public Administration Review* (September–October 1981); William M. Timmins, "Relations Between Political Appointees and Careerists," *Review of Public Personnel Administration* (Spring 1984).

See also the following entries:
APPOINTMENT CLAUSE
BRANTI V. FINKEL
CIVIL SERVICE REFORM
ELROD V. BURNS
MALEK MANUAL
MYERS V. UNITED STATES
NO-SHOW JOBS
PLUM BOOK
PUBLIC PERSONNEL POLITICS
SINECURE

patronage jokes, humorous references to the patronage system. The definitive statement on the disillusioning aspects of political patronage is credited to President William Howard Taft, who was moved to conclude that whenever he made a patronage appointment, he created "nine enemies and one ingrate." Actually, this quip is generally attributed to all sophisticated dispensers of patronage from Thomas Jefferson to Louis XIV. U.S. presidents have produced only two memorable patronage jokes (other than many of the appointees themselves). In addition to President Taft's remark, there is the story that Abraham Lincoln, while lying prostrate in the White House with an attack of smallpox, said to his attendants: "Tell all the office-seekers to come in at once, for now I have something I can give to all of them."

pattern bargaining, collective bargaining in which key contract terms agreed to by one bargaining unit are copied by other companies in the same industry during subsequent negotiations. *See* Audrey Freedman and William E. Fulmer, "Last Rites for Pattern Bargaining," *Harvard Business Review* (March–April 1982).

See also UNITED MINE WORKERS V. PENNINGTON.

patterned interview, also UNPATTERNED INTERVIEW, interview that seeks to ask the same questions of all applicants. An *unpatterned interview* does not seek such uniformity. *See* Barbara Felton and Sue Ries Lamb, "A Model for Systematic Selection Interviewing," *Personnel* (January–February 1982).

pay, *see* the following entries:
BASIC RATE OF PAY
CALL-BACK PAY
CALL-IN PAY
COMPARABLE WORTH
COMPENSATION
DOWN-TIME PAY
EQUAL PAY FOR EQUAL WORK
HAZARD PAY
HOLIDAY PAY
INCENTIVE PAY
JOURNEYMAN PAY
JURY-DUTY PAY
LONGEVITY PAY
MAKE-UP PAY
RETROACTIVE PAY
SEVERANCE PAY
STRIKE PAY
TAKE-HOME PAY
VACATION PAY
WELL PAY
WORK PREMIUM

pay-as-you-go plan, pension plan that has employers paying pension benefits to retired employees out of current income.

Pay Board, fifteen-member tripartite board consisting of business, labor, and public representatives whose function was to set and administer wage and salary policies. The Pay Board, authorized by the Economic Stabilization Act of 1970 and established by Executive Order 11627 on October 28, 1971, officially functioned under the Economic Stabilization Program of the Executive Office of the President. It was abolished by Executive Order 11695 on January 11, 1973.

pay compression, a situation where the salaries of all classes of employees are forced so close together that there cease to be meaningful differences in the various pay grades. See James W. Steele, *Paying for Performance and Position: Dilemmas in Salary Compression and Merit Pay* (New York: American Management Associations, 1982); Thomas J. Bergmann, Frederick S. Hills and Laurel Priefert, "Pay Compression: Causes, Results, and Possible Solutions," *Compensation Review* (Second Quarter 1983).

pay criteria, see WAGE CRITERIA.

pay for performance, concept of paying an employee on the basis of job performance—all bonuses, raises, promotions, etc., would be directly related to the measurable results of the employee's efforts. See Thomas H. Patten, Jr., "Pay for Performance or Placation?" *The Personnel Administrator* (September 1977); Paula Cowan, "How Blue Cross Put Pay-for-Performance to Work," *Personnel Journal* (May 1978); James W. Steele, *Paying for Performance and Position: Dilemmas in Salary Compression and Merit Pay* (New York: American Management Associations, 1982); Robert H. Rock, "Pay for Performance: Measures and Standards," *Compensation Review* (Third Quarter 1984); Karen N. Gaertner, "Performance-Contingent Pay for Federal Managers," *Administration and Society* (May 1985).

pay increase, any permanent raise in an employee's basic salary or wage level. See Linda A. Krefting and Thomas A. Mahoney, "Determining the Size of a Meaningful Pay Increase," *Industrial Relations* (February 1977); Poondi Varadarajan and Charles Futrell, "Factors Affecting Perceptions of Smallest Meaningful Pay Increases," *Industrial Relations* (Spring 1984).

paying your dues, the experiences that one must have before being ready for advancement. In effect, "you have to pay your dues" before you can be perceived as a legitimate occupant of a higher position.

pay level, see PAY GRADE.

payments in kind, noncash payments for services rendered.

pay plan, a listing of rates of pay for each job category in an organization. A *pay range,* also known as *salary* or *wage range,* indicates the minimum through maximum rates of pay for a job. The various increments that make up the pay range are known as the *pay steps.* The *pay grade* or *pay level* is the range of pay or a standard rate of pay for a specific job. The totality of the pay grades make up the *pay structure.*
While a position classification plan essentially arranges positions in classes on the basis of their similarities, a pay plan establishes rates of pay for each class of positions. Consequently, if a position is improperly classified, the corresponding salary cannot be in accord with the principle of "equal pay for equal work." See Donald E. Hoag and Robert J. Trudel, *How to Prepare a Sound Pay Plan* (Chicago: International Personnel Management Association, 1976); G. Douglass Jenkins, Jr. and Edward E. Lawler III, "Impact of Employee Participation Pay Plan Development," *Organizational Behavior and Human Performance* (August 1981).

payroll, listing of all the wages and/or salaries earned by employees within an organization for a specific time period (usually weekly, bi-monthly, or monthly).

payroll taxes, *see* EMPLOYMENT TAXES.

pay satisfaction, according to Edward E. Lawler III, in *Pay and Organizational Effectiveness: A Psychological View* (New York: McGraw-Hill, 1971), pay satisfaction "is basically determined by the difference between pay and the person's belief about what his pay should be." If employees find themselves assuming substantially similar duties and responsibilities as co-workers who, because of seniority or education, have higher paying classifications, they are going to be dissatisfied with their pay. It is very difficult to convince employees that their pay is determined fairly if they have before them on a daily basis other more highly paid employees who serve not as role models that one should strive to emulate, but rather as glaring examples of the inequities of the pay program.

pay step, each of the various increments that make up a pay range.

pay survey, *see* WAGE SURVEY.

pay system, dual, *see* DUAL PAY SYSTEM.

pay system, Foreign Service, *see* FOREIGN SERVICE PAY SYSTEM.

PBGC, *see* PENSION BENEFIT GUARANTY CORPORATION.

P-C, *see* PROGRESS CONSULTATION.

Peace Corps, group established by the Peace Corps Act of 1961. Made an independent agency by Title VI of the International Security and Development Cooperation Act of 1981, the Peace Corps consists of a Washington, D.C., headquarters; three recruitment service centers, supporting fifteen area offices; and overseas operations in more than sixty-two countries. The Peace Corps' purpose is to promote world peace and friendship and to help the peoples of other countries in meeting their needs for trained manpower.

To fulfill the Peace Corps mandate, men and women of all ages and walks of life are trained for a nine- to fourteen-week period in the appropriate local language, the technical skills necessary for their particular job, and the cross-cultural skills needed to adjust to a society with traditions and attitudes different from their own. Volunteers serve for a period of two years, living among the people with whom they work.

Peace Corps
806 Connecticut Avenue, N.W.
Washington D.C. 20526
(202) 254-5010

peaked out, negative way of referring to an employee who has reached the maximum step in his salary range or has already made his or her maximum contributions to the organization.

peak-period pricing, user pricing that charges higher rates during higher periods of demand for a service (*e.g.,* a utility), and lower rates during lower periods of demand.

pecking order, relative order of power. Ever since social psychologists discovered that chickens have a pecking order—the strongest or most aggressive fowl get to eat, or to peck, first—the term has been used to describe the comparative ranks that humans hold in their social organizations. No aspect of our society is immune from the pecking order's fowl antics. According to Lyndon Johnson's former press secretary, Geroge E. Reedy, in *The Twilight of the Presidency* (Cleveland: World Publishing, 1970),

the inner life of the White House is essentially the life of the barnyard, as set forth so graphically in the study of the pecking order among chickens which every freshman sociology student must read. It is a question of who has the right to peck whom and who must submit to being pecked. There are only two important differences. The first is that the pecking order is determined by the individual strength and forcefulness of each chicken, whereas in the White House it depends upon the relationship to the barnyard keeper. The second is that no one outside the barnyard glorifies the chickens and expects them to order the affairs of mankind. They are destined for the frying pan and that is that.

peer rating, also called MUTUAL RATING, performance evaluation technique that calls for each employee to evaluate all of the other employees in his/her work unit. *See* Allen I. Kraut, "Prediction of Managerial Success by Peer and Training-Staff Ratings," *Journal of Applied Psychology* (February 1975); R.G. Downey, F.F. Medland, and L.G. Yates, "Evaluation of a Peer Rating System for Predicting Subsequent Promotion of Senior Military Officers," *Journal of Applied Psychology* (April 1976); Kevin G. Love, "Empirical Recommendations for the Use of Peer Rankings in the Evaluation of Police Officer Performance," *Public Personnel Management* (Spring 1983); David N. Ammons, "Peer Participation in Local Government Employee Appraisal," *Administration & Society* (August 1984); Fred C. Olson, "How Peer Review Works at Control Data," *Harvard Business Review* (November-December 1984).

PEG, *see* PERSONNEL EFFECTIVENESS GRID.

Pendleton Act of 1883, the "Act to Regulate and Improve the Civil Service of the United States" that introduced the merit concept into federal employment and created the U.S. Civil Service Commission. While it was termed a commission, it was by no means independent. It was an executive agency that for all practical purposes was subject to the administrative discretion of the president. Its three bipartisan commissioners served at the pleasure of the president. The act gave legislative legitimacy to many of the procedures developed by the earlier unsuccessful Civil Service Commission during the Grant administration. Written into the act were requirements for open competitive examinations, probationary periods, and protection from political pressures. While the personnel program was to remain decentralized and in the control of

the departments, the Commission was authorized to supervise the conduct of examinations and make investigations to determine the degree of departmental enforcement of its rules. Of tremendous significance was the authority given to the president to extend merit system coverage to federal employees by executive order. However, the authority to extend also carries with it the authority to retract. Theoretically the president could reintroduce spoils into those large portions of the federal service not specifically protected by other legislation at any time he wishes. Both Presidents McKinley and Eisenhower had occasion to remove positions from merit coverage by executive order. In both cases this resulted when a new party assumed power only to find that, in their opinion, a disproportionate number of positions had been "blanketed in" by the previous administration.

The Pendleton Act was hardly a total victory for the reformers. It only covered just over 10 percent of the federal service. Actually, the reformers were not at all anxious for near-universal merit system coverage. They recognized the problems of creating the appropriate administrative machinery and were concerned that the reform program would be overburdened and subject to failure if complete reform were attempted all at once. With the ensuing years federal employees would be more and more brought under the jurisdiction of the Civil Service Commission or of other federal merit systems, such as those of the Foreign Service and the Tennessee Valley Authority. *See* David H. Rosenbloom, ed., *Centenary Issues of the Pendleton Act of 1883: The Problematic Legacy of Civil Service Reform* (New York: Marcel Dekker, 1982); Paul P. Van Riper, "The Pendleton Act—A Centennial Eulogy," *American Review of Public Administration* (Spring 1983).

See also the following entries:
CIVIL SERVICE REFORM ACT OF 1978
GRANT'S CIVIL SERVICE COMMISSION
NATIONAL CIVIL SERVICE LEAGUE

penetration rate, also PENETRATION RATIO, in the context of equal employment opportunity, the proportion of a work force belonging to a particular minority group. The *penetration ratio* is the ratio of an organization's penetration rate to the penetration rate for its geographic region (usually the standard metropolitan statistical area or SMSA). The rate and ratio are derived as follows:

$$\text{Penetration Rate} = \frac{\text{Total Minority Employment}}{\text{Total Employment}}$$

$$\text{Penetration Ratio} = \frac{\text{Penetration Rate for an Organization}}{\text{Penetration Rate for the SMSA}}$$

See also REPRESENTATIVE BUREAUCRACY.

Pennhurst State School v. Halderman, 67 L.Ed. 2d 694 (1981), U.S. Supreme Court Case which held that federal law did not give the mentally retarded substantive rights to "appropriate treatment" in the "least restrictive" environment.

pension, periodic payments to an individual who retires from employment (or simply from a particular organization) because of age, disability, or the completion of a specific period of service. Such payments usually continue for the rest of the recipient's life and sometimes extend to legal survivors.

While pensions have a long history as royal beneficences, the populace did not always view such royal largess as justified. Samuel Johnson, in his 1755 *English Dictionary*, defined pension by stating, "in England it is generally understood to mean pay given to a state hireling for treason to his country." While early industrial pension plans were informal and based upon oral agreements, the first formal pension plan in the United States was the 1875 program of the American Express Company. In the public sector, the first civilian pension plans appeared just before World War I for some of the larger municipal police and fire departments. Federal civilian employees had to wait for the Retirement Act of 1920 before they were eligible for any retirement benefits.

Pension plans generally have either defined benefits or defined contributions.

In *defined benefit plans* the amount of the benefit is fixed, but not the amount of contribution. These plans usually gear benefits to years of service and earnings or a stated dollar amount. About 60 percent of all pension plan participants are covered by defined benefit plans. In *defined contribution plans,* the amount of contributions is fixed, but the amount of benefit is not. These plans usually involve profit sharing, stock bonus, or money purchase arrangements where the employer contributes an agreed percentage of profits or wages to the worker's individual account. The eventual benefit is determined by the amount of total contributions and investment earnings in the years during which the employee is covered.

For a history and analysis of pension programs, see William C. Greenough and Francis P. King, *Pension Plans and Public Policy* (New York: Columbia University Press, 1976). See also William D. Hall and David L. Landsittel, *A New Look at Accounting for Pension Costs* (Homewood, Ill.: Richard D. Irwin, 1977); Everett T. Allen, Jr., Joseph J. Melone, and Jerry S. Rosenbloom, *Pension Planning*, 3rd ed. (Homewood, Ill.: Richard D. Irwin, 1976); Abigail R. Bacon, "A Note on Selecting the Appropriate Pension Funding Method for Localities," *Public Administration Review* (May–June 1980); Wesley S. Mellow, "Health and Pension Coverage by Worker Characteristics," *Monthly Labor Review* (May 1982); Robert J. Lynn, *The Pension Crisis* (Lexington, Mass.: Lexington Books, 1983); Robert W. Hartman, *Pay and Pensions for Federal Workers* (Washington, D.C.: The Brookings Institution, 1983); Werner Paul Zorn, "Public Pension Policy: A Survey of Current Practices," *Governmental Finance* (September 1983); Robert M. Fogelson, *Pensions: The Hidden Costs of Public Safety* (New York: Cambridge University Press, 1984).

See also the following entries:
ARIZONA V. NORRIS
CITY OF LOS ANGELES, DEPARTMENT OF
    WATER & POWER V. MANHART
PORTABILITY
VARIABLE ANNUITY
VESTING

Pension Benefit Guaranty Corporation (PBGC), federal agency that guarantees basic pension benefits in covered private plans if they terminate with insufficient assets. Title IV of the Employee Retirement Income Security Act of 1974 (ERISA) established the corporation to guarantee payment of insured benefits if covered plans terminate without sufficient assets to pay such benefits. The PBGC, a self-financing, wholly-owned government corporation is governed by a Board of Directors consisting of the Secretaries of Labor, Commerce and the Treasury. The Secretary of Labor is chairman of the board and is responsible for administering the PBGC in accordance with policies established by the board. A seven-member Advisory Committee, composed of two labor, two business, and three public members appointed by the president, advises the PBGC on various matters.

Title IV of ERISA provides for mandatory coverage of most private defined benefit plans. These are those plans that provide a benefit, the amount of which can be determined from a formula in the plan; for example, based on factors such as age, years of service, average or highest salary, etc. *See* David M. Walker, "The PBGC's Role in Protecting Lump-Sum Benefit Values," *Labor Law Journal* (November 1984).

Pension Benefit Guaranty Corporation
2020 K Street, N.W.
Washington, D.C. 20006
(202) 254-4817

pension fund socialism, Peter F. Drucker's term for the phenomenon that is turning traditional thinking about the "inherent" and historical separation of capital and labor upside down—namely, that the "workers" of the United States are rapidly and literally becoming the owners of the nation's industry through their pension fund investments in diverse common stocks. According to Drucker, by 1985 pension funds "will own at least 50—if not 60—percent of equity capital." For Drucker's complete analysis, *see* his *The Unseen Revolution: How Pension Fund*

Socialism Came to America (New York: Harper & Row, 1976).

pension plan, contributory, *see* CONTRIBUTORY PENSION PLAN.

pension plan, fully funded, *see* FULLY FUNDED PENSION PLAN.

pension plan, funded, *see* FUNDED PENSION PLAN.

Pension Reform Act of 1974, *see* EMPLOYEE RETIREMENT INCOME SECURITY ACT OF 1974.

pension trust, individual-contract, *see* INDIVIDUAL-CONTRACT PENSION TRUST.

peonage, forced labor. The 13th Amendment prohibits such involuntary servitude.

per capita, Latin phrase meaning "by heads." In a per capita election each member would have one vote.

per capita income, the mean income computed for every man, woman, and child in a particular group. It is derived by dividing the total income of a particular group by the total population (including patients or inmates in institutional quarters) in that group.

per capita tax, tax on each head and the regular payment made on the basis of membership by a local union to its national organization.

percentile, that point or score in a distribution below which falls the percent of cases indicated by the given percentile. Thus the 15th percentile denotes the score or point below which 15 percent of the scores fall.

percentile band, interval between percentiles, corresponding to score limits one standard error of measurement above and below an obtained score. The chances are approximately two out of three that the true score of an examinee with a particular obtained score is within these score limits.

397

percentile rank, percent of scores in a distribution equal to or lower than a particular obtained score.

per diem, Latin for "by the day." Temporary employees may be paid a "per-diem" rate or a travel expense program may reimburse employees using a flat "per-diem" amount.

performance, demonstration of a skill or competence.

performance appraisal, also called PERFORMANCE EVALUATION and PERFORMANCE REPORTING, title usually given to the formal method by which an organization documents the work performance of its employees. Performance appraisals are designed to serve a variety of functions, such as:
1. changing or modifying dysfunctional work behavior;
2. communicating to employees managerial perceptions of the quality and quantity of their work;
3. assessing future potential of an employee in order to recommend appropriate training or developmental assignments;
4. assessing whether the present duties of an employee's position have an appropriate compensation level; and
5. providing a documental record for disciplinary and separation actions.

For a classic analysis of the problems of performance appraisal, *see* Douglas McGregor, "An Uneasy Look at Performance Appraisal," *Harvard Business Review* (May-June 1957; reprinted May-June 1975). For legal analyses, *see* William H. Holley and Hubert S. Feild, "Performance Appraisal and the Law," *Labor Law Journal* (July 1975); Dena B. Schneier, "The Impact of EEO Legislation on Performance Appraisals," *Personnel* (July-August 1978); Gary L. Lubben *et al.,* "Performance Appraisal: The Legal Implications of Title VII," *Personnel* (May-June 1980); Patricia Linenberger and Timothy J. Keaveny, "Performance Appraisal Standards Used by the Courts," *Personnel Administrator* (May 1981); William Holley and Hubert S. Field, "Will Your Performance Appraisal System Hold Up in Court?" *Personnel* (January-February, 1982); David H. Rosenbloom, "Public Sector Performance Appraisal in the Contemporary Legal Environment," *Public Personnel Management* (Winter 1982). For overviews, *see* Alan H. Locher and Kenneth S. Teel, "Performance Appraisal—A Survey of Current Practices," *Personnel Journal* (May 1977); Albert C. Hyde and Wayne F. Cascio, eds., "Special Issue: Performance Appraisal," *Public Personnel Management* (Winter 1982); Richard I. Henderson, *Performance Appraisal,* 2nd ed. (Reston, Va.: Reston/Prentice-Hall, 1983). *Also see* Peter Allan and Stephen Rosenberg, "Getting a Managerial Performance Appraisal System Under Way: New York City's Experience," *Public Administration Review* (July-August 1980); Ann M. Morrison and Mary Ellen Kranz, "The Shape of Performance Appraisal in the Coming Decade," *Personnel* (July-August 1981); Fred C. Thayer, "Civil Service Reform and Performance Appraisal: A Policy Disaster," *Public Personnel Management,* Vol. 10, No. 1 (1981); Stephen J. Carrol and Craig E. Schneier, *Performance Appraisal and Review Systems: The Identification, Measurement, and Development of Performance in Organizations* (Glenview, IL.:

The Ultimate Performance Appraisal Scale

Check One
1. Individual is inept *within* tolerable organizational standards. ___
2. Individual is inept *beyond* tolerable organizational standards. ___
3. Individual is *hopelessly* inept. ___
4. Individual is a *classic case* of *dysfunctional ineptness.* ___
5. Individual is so *totally* and *completely inept* that even the *ineptitude* is marred by *ineptness.* ___

Scott, Foresman and Co., 1982); Robert L. Taylor and Robert A. Zawacki, "Trends in Performance Appraisal: Guideline for Managers," *Personnel Administrator* (March 1984); Robert G. Pajer, "Performance Appraisal: A New Era for Federal Government Managers," *Personnel Administrator* (March 1984); Edward E. Lawler III, Allan M. Mohrman, Jr., and Susan M. Resnick, "Performance Appraisal Revisited," *Organizational Dynamics* (Summer 1984).

See also the following entries:
BEHAVIORALLY ANCHORED RATING SCALES
EFFICIENCY RATING
SCHLESINGER V. BALLARD
SELF-APPRAISAL

performance budgeting, see BUDGETING, PERFORMANCE.

performance evaluation, see PERFORMANCE APPRAISAL.

performance incentive, see INCENTIVE.

performance objective, also called CRITERION OBJECTIVE, statement specifying exactly what behavior is to be exhibited, the conditions under which behavior will be accomplished, and the minimum standard of acceptable performance. See Roger B. Parks, "Linking Objective and Subjective Measures of Performance," *Public Administration Review* (March–April 1984).

performance reporting, see PERFORMANCE APPRAISAL.

performance standards, see STANDARDS OF PERFORMANCE.

performance test, examination that has candidates perform a sample of the actual work that would be found on the job. See Roscoe W. Wisner, "Constructon and Use of Performance Tests," J. J. Donovan, ed., *Recruitment and Selection in the Public Service* (Chicago: Public Personnel Association, 1968); Wayne F. Cascio and Neil F. Phillips, "Performance Testing: A

Rose Among Thorns?" *Personnel Psychology* (Winter 1979).

periodic increase, see WITHIN-GRADE INCREASE.

peripheral employees, according to Martin J. Gannon, "The Management of Peripheral Employees," *Personnel Journal* (September 1975), those that
are not totally committed to the organization and, in fact, view their work, not as a career, but as a job which can be easily discarded. Included in this segment of the labor force would be part-time employees, temporary employees, working students, moonlighters and women who decide to take a job only for a short period of time.
See also Dean Morse, *The Peripheral Worker* (New York: Columbia University Press, 1969).

Perkins, Frances (1882–1965), Secretary of Labor from 1933 to 1945 and the first woman to hold a cabinet post in the U.S. government. For a biography, see George Martin, *Madam Secretary: Frances Perkins* (Boston: Houghton Mifflin, 1976).

perks, see PERQUISITES.

permanent arbitrator, arbitrator who hears all disputes during the life of a contract or other stipulated term.

permanent injunction, see INJUNCTION.

perquisites, also called PERKS, the special benefits, frequently tax exempt, made available only to the top executives of an organization. There are two basic kinds of executive perquisites: (1) those with "take-home" value (such as company cars, club memberships, etc.) and (2) those that have no "take-home" value, but serve mainly to confer status (such as the proverbial executive washroom, office size and decor, etc.). Historically, the U.S. Internal Revenue Service has striven to restrict the tax exempt status of executives perquisites. According to Robert C. Coffin, in "Developing A Program of Executive Benefits and Perquisites," *The Personnel Administrator* (February 1977),

the possibilities of executive benefits are numerous. Some are clearly tax advantaged. Some are tax advantaged under certain circumstances—conceivably they could be tax advantaged for some executives and not for others. Some executive benefits, though valuable, have no tax advantage—their value is the same as the equivalent in direct pay. Remember, however, that the legal niceties are not always observed by small companies not heavily subject to public, stockholder, or IRS scrutiny, that certain perquisites are easily hidden even by large, exposed corporations and that in some cases (expense accounts, for example), the tax aspect is a private matter between the beneficiary of the perquisites and IRS.

Also see Michael F. Klein, "Executive Perquisites," *Compensation Review* (Fourth Quarter 1979); Bruce R. Ellig, "Perquisites: The Intrinsic Form of Pay," *Personnel* (January-February 1981); Karen M. Evans, "The Power of Perquisites," *Personnel Administrator* (May 1984).

Perry v. *Sinderman,* 408 U.S. 593 (1972), U.S. Supreme Court case which held that while a teacher's subjective "expectancy" of tenure is not protected by procedural due process, an allegation that a school had a *de facto* tenure policy entitles one to an opportunity of proving the legitimacy of a claim to job tenure. Such proof would obligate a school to hold a requested hearing when the teacher could both be informed of the grounds for non-retention and challenge the sufficiency of those grounds.

persona, term developed by Carl Jung that refers to the personality or façade that each individual shows to the world. The persona is distinguished from our inner being because it is adopted and put on like a mask to meet the demands of social life. Persona is the word for the masks that actors wore in ancient Greece.

personality inventory, also called SELF-REPORT INVENTORY, questionnaire concerned with personal characteristics and behavior that an individual answers about himself/herself. Then, the individual's self-report is compared to norms based upon the responses given to the same questionnaire by a large representative group.

personality test, test designed to measure any of the non-intellectual aspects of an individual's psychological disposition. It seeks information on a person's motivations and attitudes as opposed to his or her abilities.

personal property tax, *see* TAX, PERSONAL PROPERTY.

personal-rank system, *see* RANK-IN-MAN SYSTEM.

personal space, the area that individuals actively maintain around themselves, into which others cannot intrude without arousing discomfort. *See* Leslie Alec Hayduk, "Personal Space: An Evaluative and Orienting Overview," *Psychological Bulletin* (January 1978).

personal time, that time an employee uses to tend to personal needs. This time is usually separate from lunch and rest breaks and is sometimes written into union contracts.

personnel, collective term for all of the employees of an organization. The word is of military origin—the two basic components of a traditional army being materiel and personnel. Personnel is also commonly used to refer to the personnel management function or the organizational unit responsible for administering personnel programs. *See* Cyril Curtis Ling, *The Management of Personnel Relations: History and Origins* (Homewood, Ill.: Richard D. Irwin, 1965).

Personnel, bimonthly magazine of the American Management Associations which contains articles by scholars and practitioners on every phase of human resource management and personnel administration.

Personnel
Editorial Address:
American Management Associations
135 West 50th Street
New York, NY 10020
Subscriptions:
Subscription Services
Box 319
Saranac Lake, NY 12983

Personnel Accreditation Institute, a personnel accreditation program sponsored by the American Society for Personnel Administration which is designed to raise and maintain professional standards in the field. Through testing and peer reviews, the program identifies persons who have mastered the various functions and levels of personnel and industrial relations.

Personnel Accreditation Institute
606 N. Washington Street
Alexandria, VA 22314
(703) 684-8327

personnel action, process necessary to appoint, separate, reinstate, or make other changes affecting an employee (*e.g.,* change in position assignment, tenure, etc.).

personnel administration, also PERSONNEL MANAGEMENT, that aspect of management concerned with the recruitment, selection, development, utilization, and compensation of the members of an organization. While the terms *personnel administration* and *personnel management* tend to be used interchangeably, there is a distinction. The former is mainly concerned with the technical aspects of maintaining a full complement of employees within an organization, while the latter concerns itself as well with the larger problems of the viability of an organization's human resources. For analyses of how personnel administration has been evolving into personnel management, *see* Henry Eilbirt, "The Development of Personnel Management in the United States," *Business History Review* (Autumn 1959); Edward J. Giblin, "The Evolution of Personnel,"

Human Resource Management (Fall 1978); Lawrence A. Wangler, "The Intensification of the Personnel Role," *Personnel Journal* (February 1979).
See also STAFFING.

Personnel Administrator, official monthly publication of the American Society for Personnel Administration. Its major purpose is to further the professional aims of the ASPA and the human resources management profession. Articles cover all aspects of personnel management, human resources development, and industrial relations.

Personnel Administrator
American Society for Personnel
  Administration
606 N. Washington Street
Alexandria, VA 22314

Personnel Administrator of Massachusetts v. Feeney, 442 U.S. 256 (1979), U.S. Supreme Court case which held that a state law operating to the advantage of males by giving veterans lifetime preference for state employment was not in violation of the equal protection clause of the 14th Amendment. The court found that a veterans preference law's disproportionate impact on women did not prove intentional bias.
See also VETERANS PREFERENCE.

Personnel and Guidance Journal, The, *see* JOURNAL OF COUNSELING AND DEVELOPMENT.

personnel audit, evaluation of one or more aspects of the personnel function. *See* Eugene Schmuckler, "The Personnel Audit: Management's Forgotten Tool," *Personnel Journal* (November 1973); Paul Sheibar, "Personnel Practices Review: A Personnel Audit Activity," *Personnel Journal* (March 1974).

personnel director, manager responsible for all of an organization's personnel programs. In larger corporations, the personnel director is frequently a vice president for personnel. *See* Herbert E. Myers, "Personnel Directors Are the New Corporate Heroes," *Fortune* (February 1976).

personnel effectiveness grid, a device used to assess the effectiveness of an organization's human resources management system from three dimensions: (1) top management support, (2) lower management cooperation, and (3) the perceived quality of the personnelists and their programs. *See* D. J. Petersen and R. L. Malone, "The Personnel Effectiveness Grid (PEG): A New Tool for Estimating Personnel Department Effectiveness," *Human Resource Management* (Winter 1975).

personnel examiner, job title for an individual who is a professional staff member of that unit of a personnel department which is concerned with selection.

personnel function, service to line management. As with many questions in public administration, the issue of how the overall public personnel function should be organized has been plagued by an attempt to realize several incompatible values at once. Foremost among these values have been those of "merit" or neutral competence; executive leadership, political accountability, and managerial flexibility; and representativeness. The main problem of the structure and policy thrusts of central personnel agencies has been that maximizing some of these values requires arrangements ill suited for the achievement of others. Thus, achieving neutral competence requires the creation of a relatively independent agency to help insulate public employees from the partisan demands of political executives. Yet the same structural arrangement will tend to frustrate executive leadership and the ability of political executives to manage their agencies. To facilitate executive leadership, on the other hand, the central personnel agency should be an adjunct of the president, governor, or other chief executive. Similarly, maximizing the value of representativeness may require less emphasis on traditional merit concepts and examinations, and the placement of personnel functions having an im-

pact on equal employment opportunity in an equal employment or human rights agency. So doing, however, will also complicate the possibilities of achieving a high degree of executive leadership and neutral competence, as traditionally conceived. Matters are further confused by the rise of public-sector collective bargaining which emphasizes employee-employer codetermination of personnel policy and the creation of independent public-sector labor relations authorities.

The desire to maximize simultaneously these incompatible values accounts for many of the problematic aspects of the organization of the central personnel function. Arrangements satisfying some values inevitably raise complaints that others are being inadequately achieved. As the emphasis shifts from one value to another in conjunction with changing political coalitions and different perceptions of what is required in the public sector, structural changes also take place. Yet since the process of public personnel reform is somewhat cyclical, no set of arrangements will be immutable. *See* Fred K. Foulkes and Henry M. Morgan, "Organizing and Staffing the Personnel Function," *Harvard Business Review* (May–June 1977); *also see* Harold C. White and Michael N. Wolfe, "The Role Desired for Personnel Administration," *The Personnel Administrator* (June 1980); William H. Smits, Jr., "Personnel Administration—A Viable Function in Government?" *Public Personnel Management Journal* (Summer 1982); Roy Foltz, Karn Rosenberg and Julie Foehrenbach, "Senior Management Views the Human Resource Function," *Personnel Administrator* (September 1982); Gilbert B. Siegel, "The Personnel Function: Measuring Decentralization and Its Impact," *Public Personnel Management* (Summer 1983); Harish C. Jain and V. V. Murray, "Why the Human Resources Management Function Fails," *California Management Review* (Summer 1984).
   See also
      TRASHCAN HYPOTHESIS.
      CIVIL SERVICE REFORM
      PUBLIC PERSONNEL MANAGEMENT

personnel game, the way some personnel directors, personnel officers, personnel technicians, personnel examiners, and vice presidents for personnel refer to their occupation.

personnel generalist, personnelist who, instead of concentrating on one subspeciality, is minimally competent in a variety of personnel management subspecialities.

personnel inventory, a listing of all employees in an organization by job and personal characteristics which serves as a basic reference for planning and other purposes.

personnelist, also called PERSONNEL MANAGER, one who is professionally engaged in the practice of personnel management. *See* George Ritzer and Harrison M. Trice, *An Occupation in Conflict: A Study of the Personnel Manager* (Ithaca, N.Y.: New York State School of Industrial and Labor Relations, Cornell University, 1969); Tony J. Watson, *The Personnel Managers: A Study in the Sociology of Work and Employment* (London: Routledge and Kegan Paul, 1977).

personnel jacket, file folder containing all personnel data on, and personnel actions pertaining to, an employee.

Personnel Journal, monthly that publishes articles on all aspects of industrial relations, human relations, and personnel management.
Personnel Journal
A. C. Croft, Inc.
Box 2440
Costa Mesa, CA 92628

Personnel Literature, monthly bibliography compiled by the library of the U.S. Office of Personnel Management.
Personnel Literature
Superintendent of Documents
Government Printing Office
Washington, D.C. 20402

Personnel Management Abstracts

(PMA), quarterly that abstracts major articles in personnel management magazines, journals, and books that relate to the management of people and organizational behavior.
Personnel Management Abstracts
704 Island Lake Road
Chelsa, MI 48118

personnel management evaluation, formal effort to determine the effectiveness of any or all of an organization's personnel management program. *See* Michael E. Gordon, "Three Ways to Effectively Evaluate Personnel Programs," *Personnel Journal* (July 1972); Donald J. Peterson and Robert L. Malone, "The Personnel Effectiveness Grid (PEG): A New Tool for Estimating Personnel Department Effectiveness," *Human Resource Management* (Winter 1975); Albert S. King, "A Programmatic Procedure for Evaluating Personnel Policies," *Personnel Administrator* (September 1982).

See also PROGRAM EVALUATION.

personnel manager, *see* PERSONNELIST.

personnel manual, written record of an organization's personnel policies and procedures. *See* William B. Cobaugh, "When It's Time to Rewrite Your Personnel Manual," *Personnel Journal* (December 1978).

See also FEDERAL PERSONNEL MANUAL.

personnel officer, common job title for the individual responsible for administering the personnel program of an organizational unit.

personnel planning, process that (1) forecasts future supply and demand for various categories of personnel, (2) determines net shortages or excesses, and (3) develops plans for remedying or balancing these forecasted situations.

See also HUMAN RESOURCES PLANNING.

personnel practices, prohibited, *see* MERIT SYSTEM PRINCIPLES.

personnel psychology, that branch of psychology "concerned with individual differences in behavior and job performance and with measuring and predicting such differences," according to Wayne F. Cascio, in *Applied Psychology in Personnel Management* (Reston, Va.: Reston Publishing Company, 1978). *Also see* Thelma Hunt, "Contemporary Personnel Psychology: An Overview," *Public Personnel Management* (Spring 1982); Kenneth N. Wexley and Gary A. Yukl, *Organizational Behavior and Personnel Psychology* (Homewood, Ill.: Richard D. Irwin, 1983).

See also INDUSTRIAL PSYCHOLOGY.

Personnel Psychology, quarterly aimed at operating personnel officials, personnel technicians, and industrial psychologists. The articles in each issue are confined to reports on personnel management research and reviews of books relating to industrial psychology, human resource management, personnel practices, and organizational behavior.

Personnel Psychology
P.O. Box 6965
College Station
Durham, NC 27708

personnel ratio, number of full-time employees of a personnel department (usually exclusive of clerical support) per hundred employees of the total organization. *See* Thomas L. Wood, "The Personnel Staff: What Is a Reasonable Size?" *Personnel Journal* (March 1967).

personnel records, also called PERSONNEL FILES, all recorded information about employees kept by an employer, usually in the form of, and under the name, "personnel files." *See* Mordechai Mironi, "The Confidentiality of Personnel Records: A Legal and Ethical View," *Labor Law Journal* (May 1974); Joan Johnson Schliebner and Joy Sandberg, "Record Retention and Posting Requirements of the Federal Government," *Personnel Administrator* (April 1979); John G. Fox and Paul J. Ostling, "Employee and Government Access to Personnel Files: Rights and Requirements," *Employee Relations Law Journal* (Summer 1979).

personnel research, also called INDUSTRIAL RELATIONS RESEARCH, systematic inquiry into any or all of those problems, policies, programs, and procedures growing out of the employee-employer relationship. For a summary of the origins and importance of personnel management research, *see* Thomas H. Patten, Jr., "Personnel Research: Status Key," *Management of Personnel Quarterly* (Fall 1965). *Also see* John R. Hinrichs, "Characteristics of the Personnel Research Function," *Personnel Journal* (August 1969); Allen P. O. Williams, ed., *Using Personnel Research* (Aldershot, Hants, England: Gower Publishing, 1983).

personnel runaround, what happens to job applicants who apply for positions for which individuals have been preselected.

See also REALPOLITIK.

personnel selection, also called SELECTION and EMPLOYEE SELECTION, program whose object is to choose for employment those applicants who best meet an organization's needs in particular jobs. *See* Mary Green Miner and John B. Miner, *Employee Selection Within the Law* (Washington, D.C.: The Bureau of National Affairs, Inc., 1979); Alfred J. Walker, "Management Selection Systems that Meet the Challenges of the '80s," *Personnel Journal* (October 1981); James P. Springer, "The Importance of Selection in Public Sector Administration," *Public Personnel Management* (Spring 1982); Paul R. Sackett and Michael M. Harris, "Honesty Testing for Personnel Selection: A Review and Critique," *Personnel Psychology* (Summer 1984).

personnel technician, job title for an individual who is a professional staff member of a specialized unit (recruitment, classification and pay, examinations, etc.) of a personnel department.

PERT, acronym for "program evaluation and review technique," a planning and control process that requires identification of the accomplishments of programs and the time and resources needed to go from one accomplishment to the next. A PERT diagram would show the sequence and interrelationships of activities from the beginning of a project to the end. *See* J. D. Wiest and F. K. Levy, *A Management Guide to PERT/CPM,* 2nd ed. (Englewood Cliffs, N.J.: Prentice-Hall, 1977).

Peter Principle, principle promulgated by Laurence J. Peter in his worldwide best seller, *The Peter Principle: Why Things Always Go Wrong,* with Raymond Hull (New York: William Morrow, 1969). The "principle" held that "in a hierarchy every employee tends to rise to his level of incompetence." Corollaries of the Peter Principle hold that "in time, every post tends to be occupied by an employee who is incompetent to carry out its duties." In answer to the logical question of who then does the work that has to be done, Peter asserts that "work is accomplished by those employees who have not yet reached their level of incompetence."
See also REALPOLITIK.

phantom unemployment, jobless citizens who, for a variety of reasons, fall between the statistical cracks and are never officially counted among the unemployed. They have the double misfortune of being both unemployed and "invisible" to their government. For an analysis, *see* Alan Mark Mendelson, "Phantom Unemployment: What Government Figures Don't Tell," *Washington Journalism Review* (April-May 1978).

phased testing, also called PROGRESS TESTING, testing of those in a training program after specific phases of the program.

phatic language, any language used to create an atmosphere of sociability rather than to convey information. For example, a manager might observe that "It's nice weather today," or ask an employee, "How are you?" before being critical of some aspect of the employee's work. The initial phatic language is an attempt to make the employee more receptive to the ensuing criticism.

phenomenology, frame of reference with which to view organizational phenomena. To a phenomenologist, an organization exists on two planes—in reality and in the mind of the person perceiving its actions. Phenomenology is the integrated study of reality as well as its perceptions. According to Howard E. McCurdy, in "Fiction, Phenomenology, and Public Administration," *Public Administration Review* (January-February 1973), "Under phenomenology, concepts as 'hierarchy' and 'patterned behavior' are not seen as objects; rather they are concepts created intuitively and supported by fictions in order to help us conceptualize and eventually manipulate reality." For a broad introduction to the concept, *see* Pierre Thevenaz, *What Is Phenomenology?* (Chicago: Quadrangle Books, 1962).

Philadelphia Plan, equal opportunity compliance program that requires bidders on all federal and federally-assisted construction projects exceeding $500,000 to submit affirmative action plans setting specific goals for the utilization of minority employees. The plan went into effect on July 18, 1969 in the Philadelphia area and affected six of the higher-paying trades in construction—iron work, plumbing and pipefitting, steamfitting, sheet-metal work, electrical work and elevator construction work.
The plan was issued under Executive Order 11246 of 1965, which charges the Secretary of Labor with responsibility for administering the government's policy requiring equal employment opportunity in federal contracts and federally-assisted construction work.

Philippine Journal of Public Administration, quarterly of comparative and development administration focusing on southeast Asia.
Philippine Journal of Public Administration
University of the Philippines
College of Public Administration
Box 474
Manila, The Philippines

Phillips Curve, graphic presentation of the theory put forth in 1958 by the British economist A. W. Phillips, holding that there is a measurable, direct relationship between unemployment and inflation. In short, as unemployment declines, wages and prices can be expected to rise. For analyses, *see* N. J. Simler and A. Tella, "Labor Reserve and The Phillips Curve," *Review of Economics and Statistics* (February 1968); Maurice D. Levi and John H. Makin, "Inflation Uncertainty and the Philips Curve: Some Empirical Evidence," *The American Economic Review* (December 1980).

Phillips* v. *Martin Marietta, *see* SEX PLUS.

philosophy, *see* MANAGERIAL PHILOSOPHY.

Phyrr, Peter A. (1942–   ), most successful popularizer of zero-base budgeting. Major works include: *Zero-Base Budgeting: A Practical Management Tool for Evaluating Expenses* (New York: Wiley-Interscience, 1973); "The Zero-Base Approach to Government Budgeting," *Public Administration Review* (January–February 1977).

physical examination, medical review to determine if an applicant is able to perform the duties of a position. *See* Mitchell S. Novit, "Physical Examinations and Company Liability: A Legal Update," *Personnel Journal* (January 1982).

Pickering* v. *Board of Education, 391 U.S. 563 (1968), U.S. Supreme Court case which held that when public employees' rights to freedom of speech are in question, the special duties and obligations of public employees cannot be ignored; the proper test is whether the government's interest in limiting public employees' "opportunities to contribute to public debate is . . . significantly greater than its interest in limiting a similar contribution by any member of the general public." The court identified six elements which would generally enable the state to

legitimately abridge a public employee's freedom of expression:

1. The need for maintaining discipline and harmony in the workforce.
2. The need for confidentiality.
3. The possibility that an employee's position is such that his or her statements might be hard to counter due to his or her presumed greater access to factual information.
4. The situation in which an employee's statements impede the proper performance of work.
5. The instance where the statements are so without foundation that the individual's basic capability to perform his or her duties comes into question.
6. The jeopardizing of a close and personal loyalty and confidence.

In addition to the above factors, it has been held that the nature of the remarks or expression, degree of disruption, and likelihood that the public will be prone to accepting the statements of an employee because of his or her position must be weighed. In general, however, only expressions on matters of public concern, as opposed to those primarily of interest to co-workers, are subject to constitutional protection.

picket-fence federalism, *see* FEDERALISM, PICKET-FENCE.

picketing, act that occurs when one or more persons are present at an employer's business in order (1) to publicize a labor dispute, (2) to influence others (both employees and customers) to withhold their services or business, and/or (3) to demonstrate a union's desire to represent the employees of the business being picketed.

The U.S. Supreme Court held, in the case of *Thornhill* v. *Alabama*, 310 U.S. 88 (1940), that the dissemination of information concerning the facts of a labor dispute was within the rights guaranteed by the First Amendment. However, picketing may be lawfully enjoined if it is not peaceful, for an unlawful purpose, or in violation of some specific state or federal law.

See also the following entries:
AMERICAN STEEL FOUNDRIES V. TRI-CITY CENTRAL TRADES COUNCIL
ANTI-STRIKEBREAKER ACT OF 1936
CHAIN PICKETING
COMMON SITUS PICKETING
CROSS PICKETING
LAUF V. E.G. SHINNER AND COMPANY
MASS PICKETING
ORGANIZATIONAL PICKETING
RECOGNITION PICKETING
TEAMSTERS, LOCAL 695 V. VOGT
UNFAIR LABOR PRACTICES (UNIONS)
UNITED STATES V. HUTCHESON

piece rate, also called PIECE-WORK RATE, incentive wage program in which a predetermined amount is paid to an employee for each unit of output.

See also DIFFERENTIAL PIECE RATE.

piece rate, nibbling, see NIBBLING.

piece work, differential, see DIFFERENTIAL PIECE WORK.

PIGs, see PUBLIC INTEREST GROUPS.

pilot study, method of testing and validating a survey research instrument by administering it to a small sample of the subject population. According to Sigmund Nosow, in "The Use of the Pilot Study in Behavioral Research," *Personnel Journal* (September 1974),

there is a significant latent use for the pilot study, in a sense somewhat related to feasibility, and that is the creation of a climate of acceptance for such research. For organizations which have not used such research, it is very possible that the acceptance function may be the most important one for a pilot study.

pilot testing, experimental testing of a newly devised test in order to discover any problems before it is put into operational use.

pink-collar jobs, those jobs in which non-college women form the bulk of the labor force, in which the pay is usually low in comparison to men of the same or lower educational levels, in which unionization is nil or weak, and where "equal-pay-for-equal-work" provisions are of little effect because women tend to compete only with other women for pink-collar jobs. *Pink-collar workers* include nurses, elementary school teachers, typists, telephone operators, secretaries, hairdressers, waiters and waitresses, private household workers, etc. See Louise Kapp Howe, *Pink Collar Workers* (New York: G. P. Putnam's Sons, 1977); Martin F. Payson, "Wooing the Pink Collar Work Force," *Personnel Journal* (January 1984).

Pittsburgh Press Co. v. The Pittsburgh Commission on Human Relations, 413 U.S. 376 (1973), U.S. Supreme Court case which held that a municipal order forbidding newspapers to segregate job announcements according to sex when gender is not a required qualification did not violate the constitutional freedom of the press.

placement, acceptance by an employer or hiring authority of a candidate for a position as a direct result of the efforts of an employment agency or central personnel office. See Ronald C. Pilenzo, "Placement by Objectives," *Personnel Journal* (September 1973).

planned unit development (PUD), generic name for the ability of local governments to require developers to adhere to a plan that includes public facilities, such as streets, schools, parks, etc. It is a formal legal designation requiring a set process if the developer or subsequent owners desire to change the original plan.

planning, the formal process of making decisions for the future of individuals and organizations. There are two basic kinds of planning: *strategic* and *operational*. *Strategic planning*, also known as long-range, comprehensive, corporate, integrated, overall, and managerial planning, has three dimensions: the identification and examination of future opportunities, threats, and consequences; the process of analyzing an organization's environment and developing compatible objectives along with the appropriate strategies and policies capable of achieving those objectives; and the integration of the various elements of planning into an overall structure of plans so that each unit of the organization knows in advance what must be done when and by whom. *Operational planning*, also known as divisional planning, is concerned with the implementation of the larger goals and strategies that have been determined by strategic planning; improving current operations; and the allocation of resources through the operating budget.

See John Friedmann, "The Future of Comprehensive Planning: A Critique," *Public Administration Review* (May–June 1971); Robert Anthony, "Closing the Loop Between Planning and Performance," *Public Administration Review* (November–December 1971); Naomi Caiden and Aaron Wildavsky, *Planning and Budgeting in Poor Countries* (New York: John Wiley & Sons, 1974); E. Downey Brill, Jr., "The Use of Optimization Models in Public-Sector Planning," *Management Science* (May 1979); Seymour J. Mandelbaum, "A Complete General Theory of Planning is Impossible," *Policy Sciences* (August 1979); Anthony Sutcliffe, *The History of Urban and Regional Planning* (New York: Facts on File, 1981); Marilyn Spigel Schultz and Vivian Loeb Kasen, *Encyclopedia of Community Planning and Environmental Management* (New York: Facts on File, 1983); Donald A. Krueckeberg, ed., *Introduction to Planning History in the United States* (New Brunswick, N.J.: Center for Urban Policy Research/Rutgers University, 1983); Douglas C. Eadie, "Putting a Powerful Tool to Practical Use: The Application of Strategic Planning in the Public Sector," *Public Administration Review* (September–October 1983); David C. Slater, *Management of Local Planning* (Washington, D.C.: International City Management Association, 1984).

See also the following entries:
ADMINISTRATIVE PLANNING
AMERICAN PLANNING ASSOCIATION
CITY PLANNER
LONG-RANGE PLANNING
NATIONAL PLANNING ASSOCIATION
OPERATIONAL PLANNING
PERSONNEL PLANNING
STRATEGIC PLANNING

planning, career, *see* CAREER PLANNING.

planning horizon, the time limit of organizational planning beyond which the future is considered too uncertain or unimportant to waste time on.

Planning Programming Budgeting Systems (PPBS), an elaborate version of program budgeting which requires agency directors to identify program objectives, develop methods of measuring program output, calculate total program costs over the long run, prepare detailed multi-year program and financial plans, and analyze the costs and benefits of alternative program designs.

In the 1960s PPBS took the budgeting world by storm. Widely hailed as "an exciting, new approach" to "rational decisionmaking," this acclaim prompted more cautious observers to suggest that PPBS stood for the "pristine path to budget salvation."

PPBS in fact did promise much. It began by insisting that it could interrelate and coordinate the three management processes constituting its title. Planning would be related to programs that would be keyed to budgeting. To further emphasize the planning dimension, PPBS pushed the time horizon out to half a decade, requiring five-year forecasts for program plans and cost estimates. PPBS placed a whole new emphasis on program objectives, outputs, and alternatives and stressed the new watchword of evaluation—the "effectiveness" criterion. Finally, PPBS required the use of new analytical techniques from strategic planning, systems analysis, and cost-benefit analysis to make governmental decision-making more systematic and rational.

PPBS was developed in the U.S. Department of Defense (DOD) during the late 1950s and early 1960s. Yet PPBS remained essentially a strategic planning and analysis tool until Robert McNamara's tenure as Secretary of Defense. McNamara was not pleased with what he found at DOD when he arrived in 1961. Plans were being formulated without considering costs, alternatives were not being considered, and each of the four services was submitting a separate budget delineating its own priorities. McNamara's response was an integrated (one budget for all four services) planning program budget that put him in a position of being able to make some budgetary decisions of real consequence.

PPBS succeeded admirably in DOD—both in producing quality budgetary analysis and in establishing a modicum of control for the Secretary of Defense. What remains unclear is the uniqueness of DOD's example. Aaron Wildavsky observed that numerous requisites existed in DOD that were nonexistent in the domestic sector. Among them were: lengthy staff experience with defense strategy and logistics; the prior establishment of common terminology and analytical techniques; an experienced planning staff and established planning systems; and finally, with the advent of McNamara, top leadership that actually comprehended policy analysis and was willing to make a commitment to it. Perhaps Wildavsky's most telling point for why DOD was a bad model for PPBS was the relative size of the budgets involved; cost figures for most domestic programs do not even approximate the magnitude of small defense programs. Consequently, the cost and applicability of the type of analysis employed at Defense in PPBS was neither transferable nor affordable.

Undaunted, Lyndon Johnson made PPBS mandatory for all federal agencies in 1965. Johnson—at the height of his political powers after his landslide election win—envisioned PPBS as the steering mechanism for his Great Society programs. Greatly concerned about the lack of objectives being formulated in the federal government, the nonconsideration of ends and preoccupation with means, the woeful lack of analysis and planning, and the ever-present dilemma of the lack of viable alternatives, Johnson embraced PPBS as the method and system that would ensure the success of his new programs. From this apex, PPBS became the preeminent budgeting system in U.S. government.

By 1970, PPBS, as a formal system, was expanding in some jurisdictions while contracting in others. Opposition to PPBS came from various quarters, especially from bedeviled agency administrators and staff who experienced one difficulty after another in complying with PPBS's submission requirements.

PPBS was formally abandoned in the federal government when the Nixon Administration discontinued it in 1971. State and local governments, on the other hand, were rapidly modifying their PPBS programs and installing hybrid versions. Whatever happened to PPBS? The answer, in short, was that jurisdictions all over the nation simply modified it to fit their needs.

See Fremont J. Lyden and Ernest G. Miller, eds., *Public Budgeting: Program Planning and Evaluation,* 3rd ed. (Chicago: Rand McNally, 1978); David Novick, "The Origin and History of Program Budgeting," *California Management Review,* Vol. XI, No. 1 (1968); Allen Schick, "The Road to PPB: The States of Budget Reform," *Public Administration Review* (December 1966); Allen Schick, "A Death in the Bureaucracy: The Demise of Federal PPB," *Public Administration Review* (March-April 1973); Aaron Wildavsky, "Rescuing Policy Analysis from PPBS," *Public Administration Review* (March-April 1969); August B. Trumbull III, *Government Budgeting and PPBS: A Programmed Introduction* (Reading, Mass.: Addison-Wesley Publishing Co., 1970).

See also BUDGETING.

plan termination insurance, pension insurance available through the Pension Benefit Guarantee Corporation which provides that in the event of the financial collapse of a private pension fund wherein the pension fund assets are not sufficient to meet its obligations, the interests of vested employees will be protected. *See* Powell Niland, "Reforming Private Pension Plan Administration," *Business Horizons* (February 1976).

platykurtic, frequency distribution or curve that is more flat-topped, as opposed to peaked, than a normal curve.

Plum Book, also known as the POLICY AND SUPPORTING POSITIONS BOOK, book first published in 1960 that lists the jobs that are the current leading positions in the U.S. government.

The Plum Book is often viewed as a list of "political jobs" available to a new administration to which it can make appointments. The available jobs include a large variety of positions exempt from competitive civil service rules as well as vacancies in the judiciary and jobs in the legislative branch filled by presidential appointment.

The Plum Book is prepared by the Committee on Post Office and Office of Personnel Management of the House of Representatives after every presidential election and is printed quadrennially by the U.S. Government Printing Office.

See also PATRONAGE.

plural executive, concept that has a committee assuming the normal responsibilities of an executive. For an account of this in action, *see* William H. Mylander, "Management by Executive Committee," *Harvard Business Review* (May–June 1955).

pluralism, in the U.S. context, a theory of government that attempts to reaffirm the democratic character of society by asserting that open, multiple, competing, and responsive groups preserve traditional democratic values in a mass industrial state. Thus, traditional democratic theory, with its emphasis on individual responsibility and development, is transformed into a model that emphasizes the role of the group in society.

However, power-elite theory argues that if democracy is defined as popular participation in public affairs, then pluralist theory is inadequate as an explanation of modern U.S. government. Pluralism, according to this view, offers little direct participation since the elite structure is closed, pyramidal, consensual, and unresponsive. Society is divided into two classes: the few who govern and the many who are governed. That is, pluralism is covert elitism, instead of a practical solution to preserve democracy in a mass society.

The principal pluralist work is Robert Dahl, *Who Governs?* (New Haven, Conn.: Yale University Press, 1961). For the classical statement of the elitist view, *see* C. Wright Mills, *The Power Elite* (New York: Oxford University Press, 1956). *Also see* Robert A Dahl, *Pluralist Democracy in the United States* (Chicago: Rand McNally, 1967); William E. Connally, ed., *The Bias of Pluralism* (New York: Atherton, 1971); Bruce Berg, "Public Choice, Pluralism and Scarcity: Implications for Bureaucratic Behavior," *Administration & Society* (May 1984).

See also INTEREST GROUP LIBERALISM.

pocket veto, *see* VETO.

point system, also called POINT METHOD, most widely used method of job evaluation, in which the relative worth of the jobs being evaluated is determined by totaling the number of points assigned to the various factors applicable to each of the jobs.

See also HAY SYSTEM.

police power, authority of a state to pass laws for the health, safety, and morals of its citizens.

See also HOLDEN V. HARDY.

policy, statement of goals that can be translated into a plan or program by specifying the objectives to be obtained. Goals are a far more general statement of aims than are objectives. Goal/objective ambiguity may exist for a variety of reasons. The original sponsors of the policy or program may not have had a precise idea of the end results desired. Formal statements of objectives may be intentionally ambiguous if it is easier to obtain a consensus on action. Value judgments underlying the objectives may not be shared by important groups. Consequently, the end results intended may be perceived by some as implying ill effects for them; explicit statements of objectives tend to imply a specific assignment of priorities and commitment of resources.

policy analysis, set of techniques that seek to answer the question of what the probable effects of a policy will be before they actually occur. Policy analysis involves the application of systematic research techniques, drawn largely from the social sciences and based on measurements of program effectiveness, quality, cost, and impact, to the formulation, execution, and evaluation of public policy in order to create a more rational or optimal administrative system. The literature on policy analysis is vast. For some examples, *see* Nelson Polsby, "Policy Analysis and Congress," *Public Policy* (Fall 1969); Robert H. Haveman and Julius Margolis, eds., *Public Expenditures and Policy Analysis* (Chicago: Markham, 1970); Ira Sharkansky, ed., *Policy Analysis in Political Science* (Chicago: Markham, 1970); Arnold J. Meltsner, "Political Feasibility and Policy Analysis," *Public Administration Review* (November–December 1972); Steven E. Rhoads, *Policy Analysis in the Federal Aviation Administration* (Lexington, Mass.: Lexington Books, 1974); Fred A. Kramer, "Policy Analysis as Ideology," *Public Administration Review* (September–October 1974); Arnold J. Meltsner, *Policy Analysts in the Bureaucracy* (Berkeley, Calif.: University of California Press, 1976); Charles O. Jones, "Why Congress Can't Do Policy Analysis," *Policy Analysis* (Spring 1976); Phillip Martin Gregg, ed., *Problems of Theory in Policy Analysis* (Lexington, Mass.: Lexington Books, 1976); Thomas R. Dye, *Policy Analysis* (University, Ala.: University of Alabama Press, 1976); Bruce L. R. Smith, "The Non-Governmental Policy Analysis Organization," *Public Administration Review* (May–June 1977); Norman Beckman, "Policy Analysis for the Congress," *Public Administration Review* (May–June 1977); Norman Beckman, "Policy Analysis in Government: Alternatives to Muddling Through," *Public Administration Review* (May–June 1977); Selma J. Mushkin, "Policy Analysis in State and Community," *Public Administration Review* (May–June 1977); Stuart Nagel and Marian Neef, "Finding an Optimum Choice, Level, or Mix in Public Policy Analysis," *Public Administration Review* (September–October 1978); Gordon Tullock and Richard E. Wagner, eds., *Policy Analysis and Deductive Reasoning* (Lexington, Mass.: Lexington Books, 1978); Duncan McRae and James White, *Policy Analysis for Public Decisions* (North Scituate, Mass.: Duxbury Press, 1979); Aaron Wildavsky, *Speaking Truth to Power: The Art and Craft of Policy Analysis* (Boston: Little, Brown & Co., 1979); Arlyn J. Melcher and Bonita H. Melcher, "Toward A Systems Theory of Policy Analysis: Static Versus Dynamic Analysis," *Academy of Management Review* (April 1980), William N. Dunn, *Public Policy Analysis: An Introduction* (Englewood Cliffs, N.J.: Prentice-Hall, 1981); Peter W. House, *The Art of Public Policy Analysis* (Beverly Hills, Calif.: Sage Publications, 1982); John S. Robey, *Public Policy Analysis: An Annotated Bibliography* (New York: Garland Publishing, 1982).

See also BUREAUCRATIC POLICYMAKING and POLICYMAKING.

Policy Analysis, quarterly journal of the Graduate School of Public Policy of the University of California, Berkeley. This journal ceased publication in 1981 and was succeeded by the *Journal of Policy Analysis and Management.*

policy analyst, individual employed to study the effects of a proposed or actual public policy. See Yehezkel Dror, "Policy Analysts: A New Professional Role in Government Service," *Public Administration Review* (September 1967); Arnold J. Meltsner, "Bureaucratic Policy Analysts," *Policy Analysis* (Winter 1975).

Policy and Supporting Positions Book, see PLUM BOOK.

policy evaluation, study of the "impacts of policy outputs." See David Nachmias, ed., *The Practice of Policy Evaluation* (New York: St. Martin's Press, 1980); Stuart S. Nagel, *Policy Evlauation: Making Optimum Decisions* (New York: Praeger Publishers, 1982); Stuart S. Nagel, "Productivity Improvement and Policy Evaluation," *Public Productivity Review* (June 1983).
See also PROGRAM EVALUATION.

policy implementation, see IMPLEMENTATION.

policymaking, see PUBLIC POLICYMAKING.

policy management, term used to refer to the capacity of elected officials to perform on an integrated, cross-cutting basis the needs assessment, goal setting, and evaluation functions of management; to mobilize and allocate resources; and to initiate and guide the planning, development, and implementation of policies, strategies, and programs that are related to sustaining or improving the physical, socioeconomic, or political conditions that have a bearing on the quality of life in a community. See Richard G. RuBino, "State Policy Management: A Question of the Will to Act," *Public Administration Review* (December 1975); Paul Scott and Robert J. Macdonald, "Local Policy Management Needs: The Federal Response," *Public Administration Review* (December 1975).

policy management assistance, term used to refer to any system, effort, or process—including a federal grant or contract—which has among its major objectives strengthening the capability of elected officials to exercise the strategic needs assessment, goal-setting, and evaluation functions of management on a jurisdictional or territorial basis. See Ann C. Macaluso, "Background and History of the Study Committee on Policy Management Assistance," *Public Administration Review*

(December 1975); Norman C. Paulhus, Jr., and Alfonso B. Linhares, "Policy Management Assistance in Mission Agencies," *Public Administration Review* (December 1975).

Policy Review, a conservative quarterly on policy issues.
Policy Review
The Heritage Foundation
214 Mass. Avenue, N.E.
Washington, D.C. 20002

policy sciences, according to Harold D. Lasswell, the sciences that "study the process of deciding or choosing and evaluate the relevance of available knowledge for the solution of particular problems." See his "The Emerging Conception of Policy Sciences," *Policy Sciences* (Spring 1970). *Also see* Peter deLeon, "Policy Sciences: The Discipline and the Profession," *Policy Sciences* (February 1981).
See also LASSWELL, HAROLD D.

Policy Sciences, international journal devoted to the improvement of policymaking, policy analysis, and policymaking methodology.
Policy Science
Elsevier Scientific Publishing Company
Box 211
Amsterdam
The Netherlands

policy studies, imprecise term for interdisciplinary academic programs which focus on any or all aspects of public policy. See Stuart Nagel and Marian Neef, "What Is and What Should Be in University Policy Studies?" *Public Administration Review* (July–August 1977); William D. Coplin, ed., *Teaching Policy Studies: What and How* (Lexington, Mass.: Lexington Books, 1978); Stuart S. Nagel, ed., *Encyclopedia of Policy Studies* (New York: Marcel Dekker, 1983).

Policy Studies Journal, also Policy Studies Review, journals of the Policy Studies Organization. The *Policy Studies Journal* concentrates on agenda setting and policy implementation while the *Policy*

Studies Review is more concerned with policy analysis, program evaluation and quantitative methods.

Policy Studies Journal/Review
361 Lincoln Hall
University of Illinois
Urbana, IL 61801

policy termination, cessation of a public policy or program. *See* Eugene Bardach, "Policy Termination as a Political Process," *Policy Sciences* (June 1976); Robert P. Biller, "On Tolerating Policy and Organizational Termination: Some Design Considerations," *Policy Sciences* (June 1976); Robert D. Behn, "How To Terminate a Public Policy: A Dozen Hints for the Would Be Terminator," *Managing Fiscal Stress*, ed. by Charles H. Levine (Chatham, N.J.: Chatham House, 1980); Carol L. Ellis, "Program Termination: A Word to the Wise," *Public Administration Review* (July–August 1983).

political action, any attempt to influence the political process, from lobbying legislators to seeking the election (or defeat) of particular candidates.

political culture, a community's attitudes towards the quality and vigor of its governmental operations. The only way to explain the extreme variations found in U.S. public bureaucracies is to examine the cultural context of the host jurisdictions. The quality of bureaucratic operations varies for a variety of reasons—not the least of which is the substantial disagreement as to just what constitutes a quality operation. But the quality or style of operations is determined only in the lesser part by well-meaning critics or even by the public administrators themselves; the crucial determinant is the political will of the community as expressed by its political culture and manifested by the administrative style of public programs.

James Q. Wilson, in his *Varieties of Police Behavior* (Cambridge, Mass.: Harvard University Press, 1968), has shown that the style of police operations in eight communities reflected not some abstract standard of quality or professionalism but rather the expressed and/or implied desires of the community. For example, the police were either exceedingly lenient or exceedingly strict with minor legal violations depending upon the perceived degree of community concern one way or another. A similar condition exists with personnel operations. Merit systems arrayed along a continuum tend to be tight and legalistic or open to manipulation in reflection of community attitudes. Since public personnel agencies typically have a policing role to perform, it is useful to compare their operating premises to those of police departments in the same jurisdiction. Wilson considers a police department to have a "watchman" style of performance if it is one in which order maintenance is perceived to be the prime function of the department. Such a police operation will tend to ignore law infringements that do not involve "serious" crimes, such as minor traffic violations, bookmaking, and illegal church bingo. Correspondingly, a public personnel agency exhibiting this style might knowingly accept false information from favored individuals, might encourage unsuspecting applicants to apply for a job vacancy for which a candidate has been preselected, or might allow the equal rights provisions of recent legislation to be ignored or abused. Of course, all of these activities or non-activities are subject to occasional crackdowns. Just as the police periodically shut down illegal gambling operations in response to the political needs of the police chief or mayor, "watchman" style personnel operations periodically tighten up their application procedures or pump new life into their equal employment opportunity programs in response to the political needs of the appointed executives. The thrust of the "watchman" style in both instances is to maintain order, to insure a smooth, non-disruptive running of the community or bureaucracy. Legal considerations and official operating mandates are paramount only when the "heat" is on. Of course, the standard operating procedures of a police, personnel, or any other public bureaucracy will tend to be more legalistic in communities that are so disposed.

While a community's political culture is seldom articulated, it nevertheless serves as a source of definition. By determining the values to be applied to any given problem set, the political culture insures that the decisional process is filtered through its value system prior to administrative action. Just as other aspects of culture create an individual's needs hierarchy by ordering the importance in his life of such things as new clothes, big cars, and ancestor worship, the political culture is a significant influence in establishing an individual's hierarchy of role obligation whereby his legalistic responsibilities are placed above or below his obligations to political party, kinship group, coreligionists, etc. It establishes the parameters of the systemically legitimate activities in which an individual may participate without incurring community sanctions. Even when corruption is rife, it is the cultural environment that sets the limits and direction of such corruption.

For studies that relate political culture to administrative practices, see Robert R. Alford, *Bureaucracy and Participation: Political Cultures in Four Wisconsin Cities* (Chicago: Rand McNally, 1969); Gabriel A. Almond and Sidney Verba, *The Civic Culture: Political Attitudes and Democracy in Five Nations* (Boston: Little, Brown and Co., 1965); Daniel J. Elazar, *American Federalism: A View From the States,* 2nd ed. (New York: Thomas Y. Crowell, 1972); John R. Johannes, "Political Culture and Congressional Constituency Service," *Polity* (Summer 1983); Michael Johnson, "Corruption and Political Culture in America: An Empirical Perspective," *Publius* (Winter 1983); Jay M. Shafritz, "Political Culture: The Determinant of Merit System Viability," *Public Personnel Management* (January-February 1974); Raymond E. Wolfinger and John O. Field, "Political Ethos and the Structure of City Government," *American Political Science Review* (June 1966).

political economy, the conjunction of politics and economics. Political economy is of concern to public administration because of the primacy of economic pros-perity. Maintaining economic prosperity remains the primary, though unspoken, objective of U.S. governments. Not only does the government account for one third of the gross national product, but it also regulates the basic economic conditions of society. For example, it can specify whether or not a product can be produced; regulate the minimum wages of the production workers; prescribe working conditions at the job site and establish standards for and inspect the quality of the finished products. See W. W. Heller, *New Dimensions in Political Economy* (Cambridge: Harvard University Press, 1967); Arthur M. Okum, *The Political Economy of Prosperity* (Washington, D.C.: The Brookings Institution, 1970); Warren F. Ilchman and Norman Thomas Uphoff, *The Political Economy of Change* (Berkeley: University of California Press, 1971); William B. Neenan, *Political Economy of Urban Areas* (Chicago: Markham, 1972); Gary L. Wamsley and Mayer N. Zald, "The Political Economy of Public Organizations," *Public Administration Review* (January-February 1973); Bruce L. R. Smith, ed., *The New Political Economy: The Public Use of the Private Sector* (London: Macmillan & Co., 1975); Norman Frohlich and Joe A. Oppenheimer, *Modern Political Economy* (Englewood Cliffs, N.J.: Prentice-Hall, 1978); Ferdinand E. Banks, *The Political Economy of Oil* (Lexington, Mass.: Lexington Books, 1980): Barry M. Mitnick, *The Political Economy of Regulation* (New York: Columbia University Press, 1980); Bruce Jacobs, *The Political Economy of Organizational Change* (New York: Academic Press, 1981); Peter D. McClelland and Alan L. Magdovitz, *Crisis in the Making: The Political Economy of New York State Since 1945* (New York: Cambridge University Press, 1981); P. M. Jackson, *The Political Economy of Bureaucracy* (Totowa, N.J.: Rowman & Allanheld, 1983); John Mark Hansen, "The Political Economy of Group Membership," *American Political Science Review* (March 1985).

See also ECONOMIC POLICY and FISCAL POLICY.

political executive, individual whose institutional position makes him or her formally responsible for the governance of a political community. *See* Hugh Heclo, "Political Executives and the Washington Bureaucracy," *Political Science Quarterly* (Fall 1977).

political machine, *see* BOSSISM.

political process, efforts of individuals and groups to gain and use power to achieve their goals.

political science, academic discipline that studies political phenomena. Public administration as an academic discipline grew out of political science.

Political Science Quarterly, founded in 1886, the oldest continuous journal of political science in the United States.
Political Science Quarterly
Academy of Political Science
2852 Broadway
New York, NY 10025
See also ACADEMY OF POLITICAL SCIENCE.

politics/administration dichotomy, the belief, growing out of the early administrative reform movement and its reaction against the spoils system, which held that political interference in administration would erode the opportunity for administrative efficiency, that the policymaking activities of government ought to be wholly separated from the administrative functions, and that administrators had to have an explicit assignment of objectives before they could begin to develop an efficient administrative system.

The politics/administration dichotomy is traditionally traced to these two sources: Woodrow Wilson, "The Study of Administration," *Political Science Quarterly* (June 1887); Frank J. Goodnow, *Politics and Administration: A Study in Government* (New York: Macmillan, 1900). *Also see* Edwin O. Stene, "The Politics-Administration Dichotomy," *Midwest Review of Public Administration* (April-July 1975); William Earle Klay, "Fiscal Constraints,

Trust, and the Need for a New Politics/ Administrative Dichotomy," *Review of Public Personnel Administration* (Fall 1983); James H. Svara, "Dichotomy and Duality: Reconceptualizing the Relationship Between Policy and Administration in Council-Manager Cities," *Public Administration Review* (January–February 1985).
See also GOODNOW, FRANK and WILSON, WOODROW.

poll tax, *see* TAX, POLL.

polygraph, *see* LIE DETECTOR.

population, also called SET and UNIVERSE, all of the cases in a class of things under statistical examination.
See also CANDIDATE POPULATION.

populism, recurring political theme in the U.S. that stresses the role of government in defending small voices against the powerful and wealthy. *See* Norman Pollack, ed., *The Populist Mind* (Indianapolis: Bobbs-Merrill, 1967); Raymond J. Cunningham, ed., *The Populists in Historical Perspective* (Boston: D.C. Heath, 1968); Margaret Canovan, *Populism* (New York: Harcourt Brace Jovanovich, 1981).

portability, characteristic of a pension plan that allows participating employees to have the monetary value of accrued pension benefits transfered to a succeeding pension plan should they leave their present organization. According to Susan Meredith Phillips and Linda Pickthorne Fletcher, "The Future of the Portable Pension Concept," *Industrial and Labor Relations Review* (January 1977), "the portable pension concept has been offered as a solution to the problem of providing a secure retirement income to a mobile labor force."

Porter Co. v. *National Labor Relations Board,* 397 U.S. 99 (1970), U.S. Supreme Court case which held that the National Labor Relations Board did not have the power to compel a company or union

415

to agree to a substantive provision of a collective bargaining agreement.

POSDCORB, mnemonic device invented by Luther Gulick in 1937 to call attention to the various functional elements of the work of a chief executive. POSDCORB stands for the following activities:

Planning, that is, working out in broad outline the things that need to be done and the methods for doing them to accomplish the purpose set for the enterprise;

Organizing, that is, the estabishment of the formal structure of authority through which work subdivisions are arranged, defined and co-ordinated for the defined objective;

Staffing, that is, the whole personnel function of bringing in and training the staff and maintaining favorable conditions of work;

Directing, that is, the continuous task of making decisions and embodying them in specific and general orders and instructions and serving as the leader of the enterprise;

Co-ordinating, that is, the all-important duty of interrelating the various parts of the work;

Reporting, that is, keeping those to whom the executive is responsible informed as to what is going on, which thus includes keeping himself and his subordinates informed through records, research and inspection;

Budgeting, with all that goes with budgeting in the form of fiscal planning, accounting and control.

Source: Luther Gulick, "Notes on the Theory of Organization," in Luther Gulick and L. Urwick, eds., *Papers on the Science of Administration* (New York: Institute of Public Administration, 1937). For a reexamination, *see* David S. Brown, "POSDCORB Revisited and Revised," *Personnel Administration* (May–June 1966).

See also GULICK, LUTHER.

position, group of duties and responsibilities requiring the full- or part-time employment of one individual. A position may, at any given time, be occupied or vacant.

position, benchmark, *see* BENCHMARK POSITION.

position analysis, a systematic method of identifying, summarizing and documenting the most important elements of an individual position, including (1) the results expected from the incumbent's work activity, (2) a summary of that work activity in terms of the tasks performed, and (3) a description of the qualifications needed to perform the necessary tasks. Position analysis is distinguished from job analysis in that the latter focuses on an analysis of a representative sample of positions included in a job classification. *See* Robert D. White, "Position Analysis and Characterization," *Review of Public Personnel Administration* (Spring 1984).

Position Analysis Questionnaire (PAQ), job analysis questionnaire that is a tool for quantitatively describing the various aspects of a job. It was developed and copyrighted by the Purdue University Research Foundation and is available from the Purdue University Book Store, 360 West State Street, West Lafayette, IN 47906. *See* Ernest J. McCormick, Angelo S. DeNisi and James B. Shaw, "Uses of Position Analysis Questionnaires in Personnel Administration," *The Personnel Administrator* (July 1978); P. R. Jeanneret, "Equitable Job Evaluation and Classification with the Position Analysis Questionnaire," *Compensation Review* (First Quarter 1980).

position ceiling, *see* JOB CEILING.

position classification, process of using formal job descriptions to organize all jobs in a given organization into classes on the basis of duties and responsibilities for the purpose of delineating authority, establishing chains of command, and providing equitable salary scales. As with other aspects of traditional public personnel administration, they often represent what Wallace Sayre has called the "triumph of techniques over purpose." In seeking to thwart the excesses of spoils politics, the reform movement instituted many civil service procedures that have inadvertently had the effect of thwarting effective management practices as well. Thus the negative role of the public personnel agency in guarding the merit system has commonly been more influential than the positive role of aiding management in the maintenance of a viable personnel system. This contradictory duality of function in public personnel operations is nowhere more evident than with position classification procedures.

All public personnel agencies have a dual role to play within their organizations. They are both the enforcer of the myriad civil service laws, rules, and regulations and a servitor to the jurisdiction's executive. There is frequently considerable conflict over what role the personnel agency should take in its activities. Is it a policing agency or a service department? Of course, it must be both at the same time. If the personnal agency makes a severe shift to one side or the other, it loses its effectiveness to either the executive or the public. And it must serve both—if not equally, at least fairly.

To a program manager, budget maker, or civil service commission, positions are neat packages that represent specific salaries. Ultimately the management of positions is a budgetary process. If position classification is thought of as essentially an accounting procedure, the whole system becomes more rational.

The principles and practices of position classification that are generally used in the public service are throwbacks to the heyday of the scientific management movement. They were conceived at a point in time—the second two decades of this century—when this school of management thought held sway, and they have never really adapted to modern currents of management thought. After all, a classification plan is essentially a time-and-motion study for a governmental function. The duties of the larger organization are divided into positions in order to prevent duplication and enhance efficiency. A position is not a person but a set of duties

and responsibilities fully equivalent to an interchangeable machine part because that is exactly what it represents—a human interchangeable part.

Current position classification practices are best thought of as being of mixed parentage, being derived more or less equally from two contemporary, early twentieth century movements—scientific management and civil service reform.

As control devices, position classifications are doubly unsuccessful. First, they prevent program managers from having the discretion essential for the optimum success of their mission. Second, they generate an astounding amount of dysfunctional activity whose sole purpose is to get around the control devices. Although the controls are frequently and successfully circumvented, the costs of such activity take away resources from the organization's prime goals. While position classifications tend to be required of public personnel programs, their allegiance to notions of the past occasions their frequent denunciation for being unreasonable constraints on top management, sappers of employee morale, and little more than polite fictions in substance. For a "how-to" text, see Harold Suskin, ed., *Job Evaluation and Pay Administration in the Public Sector* (Chicago: International Personnel Management Association, 1977). For a critical analysis, see Jay M. Shafritz, *Position Classification: A Behavioral Analysis for the Public Service* (New York: Praeger, 1973).

See also the following entries:
CLASSIFICATION AND COMPENSATION SOCIETY
CLASSIFICATION STANDARDS
FACTOR EVALUATION SYSTEM
SERIES OF CLASSES
SPECIFICATION

position classification principles, basic principles of position classification that constitute the foundation of most position classification systems in government. They were promulgated by the 1919 Congressional Joint Commission on Reclassification of Salaries. The commission's 1920 Report recommended that:

1. positions and not individuals should be classified;
2. the duties and responsibilities pertaining to a position constitute the outstanding characteristics that distinguish it from, or mark its similarity to, other positions;
3. qualifications in respect to education, experience, knowledge, and skill necessary for the performance of certain duties are determined by the nature of those duties (Therefore, the qualifications for a position are an important factor in the determination of the classification of a position.);
4. the individual characteristics of an employee occupying a position should have no bearing on the classification of the position; and
5. persons holding positions in the same class should be considered equally qualified for any other position in that class.

For the total report, see Report of the Congressional Joint Commission on Reclassification of Salaries (H. Doc. 686, 66th Cong. 2nd Sess., March 12, 1920).

position classifier, a specialist in job analysis who determines the titles, occupational groups, series, and grades of positions.

position description, formal statement of the duties and responsibilities assigned to a position.

position excepted by law/executive order/civil service rule, see EXCEPTED POSITION.

position guide, see JOB DESCRIPTION.

position management, term used to describe the key management actions involved in the process of organizing work to accomplish the missions of federal departments and agencies. It involves, essentially, the determination of the needs for positions, the determination of required skills and knowledges, and the organization, grouping, and assignment of duties and responsibilities among positions. There are no absolute rules for managers to follow in the complex and evolving art of position management; however, there are basic *system* requirements for position management in government agencies, which are designed to assure that work structures and organizational designs are systematically being assessed for improvement, that positions are correctly classified, and that the allocation of positions and deployment of people reflect the best that is known about managing human resources. See Tim E. Winchell, Sr., "Federal Position Control Programs in an Era of Cutback Management," *Public Personnel Management Journal* (Fall 1982).

position ranking, also called JOB GRADING, method of comparing jobs on a "whole job" basis in order to rank such jobs in a hierarchy from highest to lowest.

position survey, agency review of positions to determine whether the positions are still needed and, if so, whether the classification and position description are correct.

positive economics, economic analysis which limits itself to what *is* rather than to normative concerns of what *ought to be.* See James R. Wible, "Friedman's Positive Economics and Philosophy of Science," *Southern Economic Journal* (October 1982).

positive law, a law that has been passed by a legislature.

positively skewed, see SKEWNESS.

positive recruitment, aggressive action designed to encourage qualified individuals to apply for positions, as opposed to just waiting for the right person to "knock on the door."

positive reinforcement, see REINFORCEMENT.

positive strike, also NEGATIVE STRIKE, one whose purpose is to gain new benefits. A *negative strike* is one whose purpose is to prevent the loss of present benefits.

positive stroking, see STROKING.

positive transfer, see TRANSFER OF LEARNING.

Postal Rate Commission, body whose major responsibility is to submit recommended decisions to the United States Postal Service on postage rates and fees and mail classifications. The commission has appellate jurisdiction to review Postal Service determinations to close or consolidate small post offices.

Postal Rate Commission
2000 L Street, N.W.
Washington, D.C. 20268
(202) 655-4000

Postal Reorganization Act of 1970, federal statute that converted the Post Office Department into an independent establishment—within the executive branch of the government, but free from direct political pressures—to own and operate the nation's postal system, known as the United States Postal Service. The act also provided for collective bargaining by postal workers—the first instance of true collective bargaining in the federal service. See John J. Morrison, *Postal Reorganization: Managing the Public's Business* (Boston, Mass.: Auburn House Publishing, 1981).

Postal Service, United States (USPS), government corporation that provides mail processing and delivery services to individuals and businesses within the United States. It is also the responsibility of the Postal Service to protect the mails from loss or theft and to apprehend those who violate postal laws. The Postal Service is the only federal agency whose employment policies are governed by a process of collective bargaining.

The chief executive officer of the Postal Service, the Postmaster General, is appointed by the nine governors of the Postal Service, who are appointed by the president, with the advice and consent of the Senate, for overlapping nine-year terms.

The ambiguous legal status of the Postal Service has been the source of political controversy since the Service was established in 1970. It does not report to the president and is only indirectly responsible to Congress. There have been a number of bills introduced in recent Congresses to return the Postal Service to the status of a regular executive department. See Simcha B. Werner, "The Political Reversibility of Administrative Reform: A Case Study of the United States Postal Service," *Public Administration* (Autumn 1982); Joel L. Fleishman, *The Future of the Postal Service* (New York: Praeger Publishers, 1983).

USPS
475 L'Enfant Plaza West, S.W.
Washington, D.C. 20260
(202) 245-4000

postbureaucratic organizations, organizations described in 1952 by Dwight Waldo in the *American Political Science Review*. He prophesied a future society in which "bureaucracy in the Weberian sense would have been replaced by more democratic, more flexible, though more complex, forms of large-scale organization." Waldo called such a society "postbureaucratic." However, it remained for Warren G. Bennis, in the 1960s, to make the term particularly his own with a series of articles and books predicting the "end of bureaucracy." In its place, he wrote,

there will be adaptive, rapidly changing *temporary systems*. These will be task forces composed of groups of relative strangers with diverse professional backgrounds and skills organized around problems to be solved. The groups will be arranged in an organic, rather than mechanical, model, meaning that they will evolve in response to a problem rather than to preset, programmed expectations. People will be evaluated not vertically according to rank and status, but flexibly according to competence. Organizational charts will consist of project groups rather than stratified functional groups.

See Warren G. Bennis and Philip E. Slater, *The Temporary Society* (New

York: Harper & Row, 1968). *Also see* Warren G. Bennis, *Changing Organizations* (New York: McGraw-Hill, 1966). For a reader in organizational futures, *see* Jong S. Jun and William B. Storm, eds., *Tomorrow's Organizations: Challenges and Strategies* (Glenview, Ill.: Scott, Foresman and Co., 1973).

post-entry training, activities designed to upgrade the capabilities of an employee once he or she has joined an organization. Everything from executive development seminars constructed to improve the decision-making skills of top management to an orientation program which has as its objective acquainting new employees with the purposes and structure of the organization may be identified as post-entry training.

post-industrial society, term coined by Daniel Bell to describe the new social structures evolving in modern societies in the second half of the twentieth century. Bell holds that the "axial principle" of post-industrial society is the centrality of theoretical knowledge as the source of innovation and policy formation for the society. Hallmarks of post-industrial society include a change from a goods-producing to a service economy, the pre-eminence of a professional and technical class, and the creation of a new "intellectual" technology. For the definitive work to date, *see* Daniel Bell, *The Coming of Post-Industrial Society: A Venture in Social Forecasting* (New York: Basic Books, 1973). *Also see* John Schmidman, *Unions in Postindustrial Society* (University Park, Pa.: The Pennsylvania State University Press, 1979); Hank E. Koehn, "The Post-Industrial Worker," *Public Personnel Management* (Fall 1983).

post-test, test given at the end of a training program to determine if the training objectives have been met.

poverty, defined by the U.S. Bureau of the Census in 1985 as an annual cash income of less than $10,609 for a family of four.

Poverty and Human Resources Abstracts, *see* HUMAN RESOURCES ABSTRACTS.

poverty area, an urban or rural geographic area with a high proportion of low income families. Normally, low average income is used to define a poverty area, but other indicators, such as housing conditions, illegitimate birth rates, and incidence of juvenile delinquency are sometimes added to define geographic areas with poverty conditions.

power, the ability and/or right to do something. Power enables leaders to exercise influence over other people. John R. P. French and Bertram Raven, in "The Bases of Social Power," suggest that there are five major bases of power: (1) *expert power,* which is based on the perception that the leader possesses some special knowledge or expertise; (2) *referent power,* which is based on the follower's liking, admiring, or identifying with the leader; (3) *reward power,* which is based on the leader's ability to mediate rewards for the follower; (4) *legitimate power,* which is based on the follower's perception that the leader has the legitimate right or authority to exercise influence over him or her; and (5) *coercive power,* which is based on the follower's fear that noncompliance with the leader's wishes will lead to punishment. Subsequent research on these power bases has indicated that emphasis on expert and referent power are more positively related to subordinate performance and satisfaction than utilization of reward, legitimate, or coercive power. For the French and Raven study, *see* Dorwin Cartwright, ed., *Studies in Social Power* (Ann Arbor, Michigan: Institute for Social Research, University of Michigan, 1959). *Also see* Norton E. Long, "Power and Administration," *Public Administration Review* (Autumn 1949); R. G. H. Siu, *The Craft of Power* (New York: John Wiley & Sons, 1979); Karen Van Wagner and Cheryl Swanson, "From Machiavelli to Ms.: Differences in Male-Female Power Styles," *Public Administration Review* (January-February 1979); R. G. H Siu,

Transcending the Power Game: The Way to Executive Serenity (New York: John Wiley, 1980); Anthony T. Cobb, "Informal Influence in the Formal Organization: Perceived Sources of Power Among Work Unit Peers," *Academy of Management Journal* (March 1981); Jeffrey Pfiffer, *Power in Organizations* (Marshfield, Mass.: Pitman Publishing, Inc., 1981); Donald C. Hambrick, "Environment, Strategy, and Power Within Top Management Teams," *Administrative Science Quarterly* (June 1981); Carleton S. Bartlem and Edwin A. Locke, "The Coch and French Study: A Critique and Reinterpretation," *Human Relations* (July 1981); Andrew Kakabadse and Christopher Parker, *Power, Politics and Organizations: A Behavioral Science View,* (New York: Wiley, 1984).

See also LEADERSHIP.

power-elite theory, *see* PLURALISM.

power of attorney, document authorizing one person to act as attorney for, or in the place of, the person signing the document.

Power Plant and Industrial Use Act, *see* NATIONAL ENERGY ACT OF 1978.

power test, test intended to measure level of performance unaffected by speed of response—there is either no time limit or a very generous one.

PPBS, *see* PLANNING PROGRAMING BUDGETING SYSTEMS.

practice, the use of one's knowledge in a particular profession. The practice of medicine is the exercise of one's knowledge in the promotion of health and treatment of disease.

practice effect, the influence of previous experience with a test on a later administration of the same test or a similar test—usually an increase in score on the second testing that can be attributed to increased familiarity with the directions, kinds of questions, or content of particular questions. Practice effect is greatest when the interval between testings is small, when the

materials in the two tests are very similar, and when the initial test taking represents a relatively novel experience for the subjects.

precedent, a legal decision on a question of law that gives authority and direction on how similar cases should be decided in the future. *See* Gregory A. Caldeira, "The Transmission of Legal Precedent: A Study of State Supreme Courts," *American Political Science Review* (March 1985).

precinct, the smallest of political units. A precinct typically contains less than one thousand voters.

prediction, differential, *see* DIFFERENTIAL VALIDATION.

predictive efficiency, measure of accuracy of a test or other predictive device in terms of the proportion of its predictions that have been shown to be correct.

predictive validity, measure obtained by giving a test to a group of subjects and then comparing the test results with the job performance of those tested. Predictive validity is the type of validity most strongly advocated by the EEOC, because predictively valid tests are excellent indicators of future performance.

predictor, any test or other employment procedure used to assess applicant characteristics and from which predictions of future performance may be made.

preferential hiring, union security agreement under which an employer, in hiring new workers, will give preference to union members.

preferential shop, work unit where the employer must give union members preference in hiring.

pregnancy, the condition of being pregnant. According to Equal Employment Opportunity Commission guidelines,
   a written or unwritten employment policy or practice which excludes from

employment applicants or employees because of pregnancy is in prima facie violation of Title VII (of the Civil Rights Act of 1964).

See also the following entries:

GEDULDIG V. AIELLO
GENERAL ELECTRIC CO. V. GILBERT
MATERNITY LEAVE
NASHVILLE GAS CO. V. SATTY
NEWPORT NEWS SHIPBUILDING AND DRY DOCK CO V. EEOC.
SEX DISCRIMINATION
TITLE VII

Pregnancy Discrimination Act of 1978, an amendment to Title VII of the Civil Rights Act of 1964 which holds that discrimination on the basis of pregnancy, childbirth, or related medical conditions constitutes unlawful sex discrimination. The amendment was enacted in response to the Supreme Court's ruling in *General Electric Co.* v. *Gilbert,* 429 U.S. 125 (1976), that an employer's exclusion of pregnancy related disabilities from its comprehensive disability plan did not violate Title VII. The amendment asserts that:

1. A written or unwritten employment policy or practice which excludes from employment opportunities applicants or employees because of pregnancy, childbirth or related medical conditions is in prima facie violation of Title VII.

2. Disabilities caused or contributed to by pregnancy, childbirth, or related medical conditions, for all job-related purposes, shall be treated the same as disabilities caused or contributed to by other medical conditions, under any health or disability insurance or sick leave plan available in connection with employment. Written or unwritten employment policies and practices involving matters such as the commencement and duration of leave, the availability of extensions, the accrual of seniority and other benefits and privileges, reinstatement, and payment under any health or disability insurance or sick leave plan, formal or informal, shall be applied to disability due to pregnancy, childbirth, or related medical conditions on the same terms and conditions as they are applied to other disabilities. Health insurance benefits for abortion, except where the life of the mother would be endangered if the fetus were carried to term or where medical complications have arisen from an abortion, are not required to be paid by an employer; nothing herein, however, precludes an employer from providing abortion benefits or otherwise affects bargaining agreements in regard to abortion.

3. Where the termination of an employee who is temporarily disabled is caused by an employment policy under which insufficient or no leave is available, such a termination violates the Act if it has a disparate impact on employees of one sex and is not justified by business necessity.

premium pay, *see* WORK PREMIUM.

prepaid legal services, employee benefit that has the employee and/or employer contribute to a fund that pays for legal services in the same way that medical insurance pays for hospitalization. *See* Guvenc G. Alpander and Jordon I. Kobritz, "Prepaid Legal Services: An Emerging Fringe Benefit," *Industrial and Labor Relations Review* (January 1978).

pre-retirement counseling, efforts on the part of an organization to give to those of its employees who will be eligible to retire information about all of the options that retirement entails. *See* Don F. Pellicano, "Overview of Corporate Pre-Retirement Counseling," *Personnel Journal* (May 1977); William Arnone, "Preretirement Planning: An Employee Benefit That Has Come of Age," *Personnel Journal* (October 1982); Judith Raffel, "How to Select a Preretirement Consultant," *Personnel Journal* (November 1982).

See also RETIREMENT COUNSELING.

preselection, process by which a person

is informally selected for a position prior to the normal competitive selection procedures. The ensuing selection is necessarily a sham. *See* Shelby McIntyre, Dennis J. Moberg, and Barry Z. Posner, "Preferential Treatment in Preselection Decisions According to Sex and Race," *Academy of Management Journal* (December 1980).

presidency, American, the U.S. institution of presidency. The American president has been compared to an elective monarch, but there are few kings or queens today who exercise the same degree of authority as does the president of the United States. He simultaneously holds several titles that are often split among two or more incumbents in monarchies and parliamentary democracies.

He is traditionally accorded the unofficial designation "Chief of State," a position which most closely parallels that of a king or queen in a monarchy. As such, the president is recognized as the symbolic embodiment of the United States and its citizens, and thus is accorded the same honors due a reigning sovereign.

The president also performs many of the functions of a prime minister or premier in a parliamentary democracy. As chief executive, an office he holds under the Constitution, he presides over the cabinet and manages the executive branch. As political leader, he directs the operations of his party's national organization and serves as leader of its members in Congress. The Constitution also vests the President with power to make treaties, appoint ambassadors, cabinet officers, and judges of federal courts with the advice and consent of the Senate. He also holds the position of commander in chief of the Armed Forces.

Unlike a prime minister, the president is not a member of the legislature, nor is his tenure in office dependent on the approval of a majority of the legislators. Elected by the citizens, he serves a definite term from which he can be removed against his will only by the process of impeachment. At the same time, his tenure is limited to no more than two four-year

terms or ten years, which distinguishes him from hereditary monarchs, who reign for life.

Presidential Management Intern Program, program established August 25, 1977, by Executive Order 12008. The Presidential Management Intern Program provides a special means of entry into the federal service for recipients of graduate degrees in general management with a public sector focus. Each year, up to 250 interns receive two-year appointments to developmental positions throughout the executive branch of the federal government. These internships differ from most entry level positions in their emphasis on career development. Through rotational assignments, on-the-job training, seminars, discussion groups, career counseling, and other activities, interns are exposed to a variety of management areas and issues. At the successful completion of the two-year term, the interns are eligible for conversion to regular civil service appointments without further competition.

Presidential Management Intern Program
Office of Presidential Management Internships
1900 E Street, N.W.
Washington, D.C. 20415
See also INTERNSHIP.

presidential power, executive power. Article II of the Constitution vests the "executive power" in the president. There is dispute among scholars as to whether the executive power consists solely of those powers enumerated for the president or whether it includes also those powers that are implied in Article II. Most authorities lean toward the latter interpretation.

The actual powers expressly granted to the president are few in number. He is commander in chief of the Army and Navy and of the state militias when they are called into the service of the United States. He may require the written opinion of his executive officers and is empowered to grant reprieves and pardons except in the case of impeachment. He has power, by and with the advice and consent of the

Senate, to make treaties, provided that two thirds of the Senators present concur. He also nominates and, by and with the advice and consent of the Senate, appoints ambassadors, other public ministers and consuls, justices of the Supreme Court, and other federal officers whose appointments are established by law. The president has the power to fill all vacancies that occur during the recess of the Senate. Those commissions expire unless the Senate consents to them when it reconvenes. The Constitution also directs the president periodically to inform Congress on the state of the union and to recommend legislation that he considers necessary and expedient. He may, on extraordinary occasions, convene both houses of Congress, or either of them, and in case the two houses disagree as to the time of adjournment, he may adjourn them to such time as he considers proper. The president also receives ambassadors and other public ministers, must take care that the laws are faithfully executed, and commissions all officers of the United States. The president may veto acts of Congress. A two-thirds vote of those present and voting is required in both the House and Senate to override his veto.

In addition to these express powers, the chief executive derives certain implied authority from the Constitution. This implied authority, like the express powers, has been in the past and remains today a subject of dispute and debate. For example, the Constitution does not grant to the president express power to remove administrators from their offices, though until the 1930s there was general broad agreement that the president possessed this power. In the 1930s however, when President Roosevelt removed a member of the Federal Trade Commission for reasons of "policy," the Supreme Court ruled the removal invalid because Roosevelt did not follow the statutory grounds for removal. In a more recent incident, the removal of Archibald Cox by President Nixon during the Watergate investigations was ruled invalid by a U.S. district court.

Another implied constitutional power is the president's authority as commander in chief. Though the Congress has the explicit power to declare war, the president not only has the authority to protect the nation from sudden attack, but also to initiate military activities without a formal declaration of war. American presidents have used military force hundreds of times, but only on five occasions has Congress declared war: the War of 1812, the Mexican War, the Spanish-American War, and the two World Wars. On all other occasions it merely recognized, after executive initiatives, that war did in fact exist. In recent years, Congress has sought to define more clearly, most notably through the War Powers Resolution of 1973, the conditions under which presidents could take unilateral military action.

The classic scholarly analysis of presidential power is Richard E. Neustadt's *Presidential Power* (New York: Wiley, 1960), which asserts that a president's real powers are informal, that presidential power is essentially the "power to persuade." *Also see* Robert S. Hirschfield, ed., *The Power of the Presidency*, 2nd ed. (Chicago: Aldine, 1973); Erwin C. Hargrove, *The Power of the Modern Presidency* (New York: Knopf, 1974); Harry A. Bailey, Jr., ed., *Classics of the American Presidency* (Oak Park, Ill.: Moore Publishing Co., 1980).

See also the following entries:
> PECKING ORDER
> UNITED STATES V. CURTIS-WRIGHT EXPORT CORP.
> UNITED STATES V. NIXON
> YOUNGSTOWN SHEET AND TUBE V. SAWYER.

Presidential Studies Quarterly, scholarly journal that offers an historic, present, and projective view of the American presidency.
> *Presidential Studies Quarterly*
> 926 Fifth Avenue
> New York, NY 10021

presidential succession, the order of successors to the presidency. Under Article II, Section 1, the vice president exercises the power and duties of the president in the event of the death, resignation, or disability of the chief executive, or his removal from office. The 25th Amendment, ratified by the required three fourths of the states on February 10, 1967, provides: (1) that a vice president who succeeds a president acquires all powers of the office; (2) that when the vice-presidency is vacant, the president shall nominate a vice president who shall take office when confirmed by a majority vote of both houses of Congress; (3) that when the president informs Congress in writing that he is unable to discharge his duties and until he informs Congress in writing otherwise, the vice president shall be the acting president; (4) a procedure by which Congress would settle disputes between a vice president and a president as to the latter's ability to discharge the powers and duties of his office. A law of July 18, 1947 establishes the order of succession after the vice president as follows: the speaker of the House of Representatives, the president *pro tempore* of the Senate, and certain members of the cabinet, beginning with the Secretary of State.

Two vice presidents have been appointed under the provisions of this amendment: Gerald R. Ford, installed on December 8, 1973, and Nelson A. Rockefeller, installed on December 16, 1974.

On August 9, 1974, President Richard M. Nixon resigned and was succeeded by Gerald R. Ford. Mr. Nixon was the first president in history to resign from the presidency and Mr. Ford was the first to succeed to that office without being elected either president or vice president.

president's budget, see BUDGET, PRESIDENT'S.

President's Commission on Executive Interchange, federal government program established in 1969 by Executive Order 11451 which arranges for managers from the public and private sector to work in a different sector for a year or more. *See* Herman L. Weiss, "Why Business and Government Exchange Executives," *Harvard Business Review* (July–August 1974).

President's Commission on Executive Interchange
144 Jackson Place, N.W.
Washington, D.C. 20503
(202) 395-4616

President's Committee on Administrative Management, see BROWNLOW COMMITTEE.

pressure bargaining, see PRODUCTIVITY BARGAINING.

pressure group, also called INTEREST GROUP, less kind ways of referring to legitimate lobbying organizations.
See also INTEREST GROUP THEORY.

Presthus, Robert G. (1917-), founding editor of *Administrative Science Quarterly* from 1957 to 1964, Presthus is well known for his research on organizations, community power structures, and political elites. Major works include: *The Turkish Conseil d'Etat* (Ithaca, New York: Cornell University Press, 1958); *Men at the Top: A Study in Community Power* (New York: Oxford University Press, 1964); *The Organizational Society* (New York: Knopf, 1962; rev. ed., New York: St. Martin's Press, 1978); *Behavioral Approaches to Public Administration* (University, Ala.: University of Alabama Press, 1965); *Elites in the Policy Process* (New York: Cambridge University Press, 1974); *Elite Accommodation in Canadian Politics* (New York: Cambridge University Press, 1974); *Public Administration* (New York: Ronald Press, 1975).

pre-test, test given before training in order to measure existing levels of proficiency. Such levels should later be compared to end-test scores in order to evaluate the quality of the training program as well as the attainments of the individuals being trained. Also, a test designed for the purpose of validating new items and obtaining statistics for them before they are used in a final form.

prevailing wage, average pay for a specific job in a given geographical region.

Because wages in the private sector are determined to a large extent by market forces, the prevailing wage concept is used more extensively in the public sector where wage "comparability" is frequently mandated by law. For an analysis, *see* David Lewin, "The Prevailing-Wage Principle and Public Wage Decisions," *Public Personnel Management* (November-December 1974).

Prevailing Wage Law, *see* DAVIS-BACON ACT OF 1931.

preventive discipline, action premised on the notion that knowledge of disciplinary policies tends to inhibit infractions. Preventive discipline seeks to heighten employees' awareness of organizational rules and policies.

preventive mediation, the use of a mediator before an impasse has been reached. In order to avoid last minute crisis bargaining, the negotiating parties sometimes seek preventive mediation.

Price, Don K. (1910-), pioneering analyst of science policy and the first to assert that decisional authority was inexorably flowing from the executive suite to the technical offices. Consequently, a major distinction had to be made between the legal authority to make a policy decision and the technical ability to make the same decision. Major works include: *Government and Science* (New York: New York University Press, 1954); *The Scientific Estate* (Cambridge, Mass.: The Belknap Press of Harvard University Press, 1965).
See also ESTATES ANALYSIS.

price support, *see* PARITY, FARM.

primary boycott, concerted effort by a union to withdraw and to induce others to withdraw from economic relationships with an offending employer.

prime rate, the rate of interest charged by commercial banks for short-term loans to their most creditworthy customers.

principles of classification, *see* POSITION CLASSIFICATION PRINCIPLES.

principles of management, fundamental truths or working hypotheses that serve as guidelines to management thinking and action. The first complete statement of the principles of management was produced by Henri Fayol in 1916. *See* his *General and Industrial Management,* trans. by Constance Storrs (London: Pitman, 1949). For a modern treatment, *see* Geroge R. Terry and Stephan G. Franklin, *Principles of Management,* 8th ed. (Homewood, Ill.: Richard D. Irwin, 1982).
  See also the following entries:
    POSDCORB
    PROVERBS OF ADMINISTRATION
    SPAN OF CONTROL

prismatic society, *see* RIGGS, FRED W.

Prisoner Rehabilitation Act of 1965, federal statute that permits selected federal prisoners to work in the community while still in an inmate status.

Privacy Act of 1974, (Public Law 93-579), federal statute that reasserts the fundamental right to privacy as derived from the Constitution of the United States and provides a series of basic safeguards for the individual to prevent the misuse of personal information by the federal government.
  The act provides for making known to the public the existence and characteristics of all personal information systems kept by every federal agency. It permits an individual to have access to records containing personal information on that individual and allows the individual to control the transfer of that information to other federal agencies for nonroutine uses. The act also requires all federal agencies to keep accurate accountings of transfers of personal records to other agencies and outsiders, and to make the accountings available to the individual. It further provides for civil remedies for the individual whose records are kept or used in contravention of the requirements of the act.

Virtually all agencies of the federal government have issued regulations implementing the Privacy Act. These regulations generally inform the public how to determine if a system of records contains information on themselves, how to gain access to such records, how to request amendment of such records, and the method of internal appeal of an adverse agency determination on such a request. The Office of the Federal Register publishes a compilation, which includes descriptions of all the systems of records maintained by each agency of the federal government, the categories of individuals about whom each record system is maintained, and the agency rules and procedures whereby an individual may obtain further information. The most recent compilation, entitled Privacy Act Issuances, 1976 Compilation, is divided into five volumes, and is available at many public libraries or from the Superintendent of Documents. For an examination of the adequacy of privacy legislation, see John Raliya, "Privacy Protection and Personnel Administration: Are New Laws Needed?" *The Personnel Administrator* (April 1979). *Also see Freedom of Information Guide: Citizen's Guide to the Use of the Freedom of Information And Privacy Acts* (Washington, D.C.: Want Publishing Co., 1982).

See also FREEDOM OF INFORMATION ACT.

private law, statute passed to affect only one person or group, in contrast to a public law.

private sector organization, all of those industries or activities considered to be within the domain of free enterprise. See Michael A. Murray, "Comparing Public and Private Management: An Exploratory Essay," *Public Administration Review* (July-August 1975); Kenneth A. Gold, "Managing for Success: A Comparison of the Private and Public Sectors," *Public Administration Review* (November-December 1982).

See also THIRD SECTOR.

privatization, the process of returning to the private sector property (such as public lands) or functions previously owned or performed by government. *See* David Heald, "Will the Privatization of Public Enterprises Solve the Problem of Control?" *Public Administration* (Spring 1985).

probability, chance of an occurrence — the likelihood that an event will occur, expressed as a number from 0 to 1.

probationary employee, also PROBATIONARY PERIOD, term for a new employee who has not yet satisfactorily completed a period of on-the-job trial — the *probationary period.* During this time the employee has no seniority rights and may be discharged without cause, so long as such a discharge does not violate laws concerning union membership and equal employment opportunity.

See also SAMPSON V. MURRAY.

probationary rate, *see* ENTRANCE RATE.

pro bono publico, Latin phrase meaning "for the public good." When abbreviated to *pro bono,* it usually stands for work done by lawyers without pay for some charitable or public purpose.

procedural rights, various protections that all citizens have against arbitrary actions by public officials.

process consultation (P-C), according to Edgar H. Schein's *Process Consultation: Its Role in Organization Development* (Reading, Mass.: Addison-Wesley Publishing Co., 1969), "a set of activities on the part of the consultant which help the client to perceive, understand, and act upon process events which occur in the client's environment."

According to Schein, P-C makes the following seven assumptions:

1. Managers often do not know what is wrong and need special help in diagnosing what their problems actually are.
2. Managers often do not know what kinds of help consultants can give to them; they need to be helped to know what kind of help to seek.

427

3. Most managers have a constructive intent to improve things but need help in identifying what to improve and how to improve it.
4. Most organizations can be more effective if they learn to diagnose their own strengths and weaknesses. No organizational form is perfect; hence every form of organization will have some weaknesses for which compensatory mechanisms need to be found.
5. A consultant could probably not, without exhaustive and time-consuming study, learn enough about the culture of the organization to suggest reliable new courses of action. Therefore, he must work jointly with members of the organization who do know the culture intimately from having lived within it.
6. The client must learn to see the problem for himself, to share in the diagnosis, and to be actively involved in generating a remedy. One of the process consultant's roles is to provide new and challenging alternatives for the client to consider. Decisionmaking about these alternatives must, however, remain in the hands of the client.
7. It is of prime importance that the process consultant be expert in how to diagnose and how to establish effective helping relationships with clients. Effective P-C involves the passing on of both these skills.

Also see Robert E. Kaplan, "The Conspicuous Absence of Evidence that Process Consultation Enhances Task Performance," *Journal of Applied Behavioral Science* (July-August-September 1979).

process evaluation, also IMPACT EVALUATION, according to David Nachmias, *Public Policy Evaluation: Approaches and Methods* (New York: St Martin's Press, 1979), activity "concerned with the extent to which a particular policy or program is implemented according to its stated guidelines," while *impact evaluation* "is concerned with examining the extent to

which a policy causes a change in the intended direction."

Producer Prices and Price Indexes, U.S. Bureau of Labor Statistics' comprehensive monthly report on price movements of both farm and industrial commodities, by industry and stage of processing.

Producer Prices and Price Indexes
Superintendent of Documents
Government Printing Office
Washington, D.C. 20402

production bonus, regularly scheduled additional payments to workers for exceeding production quotas.

production workers, those employees directly concerned with the manufacturing or operational processes of an organization, as opposed to supervisory and clerical employees.

productivity, measured relationship between the quantity (and quality) of results produced and the quantity of resources required for production. Productivity is, in essence, a measure of the work efficiency of an individual, a work unit, or a whole organization.

Productivity can be measured in two ways. One way relates the output of an enterprise, industry, or economic sector to a single input such as labor or capital. The other relates output to a composite of inputs, combined so as to account for their relative importance. The choice of a particular productivity measure depends on the purpose for which it is to be used.

The most generally useful measure of productivity relates output to the input of labor time—output per hour, or its reciprocal, unit labor requirements. This kind of measure is used widely because labor productivity is relevant to most economic analyses, and because labor is the most easily measured input. Relating output to labor input provides a tool not only for analyzing productivity, but also for examining labor costs, real income, and employment trends.

Labor productivity can be measured readily at several levels of aggregation: the business economy, its component sectors, industries, or plants. Depending on the components of the measure used and the context, labor productivity will be called output per hour of all persons engaged in the productive process, output per employee hour, or just output per hour.

The use of labor productivity indexes does not imply that labor is solely or primarily responsible for productivity growth. In a technologically advanced society, labor effort is only one of many sources of productivity improvement. Trends in output per hour also reflect technological innovation, changes in capital stock and capacity utilization, scale of production, materials flow, management skills, and other factors whose contribution often cannot be measured.

The output side of the output per hour ratio refers to the finished product or the amount of real value added in various enterprises, industries, sectors, or the economy as a whole. Few plants or industries produce a single homogeneous commodity that can be measured by simply counting the number of units produced. Consequently, for the purpose of measurement, the various units of a plant's or an industry's output are combined on some common basis—either their unit labor requirements in a base period or their dollar value. When information on the units produced is not available, as is often the case, output must be expressed in terms of the dollar value of production, adjusted for price changes.

See Solomon Fabricant, *A Primer on Productivity* (New York: Random House, 1969); Marc Holzer, ed., *Productivity in Public Organizations* (Port Washington, N.Y.: Kennikat Press, 1976); Allan S. Udler, "Productivity Measurement of Administrative Services," *Personnel Journal* (December 1978); Walter L. Balk, Symposium Editor, "Productivity in Government," *Public Administration Review* (January-February 1978); Anna C. Goldoff with David C. Tatage, "Joint Productivity Committees: Lessons of Recent Initiatives," *Public Administration Review* (March-April 1978); John W. Kendrick, *Understanding Productivity: An Intro-*

duction to the Dynamics of Productivity Change (Baltimore: Johns Hopkins Press, 1978); Selma J. Mushin and Frank H. Sandifer, *Personnel Management and Productivity in City Government* (Lexington, Mass.: Lexington Books, 1979); George J. Washnis, ed., *Productivity Handbook for State and Local Government* (New York: John Wiley, 1980); John Greiner et al., *Productivity and Motivation: A Review of State and Local Government Initiatives* (Washington, D.C.: The Urban Institute Press, 1981); Jerome A. Mark, "Measuring Productivity in Service Industries," *Monthly Labor Review* (June 1982); Arnold S. Judson, "The Awkward Truth About Productivity," *Harvard Business Review* (September-October 1982); Donald M. Fisk, "Measuring Productivity in State and Local Government," *Monthly Labor Review* (June 1984).

See also the following entries:

NATIONAL ASSOCIATION OF SUGGESTION SYSTEMS

NATIONAL CENTER FOR PRODUCTIVITY AND QUALITY OF WORKING LIFE

SUGGESTION SYSTEM

TURKEY FARM

productivity bargaining, collective bargaining that seeks increases in productivity in exchange for increases in wages and benefits. There are two basic approaches to productivity bargaining—integrative bargaining and pressure bargaining. The latter is the stuff of confrontation and is best illustrated by the adversary model of labor relations—the most commonly adopted model in the United States. Its dysfunctional consequences—strikes and hostility—are well known. The other approach—integrative bargaining—is, in essence, participative management. It is premised upon the notions that a decrease in hostility is mutually advantageous and that management does not have a natural monopoly on brains. The crucial aspect of integrative bargaining is its joint procedures in defining problems, searching for alternatives, and selecting solutions.

The two productivity bargaining strategies are not mutually exclusive. Each side develops what it believes to be the best mix of both approaches for any given situation. While the end of labor-management conflict is far from at hand, mixed strategies are a step in the right direction. Since financial resources are finite and imagination is frequently infinite, a mixed approach to productivity bargaining holds out more hope for radical changes in job design and organization environment than for radical changes in salaries.

The best survey of productivity bargaining tactics in the private sector is R. B. McKersie and L. C. Hunter, *Pay, Productivity and Collective Bargaining* (London: The Macmillan Press, 1973). For a public sector analysis, *see* Raymond D. Horton, "Productivity and Productivity Bargaining in Government: A Critical Analysis," *Public Administration Review* (July–August 1976).

The Little Red Hen: A Productivity Fable

Once upon a time there was a little red hen who scratched about the barnyard until she uncovered some grains of wheat. She turned to other workers on the farm and said: "If we plant this wheat, we'll have bread to eat. Who will help me plant it?"

"We never did that before," said the horse, who was the supervisor.

"I'm too busy," said the duck.

"I'd need complete training," said the pig.

"It's not in my job description," said the goose.

"Well, I'll do it myself," said the little red hen. And she did. The wheat grew tall and ripened into grain. "Who will help me reap the wheat?" asked the little red hen.

"Let's check the regulations first," said the horse.

"I'd lose my seniority," said the duck.

"I'm on my lunch break," said the goose.

"Out of my classification," said the pig.

"Then I will," said the little red hen, and she did.

At last it came time to bake the bread. "Who will help me bake the bread?" asked the little red hen.

"That would be overtime for me," said the horse.

"I've got to run some errands," said the duck.

"I've never learned how," said the pig.

"If I'm to be the only helper, that's unfair," said the goose.

"Then I will," said the little red hen.

She baked five loaves and was ready to turn them in to the farmer when the other workers stepped up. They wanted to be sure the farmer knew it was a group project.

"It needs to be cleared by someone else," said the horse.

"I'm calling the shop steward," said the duck.

"I demand equal rights," yelled the goose.

"We'd better file a copy," said the pig.

But the little red hen turned in the loaves by herself. When it came time for the farmer to reward the effort, he gave one loaf to each worker.

"But I earned all the bread myself!" said the little red hen.

"I know," said the farmer, "but it takes too much paperwork to justify giving you all the bread. It's much easier to distribute it equally, and that way the others won't complain."

So the little red hen shared the bread, but her co-workers and the farmer wondered why she never baked any more.

SOURCE: Federal News Clip Sheet *(June 1979).*

---

productivity measurement, assessment of productivity. Measuring the productivity of any jurisdiction, organization, program, or individual is particularly problematic in the public sector because of the problem of defining outputs and of quantifying measures of efficiency, effectiveness, and impact.

Organizations that provide public services often have multiple and sometimes intangible outputs. In evaluating efficiency, selecting from among the many possible input/output ratios is troublesome. A considerable danger exists in selecting only certain input and output variables because a single efficiency measure may be, in truth, a meaningless or oversimplified measure of performance.

The productivity measurement issue is further complicated by the fact that different efficiency and effectiveness measures must be selected depending upon certain organizational variables: highly routine work vs. non-routine work; high or low degrees of employee discretion; outputs that are standard or novel; or a work process which is simple vs. complex. Another way of stating this problem is that from the variety of available productivity measures, those selected must differentiate between intermediate outputs (outputs used by other members of the organization) and final outputs (those absorbed by the outside environment) and between staff and line functions (some individuals/units perform support functions whose impact can be assessed only in terms of increased performance of line departments). The question remains: how can these varied contributions be isolated and measured? Productivity measurement is beset by many obstacles, not the least of which is the insecurity felt by managers attempting to undertake productivity assessments.

See Elinor Ostrom, "The Need for Multiple Indicators in Measuring the Output of Public Agencies," Policy Studies Journal (Winter 1973); Walter L. Balk, "Technological Trends in Productivity Measurement," Public Personnel Management (March-April 1975); Michael E. O'Neill and Ernest A. Unwin, "Productivity Measurement: A Challenge for Implementation," Public Productivity Review (Fall 1977); Harry P. Hatry, "The Status of Productivity Measurement in the Public Service," Public Administration Review (January-February 1978); Lawrence S. Aft, Productivity Measurement and Improvement (Reston, Va.: Reston/Prentice-Hall, 1983).

profession, occupation requiring specialized knowledge that can only be gained after intensive preparation. Professional occupations tend to possess three features: (1) a body of erudite knowledge which is applied to the service of society; (2) a standard of success measured by accomplishments in serving the needs of society rather than purely serving personal gain; and (3) a system of control over the professional practice which regulates the education of its new members and maintains both a code of ethics and appropriate sanctions. The primary characteristic that differentiates it from a vocation is its

theoretical commitment to rendering a public service. See Kenneth S. Lynn, ed., The Professions in America (Boston: Houghton Mifflin, 1965); Edgar H. Schein, Professional Education (New York: McGraw-Hill, 1972); Judith V. May, Professionals and Clients: A Constitutional Struggle (Beverly Hills, Calif.: Sage Publications, 1976). For accounts of professions in public administration, see Frederick C. Mosher and Richard Stillman, Jr., Symposium Editors, "The Professions in Government," Public Administration Review (November-December 1977); Frederick C. Mosher and Richard Stillman II, Symposium Editors, "The Professions in Government II," Public Administration Review (March-April 1978); Richard Schott, "Public Administration as a Profession: Problems and Prospects," Public Administration Review (May-June 1976); Marina Angel, "White-Collar and Professional Unionization," Labor Law Journal (February 1982).

Professional and Administrative Careers Examination (PACE), formerly the principal means of entry into the federal government for liberal arts graduates, although it was open to all majors and applicants with equivalent experience. Each year, thousands of hires were made through this route for more than one hundred different positions and career fields. PACE replaced the Federal Service Entrance Examination (FSEE) in 1975, but suffered a similar fate in 1982. It was discontinued in response to a legal challenge to its validity as a selection tool by the NAACP.

See also FEDERAL SERVICE ENTRANCE EXAMINATION.

professionalism, conduct of one's self in a manner that characterizes a particular occupation. For example, a professional fireman is a full-time fireman who is thoroughly skilled in his trade. Nevertheless, a fireman is not a "professional" in the traditional sense. See Kathryn M. Bartol, "Professionalism as a Predictor of Organizational Commitment, Role Stress, and Turnover: A Multidimensional Approach," *Academy of Management Journal* (December 1979); Philip J. Cooper, "Defining PA Professionalism," *The Bureaucrat* (Spring 1982); Cheryl Haigley, "Professionalism in Personnel," *Personnel Administrator* (June 1984); William I. Sauser, Jr., and Elton C. Smith, "Toward An Empirical Definition of Public Sector Professionalism," *Review of Public Personnel Administration* (Spring 1984).

professionalization, process by which occupations acquire professional status. For example, U.S. police departments are becoming more professional as increasing numbers of their members gain advanced degrees and take their ethical responsibilities more seriously. This process of professionalization will be complete only when the overwhelming majority of police officers meet the high standards of the present minority. *See* M. S. Larson, *The Rise of Professionalism: A Sociological Analysis* (Berkeley, Calif.: University of California Press, 1977); Robert T. Golembiewski, "Professionalization, Performance and Protectionism," *Public Productivity Review* (September 1983).

proficiency test, device to measure the skill or knowledge that a person has acquired in an occupation.

pro forma, Latin phrase meaning "as a matter of form" or "a mere formality."

program, major organizational endeavor, mission oriented, that fulfills statutory or executive requirements and is defined in terms of the principal actions required to achieve a significant objective. A program is an organized set of activities designed to produce a particular result or set of results that will have a certain impact upon a problem.

program, also PROGRAMMER and PROGRAMMING, in computer terminology, a set of instructions telling the computer what to do. A *programmer* is a person who writes a computer program. As the programmer does his or her job, he or she can be said to be *programming* the computer.

program authorization, statutory basis of an agency function.

program budgeting, *see* BUDGETING, PERFORMANCE.

program evaluation, systematic examination of any activity or group of activities undertaken by government to make a determination about their impact or effects, both short and long range. A program evaluation should be distinguished from a management evaluation or an organization evaluation because these are limited to concentrating on a program's internal administrative procedures. While program evaluations will use information such as workload measures, staffing levels, or operational procedural data, the main thrust is necessarily on overall program objectives and impact.

The concepts of efficiency and effectiveness are the standard criteria against which programs are pitted by evaluation. In addition, these concepts helped to forge a workable distinction between audits and evaluations. Audits, primarily financial accounting audits, are geared to control—to insure that every dime of public funds is accounted for and that every regulation is complied with. This law enforcement style of management is being increasingly displaced by program evaluation—a far more comprehensive management tool. We still expect programs to be administered efficiently, just as we expect complete fiscal accountability for funds and receipts. But efficiency isn't enough. A work unit could be terribly efficient while working toward the wrong goals. Because of this, evaluations, if they are themselves to be effective, must also deal with the questions of effectiveness and relevance. It is not unreasonable to demand that programs have an effect on problems, and the right problems at that. Simply put, the most basic objective of a program evaluation is to assay the impact of a program on its target problem.

Program evaluation is not the sole province of any branch of government. Evaluations are even being done by the courts in response to petitions by client groups. Of course, the press conducts evaluations with every exposé of a mismanaged agency. However, accurate or not, journalistic evaluations often tend to be too superficial to serve as instruments of reform, although they do serve to provide impetus for full scale evaluation efforts by objective outsiders.

At any given time an agency may subject its Program X to the scrutiny of an evaluation. This is no way inhibits the budget office of the jurisdiction's chief executive from deciding that it will conduct a separate evaluation of Program X. Meanwhile, an appropriations committee of the jurisdiction's legislature may feel the need for an "unbiased" evaluation of that same Program X. None of this earlier activity would automatically constrain the U.S. General Accounting Office or a similar audit commission of a state legislature from also choosing to evaluate Program X at the same time.

Each of these evaluators necessarily represents different rationales that will tend to permeate the perspective of the evaluating body. Executive branch internal evaluation, essentially a "self" evaluation, is normally incorporated into the management process. Agencies need to be sure that they are accomplishing their objectives, that they are making progress. Of course, this "thirst" for evaluation may be induced from various motives. The noblest is the good management practice of assessing progress in order to induce corrective action. Many a sophisticated management information system has been designed to focus management's attention on problem areas so that remedial action can be taken. Equally necessary, though considerably less noble, are program evaluations undertaken for political considerations. A common gambit here is the "defensive program evaluation" whereby possibly controversial programs are evaluated to "in effect" create "good" report cards to show legislative committees, or at least to provide some counterarguments to evaluations by others that portend less favorable results. The imprecision inherent in the "state of the art" of program evaluation

both tolerates such tactics and constitutes a great temptation.

See Marcia Guttentag and Elmer L. Struening, eds., *Handbook of Evaluation Research* (Beverly Hills: Sage Publications 1975); Harry Hatry et al., *Program Analysis for State and Local Governments* (Washington, D.C.: The Urban Institute, 1976); Harry Hatry et al., *Practical Program Evaluation for State and Local Government Officials* (Washington, D.C.: The Urban Institute, 1973); Jerome T. Murphy, *Getting the Facts: A Fieldwork Guide for Evaluators & Policy Analysts* (Santa Monica, Calif.: Goodyear Publishing Co., 1980); A. C. Hyde and J. M. Shafritz, eds., *Program Evaluation in the Public Sector* (New York: Praeger Publishers, 1979); Carol H. Weiss, *Evaluation Research* (Englewood Cliffs, N.J.: Prentice-Hall, 1972); Alice Rivlin, *Systematic Thinking for Social Action* (Washington, D.C.: The Brookings Institution, 1971); Aaron Wildavsky, "The Self-Evaluating Organization," *Public Administration Review* (September–October 1972); Theodore H. Poister, James C. McDavid, and Anne H. Magoun, *Applied Program Evaluation in Local Government* (Lexington, Mass.: Lexington Books, 1979); Judith R. Brown, "Legislative Program Evaluation: Defining a Legislative Service and a Profession," *Public Administration Review* (May–June 1984); Eleanor Chelimsky, ed., *Program Evaluation: Patterns and Directions* (Washington, D.C.: American Society for Public Administration, 1984).

See also the following entries:
AUDIT
EVALUATION
PERSONNEL MANAGEMENT EVALUATION
SUNSET LAWS
TRAINING EVALUATION

Program Evaluation and Review Technique, see PERT.

program management, see PROJECT MANAGEMENT.

programmed learning, also called PROGRAMMED INSTRUCTION, technique that has learning materials presented in a predetermined order, with provisions that permit the learner to proceed at his/her own pace and gain immediate feedback on his/her answers. Programmed learning usually requires the use of a teaching machine (computer) or programmed text. The rationale for and methodology of programmed learning is generally credited to B. F. Skinner. *See* J. G. Holland and B. F. Skinner, *The Analysis of Behavior: A Program for Self-Instruction* (New York: McGraw-Hill, 1961). For a report of the efficacy of programmed instruction, *see* J. W. Buckley, "Programmed Instruction in Industry," *California Management Review* (Winter 1967). *Also see* Angus Reynolds, "An Introduction to Computer-Based Learning." *Training and Development Journal* (May 1983).

program results audits, audits which determine (1) whether the desired results or benefits established by the legislature or other authorizing body are being achieved and (2) whether the agency has considered alternatives that might yield desired results at a lower cost.

progression line charts, lists of job titles in a broad job family, generally starting with the less difficult, lower paying jobs and progressing to the more difficult, higher paying jobs.

progression sequences, a hierarchy of job titles through which an employee may progress in following a career path or ladder. Such sequences generally begin with lower paying job titles and ascend through intermediate job titles to higher paying job titles.

progressive discipline, concept predicated on the notion that employees are both aware of the behavior expected of them and subject to disciplinary action to the extent that they violate the norms of the organization. A policy of progressive discipline would then invoke penalties appropriate to the specific infraction and its circumstances.

progressive movement, also called REFORM MOVEMENT, movement that centered on reforming political institutions during the rapid urbanization and industrialization of the United States in the period from the 1870s to World War I. It sought to improve governing institutions by bringing science to bear on public problems. It was a disparate movement, with each reform group targeting a level of government, a particular policy, etc. At the national level it achieved civil service reform; at the local level it spawned the commission and council/manager forms of government. For histories, *see* Frank M. Stewart, *A Half Century of Municipal Reform* (Berkeley, Calif.: University of California Press, 1950); Richard Hofstadter, *The Age of Reform* (New York: Knopf, 1955); Robert H. Wiebe, *Businessmen and Reform: A Study of The Progressive Movement* (Cambridge, Mass.: Harvard University Press, 1962); Richard Hofstadter, *The Progressive Movement, 1900-1915* (Englewood Cliffs, N.J.: Prentice-Hall, 1963); Samuel P. Hays, "The Politics of Reform in Municipal Government in the Progressive Era," *Pacific Northwest Quarterly* (October 1964); Robert L. Lineberry and Edmund P. Fowler, "Reformism and Public Policy in American Cities," *American Political Science Review* (September 1967); Zane I. Miller, *Boss Cox's Cincinnati: Urban Politics in the Progressive Era* (New York: Oxford University Press, 1968); Otis A. Pease, "Urban Reformers in the Progressive Era: A Reassessment," *Pacific Northwest Quarterly* (April 1971); John M. Dobson, *Politics in the Gilded Age: A New Perspective on Reform* (New York: Praeger, 1972); John D. Buenker, *Urban Liberalism and Progressive Reform* (New York: Scribner's, 1973); Richard M. Bernard and Bradley R. Rice, "Political Environment and the Adoption of Progressive Municipal Reform," *Journal of Urban History* (February 1975); Martin J. Schiesl, *The Politics of Municipal Reform: Municipal Administration and Reform in America 1880-1920* (Berkeley: University of California Press, 1977); Robert M. Crunden, *Ministers of Reform: The Progressives' Achievement in American Civilization, 1889-1920* (New York: Basic

Books, 1982); Laurence J. O'Toole, Jr., "American Public Administration and the Idea of Reform," *Administration & Society* (August 1984).

See also CIVIL SERVICE REFORM.

progressive tax, see TAX EQUITY.

progress testing, see PHASED TESTING.

prohibited personnel practices, see MERIT SYSTEM PRINCIPLES.

project categorical grant, see GRANT.

projective test, also called PROJECTIVE TECHNIQUE, any method which seeks to discover an individual's attitudes, motivations, and characteristic traits through responses to unstructured stimuli such as ambiguous pictures or inkblots. See D. L. Grant, W. Katkovsky, and D. W. Bray, "Contributions of Projective Techniques to Assessment of Management Potential," *Journal of Applied Psychology* (June 1967).

See also RORSCHACH TEST and THEMATIC APPERCEPTION TEST.

project management, also called PROGRAM MANAGEMENT, management of an organizational unit created to achieve a specific goal. While a project may last from a few months to a few years, it has no further future. Indeed, a primary measure of its success is its dissolution. The project staff necessarily consists of a mix of skills from the larger organization. The success of project management is most dependent upon the unambiguous nature of the project's goal and the larger organization's willingness to delegate sufficient authority and resources to the project manager. Project or program management is an integral part of matrix organizations. See Charles C. Martin, *Project Management: How to Make it Work* (New York: AMACOM, 1976); Arthur G. Butler, "Project Management: A Study in Organizational Conflict," *Academy of Management Journal* (March 1973); Clifford F. Gray, *Essentials of Project Management* (Princeton, N.J.: Petrocelli, 1981); Harold Kerzner, *Project*

Management for Executives (New York: Van Nostrand Reinhold, 1982); David I. Cleland, *Systems Analysis and Project Management,* 3rd ed. (New York: McGraw-Hill, 1983). For a comparative focus, see Per Jonason, "Project Management, Swedish Style," *Harvard Business Review* (November-December 1971).

See also MATRIX ORGANIZATION and TASK FORCE.

project manager, manager whose task is to achieve a temporary organizational goal using as his/her primary tool the talents of diverse specialists from the larger organization. The authority and responsibility of a project manager varies enormously with differing projects and organizations. See Paul O. Gaddis, "The Project Manager," *Harvard Business Review* (June 1959).

proletariat, in ancient Rome, those members of society who were so poor that they could contribute nothing to the state but their offspring. In the 19th century, Karl Marx used it to refer to the working class in general. Because of the word's political taint, it should not be used to refer simply to workers, but only to the "oppressed" workers.

promotion, process of advancing employees to positions that usually carry more responsibility and greater salaries. For analyses of what it takes to get promoted, see Sexton Adams and Don Fyffe, *The Corporate Promotables* (Houston: Gulf Publishing Co., 1969); Vinay Kothari, "Promotional Criteria—Three Views," *Personnel Journal* (August 1976). For what to do when you can't get promoted, see Edward Roseman, *Confronting Unpromotability: How To Manage A Stalled Career* (New York: AMACOM, 1977). *Also see* Alfred W. Swinyard and Floyd A. Bond, "Who Gets Promoted?" *Harvard Business Review* (September-October 1980).

See also the following entries:
CAREER PROMOTION
COMPETITIVE PROMOTION
HORIZONTAL PROMOTION

MERIT PROMOTION

promotion certificate, list of best qualified candidates to be considered to fill a position under competitive promotion procedures.

promotion plan, a federal government plan that covers a group of positions, such as all regional positions below GS-12, or all regional supervisory positions, or all central office positions at GS-5 and below. The plan describes the methods to be followed in locating, evaluating, and selecting employees for promotion. It also explains what records will be kept, how information will be given to employees about the promotion program, etc.

property tax, see TAX, REAL-PROPERTY and TAXATION.

proportional tax, see TAX EQUITY.

Proposition 13, also called the JARVIS-GANN INITIATIVE, state constitutional amendment approved by California voters in 1978 that rolled back and set ceilings on property taxes. Proposition 13 is an important landmark in a national tax-relief movement. See U.S. Congress, Congressional Budget Office, *Proposition 13: Its Impact on the Nation's Economy, Federal Revenues and Federal Expenditures* (Washington, D.C.: U.S. Government Printing Office, July 1978); "Proposition 13: The Taxpayers' Hidden Agenda," *Public Management* (August 1978); Jeffrey I. Chapman, *Proposition 13 and Land Use: A Case Study of Fiscal Limits in California* (Lexington, Mass.: Lexington Books, 1980); Roger L. Kemp, *Coping with Proposition 13* (Lexington, Mass.: Lexington Books, 1980); Robert Kuttner, *Revolt of the Haves: Tax Rebellions and Hard Times* (New York: Simon & Schuster, 1980); Virginia Ermer-Bott and Alan Saltzstein, "The Impact of Proposition 13 on Labor-Management Relations in California," *Public Personnel Management* (Summer 1981); David B. Magleby, *Direct Legislation: Voting on Ballot Propositions in the United States* (Baltimore,

Md.: Johns Hopkins U Press, 1984); Terry Schwadron, ed., *California and the American Tax Revolt: Proposition 13 Five Years Later* (Berkeley, Calif.: University of California Press, 1984).
    See also AGE OF SCARCITY.

Proposition 2½, a 1980 tax limitation measure approved by the voters of Massachusetts which requires local governments to lower property taxes by 15 percent a year until they reach 2½ percent of fair market value.

proprietary receipts from the public, see OFFSETTING RECEIPTS.

prosecutor, attorney employed by a government agency or subunit whose official duty is to initiate and maintain criminal proceedings on behalf of the government against persons accused of committing criminal offenses.

prosecutorial agency, a federal, state, or local criminal justice agency of which the principal function is the prosecution of alleged offenders.

protected classes/groups, see AFFIRMATIVE ACTION GROUPS.

protectionism, policy of high tariffs or low import quotas in order to protect domestic industries.

Protestant ethic, also called WORK ETHIC, Max Weber's term from his 1904-05 book, *The Protestant Ethic and the Spirit of Capitalism,* which refers to his theory that modern capitalism has its origins in the Calvinistic concern for moral obligation and economic success. While some dispute Weber's historical analysis, any society whose members have a strong drive for work and the accumulation of wealth is colloquially said to have a "Protestant" or work ethic. For a history of the U.S. work ethic, see Daniel T. Rodgers, *The Work Ethic in Industrial America: 1850-1920* (Chicago: University of Chicago Press, 1978). For present-day analyses, see M. Scott Myers and Susan

S. Myers, "Toward Understanding the Changing Work Ethic," *California Management Review* (Spring 1974); Roger E. Calhoun, "The New Work Ethic," *Training and Development Journal* (May 1980); Ann Howard and James A. Wilson, "Leadership in a Declining Work Ethic," *California Management Review* (Summer 1982); Perry Pascarella, *The New Achievers: Creating a Modern Work Ethic* (New York: The Free Press, 1984).

proverbs of administration, a significant landmark in the history of administrative theory. Herbert A. Simon's refutation of the principles approach that dominated administrative thinking until after World War II asserted, in "The Proverbs of Administration," *Public Administration Review* (Winter 1946), that the principles of administration, like proverbs, almost always occur in mutually contradictory pairs:

> Most of the propositions that make up the body of administrative theory today share, unfortunately, this defect of proverbs. For almost every principle one can find an equally plausible and acceptable contradictory principle. Although the two principles of the pair will lead to exactly opposite organizational recommendations, there is nothing in the theory to indicate which is the proper one to apply.

provisional appointment, usually, government employment without competitive examination because there is no appropriate eligible list available. Most jurisdictions have a three-, six-, or twelve-month limitation on provisional appointments.

pseudo-effectiveness, according to Chris Argyris, in *Integrating the Individual and the Organization* (New York: John Wiley & Sons, 1964), "a state in which no discomfort is reported but [in] which, upon diagnosis, ineffectiveness is found." Since the underlying ineffectiveness is not evident, the true costs of continuing in such a state remain hidden by compensatory

mechanisms. Eventually, such compensatory mechanisms will require so much energy that they will influence the organization negatively and call attention to the underlying problem.

psychiatry, industrial/occupational, *see* OCCUPATIONAL PSYCHIATRY.

psychic income, *see* INTRINSIC REWARD.

psychobabble, indiscriminate use of psychological concepts and terms as an affected style of speech. R. D. Rosen, in *Psychobabble* (New York: Atheneum, 1977), says that psychobabblers

> free-float in an all-purpose linguistic atmosphere, a set of repetitive verbal formalities that kills off the very spontaneity, candor, and understanding it pretends to promote. It's an idiom that reduces psychological insight to a collection of standardized observations, that provides a frozen lexicon to deal with an infinite variety of problems. *Uptight*, for instance, is a word used to describe an individual experiencing anything from mild uneasiness to a clinical depression. . . . One is no longer fearful; one is *paranoid*. . . . Increasingly, people describe their moody acquaintances as *manic-depressives*, and almost anyone you don't like is *psychotic* or at the very least *schizzed-out*.

psychological contract, implicit agreement between worker and employer. Edgar H. Schein, in his *Organizational Psychology*, 2nd ed. (Englewood Cliffs, N.J.: Prentice-Hall, 1970) asserts that the notion of a psychological contract implies that the individual has a variety of expectations of the organization and that the organization has a variety of expectations of him. These expectations not only cover how much work is to be performed for how much pay, but also involve the whole pattern of rights, privileges, and obligations between worker and organization. For example, the worker may expect the company not to fire him after he has worked there for a certain number of years and the company may expect that the worker will not run down the company's public image or give away company secrets to competitors. Expectations such as these are not written into any formal agreement between employee and organization, yet they operate powerfully as determinants of behavior.

For a discussion of this concept in the context of employment, *see* Emanuel C. Salemi and John B. Monohan, "The Psychological Contract of Employment: Do Recruiters and Students Agree?" *Personnel Journal* (December 1970); Michael H. Dunahee and Lawrence A. Wangler, "The Psychological Contract: A Conceptual Structure for Management/Employee Relations," *Personnel Journal* (July 1974).

See also EXPECTANCY THEORY.

Psychological Review, bimonthly that publishes articles making theoretical contributions to any area of scientific psychology. Preference is given to papers that advance theory rather than review it.

Psychological Review
American Psychological Association, Inc.
1200 Seventeenth Street, N.W.
Washington, D.C. 20036

psychological stress analyzer, *see* LIE DETECTOR.

psychological test, a general term for any effort (usually a standardized test) that is designed to measure the abilities or personality traits of individuals or groups. *See* A. Anastasi, *Psychological Testing,* 4th ed. (New York: Macmillan, 1976); J. Lee Cronback, *Essentials of Psychological Testing,* 4th edition (New York: Harper & Row, 1983).

psychology, generally, the scientific study of human and animal behavior. According to Bergen Evans and Cornelia Evans, in *A Dictionary of Contemporary American Usage* (New York: Random House, 1957),

in an age which James Joyce has described as "jung and easily freudened," *psychology* is a word thrown about knowingly by about everyone capable of articulating a four-syllabled word, though not necessarily of spelling it. Basically it means the science of mind, of mental states or processes, the science of human nature.

See also the following entries:
DYNAMIC PSYCHOLOGY
INDUSTRIAL PSYCHOLOGY
PERSONNEL PSYCHOLOGY
VOCATIONAL PSYCHOLOGY

psychometrician, psychologist who deals with mental tests and their associated statistical procedures.

psychometrics, that branch of psychology that deals with mental tests and their associated statistical procedures. *See* Judson Gooding, "Psychometrics: The Use and Misuse of Psychological Tests in Executive Employment," *Across The Board* (November 1976).

psychometry, mental measurements and/or testing.

psychomotor test, *see* DEXTERITY TEST.

public administration (definition). Remember the story of the boy who went to the religious leader of his community and said, "I'll give you an apple if you tell me where God is!" The religious leader replied, "But I'll give you two apples if you tell me where he or she isn't!" It is much the same with public administration. One can hardly say where it isn't. Consequently, definitions of the field which tend to be narrow also tend to exclude significant elements. Conversely, definitions which are very broad and all-encompassing tend to be so broad as to be virtually meaningless. What to do? Some textbooks offer, in place of definition, a discussion of why formulating a definition is a futile exercise. Since a dictionary can hardly run from the challenge of defining its subject, here are a variety of definitions from respectable textbooks.

J. Bernstein and Patrick O'Hara, *Public Administration: Organizations, People, and Public Policy* (New York: Harper & Row, 1979):

> *Public administration determines the way we live through people working in organizations that function and make decisions under rules reflecting past and present societal needs and values.*

James C. Charlesworth, *Governmental Adminstration* (New York: Harper & Row, 1951):

> Governmental administration in the United States is the art and science of realizing the intent of legislators and policy-making executives. It is an art because it requires finesse, leadership, zeal, and lofty conviction. It is a science because it requires inductive analysis, methodical organization, careful planning, and ingenious devisement of procedures.

Marshall E. Dimock and Gladys O. Dimock, *Public Administration* (New York: Holt, Rinehart and Winston, 1964, 4th ed., 1969):

> Public administration is the accomplishment of politically determined objectives.

George J. Gordon, *Public Administration in America* (New York: St. Martin's Press, 1978):

> *Public administration may be defined as all processes, organizations, and individuals (the latter acting in official positions and roles) associated with carrying out laws and other rules adopted or issued by legislatures, executives, and courts.*

Harold F. Gortner, *Administration in the Public Sector* (New York: John Wiley & Sons, 1977):

> Public administration involves *the coordination of all organized activity, having as its purpose the implementation of public policy.*

Larry B. Hill and F. Ted Herbert, *Essentials of Public Administration: A Text with Readings* (North Scituate, Mass.: Duxbury Press, 1979):

> Public administration is the authoritative implementation of those policy choices that have been legitimated through political processes.

William L. Morrow, *Public Administration: Policy and the Political System* (New York: Random House, 1975):

> Public administration is the study of government decisionsmaking, the analysis of the policies themselves, the various inputs that have produced them, and the inputs necessary to produce alternative policies.

Robert Presthus, *Public Administration,* 6th ed. (New York: The Ronald Press Co., 1975):

> Public administration may be defined as the art and science of designing and carrying out public policy.

Grover Starling, *Managing the Public Sector* (Homewood, Ill.: The Dorsey Press, 1977):

> Public administration concerns the accomplishing side of government. It comprises all those activities involved in carrying out the policies of elected officials and some activities associated with the development of those policies. Public administration is, in short, all that comes after the last campaign promise and election night cheer.

Leonard D. White, *Introduction to the Study of Public Administration,* 3rd ed. (New York: Macmillan, 1950):

> Public administration consists of all these

Dual Usage of the Words "Public Administration"

A fertile source of confusion and error, closely related to the science-art controversy, is the fact that the words "public administration" have two usages. They are used to designate and delineate both (1) an area of intellectual inquiry, a discipline or study, and (2) a process of activity—that of administering public affairs. While the two meanings are of course closely related, they are nevertheless different; it is a difference similar to that between biology as the study of organisms and the organisms themselves.

Now if this distinction seems so obvious as not to warrant the making, the excuse must be that it is nevertheless a distinction often missed.

Source: Dwight Waldo, *The Study of Public Administration* (New York: Random House, 1955).

operations having for their purpose the fulfillment or enforcement of public policy.

public administration (origins). The origins of public administration can be traced back as far as the ancient Egyptians. Indeed, the rise of civilization and the increasing sophistication of administrative institutions would seem to go hand in hand.

Appropriately, it was the Roman Empire that introduced the western world to the fundamental features of modern public administration. The Roman state was depersonalized; that is, it had an existence independent of the political leader and was not "owned" by anyone. This meant that the public moneys of the state were separate from private funds of its leadership. Secondly, it made use of a centralized hierarchical structure. This consisted of the central government, the province, and the diocese, terms and concepts with which we are obviously still familiar. Finally, the Romans introduced several units of functional specialization which still form the core of most modern public administrative systems. There were organizational units for military affairs, finance, justice, and police. The latter encompassed several functions which now commonly form the basis of separate departments or ministries in and of themselves. Among these are transportation, health, education, agriculture, and commerce.

After the decline of the Roman Empire many of these administrative ideas lay dormant. Indeed, it is probably not too much to say that during the "Dark Ages" only the most elementary public services remained. As feudalism gave way to the development of the nation-state, several interrelated factors combined to bring about the rebirth of public administrative institutions in western Europe. The rise of the centralized state was the result of efforts by monarchs to wrest control of public affairs from feudal lords. This occurred in conjunction with the rise of a money economy, which contributed to pressures to facilitate trade and made it possible to build political power on the basis of economic resources. This rise of a money

economy in turn contributed to the growth of a new middle class—a natural ally for the monarch as both sought to reduce the power of the aristocracy. As the new nation-states became more centralized they took on new functions, such as education and welfare. By 1660 England, France, and Prussia had all more or less succeeded in establishing separate administrative units for finance, justice, foreign affairs, and internal affairs. Among the state functions which contributed most to the modernization of public administration were taxation, military affairs, and the related desire for the gathering of statistics.

By the late 1600s European administrative practices were making their way across the Atlantic to the American colonies. Our early experience with public administration was less than happy. Colonial America suffered much from the characteristics one might expect to find in underdeveloped, pre-modern nations. Public employment was seen largely as a commodity. As such, it could be bought and sold, inherited, rented out, or otherwise treated as an investment. Accordingly, there was constant pressure to create more and more administrative posts. Remember, the Declaration of Independence complains that King George III "erected a multitude of new offices, and sent hither swarms of officers to harass our people, and eat out their substance."

For histories, see William C. Beyer, "The Civil Service of the Ancient World," *Public Administration Review* (Spring 1959); Frederick C. Mosher, ed., *Basic Documents of American Public Administration, 1776-1950* (New York: Holmes & Meier Publishers, 1976); Michael T. Dalby and Michael S. Werthman, eds., *Bureaucracy in Historical Perspective* (Glenview, Ill.: Scott, Foresman and Co., 1971); E. N. Gladden, *A History of Public Administration* (London: Frank Cass, 1972); Edward A. Loucks, "Bureaucratic Ethics from Washington to Carter: An Historical Perspective," *Public Personnel Management*, Vol. 10, No. 1 (1981); William E. Nelson, *The Roots of American Bureaucracy, 1830-1900* (Cambridge, Mass.: Harvard University Press, 1982); Richard J. Stillman, ed., *Basic Documents of American Public Administration Since 1950* (New York: Holmes & Meier Publishers, 1982); James W. Fesler, ed., *American Public Administration: Patterns of the Past* (Washington D.C.: American Society for Public Administration, 1982); Joseph A. Uveges, Jr., *Public Administration: History and Theory in Contemporary Perspective* (New York: Marcel Dekker, 1982); Jon C. Teaford, *The Unheralded Triumph: City Government in America, 1870-1900* (Baltimore, Md.: Johns Hopkins Press, 1984).

Public Administration, leading British journal of public administration sponsored by the Royal Institute of Public Administration.
> Public Administration
> Journals Department
> Basil Blackwood
> 108 Cowley Road
> Oxford OX41JF
> England

Public Administration, see AUSTRALIAN JOURNAL OF PUBLIC ADMINISTRATION.

public administration, comparative, also DEVELOPMENT ADMINISTRATION, comparative analysis of the systems and politics of public administration in differing nation-states. *Development administration* refers to the study of the administrative development of the "underdeveloped" countries of the third world. See Ferrel Heady, *Public Administration: A Comparative Perspective,* 2nd ed. (New York: Marcel Dekker, 1979); Dwight Waldo, ed., "Symposium on Comparative and Development Administration: Retrospect and Prospect," *Public Administration Review* (November-December 1976); Mark Huddleston, *Comparative Public Administration: An Annotated Bibliography* (New York: Garland Publishing, 1982).

public administration, ecology of, view that the social, economic, and political conditions surrounding any administrative system will determine how it operates in practice; moreover, that the model of bureaucratic efficiency developed by industrialized nations, if introduced into a developing country with a different social, economic, and political heritage, will produce an administrative system that may be bureaucratic in form or structure but not in the actual functions it performs. *See* Fred W. Riggs, *The Ecology of Public Administration* (New York: Asia Publishing House, 1961); Fred W. Riggs, "The Ecology and Context of Public Administration: A Comparative Perspective," *Public Administration Review* (March-April 1980).

public administration, new, a general, mostly undefined movement inspired mainly by younger scholars who challenged several tenets of public administration, primarily the emphasis upon value-neutral administrative research and practice. It appealed to scholars and practitioners to take a more proactive role, guided not only by the search for efficiency, but by a sensitivity to the forces of change, the needs of clients, and the problems of social equity in service delivery. *See* Frank Marini, ed., *Toward A New Public Administration* (San Francisco: Chandler, 1971); Alan K. Campbell, "Old and New Public Administration in the 1970's," *Public Administration Review* (July-August 1972); York Willbern, "Is the New Public Administration Still with Us?" *Public Administration Review* (July-August 1973); George K. Najjar, "Development Administration and 'New' Public Administration: A Convergence of Perspectives?" *Public Administration Review* (November-December 1974); Gary Wamsley, "On the Problem of Discovering What's Really New In Public Administration," *Administration and Society* (November 1976); Carl J. Bellone, ed., *Organization Theory and the New Public Administration* (Boston: Allyn and Bacon, 1980); Rayburn Barton, "The New Public Administration: A Modest Look at the Feasibility of Application," *Public Administration Quarterly* (Fall 1983).

See also FREDERICKSON, H. GEORGE.

Public Administration and Development, a quarterly journal of the Royal Institute of Public Administration which reports, reviews, and assesses development administration.

> *Public Administration and Development*
> Subscription Department C
> John Wiley & Sons, Inc.
> 605 Third Avenue
> New York, NY 10158

public administration indexes, indexes, found in most university libraries, that tend to be useful for public administration research:

Business Periodicals Index
Human Resources Abstracts
Index to Legal Periodicals
Index to U.S. Government Periodicals
International Political Science Abstracts
Personnel and Training Abstracts
Personnel Management Abstracts
Public Administration Abstracts and Index of Articles
Public Affairs Information Service Bulletin
Reader's Guide to Periodical Literature
Sage Public Administration Abstracts
Sage Urban Studies Abstracts
Social Sciences Citation Index
Social Sciences Index
Urban Affairs Abstracts
Work Related Abstracts
See also DATA BASES.

public administration journals. No list of professional journals relevant to public administration can be exhaustive. The following list contains all of the "standard" journals in the field as well as a representative sample of those on the periphery. See separate entries for each of them.

Academy of Management Journal
Academy of Management Review
Administration
Administration and Society
Administrative Management
Administrative Science Quarterly
American City and County
American Journal of Public Health
American Political Science Review
American Review of Public Administration
Annals, The
Arbitration Journal
Australian Journal of Public Administration
Bureaucrat, The
Business and Society Review
Business History Review
California Management Review
Canadian Public Administration
Civil Service Journal
Compensation Review
Employee Assistance Quarterly
Federal Times
Fortune
GAO Review
Government Finance
Government Executive
Harvard Business Review
Human Relations
Human Resources Abstracts
Human Resource Management
Human Resources Planning
Indian Journal of Public Administration
Industrial and Labor Relations Review
Industrial Management
Industrial Relations
International Journal of Government Auditing
International Journal of Group Psychotherapy
International Review of Administrative Sciences
International Journal of Public Administration
Journal of Applied Behavioral Science
Journal of Counseling and Development
Journal of Human Resources
Journal of Policy Analysis and Management
Journal of Political Economy
Journal of Public Policy
Labor Law Journal
Labor Studies Journal
Management
Management Science
Midwest Review of Public Administration
Monthly Labor Review
National Civic Review
National Journal

Nation's Cities
Organizational Behavior and Human
 Performance
Organizational Dynamics
Personnel
Personnel Administrator
Personnel and Guidance Journal
Personnel Journal
Personnel Literature
Personnel Management Abstracts
Personnel Psychology
Philippine Journal of Public
 Administration
Policy Analysis
Policy Review
Policy Sciences
Policy Studies Journal
Policy Studies Review
Political Science Quarterly
Presidential Studies Quarterly
Psychological Review
Public Administration
Public Administration and Development
Public Administration Quarterly
Public Administration Review
Public Administration Times
Public Budgeting and Finance
Public Finance
Public Finance Quarterly
Public Interest, The
Public Management
Public Personnel Management
Public Policy
Public Productivity Review
Public Welfare
Publius
Review of Public Personnel
 Administration
Sloan Management Review
State Government
Training
Training and Development Journal
Urban Affairs Quarterly
Washington Monthly

Public Administration Quarterly, a
general journal of public administration;
formerly the *Southern Review of Public
Administration.*
 Public Administration Quarterly
 Editorial:
 Jack Rabin, editor
 Rider College

P. O. Box 6400
Lawrenceville, NJ 08648
Subscriptions:
Auburn University at Montgomery
Montgomery, AL 36193

Public Administration Review **(PAR),**
leading professional journal on all aspects
of managing public and nonprofit in-
stitutions.
 Editorial Address:
 Chester A. Newland
 Editor-in-Chief
 Public Administration Review
 University of Southern California,
  Sacramento
 921 11th Street, #200
 Sacramento, CA 95814-2876
 Subscriptions:
 Public Administration Review
 American Society for Public
  Administration
 1120 G Street, N.W.
 Washington, D.C. 20005

public administration schools, *see* NA-
TIONAL ASSOCIATION OF SCHOOLS OF
PUBLIC AFFAIRS AND ADMINISTRATION.

Public Administration Service (PAS),
body established in 1933 as a private, self-
supporting, not-for-profit institution
dedicated to improving the quality and
effectiveness of governmental operations.
PAS performs a wide variety of consulting
and research work in serving the special
needs of governments and other public
service institutions. Its services are provided on a cost-reimbursement basis and
range from technical studies of central
management problems to analyses of
public policy issues. Originally based in
Chicago, PAS is now located in Virginia.
 Public Administration Service
 1497 Chain Bridge Road
 McLean, VA 22101
 (703) 734-8970

public administration textbooks.
Leonard D. White's 1926 *Introduction to
the Study of Public Administration* was the
first text in the field. Until the mid-1960s
there were less than half a dozen public ad-

ministration texts in print at any one time. Today there are dozens to choose from, and it seems like a new general public administration text is announced every month. Listed below are most of the major texts and readers: Don Allensworth, *Public Administration: The Execution of Public Policy* (Philadelphia: J. B. Lippincott Co., 1973); Rayburn Barton and William L. Chappell, Jr., *Public Administration: The Work of Government* (Glenview, Ill.: Scott, Foresman, 1985); George E. Berkley, *The Craft of Public Administration,* 4th ed. (Boston: Allyn & Bacon, 1984); Samuel J. Bernstein and Patrick G. O'Hara, *Public Administration: Organizations, People, and Public Policy* (New York: Harper & Row, 1979); Barry Bozeman, *Public Management and Policy Analysis* (New York: St. Martins Press, 1979); Gerald Caiden, *The Dynamics of Public Administration: Guidelines to Current Transformations in Theory and Practice* (New York: Holt, 1971); Gordon Chase and Elizabeth C. Reveal, *How To Manage in the Public Sector* (Reading, Mass.: Addison-Wesley, 1983); Donald P. Crane and William A. Jones, Jr., *The Public Manager's Guide* (Washington, D.C.: Bureau of National Affairs, Inc., 1982); James W. Davis, *An Introduction to Public Administration* (New York: The Free Press, 1975); Marshall Edward Dimock and Gladys Ogden Dimock, *Public Administration,* 4th ed. (New York: Holt, Rinehart and Winston, 1969); James W. Fesler, *Public Administration: Theory and Practice* (Englewood Cliffs, N.J.: Prentice-Hall, 1980); Douglas M. Fox, *Managing the Public's Interest* (New York: Holt, Rinehart & Winston, 1979); Robert C. Fried, *Performance in American Bureaucracy* (Boston: Little, Brown, 1976); G. David Garson and J. Oliver Williams, *Public Administration: Concepts, Readings, Skills* (Boston: Allyn and Bacon, 1982); Robert T. Golembiewski, Frank Gibson, and Geoffrey Y. Cornog, eds., *Public Administration: Readings in Institutions, Processes, Behavior, Policy,* 3rd ed. (Chicago: Rand McNally, 1976); Charles T. Goodsell, *The Case for Bureaucracy: A Public Administration Polemic* (Chatham, N.J.: Chatham House Publishers, 1983); George J. Gordon, *Public Administration in America,* 2nd ed. (New York: St. Martins, 1982); Harold F. Gortner, *Administration in the Public Sector,* 2nd ed. (New York: John Wiley & Sons, 1981); Nicholas Henry, *Public Administration and Public Affairs,* 2nd ed. (Englewood Cliffs, N.J.: Prentice-Hall, 1980); Larry B. Hill and F. Ted Herbert, *Essentials of Public Administration* (North Scituate, Mass.: Duxbury Press, 1979); Donald E. Klingner, *Public Administration: A Management Approach* (Boston, Mass.: Houghton Mifflin, 1983); Fred A. Kramer, *Dynamics of Public Bureaucracy,* 2nd ed. (Cambridge, Mass.: Winthrop, 1981); Robert S. Lorch, *Public Administration* (New York: West Publishing, 1978); Frederick S. Lane, ed., *Current Issues in Public Administration,* 2nd ed. (New York: St. Martins Press, 1982); Carol E. Lutrin and Allen S. Settle, *American Public Administration: Concepts and Cases,* 2nd ed. (Palo Alto, Calif.: Mayfield, 1980); Jerome B. McKinney and Lawrence C. Howard, *Public Administration: Balancing Power and Accountability* (Oak Park, Ill.: Moore Publishing Company, 1979); James L. Mercer and Edwin H. Koester, *Public Management Systems: An Administrator's Guide* (New York: AMACOM, 1978); John D. Millet, *Organization for the Public Service* (New York: D. Van Nostrand, 1966); Robert D. Miewald, *Public Administration: A Critical Perspective* (New York: McGraw-Hill, 1978); William L. Morrow, *Public Administration: Politics, Policy, and the Political System,* 2nd ed. (New York: Random House, 1980); F. C. Mosher, ed., *American Public Administration: Past, Present, Future* (University, Ala.: University of Alabama Press, 1975); Fritz Morstein Marx, *The Administrative State* (Chicago: University of Chicago Press, 1957); Fritz Morstein Marx, ed., *Elements of Public Administration,* 2nd ed. (Englewood Cliffs, N.J.: Prentice-Hall, 1959); Howard E. McCurdy, *Public Administration: A Synthesis* (Menlo Park, Calif.: Cummings Publishing Co., 1977); Felix A. Nigro and Lloyd C. Nigro,

Modern Public Administration, 6th ed. (New York: Harper & Row, 1984); Robert Presthus, *Public Administration,* 6th ed. (New York: Ronald Press, 1975); Robert D. Pursley and Neil Snortland, *Managing Government Organizations* (North Scituate, Mass.: Duxbury Press, 1980); John Rehfuss, *Public Administration As a Political Process* (New York: Charles Scribner's Sons, 1973); Ivan L. Richardson and Sidney Baldwin, *Public Administration: Government in Action* (Columbus, Ohio: Charles E. Merrill, 1976); Stephen R. Rosenthal, *Managing Government Operations* (Glenview, Ill.: Scott, Foresman, 1982); Jay M. Shafritz and Albert C. Hyde, eds., *Classics of Public Administration* (Oak Park, Ill.: Moore Publishing Co., 1978); Ira Sharkansky, *Public Administration: Policymaking in Government Agencies,* 4th ed. (Chicago: Markham, 1978); Ira Sharkansky, *Public Administration: Agencies, Policies, and Politics* (San Francisco: W. H. Freeman, 1982); Robert H. Simmons and Eugene P. Dvorin, *Public Administration: Values, Policy, and Change* (Port Washington, N.Y.: Alfred Publishing, 1977); Herbert A. Simon, David W. Smithburg, and Victor A. Thompson, *Public Administration* (New York: Knopf, 1950); Grover Starling, *Managing the Public Sector,* rev. ed. (Homewood, Ill.: The Dorsey Press, 1982); Richard J. Stillman II, *Public Administration: Concepts and Cases,* 3rd ed. (Boston: Houghton Mifflin, 1984); Joseph A. Uveges, Jr., ed., *The Dimensions of Public Administration,* 3rd ed. (Boston: Allyn & Bacon, 1979); Dwight Waldo, ed., *Ideas and Issues in Public Administration* (New York: McGraw-Hill, 1953); Dwight Waldo, *Public Administration in a Time of Turbulence* (Scranton, Pa.: Chandler Publishing Co., 1971); Dwight Waldo, *The Study of Public Administration* (New York: Random House, 1955); Leonard D. White, *Introduction to the Study of Public Administration,* 4th ed. (New York: Macmillan Co., 1955); J. D. Williams, *Public Administration: The People's Business* (Boston: Little, Brown, 1980); Peter Woll, ed., *Public Administra-*

tion and Policy (New York: Harper & Row, 1966).

Public Administration Times, biweekly newsletter of the American Society for Public Administration.
PA Times
1120 G Street, N.W.
Washington, D.C. 20005

Public Budgeting and Finance, quarterly co-sponsored by the American Society for Public Administration Section on Budgeting and Financial Management and the American Association for Budget and Program Analysis.
Public Budgeting & Finance
Editorial:
Jesse Burkhead, editor
The Maxwell School
Syracuse University
Syracuse, NY 13210
Subscriptions:
Transactions Periodicals Consortium
Dept. 8010
Rutgers University
New Brunswick, NJ 08903

public bureaucracy, see BUREAUCRACY.

public-choice economics, an approach to public administration based on microeconomic theory which views the citizen as a consumer of government goods and services and would attempt to maximize administrative responsiveness to citizen demand by creating a market system for governmental activities in which public agencies would compete to provide citizens with goods and services. This would replace the current system under which administrative agencies in effect act as monopolies under the influence of organized pressure groups which, the public-choice economists argue, are institutionally incapable of representing the demands of individual citizens. See Gordon Tulloch, "Problems in the Theory of Public Choice: Social Cost of Government Action," *American Economic Review* (May 1969); Dennis C. Mueller, *Public Choice* (New York: Cambridge University Press, 1979); Nicholas P. Lovrich and

Max Neiman, *Public Choice Theory in Public Administration: An Annotated Bibliography* (New York: Garland Publishing, 1982); Louis F. Weschler, "Public Choice: Methodological Individualism in Politics," *Public Administration Review* (May-June 1982).

public defender, attorney employed by a governmental agency or subdivision whose official duty is to represent defendants unable to hire private counsel.

public defender's office, federal, state, or local criminal justice agency or subunit of which the principal function is to represent defendants unable to hire private counsel.

public domain, land owned by the government or any property right that is held in common by all citizens; for example, the content of U.S. government publications, expired copyrights, or expired patents. *See* Paul J. Culhane, *Public Lands Politics: Interest Group Influence on the Forest Service and the Bureau of Land Management* (Baltimore: The Johns Hopkins University Press, 1981).

public employee, any person who works for a governmental agency.

Public employees constitute the core of government in developed nations. They carry on the day-to-day business of government with expertise that is generally unavailable elsewhere in the society. Although many public service tasks are technical and highly structured in nature, a substantial proportion of civil servants are inevitably engaged in making decisions which have a fundamental impact on the general direction and content of public policy. For example, the use of "affirmative action" in the sense of quotas or goals has been an important political issue in the United States for almost two decades, yet it is a policy which has been created by administrative fiat and has yet to be mandated fully either by legislation or executive order. The U.S. political system enhances the policymaking role of the public service in several ways. Elected officials often prefer to avoid making decisions on hotly contested political issues. In consequence, these matters are often thrust upon the judicial and administrative arms of government. The Congress, recognizing both its own limitations and the expertise of career administrators, has in recent decades delegated authority in a vast array of policy areas to the bureaucracy.

public employee relations, labor-management relations in the public sector. For texts, *see* Hugh D. Jascourt, ed., *Government Labor Relations* (Oak Park, Ill.: Moore Publishing Co., 1979); Marvin J. Levine and Eugene C. Hagburg, *Public Sector Labor Relations* (St. Paul, Minn.: West Publishing, 1979); Richard C. Kearney, *Labor Relations in the Public Sector* (New York: Marcel Dekker, 1984).

Public Employees' Fair Employment Act, *see* TAYLOR LAW.

public enterprise (revolving) funds, federally owned funds that are credited with receipts, primarily from the public, generated by and earmarked to finance a continuing cycle of business-type operations (*e.g.,* the Federal Deposit Insurance Corporation).

public finance, imprecise term that refers to the totality (1) of the gaining and spending of funds by governments and (2) of the management of government debt. *See* L. L. Ecker-Racz, *The Politics and Economics of State-Local Finance* (Englewood Cliffs, N.J.: Prentice-Hall 1970); Richard A. Musgrave and Peggy B. Musgrave, *Public Finance in Theory and Practice* (New York: McGraw-Hill, 1973); Alan S. Blindner *et al., The Economics of Public Finance* (Washington, D.C.: The Brookings Institution, 1974); Lennox L. Moak and Albert M. Hillhouse, *Concepts and Practices in Local Government Finance* (Chicago: Municipal Finance Officers Association, 1975); James A. Maxwell and J. Richard Aaronson, *Financing State and Local Governments,* 3rd ed. (Washington, D.C.: Brookings Institution, 1977); John Meyer and John Quigley, eds., *Local Public Finance and the Fiscal*

Squeeze (Cambridge, Mass.: Ballinger, 1977); Wayland D. Gardner, *Government Finance: National, State and Local* (Englewood Cliffs, N.J.: Prentice-Hall, 1978); Bernard P. Herber, *Modern Public Finance* (Homewood, Ill.: Richard D. Irwin, Inc., 1979); Otto Eckstein, *Public Finance*, 4th ed. (Englewood Cliffs, N.J.: Prentice-Hall, 1979); James M. Buchanan and Marilyn R. Flowers, *The Public Finances: An Introductory Textbook*, 5th ed. (Homewood, Ill.: Richard D. Irwin, Inc., 1980); Robert T. Golembiewski, *Public Budgeting and Finance: Behavioral, Theoretical, and Technical Perspectives*, 3rd ed. (New York: Marcel Dekker, 1983); Richard Goode, *Government Finance in Developing Countries* (Washington, D.C.: The Brookings Institution, 1984).

See also the following entries:
DEFAULT
DEBT FINANCING
FEDERAL DEBT
FEDERALISM, FISCAL
INTERGOVERNMENTAL FUNDS
MUNICIPAL BONDS

Public Finance, international quarterly devoted to fiscal policy and theory. Text in English, French, or German.
Public Finance
Goethestr. 13/D-6240
Konigstein
Federal Republic of Germany

Public Finance Quarterly, journal devoted to the theory and practice of public financial management.
Public Finance Quarterly
Sage Publications, Inc.
275 South Beverly Drive
Beverly Hills, CA 90212

public goods, commodities typically provided by government that cannot, or would not, be separately parceled out to individuals since no one can be excluded from their benefits. Public goods such as national defense, clean air, or public safety are neither divisible nor exclusive. *See* Mancur Olson, Jr., *The Logic of Collective Action: Public Goods and the Theory of Groups* (Cambridge, Mass.: Harvard University Press, 1965).

public health, the science dealing with the protection and improvement of community health by organized community effort. Public health activities are generally those which are less amenable to being undertaken or less effective when undertaken on an individual basis, and which do not typically include direct personal health services. Immunizations, sanitation, preventive medicine, quarantine, and other disease control activities, occupational health and safety programs, assurance of the healthfulness of air, water, and food, health education and epidemiology are recognized public health activities.

public health administration, that area of public administration generally concerned with preventing disease, prolonging life, and promoting health by means of organized community efforts.

public interest, universal label in which political actors wrap the policies and programs that they advocate. Would any public manager, legislator, or chief executive ever propose a program that was not "in the public interest?" Because "the public interest" is generally taken to mean a commonly accepted good, the phrase is used both to further policies that are indeed for the common good as well as to obscure policies that may not be so commonly accepted as good. A considerable body of literature has developed about this phrase because it represents an important philosophic point that, if found, could provide considerable guidance for public administrators. *See* E. Pendleton Herring, *Public Administration and the Public Interest* (New York: Russell & Russell, 1936); Martin Meyerson and Edward C. Banfield, *Politics, Planning and the Public Interest: The Case of Public Housing in Chicago* (New York: Free Press, 1955); Glendon A. Schubert, Jr., " 'The Public Interest' in Administrative Decisionmaking," *American Political Science Review* (June 1957); Frank J. Sorauf, "The Public Interest Reconsidered," *The Journal of*

Politics (November 1957); Glendon A. Schubert, *The Public Interest* (New York: Free Press, 1960); Michael Mount Harmon, "Administrative Policy Formulation and the Public Interest," *Public Administration Review* (September–October 1969); Virginia Held, *The Public Interest and Individual Interests* (New York: Basic Books, 1970); John Guinther, *Moralists and Managers: Public Interest Movements in America* (Garden City, N.Y.: Anchor Books, 1976); Barry Mitnick, "A Typology of Conceptions of the Public Interest," *Administration and Society* (May 1976); Edgar Shor, Symposium Editor, "Public Interest Representation and the Federal Agencies," *Public Administration Review* (March–April 1977); A. W. McEachern and Jawad Al-Arayed, "Discerning the Public Interest," *Administration & Society* (February 1984).

Public Interest, The, quarterly journal of public affairs.
> The Public Interest
> National Affairs, Inc.
> 10 East 53rd Street
> New York, NY 10022

public interest group, an organized pressure group seeking to develop positions and support national causes relating to a broader definition of the public good as opposed to any specific social or economic interest. Such groups are often characterized by efforts to obtain a national membership with a high level of participation by members and dissemination of information and authority. Examples of public interest groups are Common Cause, the Nader organizations, the League of Women Voters, the Sierra Club, and Consumer's Union.
> See also INTEREST GROUP.

Public Interest Groups, national network of quasi-public voluntary associations. The so-called Big Seven include the Council of State Governments (CSG), the National Governors Association (NGA), the National Conference of State Legislatures, the National Association of Counties (NACo), the National League of Cities (NLC),

United States Conference of Mayors (USCM), and the International City Management Association (ICMA). In addition to NGA, the CSG has several relevant affiliated organizations: associations of attorneys general, lieutenant governors, state budget officers, state purchasing officials, and state planning agencies. The state leagues of municipalities are constituent bodies of the NLC. In addition, the American Society for Public Administration (ASPA), the National Academy of Public Administration (NAPA), and the National Association of Schools of Public Affairs and Administration (NASPAA) are the principal important inputs into the intergovernmental network. More specialized are the associations of planning, personnel, and finance officials.

public-interest law, that portion of legal practice devoted to broad societal interests rather than the problems of individual clients.

public law, any legislative enactment which relates to the public as a whole; the term also refers to that part of the law which is concerned with the state in its capacity as sovereign. *See* A. Chayes, "The Role of the Judge in Public Law Litigation," *Harvard Law Review*, Vol. 89 (1976); David H. Rosenbloom, *Public Administration and Law* (New York: Marcel Dekker, 1983).

public management, a general term referring to a major segment of public administration. Typically, the phrase "public management" is used to identify those functions of public and nonprofit organizations which are more internally than externally oriented, such as personnel management, procedures management, and organizational control functions. Whereas "policy management" typically focuses on policy formation and the selection of basic strategies, "public management" focuses on the organizational "machinery" for achieving policy goals.

Planning, organizing, and controlling are the major means or functions by which the public manager shapes government services (*see* POSDCORB). These functions constitute the primary knowledge and skills of the public manager and are applied in the form of budgets, performance appraisals, management information systems, program evaluations, organizational charts, cost/benefit analyses, and similar management tools. Public management also requires behavioral skills. Communications, negotiation, motivation, lead-

An Assessment of the Elements of Public Management

Public Management Function / Assessment Criteria	Policy Management (PM)	Resource Management (RM)	Program Management (PG)
Functional Emphasis	*Strategic* functions of providing *guidance* and *leadership*.	*Routine* support functions to ensure *organizational maintenance*, a capacity for *adaptation* and *compliance* with environmental constraints.	*Tactical* functions of *executing* administrative directives and policy guidance in the form of programs, activities, and services.
Purpose	To *clarify* and *articulate* community and social *values* and *to develop priorities* and *establish commitments* designed to meet community needs and aspirations.	To develop and maintain a human, material, financial, and informational *resource base that is maximally responsive to the demands* of the Policy and Program components of the organization and to ensure that all organizational elements comply with established administrative and regulatory procedures—both internal and external.	To design operating programs, services, and activities that reflect general policy guidance and are responsive to the unique and/or changing needs of clientele.
Major Concerns	*What should* be done and *why should* it be done?	*How can* it be done?	How *to do* it?
Participants and Arenas	*Elected officials* and their immediate staffs; dominated by "generalists."	*Administrative officers;* professionals specialized in budgeting, accounting, data processing, statutory and administrative law, drafting, materials procurement, personnel, recruitment and training, property management, and other similar areas. Dominated by "specialists"; "generalists" are likely to be found in the staff elements devoted to legal matters or to budgeting	*Department or agency heads,* their staffs, and the heads of organizational subunits. Some "generalists," though dominated by professionals and para-professionals specialized in some *substantive* aspect of a functional program area (e.g., mass transportation, health care, etc.), related *methodologies* (e.g., R&D, institutional development, etc.), or in *Resource Management skills specifically required to develop, operate, and manage a major program, project, or service.*

Source: Study Committee on Policy Management Assistance, Office of Management and Budget, *Strengthening Public Management in the Intergovernmental System* (Washington, D.C.: Government Printing Office, 1975), p. 6.

ership, and interpersonal skills are equally important aspects of the job of the public manager in securing resources and achieving public goals.

Public management, according to James Perry and Kenneth Kraemer in *Public Management: Public and Private Perspectives* (Palo Alto, Calif.: Mayfield Publishing, 1983), "is a merger of the normative orientation of traditional public administration and the instrumental orientation of generic management." Public management is often compared to its successful counterpart, public policy, and to the formulation and implementation of public goals. Both policy and management are part of the larger field of public administration, but contemporary public management is arguably closer to Woodrow Wilson's original formulation of administration as a field of business. The characteristics that distinguish public management from public policy and administration appear to be: (1) a focus on the public organization in lieu of a focus on laws or political institutions; (2) an instrumental orientation favoring criteria of efficiency and effectiveness in lieu of consideration of social values or conflicts of bureaucracy and democracy; (3) a pragmatic focus on mid-level managers in lieu of political or policy elites; and (4) an applied problem-solving perspective.

According to David Garson and E. Samuel Overman in *Public Management Research in the United States* (New York: Praeger Publishers, 1983), public management is not exactly scientific management or administrative science, though it is still heavily influenced by them. Nor is it policy analysis, new public administration, or generic management. Public management reflects the tensions between the rational-instrument orientations, on the one hand, and political-policy orientations on the other. Public management is the interdisciplinary study of the generic aspects of public administration. It is a blend of the planning, organizing, leadership, and controlling functions of management with the management of human, financial, physical, information, and political resources.

See Joseph Bower, "Effective Public Management," *Harvard Business Review* (March–April 1977); James Mercer and Edwin Koester, *Public Management Systems: An Administrator's Guide* (New York: AMACOM, 1978); Michael White et al., *Managing Public Systems; Analytic Techniques for Public Administration* (North Scituate, Mass.: Duxbury Press, 1980); Lawrence Lynn, *Managing the Public's Business* (New York: Basic Books, 1981); Stephen Rosenthal, *Managing Government Operations* (Glenview, Ill.: Scott, Foresman, 1982); Alan W. Steiss, *Management Control in Government* (Lexington, Mass.: D.C. Heath, 1982); E. Samuel Overman and G. David Garson, "Contemporary Public Management," *Public Administration Quarterly* (1983); E. Samuel Overman, "Public Management: What's New and Different?" *Public Administration Review* (May–June 1984).

Public Management (PM), monthly magazine for city managers published by the International City Management Association.
   PM
   1120 G Street, N.W.
   Washington, D.C. 20005

Public Personnel Association, *see* INTERNATIONAL PERSONNEL MANAGEMENT ASSOCIATION.

public personnel management, personnel management in government. The essential difference between personnel management in the private sector and personnel management in the public sector can be summed up in one word—politics. The public personnel process is a political process; except in the most sophisticated jurisdictions, management processes are decidedly subordinate to political considerations. For texts, *see* Jonathan Brock, *Managing People in Public Agencies* (Boston: Little, Brown, 1984); N. Joseph Cayer, *Public Personnel Administration in the United States* (New York: St. Martin's Press, 1975); N. Joseph Cayer, *Managing Human Resources: An Introduction to Public Personnel Administration* (New

York: St. Martin's Press, 1980); Michael Cohen and Robert T. Golembiewski, eds., *Public Personnel Update* (New York: Marcel Dekker, 1984); Winston W. Crouch, ed., *Local Government Personnel Administration* (Washington, D.C.: International City Management Association, 1976); Dennis L. Dresang, *Public Personnel Management and Public Policy* (Boston, Mass.: Little, Brown, 1984); Robert H. Elliott, *Public Personnel Administration: A Values Perspective* (Reston, Virginia: Reston/Prentice-Hall, 1985); Donald E. Klingner, ed., *Public Personnel Management: Readings in Contexts and Strategies* (Palo Alto, Calif.: Mayfield Publishing Co., 1981); Marvin J. Levine, ed., *Public Personnel Management: Readings, Cases and Contingency Plans* (Salt Lake City: Brighton Publishing Co., 1980); John Matzer, Jr., ed., *Creative Personnel Practices: New Ideas for Local Government* (Washington, D.C.: International City Management Association, 1984); Perry Moore, *Public Personnel Management: A Contingency Approach* (Lexington Mass.: Lexington Books, 1985); O. Glenn Stahl, *Public Personnel Administration*, 8th ed. (New York: Harper & Row, 1983); Jack Rabin, C. E. Teasley III, Arthur Finkle, and Luther F. Carter, *Personnel: Managing Human Resources in the Public Sector* (New York: Harcourt Brace Jovanovich, 1985); Jay M. Shafritz, ed., *The Public Personnel World: Readings on the Professional Practice* (Chicago: International Personnel Management Association, 1977); Jay M. Shafritz, Albert C. Hyde, and David H. Rosenbloom, *Personnel Management in Government: Politices and Process,* 3rd ed. (New York: Marcel Dekker, 1986); Gilbert B. Siegel and Robert C. Myrtle, *Public Personnel Administration: Concepts and Practices* (Boston: Houghton Mifflin, 1985); Frank J. Thompson, ed., *Classics of Public Personnel Policy* (Oak Park, Ill.: Moore Publishing Company, 1979).

See also the following entries:
CIVIL SERVICE REFORM
CIVIL SERVICE REFORM ACT OF 1978
PATRONAGE
PENDLETON ACT
POSITION CLASSIFICATION
PUBLIC PERSONNEL POLITICS

***Public Personnel Management* (PPM),** quarterly journal of the International Personnel Management Association which offers articles dealing with all aspects of personnel management in government.
Public Personnel Management
Suite 870
1850 K Street, N.W.
Washington, D.C. 20006

public personnel politics, the perversion of most civil service merit systems for private, administrative, and especially partisan ends. This is one of the worst-kept, yet least-written-about, secrets in government. While the general textbooks on state and local government frequently take cognizance of this situation, traditional texts on public personnel administration have tended to deal with this subject as if it were an abnormal malignancy instead of an inherent and frequently beneficial part of governmental personnel management. This is faulty perspective. Senator Daniel P. Moynihan (N.Y.) long ago noted that corruption must be recognized as "a normal condition of American local government." Similarly, it must be recognized that the perversion of merit system principles is a normal condition of the public personnel process. This latter situation is not necessarily as unhealthy and undesirable as the former. Frequently such "perversions" are essential if actual merit is to be rewarded within the "merit" system. Unfortunately, other considerations seem just as likely to apply.

Throughout the United States, public personnel merit systems tend to operate on two different planes within the same jurisdiction. The great majority of civil service employees within merit systems are able to enter and advance on the basis of their own talents and the design of the system. However, at the same time and within the same system there are two groups of individuals that enter and advance according to criteria other than that provided for in the merit system regulations.

The first group of employees consists of all those who were appointed for considerations other than personal fitness. Here are hidden the political appointees in excess of those policymaking and confidential positions that are usually the executive's legal prerogative. The extent of such placements depends upon such factors as the strength and longevity of the merit system, the political culture of the community, and the integrity of the executive who, having taken an oath to uphold all the laws of his jurisdiction, can only make such appointments in violation of the spirit, if not the letter, of his oath.

While the merit system is frequently perverted for traditional political ends, it is similarly abused for more scrupulous purposes. The excessively rigid procedures for entering and advancing in most merit systems have long been recognized as a decided hindrance to effective management practices. In order to compensate for the lack of managerial discretion occasioned by such rigidities, career civil servants as well as other highly qualified individuals have either been advanced or initially installed through a fudging of the civil service regulations—this is the same process by which politicos are foisted upon the merit system. The procedural morass designed to keep out the bad is frequently as effective in keeping out the good. In consequence, what exists in fact, although it is nowhere de jure, is a first-class and second-class civil service. This classification is not a reflection on the quality of any given individual or of the productive value of each class, but merely a reference as to how they are treated by those who work the merit system. While the members of the civil service proletariat must be content with careers bounded by the full force of the frequently unreasonable and always constraining regulations, others—those fortunate enough to be recognized for their talents as well as those recognized in spite of their talents—benefit markedly by having these same regulations waived, fraudulently complied with, or simply ignored when it is to their advantage. *See* Jay M.

Shafritz, *Public Personnel Management: The Heritage of Civil Service Reform* (New York: Praeger, 1975); Frank J. Thompson, *Personnel Policy in the City: The Politics of Jobs in Oakland* (Berkeley, Calif.: University of California Press, 1975); Wilbur C. Rich, *The Politics of Urban Personnel Policy: Reformers, Politicians, and Bureaucrats* (Port Washington, N.Y.: Kennikat Press, 1981).

See also the following entries:
CIVIL SERVICE REFORM
CIVIL SERVICE REFORM ACT OF 1978
GRANT'S CIVIL SERVICE COMMISSION
JACKSON, ANDREW
PATRONAGE

public policy, according to David Easton, *A Systems Analysis of Political Life* (New York: John Wiley & Sons, 1965), a policy made by certain "occupants" who are the "authorities" in a system of government; those who "engage in the daily affairs of a political system" and are "recognized by most members of the system as having the responsibilities for these matters," and whose actions are "accepted as binding most of the time by most of the members as long as they act within the limits of their roles."

There are essentially two kinds of literature on public policy. One is process oriented and attempts to understand and explore the dynamic social and political mechanics and relationships of how policies are made. The other is basically prescriptive and attempts to examine how rational analysis can produce better policy decisions. *See* Raymond Bauer, Ithiel de Sola Pool, and Lewis A. Dexter, *American Business and Public Policy: The Politics of Foreign Trade* (New York: Atherton, 1963); Raymond A. Bauer and Kenneth J. Gergen, eds., *The Study of Policy Formulation* (New York: The Free Press, 1968); Michael D. Reagan, ed., *The Administration of Public Policy* (Glenview, Ill.: Scott, Foresman, 1969); L. L. Wade and R. L. Curry, *A Logic of Public Policy: Aspects of Political Economy* (Belmont, Calif.: Wadsworth, 1970); Robert Eyestone, *The Threads of Public Policy: A Study in Policy Leadership* (Indianapolis:

Bobbs-Merrill, 1971); Larry L. Wade, *The Elements of Public Policy* (Columbus, Ohio: Merrill, 1972); Ida Hoos, *Systems Analysis in Public Policy* (Berkeley, Calif.: University of California Press, 1972); Michael P. Smith, ed., *American Politics and Public Policy* (New York: Random House, 1973); Richard I. Hofferbert, *The Study of Public Policy* (Indianapolis, Indiana: Bobbs-Merrill Co., 1974); Randall B. Ripley, *American National Government and Public Policy* (New York: The Free Press, 1974); Peter Woll, *Public Policy* (Englewood Cliffs, N.J.: Prentice-Hall, 1974); Jay A. Sigler and Benjamin R. Beede, *The Legal Sources of Public Policy* (Lexington, Mass.: Lexington Books, 1977); George D. Greenberg *et al.,* "Developing Public Policy Theory," *American Political Science Review* (December 1977); Charles O. Jones, *An Introduction to the Study of Public Policy*, 2nd ed. (North Scituate, Mass.: Duxbury Press, 1977); David Nachmias, *Public Policy Evaluation: Approaches and Methods* (New York: St. Martin's Press, 1978); Thomas R. Dye, *Understanding Public Policy*, 3rd ed.(Englewood Cliffs, N.J.: Prentice-Hall, 1978); Fred M. Frohock, *Public Policy: Scope and Logic* (Englewood Cliffs, N.J.: Prentice-Hall, 1979); Elizabeth Markson and Gretchen Batra, eds., *Public Policies for an Aging Population* (Lexington, Mass.: Lexington Books, 1980); Kenneth M. Dolbeare, *American Public Policy: A Citizen's Guide* (New York: McGraw-Hill, 1982); John W. Kingdom, *Agendas, Alternatives, and Public Policies* (Boston, Mass.: Little, Brown, 1984); Stuart S. Nagel, *Public Policy: Goals, Means, and Methods* (New York: St. Martin's Press, 1984).

Public Policy, quarterly journal of policy analysis of the Kennedy School of Government, Harvard University. This journal ceased publication in 1981 and was succeeded by the *Journal of Policy Analysis and Management.*

public policymaking, totality of the decisional processes by which a government decides to act or deliberately not act to deal with a particular problem or concern.

In seeking an explanation for the mechanisms that produce policy decisions or non-decisions, one is immediately confronted with two early, distinct, and opposite theories. What might be called the rational decision-making approach generally has been attributed to Harold Lasswell's *The Future of Political Science* (New York: Atherton, 1963), which posited seven significant phases for every decision:

1. the intelligence phase, involving an influx of information,
2. the promoting or recommending phase, involving activities designed to influence the outcome,
3. the prescribing phase, involving the articulation of norms,
4. the invoking phase, involving establishing correspondence between prescriptions and concrete circumstances,
5. the application phase, in which the prescription is executed,
6. the appraisal phase, assessing intent in relation to effect, and
7. the terminating phase, treating expectations (rights) established while the prescription was in force.

The rejection of this approach was urged by Charles E. Lindblom, who proposed the incremental decision-making theory popularly known as the "science of muddling through." Lindblom sees a rational model as unrealistic. The policymaking process was above all, he asserted, complex and disorderly. Disjointed incrementalism as a policy course was in reality the only truly feasible route, since incrementalism "concentrated the policymaker's analysis on familiar, better-known experiences, sharply reduced the number of different alternative policies to be explored, and sharply reduced the number and complexity of factors to be analyzed."

The rational and incremental models, despite their opposite contentions, seemingly have produced no real obstacles for subsequent study of policymaking. One later policy analysis scholar simply has contended that the reality of the policy process should not negate attempts to establish ideal models. Charles O. Jones, in *An Introduction to the Study of Public Policy* (Belmont, Calif.: Wadsworth, 1970), finds that while Lindblom's thesis accurately describes most policy processes, there is "no particular reason why those who want change should limit their actions because the system is 'incremental.'"

A question then remains—how can one accept the incremental model as a reality but use the rational model as a conceptual framework for policy analysis? There is no ready answer to such a question other than to go back to Jones' contention about the utility of the rational model in producing change, or more information oriented policy action. Scholars will use the rational model because it affords a dissective capability that can be used to focus on policy specifics and stages, regardless of how well constructed or formulated any given decisions may be.

Another significant theorist, Theodore J. Lowi, holds that different models should be constructed for different types of public policies. His now classic article in *World Politics* (July 1964), "American Business, Public Policy, Case Studies and Political Theory," argued that policy contents should be an independent variable and that it be recognized that there are three major categories of public policies: distribution, regulation, and redistribution. "Each arena tends to develop its own characteristic political structure, political process, elites, and group relations." As one might expect, distribution policies involve actions that provide services and products to individuals and groups; regulatory policies involve controls and prohibitions on certain actions; and redistributive policies involve transfers or transactions that take from one party and provide to another.

It seems fair to conclude that there is no single policymaking process that produces all policies. Rather, there are numerous policy processes, each capable of producing different policy contents and applicable only in a particular environment. *See* William W. Boyer, *Bureaucracy on Trial: Policymaking by Government Agencies* (Indianapolis: Bobbs-Merrill, 1964); Charles E. Lindblom, *The Policy-Making Process* (Englewood Cliffs, N.J.: Prentice-Hall, 1968); Yehezkel Dror, *Public Policymaking Reexamined* (San Francisco: Chandler, 1968); John C. Donovan, *The Policy Makers* (New York: Pegasus, 1970); Lewis Friedman, *Budgeting Municipal Expenditures: A Study in Comparative Policy Making* (New York: Praeger, 1975); David A. Caputo, ed., *The Politics of Policy Making in America: Five Case Studies* (San Francisco: W. H. Freeman & Co., 1977); John Brigham, *Making Public Policy: Studies in American Politics* (Lexington, Mass.: D. C. Heath & Co., 1977); Carol H. Weiss, ed., *Using Social Research for Public Policy Making* (Lexington, Mass.: Lexington Books, 1977); George C. Edwards III and Ira Sharkansky, *The Policy Predicament: Making and Implementing Public Policy* (San Francisco: W. H. Freeman & Co., 1978); James E. Anderson, *Public Policymaking,* 3rd ed. (New York: Holt, Rinehart & Winston, 1984); Nelson W. Polsby, *Political Innovation in America: The Politics of Policy Initiation* (New Haven, Conn.: Yale University Press, 1984).

See also BUREAUCRATIC POLICY-MAKING and DECISION-MAKING.

public power, energy produced by government owned and operated power plants such as those of the Tennessee Valley Authority.

Public Productivity Review, quarterly devoted to all of the concerns of productivity enhancement in the public sector.
Public Productivity Review
National Center for Public
  Productivity
John Jay College of Criminal Justice
City University of New York
445 West 59th Street
New York, NY 10019

public relations, the totality of informing and influencing the public about the jurisdiction's activities as well as measuring public attitudes towards the jurisdiction's activities in order to modify existing programs.

public sector organization, any agency or institution funded, directly or indirectly, by public taxation.

See also PRIVATE SECTOR ORGANIZATION and THIRD SECTOR.

public utilities, legal designation encompassing those organizations producing essential services, usually in a monopolistic fashion. The designation requires these organizations to be highly regulated by government. Examples are electricity, natural gas, etc. *See* William T. Gormley, Jr., *The Politics of Public Utility Regulation* (Pittsburgh, Pa.: University of Pittsburgh Press, 1985).

public utilities commission (PUC), state agency that regulates power companies, railroads, etc.

Public Utility Regulatory Policies Act, *see* NATIONAL ENERGY ACT OF 1978.

public welfare, support of and assistance to needy persons contingent upon their need. *See* Gilbert Steiner, *Social Insecurity: The Politics of Welfare* (Chicago: Rand McNally, 1966); Gilbert Steiner, *The State of Welfare* (Washington, D.C.: The Brookings Institution Press, 1971); Francis Fox Piven and Richard A. Cloward, *Regulating the Poor: The Functions of Public Welfare* (New York: Random House, 1971).

See also RELIEF and WELFARE.

Public Welfare, quarterly journal of the American Public Welfare Association.
Public Welfare
1125 15th Street, N.W.
Washington, D.C. 20036

public works, generic term for government sponsored construction projects. *See* Ellis Armstrong, ed., *History of Public Works in the United States: 1776-1976* (Chicago: American Public Works Association, 1976); F. Burke Sheeran, *Management Essentials for Public Works Administrators* (Chicago: American Public Works Association, 1976); William E. Korbitz, ed., *Urban Public Works Ad-*

ministration (Washington, D.C.: International City Management Association, 1976).
See also BENEFIT DISTRICT.

Publius, journal of federalism that deals with all aspects of intergovernmental relations.
Publius
Center for the Study of Federalism
Temple University
Philadelphia, PA 19122

PUC, *see* PUBLIC UTILITIES COMMISSIONS.

PUD, *see* PLANNED UNIT DEVELOPMENT.

pyramid, also called ORGANIZATIONAL PYRAMID, colloquial term for an organization's hierarchy. According to Vance Packard, *The Pyramid Climbers* (New York: McGraw-Hill, 1962),

> The number of ledges—or steps—in a company's hierarchy varies of course with the company's size and philosophy of organization. Some like tall, slender pyramids, with only a few people under each leader; others prefer short, squat pyramids. Occasionally, one literally sees these modern pyramids in brick and mortar, where the home office occupies a skyscraper with the suites of the highest officers at the pinnacle.
>
> This is equally true for government. For example, in the U.S. State Department, the highest officials occupy the seventh and highest floor of their building. Policy is frequently said to come—not from any particular official—but simply from the "seventh floor."

See also FLAT ORGANIZATION.

Q

qualification requirements, education, experience, and other prerequisites to employment or placement in a position.

Qualifications Review Board, panel attached to the federal government's Office of Personnel Management (OPM) that determines whether a candidate for career appointment in the Senior Executive Service meets the managerial criteria established by law.

qualified handicapped individual, *see* HANDICAPPED INDIVIDUAL.

qualifying test, examination used to simply qualify or disqualify individuals for employment or promotion, in contrast to tests that rank order individuals in terms of their scores.

qualitative research methods, a general term that incorporates a wide array of research methodologies which do not use quantitative data or analytical procedures. As applied to the study of organizations, qualitative research has been rooted in the tradition of cultural anthropology's "ethnographic paradigms" —see P. R. Sanday, "The Ethnographic Paradigms," in John VanMannen, ed., *Qualitative Methodology* (Beverly Hills, Calif.: Sage Publications, 1979). During the late 1970's and 1980's, qualitative research methods have been experiencing a rebirth of interest and attention for studying organizations, largely because of dissatisfaction with the lack of useful knowledge produced during the last two decades through such quantitative research methods such as experimental and quasi-experimental designs. *See also* B. G. Glaser and A. L. Strauss, *The Discovery of Grounded Theory: Strategies for Qualitative Research* (New York: Aldine Publishing Company, 1967) and M. B. Miles and A. M. Huberman, *Qualitative Data Analysis: A Sourcebook of New Methods* (Beverly Hills, Calif.: Sage Publications, 1984).

quality circles, small groups of employees working in the same organizational unit who, with the approval of management, voluntarily meet on a regular basis to identify and solve problems that directly affect their work. *See* Elaine Rendall, "Quality Circles—A 'Third Wave' Intervention," *Training and Development Journal* (March 1981); Edwin G. Yager, "The Quality Control Circle Explosion," *Training and Development Journal* (April 1981); Kenneth M. Jenkins and Justin Shimada, "Quality Circles in the Service Sector," *Supervisory Management* (August 1981); Philip C. Thompson, *Quality Circles: How to Make Them Work in America* (New York: AMACOM, 1982); John D. Blair, Stanley L. Cohen, and Jerome V. Hurwitz, "Quality Circles," *Public Productivity Review* (March–June 1982); Joyce Roll and David Roll, "The Potential For Application of Quality Circles in the American Public Sector," *Public Productivity Review* (June 1983).

quality control, the totality of concern for, including the inspection of, the goods and services that are produced by an organization.

quality increase, additional within-grade increase granted to federal General Schedule employees for high quality performance above that ordinarily found in the type of position concerned.

quality of working life, area of concern that addresses the problem of creating more humane working environments. For a summary of the "state of the art," *see* Louis E. Davis & Albert B. Cherns, eds., *The Quality of Working Life* (New York: The Free Press, 1975). For analyses of cooperative union-management projects, *see* Edward E. Lawer III and John A. Drexler, Jr., "Dynamics of Establishing Cooperative Quality-of-Worklife Projects," *Monthly Labor Review* (March 1978); William H. Holley, Hubert S. Feild and James C. Crowley, "Negotiating Quality of Worklife, Productivity and Traditional Issues: Union Members' Preferred Roles of Their Union," *Personnel Psychology* (Summer 1981); David Lewin, "Collective Bargaining and the Quality of Worklife," *Organizational Dynamics* (Autumn 1981); Michael Maccoby, "Helping Labor and a Firm Set Up a Quality-of-Worklife Plan," *Monthly Labor Review* (March 1984). *Also see* Robert H. Guest, "Quality of

Work Life—Learning From Tarrytown," *Harvard Business Review* (July–August 1975); Jerome M. Rosow, "Quality of Work Life Issues for the 1980s," *Training and Development Journal* (March 1981); David A. Nadler and Edward E. Lawler III, "Quality of Work Life: Perspectives and Directions," *Organizational Dynamics* (Winter 1983); Rupert F. Chisholm, "Quality of Working Life," *Public Productivity Review* (March 1983); Leonard A. Schlesinger and Barry Oshry, "Quality of Work Life and the Manager: Muddle in the Middle," *Organizational Dynamics* (Summer 1984).

See also NATIONAL CENTER FOR PRODUCTIVITY AND QUALITY OF WORKING LIFE.

quartile, one of three points that divide the test scores in a distribution into four equal groups.

quasi-experimental design, use of experimental methods and modes of analysis in situations lacking the full requirements of experimental control. The methodology for research in many social organizations is necessarily quasi-experimental.

quasi-judicial agency, agency such as a regulatory commission that may perform many courtlike functions in the course of enforcing its rules. For example, it may bring charges, hold hearings and render judgments. *Quasi* is Latin for "sort of" or "analogous to."

quasi-legislative, rule-making functions of administrative agencies.

questionnaire, set of questions to be answered by a subject. *See* J. L. Stone, "The Use of an Applicant Service Questionnaire," *Public Personnel Management* (March–April 1974); Donald P. Warwick and Charles A. Lininger, *The Sample Survey* (New York: McGraw-Hill, 1975).

questionnaire, exit, *see* EXIT INTERVIEW.

queuing theory, mathematical technique used in simulation and operations research that allows an analyst to identify the op-

timal use of agency personnel and equipment in situations that have the characteristics of a waiting line.

quickie strike, spontaneous or unannounced strike of short duration.

quid pro quo, Latin meaning "something for something"; the giving of one valuable thing for another.

quit, volunteered resignation. According to Ken Jennings, in "When A Quit Is Not a Quit," *Personnel Journal* (December 1971), a quit can be considered a discharge for the purposes of arbitral review if "intent to resign is not evidenced." Arbitrators have reasoned that "if this treatment of quit as discharge were not applied, management could escape from the 'just cause' provisions of the labor contract by insisting that an undesirable employee's quit (voluntary or coerced) was not subject to the grievance procedure." *Also see* Francine D. Blau and Lawrence M. Khan, "Race and Sex Differences in Quits by Young Workers," *Industrial and Labor Relations Review* (July 1981); Gary Solon, "The Effects of Unemployment Insurance Eligibility Rules on Job Quitting Behavior," *Journal of Human Resources* (Winter 1984).

quota, *see* GOAL.

R

r, see CORRELATION COEFFICIENT.

race, according to the United Nations publication *Race and Science* (New York: UNESCO, 1961),

a group or population characterized by some concentrations, relative as to frequency and distribution, of hereditary particles (genes) or physical characters, which appear, fluctuate, and often disappear in the course of time by reason of geographic and/or cultural isolation. The varying manifestations of these traits in different populations are perceived in different ways by each group. What is perceived is largely preconceived, so that each group arbitrarily tends to misinterpret the variability which occurs as a fundamental difference which separates that group from all others.

A more expansive definition is provided by G. E. Simpson and J. M. Yinger in *Racial and Cultural Minorities,* 3rd ed. (New York: Harper & Row, 1965). They find that there are really three basic approaches to race: (1) the "mystical" or "political" approach "has been the stock in trade in the chicanery of rabble rousers, fanatics, demagogues, adventurers, and charlatans (rational or psychopathic)," (2) the "administrative conception of race" has government actions based on certain "racial" categories established by legislative act or bureaucratic practice; and (3) the biological approach based on crude observations of obvious physical differences. *Also see* Anne Wortham, *The Other Side of Racism: A Philosophical Study of Black Race Consciousness* (Ohio State University Press, 1981); Thomas S. Sowell, *The Economics and Politics of Race* (New York: Morrow, 1983).

race categories, *also* ETHNIC CATEGORIES, the race/ethnic categories that the Equal Employment Opportunity Commission insists to be used for EEO reporting purposes, as follows:

White, not of Hispanic Origin. Persons having origins in any of the original peoples of Europe, North Africa, or the Middle East.

Black, not of Hispanic Origin. Persons having origins in any of the black racial groups of Africa.

Hispanic. Persons of Mexican, Puerto Rican, Cuban, Central or South American or other Spanish culture or origin, regardless of race.

American Indian or Alaskan Native. Persons having origins in any of the original peoples of North America and who maintain cultural identification through tribal affiliation or community recognition.

Asian or Pacific Islander. Persons having origins in any of the original peoples of the Far East, Southeast Asia, the Indian subcontinent, or the Pacific Islands. This area includes, for example, China, Japan, Korea, the Philippine Islands, and Samoa.

race differential, *see* SEX DIFFERENTIAL.

racist, any person or oragnization that consciously or unconsciously practices racial discrimination. *See* Benjamin P. Bowser and Raymond G. Hunt, eds., *Impacts of Racism on White Americans* (Beverly Hills, Calif.: Sage Publications, Inc., 1981); John P. Fernandez, *Racism and Sexism in Corporate Life: Changing Values in American Business* (Lexington, Mass.: D.C. Heath and Co., Lexington Books, 1981); Terry L. Leap and Larry R. Smeltzer, "Racial Remarks in the Workplace: Humor or Harassment?" *Harvard Business Review* (November-December 1984).

raiding, generally, efforts by one organization to gain members of a competing organization for their own. As a tactic, raiding is used by both management and labor.

Railroad Retirement Act of 1934, act declared unconstitutional by the U.S. Supreme Court in *Railroad Retirement Board* v. *Alton Railroad Company,* 295 U.S. 330 (1935). The Railroad Retirement Act of 1935, as amended, provides for a federal retirement program for employees in the railroad industry and their families.

Railroad Retirement Board (RRB), federal agency that administers retirement-survivor and unemployment-sickness benefit programs provided by federal laws for the nation's railroad workers and their families. Under the Railroad Retirement Act, annuities are paid by the RRB to rail employees with at least ten years of service who retire because of age or disability and to their eligible spouses. Under the Railroad Unemployment Insurance Act, biweekly benefits are payable by the RRB to workers with qualifying railroad earnings who become unemployed or sick. About one hundred field offices are maintained across the country.

The RRB is composed of three members appointed by the president by and with the advice of the Senate—one upon recommendations of representatives of employees, one upon recommendations of carriers, and one, the chairman, as a public member.

Railroad Retirement Board
844 Rush Street
Chicago, IL 60611
(312) 751-4776
Washington Liaison Office
Room 630
425 Thirteenth Street, N.W.
Washington, D.C. 20004
(202) 724-0787

Railroad Retirement Board* v. *Alton Railroad Co., *see* RAILROAD RETIREMENT ACT.

Railroad Unemployment Insurance Act of 1938, federal statute that created a national system to provide railroad employees with unemployment and sickness benefits.

Railway Labor Act of 1926, federal statute, amended in 1934 to include airlines, that protects the collective bargaining rights of employees and established the National Railroad Adjustment Board to arbitrate grievances that arise from labor-management contracts. *See* Leonard A. Lecht, *Experience Under Railway Labor Legislation* (New York: AMS Press, 1955, 1968); George S. Roukis, "Should the Railway Labor Act Be Amended?" *The Arbitration Journal* (March 1983).

RAND Corporation, leading "think tank" that periodically issues analyses of public policies and problems.
RAND Corporation
1700 Main Street

Santa Monica, CA 90406
(213) 393-0411

R & D, *see* RESEARCH AND DEVELOPMENT.

random sample, sample of members of a population drawn in such a way that every member of the population has an equal chance of being included in the sample.

random selection, research procedure in which every potential subject has an equal chance to be included in the research sample. Random selection is a process that allows the scientist to collect information from a sample of subjects who represent the total population and then to generalize the findings to the entire population. By employing the techniques of random selection, the scientist saves time, energy, and money.

range, difference between the lowest and highest scores obtained on a test by some group.

rank, place in a hierarchical ordering of positions.

rank and file, colloquial expression referring to the masses. When used in an organizational context, it refers to those members of the organization who are not part of management. The term is frequently used to describe those members of a union having no status as officers or shop stewards. Rank and file was originally a military term referring to the enlisted men who had to line up in ranks, side by side, and files, one behind the other. Officers, being gentlemen, were spared such indignities. *See* George W. Bohlander, "How the Rank and File Views Local Union Administration—A Survey," *Employee Relations Law Journal* (Autumn 1982); Samuel R. Friedman, *Teamster Rank and File: Power, Bureaucracy, and Rebellion at Work and in a Union* (New York: Columbia University Press, 1982).

ranking, *see* JOB RANKING.

ranking test, examination used to rank individuals according to their scores so that those with the higher scores have an advantage in gaining employment or promotion.

rank-in-man system, also called PERSONAL-RANK SYSTEM, method of establishing pay primarily on the basis of an employee's qualifications without consideration given to the specific duties and responsibilities that would be performed by the employee. Such personal rank systems tend to be restricted to the military, the U.S. Foreign Service, and other similar officer corps systems. *See* Harold H. Leich, "Rank in Man or Job? Both!" *Public Administration Review* (Spring 1960).

rank performance rating, method of performance appraisal that requires superiors to rank order employees according to their merit.

rate, beginner's, *see* BEGINNER'S RATE.

rate, incentive, *see* INCENTIVE RATE.

rate, trainee, *see* BEGINNER'S RATE.

ratebuster, also called JOB SPOILER, general term for any employee whose production level far exceeds the norms established by the majority of the work force. Ratebusters usually face considerable peer pressure to conform to average production levels and sometimes this pressure can be physical. A *job spoiler* is a British ratebuster. For a study of the personality traits of ratebusters, *see* Melville Dalton, "The Industrial 'Ratebuster': A Characterization," *Applied Anthropology* (Winter 1948).

rate fixing, the power of some administrative agencies—public utility commissions, for example—to set the prices a company may charge for its services. This differs from price fixing which is done by sellers of goods or services and may be illegal.

ratification, formal confirmation by the union membership of a contract that has been signed on their behalf by union representatives.

rating, efficiency, *see* EFFICIENCY RATING.

rating, rank-performance, *see* RANK-PERFORMANCE RATING.

rating chart, graphic, *see* GRAPHIC RATING CHART.

rating system, deferred, *see* DEFERRED RATING SYSTEM.

ratio, efficiency, *see* EFFICIENCY.

ratio delay, work sampling technique that uses a large number of observations taken at random intervals in order to determine the parts of the work day (expressed in minutes or hours) during which an employee is working productively or is engaged in activities other than productive work. *See* L.H.C. Tippett, "The Ratio-Delay Technique," *Time and Motion Study* (May 1953).

rational-comprehensive approach, decision-making model requiring a complete assessment of all factors (costs, benefits, alternatives, etc.) in order to discover the best possible decision.

rational validity, measure that involves the use of a detailed job analysis to determine the knowledges, skills, and abilities that are necessary for effective performance in a particular job. Measurement instruments are then designed to measure such factors. For example, if a job requirement is the ability to type errorless copy at fifty words a minute, a test can be designed to measure that ability.

rat race, slang phrase for the relentless pursuit of success. The "race" is usually engaged in and won by workaholics who can't think of anything better to do anyway. Vermin lovers consider the phrase a gross libel of a species that would be innocent save for the bubonic plague. *See also* WORKAHOLIC.

raw score, also called CRUDE SCORE, number of items correct when there is no correction for guessing, or the formula score when a correction for guessing has been applied.

reaction management, management posture that is limited to responding to immediate problems and pressures. *See* Robert P. McGowan and John M. Stevens, "Local Government Management: Reactive or Adaptive?" *Public Administration Review* (May-June 1983).

reading assistant, reader for a blind employee. Public Law 87-614 of 1962 authorizes the employment of readers for blind federal employees. These reading assistants serve without compensation from the government, but they can be paid by the blind employees, nonprofit organizations, or state offices of vocational rehabilitation. They may also serve on a volunteer basis.

Reaganomics, *see* SUPPLY-SIDE ECONOMICS.

reallocate, *see* ALLOCATE.

reallocation, also called RECLASSIFICATION, change in the position classification of an existing position resulting from significant changes in assigned duties and responsibilities.

Realpolitik, originally a German word meaning "realist politics." Applied to politics—whether of the organizational or societal variety—that are premised upon material or practical factors rather than theoretical or ethical considerations. According to John E. Fisher in "Playing Favorites in Large Organizations," *Business Horizons* (June 1977),

the realpolitiks of business offices may be overlooked by students of business administration who are surfeited with the literature of management techniques. Yet the literature actually reveals far less about how organizations operate internally than can be learned from studying office patronage and politics.

Pre-occupation with management techniques may be misleading to callow youth just coming from the halls of academe into the occupational armies of business. Unsophisticated tyros are led to believe that their technical qualifications will be highly regarded and will play a significant role in their advancement. And so it may, in some instances. In organizations dominated by authoritarians, however, office patronage and politics hold the key to what is to be accomplished and what is forbidden. Office patronage provides a means for people of indifferent ability who have acquired power to be secure in its exercise.

Also see Albert Somit, "Bureaucratic Realpolitik and Teaching of Administration," *Public Administration Review* (Autumn 1956); Nestor Cruz, " 'Realopolitik' and Affirmative Action," *Public Personnel Management,* Vol. 9, No. 3, 1980); Gerald F. Cavanagh, Dennis J. Moberg, and Manuel Velasquez, "The Ethics of Organizational Politics," *Academy of Management Review* (July 1981); Frank M. Machovec and Howard R. Smith, "Fear Makes the World Go Round: The 'Dark' Side of Management," *Management Review* (January 1982); Manuel Velasquez, Dennis J. Moberg, and Gerald F. Cavanagh, "Organizational Statesmanship and Dirty Politics: Ethical Guidelines for the Organizational Politician," *Organizational Dynamics* (Autumn 1983); Andrew Kakabadse, *The Politics of Management* (New York: Nichols, 1984).

real-property tax, *see* TAX, REAL-PROPERTY.

real wages, wages after they have been adjusted for changes in the level of prices. The buying power of wages, the "real" wages, are computed by dividing the dollar amount by an index measuring changes in prices (such as the Consumer Price Index).

reappropriation, legislative action to restore or extend the obligational availability, whether for the same or different purposes, of all or part of the unobligated portion of budget authority which otherwise would lapse.

reasonable accommodation, reasonable steps to accommodate a handicapped employee's disability, required of an employer unless such steps would cause the employer undue hardship. Examples of "reasonable accommodations" include providing a reader for a blind employee, an interpreter for a deaf person requiring telephone contacts, or adequate work space for an employee confined to a wheelchair. *See* Janet Asher and Jules Asher, "How To Accommodate Workers in Wheelchairs," *Job Safety and Health* (October 1976); Leslie Milk, "What Is Reasonable Accommodation?" *Civil Service Journal* (October-December 1978); Dorothy J. Steffanic, *Reasonable Accommodation for Deaf Employees in White Collar Jobs* (Washington, D.C.: U.S. Office of Personnel Management, 1982).

reassignment, transfer of an employee while serving continuously within the same organization from one position to another without promotion or demotion.

recall, (1) procedure that allows citizens to vote officeholders out of office between regularly scheduled elections or (2) the rehiring of employees from a layoff. In an employee recall, union contracts usually require that the union be given both notice of the recall and the names of the employees to be recalled. This enables the union to determine if employees are being called back in the order required by the agreement. *See* Bureau of Labor Statistics, U.S. Department of Labor, *Major Collective Bargaining Agreements: Layoff, Recall, and Worksharing Procedures* (Washington, D.C.: U.S. Government Printing Office, Bulletin 1425-13, 1972).

recall item, test question that requires the examinee to supply the correct answer from memory, in contrast to a recognition item, where the examinee need only identify the correct answer.

receipts from off-budget federal agencies, *see* OFFSETTING RECEIPTS.

receiver, person appointed by a court to manage the affairs of an organization facing litigation and/or reorganization.

recess appointment, a presidential appointment to federal office of a person to fill a vacancy while the Senate is not in session.

A person appointed to office while the Senate is in recess may begin his or her duties before his or her name has been submitted to the Senate. However, the president must submit the nomination when the Senate reconvenes, and the recess appointment expires at the end of the next session unless the Senate has confirmed the appointment by a majority vote. Moreover, the recess appointment expires and the office is declared vacant even earlier than the end of the next session if the Senate acts before that time to reject the nominee.

recession, a decline in overall business activity that is pervasive, substantial, and of at least several months' duration. Historically, a decline in real gross national product for at least two consecutive quarters has been considered a recession.

reciprocity, the giving of privileges to the citizens of one jurisdiction by the government of another and vice versa.

reclassification, *see* REALLOCATION.

reclassify, *see* CLASSIFY.

recognition, employer's acceptance of a union as the bargaining agent for all of the employees in a particular bargaining unit. *See also* EXCLUSIVE RECOGNITION.

recognition item, test question that calls for the examinee to recognize or select the correct answer from among two or more alternatives.

recognition picketing, picketing to encourage an employer to recognize a particular union as the bargaining agent for his or her employees.

recognition strike, work stoppage that seeks to force an employer to formally recognize and deal with a union.

reconciliation, the process used by Congress to reconcile amounts determined by tax, spending, and debt legislation for a given fiscal year with the ceilings enacted in the second required concurrent resolution on the budget for that year. Changes to laws, bills, and resolutions, as required to conform with the binding totals for budget authority, revenues, and the public debt, are incorporated into either a reconciliation resolution or reconciliation bill.

record, written account of a case containing the complete history of all actions taken concerning it.

record, public, document filed with, or put out by, a government agency and open for public review.

record copy, copy of a document that is regarded by an organization as the most important or the key official copy.

recorder of deeds, official who is responsible for properly filing public land records.

recruitment, total process by which an organization gathers individuals to occupy its various positions. *See* Robert M. Guion, "Recruiting, Selection, and Job Placement," in Marvin D. Dunnett, ed., *Handbook of Industrial and Organization Psychology* (Chicago: Rand McNally, 1976); Erwin S. Stanton, *Successful Personnel Recruiting and Selection within EEO/Affirmative Action Guidelines* (New York: AMACOM, 1977); John P. Wanous, *Organizational Entry: Recruitment, Selection, and Socialization of Newcomers* (Reading, Mass.: Addison-Wesley, 1980); Christine White and Abbie Willard Thorner, *Managing the Recruitment Process* (New York: Law & Business, Inc., 1982); Bernard S. Hodes, *The Principles and Practices of Recruit-*

ment Advertising: A Guide for Personnel Professionals (New York: F. Fell Publishers, 1982).
See also POSITIVE RECRUITMENT.

red circle (position classification), *see* EAR-MARK.

red-circle rate, also called RINGED RATE, rate of pay that is higher than the established rate for a particular job.

Redford, Emmette S. (1904-), political scientist who holds that because a technological society can operate "only in part under directives from organizations directly representative of the people," the best that can be hoped for is a "workable democracy" in which groups are forced to compete with each other for influence. In such a context the successful public administrators will be those able to work with the competing forces to achieve enough of a consensus to move ahead. Major works include: *Administration of National Economic Control* (New York: Macmillan, 1952); *Ideal and Practice in Public Administration* (University, Ala.: University of Alabama Press, 1958); *American Government and the Economy* (New York: Oxford University Press, 1966); *Democracy in the Administrative State* (New York: Oxford University Press, 1969); *The Regulatory Process* (Austin: University of Texas Press, 1969).

redlining, practice allegedly followed by urban financial institutions in which they refuse loans for home mortgages and home improvements to areas thought to be poor risks. Consequently, people living or wishing to live in these designated areas are denied such loans regardless of their particular financial situation. The name, redlining, derives from the drawing of red lines around such areas on a map. *See* John Tomer, "The Mounting Evidence on Mortgage Redlining," *Urban Affairs Quarterly* (June 1980); Joe T. Darden, "State Anti-Redline Laws: A Comparative Analysis," *State Government,* Vol. 56, No. 1 (1983).

red rash, job action by firefighters who, because they cannot legally strike, call in sick. When police suffer from this affliction, it is called the "blue flu."

See also BLUE FLU and STRIKE.

red tape, despised symbol of excessive formality and attention to routine that has its origins in the red ribbon with which clerks bound official documents in the last century. The ribbon has disappeared, but the practices it represents linger on.

Herbert Kaufman's *Red Tape: Its Origins, Uses, and Abuses* (Washington, D.C.: The Brookings Institution, 1977) finds that the term "is applied to a bewildering variety of organizational practices and features." After all, "one person's 'red tape' may be another's treasured procedural safeguard." Kaufman concludes that "red tape turns out to be at the core of our institutions rather than an excresence on them."

reduction in force, *see* RIF.

redundant, no longer needed; to be laid off. *See* Peter F. Drucker, "Planning for 'Redundant' Workers," *Personnel Administrator* (January 1980); Edward Yemin, ed., *Workforce Reductions in Undertakings: Policies and Measures for the Protection of Redundant Workers in Seven Industrialized Market Economy Countries* (Geneva: International Labour Office, 1982).

re-employed annuitant, employee who, having retired with a pension from an organization, is again employed by that same organization. Most of the re-employed annuitants working for the federal government (about three thousand in 1975) are subject to a law that has their salary reduced by the amount of the annuity.

re-employment list, also called RE-EMPLOYMENT ELIGIBILITY LIST, list required by most merit systems and union contracts. In the event of layoffs, employees will be ranked on a re-employment list in order of their seniority. Usually, re-employment

lists must be exhausted before new hires can be considered.

See also the following entries:
LAYOFF
RECALL
RIF

reference checking, verifying information provided by a job applicant. *See* Edward L. Levine, "Legal Aspects of Reference Checking for Personnel Selection," *The Personnel Administrator* (November 1977); John D. Rice, "Privacy Legislation: Its Effect on Pre-employment Reference Checking," *The Personnel Administrator* (February 1978); Edward L. Levine and Stephone M. Rudolph, *Reference Checking for Personnel Selection: The State of the Art* (Berea, Ohio: American Society for Personnel Administration, 1978); Paula Lippin, "The Delicate Art of Checking References," *Administrative Management* (August 1979); James D. Bell, James Castagnera, and Jane Patterson Young, "Employment References, Do You Know the Law?" *Personnel Journal* (February 1984).

reference group, also called SOCIAL REFERENCE GROUP, social group with which an individual identifies to the extent that his/her personal values are derived from the group's norms and attitudes. *See* Herbert H. Hyman and Eleanor Singer, eds., *Readings in Reference Group Theory and Research* (New York: The Free Press, 1968).

referendum, procedure for submitting proposed laws to the voters for ratification. *See* Stanley Scott and Harriet Nathan, "Public Referenda: A Critical Appraisal," *Urban Affairs* (March 1970); Darold T. Barnum and I. B. Helburn, "Influencing the Electorate: Experience with Referenda on Public Employee Bargaining," *Industrial and Labor Relations Review* (April 1982).

reform movement, *see* PROGRESSIVE MOVEMENT.

refunding, issuance of long-term debt in exchange for, or to provide funds for, the retirement of long-term debt already outstanding.

Regents of the University of California v. Allan Bakke, 438 U.S. 265 (1978), U.S. Supreme Court case which upheld a white applicant's claim of reverse discrimination because he was denied admission to the University of California Medical School at Davis when sixteen out of the school's one hundred class spaces were set aside for minority applicants. The court ruled that Bakke must be admitted to the Davis Medical School as soon as possible, but that the university had the right to take race into account in its admissions criteria. The imprecise nature of taking race into account as one factor among many has created considerable speculation about the potential impact this case may have on voluntary affirmative action programs concerning employment. *See* Allan P. Sindler, *Bakke, Defunis, and Minority Admissions: The Quest for Equal Opportunity* (New York: Longman, 1978); Joel Dreyfuss and Charles Lawrence III, *The Bakke Case: The Politics of Inequality* (New York: Harcourt, Brace, Jovanovich, 1979); J. Harvie Wilkinson III, *From Brown to Bakke: The Supreme Court and School Integration 1954-1978* (New York: Oxford University Press, 1979); C. G. Bakaly and G. E. Krischer, "Bakke: Its Impact on Public Employment Discrimination," *Employee Relations Law Journal* (Spring 1979); William Kelso, "From Bakke to Fullilove: Has the Supreme Court Finally Settled the Affirmative Action Controversy?" *Review of Public Personnel Administration* (Fall 1980); Timothy J. O'Neill, *Bakke and the Politics of Equality: Friends and Foes in the Classroom of Litigation* (Middletown, CT: Wesleyan University Press, 1984).
See also the following entries:
DEFUNIS V. ODEGAARD
REVERSE DISCRIMINATION
UNITED STEEL WORKERS OF AMERICA V. WEBER, ET AL.

regional bargaining, collective bargaining between a union and the representatives of an industry in a given region.

regional science, comprehensive study of natural and human resources of a discrete geographic area. *See* Gill C. Lim, ed., *Regional Planning: Evolution, Crisis and Prospects* (Totowa, N.J.: Rowman & Allanheld, 1983).

Regional Science Association (RSA), organization of academics and professionals (usually planners) concerned with urban and regional analysis.
RSA
3718 Locust Walk
University of Pennsylvania
Philadelphia, PA 19104
(215) 898-8412

register, also called REGISTRY, any book of public facts, such as births, deaths, and marriages. Other examples of public record books are the register of patents, the register of ships, the register of deeds, and the register of wills.

registered bonds, bonds that require registration of the owner with the jurisdiction issuing the bond.

register of eligibles, see ELIGIBLE LIST.

registration, see OCCUPATIONAL REGISTRATION.

regression analysis, also MULTIPLE REGRESSION ANALYSIS, method for describing the nature of the relationship between two variables so that the value of one can be predicted if the value of the other is known. *Multiple regression analysis* involves more than two variables. *See* James L. Danielson and Russ Smith, "The Application of Regression Analysis to Equality and Merit in Personnel Decisions," *Public Personnel Management,* Vol. 10, No.1 (1981); Walter W. Hudson, "Simplified Multiple Regression for Applied Behavioral Science," *The Journal of Applied Behavioral Science,* Vol. 18, No. 4 (1982).

regressive tax, see TAX EQUITY.

regulation, the rulemaking process of those administrative agencies charged with the official interpretation of a statute. These agencies (most typically independent regulatory commissions), in addition to issuing rules, also tend to administer their implementation and adjudicate interpretative disputes. *See* Henry M. Peskin, Paul R. Portney, and Allen V. Kneese, eds., *Environmental Regulation and the U.S. Economy* (Baltimore: Johns Hopkins University Press, 1981); Lawrence J. White, *Reforming Regulation: Processes and Problems* (Englewood Cliffs, N.J.: Prentice-Hall, 1981); Robert A. Katzmann, *Regulatory Bureaucracy: The Federal Trade Commission and Antitrust Policy* (Cambridge, Mass.: M.I.T. Press, 1981); M. Elizabeth Sanders, *The Regulation of Natural Gas: Policy and Politics, 1938-1978* (Philadelphia, Pa.: Temple University Press, 1981); Eugene Bardach and Robert A. Kagan, *Going by the Book: The Problem of Regulatory Unreasonableness* (Philadelphia, Pa.: Temple University Press, 1981); Frederick C. Thayer, Jr., *Rebuilding America: The Case for Economic Regulation* (New York: Praeger Publishers, 1984); Ted Greenwood, *Knowledge and Discretion in Government Regulation* (New York: Praeger Publishers, 1984); Thomas K. McCraw, "Regulation in America: A Historical Overview," *California Management Review* (Fall 1984); Andrew S. Carron, *Reforming the Bank Regulatory Structure* (Washington, D.C.: The Brookings Institution, 1985); Kenneth J. Meier, *Regulation: Politics, Bureaucracy, and Economics* (New York: St. Martin's Press, 1985).

See also following entries:
RULEMAKING
HUMPHREY'S EXECUTOR V. UNITED STATES
INDEPENDENT AGENCY
CONSENT ORDER
DELEGATION OF POWER
NATIONAL ASSOCIATION FOR THE ADVANCEMENT OF COLORED PEOPLE V. FEDERAL POWER COMMISSION
UNITED STATES V. STUDENTS CHALLENGING REGULATORY AGENCY PROCEDURES

regulatory tax, *see* TAX, REGULATORY.

rehabilitants, emotional, *see* EMOTIONALLY HANDICAPPED EMPLOYEES.

Rehabilitated Offender Program, federal government's program to assure fair federal employment opportunity for qualified applicants convicted of a crime who are subsequently declared rehabilitated offenders. The federal government seeks to selectively hire rehabilitated offenders for jobs where they are needed and for which they are qualified by experience, education, and training, as determined by normal competitive examining procedures. Rehabilitated offenders who are mentally retarded or otherwise severely handicapped are appointed under the same procedures used for other such handicapped persons, with appointing officials taking into account their record, conduct, and rehabilitative efforts. In both competitive and excepted appointments, the hiring agency makes the final decision on whether an applicant would be the right person for a particular opening.

Reid* v. *Covert, *see* EXECUTIVE AGREEMENT.

reindustrialization, a loose term for public and private efforts to make American industry more competitive in world markets by rejuvenating its physical plant. *See* Milton D. Lower, "The Reindustrialization of America," *Journal of Economic Issues* (June 1982).

reinforcement, also POSITIVE REINFORCEMENT and NEGATIVE REINFORCEMENT, inducement to perform in a particular manner. *Positive reinforcement* occurs when an individual receives a desired reward that is contingent upon some prescribed behavior. *Negative reinforcement* occurs when an individual works to avoid an undesirable reward. *See* B. F. Skinner, *Contingencies of Reinforcement: A Theoretical Analysis* (New York: Appleton-Century-Crofts, 1969); Harry Wiard, "Why Manage Behavior? A Case for Positive Reinforcement," *Human Resource Management* (Summer 1972); Jerry A. Wallinand and Ronald D. Johnson, "The Positive Reinforcement Approach to Controlling Employee Absenteeism," *Personnel Journal* (August 1976); Norman C. Hill, "The Need For Positive Reinforcement in Corrective Counseling," *Supervisory Management* (December 1984).

reinstatement, restoration of an employee to his/her previous position without any loss of seniority or other benefits. In a governmental context, reinstatement is the noncompetitive reentrance into the competitive service of a person who acquired eligibility for such action as a result of previous service. Reinstatement is a privilege accorded in recognition of and on the basis of former service and is not a "right" to which one is entitled.

relevance, *see* CRITERION RELEVANCE.

relevant labor market, in the context of equal employment opportunity, the geographic area from which an organization should recruit in order to satisfy affirmative action requirements. *See* Howard R. Bloch and Robert L. Pennington, "Measuring Discrimination: What is a Relevant Labor Market," *Personnel* (July-August 1980).

reliability, dependability of a testing device, as reflected in the consistency of its scores when repeated measurements of the same group are made. When a test is said to have a high degree of reliability, it means that an individual tested today and tested again at a later time with the same test and under the same conditions will get approximately the same score. In short, a test is reliable if it gives a dependable measure of whatever it seeks to measure.
    See also INTERNAL CONSISTENCY RELIABILITY and INTERRATER RELIABILITY.

reliability coefficient, numerical index of reliability that is obtained by correlating scores on two forms of a test, from statistical data on individual test items, or

by correlating scores on different administrations of the same test. A reliability coefficient can be a perfect 1.00 or a perfectly unreliable -1.00. A reliability of .90 or greater is generally considered adequate for a test used as a personnel selection device.

relief, also WORK RELIEF, terms that usually refer to the public assistance programs available during the depression of the 1930s. *Relief* or *direct relief* referred to straight welfare payments. *Work relief* referred to any of the numerous public works projects initiated specifically to provide jobs for the unemployed. *See* Bruno Stein, *On Relief: The Economics of Poverty and Public Welfare* (New York: Basic Books, 1971).

religious discrimination, any act that manifests unfavorable or inequitable treatment toward employees or prospective employees because of their religious convictions. Because of section 703(a) (1) of the Civil Rights Act of 1964, an individual's religious beliefs or practices cannot be given any consideration in making employment decisions. The argument that a religious practice may place an undue hardship upon an employer—for example, where such practices require special religious holidays and hence absence from work—has been upheld by the courts. However, because of the sensitive nature of discharging or refusing to hire an individual on religious grounds, the burden of proof to show that such a hardship exists is placed upon the employer. *See* Charles J. Hollon and Thomas L. Bright, "Avoiding Religious Discrimination in the Workplace," *Personnel Journal* (August 1982); I. B. Helburn and John R. Hill, "The Arbitration of Religious Practice Grievances," *Arbitration Journal* (June 1984).

relocation allowance, payment by an employer of all or part of the cost of moving one's self and one's household to a distant place of employment. *See* Peter J. DiDomenico, Jr., "Relocation Benefits for

New Hires," *The Personnel Administrator* (February 1978).

removal, separation of an employee for cause or because of continual unacceptable performance.

remuneration, *see* COMPENSATION.

Renegotiation Board, federal agency that from 1951 to 1979 sought the elimination of excessive profits on defense and space contracts and related subcontracts. This was accomplished through informal and nonadversary proceedings before the board. Contractors not agreeing with board determinations had the right to petition the Court of Claims for redetermination.

rent control, local laws that regulate the amount by which landlords can raise rents on residential rental properties. *See* Peter Navarro, "Rent Control in Cambridge, Mass.," *The Public Interest* (Winter 1985).

reopener clause, also WAGE REOPENER CLAUSE, provision in a collective bargaining agreement stating the circumstances under which portions of the agreement, usually concerning wages, can be renegotiated before the agreement's normal expiration date. Typically such clauses provide for renegotiation at the end of a specified time period (such as one year) or when the Consumer Price Index increases by an established amount.

reorganization, changes in the administrative structure or formal procedures of government, traditionally in the areas of departmental consolidation, executive office expansion, budgetary reform, and personnel administration, generally for the purpose of promoting bureaucratic responsiveness to central executive control and, secondly, to simplify or professionalize administrative affairs.

Frederick C. Mosher in *Government Reorganizations: Cases and Commentary* (Indianapolis: Bobbs-Merrill, 1967) holds that the following generalities can be made about reorganizations:

1. that the tensions underlying reorganization efforts are already in existence and have been for some time;
2. that the majority of reorganization efforts are unsuccessful or only partially successful in reducing the tensions underlying them;
3. that the understanding of a single reorganization effort requires comprehension of the organization's prior history;
4. that a reorganization effort is not a "one time thing" but a step in a progressive history.

See Herbert Emmerich, *Essays on Federal Reorganization* (University, Ala.: University of Alabama Press, 1950); Barry Dean Karl, *Executive Reorganization and Reform in the New Deal: The Genesis of Administrative Management, 1900-1939* (Cambridge, Mass.: Harvard University Press, 1963); Richard Polenberg, *Reorganizing Roosevelt's Government: The Controversy Over Executive Reorganization, 1936-1939* (Cambridge, Mass.: Harvard University Press, 1966); Harvey C. Mansfield, "Federal Executive Reorganization: Thirty Years of Experience," *Public Administration Review* (July-August 1969); Harvey C. Mansfield, "Reorganizing the Federal Executive Branch: The Limits of Institutionalization," *Law and Contemporary Problems* (Summer 1970); Alan L. Dean, "The Goals of Departmental Reorganization," *The Bureaucrat* (Spring 1972); Peri E. Arnold, "Reorganization and Politics: A Reflection on the Adequacy of Administrative Theory," *Public Administration Review* (May-June 1974); Rufus E. Miles, Jr., "Considerations for a President Bent on Reorganization," *Public Administration Review* (March-April 1977); Rochelle L. Stanfield, "The Best Laid Reorganization Plans Sometimes Go Astray," *National Journal* (January 20, 1979); John M. Boyle, "Reorganization Reconsidered: An Empirical Approach to the Departmentalization Problem," *Public Administration Review* (September-October 1979); James L. Garnett, *Reorganizing State Government: The Executive Branch*

(Boulder, Colo.: Westview Press, 1980); Louis Fisher and Ronald C. Moe, "Presidential Reorganization Authority: Is It Worth the Cost?" *Political Science Quarterly* (Summer 1981); Vera Vogelsang-Coombs and Marvin Cummins, "Reorganizations and Reforms: Promises, Promises," *Review of Public Personnel Administration* (Spring 1982).

report, auditor's report in a financial audit, the medium through which an auditor expresses an opinion or, if circumstances require, disclaims an opinion. In either case, the auditor states whether the examination was made in accordance with generally accepted auditing standards. These standards require a statement as to whether, in the auditor's opinion, the financial statements are presented in conformity with generally accepted accounting principles and whether such principles have been consistently applied in the preparation of the financial statements of the current period in relation to those of the preceding period. *See* Roger Mansfield, "The Financial Reporting Practices of Government: A Time for Reflection," *Public Administration Review* (March–April 1979); Ronell B. Raaum, "A Recipe for Writing Management Audit Reports," *Government Accountants Journal* (Summer 1982).

reporting pay, *see* CALL-IN PAY.

representation election, *see* AUTHORIZATION ELECTION and EXCELSIOR RULE.

representative bureaucracy, concept originated by J. Donald Kingsley, in *Representative Bureaucracy* (Yellow Springs, Ohio: Antioch Press, 1944), which asserts that all social groups have a right to participation in their governing institutions. In recent years, the concept has developed a normative overlay—that all social groups should occupy bureaucratic positions in direct proportion to their numbers in the general population. For defenses of this normative position, *see* Samuel Krislov, *Representative Bureaucracy* (Englewood Cliffs, N.J.: Prentice-Hall, 1974); Harry Kranz, *The*

Participatory Bureaucracy: Women and Minorities in a More Representative Public Service (Lexington, Mass.: Lexington Books, 1976); Samuel Krislov and David H. Rosenbloom, *Representative Bureaucracy and the American Political System* (New York: Praeger, 1981); Dennis Daley, "Political and Occupational Barriers to the Implementation of Affirmative Action: Administrative, Executive, and Legislative Attitudes Toward Representative Bureaucracy," *Review of Public Personnel Administration* (Summer 1984).

representative sample, sample that corresponds to or matches the population of which it is a sample with respect to characteristics important for the purposes under investigation. For example, a representative national sample of secondary school students should probably contain students from each state, from large and small schools, and from public and independent schools in approximately the same proportions as these exist in the nation as a whole.

reprimand, formal censure for some job related behavior. A reprimand is less severe than an adverse action, more forceful than an admonition.

reprivatization, assignment of functions to the private sector that were previously performed by government (*i.e.,* trash collection, fire protection, etc.). *See* E. S. Savas, *Privatizing the Public Sector* (Chatham, N.J.: Chatham House, 1982).

reprogramming, procedure by which executive branch officials shift congressionally appropriated funds *within* an appropriation account from one program to another or from one activity to another. In the reprogramming procedure, the total amount of money appropriated to a specific account remains the same; only the purpose to which the money is put changes. Funds would be reprogrammed, for example, if the Department of Defense moved moneys within an account appropriated for the design stage of a new tank to the production stage. Reprogramming of funds does not require statutory authority. Usually the appropriate executive department or agency need only clear with the pertinent congressional committee or subcommittee. Reprogramming of funds is permitted to the executive by Congress on the assumption that circumstances unforseen at the time of appropriation may warrant limited but new applications of such funds. The reprogramming variant of presidential spending power became widely known after Louis Fisher published his *President and Congress: Power and Policy* (New York: The Free Press, 1972). *Also see* Fisher's *Presidential Spending Power* (Princeton, N.J.: Princeton University Press, 1975).

requisite skills, those skills that make a person eligible for consideration for employment in a particular job.

rescission, bill or joint resolution that provides for cancellation in whole or in part of budget authority previously granted by the Congress. Rescissions proposed by the president must be transmitted in a special message to the Congress. Congress must approve such proposed rescissions under procedures in the Budget and Impoundment Control Act of 1974 for them to take effect.

research and development, the systematic and intensive study of a subject in order to direct that knowledge toward the production of new materials, systems, methods, or processes. Corporate research uncovers facts and principles in order to benefit development. *Pure* or *basic* research attempts to uncover new scientific knowledge and understanding with little regard to when, or specifically how, the new facts will be used; and *applied* research is conducted with a special purpose in mind. It is usually directed toward a specific problem, or toward a series of problems that stand in the way of progress in a particular area. *See* Edward F. O'Keefe, Jr., "A Framework for Auditing Department of Defense Research and Development Programs," *Government Accountants Journal* (Fall 1978); Peter

House, "Making Federal R & D Useful— A Study of the Implementation Process," *The Bureaucrat* (Summer 1979); David B. Balkin and Luis R. Gomez-Mejia, "Determinants of R and D Compensation Strategies in The High Tech Industry," *Personnel Psychology* (Winter 1984).

Research Center for Group Dynamics, *see* INSTITUTE FOR SOCIAL RESEARCH.

research design, plan of investigation developed by a scientist to provide an answer to a research question. It is important that the plan meet the basic requirements of the scientific approach and that the selected procedures for gathering information are appropriate to the purposes of the research effort.

reserved powers, principle of federalism embodied in the Tenth Amendment of the U.S. Constitution that reserves for the states the residue of powers not granted to the federal government or withheld from the states.

reserved rights, *see* MANAGEMENT RIGHTS.

reserve requirements, the percentage of deposit liabilities that U.S. commercial banks are required to hold as a reserve at their Federal Reserve bank, as cash in their vaults, or as directed by state banking authorities. The reserve requirement is one of the tools of monetary policy. Federal Reserve officials can control the lending capacity of the banks (thus influencing the money supply) by varying the ratio of reserves to deposits that commercial banks are required to maintain.

residency requirement, *see* the following entries:
  DOMICILE
  HICKLIN V. ORBECK
  MCCARTHY V. PHILADELPHIA CIVIL
    SERVICE COMMISSION

residual unemployment, the fact that no matter how many jobs are available, there will always be some people out of work because of illness, indolence, movement from one job or community to another, etc. The total number of these individuals is a measure of residual unemployment.

resignation, employee's formal notice that his or her relationship with the employing organization is being terminated.

resignation, volunteered, *see* QUIT.

response rate, in survey research, the percentage of those given questionnaires who complete and return them.

responsibility, full, *see* FULL RESPONSIBILITY.

rest period, recuperative pause during working hours. *See* Stephen E. Bechtold, Ralph E. Janaro, and DeWitt L. Sumners, "Maximization of Labor Productivity Through Optimal Rest-Break Schedules," *Management Science* (December 1984).

restraining order, temporary, *see* INJUNCTION.

restriction of output, reduced productivity on the part of a worker or work force because of informal group norms, personal grievances, or sloth. For the classic study of this phenomenon, *see* Stanley B. Mathewson, *Restriction of Output Among Unorganized Workers* (Carbondale, Ill.: Southern Illinois University Press, 1931, 1969). *Also see* Harry Cohen, "Dimensions of Restriction of Output," *Personnel Journal* (December 1971).

restrictive credentialism, general term for any selection policy adversely affecting disadvantaged groups because they lack the formal qualifications for positions that, in the opinion of those adversely affected, do not truly need such formal qualifications.

resume, also CURRICULUM VITA, brief account of one's education and experience that job applicants typically prepare for prospective employers to review. In the academic world, a resume is more pompously called a *curriculum vita. See* Robert

P. Vecchio, "The Problem of Phony Resumes: How to Spot a Ringer Among the Applicants," *Personnel* (March-April 1984).

retention period, stated period of time during which personnel records are to be retained.

retention preference, relative standing of employees competing in a reduction-in-force. Their standing is determined by veterans preference, tenure group, length of service, and performance appraisal.

retention register, federal government's record of employees occupying positions in a competitive level. Employees on the register are arranged by tenure groups and subgroups and according to their relative retention standing within the subgroups.

retention standing, precise rank among employees competing for a position in the event of a reduction-in-force or layoff.

retirement, voluntary or involuntary termination of employment because of age, disability, illness, or personal choice. *See* James W. Walker and Harriet L. Lazer, *The End of Mandatory Retirement: Implications for Management* (New York: John Wiley, 1978); Thomas S. Litras, "The Battle over Retirement Policies and Practices," *Personnel Journal* (February 1979); William Graebner, *A History of Retirement: The Meaning and Function of an American Institution, 1885-1978* (New Haven: Yale University Press, 1980); James B. Shaw and Lisa L. Grubbs, "The Process of Retiring: Organizational Entry in Reverse," *Academy of Management Review* (January 1981); Malcolm H. Morrison, "Retirement and Human Resource Planning for the Aging Work Force," *Personnel Administrator* (June 1984).
    See also the following entries:
        ALLIED CHEMICAL WORKERS V. PITTSBURGH PLATE GLASS CO.
        CANNON V. GUSTE
        CIVIL SERVICE RETIREMENT AND DISABILITY FUND

retirement age, age at which workers must retire. A 1978 amendment to the Age Discrimination in Employment Act raised the minimum mandatory retirement age to seventy years for workers in private companies and state and local governments. It banned forced retirement at any age for federal workers.

retirement counseling, systematic efforts by an organization to help its employees who are retiring to adjust to their new situation. For how to establish a retirement counseling program, *see* Douglas M. Bartlett, "Retirement Counseling: Make Sure Employees Aren't Dropouts," *Personnel* (November–December 1974); Don Pellicano, "Retirement Counseling," *Personnel Journal* (July 1973); Don Underwood, "Toward Self-Reliance in Retirement Planning," *Harvard Business Review* (May–June 1984).

Retirement Equity Act of 1984, act that broadens the conditions under which spouses receive retirement benefits. Under the act, spouses of employees who die after attaining eligibility for pensions are guaranteed a benefit beginning at age fifty-five; a prospective survivor must agree in a signed, notarized statement before a pension plan member can waive the option of providing a survivorship benefit (previously, the plan member had the sole right to decide); and the divorced spouse of a plan member is entitled to part of a pension, if stipulated in the separation papers or ordered by a judge.

Also, the new act:
- Requires employers to count all service from age eighteen in calculating when an employee becomes vested (legally entitled to a pension, which usually requires ten years of service). In computing the amount of benefits, all employee earnings from age twenty-one must be considered. (Previously, service accrual toward vesting began at age twenty-two and benefits were based on earnings from age twenty-five.)
- Permits pension plan members to leave the work force for up to five consecutive years without losing pension credits.
- Allows plan members to take maternity or paternity leave of up to one year without loss of service credit for the period.
- Permits employees of companies that have thrift (savings) plans to join as early as age twenty-one. These plans generally provide for employers to match some of the money the employee invests.
- Requires employers to explain to employees the tax consequences of taking lump-sum amounts from pension or profit-sharing plans.

The new provisions, which amend the Employee Retirement Income Security Act of 1974, became effective December 31, 1984. For pension plans established through collective bargaining, provisions take effect when the contract pertaining to the pension plan expires, or January 1, 1987, whichever comes first.

retirement plan, fixed-benefit, *see* FIXED-BENEFIT RETIREMENT PLAN.

retreating, assigning an employee to a position from or through which the employee was promoted, when the position is occupied by someone with lower retention standing.

retroactive pay, wages for work performed during an earlier time at a lower rate. Retroactive pay would make up the difference between the new and old rates of pay.

retroactive seniority, seniority status that is retroactively awarded back to the date that a woman or minority group member was proven to have been discriminatorily refused employment. The U.S. Supreme Court has interpreted the "make whole" provision of Title VII of the Civil Rights Act of 1964 to include the award of retroactive seniority to proven discriminatees; however, retroactive seniority cannot be awarded further back than 1964—the date of the act. *See* Hindy Lauer Schachter, "Retroactive Seniority and Agency Retrenchment," *Public Administration Review* (January-February 1983).

Also see INTERNATIONAL BROTHERHOOD OF TEAMSTERS V. UNITED STATES.

retrospective study, an inquiry planned to observe events that have already occurred (a case-control study is usually retrospective); compare with a prospective study, which is planned to observe events that have not yet occurred.

revenue, also GROSS RECEIPTS, receipts of a jurisdiction or government body from all sources including, but not limited to, taxes, fees, licenses, fines, user charges, sale of assets, lotteries, etc. Unless otherwise stated, such receipts represent *gross receipts* or receipts prior to the deduction of expenses. *See* Arnold Meltsner, *The Politics of City Revenue* (Berkeley, Calif.: University of California Press, 1971); John L. Mikesell, "Administration and the Public Revenue System: A View of Tax Administration," *Public Administration Review* (November-December 1974).

revenue anticipation notes, also TAX ANTICIPATION NOTES, forms of short-term borrowing used by a jurisdiction to resolve a cash flow problem occasioned by a shortage of necessary revenues or taxes to cover planned or unplanned expenditures.

revenue bonds, municipal bonds whose repayment and dividends are guaranteed by revenues derived from the facility constructed from the proceeds of the sale of the bonds (*e.g.*, stadium bonds, toll road bonds, etc.). As revenue bonds are not pledged against the tax base of the issuing jurisdiction, they are usually not regulated by the same debt limitations imposed

by most states on the sale of general obligation bonds. Additionally, revenue bond questions usually do not have to be submitted to the voters for approval as they do not commit the full-faith-and-credit of the jurisdiction. *See* Philip J. Fisher, Ronald W. Forbes, and John E. Peterson, "Risk and Return in the Choice of Revenue Bond Financing," *Governmental Finance* (September 1980).

revenue gainers, also REVENUE ENHANCEMENT, euphemisms for tax increases.

revenue sharing, sharing of federal tax revenues among subnational levels of government. First proposed in its present form in the early 1960's by Walter Heller, then chairman of President Kennedy's Council of Economic Advisors, revenue sharing was designed to arrest the rising fiscal burdens of many state and local governments. Part of its original rationale was the concern of some economists about the accumulation of federal budget surpluses. Given today's record federal deficits, this sounds a bit unreal; nevertheless, it was a true concern of the early 1960s. The theory was that a budget surplus would produce a "fiscal drag" effect on the economy and that the money ought to be put back into the economy in some efficient way. Revenue sharing was a "natural." Another justification for revenue sharing was its ability to mitigate fiscal imbalances among the states where variances in per capita personal income are significant. Finally, the argument was made that revenue sharing is economically justified by the federal government's monopolization of the most efficient and progressive tax source—the federal income tax. It was contended that both efficiency and equity would be furthered by an increasing reliance on the best tax source and a corresponding passing down of revenues to those less affluent jurisdictions providing services directly to the people.

In 1972 revenue sharing was introduced to the nation with the passage of the State and Local Fiscal Assistance Act.

The heart of the revenue sharing concept is its distribution formula for funds.

Congress provided for two separate distribution formulas. Each *state* can opt for the formula which provides it with the most generous funding. As one might have expected, the formula recommended by the House favored the more populous states. The political realities were such that both formulas were accepted. The congressional debate left few satisfied. One House Ways and Means Committee member, Representative Corman of California, reported on the floor of the House, "We finally quit, not because we hit on a rational formula, but because we were exhausted. And finally we got one that almost none of us could understand at the moment." Once the state share is calculated, shares for each locality are allocated by the state governments. One third of the total state share is retained by the state and the remaining two thirds are divided among localities. Revenue sharing began in 1972 amid much fanfare. But even before the first year of the program was over, criticism started to mount. There were three main threads to opposition arguments. The first was that revenue sharing breached the most sacred doctrine of government finance by separating expenditure decisions from revenue decisions. The second was a rephrasing of an argument initially put forth by Congressman Henry Reuss of Wisconsin, who maintained that the current organization of fiscal federalism is not efficient and that massive change is needed. Revenue sharing, it was argued, would perpetuate the existing structure of governments; delay reform, consolidation, and reorganization; and pass revenues on to government units whose existence was premised on neither need nor effective management, but on historical accident. The third contention involves the relationship between revenue sharing and other federal grant programs. Revenue sharing was supposed to augment existing programs, not be a substitute for them. However, the early years of revenue sharing were highlighted by impoundment controversies involving highway and water-sewer construction grants and cuts in federal grants for social service programs. State and local officials were naturally skeptical.

Yet this third point is somewhat groundless; from the beginning it was intended that general revenue sharing be complemented by other grant programs.

The problems with revenue sharing are now centered on evaluation—a seemingly simple matter given the fact that localities have to report planned and actual use of revenue sharing funds and maintain separate fiscal accounting procedures. However, the problem is made more complex because there are no specified objectives as to what revenue sharing should accomplish. The town of Redding, Connecticut, narrowed its decision on how to spend its first revenue sharing check of $69,000 down to either a dog pound or tennis courts and a bridle path. While this was totally legal, it made headlines and the question of appropriateness began to emerge. In Pittsburgh, revenue sharing funds were used to decrease real estate taxes. Providing tax relief attracted additional controversy—legal, yes; appropriate, debatable. The crux of the issue is what problems should revenue sharing ameliorate?

With the advent of the Reagan administration, general revenue sharing was subject to increased scrutiny. The current General Revenue Sharing program is slated to expire. The burgeoning of federal budget deficits stands as one obstacle to renewal. Another obstacle seems to be the preference of the Reagan administration for some type of tax or revenue turnback program which would have the federal government relinquish its use of a specific tax or taxes in favor of state or local government adoption. A turn-back program seems to be viewed by the Reagan administration as a potentially more effective mechanism by which to devolve authority from the federal government to state and local governments.

See Henry S. Reuss, *Revenue-sharing* (New York: Praeger Publishers, 1970); Otto G. Stolz, *Revenue Sharing: Legal and Policy Analysis* (New York: Praeger, 1974); Paul R. Dommel, *The Politics of Revenue Sharing* (Bloomington, Ind.: Indiana University Press, 1974); Richard P. Nathan, Allen D. Manvel, and Susannah

E. Calkans, *Monitoring Revenue Sharing* (Washington, D.C.: The Brookings Institution, 1975); David A. Caputo, Symposium Editor, "General Revenue Sharing," *Public Administration Review* (March–April 1975); Samuel H. Beer, "The Adoption of General Revenue Sharing: A Case Study in Public Sector Politics," *Public Policy* (Spring 1976); David A. Caputo and Richard L. Cole, "City Officials and General Revenue Sharing," *Publius* (Winter 1983).

See also GRANT.

revenue systems, *see* TAXATION.

reverse collective bargaining, activity that occurs when economic conditions force collective bargaining agreements to be renegotiated so that employees end up with a less favorable wage package. *See* Peter Henle, "Reverse Collective Bargaining? A Look at Some Union Concession Situations," *Industrial and Labor Relations Review* (April 1973).

reverse discrimination, practice generally understood to mean preferential treatment for women and minorities as opposed to white males; the practice has no legal standing. Indeed, Section 703 (j) of Title VII of the Civil Rights Act of 1964 holds that nothing in the title shall be interpreted to require any employer to "grant preferential treatment to any individual or group on the basis of race, color, religion, sex or national origin." Yet affirmative action programs necessarily put some otherwise innocent white males at a disadvantage that they would not have otherwise had. The whole matter may have been summed up by George Orwell in his 1945 novella, *Animal Farm,* when he observed that "All animals are equal, but some animals are more equal than others." For analyses of the problem, *see* Gopal C. Pati, "Reverse Discrimination: What Can Managers Do?" *Personnel Journal* (July 1977); Alan H. Goldman, *Justice and Reverse Discrimination* (Princeton, N.J.: Princeton University Press, 1979); Robert K. Fullinwider, *The Reverse Discrimination Controversy: A Moral And Legal Analysis* (Totowa, N.J.:

Rowman and Littlefield, 1980); Ralph A. Rossum, *Reverse Discrimination: The Constitutional Debate* (New York: Marcel Dekker, 1980). For a political analysis, *see* Nathan Glazer, *Affirmative Discrimination* (New York: Basic Books, 1975). For a defense, *see* Boris Bittker, *The Case for Black Reparations* (New York: Random House, 1973). For a philosophic approach, *see* Barry R. Gross, *Discrimination in Reverse: Is Turnabout Fair Play?* (New York: New York University Press, 1978). *Also see* Marianne A. Ferber and Carole A. Green, "Traditional or Reverse Sex Discrimination? A Case Study of a Large Public University," *Industrial and Labor Relations Review* (July 1982); R. Kent Greenawalt, *Discrimination and Reverse Discrimination* (New York: Knopf, 1983).

See also the following entries:
DEFUNIS V. ODEGAARD
REGENTS OF THE UNIVERSITY OF CALIFORNIA V. ALLAN BAKKE
UNITED STEELWORKERS OF AMERICA V. WEBER, ET AL.

Review of Public Personnel Administration, a journal of public personnel management and labor relations.
Review of Public Personnel Administration
Bureau of Governmental Research and Service
University of South Carolina
Columbia, SC 29208

revolving fund, fund established to finance a cycle of operations through amounts received by the fund. There are three types of revolving funds: public enterprise, intragovernmental, and trust revolving funds.

Ricardo, David (1772-1823), the English economist who developed the first comprehensive economic model, formulated the concept of comparative advantage in international trade, and promulgated the iron law of wages.

rider, extraneous provision incorporated into a bill with the idea of its "riding" through to enactment on the merits of the main measure.

RIF, acronym for "reduction in force"—the phrase the federal government uses when it eliminates specific job categories in specific organizations. While an employee who has been "riffed" has not been fired, he or she is nevertheless without a job. This acronym has become so common that it is often used as a verb and seems to be spreading well beyond the federal bureaucracy. *See* Robert Rudary and J. Garrett Ralls, Jr., "Manpower Planning for Reduction-in-Force," *University of Michigan Business Review* (November 1978); George H. Cauble, Jr., "Alternative to a Reduction in Force," *Public Personnel Management* (Spring 1982); Harry C. Dennis, Jr., "Reductions in Force: The Federal Experience," *Public Personnel Management* (Summer 1983); Richard I. Lehr and David J. Middlebrooks, "Work Force Reduction: Strategies and Options," *Personnel Journal* (October 1984).

See also the following entries:
LAYOFF
RECALL
RE-EMPLOYMENT LIST
REINSTATEMENT
RETENTION REGISTER
RETENTION STANDING

Riggs, Fred W. (1917-), leading authority on comparative and development administration noted for his theory of prismatic society, which uses the prism as an analogy to explain the paradoxical nature of public administration in transitional societies. Major works include: *The Ecology of Public Administration* (New York: Asia Publishing House, 1961); *Administration in Developing Countries: The Theory of Prismatic Society* (Boston: Houghton Mifflin, 1965); *Thailand: The Modernization of a Bureaucratic Polity* (Honolulu: East-West Center Press, 1965); *Frontiers of Development Administration,* ed. (Durham, N.C.: Duke University Press, 1971); *Prismatic Society Revisited* (Morristown, N.J.: General Learning Press, 1973).

rightful place, judicial doctrine that an individual who has been discriminated against should be restored to the job—to his or her "rightful place"—as if there had been no discrimination and given appropriate seniority, merit increases, and promotions.

right-of-way, also EASEMENT and SCENIC EASEMENT, legal right to use the land of another, typically for right of passage of a person or vehicle. In the case of *scenic easement,* it is the right to a view and therefore controls the land over which easement is held.

rights arbitration, *see* GRIEVANCE ARBITRATION.

right-to-work laws, state laws that make it illegal for collective bargaining agreements to contain maintenance of membership, preferential hiring, union shop, or any other clauses calling for compulsory union membership. A typical "right-to-work" law might read: "No person may be denied employment and employers may not be denied the right to employ any person because of that person's membership or nonmembership in any labor organization."

It was the Labor-Management Relations (Taft-Hartley) Act of 1947 that authorized right-to-work laws when it provided in section 14(b) that "nothing in this Act shall be construed as authorizing the execution or application of agreements requiring membership in a labor organization as a condition of employment in any State or Territory in which such execution or application is prohibited by State or Territorial law."

The law does not prohibit the union or closed shop; it simply gives each state the option of doing so. Twenty states have done so: Alabama, Arizona, Arkansas, Florida, Georgia, Iowa, Kansas, Louisiana, Mississippi, Nebraska, Nevada, North Carolina, North Dakota, South Carolina, South Dakota, Tennessee, Texas, Utah, Virginia, and Wyoming.

See also NATIONAL RIGHT TO WORK COM-

MITTEE and OIL WORKERS V. MOBIL OIL COMPANY.

ringed rate, see RED-CIRCLE RATE.

ring theory of urban development, theory depicting growth of urban areas in concentric rings, much like ripples in a pond.

risk management, all of an organization's efforts to protect its assets and its human resources against accidental loss; accordingly, the major elements of risk management are safety and insurance management. See W. Bartley Hildreth, "Errors, Liability, and Risk Management," *The Bureaucrat* (Fall 1981).

rival unionism, competition between two or more unions for the same prospective members.

Rivlin, Alice M. (1931-), economist and authority on fiscal policy and program evaluation who was the first director of the U.S. Congressional Budget Office. Major works include: *The Role of the Federal Government in Financing,* with others (Washington, D.C.: The Brookings Institution, 1961); *Microanalysis of Socioeconomic Systems: A Simulation Study,* with others (New York: Harper & Bros., 1961); *The United States Balance of Payments in 1968* (New York: Harper & Row, 1968); *Systematic Thinking for Social Action* (Washington, D.C.: Brookings Institution, 1971); *Ethical and Legal Issues of Social Experimentation,* edited with P. Michael Timpane (Washington, D.C.: Brookings Institution, 1975); *Planned Variation in Education: Should We Give Up Or Try Harder?,* ed. with P. Michael Timpane (Washington, D.C.: Brookings Institution, 1975)

Robinson v. Lorrilard Corp., see BUSINESS NECESSITY.

robot, general term for any machine that does the work that a person would otherwise have to do. The word comes from *robotnik,* the Czech word for slave. See

S. A. Levitan and C. M. Johnson, "The Future of Work: Does it Belong to Us or to the Robots?" *Monthly Labor Review* (September 1982); James Lambrinos and W. G. Johnson, "Robots to Reduce the High Cost of Illness and Injury," *Harvard Business Review* (May-June 1984); F. K. Foulkes and J. L. Hirsch, "People Make Robots Work," *Harvard Business Review* (January-February 1984).

robotics, the use of robots. See H. Allan Hunt and Timothy L. Hunt, *Human Resource Implications of Robotics* (Kalamazoo, Mich.: The W. E. Upjohn Institute for Employment Research, 1983); Linda Argote, Paul S. Goodman, and David Schkade, "The Human Side of Robotics: How Workers React to a Robot," *Sloan Management Review* (Spring 1983); A. J. Hughes, "Robotics: Effect on Japanese and American Labor and a Practical Application in the New York City Department of Sanitation," *Public Productivity Review* (June 1983).

Roethlisberger, Fritz J. (1898-1974), with Elton Mayo, one of the founders of the human relations movement in industry. As one of the prime researchers of the Hawthorne experiments, he co-authored the definitive report on them—*Management and the Worker,* with William J. Dickson (Cambridge, Mass.: Harvard University Press, 1939). Other major works include: *Management and Morale* (Cambridge, Mass.: Harvard University Press, 1941); *Man-in-Organization* (Cambridge, Mass.: Harvard University Press, 1968); *The Elusive Phenomena: An Autobiographical Account of My Work in the Field of Organizational Behavior at the Harvard Business School,* ed. by George F. F. Lombard (Cambridge: Harvard University Press, 1977). Also see George F. F. Lombard, ed., *The Contributions of F. J. Roethlisberger to Management Theory and Practice* (Cambridge, Mass.: Harvard University Graduate School of Business, 1976).

Rogers Act of 1924, federal statute that created a merit-based career system for the

Foreign Service of the U.S. Department of State.

role, also ROLE PLAYING, in social psychology, term used to describe the behavior expected of an individual occupying a particular position. Just as an actor acts out his role on the stage, a personnel manager, for example, performs his role in real life. Role playing is a very common training technique and is based on the assumption that the process of acting out a role will enable an individual to gain insights concerning the behavior of others that cannot be realized by reading a book or listening to a lecture. *See* R. J. Corsini, M. Shaw, and R. Blake, *Roleplaying in Business and Industry* (New York: Free Press, 1961); Norman R. F. Maier, Allen Solem, and Ayesha A. Maier, *The Role-Play Technique: A Handbook for Management and Leadership Practice* (La Jolla, Calif.: University Associates, 1975); Frank Sherwood, "The Role Concept in Administration," *Public Personnel Review* (January 1964); George Graen, "Role-Making Processes within Complex Organizations," in Marvin D. Dunnette, ed., *Handbook of Industrial and Organizational Psychology* (Chicago: Rand McNally, 1976).

See also STRUCTURED ROLE PLAYING.

role conception, *see* ROLE PERCEPTION.

role conflict, the state that occurs when an individual is called upon to perform mutually exclusive acts by parties having legitimate "holds" on him/her. For example, a rising young manager may not make it to the "big" meeting if he must at that moment rush his child to the hospital for an emergency appendectomy. When such conflicts arise, most individuals invoke a hierarchy of role obligation that gives some roles precedence over others. To most fathers, their child's life would be more important than a business meeting—no matter how "big." Real life is not always so unambiguous, however, and role conflict is a common dilemma in the world of work. *See* J. R. Rizzo, R. J. House, and S. I. Lirtzman, "Role Conflict and Am-

biguity in Complex Organizations," *Administrative Science Quarterly* (June 1970); R. H. Miles and W. D. Perreault, Jr., "Organizational Role Conflict: Its Antecedents and Consequences," *Organizational Behavior and Human Performance* (October 1976); James H. Morris, Richard M. Steers, and James L. Koch, "Influence of Organizational Structure on Role Conflict and Ambiguity for Three Occupational Groupings," *Academy of Management Journal* (March 1979); Mary Van Sell, Arthur P. Brief, and Randall S. Schuler, "Role Conflict and Role Ambiguity: Integration of the Literature and Directions for Future Research," *Human Relations* (January 1981).

role perception, also called ROLE CONCEPTION, mental perception that delineates the position that the individual occupies in his/her organization and establishes for the individual the minimum and maximum ranges of permissible behavior in "acting" out his/her organizational role. For empirical studies, *see* Andrew D. Szilagyi, "An Empirical Test of Causal Inference between Role Perceptions, Satisfaction with Work, Performance and Organizational Level," *Personnel Psychology* (Autumn 1977); Randell S. Schuler, "The Effects of Role Perceptions on Employee Satisfaction and Performance Moderated by Employee Ability," *Organizational Behavior and Human Performance* (February 1977); Barbara Ley Toffler, "Occupational Role Development: The Changing Determinants of Outcomes for the Individual," *Administrative Science Quarterly* (September 1981); Kevin W. Mossholder, Arthus G. Bedeian, and Achilles A. Armenakis, "Role Perceptions, Satisfaction, and Performance: Moderating Effects of Self Esteem and Organizational Level," *Organizational Behavior and Human Performance* (October 1981).

role playing, *see* ROLE and STRUCTURED ROLE PLAYING.

romance, *see* LOVE.

Rorschach test, also called INK-BLOT

TEST, projective test in which the responses to standard ink blots are interpreted to gain clues to the subject's personality. Developed by the Swiss psychiatrist Hermann Rorschach (1884-1922), the Rorschach test is no longer considered to be a valid tool for predicting vocational success.

See also PROJECTIVE TEST and THEMATIC APPERCEPTION TEST.

Rosenbloom, David H. (1943-), the leading authority on the constitutional aspects of public employment. His major works include *Federal Service and the Constitution* (Ithaca: Cornell University Press, 1971), *Federal Equal Employment Opportunity* (New York: Praeger, 1977) and *Public Administration and Law: Bench v. Bureau in the United States* (New York: Marcel Dekker, 1983).He is coauthor of *Bureaucratic Culture: Citizens and Administrators in Israel* (New York: St. Martin's Press, 1978); *Bureaucratic Government, USA* (New York: St. Martin's Press, 1980); *Representative Bureaucracy and the American Political System* (New York: Praeger, 1981); *Personnel Management in Government: Politics and Process*, 3rd ed. (New York: Marcel Dekker, Inc., 1986).

roster of elegibles, see ELIGIBLE LIST.

Rostker v. Goldberg 69 L.Ed. 2d 478 (1981), U.S. Supreme Court case which held that the registration of males and not females for potential military draft was not in violation of equal protection of law.

rotating shift, work schedule designed to give employees an equal share of both day and night work.

Roth decision, see BOARD OF REGENTS V. ROTH.

Royal Institute of Public Administration, non-political body whose objects are to advance the study of public administration and to promote the exchange of information and ideas on all aspects of the subject. It issues publications, arranges conferences, courses, and lectures, undertakes research, and maintains a reference library.

> *Royal Institute of Public Administration*
> Hamilton House
> Mabledon Place
> London WCIH 9BD
> UNITED KINGDOM

RRB, see RAILROAD RETIREMENT BOARD.

RSA, see REGIONAL SCIENCE ASSOCIATION.

rule, a regulation made by an administrative agency.

rule-making authority, powers exercised by administrative agencies that have the force of law.

Agencies begin with some form of legislative mandate and translate their interpretation of that mandate into policy decisions, specifications of regulations, and statements of penalties and enforcement provisions. The exact process to be followed in formulating regulations is only briefly described in the federal Administration Procedure Act (APA). There are no more constitutional procedural requirements for enacting rules than for legislatures enacting statutes. Agencies are required only to provide advance notice of their intent to formulate new rules or changes in existing rules.

The APA does distinguish between rule-making requiring a hearing and rule-making requiring only notice and opportunity for public comment. Bernard Schwartz sees these categories as two different procedural requirements: formal rule-making, which must be preceded by a trial-type hearing, and informal rule-making, which is termed "notice and comment rule-making." But the test of whether the formal or informal procedure will be used is the specification in the enabling statute. This was affirmed in the Supreme Court's decision in *United States v. Florida East Coast Railway*, 410 U.S. 224 (1973), that formal rule-making need only be followed when the enabling statute expressly requires an agency hearing prior to rule formulation.

What remains in the APA provisions for rule-making is the requirement that rules be published thirty days before their effective date and that agencies afford any interested party the right to petition for issuance, amendment, or repeal of a rule. In effect, while APA establishes a process of notice and time for comment, it accords administrative rule-making the same prerogatives as legislatures have in enacting statutes. There is, of course, the additional requirement that the rule enacted be consistent with the enabling statute directing the rule-making. *See* J. Skelly Wright, "Court of Appeals Review of Federal Agency Rulemaking," *Administrative Law Review* (Winter 1974); Bernard Schwartz, "Administrative Law in the Next Century," *Ohio State Law Journal* (1978); William F. Kent, "The Politics of Administrative Rulemaking," *Public Administration Review* (September-October 1982); Jurgen Schmandt, "Managing Comprehensive Rule Making: EPA's Plan for Integrated Environmental Management," *Public Administration Review* (March-April 1985).

See also ABBOTT LABORATORIES V. GARDNER and INDEPENDENT AGENCY.

rule of three, *also* RULE OF ONE and RULE OF THE LIST, practice of certifying to an appointing authority the top three names on an eligible list. The rule of three is intended to give the appointing official an opportunity to weigh intangible factors, such as personality, before making a formal offer of appointment. The *rule of one* has only the single highest ranking person on the eligible list certified. The *rule of the list* gives the appointing authority the opportunity to choose from the entire list of eligibles.

See also APPOINTMENT CLAUSE.

run-off election, second election held when no single union receives a majority in a representation election. Participants choose between the two unions that got the most votes in the first election.

S

sabbath, *see* TRANS WORLD AIRLINES V. HARDISON.

sabbatical, lengthy paid leave for professional, intellectual, or emotional refurbishment. It was an ancient Hebrew tradition to allow fields to lie fallow every seventh year. The words sabbath and sabbatical both come from the Hebrew word *shabath,* meaning to rest. In modern times, a sabbatical has been a period of paid leave and rejuvenation for teachers at colleges and universities, but it has recently gained a broader meaning. *See* Angelos A. Tsaklanganos, "Sabbaticals for Executives," *Personnel Journal* (May 1973).

sabotage, deliberate destruction of property or the slowing down of work in order to damage a business. During a 1910 railway strike in France, strikers destroyed some of the wooden shoes or *sabots* that held the rails in place. Sabotage soon came into English, but it wasn't until World War II that the word gained widespread popularity as a description of the efforts of secret agents to hinder an enemy's industrial/military capabilities.

There is also the story of the French wool finishers who, in the 1820s, rioted to protest the use of machinery that might supplant them. They were said to have used their wooden shoes or *sabots* to kick the machines to pieces. While this may have been the first instance of sabotage, the use of the word in English dates from the 1910 railway strike.

sack, *see* GET THE SACK.

safety, also SAFETY DEPARTMENT, an organization's total effort to prevent and eliminate the causes of accidents. Some organizations have a safety department responsible for administering the various aspects of the safety program. For a text, *see* John V. Grimaldi and Rollin H. Simonds, *Safety Management,* 4th ed. (Homewood, Ill.: Richard D. Irwin, Inc., 1984). For how to staff a safety department, *see* Robert E. McClay, "Professionalizing the Safety Function," *Personnel Journal* (February 1977). *Also see* Robert W. Crandall and Lester B. Lave, eds., *The Scientific Basis of Health and Safety Regulations* (Washington, D.C.: Brookings Institution, 1981); Allan J. Harrison, "Managing Safety and Health," *Labor Law Journal* (September 1981); L. Parmeggiani, "State of the Art: Recent Legislation on Workers' Health and Safety," *International Labour Review* (May-June 1982); Kathryn A. Gellens, "Resolving Industrial Safety Disputes: To Arbitrate or Not to Arbitrate," *Labor Law Journal* (March 1983).

See also the following entries:
NATIONAL SAFETY COUNCIL
OCCUPATIONAL SAFETY AND HEALTH
ADMINISTRATION

safety net, President Ronald Reagan's term for the totality of social welfare programs which, in his opinion, assure at least a subsistence standard of living for all Americans.

salary, *see* WAGES.

salary, straight, *see* STRAIGHT SALARY.

salary compression, also called WAGE COMPRESSION, according to M. Sami Kassem, in "The Salary Compression Problem," *Personnel Journal* (April 1971), "the shrinking difference of pay being given newcomers as opposed to the amount paid to the experienced regulars."
See also PAY COMPRESSION.

salary curve, *see* MATURITY CURVE.

salary range, *see* PAY PLAN.

Salary Reform Act of 1962 (Public Law 87-793), federal statute that provided that "federal salary rates shall be comparable

with private enterprise salary rates for the same levels of work."

salary review, formal examination of an employee's rate of pay in terms of his or her recent performance, changes in the cost of living, and other factors.

salary structures, according to Robert E. Sibson, in "New Practices and Ideas in Compensation Administration," *Compensation Review* (Third Quarter 1974), originally
largely conceived as boxes within which salaries must be paid. Increasingly, though, companies are viewing their salary structures essentially as a uniform accounting system, intended primarily as an information source, rather than a control mechanism. Furthermore, the use of salary structures is changing in very fundamental ways. For instance, . . . the bottom part of the salary range in management positions is seldom used in many companies today, because paying managers at the bottom part of the range suggests that they are trainees or not qualified to do the work.

salary survey, *see* WAGE SURVEY.

salary survey, community, *see* COMMUNITY WAGE SURVEY.

SAM, *see* SOCIETY FOR THE ADVANCEMENT OF MANAGEMENT.

SAM Advanced Management Journal, quarterly offering articles on all phases of management and career development.
SAM Advanced Management Journal
Society for Advancement of
Management
135 West 50th Street
New York, NY 10020

sample, any deliberately chosen portion of a larger population that is representative of that population as a whole. *See* Donald P. Warwick and Charles A. Lininger, *The Sample Survey: Theory and Practice* (New York: McGraw-Hill, 1975).

Sampling Error

See also BIASED SAMPLE, RANDOM SAMPLE, and REPRESENTATIVE SAMPLE.

sampling error, error caused by generalizing the behavior of a population from a sample of that population that is not representative of the population as a whole.

Sampling

The devastating effect of biased sampling is illustrated by an incident which attracted national attention a third of a century ago. The summer before the 1936 Presidential election, the *Literary Digest* undertook an extensive poll of the U.S. population to determine who the next President would be. The *Digest* did things in a big way. More than 10 million double postcards were mailed to persons living in every county in the United States. The list was made up of names taken from every telephone book in the United States, from the rosters of clubs and associations, from state directories, lists of registered voters, mail order lists, etc. The recipients were asked to indicate whether they intended to vote for Franklin D. Roosevelt or Alfred M. Landon for President. A sampling of 10 million people established an all-time record. The response was disappointing: Only 2 million cards were returned. Tabulating the returned cards, the *Digest* predicted the election of Landon by a substantial majority. When the votes were counted, Governor Landon carried only two states. The debacle was fatal to the *Digest*. It went out of business shortly thereafter.

This gargantuan poll suffered from two fatal deficiencies. In the first place, the list was made up predominantly of persons who had telephones or who belonged to clubs and associations. Millions of other citizens who did not enjoy the blessings of either a telephone or a membership were underrepresented in the sample. Those who did not get cards comprised a very different "statistical universe" from those who did. In the second place, the one-fifth of those polled who did respond doubtless also represented a different "universe" from the four-fifths who did not bother to answer, thus contributing a further—and unmeasurable—source of error.

The *Digest* discovered the hard way that mere size of a sample carries no guarantee of producing a representative response. Only if care is taken to assure that the sample drawn constitutes a true cross section of the entire population can it be relied on to produce usefully accurate information.

Source: Charles P. Kaplan and Thomas L. Van Valey, Census '80: Continuing the Fact-finder Tradition *(Washington, D.C.: U.S. Department of Commerce, Bureau of the Census, 1980), p. 27.*

sampling population, entire set or universe from which a sample is drawn.

Sampson v. Murray, 415 U.S. 61 (1974), U.S. Supreme Court case which held that the federal courts did not have the authority to issue a temporary restraining order (pending an administrative appeal to the U.S. Civil Service Commission) on behalf of a probationary federal government employee who had been discharged. A federal court's authority to review agency action does not come into play until it may be authoritatively said that the administrative decision to discharge an employee does, in fact, fail to conform to the applicable regulations. Until administrative action has become final, no court is in a position to say that such action did or did not conform to the regulations.

Samuelson, Paul Anthony (1915-), Nobel Prize-winning economist who advanced the use of mathematics in economic analysis. His introductory textbook, *Economics*, 12th ed. (N.Y.: McGraw-Hill, 1985), has since 1947 been providing a Keynesian perspective to several generations of college students and has become a publishing phenomenon by selling over four million copies.

sandwich management, humorous term for an ineffective management style. This technique is one that is adopted most innocently. In fact, it has been perpetrated for years as managers have been encouraged to manipulate people rather than level with them. A typical statement by a sandwich manager, taken from William Thomas, "Humor for Hurdling the Mystique in Management," *Management of Personnel Quarterly* (Winter 1970), goes something like this: "Fred, you've been doing a splendid job in many respects since you came aboard. On the other hand, there have been times when your work was so late, it caused problems for the whole department. You will have to get on the ball, son, or else we might have to transfer you to a job you can handle for sure. But I am sure we can count on you to do the right thing. Your past history indicates you have a great potential." Upon analyzing that statement closely you can see a loss of "bread," neatly sandwiched between two slices of baloney.

satisfactory-performance increase, annual incremental salary increase awarded for satisfactory performance within a single salary grade.

satisficing, also called BOUNDED RATIONALITY, term coined by Herbert A. Simon in *Administrative Behavior* (New York: Macmillan, 1947), while explaining his concept of *bounded rationality*. Simon asserts that it is impossible to ever know "all" of the facts that bear upon any given decision. Because truly rational research on any problem can never be completed, humans put "bounds" on their rationality and make decisions, not on the basis of optimal information, but on the basis of satisfactory information. Humans tend to make their decisions by satisficing—choosing a course of action that meets one's minimum standards for satisfaction. *See* John Forester, "Bounded Rationality and the Politics of Muddling Through," *Public Administration Review* (January-February 1984).

Sayre Model of Decision Making, model that views bureau leaders as representing the federal executive branch level at which many significant decisions are made. The model identifies nine power structures which surround bureau leaders and influence the decision-making system. *See* Walter G. Held, *Decisionmaking in the Federal Government: The Wallace S. Sayre Model* (Washington, D.C.: The Brookings Institution, 1979).

SBA, *see* SMALL BUSINESS ADMINISTRATION.

scab, also called BLACKLEG, generally, an employee who continues to work for an organization while it is being struck by coworkers. Since the 1500s, scab has been used as a term for a rascal or scoundrel. Early in the 1800s, Americans started using it to refer to workers who refused to support organized efforts on behalf of their trade. A scab should be distinguished from a fink or strikebreaker who is brought into an organization only after a strike begins. Samuel Gompers, the first president of the American Federation of Labor, said that "a 'scab' is to his trade what a traitor is to his country. He is the first to take advantage of any benefit secured by united action, and never contributes anything toward its achievement." *Blackleg* is the British word for scab.

See also OLD DOMINION BRANCH NO. 496, NATIONAL ASSOCIATION OF LETTER CARRIERS V. AUSTIN and STRIKEBREAKER.

scalar chain, also LINE OF AUTHORITY, according to Henri Fayol, *General and Industrial Management*, trans. by Constance Storrs (London: Pitman Publishing, Ltd., 1949),

the chain of supervisors ranging from the ultimate authority to the lowest ranks. The *line of authority* is the route followed—via every link in the chain—by all communications which start from or go to the ultimate authority. This path is dictated both by the need for some transmission and by the principle of unity of command, but it is not always the swiftest. It is even at times disastrously lengthy in large concerns, notably in governmental ones.

scaled score, score on a test when the raw score obtained has been converted to a number or position on a standard reference scale. Test scores reported to examinees and users of tests are usually scaled scores. The purpose of converting scores to a scale is to make reported scores as independent as possible of the particular form of a test an examinee has taken and of the composition of the candidate group at a particular administration. For example, the College Board Achievement tests are all reported on a scale of 200 to 800. A score of 600 on a College Board Achievement test is intended to indicate the same level of ability from year to year.

Scanlon Plan, employee incentive plan developed in the 1930s by Joseph N. Scanlon (then an officer of the United Steelworkers of America) which seeks to enhance productivity and organizational harmony through bonus and suggestion systems. The suggestion system demanded by a "true" Scanlon Plan is so sophisticated that it is more properly considered a form of participatory management. For details, see Frederick G. Lesieur, *The Scanlon Plan: A Frontier in Labor-Management Cooperation* (N.Y. and Cambridge: John Wiley and the Technology Press of M.I.T., 1958); Frederick G. Lesieur and Elbridge Pluckett, "The Scanlon Plan Has Proved Itself," *Harvard Business Review* (October 1969); Brian E. Moore and Timothy L. Ross, *The Scanlon Way to Improved Productivity: A Practical Guide* (New York: John Wiley & Sons, 1978); Michael Schuster, "The Scanlon Plan: A Longitudinal Analysis," *The Journal of Applied Behavioral Science,* Vol. 20, No. 1 (1984).

scapegoating, shifting the blame for a problem or failure to another person, group or organization—a common bureaucratic and political tactic. *See* Jeffrey Eagle and Peter M. Newton, "Scapegoating in Small Groups: An Organizational Approach," *Human Relations* (April 1981).

scatter diagram, display of the relationship between variables using dots on a graph.

scenic easement, *see* RIGHT-OF-WAY.

Schecter Poultry Corp.* v. *United States, 295 U.S. 495 (1935), Supreme Court case concerning the constitutionality of congressional delegations of authority. The court held that the separation of powers provided for in the Constitution means that "Congress is not permitted to abdicate or to transfer to others the essential legislative functions with which it is . . . vested." Consequently, legislative delegations would be constitutional only if Congress "has itself established the standards of legal obligation." Based upon these premises the court held that the promulgation of a "Live Poultry Code" under the National Industrial Recovery Act was constitutionally defective. Although *Schecter* has never been directly overruled, the courts have subsequently taken a more flexible view of legislative delegations. Had the *Schecter* rule been forcefully applied since 1935, the discretion exercised by the federal bureaucracy would have been severely constricted.

Schedule A, category used by the Office of Personnel Management (OPM) for those excepted federal positions for which it is not practicable to hold any examinations and which are not of a confidential or policy determining nature. Included here are teachers in dependent school systems overseas, faculty members of the service academies, narcotics agents for undercover work, certain part-time positions at isolated localities, positions on vessels operated by the Military Sealift Command, and many purely seasonal positions not of a continuing nature. In addition, because the OPM is forbidden by law to examine for attorneys, they have also been placed in Schedule A. There are about 75,000 positions in this schedule. (This number increases during the summer months to include temporary seasonal personnel).

Schedule B, category used by the Office of Personnel Management for those excepted federal positions for which competitive examinations are impracticable, but for which the person must pass a *noncompetitive* examination. Included here are positions assigned to Navy or Air Force Communications Intelligence activities and national bank examiners in the Treasury Department. Only about three thousand positions are covered by Schedule B.

Schedule C, category used by the Office

of Personnel Management (OPM) for the excepted positions which are policy-determining or which involve a close personal relationship between the incumbent and the agency head or his/her key officials. It contains key positions that should be filled by the administration in power with persons who will fully support its political aims and policies as well as the positions of secretaries, special assistants, and other members of the immediate staffs of key officials. There are about 1,200 positions in Schedule C.

No examination is required for appointment to Schedule C jobs. Departments and agencies may recommend to OPM that a position be placed in Schedule C if they feel the duties assigned are either policy-determining or require the incumbent to serve in a confidential relationship to a key official. If OPM considers the duties of the position are actually policy-determining in nature of if they establish a confidential relationship to a key official, it places the position in Schedule C. If not, OPM rejects the recommendation. Each job is considered on an individual basis.

Schein, Edgar H. (1928-), psychologist who has written some of the most influential work on organizational psychology, organization development, and career management. Major works include: *Personnel and Organizational Change Through Group Methods: The Laboratory Approach*, with Warren Bennis (New York: John Wiley, 1965); *Process Consultation: Its Role in Organization Development* (Reading, Mass.: Addison-Wesley, 1969); *Organizational Psychology*, 3rd. ed. (Englewood Cliffs, N.J.: Prentice-Hall, 1980); *Professional Education: Some New Directions* (New York: McGraw-Hill, 1972); *Career Dynamics: Matching Individual and Organizational Needs* (Reading, Mass.: Addison-Wesley, 1978).

Scheuer v. Rhodes, 416 U.S. 232 (1974), Supreme Court case holding that officers of the executive branch of state governments had a qualified immunity from civil suits for damages.

Schick, Allen (1934-), leading chronicler of public budgeting systems. When new budgeting concepts such as PPBS and ZBB became significant to public administration, Schick wrote of their origins and utility; when these same concepts failed in practice, he wrote their obituaries. He has even written a poem on the rise and fall of budget systems, which reads in part:

Reforms come, reforms go,
I've seen them all—PPB, ZBB, MBO.
ZBB's the latest, won't be the last,
What is now, someday will be past.
Only to be followed by a new fashion,
Exciting our innovative passion.
Yet the budget goes up and up some more,
Always higher than the year before.
So every generation's budget expectation,
Ends up just another bureaucratic frustration.

[*Source:* "Budget Gap," *Public Administration Review* (September-October 1977).]

Schick's major works include: "The Road to PPB: The Stages of Budget Reform," *Public Administration Review* (December 1966); "Systems Politics and Systems Budgeting," *Public Administration Review* (March-April 1969); "The Budget Bureau that Was: Thoughts on the Rise, Decline and Future of a Presidential Agency," *Law and Contemporary Problems* Vol. 25 (1970); "A Death in the Bureaucracy: The Demise of Federal PPB," *Public Administration Review* (March-April 1973); *Budget Innovation in the States* (Washington, D.C.: The Brookings Institution, 1971); "Zero-Base Budgeting and Sunset: Redundancy or Symbiosis," *The Bureaucrat* (Spring 1977); "The Road from ZBB," *Public Administration Review* (March-April 1978); *Congress and Money: Budgeting, Spending & Taxing* (Washington, D.C.: The Urban Institute, 1980).

Schlesinger v. Ballard, 419 U.S. 498

(1975), U.S. Supreme Court case which held that women could be judged by a more lenient standard than men in measuring their performance in the military services because their promotional opportunities were fewer.

schmoozing, collective term for all of the social interactions engaged in by employees that are seemingly unrelated to their organization's productivity.

science policy, generic term referring to government decision-making, usually at the national level, which relates to the furtherance, uses, and implications of science and scientific research. The beginnings of modern science policymaking are traditionally dated at the beginning of World War II with the establishment of the Office of Scientific Research and Development, which was responsible, among other things, for the development of the atomic bomb. The establishment of the National Science Foundation in 1951 institutionalized federal concerns for the control and direction of scientific research, and led to the development of a huge and growing number of agencies in the federal bureaucracy concerned with science and technology issues. *See* Don K. Price, *Government and Science* (New York: New York University Press, 1954); Daniel S. Greenberg, *The Politics of Pure Science* (New York: New American Library, 1967); Michael D. Reagan, *Science and the Federal Patron* (New York: Oxford University Press, 1969); James Penick, ed., *The Politics of American Science* (Cambridge, Mass.: M.I.T. Press, 1972); W. Henry Lambright, *Governing Science and Technology* (New York: Oxford University Press, 1976); Anton Jachim, *Science Policy Making in the United States* (Carbondale, Ill.: Southern Illinois University Press, 1975); James E. Katz, *Presidential Politics and Science Policy* (New York: Praeger, 1978); Barry Bozeman and Ian Mitroff, Symposium Editors, "Managing National Science Policy," *Public Administration Review* (March–April 1979).
    See also the following entries:

    ESTATES ANALYSIS
    TECHNOLOGY ASSESSMENT
    PRICE, DON K.

scientific approach, procedure for collecting and analyzing data in a systematic and unbiased manner. The three major steps in the scientific approach are observation, measurement, and prediction.

scientific management, systematic approach to managing that seeks the "one best way" of accomplishing any given task by discovering the fastest, most efficient, and least fatiguing production methods. The job of the scientific manager, once the "one best way" was found, was to impose this procedure upon the work force. Frederick W. Taylor is considered to be the "father" of scientific management. *See* his *Principles of Scientific Management* (New York: Harper & Bros., 1911). *Also see* Samuel Haber, *Efficiency and Uplife: Scientific Management in the Progressive Era 1890-1920* (Chicago: University of Chicago Press, 1964).
    See also the following entries:
    GILBRETH, FRANK BUNKER AND LILLIAN
      MOLLER
    MOTION STUDY
    TAYLOR, FREDERICK W.
    TIME STUDY

scope of bargaining, those issues over which management and labor negotiate during the collective bargaining process. *See* Joan Weitzman, *The Scope of Bargaining in Public Employment* (New York: Praeger, 1975); Robert M. Tobias, "The Scope of Bargaining in the Federal Sector: Collective Bargaining or Collective Consultation," *The George Washington Law Review* (May 1976); Stephen A. Woodbury, "The Scope of Bargaining and Bargaining Outcomes in the Public Schools," *Industrial & Labor Relations Review* (January 1985).

score, crude/raw, *see* RAW SCORE.

score, formula, *see* FORMULA SCORE.

score, scaled, *see* SCALED SCORE.

score, standard, see STANDARD SCORE.

Scott, Walter Dill (1869-1955), psychologist who was one of the pioneers of modern personnel management and industrial psychology. He is generally credited with having convinced the U.S. Army to use psychological techniques for the classification and assignment of men during World War I. For a biography, see Edmund C. Lynch, *Walter Dill Scott: Pioneer in Personnel Management* (Austin, Texas: Bureau of Business Research, The University of Texas at Austin, 1968); Edmund C. Lynch, "Walter Dill Scott: Pioneer Industrial Psychologist," *Business History Review* (Summer 1968).

Scott, William G. (1926-), a leading authority on organizational theory and behavior. Major works include: *Human Relations in Management* (Homewood, Ill.: Richard D. Irwin, 1962); *The Management of Conflict: Appeal Systems in Organizations* (Homewood, Ill.: Richard D. Irwin, 1965); *Organizational Concepts and Analysis* (Belmont, Calif.: Dickenson, 1969); *Organization Theory: A Structural and Behavioral Analysis,* rev. ed. (Homewood, Ill.: Richard D. Irwin, 1972).

screening interview, initial interview for a job that serves to determine which applicants are to be given further consideration. See Jack Bucalo, "The Balanced Approach to Successful Screening Interviews," *Personnel Journal* (August 1978).

SCSA, see STANDARD CONSOLIDATED STATISTICAL AREA.

seasonal adjustments, statistical modifications made to compensate for fluctuations in a time series which recur more or less regularly each year. The cause of these movements may be climatic (farm income, for example, is highest in the fall) or institutional (retail sales reach a peak just before Christmas). These seasonal movements are often so strong that they distort the underlying changes in economic data and tend to obscure trends that might be developing.

seasonal employment, also SEASONAL UNEMPLOYMENT, work that is available only during certain times of the year, such as jobs picking or canning fruit in the fall, playing Santa Claus in a shopping mall, or lifeguarding at summer resorts. *Seasonal unemployment* is unemployment occasioned by the seasonal variations of particular industries. Jobs affected by the weather, such as construction and agriculture, are particularly susceptible to seasonable unemployment.

SEC, see SECURITIES AND EXCHANGE COMMISSION.

secondary boycott, concerted effort by a union engaged in a dispute with an employer to seek another union to boycott a fourth party (usually their employers) who, in response to such pressure, might put like pressure on the original offending employer. Secondary boycotts are forbidden by the Labor-Management Relations (Taft-Hartley) Act of 1947. For a legal analysis, see Ralph M. Dereshinsky, *The NLRB and Secondary Boycotts* (Philadelphia: University of Pennsylvania Press, 1972).
See also the following entries:
    BOYCOTT
    NATIONAL WOODWORK MANUFACTURES
        ASSOCIATION V. NATIONAL LABOR
        RELATIONS BOARD
    UNFAIR LABOR PRACTICES (UNIONS)

secondary strike, strike against an employer because it is doing business with another employer whose workers are on strike.

second career, see CAREER CHANGE.

Second Hoover Commission, see HOOVER COMMISSION OF 1953-55.

second-order effects, also called SECOND-ORDER CONSEQUENCES, side effects from a program or project.

Secret Service, United States, service authorized to detect and arrest any person committing any offense against U.S. laws relating to coins, currency, and other obligations, and securities of the United States and of foreign governments. In addition, subject to the direction of the Secretary of the Treasury, the Secret Service is authorized to protect the person of the president of the United States, the members of his immediate family, the president-elect, the vice president or other officer next in the order of succession to the presidency, the immediate family of the vice president, the vice president-elect, major presidential and vice-presidential candidates, former presidents and their wives during his lifetime, widows of former presidents until their death or remarriage, minor children of a former president until they reach age sixteen, and visiting heads of a foreign state or foreign government.

U.S. Secret Service
1800 G Street, N.W.
Washington, D.C. 20223
(202) 535-5708

Securities and Exchange Commission (SEC), federal commission that seeks the fullest possible disclosure to the investing public and seeks to protect the interests of the public and investors against malpractices in the securities and financial markets.

SEC
450 Fifth Street, N.W.
Washington, D.C. 20549
(202) 272-3100

security assistance, term that refers to the programs of various agencies in the U.S. government relating to international defense cooperation. U.S. security assistance (sometimes called military assistance) has five components: the Military Assistance Program (MAP), in which defense articles and defense services are provided to eligible foreign governments on a grant basis; International Military Education and Training (IMET), which provides grant military training in the United States and U.S. territories to foreign military and civilian personnel; Foreign Military Sales (FMS), which provides credits and loan repayment guarantees to enable eligible foreign governments to purchase defense articles and defense services; Security Supporting Assistance (SSA), which promotes economic and political stability in areas where the United States has special foreign policy security interests; and the Peacekeeping Operations Program, which funds the Sinai Support Mission and the U.S. contribution to the U.N. forces in Cyprus.

select committee, also JOINT COMMITTEE and CONFERENCE COMMITTEE, committee established by the House or Senate, usually for a limited period and generally for a strictly temporary purpose. When that function has been carried out the select committee automatically expires. A *standing committee*, on the other hand, is a regular, permanent unit in Congress.

Joint committees are those which have members chosen from both the House and Senate, generally with the chairmanship rotating between the most senior majority party senator and representative. These committees can be created by statute, or by joint or concurrent resolution. However, all existing joint committees have been established by statute, the oldest being the Joint Committee on the Library, which dates from 1800.

From the earliest days, differences of opinion between the two houses have been committed to *conference committees* to work out a settlement. The most usual case is that in which a bill passes one house with amendments unacceptable to the other. In such a case, the house which disagrees generally asks for a conference, and the speaker (and the vice president for the Senate) appoints the "managers," as the conferees are called. Generally they are selected from the committee having charge of the bill and they usually represent majority and minority positions on the bill. After attempting to resolve the points in disagreement, the conference committee issues a report to each house. If the report is accepted by both houses, the bill is then signed and sent to the president. If rejected by either house, the matter in disagreement comes up for disposition anew as if there had been no conference. Unless all differences between the houses are finally adjusted, the bill fails.

See also AUTHORIZING COMMITTEE and STANDING COMMITTEE.

selection, *see* PERSONNEL SELECTION.

selection guidelines, *see* UNIFORM GUIDELINES ON EMPLOYEE SELECTION.

selection interview, *see* INTERVIEW.

selection out, euphemism for terminating an employee from a training program or employment.

selection procedure, according to the "Uniform Guidelines on Employee Selection,"

any measure, combination of measures, or procedures used as a basis for any employment decision. Selection procedures include the full range of assessment techniques from traditional paper and pencil tests, performance tests, training programs, or probationary periods and physical, educational, and work experience requirements through informal or casual interviews and unscored application forms.

See also UNIFORM GUIDELINES ON EMPLOYEE SELECTION.

selection ratio, number of job applicants selected compared to the number of job applicants who were available.

self-actualization, apex of Abraham Maslow's needs hierarchy, where an individual theoretically reaches self-fulfillment and becomes all that he or she is capable of becoming. The importance of the concept of self-actualization was established long before Maslow gave it voice. The 19th-century poet Robert Browning described its essence when he said, "A man's reach should exceed his grasp, or what's a heaven for?" Maslow's needs hierarchy was originally presented in "A Theory of Human Motivation," *Psychological Review* (July 1943). For a technique to measure self-actualization, *see* Charles Bonjean and Gary Vance, "A Short Form Measure of Self-Actualization," *Journal of Applied Behavioral*

Science (July-August-September 1968). *Also see* Harold R. McAlindon, "Education for Self-Actualization," *Training and Development Journal* (October 1981).

self-appraisal, performance evaluation technique in which the employee takes the initiative in appraising his/her own performance. *See* Kenneth S. Teel, "Self-Appraisal Revisited," *Personnel Journal* (July 1978); Robert P. Steel and Nestor K. Ovalle 2nd, "Self-Appraisal Based Upon Supervisory Feedback," *Personnel Psychology* (Winter 1984).

self-employed, members of the workforce who work for themselves—in their own trade or business—as opposed to wage earners who are in the employ of others.

self-employment tax, means by which persons who work for themselves are provided social security coverage. Each self-employed person must pay self-employment tax on part or all of his or her income to help finance social security benefits, which are payable to self-employed persons as well as wage earners.

See also TAXATION.

self-fulfilling prophecy, causing something to happen by believing it will. If a manager or teacher believes that his or her employees or students are not capable, they will eventually live up (or down) to the manager's or teacher's expectations. For a case study of how a manager's expectations about employee performance become a self-fulfilling prophecy, *see* J. Sterling Livingston, "Pygmalion in Management," *Harvard Business Review* (July-August 1969).

Selznick, Philip (1919-), sociologist best known to public administration for his account of the Tennessee Valley Authority's use of cooptation. Major works include: "Foundations of the Theory of Organization," *American Sociological Review,* Vol. 13 (1948); *TVA and the Grass Roots* (Berkeley, Calif.: University of California Press, 1949); *Leadership in Admin-*

istration (New York: Row, Peterson, 1957).

semiskilled workers, employees whose jobs are confined to well-established work routines, usually requiring a considerable degree of manipulative ability and a limited exercise of independent judgment.

senior civil service, a civil service corps recommended by the Hoover Commission of the 1950s. The federal government, according to the commission, should establish a senior civil service "consisting of career administrators selected from all agencies of the Government solely on the basis of demonstrated competence to fill positions requiring a high degree of managerial competence." The senior civil service concept was only realized when the Civil Service Reform Act of 1978 created the Senior Executive Service. *See* Leonard D. White, "The Senior Civil Service," *Public Administration Review* (Autumn 1955); Paul P. Van Riper, "The Senior Civil Service and the Career System," *Public Administration Review* (Summer 1958); William Pincus, "The Opposition to the Senior Civil Service," *Public Administration Review* (Autumn 1958).

Senior Executive Service (SES), federal government's top management corps, established by the Civil Service Reform Act of 1978. The large majority of SES executives are career managers; there is a 10 percent government-wide ceiling on the number who may be noncareer. In addition, about 45 percent of SES positions are career-reserved; that is, they can be filled only by career executives. *See* "All You Ever Wanted to Know About SES," *Civil Service Journal* (April-June 1979); Bruce Buchanan, "The Senior Executive Service: How Can We tell If It Works," *Public Administration Review* (May-June 1981); Norton E. Long, "The S.E.S. and the Public Interest," *Public Administration Review* (May-June 1981); Bernard Rosen, "Uncertainty in the Senior Executive Service," *Public Administration Review* (March-April 1981); William J. Lanouette, "SES In Flames," *National Journal* (July 18, 1981); Patricia W. Ingraham and Peter W. Colby, "Individual Motivation and Institutional Changes Under the Senior Executive Service," *Review of Public Personnel Administration* (Spring 1982); Patricia W. Ingraham and Charles Barrilleaux, "Motivating Government Managers for Retrenchment: Some Possible Lessons from the Senior Executive Service," *Public Administration Review* (September-October 1983); Michael A. Pagano, "The SES Performance Management System and Bonus Awards," *Review of Public Personnel Administration* (Spring 1984).

See also CIVIL SERVICE REFORM ACT OF 1978.

seniority, social mechanism that gives priority to the individuals who are the most senior—have the longest service—in an organization. Seniority is often used to determine which employees will be promoted, subjected to layoff, or given/denied other employment advantages. For a legal analysis, *see* Barry A. Friedman, "Seniority Systems and the Law," *Personnel Journal* (July 1976). For contractual provisions, *see* Winston L. Tillery, "Seniority Administration in Major Agreements," *Monthly Labor Review* (December 1972). *Also see* Maryellen R. Kelley, "Discrimination in Seniority Systems: A Case Study," *Industrial and Labor Relations Review* (October 1982); Gene M. Grossman, "Union Wages, Temporary Layoffs, and Seniority," *The American Economic Review* (June 1983); Elaine Gale Wrong, "Arbitrator's Decisions in Seniority-Discrimination Cases," *Arbitration Journal* (December 1984).

See also the following entries:
BENEFIT SENIORITY
COMPETITIVE SENIORITY
DEPARTMENTAL SENIORITY
DOVETAIL SENIORITY
FIRE FIGHTERS LOCAL UNION NO. 1784 V. STOTTS
INTERNATIONAL BROTHERHOOD OF TEAMSTERS V. UNITED STATES
INVERSE SENIORITY
RETROACTIVE SENIORITY

sensitivity analysis, a procedure employed because of uncertainty about the actual value of a parameter or parameters included in an analysis. The procedure is to vary the value of the parameters in question and examine the extent to which these changes affect the results of the analysis. For example, if an analysis indicates that Project A is preferable to Project B, sensitivity analysis might be performed by increasing the cost of one factor and then examining the results of the analysis under this change.

sensitivity training, *see* LABORATORY TRAINING and BRADFORD, LELAND P.

separation, termination of an individual's employment for whatever reason.

separation interview, *see* EXIT INTERVIEW.

separation pay, *see* SEVERANCE PAY.

separation rate, ratio of the number of separations per hundred employees over a specified time span.

serial bonds, also TERM BONDS, bonds that are sold in such a way that a certain number of them are retired each year. *Term bonds,* in contrast, all mature on the same date.

series of classes, all classes of positions involving the same kind of work, but which may vary as to the level of difficulty and responsibility and have differing grade and salary ranges. The classes in a series either have differing titles (*e.g.*, assistant accountant, associate accountant, senior accountant) or numerical designations (*e.g.*, Accountant I, Accountant II, Accountant III). Be wary of numerical designations, however. There is no uniformity in their use; an Accountant I could be either the most junior or most senior level.
See also POSITION CLASSIFICATION.

service contract, also called LAKEWOOD PLAN, agreement between locɑ government for one unit (usually to provide a service for another (usս smaller). It is often called the *Lakewoᴏ ı Plan* because it was first extensively used in the Los Angeles area between the County of Los Angeles and the City of Lakewood.

service delivery system, deliberately established set of social, economic, political, and/or cultural arrangements designed to provide a designated set of goods and/or services to consumers who are adjudged to have particular needs.

service fee, money (usually the equivalent of union dues) that nonunion members of an agency shop bargaining unit pay the union for negotiating and administering the collective bargaining agreement.
See also ABOOD V. DETROIT BOARD OF EDUCATION.

SES, *see* SENIOR EXECUTIVE SERVICE.

set, *see* POPULATION.

set-up time, time during the normal work day when a worker's machine is being set up (usually by the machine's operator) prior to commencing production. Union contracts frequently provide time standards for set-up operations.

706 agency, state and local fair employment practices agency named for Section 706(c) of Title VII of the Civil Rights Act of 1964, which requires aggrieved individuals to submit claims to state or local fair employment practices agencies before they are eligible to present their cases to the federal government's Equal Employment Opportunity Commission. State and local agencies that have the ability to provide the same protections provided by Title VII as would the EEOC are termed 706 agencies. The EEOC maintains a list of the 706 agencies that it formally recognizes.

70-percent syndrome, *see* CUTTING SCORE.

ed DISMISSAL PAY, TERMINATION PAY, an employer to an been permanently ganization because on, the introduction ery, or for any rea- :." The amount of a usually determined by a schedule based on years of service and earnings. About 40 percent of all union contracts contain provisions for severance pay.

Eligible federal government employees have severance pay computed on the basis of one week's salary for each year of the first ten years of service and two weeks' salary for each year of service after ten years. For employees over age forty, an age adjustment allowance is added to the basic allowance by computing 10 percent of the basic allowance of each year over age forty. The total severance pay that a federal employee may receive is limited to one year's pay at the rate of pay received immediately prior to separation.

See also NOLDE BROTHERS, INC. V. LOCAL NO. 358, BAKERY WORKERS.

severance tax, *see* TAX, SEVERANCE.

sewer taps, *see* WATER RIGHTS.

sex differential, also RACE DIFFERENTIAL, lower than "regular" wage rate paid by an employer to female and/or black employees. Such differentials were paid before the advent of current equal employment opportunity laws and are now illegal.

sex discrimination, any disparate or unfavorable treatment of an individual in an employment situation because of his or her sex. The Civil Rights Act of 1964 makes sex discrimination illegal except where a bona fide occupational qualification is involved. For a legal analysis, *see* Jerri D. Gilbreath, "Sex Discrimination and Title VII of the Civil Rights Act," *Personnel Journal* (January 1977). *See also* Paul Osterman, "Sex Discrimination in Professional Employment: A Case Study," *In-*

dustrial and Labor Relations Review (July 1979); Joan Acker and Donald R. Van Houten, "Differential Recruitment and Control: The Sex Structuring of Organizations," *Administrative Science Quarterly* (June 1974); Sandra Sawyer and Arthur A. Whatley, "Sexual Harassment: A Form of Sex Discrimination," *The Personnel Administrator* (January 1980).

See also the following entries:
CITY OF LOS ANGELES, DEPARTMENT OF WATER & POWER V. MANHART
DAVIS V. PASSMAN
DISCRIMINATION
GOESAERT V. CLEARY
PITTSBURGH PRESS CO. V. THE PITTSBURGH COMMISSION ON HUMAN RELATIONS
PREGNANCY DISCRIMINATION ACT OF 1978
SCHLESINGER V. BALLARD

sexist, person or organization that consciously or unconsciously practices sex discrimination. *See* Betty J. Collier and Louis N. Williams, "Towards a Bilateral Model of Sexism," *Human Relations* (February 1981).

sex plus, situation where an employer does not discriminate against all males or all females, but discriminates against a subset of either sex. *Phillips* v. *Martin Marietta,* 400 U.S. 542 (1971), is the U.S. Supreme Court case that dealt with the "sex plus" criterion for evaluating applicants for employment. Martin Marietta had a policy of hiring both sexes for a particular job but refused to hire any women with preschool-aged children. The court found this "sex plus" policy to be in violation of Title VII of the Civil Rights Act of 1964.

sexual harassment, action of an individual in a position to control or influence another's job, career, or grade who uses such power to gain sexual favors or punish the refusal of such favors. Sexual harassment on the job varies from inappropriate sexual innuendo to coerced sexual relations.

Everyone copes with sexual harassment differently. What one person finds offensive another may find flattering. A physical touch or a suggestion of intimacy might be objectionable to some but humorous to others. We all cope in the way that is most comfortable to us. Some simply run away. Some stay and fight through the courts or with their fists. Others cope by not seeing sexual harassment as a problem at all. Phyllis Schlafly, the anti-feminist crusader, testified before a congressional committee in 1981 that "sexual harassment on the job is not a problem for virtuous women, except in the rarest of cases. Men hardly ever ask sexual favors of women from whom the certain answer is 'no.' "

Can professional relationships remain successful once they turn sexual? Can the person on whose impartial professional judgment you depend also be your lover? Is it normal, healthy, or ethical to continue a professional relationship in bed? Not often. But that has certainly not stopped great numbers of people from trying. The problem is all the worse when the couple involved have unequal status. Then it is argued just as rape may be more a crime of violence than of passion—that sex at work may be more an act of power than of lust.

The courts are only gradually giving us a general idea of what behavior should not be permitted on the job. Sex discrimination was by no means a significant concern of the civil rights advocates of the early 1960s. Its prohibition only became part of the Civil Rights Act of 1964 because of Congressman Howard "Judge" Smith. As the leader of the South's fight against civil rights in the U.S. House of Representatives, he added one small word—sex—to prohibitions against race, color, religion and national origin. He felt confident this amendment would make the proposed law ridiculous and cause its defeat. Smith was an "old style" bigot: to his mind, the one thing more ridiculous than equal rights for blacks was equal rights for women.

When the Civil Rights Act of 1964 prohibited sex discrimination in employment there wasn't anybody who would have said or implied that the new law had anything to do with sexual harassment. The phrase "sexual harassment" wasn't even in the language. Yet today, for all legal purposes, sex discrimination includes sexual harassment. A few courageous women enlarged the meaning of the law because they were mad enough about unwarranted sexual pressures to "go public" and test their novel interpretation of sex discrimination in federal court.

Although there was universal agreement that sexual harassment was bad, there was no agreement as to where the normal give and take between the sexes ended and sexual harassment began. An old maxim of the law in such situations was that "there is no harm in asking!" But the harm was always there. Countless women left jobs rather than submit to sexual requests. Countless others, out of sheer economic necessity, continued on in humiliation and fear.

In 1974 Paulette Barnes started the first major case linking sexual harassment to violations of the federal civil rights law. She was an administrative aide in the Environmental Protection Agency when her supervisor began a "campaign to extract sexual favors." This included suggestions that sexual cooperation would advance her career and repeated requests for dates despite her consistent refusals.

After Barnes' supervisor finally gave up hope of seducing her, he initiated an "administrative consolidation" of his office which, as a byproduct, eliminated the need for her job. A federal judge ruled that it was sex discrimination to abolish a woman's job because she refused her male supervisor's sexual advances. The Court of Appeals left no doubt that sexual harassment was sex discrimination when a woman's job "was conditional upon submission to sexual relations—an exaction which the superior would not have sought from any male." Paulette Barnes was awarded $18,000 in damages. See *Barnes v. Costle*, 561 F. 2d. 983 (D.C. Cir 1977).

Over the next few years a variety of similar cases were successfully brought to court. They all involved women who had lost their jobs because of sexual harassment. These women were not suing their actual harassers; they were suing the companies that had employed them.

In 1980, after the federal courts had decided that sexual harassment was sex discrimination in a variety of cases, the Equal Employment Opportunity Commission—the federal agency responsible for enforcing sex discrimination prohibitions—took formal action. It issued legally binding rules clearly stating that an employer has a responsibility to provide a place of work that is free from sexual harassment or intimidation. And an agency can be held responsible for sexual harassment by its employees whether or not supervisors knew of the harassment.

See Constance Backhouse and Leah Cohen, *The Secret Oppression: Sexual Harassment of Working Women* (Toronto: Macmillan of Canada, 1978); Lin Farley, *Sexual Shakedown: The Sexual Harassment of Women on the Job* (New York: McGraw-Hill, 1978); Catharine A. MacKinnon, *Sexual Harassment of Working Women* (New Haven, Conn.: Yale University Press, 1979); Dail Ann Neugarten and Jay M. Shafritz, eds., *Sexuality in Organizations* (Oak Park, Ill.: Moore Publishing Co., 1980); Mary Coeli Meyer et al., *Sexual Harassment* (New York: Petrocelli, 1981); U.S. Merit Systems Protection Board, *Sexual Harassment in the Federal Workplace: Is It a Problem?* (Washington, D.C.: U.S. Government Printing Office, 1981); Patrice D. Horn and Jack C. Horn, *Sex in the Office: Power and Passion in the Workplace* (Reading, Mass.: Addison-Wesley, 1982); Robert E. Quinn and Patricia L. Lees, "Attraction and Harassment: Dynamics of Sexual Politics in the Workplace," *Organizational Dynamics* (Autumn 1984).

**NATIONAL AERONAUTICS AND SPACE ADMINISTRATION
JOHNSON SPACE CENTER
POLICY STATEMENT AND DEFINITION ON SEXUAL HARASSMENT**

Federal employees have a grave responsibility under the Federal code of conduct and ethics for maintaining high standards of honesty, integrity, impartiality and conduct to assure proper performance of the Government's business and the maintenance of confidence of the American people. Any employee conduct which violates this code will not be condoned.

Sexual harassment is a form of employee misconduct which undermines the integrity of the employment relationship. All employees must be allowed to work in an environment free from unsolicited and unwelcome sexual overtures. Sexual harassment debilitates morale and interferes in the work productivity of its victims and co-workers.

Sexual harassment is a form of sex discrimination because it involves actions taken for or against an employee on the basis of conduct not related to performance, such as the taking or refusal to take a personnel action, including the promotion of employees who submit to sexual advances or the refusal to promote employees who resist or protest sexual overtures.

Specifically, sexual harassment is deliberate or repeated unsolicited verbal comments, gestures, or physical contact of a sexual nature which are unwelcome.

Within the Federal Government, a supervisor, who uses implicit or explicit coercive sexual behavior to control, influence, or affect the career, salary, or job of an employee is engaging in sexual harassment. Similarly, an employee of an agency who behaves in this manner in the process of conducting agency business is engaging in sexual harassment.

Finally, any employee who participates in deliberate or repeated unsolicited verbal comments, gestures, or physical contact of a sexual nature which are unwelcome and interfere in work productivity is also engaging in sexual harassment.

It is the policy of the Johnson Space Center that sexual harassment is unacceptable conduct in the workplace and will not be condoned. At the same time, it is not the intent of Johnson Space Center to regulate the social interaction of relationships freely entered into by its employees.

Complaints of harassment should be brought to the attention of the appropriate supervisory level, the Personnel Office, or the Equal Opportunity Programs Office.

Shakespeare, William (1564-1616), English writer who created now-classic studies in personnel management and organizational behavior. His more famous works include:

Macbeth—the story of a ruthless workaholic who allows his too-ambitious wife to egg him on to the top only to find that he can't hack it when up against a "C" section rival.

Romeo and Juliet—illustrates the dysfunctional aspects of a breakdown in communications between two competing paternalistic organizations. This situation is only temporarily rectified when informal inter-organizational communications are established at the employee level—unfortunately with poisonous results.

Hamlet—poignant case study of a sensitive young executive who fails to move up in the organizational hierarchy because of his inability to make decisions.

Othello—minority employee makes it to the top, only to find that jealousy at the office leads to murder.

King Lear—chief executive of a family business learns the perils of early retirement.

Sharkansky, Ira (1938-   ), leading voice on policy analysis, urban politics, and inter-governmental relations who wrote the first public administration text that took a systems approach—*Public Administration: Policy-Making in Government Agencies*, 4th ed. (Chicago: Rand McNally, 1978). Other major works include: *Spending in the American States* (Chicago: Rand McNally, 1968); *The Politics of Taxing and Spending* (Indianapolis: Bobbs-Merrill, 1969); *Regionalism in American Politics* (Indianapolis: Bobbs-Merrill, 1969); *The Routines of Politics* (Princeton, N.J.: Van Nostrand, 1970); *Urban Politics and Public Policy*, with Robert Lineberry (New York: Harper & Row, 1971, 1974); *The Maligned States* (New York: McGraw-Hill, 1972); *The United States: A Study of a Developing Country* (New York: McKay, 1975); *Whither the State: Politics and Public Enterprise in Three Countries* (Chatham, N.J.: Chatham House Publishers, 1979); *Public Administration: Agencies, Policies, & Politics* (San Francisco: W. H. Freeman, 1982).

Shaw, Lemuel (1781-1861), chief justice of the Supreme Judicial Court of Massachusetts from 1830 to 1860 who wrote a landmark decision in the case of *Commonwealth* v. *Hunt*, 4 Metcalf, 45 Mass., Ill (1842), which held that it was not a criminal act of conspiracy for a combination of employees or a union to refuse to work for an employer who hires nonunion labor. This decision established the legality of the right to strike for higher wages. For a biography, *see* Leonard W. Levy, *Law of the Commonwealth and Chief Justice Shaw* (Cambridge, Mass.: Harvard University Press, 1957).

sheepskin psychosis, *see* CREDENTIALISM.

Sheldon, Oliver (1894-1951), English businessman who was the first to provide a philosophical basis for the identification of management as a profession. In *The Philosophy of Management* (London: Pitman, 1923), he asserted that management was separate from both capital and labor; and that, as a profession, its primary responsibility was "social and communal."

sheltered workshop, place of employment that offers a controlled, noncompetitive environment for persons unable to compete in the regular world of work because of physical or mental disabilities. For a history, *see* Nathan Nelson, *Workshops for the Handicapped in the United States: An Historical and Developmental Perspective* (Springfield, Ill.: Charles C. Thomas, 1971).

See also WAGNER-O'DAY ACT.

Shelton v. Tucker, 364 U.S. 479 (1960), U.S. Supreme Court case which dealt with the question of whether public employees could have membership in subversive organizations, organizations with illegal objectives, and unions. Their right to join the last was upheld. With regard to the first two, it was held that there could be no general answer. Rather, each case has to be judged on the basis of whether a public employee actually supports an organization's illegal aims, because, as the Supreme Court expressed it, "Those who join an organization but do not share its unlawful purposes and who do not participate in its unlawful activities surely pose no threat, either as citizens or as public employees." Consequently, it is incumbent upon public employers seeking to dismiss employees for membership in subversive organizations or those with illegal purposes to prove that the employees actually shared in the subversive organization's objectionable aims and activities.

Sherbert v. Verner, 374 U.S. 398 (1963), U.S. Supreme Court case which held it unconstitutional to disqualify a person for unemployment compensation benefits solely because that person refused to accept employment that would require working on Saturday contrary to his or her religious belief.

Sherman Antitrust Act of 1890, also called SHERMAN ACT, federal statute that held "every contract, combination in the form of trust or otherwise, or conspiracy, in restraint of trade or commerce. . . is hereby declared to be illegal." While the statute was directed at industrial monopolies, the courts used the act punitively against the budding union movement. Subsequent legislation (the Clayton Act of 1914) exempted unions from the Sherman Act prohibitions on the restraint of trade.
See also the following entries:
BEDFORD CUT STONE COMPANY V. JOURNEYMEN STONE CUTTERS' ASSOCIATION
LAWLOR V. LOEWE
UNITED MINE WORKERS V. PENNINGTON
UNITED STATES V. HUTCHESON

shift, fixed, see FIXED SHIFT.

shift, split, see BROKEN TIME.

shift premium, also called SHIFT DIFFEREN-

TIAL, extra compensation paid as an inducement to accept shift work.

shift work, formal tour of duty that is mostly outside of "normal" daytime business hours. According to Richard A. Edwards, in "Shift Work: Performance and Satisfaction," *Personnel Journal* (November 1975), an examination of the research on the efficiency of night or shift workers seems to indicate that it is "a physiological fact of life that night shift workers will never perform with the same efficiency as the other two shifts." *Also see* Peter Finn, "The Effects of Shift Work on the Lives of Employees," *Monthly Labor Review* (October 1981); Jane C. Hood and Nancy Milazzo, "Shiftwork, Stress and Well-being," *Personnel Administrator* (December 1984); Gerald A. Benjamin, "Shift Workers," *Personnel Journal* (June 1984).

shop committee, group of union members in the same organizational unit who have been selected to speak for the union membership on any of a variety of issues.

shop steward, see STEWARD.

short-term debt, interest-bearing debt to be paid off within one year from date of issue, such as bond anticipation notes, bank loans, and tax anticipation notes and warrants. Includes obligations having no fixed maturity date if payable from a tax levied for collection in the year of their issuance.

showing of interest, evidence of membership—the requirement that a union must show that it has adequate support from employees in a proposed bargaining unit before a representation election can be held. A "showing of interest" is usually demonstrated by signed authorization cards.

sick leave, leave of absence, usually with pay, granted to employees who cannot attend work because of illness. See Charles N. Weaver, "Influence of Sex, Salary and

Age on Seasonal Use of Sick Leave," *Personnel Journal* (August 1970); Maureen Heneghan and Sigmund G. Ginsberg, "Use of Sick Leave," *Personnel Administration* (September–October 1970).

sick-leave bank, arrangement that allows employees to pool some of their paid sick-leave days in a common fund so that they may draw upon that fund if extensive illness uses up their remaining paid time off. Sick-leave banks have tended to discourage absenteeism because, with everyone jointly owning days in the bank, there is some psychological pressure on workers not to use their sick-leave unless they are really sick.

significance, also called STATISTICAL SIGNIFICANCE, degree to which one can be confident in the reliability of a statistical measure. For example, a confidence level of .05 means that the statistical finding would occur by chance in only one sample out of every twenty.

silver-circle rate, higher than standard pay rate based upon length of service.

Simon, Herbert A. (1916-), awarded the Nobel Prize for Economics in 1978 for his pioneering work in management decision making, Simon is best known to the administrative world for his equally impressive contributions to our understanding of organizational behavior. Major works include: *Administrative Behavior* (New York: Macmillan, 1947); *Public Administration*, with D. Smithburg and V. Thompson (New York: Knopf, 1950); *Models of Man: Social and Rational* (New York: John Wiley, 1958); *The New Science of Management Decision* (New York: Harper & Row, 1960); *The Shape of Automation for Men and Management* (New York: Harper & Row, 1965); *Human Problem Solving*, with Allen Newell (Englewood Cliffs, N.J.: Prentice-Hall, 1972).

See also PROVERBS OF ADMINISTRATION and SATISFICING.

simulation, see GAMING SIMULATION.

sinecure, any position for which a salary is extracted but little or no work is expected. This was originally an ecclesiastical term, which meant a church office that did not require the care of souls. Sinecure is Latin for "without care."

single rate, see FLAT RATE.

Singleton v. Wulff, 428 U.S. 106 (1976), Supreme Court case granting standing to sue to medical doctors challenging a state law forbidding the use of Medicaid funds for abortions. The court held that the doctors could assert the rights of the women who could be injured by this statute.

single-use plans, plans used up or defunct when the goals are accomplished for which that plan was designed (*e.g.*, construction projects, research and development projects, fabrication of equipment or structures, etc.).

sit-down strike, also STAY-IN STRIKE, any work stoppage during which the strikers remain at their work stations and refuse to leave the employer's premises in order to forestall the employment of strikebreakers. This kind of strike gained widespread publicity in the 1930s as a tactic of the unions in the rubber and automobile industries. A sit-down strike that lasts for a substantial period of time is then called a *stay-in strike*. For a history, see Daniel Nelson, ed., "The Beginning of the Sit-Down Era: The Reminiscences of Rex Murray," *Labor History* (Winter 1974); Sidney Fine, *Sit-Down: The General Motors Strike of 1936-1937* (Ann Arbor: University of Michigan Press, 1969).

In 1939, the U.S. Supreme Court, in *National Labor Relations Board v. Fansteel Metallurgical Corp.*, 306 U.S. 240 (1939), ruled that the right to strike did not extend to the use of sit-down strikes and that employees discharged under such circumstances had no reinstatement rights under the National Labor Relations (Wagner) Act of 1935. The Court held that a sit-down strike

was an illegal seizure of the buildings in order to prevent their use by the employer in a lawful manner and thus by acts of force and violence to compel the employer to submit. When the employees resorted to that sort of compulsion they took a position outside the protection of the statute and accepted the risk of the termination of their employment upon grounds aside from the exercise of the legal rights which the statute was designed to conserve.

situational management, see CONTINGENCY MANAGEMENT.

skewness, tendency of a distribution to depart from symmetry or balance around the mean. If the scores tend to cluster at the lower end of the distribution, the distribution is said to be positively skewed; if they tend to cluster at the upper end of the distribution, the distribution is said to be negatively skewed.

skill differential, differences in wage rates paid to workers employed in occupational categories requiring varying levels of skill.

skilled labor, workers who, having trained for a relatively long time, have mastered jobs of considerable skill requiring the exercise of substantial independent judgment. See W. Franke and D. Sokel, *The Shortage of Skilled and Technical Workers* (Lexington, Mass.: Lexington Books, 1970).

skills, physical or manipulative activities requiring knowledge for their execution.

skills survey, also called SKILLS AUDIT and SKILLS INVENTORY, comprehensive collection and examination of data on the work force to determine the composition and level of employees' skills, knowledges, and abilities so that they can be more fully utilized and/or developed to fill the staffing needs of an organization. A skills survey or inventory may at times be the process

of collecting data and at other times the product as represented by a collection of data in a variety of forms. To be effective, skills data must also be arranged in such a manner that the information gathered can be readily accessible for management use. See John A. R. Jons, "A Skills Audit," *Training and Development Journal* (September 1980).

Skinner, B. F. (1904-), full name FREDERIC BURRHUS SKINNER, one of the most influential of behavioral psychologists, inventor of the teaching machine, and generally considered to be the "father" of programmed instruction. Major works include: *Waldon Two* (New York: Macmillan 1948, 1966); *Science and Human Behavior* (New York: Free Press, 1953, 1965); *The Technology of Teaching* (New York: Appleton-Century-Crofts, 1968); *Beyond Freedom and Dignity* (New York: Knopf, 1971).

slide-rule discipline, approach to discipline that eliminates supervisory discretion and sets very specific quantitative standards as the consequences of specific violations. For example, a discipline policy based on this concept might hold that any employee who is late for work more than four times in a thirty-day period would be "automatically" suspended for three days.

Sloan Management Review, professional management journal of the Alfred P. Sloan School of Management at the Massachusetts Institute of Technology. It is published three times each academic year (Fall, Winter, and Spring) and has as its principal goal the exchange of information between the academic and business communities.

Sloan Management Review
Alfred P. Sloan School of Management
Massachusetts Institute of Technology
Cambridge, MA 02139

slot, position in an organization.

slowdown, deliberate reduction of output by employees. Such efforts are usually designed to bring economic pressure upon an employer without incurring the costs of a strike. *See* Richard S. Hammett, Joel Seidman, and Jack London, "The Slow-down as a Union Tactic," *Journal of Political Economy* (April 1957).

Small Business Administration (SBA), federal agency whose purposes are to aid, counsel, assist, and protect the interests of small business; ensure that small business concerns receive a fair proportion of government purchases, contracts, and subcontracts, as well as of the sales of government property; make loans to small business concerns, state and local development companies, and the victims of floods or other catastrophes, or of certain types of economic injury; license, regulate, and make loans to small business investment companies; improve the management skills of small business owners, potential owners, and managers; conduct studies of the economic environment; and guarantee surety bonds for small contractors.

SBA
1441 L Street, N.W.
Washington, D.C. 20416
(202) 653-6565

small-group research, also GROUP, study of small groups. A *group* consists of a number of individuals who interact with each other in a particular social setting. Generally, groups are classified as "small" when each member can at least take personal cognizance of all other members. This distinguishes small groups from social units that are so large that it is impossible for each member to be aware of all others. For the pioneering concepts of small-group research, *see* George C. Homans, *The Human Group* (New York: Harcourt, Brace Jovanovich, 1950); Robert T. Golembiewski, *The Small Group: An Analysis of Research Concepts and Operations* (Chicago: University of Chicago Press, 1962); A. Paul Hare, *Handbook of Small Group Research*, 2nd ed. (New York: The Free Press, 1976).

See also GROUP DYNAMICS and ORGANIZATION DEVELOPMENT.

Smith, Adam (1723-1790), the Scottish economist who provided the first systematic analysis of economic phenomena and the intellectual foundation for laissez-faire capitalism. In *The Wealth of Nations* (1776) Smith discovered an "invisible hand" that automatically promotes the general welfare so long as individuals are allowed to pursue their self-interest. It has become customary for organization theorists to trace the lineage of present-day theories to Smith's concept of the division of labor. Greater specialization of labor was one of the pillars of the "invisible hand" market mechanism with which the greatest rewards would go to those who were the most efficient in the competitive marketplace. As Smith's work marks the beginning of economics as an identifiable discipline, he is often referred to as the "father" of economics. *See* N. R. Goodwin and Bruce Mazlish, "The Wealth of Adam Smith," *Harvard Business Review* (July-August 1983).

Smith Act, *see* ALIEN REGISTRATION ACT OF 1940.

Smith-Hughes Act of 1917, federal vocational educational act that established the principles of federal financial aid and cooperation with the states in promoting public vocational education.

Smithsonian Institution, institution created by an act of Congress in 1846 to carry out the terms of the will of James Smithson of England, who in 1829 bequeathed his entire estate to the United States "to found at Washington, under the name of the Smithsonian Institution, an establishment for the increase and diffusion of knowledge among men."

To carry out Smithson's mandate, the Institution, as an independent trust establishment, performs fundamental research; publishes the results of studies, explorations, and investigations; preserves for study and reference over seventy million items of scientific, cultural, and historical interest; maintains exhibits representative of the arts, U.S. history, technology, aeronautics and space explorations, and natural history; participates in the international exchange of learned publications; and engages in programs of education and national and international cooperative research and training, supported by its trust endowments and gifts, grants and contracts, and funds appropriated to it by Congress.

Smithsonian Institution
1000 Jefferson Drive, S.W.
Washington, D.C. 20560
(202) 357-1300

Smith v. Arkansas State Highway Employees, Local 1315, 441 U.S. 463 (1979), U.S. Supreme Court case which held that the Arkansas State Highway Commission's refusal to consider a Highway Department employee's grievance when submitted by a union rather than by the employee did not violate First Amendment rights.

smoking, a form of worksite air pollution. For the controversy, *see* Robert L. Jauvtis, "The Rights of Nonsmokers in the Workplace: Recent Developments," *Labor Law Journal* (March 1983); William L. Weis, Horace R. Kornegay, and Lewis Solomon, "The Fiery Debate Over Smoking At Work," *Business and Society Review* (Fall 1984).

smorgasbord benefits plan, *see* CAFETERIA BENEFITS PLAN.

SMSA, *see* STANDARD METROPOLITAN STATISTICAL AREA.

social audit, audit defined by Raymond A. Bauer and Dan H. Fenn, Jr., in "What is a Corporate Social Audit?" *Harvard Business Review* (January-February 1973), as "a commitment to systematic assessment of and reporting on some meaningful, definable domain of a company's activities that have social impact." *Also see* John William Humble, *Social Responsibility Audit: A Management Tool for Survival* (New York: AMACOM, 1973); Clark C. Abt, *The Social Audit for Management* (New York: AMACOM, 1977).

social benefits, gains, both quantifiable and nonquantifiable, which result from a specific program or project.

social costs, prices, both quantifiable and nonquantifiable, paid for undertaking a specific program or project.

social darwinism, Charles Darwin's concept of the "survival of the fittest" applied to human society.

social equity, normative standard holding that equity, rather than efficiency, is the major criterion for evaluating the desirability of a policy or program. *See* H. George Frederickson, Symposium Editor, "Social Equity and Public Administration," *Public Administration Review* (January-February 1974); Arthur M. Oken, *Equity and Efficiency: The Big Tradeoff* (Washington, D.C.: Brookings Institution, 1975).
See also PUBLIC ADMINISTRATION, NEW.

social indicators, statistical measures that aid in the description of conditions in the social environment (*i.e.*, measures of income distribution, poverty, health, physical environment). *See* Raymond Bauer, *Social Indicators* (Cambridge, Mass.: M.I.T. Press, 1967); Raymond D. Gastil, "Social Indicators and Quality of Life," *Public Administration Review* (November-December 1970); Bureau of the Census, U.S. Department of Commerce, *Social Indicators 1976; Selected Data on Social Conditions and Trends in the United States* (Washington, D.C.: Government Printing Office, 1977); W. A. McIntosh, G. E. Klonglan, and L. D. Wilcox, "Theoretical Issues and Social Indicators: A Societal Process Approach," *Policy Sciences* (September 1977); Fremont Kast, "Scanning the Future Environment: Social Indicators," *California Management Review* (Fall 1980).

social insurance, any benefit program that a state makes available to the members of its society in time of need and as a matter of right.

socialism, a system of government in

which many of the means of production and trade are owned or run by the government and in which many human welfare needs are provided directly by the government. *Socialism* may or may not be democratic.

socialized medicine, a medical care system where the organization and provision of medical care services are under direct government control, and providers are employed by or contract for the provision of services directly with the government; also a term used more generally, without recognized or constant definition, referring to any existing or proposed medical care system believed to be subject to excessive governmental control.

social reference group, *see* REFERENCE GROUP.

social security, program once defined by Britain's Lord Beveridge as "a job when you can work and an income when you can't." In the United States, social security is the popular name for the Old Age, Survivors, and Disability Insurance (OASDI) system established by the Social Security Act of 1935. At first, social security only covered private sector employees upon retirement. In 1939, the law was changed to pay survivors when the worker died, as well as certain dependents when the worker retired. In the 1950s, coverage was extended to include most self-employed persons, most state and local employees, household and farm employees, members of the armed forces, and members of the clergy. Today, almost all U.S. jobs are covered by social security.

Disability insurance was added in 1954 to give workers protection against loss of earnings due to total disability. The social security program was expanded again in 1965 with the enactment of Medicare, which assured hospital and medical insurance protection to people sixty-five and over. Since 1973, Medicare coverage has been available to people under sixty-five who have been entitled to disability checks for two or more consecutive years and to people with permanent kidney failure who need dialysis or kidney transplants. Amendments enacted in 1972 provide that social security benefits will increase automatically with the cost of living. *See* Alicia H. Munnell, *The Future of Social Security* (Washington, D.C.: The Brookings Institution, 1977); Robert M. Ball, *Social Security: Today and Tomorrow* (New York: Columbia University Press, 1978); Martha Derthick, *Policymaking for Social Security* (Washington, D.C.: The Brookings Institution, 1979); Edward Wynne, *Social Security: A Reciprocity System Under Pressure* (Boulder, Colo.: Westview Press, 1980); Henry J. Aaron, *Economic Effects of Social Security* (Washington, D.C.: The Brookings Institution, 1982).

See also the following entries:
HELVERING V. DAVIS
MEDICARE
OLD AGE, SURVIVORS, AND DISABILITY INSURANCE

Social Security Act of 1935, federal statute that, as amended, is the foundation of the nation's social insurance program. For histories, *see* Edwin E. White, *The Development of the Social Security Act* (Madison: University of Wisconsin Press, 1963); Roy Lubove, *The Struggle for Social Security: 1900-1935* (Cambridge, Mass.: Harvard University Press, 1968); J. Douglas Brown, *An American Philosophy of Social Security: Evolution and Issues* (Princeton: Princeton University Press, 1972).

Social Security Administration (SSA), U.S. government agency, part of the Department of Health and Human Services, that administers the national program of contributory social insurance whereby employees, employers, and the self-employed pay contributions that are pooled in special trust funds.

Social Security Administration
6401 Security Boulevard
Baltimore, MD 21235
(301) 594-1234

social work, governmental or non-profit administration of services for the old or those who are socially handicapped. For a history, *see* Roy Lubove, *The Professional Altruist: The Emergence of Social Work as a Career, 1880-1930* (Cambridge, Mass.: Harvard University Press, 1965).

social worker, a professionally trained person providing social services, either as a member of a health team, a social service section of a health or welfare facility, or on a consultant basis. Most trained social workers now hold a master's degree in social work (MSW).

Society for Personnel Administration, *see* INTERNATIONAL PERSONNEL MANAGEMENT ASSOCIATION.

Society for the Advancement of Management (SAM), group formed in 1912 by colleagues of Frederick W. Taylor as a professional society dedicated to the discussion and promotion of scientific management. SAM is now a peer training organization "devoted to helping managers develop professionally through communication and interaction with other managers."

> Society for the Advancement of Management
> 135 West 50th Street
> New York, NY 10020
> (212) 586-8100

sociogram, diagram showing the interactions between members of a group. Typically, it has circles representing people and arrows extending from those circles pointing out the other people (circles) that are liked, disliked, etc.

sociology, occupational, *see* OCCUPATIONAL SOCIOLOGY.

sociology of work, *see* OCCUPATIONAL SOCIOLOGY.

sociometry, technique for discovering the patterns of interpersonal relationships that exist within a group. A sociometric analysis typically has each member of the group express his or her choices for or against other members of the group. A common question on such surveys is "who should be the leader of the group?" The ensuing preference and rejection patterns can be used to construct sociograms or social maps. For the pioneering work in sociometric methodologies, *see* J. L. Moreno, "Contributions of Sociometry to Research Methodology in Sociology," *American Sociological Review* (June 1947); J. L. Moreno, ed., *The Sociometry Reader* (Glencoe, Ill.: The Free Press, 1960). For an evaluation of its usefulness, *see* B. J. Speroff, "Sociometry: A Key to the Informal Organization," *Personnel Journal* (February 1968).

socio-technical systems, concept that a work group is neither a technical nor a social system, but an interdependent socio-technical system. Research on this concept was pioneered in the early 1950s by the Tavistock Institute of Human Relations in London. For accounts by the original researchers, *see* F. E. Emery and E. L. Trist, "Socio-Technical Systems," in C. W. Churchman and M. Verhulst, eds., *Management Science, Models, and Techniques* (London: Pergamon, 1960); Fred E. Emery, "Characteristics of Socio-Technical Systems," in Louis E. Davis and Jamess C. Taylor, eds., *Design of Jobs* (Baltimore: Penguin Books, 1972). *Also see* Thomas G. Cummings and Suresh Srivastva, *Management of Work: A Socio-Technical Systems Approach* (Kent State University Press, 1977); William A. Pasmore and John J. Sherwood, *Socio-technical Systems: A Sourcebook* (La-Jolla, Calif.: University Associates, 1978). *See also* HUMAN-FACTORS ENGINEERING.

socio-technology, W. Henry Lambright's term for technological projects specifically aimed at producing immediate benefits to society at large. As opposed to basic research, socio-technological projects are "targeted" or "mission"-oriented research aimed at specific problems requiring technological solutions. *See* W. Henry Lambright, *Governing Science and Technology* (New York: Oxford University Press, 1976).

Socrates (470–399 B.C.), ancient Greek philosopher who established the intellectual foundations of modern employment testing when he asserted that "the unexamined life is not worth living."

soft match, *see* IN-KIND MATCH.

soldier, in the industrial world, to malinger, to shirk one's duty, to feign illness, or to make a pretense of working. The usage comes from naval history. In earlier centuries, soldiers aboard ship did not have duties as arduous as those of the regular ship's company, so the sailors made soldiering synonymous with loafing and other nonproductive activities.

solid waste management, methods used to deal with the residential and commercial solid byproducts of consumption and production. Management techniques include solid waste reduction (*e.g.,* returnable beverage bottles), recycling (*e.g.,* the remanufacture of a new product from an old one, such as paper), burning (*e.g.,* waste heat from incinerators used to heat buildings) and burial (*e.g.,* landfills). In contrast to air and water pollution, there is little national legislation in this field except for federal planning grants and hazardous waste management.

Southern Review of Public Administration, general quarterly of public affairs.
Southern Review of Public Administration
Southern Public Administration Education Foundation, Inc.
Auburn University at Montgomery
Montgomery, AL 36193

sovereign immunity, a government's freedom from being sued for damages in all but special situations where it consents to suit by passing statutes allowing it.
See also IMMUNITY.

sovereignty, the quality of being supreme in power, rank, or authority. In the United States the people are sovereign and government is considered their agent. The sovereignty of the sovereign states of the United States is largely a myth, however, because so much power on most crucial issues now lies with the federal government. The literature on sovereignty is immense and fraught with philosophy. Two examples: Charles E. Merriam, Jr., *History of the Theory of Sovereignty Since Rousseau* (New York: Garland Publishing, 1972); Julian H. Franklin, *John Locke and the Theory of Sovereignty* (Cambridge, U.K.: Cambridge University Press, 1978).

Spalding* v. *Vilas, 161 U.S. 483 (1896), Supreme Court case granting absolute immunity from civil suit for damages to the Postmaster General of the United States and, by implication, to the heads of other federal departments.
See also the following entries:
BARR V. MATTEO
BUTZ V. ECONOMOU
WOOD V. STRICKLAND

Spanish Speaking Program, also HISPANIC EMPLOYMENT PROGRAM, federal government program established on November 5, 1970 to call attention to the needs of the Spanish-speaking in federal employment. It is an integral part of the government's total EEO effort and is designed to assure equal employment opportunity for the Spanish-speaking in all aspects of federal employment. In March 1978, the name of the Spanish Speaking Program was changed to the Hispanic Employment Program. *See* Office of the Spanish Speaking Program, U.S. Civil Service Commission, *Spanish Speaking Program: A Guidebook for Coordinators* (Washington, D.C.: U.S. Government Printing Office, 1975). *See also* Harry P. Pachon, "Hispanics in Local Government: A Growing Force," *Public Management* (October 1980).

span of control, extent of a manager's responsibility. The span of control has usually been expressed as the number of subordinates that a manager should supervise. Sir Ian Hamilton, in *The Soul and Body of an Army* (London: Edward Arnold & Co., 1921), is generally credited with having first asserted that the "average human brain finds its effective scope in handling from three to six other brains." A.V. Graicunas took a mathematical approach to the concept and demonstrated, in "Relationship in Organization," in Luther Gulick and Lyndall Urwick, eds., *Papers on the Science of Administration* (New York: Institute of Public Administration, 1937), that as the number of subordinates reporting to a manager increases arithmetically, the number of possible interpersonal interactions increases geometrically. Building upon Graicunas' work, Lyndall F. Urwick boldly asserts, in "The Manager's Span of Control," *Harvard Business Review* (May–June 1956), that "no superior can supervise directly the work of more than five or, at the most, six subordinates whose work interlocks." Studies on the concept of span of control abound, but there is no consensus on an "ideal" span. *Also see* John Udell, "An Empirical Test of Hypotheses Relating to Span of Control," *Administrative Science Quarterly* (December 1967); Michael Keren and David Levhari, "The Optimum Span of Control in a Pure Hierarchy," *Management Science* (November 1979); Robert D. Dewar and Donald P. Simet, "A Level Specific Prediction of Spans of Control Examining the Effects of Size, Technology, and Specialization," *Academy of Management Journal* (March 1981).

special assessment, a real estate tax on certain landowners to pay for improvements that will, at least in theory, benefit them all; for example, a paved street.
See also BENEFIT DISTRICT.

special district, unit of government typically performing a single function and overlapping traditional political boundaries. Examples include transportation districts, water districts, sewer districts, etc. *See* Robert G. Smith, *Public Authorities, Special Districts and Local Government* (Washington: National Association of Counties, 1964); John C. Bollens, *Special District Governments in the United States* (Berkeley: University of California Press, 1957); Thomas J. DiLorenzo, "Special

Districts and Local Public Services," *Public Finance Quarterly* (July 1981).

special funds, federal funds credited with receipts that are earmarked by law for a specific purpose (*e.g.,* Land and Water Conservation Fund of the Bureau of Outdoor Recreation, Department of Interior). Generally, if the purpose of the fund is to carry out a continuing cycle of business-type operations, it will be classified as a public enterprise fund rather than a special fund.

special revenue sharing, *see* GRANT.

specification, also called JOB SPECIFICATION and CLASS SPECIFICATON, written description of the duties and responsibilities of a class of positions. Specifications usually include the title of the position; a general statement of the nature of the work; examples of typical tasks; the minimum requirements and qualifications for the position; the knowledges, skills, and abilities essential for satisfactory performance; and the assigned salary range.

Specifications are designed to highlight those aspects of a position that are significant for classification purposes. They are descriptive, not restrictive. They are not expected to include all of the possible duties that might make up an individual position.
See also POSITION CLASSIFICATION.

specific tax, *see* TAX BASE.

speededness, appropriateness of a test in terms of the length of time allotted. For most purposes, a good test will make full use of the examination period but not be so speeded that an examinee's rate of work will have an undue influence on the score received.

speed rating, performance rating that compares the speed with which an employee performs specific tasks against an observer's standard or norm.

speed test, term loosely applied to any test that few can complete within the allotted time or, more technically, a test consisting of a large number of relatively easy items so that a high score depends on how fast an examinee can work within a time limit.

speed-up, also STRETCH-OUT, terms referring to any effort by employers to obtain an increease in productivity without a corresponding increase in wages.

spending authority, designation for contract, borrowing, or entitlement authorities for which budget authority is not provided in advance by appropriation acts.
See also BACKDOOR AUTHORITY.

spillover effect, also EXTERNALITIES, benefits or costs that accrue to parties other than the buyer of a good or service. For the most part, the benefits of private goods and services inure exclusively to the buyer (e.g., new clothes, a television set, etc.). In the case of public goods, however, the benefit or cost usually spills over onto third parties. A new airport, for example, not only benefits its users but spills over onto the population at large in both positive and negative ways. Benefits might include improved air service for a community, increased tourism, and attraction of new businesses, while costs might include noise pollution and traffic congestion. *See* E.J. Mishan, "The Postwar Literature on Externalities: An Interpretive Essay," *Journal of Economic Literature* (March 1971); Guy Black, "Externalities and Structure in PPB," *Public Administration Review* (November–December 1971).

spiral-omnibus test, test in which the various kinds of tasks are distributed throughout the test (instead of being grouped together) and are in cycles of increasing difficulty. There is only one timing and one score for such a test.

split-dollar life insurance, also called SUPPLEMENTAL LIFE INSURANCE, life insurance for employees paid for by an employer. In the event of the covered employee's death, the employer totally recovers the paid premiums from the bene-

fit sum with the remainder distributed to the employee's beneficiaries. *See* Robert B. Morley, "New Uses of Supplemental Life Insurance," *The Personnel Administrator* (May 1975).

split-half reliability, measure of the reliability of a test obtained by correlating scores on one half of a test with scores on the other half and correcting for the reduced size.

split labor market, according to Edna Bonacich, in "A Theory of Ethnic Antagonism: The Split Labor Market," *American Sociological Review* (October 1972), a labor market with "at least two groups of workers whose price of labor differs for the same work, or would differ if they did the same work."

split shift, *see* BROKEN TIME.

split-the-difference, collective bargaining tactic in which both sides agree to a settlement halfway between their bargaining positions. For a lesson on strategy, *see* Roger L. Bowlby and William R. Schriver, "Bluffing and the 'Split-the-Difference' Theory of Wage Bargaining," *Industrial and Labor Relations Review* (January 1978).

spoils system, *see* CIVIL SERVICE REFORM.

spot zoning, changing the zoning of a parcel of land without regard for the zoning plan of the entire area.

SSI, *see* SUPPLEMENTAL SECURITY INCOME.

stabilization, maintenance of economic activity with an absence of serious cyclical fluctuations.

staff, specialists who assist line managers in carrying out their duties. Generally, staff units do not have the power of decision, command, or control of operations. Rather, they make recommendations (which may or may not be adopted) to the line personnel.

staffer, originally, any full time employee of a politician's campaign or elected public office. The term has grown to include all legislative committee staffs as well. *See* Harrison W. Fox, Jr., and Susan Webb Hammond, *Congressional Staff: The Invisible Force in American Lawmaking* (New York: The Free Press, 1975); Michael J. Malbin, "Congressional Committee Staffs: Who's in Charge Here?" *The Public Interest* (Spring 1977); Michael J. Malbin, *Unelected Representatives: Congressional Staff and the Future of Representative Government* (New York: Basic Books, 1980); Barry A. Kinsey, "Congressional Staff: The Cultivation and Maintenance of Personal Networks in an Insecure Work Environment," *Urban Life* (January 1985).

staffing, one of the most basic functions of management and usually considered synonymous with employment—that is, the process of hiring people to perform work for the organization. Staffing defines the organization by translating its objectives and goals into a specific work plan. It structures the responsibilities of the organization's human resources into a work system by establishing who will perform what function and have what authority. Staffing must also make the employment, advancement, and compensation processes satisfy the criteria of equity and due process while at the same time relating their processes to the overall organizational structure in order to ensure their relevance. Staffing is the essence of the personnel management process. *See* Benjamin Schneider, *Staffing Organizations* (Pacific Palisades, Calif.: Goodyear Publishing Co., 1976); William I. Bacchus, *Staffing for Foreign Affairs: Personnel Systems for the 1980's and 1990's* (Princeton, N.J.: Princeton University Press, 1983); Judy D. Olian and Sara L. Rynes, "Organizational Staffing: Integrating Practice with Strategy," *Industrial Relations* (Spring 1984).

staffing dynamics, phrase used by those who are not content with calling turnover turnover.

staffing plan, planning document that minimally (1) lists an organization's projected personnel needs by occupation and grade level and (2) identifies how these needs will be met.

staffing program planning, determination by organization personnel management of the numbers and kinds of personnel management actions necessary during each stage of the planning period to staff the work force required in management's program plan.

staff organization, those segments of a larger organization that provide support services and have no direct responsibilities for line operations or production. Personnel administration has traditionally been a staff function. *See* Ernest Dale and Lyndall F. Urwick, *Staff in Organization* (New York: McGraw-Hill, 1960).

staff out, process that involves soliciting a variety of views or recommendations on an issue so that a decision-maker will be aware of all reasonable options.

staff principle, the principle of administration which states that the executive should be assisted by officers who are not in the line of operations but are essentially extensions of the personality of the executive and whose duties consist primarily of assisting the executive in controlling and coordinating the organization and, secondly, of offering advice.

stagflation, high levels of unemployment and inflation at the same time. *See* Martin L. Weitzman, *The Share Economy: Conquering Stagflation* (Cambridge, Mass.: Harvard University Press, 1984). *See also* PHILLIPS CURVE.

Stahl, O. Glenn (1910-   ), until his retirement in 1969, the director of the Bureau of Policies and Standards, U.S. Civil Service Commission, and the author of one of the leading texts on public personnel administration. Major works include: *The Personnel Job of Government Managers* (Chicago: International Personnel Management Association, 1971); *Public Personnel Administration*, 8th ed. (New York: Harper & Row, 1983).

Stakhanovite, decidedly dated term for a ratebuster. Alexei Stakhanov was a Russian miner who regularly exceeded his production quota. During Stalin's regime, he was a well-publicized example of the "ideal" Russian worker. Rumor has it that Stakhanov increased his production output on secret orders from the Communist Party. For his efforts, he was promoted from worker to commissar and even awarded the Order of Lenin.

standard, employment, *see* EMPLOYMENT STANDARD.

standard allowance, established amount of time by which the normal time for employees to complete their tasks is increased in order to compensate for the expected amount of personal and/or unavoidable delays.

Standard Consolidated Statistical Area (SCSA), creation of the U.S. Census Bureau combining contiguous standard metropolitan statistical areas in order to more accurately portray urban population patterns.

standard deviation, measure of the variability of a distribution about its mean or average. In distributions of test scores, for example, a low standard deviation would indicate a tendency of scores to cluster about the mean; a high standard deviation would indicate a wide variation in scores. In a normal distribution, approximately 68 percent of the cases lie between + 1 S.D. and − 1 S.D. from the mean and approximately 96 percent of the cases between + 2 S.D. and − 2 S.D. from the mean.

standard error of measurement, number expressed in score units that serves as another index of test reliability. It can be interpreted as indicating the probability that if an error of measurement of a test is twenty points, there are approximately two chances out of three that an individual's "true score" will be within ± 20 points of his/her "obtained score" on the test. Similarly, the chances are approximately 96 out of 100 that his/her "true score" will be within ± 40 points of his/her "obtained score."

standard federal regions, geographic subdivisions of the U.S. established to achieve more uniformity in the location and geographic jurisdiction of federal field offices as a basis for promoting more systematic coordination among agencies and among federal-state local governments and for securing management improvements and economies through greater interagency and intergovernmental cooperation. Boundaries were drawn and regional office locations designed for ten regions, and agencies are required to adopt the uniform system when changes are made or new offices established.

Standard Form 171, the federal government's "Personal Qualifications Statement" and its universal employment application.

standard hour, the normally expected amount of work to be done in an hour. It is a unit of measurement for use in nearly all production activities. Standard hours do not correspond to clock times; the standard hour notation on an incoming job order may indicate that the job will require forty standard hours, but this does not mean that the job can be completed by one person in a regular forty-hour work week. The available clock time of a facility does not take into account, for example, personal time, absenteeism, stoppages, and reduced efficiency. The only way to correlate standard hours and maximum gross hours is to reduce the maximum gross hours available by total lost time.

standard-hour plan, incentive plan that rewards an employee by a percent premium that equals the percent by which performance beats the standard.

standardization, specification of consistent procedures to be followed in administering, scoring, and interpreting tests.

standardized test, any objective test given under constant conditions and/or any test for which a set of norms is available.

Standard Metropolitan Statistical Area (SMSA), creation of the U.S. Census Bureau so as to more accurately portray urban population. It includes the population in all counties contiguous to an urban county (that is one with a city over fifty thousand in a common total) if the population of those counties is involved in the urban-county work force. Being designated an SMSA is important to cities and counties because only SMSAs are eligible for certain federal government grants.

standard of living, measure of the material affluence enjoyed by a nation or by an individual. *See* Victor R. Fuchs, *How We Live: An Economic Perspective on Americans from Birth to Death* (Cambridge, Mass.: Harvard University Press, 1984).

standard rate, see FLAT RATE.

standards, *see* CLASSIFICATION STANDARDS.

standard score, any transformed test score in terms of which raw scores are expressed for convenience and ease of interpretation.

standards of conduct, an organization's formal guidelines for ethical behavior. For example, the standards of conduct for National Aeronautics and Space Administration employees require that
> each NASA employee will refrain from any use of his official position which is motivated by, or has the appearance of being motivated by, the desire for private gain for himself or other persons. He must conduct himself in such a manner that there is not the slightest suggestion of the extracting of private advantage from his Government employment.

See also ETHICS and CODE OF ETHICS.

Standards of Conduct For Labor Or-

ganization, in the federal sector, a code governing internal democratic practices, fiscal responsibility, and procedures to which a labor organization must adhere to be eligible to receive any recognition.

standards of performance, statements that tell an employee how well he or she must perform a task to be considered a satisfactory employee. Standards cover how much, how accurately, in what time period, or in what manner the various job tasks are to be performed. The performance standards, whether written or unwritten, will specify the minimum level of performance at which an employee must work in order to attain a satisfactory performance rating.

standing, a person's right to initiate legal action because he or she is directly affected by the issues raised. *See* Karen Orren, "Standing to Sue: Interest Group Conflict in the Federal Courts," *American Political Science Review* (September 1976).
> *See also* the following entries:
> FLAST V. COHEN
> MASSACHUSETTS V. MELON
> SINGLETON V. WULFF
> UNITED STATES V. RICHARDSON
> VALLEY FORGE CHRISTIAN COLLEGE V. AMERICANS UNITED FOR SEPARATION OF CHURCH AND STATES

standing committee, a regular committee of a legislature that deals with bills within the committee's subject area.

In the U.S. Congress, each of the two principal parties has a Committee on Committees which recommends committee assignments subject to caucus or conference approval. At the beginning of each Congress, members can express assignment preferences to their respective Committee on Committees. The Committee on Committees then prepares and approves an assignment slate of members for each committee and submits it to the caucus or conference for approval. Normally, the assignment recommendations are approved without challenge, but procedures exist by which other members can be nominated for vacant committee posts. The House, generally by strict party vote, adopts the slates presented by the two parties. The proportion of Republicans to Democrats is fixed by the majority party of the House. A similar method is used in the Senate.

The standing committees of the Congress are:

HOUSE
Agriculture
Appropriations
Armed Services
Banking, Finance and Urban Affairs
Budget
District of Columbia
Education and Labor
Energy and Commerce
Foreign Affairs
Government Operations
House Administration
Interior and Insular Affairs
Judiciary
Merchant Marine and Fisheries
Post Office and Civil Service
Public Works and Transportation
Rules
Science and Technology
Small Business
Standards of Official Conduct
Veterans' Affairs
Ways and Means

SENATE
Agriculture, Nutrition and Forestry
Appropriations
Armed Services
Banking, Housing and Urban Affairs
Budget
Commerce, Science and Transportation
Energy and Natural Resources
Environment and Public Works
Finance
Foreign Relations
Governmental Affairs
Judiciary
Labor and Human Resources
Rules and Administration
Small Business
Veterans' Affairs

See William L. Morrow, *Congressional Committees* (New York: Charles Scribner's Sons, 1969); Roger H. Davidson, "Congressional Committees: The Toughest Customers," *Policy Analysis* (Spring 1976); Leroy N. Rieselbach and

Joseph K. Unekis, *Congressional Committee Politics* (New York: Praeger Publishers, 1983); Steven S. Smith and Christopher J. Deering, *Committees in Congress* (Washington, D.C.: Congressional Quarterly Press, 1984).

See also SELECT COMMITTEE.

standing plans, also called CONTINUING PLANS, plans designed to guide organizations in policies, standard methods, or procedures when dealing with objectives or problems of a recurring nature.

starvation wages, *see* LIVING WAGE.

State, Department of, cabinet-level department of the federal government. This department's primary objective is the execution of foreign policy to promote the long-range security and well-being of the United States.

Department of State
2201 C Street, N.W.
Washington, D.C. 20520
(202) 655-4000

State and Local Fiscal Assistance Act, *see* REVENUE SHARING.

state government, government that consists of its legislative, executive, and judicial branches and all departments, boards, commissions, and other organizational units thereof. It also includes any semi-autonomous authorities, institutions of higher education, districts, and other agencies that are subject to administrative and fiscal control by the state through its appointment of officers, determination of budgets, approval of plans, and other devices.

State Government, quarterly journal of the Council of State Governments.

State Government
P.O. Box 11910
Lexington, KY 40511

state of the art, level of development in a given scientific or technological field at a given time, usually the present. *See* Edward M. Glaser, "Using Behavioral Science Strategies for Defining the State-of-the-Art," *Journal of Applied Behavioral Science* (January-February-March 1980).

State of the Union Message, annual message of the president of the United States to Congress wherein he usually proposes legislative initiatives. Article II, secton 3 of the Constitution requires that the president "shall from time to time give to the Congress information of the state of the Union, and recommend to their consideration such measures as he shall judge necessary and expedient."

Presidents George Washington and John Adams appeared before the two houses in joint session to read their messages. Thomas Jefferson discontinued the practice in 1801, transmitting his message to the Capitol to be read by clerks in both houses. Jefferson's procedure was followed for a full century. On April 8, 1913, Woodrow Wilson revived the practice of delivering the State of the Union Message in person. With the exception of President Herbert Hoover, the practice has been followed generally by subsequent presidents.

static system, *see* DYNAMIC SYSTEM.

statistical inference, use of information observed in a sample to make predictions about a larger population.

statistical signficance, *see* SIGNIFICANCE.

statistical validation, also called CRITERION RELATED VALIDATION, validation that involves definition of what is to be measured (*i.e.,* criterion) by some systematic method based upon observations of the job behavior of individuals. Possible measures of the knowledges, skills, abilities, and other employee characteristics are then obtained for individuals. Through statistical means, the strength of the relationship between the criterion and the measures is evaluated (validity).

If the criterion has been defined rationally through a careful empirical analysis of job duties, job-relatedness of the appraisal procedure is considered to be present. If the criterion has not been defined in this way, job-relatedness is inferred but not assured.

See also VALIDATION and VALIDITY.

statistics, any gathered numerical data and any of the processes of analyzing and of making inferences from the data. While there are innumerable works on the collection and interpretation of statistics, the classic work on statistical presentation is Darrell Huff, *How to Lie with Statistics* (New York: W.W. Norton & Co., 1954). This work is valuable for those who would lie, those who would not, and those who would like not to be lied to. *Also see* Stanley Vanagunas, "Statistical Methods and the City Management Community," *Public Productivity Review* (March-June 1982); Robert Hooke, *How to Tell the Liars from the Statisticians* (New York: Marcel Dekker, 1983).

status, abstraction of one's relative position or ranking within an organization or society. *See* Wilber Rich, "The Effects of Status Conflicts on Productivity and Communication in Public Organizations," *Public Productivity Review* (March-June 1982).

status symbols, visible signs of an individual's social status or importance in an organization. Status symbols are a significant element of the psychic compensation of every job. Under varying circumstances almost anything can be a status symbol—a private secretary, a key to the executive washroom, an assigned parking space, wood as opposed to metal office furniture, etc. For an account of the relentless search for greater status, *see* Vance Packard, *The Status Seekers* (New York: David McKay Co., 1959).

statutes at large, a collection of all statutes passed by a particular legislature (such as the U.S. Congress), printed in full and in the order of their passage.

stay-in strike, *see* SIT-DOWN STRIKE.

Steelworkers' Trilogy, three decisions of the U.S. Supreme Court which held that (1) a labor-management dispute could not be judged to be nonarbitrable unless the parties specifically excluded the subject from the arbitration process; (2) the role of the federal courts is limited when the parties have agreed to submit all questions of contract interpretation to an arbitrator; and (3) the interpretation of a collective bargaining agreement is a question for the arbitrator and the courts do not have the right to overrule the arbitrator because of his interpretation.

The trilogy cases are, respectively: *United Steelworkers of America v. Warrior and Gulf Navigation Co.,* 363 U.S. 574 (1960); *United Steelworkers of America v. American Manufacturing Co.,* 363 U.S. 564 (1960); and *United Steelworkers of America v. Enterprise Wheel and Car Corp.,* 363 U.S. 593 (1960).

step bonus, feature of wage incentive plans that calls for a substantial increase in incentive payments when the quantity and/or quality of output reaches a specified level.

step increases, *see* INCREMENT and WITHIN-GRADE INCREASE.

steward, also called SHOP STEWARD and UNION STEWARD, local union's most immediate representative in a plant or department. Usually elected by fellow employees (but sometimes appointed by the union leadership), the shop steward handles grievances, collects dues, solicits new members, etc. A shop steward usually continues to work at his or her regular job and handles union matters on a part-time basis, frequently on the employer's time. According to the *AFL-CIO Manual for Shop Stewards* (July 1978),

> it is important that the steward understands his relationship with management. Although the foreman, forelady or supervisor exercises certain authority over him in his role as a worker in the

department, when they meet to discuss grievances the steward acts as an official representative of the union and, therefore, has equal status. He has every right to expect to be treated as an equal as well as the right to express himself fully on the problem under discussion.

See Allan N. Nash, *The Union Steward: Duties, Rights, and Status,* 2nd ed. (Ithaca, N.Y.: New York State School of Industrial and Labor Relations, Cornell University, 1983).

steward chief, union representative who supervises the activities of a group of shop stewards.

Stigler, George Joseph (1911-), Nobel Prize winning economist of the Chicago School. He once responded to the question of a political scientist as to why there were no Nobel Prizes in the other social sciences by asserting that "they already had a Nobel Prize in literature."

Also see CHICAGO SCHOOL.

stimulative, term used to describe a grant that increases the expenditures of the grantee for the specified activities over and above what they would have been in the absence of the grant.

stint-plan wage system, system that assigns a definite output as an employee's day's work; if the work is completed in less than normal time, the employee is credited with a full day's work and allowed to go home.

stranger laboratory, laboratory experience for individuals from differing organizations.

stranger pickets, workers who picket an employee who has never employed them.
See also AMERICAN FEDERATION OF LABOR V. SWING.

strategic management, a decisional process that combines an organization's capabilities with the opportunities and threats found in both the internal and external organizational environment. *See*

Jeffrey Bracker, "The Historical Development of the Strategic Management Concept," *Academy of Management Review* (April 1980); Edward H. Bowman, "A Risk/Return Paradox for Strategic Management," *Sloan Management Review* (Spring 1980); J. Krieken, "Formulating and Implementing a More Systematic Approach to Strategic Management," *Management Review* (July 1980); Alan J. Rowe, Richard O. Mason, and Karl Dickel, *Strategic Management & Business Policy: A Methodological Approach* (Reading, Mass.: Addison-Wesley, 1982); Noel M. Tichy, "Managing Change Strategically: The Technical, Political, and Cultural Keys," *Organizational Dynamics* (Autumn 1982); Max S. Wortman, Jr., "Strategic Management and Changing Leader-Follower Roles," *The Journal of Applied Behavioral Science,* Vol. 18, No 3 (1982); Lee Dyer, "Studying Human Resources Strategy: An Approach and an Agenda," *Industrial Relations* (Spring 1984).

strategic planning, according to William R. King and David I. Cleland, *Strategic Planning and Policy* (New York: Van Nostrand Reinhold Co., 1978), process that "provides procedures, processes, information support, and a facilitative organizational structure to permit managers to 'break out' of an emphasis on day-to-day operating problems and give appropriate attention to the development of *controlled organizational change." Also see* Peter Lorange and Richard F. Vancil, *Strategic Planning Systems* (Englewood Cliffs, N.J.: Prentice-Hall, 1977); Michael H. Moskow, *Strategic Planning in Business and Government* (New York: Committee for Economic Development, 1978); Lewis F. McLain, Jr., "How Strategic Planning Can Help Put Budgeting in Perspective," *Governmental Finance* (June 1981); Eddie C. Smith, "Strategic Business Planning and Human Resources: Part 1," *Personnel Journal* (August 1982); Laurence J. Styble, "Linking Strategic Planning and Management Manpower Planning," *California Management Review* (Fall 1982); Douglas C. Eadie and Roberta

Steinbacher, "Strategic Agenda Management: A Marriage of Organizational Development and Strategic Planning," *Public Administration Review* (May-June 1985).

straw boss, colloquial term for a supervisor who has no real authority, power, or status with which to back up his orders.

stress, engineering term applied to humans in reference to any condition or situation that forces the body to respond to it. Prolonged stress can overtax an individual's emotional and/or physical ability to cope with it. The pioneering work on "stress on the whole person" was done by Hans Seyle in *The Stress of Life,* rev. ed. (New York: McGraw-Hill, 1976). *Also see* David E. Morrison, "Stress and the Public Administrator," *Public Administration Review* (July-August 1977); John E. Newman and Terry A Beehr, "Personal and Organizational Strategies for Handling Job Stress: A Review of Research and Opinion," *Personnel Psychology* (Spring 1979); Michael T. Matteson and John M. Ivancevich, "Organizational Stressors and Heart Disease: A Research Model," *Academy of Management Review* (July 1979); Manfred F. R. Kets de Vries, "Organizational Stress: A Call for Management Action," *Sloan Management Review* (Fall 1979); Randell S. Schuler, "Definition and Conceptualization of Stress in Organizations," *Organizational Behavior and Human Performance* (April 1980); Herbert Benson and Robert L. Allen, "How Much Stress Is Too Much?" *Harvard Business Review* (September-October 1980); John M. Ivancevich and Michael T. Matteson, "Optimizing Human Resources: A Case for Preventive Health and Stress Management," *Organizational Dynamics* (Autumn 1980); Kim R. Kanaga and Mark Flynn, "The Relationship Between Invasion of Personal Space and Stress," *Human Relations* (March 1981); Robert L. Kahn, "Work, Stress, and Individual Well-Being," *Monthly Labor Review* (May 1981); Cary L. Cooper and Marilyn J. Davidson, "The High Cost of Stress on Women Managers," *Organizational Dynamics*

(Spring 1982); Srinika Jayaratne and Wayne A. Chess, "The Effects of Emotional Support on Perceived Job Stress and Strain," *The Journal of Applied Behavioral Science,* Vol. 20, No. 1 (1984); James C. Quick and Jonathan D. Quick, "Preventive Stress Management at the Organizational Level," *Personnel* (September-October 1984).

The definitive compendium on occupational stress is the 1980 Addison-Wesley series of six books on the subject. Titles include: *Work Stress* by Alan McLean, *Managing Stress* by Leon Warshaw, *Blue-Collar Stress* by Arthur B. Shostak, *Work Stress and Social Support* by James S. House, *Management and Stress* by Leonard Moss, and *Preventing Work Stress* by Lennart Levi.

See also the following entries:
MID-CAREER CRISIS
NERVOUS BREAKDOWN
OCCUPATIONAL NEUROSIS

stress carriers, fellow workers who are crisis oriented and tend to induce stress in others in addition to suffering from it themselves.

stress interview, interview in which the interviewer deliberately creates a stressful situation for the interviewee in order to see how the interviewee might behave under such pressure. Common tactics used to induce stress include critically questioning the opinions of the interviewee, frequent interruptions of interviewee's answers to possibly hostile questions, silence on the part of the interviewer for an extended period, etc.

stretch-out, see SPEED-UP.

strike, also called WALKOUT, mutual agreement among workers (whether members of a union or not) to a temporary work stoppage in order to obtain or resist a change in their working conditions. The term is thought to have nautical origins, because sailors would stop work by striking or taking down their sails. A strike or potential strike is considered an essential element of the collective bargaining pro-

cess. Many labor leaders would claim that collective bargaining can never be more than a charade without the right to strike. For histories, *see* P. K. Edwards, *Strikes in the United States, 1881-1974* (New York: St. Martin's Press, 1981); Bruce E. Kaufman, "The Determinants of Strikes in the United States, 1900-1977," *Industrial and Labor Relations Review* (July 1982).

For a defense of the right to strike, *see* T. Kennedy, "Freedom to Strike Is in the Public Interest," *Harvard Business Review* (July-August 1970); Grace Sterrett and Antone Aboud, *The Right to Strike in Public Employment* (Ithaca, N.Y.: Cornell University, New York State School of Industrial and Labor Relations, 1982). To prepare for a strike, *see* Lee T. Paterson and John Liebert, *Management Strike Handbook* (Chicago: International Personnel Management Associations, 1974). For alternatives, *see* Theodore E. Kheel *et al.,* "Exploring Alternatives to the Strike," *Monthly Labor Review* (September 1973); Thomas P. Gies, "Employer Remedies for Work Stoppages that Violate No-Strike Provisions," *Employee Relations Law Journal* (Autumn 1982). *Also see* Robert B. Fouler, "Normative Aspects of Public Employee Strikes," *Public Personnel Management* (March-April 1974); Eugene H. Becker, "Analysis of Work Stoppages in the Federal Sector, 1962-81," *Monthly Labor Review* (August 1982); Woodruff Imberman, "Who Strikes—and Why," *Harvard Business Review* (November-December 1983); Peter A. Veglahn, "Public Sector Strike Penalties and Their Appeal," *Public Personnel Management* (Summer 1983); Edward Levin and Candace Reid, "Arbitration of Strike Misconduct Cases Arising out of Legal Strikes," *Arbitration Journal* (September 1984).

See also the following entries:
AIR TRAFFIC CONTROLLER'S STRIKE
APEX HOSIERY CO. V. LEADER
BATTERTON V. FRANCIS
BLUE FLU
BOSTON POLICE STRIKE
BOYS MARKET V. RETAIL CLERKS LOCAL 770
BUFFALO FORGE V. UNITED STEELWORKERS

strike authorization, also called STRIKE VOTE, formal vote by union members that (if passed) invests the union leadership with the right to call a strike without additional consultation with the union membership.

strike benefits, payments by a union to its striking members or to non-members who are out on strike in support of the union. The U.S. Supreme Court has held, in *United States* v. *Allen Kaiser,* 363 U.S. 299 (1960), that for tax purposes strike benefits are to be considered as gifts and thus not taxable as part of a worker's gross income. *See* Sheldon M. Kline, "Strike Benefits of National Unions," *Monthly Labor Review* (March 1975); John Gennard, *Financing Strikers* (New York: John Wiley, 1977).

strike-bound, any organization that is be-ing struck by its employees and/or attempting to function in spite of the strike.

strikebreaker, person who accepts a position vacated by a worker on strike, or a worker who continues to work while others are on strike. The Labor-Management Relations (Taft-Hartley) Act of 1947 guarantees a strikebreaker's right to work and makes it illegal for unions to attempt to prohibit strikebreakers from crossing picket lines.

See also the following entries:

strike counselors, *see* UNION COUNSELORS.

strike duty, tasks assigned to union members by the union leadership during the course of a strike (*e.g.,* picketing, distributing food, preventing violence, creating violence, etc.).

strike fund, moneys reserved by a union to be used during a strike to cover costs such as strike benefits or legal fees. Strike funds are not necessarily separate from a union's general fund. The amount of strike funds available may mean the success or failure of a strike.

strike notice, formal notice of an impending work stoppage that is presented by a union to an employer or to an appropriate government agency. *See* John G. Kruchko and Jay R. Fries, "Hospital Strikes: Complying with NLRA Notice Requirements," *Employee Relations Law Journal* (Spring 1984).

strike pay, union payments to union members as partial compensation for income loss during a strike.

strike vote, see STRIKE AUTHORIZATION.

stroking, also POSITIVE STROKING and NEGATIVE STROKING, feedback. Eric Berne, in *Games People Play: The*

Psychology of Human Relationships (New York: Grove Press, 1964), took the intimate physical act of stroking and developed its psychological analogy in conversation. All of human intercourse can be viewed from the narrow perspective of the giving and receiving of physical and psychological strokes. In an organizational context, *positive stroking* consists of the laying of kind words on employees. *Negative stroking* involves using less than kind words—being critical. *See* Thomas C. Clary, "Motivation Through Positive Stroking," *Public Personnel Management* (March–April 1973).

See also MOTIVATION.

strong mayor, *see* MAYOR-COUNCIL SYSTEM.

structure, formal arrangement of positions, authority relations, and information flows in an organization.

structural change, alterations in the relative significance of the productive components of a national or international economy that take place over time. Expansion in the economy as a whole or temporary shifts in the relationship of its components as a result of cyclical developments would *not* be considered structural changes. Since the industrial revolution, structural change in most countries has resulted principally from changes in comparative advantage associated with technological advance, but also (to a lesser degree) from changes in consumer preference. It has involved shifts from subsistence agriculture to commercial agriculture, an increase in the relative significance of manufacturing, and, at a later stage, a further shift toward service industries. Other major structural changes involve shifts in economic importance between various industries, shifts between regions of large national economies, and changes in the composition of exports and imports.

structural-functional theory, also called STRUCTURAL-FUNCTIONALISM, an approach in sociology in which societies, communities, or organizations are viewed as

systems; then their particular features are explained in terms of their contributions—their functions—in maintaining the system. This approach is generally credited to Talcott Parsons. *See* his *The Social System* (New York: The Free Press, 1951).

structural unemployment, unemployment resulting from changes in technology, consumption patterns, or government policies—a mismatch between available labor and demand for skills. Structural unemployment can be said to be an inherent part of a dynamic economic system. The "cure" for structural unemployment is worker retraining. *See* Eleanor G. Gilpatrick, *Structural Unemployment And Aggregate Demand* (Baltimore: Johns Hopkins Press, 1966); Paul G. Schervish, *The Structural Determinants of Unemployment: Vulnerability and Power in Market Relations* (New York: Academic Press, 1983).

structured role playing, role-play exercise or simulation in which the players receive oral or written instruction giving them cues as to their roles.

Stump v. Sparkman, 435 U.S. 349 (1978), Supreme Court case reaffirming the principle of *Bradley v. Fisher*, 13 Wall 335 (1872), that judges have absolute immunity from liability in civil suits based upon their official acts.

SUB, *see* SUPPLEMENTAL UNEMPLOYMENT BENEFIT.

subemployment, concept that tries to capture two major dimensions of labor market functioning that produce and reproduce poverty—the lack of opportunity for work and sub-standard wage employment. *See* T. Vietorisz, R. Mier, and J. Giblin, "Subemployment: Exclusion and Inadequacy Indexes," *Monthly Labor Review* (May 1975).

subordinate rating, evaluation of an organizational superior by someone of lesser rank.

subpoena, written order issued by a judicial officer requiring a specified person to appear in a designated court at a specified time in order to serve as a witness in a case under the jurisdiction of that court, or to bring material to that court.

subsistence allowance, payments for an employee's reasonable expenses (meals, lodging, transportation, etc.) while traveling on behalf of his employer.

subsistence theory of wages, see IRON LAW OF WAGES.

substandard rate, wage rate below established occupational, prevailing, or legal levels.

substantive bill clearance, see CENTRAL CLEARANCE.

substantive law, the basic law of rights and duties (contract law, criminal law, accident law, law of wills, etc.), as opposed to procedural law (law of pleading, law of evidence, law of jurisdiction, etc.).

substitutive, term that describes a grant that is used by the recipient to reduce spending from the recipient's own sources for the aided activity, freeing these own-source funds for other programs or for tax stabilization or reduction.

Sugarman* v. *Dougall, 413 U.S. 634 (1973), U.S. Supreme Court case which held that a ban on the employment of resident aliens by a state was unconstitutional because it encompassed positions that had little, if any, relation to a legitimate state interest in treating aliens differently from citizens. However, the court also stated that alienage might be reasonably taken into account with regard to specific positions.
 See also the following entries:
  AMBACH V. NORWICK
  CITIZENSHIP, U.S.
  FOLEY V. CONNELIE
  HAMPTON V. MOW SUN WONG

suggestion system, formal effort to encourage employees to make recommen-

dations that would improve the operations of their organizations. *See* Charles Foos, "How to Administer A Suggestion System," *Management Review* (August 1968); Edward H. Downey and Walter L. Balk, *Employee Innovation and Government Productivity: A Study of Suggestion Systems in the Public Sector* (Chicago: International Personnel Management Association, 1976); Paul S. Greenlaw, "Suggestions Systems: An Old Approach to a New Problem," *The Personnel Administrator* (January 1980). For a history, *see* Stanley J. Seimer, *Suggestion Plans in American Industry* (Syracuse, N.Y.: Syracuse University Press, 1959).
 See also SCANLON PLAN.

summons, written order issued by a judicial officer requiring a person who is a party to a lawsuit to appear in a designated court at a specified time.

sumptuary laws, laws which attempt to control the sale or use of socially undesirable, wasteful, or harmful products.

sunk costs, resources committed to the achievement of an organizational objective that cannot be regained if the objective is abandoned.

sunset laws, laws pioneered by Colorado and encouraged by a major lobbying effort by Common Cause. Many jurisdictions are enacting "sunset laws" which fix termination dates on programs or agencies. Formal evaluations and subsequent affirmative legislation are required if the agency or program is to continue. Although the purpose of a finite life span of, say, five years is to force evaluation and toughen legislative oversight, the effect is to subject programs to automatic termination unless the "clock" is reset.
 Despite its widespread popularity, this type of "time bomb" evaluation mentality is not without risks. There are limits to the abilities of any legislatures' staffs to do the kind of thorough evaluation required to make "sunset" meaningful. And of course, the political reality always exists that it might become a tool of bipartisan political

infighting. In fairness, however, the verdict is not in on how sunset has worked in Colorado or other early users. Initial reports are enthusiastic. A few states, such as Alabama and Louisiana, have legislated "sunset" in totality. The Alabama Sunset Law is popularly called the "High Noon" law because it subjects all state agencies to a sunset review over a four-year period; to survive, an agency must win a resolution from the legislature. Given the workload, the time allotted, and Alabama's evaluation staffing capability, it is very doubtful that serious effective organizational change will result. Merely requiring organizations to submit evaluation data for review and to justify their programs may amount to little more than burying the legislature in an avalanche of insignificant paper—something at which agencies have a demonstrated prowess. Naturally, some agencies, such as prisons, mental health institutions, public safety, etc., will be rightly skeptical of the chances of their programs being shut down.

See Bruce Adams, "Sunset: A Proposal for Accountable Government," *Administrative Law Review* (Summer 1976); Allen Schick, "Zero-Base Budgeting and Sunset: Redundancy or Symbiosis?" *The Bureaucrat* (Spring 1977); Robert D. Behn, "The False Dawn of the Sunset Laws," *The Public Interest* (Fall 1977); Bruce Adams and Betsy Sherman, "Sunset Implementation: A Positive Partnership to Make Government Work," *Public Administration Review* (January-February 1978); Glen E. Deck, "Sunset Laws and Performance Audits: A Partnership for Improving Government," *The GAO Review* (Summer 1981); David C. Nile, "Sunset Laws and Legislative Vetoes in the States," State Government (Spring 1985).

See also PROGRAM EVALUATION.

sunshine bargaining, also called GOLD-FISH-BOWL BARGAINING, collective bargaining sessions open to the press and public. This process is more likely to be used in public sector negotiations (in response to the assertion that since the spending of public funds are the essence of the nego-

tiations, the negotiating process should be open to public scrutiny).

sunshine laws, any requirement that government agencies hold their formal business meetings open to the public. See Jerry W. Markham, "Sunshine on the Administrative Process: Wherein Lies the Shade," *Administrative Law Review* (Summer 1976).

superannuated rate, pay rate below the prevailing rate that is paid to older employees who are in need or are needed because of a labor shortage. A ratio for superannuated workers is sometimes provided for in union agreements. The lower rate is justified on the theory that these older, otherwise retired workers are not as productive as younger employees. Some superannuated rate policies may be in violation of age discrimination laws.

superbureaucrat, according to Colin Campbell and George J. Szablowski in their *The Superbureaucrats: Structure and Behavior in Central Agencies* (Toronto: Macmillan of Canada, 1979), administrators who "turn their backs on mere 'red tape'—on the simple carrying out of policy. Superbureaucrats help *make* policy."

supergrades, federal government executives in grades GS-16, 17, and 18.

supernumerary income, that portion of a worker's income which is not needed for the essentials of everyday life and consequently is available for luxuries and other optional spending. See Fabian Linden, "Supernumerary Income: A Statistical Measure of Consumer Affluence," *Conference Board Record* (April 1968).

superseniority, also called SYNTHETIC SENIORITY, seniority that supersedes ordinary seniority, which is dependent on an individual's length of service. Because a union may be detrimentally affected if its key union officials are subject to layoffs, union contracts often grant them superseniority. This synthetic seniority is designed to ensure continued representation for workers remaining following a reduction in force. Superseniority also provides an advantage to management, since established lines of communication with the union and its members continue without interruption. Sometimes union contracts provide for superseniority for special categories of employees (such as the aged or physically handicapped and key personnel essential if production is to be maintained). *See* Max S. Wortman, "Superseniority—Myth or Reality?" *Labor Law Journal* (April 1967); George K. Leonard, "Practical Applications of Superseniority," *Labor Law Journal* (January 1975).

supervision, directing the performance of one or more workers towards the accomplishment of organizational goals. *See* Robert M. Fulmer, *Supervision: Principles of Professional Management* (Beverly Hills, Calif.: Glencoe Press, 1976); Fred Luthans and Mark J. Martinko, *The Practice of Supervision and Management* (New York: McGraw-Hill, 1979); Andrew J. DuBrin, *The Practice of Supervision: Achieving Results Through People* (Dallas: Business Publications, 1980); Michael J. Austin, *Supervisory Management for Human Services* (Englewood Cliffs, N.J.: Prentice-Hall, 1981); Jack Halloran, *Supervision: The Art of Management* (Englewood Cliffs, N.J.: Prentice-Hall, 1981); Leonard A. Schlesinger, *The Quality of Work Life and the Supervisor* (New York: Praeger, 1982); Edward E. Scannell, *Supervisory Communications* (Dubuque, Iowa: Kendall/Hunt, 1982); Ann Majchrzak, *The Manipulation of Supervisory Behaviors: Results of a Field Experiment* (West Lafayette, Ind.: Krannert Graduate School of Management, Purdue University, 1984).

supervisor, according to Section 2(11) of the National Labor Relations Act, as amended,

> any individual having authority, in the interest of the employer, to hire, transfer, suspend, lay off, recall, promote, discharge, assign, reward, or discipline other employees, or responsibly to direct them, or to adjust their grievances, or

effectively to recommend such action, if in connection with the foregoing the exercise of such authority is not of a merely routine or clerical nature, but requires the use of independent judgment. *See also* FLORIDA POWER & LIGHT COMPANY V. BROTHERHOOD OF ELECTRICAL WORKERS and HANNA MINING CO. V. DISTRICT 2, MARINE ENGINEERS.

supervisors, board of, governing body for a county unit of government in which membership on the board is determined by election or appointment to a particular office. For example, in some counties the board includes officials such as county judges.

supplemental appropriation, appropriation enacted as an addition to a regular annual appropriation act. Supplemental appropriations provide additional budget authority beyond original estimates for programs or activities (including new programs authorized after the date of the original appropriation act) for which the need for funds is too urgent to be postponed until the next regular appropriation.

supplemental bill, *see* DEFICIENCY BILL.

supplemental compensation, *see* BONUS and FEDERAL SUPPLEMENTAL COMPENSATION.

supplemental dental insurance, *see* SUPPLEMENTAL MEDICAL INSURANCE.

supplemental life insurance, *see* SPLIT-DOLLAR LIFE INSURANCE.

supplemental medical insurance, also SUPPLEMENTAL DENTAL INSURANCE, fringe benefit usually offered only to top management whereby all expenses from medical and/or dental care not covered by the general medical/dental policy offered by the company are reimbursable.

Supplemental Security Income (SSI), federal program that assures a minimum monthly income to needy people with limited income and resources who are sixty-five or older, blind, or disabled. Eligibility is based on income and assets. Although the program is administered by the Social Security Administration, it is financed from general revenues, not from social security contributions. *See* Marilyn Moon, "Supplemental Security Income, Asset Tests, and Equity," *Policy Analysis* (Winter 1980).

supplemental unemployment benefit (SUB), payments to laid-off workers from private unemployment insurance plans that are supplements to state unemployment insurance compensation. The first SUB plan was negotiated by the Ford Motor Company and the United Auto Workers in 1955. By 1973, about 29 percent of the members of major unions worked under contracts containing SUB plans. There are two basic SUB plans—the individual account and the pooled fund. With the former, contributions are credited to each employee's account and a terminated employee may take his benefits with him. With the latter, benefits are paid from a common fund and individual employees have no vested rights should they leave the company. For the history of SUB, *see* Joseph M. Becker, *Guaranteed Income for the Unemployed: The Story of SUB* (Baltimore: Johns Hopkins Press, 1968). For a financial analysis, *see* Emerson H. Beier, "Financing Supplemental Unemployment Benefits," *Monthly Labor Review* (November 1969). *Also see* Audrey Freedman, *Security Bargains Reconsidered: SUB, Severance Pay, Guaranteed Work* (New York: The Conference Board, 1978).

supply, in economics, the quantity of goods and services available for purchase if income and other factors are held constant. Increases in price either induce increases in supply or serve to ration the supply.

supply-side economics, also called Reaganomics, belief that lower tax rates, especially on marginal income, will encourage fresh capital to flow into the economy, which will in turn generate jobs and growth

and new tax revenue. Because this concept was adopted by President Reagan and his advisors, it has been popularly called "Reaganomics." Economist Arthur Laffer is generally credited with having "discovered" supply-side economics. *See* Bruce R. Bartlett, *Reaganomics: Supply-Side Economics in Action* (Westport, Conn.: Arlington House, 1981); R. T. McNamar, "President Reagan's Economic Program," *Presidential Studies Quarterly* (Summer 1981); Paul Craig Roberts, "Will Reaganomics Unravel?" *Fortune* (November 16, 1981); John Kenneth Galbraith, "Why Reaganomics Can't Work," *The New Republic* (September 23, 1981); Robert B. Reich, "Beyond Reaganomics," *The New Republic* (November 18, 1981); Robert Lekachman, *Greed is Not Enough: Reaganomics* (New York: Pantheon, 1982); Michael J. Boskin, *Reaganomics Examined: Successes, Failures, Unfinished Agenda* (San Francisco: Institute for Contemporary Studies, 1985).

See also LAFFER CURVE and TRICKLE-DOWN ECONOMICS.

supported work, jobs or job training that is subsidized by welfare or other benefits paid to (or on behalf of) a disadvantaged person; any employment for the hard core unemployed that is not totally generated by free market forces; government "make work" employment.

supportive, said of a grant when a reduction or withdrawal of the grant is unlikely to weaken support for the aided activity from the recipient's own resources.

Supreme Court, United States, the highest United States court. Since 1869, the Court has been composed of the chief justice of the United States and eight associate justices. Congress, which governs its organization by legislation, has varied the number of associate justices from six to ten. Congress now requires six justices for a quorum.

Power to nominate the justices is vested in the president of the United States, and appointments are made by and with the advice and consent of the Senate. Article

III, section 1 of the Constitution further provides that "the Judges, both of the supreme and inferior Courts, shall hold their Offices during good Behaviour, and shall, at stated Times, receive for their Services, a Compensation, which shall not be diminished during their Continuance in Office." A justice may, if he so desires, retire at the age of seventy after serving for ten years as a federal judge or at age sixty-five after fifteen years of service.

The Constitution provides that "in all cases affecting ambassadors (to the United States), other public ministers and consuls, and those in which a State shall be party," the Supreme Court has original jurisdiction. This was modified by the 11th Amendment to preclude citizens from suing a state. Additionally, the Constitution provides that Congress may regulate the appellate jurisdiction of the Court. Congress has authorized the Supreme Court to, *among other things,* review decisions of the lower federal courts and the highest courts of the states.

The internal review process of the Court has largely evolved by custom while the procedures to be followed by petitioners to the Court are established in rules set forth by the Court.

After individually examining each case submitted, the justices hold a private conference to decide which cases to schedule for oral argument, which to decide without argument, and which to dismiss. If at least four justices agree, a case will be taken by the Court for a decision, with or without oral argument, and the other requests for review will be dismissed. If oral argument is heard, a total of one hour is generally allowed the parties to argue the issues and respond to questions of the justices. Later, in conference, the justices make their decision by simple majority or plurality vote. A tie vote means that the decision of the lower court is allowed to stand. Such a vote could occur when one or three justices do not take part in a decision.

When the justices have decided a case, the chief justice, if he voted with the majority, will assign an associate justice to write the opinion of the Court. If the chief justice is in the minority, the senior associate justice in the majority will make the assignment. The individual justices may, of course, write their own opinions in any decision.

Article VI of the Constitution provides that the Constitution and the laws of the United States made "in pursuance thereof" shall be the supreme law of the land. Thus when the Supreme Court decides a case, particularly on constitutional grounds, it becomes guidance for all the lower courts and legislators when a similar question arises.

Each year the Court receives for review nearly four thousand decisions from lower state and federal courts. The justices examine each case submitted and agree to hear arguments on less than two hundred each term. Another one hundred or so lower court decisions are disposed of by decision of the Court without oral argument, and the rest of the petitions for review are either denied or dismissed.

United States Supreme Court
United States Supreme Court Building
1 First Street, N.E.
Washington, D.C. 20543
(202) 252-3000

supreme law of the land, the Constitution, laws of the United States made "in pursuance of" the Constitution, and treaties made under authority of the United States. Judges throughout the country are bound by them, regardless of anything in separate state constitutions or laws.

surtax, an additional tax on what has already been taxed; that is, a tax on a tax. For example, if you must pay a $1,000 tax on a $10,000 income (ten percent), a ten percent surtax would be an additional $100.

Survey Research Center, *see* INSTITUTE FOR SOCIAL RESEARCH.

survivors benefits, totality of the benefits that are paid upon the death of an employee to his/her legal survivors. Employees are frequently required to make a decision at the time of retirement whether or not to take a reduced pension that allows for survivors benefits.

suspension, removing an individual from employment for a specified period. Suspensions, by their nature temporary, are disciplinary acts—more severe than a reprimand yet less severe than a discharge.

sweat shop, work site where employees work long hours for low wages, usually under unsanitary conditions. While sweat shop conditions have been mostly eliminated in the United States because of the union movement and labor legislation, the term is still used informally to refer to various working conditions that employees might find distasteful. For a description of real sweat shops, *see* Leon Stein, ed., *Out of the Sweat Shop: The Struggle for Industrial Democracy* (New York: Quadrangle, 1977).

sweetheart agreement, also called SWEETHEART CONTRACT, expression for any agreement between an employer and a union or union official that benefits them but not the workers. Incidences of employer bribes to labor officials in order to gain their agreement to substandard or "sweetheart" contracts are well known in American labor history.

sweetheart clause, that portion of a union contract that makes a general policy statement about the harmonious manner in which both sides will live up to the spirit and letter of the agreement.

sweetheart contract, *see* SWEETHEART AGREEMENT.

swing shift, extra shift of workers in an organization operating on a continuous or seven-day basis. The swing crew rotates among the various shifts to compensate for those employees who are absent, sick, on vacation, etc.

symbols, signs. Since prehistory people have been effectively controlled by their leaders by means of announced taboos and mandated rituals. The associated symbolism portends either terror or hope. Political leaders in the United States have evoked terror with dire predictions about the "international communist conspiracy" and hope with a call to arms to fight the "war on poverty." Similarly, U.S. business leaders evoke terror by reminding us of the perils of bad breath, dull teeth, and unsprayed bodily areas. These fears fade when the various sprays, creams, gels, and pastes are purchased and used. The public is assured that they too can be "beautiful people" if they take the right vitamin supplements, drive the appropriate car, and drink the correct diet cola. We are all subliminally (if not consciously) aware of symbolism utilized in political rhetoric and business advertising. However, the vital role that symbolism plays in policymaking and managerial control in organizational and political situations is frequently unnoticed.

A political executive wishing to impose a sanction upon a congressional committee that is holding up the funding of his programs might suggest that the committee is not acting in "the national interest." The notion of "the national interest," while vague, is a powerful symbol because it represents a commonly accepted good. Because it is so widely revered it has great legitimacy. By wrapping his program in a symbol of hefty weight and using that symbol punitively against legislators in opposition to his program, a political executive may succeed in influencing those legislators. The success or failure of such a calculated gambit depends upon a large variety of interrelated factors. How susceptible to this particular symbol are the legislators that he is trying to influence? Is the symbol of appropriate weight in comparison to the symbols of the opposition? While the political executive might wish to use a heavier symbol, such a tactic might also backfire. One does not fight the opposition's symbol of "economy and efficiency" by calling them "communist dupes."

Conversely, symbols can be used to reward favorable action. After the political executive gets his desired appropriations, he might applaud the congressional committee members involved by publicly stating that they have shown "fiscal responsibility." In order to apply the above discussion on a smaller scale, simply substitute "the good of the organization" or "the best interests of the city" for "the national interest." The difference between symbol usages in political and organizational contexts is merely one of vocabulary. Essentially the same considerations and tactics apply.

See Thurman W. Arnold, *The Symbols of Government* (New Haven, Conn.: Yale University Press, 1935); Murray Edelman, *The Symbolic Uses of Politics* (Urbana, Ill.: University of Illinois Press, 1967); Roger W. Cobb and Charles D. Elder, "The Political Uses of Symbolism," *American Politics Quarterly* (July 1973); Thomas C. Dandridge, Ian I. Mitroff and William F. Joyce, "Organizational Symbolism: A Topic to Expand Organizational Analysis," *Academy of Management Review* (January 1980); James G. March and Martha S. Feldman, "Information in Organizations as Signal and Symbol," *Administrative Science Quarterly* (June 1981).

sympathy strike, also called SYMPATHETIC STRIKE, strike by one union undertaken solely to support the aims of another union in an effort to exert indirect pressure upon an employer. The Labor-Management Relations (Taft-Hartley) Act of 1947 made sympathy strikes illegal. See Elvis C. Stephens and Donna Ledgerwood, "Do No-Strike Clauses Prohibit Sympathy Strikes?" *Labor Law Journal* (May 1982).

syndicalism, the theory that trade unions should control the means of production and, ultimately, the government.

synectics, originally a Greek word meaning the joining together of different and apparently irrelevant elements. It is now used to describe an experimental process of observing and recording the unrestrained exchange of ideas among a group in order to methodically develop new ideas, solve problems, and/or make discoveries. As an effort to induce creativity, it is akin to brain-

storming. See William J. J. Gordon, *Synectics: The Development of Creative Capacity* (New York: Harper & Row, 1961).

synthetic basic-motion times, time standards for fundamental motions and groups of motions.

synthetic seniority, see SUPERSENIORITY.

synthetic time study, time study not dependent upon direct observation, in which time elements are obtained from other sources of time data.

synthetic validity, also called INDIRECT VALIDITY, inferring validity by means of a systematic analysis of a job and its elements, obtaining test validity for the various elements, then combining the elemental validities into a whole synthetic validity. See M. J. Balma, "The Development of Processes for Indirect or Synthetic Validity," *Personnel Psychology* Vol. 12 (1959).

system, any organized collection of parts that is united by prescribed interactions and designed for the accomplishment of a specific goal or general purpose. According to William Exton, Jr., in *The Age of Systems: The Human Dilemma* (New York: American Management Association, 1972), term that

represents the principle of functional combination of resources to produce intended result of effects. The combination may be great or small, simple or enormously complex, active or potential, solitary or parallel, new or old, static or dynamic. The intended effect may be fixed or otherwise, unique or repetitive or continuous, geographically or spatially defined or unlimited in territorial scope, physical or symbolic, tangible or intangible.

system, career, see CAREER SYSTEM.

System 4, Rensis Likert's term for a participative-democratc managerial style. See his *The Human Organization* (New York: McGraw-Hill, 1967).

systemic discrimination, use of employment practices (recruiting methods, selection tests, promotion policies, etc.) that have the unintended effect of excluding or limiting the employment prospects of women and minorities. Because of court interpretations of Title VII of the Civil Rights Act of 1964, all such systemic discrimination, despite its "innocence," must be eliminated where it cannot be shown that such action would place an unreasonable burden on the employer or that such practices cannot be replaced by other practices which would not have such an adverse effect.

systemism, belief that systems can actually be designed and managed to achieve their expressed goals. For the counterarguments that "systems in general work poorly or not at all," *see* John Gall, *"Systematics: How Systems Work and Especially How They Fail* (New York: Quadrangle, 1975)

systems analysis, methodologically rigorous collection, manipulation, and evaluation of organizational data in order to determine the best way to improve the functioning of the organization (the system) and to aid a decision maker in selecting a preferred choice among alternatives. According to David I. Cleland and William R. King, in *Management: A Systems Approach* (New York: McGraw-Hill, 1972),

systems analysis is a way of reaching decisions which contrasts with intuition-based and unsystematic approaches; the techniques of systems analysis help to make a complex problem understandable and manageable in the sense of offering possible strategies and solutions and establishing, to the maximum extent practical, criteria for selecting the best solution.

Also see David Easton, *A Systems Analysis of Political Life* (New York: John Wiley & Co., 1965); Guy Black, *The Application of Systems Analysis to Government Operations* (New York: Praeger, 1968); E. S. Quade and W. I. Boucher, eds., *Systems Analysis and Policy Planning* (New York: American Elsevier Publishing Co., 1968); Ida R. Hoos, *Systems Analysis in Public Policy: A Critique* (Berkeley: University of California Press, 1972); David Cleland and William King, *Systems Analysis and Project Management* (New York: McGraw-Hill, 1975); Chris Game and Trish Sarson, *Structured Systems Analysis: Tools and Techniques* (Englewood Cliffs, N.J.: Prentice-Hall, 1979); Hugh J. Miser and Edward S. Quade, eds., *Handbook of Systems Analysis* (New York: Elsevier Science Publishing, 1985).

See also PARETO OPTIMALITY.

systems analyst, specialist in systems analysis.

systems approach, also called SYSTEMS PHILOSOPHY, approach or philosophy that can help a manager cope with complex situations by providing an analytical framework which conceives of an enterprise as a set of objects with a given set of relationships and attributes all connected to each other and to their environment in such a way as to form an entirety. Because organizations (as well as the whole world) are constantly changing, approaches to dealing with such systems must necessarily have a corresponding evolution. According to C. West Churchman, in *The Systems Approach* (New York: Delacorte Press, 1968),

we must admit that the problem—the appropriate approach to systems—is not solved, but this is a very mild way of putting the matter. This is not an unsolved problem in the sense in which certain famous mathematical problems are unsolved. It's not as though we can expect that next year or a decade from now someone will find the correct systems approach and all deception will disappear. This, in my opinion, is not in the nature of systems. What is in the nature of systems is a continuing perception and deception, a continuing reviewing of the world, of the whole system, and of its components. The essence of the systems approach, therefore, is confusion as well as enlightenment. The two are inseparable aspects of human living.

systems management, according to Richard A. Johnson, Fremont E. Kast, and James E. Rosenzweig, in *The Theory and Management of Systems,* 3rd ed. (New York: McGraw-Hill, 1973), management that

involves the application of systems theory to managing organizational systems or subsystems. It can refer to management of a particular function or to projects or programs within a larger organization. An important point is that systems theory is a vital ingredient in the managerial process. It involves recognizing a general model of input-transformation-output with identifiable flows of material, energy, and information. It also emphasizes the interrelationships among subsystems as well as the supra-system to which a function, project, or organization belongs.

systems philosophy, *see* SYSTEMS APPROACH.

systems theory, *see* GENERAL SYSTEMS THEORY.

T

TA, *see* TRANSACTIONAL ANALYSIS.

Taft-Hartley Act, *see* LABOR-MANAGEMENT RELATIONS ACT OF 1947.

take-home pay, also called NET PAY, employee's wages minus deductions that are either required (such as taxes) or requested (such as savings bonds).

tall organization, *see* FLAT ORGANIZATION.

tangible objective, *see* OBJECTIVE.

tardiness, reporting to work later than the scheduled time.

target, expected earnings under a piece-rate wage system. The earnings target is usually set at a fixed percentage (10 to 15 percent) above the base rate.

targeted, term that describes a grant when its eligibility and allocation provisions are drawn tightly, so that only the most "needy" cases are assisted and the amounts of aid are directly proportional to program needs.
  See also GRANT.

tariff, *see* DUTY.

Tariff Commission, United States, *see* INTERNATIONAL TRADE COMMISSION, UNITED STATES.

task, unit of work.

task analysis, identifying the various elements essential to the accomplishment of a task. *See* Ricky W. Griffin, *Task Design: An Integrative Approach* (Glenview, Ill.: Scott, Foresman and Co., 1982).

task-and-bonus plan, wage incentive plan paying a specific percent of the base wage rate (in addition to the base wage rate) when a specified level of production is maintained or exceeded for a specified period of time.

task force, also called INTERDISCIPLINARY TEAM, temporary organizational unit charged with accomplishing a specific mission. Committees tend to be chiefly concerned with the assessment of information in order to reach a conclusion. In contrast, a task group, task force, or interdisciplinary team is aggressively oriented. According to Lawrence W. Bass, in *Management By Task Forces: A Manual on the Operation of Interdisciplinary Teams* (Mt. Airy, Md.: Lomond Books, 1975), the great benefit of task forces is the great improvement that they bring about in information transfer: The members develop needed information in their respective spheres. They communicate their findings and conclusions to their colleagues on a timely schedule in order that the others may take them into consideration in carrying out their own missions. Their contacts are frequent and mutually helpful. They participate in discussions to dovetail their common and individual progress toward main objectives. They are an integrated community.

Also see Robert J. Butler and Lyle Yorks, "A New Appraisal System as Organizational Change: GE's Task Force Approach," *Personnel* (January-February 1984); Deborah L. Gladstein, "Groups in Context: A Model of Task Force Effectiveness," *Administrative Science Quarterly* (December 1984).

task group, *see* WORK GROUP.

TAT, *see* THEMATIC APPERCEPTION TEST.

tax, compulsory contribution exacted by a government for public purposes, except employee and employer assessments for retirement and social insurance purposes, which are classified as insurance trust revenue. All tax revenue is classified as general revenue and comprises amounts received (including interest and penalties but excluding protested amounts and refunds) from all taxes imposed by a government. *See* Joseph Pechman, "The Rich, the Poor and the Taxes They Pay," *The Public Interest* (Fall 1969); Advisory Commission on Intergovernmental Relations, *Changing Public Attitudes on Governments and Taxes, 1977* (Washington, D.C.: Government Printing Office, 1977).

See also REVENUE and TAXATION.

tax, earmarked, tax whose revenues must, by law, be spent for specific purposes.

tax, employment/payroll, *see* EMPLOYMENT TAXES.

tax, estate, tax on a deceased person's estate made prior to the estate's distribution.

tax, excess profits, a supplement to corporate income taxes usually imposed during a national emergency.

tax, excise, tax on the manufacture, sale, or consumption of a product.

tax, exported, tax paid by nonresidents of a community.

tax, flat, a tax that charges the same rate to each taxpayer. This term is also used to refer to any of a wide variety of proposals for reform of the federal income tax. *See* Robert E. Hall and Alvin Rabushka, *The Flat Tax* (Stanford, Calif.: Hoover Institution Press, 1985).

tax, inheritance, tax, usually progressive, on an individual's share of a deceased person's estate.

tax, license, tax exacted (either for revenue raising or for regulation) as a condition to the exercise of a business or non-business privilege, at a flat rate or measured by such bases as capital stock, capital surplus, number of business units, or capacity. Excludes taxes measured directly by transactions, gross or net income, or value of property except those to which only nominal rates apply. "Licenses" based on these latter measures, other than those at nominal rates, are classified according to the measure concerned. Includes "fees" related to licensing activities, automobile inspection, gasoline and oil inspection, professional examinations and licenses, etc.—as well as license taxes producing substantial revenues.

tax, negative income, welfare program in which citizens with incomes below a specified level would receive cash payments.

tax, personal property, tax on the assessed value (1) of tangible property such as furniture, animals, or jewelry, or (2) of intangible property such as stocks and bonds.

tax, poll, tax required of voters. The 24th Amendment prohibits denial of the right to vote for federal officials because a person has not paid a tax. This amendment was designed to abolish the requirement of a poll tax which, at the time of its ratification, was imposed by five states as a condition to voting.

The Supreme Court subsequently held that poll taxes were unconstitutional under the Equal Protection Clause of the 14th Amendment on the basis that the right to vote should not be conditioned on one's ability to pay a tax. Accordingly, poll taxes are now prohibited in all state and federal elections.

tax, real-property, any tax on land and its improvements; usually referred to simply as "property tax."

tax, regulatory, tax levied for a purpose other than that of raising revenue.

tax, severance, tax imposed by about half of the states for the privilege of "severing" natural resources from the land. *See* Albert M. Church, *Taxation of Nonrenewable Resources* (Lexington, Mass.: Lexington Books, 1981).

tax, stamp, a tax on certain legal documents, such as deeds, when it is required that revenue stamps be bought and put on the documents in order to make them valid.

tax, transfer, a tax on large transfers of property or money which are made without something of value given in return. Often called a "gift tax."

tax, unitary, a business tax of a percentage of world-wide profits, not just profits earned in the taxing jurisdiction. For example, if a corporation has twenty percent of its payroll, property and sales in a given state, that state might tax twenty percent of the corporation's world-wide income.

tax, value-added, *see* VALUE-ADDED TAX.

tax, withholding, sums of money that an employer takes out of an employee's pay and turns over to a government as prepayment of the employee's income tax obligation.

taxable income, under federal tax law, either the "gross income" of businesses or the "adjusted gross income" of individuals minus deductions and exemptions. It is the income against which tax rates are applied in order to compute one's tax obligation.

tax anticipation notes, *see* REVENUE ANTICIPATION NOTES.

taxation, governmental revenue collection. There are major differences between the federal and state/local revenue systems. The federal system has experienced a trend towards less diversity. Over two thirds of its general revenue are provided by the federal income tax and the several insurance trust funds (*i.e.,* social security). State and local revenue systems, in contrast, depend on a greater variety of revenue sources, such as property taxes, income taxes, sales taxes, user charges, lotteries, and federal grants. While local governments still rely primarily on the property tax, their states—with a few exceptions—rely largely on the state personal income tax. In addition, state sales and business taxes provide a significant source of income. This melange of taxing authorities creates great disparities for the taxpayer. There is significant variance in the state-local tax burden. A resident of New York may pay hundreds or thousands of dollars in state income taxes while a resident of Texas—which has no state income tax—will pay none. Virginians have to pay more than double the sales taxes paid by Vermonters. There are even greater variations in property taxes. The identical house assessed X dollars in one jurisdiction may be taxed three times that amount in another.

These are the major methods of taxation:

1. *Personal Income Tax.* Based on ability to pay in that the tax rate is applied against income. But income is more than just money; it is any asset that increases one's net worth. But income taxes are not necessarily a straight tax on all of one's income in a given year. Remember all of those millionaires that the press annually discovers who do not pay any tax on their income? They are able to do this because it is not their large incomes that are subject to taxation, but their adjusted gross incomes. All taxpayers have the right to exclude certain kinds of incomes from their gross incomes for tax purposes. For example, interest from state and local bonds is exempt from federal taxation. Thus, a millionaire whose sole income came from investments in such bonds would pay no federal income tax. Once adjusted gross income is realized, the taxpayer may subtract deductions and exemptions from his taxable income. Exemptions of so many dollars each are counted for the individual taxpayer(s) and his (their) exemptions. Then the taxpayer can deduct a host of expenses as long as they are allowed by the tax laws. Common deductions are those for medical care, state and local taxes (if a federal return), home mortgage interest, child care, and charitable contributions. A taxpayer can itemize his various deductions or take a minimum standard deduction, a pre-calculated weighted average. Progressive tax rates are then applied to the taxable income to determine how much tax is due.
2. *Corporation Income Tax.* A tax on the privilege of operating a business. Various deductions can be made for depreciation, capital gains, research and development costs, etc., to finally determine taxable income.
3. *Capital Gains Tax.* According to the 1984 Tax Act, the profits from investments (*i.e.,* capital gains) held more than six months are taxed at a 40 percent rate by the federal government. Capital gains achieved in less than six months are taxed as ordinary income.
4. *Sales Tax.* A favorite of many state and local governments, this is a tax on consumption, rather than income. Some fixed tax rate, ranging from 2 to 9 percent, is charged on most purchases. A variety of items tend to be excluded from sales taxation—medicine, clothing, foods. The major difficulty with the sales tax is its equity. Sales taxes tend towards regressivity since higher income groups pay a lesser percentage of their income in tax than do lower income groups. For example, a family of four with an income of $8,000 would spend half of that in direct consumption and might pay a 5 percent sales tax of $200, or 2.5 percent of their income. But another family of four with an $80,000 income will have a much lower percentage of direct consumption (say 25 percent) and although they pay 5 percent on $20,000, or $1,000, the proportion of their income taken by the sales tax is 1.2 percent, or half that of the lower income family.
5. *Property Tax.* The mainstay of most local governments; provides nearly half of the revenues that local governments get from their own sources. To administer a property tax, the tax base must first be defined—*i.e.,* housing and land, automobiles, other assets, whatever. Then an evaluation of the worth of the tax base must be made—this is the assessment. Finally, a tax rate, usually an amount to be paid per $100 value of the tax base, is levied. Since the value of the tax base will appreciate or depreciate substantially over time, continuing assessments must be made.

Arguments for the property tax resemble a good news/bad news joke. The good news is that the property tax provides a stable revenue source and has a good track record as a strong revenue raiser. The bad news is that its stability can also be considered inflexibility, as it does not keep pace with income growth. The good news is that since property is generally unmovable, it is hard to miss and therefore provides a good visible tax base for "relatively unskilled" local tax offices to administer. The bad news is that the administration and assessment of property tax is at best erratic and at worst a horrendous mess. The result is that the property tax base tends to erode over time; that most errors are made undervaluing the property of the wealthy or the politically influential; that there is a strong incidence effect on new people; and that old people are being increasingly pressed to meet property tax burdens.

See William H. Anderson, *Financing Modern Government* (Boston: Houghton Mifflin, 1973); Henry J. Aaron, *Who Pays the Property Tax? A New View* (Washington, D.C.: The Brookings Institution, 1975); James A. Maxwell and J. Richard Aronson, *Financing State and Local Government,* 3rd ed. (Washington, D.C.: The Brookings Institution, 1977); Diane B. Paul, *The Politics of the Property Tax* (Lexington, Mass.: D.C. Heath, 1975); Joseph A. Pechman, *Federal Tax Policy,* 3rd ed. (Washington D.C.: The Brookings Institution, 1977); Clarence G. McCarthy, *The Federal Income Tax: Its Sources and Applications* (Englewood Cliffs, N.J.: Prentice-Hall, 1979); Warren J. Samuels and Larry L. Wade, eds., *Taxing and Spending Policy* (Lexington, Mass.: Lexington Books, 1980); Henry J. Aaron and Michael J. Boskin, eds., *The Economics of Taxation* (Washington, D.C.: Brookings Institution, 1980); Henry J. Aaron and Joseph A. Pechman, eds., *How Taxes Affect Economic Behavior* (Washington, D.C.: Brookings Institution, 1981); Susan B. Hansen, *The Politics of Taxation: Revenue Without Representation* (New York: Praeger Publishers, 1983); Barry P. Bosworth, *Tax Incentives and Economic Growth* (Washington, D.C.: The Brook-

ings Institution, 1984); Joseph A. Pechman, *Who Paid the Taxes, 1966-85?* (Washington, D.C.: The Brookings Institution, 1985).

See related entries under REVENUE, TAX, and the following entries:

ABILITY TO PAY
CONSUMER TAXES
DIRECT TAX
DOCUMENT AND STOCK TRANSFER
 TAXES
DUTY
SELF-EMPLOYMENT TAX

tax avoidance, planning one's personal finances carefully so as to take advantage of all legal tax breaks, such as deductions and exemptions.

tax base, also AD VALOREM TAX, the thing or value on which taxes are levied. Some of the more common tax bases include: individual income, corporate income, real property, wealth, motor vehicles, sales of commodities and services, utilities, events, imports, estates, gifts, etc. The rate of a tax to be imposed against a given tax base may be either specific or *ad valorem.* Specific taxes, for example, raise a specific, non-variable amount of revenue from each unit of the tax base (*e.g.,* 10¢ per gallon of gasoline). *Ad valorem* taxes, on the other hand, are expressed as a percentage and the revenue yield varies according to the value of the tax base (*e.g.,* mill levy against real property).

tax bracket, *see* TAX RATE.

tax collections, *see* TAX YIELD.

tax credits, any provisions of law that allow a dollar-for-dollar reduction in tax liabilities that would otherwise be due.

tax deferred annuity, also called TAX SHELTERED ANNUITY, annuity whose employee contributions are not subject to taxes at the time that the contributions are made. Contributions are later taxed as they are paid out after retirement when the annuitant is presumably in a lower tax bracket.

tax efficiency, also TAX ELASTICITY, construed as a basic productivity measurement; specifically, how much does it cost to collect the tax, what is its political practicality, what is its long range and short range ability to raise revenue? This time dimension incorporates yet another concept, tax elasticity, which is simply the percentage of tax revenue raised compared to the percentage of change in personal income. A perfectly elastic tax would always be able to collect the same percentage of its jurisdiction's income. Elasticity is an important feature of efficient taxation since, in the short run, high elasticity can provide economic stability through a countering of cyclical effects. In the long run, elasticity should guarantee steadily increasing revenues. This is not to say that no case can be made for inelasticity. For example, the property tax tends to be inelastic in that major changes in personal income will not significantly increase property tax revenues. On the negative side, this means that property tax revenues will lag considerably behind increases in income. However, on the positive side is its stability. For small localities interested in steady tax revenues through times of recession and expansion, the relatively inelastic property tax could be viewed as an ideal revenue source.

The bottom line in evaluating tax and revenue mechanisms is the cost of collection. The smaller the governmental unit, the more restrained is the choice of revenue collection mechanisms. Obviously, it is not feasible for small localities to support a computerized personal income tax system, since the costs of collecting the tax would far exceed the revenues produced. One obvious response to this problem is consolidation of tax collection efforts, or piggybacking. The objective of consolidation is to achieve economics of scale. But problems of political control mitigate against the consolidation concept.

tax equity, also HORIZONTAL EQUITY and VERTICAL EQUITY, insuring that taxes treat equals as equals, and that unequals are treated unequally, or comparably. An equitable tax system would be one that requires all taxpayers with equal incomes to pay the same amount of taxes—this is horizontal equity. But since all citizens don't have the same income, vertical equity is applied—as personal income gets higher, so does the percentage of taxes. The degree or percentage of tax increase compared to the increase in the tax base yields another criterion with which to judge the equity of fiscal institutions: their use of progressive, proportional, and regressive taxes. All three criteria can satisfy vertical equity, in a very simple sense, if the only requirement is higher taxes for higher incomes. But it is the comparison of the increase in tax rate against the increase in the tax base that establishes progressive taxation as the only true vertical equity criterion. The federal graduated personal income tax is the best example of progressive taxation. Each successive higher income bracket pays a progressively higher tax rate. Proportional taxes are those that require an identical percentage increase in tax rates. Regressive taxes are those where the tax rate falls as the tax base increases. Some taxes that are actually proportional in structure, such as sales taxes or property taxes, function as regressive taxes when the tax paid is compared against income; the point being that individuals in a low income bracket will pay a higher percentage of their incomes for sales tax than will individuals with higher incomes.

Equity is premised on two classical economic concepts by which taxation is justified. The first concept is benefit—those who benefit from a public service should pay for it. A common example is the earmarking of gasoline taxes to finance highway construction and maintenance costs. The benefit concept is much more difficult to apply to national defense, clean air, prisons, and other public services where there is no direct link from usage to revenue source. The second concept is ability to pay—that the amount of tax should consider income, wealth, or other factors that determine how much an individual can afford. This is the essence of progressive taxation: higher incomes are taxed more, proportionately, than lower incomes. Here it is assumed that even the burden of paying fifty percent on taxable incomes over $80,000 will not deprive any individuals of the basic necessities of life. *See* David Lowery, "Tax Equity Under Conditions of Fiscal Stress: The Case of the Property Tax," *Publius* (Spring 1984).

tax-exempt municipal bonds, *see* MUNICIPAL BONDS.

tax expenditures, losses of tax revenue attributable to provisions of the federal tax laws that allow a special exclusion, exemption, or deduction from gross income or that provide a special credit, preferential rate of tax, or deferral of tax liability. *See* Ronald F. King, "Tax Expenditures and Systematic Public Policy: An Essay on the Political Economy of the Federal Revenue Code," *Public Budgeting & Finance* (Spring 1984).

tax-expenditures budget, *see* BUDGET, TAX-EXPENDITURES.

Tax Foundation, organization devoted to non-partisan research and public education on the fiscal aspects of government.
Tax Foundation
1875 Connecticut Avenue, N.W.
Washington, D.C. 20009
(202) 328-4500

tax incidence, the effects of a particular tax burden on various socioeconomic levels.

tax-increment financing, the ability of local government to finance large-scale development through the expected rise in the property tax to be collected after the development is completed. This permits the issuance of bonds based on the expected tax increase.

tax loophole, an inconsistency in the tax laws, intentional or unintentional, that allows the avoidance of some taxes.

tax rate, also TAX BRACKET, the percentage of taxable income (or of inherited money, things purchased subject to sales tax, etc.) paid in taxes. The federal income tax has a graduated tax rate. This means that the first ten thousand dollars of a person's taxable income might be taxed at a 20 percent rate (or two thousand dollars) and the next one thousand to two thousand dollars at a 25 percent rate. This percentage rate is what most people think of as their "tax bracket."

tax reform, the recurrent effort to produce a more equitable tax system. For analyses, *see* Joseph A. Pechman and Benjamin A. Okner, *Who Bears the Tax Burden* (Washington, D.C.: Brookings Institution, 1974); Philip Stern, *The Rape of the Taxpayer* (New York: Random House, 1974); Joseph A. Pechman, ed., *Options for Tax Reform* (Washington, D.C.: The Brookings Institution, 1984); Henry J. Aaron and Harvey Calper, *Assessing Tax Reform* (Washington, D.C.: The Brookings Institution, 1985).

tax shelter, investment in which any profits are fully or partially tax free; or an investment which creates deductions and credits that reduce one's overall taxes.

tax sheltered annuity, *see* TAX DEFERRED ANNUITY.

tax subsidy, tax advantage designed to encourage specific behavior that furthers public policy; for example, mortgage interest deductions to encourage citizens to buy houses, investment tax credits to encourage businesses to expand and create new jobs, etc.

tax yield, also TAX COLLECTIONS, the amount of tax which could potentially be collected. *Tax collections* are the portion of the tax yield that is actually collected.

Taylor, Frederick W. (1856–1915), originally an engineer, now considered the "father of scientific management." He did pioneering work on time-and-motion studies and led the search for the "one best way" of accomplishing any given task. Major works include: *Shop Management* (New York: Harper & Bros., 1903); *The Principles of Scientific Management* (New York: Harper & Bros., 1911). For biographies, *see* Frank Barkley Copley, *Frederick W. Taylor: Father of Scientific Management* (New York: Harper & Bros., 1923; reprinted by Augustus M. Kelley, 1969); Subhir Kakar, *Frederick Taylor: A Study in Personality and Innovation* (Cambridge, Mass.: M.I.T. Press, 1970). *Also see* Edwin A. Locke, "The Ideas of Frederick W. Taylor: An Evaluation," *Academy of Management Review* (January 1982).

See also SCIENTIFIC MANAGEMENT.

Taylor Differential Piece-Rate Plan, also DIFFERENTIAL PIECE RATE PLAN, incentive plan where different piece rates are established for substandard, standard, and higher than standard production.

Taylorism, term used to describe the "scientific management" advocated by Frederick W. Taylor; also used as a general description for the mechanistic and authoritarian style of management common in American industry.

Taylor Law, also PUBLIC EMPLOYEES' FAIR EMPLOYMENT ACT, New York State's law governing the unionization of state, county, and municipal employees. It grants all public employees the right to organize and be recognized, provides for a Public Employment Relations Board for the resolution of impasses, prohibits strikes, and provides a schedule of penalties for both striking individuals and their unions. The Taylor Law owes its name to George W. Taylor, a University of Pennsylvania Wharton School professor who chaired the Governor's Committee on Public Employee Relations that recommended the enacting legislation in 1966. *See* Lynn Zimmer and James B. Jacobs, "Challenging the Taylor Law: Prison Guards on Strike," *Industrial and Labor Relations Review* (July 1981).

tea break, *see* COFFEE BREAK.

Teachers Insurance and Annuity Association (TIAA), organization that manages portable pension plans for pro-

fessional employees of colleges and universities.
TIAA
730 Third Ave.
New York, NY 10017
(212) 490-9000

Tead, Ordway (1891–1973), pioneer in applying psychology to industry and co-author of one of the first personnel management texts. Major works include: *Instincts in Industry* (Boston: Houghton Mifflin, 1918); *Personnel Administration: Its Principles and Practice,* with Henry C. Metcalf (New York: McGraw-Hill, 1920); *The Art of Leadership* (New York: McGraw-Hill, 1935); *The Art of Administration* (New York: McGraw-Hill, 1951); *Administration: Its Purpose and Performance* (New York: Harper & Bros., 1959).

team building, any planned and managed change involving a group of people in order to improve communications and working relationships. Team building is most effective when used as a part of a long-range strategy for organizational and personal development. *See* Richard Beckhard, "Optimizing Team-Building Efforts," *Journal of Contemporary Business* (Summer 1972); Thomas H. Patten, Jr., and Lester E. Dorey, "Long-Range Results of a Team Building OD Effort," *Public Personnel Management* (January–February 1977); Patricia Palleschi and Patricia Heim, "The Hidden Barriers to Team Building," *Training and Development Journal* (July 1980).

Teamsters, Local 695* v. *Vogt, 354 U.S. 284 (1957), U.S. Supreme Court case which held that a state, in enforcing a public policy, may constitutionally enjoin peaceful picketing aimed at preventing effectuation of that policy.

technical assistance, term used to refer to the programs, activities, and services provided by the federal government, a public interest group, or another third party to strengthen the capacity of recipients to improve their performance with respect to an inherent or assigned function.

technocrat, an individual in a decision-making position of a technoscience agency whose background includes specialized technical training in a substantive field of science and/or technology. Sometimes used disparagingly.

See also TECHNOSCIENCE AGENCIES.

technological unemployment, unemployment that results from the displacement of workers by machinery or by the introduction of more efficient methods of production. See Guy Standing, "The Notion of Technological Unemployment," International Labour Review (March-April 1984).

technology assessment, planning and evaluation device with which to judge the impact of technology in society. It is a tool that can be used to empirically evaluate the performance and the physical, ecological, political, and economic effects of any particular technology either presently in use or contemplated in the future. See Marvin J. Cetron, ed., Technology Assessment in a Dynamic Environment (London: Gardon and Breach Science Pubs., 1973); John W. Dickey et al., Technology Assessment: Its Application to the Solid Waste Programs of Urban Governments (Lexington, Mass.: Lexington Books, 1973); Gerhard J. Stober and Dietar Schumacher, Technology Assessment and the Quality of Life (Amsterdam: Elsevier Scientific, 1973); Engineers Joint Council, Technology Assessment: State of the Field (New York: The Council, 1976); Erasmus H. Kloman, ed. (mini-symposium), "Public Participation in Technology Assessment," Public Administration Review (January-February 1975); Giandomenico Majone, "Technology Assessment in a Dialectic Key," Public Administration Review (January-February 1978).

Technology Assessment Act of 1972, see OFFICE OF TECHNOLOGY ASSESSMENT.

technology forecasting, use of techniques such as surveys of experts or the assessment of a future demand to anticipate technological developments. See Daniel D. Roman, "Technological Forecasting in the Decision Process," Academy of Management Journal (June 1970); James R. Bright, A Brief Introduction to Technology Forecasting (Austin, Tex.: Permaquid Press, 1972); Joseph P. Martino, Technology Forecasting for Decisionmaking (New York: American Elsevier, 1975).

technology transfer, application of technologies developed in one area of research or endeavor to another, frequently involving a concomitant shift in institutional setting (e.g., from one federal agency to another). Examples include the application of space technology developed under the auspices of NASA to the problems of public transportation or weather prediction. Claims regarding the future possibilities for transfer frequently are factors in decisions concerning continuing financial support for technology development. See Samuel I. Doctors, The Role of Federal Agencies in Technology Transfer (Cambridge, Mass.: M.I.T. Press, 1969); W. Henry Lambright and Albert H. Teich, Federal Laboratories and Technology Transfer: Institutions, Linkages, and Processes (Syracuse and Binghamton, N.Y.: Syracuse University Research Corporation and the State University of New York at Binghamton Press, 1974); National Academy of Engineering, Technology Transfer and Utilization (Washington, D.C.: National Academy of Engineering, 1974).

technoscience agencies, federal government agencies involved with science and technology policymaking. These agencies generate ideas for scientific research and technological development, sponsor research in universities, corporations, and federal laboratories, and direct deployment projects. Examples include: National Science Foundation, National Aeronautics and Space Administration, Office of Science and Technology, Department of Defense, and Department of Energy (DOE).

technostructure, term that implies a growing influence of technical specialists in policy decisions. Technostructure is increasingly used as a technical term in the study of science and technology policy-making to refer to the decision-making structure in private and public organizations.

temporary appointment, *see* APPOINTMENT.

temporary restraining order, *see* INJUNCTION.

Tennessee Valley Authority (TVA), government-owned corporation that conducts a unified program of resource development for the advancement of economic growth in the Tennessee River Valley region. The authority's program of activities includes flood control, navigation development, electric power production, fertilizer development, recreation improvement, and forestry and wildlife development. While its power program is financially self-supporting, other programs are financed primarily by appropriations from Congress.

TVA
400 West Summit Hill Dr.
Knoxville, TN 37902
(615) 632-2101
or
Capital Hill Office Building
412 First Street, S.E.
Washington, D.C. 20444
(202) 245-0101

For histories of the TVA, *see* Philip Selznick, *T.V.A. and the Grass Roots* (Berkeley: University of California Press, 1949); David Lilienthal, *TVA—Democracy on The March* (New York: Harper & Row, 1944); Gordon Clapp, *T.V.A.* (Chicago: University of Chicago Press, 1955); Preston J. Hubbard, *Origins of the TVA: The Muscle Shoals Controversy, 1920-1932* (New York: W. W. Norton, 1961); Thomas K. McCraw, *TVA and the Power Fight 1933-1939* (Philadelphia: J. B. Lippincott, 1971); Steven M. Neuse, "TVA at Age Fifty—Reflections and Retrospect," *Public Administration Review* (November-December 1983); Michael K. Fitzgerald and Steven M. Neuse, eds., "Symposium: TVA: The Second Fifty Years," *Public Administration Quarterly* (Summer 1984).

tenure, period of time that one occupies a position. In the academic world and in some government jurisdictions, to have "tenure" means that an individual may continue in his or her position until retirement, subject, of course, to adequate behavior and the continued viability of the organization. *See* Michael T. Bolger and David D. Wilmoth, "Dismissal of Tenured Faculty Members for Reasons of Financial Exigency," *Marquette Law Review* (Spring 1982).
See also PERRY V. SINDERMAN.

term appointment, *see* APPOINTMENT.

term bonds, *see* SERIAL BONDS.

terminal arbitration, arbitration that is called for as the final step in a grievance procedure.

terminal earnings formula, a formula that bases pension benefits on average earnings in the final years of credited service—often the last three or five years.

termination, dismissal from employment.
There is no general law which prohibits private and nonprofit employers from discharging employees without good cause. Employers have historically had the right to fire employees at will, unless there was a written contract which protected against it. This broad right to discharge employees at will has been limited by a number of federal laws which prohibit discrimination based on sex, race, color, religion, national origin, age, physical or mental handicap, union or other protected concerted activities, wage garnishment, and filing complaints or assisting in procedures related to enforcing these laws.
In addition, some states and municipalities have passed laws which prohibit discharge for serving on jury duty, filing workers' compensation claims, refusing to take lie detector tests, or for discrimination based on marital status or sexual orientation. Collective bargaining agreements be-

tween employers and unions and employee complaint procedures also impose limitations on the absolute right of an employer to fire workers.

Some employees have challenged their discharges in courts, and in a few cases have succeeded in placing additional limitations on employers' right to discharge. Courts in some states have ruled in favor of discharged employees when the discharge was contrary to public policy, such as refusal to commit perjury or to approve market testing of a possibly harmful drug; when it was not based on good faith and fair dealing, such as discharge for refusal to date a supervisor, or to avoid paying a large commission; or when there was an implied promise of continued employment. An implied promise of continued employment might be demonstrated by the personnel policies or practices of an employer, an employee's length of service, the nature of the job, actions or communications by the employer, and industry practices. See Stuart A. Youngblood and Gary L. Tidwell, "Termination at Will: Some Changes in the Wind," Personnel (May-June 1981); Stuart R. Korshak, "Arbitrating the Termination of a Union Activist," Personnel Journal (January 1982); William J. Holloway and Michael J. Leech, Employment Termination: Rights and Remedies (Washington, D.C.: Bureau of National Affairs, Inc., 1985).
Also see DISMISSAL, FIRE.

termination contract, agreement between an employer and a new employee that provides for salary continuation for the employee in the event of termination. The length of time that compensation continues to be paid typically varies from six months to two years. See Frank R. Beaudine, "The Termination Contract as a Recessionary Employment Tool," Personnel Journal (June 1975).

termination pay, see SEVERANCE PAY.

term life insurance, temporary insurance that offers protection for a limited number of years and has no cash value.

terms and conditions of employment, the entirety of the environment in which an employee works; all aspects of an employee's relationship with his or her employer and fellow employees, including compensation, fringe benefits, physical environment, work-related rules, work assignments, training and education, and opportunities to serve on committees and decision-making bodies.

test anxiety, nervousness that an examinee experiences before and during the administration of a test. For a study concluding that test anxiety is, except for extremes, inversely correlated with test performance, see C. S. Berkely and C. F. Sproule, "Test Anxiety and Test Unsophistication: The Effects and Cures," Public Personnel Management (January 1973).

test fidelity, extent to which a test represents the actual duties of a job.

test-retest reliability, measure of the reliability obtained by giving individuals the same test for a second time after an interval and correlating the sets of scores.

tests and testing, see the following entries:
CONFIDENCE TESTING
CREATIVITY TEST
CRITERION-REFERENCED TEST
CULTURE-FAIR TEST
DETROIT EDISON COMPANY V. NATIONAL LABOR RELATIONS BOARD
DEXTERITY TEST
DIAGNOSTIC TEST
EMPLOYMENT TESTING
FREE-RESPONSE TEST
HANDS-ON TEST
INDIVIDUAL TEST
INTELLIGENCE TEST
INTEREST TEST
MULTIPLE-CHOICE TEST
NORM-REFERENCED TEST
PERFORMANCE TEST
PERSONALITY TEST
POST-TEST
POWER TEST
PRE-TEST
PROFICIENCY TEST
PSYCHOLOGICAL TEST

QUALIFYING TEST
RANKING TEST
RORSCHACH TEST
SPEED TEST
SPIRAL-OMNIBUS TEST
STANDARDIZED TEST
TEST ANXIETY
TEST FIDELITY
TEST-RETEST RELIABILITY
TOWER AMENDMENT

Texas and New Orleans Railway* v. *Brotherhood of Railway and Steamship Clerks, 281 U.S. 548 (1930), U.S. Supreme Court case which denied a company the option of bargaining with its "company union" and required it to bargain with the self-organized union of its employees.

Texas Department of Community Affairs* v. *Joyce Ann Burdine, 67 L.Ed. 2d 207 (1981), U.S. Supreme Court case which held that a clear explanation of non discriminatory reasons for an employer's action may be sufficient to rebut an employee's prima facie case alleging job discrimination under Title VII of the Civil Rights Act of 1964.

Textile Workers* v. *Darlington Manufacturing Company, also called DARLINGTON CASE, 380 U.S. 263 (1965), U.S. Supreme Court case which held that while an employer has an absolute right to terminate his entire business for any reason, he does not have the right to close or move part of his business if he is motivated by anti-union bias. *See* Sherman F. Dallas and Beverly K. Schaffer, "Whatever Happened to the Darlington Case?" *Labor Law Journal* (January 1973); Robert A. Bedolis, "The Supreme Court's Darlington Mills Opinion," *The Conference Board Record* (June 1965).

Textile Workers* v. *Lincoln Mills 353 U.S. 448 (1957), U.S. Supreme Court case which held that the arbitration clause in a collective bargaining agreement is the *quid pro quo* given by the employer in return for the non-strike clause agreed to by a union.

T-Group, *see* LABORATORY TRAINING.

T-Group, family, *see* FAMILY T-GROUP.

Thematic Apperception Test (TAT), projective test that uses a standard set of pictures and calls for the subject to reveal his or her personality by making up stories about them. Variations of the TAT have been successfully used for vocational counseling and executive selection, as well as for determining attitudes toward labor problems, minority groups, and authority. *See* P. C. Cummin, "TAT Correlates of Executive Performance," *Journal of Applied Psychology* (February 1967).

Theory X and Theory Y, contrasting sets of assumptions made by managers about human behavior that Douglas McGregor distilled and labeled in *The Human Side of Enterprise* (New York: McGraw-Hill, 1960).

Theory X holds that:

1. The average human being has an inherent dislike of work and will avoid it if possible.

2. Because of this human characteristic of dislike of work, most people must be coerced, controlled, directed, or threatened with punishment to get them to put forth adequate effort toward the achievement of organizational objectives.

3. The average human being prefers to be directed, wishes to avoid responsibility, has relatively little ambition, wants security above all.

Theory X assumptions are essentially a restatement of the premises of the scientific management movement, not a flattering picture of the average citizen of modern industrial society. While McGregor's portrait can be criticized for implying greater pessimism concerning the nature of man on the part of managers than is perhaps warranted, Theory X is all the more valuable as a memorable theoretical construct because it serves as such a polar opposite of Theory Y. (McGregor would later deny that the theories were polar opposites and assert that they were "simply different cosmologies.")

Theory Y holds that:

1. The expenditure of physical and mental effort in work is as natural as play or rest. The average human being does not inherently dislike work. Depending upon controllable conditions, work may be a source of satisfaction (and will be voluntarily performed) or a source of punishment (and will be avoided if possible).

2. External control and the threat of punishment are not the only means for bringing about effort toward organizational objectives. Men and women will exercise self-direction and self-control in the service of objectives to which they are committed.

3. Commitment to objectives is a function of the rewards associated with their achievement. The most significant of such rewards (*e.g.*, the satisfaction of ego and self-actualization needs) can be direct products of effort directed toward organizational objectives.

4. The average human being learns, under proper conditions, not only to accept but to seek responsibility. Avoidance of responsibility, lack of ambition, and emphasis on security are generally consequences of experience, not inherent human characteristics.

5. The capacity to exercise a relatively high degree of imagination, ingenuity, and creativity in the solution of organizational problems is widely, not narrowly, distributed in the population.

6. Under the conditions of modern industrial life, the intellectual potentialities of the average human being are only partially utilized.

While McGregor admitted that the assumptions of Theory Y were not finally validated, he found them "far more consistent with the existing knowledge in the social sciences than are the assumptions of Theory X." A central motif in both Theory X and Theory Y is control. With Theory X, control comes down from management via strict supervision. Theory Y, on the contrary, assumes that employees will be internally rather than externally controlled. Such internal control presumably comes from an inward motivation to perform effectively.

Theory Z, an approach to management generally associated with the Japanese that emphasizes participative management from employees who are committed to their work through cultural tradition, shared socioeconomic values, and communal forms of decision making. Theory Z personnel policies are characterized by high levels of trust, lifetime or long-term job security, and holistic career planning.

See William Ouchi, *Theory Z: How American Business Can Meet the Japanese Challenge* (Reading, Mass.: Addison-Wesley, 1981); William G. Ouchi, "Organizational Paradigms: A Commentary on Japanese Management and Theory Z Organizations," *Organizational Dynamics* (Spring 1981); Ronald Contino and Robert M. Lorusso, "The Theory Z Turnaround of a Public Agency," *Public Administration Review* (January-February 1982); Grover Starling, "Performance Appraisal in the Z Organization," *Public Personnel Management* (Winter 1982); Stephen P. Robbins, "The Theory Z Organization from a Power-Control Perspective," *California Management Review* (January 1983).

therblig, basic elements of work motions first classified by the "inventor" of motion study, Frank G. Gilbreth. Therbligs (Gilbreth spelled backward) came in seventeen varieties and remain the foundation of the science of motion study. The basic therbligs, as modified by the Society for the Advancement of Management, are: search, select, grasp, reach, move, hold, release, position, pre-position, inspect, assemble, disassemble, use, unavoidable delay, avoidable delay, plan, and rest to overcome fatigue.

think tank, colloquial term that refers to an organization or organizational segment whose sole function is research. Some of the better known "think tanks" include: The RAND Corporation, The Hudson Institute, and The Stanford Research Institute. For a complete account, *see* Paul Dickson, *Think Tanks* (New York: Atheneum, 1971).

third-party allegations of discrimination, allegations of discrimination in employment brought by third parties—that is, groups or individuals not alleging discrimination against themselves and not seeking relief on their own behalf. The purpose of third-party procedures is to permit organizations with an interest in furthering equal opportunity to call attention to equal employment opportunity problems that appear to require correction or remedial action and that are unrelated to individual complaints of discrimination.

third sector, all those organizations that fit in neither the public sector (government) nor the private sector (business). Theodore Levitt, in *The Third Sector: New Tactics for a Responsive Society* (New York: AMACOM, 1973), defines the third sector as comprising "those organizations which have risen to institutionalize activism in order to meet problems ignored by the other two sectors." For a symposium, *see* Michael E. McGill and Leland M. Wooton, eds., "Management in the Third Sector," *Public Administration Review* (September-October 1975). *Also see* James T. Evans, "Third Sector Management: The Museum in the Age of Introspection— Survival and Redefinition for the 1980s," *Public Administration Review* (September-October 1982).

Thomas v. Review Board of the Indiana Employment Security Division, 67 L.Ed. 2d 624 (1981), U.S. Supreme Court case which held the denial of unemployment compensation to a member of Jehovah's Witnesses who voluntarily quit his job because of his religious beliefs was violative of the free exercise clause of the First Amendment.

Thompson, James D. (1919-73), sociologist whose landmark book in organ-

izational analysis and theory, *Organizations in Action* (New York: McGraw-Hill, 1967), found organizations to be primarily open systems. But Thompson suggested that the closed system approach might be more realistic at the technical level of operations. He sought to bridge the gap between open and closed systems by suggesting that organizations deal with the uncertainty of their environment by creating specific elements designed to cope with the outside world while other elements are able to focus on the rational nature of technical operations.

Thompson, Victor A. (1912-   ), one of the most gifted stylists in the literature of public administration. Thompson is best known for dealing deftly with bureaucratic interactions and dysfunctions. In his most influential work, *Modern Organization* (New York: Knopf, 1961), he reminds us that "one must not forget that clients are notoriously insensitive to the needs of bureaucrats." Other major works include: *Public Administration,* with Herbert A. Simon and Donald W. Smithburg (New York: Knopf, 1950); *Bureaucracy and Innovation* (University, Ala.: University of Alabama Press, 1969); *Without Sympathy or Enthusiasm: The Problem of Administrative Compassion* (University, Ala.: University of Alabama Press, 1975); *Bureaucracy and the Modern World* (Morristown, N.J.: General Learning Press, 1976).

Thornhill v. Alabama, *see* PICKETING.

threshold effect, total impression a job applicant makes by his or her bearing, dress, manners, etc., as he or she "comes through the door."

throughput, middle step in data processing or a system's operation; it comes after input and before output.

Thurstone Scale, attitude scale created by Louis L. Thurstone that has judges rate the favorability of statements, then has subjects select those statements with which they agree. *See* L. L. Thurston and E. J.

Chave, *The Measurement of Attitude* (Chicago: University of Chicago Press, 1929).

TIAA, *see* TEACHERS INSURANCE AND ANNUITY ASSOCIATION.

tiger team, a task force or work group assigned to solve a specific problem or generate new ideas.

time, broken, *see* BROKEN TIME.

time card, most basic payroll form on which is recorded, either manually or by means of a mechanical time clock, the hours that an employee has worked during a particular pay period. For an analysis, *see* E. B. Helin, "Sophisticating the Antiquated Time Card," *Personnel Journal* (June 1971).

time horizon, that distance into the future to which a planner looks when seeking to evaluate the consequences of a proposed action. *See* Ronald J. Ebert and DeWayne Piehl, "Time Horizon: A Concept for Management," *California Management Review* (Summer 1973).

time-in-grade restriction, requirement intended to prevent excessively rapid promotions in the federal government's General Schedule. Generally, an employee may not be promoted more than two grades within one year to positions up to GS-5. At GS-5 and above, an employee must serve a minimum of one year in grade, and cannot be promoted more than one grade (or two grades if that is the normal progression).

time-sharing, simultaneous use of a central computer by two or more remote users, each of whom has direct and individual use of the central computer through the use of a terminal. The first commercial computer time-sharing services began in 1965.

time study, according to Benjamin W. Niebel, in *Motion and Time Study,* 7th ed. (Homewood, Ill.: Richard D. Irwin, 1982),

technique of establishing an allowed time standard to perform a given task, based upon measurement of the work content of the prescribed method, with due allowance for fatigue and for personal and unavoidable delays. The time study analyst has several techniques that can be used to establish a standard: stopwatch time study, standard data, fundamental motion data, work sampling, and estimates based upon historical data.
See also the following entries:
GILBRETH, FRANK BUNKER AND LILLIAN MOLLER
MOTION STUDY
SYNTHETIC TIME STUDY
THERBLIG
WORK SAMPLING

timetable, *see* GOAL.

time wage rate, any pay structure providing for wage payments in terms of an hourly, weekly, or monthly time interval. This is in contrast to a piece-rate structure where an employee is paid only for the amount that he or she produces.

title, also called CLASS TITLE, the "label" used to officially designate a class. It is descriptive of the work performed and its relative level.

titles, formal job descriptions. Titles are useful management tools (and cheap, too). The appropriate title can provide incalculable psychic income and a decided advantage when dealing with the outside world. A sales representative may be more effective as a vice president for sales. A secretary may be more effective as an administrative assistant. Shakespeare's Juliet was wrong. A rose by any other name would not necessarily smell as sweet; sometimes it smells better!

Title VII, in the context of equal employment opportunity, almost invariably refers to Title VII of the Civil Rights Act of 1964 (as amended)—the backbone of the nation's EEO effort. It prohibits employment discrimination because of race, color, religion, sex, or national origin and created the Equal Employment Opportunity Commission as its enforcement vehicle. The federal courts have relied heavily upon Title VII in mandating remedial action on the part of employers. *See* Paul J. Speigelman, "Bona Fide Seniority Systems and Relief from 'Last Hired, First Fired' Layoffs under Title VII," *Employee Relations Law Journal* (Autumn 1976); Gary L. Lubben, Duane C. Thompson, and Charles R. Klasson, "Performance Appraisal: The Legal Implications of Title VII," *Personnel* (May–June 1980); David G. Karro, "The Importance of Being Earnest: Pleading and Maintaining a Title VII Class Action for the Purpose of Resolving the Claims of Class Members," *Fordham Law Review* (May 1981); Elaine Gale Wrong, "The Social Responsibility of Arbitrators in Title VII Disputes," *Labor Law Journal* (September 1981); Nestor Cruz, "Abuse of Rights in Title VII Cases: The Emerging Doctrine," *Labor Law Journal* (May 1981); Kenneth Kirschner, "The Extraterritorial Application of Title VII of the Civil Rights Act," *Labor Law Journal* (July 1983); Ann W. Hart, "Intent vs. Effect: Title VII Case Law That Could Affect You (Part 1)," *Personnel Journal* (March 1984).

See also the following entries:

FAIRS V. JOYCE ANN BURDINE
TOWER AMENDMENT

title-structure change, elimination of a title by substitution of a more appropriate title without any change in duties or responsibilities of the position involved.

tokenism, in the context of Equal Employment Opportunity, an insincere EEO effort by which a few minority group members are hired in order to satisfy government affirmative action mandates or the demands of pressure groups.

tool-handling time, that time during the normal work day that the worker devotes to tending to the tools that are the necessary instruments of his or her work.

Torcaso* v. *Watkins, 367 U.S. 488 (1961), U.S. Supreme Court case which held that a state requirement of a declaration of a belief in God as a qualification for office was unconstitutional because it invades one's freedom of belief and religion guaranteed by the First Amendment and protected by the 14th Amendment from infringement by the states.

total compensation comparability, major means of incorporating fringe benefits into overall pay policy. The comparability principle, which holds that public employees should be paid wages comparable to those of similar workers in the economy, has not kept pace with changing conditions. Consequently, in some jurisdictions, while actual wages and salaries may be comparable to those of private-sector counterparts, the total package of pay plus fringe benefits often gives the public sector employee a greater total return than that gained by a private sector counterpart. In response to this situation jurisdictions are increasingly calling for total compensation comparability. This, in essence, calls for both pay and benefits to be included in comparability surveys, rather than pay alone. This move toward total compensation comparability nicely dovetails with governmental concerns for steadily rising inflation, dwindling fiscal resources, and the mood of taxpayers to hold down governmental spending. *See* Pierre Martel, "A Model of Total Compensation in a Market-Comparability Framework," *Public Personnel Management* (Summer 1982); Bruce R. Eillig, "Total Compensation Design: Elements and Issues," *Personnel* (January–February 1984).

total labor force, *see* LABOR FORCE.

total obligational authority, the sum of all budget authority granted (or requested) from the Congress in a given year, plus amounts authorized to be credited to a specific fund, and the balances of unused budget authority from previous years which remain available for obligation. In practice, this term is used primarily in discussing the Department of Defense budget, but could be applied to other agencies' budgets as well.

totem-pole ranking, rank ordering of employees, usually for purposes of evaluation, where each is placed above or below another with no more than one individual per rank.
    See also LOW MAN ON THE TOTEM POLE.

tour of duty, hours that an employee is scheduled to work.

Tower Amendment, portion of Title VII of the Civil Rights Act of 1964 that was introduced by Senator John Tower of Texas during Senate debate on the act. The Tower Amendment, Section 703 (h), had the effect of establishing, in legal terms, the right of an employer to give "professionally developed ability tests" as long as they were not intentionally discriminatory. The amendment reads as follows:
    Nor shall it be an unlawful employment practice for an employer to give and to act upon the results of any professionally developed ability test provided that such test, its administration or action upon the results is not designed, intended or used to discriminate because of race, color, religion, sex, or national origin.

town, also BOROUGH and VILLAGE, urban entities with powers less than those possessed by cities. They are strictly controlled by state statutes.

Towne, Henry Robinson (1844–1924), an early scientific management advocate whose efforts predated and influenced Frederick W. Taylor. His most famous paper, "The Engineer as an Economist" (ASME *Transactions,* Vol. 7, pp. 428–432), presented at the 1886 meeting of the American Society of Mechanical Engineers, called on his fellow engineers to become interested in management because "the matter of shop management is of equal importance with that of engineering."

town meeting, a method of self government, now suitable for only the smallest jurisdictions, where the entire citizenry meets to decide local issues of public policy.

township, a division of state land having six miles on each side and varying in importance as a unit of government from state to state.

track record, athletic metaphor for an individual's history of performance in any given field or endeavor.

trade union, *see* CRAFT UNION.

Tragedy of the Commons, a story illustrative of the principle that the maximization of private gain will not result in the maximization of social benefit. When herdsmen sought to maximize individual gain by adding more and more cattle to a common pasture, this overgrazed the common. The resulting tragedy was that no one was able to effectively use the common for grazing. The concepts involved with the tragedy of the commons apply to societal problems such as pollution, overpopulation, etc. *See* Garrett Hardin, "The Tragedy of the Commons," *Science* (December 13, 1968).

trainee rate, *see* BEGINNER'S RATE.

trainerless laboratory, laboratory training experience conducted by the participants themselves.

training, organized effort to increase the capabilities of individuals and modify their behavior in order to achieve previously determined objectives. For texts, *see* I. L. Goldstein, *Training: Program Development and Design* (Monterey, Calif.: Brooks/Cole, 1974); Kenneth T. Byers, ed., *Employee Training and Development in the Public Sector,* rev. ed. (Chicago: International Personnel Management Association, 1974); Robert L. Craig, ed., *Training and Development Handbook,* 2nd ed. (New York: McGraw-Hill, 1976); Dugan Laird, *Approaches To Training and Development* (Reading, Mass.: Addison-Wesley, 1978); Kenneth N. Wexley and Gary P. Latham, *Developing and Training Human Resources in Organizations* (Glenview, Ill.: Scott, Foresman and Co., 1981).

See also the following entries:
AMERICAN SOCIETY FOR TRAINING AND DEVELOPMENT
ASSERTIVENESS TRAINING
COLD-STORAGE TRAINING
COMPREHENSIVE EMPLOYMENT AND TRAINING ACT OF 1973
GOVERNMENT EMPLOYEES TRAINING ACT OF 1958
IN-SERVICE TRAINING
JOINT TRAINING
LABORATORY TRAINING
NATIONAL TRAINING LABORATORIES INSTITUTE FOR APPLIED BEHAVIORAL SCIENCE
POST-ENTRY TRAINING
RADIUS CLAUSE
ROLE
TRANSFER OF TRAINING
VERTICAL TRAINING
VESTIBULE TRAINING
VOCATIONAL TRAINING

Training and Development Journal, monthly journal of the American Society for Training and Development, Inc. Articles written by both practitioners and academics emphasize all phases of training and organization development. Selections tend to be more practical than theoretical.
Training and Development Journal
ASTD, Suite 305
600 Maryland Ave., S.W.
Washington, D.C. 20024

training by objectives, method that allows employees to establish their own developmental goals (compatible with organizational goals) and direct their activities toward these goals much as a management by objectives system establishes objectives and breaks down all subordinate activity into subdivisions that contribute to the overall objectives. For the most comprehensive treatment of this concept, *see* George S. Odiorne, *Training by Objectives: An Economic Approach To Management Training* (New York: Macmillan, 1970).

training demand, also TRAINING NEED, expressed preferences for training programs by individuals. *Training need* reflects some form of skill deficit that is directly related to job performance. If an organization's sole criterion for initiating a training program is demand, the danger will persist that what is demanded is not necessarily what is needed. *See* Richard A. Morano, "Determining Organizational Training Needs," *Personnel Psychology* (Winter 1973); Richard F. Fraser, John W. Gore, and Chester C. Cotton, "A System for Determining Training Needs," *Personnel Journal* (December 1978); Stephen V. Steadham, "Learning to Select a Needs Assessment Strategy," *Training and Development Journal* (January 1980); Ron Zemke, "How To Conduct a Needs Assessment For Computer Literacy Training," *Training* (September 1983); John P. Bucalo, Jr., "An Operational Approach to Needs Analysis," *Training and Development Journal* (April 1984); Vicki S. Kaman and John P. Mohr, "Training Needs Assessment in the Eighties: Five Guideposts," *Personnel Administrator* (October 1984).

training evaluation, also TRAINING MEASUREMENT, determination of the extent to which a training program is justified by its results. *Training measurement* must precede training evaluation, because it reveals the changes that may have occurred as a result of training. The essential question is whether or not a training effort has met its objective. Annual reports frequently boast of the number of employees trained during the preceding year, but such "facts" should be looked upon with great suspicion. It is a common mistake to assume that the number of people who have been subjected to training is equal to the number who have been trained. No statement of training accomplishment can confidently be made unless it is supported by sophisticated measures of evaluation. *See* Irwin L. Goldstein, *Training: Program Development and Evaluation* (Monterey, Calif.: Brooks/Cole, 1974); Richard Morano, "Measurement and Evaluation of Training," *Training and Development Journal* (July 1975); Donald Kirkpatrick, *Evaluating Training Programs* (Madison, Wis.: American Society for Training and Development, 1975); John W. Newstrom, "Evaluating the Effectiveness of Training Methods," *The Personnel Administrator* (January 1980); Jonathan S. Monat, "A Perspective on the Evaluation of Training and Development Programs," *Personnel Administrator* (July 1981); A. R. Hoyle, "Evaluation of Training: A Review of the Literature," *Public Administration and Development* (July-September 1984); Darlene Russ-Eft and John H. Zenger, "Common Mistakes in Evaluating Training Effectiveness," *Personnel Administrator* (April 1985).

training measurement, *see* TRAINING EVALUATION.

training need, *see* TRAINING DEMAND.

Training: The Magazine of Human Resources Development, monthly trade magazine dealing with all aspects of training and human resource development. Articles tend to be written by practitioners in order to help managers of training development functions use the behavioral sciences to solve human performance problems.

> *Training: The Magazine of Human Resources Development*
> 731 Hennepin Avenue
> Minneapolis, MN 55403

transactional analysis (TA), approach to psychotherapy first developed by Eric Berne. Transactional analysis defines the basic unit of social intercourse as a "transaction." There are three "ego states" from which transactions emanate—that of a "parent," an "adult," or a "child." The transactions between individuals can be classified as complementary, crossed, simple, or ulterior, based upon the response that an individual receives to a "transactional stimulus"—any action that consciously or unconsciously acknowledges the presence of other individuals. The transactional analysis framework has become a popular means of helping managers to assess the nature and effectiveness of their interpersonal behavior. By striving for more adult-to-adult transactions, managers may eliminate many of the "games people play." For the first published account, *see* Eric Berne, "Transactional Analysis: A New and Effective Method of Group Therapy," *American Journal of Psychotherapy* (October 1958). For the best-seller that made transactional analysis a household term, *see* Eric Berne, *Games People Play: The Psychology of Human Relationships* (New York: Grove Press, 1964). For a general treatment, *see* Thomas A. Harris, *I'm OK—You're OK* (New York: Harper & Row, 1969). For an application to personnel, *see* A. J. Tasca, "Personnel Management: A T/A Perspective," *Personnel Journal* (November 1974).

transactional avoidance, "management theory" described by Norman A. Parker, in "The Tongue-in-Cheek Approach To Management Theories," *Personnel Journal* (July 1978):

> The psychologists have put a lot of time into analyzing relationships between people. They have observed that many of these relationships, or transactions,

take place between two people playing combinations of roles as parent, child or adult. The conclusion usually reached is that in a work situation, the optimal transaction is conducted by two people playing the role of adult. This is nice if you can get everyone involved to agree to act like an adult. Unfortunately, such is not always the case. Some days, when the planets are right, two people might interact that way. Most of the time there is just too much going on to bother. You then have the transactor making a real college try to be "OK," while the transactee is sucking his or her thumb or acting like a wounded parent. What this leads to is ambivalence in the transaction process, and that is bad and almost incurable. Transactional Avoidance, however, neatly side-steps all the pitfalls.

The basic concept of Transactional Avoidance was devised by an exhermit. His thesis is that in any kind of confrontation, somebody usually loses and therefore any avoidance of transaction is a plus. The elements of the technique involve free delegation of everything, and since almost everyone is familiar with the rudiments of delegation, there is no long learning process involved. The originator of this system refuses to teach any classes and little has been published on this promising concept.

transcendental meditation, technique utilizing biofeedback which seeks to expand an individual's intellectual growth and consciousness. For the methodology, see Robert B. Kory, *The Transcendental Meditation Program for Business People* (New York: AMACOM, 1976).

transfer, also called LATERAL TRANSFER, job reassignment in which the employee retains approximately the same pay, status, and responsibility as in his or her previous assignment. See Edward J. Bardi and Jack L. Simonetti, "The Game of Management Chess—Policies and Perils of Management Transfers," *Personnel Journal* (April 1977).

transfer authority, statutory power granted the executive to shift congressionally appropriated funds from one appropriation account to another.

Under the transfer authority money appropriated to a specific account changes as the new account gains and the old account loses. Funds would be transferred, for example, if the State Department moved money from an aid program appropriated to Uganda to one for Zimbabwe. In some instances of transfer authority, pertinent congressional committees must be notified in advance and have the option of approving or denying the transfer of funds. For details, see Louis Fisher, *Presidential Spending Power* (Princeton, N.J.: Princeton University Press, 1975).

transfer of training, theory that knowledge or abilities acquired in one area aid the acquisition of knowledge or abilities in other areas. When prior learning is helpful, it is called *positive transfer*. When prior learning inhibits new learning, it is called *negative transfer*.

transfer payments, payments by government made to individuals who provide no goods or services in return. See Robert H. Michel, "The Future Direction of Income Transfer Programs," *Public Administration Review* (September–October 1976).

transition quarter, the three-month period (July 1 to September 30, 1976) between fiscal year 1976 and fiscal year 1977 resulting from the change from a July 1 through June 30 fiscal year to an October 1 through September 30 fiscal year beginning with fiscal year 1977.

Transportation, Department of (DOT), cabinet-level department of the U.S. federal government.

DOT establishes the nation's overall transportation policy. Under its umbrella there are eight administrations whose jurisdictions include highway planning, development, and construction; urban mass transit; railroads, aviation; and the safety of waterways, ports, highways, and oil and gas pipelines.

DOT
400 Seventh St., S.W.
Washington, D.C. 20590
(202) 426-4000

Trans World Airlines v. Hardison, 432 U.S. 63 (1977), U.S. Supreme Court case which ruled

that an employer is not required to arrange Saturdays off for an employee so that he may observe his Sabbath, if in doing so the employer would incur more than minimal costs—such as overtime pay for a replacement. The Court also ruled that, if employees' work schedules are determined on the basis of seniority, an employer is not required to violate the seniority privileges of others so that an employee can observe a Saturday Sabbath.

trashcan hypothesis, assertion that the personnel department is the dumping ground of management. According to Dalton E. McFarland, in *Cooperation and Conflict in Personnel Administration* (New York: American Foundation for Management Research, 1962),

in the assignment of functions to employee relations executives, chief executives or members of organizing committees have no systematic basis for determining the degree of appropriateness of the function for this department. Consequently, they view the personnel department as a dumping ground for a broad array of functions having little to do with the major goals of personnel administration. These decisions have a potential for weakening the performance of major employee relations functions. Personnel executives dislike this extension of their duties and the resulting thinning out of time and available resources.

Treasury, Department of the, cabinet-level department of the U.S. federal government.

The Department of the Treasury formulates and recommends financial, tax, and fiscal policies; serves as financial agent for the U.S. Government; manufactures coins and currency; and enforces related laws.

Department of the Treasury
Fifteenth St. & Pennsylvania Avenue, N.W.
Washington, D.C. 20220
(202) 566-2000

treasury bills, the shortest term federal security. Treasury bills have maturity dates normally varying from three to twelve months and are sold at a discount from face value rather than carrying an explicit rate of interest.

trend projections, the examination and study of the behavioral patterns of both past and present statistical data; also, the projecting or predicting of the possible range of that data over a future period of time. Predicting trends consists of using (usually) quantitative methods for plotting data as a function of time to see what did happen to it in the past and determine if the trend or character of the (plotted) data will continue unchanged for some future period. The three major types of predictions used are:

1. *Cyclic predictions,* which may be based on the principle that history repeats itself. Such data when displayed may show periodic fluctuations, such as temperature changes throughout the year or the use of electricity in the same period. This can be used only when you are sure how the periodicity comes about and why.
2. *Trajectory predictions,* which are based on changes that occur in data that remain stable in character (*e.g.,* population growths, gross national product, etc.).
3. *Associative predictions,* which are data from one event that are used to predict a second event. "Cause and effect" relationships must exist to predict these situations (*e.g.,* unemployment vs. increase in the welfare rolls).

trickle-down economics, description for

government policies that seek to benefit the wealthy in hopes that prosperity will in turn "trickle down" to the middle and lower economic classes. The term was first coined by humorist Will Rogers (1879–1935) when he analyzed some of the depression remedies of the Hoover administration and noted that "the money was all appropriated for the top in the hopes it would trickle down to the needy."

See also SUPPLY-SIDE ECONOMICS.

trickle-down housing theory, belief that housing would be upgraded for all groups as they move through housing left vacant by other groups as they progressed up the economic ladder.

Trilateral Commission, organization of approximately two hundred private citizens from Japan, Western Europe, and North America which was created in 1973 for the purpose of debating the common political and economic and security issues of the three regions. Many of the commission's activities make use of the number "three": it meets for three days every nine months, rotating between the trilateral regions; its newsletter is called the *Trialogue;* and its trilateral task forces composed of three rapporteurs each produce a series of topical reports called Triangle Papers.

trilogy cases, *see* STEELWORKER'S TRILOGY.

true score, score entirely free of measurement errors. True scores are hypothetical values never obtained in actual testing, which always involves some measurement error. A true score is sometimes defined as the average score that would result from an infinite series of measurements with the same or exactly equivalent tests, assuming no practice or change in the examinee during the testings.

trusteeship, also called UNION TRUSTEESHIP, situation whereby a labor organization (usually a national or international union) suspends the authority of a subordinate organization (usually a local

union) and takes control of the subordinate organization's assets and administrative apparatus. Trusteeships are commonly authorized by the constitutions of international unions in order to prevent and, if necessary, remedy corruption and mismanagement by local union officials. Title III of the Labor-Management Reporting and Disclosure (Landrum-Griffin) Act of 1959 prescribes the conditions under which union trusteeships may be established and continued. *See* Daniel L. Schneidman, "Union Trusteeships and Section 304 (a) of the Landrum-Griffin Act," *Labor Law Journal* (June 1963).

trust funds, funds collected and used by the federal government for carrying out specific purposes and programs according to terms of a trust agreement or statute, such as the social security and unemployment trust funds. Trust funds are administered by the government in a fiduciary capacity and are not available for the general purposes of the government. Trust fund receipts that are not anticipated to be used in the immediate future are generally invested in interest-bearing government securities and earn interest for the trust fund. A special category of trust funds called *trust revolving funds* is used to carry out a cycle of business-type operations (*e.g.,* Federal Deposit Insurance Corporation).

trust intrafund transactions, *see* OFFSETTING RECEIPTS.

tuition aid, also TUITION REFUND, training program that partially or fully reimburses employees for the expenses of taking job-related part-time courses at local colleges or universities. For an analysis, *see* Richard A. Kaimann and Daniel Robey, "Tuition Refund—Asset or Liability?" *Personnel Journal* (August 1976). *Also see* Milwaukee Personnel Department Training Unit, "Tuition Reimbursement in Employee Productivity and OD: A Survey," *Public Personnel Management* (May–June 1977).

turkey farm, also called TURKEY OFFICE

and TURKEY DIVISION, government office having little work and slight, if any, responsibility. Government managers frequently find it easier to place troublesome or incompetent employees on turkey farms rather than go through the hassle of adverse action proceedings. *See* Richard E. Miller, "Recipes for Turkey Turnover," *The Bureaucrat* (Winter 1979-80).

turnover, movement of individuals into, through, and out of an organization. Turnover can be statistically defined as the total number (or percentage) of separations that occur over a given time period. The turnover rate is an important indicator of the morale and health of an organization. For analyses of turnover, *see* James L. Price, *The Study of Turnover* (Ames, Iowa: Iowa State University Press, 1977); Barrie O. Pettman, ed., *Labour Turnover and Retention* (New York: John Wiley and Sons, 1975); Dan R. Dalton, "Turnover Turned Over: An Expanded and Positive Perspective," *Academy of Management Review* (April 1979); J. Thomas Horrigan, "The Effects of Training on Turnover: A Cost Justification Model," *Training and Development Journal* (July 1979); Catherine Begnoche Smith, "Influence of Internal Opportunity Structure and Sex of Worker on Turnover Patterns," *Administrative Science Quarterly* (September 1979); Leonard Greenhalgh, "A Process Model of Organizational Turnover: The Relationship with Job Security as a Case in Point," *Academy of Management Review* (April 1980); William N. Cooke, "Turnover and Earnings: The Scientist and Engineer Case," *Journal of Human Resources* (Summer 1980); Stephen A. Stumpf and Patricia Kelly Dawley, "Predicting Voluntary and Involuntary Turnover Using Absenteeism and Performance Indices," *Academy of Management Journal* (March 1981); David Krackhardt *et al.*, "Supervisory Behavior and Employee Turnover: A Field Experiment," *Academy of Management Journal* (June 1981); Thomas E. Hall, "How to Estimate Employee Turnover Costs," *Personnel* (July-August 1981); John W. Seybolt, "Dealing with Premature Employee Turnover," *Cali-*

fornia Management Review (Spring 1983); Ellen F. Jackofsky, "Turnover and Job Performance: An Integrated Process Model," *The Academy of Management Review* (January 1984); Russ Winn, "A Comparison of Internal and External Factors Affecting Voluntary Turnover," *Review of Public Personnel Administration* (Fall 1984).

See also STAFFING DYNAMICS and WORK PREVIEW.

TVA, *see* TENNESSEE VALLEY AUTHORITY.

two-career couple, *see* DUAL-CAREER COUPLE.

Two-Factor Theory, *see* MOTIVATION-HYGIENE THEORY.

Type I error, rejection of a statistical test or assumption that should be accepted in this case.

Type II error, acceptance of a statistical test or assumption that should be rejected in this case.

U

unaffiliated union, union not affiliated with the AFL-CIO.

unassembled examination, examination in which applicants are rated solely on their education, experience, and other requisite qualifications as shown in the formal application and on any supporting evidence that may be required.

unauthorized strike, *see* WILDCAT STRIKE.

unclassified positions, *see* EXCEPTED POSITIONS.

uncontrollable expenses, *also* UNCON-

TROLLABLE SPENDING, one of two kinds of expenses. The first are contractual obligations, where the government has granted long term contracts or is obligated to pay, as in the case of interest on the national debt. The second category consists of entitlement programs, which covers payments or aid granted to individuals or state and local governments. Obviously, once such a program is created and individuals or governments qualify for payment, they must be paid. The end result is a drastic loss of fiscal flexibility for controlling federal spending. *See* Martha Derthick, *Uncontrollable Spending for Social Services Grants* (Washington, D.C.: The Brookings Institution, 1975).

underachievement, *see* OVERACHIEVEMENT.

underemployment, those workers who are involuntarily working less than a normal work week and those who are situated in jobs that do not make efficient use of their skills and educational backgrounds. Examples of the latter would include a Ph.D. driving a taxi or an engineer working as a file clerk. *See* Lewis C. Solmon *et al., Underemployed Ph.D.'s* (Lexington, Mass.: Lexington Books, 1981); H. G. Kaufman, *Professionals in Search of Work: Coping with the Stress of Job Loss and Underemployment* (New York: Wiley, 1982).

underground economy, the totality of economic activity undertaken in order to evade tax obligations. *See* Richard J. McDonald, "The 'Underground Economy' and BLS Statistical Data," *Monthly Labor Review* (January 1984); Carol S. Carson, "The Underground Economy: An Introduction," *Survey of Current Business* (May 1984).

understudy, individual who is engaged in on-the-job training under the direction of a journeyman, or an individual who is specifically hired to replace someone planning to retire.

underutilization, in the context of equal employment opportunity, instance of fewer minorities or women in a particular job classification than would be reasonably expected by their general availability.

undistributed offsetting receipts, *see* OFFSETTING RECEIPTS.

undocumented workers, *see* ILLEGAL ALIENS.

unemployed, experienced, *see* EXPERIENCED UNEMPLOYED.

unemployed, hard-core, *see* HARD-CORE UNEMPLOYED.

unemployed, hidden, *see* DISCOURAGED WORKERS.

unemployment, persons able and willing to work who are actively (but unsuccessfully) seeking to work at the prevailing wage rate. The unemployment rate is probably the most significant indicator of the health of the economy. U.S. economists tend to consider an unemployment rate of about four percent of the total labor force as "full employment." Unemployment statistics are compiled monthly by the Bureau of Labor Statistics. These figures are obtained by surveys of a sample of all U.S. households. The Bureau of the Census, which actually conducts the surveys, defines an unemployed person as a civilian over sixteen years old who, during a given week, was available for work but had none, and (1) had been actively seeking employment during the past month, or (2) was waiting to be recalled from a layoff, or (3) was waiting to report to a new job within thirty days. For the most comprehensive history on the concept of unemployment, *see* John A. Garraty, *Unemployment In History: Economic Thought and Public Policy* (New York: Harper & Row, 1978). Also *see* Philip L. Rones, "Recent Recessions Swell Ranks of the Long Term Unemployed," *Monthly Labor Review* (February 1984); Donald C. Baumer and Carl E. Van Horn, *The Politics of Unemployment* (Washington,

D.C.: Congressional Quarterly Press, 1984).

See also the following entries:
FRICTIONAL UNEMPLOYMENT
PHANTOM UNEMPLOYMENT
PHILLIPS CURVE
RESIDUAL UNEMPLOYMENT
SEASONAL UNEMPLOYMENT
STRUCTURAL UNEMPLOYMENT
TECHNOLOGICAL UNEMPLOYMENT

unemployment benefits, also called UNEMPLOYMENT COMPENSATION, specific payments available to workers from the various state unemployment insurance programs. Unemployment benefits are available as a matter of right (without a means test) to unemployed workers who have demonstrated their attachment to the labor force by a specified amount of recent work and/or earnings in covered employment. To be eligible for benefits, the worker must be ready, able, and willing to work and must be registered for work at a public employment office. A worker who meets these eligibility conditions may still be denied benefits if he or she is disqualified for an act that would indicate the worker is responsible for his or her own unemployment.

A worker's monetary benefit rights are determined on the basis of employment in covered work over a prior reference period (called the "base period"). Under all state laws, the weekly benefit amount— that is, the amount payable for a week of total unemployment—varies with the worker's past wages within certain minimum and maximum limits. In most of the states, the formula is designed to compensate for a fraction of the usual weekly wage, subject to specified dollar maximums.

The requirements for getting unemployment insurance benefits are generally as follows:

1. The worker must register for work at a public employment office and file a claim for benefits.
2. He or she must have worked previously on a job covered by the state law.
3. He or she must have a prescribed amount of employment or earnings in covered employment during a specified "base period," generally a year, prior to the time benefits are claimed.
4. He or she must be able to work. In general, unemployment insurance benefits are not payable to workers who are sick or unable to work for any other reason, although a few states continue to pay the benefits (within the legal limits) to workers who became ill after they had established their claims, so long as no offer of suitable work is refused.
5. The worker must be available for work and must be ready and willing to take a suitable job if one is offered.
6. The worker must not have:
   a. quit his or her job voluntarily without good cause. (In some states, the law says "without good cause attributable to the employer" or "connected with the work.")
   b. been discharged for misconduct in connection with his or her work.
   c. refused or failed, without good cause, to apply for or accept an offer of suitable work. (What is "suitable" work is generally decided by the state. However, under federal law, no worker may be denied benefits for refusing to accept a new job under substandard labor conditions, where a labor dispute is involved, or where the worker would be required to join a company union or to resign from or refrain from joining any bona fide labor organization.)
   d. become unemployed because of a stoppage of work as the result of a labor dispute, in which he or she is interested or participating, that occurred at the establishment where the worker was last employed.

See Joe A. Stone, "The Impact of Unemployment Compensation on the Occupation Decisions of Unemployed Workers," *The Journal of Human Resources* (Spring 1982); Peter S. Saucier and John A. Roberts, "Unemployment Compensation: A Growing Concern for Employers," *Employee Relations Law Journal* (Spring 1984).

See also the following entries:

unemployment insurance, programs designed to provide cash benefits to regularly employed members of the labor force who become involuntarily unemployed and who are able and willing to accept suitable jobs.

The first unemployment insurance law in the United States was passed by Wisconsin in 1932 and served as a forerunner for the unemployment insurance provisions of the Social Security Act of 1935. Unlike the old-age provisions of the social security legislation, which are administered by the federal government alone, the unemployment insurance system was made federal-state in character.

The Social Security Act provided an inducement to the states to enact unemployment insurance laws by means of a tax offset. A uniform national tax was imposed on the payrolls of industrial and commercial employers who in twenty weeks or more in a calendar year had eight workers or more. Employers who paid a tax to a state with an approved unemployment insurance law could credit (offset) the state tax against the national tax (up to 90 percent of the federal levy). Thus, employers in states without an unemployment insurance law would not have an advantage in competing with similar businesses in states with such a law, because they would still be subject to the federal payroll tax. Furthermore, their employees would not be eligible for benefits. In addi-

tion, the Social Security Act authorized grants to states to meet the full costs of administering the state systems. By July, 1937, all forty-eight states, the territories of Alaska and Hawaii, and the District of Columbia had passed unemployment insurance laws. Much later, Puerto Rico adopted its own unemployment insurance program, which was incorporated into the federal-state system in 1961.

Federal law provides that a state unemployment insurance program has to meet certain requirements if employers are to get their offset against the federal tax and if the state is to receive federal grants for administration. These requirements are intended to assure that a state participating in the program has a sound and genuine unemployment insurance system, fairly administered and financially secure. One of these requirements is that all contributions collected under the state laws be deposited in the unemployment trust fund in the U.S. Treasury. The fund is invested as a whole, but each state has a separate account to which its deposits and its share of interest on investments are credited. Aside from certain broad federal standards, each state has responsibility for the content and development of its unemployment insurance law. The state itself decides what the amount and duration of benefits shall be and, with minor limitations, what the coverage and contribution rates shall be, and what the eligibility requirements and disqualification provisions shall be. The states also directly administer the laws—collecting contributions, maintaining wage records (where applicable), taking claims, determining eligibility, and paying benefits to unemployed workers. For a history, see William Haber & Merrill G. Murray, *Unemployment Insurance in the American Economy: An Historical Review and Analysis* (Homewood, Ill.: Richard D. Irwin, 1966). For critiques, see Martin S. Feldstein, "Unemployment Insurance: Time for Reform," *Harvard Business Review* (March–April 1975); Arthur Padilla, "The Unemployment Insurance System: Its Financial Structure," *Monthly Labor Review* (December 1981); Murray Rubin, *Federal-State Relations in Unemployment*

Insurance: A Balance of Power (Kalamazoo, Mich.: W. E. Upjohn Institute for Employment Research, 1983); Diana Runner, "Changes in Unemployment Legislation During 1983," *Monthly Labor Review* (February 1984).

unfair labor practices (employers), certain employer practices that are specifically forbidden by the National Labor Relations (Wagner) Act of 1935. The prohibitions, which serve to protect the right of employees to organize themselves in labor unions, are as follows:

Section 8(a) (1) forbids an employer "to interfere with, restrain, or coerce employees." Any prohibited interference by an employer with the rights of employees to organize, to form, join, or assist a labor organization, to bargain collectively, or to refrain from any of these activities, constitutes a violation of this section. This is a broad prohibition on employer interference, and an employer violates this section whenever it commits any of the other employer unfair labor practices. In consequence, whenever a violation of Section 8 (a) (2), (3), (4), or (5) is committed, a violation of Section 8 (a) (1) is also found. This is called a "derivative violation" of Section 8 (a) (1).

Section 8(a) (2) makes it unlawful for an employer "to dominate or interfere with the formation or administration of any labor organization or contribute financial or other support to it." This section not only outlaws "company unions" that are dominated by the employer, but also forbids an employer to contribute money to a union it favors or to give a union improper advantages that are denied to rival unions.

Section 8(a) (3) makes it an unfair labor practice for an employer to discriminate against employees "in regard to hire or tenure of employment or any term or condition of employment" for the purpose of encouraging or discouraging membership in a labor organization. In general, the act makes it illegal for an employer to discriminate in employment because of an employee's union or other group activity within the protection of the Act. A banding together of employees, even in the absence of a formal organization, may constitute a labor organization for purposes of Section 8 (a) (3). It also prohibits discrimination because an employee has refrained from taking part in such union or group activity except where a valid union-shop agreement is in effect. Discrimination within the meaning of the act would include such action as refusing to hire, discharging, demoting, assigning to a less desirable shift or job, or withholding benefits.

Section 8(a) (4) makes it an unfair labor practice for an employer "to discharge or otherwise discriminate against an employee because he has filed charges or given testimony under this Act." This provision guards the right of employees to seek the protection of the act by using the processes of the NLRB. Like the previous section, it forbids an employer to discharge, lay off, or engage in other forms of discrimination in working conditions against employees who have filed charges with the NLRB, given affidavits to NLRB investigators, or testified at an NLRB hearing. Violations of this section are in most cases also violations of Section 8 (a) (3).

Section 8(a) (5) makes it illegal for an employer to refuse to bargain in good faith about wages, hours, and other conditions of employment with the representative selected by a majority of the employees in a unit appropriate for collective bargaining. A bargaining representative seeking to enforce its right concerning an employer under this section must show that it has been designated by a majority of the employees, that the unit is appropriate, and that there has been both a demand that the employer bargain and a refusal by the employer to do so.

See also the following entries:

BOULWAREISM

MASTRO PLASTICS CORP. V. NATIONAL LABOR RELATIONS BOARD

WILLIAM E. ARNOLD CO. V. CARPENTERS DISTRICT COUNCIL OF JACKSONVILLE

unfair labor practices (unions), forbidden union practices. Twelve years after the passage of the National Labor Relations Act, the Congress became convinced that both employees and employers needed additional legal protections against unfair labor practices of unions, so the Labor-Management Relations (Taft-Hartley) Act of 1947 amended the National Labor Relations Act to include the following major prohibitions:

Section 8(b) (1) (A) forbids a labor organization or its agents "to restrain or coerce employees." The section also provides that it is not intended to "impair the rights of a labor organization to prescribe its own rules" concerning membership in the labor organization. A union may violate this section by coercive conduct of its officers or agents, of pickets on a picket line endorsed by the union, or of strikers who engage in coercion in the presence of union representatives who do not repudiate the conduct. Unlawful coercion may consist of acts specifically directed at an employee, such as physical assaults, threats of violence, and threats to affect an employee's job status. Coercion also includes other forms of pressure against employees, such as acts of a union while representing employees as their exclusive bargaining agent. A union that is a statutory bargaining representative owes a duty of fair representation to all the employees it represents. It may exercise a wide range of reasonable discretion in carrying out the representative function, but it violates Section 8 (b) (1) (A) if, while acting as the employees' statutory bargaining representative, it takes or withholds action in connection with their employment because of their union activities or for any irrelevant or arbitrary reason, such as an employee's race or sex.

Section 8(b) (1) (B) prohibits a labor organization from restraining or coercing an employer in the selection of a bargaining representative. The prohibition applies regardless of whether the labor organization is the majority representa-

tive of the employees in the bargaining unit.

Section 8(b) (2) makes it an unfair labor practice for a labor organization to cause an employer to discriminate against an employee. (Section 8(a) (3) prohibits an employer from discriminating against an employee in regard to wages, hours, and other conditions of employment for the purpose of encouraging or discouraging membership in a labor organization.)

Section 8(b) (3) makes it illegal for a labor organization to refuse to bargain in good faith with an employer about wages, hours, and other conditions of employment if it is the representative of that employer's employees. This section imposes on labor organizations the same duty to bargain in good faith that is imposed on employers by Section 8(a) (5).

Section 8(b) (4) prohibits a labor organization from engaging in a strike, or to induce or encourage a strike, work stoppage, or a refusal to perform services by "any individual employed by any person engaged in commerce or in an industry affecting commerce" in order to foster a secondary boycott, a strike against certification, a jurisdictional strike, or a "hot cargo" agreement.

Section 8(b) (5) makes it illegal for a union to charge employees covered by an authorized union-security agreement a membership fee in an amount the NLRB "finds excessive or discriminatory under all the circumstances."

Section 8(b) (6) forbids a labor organization "to cause or attempt to cause an employer to pay or deliver or agree to pay or deliver any money or other thing of value, in the nature of an exaction, for services which are not performed or not to be performed."

Section 8(b) (7) prohibits a labor organization that is not currently certified as the employees' representative from picketing or threatening to picket with an object of obtaining recognition by the employer (recognitional picketing) or acceptance by his or her employees as their representative (organizational picketing).

See Myron Roomkin, "A Quantitative Study of Unfair Labor Practice Cases," *Industrial and Labor Relations Review* (January 1981); Howard J. Parker and Harold L. Gilmore, "The Unfair Labor Practice Caseload: An Analysis of Selected Remedies," *Labor Law Journal* (March 1982); William J. Payne and Donald F. Sileo, "Self-Enforcement Under the National Labor Relations Act: Disavowals of Unfair Labor Practice Conduct," *Labor Law Journal* (December 1982); Morris M. Kleiner, "Unionism and Employer Discrimination: Analysis of 8(a) (3) Violations," *Industrial Relations* (Spring 1984).

See also BOOSTER LODGE NO. 405, MACHINISTS V. NATIONAL LABOR RELATIONS BOARD and WILLIAM E. ARNOLD CO. V. CARPENTERS DISTRICT COUNCIL OF JACKSONVILLE.

unicameral, see BICAMERAL.

unified budget, see BUDGET, UNIFIED.

Uniformed Sanitation Men's Ass'n v. Commisssioner of Sanitation of the City of New York, see GARDNER V. BRODERICK.

Uniform Guidelines on Employee Selection, guidelines adopted in 1978 by the four federal agencies most concerned with employee selection processes: the Equal Employment Opportunity Commission, the Civil Service Commission, the Department of Justice, and the Department of Labor. The guidelines are designed to assist employers, labor organizations, employment agencies, and licensing and certification boards to comply with requirements of federal law prohibiting employment practices that discriminate on grounds of race, color, religion, sex, or national origin. See James Ledvinka, "The Statistical Definition of Fairness in the Federal Selection Guidelines and Its Implications for Minority Employment," *Personnel Psychology* (Autumn 1979); Marilyn Koch Quaintance, "The Impact of the Uniform Selection Guidelines on Pub-

lic Merit Systems," *Public Personnel Management* (Vol. 9, No. 3, 1980); Charles F. Schanie and William L. Holley, "An Interpretive Review of the Federal Uniform Guidelines on Employee Selection Procedures," *The Personnel Administrator* (June 1980); Ad Hoc Group on the Uniform Selections Guidelines, *A Professional and Legal Analysis of the Uniform Guidelines on Employee Selection Procedures* (Berea, Ohio: American Society for Personnel Administration, 1981).

See also SELECTION PROCEDURE.

uniform user charge, any user charge that makes no pricing distinctions among different kinds of customers, their levels of service, etc.

unincorporated area, an urban area that has not become a city and therefore has no local governmental structure of its own other than its county.

union, see the following entries:
BONA FIDE UNION
BREAD-AND-BUTTER UNIONS
BUSINESS UNIONS
CENTRAL LABOR UNION
CLOSED UNION
COMPANY UNION
CRAFT UNION
GENERAL LABOR UNION
INDEPENDENT UNION
INDUSTRIAL UNION
INTERNATIONAL UNION
LABOR ORGANIZATION
LOCAL INDEPENDENT UNION
LOCAL INDUSTRIAL UNION
LOCAL UNION
MULTICRAFT UNION
NATIONAL UNION
OPEN UNION
UNAFFILIATED UNION
WHITE-COLLAR UNION

union counselor, also called STRIKE COUNSELOR, under ordinary circumstances, a union member who has volunteered to take a training course on the work of his or her community's social agencies. Training completed, the counselor serves as a referral agent in the local union, supplying information about the location, specific services, eligiblity requirements, and application procedures to fellow union members who seek help in resolving some personal or family problem. In the event of a strike, the counselor advises strikers how they may best avail themselves of their community's social welfare programs. *See* Armand J. Thiebolt, Jr., and Ronald M. Cowin, *Welfare and Strikes: The Use of Public Funds to Support Strikers* (Philadelphia: The Wharton School of the University of Pennsylvania, 1972).

union dues, *see* DUES.

unionism, dual, *see* DUAL UNIONISM.

union organizer, *see* ORGANIZER.

union scale, *see* JOURNEYMAN PAY.

union security, any agreement between an employer and a union that requires every employee in the bargaining unit, as a condition of employment, to be a member of the union or to pay a specified sum to the union for its bargaining services. *See* Patricia N. Blair, "Union Security Agreement in Public Employment," *Cornell University Law Review* (January 1975).

union-security clause, provision in a collective bargaining agreement that seeks to protect the union by providing for a constant flow of funds by any of a variety of means. Union-security clauses typically provide for such things as the checkoff, the closed shop, the union shop, the agency shop, preferential hiring, etc. *See* Thomas R. Haggard, *Compulsory Unionism, the NLRB, and the Courts: A Legal Analysis of Union Security Agreements* (Philadelphia: The Wharton School, University of Pennsylvania, 1977); Glenn A. Zipp, "Rights and Responsibilities of Parties to a Union-Security Agreement," *Labor Law Journal* (April 1982).

union shop, union-security provision found in some collective bargaining agreements that requires all employees to become members of the union within a specified time (usually 30 days) after being hired (or after the provision is negotiated) and to remain members of the union as a condition of employment.
See also MODIFIED UNION SHOP.

union steward, *see* STEWARD.

union trusteeship, *see* TRUSTEESHIP.

unit, *see* BARGAINING UNIT.

unit, employer, *see* EMPLOYER UNIT.

unitary tax, *see* TAX UNITARY.

United Airlines v. Evans, 431 U.S. 553 (1977), U.S. Supreme Court case that limited an employer's liability for prior violations under Title VII. The court ruled that an employee who was illegally discriminated against after Title VII took effect could lose her right to retroactive seniority if she fails to file charges within the specified period (now 180 days) after the violation occurred. For an analysis, *see* Stephen L. Swanson, "The Effect of the Supreme Court's Seniority Decisions," *Personnel Journal* (December 1977).

United Airlines v. McMann, 434 U.S. 192 (1977), U.S. Supreme Court case which upheld the Age Discrimination in Employment Act of 1967. The court held that the law, designed to protect the rights of workers age forty to sixty-five, does not prohibit "bona fide" retirement plans that require involuntary termination before the age of sixty-five. However, the act's 1978 amendments overturned the court's decision.

United Mine Workers v. Pennington, 381 U.S. 657 (1965), U.S. Supreme Court case which held that pattern bargaining may leave both employers and unions liable for damages under the Sherman Anti-Trust Act of 1890 if it can be shown that the parties who wrote the pattern-setting contract conspired to impose it on others. *See* Herman A. Gray, "Pennington and the 'Favored Nation' Clause," *Labor Law Journal* (November 1965).

United Public Workers v. Mitchell, *see* UNITED STATES CIVIL SERVICE COMMISSION V. NATIONAL ASSOCIATION OF LETTER CARRIERS.

United States Civil Service Commission, the central personnel agency of the United States from 1883 to 1978. It was abolished by the Civil Service Reform Act of 1978.

See also SERVICE REFORM ACT OF 1978, OFFICE OF PERSONNEL MANAGEMENT, and MERIT SYSTEMS PROTECTION BOARD.

United States Civil Service Commission v. National Association of Letter Carriers, 413 U.S. 548 (1973), U.S. Supreme Court case which upheld the Hatch Act's limitations on the political activities of federal employees.

The *Letter Carriers* decision reaffirmed an earlier court ruling, *United Public Workers* v. *Mitchell,* 330 U.S. 75 (1947), which had held that the ordinary citizen rights of federal employees could be abridged by Congress in the interest of increasing or maintaining the efficiency of the federal service.

In the 1972 case, *National Association of Letter Carriers* v. *United States Civil Service Commission,* the Court of Appeals for the District of Columbia Circuit declared the Hatch Act to be unconstitutional because its vague and "overboard" language made it impossible to determine what it prohibited. When this case was appealed to the Supreme Court the court reasoned that, despite some ambiguities, an ordinary person using ordinary common sense could ascertain and comply with the regulations involved. It also argued that its decision did nothing more than to confirm the judgment of history that political neutrality was a desirable, or even essential, feature of public employment in the United States.

United States Code (U.S.C.), official law-books that contain all federal laws.

United States Conference of Mayors (USCM), an organization of city governments founded in 1933. It is a national forum through which this country's larger cities express their concerns and actively work to meet U.S. urban needs. By limiting membership and participation to the 750 cities with over 30,000 population and by concentrating on questions of federal-city relationships, the Conference seeks to become a focus for urban political leadership.

> United States Conference of Mayors
> 1620 I Street, N.W.
> Washington, D.C. 20006
> (202) 293-7330

United States Court of Appeals, *see* COURT OF APPEALS.

United States District Court, *see* DISTRICT COURT.

United States Employment Service (USES), federal agency within the U.S. Department of Labor which provides assistance to states and territories in establishing and maintaining a system of over 2,500 local public employment offices. Established by the Wagner-Peyser Act of 1933, the USES is responsible for providing job placement and other employment services to unemployed individuals and other jobseekers; providing employers and workers with job development, placement, recruitment, and similar assistance, including employment, counseling and special services to youth, women, older workers, and handicapped persons; and related supportive services. The USES is also responsible for the development of state and local information on employment and unemployment, and on occupational demand and supply necessary for the planning and operation of job training and vocational education programs throughout the country.

The USES develops policies and procedures to provide a complete placement service to workers and employers in rural areas. Migrant and seasonal farm workers receive assistance to help them maintain year-round employment through the federal-state employment services interstate clearance system. The USES is responsible for insuring that, in the interstate recruitment of farm and woods workers, applicable standards and regulations relating to housing, transportation, wages, and other conditions are met.

Other USES services include: certifying aliens who seek to immigrate to the United States for employment; providing employment services and adjustment assistance to U.S. workers adversely affected by foreign imports under the Trade Act of 1974; issuing *Exemplary Rehabilitation Certificates* to qualified persons discharged from the armed services under conditions other than honorable; providing job search guidance and aptitude testing services to workers; giving specialized recruitment assistance to employers; providing labor market information to other federal or state agencies to meet various program responsibilities and to the public on state and local employment conditions; providing guidance, counseling, referral, and placement in apprenticeship opportunities through *Apprenticeship Information Centers* located in selected state employment service offices; reviewing rural industrialization loan and grant certification applications under the Rural Development Act of 1972; maintaining an occupational research program for the compilation of the *Dictionary of Occupational Titles;* and providing bonding assistance to individuals who have been unable to obtain it on their own. *See* Henry P. Guzda, "The U.S. Employment Service at 50: It Too Had to Wait Its Turn," *Monthly Labor Review* (June 1983).

United States Government Manual, annual publication of the federal government that provides detailed information on all agencies of the executive, legislative, and judicial branches of government. The *Manual* includes the names of major federal office holders.

United States International Trade Commission, *see* INTERNATIONAL TRADE COMMISSION, UNITED STATES.

United States Reports, official record of cases decided by the U.S. Supreme Court. When cases are cited, *United States Reports* is abbreviated to "U.S." For example, the legal citation for the case of *Pickering* v. *Board of Education* is 391 U.S. 563 (1968). This means that the case will be found on page 563 of volume 391 of the *United States Reports* and that it was decided in 1968.

United States Statutes at Large, bound volumes issued annually containing all public and private laws and concurrent resolutions enacted during a session of Congress; reorganization plans; proposed and ratified amendments to the Constitution; and presidential proclamations.

United States Tariff Commission, *see* INTERNATIONAL TRADE COMMISSION, UNITED STATES.

United States Treaties and Other International Agreements, *see* EXECUTIVE AGREEMENT.

United States v. **Allen Kaiser,** *see* STRIKE BENEFITS.

United States v. **Belmont,** *see* EXECUTIVE AGREEMENT.

United States v. **Curtis-Wright Export Corporation,** 299 U.S. 304 (1936), Supreme Court case defining the president's constitutional position in foreign affairs. In 1934 Congress adopted a joint resolution authorizing the president by proclamation to prohibit the sale (within the United States) of arms to some South American nations. The president issued such a proclamation. Curtis-Wright attacked the constraint on its business on the grounds that the joint resolution constituted an unconstitutional delegation of legislative authority to the president. The Supreme Court upheld the resolution and proclamation on the grounds that the Constitution created the "very delicate, plenary and exclusive power of the president as the sole organ of the federal government in the field of international relations" and that in the international sphere the president must be accorded "a degree of discretion and freedom from statutory restriction which would not be admissible were domestic affairs alone involved."

United States v. Darby Lumber, 312 U.S. 100 (1941), U.S. Supreme Court case that upheld the Fair Labor Standards Act of 1938, which established minimum wages and maximum hours for workers in businesses engaged in, or producing goods for, interstate commerce.

United States v. Guy W. Capps, Inc., see EXECUTIVE AGREEMENT.

United States v. Hutcheson, 312 U.S. 219 (1941), U.S. Supreme Court case which held that criminal liability could not be imposed, under the Sherman Antitrust Act of 1890, on a union that calls for picketing and/or a boycott against an employer because of a jurisdictional dispute with another union.

United States v. Lee, 106 U.S. 196 (1882), Supreme Court case dealing with the nature of sovereign immunity in the United States.

United States v. Lovett, 328 U.S. 303 (1946), Supreme Court case holding that a congressional effort to dismiss three allegedly "irresponsible, unrepresentative, crackpot, radical bureaucrats" from the executive branch by passing legislation prohibiting the payment of their salaries amounted to an unconstitutional bill of attainder.

United States v. Nixon, 418 U.S. 683 (1974), Supreme Court case dealing with President Nixon's claim that the Constitution provided the president with an absolute and unreviewable executive privilege; that is, the right not to respond to a subpoena in connection with a judicial trial. The court held that "neither the doctrine of separation of powers, nor the need for confidentiality of high-level communications, without more, can sustain an absolute, unqualified, presidential immunity from judicial process under all circumstances." The court allowed that there was a limited executive privilege which might pertain in the areas of military, diplomatic, or security affairs and where confidentiality was related to the president's ability to carry out his constitutional mandates.

See also EXECUTIVE PRIVILEGE.

United States v. Richardson, 418 U.S. 166 (1974), Supreme Court case holding that a taxpayer did not have standing to challenge the Central Intelligence Act of 1949 on the grounds that one of its provisions violates Article I, Section 9, Clause 7 of the Constitution, which requires the government to publish from time to time a "regular statement and account of the receipts and expenditure of all public money." The court reasoned that the challenger was unable to show any concrete injury other than the federal taxes he paid. The challenger, however, could not show any such injury in the absence of published accounts of how the Central Intelligence Agency spent funds derived from taxation.

United States v. Students Challenging Regulatory Agency Procedures (SCRAP), 412 U.S. 669 (1973), Supreme Court case granting standing to five law school students challenging an Interstate Commerce Commission-sanctioned increase in freight rates on the grounds that the increase might reduce the recycling of cans which in turn might pollute the national parks in the Washington, D.C., area and consequently injure the students who use these parks. The case suggests that under present standards one who is injured by governmental activity will have standing to challenge it in court.

United Steelworkers of America v. American Manufacturing Co., 363 U.S. 564 (1960), U.S. Supreme Court case which held that the role of the federal courts is limited when the parties have agreed to submit all questions of contract interpretation to an arbitrator.

See also STEELWORKERS' TRILOGY.

United Steelworkers of America v.

Enterprise Wheel and Car Corp., 363 U.S. 593 (1960), U.S. Supreme Court case which held that the interpretation of a collective bargaining agreement is a question for an arbitrator and the courts do not have the right to overrule an arbitrator because of his interpretation.

See also STEELWORKERS' TRILOGY.

United Steelworkers of America v. Warrior and Gulf Navigation Co., 363 U.S. 574 (1960), U.S. Supreme Court case which held that a labor-management dispute could not be judged to be non-arbitrable unless the parties specifically excluded the subject from the arbitration process.

See also ARBITRABILITY and STEELWORKERS' TRILOGY.

United Steelworkers of America v. Weber, et al., 443 U.S. 193 (1979), decided together with KAISER ALUMINUM & CHEMICAL CORP V. WEBER, ET AL., U.S. Supreme Court decision that upheld an affirmative action program giving blacks preference in selection of employees for a training program.

In 1974, the United Steelworkers of America and Kaiser Aluminum & Chemical Corporation entered into a master collective bargaining agreement covering terms and conditions of employment at fifteen Kaiser plants. The agreement included an affirmative action plan designed to eliminate conspicuous racial imbalances in Kaiser's then almost exclusively white craft work forces. It reserved 50 percent of the openings in in-plant craft training programs for blacks until the percentage of black craft workers in a plant became commensurate with the percentage of blacks in the local labor force. This litigation arose from the operation of the affirmative action plan at one of Kaiser's plants where, prior to 1974, only 1.83 percent of the skilled craft workers were black even though the local work force was approximately 39 percent black. Pursuant to the national agreement, Kaiser, rather than continuing its practice of hiring trained outsiders, established a training program to train its production workers to fill craft openings. Trainees were selected on the basis of seniority, with the proviso that at least 50 percent of the trainees were to be black until the percentage of black skilled craft workers in the plant approximated the percentage of blacks in the local labor force. During the plan's first year of operation, seven black and six white craft trainees were selected from the plant's production work force. The most junior black trainee had less seniority than several white production workers whose bids for admission were rejected. Thereafter, Brian Weber, one of those white production workers, instituted a class action in a federal district court. The suit alleged that because the affirmative action program had resulted in junior black employees receiving training in preference to more senior white employees, Weber and other similarly situated white employees had been discriminated against in violation of Title VII of the Civil Rights Act of 1964 (which makes it unlawful to discriminate because of race in hiring and in the selection of apprentices for training programs).

The district court ruled in favor of Weber. The court of appeals affirmed, holding that all employment preferences based upon race—including those preferences incidental to bona fide affirmative action plans—violated Title VII's prohibition of racial discrimination in employment. The U.S. Supreme Court reversed the lower court rulings. Justice Brennan, in delivering the majority opinion of the court, stated that "the only question before us is the narrow statutory issue of whether Title VII *forbids* private employers and unions from voluntarily agreeing upon bona fide affirmative action plans that accord racial preferences." The court concluded that "Congress did not intend to limit traditional business freedom to such a degree as to prohibit all voluntary, race-conscious affirmative action." Brennan went on to add that because Kaiser's preferential scheme was legal, it was unnecessary to "define in detail the line of demarcation between permissible and impermissible affirmative action plans." See David H. Rosenbloom, "Kaiser vs. Weber: Perspective From the Public Sector," *Pub-*

lic Personnel Management (November-December 1979); Andrew J. Ruzicho, "The *Weber* Case—Its Impact on Affirmative Action," *The Personnel Administrator* (June 1980); David E. Robertson and Ronald D. Johnson, "Reverse Discrimination: Did *Weber* Decide the Issue?" *Labor Law Journal* (November 1980); Ronald D. Johnson, "Voluntary Affirmative Action in the Post-*Weber* Era: Issues and Answers," *Labor Law Journal* (September 1981); William A. Simon, Jr., "Voluntary Affirmative Action After *Weber*," *Labor Law Journal* (March 1983).

See also the following entries:
AFFIRMATIVE ACTION
CIVIL RIGHTS ACT OF 1964
REGENTS OF THE UNIVERSITY OF CALIFORNIA V. ALLAN BAKKE
REVERSE DISCRIMINATION
TITLE VII

unit labor cost, *see* LABOR COSTS.

unit seniority, *see* DEPARTMENTAL SENIORITY.

unity of command, concept that each individual in an organization should be accountable to only a single superior.

unity of direction, concept that there should be only one head and one plan for each organizational segment.

universe, *see* POPULATION.

unobstrusive measures, measures taken without the subject being aware that he or she is being observed. *See* Eugene J. Webb *et al., Unobstrusive Measures: Nonreactive Research in the Social Sciences* (Chicago: Rand McNally, 1966); Eugene Webb and Karl E. Weick, "Unobstrusive Measures in Organization Theory: A Reminder," *Administrative Science Quarterly* (December 1979).

unpatterned interview, *see* PATTERNED INTERVIEW.

unskilled workers, employees whose jobs are confined to manual operations limited to the performance of relatively simple duties requiring only the slightest exercise of independent judgment.

unstructured role playing, role-play exercise or simulation in which the players are not given specific information on the character of their roles.

Upjohn Institute for Employment Research, private, nonprofit organization founded in 1945 to foster "research into the causes and effects of unemployment and to study and investigate the feasibility and methods of insuring against unemployment and devise ways and means of preventing and alleviating the distress and hardship caused by unemployment."

Upjohn Institute for Employment
Research
Kalamazoo, MI 49007
(616) 343-5541

up-or-out system, career system that terminates individuals who do not qualify themselves for the next higher level of the system within a specified time period. The U.S. military officer corps and Foreign Service are two examples of up-or-out systems.

upward-mobility program, systematic management effort that focuses on the development and implementation of specific career opportunities for lower-level employees who are in positions or occupational series which do not enable them to realize their full work potential. An upward-mobility program is usually just one aspect of an organization's overall EEO effort. *See* Thomas E. Diggin, "Upward Mobility—TECOM puts it all Together," *Public Personnel Management* (May-June 1974); Gary Gemmill, "Reward Mapping and Upward Mobility," *Management of Personnel Quarterly* (Winter 1970); Carlene Jackson, "Upward Mobility in State Government," *Training and Development Journal* (April 1979); William T. McCaffrey, "Career Growth Versus Upward Mobility," *Personnel Administrator* (May 1981).

Urban Affairs Quarterly, journal devoted to the social and political aspects of urban life.

Urban Affairs Quarterly
Department of Political Science
Wayne State University
Detroit, MI 48202

urban development, *see* RING THEORY OF URBAN DEVELOPMENT.

urban enterprise zone, *see* ENTERPRISE ZONE.

urban homesteading, programs that give a family a substandard home in a distressed urban area on condition that it be renovated and lived in by that family. Sometimes these programs provide for low-interest home improvement loans and/or sell the homes for token amounts. *See* James W. Hughes and Kenneth Bleakly, Jr., *Urban Homesteading* (New Brunswick, N.J.: Center for Urban Policy Research, 1975); Anne Clark and Zelma Rivin, "The Administrative Models of Urban Homesteading," *Public Administration Review* (May–June 1977).

Urban Institute, research organization founded in 1968 to provide independent studies of and solutions to urban problems.

Urban Institute
2100 M Street, N.W.
Washington, D.C. 20037
(202) 223-1950

Urban League, *see* NATIONAL URBAN LEAGUE.

urban park movement, part of the general movement of the turn of the century that attempted to create urban parks. The major premise of the movement was that parks created an environment that helped to ameliorate the immoral and squalid conditions of urban life occasioned by the industrialization of the United States.

urban planning, formal process of guiding the physical and social development of cities and their regions. *See* James Q.

Wilson, "Planning and Politics: Citizen Participation in Urban Renewal," *Journal of the American Institute of Planners* (November 1963); Darwin Stuart, *Systematic Urban Planning* (New York: Praeger, 1976); W. G. Roeseler, *Successful American Urban Plans* (Lexington, Mass.: Lexington Books, 1981).
See PLANNING.

urban renewal, also called URBAN REDE-VELOPMENT, national program started in 1949 to rejuvenate urban areas through large-scale physical projects. Originally a loan program primarily for housing, it was quickly transformed by political pressures into a grant program for redoing large sections of the central business district or other commercial areas. It has been severely criticized for its uprooting of communities, especially black neighborhoods, and replacing them with commercial developments. *See* Martin Anderson, *The Federal Bulldozer: A Critical Analysis of Urban Renewal* (Cambridge, Mass.: M.I.T. Press, 1964), James Q. Wilson, ed., *Urban Renewal* (Cambridge, Mass.: M.I.T. Press, 1966).

Urwick, Lyndall F. (1891–1983), one of the pioneers of the classical school of organization theory. Major works include: *Papers on the Science of Administration,* with Luther Gulick (New York: Institute of Public Administration, 1937); *Scientific Principles of Organization* (New York: American Management Association, 1938); *The Elements of Administration* (New York: Harper & Bros., 1944); *The Pattern of Management* (Minneapolis: University of Minnesota Press, 1956); *Staff in Organization,* with Ernest Dale (New York: McGraw-Hill, 1960).

U.S., *see* UNITED STATES REPORTS.

U.S.C., *see* UNITED STATES CODE.

USCM, *see* UNITED STATES CONFERENCE OF MAYORS.

USDA, *see* AGRICULTURE, DEPARTMENT OF.

user charges, also called USER FEES, specific sums that users or consumers of a government service pay in order to receive that service. For example, a homeowner's water bill, if based upon usage, would be a user charge. *See* Calvin A. Kent, "Users' Fees for Municipalities," *Governmental Finance* (February 1972); Bruce A. Webber, "User Charges, Property Taxes, and Population Growth: The Distributional Implications of Alternative Municipal Financing Strategies," *State and Local Government Review* (January 1981); Timothy B. Clark, "Users Pay More," *National Journal* (May 30, 1981).

Usery v. Turner Elkhorn Mining Co., 428 U.S. 1 (1976), U.S. Supreme Court case which upheld that portion of the Federal Coal Mine Health and Safety Act of 1969 making coal mine operators liable for benefits to former miners (and their dependents) who have suffered from black-lung disease (pneumoconiosis).

USES, *see* UNITED STATES EMPLOYMENT SERVICE.

USPS, *see* POSTAL SERVICE, UNITED STATES.

V

VA, *see* VETERANS ADMINISTRATION.

vacancy, available position for which an organization is actively seeking to recruit a worker.

vacating an award, court's setting aside of an arbitration award.

vacation pay, pay for specified periods of time off work. The vacation or leave time that an employee earns frequently varies with length of service.

valence, in Victor H. Vroom's "Expectancy Theory of Motivation," the value an employee places on an incentive or reward. For a full account of Vroom's theory, *see* his *Work and Motivation* (New York: John Wiley & Sons, 1964). For a test of it, *see* Robert Pritchard, Philip DeLeo, and Clarence Von Bergen, Jr., "The Field Experimental Test of Expectancy—Valence Incentive Motivation Techniques," *Organizational Behavior and Human Performance* (April 1976).
See also EXPECTANCY THEORY.

validation, process of investigation by which the validity of a particular type of test use is estimated. What is important here is to identify an ambiguity in the term "to validate," which is responsible for much confusion in the area of employment testing. To validate in ordinary language may mean to mark with an indication of official approval. In this sense, it is also possible to "invalidate," or to indicate official disapproval. In the technical vocabulary of employment testing, to validate is to investigate, to conduct research. Thus, in validating a test (more properly, in validating a use of a test), one is conducting an inquiry. In this context, the term "invalidating" has no meaning at all. *See* Douglas D. Baker and David E. Terpstra, "Employee Selection: Must Every Job Test Be Validated?" *Personnel Journal* (August 1982).
See also the following entries:
CONSENSUAL VALIDATION
CRITERION RELATED VALIDATION
CROSS VALIDATION
DIFFERENTIAL VALIDATION
GRIGGS V. DUKE POWER CO.
STATISTICAL VALIDATION
VALIDITY

validity, extent to which a test measures what it is supposed to measure or the accuracy of inferences drawn from test scores.
See also the following entries:
CONCURRENT VALIDITY
CONSTRUCT VALIDITY
CONTENT VALIDITY

CONVERGENT VALIDITY
CURRICULAR VALIDITY
DISCRIMINANT VALIDITY
EMPIRICAL VALIDITY
FACE VALIDITY
ITEM VALIDITY
OPERATIONAL VALIDITY
PREDICTIVE VALIDITY
RATIONAL VALIDITY
SYNTHETIC VALIDITY
VALIDATION

validity coefficient, correlation coefficient that estimates the relationship between scores on a test (or test battery) and the criterion.

Valley Forge Christian College* v. *Americans United for Separation of Church and State, 70 L.Ed. 2d 700 (1982), U.S. Supreme Court case which held that a taxpayers' organization dedicated to separation of church and state was without standing to challenge "no-cost transfer of surplus" U.S. property to religious educational institutions.

value-added tax (VAT), type of national sales tax imposed by almost all Western European countries as a major source of revenue, levied on the value added at each stage of production and distribution.
Proponents of VAT in the United States argue that VAT rewards efficiency, and thus is superior to the corporate income tax in allocating economic resources; it can encourage savings and capital formation because it is a tax solely on consumption; it can help balance-of-payments problems because it can be imposed on imports and rebated on exports; and it can be a major new source of revenue of meeting domestic spending needs, especially social security costs. Opponents of VAT in the United States charge that it is a regressive tax (*i.e.,* it falls most heavily on the poor); think it is inflationary, in that prices to consumers go up; and fear it will be an additional tax rather than a substitute for present taxes. *See* Henry J. Aaron, ed., *The Value-Added Tax: Lessons from Europe* (Washington, D.C.: The Brook-

ings Institution, 1981); William J. Turnier, "Designing an Efficient Value Added Tax," *Tax Law Review* (Summer 1984).

Vance* v. *Bradley, 440 U.S. 93 (1979), U.S. Supreme Court case which held that requiring officers of the U.S. Foreign Service to retire at age sixty did not violate the equal protection component of the due process clause of the Fifth Amendment, even though other federal employees do not face mandatory retirement at such an early age.

variable, any factor or condition subject to measurement, alteration, and/or control.

variable, contextual, *see* CONTEXTUAL VARIABLE.

variable annuity, also called ASSET-LINKED ANNUITY, annuity that varies with the value of assets. In an effort to protect the purchasing power of a pensioner, some pension plans link benefit accruals to the value of an associated asset portfolio. Upon retirement, the pensioner may have the option of continuing to receive asset-linked benefits or to convert total benefits to a conventional fixed-income annuity.

variable life insurance, form of life insurance whose death benefit is dependent upon the performance of investments in a common portfolio.

variance, difference between an expected or standard value and an actual one.

variance analysis, *see* ANALYSIS OF VARIANCE.

velvet ghetto, organizational unit (such as a public relations department) that is overloaded with women in response to an affirmative action program and in compensation for their scarcity in other professional or management categories. For a discussion, *see* "PR: 'The Velvet

Ghetto' of Affirmative Action," *Business Week* (May 8, 1978).

vertical communication, *see* COMMUNICATION.

vertical conflict, bureaucratic conflict between differing hierarchical levels of an agency.

vertical equity, *see* TAX EQUITY.

vertical federalism, *see* FEDERALISM, HORIZONTAL.

vertical loading, *see* JOB LOADING.

vertical occupational mobility, *see* OCCUPATIONAL MOBILITY.

vertical training, simultaneous training of people who work together, irrespective of their status in the organization.

vertical union, *see* INDUSTRIAL UNION.

vertical work group, work group containing individuals whose positions differ in rank, prestige, and level of skill.

vested benefit, *see* VESTING.

vestibule training, training that prepares a new employee for an occupation after acceptance for employment but before the assumption of the new job's duties, for example, rookie training for new police.

vesting, granting an employee the right to a pension at normal retirement age even if the employee leaves the organization before the age of normal retirement. A vested benefit is usually based on accrued pension credit, as opposed to the pension for which the employee would have been eligible had he/she remained in the organization until retirement.
See also DEFERRED FULL VESTING, DEFERRED GRADED VESTING, and IMMEDIATE FULL VESTING.

veteran, disabled, *see* DISABLED VETERAN.

Veterans Administration (VA), federal agency that administers benefits for veterans and their dependents. These benefits include compensation payments for disabilities or death related to military service; pensions based on financial need for totally disabled veterans or certain survivors for disabilities or death not related to military service; education and rehabilitation; home loan guaranty; burial, including cemeteries, markers, flags, etc.; and a comprehensive medical program involving a widespread system of nursing homes, clinics, and more than 170 medical centers.
VA
810 Vermont Avenue, N.W.
Washington, D.C. 20420
(202) 393-4120

veterans preference, concept that dates from 1865, when Congress, toward the end of the Civil War, affirmed that "persons honorably discharged from the military or naval service by reason of disability resulting from wounds or sickness incurred in the line of duty, shall be preferred for appointments to civil offices, provided they are found to possess the business capacity necessary for the proper discharge of the duties of such offices." The 1865 law was superseded in 1919, when preference was extended to all "honorably discharged" veterans, their widows, and wives of disabled veterans. The Veterans Preference Act of 1944 expanded the scope of veterans preference by providing for a five-point bonus on federal examination scores for all honorably separated veterans (except for those with a service-connected disability, who are entitled to a ten-point bonus). Veterans also received other advantages in federal employment (such as protections against arbitrary dismissal and preference in the event of a reduction-in-force).

All states and many other jurisdictions have veterans preference laws of varying intensity. New Jersey, an extreme example, offers veterans absolute preference: if a veteran passes an entrance examination, he/she must be hired (no matter what his/her score) before nonveterans can be hired. Veterans competing with each other are rank ordered, and all disabled veterans receive preference over other veterans. Veterans preference laws have been criticized because they have allegedly made it difficult for government agencies to hire and promote more women and minorities. Although the original version of the Civil Service Reform Act of 1978 sought to limit veterans preference in the federal service, the final version contained a variety of new provisions *strengthening* veterans preference. *See* Charles E. Davis, "Veterans' Preference and Civil Service Employment: Issues and Policy Implications," *Review of Public Personnel Administration* (Fall 1982).

See also PERSONNEL ADMINISTRATOR OF MASSACHUSETTS V. FEENEY and MILITARY SERVICE.

Veterans Readjustment Assistance Act of 1974, federal statute that required contractors with federal contracts of $10,000 or more to establish programs to take "affirmative action" to employ and advance in employment all disabled veterans (with thirty percent or more disability) and other veterans for the first forty-eight months after discharge.

veterans reemployment rights, reemployment rights program, under provisions of Chapter 43 of Title 38, U.S. Code, for men and women who leave their jobs to perform training or service in the armed forces. The Office of Veterans Reemployment Rights of the Labor-Management Services Administration of the U.S. Department of Labor has responsibility for the program. In general terms, to be entitled to reemployment rights a veteran must leave a position (other than a temporary position) with a private employer, the federal government, or a state or local government for the purpose of entering the armed forces, voluntarily or involuntarily. The employer is generally obligated to reemploy the veteran within a reasonable time after he/she makes application for the position he/she would have occupied if he/she had remained on the job instead

of entering military service.
See also FOSTER V. DRAVO CORP.

veto, also ITEM VETO and POCKET VETO, word derived from the Latin meaning "I forbid." The president is authorized by the Constitution to refuse his assent to any measure presented by Congress for his approval. In such case, he returns the measure to the house in which it originated, at the same time indicating his objections—the so-called veto message. The veto goes to the entire measure; the president is not authorized, as are the governors of some states, to veto separate items in a bill. This power to veto separate items is called the *item veto*.

By the Constitution the president is allowed ten days (exclusive of Sundays) from the date of receiving a bill within which to give it his approval; if within ten days Congress adjourns and so prevents the return of a bill to which the president objects, that bill does not become law. In many cases, where bills have been sent to him toward the close of a session, the president has taken advantage of this provision, and has held until after adjournment measures of which he disapproved but which for some reason did not wish to return with his objections to Congress for their further action. This action is the so-called *pocket veto*. It is also used by state governors. *See* Ray L. Brown, "A Route to Increased Federal Fiscal Control: Line Item Veto," *Government Accountants Journal* (Fall 1984); Glenn Abney and Thomas P. Lauth, "The Line-Item Veto in the States: An Instrument for Fiscal Restraint or an Instrument of Partisanship?" *Public Administration Review* (May–June 1985).

See also CONGRESSIONAL VETO.

Vietnam Era Veterans Readjustment Act of 1974, *see* VETERANS READJUSTMENT ACT OF 1974.

village, *see* TOWN.

VISTA, *see* ACTION.

vocational behavior, total realm of

human actions and interactions related to the work environment, including preparation for work, participation in the workforce, and retirement. For a text, *see* Donald G. Zytowski, *Vocational Behavior: Readings in Theory and Research* (New York: Holt, Rinehart and Winston, 1968).

vocational counseling, any professional assistance given to an individual preparing to enter the workforce concerning the choice of occupation.

Vocational Education Act of 1963, federal statute that authorized federal grants to states to assist them to maintain, extend, and improve existing programs of vocational education; to develop new programs of vocational education; and to provide part time employment for youths who need the earnings from such employment to continue their vocational training on a full time basis.

See also SMITH-HUGHES ACT OF 1917.

vocational maturity, term premised upon the belief that vocational behavior is a developmental process; it implies a comparison of an individual's chronological and vocational ages. For a model of vocational maturity, *see* John O. Crites, "Career Development Processes: A Model of Vocational Maturity," in Edwin Herr, ed., *Vocational Guidance and Human Development* (Boston: Houghton Mifflin Co., 1974).

vocational maturity quotient, ratio of vocational maturity to chronological age.

vocational psychology, scientific study of vocational behavior and development. According to John O. Crites, in *Vocational Psychology* (New York: McGraw-Hill, 1969):

Historically the field of vocational psychology grew out of the practice of vocational guidance. It seems desirable to differentiate between them, however, if vocational psychology is to become firmly established as the science of vocational behavior and development— unconfounded with the purposes and

procedures of vocational guidance, which is still largely an art. There is one important area of overlap (approximately 10 percent) which should be mentioned. To the extent that vocational guidance, as a stimulus or treatment condition, is functionally related to vocational behavior, then it falls within the purview of vocational psychology as a field of study.

vocational rehabilitation, restoration of the handicapped to the fullest physical, mental, social, vocational, and economic usefulness of which they are capable. *See* Ronald W. Conley, *The Economics of Vocational Rehabilitation* (Baltimore: Johns Hopkins Press, 1965).

Vocational Rehabilitation Act of 1973, federal statute that requires federal contractors with contracts in excess of $2,500 to "take affirmative action to employ and advance in employment qualified handicapped individuals." The act also established within the federal government an Interagency Committee on Handicapped Employees whose purpose is "(1) to provide a focus for Federal and other employment of handicapped individuals, and to review, on a periodic basis, in cooperation with the Civil Service Commission [now Office of Personnel Management] the adequacy of hiring, placement, and advancement practices with respect to handicapped individuals, by each department, agency, and instrumentality in the executive branch of Government, and to insure that the special needs of such individuals are being met; and (2) to consult with the Civil Service Commission to assist the Commission to carry out its responsibilities" in implementing affirmative action programs for the handicapped.

vocational training, formal preparation for a particular business or trade.

voice stress analyzer, *see* LIE DETECTOR.

voluntary arbitration, arbitration agreed

to by two parties in the absence of any legal or contractual requirement.

voluntary bargaining items, those items over which collective bargaining is neither mandatory nor illegal

voluntary demotion, see DEMOTION.

Von Bertalanffy, Ludwig, see BER-TALANFFY, LUDWIG VON.

voucher, in staffing terms, a formal inquiry to employers, references, professors, and others who presumably know a job applicant well enough to describe his job qualifications and personal character.

Vroom, Victor H. (1932-), industrial psychologist and a leading authority on organizational motivation and leadership. His major work on expectancy theory is *Work and Motivation* (New York: John Wiley, 1964).
　See also VALENCE.

vulnerability assessment, an evaluation of the susceptibility of organization functions, programs, or projects in question to future loss of revenues or budgetary reductions.

W

wage, guaranteed annual, see GUARANTEED ANNUAL WAGE.

wage, living, see LIVING WAGE.

wage and hour laws, the federal and state laws which set minimum wages and maximum hours for workers. See FAIR LABOR STANDARDS ACT.

wage-and-price controls, a government's formal efforts to control inflation by

regulating the wages and prices of its economic system. For accounts of the wage-and-price controls of the 1971 to 1974 period, see George P. Shultz and Kenneth W. Dam, "Reflections on Wage and Price Controls," *Industrial and Labor Relations Review* (January 1977); Robert A. Kagan, *Regulatory Justice: Implementing a Wage-Price Freeze* (New York: Basic Books, 1978). *Also see* Hugh Rockoff, "Price and Wage Controls in Four Wartime Periods," *Journal of Economic History* (June 1981).
　See also FRY V. UNITED STATES.

Wage and Price Stability, Council on, see COUNCIL ON WAGE AND PRICE STABILITY.

wage and salary administration, according to Herbert G. Zollitsch and Adolph Langsner, in *Wage and Salary Administration,* 2nd ed. (Cincinnati, Ohio: South-Western Publishing Co., 1970), administration that "may be thought of as the planning, organizing, and controlling of those activities that relate to the direct and indirect payments made to employees for the work they perform or the services they render." *Also see* John D. McMillan and Valerie C. Williams, "The Elements of Effective Salary Administration Programs," *Personnel Journal* (November 1982); Milton L. Rock, ed., *Handbook of Wage and Salary Administration,* 2nd ed. (New York: McGraw-Hill, 1983); Leonard R. Burgess, *Wage and Salary Administration: Pay and Benefits* (Columbus, Ohio: Charles E. Merrill, 1984).

wage and salary survey, see WAGE SURVEY.

Wage and Tax Statement, see FORM W-2.

wage arbitration, referral of a wage dispute to an arbitrator.

wage area, national and/or regional areas selected on the basis of population size, employment, location, or other criteria for wage surveys. See James N. Houff, "Improving Area Wage Survey Indexes," *Monthly Labor Review* (January 1973).

wage assignment, voluntary transfer of earned wages to a third party to pay debts, buy savings bonds, pay union dues, etc.

wage compression, *see* SALARY COMPRESSION.

wage criteria, those external and internal standards or factors that determine the internal pay structure of an organization. According to David W. Belcher, in *Compensation Administration* (Englewood Cliffs, N.J.: Prentice-Hall, 1974),

> wage criteria may be used by organizations and unions to rationalize positions taken as well as to arrive at these positions. Also, strictly applying the various criteria would in many situations result in conflicting decisions. For example, if the cost of living is up 10 percent and ability to pay is down 10 percent, comparable wages in the area justify a 5 percent increase, and comparable wages in the industry call for a 5 percent decrease, what change in wage level is justified?

wage differentials, differences in wages paid for identical or similar work that are justified because of differences in work schedules, hazards, cost of living, or other factors. *See* Orel R. Winjum, "Negotiated Wage Rate Differentials," *Personnel Journal* (August 1971); Robert J. Newman, "Dynamic Patterns in Regional Wage Differentials," *Southern Economic Journal* (July 1982).

wage drift, concept that explains the gap between basic wage rates and actual earnings, which tend to be higher because of overtime, bonuses, and other monetary incentives.

Wage Earner Plan, title of Chapter 13 of the Bankruptcy Act, which allows anyone who is employed to get an extension of time to pay off debts in lieu of bankruptcy if the employee submits all earnings to court jurisdiction until all creditors have been paid. For details, *see* Irving L. Berg, "The Wage Earner Plan as an Alternative to Bankruptcy," *Personnel Journal* (March 1971).

wage floor, minimun wage established by contract or law.

wage garnishment, *see* GARNISHMENT.

wage increase, deferred, *see* DEFERRED WAGE INCREASE.

wage inequity, *see* COGNITIVE DISSONANCE.

wage parity, *see* PARITY.

wage-price freeze, *see* WAGE-AND-PRICE CONTROLS.

wage progression, progressively higher wage rates that can be earned in the same job. Progression takes place on the basis of length of service, merit, or other criteria.

wage range, *see* PAY RANGE.

wage reopener clause, *see* REOPENER CLAUSE.

wages, also SALARY, as defined by J. D. Dunn and Frank M. Rachel, in *Wage and Salary Administration: Total Compensation Systems* (New York: McGraw-Hill, 1971):

> The remuneration (pay) received by an employee (or group of employees) for services rendered during a specific period of time—hour, day, week, or month. Traditionally, the term "wages" has been used to denote the pay of a factory employee or any employee on an hourly rate, and "salary" has been used to denote the pay of an administrative, professional, clerical, or managerial employee on a weekly, monthly, or annual time basis.
> *See also* the following entries:
> BARGAINING THEORY OF WAGES
> BOOTLEG WAGES
> COMPETITIVE WAGES
> INDIRECT WAGES
> IRON LAW OF WAGES
> REAL WAGES

LIVING WAGE
PAY
SALARY

Wages and Hours Act, see FAIR LABOR STANDARDS ACT.

wage survey, also called WAGE AND SALARY SURVEY, and AREA WAGE SURVEY, formal effort to gather data on compensation rates and/or ranges for comparable jobs within an area, industry, or occupation. Wage surveys on both a national and regional bases are available from such organizations as the American Management Association, the International Personnel Management Association, and the International City Management Association. See Bruce R. Ellig, "Salary Surveys: Design to Application," *The Personnel Administrator* (October 1977); James N. Houff, "Improving Area Wage Survey Indexes," *Monthly Labor Review* (January 1973); Michael A. Conway, "Salary Surveys: Avoid the Pitfalls," *Personnel Journal* (June 1984).
See also COMMUNITY WAGE SURVEY.

wage tax, any tax on wages and salaries levied by a government. Many cities have wage taxes that force suburban commuters to help pay for the services provided to the region by the central city.

Wagner Act, see NATIONAL LABOR RELATIONS ACT OF 1935.

Wagner-O'Day Act, federal statute which provides that sheltered workshops serving blind and severely handicapped persons shall receive special preference in bidding on federal government contracts for products and services.

Wagner-Peyser Act of 1933, federal statute that established the U.S. Employment Service in the Department of Labor to assist in the development of a cooperative nationwide system of public employment offices.

Waldo, (Clifford) Dwight (1913-), pre-eminent historian of the academic discipline of public administration and editor-in-chief of *Public Administration Review* from 1966 to 1977. Waldo first became an influence in public administration when he attacked the "gospel of efficiency" that so dominated administrative thinking prior to World War II. In his landmark book, *The Administrative State: A Study of the Political Theory of American Public Administration* (New York: Ronald Press Co., 1948), he asserted that the drive for efficiency has "occasionally served the end of those whose purposes might be regarded as more or less reprehensible if stated in another idiom." Other major works include: *Ideas and Issues in Public Administration,* ed. (New York: McGraw-Hill, 1953); *The Study of Public Administration* (New York: Random House, 1955); *Perspectives on Administration* (University, Ala.: University of Alabama Press, 1956); *Public Administration in a Time of Turbulence,* ed. (Scranton, Pa.: Chandler Publishing Company, 1971); *The Enterprise of Public Administration* Novato, Calif · Chandler & Sharp Publishers, 1980).
See also POSTBUREAUCRATIC ORGANIZATIONS.

walk-around pay, pay for workers who "walk around" with federal inspectors. Occupational Safety and Health Administration inspectors must sometimes be accompanied on their plant inspections.

walkout, see STRIKE.

Walsh-Healey Public Contracts Act of 1936, federal statute establishing basic labor standards for work done on U.S. government contracts exceeding $10,000 in value.

warm-up effect, adjustment process that takes place at the start of work. The warm-up period is over when the work curve reaches its first peak.

War on Poverty, see ECONOMIC OPPORTUNITY ACT OF 1964.

warrant, a short-term obligation issued by

a government in anticipation of revenue. The instrument, or draft, when presented to a disbursing officer, such as a bank, is payable only upon acceptance by the issuing jurisdiction. Warrants may be made payable on demand or at some time in the future. Local governments, in particular, have used delayed payment of warrants as a way to protect cash flow.

Washington Monthly, The, journal that focuses on public policy and the bureaucracy.

The Washington Monthly
Washington Monthly Company
1711 Connecticut Ave., N.W.
Washington, D.C. 20009

Washington v. Davis, 426 U.S. 229 (1976), U.S. Supreme Court case which held that although the Due Process Clause of the Fifth Amendment prohibits the government from invidious discrimination, it does not follow that a law or other official act is unconstitutional *solely* because it has a racially disproportionate impact. The court ruled that, under the Constitution (as opposed to Title VII of the Civil Rights Act of 1964), there must be discriminatory purpose or intent—adverse impact alone is insufficient. *See* Carl F. Goodman, "Public Employment and the Supreme Court's 1975-76 Term," *Public Personnel Management* (September–October 1976).

wash up, *see* CLEAN-UP TIME.

Watergate, the scandal that led to the resignation of President Richard M. Nixon. "Watergate" itself refers to the hotel-office-apartment complex in Washington, D.C. When individuals associated with the Committee to Reelect the President were caught breaking into the Democratic National Committee Headquarters (then located in the Watergate complex) in 1972, the resulting cover-up and national trauma was condensed into one word—Watergate. The term has grown to refer to any political crime or instance of bureaucratic corruption that undermines confidence in governing institutions. *See* James L. Sundquist, "Reflections on Watergate:

Lessons for Public Administration," *Public Administration Review* (September–October 1974); Frederick C. Mosher *et al.,* *Watergate: Implications for Responsible Government* (New York: Basic Books, 1974); Ronald E. Pynn, ed., *Watergate and the American Political Process* (New York: Praeger, 1975).

Water Pollution Control Act, federal statute originally passed in 1948, strengthened in 1956, and significantly amended in 1972 by establishing federal responsibility for attaining fishable/swimmable waters by 1983 and for ending pollution in all U.S. waterways by 1985. To achieve their goals, industries were to install the "best practicable technology" (BPT) by 1977 and the "best available technology" (BAT) by 1983. Municipalities were to install secondary sewage treatment facilities by 1977 and BPT by 1983. These requirements were enforced through a federal permit system that specified discharge limitations and performance standards.

In 1977, the act was amended to extend industry deadlines under certain circumstances for BPT and BAT to 1979 and 1984, respectively. The new amendments permit the extension of deadline requirements for municipal treatment plants on a case-by-case basis. *See* Russell L. Culp, George Mark Wesner and Gordon L. Culp, *Handbook of Advanced Wastewater Treatment,* 2nd ed. (New York: Van Nostrand Reinhold, 1978); Joseph L. Pavoni, ed., *Handbook of Water Quality Management Planning* (New York: Van Nostrand Reinhold, 1977).

water rights, also SEWER TAPS, term used in the western states where water is scarce. The law concerning water centered on the creation of exclusive rights to a particular water source. This contrasts with the eastern system of riparian rights in which all persons having access to a water source have a right to a proportionate share. Consequently, western cities are constantly engaged in a struggle to secure rights to a sufficient supply of water. Hence water politics are very important and the ensuing struggles often lead to limitations on growth and development through the allocation of water and sewer taps; that is, the ability to connect into the local water and sewer supply lines. For a history of urban water supply, *see* Nelson M. Blake, *Water for the Cities: A History of the Urban Water Supply Problem in the United States* (Syracuse, N.Y.: Syracuse University Press, 1956).

weak mayor, *see* MAYOR-COUNCIL SYSTEM.

Weber, Max (1864-1920), German sociologist who produced an analysis of bureaucracy that is still the most influential statement—the point of departure for all further analyses—on the subject. For a biography, *see* Reinhard Bendix, *Max Weber: An Intellectual Portrait* (Garden City, N.Y.: Doubleday, 1960).

Weber decision, *see* UNITED STEELWORKERS OF AMERICA V. WEBER, ET AL.

weighted application blank, application in which weights or numeric values can be placed on the varying responses to application blank items. After a job analysis determines the knowledges, skills, and abilities necessary to perform the duties of a position, corresponding personal characteristics can be elicited. Applicants who score highest on the weighted application blank would be given first consideration. *See* H. M. Trice, "The Weighted Application Blank—A Caution," *The Personnel Administrator* (May-June 1964); Richard D. Scott and Richard W. Johnson, "Use of the Weighted Application Blank in Selecting Unskilled Employees," *Journal of Applied Psychology* (October 1967).

welfare, public financial assistance to certain categories of poor persons. *See* M. Donna Price Cofer, *Administering Public Assistance: A Constitutional and Administrative Perspective* (Port Washington, N.Y.: Kennikat Press, 1982).
See also the following entries:
BATTERTON V. FRANCIS
ENTITLEMENT PROGRAM
GOLDBERG V. KELLY

MATHEWS V. ELDRIDGE
PUBLIC WELFARE
RELIEF

welfare funds, employer contributions, agreed to during collective bargaining, to a common fund to provide welfare benefits to the employees of all of the contributing employers.

welfare state, a governing system where it is public policy that government will strive for the maximum economic and social benefits for each of its citizens short of changing the operating premises of the society. The line between an extreme welfare state and socialism is so thin that its existence is debatable. *See* Edward D. Berkowitz and Kim McQuaid, *Creating the Welfare State: The Political Economy of Twentieth Century Reform* (New York: Praeger, 1980); Roger A. Freeman, *The Wayward Welfare State* (Stanford, Calif.: Stanford University, Hoover Institution Press, 1981); Richard E. Just, Darrell L. Hueth, and Andrew Schmitz, *Applied Welfare Economics and Public Policy* (Englewood Cliffs, N.J.: Prentice-Hall, 1982); Bruce R. Scott, "Can Industry Survive the Welfare State," *Harvard Business Review* (September-October 1982).
See also PUBLIC WELFARE.

wellness program, a formal effort on the part of an employer to maintain the mental and physical health of its work force. *See* Gordon F. Shea, "Profiting From Wellness Training," *Training and Development Journal* (October 1981); John P. McCann, M.D., "Control Data's 'Staywell' Program," *Training and Development Journal* (October 1981).

well pay, also called SWEEP PAY, incentive payments to workers who are neither "sick" nor late over a specified time period. In some companies, well pay is called "sweep pay" for "Stay at Work, Earn Extra Pay." *See* Barron H. Harvey, Jerome F. Rogers, and Judy A. Schultze, "Sick Pay vs. Well Pay: An Analysis of the Impact of Rewarding Employees for Being on the Job," *Public Personnel Management* (Summer 1983).

West Coast Hotel v. Parrish, 300 U.S. 379 (1937), U.S. Supreme Court case which upheld the minimum wage law of the State of Washington by declaring that a minimum wage law did not violate the freedom of contract provided by the due process clause of the 14th Amendment. This case overruled the court's earlier decision, *Adkins v. Children's Hospital,* 261 U.S. 525 (1923), which held unconstitutional a federal law establishing minimum wages for women and children in the District of Columbia.

"When in charge, ponder. When in trouble, delegate. When in doubt, mumble," *see* INTERNATIONAL ASSOCIATION OF PROFESSIONAL BUREAUCRATS.

whipsaw strike, strike stratagem that uses one struck employer as an example to others in order to encourage them to accede to union demands without the necessity of additional strikes.

whistle blower, individual who believes the public interest overrides the interests of their organization and publicly "blows the whistle" if their organization is involved in corrupt, illegal, fraudulent, or harmful activity. For accounts of famous whistle blowers, *see* Ralph Nader, Peter J. Petkas, and Kate Blackwell, eds., *Whistle Blowing: The Report of the Conference on Professional Responsibility* (New York: Grossman Publishers, 1972); Charles Peters and Taylor Branch, eds., *Blowing The Whistle: Dissent in the Public Interest* (New York: Praeger Publishers, 1972); *also see* Kenneth D. Walters, "Your Employees' Right to Blow the Whistle," *Harvard Business Review* (July–August 1975); James S. Bowman, "Whistle-Blowing in the Public Service: An Overview of the Issues," *Review of Public Personnel Administration* (Fall 1980); Arthur L. Burnett, "Management's Positive Interest in Accountability Through Whistleblowing," *Bureaucrat* (Summer 1980); James S. Bowman, "Whistle Blowing: Literature and Resource

Materials," *Public Administration Review* (May–June 1983).
    See also FITZGERALD, A. ERNEST.

White, Leonard D. (1891–1958), author of the first public administration text in 1926, author of the standard administrative histories of the United States government in the 19th century, and one of the most significant voices in the development of public administration as an academic discipline. Major works include: *Introduction to the Study of Public Administration* (New York: Harper & Bros., 1926; 4th edition, 1955); *The City Manager* (Chicago: University of Chicago Press, 1927); *The Prestige Value of Public Employment in Chicago* (Chicago: University of Chicago Press, 1929); *Trends in Public Administration* (New York: McGraw-Hill, 1933); *The Federalists* (New York: Macmillan, 1948); *The Jeffersonians* (New York: Macmillan, 1951); *The Jacksonians* (New York: Macmillan, 1954); *The Republican Era* (New York: Macmillan, 1958). For appreciations, *see* John M. Gaus, "Leonard Dupree White 1891–1958," *Public Administration Review* (Summer 1958); H. J. Storing, "Leonard D. White and the Study of Public Administration," *Public Administration Review* (March 1965).

white-collar unions, general term for a union whose members are more likely to wear street clothes and sit at a desk than wear work clothes and stand at a lathe. *See* Adolf Sturmthal, *White-Collar Trade Unions: Contemporary Developments in Industrialized Societies* (Urbana, Ill.: University of Illinois Press, 1966); George Sayers Bain, *The Growth of White-Collar Unionism* (New York: Oxford University Press, 1970); Everett M. Kassalow, "White-Collar Unions and the Work Humanization Movement," *Monthly Labor Review* (May 1977); Nigel Nicholson, Gill Ursell, and Jackie Lubbock, "Membership Participation in a White-Collar Union," *Industrial Relations* (Spring 1981); John G. Kilgour, "Union Organizing Activity Among White-Collar Employees," *Personnel* (March–April 1983).

white-collar worker, employee whose job requires slight physical effort and allows him/her to wear ordinary clothes. *See* C. Wright Mills, *White Collar: The American Middle Class* (New York: Oxford University Press, 1951); J. M. Pennings, "Work Value Systems of White-Collar Workers," *Administrative Science Quarterly* (December 1970); Carl Dean Snyder, *White Collar Workers and the UAW* (Urbana, Ill.: University of Illinois Press, 1973); C. C. Hoop and J. N. Wolzansky, "Matching White-Collar Skills to the Work," *Harvard Business Review* (November-December 1983); Robert N. Lehrer, ed., *White Collar Productivity* (New York: McGraw-Hill, 1983).

   See also BLUE-COLLAR WORKERS.

white paper, any formal statement of an official government policy with its associated background documentation.

Whitten Amendment, amendment to the federal government's Classification Act which states that most federal employees may only be permanently appointed to one grade within a fifty-two-week period and may be promoted no more than one grade at a time.

   See also TIME-IN-GRADE RESTRICTION.

whole-job ranking, job evaluation method that simply ranks jobs as a whole. For example, a small organization might rank one person president, another as bookkeeper, two others as stock clerks, etc.

whole-man concept, philosophic attitude that management should be concerned with an employee's physical and mental health both on and off the job.

Whyte, William Foote (1914-), sociologist and one of the foremost authorities on human relations in industry. His work has often emphasized the impact of technology upon managerial behavior. Major works include: *Street Corner Society* (Chicago: University of Chicago Press, 1943); *Human Relations in the Restaurant Industry* (New York: McGraw-Hill, 1948); *Pattern for Industrial Peace* (New York:

Harper & Row, 1951); *Money and Motivation* (New York: Harper & Row, 1955); *Men at Work* (Homewood, Ill.: Richard D. Irwin, 1961).

Wiener v. United States, 357 U.S. 349 (1958), Supreme Court case holding that the president overstepped his constitutional authority in removing a member of the War Claims Commission for political reasons since the commission had judicial functions.

   See also HUMPHREY'S EXECUTOR V. UNITED STATES and MYERS V. UNITED STATES.

Wildavsky, Aaron B. (1930-), author of *The Politics of the Budgetary Process* (Boston: Little, Brown, 1964; 4th ed., 1984), which reveals the tactics public managers use to get their budgets passed and explains why rational attempts to reform the budgetary process have always failed. For this classic work alone Wildavsky would have earned his place in the pantheon of public administration. However, Wildavsky has also made landmark contributions to the study of the U.S. presidency, policy analysis, and program implementation and evaluation. Because of the volume, quality, and diversity of his work, Wildavsky is probably the nation's most widely read and influential academic analyst of public affairs. Other major works include: "Political Implications of Budgetary Reform," *Public Administration Review* (Autumn 1961); *Dixon-Yates: A Study in Power Politics* (New Haven, Conn.: Yale University Press, 1962); *Presidential Elections,* with Nelson W. Polsby (New York: Scribner's, 1964; 4th edition, 1976); "The Two Presidencies," *Trans-Action* (December 1966); "The Political Economy of Efficiency: Cost-Benefit Analysis, Systems Analysis, and Program Budgeting," *Public Administration Review* (December 1966); *American Federalism in Perspective* (Boston: Little, Brown, 1967); *Implementation,* with Jeffry Pressman (Berkeley, Calif.: University of California Press, 1973; 2nd ed., 1979); *Urban Outcomes: Schools, Streets, and Libraries,* with Frank Levy and Arnold J. Meltsner

(Berkeley, Calif.: University of California Press, 1974); *Planning and Budgeting in Poor Countries,* with Naomi Caiden (New York: John Wiley & Sons, 1974); "The Past and Future Presidency," *The Public Interest* (Fall 1975); *Budgeting: A Comparative Theory of Budgetary Process* (Boston: Little, Brown, 1975); *Speaking Truth to Power: The Art and Craft of Policy Analysis* (Boston: Little, Brown, 1979); *How to Limit Government Spending* (Berkeley, Calif.: University of California Press, 1980); *The Nursing Father: Moses as a Political Leader* (University, Ala., University of Alabama Press, 1984).

wildcat strike, also called UNAUTHORIZED STRIKE and OUTLAW STRIKE, work stoppage not sanctioned by union leadership and usually contrary to an existing labor contract. Unless it can be shown that unfair employer practices were the direct cause of the wildcat strike, the union could be liable for damages in a breach of contract suit by management. Garth L. Mangum, in "Taming Wildcat Strikes," *Harvard Business Review* (April-May 1960), holds that "wildcat strikes are management's responsibility—they continue as long as the participants find them profitable; cease when management, through disciplinary action, makes them unrewarding." For an analysis of how wildcat strikes are treated by the courts, *see* Evan J. Spelfogel, "Wildcat Strikes and Minority Concerted Activity—Discipline, Damage Suits and Injunctions," *Labor Law Journal* (September 1973). *Also see* Steven Rummage, "Union Officers and Wildcat Strikes: Freedom From Discriminatory Discipline," *Industrial Relations Law Journal, Vol. 4, No. 2 (1981).*

See also NONSUABILITY CLAUSE.

William E. Arnold Co.* v. *Carpenters District Council of Jacksonville, 417 U.S. 12 (1974), U.S. Supreme Court case which held that when an activity is arguably both an unfair labor practice prohibited by the National Labor Relations Act and a breach of a collective bargaining agreement, the National Labor Relations Board's authority "is not exclusive and

does not destroy the jurisdiction" of appropriate courts.

Williams-Steiger Act, *see* OCCUPATIONAL SAFETY AND HEALTH ACT OF 1970.

Wilson, Woodrow (1856-1924), president of the United States from 1913 to 1921. Wilson was also a president of the American Political Science Association and is considered one of the most influential early voices of both political science and public administration. His most enduring scholarly works are *Congressional Government: A Study in American Politics* (Boston: Houghton Mifflin, 1885) and "The Study of Administration," *Political Science Quarterly* (June 1887). For appreciations, *see* Louis Brownlow, "Woodrow Wilson and Public Administration," *Public Administration Review* (Spring 1956); Richard J. Stillman II, "Woodrow Wilson and the Study of Administration: A New Look at an Old Essay," *American Political Science Review* (June 1973); Jack Rabin and James S. Bowman, eds., *Politics and Administration: Woodrow Wilson and American Public Administration* (New York: Marcel Dekker, 1984).

Woodrow Wilson Invents Public Administration

In 1885 Woodrow Wilson, having not yet completed his doctoral program at Johns Hopkins University and being desperately poor as well as recently married, began his teaching career at the newly founded Bryn Mawr College for Women. He would have preferred a better appointment. He would have preferred to teach men. But, as he wrote his wife, "beggars cannot be choosers." In the following year he returned briefly to Johns Hopkins to pass the final examinations for his Ph.D. and wrote to his wife, "Hurrah—a thousand times hurrah— *I'm through I'm through*—the degree is actually secured! Oh, the relief of it!"

But young Woodrow was not happy with his situation at Bryn Mawr. His salary was barely adequate for a growing family. While reportedly a lecturer of genius, he resented having to teach women. As he told an associate, such an activity "relaxes one's mental muscle." In 1887 he summed up his life by saying, "Thirty-one years old and nothing done!" In retrospect Wilson seems to be like many another ambitious academic seemingly stuck in a post that did no justice to talent. And he chose as the way out the now traditional road to high academic fame, fortune, and position: he wrote and published and was saved!

During this time he worked on several textbooks—eventually completed, but now long forgotten; wrote fiction under a pen name—but it was all rejected; and wrote a few political essays—one of which remains his most enduring contribution as a political scientist.

In June of 1887 the fledgling *Political Science Quarterly* published Wilson's article, "The Study of Administration." While it attracted slight notice at the time, it has with the years become a distinguished and much honored essay; so much so that it is now customary to trace the origins of the academic discipline of public administration to it. Wilson attempted nothing less than to refocus political science. Rather than be concerned with the great maxims of lasting political truth, he argued that political science should concentrate on how governments are administered. In his words: "It is getting to be harder to *run* a constitution than to frame one."

Wilson wanted the study of public administration to focus not only on personnel problems, as other reformers of the time had advocated, but also on organization and management in general. But like all those concerned with the reform movement, Wilson overstated and obscured the distinction between politics and administration. This was politically necessary for the reformers because arguments that public personnel administration should be based on fitness and merit, rather than partisanship, necessarily had to assert that "politics" was out of place in the public service. In establishing what became known as the "politics-administration" dichotomy, Wilson was really referring to "partisan" politics. Thus, he wrote that public administration "is directly connected with the lasting maxims of political wisdom, the permanent truths of political progress." While this subtlety was lost on many, Wilson's main themes—that public administration should be both premised on a science of management and separate from traditional politics—fell on fertile intellectual ground. The ideas of this then obscure professor eventually became the dogma of the discipline, and remained so until after World War II.

And what happened to the young Wilson who plaintively wrote in 1888, "I have for a long time been hungry for a class of *men*"? Shortly thereafter he took up an appointment at Wesleyan University in Connecticut. From there he went to Princeton, made good, and became president of that university. In later life he found a job in Washington.

Note: Biographical information from Ray Stannard Baker, Woodrow Wilson, Life and Letters: Youth 1856–*1890 (Garden City, N.Y.: Doubleday, Page & Co. 1927).*

wink, unit of time equal to 1/2000 of a minute which is used in motion-and-time study.

withholding tax, those federal, state, or local taxes that are withheld by employers from the paychecks of their employees and paid directly to the taxing jurisdiction.

within-grade increase, also known as PERIODIC INCREASE and STEP INCREASE, a salary increase provided in certain government pay plans based upon time-in-grade and acceptable or satisfactory work performance.

womb to tomb, *see* CRADLE TO THE GRAVE.

Women's Bureau, agency of the U.S. Department of Labor that is responsible for formulating standards and policies to promote the welfare of wage-earning women, improve their working conditions, increase their efficiency, advance their opportunities for professional employment, and investigate and report on all matters pertinent to the welfare of women in industry. The Women's Bureau has regional offices established in ten areas throughout the United States.

Wood v. Strickland, 420 U.S. 308 (1975), Supreme Court ruling creating new standards for the immunity of public employees from civil suits for damages. The court held that a school board member (and by implication other public employees) is not immune from liability for damages "if he knew or reasonably should have known that the action he took within his sphere of official responsibility would violate the constitutional rights of the students affected, or if he took the action with the malicious intention to cause a de-

For reasons known mostly to themselves, three "sweet sixteens" in the tenth grade of the Mena Public High School in Mena, Arkansas, decided to "spike" the punch at a school affair. In order to operationalize this plan, they first had to drive to Oklahoma, where they purchased two twelve-ounce bottles of a malt liquor called "Right Time." The next phase of the plan called for the mixing of these twenty-four ounces with about sixty ounces of a soft drink. This was accomplished in an empty milk carton. The resulting concoction became the punch. Although, in the words of the United States Supreme Court, "the punch was served at the meeting, without apparent effect," the girls were nevertheless expelled from the Mena Public High School for their misdeed.

After confessing to a sympathetic teacher and later to a school principal in return for "leniency," the girls were expelled by a vote of the school board. Subsequently, the pranksters went to court alleging that their constitutional rights to due process had been violated.

That such a case could eventually become an important decision by the U.S. Supreme Court is a lesson in and of itself. However, equally interesting is that this rather straightforward set of facts could raise great legal complexities. Thus, the Federal District Court instructed the jury that a decision in favor of the girls had to be premised on the belief that the school board acted with malice, defined as "ill will against a person—a wrongful act done intentionally without just cause or excuse." The Court of Appeals, on the other hand, rejected this approach, arguing instead that only failure to act in good faith was required for the girls to win their point. Ultimately, the Supreme Court found both lines of reasoning inadequate and erected a new, and more controversial, standard of its own—that immunity for school board officials is not unqualified; it depends not simply on good faith but also on knowledge that officials should have concerning whether their actions violate the constitutional rights of others.

Had the constitutional rights of the "punch spikers" been violated? Had the girls' rights to procedural due process, in the form of a hearing, perhaps with counsel, been violated by the school board? Although the girls did have an opportunity to present their story, it may have been inadequate. While lower courts failed to deal with this question, the Supreme Court found it substantial enough to warrant sending the case back to the Court of Appeals.

Constitutional issues aside, did the facts of the case warrant so drastic a step as expulsion from high school? The Court of Appeals found that there was "*no* evidence that the school regulations had been violated," despite the girls' admission that they had spiked the punch. This was the result of the Court's interpretation of the words "intoxicating liquor" in the school's regulations as being identical in meaning with those words under Arkansas statutes. The latter applied to any beverage exceeding 5 percent alcoholic content by weight. The punch in question had an alcoholic content of 0.91 percent, according to the evidence presented at the trial in the District Court.

What has been the point of this recounting of a rather common—aside from its legal follow-up—teenage prank?

It shows that even the most trivial matters can result in litigation and generate important legal questions and landmark decisions. Moreover, administrative decisions and actions will increasingly be challenged in the courts as more and more individuals see the utility in bringing even minor matters before the judiciary. The problem is even more complex because, as we have seen, District Courts, Courts of Appeals, and the Supreme Court may all disagree over standards, approaches, and facts. The lesson of *Wood* v. *Strickland* is that public managers must always be cognizant of the constitutional constraints affecting their jobs. One can never fully know where an innocent question like "Who spiked the punch?" might lead!

privation of constitutional rights or other injury to the student." *See* David H. Rosenbloom, "Public Administrators' Official Immunity and the Supreme Court: Developments During the 1970s," *Public Administration Review* (March–April 1980).

work, according to Mark Twain, in *The Adventures of Tom Sawyer,* "work consists of whatever a body is obliged to do, and play consists of whatever a body is not obliged to do." For an exhaustive survey of the nature of work, *see* Report of a Special Task Force to the Secretary of HEW, *Work in America* (Cambridge, Mass.: The M.I.T. Press, 1973). *Also see* Irene M. Frank and David M. Brownstone,

The Historical Encyclopedia of Work: The Evolution of Careers, Occupations and Trades from their Origins to the Present (New York: Facts on File, 1985).
See also the following entries:
BESPOKE WORK
DEAD WORK
FAT WORK
OUT-TO-TITLE WORK

work-activities centers, centers planned and designed exclusively to provide therapeutic activities for handicapped clients whose physical or mental impairment is so severe as to make their productive capacity inconsequential. The Secretary of Labor is authorized by the Fair Labor Standards Act to allow the employment of handicapped persons in work activities centers at less than the minimum wage.

workaholic, word first used by Wayne Oates, in his *Confessions of a Workaholic: The Facts About Work Addiction* (New York: World Publishing, 1971), to describe the addiction, the compulsion, or the uncontrollable need to work incessantly. A workaholic is a person whose involvement in his/her work is so excessive that his/her health, personal happiness, interpersonal relations, and social functioning are adversely affected. *See* Wayne E. Oates, *Workaholics, Make Laziness Work for You* (Garden City. N.Y.: Doubleday, 1978); Fernando Bartolome, "The Work Alibi: When It's Harder To Go Home," *Harvard Business Review* (March–April 1983).

work curve, also called OUTPUT CURVE, graphic presentation of an organization's or individual's productivity over a specified period of time.

workday, basic, *see* BASIC WORKDAY.

work design, *see* JOB DESIGN.

work disability, *see* DISABILITY.

workers, *see* EMPLOYEE. *See also* the following entries:

BLUE-COLLAR WORKERS
DISADVANTAGED WORKERS
DISCOURAGED WORKERS
DISPLACED EMPLOYEE
EXEMPT EMPLOYEE
FULL-TIME WORKERS
HOURLY-RATE WORKERS
ILLEGAL ALIENS
ITINERANT WORKER
PINK-COLLAR JOBS
PRODUCTION WORKERS
SEMISKILLED WORKERS
UNSKILLED WORKERS
WHITE-COLLAR WORKERS

workers' compensation, also called WORKMEN'S COMPENSATION and INDUSTRIAL ACCIDENT INSURANCE, plan designed to provide cash benefits and medical care when a worker is injured in connection with his/her job and monetary payments to his/her survivors if he/she is killed on the job. It was the first form of social insurance to develop widely in the United States. There are now fifty-four different workers' compensation programs in operation. Each of the fifty states and Puerto Rico has its own workmen's compensation program. In addition, there are three federal workers' compensation programs covering federal government and private employees in the District of Columbia and longshoremen and harbor workers throughout the country.

Before the passage of workers' compensation laws, an injured employee ordinarily had to file suit against his/her employer and prove that the injury was due to the employer's negligence in order to recover damages. The enactment of workmen's compensation laws introduced the principle that a worker incurring an occupational injury would be compensated regardless of fault or blame in the accident and with a minimum of delay and legal formalitiy. In turn, the employer's liability was limited, because workmen's compensation benefits became the exclusive remedy for work-related injuries.

The usual condition for entitlement to benefits is that the injury or death "arises out of and in the course of employment." Most programs exclude injuries due to the employee's intoxication, willful misconduct, or gross negligence. Although virtually limited to injuries or diseases traceable to industrial "accidents" initially, the scope of the laws has broadened over the years to cover occupational diseases as well.

In most states, workers' compensation is paid for entirely by employers who either purchase insurance coverage or self insure—that is, assume total financial liability for the work accidents of their employees.

The Occupational Health and Safety Act of 1970 created the National Commission on State Workmen's Compensation Laws to evaluate the various state workers' compensation programs. The commission reported that "the evidence compels us to conclude that state workmen's compensation laws are in general neither adequate nor equitable." [(*Report of the National Commission on State Workmen's Compensation Laws* (Washington, D.C.: U.S. Government Printing Office, 1972).] For critiques of present programs, *see* Daniel M. Kasper, "For A Better Worker's Compensation System," *Harvard Business Review* (March-April 1977); Robert J. Paul, "Workers' Compensation—An Adequate Employee Benefit?" *Academy of Management Review* (October 1976); Mark Reutter, "Workmen's Compensation Doesn't Work or Compensate," *Business and Society Review* (Fall 1980); James R. Chelius, "The Influence of Workers' Compensation on Safety Incentives," *Industrial and Labor Relations Review* (January 1982); U.S. Chamber of Commerce, *Analysis of Workers' Compensation Laws, 1983* (Washington: U.S. Chamber of Commerce, 1983); LaVerne C. Tinsely, "Workers' Compensation: Significant Enactments in 1983," *Monthly Labor Review* (February 1984).

See also MOUNTAIN TIMBER COMPANY V. WASHINGTON and HAWKINS V. BLEAKLY.

workers' councils, also called WORKS COUNCILS, any of a variety of joint labor-management bodies serving as vehicles for the resolution of problems of mutual interest. Workers' councils are usually associated with concepts of industrial democracy and are found mostly in Europe. *See* Erland Waldenstrom, "Works Councils: The Need to be Involved," *Columbia Journal of World Business* (May-June 1968).

work ethic, *see* PROTESTANT ETHIC.

workfare, any public welfare program that requires welfare payment recipients to work (work + welfare = workfare) or enroll in a formal job-training program. *See* Linda E. Demkovich, "Does Workfare Work?" *National Journal* (July 14, 1981).

work force planning, determination by organization management of the numbers, kinds, and costs of the workers needed to carry out each stage of the organization's program plan.

See also HUMAN RESOURCES PLANNING.

work group, also called WORKING GROUP and TASK GROUP, task unit within a larger organizational social system charged with the responsibility of making a specific contribution to the goals of the larger organization. *See* Maxine Bucklow, "A New Role for the Work Group," *Administrative Science Quarterly* (June 1966); J. Stephen Heinen and Eugene Jacobson, "A Model of Task Group Development in Complex Organizations and a Strategy of Implementation," *Academy of Management Review* (October 1976); David G. Bowers and Doris L. Hausser, "Work Group Types and Intervention Effects in Organizational Development," *Administrative Science Quarterly* (March 1977); Panagiotis N. Fotilas, "Semi-Autonomous Work Groups: An Alternative in Organizing Production Work?" *Management Review* (July 1981).

See also GROUP DYNAMICS.

work group, autonomous, *see* AUTONOMOUS WORK GROUP.

work group, horizontal, *see* HORIZONTAL WORK GROUP.

work-in, form of protest demonstration in

which a group of employees report to work as usual but refuse to follow their normal routines.

See also SIT-DOWN STRIKE.

working certificate, *see* WORKING PAPERS.

working class, all who work. When the term is used politically, it tends to exclude managers, professionals, and anyone who is not at the lower end of the educational and economic scales. For an analytical description, *see* Andrew Levison, *The Working-Class Majority* (New York: Coward, McCann & Geoghegan, Inc., 1974). For a social history of the American working class, *see* Herbert G. Gutman, *Work, Culture, and Society in Industrializing America* (New York: Alfred A. Knopf, 1976). *Also see* Maurice F. Neufeld, Daniel J. Leab, and Dorothy Swanson, *American Working Class History: A Representative Bibliography* (New York: R. R. Bowker Co., 1983); Sean Wilentz, *Chants Democratic: New York City and the Rise of the American Working Class, 1788-1850* (New York: Oxford University Press, 1984).

working conditions, those factors, both physical and psychological, which comprise an employee's work environment. Included are such things as arrangement of office and factory equipment, salary or wages, fringe benefits, supervision, work routine, fair employment practices, health and safety precautions, length of work day, and relationship with co-workers. *See* Neal Q. Herrick and Robert P. Quinn, "The Working Conditions Survey as a Source of Social Indicators," *Monthly Labor Review* (April 1971); Robert P. Quinn *et al.*, "Evaluating Working Conditions in America," *Monthly Labor Review* (November 1973).

working group, *see* WORK GROUP.

working hours, flexible, *see* FLEXI-TIME.

working papers, also called WORKING CERTIFICATE and WORK PERMIT, federal certificate of age showing that a minor is above the oppressive child-labor age applicable to the occupation in which he/she would be employed. Such proof of age is required under the provisions of the Fair Labor Standards Act and the Walsh-Healey Public Contracts Act. Working papers are issued by a designee of the administrator of the Wage and Hour Division of the U.S. Department of Labor.

working permit, *see* WORKING PAPERS.

workload, the result expected from an expenditure of any employee's time and energy performing tasks or functions which can be evaluated in terms of units produced, yardsticks of progress, or through judging the application and utilization of his or her effort.

work measurement, any method used to establish an equitable relationship between the volume of work performed and the human resources devoted to its accomplishment. Concerned with both volume and time, a work measurement program is basically a means of setting standards to determine just what constitutes a fair day's work. For a presentation of methods, *see* Robert I. Stevens and Walter J. Bieber, "Work Measurement Techniques," *Journal of Systems Management* (February 1977); Frank J. Landy and James L. Farr, *The Measurement of Work Performance: Methods, Theory and Applications* (New York: Academic Press, 1983); Paul J. Stonich, "The Performance Measurement and Reward System: Critical to Strategic Management," *Organizational Dynamics* (Winter 1984).

See also MOTION STUDY and TIME STUDY.

work measurement standard, a numerical value applied to the units of work an employee or group can be expected to produce in a given period of time.

work motivation, *see* MOTIVATION.

work premium, also called PREMIUM PAY, extra compensation for work that is considered unpleasant, hazardous, or inconvenient. Overtime is the most obvious example of a work premium. *See* Janice Neipert Hedges, "Long Workweeks and Premium Pay," *Monthly Labor Review* (April 1976).

work preview, also called JOB SAMPLE and JOB PREVIEW, management technique for presenting prospective employees with realistic information about the particular job that they are considering. *See* Michael A. Raphael, "Work Previews Can Reduce Turnover and Improve Performance," *Personnel Journal* (February 1975); John P. Wanous, "A Job Preview Makes Recruiting More Effective," *Harvard Business Review* (September–October 1975); John P. Wanous, "Realistic Job Previews," *Personnel Psychology* (Summer 1978); Bernard L. Dugoni and Daniel R. Ilgen, "Realistic Job Previews and the Adjustment of New Employees," *Academy of Management Journal* (September 1981).

work-ready, term used to describe a handicapped person who, if given employment, would be able to perform adequately on the job without being a burden to others.

Work Related Abstracts, monthly that seeks to abstract the significant and the informative from over 250 management, labor, government, professional, and university periodicals.

> *Work Related Abstracts*
> Information Coordinators, Inc.
> 1435-37 Randolph Street
> Detroit, MI 48226

work relief, *see* RELIEF.

work restructuring, *see* JOB RESTRUCTURING.

work rules, formal regulations prescribing both on-the-job behavior and working conditions. Work rules are usually incorporated into a collective bargaining agreement at the insistence of the union in order to restrict management's ability to unilaterally set production standards and/or reassign employees. The union's goals are to maximize and protect the jobs available to its members, to protect their health and safety, and to maintain stable work assignments for union members. *See* Joseph B. Wollenberger, "Acceptable Work Rules and Penalties: A Company Guide," *Personnel* (July–August 1963).

work sampling, also called JOB SAMPLING, technique used to discover the proportions of total time devoted to the various components of a job. Data obtained from work sampling can be used to establish allowances applicable to a job, to determine machine utilization, and to provide the criteria for production standards. While this same information can be obtained by time-study procedures, work sampling—dependent as it is upon the laws of probability—will usually provide the information faster and at less cost. For a text on the technique, *see* Ralph M. Barnes, *Work Sampling,* 2nd ed. (New York: John Wiley & Sons, 1966).

Work sampling is also used to describe a performance test designed to be a miniature replica of behavior required on the job which attempts to measure how well an employee will perform in the particular occupation. Such tests are considered a more precise device for measuring particular occupational abilities than simple motor skills or verbal ability tests. *See* James J. Asher and James A. Sciarrino, "Realistic Work Sample Tests: A Review," *Personnel Psychology* (Winter 1974); Michael K. Mount, Paul M. Muchinsky, and Lawrence M. Hanser, "The Predictive Validity of a Work Sample: A Laboratory Study," *Personnel Psychology* (Winter 1977); Donald J. Schwartz, "A Job Sampling Approach to Merit System Examining," *Personnel Psychology* (Summer 1977).

works councils, *see* WORKERS' COUNCILS.

worksharing, procedure for dividing the available work (or hours of work) among all eligible employees as an alternative to layoffs during slow periods. Three types of worksharing procedures may be identified—reduction in hours (by far the most common), division of work, and rotation of employment. *Reduction in hours*, as its name implies, requires that weekly hours of work be reduced below normal (non-overtime) schedules, usually within stated limits, to spread the work. The second procedure — *division of work* — is normally found in agreements covering employees on piecework or incentive systems, and emphasizes earnings rather than hours of work (although reduced hours may also occur). All available work is divided equally among eligible employees; under some conditions, faster workers may work somewhat fewer hours than slower ones for the same pay. The last procedure — *rotation of employment* (or layoff) — provides that short, specific periods of layoff be rotated equally among all employees, in contrast to the more common practice of laying off junior employees for longer or indefinite periods. Worksharing provisions are often part of a union contract. *See* Bureau of Labor Statistics, U.S. Department of Labor, *Major Collective Bargaining Agreements: Layoff, Recall and Worksharing Procedures* (Washington, D.C.: U.S. Government Printing Office, Bulletin 1425-13, 1972); Nancy J. McNeff et al., "Alternatives to Employee Layoffs: Work Sharing and Prelayoff Consultation," *Personnel* (January–February 1978); Maureen E. McCarthy and Gail S. Rosenberg, with Gary Lefkowitz, *Work Sharing: Case Studies* (Kalamazoo, Mich.: W. E. Upjohn Institute for Employment Research, Inc., 1981); Ramelle MaCoy and Martin J. Moramd, eds., *Short-Time Compensation: A Formula for Work Sharing* (New York: Pergamon Press, 1984); Martin Nemirow, "Work-Sharing Approaches: Past and Present," *Monthly Labor Review* (September 1984).

See also JOB SHARING.

work simplification, the industrial engineering function which seeks to find the one best way to do each job based upon economy of time, material, effort, etc. *See* Alan D. Rowland, "Combining Quality Control Circles and Work Simplification," *"Training and Development Journal* (January 1984).

work station, specific location and immediate surrounding area in which a job is performed.

work stoppage, according to the U.S. Departments of Commerce and Labor, a concerted and complete withholding of services by employees that lasts for at least one workday or one work shift.

work to rule, work slowdown in which all of the formal work rules are so scrupulously obeyed that productivity suffers considerably. Those working to rule seek to place pressure on management without losing pay by going on strike. Work-to-rule protests are particularly popular in the public sector where most formal strikes are illegal.

work values, importance that employees place on the various aspects of work, such as pay, prestige, security, responsibility, etc. *See* Stephen Wollock et al., "Development of the Survey of Work Values," *Journal of Applied Psychology,* Vol. 55, No. 4 (1971); Charles L. Hughes and Vincent S. Flowers, "Shaping Personnel Strategies to Disparate Value Systems," *Personnel* (March–April 1973).

workweek, expected or actual period of employment for a "normal" week, usually expressed in number of hours. According to the Fair Labor Standards Act, a workweek is a period of 168 hours during seven consecutive twenty-four-hour periods. It may begin on any day of the week and any hour of the day established by the employer. For purposes of minimum wage and overtime payment, each workweek stands alone, and there can be no averaging of two or more workweeks (except for hospital or nursing home employees on an "8-and-80" schedule or seamen on U.S. vessels). Employee coverage, compliance with wage payment requirements, and the application of most exemptions are determined on a workweek basis.

See also the following entries:
BASIC WORKWEEK
FOUR-DAY WORKWEEK
GUARANTEED WORKWEEK

wrap-up clause, *see* ZIPPER CLAUSE.

Wright, Carroll Davidson (1840-1909), first head of the U.S. Bureau of Labor; considered the "inventor" of the field of labor statistics. Wright's nonpartisan tone during twenty years (1885-1905) as head of the national bureau and his philosophy that supplying facts—and not advocating particular solutions—was the proper function of a labor bureau went far to create the climate that allowed for the eventual creation of the present Department of Labor. He was also the statistical wit who first observed that "figures won't lie, but liars will figure."

See James Leiby, *Carroll Wright and Labor Reform: The Origin of Labor Statistics* (Cambridge, Mass.: Harvard University Press, 1960); Judson MacLaury, "The Selection of the First U.S. Commissioner of Labor," *Monthly Labor Review* (April 1975).

Wriston Committee, 1954 committee created by President Eisenhower and headed by Henry Wriston which studied and made recommendations for the reorganization of the U.S. Foreign Service.

writ of certiorari, *see* CERTIORARI.

writ of mandamus, *see* MANDAMUS.

W-2 Form, *see* FORM W-2.

Wurf, Jerry (1919-1981), president of the American Federation of State, County, and Municipal Employees (AFSCME) from 1964 to 1981. For biographical accounts, *see* Fred C. Shapiro, "How Jerry Wurf Walks on Water," *The New York Times Magazine* (April 11, 1976); K. Bode, "Crying Wurf," *The New Republic* (July 2, 1977).

Y

yellow-dog contract, any agreement (written or oral) between an employer and an employee that calls for the employee to resign from, or refrain from joining, a union. In the early part of this century, this was a common tactic used by employers wary of union influences. The Norris-LaGuardia Act of 1932 made yellow-dog contracts illegal.

Yerkes, Robert M. (1876-1956), president of the American Psychological Association in 1918 and one of the team of psychologists who produced the famous Army Alpha and Army Beta intelligence tests first used by the United States Army during World War I.

Yeshiva University decision, *see NATIONAL LABOR RELATIONS BOARD V. YESHIVA UNIVERSITY.*

Youngstown Sheet and Tube Co.* v. *Sawyer, 343 U.S. 579 (1952), Supreme Court case involving the constitutionality of President Truman's executive order directing the Secretary of Commerce to take possession of and operate the nation's steel mills in connection with a labor dispute that threatened to disrupt production. By a vote of six to three, the Supreme Court held that the president exceeded his constitutional powers, although there was no majority opinion. *See* John L. Blackman, Jr., *Presidential Seizure in Labor Disputes* (Cambridge, Mass.: Harvard University Press, 1967).

Z

Zander, Arnold Scheuer (1901-), organized and became the first president of the American Federation of State, County, and Municipal Employees. For biographical information, *see* Leo Kramer, *Labor's Paradox: The American Federation of State, County, and Municipal Employees, AFL-CIO* (New York: John Wiley, 1962).

zero-base budgeting (ZBB), budgeting process that is first and foremost a rejection of the incremental decison-making model of budgeting. It demands a rejustification of the entire budget submission (from ground zero), whereas incremental budgeting essentially respects the outcomes of previous budgetary decisions (collectively referred to as the budget base) and focuses examination on the margin of change from year to year. Two points of significance should be noted in the contrast between incremental and comprehensive (zero-base) budgeting. *First,* incremental budgeting has been accepted as the reality of our budgeting experience. *Second,* would-be rational decision makers over the past thirty years have been adamant in their criticism of incrementalism and laudatory of the merits and desirability of a zero-base approach.

It may be that the origins of this feud stem from the legislative-executive dichotomy in budgetary decision-making. One expects an incremental approach out of a legislature because it so appropriately fits their decision-making process. As for the executive branch, decision-making there, via the budgetary process, it is argued, need not be so constricted. The executive branch can, after all, order and reorder budgeting processes and systems in order to counter incrementalism. One cannot help but have the suspicion that the growing rapidity with which new budgeting systems are adopted and abandoned is in part a reflection of the old adage that the rules should be changed occasionally just to keep the players honest. Certainly the adoption of ZBB by a new president in 1977 has certain connotations of this.

ZBB is also keyed to another "old" concept—the idea of direct consideration of alternatives within the context of administrative control. First articulated by Verne B. Lewis in his *Public Administration Review* (Winter 1952) article, "Toward a Theory of Budgeting," the idea of budget "alternatives" centers on the preparation of incremental budget submissions that permit evaluation of various funding amounts in terms of levels or quantity of service. The administrative or managerial context of alternative budgeting provides a dual advantage. Budget submissions can be prepared in a manner that will facilitate comparison and demonstrate a range of choices for service and funding levels and, at the same time, the final choice will provide a realistic contract—that is, specific, realistic expectations for the program manager.

In 1981 federal agencies were notified that President Carter's 1978 directive requiring zero-base budgeting had been rescinded by President Reagan.

See Peter A. Phyrr, *Zero-Base Budgeting: A Practical Management Tool for Evaluating Expenses* (New York: John Wiley & Sons, 1973); Peter A. Phyrr, "The Zero-Base Approach to Government Budgeting," *Public Administration Review* (January–February 1977); Allen Schick, "The Road from ZBB," *Public Administration Review* (March–April 1978); Graeme M. Taylor, "Introduction to Zero-Base Budgeting," *The Bureaucrat* (Spring 1977); Joseph S. Wholey, *Zero-Base Budgeting and Program Evaluation* (Lexington, Mass.: Lexington Books, 1978); Charles E. Hill, "Zero-Base Budgeting: A Practical Application," *Governmental Finance* (March 1983).

See also the following entries:
BASE
CONSOLIDATED DECISION PACKAGES
CROSS AGENCY RANKING
DECISION PACKAGES
PHYRR, PETER A.

zero-defects program, formal effort at quality assurance aimed at eliminating human errors during production. *See* George E. Fouch, "Motivation for Quality—Zero Defects Program," *Industrial Quality Control* (November 1965); Gerald V. Barrett and Patrick A. Cabe, "Zero Defects Programs: Their Effects at Different Job Levels," *Personnel* (November–December 1967).

zero out, to totally destroy, budgetarily speaking.

zipper clause, also called WRAP-UP CLAUSE, portion of a collective bargaining contract that specifically states the written agreement is complete and anything not contained in it is not agreed to. A typical zipper clause might read: "This contract is complete in itself and sets forth all the terms and conditions of the agreement between the parties hereto." The main purpose of the zipper or wrap-up clause is to prevent either party from demanding a renewal of negotiations during the life of the contract. It also serves to limit the freedom of a grievance arbitrator because his rulings must be based solely on the written agreement's contents.

zone of acceptance, also called ACCEPTANCE THEORY OF AUTHORITY, concept that authority stems from the bottom up, based on the extent to which individuals are willing to hold in abeyance their own critical faculties and accept the directives of their organizational superiors. The "zone of acceptance" itself is a theoretical range of tolerance within which organization members will accept orders without question. A pioneering analysis of this concept is "The Role of Authority," Chapter VII of Herbert Simon's *Administrative Behavior* (New York: The Free Press, 1947). Note that Simon's concept admittedly built upon Chester I. Barnard's concept of the "zone of indifference."

zone of employment, the physical area (usually the place of employment and surrounding areas controlled by the employer) within which an employee is eligible for workers' compensation benefits when injured, whether on the job at the time or not.

zone of indifference, concept that comes from Chester I. Barnard's *The Functions of the Executive* (Cambridge, Mass.: Harvard University Press, 1938). According to Barnard:

> If all the orders for actions reasonably practicable be arranged in the order of their acceptability to the person affected, it may be conceived that there are a number which are clearly unacceptable, that is, which certainly will not be obeyed; there is another group some-

what more or less on the neutral line, that is, either barely acceptable or barely unacceptable; and a third group unquestionably acceptable. This last group lies within the "zone of indifference." The person affected will accept orders lying within this zone and is relatively indifferent as to what the order is so far as the question of authority is concerned.

zone of uncertainty, range or zone of test scores within which it cannot truly be said that differing scores actually represent differing levels of attainment.

zoning, the process by which local government can designate the types of structures and activities that can be built and performed in a particular area. It started in the 1920s and involves a highly complex legal process which is often impacted by local politics. *See* Richard Babcock, *The Zoning Game: Municipal Practices and Policies* (Madison, Wis.: University of Wisconsin Press, 1966); Stanislaw J. Makielski, Jr., *The Politics of Zoning* (New York: Columbia University Press, 1966); Seymour I. Toll, *Zoned America* (New York: Grossman, 1969); Richard Babcock and Fred Bosselman, *Exclusionary Zoning: Land Use Regulation and Housing in the 1970s* (New York: Praeger, 1973); R. Robert Linowes and Don Allensworth, *The Politics of Land Use* (New York: Praeger, 1973); Julia Vitullo-Martin, "Land Use Policy," *Policy Studies Journal* (Spring 1977); James H. Carr and Edward E. Duensing, eds., *Land Use Issues of the 1980s* (New Brunswick, N.J.: Center for Urban Policy Research/Rutgers University, 1983); Kenneth Pearlman, "Zoning and the First Amendment," *The Urban Lawyer* (Spring 1984).

See also AFFIRMATIVE ZONING, ENTERPRISE ZONE, EUCLIDIAN ZONING, PLANNED UNIT DEVELOPMENT, and SPOT ZONING.

zoning, inclusionary, zoning practice that requires builders to provide (at reduced rates) a portion of new housing units for moderate- and low-income families.

APPENDIX A

THE CONSTITUTION OF
THE UNITED STATES

We the People of the United States, in Order to form a more perfect Union, establish justice, insure domestic Tranquility, provide for the common defence, promote the general Welfare, and secure the Blessings of Liberty to ourselves and our Posterity, do ordain and establish this Constitution for the United States of America.

Article I

Section 1. All legislative Powers herein granted shall be vested in a Congress of the United States, which shall consist of a Senate and House of Representatives.

Section 2. The House of Representatives shall be composed of Members chosen every second Year by the People of the several States, and the Electors in each State shall have the Qualifications requisite for Electors of the most numerous Branch of the State Legislature.

No Person shall be a Representative who shall not have attained to the Age of twenty five Years, and been seven Years a Citizen of the United States, and who shall not, when elected, be an Inhabitant of that State in which he shall be chosen.

Representatives and direct Taxes shall be apportioned among the several States which may be included within this Union, according to their respective Numbers, which shall be determined by adding to the whole Number of free Persons, including those bound to Service for a Term of Years, and excluding Indians not taxed, three fifths of all other Persons. The actual Enumeration shall be made within three Years after the first Meeting of the Congress of the United States, and within every subsequent Term of ten Years, in such Manner as they shall by Law direct. The Number of Representatives shall not exceed one for every thirty Thousand, but each State shall have at Least one Representative; and until such enumerations shall be made, the State of New Hampshire shall be entitled to chuse three, Massachusetts eight, Rhode-Island and Providence Plantations one, Connecticut five, New-York six, New Jersey four, Pennsylvania eight, Delaware one, Maryland six, Virginia ten, North Carolina five, South Carolina five, and Georgia three.

When vacancies happen in the Representation from any State, the Executive Authority thereof shall issue Writs of Election to fill such Vacancies.

The House of Representatives shall chuse their speaker and other Officers; and shall have the sole Power of Impeachment.

Section 3. The Senate of the United States shall be composed of two Senators from each State, chosen by the Legislature thereof, for six Years; and each Senator shall have one Vote.

Immediately after they shall be assembled in Consequence of the first Election, they shall be divided as equally as may be into three Classes. The Seats of the Senators of the first Class shall be vacated at the Expiration of the second Year, of the second Class at the Expiration of the fourth Year, and of the third Class at the Expiration of the sixth Year, so that one third may be chosen every second

Year; and if Vacancies happen by Resignation, or otherwise, during the Recess of the Legislature of any State, the Executive thereof may make temporary Appointments until the next Meeting of the Legislature, which shall then fill such Vacancies.

No Person shall be a Senator who shall not have attained to the Age of thirty Years, and been nine Years a Citizen of the United States, and who shall not, when elected, be an Inhabitant of that State for which he shall be chosen.

The Vice President of the United States shall be President of the Senate, but shall have no Vote, unless they be equally divided.

The Senate shall chuse their other Officers, and also a President pro tempore, in the Absence of the Vice President, or when he shall exercise the Office of President of the United States.

The Senate shall have the sole Power to try all Impeachments. When sitting for that Purpose, they shall be on Oath or Affirmation. When the President of the United States is tried, the Chief Justice shall preside: And no Person shall be convicted without the concurrence of two thirds of the Members present. Judgment in Cases of Impeachment shall not extend further than to removal from Office, and disqualification to hold and enjoy any Office of honor, Trust or Profit under the United States: but the Party convicted shall nevertheless be liable and subject to Indictment, Trial, Judgment and Punishment, according to law.

Section 4. The Times, Places and Manner of holding Elections for Senators and Representatives, shall be prescribed in each State by the Legislature thereof; but the Congress may at any time by Law make or alter such Regulations, except as to the Places of chusing Senators.

The Congress shall assemble at least once in every Year, and such Meeting shall be on the first Monday in December, unless they shall by Law appoint a different Day.

Section 5. Each House shall be the Judge of the Elections, Returns and Qualifications of its own Members, and a Majority of each shall constitute a Quorum to do business; but a smaller Number may adjourn from day to day, and may be authorized to compel the Attendance of absent Members, in such Manner, and under such Penalties as each House may provide.

Each House may determine the Rules of its Proceedings, punish its Members for disorderly Behaviour, and, with the Concurrence of two thirds, expel a Member.

Each House shall keep a Journal of its Proceedings, and from time to time publish the same, excepting such Parts as may in their Judgment require Secrecy; and the yeas and Nays of the Members of either House on any question shall, at the Desire of one fifth of those Present, be entered on the Journal.

Neither House, during the Session of Congress, shall, without the Consent of the other, adjourn for more than three days, nor to any other place than that in which the two Houses shall be sitting.

Section 6. The Senators and Representatives shall receive a Compensation for their Services, to be ascertained by Law, and paid out of the Treasury of the United States. They shall in all Cases, except Treason, Felony and Breach of the Peace, be privileged from Arrest during their Attendance at the Session of their respective Houses, and in going to and returning from the same; and for any Speech or Debate in either House, they shall not be questioned in any other Place.

No Senator or Representative shall, during the Time for which he was elected, be appointed to any civil Office under the Authority of the United States, which shall have been created, or the Emoluments whereof shall have been encreased during such time; and no Person holding any Office under the United States, shall be a Member of either House during his Continuance in Office.

Section 7. All Bills for raising Revenue shall originate in the House of Representatives;

but the Senate may propose or concur with Amendments as on other Bills.

Every Bill which shall have passed the House of Representatives and the Senate, shall, before it become a Law, be presented to the President of the United States; If he approve he shall sign it, but if not he shall return it, with his Objections to that House in which it shall have originated, who shall enter the Objections at large on their Journal, and proceed to reconsider it. If after such Reconsideration two thirds of that House shall agree to pass the Bill, it shall be sent, together with the Objections, to the other House, by which it shall likewise be reconsidered, and if approved by two thirds of that House, it shall become a Law. But in all such Cases the Votes of both Houses shall be determined by yeas and Nays, and the Names of the Persons voting for and against the Bill shall be entered on the Journal of each House respectively. If any Bill shall not be returned by the President within ten Days (Sundays excepted) after it shall have been presented to him, the Same shall be a Law, in like Manner as if he had signed it, unless the Congress by their Adjournment prevent its Return, in which Case it shall not be a Law.

Every Order, Resolution, or Vote to which the Concurrence of the Senate and House of Representatives may be necessary (except on a question of Adjournment) shall be presented to the President of the United States; and before the Same shall take Effect, shall be approved by him, or being disapproved by him, shall be repassed by two thirds of the Senate and House of Representatives, according to the Rules and Limitations prescribed in the Case of a Bill.

Section 8. The Congress shall have Power To lay and collect Taxes, Duties, Imposts and Excises, to pay the Debts and provide for the common Defence and general Welfare of the United States; but all duties, Imposts and Excises shall be uniform throughout the United States;

To borrow Money on the Credit of the United States;

To regulate Commerce with foreign Nations, and among the several States, and with the Indian tribes;

To establish an uniform Rule of Naturalization, and uniform Laws on the subject of Bankruptcies throughout the United States;

To coin Money, regulate the Value thereof, and of foreign Coin, and fix the Standard of Weights and Measures;

To provide for the Punishment of counterfeiting the Securities and current Coin of the United States;

To establish Post Offices and post Roads;

To promote the Progress of Science and useful Arts, by securing for limited Times to Authors and Inventors exclusive Right to their respective Writings and Discoveries;

To constitute Tribunals inferior to the supreme Court;

To define and punish Piracies and Felonies committed on the high Seas, and offences against the Law of Nations;

To declare War, grant Letters of Marque and Reprisal, and make rules concerning Captures on Land and Water;

To raise and support Armies, but no Appropriation of Money to that Use shall be for a longer Term than two Years;

To provide and maintain a Navy;

To make rules for the Government and Regulation of the land and naval Forces;

To provide for calling forth the Militia to execute the Laws of the Union, suppress Insurrections and repel Invasions;

To provide for organizing, arming, and disciplining, the Militia, and for governing such Part of them as may be employed in the Service of the United States, reserving to the States respectively, the Appointment of the Officers, and the Authority of training the Militia according to the discipline prescribed by Congress;

To exercise exclusive Legislation in all Cases whatsoever, over such District (not exceeding ten Miles square), as may, by Cession of particular States, and the Acceptance of Congress, become the Seat of the Government of the United States, and to exercise like Authority over all Places purchased by the Consent of the Legislature of the State in which the Same shall be for the Erection of Forts, Magazines, Arsenals, dock-Yards, and other needful Buildings;—And

To make all Laws which shall be necessary and proper for carrying into Execution the foregoing Powers, and all other Powers vested by this Constitution in the Government of the United States, or in any Department or Officer thereof.

Section 9. The Migration or Importation of such Persons as any of the States now existing shall think proper to admit, shall not be prohibited by the Congress prior to the Year one thousand eight hundred and eight, but a Tax or duty may be imposed on such Importation, not exceeding ten dollars for each Person.

The Privilege of the Writ of Habeas Corpus shall not be suspended, unless when in Cases of Rebellion or Invasion the public Safety may require it.

No Bill of Attainder or ex post facto Law shall be passed.

No Capitation, or other direct, Tax shall be laid, unless in Proportion to the Census or Enumeration herein before directed to be taken.

No Tax or Duty shall be laid on Articles exported from any State.

No Preference shall be given by any Regulation of Commerce or Revenue to the Ports of one State over those of another: nor shall Vessels bound to, or from, one State, be obliged to enter, clear, or pay Duties in another.

No money shall be drawn from the Treasury, but in Consequence of Appropriations made by Law; and a regular Statement and Account of the Receipts and Expenditures of all public Money shall be published from time to time.

No Title of Nobility shall be granted by the United States: And no Person holding any Office of Profit or Trust under them, shall, without the Consent of the Congress, accept of any present, Emolument, Office, or Title, of any kind whatever, from any King, Prince, or foreign State.

Section 10. No State shall enter into any Treaty, Alliance, or Confederation; grant Letters of Marque and Reprisal; coin Money; emit Bills of Credit; make any Thing but gold and silver Coin a Tender in Payment of Debts; pass any Bill of Attainder, ex post facto Law, or Law impairing the Obligation of Contracts, or grant any Title of Nobility.

No State shall, without the Consent of the Congress, lay any Imposts or Duties on Imports or Exports, except what may be absolutely necessary for executing it's inspection Laws: and the net Produce of all Duties and Imposts, laid by any State on Imports or Exports, shall be for the Use of the Treasury of the United States; and all such Laws shall be subject to the Revision and Controul of the Congress.

No State shall, without the Consent of Congress, lay any Duty of Tonnage, keep Troops, or Ships of War in time of Peace, enter into any Agreement or Compact with another State, or with a foreign Power, or engage in War, unless actually invaded, or in such imminent Danger as will not admit of delay.

Article II

Section 1. The executive Power shall be vested in a President of the United States of America. He shall hold his Office during the Term of four Years, and, together with the Vice President, chosen for the same term, be elected, as follows

Each State shall appoint, in such Manner as the Legislature thereof may direct, a Number of Electors, equal to the whole Number of Senators and Representatives to which the State may be entitled in the Congress: but no Senator or Representative, or Person holding an Office of Trust or Profit under the United States, shall be appointed an Elector.

The Electors shall meet in their respective States, and vote by Ballot for two Persons, of whom one at least shall not be an Inhabitant of the same State with themselves. And they shall make a List of all the Persons voted for, and of the Number of Votes for each; which List they shall sign and certify, and transmit sealed to the Seat of the Government of the United States, directed to the President of the Senate. The President of the Senate shall, in the Presence of the Senate and House of Representatives, open all the Certificates, and the Votes shall then be counted. The Person having the greatest Number of Votes shall be the President, if such Number be a Majority of the whole Number of Electors appointed; and if there be more than one who have such Majority, and have an equal Number of Votes, then the House of Representatives shall immediately chuse by Ballot one of them for President: and if no Person have a Majority, then from the five highest on the List the said House shall in like Manner chuse the President. But in chusing the President, the Votes shall be taken by States, the Representation from each State having one Vote; A quorum for this Purpose shall consist of a Member or Members from two thirds of the States, and a Majority of all the States shall be necessary to a Choice. In every Case, after the Choice of the President, the Person having the greatest Number of Votes of the Electors shall be the Vice President. But if there should remain two or more who have equal Votes, the Senate shall chuse from them by Ballot the Vice President.

The Congress may determine the Time of chusing the Electors, and the Day on which they shall give their Votes; which Day shall be the same throughout the United States.

No Person except a natural born Citizen, or a Citizen of the United States, at the time of the Adoption of this Constitution, shall be eligible to the Office of President; neither shall any Person be eligible to that Office who shall not have attained to the Age of thirty five Years, and been fourteen Years a Resident within the United States.

In Case of the Removal of the President from Office, or of his Death, Resignation, or Inability to discharge the Powers and Duties of the said Office, the Same shall devolve on the Vice President, and the Congress may by Law provide for the Case of Removal, Death, Resignation or Inability, both of the President and Vice President, declaring what Officer shall then act as President, and such Officer shall act accordingly, until the Disability be removed, or a President shall be elected.

The President shall, at stated Times, receive for his Services, a Compensation, which shall neither be encreased nor diminished during the Period for which he shall have been elected, and he shall not receive within that Period any other Emolument from the United States, or any of them.

Before he enter on the Execution of his Office, he shall take the following Oath or Affirmation:—"I do solemnly swear (or affirm) that I will faithfully execute the Office of President of the United States, and will to the best of my Ability, preserve, protect and defend the Constitution of the United States."

Section 2. The President shall be Commander in Chief of the Army and Navy of the United States, and of the Militia of the several States, when called into the actual Service of the United States; he may require the Opinion, in writing, of the principal Officer in each of the executive Departments, upon any Subject relating to the Duties of their respective Offices, and he shall have Power to grant Reprieves and Pardons for Offences against the United States, except in Cases of Impeachment.

He shall have Power, by and with the Advice and Consent of the Senate, to make Treaties, provided two thirds of the Senators present concur; and he shall nominate, and by and with the Advice and Consent of the Senate, shall appoint Ambassadors, other public Ministers and Consuls, Judges of the supreme Court, and all other Officers of the United States, whose Appointments are not herein otherwise provided for, and which shall be established by Law: but the Congress may by Law vest the Appointment of such inferior Officers, as they think proper, in the President alone, in the Courts of Law, or in the Heads of Departments.

The President shall have Power to fill up all Vacancies that may happen during the Recess of the Senate, by granting Commissions which shall expire at the End of their next Session.

Section 3. He shall from time to time give to the Congress Information of the State of the Union, and recommend to their Consideration such Measures as he shall judge necessary and expedient; he may, on extraordinary Occasions, convene both Houses, or either of them, and in Case of Disagreement between them, with Respect to the Time of Adjournment, he may adjourn them to such Time as he shall think proper; he shall receive Ambassadors and other public Ministers; he shall take Care that the Laws be faithfully executed, and shall Commission all the Officers of the United States.

Section 4. The President, Vice President and all civil Officers of the United States, shall be removed from Office on Impeachment for, and Conviction of, Treason, Bribery, or other High Crimes and Misdemeanors.

Article III

Section 1. The judicial Power of the United States, shall be vested in one supreme Court, and in such inferior Courts as the Congress may from time to time ordain and establish. The Judges, both of the supreme and inferior Courts, shall hold their Offices during good Behaviour, and shall, at stated Times, receive for their Services, a Compensation, which shall not be diminished during their Continuance in Office.

Section 2. The judicial Power shall extend to all Cases, in Law and Equity, arising under this Constitution, the Laws of the United States, and Treaties made, or which shall be made, under their Authority;—to all Cases affecting Ambassadors, other public Ministers and Consuls;—to all Cases of admiralty and maritime jurisdiction;—to Controversies to which the United States shall be a Party;—to Controversies between two or more States; between a State and Citizens of another State;—between Citizens of different States;—between Citizens of the same State claiming Lands under Grants of different States, and between a State, or the Citizens thereof, and foreign States, Citizens or Subjects.

In all Cases affecting Ambassadors, other public Ministers and Consuls, and those in which a State shall be Party, the supreme Court shall have original Jurisdiction. In all the other Cases before mentioned, the supreme Court shall have appellate Jurisdiction, both as to Law and Fact, with such Exceptions, and under such Regulations as the Congress shall make.

The Trial of all Crimes, except in Cases of Impeachment, shall be by Jury; and such Trial shall be held in the State where the said Crimes shall have been committed; but when not committed within any State, the Trial shall be at such Place or Places as the Congress may by Law have directed.

Section 3. Treason against the United States, shall consist only in levying War against them, or in adhering to their Enemies, giving them Aid and Comfort. No Person shall be convicted of Treason unless on the Testimony of two Witnesses to the same overt Act, or on Confession in open Court.

The Congress shall have Power to declare the Punishment of Treason, but no Attainder of Treason shall work Corruption of Blood, or Forfeiture except during the Life of the Person attainted.

Article IV

Section 1. Full Faith and Credit shall be given in each State to the public Acts, Records, and judicial Proceedings of every other State. And the Congress may by general Laws prescribe the Manner in which such Acts, Records and Proceedings shall be proved, and the Effect thereof.

Section 2. The Citizens of each State shall be entitled to all Privileges and Immunities of Citizens in the several States.

A Person charged in any State with Treason, Felony, or other Crime, who shall flee from Justice, and be found in another State, shall on Demand of the executive Authority of the State from which he fled, be delivered up, to be removed to the State having jurisdiction of the Crime.

No person held to Service or Labour in one State, under the Laws thereof, escaping into another, shall, in Consequence of any Law or Regulation therein, be discharged from such Service or Labour, but shall be delivered up on Claim of the Party to whom such Service or Labour may be due.

Section 3. New States may be admitted by the Congress into this Union; but no new State shall be formed or erected within the Jurisdiction of any other State; nor any State be formed by the Junction of two or more States, or Parts of States, without the Consent of the Legislatures of the States concerned as well as of the Congress.

The Congress shall have Power to dispose of and make all needful Rules and Regulations respecting the Territory or other Property belonging to the United States; and nothing in this Constitution shall be so construed as to Prejudice any Claims of the United States, or of any particular State.

Section 4. The United States shall guarantee to every State in this Union a Republican Form of Government, and shall protect each of them against Invasion; and on Application of the Legislature, or of the Executive (when the Legislature cannot be convened) against domestic Violence.

Article V

The Congress, whenever two thirds of both Houses shall deem it necessary, shall propose Amendments to this Constitution, or, on the Application of the Legislatures of two thirds of the several States, shall call a Convention for proposing Amendments, which, in either Case, shall be valid to all Intents and Purposes, as Part of this Constitution, when ratified by the Legislatures of three fourths of the several States, or by Conventions in three fourths thereof, as the one or the other Mode of Ratification may be proposed by the Congress; Provided that no Amendment which may be made prior to the Year One thousand eight hundred and eight shall in any Manner affect the first and fourth Clauses in the Ninth Section of the first Article; and that no State, without its Consent, shall be deprived of its equal Suffrage in the Senate.

Article VI

All Debts contracted and Engagements entered into, before the Adoption of this Constitution, shall be as valid against the United States under this Constitution, as under the Confederation.

This Constitution, and the Laws of the United States which shall be made in Pursuance thereof; and all Treaties made, or which shall be made, under the Authority of the United States, shall be the supreme Law of the Land; and the Judges in every State shall be bound thereby, any Thing in the Constitution or Laws of any State to the Contrary notwithstanding.

Appendix A

The Senators and Representatives before mentioned, and the Members of the several
State Legislatures, and all executive and judicial Officers, both of the United States
and of the several States, shall be bound by Oath or Affirmation, to support this
Constitution, but no religious Test shall ever be required as a Qualification to any
Office or public Trust under the United States.

Article VII

The Ratification of the Conventions of nine States, shall be sufficient for the Establishment of this Constitution between the States so ratifying the Same.

> done in Convention by the Unanimous Consent of the States present
> the Seventeenth Day of September in the Year of our Lord one thou-
> sand seven hundred and Eighty seven and of the Independence of the
> United States of America the Twelfth In witness whereof We have here-
> unto subscribed our Names,

G^o Washington—Presid^t
and deputy from Virginia

New Hampshire { John Langdon
Nicholas Gilman

Massachusetts { Nathaniel Gorham
Rufus King

Connecticut { Wm Saml Johnson
Roger Sherman

New York   Alexander Hamilton

New Jersey { Wil: Livingston
David Brearley
Wm Paterson
Jona: Dayton

Pennsylvania { B Franklin
Thomas Mifflin
Robt Morris
Geo. Clymer
Thos FitzSimons
Jared Ingersoll
James Wilson
Gouv Morris

Delaware { Geo: Read
Gunning Bedford jun
John Dickinson
Richard Bassett
Jaco: Broom

Maryland { James McHenry
Dan of St Thos Jenifer
Danl Carroll

Virginia { John Blair—
James Madison Jr.

North Carolina { Wm Blount
Richd Dobbs Spaight
Hu Williamson

South Carolina { J. Rutledge
Charles Cotesworth Pinckney
Charles Pinckney
Pierce Butler

Georgia { William Few
Abr Baldwin

Amendments

(The first 10 Amendments were ratified December 15, 1791, and form what is known as the "Bill of Rights.")

Amendment 1

Congress shall make no law respecting an establishment of religion, or prohibiting the free exercise thereof; or abridging the freedom of speech, or of the press; or the right of the people peaceably to assemble, and to petition the Government for a redress of grievances

Amendment 2

A well regulated Militia, being necessary to the security of a free State, the right of the people to keep and bear Arms, shall not be infringed.

Amendment 3

No Soldier shall, in time of peace be quartered in any house, without the consent of the Owner, nor in time of war, but in a manner to be prescribed by law.

Amendment 4

The right of the people to be secure in their persons, houses, papers, and effects, against unreasonable searches and seizures, shall not be violated, and no Warrants shall issue, but upon probable cause, supported by Oath or affirmation, and particularly describing the place to be searched and the persons or things to be seized.

Amendment 5

No person shall be held to answer for a capital, or otherwise infamous crime, unless on a presentment or indictment of a Grand Jury, except in cases arising in the land or naval forces, or in the Militia, when in actual service in time of War or public danger; nor shall any person be subject for the same offence to be twice put in jeopardy of life or limb; nor shall be compelled in any criminal case to be a witnesses against himself, nor be deprived of life, liberty, or property, without due process of law; nor shall private property be taken for public use, without just compensation.

Appendix A

Amendment 6

In all criminal prosecutions, the accused shall enjoy the right to a speedy and public trial, by an impartial jury of the State and district wherein the crime shall have been committed, which district shall have been previously ascertained by law, and to be informed of the nature and cause of the accusation; to be confronted with the witnesses against him; to have compulsory process for obtaining witnesses in his favor, and to have the Assistance of Counsel for his defence.

Amendment 7

In Suits at common law, where the value in controversy shall exceed twenty dollars, the right of trial by jury shall be preserved, and no fact tried by a jury, shall be otherwise re-examined in any Court of the United States, than according to the rules of the common law.

Amendment 8

Excessive bail shall not be required, nor excessive fines imposed, nor cruel and unusual punishments inflicted.

Amendment 9

The enumeration in the Constitution, of certain rights, shall not be construed to deny or disparage others retained by the people.

Amendment 10

The powers not delegated to the United States by the Constitution, nor prohibited by it to the States, are reserved to the States respectively, or to the people.

Amendment 11

(Ratified February 7, 1795)
The Judicial power of the United States shall not be construed to extend to any suit in law or equity, commenced or prosecuted against one of the United States by Citizens of another State, or by Citizens or Subjects of any Foreign State.

Amendment 12

(Ratified July 27, 1804)
The Electors shall meet in their respective states and vote by ballot for President and Vice-President, one of whom, at least, shall not be an inhabitant of the same state with themselves; they shall name in their ballots the person voted for as President, and in distinct ballots the person voted for as Vice-President, and they shall make distinct lists of all persons voted for as President, and of all persons voted for as Vice-President, and of the number of votes for each, which lists they shall sign and certify, and transmit sealed to the seat of the government of the United States, directed to the President of the Senate;—The President of the Senate shall, in the presence of the Senate and House of Representatives, open all the certificates and the votes shall then be counted;—The person having the greatest number of votes for President, shall be the President, if such number be a majority of the whole number of Electors appointed; and if no person have such majority, then from the persons having the highest numbers not exceeding three on the list of those voted for as President, the House of Representatives shall choose immediately, by ballot, the President. But in choosing the President, the votes shall be

taken by states, the representation from each state having one vote; a quorum for this purpose shall consist of a member or members from two-thirds of the states, and a majority of all the states shall be necessary to a choice. And if the House of Representatives shall not choose a President whenever the right of choice shall devolve upon them, before the fourth day of March next following, then the Vice-President shall act as President, as in the case of the death or other constitutional disability of the President. — The person having the greatest number of votes as Vice-President, shall be the Vice-President, if such number be a majority of the whole number of Electors appointed, and if no person have a majority, then from the two highest numbers on the list, the Senate shall choose the Vice-President; a quorum for the purpose shall consist of two-thirds of the whole number of Senators, and a majority of the whole number shall be necessary to a choice. But no person constitutionally ineligible to the office of President shall be eligible to that of Vice-President of the United States.

Amendment 13

(Ratified December 6, 1865)

Section 1. Neither slavery nor involuntary servitude, except as a punishment for crime whereof the party shall have been duly convicted, shall exist within the United States, or any place subject to their jurisdiction.

Section 2. Congress shall have power to enforce this article by appropriate legislation.

Amendment 14

(Ratified July 9, 1868)

Section 1. All persons born or naturalized in the United States, and subject to the jurisdiction thereof, are citizens of the United States and of the State wherein they reside. No State shall make or enforce any law which shall abridge the privileges or immunities of citizens of the United States; nor shall any State deprive any person of life, liberty, or property, without due process of law; nor deny to any person within its jurisdiction the equal protection of the laws.

Section 2. Representatives shall be apportioned among the several States according to their respective numbers, counting the whole number of persons in each State, excluding Indians not taxed. But when the right to vote at any election for the choice of electors for President and Vice President of the United States, Representatives in Congress, the Executive and Judicial officers of a State, or the members of the Legislature thereof, is denied to any of the male inhabitants of such State, being twenty-one years of age, and citizens of the United States, or in any way abridged, except for participation in rebellion, or other crime, the basis of representation therein shall be reduced in the proportion which the number of such male citizens shall bear to the whole number of male citizens twenty-one years of age in such State.

Section 3. No person shall be a Senator or Representative in Congress, or elector of President and Vice President, or hold any office, civil or military, under the United States, or under any State, who, having previously taken an oath, as a member of Congress, or as an officer of the United States, or as a member of any State legislature, or as an executive or judicial officer of any State, to support the Constitution of the United States, shall have engaged in insurrection or rebellion against the same, or given aid or comfort to the enemies thereof. But Congress may by a vote of two-thirds of each House, remove such disability.

Section 4. The validity of the public debt of the United States, authorized by law, including debts incurred for payment of pensions and bounties for services in suppressing insurrection or rebellion, shall not be questioned. But neither the United

States nor any State shall assume or pay any debt or obligation incurred in aid of insurrection or rebellion against the United States, or any claim for the loss or emancipation of any slave; but all such debts, obligations and claims shall be held illegal and void.

Section 5. The Congress shall have power to enforce, by appropriate legislation, the provisions of this article.

Amendment 15

(Ratified February 3, 1870)

Section 1. The right of citizens of the United States to vote shall not be denied or abridged by the United States or by any State on account of race, color, or previous condition of servitude.

Section 2. The Congress shall have power to enforce this article by appropriate legislation.

Amendment 16

(Ratified February 3, 1913)

The Congress shall have power to lay and collect taxes on incomes, from whatever source derived, without apportionment among the several States, and without regard to any census or enumeration.

Amendment 17

(Ratified April 8, 1913)

The Senate of the United States shall be composed of two Senators from each State, elected by the people thereof for six years; and each Senator shall have one vote. The electors in each State shall have the qualifications requisite for electors of the most numerous branch of the State legislatures.

When vacancies happen in the representation of any State in the Senate, the executive authority of such State shall issue writs of election to fill such vacancies: Provided, That the legislature of any State may empower the executive thereof to make temporary appointments until the people fill the vacancies by election as the legislature may direct.

This amendment shall not be so construed as to affect the election or term of any Senator chosen before it becomes valid as part of the Constitution.

Amendment 18

(Ratified January 16, 1919. Repealed December 5, 1933 by Amendment 21)

Section 1. After one year from the ratification of this article the manufacture, sale, or transportation of intoxicating liquors within, the importation thereof into, or the exportation thereof from the United States and all territory subject to the jurisdiction thereof for beverage purposes is hereby prohibited.

Section 2. The Congress and the several States shall have concurrent power to enforce this article by appropriate legislation.

Section 3. This article shall be inoperative unless it shall have been ratified as an amendment to the Constitution by the legislatures of the several States as provided in the Constitution, within seven years from the date of the submission hereof to the States by the Congress.

Amendment 19

(Ratified August 18, 1920)

The right of citizens of the United States to vote shall not be denied or abridged by the United States or by any State on account of sex.

Congress shall have power to enforce this article by appropriate legislation.

Amendment 20

(Ratified January 23, 1933)

Section 1. The terms of the President and Vice President shall end at noon on the 20th day of January, and the terms of Senators and Representatives at noon on the 3d day of January, of the years in which such terms would have ended if this article had not been ratified; and the terms of their successors shall then begin.

Section 2. The Congress shall assemble at least once in every year, and such meeting shall begin at noon on the 3d day of January, unless they shall by law appoint a different day.

Section 3. If, at the time fixed for the beginning of the term of the President, the President elect shall have died, the Vice President elect shall become President. If a President shall not have been chosen before the time fixed for the beginning of his term, or if the President elect shall have failed to qualify, then the Vice President elect shall act as President until a President shall have qualified; and the Congress may by law provide for the case wherein neither a President elect nor a Vice President elect shall have qualified, declaring who shall then act as President, or the manner in which one who is to act shall be selected, and such person shall act accordingly until a President or Vice President shall have qualified.

Section 4. The Congress may by law provide for the case of the death of any of the persons from whom the House of Representatives may choose a President whenever the right of choice shall have devolved upon them, and for the case of the death of any of the persons from whom the Senate may choose a Vice President whenever the right of choice shall have devolved upon them.

Section 5. Sections 1 and 2 shall take effect on the 15th day of October following the ratification of this article.

Section 6. This article shall be inoperative unless it shall have been ratified as an amendment to the Constitution by the legislatures of three-fourths of the several States within seven years from the date of its submission.

Amendment 21

(Ratified December 5, 1933)

Section 1. The eighteenth article of amendment to the Constitution of the United States is hereby repealed.

Section 2. The transportation or importation into any State, Territory, or possession of the United States for delivery or use therein of intoxicating liquors, in violation of the laws thereof, is hereby prohibited.

Section 3. This article shall be inoperative unless it shall have been ratified as an amendment to the Constitution by conventions in the several States, as provided in the Constitution, within seven years from the date of the submission hereof to the States by the Congress.

Amendment 22

(Ratified February 27, 1951)

Section 1. No person shall be elected to the office of the President more than twice, and no person who has held the office of President, or acted as President, for more than two years of a term to which some other person was elected President shall be elected to the office of the President more than once. But this Article shall not apply to any person holding the office of President when this Article was proposed by the Congress, and shall not prevent any person who may be holding the office of President, or acting as President, during the term within which this Article becomes operative from holding the office of President or acting as President during the remainder of such term.

Section 2. This article shall be inoperative unless it shall have been ratified as an amendment to the Constitution by the legislatures of three-fourths of the several States within seven years from the date of its submission to the States by the Congress.

Amendment 23

(Ratified March 29, 1961)

Section 1. The District constituting the seat of Government of the United States shall appoint in such manner as the Congress may direct:

A number of electors of President and Vice President equal to the whole number of Senators and Representatives in Congress to which the District would be entitled if it were a State, but in no event more than the least populous State; they shall be in addition to those appointed by the States, but they shall be considered, for the purposes of the election of President and Vice President, to be electors appointed by a State; and they shall meet in the District and perform such duties as provided by the twelfth article of amendment.

Section 2. The Congress shall have power to enforce this article by appropriate legislation.

Amendment 24

(Ratified January 23, 1964)

Section 1. The right of citizens of the United States to vote in any primary or other election for President or Vice President, for electors for President or Vice President, or for Senator or Representative in Congress, shall not be denied or abridged by the United States or any State by reason of failure to pay any poll tax or other tax.

Section 2. The Congress shall have power to enforce this article by appropriate legislation.

Amendment 25

(Ratified February 10, 1967)

Section 1. In case of the removal of the President from office or of his death or resignation, the Vice President shall become President.

Section 2. Whenever there is a vacancy in the office of the Vice President, the President shall nominate a Vice President who shall take office upon confirmation by a majority vote of both Houses of Congress.

Section 3. Whenever the President transmits to the President pro tempore of the Senate and the Speaker of the House of Representatives his written declaration that he is unable to discharge the powers and duties of his office, and until he transmits to them a written declaration to the contrary, such powers and duties shall be discharged by the Vice President as Acting President.

Section 4. Whenever the Vice President and a majority of either the principal officers of the executive departments or of such other body as Congress may by law provide, transmit to the President pro tempore of the Senate and the Speaker of the House of Representatives their written declaration that the President is unable to discharge the powers and duties of his office, the Vice President shall immediately assume the powers and duties of the office as Acting President.

Thereafter, when the President transmits to the President pro tempore of the Senate and the Speaker of the House of Representatives his written declaration that no inability exists, he shall resume the powers and duties of his office unless the Vice President and a majority of either the principal officers of the executive department or of such other body as Congress may by law provide, transmit within four days to the President pro tempore of the Senate and the Speaker of the House of Representatives their written declaration that the President is unable to discharge the powers and duties of his office. Thereupon Congress shall decide the issue, assembling within forty-eight hours for that purpose if not in session. If the Congress, within twenty-one days after receipt of the latter written declaration, or, if Congress is not in session, within twenty-one days after Congress is required to assemble, determines by two-thirds vote of both Houses that the President is unable to discharge the powers and duties of his office, the Vice President shall continue to discharge the same as Acting President; otherwise, the President shall resume the powers and duties of his office.

Amendment 26

(Ratified July 1, 1971)

Section 1. The right of citizens of the United States, who are eighteen years of age or older, to vote shall not be denied or abridged by the United States or by any State on account of age.

Section 2. The Congress shall have the power to enforce this article by appropriate legislation.

APPENDIX B

NASPAA
MEMBERSHIP ROSTER,
ACADEMIC INSTITUTIONS

ALABAMA
AUBURN UNIVERSITY, AUBURN
Department of Political Science
7080 Haley Center
Auburn, AL 36849
(205) 826-5370

AUBURN UNIVERSITY,
MONTGOMERY
Department of Government
Montgomery, AL 36193
(205) 271-9696

SAMFORD UNIVERSITY
Department of History
and Political Science
Director of PADM/PAFF Programs
SU Box 2238
800 Lakeshore Drive
Birmingham, AL 35229
(205) 870-2858

UNIVERSITY OF ALABAMA,
BIRMINGHAM
Department of Political Science and
Urban Affairs
University Station
236 Ullman Building
Birmingham, AL 35294
(205) 934-9679

UNIVERSITY OF ALABAMA,
UNIVERSITY
Department of Political Science
Drawer 1
University, AL 35486
(205) 348-5980

ALASKA
UNIVERSITY OF ALASKA

School of Business & Public Affairs
3211 Providence Drive, COB330
Anchorage, AK 99504
(907) 786-1758

ARIZONA
ARIZONA STATE UNIVERSITY
Center for Public Affairs
Tempe, AZ 85287
(602) 965-3926

UNIVERSITY OF ARIZONA
Department of Management and
Policy
College of Business & Public
Administration
Harvill Building #76
Tucson, AZ 85721
(602) 621-1474

ARKANSAS
ARKANSAS STATE UNIVERSITY
Department of Political Science
P.O. Box 600
State University, AR 72467
(501) 972-3049

UNIVERSITY OF ARKANSAS
MPA Program
Department of Political Science
Communications Center 619
Fayetteville, AR 72701
(501) 575-3356

CALIFORNIA
CALIFORNIA STATE COLLEGE,
BAKERSFIELD
Public Policy & Administration
Department
School of Business & Public
Administration
9001 Stockdale Highway
Bakersfield, CA 93309
(805) 833-2323

CALIFORNIA STATE COLLEGE,
STANISLAUS
Graduate Studies in Public
Administration
801 West Monte Vista Avenue
Turlock, CA 95380
(209) 667-3388

CALIFORNIA STATE POLYTECHNIC
UNIVERSITY, POMONA

Department of Political Science
3801 West Temple Avenue
Pomona, CA 91768
(714) 598-4529

CALIFORNIA STATE UNIVERSITY,
  CHICO
Coordinator of Public Administration
Chico, CA 95929
(916) 895-5301

CALIFORNIA STATE UNIVERSITY,
  DOMINGUEZ HILLS
Department of Public Administration
1000 E. Victoria Street
Carson, CA 90747
(213) 516-3444

CALIFORNIA STATE UNIVERSITY,
  FULLERTON
Public Administration Program
800 North State College Boulevard
Fullerton, CA 92634
(714) 773-3521

CALIFORNIA STATE UNIVERSITY,
  HAYWARD
Department of Public Administration
25800 Carlos Bee Boulevard
Hayward, CA 94542
(415) 881-3282

CALIFORNIA STATE UNIVERSITY,
  LONG BEACH
Center for Public Policy and
  Administration
1250 Bellflower Boulevard
Long Beach, CA 90840
(213) 498-4177

CALIFORNIA STATE UNIVERSITY,
  LOS ANGELES
Department of Political Science
5151 State University Drive
Los Angeles, CA 90032
(213) 224-2891

CALIFORNIA STATE UNIVERSITY,
  SAN BERNARDINO
Department of Public Administration
5500 State College Parkway
San Bernardino, CA 92407
(714) 887-7704

CALIFORNIA STATE UNIVERSITY,
  SACRAMENTO
Department of Public Administration
6000 J Street

Sacramento, CA 95819
(916) 454-6752

CONSORTIUM OF CALIFORNIA
  STATE UNIVERSITY &
  COLLEGES
MPA Program
Academic Program Committee in
  Public Administration
9419 Aldea Avenue
Northridge, CA 91325
(213) 885-3488

GOLDEN GATE UNIVERSITY
Graduate School of Public
  Administration
536 Mission Street
San Francisco, CA 94105
(415) 442-7231

NAVAL POSTGRADUATE SCHOOL
Administrative Sciences Department
(COD 54)
Monterey, CA 93940
(408) 646-3407

SAN DIEGO STATE UNIVERSITY
MPA Program
School of Public Administration &
  Urban Studies
San Diego, CA 92182
(619) 265-4099

UNIVERSITY OF CALIFORNIA,
  BERKELEY
Graduate School of Public Policy
2607 Hearst Avenue
Berkeley, CA 94720
(416) 642-4670

UNIVERSITY OF CALIFORNIA,
  IRVINE
Graduate School of Management
Irvine, CA 92717
(714) 856-5840

UNIVERSITY OF CALIFORNIA,
  LOS ANGELES
Department of Political Science
3357 Bunche Hall
Los Angeles, CA 90024
(213) 825-1972

UNIVERSITY OF CALIFORNIA,
  RIVERSIDE
Graduate School of Management
Riverside, CA 92521
(714) 787-4551

UNIVERSITY OF CALIFORNIA,
SANTA BARBARA
Department of Political Science
Santa Barbara, CA 93106
(805) 961-3431

UNIVERSITY OF SOUTHERN
CALIFORNIA
School of Public Administration
University Park
Los Angeles, CA 90089-0041
(213) 743-2241

UNIVERSITY OF THE PACIFIC
School of Business & Public
Administration
3601 Pacific Avenue
Stockton, CA 95211
(209) 946-2466

COLORADO
COLORADO STATE UNIVERSITY
Department of Political Science
Fort Collins, CO 80523
(303) 491-5369

UNIVERSITY OF COLORADO
Graduate School of Public Affairs
1100 14th Street
Denver, CO 80202
(303) 629-2825

UNIVERSITY OF DENVER
School of Public Management
Denver, CO 80208
(303) 556-3435

CONNECTICUT
UNIVERSITY OF CONNECTICUT
Master of Public Affairs Program
U-106
Storrs, CT 06268
(203) 486-4518

UNIVERSITY OF NEW HAVEN
Division of Public Management
300 Orange Avenue
West Haven, CT 06516
(203) 932-9375

DELAWARE
UNIVERSITY OF DELAWARE
MPA Program
College of Urban Affairs and Public
Policy
Willard Hall

Newark, DE 19716
(302) 451-2394

DISTRICT OF COLUMBIA
THE AMERICAN UNIVERSITY
College of Public & International
Affairs
Ward 101
Washington, D.C. 20016
(202) 686-3850

GEORGE WASHINGTON
UNIVERSITY
Department of Public Administration
2129 G Street, N.W.
Washington, D.C. 20052
(202) 676-6295

HOWARD UNIVERSITY
Department of Political Science
Washington, D.C. 20059
(202) 636-6720

HOWARD UNIVERSITY
Department of Public Administration
School of Business and Public
Administration
1003 K St., N.W., 4th Floor
Washington, D.C. 20059
(202) 783-6450

FLORIDA
FLORIDA ATLANTIC UNIVERSITY
MPA Program
Department of Public Administration
Boca Raton, FL 33431
(305) 393-3000

FLORIDA INTERNATIONAL
UNIVERSITY
Department of Public Administration
School of Public Affairs & Service
North Miami Campus
North Miami, FL 33181
(305) 940-5890

FLORIDA STATE UNIVERSITY
Department of Public Administration
619 Bellamy Building
Tallahassee, FL 32306
(909) 644-3525

NOVA UNIVERSITY
3301 College Avenue
Fort Lauderdale, FL 33314
(305) 475-7646

UNIVERSITY OF MIAMI
Public Administration Program
Department of Politics and Public
Affairs
P.O. Box 248047
Coral Gables, FL 33124
(305) 284-2401

UNIVERSITY OF NORTH FLORIDA
MPA Program
4567 St. Johns Bluff Road, South
Jacksonville, FL 32216
(904) 646-2540

UNIVERSITY OF SOUTH FLORIDA
Public Administration Program
College of Social & Behavioral Science
Tampa, FL 33620

UNIVERSITY OF WEST FLORIDA
Graduate Public Administration
  Program
Department of Political Science
Pensacola, FL 32514-0102
(904) 474-2336

GEORGIA
ATLANTA UNIVERSITY
Department of Public Administration
223 Chestnut Street, S.W.
Atlanta, GA 30314
(404) 681-0251

GEORGIA COLLEGE
Department of Political Science &
  Public Administration
Milledgeville, GA 31061
(912) 453-4562

GEORGIA SOUTHERN COLLEGE
MPA Program
Political Science Department
Statesboro, GA 30460
(912) 681-5698

GEORGIA STATE UNIVERSITY
Institute of Public Administration
University Plaza
Atlanta, GA 30303
(404) 658-3350

UNIVERSITY OF GEORGIA
Department of Political Science
Baldwin Hall
Athens, GA 30602
(404) 542-2057

IDAHO
BOISE STATE UNIVERSITY
Department of Political Science
1910 University Drive
Boise, ID 83725
(208) 385-1331

IDAHO STATE UNIVERSITY
Department of Political Science
Box 8073
Pocatello, ID 83209
(208) 236-2211

ILLINOIS
DEPAUL UNIVERSITY
Management of Public Service Program
25 E. Jackson Boulevard
Chicago, IL 60604
(312) 321-8441

GOVERNORS STATE UNIVERSITY
Institute for Public Policy
  & Administration
Park Forest South, IL 60466
(312) 534-5000

NORTHEASTERN ILLINOIS
  UNIVERSITY
Department of Political Science
5500 N. St. Louis Avenue
Chicago, IL 60625
(312) 583-4050

NORTHERN ILLINOIS UNIVERSITY
Division of Public Affairs
DeKalb, IL 60115
(815) 753-0183

ROOSEVELT UNIVERSITY
Public Administration Program
430 South Michigan Avenue
Chicago, IL 60605
(312) 341-3744

SANGAMON STATE UNIVERSITY
Public Policy & Administration
  Programs
Springfield, IL 62708
(217) 786-6576

SOUTHERN ILLINOIS UNIVERSITY,
  CARBONDALE
MPA Program
Department of Political Science
Carbondale, IL 62901
(618) 536-2371

UNIVERSITY OF CHICAGO

601

Committee on Public Policy Studies
1050 East 59th Street
Chicago, IL 60637
(312) 962-8400

UNIVERSITY OF ILLINOIS AT
  CHICAGO
Graduate Program in Public
  Administration
Box 4348
Chicago, IL 60680
(312) 996-3109

UNIVERSITY OF ILLINOIS,
  URBANA-CHAMPAIGN
Public Administration
702 S. Wright Street
369 Lincoln Hall
Urbana, IL 61801
(217) 333-1682

INDIANA
BALL STATE UNIVERSITY
Department of Political Science
Muncie, IN 47306
(317) 285-1607

INDIANA STATE UNIVERSITY
MPA Program
Department of Political Science
Terre Haute, IN 47908
(812) 232-6311

INDIANA UNIVERSITY
School of Public & Environmental
  Affairs, Room 300
400 East 7th Street
Poplars 333
Bloomington, IN 47405
(812) 335-1432

PURDUE UNIVERSITY
Department of Public Policy &
  Public Administration
ENAD 323
Lafayette, IN 47907
(317) 494-5036

IOWA
DRAKE UNIVERSITY
Institute of Public Affairs
Meredith Hall, Room 209
Des Moines, IA 50311
(515) 271-2913

IOWA STATE UNIVERSITY
Department of Political Science

503 Ross Hall
Ames, IA 50011
(515) 294-7256

KANSAS
KANSAS STATE UNIVERSITY
Department of Political Science
Manhattan, KS 66506
(913) 532-6842

UNIVERSITY OF KANSAS
The E. O. Stene Grad. Program in
  Public Administration
Blake Hall
Lawrence, KS 66044
(913) 864-3527

WASHBURN UNIVERSITY
Department of Political Science
Topeka, KS 66621
(913) 295-6737

WICHITA STATE UNIVERSITY
Wichita, KS 67208
(316) 689-3737

KENTUCKY
EASTERN KENTUCKY UNIVERSITY
Department of Political Science
Richmond, KY 40475
(606) 622-5931

KENTUCKY STATE UNIVERSITY
Graduate Center/School of
  Public Affairs
Frankfort, KY 40601
(502) 227-6117

MURRAY STATE UNIVERSITY
MPA Program
Department of Political Science
Murray, KY 42071
(502) 762-2661

UNIVERSITY OF KENTUCKY
Martin Center for Public Administration
409 Commerce Building
Lexington, KY 40506
(606) 257-7664

UNIVERSITY OF LOUISVILLE
Department of Political Science
Belknap Campus
Louisville, KY 40292
(502) 588-6831

LOUISIANA
GRAMBLING UNIVERSITY

602

Department of Political Science
Grambling, LA 71245
(318) 247-6941

LOUISIANA STATE UNIVERSITY
Public Administration Institute
3139 CEBA
Baton Rouge, LA 70803
(504) 388-6645

UNIVERSITY OF NEW ORLEANS
School of Urban & Regional Studies
Lakefront
New Orleans, LA 70148
(504) 286-6277

MAINE
UNIVERSITY OF MAINE, ORONO
PAD Program
Department of Political Science
Orono, ME 04469
(207) 581-1872

MARYLAND
UNIVERSITY OF BALTIMORE
Masters in Public Administration
    Program
Charles at Mount Royal
Baltimore, Maryland 21201
(301) 625-3172

UNIVERSITY OF MARYLAND,
    BALTIMORE COUNTY
Policy Sciences Graduate Program
5401 Wilkins Avenue
Catonsville, MD 21228
(301) 455-3201

UNIVERSITY OF MARYLAND,
    COLLEGE PARK
School of Public Affairs
Suite 1218 Social Sciences Building
College Park, MD 20742
(301) 454-6193

MASSACHUSETTS
BENTLEY COLLEGE
Public Administration Program
Beaver and Forest Streets
Waltham, MA 02154
(617) 891-2946

BRANDEIS UNIVERSITY
The Florence Heller School
Waltham, MA 02254
(617) 647-2914

CLARK UNIVERSITY
950 Main Street, Room 307A
Worcester, MA 01610
(617) 793-7623

HARVARD UNIVERSITY
JFK School of Government
79 JFK Street
Cambridge, MA 02138
(617) 495-1353

NORTHEASTERN UNIVERSITY
Department of Political Science
Boston, MA 02115
(617) 437-2796

SUFFOLK UNIVERSITY
School of Management
8 Ashburton Place
Boston, MA 02108
(617) 723-4700

UNIVERSITY OF MASSACHUSETTS,
    AMHERST
MPA Program
Department of Political Science
Amherst, MA 01003
(413) 545-0410

UNIVERSITY OF MASSACHUSETTS,
    BOSTON
College of Management
Harbor Campus
Boston, MA 02125
(617) 929-8098

MICHIGAN
CENTRAL MICHIGAN UNIVERSITY
Department of Political Science
247 Anspach Hall
Mt. Pleasant, MI 48858
(517) 774-3442

MICHIGAN STATE UNIVERSITY
Department of Political Science
303 S. Kedzie Hall
East Lansing, MI 48824
(517) 355-6592

UNIVERSITY OF MICHIGAN,
    ANN ARBOR
Institute of Public Policy Studies
1516 Rackham Building
Ann Arbor, MI 48109
(313) 763-4790

UNIVERSITY OF MICHIGAN,
    DEARBORN
Public Administration

4901 Evergreen Rd.
Dearborn, MI 48128
(313) 593-5287

WAYNE STATE UNIVERSITY
MPA Program in Public Administration
Department of Public Administration
870 Mackenzie Hall
Detroit, MI 48202
(313) 577-2668

WESTERN MICHIGAN UNIVERSITY
Center for Public Administration
  Program
Kalamazoo, MI 49008
(616) 383-1937

MINNESOTA
MANKATO STATE UNIVERSITY
Urban and Regional Studies Institute
Box 25
Mankato, MN 56001
(507) 389-1714

UNIVERSITY OF MINNESOTA
H.H. Humphrey Institute of Public
  Affairs
909 Social Science Building
267 19th Avenue, South
Minneapolis, MN 55455
(612) 376-9666

MISSISSIPPI
JACKSON STATE UNIVERSITY
Department of Political Science
Ayer Hall
Jackson, MS 39217
(601) 968-2136

MISSISSIPPI STATE UNIVERSITY
Department of Political Science
PO Drawer PC
Mississippi State, MS 39762
(601) 325-2711

UNIVERSITY OF MISSISSIPPI
Department of Political Science
University, MS 38677
(601) 232-7401

MISSOURI
ST. LOUIS UNIVERSITY
MAPA Program
Department of Political Science
St. Louis, MO 63103
(314) 658-3035

UNIVERSITY OF MISSOURI,
  COLUMBIA
Department of Public Administration
315 Middlebush Hall
Columbia, MO 65211
(314) 882-3304

UNIVERSITY OF MISSOURI,
  KANSAS CITY
School of Administration
5110 Cherry Street
Kansas City, MO 64110
(816) 276-2894

UNIVERSITY OF MISSOURI,
  ST. LOUIS
Public Policy Administration Master's
  Program
8001 Natural Bridge Rd.
St. Louis, MO 63121
(314) 553-5145

MONTANA
MONTANA STATE UNIVERSITY
MPA Program
Department of Political Science
Bozeman, MT 59715
(406) 994-4141

NEBRASKA
UNIVERSITY OF NEBRASKA,
  OMAHA
College of Public Affairs and
  Community Service
60th and Dodge Street
Omaha, NE 68182
(402) 554-2276

WAYNE STATE COLLEGE
Public Affairs Institute
Wayne, NE 68787
(402) 375-2200

NEW JERSEY
FAIRLEIGH DICKINSON
  UNIVERSITY
Public Administration Institute
211 Montross Avenue
Rutherford, NJ 07070
(201) 460-5343

JERSEY CITY STATE COLLEGE
Public Administration Program
Department of Political Science
Jersey City, NJ 07309
(201) 547-3239

KEAN COLLEGE OF NEW JERSEY
Union, NJ 07083
(201) 527-3022

PRINCETON UNIVERSITY
Woodrow Wilson School of Public &
    International Affairs
Princeton, NJ 08544
(609) 452-4800

RIDER COLLEGE
Graduate Program for Administrators
Lawrence, NJ 08649
(609) 896-5352

RUTGERS UNIVERSITY
Graduate Program in Public Policy
311 N. 5th Street
Camden, NJ 08102
(609) 757-6359

RUTGERS UNIVERSITY, NEWARK
Graduate Department in Public
    Administration
360 King Boulevard
Newark, NJ 07102
(201) 648-5093

SETON HALL UNIVERSITY
Department of Political Science
400 South Orange Avenue
South Orange, NJ 07079
(201) 761-9382

NEW MEXICO
NEW MEXICO STATE UNIVERSITY
Department of Government
Box 3 BN
Las Cruces, NM 88003
(505) 646-4935

UNIVERSITY OF NEW MEXICO
Division of Public Administration
Mesa Vista Hall
Albuquerque, NM 87131
(505) 277-3312

NEW YORK
BARUCH COLLEGE, CUNY
Department of Public Administration
17 Lexington Avenue, Box 336
New York, NY 10010
(212) 725-7146

COLUMBIA UNIVERSITY
MPA Program
420 West 118th St., Room 1428

New York, NY 10027
(212) 280-2167

HUNTER COLLEGE, CUNY
Department of Urban Affairs
790 Madison Avenue
New York, NY 10021
(212) 772-5517

JOHN JAY COLLEGE OF CRIMINAL
    JUSTICE, CUNY
National Center for Public Productivity
444 West 56th Street, Room 3254,
    Northhall
New York, NY 10019
(212) 489-5183

LONG ISLAND UNIVERSITY,
    BROOKLYN
Public Administration Program
Brooklyn, NY 11201
(718) 403-1074

LONG ISLAND UNIVERSITY,
    C.W. POST CAMPUS
Business and Public Administration
Greenvale, NY 11548
(516) 299-3017

MARIST COLLEGE
MPA Program
Poughkeepsie, NY 12501
(914) 471-3240

MEDGAR EVERS COLLEGE, CUNY
Social Science Division
1150 Carroll Street
Brooklyn, NY 11225
(718) 735-1971

NEW SCHOOL FOR SOCIAL
    RESEARCH
Graduate School of Management
66 Fifth Avenue
New York, NY 10011
(212) 741-7921

NEW YORK UNIVERSITY
Graduate School of Public
    Administration
4 Washington Square North
New York, NY 10003
(212) 598-2441

PACE UNIVERSITY
Department of Public Administration
55 Church Street
White Plains, NY 10601
(914) 681-4000

RUSSELL SAGE COLLEGE
Department of Government &
Public Service
140 New Scotland Avenue
Albany, NY 12208
(518) 445-1724

STATE UNIVERSITY OF NEW
YORK, ALBANY
Nelson A. Rockefeller College of Public
Affairs and Policy
Graduate School of Public Affairs
135 Western Avenue
Albany, NY 12222
(518) 455-6201

STATE UNIVERSITY OF NEW
YORK, BINGHAMTON
Master's Program
Department of Political Science
Binghamton, NY 13901
(607) 798-2116

STATE UNIVERSITY OF NEW
YORK, COLLEGE AT
BROCKPORT
Public Administration Program
Brockport, NY 14420
(761) 395-2375

STATE UNIVERSITY OF NEW
YORK, COLLEGE AT OLD
WESTBURY
Urban Studies Program
P.O. Box 210
Old Westbury, NY 11568
(516) 876-3271

STATE UNIVERSITY OF NEW
YORK, STONY BROOK
W. Averell Harriman College for Public
Management
Stony Brook, NY 11794
(516) 246-8275

SYRACUSE UNIVERSITY
Maxwell School of Citizenship &
Public Affairs
217 Maxwell Hall
Syracuse, NY 13210
(315) 423-2252

NORTH CAROLINA
DUKE UNIVERSITY
Institute of Policy Science
4875 Duke Station

Durham, NC 27706
(919) 684-4477

EAST CAROLINA UNIVERSITY
Department of Political Science
Greenville, NC 27834
(919) 757-6030

NORTH CAROLINA CENTRAL
UNIVERSITY
Public Administration Program
Durham, NC 27707
(919) 682-6018

NORTH CAROLINA STATE
UNIVERSITY
Department of Political Science and
Public Administration
Box 8102
Raleigh, NC 27695-8102
(919) 737-2060

PEMBROKE STATE UNIVERSITY
Department of Political Science
Pembroke, NC 28372
(919) 521-4214

UNIVERSITY OF NORTH
CAROLINA, CHAPEL HILL
MPA Program
305 Hamilton Hall, 070A
Chapel Hill, NC 27514
(919) 962-3041

UNIVERSITY OF NORTH
CAROLINA, CHARLOTTE
Master of Urban Administration
Program
Department of Political Science
Charlotte, NC 28223
(704) 597-2577

UNIVERSITY OF NORTH
CAROLINA, GREENSBORO
Department of Political Science
237 Graham Building
Greensboro, NC 27412
(919) 379-5989

WESTERN CAROLINA UNIVERSITY
Department of Political Science &
Public Affairs
Cullowhee, NC 28723
(704) 227-7475

OHIO
BOWLING GREEN STATE
UNIVERSITY

Public Administration Program
Department of Political Science
Bowling Green, OH 43403
(419) 372-2921

KENT STATE UNIVERSITY
Graduate School of Management
Kent, OH 44242
(216) 672-2093

THE OHIO STATE UNIVERSITY
School of Public Administration
1775 College Road
202 Hagarty Hall
Columbus, OH 43210
(614) 422-8696

OHIO UNIVERSITY
Public Administration Program
Department of Political Science
Bentley Hall
Athens, OH 45701
(614) 594-5617

UNIVERSITY OF AKRON
Department of Urban Studies
Akron, OH 44325
(216) 375-7910

UNIVERSITY OF CINCINNATI
MPA Program
Department of Political Science
1017 Crosley Tower, Room 375
Cincinnati, OH 45221
(513) 475-3211

UNIVERSITY OF DAYTON
MPA Program
300 College Park Avenue
Dayton, OH 45469
(513) 229-3649

OKLAHOMA
UNIVERSITY OF OKLAHOMA
455 West Lindsey Street
Norman, OK 73019
(405) 325-6432

OREGON
LEWIS AND CLARK COLLEGE
Public Administration Program
Campus Box 79
Portland, OR 97219
(503) 244-6161

PORTLAND STATE UNIVERSITY
Graduate Program in Public
    Administration

730 S.W. Mill Street
P.O. Box 751
Portland, OR 97207
(503) 229-3920

UNIVERSITY OF OREGON
Public Affairs Graduate Program
Department of Planning, Public Policy
Eugene, OR 97403
(503) 686-3817

WILLAMETTE UNIVERSITY
Graduate School of Administration
315 Winter Street
Salem, OR 97301
(503) 370-6440

PENNSYLVANIA
CARNEGIE-MELLON UNIVERSITY
School of Urban & Public Affairs
Pittsburgh, PA 15213
(412) 578-2159

LEHIGH UNIVERSITY
Department of Government
Maginnes Hall #9
Bethlehem, PA 18015
(215) 861-3340

MARYWOOD COLLEGE
Department of Public Service
Scranton, PA 18509
(717) 348-6284

THE PENNSYLVANIA STATE
    UNIVERSITY, CAPITOL CAMPUS
Division of Public Affairs
Middletown, PA 17057
(717) 948-6050

THE PENNSYLVANIA STATE
    UNIVERSITY, UNIVERSITY PARK
Institute of Public Administration
211 Burrowes Building
University Park, PA 16802
(814) 865-2536

SHIPPENSBURG UNIVERSITY
Department of Government
Shippensburg, PA 17257
(717) 532-1718

SLIPPERY ROCK UNIVERSITY
Department of Public Administration
Slippery Rock, PA 16057
(412) 794-7717

TEMPLE UNIVERSITY
Department of Political Science

Gladfelter Hall, 4th Floor
Philadelphia, PA 19122
(215) 787-8628

UNIVERSITY OF PITTSBURGH
Graduate School of Public &
 International Affairs
3G07 Forbes Quadrangle
Pittsburgh, PA 15260
(412) 624-4740

SOUTH CAROLINA
COLLEGE OF CHARLESTON
Center for Metropolitan Affairs and
 Public Policy
Charleston, SC 29424
(803) 792-5737

UNIVERSITY OF SOUTH CAROLINA
Department of Government and
 International Studies
Columbia, SC 29208
(803) 777-3868

SOUTH DAKOTA
UNIVERSITY OF SOUTH DAKOTA
Department of Political Science
Vermillion, SD 57069
(605) 677-5242

TENNESSEE
MEMPHIS STATE UNIVERSITY
MPA Program
Department of Political Science
Memphis, TN 38152
(901) 454-2391

MIDDLE TENNESSEE STATE
 UNIVERSITY
MPA Program
Box 460
Murfreesboro, TN 37132
(615) 898-2719

TEXAS
NORTH TEXAS STATE UNIVERSITY
Division of Public Administration
P.O. Box 5338
NT Station
Denton, TX 76203
(817) 565-2276

SOUTHERN METHODIST
 UNIVERSITY
Graduate Program in Public
 Administration

Political Science Department
24 Storey Hall
Dallas, TX 75275
(214) 692-2929

SOUTHWEST TEXAS STATE
 UNIVERSITY
Public Administration Program
San Marcos, TX 78666
(512) 245-2141

TEXAS A & M UNIVERSITY
Department of Political Science
130 Bolton Hall
College Station, TX 77843
(713) 845-2511

TEXAS SOUTHERN UNIVERSITY
School of Public Affairs
3201 Wheeler Avenue
Houston, TX 77004
(713) 527-7313

TEXAS TECH UNIVERSITY
Center for Public Service
Box 4290
Lubbock, TX 79409
(806) 742-3125

TRINITY UNIVERSITY
Department of Urban Studies
P.O. Box 61
715 Stadium Drive
San Antonio, TX 78284
(512) 736-8101

UNIVERSITY OF HOUSTON,
 UNIVERSITY PARK
MPA Program
PGH 447
Houston, TX 77004
(713) 749-7261

UNIVERSITY OF HOUSTON AT
 CLEAR LAKE CITY
Programs in Public Affairs
2700 Bay Area Boulevard
Houston, TX 77058
(713) 488-9307

UNIVERSITY OF TEXAS,
 ARLINGTON
Institute of Urban Studies
P.O. Box 19588
Arlington, TX 76019
(817) 273-3071

UNIVERSITY OF TEXAS, AUSTIN
Lyndon Baines Johnson School of

Public Affairs
Sid Richardson Hall 3.100
Austin, TX 78712
(512) 471-4962

UNIVERSITY OF TEXAS, EL PASO
MPA Program
Benedict Hall
El Paso, TX 79968
(915) 747-5227

UTAH
BRIGHAM YOUNG UNIVERSITY
Institute of Public Management
760 TNRB
Provo, UT 84602
(801) 378-4221

UNIVERSITY OF UTAH
Center for Public Affairs &
  Administration
1141 Annex
Salt Lake City, UT 84112
(801) 581-6491

VIRGINIA
COLLEGE OF WILLIAM AND MARY
Department of Government
Williamsburg, VA 23185
(804) 253-4000

FERRUM COLLEGE
Program in Public Affairs &
  Administration
Ferrum, VA 24088
(703) 365-2121

GEORGE MASON UNIVERSITY
Department of Public Affairs
4400 University Drive
Fairfax, VA 22030
(703) 323-2272

JAMES MADISON UNIVERSITY
Department of Political Science
Harrisonburg, VA 22807
(703) 433-6149

OLD DOMINION UNIVERSITY
Department of Urban Studies & Public
  Administration
Norfolk, VA 23508-8510
(804) 440-3961

UNIVERSITY OF VIRGINIA
Public Administration Program
232 Cabell Hall

Charlottesville, VA 22903
(804) 924-3358

VIRGINIA COMMONWEALTH
  UNIVERSITY
Department of Public Administration
816 W. Franklin Street, 1st Floor
Richmond, VA 23284
(804) 257-1046

VIRGINIA POLYTECHNIC
  INSTITUTE AND STATE
  UNIVERSITY
Center for Public Administration and
  Policy
Blacksburg, VA 24061
(703) 961-5133

WASHINGTON
EASTERN WASHINGTON
  UNIVERSITY
Graduate Program in Public
  Administration
212M Patterson Hall
Cheney, WA 99004
(509) 359-2365

THE EVERGREEN STATE COLLEGE
Graduate Program in Public
  Administration
Library 2102
Olympic, WA 98505
(206) 866-6000

SEATTLE UNIVERSITY
MPA Program
Institute of Public Service
Seattle, WA 98122
(206) 626-5760

UNIVERSITY OF PUGET SOUND
School of Business & Public Affairs
1500 North Warner
Tacoma, WA 98416
(206) 756-3153

UNIVERSITY OF WASHINGTON
Graduate School of Public Affairs
DP-30
Seattle, WA 98195
(206) 543-4900

WEST VIRGINIA
WEST VIRGINIA UNIVERSITY
Department of Public Administration
302-B Woodburn Hall

Morgantown, WV 26506
(304) 293-2614

WISCONSIN
UNIVERSITY OF WISCONSIN,
  MADISON
Robert M. Lafollette Institute of Public
  Affairs
322 North Hall
Madison, WI 53706
(608) 262-3581

UNIVERSITY OF WISCONSIN,
  MILWAUKEE
Department of Political Science
P.O. Box 413
Milwaukee, WI 53201
(414) 963-4505

UNIVERSITY OF WISCONSIN,
  OSHKOSH

Master of Public Administration
  Program
N/E 101
Oshkosh, WI 54901
(414) 424-3230

UNIVERSITY OF WISCONSIN,
  PARKSIDE
MPA Program
Molinaro Hall
Kenosha, WI 53141
(414) 553-2021

VIRGIN ISLANDS
COLLEGE OF THE VIRGIN
  ISLANDS
MPA Program
St. Thomas, USVI 00801
(809) 774-1252